Flash™ MX Bible

Flash™ MX Bible

Robert Reinhardt and Snow Dowd

Wiley Publishing, Inc.

Flash™ MX Bible

Published by
Wiley Publishing, Inc.
909 Third Avenue
New York, NY 10022
www.wiley.com

Copyright © 2002 by Wiley Publishing, Inc., Indianapolis, Indiana

Manufactured in the United States of America

10 9 8 7 6 5 4 3 2 1

1B/RW/QX/QS/IN

Published by Wiley Publishing, Inc., Indianapolis, Indiana
Published simultaneously in Canada

For general information on our other products and services or to obtain technical support, please contact our Customer Care Department within the U.S. at 800-762-2974, outside the U.S. at 317-572-3993 or fax 317-572-4002.

Wiley also publishes its books in a variety of electronic formats. Some content that appears in print may not be available in electronic books.

Library of Congress Cataloging-in-Publication Data

ISBN: 0-7645-3656-7

Wiley Publishing, Inc. is a trademark of Wiley Publishing

About the Authors

After discovering Macromedia Flash while working on an art project combining film, photography, animation, and audio, Robert soon realized there was a need for more comprehensive documentation of its capabilities. In 1998, not many people had even heard of Flash and publishers were wary of the limited market, but IDG Books committed to doing the Flash 4 Bible. The rest, as they say, is history. After studying and working together for five years in Toronto, Robert Reinhardt and Snow Dowd established a multimedia consulting & design company in Los Angeles in 1999, called [the MAKERS] (www.theMakers.com). One of their first large projects was creating a broadband Web site for *Gossip* (Warner Bros. 2000), as well as screen graphics for a tie-in video with the band *Tonic*. More recently, [the MAKERS] created screen graphics for *The Pledge* (Warner Bros. 2001) and worked with Outlaw Productions and Warner Bros. Online to create previsualization graphics and the Flash site (www.trainingday.net) for the Oscar-nominated film *Training Day* (Warner Bros. 2001). In addition to work for entertainment companies, [the MAKERS] has done work for independent artists and nonprofit organizations, including the Teachers Documentary Project (www.pbs.org/firstyear)

Robert Reinhardt — After studying psychology (University of Toronto) and photography (Ryerson University), Robert's autodidactic energy carried him to new media development, teaching, and writing. Although his head often leads him into the land of scripting and programming, he remains dedicated to the world of images. Before leaving Toronto, Robert worked as a collage and video artist, creating set and screen art during the production of *Gossip*.

While establishing [the MAKERS] in Los Angeles, Robert also worked as Senior Art Director and Program Developer with Rampt.com to create a ground-breaking Flash interface and search engine, launched in November 1999. After being recognized as a Macromedia Site of the Day and nominated in the FlashForward film festival in New York, Rampt received the Bandies 2000 award for Best Interface Application, as well as an award of excellence from the New Media Invision Awards 2000.

In addition to design and content creation through [the MAKERS], Robert continues to teach and write about Flash. He has developed and taught Flash workshops for education centers in California including Lynda.com and Art Center College of Design, as well as doing on-site training and seminars for clients in the United States and Canada. Robert presented topics at FlashForward conferences in 2000, 2001, and 2002, and was proud to be a speaker at the first Flash conference organized in Canada, FlashintheCan 2002. Robert is a member of the inaugural Web Graphics sub-committee for SIGGRAPH 2002.

Snow Dowd — After finishing her primary education in only five years, Snow was awarded a two-year scholarship to attend Lester B. Pearson College of the Pacific where she completed the International Baccalaureate in a class with 125 other scholarship students from 72 countries.

Snow initially collaborated with Robert Reinhardt on multimedia, film, and photography-based installation projects while earning a BFA in Image Arts at Ryerson University. During this time, she was also the production manager for Design Archive, one of Canada's preeminent architectural photography studios (www.designarchive.com). Working with renowned photographers and an exacting international client base of architects and designers helped her gain a deeper appreciation for architecture and industrial design. She also learned to love color printing, but the novelty of darkroom chemicals quickly faded. Fortunately, multimedia design offered a rewarding alternative to the health-hazards of traditional photography.

Now fully immersed in digital production, Snow is able to synthesize her background in visual arts and communication theory with an ever-expanding software toolkit. While continuing to study advanced typography and graphic design, Snow strives to make print and Web projects that are beautiful, functional, and memorable.

About the Technical Editor

Simon Allardice — A Web developer, trainer, and writer with seventeen years programming experience, Simon has pretty much done everything you can do with a computer: developed systems that range from games, to financial applications, to safety routines for nuclear reactors, to designed databases for banks and for supermarkets, and has programmed in everything from mainframe assembly language to C++, Java and .NET. Recent clients have included Emmy award-winning visual effects company Foundation Imaging, Arizona State University's Institute for Studies in the Arts, and the FlashForward conference Web sites for London, San Francisco and New York.

Simon is the author of *Building Web Applications with Dreamweaver MX* from O'Reilly & Associates, and he created the Learning UltraDev CD-ROM for Lynda.com.

As a trainer, Simon has taught advanced Flash and advanced Dreamweaver classes at Ojai Digital Arts Center and Stanford University's New Media Academy. He was a featured speaker at Macromedia UCON 2001, the FlashForward 2001 conferences in New York and Amsterdam, and has been featured in *Computer Graphics World* and the *Wall Street Journal Online*.

Simon created the inaugural Web Graphics program for SIGGRAPH 2002, the world's premier conference on computer graphics and interactive techniques.

Currently, Simon works on `www.clingfish.com`, creating extensions that make it easier, faster, and smoother to build database-driven Web sites.

Chapter Contributors

Simon Allardice

Andrew Bazar

Véronique Brossier

Jen and Peter deHaan

Dermot Glennon

David Lee

Scott Mebberson

William Moschella

For a list of chapters by title, refer to Contents at a Glance. For a list of contact and background information by author's last name, refer to Appendix D.

Guest Experts

Richard Bazley

Scott Brown

Sandro Corsaro

Brock deChristopher

Jen deHaan

Doug Downey

MD Dundon

Shane Elliott

Chris Honselaar

Justin Jamieson

Eric Jordan

Craig Kroeger

Timothy Lo

Colin Moock

Dorian Nisinson

Jane Nisselson

Vish Parameswaran

Darrel Plant

Todd Purgason

Arena Reed

Mike Richards

James Robertson

Gregg Spiridellis

Bill Turner

Bentley Wolfe

Sascha Wolter

For a list of guest expert tutorials by title, refer to Tutorials at a Glance. For a list of contact and background information by expert's last name, refer to Appendix D.

Special Thanks

Thanks to Tom Winkler of doodie.com for his expert animation examples in Chapter 10 and to Jonathan Brzyski for creating illustrations for the Flash game in Chapter 33. Last but not least, thanks to Jen deHaan for being cheerful, reliable and willing to do so many vital tasks that would have otherwise slipped through the cracks.

Credits

Senior Acquisitions Editor
Michael Roney

Project Editor
Mica Johnson

Development and Copy Editors
Eric Dafforn, Elizabeth Kuball,
Kenyon Brown

Technical Editor
Simon Allardice

Editorial Manager
Rev Mengle

Vice President and Executive Group Publisher
Richard Swadley

Vice President and Publisher
Barry Pruett

Project Coordinator
Regina Snyder

Graphics and Production Specialists
Beth Brooks, Sean Decker,
LeAndra Johnson, Kristin McMullan,
Laurie Petrone, Janet Seib,
Julie Trippetti

Quality Control Technician
Andy Hollandbeck, Susan Moritz,
Carl Pierce, Linda Quigley

Senior Permissions Editor
Carmen Krikorian

Media Development Specialists
Marisa Pearman, Megan Decraene

Proofreading and Indexing
TECHBOOKS Production Services

Cover Image
Anthony Bunyan

Special Help
Jen deHaan, Beth Taylor,
Diana Conover, Tim Borek

This version of the *Flash Bible* is based, in part, on ideas and content originally developed by Jon Warren Lentz, jwl@flash-guru.com.

*To my mom...for letting me believe that I know
what's best, and for backing me up when I don't.*

RJR

*To Bob for teaching me how much can get done
when you work all night and get up early.*

*To Rob for making work so much fun,
and for believing that the whole is
greater than the sum of the parts.*

SD

Foreword

Flash has turned the Web into the ultimate public access station. From desktops every-where, people are creating content that is professional, personal, political, humorous, and occasionally just plain weird. What do you think of when you think of Macromedia Flash? Some obvious answers include highly interactive Web sites or cartoon-like animation. But you only have to browse the Web for a short while to find many other answers.

Although a whole range of incredible content is created entirely in Flash, developers can easily leverage their skills with other image creation tools and media to enhance their Flash projects. Flash shows up in database-driven Web sites, scientific visualizations, educational applications, all manner of games, experimental animation, and more.

All of this makes it obvious, at least to me, that there is something unique about this tool that has encouraged its unprecedented influence on media production. Part of the fun is to see what happens next, which is where you come in.

If you are just getting started, you will soon learn the addictive nature of making things that not only look good, but also work. The first button that "clicks" is probably the most satisfy-ing, but the second, third and fourth also give a feeling of accomplishment; and after you have that down, basically it just gets cooler from there.

If you have just upgraded from Flash 5, you're probably realizing how much more there is for you to know, not only in Flash MX, but in general. Flash has continued to mature from an effi-cient animation program to a sophisticated authoring environment for multimedia. As such, Flash designers have the ability to make rich, multi-layered work using sound, video, as well as animation and interactivity. As Flash expands to handle many of today's most compelling media formats, the designer too must learn to use these formats in an efficient and engaging manner. The *Flash MX Bible* covers the creation, optimization, and management of these media types. Many of the practices discussed in this book are useful not only as they pertain to Flash MX, but to media acquisition and content creation in general.

Flash is being used for many purposes, some which may not have been anticipated or even imagined by its original makers. And you now have the information to start using Flash MX effectively and creatively for your own purposes. In 45 chapters, the *Flash MX Bible* covers every contingency, including information you don't even know you need now, but which will prove invaluable when you reach the next level in your project.

Dena Slothower
Academic Technology Specialist
Stanford University

Preface

In 1997, Macromedia acquired a small Web graphics program, FutureSplash, from a company named FutureWave. FutureSplash was a quirky little program with the astounding ability to generate compact, vector-based graphics and animations for delivery over the Web. With Macromedia's embrace, Flash blossomed. Now Flash has obtained ubiquity. The Flash Player plug-in ships with most major browsers and operating systems. Now Flash graphics appear all over the Web, and the number of Flash users continues to increase at an astonishing pace.

As the Web-surfing public and the development community have continued to demand more of Flash, Macromedia has delivered. The MX Studio family offers unparalleled support for multimedia production of all shapes and sizes. The tight integration of specialized programs makes it easier than ever to get the best out of each program, while maintaining a seamless, optimized workflow. Flash MX is by far the biggest leap in the evolution of Flash to date. If you liked Flash 5, you're in big trouble because you will be infatuated with Flash MX. If you stuck with Flash 4 (like certain stubborn animators we know), then you can't afford to miss the new features of Flash MX that make production so intuitive and efficient — you'll wonder how you survived before. The Flash drawing tools continue to mature — pixel-level snapping and the new Free transform and Transform fill tools are just some of the MX enhancements that empower illustrators and animators alike to create sophisticated effects with greater ease.

Flash MX has greatly expanded the interactive and programmatic features of Flash movies. Flash movies can communicate directly with server-side scripts and programs, using standard URL-encoded variables or XML-formatted structures. Sounds can be imported and exported as MP3 audio for high-quality music on the Web at the smallest file sizes. Flash MX now supports nearly every file format you'll ever come across, and native JPEG loading streamlines production and maintenance of dynamic high-volume image sites. The evolution of Smart Clips has resulted in some exciting possibilities for Flash users of all skill levels. Flash MX components offer all the flexibility and portability of Smart Clips, but the ActionScript options are more extensive and easy to access and customize.

The Flash MX interface is now consistent with other Macromedia MX products, with tool options and other editing features contained in newly streamlined panels. Evidence of the dominance of the Flash format can be found in the wide range of third-party developers creating applications that output to the Flash movie format (.swf files). Flash has fulfilled its promise of becoming the central application for generating hot, low-bandwidth, interactive content for delivery on the Web and beyond.

Is there any other Flash book for you?

The *Flash*™ *MX Bible* is the most comprehensive and exhaustive reference on Flash. It helps you get started on your first day with the program and will still be a valuable resource when you've attained mastery of the program. When you're looking for clues on how to integrate Flash with other programs so that you can deliver unique and compelling content in the Flash format, you'll know where to turn.

✦ Holistic coverage of Flash: The first two parts of the book are entirely dedicated to project planning and getting familiar with the Flash interface. Parts III and IV explain how to integrate animations and other media files into your Flash movies. Parts V through VIII gradually introduce you to the power of ActionScript. Finally, Part IX covers other programs and techniques that will enhance your Flash projects.

✦ Flash is not just one tool: You can think of Flash as a multitasking application. It's an illustration program, an image and sound editor, an animation machine, and a scripting engine, all rolled into one. In this book, we look at each of these uses of Flash and explain how all the features work together.

✦ This is a real-world book: We've worked hard to ensure that our lessons, examples, and explanations are based on professional production conventions. We have also continued the use of expert tutorials to bring you tips and techniques from some of the top names in the Flash industry, so that you can benefit from their specialized expertise.

✦ The CD-ROM that accompanies this book contains many of the source Flash project files (.fla), with original artwork and ActionScript for the examples and lessons in the book. It also includes 14 additional expert tutorials and the section of the book dedicated to optimizing and troubleshooting Flash movies. To help you get started, we've also included trial versions of Flash MX, as well as many of the Flash-friendly applications and plug-ins discussed in this edition.

✦ The book's Web site: In order to create a forum for the delivery of updates, notes, and additional sample files, we have established a Web site specifically for the *Flash MX Bible*: www.flashMXbible.com

At the Web site, you'll find new material and corrections that may be added after the book goes to print and a detailed evaluation form for the *Flash MX Bible*. We invite you to contribute your comments and suggestions for this edition, so that we can continue to improve the material.

How to Get the Most Out of This Book

Here are two things to know so you can get the most out of this book:

First, regarding menu and keyboard commands, here's the convention for indicating that you're going to need to select a command from a menu: The menu and command are separated by an arrow symbol. For example, if we tell you to select the default panel layout from the Flash application menu, the instructions will say to choose Window ➪ Panel Sets ➪ Default Layout.

Second, jump in anywhere. Although this book was written to take a beginner by the hand, starting from page one, you can also use it as a reference. Use the index and the table of contents to find what you're looking for, and just go there. If you already know Flash and want to get some details on sound, for example, just go to the Integrating Media Files with Flash section.

Icons: What Do They Mean?

Although the icons are pretty standard and self-explanatory (they have their names written on them!), here's a brief explanation of what they are and what they mean.

Tip

Tips offer you extra information that further explains a given topic or technique, often suggesting alternatives or workarounds to a listed procedure.

Note

Notes provide supplementary information to the text, shedding light on background processes or miscellaneous options that aren't crucial to the basic understanding of the material.

Caution

When you see the Caution icon, make sure you're following along closely to the tips and techniques being discussed. Some external applications may not work exactly the same with Flash on different operating systems.

Cross-Reference

If you want to find related information to a given topic in another chapter, look for the cross-reference icons.

New Feature

The New Feature icons point out any differences between Flash MX and previous versions of Flash.

RIP

The RIP icons note features or techniques that are deprecated or no longer relevant to Flash MX.

On the CD-ROM

This icon indicates that the CD-ROM contains a related file and points you to the folder location.

How This Book Is Organized

We thought the *Flash 5 Bible* was about as comprehensive as one book could be, but Flash MX has introduced so many new features and Flash production has matured enough to warrant two Bibles. In addition to the expanded *Flash MX Bible*, Robert Reinhardt has co-authored a *Flash MX ActionScript Bible* with Joey Lott, to cover more advanced Flash techniques. Even so, nearly every page of the *Flash MX Bible* has new information, and we still had to move some material to the CD-ROM.

This book has been written in a format that gives you access to need-to-know information very easily in every section (or Part) of the book. If you are completely new to Flash, then you'll want to read Parts I through V. After you have developed a familiarity with the Flash interface, then you can proceed to VII and VIII. Based on reader feedback that there was too much of a "leap" from the intro topics to the advanced topics in the Flash 5 Bible, we've added more step-by-step descriptions of real Flash projects. These sections of the book guide you through the production process, helping you to apply ActionScript and production techniques that may be new to you.

If you've already used Flash 5, then you may want to review the changes to the Flash MX interface in Part I, and then jump right into other specific parts to learn more about character animation, ActionScript, creating artwork and content in other applications, and integrating Flash with HTML. Part IX is especially useful if you have a favorite application such as Dreamweaver or Director in which you want to use Flash movies.

Part I — An Introduction to Flash Web Production

The first part of this book explores the Flash file format and how Flash MX fits into the evolution of the program (Chapter 1), explains the context in which Flash movies interact on the Web (Chapter 2), and gives an overview of multimedia planning and some specific techniques and suggestions that will make your Flash project development less painful and more productive (Chapter 3).

Part II — Mastering the Flash Environment

This part gives you all the information you need to feel comfortable in the Flash MX authoring environment. Get an introduction to, and some tips for customizing, the new Flash MX UI (Chapter 4). Learn where to find your drawing tools and how to use them efficiently (Chapter 5), then discover all the ways that Flash helps you to organize and optimize project assets (Chapter 6). Learn key color concepts relevant to multimedia production and find out why Flash MX has the best color tools yet (Chapter 7). Jump into using all the amazing new text editing tools and see how to get the best looking type and the smallest file sizes in your Flash projects (Chapter 8). Finally, learn how to modify text and graphics to get the most out of your Flash artwork (Chapter 9).

Part III — Creating Animation and Effects

After you've learned how to find your way around the Flash interface and to create static graphics, you can get some perspective on animation strategies (Chapter 10), learn to make things move, work with different symbol types to optimize your animation workflow (Chapter 11), use layers for organization and special effects (Chapter 12), and get special production tips for professional character animation and broadcast-quality graphics (Chapter 13). Finally, learn the process for tailoring animation output to a variety of viewing environments (Chapter 14).

Part IV — Integrating Media Files with Flash

Now that you're fluent in the Flash workspace, take your projects to the next level by adding sound, special graphics, and video assets. In Chapter 15, you learn the basics of digital sound, see which file formats can be imported into Flash, and how to import, optimize, and export high-quality sound for different types of projects. Chapter 16 gives an overview of how to bring vector or raster artwork from other programs into Flash and how to protect image quality while optimizing your Flash movies. Chapter 17 introduces the exciting new video embedding features of Flash MX.

Part V – Adding Basic Interactivity to Flash Movies

Learn how to start using Flash actions to create interactive and responsive presentations. Get oriented in the Flash MX Actions panel, which has an improved interface (Chapter 18). Use ActionScript in Flash movies to control internal elements on multiple timelines, such as nested Movie Clips (Chapter 19). Use some of the new features of Flash MX, including components and named anchor keyframes to create fast, clean interfaces for multipart presentations that also include some of the new Accessibility options (Chapter 20).

Part VI – Distributing Flash Movies

Finally, you need to learn how to export (or publish) your Flash presentations to the SWF file format for use on a Web page, or within presentations on other formats. Chapter 21 details every option in the Publish Settings of Flash MX, as well providing tips for optimizing your Flash movies in order to achieve smaller file sizes for faster download performance. If you prefer to hand-code your HTML, then read Chapter 22, which describes how to use the `<EMBED>` and `<OBJECT>` tags, how to load Flash movies into framesets, and how to create plug-in detection systems for your Flash movies. If you want to find out how to create a Flash standalone projector, or use the Flash standalone player, then check out Chapter 23.

Part VII – Approaching ActionScript

Learn the basic elements of ActionScript syntax (Chapter 24), and how to use ActionScript to control properties and methods of `MovieClip` objects (Chapter 25). Learn about making functions and arrays (Chapter 26), detecting Movie Clip collisions, and using the `Color` and `Sound` objects for dynamic control of movie elements (Chapter 27). Flash MX has broadened the possibilities for dynamic data loading. Get an introduction to runtime MP3 and JPEG loading features as well as how to share and load assets in multiple SWF files (Chapter 28). Find out how to use the pre-built components that ship with Flash MX to enhance your Flash projects (Chapter 29). Start creating Flash forms that send data with the new `LoadVars` object and learn to integrate XML data with Flash movies (Chapter 30). Take control of text fields using HTML tags and the new `TextFormat` object (Chapter 31). Part VII ends with two detailed chapters dedicated to building real Flash projects from the ground up (Chapters 32 and 33).

Part VIII – Optimizing and Troubleshooting Flash Movies

Part VIII is in PDF format on the CD-ROM in the Bonus_Chapters folder. When you've put all the pieces together and realize you need to drastically reduce your files' size, refer to Chapter 34 for a quick review of all the techniques you can use to optimize your files. As you start to delve into more complex ActionScript, Chapter 35 will help you to work efficiently and keep your code clean. If you've done everything right and still run into production snags with your final project, Chapter 36 will give you some tips on how to isolate and analyze the problem.

Part IX—Expanding Flash

Every multimedia designer uses Flash with some other graphics, sound, and authoring application to create a unique workflow that solves the problems of daily interactive project development. Part IX shows you how to manage raster graphics and vector graphics and how to create content in popular applications such as Macromedia Fireworks, FreeHand, and Adobe Photoshop. This part also covers topics relevant to Flash production using SoundForge, Discreet 3ds, Dreamweaver MX, and Director—just to name a few. Chapter 44 is dedicated to examples of Flash movies that work with ColdFusion MX to process user input (such as guest books and feedback forms). In Chapter 45, some of the production issues specific to developing Flash content for the Pocket PC are discussed.

Appendixes

In the printed appendixes, you'll find a table of common and updated Flash MX keyboard shortcuts (Appendix A), information on Digital Sound Basics that explains sound sampling rates and bit-depths (Appendix B), directions for Using the CD-ROM (Appendix C), and a listing of contact and bio information for the contributors and guest experts (Appendix D). There are also three Bonus Appendixes that you will find on the CD-ROM that include a listing of Flash-Compatible Media Formats (CD-BAA), a tutorial on Multilingual Content in Flash by Vish Parmaswaren (CD-BAB), and a comprehensive list of Flash Player–Compatible Actions (CD-BAC).

Getting in Touch with Us

The official Web site for the Flash MX Bible is at www.flashMXbible.com, but you can find additional information, resources, and feedback from the authors and other readers at: www.flashsupport.com.

If you have a great tip or idea that you want to share with us, we'd like to hear from you. You can also send comments about the book to: robert@theMakers.com or snow@theMakers.com.

Also, check Appendix D for more information on contacting this book's various contributors, guest experts, and our brilliant technical editor.

Macromedia Wants to Help You

The latest version of Flash is more powerful, has more robust capabilities, and is easier to use than any previous version of Flash. It's also the best program for creating compact, vector-based content and interactive presentations. But we know that Macromedia is already planning how to make the next version even better.

Macromedia has created a new Feature Request form to make it easier to process suggestions and requests from Flash users. If you have an idea or feature request for the next version, let the folks at Macromedia know. You can find the online form at: www.macromedia.com/software/flash/contact/wishlist.

The simple fact is this: If more users request a specific feature or improvement, it's more likely that Macromedia will implement it.

To support the Flash community Macromedia has created a searchable registry that allows clients to find Flash developers by location or by services offered. To create a custom developer profile, register yourself at: www.macromedia.com/locator.

Regardless of your geographic location, you always have access to the global Flash community for support and the latest information through the Macromedia Online Forums: http://webforums.macromedia.com/flash.

For inspiration and motivation check out the Site of the Day, weekly features and case studies at: www.macromedia.com/showcase.

Acknowledgments

This book would not have been possible without the dedication and talent of many people. We are grateful for the added breadth and depth the tutorials from our guest experts bring to this third edition. First and foremost, we would like to thank the Flash development community. In our combined experiences in research and multimedia production, we haven't seen another community that has been so open, friendly, and willing to share advanced tips and techniques. It has been gratifying to be involved as the community keeps expanding and to see the innovators in the first wave of Flash development become mentors to a whole new generation. Thank you all for continuing to inspire and challenge audiences and each other with the possibilities for Flash.

We would like to thank everyone at John Wiley & Sons and Hungry Minds (formerly IDG Books Worldwide) who supported us as we researched and added page after page after page. Rev Mengle, our editorial manager, was resourceful in navigating the many production hurdles that come with a book this size. As always, our endless gratitude goes to Michael Roney, our acquisitions editor. Steadfast, optimistic, and supportive, Mike was willing to trust us even as we pushed deadlines to overhaul a best-selling book.

Simon Allardice, our technical editor, was everything we hoped he would be, and more — thorough, concise, fast, friendly, funny, and, most importantly, committed to making this the best edition yet. He is one of those very rare people who balance advanced technical knowledge with an understanding and concern for others just beginning to learn. Every comment and correction he made was with our readers in mind.

David Fugate, our literary agent at Waterside Productions, has been through every revision of the Flash Bible series, and honestly none of them could have happened without him — at least, not without loss of life and limb. David, you made every step just a little bit easier and kept the light at the end of the tunnel in sight. Although we know a few people who get by without an agent, we've noticed that they tend to age faster than everyone else.

Of course, this book about Flash wouldn't even exist without the hard work of the people at Macromedia who make it all possible. Many thanks to the developers, engineers, and support staff at Macromedia, especially Jeremy Clark, Gary Grossman, Peter Santangeli, and Erica Norton, who answered our questions during the development of Flash. We would have had a hard time researching this book without software assistance from Jennipher Tchejeyan and Henriette Cohn. We're also indebted to all our intrepid fellow developers and authors, who helped us to get our bearings in early versions of Flash MX.

Tutorials at a Glance

Chapter tutorials

1: Designing for Usability, *by Scott Brown* 57
2: Interface Design, *by Eric Jordan* 64
3: Using Miniml Fonts (sidebar), *by Craig Kroeger* 238
4: JibJab.com's Collage Animation Workflow, *by Gregg Spiridellis* 362
5: Flash Character Design Strategies, *by Sandro Corsaro* 373
6: Lip-Syncing Cartoons, *by Bill Turner* 380
7: Creating Printable Paper Airplanes, *by Mike Richards* 786
8: Using Embedded Fonts with Components, *by Jen deHaan* 845
9: Introduction to XML and Flash, *by Chris Honselaar* 862
10: Using XML Sockets with a Flash Movie, *by Shane Elliott* 865
11: Unifying the Web, *by Colin Moock* 870
12: Leveraging Fireworks to Streamline Production, *by Scott Brown* 950
13: Streamlined Workflow: FreeHand and Flash, *by Todd Purgason* 986
14: Using Propellerhead's Rebirth to Create Loops for Flash, *by Justin Jamieson* 1012

Bonus tutorials (on the CD-ROM)

1: Storyboarding and Planning Interactivity, *by MD Dundon* CDBT-1
2: The Human Interface, *by Jane Nisselson* CDBT-11
3: Creating Faux 3D, *by Dorian Nisinson* CDBT-19
4: 2D Character Animation, *by Richard Bazley* CDBT-29
5: Comparing Video Compression, *by Jen deHaan* CDBT-37
6: Filling the Browser Window Using the <FRAMESET> Tag, *by Colin Moock* CDBT-43
7: Scriptless Flash Player Detection, *by Sascha Wolter* CDBT-47
8: Complex Hit Detection on the Z Axis, *by James Robertson* CDBT-57
9: Dynamic Sound Design, *by Brock deChristopher* CDBT-61
10: Animation on Bézier Curves, *by Darrel Plant* CDBT-63
11: Interfacing Miva with Flash Movies, *by Timothy Lo* CDBT-69
12: Combining Flash with the Natural Beauty of Painter 7, *by Arena Reed* CDBT-75
13: Animation in CorelDRAW 10 Graphics Suite, *by Doug Downey* CDBT-83
14: Using FreeHand with Flash, *by Bentley Wolfe* CDBT-93

Contents at a Glance

Foreword xi
Preface xiii
Acknowledgments xxi

Part I: An Introduction to Flash Web Production 1
QuickStart: Flash in a Flash 3
Chapter 1: Understanding the Flash Framework 27
Chapter 2: Exploring Web Technologies 39
Chapter 3: Planning Flash Projects 49

Part II: Mastering the Flash Environment 83
Chapter 4: Interface Fundamentals 85
Chapter 5: Drawing in Flash 123
Chapter 6: Symbols, Instances, and the Library 163
Chapter 7: Applying Color 193
Chapter 8: Working with Text 219
Chapter 9: Modifying Graphics 253

Part III: Creating Animation and Effects 293
Chapter 10: Science of Motion 295
Chapter 11: Timeline Animation Fundamentals 311
Chapter 12: Applying Layer Types 341
Chapter 13: Character Animation Techniques 361
Chapter 14: Exporting Animation 391

Part IV: Integrating Media Files with Flash 417
Chapter 15: Adding Sound 419
Chapter 16: Importing Artwork 451
Chapter 17: Embedding Video 489

Part V: Adding Basic Interactivity to Flash Movies 529
Chapter 18: Understanding Actions and Event Handlers 531
Chapter 19: Navigating Flash Timelines 553
Chapter 20: Making Your First Flash MX Project 581

Part VI: Distributing Flash Movies **607**

Chapter 21: Publishing Flash Movies 609
Chapter 22: Integrating Flash Content with HTML 635
Chapter 23: Using the Flash Player and Projector 659

Part VII: Approaching Actionscript **671**

Chapter 24: Knowing the Nuts and Bolts of Code 673
Chapter 25: Controlling Movie Clips 705
Chapter 26: Using Functions and Arrays 741
Chapter 27: Interacting with Movie Clips 763
Chapter 28: Sharing and Loading Assets 793
Chapter 29: Using Components 827
Chapter 30: Sending Data In and Out of Flash 849
Chapter 31: Applying HTML and Text Field Formatting 873
Chapter 32: Creating a Portfolio Site in Flash MX 885
Chapter 33: Creating a Game in Flash 919

Part VIII: Optimizing and Troubleshooting Flash Movies **937**

Bonus Chapter 34: Optimizing Your Movies CDBC-1
Bonus Chapter 35: Getting Your Code Under Control CDBC-23
Bonus Chapter 36: Solving Problems in Your Movies CDBC-43

Part IX: Expanding Flash **939**

Chapter 37: Working with Raster Graphics 941
Chapter 38: Working with Vector Graphics 969
Chapter 39: Working with Audio Applications 997
Chapter 40: Working with 3D Graphics 1019
Chapter 41: Working with QuickTime 1057
Chapter 42: Working with Dreamweaver MX 1079
Chapter 43: Working with Director 1097
Chapter 44: Working with ColdFusion MX 1117
Chapter 45: Making Movies for the Pocket PC 1149

Part X: Appendixes **1163**

Appendix A: Keyboard Shortcuts 1165

Appendix B: Digital Sound Basics 1171

Appendix C: Using the CD-ROM? 1179

Appendix D: Contact and Bibliography Information 1185

Bonus Appendix A: Flash-Compatible Media Formats CDBA-1

Bonus Appendix B: Multilingual Content in Flash CDBA-11

Bonus Appendix C: Flash Player–Compatible Actions CDBA-25

Index 1195

End-User License Agreement 1271

Contents

• •

Foreword xi

Preface xiii

Acknowledgments xxi

Part I: An Introduction to Flash Web Production   1

QuickStart: Flash in a Flash 3

Feature Roundup 3
Examples for Designers 4
    Using templates 5
    Components and the Property Inspector 8
    Quick Animation 9
Examples for Developers 12
    The ComboBox Component 12
    Customizable Actions panel 15
    Named anchors 17
    Dynamic bitmap and sound loading 18
    Streaming video 19
    Scriptable text fields 23
    ActionScript event model and the drawing API 24
    Summary 26

Chapter 1: Understanding the Flash Framework 27

It's a (Flash) MX World 27
    The topography of Flash MX 29
    File types in Flash MX 29
The Many Faces of Flash MX 33
    Bitmap handler 34
    Vector-based drawing program 34
    Vector-based animator 34
    Video compressor 34
    Multimedia authoring program 35
    Animation sequencer 35
    Programming and database front end 36
Summary 37

Chapter 2: Exploring Web Technologies 39

Contextualizing Flash in the Internet Evolution 39
    High expectations for Web experiences 39
    To Flash or not to Flash? 40
    Alternative methods of multimedia authoring 43

Exploring Companion Technologies 45
   HTML is here to stay 45
   Client-side scripting using JavaScript 45
Recognizing Project Potential 46
   Linear presentations 46
   Interactive presentations 46
   Data-driven presentations 47
   Data-driven applications 47
Summary 47

Chapter 3: Planning Flash Projects **49**

Workflow Basics 49
   Phase I: Establishing the concept and goals 50
   Phase II: Producing, testing, and staging the presentation 62
Using Visio to Create Flowcharts 72
   Creating an organizational chart 72
   Making a process chart for a Web site 76
   Mapping the structure of a live site 79
Summary 81

Part II: Mastering the Flash Environment   **83**

Chapter 4: Interface Fundamentals **85**

Getting Started 85
   Welcome to Flash MX 85
   Help menu options 86
   The MX interface on Macintosh and Windows 87
   MX introduces the Property inspector 90
Managing Windows and Panels 91
   Contextual menus 93
   Focus: Making panels or windows active 93
   Keyboard shortcuts 94
The Toolbox 96
   Controlling the Toolbox 96
   Reading the Toolbox 97
   Using tool options 97
The Document Window 98
   Controlling the Document window 99
   Reading the Document window 100
   Using scenes 101
   Using Document window options 103
The Timeline Window 106
   Controlling the Timeline window 106
   Reading the Timeline 107
   Editing frames and layers 111
   Using Frame View options 119
Printing 121
Summary 122

Chapter 5: Drawing in Flash 123

Using the Primary Drawing Tools 123
    Geometric shapes 124
    Freehand lines and strokes 126
Optimizing Drawings 134
Putting Selection Tools to Work 134
    The Arrow tool 135
    The Lasso tool 142
    The Subselection tool 144
Creating Precise Lines with the Pen Tool 146
Choosing Colors 149
Choosing Line Styles 151
    Hairline 153
    Solid 153
    Dashed 154
    Dotted 154
    Ragged 154
    Stippled 154
    Hatched 154
Designing and Aligning Elements 155
Drawing Panels 155
    The Info panel 155
    The Align panel 157
    The Transform panel 158
    The Edit menu 159
Summary 161

Chapter 6: Symbols, Instances, and the Library 163

Understanding the Document Library 163
    Reading the Library 165
    Organizing the Library 169
Working with Shared Assets and Fonts 170
Defining Content Types 170
    Raw data 171
    Groups 171
    Native symbols 171
    Imported media elements 172
Editing Symbols 175
    Editing a symbol in Symbol Editing mode 175
    Editing a symbol in a new window 175
    Editing a symbol in place 175
    Editing symbols in the Library 175
    Returning to the Main Timeline or scene 176
Modifying Instance Properties 177
    Applying color effects to symbol instances 177
    Changing the symbol behavior of an instance 179
    Swapping symbols 179
Building Nested Symbol Structures 180
    Converting a raw shape into a Graphic symbol 180
    Using Graphic symbols in a button 181

Animating Graphic symbols in a Movie Clip 183
Adding a Movie Clip to a Button symbol 184
Modifying a Movie Clip instance 185
Using the Movie Explorer 188
Filtering buttons 188
The Display list 188
The Movie Explorer Options menu 190
The contextual menu 191
Summary 192

Chapter 7: Applying Color **193**

Introducing Color Basics 193
Discussing Web-Safe color issues 194
Using hexadecimal values 195
Using custom Web-Safe colors 195
Using color effectively 196
Working in the Color Swatches Panel 200
Color Swatches panel options 201
Importing custom palettes 203
Using the Color Mixer Panel 205
Adjusting fill and stroke transparency 208
Working with gradient fills 209
Controlling gradient fill colors 211
Using alpha settings with gradients 213
Selecting bitmap fills 215
Working with Droppers, Paint Buckets, and Ink Bottles 216
Summary 217

Chapter 8: Working with Text **219**

Considering Typography 219
Text Field Types in Flash 220
Static text blocks 221
Editable text fields: Dynamic and Input 223
The Text Tool and Property Inspector 224
The Text tool 224
Setting text attributes in the Property inspector 227
Font Export and Display 233
Specifying device fonts 234
The Use Device Fonts option 235
Troubleshooting font display 235
Font substitution 236
Font Symbols and Shared Font Libraries 240
Creating a Font symbol 241
Modifying Text 248
Sampling and sharing text attributes 249
Converting text into vector shapes 249
Summary 251

Chapter 9: Modifying Graphics **253**

Sampling and Switching Fills and Strokes 254
The Eyedropper tool 254
The Ink Bottle tool 256

The Paint Bucket tool 257
Using the Paint Bucket Gap Size option 259
Using the Paint Bucket Lock Fill option 259
Transforming Fills 260
Adjusting the center point with the Transform Fill tool 262
Rotating a fill with the Transform Fill tool 262
Adjusting scale with the Transform Fill tool 262
Skewing a bitmap fill with the Transform Fill tool 263
Transform Fill Used for Effects 264
Modify Shape Menu Commands 265
Lines to Fills 265
Expand Fill 267
Soften Fill Edges 268
Free Transform Commands and Options 270
The Transform panel 270
The Modify Transform menu 270
The Free Transform tool 271
Transforming shapes and symbols, text, or groups 272
Modifying Item Types 275
Stacking order 275
Grouping 276
Applying Break Apart 277
About the Magic Wand option 281
Tracing bitmaps 282
Using Distribute to Layers 284
Working with Compound Shapes 286
Using Advanced Color Effects for Symbol Instances 288
Relative color control 289
Absolute color control 289
Summary 290

Part III: Creating Animation and Effects   293

Chapter 10: Science of Motion 295

Establishing Ground Rules 295
Defining Variables 296
The environment 297
The materials 297
The motion 298
Adding Personality 299
Manipulating Perception and Illusion 300
Viewpoint, framing, and depth 301
Anticipation 304
Secondary motion 305
Understanding the Laws of Nature 306
Law #1: Inertia 307
Law #2: Acceleration 307
Law #3: Action/reaction force pairs 308
Summary 310

Chapter 11: Timeline Animation Fundamentals 311

Basic Methods of Flash Animation 311
Frame-by-Frame Animation 312
    Adding keyframes 313
    Creating frame-by-frame animation 314
Modifying Multi-Frame Sequences 314
    Editing multiple frames 315
    Onion skinning 316
Tweening 317
    Shape tweening 318
    Adding Shape Hints 322
    Motion tweening 325
Integrating Multiple Animation Sequences 330
    Moving tweens onto symbol timelines 330
Organizing Symbol Instances on the Main Timeline 333
Reusing and Modifying Symbol Instances 335
Summary 339

Chapter 12: Applying Layer Types 341

Guide Layers 342
Motion Guides 344
    Applying a Motion Guide 344
    Adding control to animation along a path 347
    Using Orient to path 347
    Registration and center point alignment 347
Mask Layers 348
    Masking with a filled shape 349
    Masking with a group 351
    Masking with a symbol instance 351
    Masking text 352
Motion Guides and Movie Clip Masks 355
Summary 359

Chapter 13: Character Animation Techniques 361

Working with Large File Sizes 361
The Storyboard 364
Some Cartoon Animation Basics 366
    Expressing motion and emotion 366
    Anticipation 367
    Weight 367
    Overlapping actions 367
    Blurring to simulate motion 368
Animator's Keys and Inbetweening 368
    Walk cycles (or walk loops) 369
    Repeaters 371
    Types of walks 372
Coloring the art 372

Flash Tweening 376
    Panning 377
    Instance swapping 377
Lip-Syncing 378
    Shape morphing is not for lip-syncing 379
    Expression and lip-syncing 379
    Lip-sync tricks 379
    Syncing with music and sound effects 380
Backgrounds and Scenery 384
    Bitmaps 385
    QuickTime limitations 385
    Building layered backgrounds in Photoshop 385
    Flash Mask layers 386
    Long pans 386
    Multiplane pans 387
    Blurring to simulate depth 387
Finishing Up 388
    Final output 388
Summary 389

Chapter 14: Exporting Animation **391**

High-Quality Video Output from Flash 391
A Quick Video Primer 392
    A brief history of digital video 392
Adjusting Flash Movies for Video Output 395
Creating Sequences from Flash Movies 401
    Export process in Flash 402
    Uses of each sequence format 404
Creating AVI Files on Windows 406
    Dimensions 407
    Video format 407
    Sound format 407
    Video compression 407
Exporting Audio from a Flash Document 408
Importing Image Sequences into After Effects 409
Summary 416

Part IV: Integrating Media Files with Flash   417

Chapter 15: Adding Sound **419**

Sound File Import Formats 419
Sound Export Formats 421
Importing Sounds into Flash 423
Assigning a Sound to a Button 425
Adding Sound to the Timeline 427

Organizing sounds on the Timeline 428
Enhanced viewing of sound layers 428
Organizing sound layers with a layer folder 429
Synchronizing Audio to Animations 429
Event 429
Start 429
Stop 430
Stream 430
Stopping Sounds 431
Stopping an Event sound 431
Stopping a single instance of a Stream sound 433
Stopping all sounds 433
Editing Audio in Flash 434
Sound-editing controls 434
Applying effects from the Effect menu of the Property inspector 435
Sound Optimization Overview 437
Publish Settings for Audio 438
The Set options 439
Supporting audio and MP3 playback 442
Fine-Tuning Sound Settings in the Library 443
Settings for audio in the Library 443
Combining methods for controlling sounds 445
Final Sound Advice and Pointers 445
VBR (Variable Bit Rate) MP3 445
Optimizing sounds for bandwidth usage 446
Extracting a sound from a FLA editor file 449
Summary 450

Chapter 16: Importing Artwork 451

Defining Vectors and Bitmaps 451
Knowing the File Formats for Import to Flash 453
Preparing Bitmaps 456
Preserving Bitmap Quality 458
Importing and Copying Bitmaps 459
Importing a bitmap file into Flash 460
Importing sequences 461
Copying and pasting a bitmap into Flash 461
Setting Bitmap Properties 462
Being Prepared for Common Problems 464
Bitmap shift 466
Cross-browser consistency 466
JPEG rotation 466
Using the Bitmap Buttons in the Property Inspector 467
Swap 467
Edit 467
Making Sense of Bitmap Compression 467
24-bit or 32-bit lossless source files 468
8-bit lossless source files 468
Source files with lossy compression 470
Converting Rasters to Vectors 471

Using External Vector Graphics 473
Importing Vector Artwork 474
Importing Groups and Layers 475
    Importing Macromedia Fireworks files 476
    Importing Macromedia FreeHand files 476
    Importing Adobe Illustrator files 478
Optimizing Vectors 482
    Tracing complex vector artwork 482
    Converting text to outlines 483
    Optimizing curves 484
    Replacing blends with gradient fills 485
Summary 487

Chapter 17: Embedding Video 489

Preparing a Video File 489
    Garbage in, garbage out 489
    Editing footage 495
    Choosing an import format 496
Importing the Video 498
    Linked versus embedded video 498
    Spark compression options 499
    Adjusting audio compression 502
    Compressing video with Flash MX 502
Using Video in a Timeline 504
    Controlling playback of video 504
    Placing and controlling video within a Movie Clip 507
Publishing Flash Movies with Video 508
    Storing video in a separate Flash movie 509
    Using named anchors with video timelines 512
Using Sorenson Squeeze for Flash Video 514
    Choosing a Flash output file type 515
    Choosing a compression setting 517
    Customizing a Compression Setting 520
    Compressing video with Sorenson Spark Pro 525
Summary 528

Part V: Adding Basic Interactivity to Flash Movies   529

Chapter 18: Understanding Actions and Event Handlers 531

Actions and Event Handlers 531
    What is ActionScript? 532
    Setting up the Actions panel 532
    Normal versus Expert mode 533
Your First Five Actions 536
    goto 536
    play 539
    stop 540
    stopAllSounds 540
    getURL 540

Making Actions Happen with Event Handlers 542
   Combining an action with an event handler to make
     a functioning button 542
   The Flash event handlers 544
   Working with mouse events and buttons 545
   Capturing keyboard input 546
   Capturing time events with keyframes 547
Creating Invisible Buttons and Using getURL 548
Summary 552

Chapter 19: Navigating Flash Timelines 553

Movie Clips: The Key to Self-Contained Playback 553
   How Movie Clips interact within a Flash movie 554
   One movie, several timelines 555
Targets and Paths Explained 556
   Paths: Absolute and relative modes 557
Targeting Movie Clips in Flash MX 560
Using Movie Clips to Create Sound Libraries 565
   Overview of the pianoKeys Movie Clip 565
   Making sound Movie Clips 566
   Nesting sounds into a sound library Movie Clip 572
   Targeting sounds with ActionScript syntax 574
   Using other features of the sound library 578
Summary 579

Chapter 20: Making Your First Flash MX Project 581

The Main Timeline as the Site Layout 581
   Creating a plan 583
   Determining Flash movie properties 583
   Mapping presentation areas to keyframes 584
   Creating content for each area 586
Adding Navigation Elements to the Main Timeline 591
   Creating text buttons for a menu 591
   Browsing the video items 593
Text Scrolling with the ScrollBar Component 595
Using the Custom Fade Component 599
Adding Named Anchors 601
Making the Movie Accessible 602
Summary 605

Part VI: Distributing Flash Movies   607

Chapter 21: Publishing Flash Movies 609

Testing Flash Movies 609
   Using the Test Scene or Movie command 610
   How to use the Bandwidth Profiler 612
   Using the size report 616
Publishing Your Flash Movies 616

Publish Settings 617
    Selecting formats 617
    Using the Flash settings 618
    Using the HTML settings 621
    Using the GIF settings 626
    Using the JPEG settings 629
    Using the PNG settings 630
    Creating Windows and Macintosh projectors 633
    Using the QuickTime settings 633
Publish Preview and Publish Commands 633
    Using Publish Preview 633
    Using Publish 634
Summary 634

Chapter 22: Integrating Flash Content with HTML **635**

Writing Markup for Flash Movies 635
    Using the <OBJECT> tag 636
    Using the <EMBED> tag 640
Detecting the Flash Player 642
    Plug-in versus ActiveX: Forcing content without a check 642
    JavaScript and VBScript player detection 644
    Using a Flash sniffer movie 646
Using Flash Movies with JavaScript and DHTML 650
    A word of caution to Web developers 650
    How Flash movies work with JavaScript 651
    Changing HTML attributes 651
    Using the PercentLoaded() method 655
Summary 657

Chapter 23: Using the Flash Player and Projector **659**

The Stand-Alone Flash Player and Projector 659
    Creating a projector 660
    Distribution and licensing 662
    Distribution on CD-ROM or floppy disk 662
    fscommand actions 662
Stand-Alone Limitations and Solutions 664
Using the Flash Player Plug-In for Web Browsers 665
    Supported operating systems 665
    Supported browsers 665
    Plug-in and Flash movie distribution on the Web 666
    Plug-in installation 666
Alternative Flash-Content Players 668
    RealOne Player with Flash playback 668
    QuickTime Player 668
    Shockwave Player 669
Player Utilities 669
Summary 670

Part VII: Approaching Actionscript   671

Chapter 24: Knowing the Nuts and Bolts of Code 673

Breaking Down the Interactive Process 673
   Define your problems 674
   Clarify the solution 674
   Translate the solution into the interactive language 675
The Basic Context for Programming in Flash 677
   Normal mode 677
   Expert mode 677
   Accessing ActionScript commands 678
   Actions list organization in the Actions panel 678
   The Reference panel 678
One Part of the Sum: ActionScript Variables 680
   String literals 682
   Expressions 682
   Variables as declarations 684
   Variables as text fields 685
Declaring Variables in ActionScript 686
   Using actions to define variables 686
   Loading variables from a predefined source 686
   Sending variables to URLs 687
   Establishing variables with HTML 688
Creating Expressions in ActionScript 688
   Operators 689
   Checking conditions: if. . .else actions 690
   Branching conditions with switch() and case. 692
   Loops 694
   Properties 698
   Built-in functions 698
   Creating and calling subroutines 698
Make a Login Sequence with Variables 699
Summary 702

Chapter 25: Controlling Movie Clips 705

Movie Clips: The Object Overview 705
   Movie Clip properties 706
   Movie Clip methods 707
   onClipEvent: The original Movie Clip handler 711
   Event methods: The MX Movie Clip handler 716
   Other objects and functions that use the MovieClip object 721
Working with Movie Clip Properties 721
   Positioning Movie Clips 722
   Scaling Movie Clips 723
   Rotating Movie Clips 724
Creating Draggable Movie Clips 725
   Drag-and-drop basics 725
   Detecting the drop position: Using _droptarget 727
   Making alpha and scale sliders 730
Summary 739

Chapter 26: Using Functions and Arrays 741

What Are Data Types? 741
   string 741
   number 742
   boolean 743
   movieclip 744
   object 744
   function 744
   undefined 744
   Checking data types with typeof 745
   Checking class type with instanceof 745
Overview of Functions as Procedures 746
   What functions do 746
   When to create a function 747
   How to define a function 747
   How to execute a function 748
Managing Related Data: The Array Object 748
Creating a Dynamic Reusable Flash Menu 750
Functions as Methods of Objects 755
Functions as Constructors for Objects 759
   Function definition 760
   Object creation and assignment 760
   Sound object method execution 760
Summary 761

Chapter 27: Interacting with Movie Clips 763

Movie Clip Collision Detection 763
   Using _droptarget 763
   Collision detection with hitTest() 764
Using the Mouse Object 766
Manipulating Color Attributes 768
   Creating a Color object 770
   Creating a Transform object 772
Enabling Sound with ActionScript 775
   Creating sound libraries with ActionScript 777
   Creating a soundTransformObject 782
   Creating volume and balance sliders for sounds 783
Printing with ActionScript 785
Summary 790

Chapter 28: Sharing and Loading Assets 793

Managing Smooth Movie Download and Display 793
Preloading a Flash Movie 794
Loading Flash Movies 799
   Basic overview of Flash site architecture 800
   Storing multiple movies 801
   Loading an external SWF file into a movie 801
   How Flash handles loaded movies of differing dimensions 805
   Placing, scaling, and rotating externally loaded Flash movies 805

Communicating between multiple movies on different levels 809
Unloading movies 810
loadMovie() as a method for Movie Clip targets 810
Loading JPEG Images into Flash Movies 811
Loading MP3 Audio into Flash Movies 814
Using a Preloader for External Assets 816
Accessing Items in Shared Libraries 820
Setting up a Shared library file 820
Assigning names to assets 822
Specifying the Shared library's location 822
Publishing the Shared library movie file 822
Linking to assets from other movies 823
Updating shared assets 824
Summary 825

Chapter 29: Using Components 827

What Are Components? 827
Why Use Components? 828
What makes up a component 829
How to add a component 829
Modifying component color properties and parameters 832
Removing components from your movie 832
Components in Flash MX 832
CheckBox component 833
ComboBox component 833
ListBox component 834
PushButton component 835
RadioButton component 835
ScrollBar component 836
ScrollPane component 837
Using components in your movie 837
Modifying Components 840
Changing graphics and fonts 841
Changing button or label fonts 843
Custom Components 847
Live Preview 847
Exchanging and acquiring components 847
Summary 848

Chapter 30: Sending Data In and Out of Flash 849

Using Text Fields to Store and Display Data 849
Input text fields 849
Dynamic text fields 851
Defining a Data Process with States 852
Input state 853
Send state 853
Wait state 854
Output state 855

Creating a Flash Form 855
Using XML Data in Flash Movies 860
    Understanding XML 860
    Loading an XML document into a Flash movie 861
Summary 872

Chapter 31: Applying HTML and Text Field Formatting 873

Exploring HTML Usage in Text Fields 873
    Supported HTML tags 873
    Formatting text with the Property inspector 875
    Inserting HTML tags into text fields with ActionScript 877
    Formatting fields with the TextFormat object 878
    Using asfunction in <A HREF> tags 880
Controlling Text Field Properties 881
Manipulating Text with the Selection Object 882
Summary 884

Chapter 32: Creating a Portfolio Site in Flash MX 885

Creating an Extensible Site Structure 885
    Planning the basic site structure 886
    Establishing key elements 888
    Organizing the document 889
Preparing Graphics 891
    Acquiring original portfolio images 891
    Preparing image assets for loading 895
    Formatting logo graphics and other vector art 899
Putting It All Together 902
    Placing static elements and text 903
    Basic timeline navigation 904
    Load functions and intro animation 906
    Navigation for loaded assets 908
    Duplicating the functionality 911
    Setting up placeholders for loaded JPEGs 912
    ActionScript for final functionality 913
    Fixing details for final Flash movie 915
    Uploading the final files to the Web server 916
Summary 917

Chapter 33: Creating a Game in Flash 919

The Game Plan: Four Phases of Game Design 919
    Game design 919
    Interaction design 920
    Visual and sound design 920
    Programming 921
Building the Project 921
Scripting the Game 923
Initializing Variables and Creating Sound Objects 923

Building the Interface 924
Creating text fields 924
Creating the alphabet 925
Starting the Game 926
Display the letters of the alphabet 927
Choose a random word 927
Create the slots for the letters of the word 928
The User Input 929
Interpreting the User Input 929
Was the letter selected before? 930
Is the letter part of the word? 930
The letter is not part of the word 931
Checking the Status of the Game 931
Is the word complete? 931
The word is complete 931
Is the alien complete? 932
Is the word selection empty? 932
There are more words to guess 932
Adding a delay before the next round 932
Added Feature: Storing User and Game Information 933
Summary 936

Part VIII: Optimizing and Troubleshooting Flash Movies   937

Bonus Chapter 34: Optimizing Your Movies CDBC-1

Dealing With Problematic Elements CDBC-1
Flash Deployment and Data Types CDBC-2
Image data CDBC-2
Sound data CDBC-2
Text CDBC-3
Optimizing and Preloading CDBC-4
Frame rate CDBC-5
Bandwidth Profiler and Size Report CDBC-5
Vector Artwork CDBC-8
Vector optimization CDBC-8
Bitmap Graphics CDBC-10
Sound Files CDBC-10
Using the loadMovie Action CDBC-11
High and low quality CDBC-12
Preloading Techniques CDBC-13
Preloading symbols CDBC-13
Preloading frames CDBC-14
Using Shared Libraries CDBC-15
Author-time sharing CDBC-16
Runtime sharing CDBC-16
Converting a font to a Shared library element CDBC-16
Notes on Shared library symbols CDBC-17
Optimization Tips CDBC-18
Advanced Techniques CDBC-18
Replacing timeline-based animation with scripting CDBC-18
Employing CPU and bandwidth sniffer scripts CDBC-19
Summary CDBC-21

Bonus Chapter 35: Getting Your Code Under Control CDBC-23

Planning Your Project CDBC-23
Customizing the Working Environment CDBC-24
    Panel layout CDBC-24
    The Actions panel CDBC-26
Storing Code in External Files CDBC-31
    The #include command CDBC-32
Managing Your Code CDBC-34
    Using Search and Replace CDBC-35
    How and where to place your code CDBC-36
    Centralized code CDBC-37
    Naming conventions CDBC-37
    Commenting CDBC-38
    Definitions CDBC-38
    Flash 5 events versus Flash MX events CDBC-40
    Using other technologies CDBC-41
Summary CDBC-41

Bonus Chapter 36: Solving Problems in Your Movies CDBC-43

Defining Streaming Media CDBC-43
Using the Output Window CDBC-46
    trace() action CDBC-46
    List Objects & List Variables CDBC-50
Knowing the Flash MX Debugger panel CDBC-51
    Activating the Debugger CDBC-51
    Displaying and modifying variables CDBC-52
    The Watch list CDBC-53
    Editing and displaying movie properties CDBC-54
Assigning Breakpoints CDBC-55
    Breakpoints in the Actions panel CDBC-55
    Breakpoints in the Debugger panel CDBC-57
    Stepping through your code CDBC-57
Debugging a Flash Movie Remotely CDBC-59
    Testing across mediums CDBC-61
Troubleshooting Guidelines CDBC-62
    Good practices CDBC-63
    General troubleshooting checklist CDBC-64
    Designer troubleshooting checklist CDBC-64
    Developer troubleshooting guidelines CDBC-65
Community Help CDBC-66
Summary CDBC-67

Part IX: Expanding Flash   939

Chapter 37: Working with Raster Graphics 941

Preparing Bitmaps for Use in Flash MX 941
Enhancing Web Production with Fireworks MX 942
    Transferring Fireworks images with transparency
        to the Flash authoring environment 945
    Preparing other bitmap formats in Fireworks 948

Preparing Images for Flash with Photoshop 7 956
Creating alpha channels for PNG files 956
Exporting Raster Images from Flash 961
General export options in raster formats 963
Other raster file format options 964
Using Raster Animation Tools 966
Summary 967

Chapter 38: Working with Vector Graphics 969

Optimizing Vector Graphics for Use in Flash 969
Converting text to outlines 970
Controlling color output 970
Tracing to convert rasters to vectors 971
Reducing vector complexity 974
Enhancing Flash Production with Macromedia FreeHand 977
Setting up preferences in FreeHand 978
Creating custom type layouts in FreeHand 979
Moving artwork from FreeHand to Flash 983
Exporting Artwork from Illustrator 990
Using SWF Export from Illustrator 9 or 10 990
Exporting Vector Graphics from Flash 994
A word of caution: Using vector formats from Flash 995
Summary 996

Chapter 39: Working with Audio Applications 997

Sound-Editing and Creation Software 997
Sonic Foundry's suite (PC only) 998
Syntrillium Software 998
Bias suite (Mac only) 999
Cakewalk Pro suite (PC only) 1000
Studio Vision Pro (Mac only) 1000
Cubase (Mac/PC) 1000
Macromedia SoundEdit 16 (Mac only) 1000
Digidesign's Pro Tools (Mac/PC) 1000
Capturing Your Own Sound: Building Your Own Recording Studio 1001
Instrument of choice 1001
Choosing a sound card 1001
Getting your sound in 1001
Getting your sound out 1002
Conclusion 1002
Basic Functions of Audio Editing 1002
Making your audio selection 1002
Setting In and Out points 1002
Fade in and fade out 1003
Normalizing Audio Levels 1004
Optimizing Sound for Flash in Sound Forge 1006
Normalizing a sound file 1006
Resampling 1007
Final notes 1007

Optimizing a Sound File Step by Step 1008
Effects 1010
    Creating a reverb effect 1010
    Creating your own custom sound effects. 1010
    Other effects 1012
ACID Loops to and from Flash 1017
    About the library disks 1017
    Choosing the loops 1017
    Tempo and key changes 1017
    Mixing 1018
    Exporting 1018
Summary 1018

Chapter 40: Working with 3D Graphics **1019**

Introduction to the 3D Environment 1019
    3D basics 1020
    File formats 1025
3D Exports and Imports 1025
    EPS files, alpha channels, and image compression 1026
    Flash and 3D 1026
    Things to consider before creating 3D models 1028
Using 3ds max to Create 3D Models 1030
    Planning and design 1031
    Building your objects 1033
    Adding additional detail to the base 1035
    Creating the chessboard 1036
    Adding materials 1038
    Preparing your object for animation 1040
    Setting up your scene 1042
Swift 3D Animation and Rendering for Flash 1047
    Timing and rendering intro animation 1047
    Exporting the single pawn object 1049
    Isolating exports for optimized animation 1052
Importing and Creating the Final Flash Piece 1055
Summary 1056

Chapter 41: Working with QuickTime **1057**

QuickTime versus Windows AVI 1058
QuickTime Support in Flash 1059
Importing QuickTime into Flash 1060
Combining Flash and QuickTime Movies 1062
    Creating QuickTime Flash movies 1062
    Creating QuickTime video with Flash 1067
    A word about QuickTime VR movies 1069
Using Bitmap Sequences from Video 1071
    Extracting frames from digital video clips 1072
    Importing a sequence into Flash 1076
Summary 1077

Chapter 42: Working with Dreamweaver MX 1079

Why Use Dreamweaver? 1079
Dreamweaver MX 1079
    Installing Dreamweaver MX 1080
    What's new in Dreamweaver MX? 1080
    Dreamweaver MX and Flash MX integration 1080
Importing Flash into Dreamweaver 1081
    Working with your Flash movie 1081
    Positioning your movie 1083
    Specifying Window Mode 1083
Using the Built-In Flash Functions 1084
    Adding a Flash Button 1085
    Editing a Flash Button 1086
    Inserting a Flash Text object 1086
    Editing a Flash Text object 1087
    Launch and edit Flash from Dreamweaver 1087
Adding Dreamweaver Behaviors 1088
    Check Plugin behavior 1088
    Control Shockwave or Flash behavior 1089
Using the Flash Deployment Kit 1090
    Downloading and installing the Deployment Kit 1090
Link Checker 1093
Writing ActionScript with Dreamweaver 1094
Summary 1096

Chapter 43: Working with Director 1097

Advantages of Director over Flash 1097
Advantages of Flash MX over Director 1098
Benefits and Limitations of Flash Assets in Director 1099
Creating Director-Specific Actions in Flash 1099
    Standard getURL command 1100
    event: command 1101
    lingo: command 1102
Controlling Flash Movies in Director 1102
    The Flash Asset Xtra: Importing Flash movies 1102
    Using Director's Property Inspector 1108
    Flash movies as Sprites 1108
Controlling Flash Movies with Lingo 1110
    Lingo and ActionScript 1110
    Changing the size and rotation of Flash Sprites 1113
Summary 1115

Chapter 44: Working with ColdFusion MX 1117

An Overview of ColdFusion 1117
    Why ColdFusion? 1117
    What's new in ColdFusion MX? 1118
How Does ColdFusion Work? 1119
    How does ColdFusion work with Flash? 1120
    HTML text editors and CFML 1120

Using ColdFusion 1122
    Your First ColdFusion page 1122
    A simple feedback form 1123
    Integrating your feedback form with Flash MX 1124
Turning your Feedback Form into a Guestbook 1127
    Working with databases 1127
Creating the Guestbook 1131
    Understanding the code 1132
    Retrieving comments from the guestbook 1133
    Understanding the code 1133
    Integrate your guestbook with a Flash interface 1134
Creating the Login Form 1139
    Using cookies with ColdFusion and Flash MX 1141
    Connecting your login to a Flash interface 1145
Summary 1147

Chapter 45: Making Movies for the Pocket PC **1149**

What Is A Pocket PC? 1149
    Basic information about the Pocket PC 1149
Why Flash on the Pocket PC? 1151
    Small file size 1151
    Recycle, Repurpose, and Redeploy—the three R's of Flash . . . 1152
    Rapid development time and low barrier to entry 1152
    Pocket PC and Flash resources 1153
Getting Flash Content onto Your Device 1154
    Flash MX and the Pocket PC 1155
Mac Users and Pocket PCs 1159
    Wireless connectivity 1159
    Storage cards 1160
    PocketMac 1161
    Connectix Virtual PC 1161
Summary 1162

PART X: Appendixes   **1163**

Appendix A: Keyboard Shortcuts **1165**

Appendix B: Digital Sound Basics **1171**

Appendix C: Using the CD-ROM? **1179**

Appendix D: Contact and Bibliography Information **1185**

Bonus Appendix A: Flash-Compatible Media Formats **CDBA-1**

Bonus Appendix B: Multilingual Content in Flash **CDBA-11**

Bonus Appendix C: Flash Player–Compatible Actions **CDBA-25**

Index. 1195
End-User License Agreement 1271

An Introduction to Flash Web Production

✦ ✦ ✦ ✦

In This Part

Chapter QS
Flash in a Flash

Chapter 1
Understanding the
Flash Framework

Chapter 2
Exploring Web
Technologies

Chapter 3
Planning Flash
Projects

✦ ✦ ✦ ✦

If you're new to Flash or to multimedia production this section will get you started on the right foot. If you are a veteran Flash user, this section will give you some perspective on the evolution of Flash and the new workflow options brought about by the Macromedia Studio Family of programs.

Chapter 1 provides a comprehensive overview of the strengths and weaknesses of the Flash format and some background on where Flash came from and how it has evolved. Chapter 2 explores the various ways that Flash movies interact with other Web formats and introduces some of the issues that need to be considered when planning for specific audiences. Chapter 3 has expanded coverage of tools and strategies for multimedia project planning, including detailed descriptions of how to create flowcharts, site maps, and functional specification documents.

QuickStart:
Flash in a Flash

◆ ◆ ◆ ◆

In This Chapter

Feature roundup

Examples for designers

Examples for developers

Summary

◆ ◆ ◆ ◆

Jumping straight into Flash MX, we take a look at some of the new features that can be found in the latest release from Macromedia, just to whet your appetite.

Working through a range of simple examples, you'll get the chance to familiarize yourself with Flash MX. These small projects are designed to bring you up to speed with, among other features, the new Flash MX user interface (or GUI, for Graphic User Interface).

While we cover new features for both designers and developers, it is recommended you work through both sections to get an overall feel of Flash MX. You don't need to worry; all examples are step by step and very easy to follow.

Feature Roundup

Here is a quick introduction to some of the new features of Flash MX that we examine in this chapter:

- ✦ **Templates:** Flash MX ships with a set of standard templates covering a wide range of categories. You can use a template to quick-track your next project.

- ✦ **Components:** New to Flash MX are components, making Smart Clips a thing of the past. Smart Clips have been replaced with components, although components are much more powerful and flexible then Smart Clips. Components are reusable user interface elements like scroll bars, push buttons, check boxes, radio buttons, among others that ship with Flash MX.

- ✦ **Layer folders:** A few needed improvements to Flash's timeline greatly enhance document management capabilities. You can place any number of layers into Layer folders that you can then lock or hide.

- ✦ **Library:** Imagine the ability to drag a vector shape from the Stage to the Library panel to create a symbol. Well, stop dreaming and get to it! This is just one of the many improvements to the Library.

✦ **Property inspector:** An enhancement to usability within Flash MX comes in the form of a Property inspector. This inspector behaves much like the beloved Property inspector in Macromedia Dreamweaver MX.

✦ **Envelope modifier:** This neat little addition gives you the flexibility to warp any shape on the Stage. Although it is limited to vector shapes, you can create some interesting effects.

✦ **Break apart:** You can now break a text field into individual text fields per letter. This allows you to create simple text animations upon individual letters more easily.

✦ **Distribute to layers:** This new feature goes hand in hand with the text field Break Apart command. Once you have broken a text field apart, you can distribute each letter to a different layer. You can also use Distribute to layers on any layer with multiple items — the items will be assigned to separate layers once the Distribute to layers command is selected.

✦ **Animated masks:** Masking is a great technique that has been vastly improved in Flash MX. You can now create an animated mask, as simply as you'd create a Motion or Shape tween and use it in ActionScript.

✦ **Customizable Actions panel:** The Actions panel, used to create ActionScript code, has had a major overhaul in Flash MX. You now have the option to customize it to suit your working conditions.

✦ **Named anchors:** A great improvement to the usability of Flash movies in browsers is the ability to have the Back and Forward buttons recognize markers within your Flash MX movies.

✦ **Dynamic bitmap and sound loading:** You can dynamically load sound and bitmaps into your Flash movie at runtime. For example, you download a JPEG image right into a Movie Clip instance in the Flash movie (.swf file) as it plays within the Web browser. This is another great improvement that will dramatically extend the dynamic capabilities of Flash MX, taking over some of the powerful features of Macromedia Generator (which is no longer available for Flash MX production tasks).

✦ **Streaming video:** Flash MX has the ability to load and stream video, using Flash Player 6's native video codec, Sorenson Spark.

✦ **Scriptable text fields:** One of the major improvements to ActionScript's object model is the inclusion of the Button and TextField objects. We take a closer look at text fields in this quick start.

✦ **Improved ActionScript event model:** You can now directly set an event on an object entirely through ActionScript. Events can be applied and removed as needed.

✦ **Drawing API:** Macromedia has improved the power of ActionScript by giving us the ability to draw vector shapes, using new methods and properties of the MovieClip object.

Examples for Designers

Delving into the designer section, developers and designers alike will find many ways to improve the layout and management of their Flash documents. Macromedia has made huge leaps with the usability of the Flash MX authoring interface, which we explore in this section.

Using templates

You can now quickly and easily create a new project based on one of the templates. There is quite a wide range of categories and corresponding templates that ship with Flash MX.

We take a closer look at the PhotoSlideshow template and learn how to easily customize it to include your own photos.

Note Before we start this tutorial, you should prepare some photos that you want to use in the PhotoSlideshow. Use Macromedia Fireworks or another bitmap editor of your choice to prepare the images.

Use the following checklist to prepare your images for best results.

✦ Your images should have a size of 640 × 480 pixels. You will need four images for this exercise.

✦ Make sure your images are either JPEG or GIF files so they are suitable to use in Flash MX and on the Web.

✦ Name your photos in sequence. An example of this is photo1.jpg, photo2.jpg, photo3.jpg, and photo4.jpg.

On the CD-ROM Rather than preparing your own images you can use a set of images located in the chQS\ images folder on the *Flash MX Bible* CD-ROM. Copy these files to a location on your hard drive.

1. Open Flash MX.

2. Start a new template by selecting File ➪ New From Template. As you can see in Figure QS-1, there are many templates that make creating projects really simple. Some of the more complete templates contain their own components, which provide interactivity.

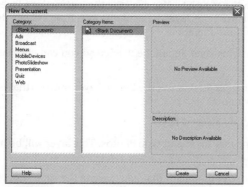

Figure QS-1: Viewing the PhotoSlideshow template from the New Document dialog box

3. In the Category panel select PhotoSlideshow. You should take a look at the other categories. When you choose an item in the Category list, you will see all the templates for that category in the Category Items pane.

4. Select PhotoSlideshow_style1 from the Category Items pane and select Create. A new Flash document will open in Flash MX, showing instructions on the Stage. (See Figure QS-2.) Many of the instruction panels of other templates contain an URL to a page on Macromedia's Web site where you can find more information about the template or Category you have chosen.

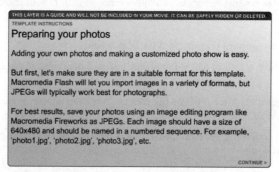

THIS LAYER IS A GUIDE AND WILL NOT BE INCLUDED IN YOUR MOVIE. IT CAN BE SAFELY HIDDEN OR DELETED.
TEMPLATE INSTRUCTIONS

Preparing your photos

Adding your own photos and making a customized photo show is easy.

But first, let's make sure they are in a suitable format for this template. Macromedia Flash will let you import images in a variety of formats, but JPEGs will typically work best for photographs.

For best results, save your photos using an image editing program like Macromedia Fireworks as JPEGs. Each image should have a size of 640x480 and should be named in a numbered sequence. For example, 'photo1.jpg', 'photo2.jpg', 'photo3.jpg', etc.

CONTINUE >

Figure QS-2: Each template has its own set of instructions.

5. Save the Flash document (.fla file) to the location on your hard drive where your images are. Name it slide_slow.fla. The topmost layer of the PhotoSlideshow template is named _instructions. This layer contains instructions on how to use the template. There are often two, three, or more frames of instructions that you can browse using the continue and back buttons. These should work within the authoring environment — if they don't, make sure Control ➪ Enable Simple Buttons is selected.

The instructions with this template are a little vague. This tutorial is a complete guide ensuring your success with the template. You can hide the instructions layer by clicking the small dot on the _instructions layer, beneath the eye. However, we do suggest that you peruse the instructions sometime.

6. Select the Old Photos layer. This layer should be deleted so you can personalize the PhotoSlideshow.

7. With the Old Photos layer highlighted, press the Delete Layer button (that is the trashcan icon) in the Timeline window.

8. Create a new layer by selecting Insert ➪ Layer.

9. Double click the name of the new layer and type Photos. This layer will be used for your imported images.

10. Select File ➪ Import to choose your images that you'll use in the slide show. Navigate to the folder where you have saved your sequentially named images. Highlight the first image and select OK.

11. If you have sequentially named your images, a dialog box will appear, asking if you want to import all images in the sequence. Select Yes.

12. If you have named your images image1.jpg, image2.jpg, and so on, another dialog box, shown in Figure QS-3, will display, stating there has been a library conflict. This is because the images in the template have the same name as the images you are importing. Select the Replace Existing Items option and press OK. This is a new feature in Flash MX — previous versions of Flash would add the new elements while still retaining the existing ones.

Flash MX will import all of the images in the sequence and create a keyframe for each of them on the Photos layer. All you have to do now is personalize the caption for each image and set the appropriate date and title.

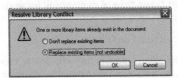

Figure QS-3: The Resolve Library Conflict dialog box

13. Once you have imported your images, it is safe to remove the old images from the Library. Open the Library panel (Windows ⇨ Library). Select each of the old images, and press the trashcan icon at the bottom of the Library panel to delete the images.

14. Select frame 1 of the Title, Date layer.

15. Replace the title Visiting the aquarium with an appropriate title for your images.

16. Replace the date February 2, 2002 with a relevant date for your images.

17. Select frame 1 of the Captions layer. At the bottom left of the document's Stage, you should see the text The elegant seahorse with a blue box around it; double-click this text to edit it. Type a relevant caption for the first image. Repeat this step for the remaining images so each caption has been personalized. You will need to select each frame individually and type each caption.

18. Test your slide show by selecting Control ⇨ Test Movie. Use the buttons in the Photoshow Controller to navigate through your images. Pushing the Autoplay button will automatically run through your images, re-starting from the first image when it reaches the end.

As you can see some of the templates will be more useful than others. Pick and choose at your will to select the template that is best suited to your needs.

Note Not all of the templates are as complete as the one we used in this exercise. Some of them are simply movies with pre-established Stage sizes with general instructions for their use.

Components and the Property inspector

A major upgrade to Smart Clips comes in the form of components. Components allow you to set parameters in the authoring environment of Flash MX, similar to Smart Clips in Flash 5. However, using ActionScript code, you can modify a component's functionality at runtime.

On the Macromedia Exchange site, you can find many components that have been designed by Flash MX developers. Visit www.macromedia.com/exchange for more information.

There are seven standard UI (user interface) components that ship with Flash MX: Checkbox, ComboBox, ListBox, PushButton, RadioButton, ScrollBar and ScrollPane. These can be used to instantly create a simple interface for user interaction.

We take a look at creating a scroll bar for a text field. The best thing about this component is you don't need any ActionScript. The component takes care of everything for you. We'll take a look at exactly how it is done and demonstrate how simple it is to use components.

1. Open Flash MX and create a new file by selecting File ➪ New.

2. Make sure you have the Property inspector open by selecting Window ➪ Properties. The Property inspector, new to Flash MX, is used to alter properties of objects in the Flash MX authoring environment. Using the Property inspector you can modify the properties of text fields, symbols, Movie Clips, graphics, buttons, sound, video, frames and vector shapes.

3. Select the Text tool. In the Property inspector select Input Text from the Text type drop-down list.

4. On the Stage click and drag to create a 100 × 100 pixel square. You needn't worry about the exact size of the square.

5. Using the Property inspector select Multiline from the Line Type menu, and press the Show Border button to apply a border to the text field. In the <Instance Name> field, type myText.

6. You can embed a font in your Flash movie, so the text in the text field will be anti-aliased by pressing the Character button in the Property inspector. In the Character Options dialog box, select the All Characters option and close the dialog box. The text field is now complete. Compare your text field's settings to those of Figure QS-4. You are now ready to apply the pre-made Scrollbar component.

Figure QS-4: The Property inspector shows the correct settings for the text field.

7. Open the Components panel by choosing Window ➪ Components.

8. Select the ScrollBar component and drag an instance of it to the document's Stage. While dragging, release it over the inside right edge of the text field. In other words, drop it on top of the text field.

9. When you release the component you should see the scroll bar snap into position and dynamically resize itself. The hard part is done. All you have to do now is test your movie and type some text into the text field.

10. Save your Flash document (File ➪ Save), and test the movie by selecting Control ➪ Test Movie.

11. Place the cursor inside the text field and type a couple of lines.

12. Select the lines you have just type by pressing Ctrl+A (Windows) or ⌘+A (Macintosh).

13. Paste the text from your clipboard into the text field by pressing Ctrl+V (Windows) or ⌘+V (Macintosh). Repeat this step as many times as you need to entirely fill the text field. Once you have filled the text box, paste the text a couple of more times to make sure you have enough text to scroll.

    Once you have filled the text box you should see the scroll bar start to respond and resize itself. You can drag the scroll bar up and down or click the up and down arrow buttons to scroll through the text.

You now know how to use the ScrollBar component. The new Flash MX UI components make it very quick and easy to add interactivity to your Flash movie.

Cross-Reference

We discuss the ScrollBar component once again in Chapter 20, "Making Your First Flash MX Project". Other components are discussed in Chapter 29, "Using Components."

Quick Animation

In this example you create a small animation. It has been designed to use a number of new features of Flash MX. We discuss Layer folders, the Library panel, Envelope modifiers, Break Apart and Distribute to Layers.

The features we are exploring have been a major focus for Macromedia. Flash MX has been enhanced and usability where designers and animators are concerned has been much improved.

On the CD-ROM

You can find quick_animation_start.fla in the chQS folder of the *Flash MX Bible* CD-ROM. Make a copy of this file to a location on your hard drive. We have prepared the basic layout for you so you can focus on using the new features of Flash MX.

1. Select the first frame of the Flash text layer. This layer contains the word Flash.

2. Position the Playhead at frame 20 and insert a keyframe by selecting Insert ➪ Keyframe.

3. Make sure frame 20 on the Flash text layer is selected and break the text apart by selecting Modify ➪ Break Apart. Once the text has broken apart you should notice that each letter is still a text box, making it easy to change each letter individually as needed. This is one of the major text improvements in Flash MX.

4. Break the text apart once again, so it becomes a simple vector shape.

5. Select Modify ➪ Transform ➪ Envelope. The Envelope Modifier tool is a new addition to the drawing tools in Flash MX. Use the Envelope Modifier to distort vector shapes on your stage. You can also use the Envelope Modifier by selecting the icon from the options section of the toolbar, when an eligible object is selected.

6. Using the Envelope Modifier tool, drag some of the nodes surrounding the text to push and squash the word similar to Figure QS-5.

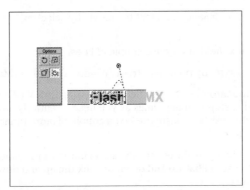

Figure QS-5: The Envelope Modifier can be used to alter vector shapes on the Stage.

7. Once you are happy with the modifications you have made with the Envelope Modifier tool, position the Playhead at frame 1 and select the first keyframe of the Flash text layer.

8. Break the text apart by selecting Modify ➪ Break Apart. Break the text apart a second time by selecting Modify ➪ Break Apart. As we are going to create a shape tween, both of these frames need to contain primitive shapes.

9. Make sure the Property inspector is open by selecting Window ➪ Properties. Create a shape tween by selecting Shape from the Tween menu in the Property inspector.

10. Right-click (Windows) or Control-click (Macintosh) on the Flash text layer icon and select Mask. This will turn the layer into a Mask layer, nesting the layer beneath it, "green bar." The contents of a Mask layer will determine what is revealed of any nested layers.

11. Select the first frame of the MXText layer. Break the text apart by selecting Modify ➪ Break Apart.

12. Distribute the text to layers by selecting Modify ➪ Distribute to Layers. The Distribute to Layers command is a new feature of Flash MX, allowing you to take multiple elements on one layer and spread them across several individual layers. You will notice the new layers have even been correctly named for you.

13. Open the Library panel by choosing Window ➪ Library.

14. Select the M text on the Stage of the M layer. Drag it over the Library panel, and release the mouse button. You should see the Convert to Symbol dialog box appear. This action is performed typically by selecting an element on the Stage and then choosing Insert ➪ Convert to Symbol. The ability to drag and drop onto the Library panel is another great timesaving addition to Flash MX.

15. In the Convert to Symbol dialog box, select the Graphic behavior, name it M and press the OK button.

16. Position the Playhead at frame 20 and select the M layer. Insert a keyframe by selecting Insert ⇨ Keyframe.

17. Select frame 1 of the M layer and create a Motion Tween by selecting Insert ⇨ Create Motion Tween.

18. Select the M on the M layer in the first keyframe. Using the Property inspector (Window ⇨ Properties), select Alpha from the Color menu. The slider and value of Alpha should automatically set itself to 0%, yet another timesaving feature in Flash MX.

19. Repeat Steps 13 to 17 for the X on the X layer.

20. In Flash 5, this may have been the end to the project. However, Flash MX has a few new features that will help tidy your Flash movie even further. You can create Layer Folders and split the sections of the animation. This technique is better used on large projects where you may have 40 – 90 layers on a timeline.

21. In the Timeline window, click the Insert Layer Folder icon (located in the lower left toolbar of the window). Rename the folder by double-clicking on the name, assigning the name Motion Tween.

Bitmaps and the Envelope Modifier

Using the Envelope modifier you can create some really nice effects. You can extend this to bitmaps. Follow these steps to manipulate a bitmap:

1. Open Flash and create a new File by selecting File ⇨ New.

2. Import a bitmap file from a location on your hard drive by selecting File ⇨ Import. Navigate to a bitmap on your hard drive, highlight it and select OK.

3. Select the bitmap on the Stage and break it apart by selecting Modify ⇨ Break Apart.

4. Making sure you have the bitmap selected, select Modify ⇨ Transform ⇨ Envelope. You can now drag the nodes around just as if it were a vector shape. It does act a little differently though — it looks as though a mask has been created on a tiled layer of the bitmaps — refer to the following figure for an example. Nonetheless, you can create some nice effects.

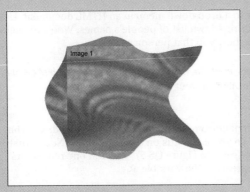

Figure SB-1: An example of applying the Envelope Modifier tool to a bitmap.

22. Drag both the M and X layers over the Motion Tween layer folder and release your mouse button. This will move the layers into the Motion Tween layer folder. Using the small triangle (to the left of the folder icon), you can close the folder, which hides all layers inside it. At this point, delete the MXText layer because it isn't needed any longer. You can do this by selecting it and pressing the Delete Layer button (the trashcan icon) located in the toolbar of the Timeline window.

23. Create another Layer Folder by clicking on the Insert Layer Folder icon in the Timeline panel. Rename it in the layer folder to `Animated Mask`.

24. Drag the Mask layer named Flash Text onto the Animated Mask layer folder and release it. All of the masked layers will be moved into the Animated Mask folder. Proceed to close the Animated Mask Layer folder.

25. Save your Flash document (File ➪ Save), and test it by choosing Control ➪ Test Movie. Watch the animation of the letters unfold.

You can find the completed file, **quick_animation_complete.fla,** in the chQS folder of the Flash MX Bible CD-ROM.

You have now created a simple animation using the new organization and management features of Flash MX. These features help you make quick animations that would have taken a fair amount of time in Flash 5 — particularly the improved Break Apart command and the new Distribute to Layers command.

Examples for Developers

In addition to the excellent enhancements for designers in Flash MX, improvements have also been made to benefit developers. ActionScript has been significantly remodeled and reworked, thus extending the capabilities of Flash development. In this section, we will look at some of these improvements.

The ComboBox component

The ComboBox component is very similar to a drop-down menu in an HTML document. Using the ComboBox component, you'll create a drop-down list of people's names. When you select the name, the Output window will open to show you that person's age.

You can find the starter file, **components_start.fla**, in the chQS folder of the *Flash MX Bible* CD-ROM. Make a copy of this file to a location on your hard drive.

1. Open the components_start.fla document from the location on your hard drive. The graphics have already been created so you can focus on the ComboBox. Notice that there are two text fields on the Stage (refer to Figure QS-6). The first one represents the variable `name` and the second represents the variable `age`.

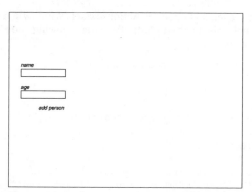

Figure QS-6: The starter document's Stage

2. Select the first frame of the Component layer. Open the Components panel by selecting Window ➪ Components and drag an instance of the ComboBox component onto the Stage.

3. Open the Property inspector by choosing Window ➪ Properties.

4. In the Property inspector you will see the options for the ComboBox component. Name this instance of the ComboBox by replacing the text <Instance Name> with dropdown. This name can now be used to target this instance of the ComboBox in ActionScript code.

5. By default the Parameters tab of the Component instance will be displayed in the Property inspector. Select the Labels field. Click the white box which appears around the [ ] symbols. The Values dialog box will open. All values for the current parameter can be entered here. The Labels field is an array used to hold the labels for display in the ComboBox.

6. Click the + button in the top corner of the Values dialog box. When the new item appears in the value table, select it and type a person's name of your choice. The person's name will appear as a label in the ComboBox once the document is exported to a Flash movie (.swf file). Repeat the process to add as many names as you like. Select OK.

7. Select the Data field in the Property inspector and open the Value dialog box by clicking on the white box surrounding the field.

8. Add an item by pressing the + button and enter the age of your imaginary person(s). The values you enter must be in the same order as the values from the Labels field.

9. Modify the Change Handler field. Select it and type dropDownChanged. dropDownChanged is a function which will be executed every time a selection is made from the ComboBox. When you've finished with this step, your component's settings should match those that appear in Figure QS-7.

Figure QS-7: The settings in the Parameters tab on the Property inspector should match this figure.

10. Select frame 1 of the Actions layer, and open the Actions panel (Window ➪ Actions). In the options menu of the panel, select Expert Mode. Type the following code into the Script pane of the Actions panel:

```
// This function will be called when a selection is made
// from the ComboBox.
function dropDownChanged(obj) {

    // Get the label and value of the selected item.
    var name = obj.getSelectedItem().label;
    var age = ob.getSelectedItem().data;

    // Send the persons name and age to the Output window.
      trace("You have selected "+name+", who is "+age+" years old.");
}
```

The function `dropDownChanged` is a callback method of the ComboBox instance, and is executed every time a selection is made from the ComboBox instance.

 Note

The `trace()` action will only work in Test Movie mode. It simply retrieves the name and age of the selected person and sends these values to the Output window.

11. Select the add person button on the Stage and open the Actions panel by choosing Window ➪ Actions. Enter the following lines of code:

```
on (press) {

    // Add the person's name and age to the
    // ComboBox instance.

    dropDown.addItem(name, age);

}
```

This code will add the person's name and age to the CombBox instance, `dropDown`. It uses the values from the text fields on the Stage whose variable names are `name` and `age`.

12. Save the Flash document, and test it by selecting Control ➪ Test Movie. Select the down arrow of the ComboBox instance and choose a name. The Output window will open with the selected person's name and age.

13. In the name text field type your own name and age in the text fields. Click the add person button. Your name and age have now been added to the ComboBox instance.

14. Select the down arrow of the ComboBox and select your name. Your name and age will appear in the Output window.

You can extend this example and apply another use of the ComboBox instance. Follow these remaining steps to update a text field displaying the current selection of the ComboBox.

15. Exit Test Movie mode by closing the SWF window.

16. Add this code to the end of the `dropDownChanged` function:

```
currentSelection.text = name;
```

This code will update the text within the `currentSelection` text field. Follow Steps 12 through 14 to see the updated version.

You can find the completed document, **components_complete.fla**, in the chQS folder of the *Flash MX Bible* CD-ROM.

You've just completed a simple example using the Property inspector to modify a component in the authoring environment and using simple ActionScript commands to alter a ComboBox component at runtime.

In this exercise, we use the Var name of an Input Text field to retrieve the contents of the text field. Flash MX allows you to assign instance names to text fields as well. In later chapters, we will use the instance name and properties of the TextField object to work with components and other interface elements. While the Var name allows you to simply access the contents of a text field, we do not recommend that you assign a Var name for projects designed to work with Flash Player 6.

Customizable Actions panel

Macromedia has focused heavily on improving Flash MX for developers. One of the major disappointments in Flash 5 was the limited Actions panel which was difficult to use when writing many lines of ActionScript. Flash MX has a very advanced and customizable Actions panel helping to make you more comfortable when writing ActionScript.

We take a look at configuring the Actions panel to suit your needs.

1. Open Flash MX and create a new file by selecting File ➪ New.

2. Open the Preferences window by selecting Edit ➪ Preferences. Select the ActionScript Editor tab (refer to Figure QS-8).

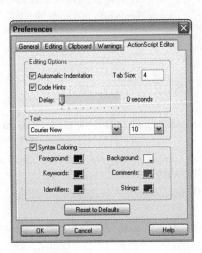

Figure QS-8: The Preferences window can be used to customize most aspects of Flash MX.

3. In the Editing Options section, we recommend you use the default options for the Automatic Indentation and Code Hints check boxes. You can set Delay slider for the Code Hints to whatever you like; we suggest using 0 because there is little point in having a code suggestion if you've already typed the function you want.

4. The Tab Size should be set to whatever you prefer; it would be a good idea to use the same setting that you might use in other code editing programs.

5. Pick whichever text you are most comfortable with. Choosing a fixed width font makes if it easy to see all of the ; : - and i characters, which are often used in programming languages.

6. Syntax Coloring is a great addition to the Actions panel in Flash MX. You should pick colors you use in other code editing packages. If you are new to typing code then experiment a little and find something you are comfortable with.

7. Open the Actions panel by selecting Window ➪ Actions. The Actions panel has undergone a radical facelift. Many options for customizing the look and feel of the Actions panel can be found in the options menu at the top-right corner of the panel. There are many options including Check Syntax, which will find syntax errors in your code. View Numbers will add line numbers to the gutter of the Script pane. You can also switch from Normal editing mode to Expert editing mode.

Note   For more advanced users, you can edit the ActionsPanel.xml file in the First Run\ActionsPanel folder within the Flash MX program folder to alter the ActionScript editor. This should be done with extreme care and we suggest that you make a backup copy of the file before proceeding to alter it. You can learn more about this advanced functionality in the *ActionScript Bible* by Robert Reinhardt and Joey Lott.

Using the ListBox Component

The ListBox component and the ComboBox components are very similar. Follow these instructions to replace the ComboBox component with the ListBox component. Make sure you have completed all steps in the ComboBox tutorial first.

1. Select the ComboBox instance on the Stage and delete it by pressing the "Delete" key on your keyboard.

2. Open the Components panel by selecting Window ➪ Components.

3. Drag an instance of the ListBox component on the stage.

4. The Resolve Component Conflict dialog box will appear. Select the Replace existing component option and select OK.

5. Follow Steps 4 through 9 of the ComboBox Component tutorial. The only difference is you'll be using the ListBox component rather than the ComboBox.

6. Test the movie by selecting Control ➪ Test Movie. All of the same functionality will occur as it did with the ComboBox.

This is just a quick example, demonstrating how easy it is to use and modify the Flash MX UI Components.

Named anchors

Improving usability of the Flash Player, Macromedia has developed methods for making the Back and Forward buttons in Web browsers control your Flash movie, and it couldn't be easier to implement. There are no excuses for Flash Websites that don't live up to a few usability rules anymore.

Caution

Named anchors are only supported in Web browsers that support JavaScript and `fscommand` action interactivity. This means that Internet Explorer for Macintosh and Netscape 6.0 or higher will not work with named anchors.

We create a simple example to demonstrate the use of named anchors within Flash; a simple slide show presentation that interacts with Forward and Back buttons of a browser.

On the CD-ROM

You can find **named_anchors_start.fla** in the chQS folder of the *Flash MX Bible* CD-ROM. Make of a copy of this file to a location on your hard drive.

1. Open Flash MX.

2. Open named_anchors_start.fla by selecting File ➪ Open. Browse to the file that you have saved on your hard drive, highlight it and select OK. The basic graphics and frame layout have been created. All you have to do is create the named anchors and test the movie in a browser.

3. Select the first keyframe on the Labels layer.

4. Make sure the Property inspector is open by selecting Window ➪ Properties.

5. Remove `// introduction` from the Frame Label field and type `intro`.

6. Select the Named Anchor check box. Once you have selected the Named Anchor check box, the icon on the frame in the timeline panel will change to a small anchor notifying you that it is a named anchor. Figure QS-9 shows the Named Anchor icons.

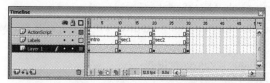

Figure QS-9: The timeline from named_anchors_start.fla shows the icon that is used to denote a named anchor.

7. Repeat Steps 5 and 6 for each commented frame on the Labels layer, including the last one. Name them in the following order: `intro`, `sec1`, `sec2` and `end`. The buttons already have the appropriate ActionScript to go to each page using the frame names above, so make sure you have typed them correctly. All that's left to do is publish the page.

8. Open the Publish settings dialog box by selecting File ➪ Publish Settings...

9. On the Formats tab make sure the Flash check box and the HTML check box are selected.

10. Select the HTML tab. The default settings on the Flash tab don't need to be modified.

11. In the Template menu, select Flash with Named Anchors. Anytime you want to use Named Anchors in Flash you must select this option when publishing.

12. Once you have modified any other settings you wish to change, select Publish and then OK.

13. The last step is to open the file you've just created in a browser. Using a browser of your choice open the HTML you just created. Click on a few of the buttons: the Flash movie will move to the different sections. When you are ready, hit the Back and Forward buttons from the browser, the flash movie should respond and cycle back or forward through the browser history.

To see a fully functional version of this example, refer to the **named_anchors_complete.fla** document in the chQS folder of the *Flash MX Bible* CD-ROM

Dynamic bitmap and sound loading

Macromedia Flash has been, for a long time, a great tool to dynamically update your Web site. You can load in XML, text files and variables to help speed updating of your site. Now you can dynamically load in bitmaps and sound files too. Using Generator, or a similar program, was the only way to do this in Flash 5. With Generator being discontinued Macromedia has given us the option to do this directly with Flash MX.

In this tutorial we create a simple example that loads in an MP3 file and a JPEG file.

You can find atmospheres_1.mp3 in the ch28 folder and image1.jpg in the chQS\images folder of the *Flash MX Bible* CD-ROM. Copy these files to a location on your hard drive. You will be saving a new Flash MX file to the same location.

1. Open Flash MX and create a new file by selecting File ➪ New. There is no graphics to draw, this example is using only ActionScript.

2. Save the file to the same directory on your hard drive where you saved theMP3 file and name it **dynamic_loading.fla**.

3. Double click Layer 1 and name the layer **actions**.

4. Select the first frame of the Actions layer.

5. Open the Actions panel by selecting Window ➪ Actions and insert the following code. Make sure the panel is in Expert mode.

```
// create an empty move clip to hold the sound object
_root.createEmptyMovieClip("bgSoundHolder", 1);
```

This code creates an empty Movie Clip. Use this Movie Clip to hold the sound. We do this so you can have multiple sounds playing at the same time, each with individual volume controls and settings.

6. On the same frame insert this code:

```
// create the new Sound object in bgSoundHolder
bgSound = new Sound("bgSoundHolder");

// load in the specified mp3 file
bgSound.loadSound("atmospheres_1.mp3", true);
```

This code creates a new instance of the Sound object named bgSound. The second line uses the new loadSound() method to dynamically load and stream the MP3 file.

7. Test the movie by selecting Control ⇨ Test Movie. Once the Flash movie (.swf file) has been generated, you should start to hear the MP3 file play.

Make sure you have copied the atmospheres_1.mp3 file into the same directory as the Flash movie. It will not work unless it is in the same directory. Alternatively, you can use your own MP3 file, but you must remember to edit the sound file name in the loadSound() method.

8. Now that you have finished importing the sound, you will dynamically load a JPEG image into the same Flash movie.

9. Select the first frame of the Actions layer.

10. If it isn't already visible, open the Actions panel by selecting Window ⇨ Actions and insert the following lines of code:

```
// create an empty movie clip to hold the bitmap
_root.createEmptyMovieClip("bitmapHolder", 2);

// load in the bitmap
bitmapHolder.loadMovie("image1.jpg");
```

The first line of code creates a new empty Movie Clip for holding the bitmap which will be dynamically loaded at runtime. The second line of code uses the improved loadMovie function to directly reference a JPEG file to load.

11. Test the movie by selecting Control ⇨ Test Movie. Once the Flash movie (.swf file) has been generated, you should see the bitmap load at the top-right corner of the Flash movie and the sound should start to play.

You can see how easy it is to use dynamic elements within Flash MX. This is a powerful new feature which will allow Flash MX developers to go down many new paths.

Streaming video

Flash MX has the ability to natively import and stream video. Flash MX uses the Sorenson Spark codec for encoding video for use in Flash MX. You can have full control over the video; enabling you to start, stop, and rewind the video with your own custom buttons.

We create a simple example of importing a Windows video file (.avi file) and streaming the video within a Flash movie.

On the CD-ROM
You will find the **robertSpin.avi** file, in the ch17 folder of the *Flash MX Bible* CD-ROM. Make a copy of this file to a location on your hard drive.

Importing the video file

In this part of the lesson, you will import a digital video file into a Flash MX document. You can use the AVI file provided on the CD-ROM or use one of your own.

1. Open Flash MX and create a new file by selecting File ➪ New.

2. Save the file to a location on your hard drive naming it video_import.fla; make sure it is in the same directory where you saved the robertSpin.avi file.

3. Create a new Movie Clip symbol to nest the video by selecting Insert ➪ New Symbol.

4. In the Create New Symbol dialog box, type **video** in the Name field.

5. Make sure the Movie Clip behavior is selected and press OK. Flash MX will enter Symbol Editing Mode inside the new Movie Clip.

6. Import the AVI file by selecting File ➪ Import. Browse to the robertSpin.avi file, highlight the file and select OK.

7. The Import Video Settings dialog box appears, as shown in Figure QS-10. You can change the properties of the imported video—manipulating the file size and quality. Flash uses the Sorenson Spark video codec.

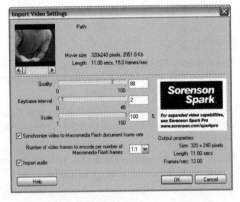

Figure QS-10: The Import Video Settings dialog box

8. Set the Quality slider to 80%, the Keyframe interval slider to 2, and the scale slider to 80%. You can alter these settings as you like; using the Quality slider you can choose a setting which best suits your needs, keeping file size in mind.

9. Select the Import Audio check box to import the sound with your video. Select OK. Flash will compress the video into the Sorenson Spark codec; this may take some time, depending on the speed of your machine.

10. A dialog box will open asking if you would like Flash MX to automatically create the frames needed for the length of video you are importing, select Yes. Flash MX will insert the video on to the document's timeline.

11. Save the Flash document as **embeddedVideo.fla**.

Placing the video

In this part of the lesson, you will learn how to place the video footage into Scene 1.

1. Return to the Main Timeline (that is, Scene 1) of the embeddedVideo.fla document by selecting Scene 1 at the bottom of the Timeline window or by selecting Scene 1 from the Scene panel. You may need to open the Scene panel by selecting Window ➪ Scenes.

2. Open the Library by choosing Window ➪ Library.

3. Drag an instance of the video Movie Clip to the Stage, by clicking and dragging the video symbol to the Stage.

4. Make sure the Property inspector is open by choosing Window ➪ Properties.

5. Select the instance of video Movie Clip on the Stage. In the Property inspector, type video in the <Instance Name> field.

6. Use the Property inspector to position the Video movie clip at X: 150 and Y: 105.

7. Save your Flash document again (File ➪ Save).

Controlling the video

Now that a video instance is on the Main Timeline, you can target the instance with ActionScript in order to control the video's playback.

1. The video has now been prepared and ready to use. The next step is to set up controls to interact with the video. Select Window ➪ Common Libraries ➪ Buttons. You can use buttons from the Buttons library to create the stop, play, and rewind and fast-forward buttons.

2. Open the Playback folder in the Buttons library.

3. Drag an instance of the gel Rewind Button symbol onto the stage.

4. The following Button symbols should also be dragged onto the Stage: gel stop, gel right and gel Fast Forward.

5. Make sure the Property inspector is open by selecting Window ➪ Properties and use it to position the buttons in the following order (refer to Figure QS-11 for an indication of the suggested layout):

   • gel Rewind; X: 210 and Y: 300

   • gel Stop; X: 244 and Y: 300

   • gel Right; X: 279 and Y: 300

   • gel Fast Forward; X: 313 and Y: 300

6. Select the gel Rewind button and open the Actions panel by selecting Window ➪ Actions.

7. Change to Expert mode by choosing Expert mode in the top-right options menu of the Actions panel.

8. Enter the following code of ActionScript:

```
on (release) {
  video.gotoAndStop(1);
}
```

This code will set the video footage back to the first frame. You interact with the `video` Movie Clip as if it was any other Movie Clip, thus making video controls a very easy task to achieve.

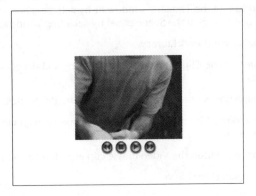

Figure QS-11: After you have completed Step 5, your movie should match this figure.

9. Select the gel Stop button and use the Actions panel to enter the following ActionScript:

```
on (release) {
   video.stop();
}
```

This code will simply stop the video footage at which ever frame it is on when the button is pressed. This is similar to a pause command.

10. Select the gel Right button and enter the following ActionScript into the Actions panel:

```
on (release) {
   video.play();
}
```

This code will start the video playing from its current position.

11. Enter the following ActionScript using the Actions panel on the last button, gel Fast Forward:

```
on (release) {
   video.gotoAndStop(video._totalframes);
}
```

This code moves the video to the last frame. The `_totalframes` property of the MovieClip object is used to find out how many frames exist in the `video` instance.

12. You have now entered all the ActionScript needed to control your movie.

13. Test your movie by selecting Control ⇨ Test Movie. You can use the rewind, stop, stop and fast-forward buttons to control the playback of the video.

Look at the size of the exported SWF containing your video footage — you can see that Flash MX does a pretty good job of optimizing the video.

Cross-Reference If you would like to use video in your Flash MX movies, read Chapter 17, "Embedding Video" for more information about Sorenson Spark Pro.

Scriptable text fields

In Flash MX you can dynamically create and draw a text field, all with ActionScript. This is one of the many improvements and additions to the ActionScript language. In this tutorial we create a simple example where you dynamically create a text field and fill the field with text loaded from a .txt file.

1. Open Flash MX and create a new file by selecting File ⇨ New. This example doesn't use any graphics; it is totally created by ActionScript.

2. Save the file to a location on your hard drive and name it **text_field.fla**.

3. Use your favorite text editor and create a new TXT file and save it to your hard drive in the same folder where you saved the Flash document (.fla file). Name the new file **text.txt**.

4. Insert the following line into the new text file:

```
textMessage=this+is+the+information+in+the+text+field
```

This is the text that will be displayed in the text field after it has been created in Flash.

5. Make sure you are back in Flash MX and select the first frame on Layer 1.

6. Open the Actions panel by choosing Window ⇨ Actions. Insert the following code using the Actions panel:

```
// Create an empty movie clip to hold the text field
_root.createEmptyMovieClip("textFieldHolder", 1);
```

This code simply creates an empty Movie Clip to hold the text field that you will create in the next step.

7. Beneath the code you have just inserted, insert the following code:

```
// Create a new LoadVars object
info = new LoadVars();

// Call the writeTextField function once the data
// has loaded
info.onLoad = writeTextField;

// Load the text file into Flash
info.load("text.txt");
```

The first line of this code creates a new LoadVars object, which is new in Flash MX. The second lines binds the writeTextField function to the onLoad event. The onLoad event is executed once the text file has been loaded into Flash. The third line loads the information from the specified text file into Flash.

8. Insert the following code directly beneath the previous block of code. Do not type ⊃ as it indicates a continuation of the same line of code.

```
// FUNCTION: used to create a text field
function writeTextField (success) {

    // Check if the information was correctly loaded
```

```
if (success == true) {

    // attach a text field to a new Movie Clip
    textFieldHolder.createTextField("myTextField", ⊃
      2, 0, 0, 200, 20);

    // turn on borders
    textFieldHolder.myTextField.border = true;

    // set the text field to the variable textMessage
    // from the loaded text file
    textFieldHolder.myTextField.text = ⊃
      this.textMessage;
  }
}
```

The `writeTextField` function is executed once the information has been loaded. It checks to see if the content of the file was loaded correctly, if so it creates the text field and sets its text to `textMessage`; the variable which was loaded into Flash from the text (TXT) file.

9. Test the movie by selecting Control ➪ Test Movie. You should see a text box appear with the loaded text, from the TXT file, in the upper left corner of the Flash movie.

The extension of Flash's document object model is a great enhancement to the capabilities of Flash MX.

ActionScript event model and the drawing API

A major improvement to the ActionScript language in Flash MX is the enhancement of the event model. You can now apply an event to an object dynamically through ActionScript. This will give developers a lot of power for creating applications in Flash.

Another major improvement is that Macromedia has allowed us to interface with the drawing API. Using this you can dynamically create vector graphics at runtime.

In this tutorial we create an empty movie clip, draw a 50 pixel black square and animate it across the screen, all with ActionScript.

1. Open Flash MX and create a new file by selecting File ➪ New.

2. Save the file to a location on your hard drive and name it **drawing_api.fla**.

3. Select the first frame of the layer and enter the following code using the Actions editor:

```
// create an empty movie clip to draw a square in
_root.createEmptyMovieClip("square", 1);
```

This code creates a new Movie Clip. The Movie Clip will be used to "draw" the vector graphics (refer to Figure QS-12 for a list of the drawing API methods).

Figure QS-12: The Drawing Methods in Flash MX are part of the MovieClip object.

4. The following lines of code use the new drawing API to draw a simple black square at 50 pixels in length and height.

```
// draw a 50 pixel black square
square.beginFill(0x000000, 100);
square.lineTo(0, 50);
square.lineTo(50, 50);
square.lineTo(50, 0);
square.endFill();
```

beginFill is used to start a vector graphic. This method and the endFill method are necessary when drawing with ActionScript. However there are other methods, such as curveTo, which are used to actually "draw."

5. We now assign an enterFrame event to the square Movie Clip using the following code:

```
// assign the enterFrame event to move the square along
// returning to the start when it reaches the end
square.onEnterFrame = function () {

  if (this._x <= Stage.width) this._x += 10;
  if (this._x > Stage.width) this._x = 0;

}
```

This code is an example of using ActionScript to dynamically set the enterFrame event on a new Movie Clip, also created through ActionScript. This technique is new in Flash MX.

6. Test the movie to see the end result by selecting Control ⇨ Test Movie. You will see a black square, 50 × 50 pixels moving across the screen then returning to the beginning of the canvas when it reaches the end (refer to Figure QS-13 to see it in action).

There are quite a few new techniques and objects used in this example including Stage, the drawing API and the dynamic event handlers.

This is a quick example of how powerful the ActionScript language has become. It is now quick and easy to implement some things that were impossible to accomplish in the previous version of Flash.

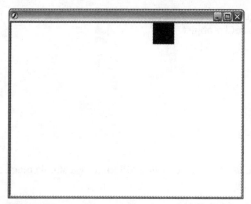

Figure QS-13: The completed movie playing in Test Movie mode.

Summary

✦ Making Flash much more dynamic has been a huge focus for Macromedia and is a big area of growth for Flash MX. ActionScript is very powerful and well-suited for creating advanced Web applications.

✦ Many timesaving features have been introduced in Flash MX, which will appeal to designers. The Timeline enhancements will help to make your Flash MX movies much more manageable and presentable; including Layer folders, the Distribute to Layers command and the improved Break Apart command.

✦ With the dynamic enhancements in Flash MX and the extension of many objects, developers will be able to take advantage of these features and use them to create some powerful applications.

✦ We limited this introduction to showing you simple examples that demonstrate several new features of Flash. There are many more features, such as interacting with Web cams, using microphones, and the ability to create cookie-like material. Features such as these will definitely help to make Flash suitable for creating Web applications.

✦ The rest of the chapters in this book delve into Flash even further, covering topics that we discussed here but in much more detail. You will also find many more topics and areas of Flash MX that are very interesting and worthwhile for creating Flash projects.

✦   ✦   ✦

CHAPTER

In This Chapter

Exploring the uses
of Flash MX

Introducing the structure
of Flash documents

Identifying Flash
file types

Understanding the Flash Framework

Since its humble beginnings as FutureSplash in 1997, Macromedia Flash has matured into a powerful tool for deploying a wide range of media content. With every new version released, the possibilities have increased for imaginative, and dynamic content creation — for the Web and beyond. Macromedia has responded to the development community's unprecedented embrace of Flash by expanding advanced features and enhancing tools for new users. Never before has Flash incorporated so many new features in a single release.

In this chapter, we introduce Flash MX and explore the many possibilities it will open up for your productions. We also discuss how Flash compares to or enhances other programs that you may be familiar with.

Flash movies are usually viewed in a few different ways. The most common method is from within a Web browser, either as an asset within an HTML page or as a Web site completely comprised of a master Flash movie (.swf) using several smaller Flash movies as loaded (.swf) assets. The Flash Player is also available as a stand-alone application (known as a *projector*), which can be used to view movies without needing a Web browser or the plug-in. This method is commonly used for deployment of Flash movies on CD-ROMs, floppy disks, or other offline media formats.

 You can learn more about projectors and standalones in Chapter 23, "Using the Flash Player and Projector."

It's a (Flash) MX World

Flash has seen significant development over the years in both capability and design. What has been consistently proven with each new release is that developers will continue to push the technology into new territory. In its current iteration, Flash MX is hitting its stride as a fully mature and globally popular authoring tool.

However, Flash MX is not alone. Macromedia, in its boldest move ever, has released an entire MX family of products: Flash MX, Dreamweaver MX, Fireworks MX, and ColdFusion MX. Along with FreeHand 10, these five software applications comprise Macromedia Studio MX. The user interfaces for Flash, Dreamweaver and Fireworks are nearly identical, each touting a Property inspector, dockable panel sets, and specialized tools to integrate the products with one another.

Cross-Reference

To learn more about each of these products and how they can enhance your Flash production, refer to Part IX, "Expanding Flash."

Note

At the time of this writing, Macromedia had announced that it would release a new Macromedia communication server technology that will provide two-way audio and video as well as real-time data transfer with Flash Player 6. This technology is not part of Studio MX.

Although the broad array of Flash work already speaks for itself, the sleek interface and the powerful additional features of Flash MX will surely inspire a whole new wave of challenging, functional, entertaining, informative, bizarre, humorous, beautiful, fascinating experiments and innovations.

There are probably more ways to use Flash than there are adjectives to describe them, but here are just a few examples:

✦ Forms for collecting user information and dynamically loading custom content based on this interaction

✦ A video portfolio using native MX video import capabilities and dynamic loading of content

✦ Animated I.D. spots and loading screens with built-in download detection

✦ A practical Web utility, such as a mortgage calculator or a search tool

✦ Robust chat rooms based on XML and server-socket technology

✦ An audio interface dynamically pulling in requested songs using native MX support for MP3 loading

✦ Interactive conceptual art experimentations involving several users, 3D or recording and playback of user interaction

✦ Shopping and e-commerce solutions built entirely using Flash and server-side technology

✦ Alternative content or movie attributes based on system capability testing using Flash MX

✦ Projectors used for creating slide show presentations in the style of PowerPoint, on either CD-ROM or an alternative storage device

✦ Broadcast quality cartoons, advertising, or titling

✦ Optimized animations for the Web, and for portable devices such as cell phones or Pocket PCs

✦ An interface that addresses accessibility issues by modifying certain elements when a screen reader is active

✦ Flash movies that are specifically exported for use in digital video projects requiring special effects and compositing

This list is obviously far from complete and is ever-expanding with each new release of the program. As you can tell from this list, if you can imagine a use for Flash, it can probably be accomplished.

The topography of Flash MX

Before you attempt to construct interactive projects in Flash, you should be familiar with the structure of the authoring environment. Even if you already know Flash 5, this is advisable. That's because with the release of Flash MX, Macromedia has again added many new features to the interface and either moved or improved other features and functionalities. So, to get a firm footing in the new interface, we strongly suggest that you work your way through this book — from the beginning.

Chapter 4, "Interface Fundamentals" introduces the new MX interface and gives you tips for customizing your workspace and optimizing your workflow.

Moreover, you need to proactively plan your interactive projects before you attempt to author them in Flash. An ounce of preplanning goes a long way during the production process. Don't fool yourself — the better your plan looks on paper, the better it will perform when it comes to the final execution.

The foundation for planning interactive Flash projects is detailed in Chapter 3, "Planning Flash Projects," and you will find these concepts reiterated and expanded in chapters that discuss specific project workflows. Chapter 20, "Making Your First Flash MX Project" is a great place to start applying these planning strategies.

In this edition of the *Flash MX Bible*, we've consolidated the overview of interactive planning in the early chapters of the book. In later chapters, we've included step-by-step descriptions of real-world projects that allow you to see how all the theory and planning suggestions apply to the development of specific projects.

Chapter 32, "Creating a Portfolio Site in Flash," describes the process for creating a site that includes a variety of source images. Chapter 33, "Creating a Game in Flash," walks through the logic required to design and script a functional and engaging game.

There are two primary files that you create during Flash development: Flash documents (.fla files) and Flash movies (.swf files). We discuss both of these formats next.

File types in Flash MX

Flash documents (.fla files) are architected to provide an efficient authoring environment for projects of all sizes. Within this environment, content can be organized into scenes, and the ordering of scenes can be rearranged throughout the production cycle. Layers provide easy separation of graphics within each scene, and, as Guide or Mask layers, they can also aid drawing or even provide special effects. The Timeline shows keyframes, motion and shape tweens, labels, and comments. The Library (which can be shared amongst movies at author-time or at runtime) stores all the symbols in your project such as graphics, fonts, animated elements, sounds or video, and components.

Flash MX Components are an evolution of the Smart Clips that many Flash developers used to make it easier to reuse ActionScript. The pre-built components that ship with Flash MX are explained in Chapter 29, "Using Components." We also introduce some custom components in the various projects that are described in other parts of the book.

Flash documents

Throughout this book, you will see us refer to Flash documents, which are the .fla files created by Flash MX when you choose File ➪ Save or File ➪ Save As. Unlike some graphic applications such as Macromedia FreeHand or Adobe Illustrator, the file extension for Flash documents does not reflect the version of the authoring tool. For example, Flash 5 and Flash MX will save Flash documents as .fla files. You cannot open later version documents in previous versions of the authoring tool. You do not use Flash documents with the Flash Player, nor do you need to upload these files to your Web server. Always keep a version (and a backup!) of your Flash document.

New Feature   Flash MX allows you to resave your Flash MX document (.fla file) as a Flash 5 document (.fla file). Choose File ➪ Save As and select Flash 5 Document in the Save as type menu. If you save the document in this manner, you can open the Flash document (.fla file) in the Flash 5 authoring application.

Figure 1-1 shows how Flash documents are comprised of individual scenes that contain keyframes to describe changes on the Stage. What you can't see in this figure is the efficiency of sharing Flash Libraries among several Flash documents, loading other Flash movies into a parent or "master" Flash movie using the loadMovie() action, or creating interactive elements with scripting methods.

Cross-Reference   Part VII of this book, "Approaching ActionScript," addresses the topic of sharing and loading Flash movies. This part will prepare you for taking on more advanced ActionScript development.

Flash movies

When you publish or test a Flash document, Flash MX will create a Flash movie file with the .swf file extension. This file format is an optimized version of the Flash document, retaining only the elements from the project file that are actually used. Flash movies are uploaded to your Web server where they are usually integrated into HTML documents for other Web users to view. You can protect your finished Flash movies from being easily imported or edited in the authoring environment by other users.

Caution   The Protect from import option in the Publish Settings does not prevent third-party utilities from stripping artwork, symbols, sounds and ActionScript code from your Flash movies. For more information, read Chapter 21, "Publishing Flash Movies."

Much of the information contained originally within a Flash document (.fla file) is discarded in the attempt to make the smallest file possible when exporting a Flash move (.swf file). When your movie is exported, all original elements remain but layers are essentially flattened and run on one timeline, in the order that was established in the Flash document. Practically all information originally in the file will be optimized somehow, and any unused Library elements are not exported with the Flash movie. Library assets are loaded into and stored in the first frame they are used in. For optimization, reused assets are only saved to the file once and are referenced throughout the movie from this one area. Bitmap images and sounds can be compressed with a variety of quality settings as well.

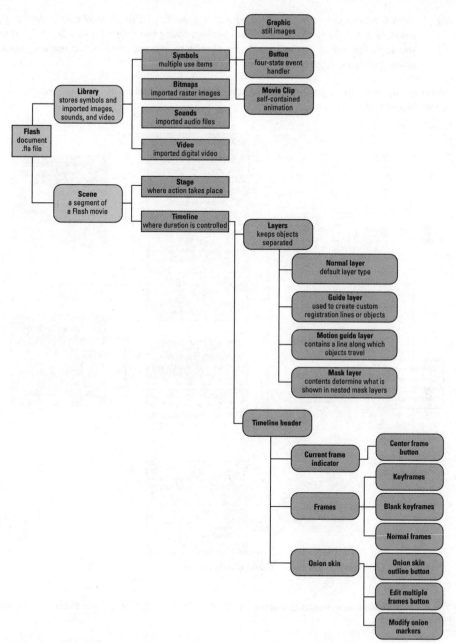

Figure 1-1: Elements of a Flash document (.fla) in the authoring environment

New Feature

Flash 6 movies can now be optimized with a specialized **Compress Movie** option that is available in the Flash tab of the Publish Settings dialog box (File ➪ Publish Settings). When you apply this option, you will see drastic file-size savings with movies that use a significant amount of ActionScript code.

Refer to Figure 1-2 for a graphic explanation of the characteristics of the Flash movie (.swf file) format.

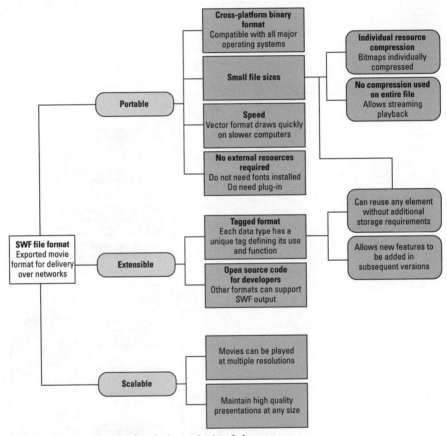

Figure 1-2: Overview of the Flash movie (.swf) format

Cross-Reference

Flash Player detection is discussed in detail in Chapter 22, "Integrating Flash Content with HTML."

Cross-Reference

Guidelines for creating accessible content for the Flash Player 6 are introduced in Chapter 20, "Making Your First Flash MX Project."

Introducing Flash Player 6

The difference between the naming conventions of the Flash Player plug-in and the Flash authoring software is potentially confusing. Macromedia is now referring to its latest release of the player as Flash Player 6, tagging the version number at the end of the name instead of following in the naming convention of its predecessors. One reason the Flash Player is numbered, rather than dubbed "MX" like the authoring software, is because a standard sequential number is required for plug-in detection.

The Flash Player now integrates MSAA technology to support assistive technologies, such as screen readers to make Flash content more accessible to people with disabilities. Macromedia developers have also written XML technology directly into the player, significantly speeding up transmissions. Playback on the Macintosh has been improved, while the file size of the player download has been kept small (despite the additions).

There are several other ways in which Flash movies, or their parts, can be played back or displayed. Since Flash 4, the Publish feature has offered provisions for the export of movies or sections of movies to either the QuickTime digital video format, the QuickTime Flash layer vector format, or to the Animated GIF format. Parts of movies can also be exported as a series of individual bitmaps or as vector files. Single frames can also be exported to these formats.

The Many Faces of Flash MX

Flash is a hybrid application that is like no other application. On the immediate surface, it may seem (to some) to be a simple hybrid between a Web-oriented bitmap handler, and a vector-drawing program, such as Macromedia FreeHand or Adobe Illustrator. But while Flash is indeed such a hybrid, it's also capable of much, much more. It's also an interactive multimedia-authoring program and a sophisticated animation program suitable for creating a range of animations — from simple Web ornaments to broadcast-quality cartoons. As if that weren't enough, it's also the host of a powerful and adaptable scripting language.

ActionScript has evolved from a limited drag-and-drop method of enabling animation to a full-fledged object-oriented programming language very similar to JavaScript. Flash ActionScript can work in conjunction with XML (Extensible Markup Language), HTML, and many other applications and parts of the Web. Flash content now can be integrated with many server-side technologies, and the Flash Player offers built-in support for dynamically loading images, MP3s, movies, and other data. Flash can work seamlessly with ColdFusion MX and XML socket servers to deliver streamlined dynamic interactive experiences.

So, what's this evolving hybrid we call Flash really capable of? That's a question that remains to be answered by developers such as you. In fact, we're hoping that you will master this application and show us a thing or two. That's why we've written this book: to put the tool in your hands and get you started on the road to your own innovations.

Because Flash is a hybrid application capable of just about anything, a good place to start working with this powerhouse is to inquire: What are the components of this hybrid? And if they were separated out, how might their capabilities be described? Those are the questions that we answer in this chapter.

Bitmap handler

In truth, Flash has limited capabilities as an image-editing program. It is more accurate to describe this part of the Flash application as a bitmap *handler*. Bitmap images are composed of dots on a grid of individual pixels. The location (and color) of each dot must be stored in memory, which makes this a memory-intensive format and leads to larger file sizes. Another characteristic of bitmap images is that they cannot be scaled without compromising quality (clarity and sharpness). The adverse effects of scaling an image up are more pronounced than when scaling down. Because of these two drawbacks — file sizes and scaling limitations — bitmap images are not ideal for Web use. However, for photographic-quality images, bitmap formats are indispensable and will often produce better image quality and lower file sizes than vector images of equivalent complexity.

Vector-based drawing program

The heart of the Flash application is a vector-based drawing program, with capabilities similar to either Macromedia FreeHand or Adobe Illustrator. A vector-based drawing program doesn't rely upon individual pixels to compose an image. Instead, it draws shapes by defining points that are described by coordinates. Lines that connect these points are called paths, and vectors at each point describe the curvature of the path. Because this scheme is mathematical, there are two distinct advantages: Vector content is significantly more compact, and it's thoroughly scalable without image degradation. These advantages are especially significant for Web use.

Vector-based animator

The vector animation component of the Flash application is unlike any other program that preceded it. Although Flash is capable of handling bitmaps, its native file format is vector-based. So, unlike many other animation and media programs, Flash relies on the slim and trim vector format for transmission of your final work. Instead of storing megabytes of pixel information for each frame, Flash stores compact vector descriptions of each frame. Whereas a bitmap-based animation program (such as Apple's QuickTime) struggles to display each bitmap in rapid succession, Flash quickly renders the vector descriptions as needed and with far less strain on either the bandwidth or the recipient's machine. This is a huge advantage when transmitting animations and other graphic content over the Web.

Video compressor

The latest release of Flash includes a built-in video compressor — the Sorenson Spark codec. You can now import source video files directly into Flash MX documents (.fla files). More importantly, Flash Player 6 includes the Sorenson Spark codec as well! This means that the Flash Player 6 plug-in can now be considered one of the world's smallest video plug-ins. Users do not need to have Apple QuickTime, RealSystems RealOne, or Microsoft Windows Media Player installed in order to view video in a Flash movie. Unlike Director Shockwave, which accommodates video but still requires Apple QuickTime to be installed to playback the video, the Flash Player 6 provides a seamless solution.

Cross-Reference

To learn more about this exciting new development in Flash MX, refer to Chapter 17, "Embedding Video." We also discuss Sorenson Squeeze, a brand new application designed to create the highest-quality Flash video content.

You can manipulate video content and/or include them in your productions, but you could also use Flash MX to directly export high-quality video content for broadcast video production.

You can learn how to transfer Flash animations to high-quality video in Chapter 14, "Exporting Animation."

Multimedia authoring program

If the heart of Flash is a vector-based drawing program, then the body of Flash is a multimedia-authoring program (or authoring *environment*). Flash documents (.fla files) can contain multiple media assets, including sound, still graphics, animation and video. Moreover, Flash is a powerful tool for creating truly interactive content because it allows you to add (ActionScript) commands to dynamically control movie (.swf file) playback. Whether you are designing simple menu systems or customized and intuitive experimental interfaces, Flash content can be authored to recognize and respond to user-input.

Animation sequencer

Most multimedia-authoring programs have a component for sequencing content as animation, and Flash is no exception. But in Flash, the animation sequencer is the core of the application. The Timeline window controls the display of all content — static or animated — within your Flash project. Within the Timeline window, there are two areas that allow you to organize content in visual space and in linear time.

Layers and layer folders allow you to keep track of content that has been placed into your Flash document. The visibility of each layer can be controlled independently to make it easier to isolate specific elements as you are authoring. Layers are viewed from front to back within each frame of the timeline — items on upper layers will overlay other items on lower layers. Any number of items can be placed on a single layer, but you have less control over the stacking order within a layer. Within the same layer, ungrouped vector lines and shapes will always be on the bottom level, while bitmaps, text, grouped items, and symbol instances will be on the upper level.

Flash MX now includes the option for Layer folders. This is invaluable for organizing projects that involve many separate elements.

For a detailed "tour" of the Flash MX environment, refer to Chapter 4, "Interface Fundamentals." The process of making artwork and managing groups and symbols is discussed in Chapter 5, "Drawing in Flash," and in Chapter 6, "Symbols, Instances, and the Library," respectively.

The structure that creates the illusion of movement in a Flash movie is a series of frames. Each frame represents a still moment in time and by controlling how the Playhead moves through these frames, you can control the speed, duration, and order of an animated sequence.

By changing the content in your layers on each frame, you can manually create frame-by-frame animation. However one of the things that makes Flash such a popular animation machine is its ability to auto-interpolate or *tween* animation. By defining the content on a beginning and an end keyframe and applying a Motion tween or a Shape tween, you can quickly create or modify animated shape transformations and the movement of elements on the Stage.

The many ways of creating Flash animation are discussed in Part III: "Creating Animation and Effects."

Within one Flash document you can also set up a series of separate scenes, each scene is a continuation of the same Main Timeline, but scenes can be named, and reordered at any time. Scenes play through from first to last without interruption unless Flash's interactive commands ("actions") dictate otherwise.

The steps for using ActionScript for simple control of movie playback are introduced in Part V: "Adding Basic Interactivity to Flash Movies."

Programming and database front end

The past two versions of Flash brought vast expansion of the possibilities for integrating Flash interfaces with server-side technology and dynamic loading of content using XML, ColdFusion, and Generator. These improvements largely came out of the development and maturity of ActionScript as a viable programming language. Flash developed into an alternative front end for large databases, which meant it could serve as an online store, MP3 player, or weather channel — an amazing feat for an "animation program"!

With Flash MX there are even more possibilities at our fingertips. One of the exciting new functionalities in this version is the incorporation of components supporting features only Generator or third-party applications offered in the past. Now you can load JPEGs and MP3s into Flash at runtime (or "on the fly"), without having to use Generator. Support for XML has been dramatically improved due to coding enhancements in Flash Player 6. Now information can be transferred in a fraction of the time it took with Flash 5.

There are many other enhancements to the programming environment and functionality of Flash that experienced users will appreciate and new users will come to value. Here are just a few of the new programming features you'll find in Flash MX:

✦ Although the improvements to ActionScript between Flash 5 and Flash MX are not as obvious as the leap made from Flash 4 to Flash 5, there are still some significant alterations. These changes support ActionScript's move toward acceptance as a standard, object-oriented programming (OOP) language on its own. One of the new features that advanced and beginning programmers alike will enjoy is a robust drawing API that allows developers to create complex graphics entirely from code.

✦ Flash Player 6 now offers improved support of XML. Support for the language has been more fully integrated with the player to improve parsing rates, eliminating the need for many of the troublesome work-arounds that were required with the Flash 5 Player.

✦ System capability checking is now built into ActionScript.

✦ The new `LoadVars` object improves upon the `loadVariables()` action by expanding upon and simplifying the process of sending and retrieving data from servers.

✦ Buttons can now be the target of actions.

✦ Shared objects can be used a lot like cookies, allowing you to store data on an end user's computer.

✦ A new object and event model is added to Flash MX ActionScript, where an object listens for and responds to specific events, such as a certain type of user input.

✦ The ActionScript editor (also known as the Actions panel) is vastly improved with new features including code hints, breakpoints and formatting control.

Summary

✦ Flash combines many of the key tools for multimedia authoring into one nimble program. The integration it facilitates with other programs and languages promotes better Web content and more advanced applications.

✦ Flash content is not only found on the Web. For example, it is also used for CD-ROM authoring, broadcast graphics, offline interfaces, and business presentations.

✦ Flash MX is a multifaceted application that can create a wide range of interactive products for the ever-growing variety of Web-enabled devices that surfers use to access the Internet.

✦ Careful planning of Flash development will undoubtedly save you time and effort in the long run.

✦ ✦ ✦

Exploring Web Technologies

✦ ✦ ✦ ✦

In This Chapter

Using Flash for
Web deployment

Understanding the
limitations of Flash

Looking at competing
technologies

Preparing to develop
Flash content

✦ ✦ ✦ ✦

Over the years, many technologies have been developed to work in conjunction with Macromedia Flash. Understanding the process of integrating these technologies will no doubt enable you to create more interactive and complex productions. If you're new to Flash, or you're looking for new ways to enhance or broaden your movies, you'll benefit from reading this chapter. It looks at the placement of Flash within the ever growing and developing toolset for Web development today.

Contextualizing Flash in the Internet Evolution

If you follow the development of "bleeding edge" technology, you may have noticed how often software is created, updated, and made obsolete. At times, this seems to happen almost on a daily basis. But exactly how many practical (and affordable) options exist for Web development, and how can everyone develop standardized methods of using these vast options? In this section, we examine how Flash MX continues to push the direction and limits of the Internet.

High expectations for Web experiences

These days the people visiting your Web sites and the clients who hire you for your expertise want to experience engaging interfaces with amazing graphics and sound. Clients may believe that everyone will be able to visit the site, download material instantaneously (regardless of connection speed limitations), and that every visitor will be having the same experience.

With every release of a new version of Flash, Web developers have access to bigger and better capabilities. We've seen a vast evolution from the early days in 1997 of mere vector animations, which vastly reduced file sizes of standard GIF animations. In 1998, Flash 3 made a marked improvement by introducing more control over these animations. At this time, Web sites and small games started to arrive on the development scene. That was also the year when Macromedia Generator was introduced, enabling dynamic graphics and data for Flash movies. Many companies were apprehensive about investing in Flash development, because Flash was relatively new and gaining ground as an accepted form of Web delivery.

In 1999, when Flash 4 was introduced, this attitude changed a great deal. The new version was much more powerful, and could accomplish many of the tasks that Generator provided in the past. Database interaction and dynamic content was suddenly possible in real time. However, Flash 4 was still a difficult application for developers to use; the programming interface for ActionScript code was limited by drag-and-drop functionality (which was only avoidable by using third-party software). This problem was no longer true in the 2000 release of version 5. Flash 5 incorporated XML data, and ActionScript became an object-oriented programming language (OOP) that strongly resembled JavaScript.

Finally in 2002, Web designers and developers have been handed the sixth version of Flash, now called MX. With the new software and player, we find XML is now processed remarkably faster, movies can be made accessible, and Macromedia Generator is no longer used. Developers can create reusable components that greatly decrease development time. Also, Flash Player 6 introduced support for video playback. Flash movies have become more browser-friendly with named anchors that allow specific sections of Flash movies to be bookmarked. With the support of programmers, ActionScript has continued its development into more of a "real" programming language.

 Cross-Reference You can find out more about new features such as video importing in Chapter 17, "Embedding Video," and components in Chapter 29, "Using Components."

In the span of about six years, we have seen an incredible evolution from Flash's predecessor known as FutureSplash, to the most widely installed Web-based plug-in technology. When Flash 5 was released, Flash was undoubtedly the key for Web branding, and it seemed as though every company wanted Flash content on their Web sites. Flash has continued to enjoy this popularity, despite opponents calling the technology "unusable." You could almost compare the introduction of Flash to that of color television. It's difficult to return to largely static HTML pages after the interactivity, animation, eye candy, and innovation Flash sites offer to Web surfers—even those on slow connections or portable devices. Because of Macromedia's efforts to keep the file size of the Flash Player smaller than most browser plug-ins, and the fact it has been preinstalled on most systems for some time now, Flash remains a widely accessible and acceptable technology for Web deployment.

 Note Currently, the file size of the latest release of Flash Player 6 (r23) is 383KB for Windows (as an ActiveX control) and 900KB (as a .bin file) for Macintosh OS X.

To Flash or not to Flash?

It is an important part of the developer's job to decide if Flash is the most appropriate tool to achieve the goals of any given project. Consider why you want—or need—to employ Flash in your work, because there are occasions when it may *not* be the best choice. It may not be wise to use this technology merely because it is "the thing to do" or "cool." If you're pitching Flash projects to clients, it's a good idea to be prepared with reasons why Flash is the best tool to use to get the job done. Later, we consider the benefit of other technologies, but for now consider what Flash can (and cannot) offer to your projects.

Effective use of Flash

With the Flash MX authoring tool, you can create a wide range of presentation material or develop fully functional applications that run in Web browsers or handheld devices:

✦ **Flash generates very small file sizes while producing high-quality animation with optimal sound reproduction.** Companies making world-renowned cartoons, such as Disney, even use Flash for some of their work. Because of these small file sizes, Flash movies (such as cards or announcements) can even be sent via e-mail.

✦ **Nearly any multimedia file format can be integrated into Flash.** Vector images (such as EPS and FreeHand or Illustrator files), bitmaps (GIF, PCT, TIF, PNG, and JPG), sound files (like WAV, AIF, or MP3), and now video (such as AVI and MOV) are all importable into your movies. Plug-ins or third-party software is not required (although it does exist) to accomplish these imports. Nor is it required to play back your movies in Flash Player 6. Significant editing advantages sometimes exist when using imported files, such as symbol and layer formatting from FreeHand and Fireworks files. These features can be beneficial if you will be working with a client's raw resources.

✦ **Precise layouts with embedded fonts are possible with Flash.** Formatting is usually inconsistent when using HTML and can easily vary amongst browsers. You can be confident your movies will format and display consistently when viewed with the Flash Player.

✦ **Text, movies, and now images can be displayed in your movie from a remote database.** You can incorporate dynamic content into your movie as long as the database can be connected via the Web and the data is formatted correctly.

✦ **Just as you can send information from a database to your movie, you can send data from your movie to the database.** Flash movies can accept user input and send the data to a server. Built-in components make it easier and faster than ever before to build interactive elements, which do not require an advanced knowledge of ActionScript from the part of the developer. Your forms have the potential to be much more engaging with animation or sound additions. Another use of this technology is to track user progression throughout your site and send the information to a database.

✦ **With the proper server-side software you can produce multi-user interactivity with backward compatibility.** Since Flash 5, we have been able to use XML sockets for transmission between a socket server and the movie. XML operates much faster using Flash Player 6. Emerging technologies integrating with Flash MX will make this kind of development easier to develop in the future.

✦ **Several Flash movies can be loaded into one large container movie.** For instance, you can create a movie and then load many Flash assets into it for each individual area. Using this method will allow you to delegate tasks to different designers and developers if you're working with others. This also allows you to create large Web sites, which are both manageable and only download what is called for by the end user.

✦ **While you can break up a large Web site by loading many Flash assets into a container movie, you can also dynamically load images and MP3 files using Flash Player 6.** This is also possible if you're working in Flash 5 and using Macromedia Generator or other server applications.

✦ **Creating components in Flash MX allows developers to form reusable template interfaces or assets for Flash movies.** The components that ship with Flash MX greatly reduce the development time of interfaces that require scrollbars or radio buttons. Components can be easily customized in the new Property inspector, and many settings can change without the use of ActionScript.

✦ **The Flash Player is available on many different platforms and devices including Windows, Macintosh, Solaris, Linux, OS/2, SGI IRIX, Pocket PC, and even some mobile telephones.** Refer to www.macromedia.com/shockwave/download/alternates for the latest version player available for these and other alternative platforms. Just about any Web surfer will be able to view Flash content by downloading and installing the latest version of the Flash Player.

✦ **Movies can be developed to run presentations of their own, commonly known as Projectors.** Projectors are Flash movies running on an embedded player, so you do not need a browser to run them. They can be burned onto DVDs, CD-ROMs, or any other media-storage device.

✦ **Like HTML pages, content from Flash movies can be sent to a printer.** ActionScript offers you the ability to precisely control the layout of the printed page. The quality of the printed artwork and text from Flash movies is remarkable.

Obviously, these are only some of the things that Flash movies can do. Regardless of the intent of your production, verifying the use of this software is usually a good idea during pre-production. In the following section, we consider situations in which you may not want to use Flash to develop your content.

When not to use Flash

If you're enthusiastic about Flash and have used Flash for previous Web projects, you can easily develop a bias in favor of Flash. It may be hard to even consider that other options could be better for development. Knowing what technology is best for each solution will assist you in offering the best quality product to clients.

✦ **Flash movies play in a Web browser using a plug-in.** Despite the near ubiquity of the Flash Player, there are still some users who may need to download the player. If you're using Flash MX to create Flash 6 movies, many surfers trying to view your site may need to update their players. It is also important to keep in mind that some workplaces or institutions (such as schools) will not allow their workers or students to install applications on the systems.

✦ **The type and version of the Web browser can affect the functionality of a Flash movie.** While internal ActionScript code should largely remain unaffected by browser variation, some scripting and interactivity with HTML documents (using JavaScript or VBScript) may be browser-dependent.

✦ **Web browsers will not automatically redirect to alternative content if the Flash Player is not installed.** You as a developer are required to create detection mechanisms for the Flash Player.

Cross-Reference

To learn how to create detection methods for the Flash Player, refer to Chapter 22, "Integrating Flash Content with HTML." We also discuss the Macromedia Flash Deployment Kit in Chapter 42, "Working with Dreamweaver MX."

✦ **3D file formats cannot be directly imported or displayed in Flash movies.** To achieve 3D-style effects, frame-by-frame animation or ActionScript is required. Macromedia Director 8.5, however, has built-in features for creating 3D content.

✦ **Typical search engines (or spiders) have a difficult time indexing the content of Flash movies.** When you make Flash-based sites, you should create some alternate HTML content that can be indexed by search engines. If you simply place Flash movies in an otherwise empty HTML document, your Web site will not likely be indexed.

✦ **Flash sites were never meant to completely replace text-based HTML sites.** For sites largely based on textual information with basic or simple graphics, there is little point to using Flash. Selecting and printing text content from Flash movies is not always as intuitive as that of standard HTML sites. At this time, the Accessibility features of Flash Player 6 are only supported by Internet Explorer for Windows when used in conjunction with the Window-Eyes reader. A greater number of assistive technologies support HTML pages.

✦ **In many circumstances, HTML is quicker, easier, and cheaper to develop than Flash content.** There are many established applications supporting HTML development.

Of course, there are always exceptions to any "rule," and these suggestions should be considered as guidelines or cautions to be examined before you embark on any Flash development. In the following section, we examine other tools used to create multimedia content.

Alternative methods of multimedia authoring

Now, let's focus on Flash's competition in the multimedia authoring arena. This section is not intended to give you a comprehensive background on these technologies. Rather, we seek to simply give you some context of Flash as it exists in the rest of the multimedia world.

Dynamic HTML

DHTML or Dynamic HTML, is a specialized set of markup tags that tap into an extended document object model (DOM) that version 4.0 browsers or higher can utilize. Using <LAYER> or <DIV> tags, you can create animations and interactive effects with Web-authoring tools ranging from Notepad or SimpleText to Macromedia Dreamweaver. You can actually combine Flash content with DHTML to create Flash layers on top of other HTML content. One problem with DHTML is that Netscape and Internet Explorer do not use it in the same way. Usually, you need to make sure you have a specialized set of code (or minor modifications) for each browser type.

XML and XSL

XML stands for e*X*tensible *M*arkup *L*anguage. XML looks like HTML, but it's really a language that can manage structured or related data such as pricing information, contact information, or anything else that you would store in a database. XSL stands for e*X*tensible *S*tylesheet *L*anguage. XSL documents apply formatting rules to XML documents. Together, XML and XSL documents can create interactive data-driven Web sites. However, only newer browsers can read and display XML and XSL documents. The Flash Player can be installed on just about every graphical Web browser available, regardless of the browser's version. As such, you can potentially reach more users with Flash content than you can with XML and XSL content. As you see later in this chapter, XML can also be used to supply data to Flash.

Macromedia Director

Originally Macromedia's flagship product, Director is *the* multimedia powerhouse authoring solution. Since its inception in the 1980s, Director has had the benefit of many years to establish its mature interface and development environment. Director can integrate and control many media types, including video, audio, and entire Flash movies. Director also has an Xtras plug-in architecture, which allows third-party developers to expand or enhance Director's capabilities. More recently, Director 8.5 has added true 3D modeling support. Now, you can create Shockwave games with textured models and lighting effects! However, there are two major drawbacks to Shockwave Director: It requires a large download for the full player installation, and the player is available only for Windows and Macintosh platforms. Director remains a primary authoring tool for CD-ROM and DVD-ROM development.

Macromedia Authorware

Authorware, like Flash, was technology developed by another company and then bought by Macromedia to add to its software lineup. Since this acquisition, Macromedia has significantly developed the features and capabilities of Authorware. It is an authoring application and a companion plug-in technology, with similar audio-video integration capabilities as Macromedia Director. However, Authorware was developed with e-learning in mind. You can structure training solutions and monitor student learning with Authorware. We mention Authorware as a potential competitor to Flash because many Flash developers use Flash to create Web-training modules that interact with server-side databases.

Scalable Vector Graphics

The Scalable Vector Graphics (SVG) format is widely supported by some of the largest names in the industry, such as Microsoft and Adobe. This format has even been proposed as a graphics standard for the Web by the World Wide Web Consortium (W3C), whose purpose is to form universal protocols regarding Web standards. SVG is much more than a graphics format; it is also an XML-based development language. Adobe Illustrator and LiveMotion 1.0 both create files based on this technology, so understandably Adobe is the strongest supporter of development in SVG. Adobe also creates the plug-in for using this file format on the Web, but the W3C is pushing for all browsers to provide built-in support for the format so that a third-party download is unnecessary. This may be necessary if it is ever to become a viable content format, because Web surfers have been quite slow to adopt the SVG plug-in. For more information on this topic, you can refer to www.w3c.org/Graphics/SVG and www.adobe.com/svg.

Note   Even Adobe is quietly abandoning support of the SVG format. The latest release of Adobe LiveMotion 2.0 does not create SVG files—it only outputs Flash movies (.swf files).

Microsoft PowerPoint

PowerPoint is usually considered a tool for making offline presentations shown in business meetings, conferences and seminars. What is perhaps not as well known is how PowerPoint is sometimes used online for presenting such content. A PowerPoint Viewer plug-in allows your browser to handle these files. While PowerPoint allows anyone from a designer to a programmer to easily create slide-show presentations, Flash can be considered a more robust tool for creating dynamic high-impact presentations.

SMIL, Real Systems RealPlayer, and Apple QuickTime

SMIL is the *S*ynchronized *M*ultimedia *I*ntegration *L*anguage, and it also looks a lot like HTML markup tags. SMIL allows you to layer several media components in SMIL-compatible players such as the RealOne Player and the QuickTime Player. You probably have seen SMIL at work when you load the RealOne Player and see the snazzy graphics that comprise the channels interface. With SMIL, you can layer interactive buttons and dynamic text on top of streaming video or audio content. You may not even think of SMIL as a competing technology, but rather a complementary one—Flash can be one of the multimedia tracks employed by SMIL! You can even use Flash as a track type in QuickTime alone, without the use of SMIL. With Flash 4, Macromedia and Apple announced QuickTime Flash movies, which allow you to create Flash interfaces that layer on top of audio-video content. The RealOne Player will also play "tuned" Flash files directly, without the use of SMIL. A tuned Flash file is weighted evenly from frame to frame to ensure synchronized playback. Note, however, that tuned files usually need to be strict linear animations without any interactive functionality.

There are several multimedia companies developing proprietary plug-in-based authoring tools for Web multimedia. To participate in a discussion of multimedia formats, check out the forums at www.flashsupport.com.

Exploring Companion Technologies

Now that you have clear understanding of how Flash fits into the current World Wide Web, we can begin to discuss the technologies that contribute to Flash's well-being. In today's world of the developer, you not only need to know how to create your Flash movies, but you also need to know how to implement Flash into existing environments, such as a Web browser or your business client's Web-ready (or not-so-Web-ready) databases.

HTML is here to stay

HTML is not going anywhere, regardless of the prolific nature of Flash on the Web. Using HTML to your advantage is very important, because it is undeniably the best solution for certain forms of Web deployment. In addition, sites constructed entirely in Flash often require HTML to function properly. Here's how HTML works with Flash:

✦ **Displaying and formatting the movie on a Web page requires HTML.** It isn't always easy to hand-code HTML to work with ActiveX for Internet Explorer and the plug-in for Netscape at the same time.

✦ **HTML is required to construct framesets correctly displaying scalable Flash movies in a browser.** Flash is able to scale to the size of the browser window, thus allowing movies to be viewed at sizes correlating to the size of the end user's monitor.

✦ **Placing some content within a Flash movie is not possible, so you will sometimes need to link it from your movie to an HTML page.** For instance, PDF files cannot be displayed within a movie and will need to be linked from the Flash movie and viewed separately with the Acrobat Reader. Or, you may need to access video files created for the RealOne Player or Windows Media Player. You can place links to these source files, or link to an HTML document that embeds the source file.

✦ **If your end user is not willing or able to view your Flash content, HTML allows you to provide an alternate version of your Web site.** Despite the addition of Accessibility into the Flash player allowing screen-reader interaction, not all screen readers are currently able to facilitate the built-in support. An HTML version is sure to reach most of this potential audience.

Many people find learning, and perhaps even using, HTML, to be painful and tedious. Accommodating the differences among browsers can sometimes be time-consuming and dry work. However, knowing some HTML is highly recommended and well worth the effort. HTML should be understood by any Web professional. If you are uncomfortable with the code, using Macromedia Dreamweaver MX will help your transition into the HTML world.

Client-side scripting using JavaScript

ActionScript and JavaScript are similar beasts, especially since Flash 5. Flash MX increases the similarity between the two languages, so by learning one language you will be able to translate this knowledge with relative ease. Already knowing some JavaScript when entering the Flash realm will definitely put you at a strong advantage. However, JavaScript itself is frequently used in conjunction with Flash, which we will look at in this section.

With JavaScript, you can create customized browser pop-up windows that open from Flash movies. By "customized," we mean browser windows that don't have any scrollbars, button bars, or menu items across the top of the browser window.

JavaScript can pass data into the Flash movie when the Web page containing the movie loads. Some browsers allow you to continually pass data back and forth between Flash and JavaScript. Also, you are able to dynamically pass variables from JavaScript right into the Flash movie.

JavaScript can be used to detect the presence or absence of the Flash Player plug-in in the user's Web browser. Likewise, you can VBScript on Internet Explorer for Windows to detect the Flash Player ActiveX control. JavaScript (or VBScript) can redirect the Web browser to alternative content if the player is not installed.

Flash movie properties such as width and height can be written on the fly using JavaScript. You can also detect various system properties (which is also possible using ActionScript in Flash MX) in JavaScript code, and pass this information into Flash.

 The *JavaScript Bible* by Danny Goodman (published by Wiley Publishing) is a highly respected resource on JavaScript. If you require more information on this language, this book is highly recommended.

Recognizing Project Potential

In this final section, we provide an overview of the types of Flash projects that are possible. This is just a starting point to prime your creative juices and break through any self-imposed limiting perceptions that you have garnered about Flash media. The categories we have devised here are by no means industry standards — they're broad generalized groups into which most Flash development will fall.

Linear presentations

In the early days when the Internet was growing, Flash shorts (cartoons) were the media buzz. These cartoons generally played from start to finish in a very linear fashion. Generally speaking, these movies load and then play — and count on catching the user's attention through the story and animation. These movies sometimes contain advanced ActionScript for animation, including randomized movement or content.

Interactive presentations

Interactive presentations represent the next step up from linear presentations. They provide the user control of the way information is presented, the flow, or the experience altogether. Usually Web sites of any construct will be considered an interactive presentation. If you have information or content in a section somewhere in a movie or Web site, then you probably have an interactive presentation. An interactive presentation will allow end users to choose the content they see, by allowing them to navigate throughout a site, bypassing some content while accessing other content. A Flash movie in this category may have all the viewable content stored in a container movie, or across several Flash files linked to a main site.

Data-driven presentations

This category of Flash development represents any movies that load external data (either dynamic or static) to drive the presentation to the user. For example, a weather site that uses Flash may download dynamic Flash graphics of precipitation maps to display to the site's visitors. These graphics may be customized for each user of the site, depending on where he lives. Data-driven may even simply mean that text information within the Flash movie changes from time to time. Simply put, when information data is separated from the actual Flash movie, it is considered data-driven.

Data-driven applications

This category is somewhat loosely defined as those Flash movies that allow the user to accomplish some sort of task or enable a transaction from the Flash movie to an external remote data source. For example, an online Flash ATM (that is, bank machine) could allow a bank customer to log in to the bank's secure server, and transfer funds to another account or pay a bill. All of these tasks would require a transaction from the Flash movie to the bank's server. Another example could be an online Flash shopping cart, in which visitors add products to their virtual carts, and check out with their final order. Again, these tasks would require data to be sent from and received by the Flash movie.

Summary

✦ Expectations of Web sites produced by Flash developers and designers grow with every new version of Flash. With an ever-increasing tool base, sites not facilitating new technology (such as new forms of interaction or media content) can easily become overlooked or considered uninteresting.

✦ Flash has many features making it useful authoring software for online deployment. Some of the main reasons to use it include small movie file sizes and the ability to precisely control layout.

✦ Flash is not always the best tool for the job. End users need a plug-in to view Flash movies, and Flash sites are not indexed well by search engines.

✦ There are several multimedia file formats available on the Web today. Although most users have many of the popular plug-ins installed, some users have restricted bandwidth and computer system environments. Flash has the capability to produce small movie files that can play identically on several devices.

✦ In order to develop advanced Flash projects, one should know the necessary HTML, JavaScript, and data-formatting standards allowing Flash to interact with other environments and data sources. These languages broaden the capabilities for interactivity and access to large amounts of data.

✦ Flash movies loosely fall into several different categories, which are based on the type of experience they provide the end user. These categories provide a basis to visualize future projects for the benefit of your clients.

✦ ✦ ✦

Planning Flash Projects

✦ ✦ ✦ ✦

In This Chapter

Knowing your workflow

Managing Flash
content production

Creating a functional
specification document

Using Microsoft
Visio 2002

✦ ✦ ✦ ✦

One of the most important steps — if not *the* most important step — to producing great Flash content is *knowing* what steps you'll have to take to move from the concept or idea of the Flash movie to the finished product. This chapter explores the basics of Flash production, and shows you how to use Visio to build flowcharts. Whether you are a freelance Web consultant (or designer) or a member of a large dot-com creative department, knowing how to manage the Flash content production will save you plenty of headaches, time, and money.

Workflow Basics

No matter what the size or scope, every project in which you choose to participate should follow some type of planned workflow. Whether it's for print, film, video, or Web delivery (or all four!), you should establish a process to guide the production of your presentation.

Before we can explore the way in which Flash fits into a Web production workflow, we need to define a holistic approach to Web production in general. Figure 3-1 shows a typical example of the Web production process within an Internet production company.

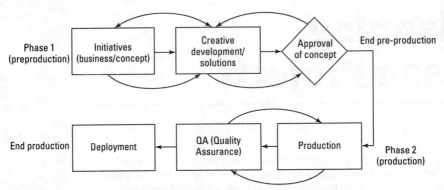

Figure 3-1: Two of the most common phases to generating Web content are pre-production and the actual production phase.

Phase I: Establishing the concept and goals

As a Web developer or member of a creative team, you will be approached by companies (or representatives for other departments) to help solve a problem with a project. The problem may or may not be well defined by the parties coming to you. The goal of Phase I is to thoroughly define the problem, offer solutions for the problem, and approve one (or more) solutions for final production.

Defining the problem

Before you can help someone solve a problem, you need to determine what the problem is, and whether there is more than one problem. When we say *problem,* we don't mean something that's necessarily troublesome or irritating. Think of it more as a math problem, where you know what you want—you're just not sure how to get there. When you're attempting to define a client's problem, start by asking them the following questions:

✦ What's the message they want to deliver? Is it a product that they want to feature on an existing Web site?

✦ Who's their current audience?

✦ Who's their ideal audience? (Don't let them say, "Everyone!")

✦ What branding materials (logos, colors, and identity) do they already have in place?

✦ Who are their competitors? What do they know about their competitors?

The last question points to a bigger picture, one in which the client may already have several emotive keywords that define their brand. Try to define the emotional heart and feeling of their message—get them to be descriptive. Don't leave the meeting with the words *edgy* or *sexy* as the only descriptive terms for the message.

Tip　　Never go into a meeting or a planning session without a white board or a big pad of paper. Documenting everyone's ideas and letting the group see the discussion in a visual format is always a good idea.

Information Architects

You may have already been bombarded by the idea of *information architecture*. Information architecture is the method by which sought data is represented and structured. Good information architecture is usually equivalent to intuitive user interface design — visitors to a well-organized Web site won't spend much time finding what they came for.

We mention information architecture because the steps in Phase I are similar to the steps that traditional architects take to build a comprehensive design and production strategy *before* they start building any structure. Although this may seem obvious enough, the sad fact remains that most Internet sites (or projects) are planned as they're constructed. Indeed, we're told that production must move at Internet speed — directives can be given without thorough research into other solutions to the problem.

You can also start to ask technical questions at this point:

✦ What type of browser support do you want to have?

✦ Do you have an idea of a Web technology (Shockwave, Flash, DHTML, SVG) that you want to use?

✦ Does the message need to be delivered in a web browser? Can it be in a downloadable application such as a standalone player? A CD-ROM? A DVD?

✦ What type of computer processing speed should be supported? What other types of hardware concerns might exist (for example, hi-fi audio)?

Of course, many clients and company reps will look to *you* for the technical answers. If this is the case, the most important questions are:

✦ Who's your audience?

✦ Who do you *want* to be your audience?

Your audience will determine, in many ways, what type of technology to choose for the presentation. If they say that Ma and Pa from a country farm should be able to view the Web site with no hassle, then you may need to consider a non-Flash presentation (such as HTML 3.0 or earlier), unless it's packaged as a standalone player that's installed with a CD-ROM (provided by the client to Ma and Pa). However, if they say that their ideal audience is someone who has a 56K modem and likes to watch mature cartoons, then you're getting closer to a Flash-based presentation. If they have any demographic information for their user base, ask for it up front. Putting on a show for a crowd is difficult if you don't know who's *in* the crowd.

Cross-Reference   Standalone players are discussed in Chapter 23, "Using the Flash Player and Projector."

Determine the project's goals

The client or company rep came to you for a reason — they want to walk away with a completed project. As you initially discuss the message and audience for the presentation, you also need to get a clear picture of what the client expects to get from you.

✦ Will you be producing just one piece of a larger production?

✦ Do they need you to host the Web site? Or do they already have a Web server and a staff to support it?

✦ Do they need you to maintain the Web site after handoff?

✦ Do they expect you to market the presentation? If not, what resources are in place to advertise the message?

✦ When does the client expect you to deliver proposals, concepts, and the finished piece? These important dates are often referred to as *milestones*. The payment schedule for a project is often linked to production milestones.

✦ Will they expect to receive copies of all the files you produce, including your source .fla files?

✦ What are the costs associated with developing a proposal? Will you do work on specu-lation of a potential project? Or will you be paid for your time to develop a concept pitch? (You should determine this *before* you walk into your initial meeting with the client.) Of course, if you're working with a production team in a company, you're already being paid a salary to provide a role within the company.

At this point, you'll want to plan the next meeting with your client or company rep. Give them a realistic timeframe for coming back to them with your ideas. This amount of time will vary from project to project and will depend on your level of expertise with the materials involved with the presentation.

Creative exploration: Producing a solution

After you leave the meeting, you'll go back to your design studio and start cranking out mate-rials, right? Yes and no. Give yourself plenty of time to work with the client's materials (what you gathered from the initial meeting). If your client sells shoes, read up on the shoe business. See what the client's competitor is doing to promote their message — visit their Web site, go to a store and compare the products, and read any consumer reports that you can find about your client's products or services. You should have a clear understanding of your client's market, and a clear picture of how your client distinguishes their company or their product from their competitors'.

After you (and other members of your creative team) have completed a round of research, sit down and discuss the findings. Start defining the project in terms of mood, response, and time. Is this a serious message? Do you want the viewer to laugh? How quickly should this presentation happen? Sketch out any ideas you and any other member of the team may have. Create a chart that lists the emotional keywords for your presentation.

At a certain point, you need to start developing some visual material that articulates the message to the audience. Of course, your initial audience will be the client. You are preparing materials for them, not the consumer audience. We assume that you are creating a Flash-based Web site for your client. For any interactive presentation, you need to prepare the following:

✦ An organizational flowchart for the site

✦ A process flowchart for the experience

✦ A functional specification for the interface

✦ A prototype or a series of comps

To see how Visio can be used to make flowcharts, skip to the "Using Visio to Create Flowcharts" section later in this chapter.

An *organizational flowchart* is a simple document that describes the scope of a site or presentation. Other names for this type of chart are *site chart, navigation flowchart,* and *layout flowchart.* It will include the major sections of the presentation. For example, if you're creating a Flash movie for a portfolio site, you might have a main menu and four content areas: about, portfolio, resume, and contact. In an organizational flowchart, this would look like Figure 3-2.

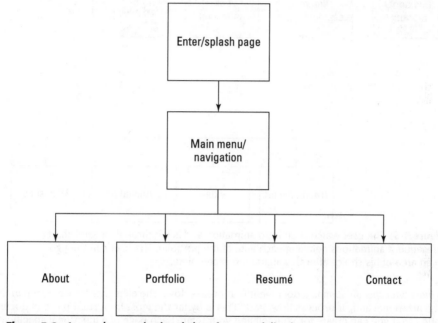

Figure 3-2: A sample organizational chart for a portfolio site

A *process flowchart* constructs the interactive experience of the presentation and shows the decision-making process involved for each area of the site. There are a few types of process charts. A basic process flowchart will display the decision-making of the end user (for example, what type of options does a user have on any given page of the site?). Another type of flowchart will show the programming logic involved for the end-user process chart. For example, will certain conditions need to exist before a user can enter a certain area of the site? Does he have to pass a test, finish a section of a game, or enter a username and password? Refer to Figure 3-3 for a preliminary flowchart for a section of our portfolio Web site. We discuss the actual symbols of the flowchart later in this chapter.

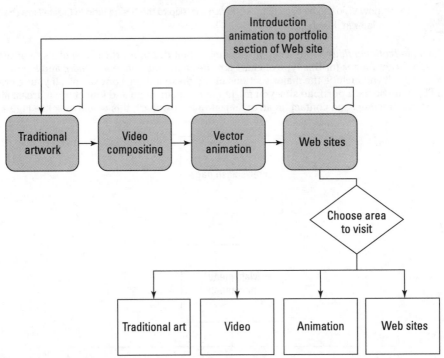

Figure 3-3: The user watches an intro animation and is led through several short subsequent animations detailing each area of the portfolio. The user can then go to an area of his choice after this animation is complete.

A *functional specification* is a document that breaks down the elements for each step in the organizational and/or process flowchart. This is by far the most important piece of documentation that you can create for yourself and your team. Each page of a functional specification (functional spec, for short) will list all the assets used on a page (or Flash scene, keyframe, Movie Clip) and indicate the following information for each asset:

✦ **Item ID:** This is part of the naming convention for your files and assets. It should be part of the filename, or Flash symbol and instance name. It should also be used in organizational and process flowcharts.

✦ **Type:** This part of the spec defines the name you're assigning to the asset, in more natural language, such as Home Button.

✦ **Purpose:** You should be able to clearly explain why this element is part of the presentation. If you can't, then you should consider omitting it from the project.

✦ **Format:** This column will indicate what technology (or what component of the technology) will be utilized to accomplish the needs of the asset. In an all-Flash presentation, list the symbol type or timeline component (frames, scene, nested Movie Clips) necessary to accomplish the goals of the asset.

Project:		Flash interface v2.0	Section:	1 of 5 (Main Menu)
No.	Type	Purpose	Content	Format
1.A	Navigation bar	To provide easier access to site content.		A menu bar fixed at the top left of the browser window.
1.A.1	Directory buttons	To provide a means for accessing any of the portfolio sections.	Names each content area - e.g., video, audio, graphics.	A horizontal row of buttons or a skinned ComboBox component.
1.A.2	Home button	So the user can always jump back to the main page.	The text: "home."	A skinned PushButton component.
1.A.3	Search field	So a specific word can be entered to search site content.	An empty text input area with the label "search."	A Dynamic text field.
1.A.4	Sign up	Captures the user's e-mail address for the site's mailing list.	Text input fields for name and e-mail address.	A PushButton opens a browser window. ColdFusion and Access used for data transfer.
1.A.5	Back button	Allows the user to jump to the previously visited page.	Button labeled with the text "back."	A skinned PushButton component.
1.A.6	Logo or ID	Provides a means of personal branding.	A spider web with the name of the Web site in Arial Narrow text.	Graphics in Flash and Illustrator.

Figure 3-4: This functional spec displays the six components of a Flash-based navigation bar, which will appear on the main menu of our portfolio content site.

Finally, after you have a plan for your project, you'll want to start creating some graphics to provide an atmosphere for the client presentation. Gather placement graphics (company logos, typefaces, photographs) or appropriate "temporary" resources for purposes of illustration. Construct one composition (or *comp*) that represents each major section or theme of the site. In our portfolio content site example, you might create a comp for the main page and a comp for one of the portfolio work sections, such as "Animation." Don't create a comp for each page of the portfolio section. You simply want to establish the feel for the content you will create for the client. We recommend that you use the tool(s) with which you feel most comfortable creating content. If you're better at using FreeHand or Photoshop to create layouts, then use them. If you're comfortable with Flash for assembling content, then use it.

Caution   Do not use copyrighted material for final production use, unless you have secured the appropriate rights to use the material. However, while you're exploring creative concepts, use whatever materials you feel best illustrate your ideas. When you get approval for your concept, improve upon the materials that inspired you.

Then you'll want to determine the time and human resources required for the entire project or concept. What role will you play in the production? Will you need to hire outside contractors to work on the presentation (for example, character animators, programmers, and so on)? Make sure you provide ample time to produce and thoroughly test the presentation. When you've determined the time and resources necessary, you'll determine the costs involved. If this is an internal project for your company, then you won't be concerned about cost so much as the time involved—your company reps will want to know what it will cost the company to produce the piece. For large client projects, your client will probably expect a project rate—not an hourly or weekly rate. Outline a time schedule with milestone dates, at which point you'll present the client with updates on the progress of the project.

Exploring the details of the workflow process any further is beyond the scope of this book. However, there are many excellent resources for project planning. One of the best books available for learning the process of planning interactive presentations is Nicholas Iuppa's *Designing Interactive Digital Media*. We strongly recommend that you consult the *Graphic Artists Guild Handbook of Pricing and Ethical Guidelines* and the *AIGA Professional Practices in Graphic Design,* edited by Tad Crawford, for information on professional rates for design services.

Note   You can search for other design, computer, and art books recommended by the authors at www.theMakers.com/resources.

Approving a final concept and budget

After you have prepared your design documents for the client, it's time to have another meeting with the client (or company rep). Display your visual materials (color laser prints, inkjet mockups, and so on), and walk through the charts you've produced. In some situations, you may want to prepare more than one design concept. Always reinforce how the presentation addresses the client's message and audience.

Cross-Reference   See Todd Purgason's tutorial on Flash and FreeHand, in Chapter 38, "Working with Vector Graphics." He offers some excellent suggestions for creating high-impact presentation boards in FreeHand and tips on how to reuse graphics in print and Web projects.

When all is said and done, discuss with the client the options that you presented. Gather feedback. Hopefully, the client prefers one concept (and its budget) and gives you the approval to proceed. It's important that you leave this meeting knowing one of two things:

✦ The client has signed off on the entire project or presentation.

✦ The client wants to see more exploration before committing to a final piece.

In either case, you shouldn't walk away not knowing how you'll proceed. If the client wants more time or more material before making a commitment, negotiate the terms of your fees that are associated with further conceptual development.

Designing for Usability, *by Scott Brown*

As mentioned earlier in this chapter, the first step in developing a Flash site, or any other type of site, is to define the information architecture. In this tutorial, you find out how to define the goals and mission of the site.

Defining the goals and mission of the site

Defining the mission and goals is laying the foundation upon which to build your project. To create a solid project foundation, we must begin by questioning everything, especially the company's business model. Start with these questions:

- ✦ What is the mission or purpose of the organization?
- ✦ Why does this organization want a Web site?
- ✦ Will the Web site support the mission of the organization?
- ✦ What are the short– and long-term goals of the Web site?
- ✦ Who are the intended audiences?
- ✦ Why will people come to the site?
- ✦ Are we trying to sell a product?
- ✦ What is the product or products?
- ✦ Do we have a unique service?
- ✦ What makes the service different?
- ✦ Why will people come to the site for the first time?
- ✦ Will they ever come back?
- ✦ Why would they come back?

The list of questions can go on forever. After you have gathered a list of questions, you need to get the answers. Ask around the organization, ask your friends, ask strangers, ask anyone. After the answers have been collected, you need to filter through them to create a list of goals that are based on the responses. From this list of goals, you must define further the answer to the question, "Who is the audience?"

Defining the audience

The audience can be defined as the potential users of the site and by their intentions or tasks that they may have when they come to your site. Are they kids or adults? Are they Generation X, Y, or Z? Are they into rave music or country music?

So, who is your audience? It's not an easy question, because there are so many possibilities. Start with a list of all the possible audiences that the organization would like to reach, and then rearrange the list in a ranking order of most important audience to least important audience. From the audience-ranking list, create a list of possible goals and needs of each audience.

Creating character scenarios

With the list of possible goals take the process one step further by creating scenarios of the users. Think of it as writing a screenplay for your Web site. Create multiple characters that represent the majority of visitors with hobbies, likes, dislikes, and, most importantly, a task to complete on the site. The object of the scenario game is to get into the characters' heads to learn why and how they would use your site. From their viewpoint you will have an easier time creating a list of needs and wants for the character, a wish list if you will.

After the scenarios are written, the next step in the process is to gather the team together and analyze the Web sites of the competition.

Analyzing the competition

Studying the competition gives you the chance to generate a list of what kind of features they are offering and to determine whether your feature list, the one that you created from the scenarios, is missing anything. If your wish list is lacking anything in comparison to your competition, now is a good time to expand the user's functionality requirements, and to return to the scenarios to determine whether the competition's functionality matches your character's needs. If it does, you should try to elaborate on their functions and create new functions of your own — the classic case of outdoing your competition.

Reaching a consensus on what good design is

At this time in the process, have the team come together to develop a definition of what is "good site design." This step is most beneficial for any contract designer trying to gain an understanding of his client's design viewpoint. To create this "good design" definition, the team should observe a good number of sites and document everybody's likes and dislikes for each site. From the documentation of this exercise, everyone on the team will have a better understanding of what to strive for and what to try to avoid.

Structuring the content

Now you should have several documents to refer to — the project mission statement, the user functionality needs (wish list), and the organization's definition of good design. With these three documents in hand, the next step is to blend them into one master menu of content inventory. Think of each item on this list as a building block. You now have all the blocks needed to construct the site. The only problem is that these blocks are in a big pile with no organization (structure). Naturally, the next step is to begin creating layouts of the site, providing structure. But before you can begin the page layout process, you need to educate yourself on some Web site usability issues.

Identifying factors of usability

Usability is a much-debated concept, but generally it means creating a site/project/interface that is functional and that your audience will understand. A usable site aims to be a natural extension of a user's expectations and needs. A user-friendly site will try to mirror its structure to that of the user's experience and goals. Just to make the task at hand a little more complex, keep in mind that user expectations learned in other areas of life affect how the user will think your site works. So, how can you design a site to meet your user's expectations? Well, if you did your homework on your audience and wrote the character scenarios, you should have a pretty good idea of the target audience's expectations. By knowing the general background of a user, you could include metaphors into the structure of the site. Using metaphors is a great way to help users draw upon knowledge they already have, thereby making the site easier to use. By matching the site structure to the user's experience, the amount of time it takes for the user to learn how to operate or navigate the site is minimized. The shorter the learning curve for the site, the better. If you come to a site when you have a specific goal in mind, and it takes you ten minutes to figure out how to achieve your goal, would you call that a positive experience? Most likely not!

The goal of the designer is to create an attractive site without distracting the users from their goals. Forcing the users to spend a noticeable amount of time trying to learn how to achieve their goals is very taxing on their patience, and is a good way to create a negative experience. If you're trying to sell something, chances are you want customers to be happy not annoyed. One way to make your customers' experience more enjoyable is to make their experience as easy as possible. So, how do you create a positive experience? Let's start with the most basic of user needs, the ability to navigate.

Users need to know at all times where they are in the site, where they have been, and where they can go. When developing a navigation system, be sure to keep the navigation visually consistent. Inconsistency in the navigation can cause the user to be confused and frustrated. A great concept for a navigational aid is the use of a breadcrumb trail. The breadcrumb system is a visual way to show the user the path they took to get to their current position in the site. This navigational convention is used on many resource sites and even in the Flash authoring environment itself — as you click in to edit grouped shapes or symbols, the steps you've taken are shown as text labels on the bar above the Stage. Beyond displaying the path of the user, this system gives the user the ability to backtrack to any page displayed in the path. However, remember that navigation is not the goal of the user, only an aid. The user is there to find or buy something; the user is there for the content. So, make the content the first read on all your pages. Navigational elements are there to support the content, not eclipse it.

Of course, navigation isn't the only factor to consider when designing for usability. Other variables, such as the length of text on a page, can affect the usability of a site tremendously. It's a fact that reading text on a monitor is far more taxing on the eyes than reading text on paper. Therefore, people are less inclined to read large amounts of text on the Web. As designers, we must accommodate these changes in reading patterns. Keep these simple guidelines in mind when writing text for the Web. Try to make the text scanable, because readers skim Web content. Bold the important ideas or put key information in bulleted lists. But most of all, keep the text short.

In addition to the treatment of text, there are several other tips to help improve the usability of a site. The concept of redundant links is an excellent method to support users with different backgrounds and goals. With redundant links, a user has more than one way to get to the desired content. The user may have the option to click a text link, a graphic link, or even a text link that is worded differently. Each redundant link should be designed to accommodate a wide range of users. So, where on the page should all these usability elements go?

I can't tell you where you should place your navigation system or your redundant links. However, I can provide you with some information on eye-tracking studies that will help you make an educated decision. Yes, it is true that usability researchers are able to actually monitor and record what you're looking at when viewing a Web site. Based on the research they've found that when a Web page loads, our eyes are looking at the center of the page, then move over to the left, and then sometimes to the right. Of course, these findings are dependent on the user's cultural background. Nevertheless, the scary finding is that the users rarely look to the right! This is most likely because most sites use the right side of the page as a place to add sidebar elements, items of lesser importance. This is also a good example of how a user's past experience can affect his future experiences. So, how does Flash fit into Web site usability considerations?

Flash is a great design tool to create amazing interfaces. Flash gives the designer the freedom to create almost anything he desires. But the flexibility given to the designer is also Flash's greatest weakness from a usability perspective. Flash is a great tool for creating animation, however, inexperienced Web designers can easily go overboard. Just because you can animate an object doesn't mean that you should. The eye is very sensitive to the smallest amount of animation or movement in its peripheral view, pulling the eyes' attention away from the site's main content. On the plus side, animation used as a transitional element is very beneficial for the user. Animated transitions enable the user to follow the navigation process, gaining a better understanding of how the site might work.

Along with the problems of animation abuse, Flash enables the designers to create their own graphical user interface (GUI) elements. This is great for the designers, but the users are often left out in the cold with all this newfound freedom. This design freedom is forcing the user to learn, almost from scratch, how to operate a scroll bar or a navigation bar. If you recall, earlier we mentioned the importance of a short learning curve for the users. These extreme creative versions of standardized GUI elements might rank high on the "cool" scale, but they really throw a monkey wrench into the user's goal and expectations. GUI standards are developed to help create a consistent experience across all platforms in an effort to eliminate any unpleasant surprises. Again, these usability problems can be avoided in Flash by educating the designers about the issues at hand and finding solutions based on the set standards.

Other usability issues with Flash arise from the actual plug-in nature of Flash. Unfortunately, because Flash requires a plug-in to work in Web browsers, Flash movies are unable to take advantage of some of the browser's built-in capabilities such as the Back button and the capability to display history for the links by changing the color of the links that have been clicked. The problem with the browser's Back button is that when the button is pressed, the browser will take the user back to the previous HTML page, not to the previous state in the Flash movie. It's not a nice surprise for unsuspecting users. One solution to this problem is to pop up the Flash movie in a new browser window (via JavaScript) with all the browser's navigation elements removed (in other words, no toolbar, no location bar, no menus, and so on). No Back button on the browser, no problem right?

Fortunately, ActionScript can often smooth out the discrepancies between the default browser behaviors and Flash movie functionality. For an introduction to some ActionScript solutions, refer to Part VI, "Distributing Flash Movies".

Named anchor keyframes is a new Flash MX feature that makes it easier for users to navigate a Flash movie using keystrokes. For an example of named anchors in action, refer to Chapter 20, "Making Your First Flash MX Project."

Building mockups of the site

You're now ready to begin mocking up the site structure using index cards, sticky notes, and other common office supplies. Creating these paper mockups will save the development team a large amount of time. The beauty of the paper mockups is that you can quickly create a navigational system and find the major flaws without spending long hours developing a beautiful rendering of a structure that may be flawed. There is nothing worse than spending months developing a product with a faulty structure only to discover the mistake just before launch!

Testing the site on real users

Testing the site is the most important step in creating a usable site. The key to testing the site is *not* to test it on people of the organization, but to test it on people in the target audience. Test the site on the real users. It's usually easier to test the site by using people who are familiar with the project. The problem with that practice is that the people are familiar with the project. You want to test fresh eyes and minds in order to get optimum feedback. For testing purposes, create a list of several tasks to complete on the site. The tasks should be pulled from the list of possible users' goals defined in the early steps of the project. As the test subjects navigate through your project, pay close attention to how long it takes them. How many times did they have to click to find what they were looking for? How many had to resort to using a search feature (or wished that they could)? What elements seemed to cause confusion or delay? What elements attracted or held the users' attention? After each test subject has completed a task, or tried, give her a post-task questionnaire with questions such as:

"How would you rate the quality of the content on this site?"

Unacceptable −3 −2 −1 0 1 2 3 Excellent

Also, leave some room for the test subject to elaborate on the questions. After the testing is finished, review your findings and determine what needs to be fixed. After the problems are fixed, test the site again, but on new users. Repeat the process until you have a product that meets the defined goals of the organization and the users. Keep asking yourself this question "Is the interface helping the users accomplish their goals?" When all else fails, you can always depend on the greatest guideline of the century, keep it simple. Oh, how true.

Tip   If this process is new to you, don't waste time "reinventing the wheel" when there are plenty of resources on this topic that can get you started. Jakob Nielsen has achieved near-celebrity status as a result of his strong opinions on this topic and he has written several books that some consider definitive. Another popular book on this topic is *Don't Make Me Think: A Common Sense Approach to Web Usability,* by Steve Krug and Roger Black.

Phase II: Producing, testing, and staging the presentation

When your client or company executives have signed off on a presentation concept, it's time to rock and roll! You're ready to gather your materials, assemble the crew, and meet an insane production schedule. This section provides a brief overview of the steps you need to take to produce material that is ready to go live on your Web site.

Assembling assets

The first step is to gather (or start production of) the individual assets required for the Flash presentation. Depending on the resources you included in your functional spec and budget, you may need to hire a photographer, illustrator, animator, music composer (or all four!) to start work on the production. Or, if you perform any of these roles, then you'll start creating rough drafts for the elements within the production. At this stage, you'll also gather high-quality images from the client for their logos, proprietary material, and so on.

Making the Flash architecture

Of course, we're assuming that you're creating a Flash-based production. All the resources that you've gathered (or are working to create) in Step 1 will be assembled into the Flash movie(s) for the production. For large presentations or sites, you'll likely make one master Flash movie that provides a skeleton architecture for the presentation, and use `loadMovie()` to bring in material for the appropriate sections of the site.

Before you begin Flash movie production, you should determine two important factors: frame size and frame rate. You don't want to change either of these settings midway through your project. Any reductions in frame size will crop elements that weren't located near the top-left portion of the Stage — you'll need to recompose most of the elements on the Stage if you used the entire Stage. Any changes in your frame rate will change the timing of any linear animation and/or sound synchronization that you've already produced.

Staging a local test environment

As soon as you start to author the Flash movies, you'll create a local version of the presentation (or entire site) on your computer, or a networked drive that everyone on your team can access. The file and folder structure (including the naming conventions) will be consistent with the structure of the files and folders on the Web server. As you build each component of the site, you should begin to test the presentation with the target browsers (and Flash Player plug-in versions) for your audience.

HTML page production

Even if you're creating an all-Flash Web site, you need a few basic HTML documents, including:

✦ **HTML frameset document** (if you're creating a scalable Flash movie). The frameset has two frames: One displays the Flash movie at 100 percent of the browser window size, and the other one is hidden.

Colin Moock explains this browser window technique in his tutorial, found in the Bonus_Tutorials folder on the *Flash MX Bible* CD-ROM.

✦ **A plug-in detection page** that directs visitors without the Flash Player plug-in to the Macromedia site to download the plug-in.

✦ **HTML page(s) to display any non-Flash material** in the site within the browser.

You will want to construct basic HTML documents to hold the main Flash movie as you develop the Flash architecture of the site.

Staging a server test environment

Before you can make your Flash content public, you'll need to set up a Web server that is publicly accessible (preferably with login and password protection) so that you can test the site functionality over a non-LAN connection. This also enables your client to preview the site remotely. After quality assurance (QA) testing has finished (the next step that follows), you'll move the files from the staging server to the live Web server.

We've noticed problems with larger .swf files that weren't detected until we tested them from a staging server. Why? When you test your files locally, they're loaded instantly into the browser. When you test your files from a server (even over a fast DSL or cable modem connection), you have to wait for the .swf files to load over slower network conditions. Especially with preloaders or loading sequences, timing glitches may be revealed during tests on the staging server, that were not apparent when testing locally.

Quality assurance testing

In larger corporate environments, you'll find a team of individuals whose sole responsibility is to thoroughly test the quality of a nearly finished production (or product). If you're responsible for QA, then you should have an intimate knowledge of the process chart for the site. That way, you know how the site should function. If a feature or function fails in the production, QA will report it to the creative production team. QA teams will test the production with the same hardware and conditions as the target audience, accounting for variations in:

✦ Computer type (PC versus Mac)

✦ Computer speed (top-of-the-line processing speed versus minimal supported speeds, as determined by the target audience)

✦ Internet connection speeds (as determined by the target audience)

✦ Flash Player plug-in versions (and any other plug-ins required by the production)

✦ Browser application and version (as determined by the target audience)

Tip   If you're a freelance designer or operate a small company, keep in mind that there is no such thing as a useless computer—recycle your older computers as test platforms for target audiences.

After QA has finished rugged testing of the production, then, pending approval by the client (or company executives), the material is ready to go live on the site.

Maintenance and updates

After you've celebrated the finished production, your job isn't over yet. If you were contracted to build the site or presentation for a third party, then you may be expected to maintain and address usability issues provided by follow-ups with the client and any support staff they might have. Be sure to account for periodic maintenance and updates for the project in your initial budget proposal. If you don't want to be responsible for updates, make sure you advise your clients ahead of time to avoid any potential conflicts after the production has finished.

You should have a thorough staging and testing environment for any updates you make to an all-Flash site, especially if you're changing major assets or master architecture files. Repeat the same process of staging and testing with the QA team that you employed during original production.

Interface Design, *by Eric Jordan*

Macromedia Flash has been present in the industry for some time now as the preferred mechanism by which a Web site is designed and engineered. Not limited by the rigid constraints of HTML, it allows for the construction of more sophisticated components, which better streamline and enhance the user experience. The Web is now a far more familiar and common platform for delivering and retrieving information, and users are becoming more accustomed to its interactive nature. The job of the interface designer is to create and mold a platform by which the user can complete a specific task, and ultimately gain knowledge or information about a specific topic. It is important to note that, out of the depths, two competing visions of interface design have arisen and present us with an ongoing struggle to define the way Web sites should be conceived and engineered:

✦ **Structuralists** are advocates of a conservative Web, a Web based on the ultimate goal of simply driving information to the user, a tool void of artistic impositions that may inhibit the reception of pure information. Structuralists maintain that the Web is intended as a universal platform for delivering standardized content, and that document presentation is better left up to the desires and preferences of the end user or the device on which it is being presented.

✦ **Presentationalists** see the Web platform in a slightly different light. Advocates of this viewpoint maintain that the presentation of information is best delivered as an experience, rich with sensory feedback and interactive metaphors.

At 2advanced Studios, we are believers in the latter view; that the Web is a diverse platform in which artistic expression can enhance the delivery of complex messages or information. This involves the fusing of a sort of "narrative" with the content, which ultimately gives life to the presentation of information. It is a way of translating the intricacy of our experience into something we can better understand and soak up. Because you're reading a book about Flash technology, we're going to assume that you either share, or are open to, the same viewpoint. Thus, in this tutorial we highlight the use of Flash MX, Macromedia's latest installment of the powerful authoring tool, as it applies to the design and development of interactive interfaces with narrative expression.

Flash MX now empowers designers and developers with the ability to create rich Web-based environments that are more interactive and sophisticated than ever before. In the pursuit of wrapping an artistic narrative around the presentation of information, Flash designers seek to develop rich and engaging interfaces, which the user can navigate through and react with on a more challenging interactive level. By tapping the new enhancements built into Flash MX, designers now have a much more efficient and opportunistic approach to the conception and implementation of this new breed of interfaces.

Conceptualization and implementation

Whenever you begin the process of creating a Flash interface, it's important to consider one important factor: After an interface is animated, it is intensely difficult to backtrack if the client wants a change in the overall design layout. Although the greatest impact of a Flash site normally comes from its animated elements, it's important to lock down an interface design that pleases the client from the very start. We have created a development process at 2advanced Studios that works very effectively for conceptualizing and finalizing an interface design before moving onto the actual use of Flash. This process normally begins with three roughs, which are three stylistically different interface concepts envisioned by the designer. These designs vary in look and feel, to give the client an opportunity to settle on a general aesthetic style for the Web site. Then we move onto the next phase, in which we provide three comprehensive designs that follow the same aesthetic theme of the chosen rough, yet vary in their execution of the layout structure. After the client has selected the final comprehensive, we then proceed to create a working model of the interface that includes the use of animated elements and functionality.

Aesthetic considerations

Specializing in Flash technology, 2advanced Studios has had the opportunity to develop a variety of interfaces, with a wide range of navigation types, thematic approaches, and bandwidth considerations. Based on the individual requirements of each project we undertake, we attempt to infuse as much artistic narrative as we can, while still maintaining control over the usability guidelines that have been set forth. Technical requirements aside, the visual appearance of an interface is a creative endeavor that is entirely subjective. It is a matter of one's style. Although our imaginations tend to run wild at times, it is a designer's duty to execute a site design that properly presents its content based on the branding strategy, corporate mentality, and goals of the client. At 2advanced Studios, our strength lies in the ability to implement interfaces that organize content in an engaging, yet usable manner. To better showcase these abilities, we began translating the latest installment of our Web site (www.2advanced.com) using the enhancements of Flash MX. The 2advanced interface (shown in Figure 3-5) uses many of the metaphors that we build for our clients. Components such as animated drop-down menus and conveniently swappable modules provide the user with rich interactive navigation and a sense of control, and enhancing usability within the environment. These elements are by no means a requirement for an interface design; they are simply consistent with our understanding of design/layout and usability. The key is to provide the user with a straightforward metaphor for navigating the content, coupled with a visually compelling environment.

Figure 3-5: The 2advanced Studios Web site, after the opening animation has completed and the interface has peaked

Color is also an indispensable factor for successful interface design. It's an integral part of the visual appeal, and it plays a crucial role in highlighting functionality or important areas of content. The correct colors attract the eye to the most important areas of the interface. They enhance readability and diminish optical exhaustion. Incorrect colors distract the user and decrease the level of comprehension. Paying close attention to color theory as it applies to interface design will help you to better communicate the message to the audience and aid the users in their experience.

Beginning the design process and understanding the tools

Typically, we create our conceptual layouts using Macromedia Flash MX, Macromedia FreeHand, or Adobe Photoshop. Flash MX improves the design process with a workspace that is both flexible and intuitive. The new application environment allows for complex customization, which accelerates the productivity for both designers and developers. In addition, new pre-developed interface components have been included in order to rapidly increase the time it takes to implement customizable scroll bars, form elements, list menus, and so on. This allows us to save a lot of time and effort by reusing the custom components across multiple interface projects.

At 2advanced Studios, we are very visual people. We believe that if a picture is worth a thousand words, a video is worth a million. Flash MX's video support has given us the ability to enhance our narrative style by making use of full-motion video-formats such as QuickTime and AVI. The opportunity for complete control over the look and feel of these components helps us to better refine the user experiences we develop.

With the addition of the new graphic design tools in Flash MX, sophisticated interfaces can be created easily, even without the aid of an illustration program such as FreeHand. Generally, we find that the Flash MX drawing tools are more than sufficient for creating the overall interface. However, if we choose to make use of raster graphics in combination with the vector graphics of Flash, then we have to use a raster-based authoring application such as Photoshop. With direction from the client, the design team begins the creation of three rough designs, keeping in mind the various aspects of the decided GUI guidelines, which include:

✦ Target resolution (640x480, 800x600, and so on)

✦ Navigational metaphors (horizontal, vertical, drop-down, draggable, sliding, and so on)

✦ Technical requirements such as cross-browser compatibility, frames, and so on

✦ Color palette support (16-bit, 32-bit, and so on)

✦ Color usage guidelines

When these requirements have been established, we begin laying out interface concepts using the drawing tools in Flash MX. However, constant attention is paid to every factor that may affect the outcome of the final file. The most prominent advantage of using Flash to develop an interactive environment is its combined capability to carry out the construction of graphical layout, content delivery, and functionality, all in one place. This does, however, require careful planning on the part of the designer to ensure that he doesn't get backed into a corner by making a few wrong turns during the design process. Without forethought, a Flash site can quickly become an ill-fated nightmare full of unforeseen hurdles such misplaced elements on keyframes and bloated file sizes.

Roughs

Although the three roughs that we create are simply conceptual approaches to the interface, we still maintain constant scrutiny of the file size during the design process. Our design team is well aware that two of the three designs are likely to be thrown out completely, but if we don't pay attention to the optimization of the file from the very start, the chosen rough may have to be redesigned and restructured in order to ensure that it makes efficient use of symbols, and other elements that ultimately affect the size of the file.

While designing the latest version of the 2advanced Studios Web site, our main concern was file size. Although this site was a project of our own undertaking, and would not come under the scrutiny of a client, we used the same rough-and-comp approach to ensure that we thoroughly explored the possibilities for our own branding in a strategic way. As we envisioned the site, the main background of the interface would consist of a large raster graphic that would add a great deal of size to the Flash file. The upper and lower portions of the interface would be built with vectors to accommodate navigation and so on. To avoid further bloating the file size, we focused our efforts on efficient use of symbols wherever possible. This included reusing simple shapes such as rectangles, lines, and circles within the upper and lower interface bars. Although these areas of the interface appear to consist of 13 blue rectangular shapes, each was derived from a singular symbol. If some rectangles needed to be a different color or size, we didn't go in and draw another rectangle. (This is what eventually causes the file size of a Flash movie to inflate.) Instead, we simply used instances of the same rectangle symbol, while changing the tint (in the Color Effect panel) and size (in the Info or Transform panel) of its instance. The advantage of this method is that the final movie needs to load only 1 shape during playback, rather than 13 different shapes of various colors and sizes. We used the same technique with lines. Everywhere a line appears, no matter what color or size, it's always an instance of the same symbol. Changes are only made to each particular instance, by using the Effect panel to modify the tint color and by using the Info panel to modify the length. If you pay close attention to these details, you can eliminate many design headaches. Thus, we end up with three optimized designs that are ready to be refined and built out.

Comprehensives

When a rough has been chosen, we move onto the comprehensive phase. In this stage, we develop three new designs that have their aesthetic roots based in the stylistic elements of the selected rough. The only variance is the way in which these elements are structured. Using the symbols that are already created, we shift the layout around and come up with three distinctly different renditions of the same basic theme. In this phase, we have already locked down the visual feel of the site, and we're developing options to offer the client further choices for the way in which that feel will be executed. A comprehensive can be thought of as the peak of the Web site, where animation ceases and the full interface is revealed in all its glory.

Figure 3-6 is a view of the source FLA for the completed 2advanced Web site. Note how many layers appear in the Main Timeline, yet how many more are obscured — as evinced by the scroll bar to the far right of the timeline. In this shot, the play head is halfway to the peak of the interface animation.

Fortunately, Flash MX now includes an efficient method for organizing large amounts of layers. Folders enable multiple layers to be condensed into organized categories or sets, similar to the way a file manager organizes files.

Figure 3-7 is another view of the source FLA file for the completed 2advanced Web site after all layers have been reorganized using the Folders feature in Flash MX. Now note how the layers appear in the Main Timeline. All layers have been re-organized into Folder sets that allow us to more easily understand how the interface is structured. This helps our designers to pass the files back and forth, without confusing one another with hundreds of unorganized layers.

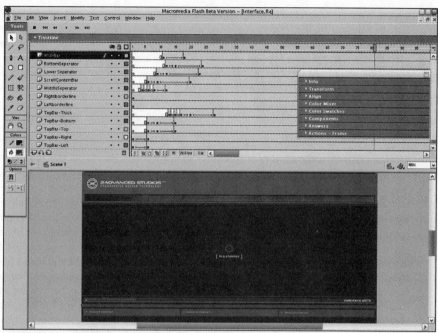

Figure 3-6: The Main Timeline of the source Flash document

Figure 3-7: The reorganized Main Timeline in Flash MX

We use layers to design the basic levels of the interface elements so that when it comes time to animate the site, everything is organized on its own layer in a categorized folder set and ready for movement and/or functionality. As we add elements to the timeline, each layer and/or folder is labeled in order to provide clarity for the execution of the animation process. At the end of this phase, we will have a series of folders, each of which contain several layers with one keyframe on each. Each keyframe consists of a single symbol instance that makes up a different part of the interface.

Build-out

After our client has chosen one of the three comprehensives, we begin the process of Flash-ing the interface. In this phase, we add motion and functionality to the site design. Because we have placed each element of the layout on a different layer, it is easy for us to now animate each symbol so that the design will move and manifest into the peak design that we've created. It's almost like deconstructing the interface in reverse, so that it may reconstruct itself through animation when played back. We typically insert a set of new keyframes about 100 frames deep in our Flash timeline to be the predetermined peak moment when the site will have achieved its full manifestation. We then proceed to set the properties for the symbol instances at frame 1. This is the very beginning of the animation, where the interface begins to manifest itself. Usually, we set items to have an alpha value of 0, a tint value similar to that of the background, or — if we want the element to slide into place — a position off stage. After we create our Motion Tweens for each animated element of the interface, we then set values for easing in the Frame Panel to ensure fluid motion of each symbol. For aggressive and energetic interfaces, we usually set elements to Ease In and use short Motion Tweens to simulate fast movement. For calmer, more conservatively animated interfaces, we set elements to Ease out and use longer Motion Tweens to simulate softer motion. These techniques are, of course, completely subjective, and each project may follow a different style and/or feel. Of course, some interfaces may not require animation at all, and some interfaces may only use Flash for its implementation of functionality through ActionScripting.

Now that we have a semi-animated site, with a key moment in time acting as the peak of the interface, we begin developing content sections either within the main movie (using scenes) or externally for sections that will be loaded into the main movie (using the loadMovie() command). The 2advanced interface requires the use of loadMovie() to introduce additional content into the host Flash movie. Thus, the steps that were pursued during the design and build-out process differed from the normal process. The navigation and content windows for the various sections of the 2advanced Web site were intended to consist of separately loaded modules, and would be externally loaded into the host movie in order to avoid bloating the file size. Instead of designing the content windows blindly in a separate movie file, we have developed a technique by which we design and animate them on their own layers within the host movie. This type of workflow enabled us to see how the content sections would appear aesthetically within the main interface. During build-out, we simply copy the frames being used by the navigation and content sections and paste them into their own Flash file (with the same dimensions as the host movie), which is then saved out as a separate SWF file to be externally loaded using button triggers in the main movie. By copying and pasting the frames, we are able to retain all positioning or animation properties they possessed while in the main movie.

After the layout is completed and the file structures are established for the externally loaded interface elements (the navigation and content sections), we begin using ActionScript to make everything function, such as the navigational elements or the loading of the external SWFs into the host movie.

Within the interface, we created a top panel to house the navigation of the main movie, a middle area in which external SWFs would be loaded/positioned, and a larger lower panel that contains controls for audio and modules for important content such as dynamic news, downloads, and other related data. In certain sections (the Contact movie, for instance), we implemented interface components such as drop-down selection menus. Using drop-down menus (as shown in Figure 3-8) is an effective way to organize an interface because they avoid cluttering the main GUI. Features such as these are important for providing an intuitive interface that is easily navigable and that does not overwhelm the user with too many options at once.

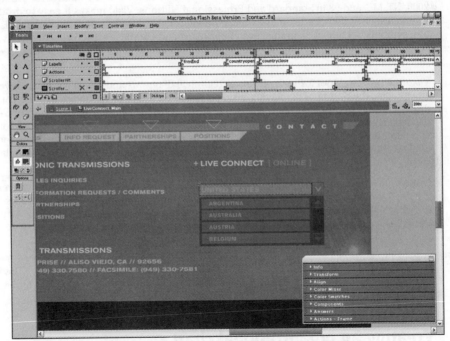

Figure 3-8: Drop-down menus save valuable real estate in the interface.

Reflection

Interface design within Flash concerns two factors:

✦ How effectively users complete tasks (in other words, comprehend content)

✦ How well-represented the content is aesthetically

Flash MX has accelerated our ability to create new forms of advanced interactive environments. Without a fundamental understanding of interfaces in general, however, it can be difficult to make these environments become a reality. Our current understanding of interface design, usability, and layout in non–Web-based interfaces can be applied and expanded to maximize the impact and comprehension of information on the Web. To take full advantage of Web efficiency, it's important to explore the use of guidelines, develop new methods of interactivity, and push beyond the existing boundaries of conventional interface design.

Using Visio to Create Flowcharts

Microsoft Visio 2002 is a flowcharting application for Windows. It is available for Windows XP, 2000, NT, ME, and 98 in Standard and Professional editions. Visio makes it easy to produce a diverse range of flowcharts and technical drawings using a variety of artwork symbols, custom symbols, technical diagrams, even floor plans and database structuring diagrams. The utility of Visio extends far beyond the organizational and process flowcharts discussed in this chapter.

Visio is a powerful tool for many forms of technical diagrams and drawings. It has several advantages, the option of displaying Visio diagrams on the Internet (much like you can display PowerPoint presentations) through the use of a plug-in for Internet Explorer 5+ is particularly relevant to web designers. It is also possible to export your diagrams to other Microsoft programs such as Word, Excel, Access, and even SQL Server. Many downloadable add-ins and toolsets are available to expand the capabilities and graphical icons available within Visio.

In the following sections of this chapter, we will use Visio 2002 to show you how to create a site map—also referred to as an organizational chart (or **orgchart**)—and a process flowchart. These simple tools will help you to design and develop solid project structures. We will also go through the steps for creating site maps of existing web projects.

Note   You can obtain a trial of Visio Standard or Professional 2002 by requesting a copy from Microsoft at www.microsoft.com/office/visio/evaluation/trial.asp. This location handles US and Canadian requests only. There are links from this location for international requests as well.

Creating an organizational chart

To create an organizational chart (site chart) for your Flash or Web concepts, you need to have a list of all the sections included in the concept. For the portfolio site that we'll use as an example, we'll create a chart that diagrams the following elements:

✦ A **Main Page** area containing navigation/links to sub-areas.

✦ Sections dedicated to each type of work in the **Portfolio: Video** work, **Animation**, **Web sites**, **Graphic design**, and **Audio**.

✦ A featured **Current Project** loaded into the main menu screen (or main page) of the site.

✦ A **Feedback form** for visitors that allows input of name, e-mail, and comments.

✦ An **About** section containing resumé, pricing information, and contact information.

Now you're ready to build an organizational chart in Visio.

1. Open Visio 2002. For this example, you only need to use a Basic Flowchart template.

2. When you first open the program, you'll have a **Category** menu, where you can choose the **Flowchart** link, and then the **Basic Flowchart** button. If Visio is already open, navigate to File ➪ New ➪ Flowchart ➪ Basic Flowchart. You're provided a blank template (the **Drawing** page) and Basic Shapes, Background, and Pattern tools in the Stencil window. These shapes are more than enough for you to get started; you add them to the document by clicking and dragging. Refer to Figure 3-9 for the elements comprising the main interface.

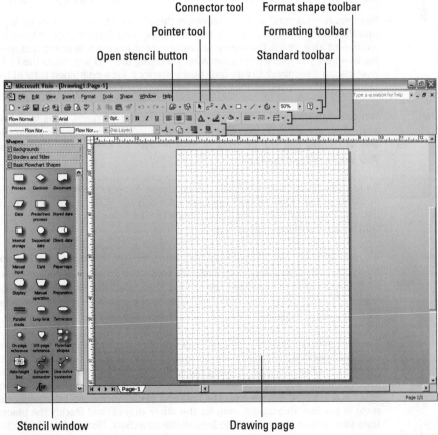

Figure 3-9: The Visio 2002 interface is intuitive and easy to use. The specific toolbars we use in our examples are referenced in this figure.

Note   An easy way to add formatting to shapes is by going to View ➪ Toolbars ➪ Format Shape, which will add buttons used to customize edges, fill, and drop shadows. You can open new shapes by clicking on the **Open Stencil** button on the Standard toolbar and selecting one of the many sets.

3. In File ➪ Page Setup, under the Page size tab you can set your page orientation to Portrait or Landscape. After choosing the **Pre-defined size** option, the **Portrait** and **Landscape** options become active. Select the Landscape option to change the Drawing page's orientation. This option is also available under the Print setup tab.

4. Make sure your Basic Flowchart Shapes window is open. Select and drag the rectangle called **Process** to the Drawing page.

5. When you double-click shapes on the Drawing page, a text entry cursor will appear. You can format your font attributes and justification in the Formatting toolbar (if it is not visible, go to View ➪ Toolbars ➪ Formatting). Type **Main Page** into this shape.

6. Now you need several more instances of this shape. The easiest way to duplicate the first Process rectangle is by holding the Ctrl key and dragging the original instance to a different area on the Drawing page. Subsequent images will space themselves according to where you move the shape. After releasing the Ctrl key, press the F4 key for each new instance required. Create four new instances, for a combined total of five. Refer to Figure 3-10 if you need an idea of how to set up your flowchart.

Tip   You can align several shapes at once by Shift-selecting them and going to Shape Menu ➪ Align Shapes, which will open a new dialogue box. Select the alignment style you require, and hit OK. The grid and snapping features in Visio are often enough to adequately align your shapes without this feature.

7. You're now ready to enter text into each shape. Simply double-click each shape, and add descriptive titles for each area of your Flash site. Referring back to our example list, you can add sections for a portfolio, a feedback form, a current project, and a section for information about your site.

Tip   If you've formatted one of your rectangles using the Format Shapes tools mentioned after Step 2, there is an easy way to duplicate the formatting instead of repeating the actions for each shape. Select the formatted shape, and then select the **Format Painter** icon in the Standard toolbar. Select each shape you want to apply this formatting to, and deselect the icon after you're finished.

8. The next step is to add connecting lines between the Main Page shape, and the rest of the site section symbols on the Drawing page. Select the Connector tool in the Standard toolbar. On your Drawing page, click on one symbol and drag the tool to the second symbol you want to join it to. A line will be formed, which you can reshape when it is selected. Mouse over the line, and use the arrow tool to modify the placement of the line. Repeat this step for the other shapes, and modify the placement of the lines until you're happy with the look of the flowchart. Next, select the Pointer tool.

9. Depending on what default or state your Connector tool was set to, you may need to modify the lines you just created. If your lines end with arrowheads, select each line and go to the Formatting tool bar. Select the **Line Ends** button, and then the **No line ends** option on the drop-down menu.

Note Org charts like the one you're creating don't need to display the arrows that indicate flow directions like a process chart.

10. At this stage, your organizational chart has been set up to reflect several areas of your Flash site, all linking from one main page. Refer to Figure 3-10 for an idea of what your Visio file may now look like.

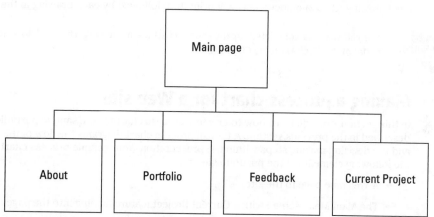

Figure 3-10: This is what our stage looks like after duplicating several instances of the rectangle box on our Drawing page in Visio.

11. Save your document as **org_chart.vsd**.

12. Next, you will create a new page for one of the areas of your site. You can start with the Portfolio area. Go to Insert ➪ New Page. The dialog box will ask you to name the page, which we named **Portfolio**.

13. In the new diagram, select the Process box, and then duplicate it five times as you did in Step 6. For each of these boxes, you need to provide names for each area of your Portfolio: **Video**, **Animation**, **Web sites**, **Graphic design** and **Audio** (as shown in Figure 3-11).

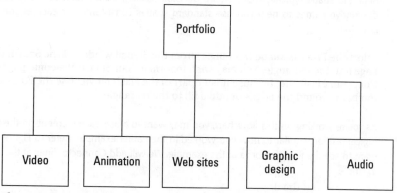

Figure 3-11: Each main section of the site has several subsections.

By now you should be comfortable using these features of Visio. You can easily repeat Steps 12 and 13 for each area of the movie to define the content of in these sections. When you're finished, you can print out the documents, and each area of the site will have its own diagram detailing the structure and content you need to cover.

14. Save your Visio document.

That's all there is to building an organizational chart. When you print the document, the top-level drawing (the main document) will print first, followed by each drawing in the document.

On the CD-ROM

You can view the completed organizational chart file named org_chart.vsd, located in ch03 folder of the *Flash MX Bible* CD-ROM.

Making a process chart for a Web site

In this section, you will learn how to create a process chart for the sample portfolio site we described in the previous section. A typical process chart diagrams the flow of the experience and the decision-making steps within the presentation. Your sample process chart will show the following elements of the portfolio site:

✦ A Welcome page to the site

✦ The Main Menu screen with a Current Project feature loading into the page

✦ A navigation menu linking to other areas of the site (Feedback, About, and Portfolio)

✦ A page containing a form to submit feedback to the Webmaster

For this example, you will *not* continue with the org_chart.vsd file you created in the last section. You will need to start a brand new file in Visio 2002.

1. Open Visio and open a new Basic Flowchart as you did in the previous exercise. Save it as **process_chart.vsd**. Make sure you have the Basic Flowchart Shapes stencil open. If it isn't open, select the Open Stencil button in the Standard toolbar and go to Flowchart ➪ Basic Flowchart Shapes.

Note

As you've probably noticed already in the Visio stencil window, different shapes are commonly used for certain functions. For instance, a square typically refers to a process, while a diamond shape typically represents a decision. Luckily, Visio references each symbol with descriptive names to help you use standard shapes consistently for each element of your flowchart.

2. Select the Process shape (rectangle) from the Stencil window. Type Splash or Welcome page into the rectangle. You may wish to format your Splash/Welcome page differently from your Flash site, because it isn't part of the Flash movie. Use the Format shape toolbar to round the edges or add a fill to the rectangle.

Note

As you're working on this flowchart, you may want to place each element on the Stage in a logical fashion, similar to how you worked in the earlier example. Refer to Figure 3-8 if you want to see the final outcome of the example. We will add Connector lines at the end of the example.

3. Because you will give the user the option to enter/load the site, you will insert a decision point into the process chart. Drag a Decision shape (diamond) from the Stencil window to the Drawing page. Select the shape and type **Enter** into this shape.

4. Next you will want to add two Process shapes from the Stencil window for your Main page and the Current project page loading onto the main page and type descriptive names into them. Following this, add another decision box to the Drawing page. Because the navigation is on the Main page, the user has a choice of where to navigate on the site, which is represented by the Menu navigation symbol.

5. Now you will need to add Process shapes for the next three content areas of your site. Referring to the earlier exercise and the list at the beginning of the exercise, you will require areas for feedback, about the site, and the portfolio. Remember: You can duplicate instances by selecting one, and while pressing Ctrl, dragging the instance to another area of the stage and pressing F4. Add these descriptions into the rectangle instances you create.

6. The next thing you need to do is create shapes for each area you have within the feedback, contact, and portfolio sections of your site. You may want to use a different shape for these areas as well. Because you will probably have several links or content within each area of the portfolio and perhaps even the contact and about sections, a Document symbol is perhaps a wise choice in this situation (which signifies a continuation of the process chart). Name these shapes for each area of your portfolio and contact areas. Refer to the initial list of areas or Figure 3-12 if necessary.

7. Your feedback form will contain three elements for input data, which will be sent back to your email server. First, because this is a decision, use a diamond shape from the Stencil window before these elements to notify this process. You should also use a different shape for the name, e-mail, and comments symbols (in our diagram we use an oval). Drag these from your Stencil window, modify if necessary, and label with descriptive names. Because data is sent from these elements to the server, use a Data symbol in this area, and if you want, another for the server (perhaps Stored data).

8. Now you're ready to create your Connector lines. The flow should be somewhat obvious to you by now. Select the Connector tool button in the Standard toolbar. Then go to the Line ends button in the Formatting toolbar and select an arrow that points right. You're now ready to create connections between the instances.

9. Start with the Splash/Welcome page symbol, and link it to the diamond shaped Enter symbol. This will then link to your Main page. Loading into your Main page is the Current production, so perhaps connect these two pages with an arrow going from the Current production page to the Main page.

10. From the Main page, your user can make a decision to go to your three other main areas, so create an arrow leading to the Menu selection decision box, and then from this one symbol to your three main areas. Each of these areas then points to many sub-regions of your site. Make arrows stemming from each of these primary pages to their sub-areas. For the Feedback region, you may want to link name, e-mail, and comments without arrows, as they would logically be placed on one page. Link these three symbols to the Data symbol, and Data to the server instance.

11. At this point, your flowchart should be complete. Refer to the diagram in Figure 3-12 if you need some ideas on how to format your instances and connector lines. Save your file as process_chart.vsd.

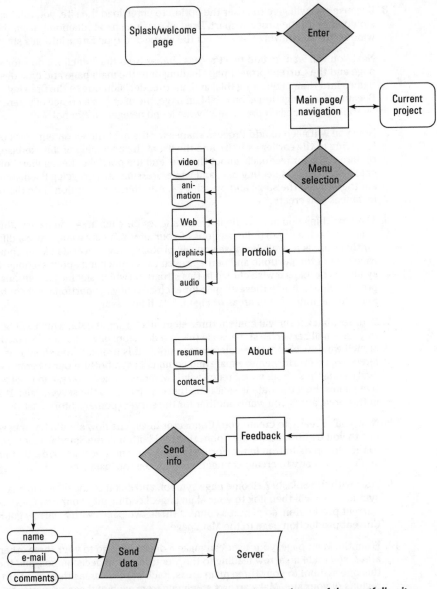

Figure 3-12: This process flowchart maps the user's experience of the portfolio site.

As soon as you have developed a process flowchart, construction of the functional specification for your Flash movie is the next logical step. Refer to the earlier sections of this chapter for more information on this subject.

You will find the completed process chart file, process_chart.vsd, in the ch03 folder of the *Flash MX Bible* CD-ROM.

Mapping the structure of a live site

Visio 2002 makes it extremely easy to diagram the structure of existing Web sites, which can aid in updates and site maintenance. Using built-in functionality, you can take a local or live Web site and generate a flowchart showing the site's architecture. This can be very useful if you need to map a Web site using Flash within HTML architecture. Custom Visio settings allow you to generate flowcharts of varying complexity. Visio can track different numbers of levels (1 through 12) and file types, which can be useful when dealing with Web sites with repetitive pages, such as message board sites. Take a look at how to use this function in Visio:

1. Open up Visio 2002 and select File ⇨ New ⇨ Web Diagram ⇨ Web Site Map.

If you want a standard example of a Web site flowchart, we've provided a file called flowchart.html in the HTML folder within the ch03 folder on the *Flash MX Bible* CD-ROM. To view the sample files, copy the folder and contained files onto your hard drive.

2. The Generate Site Map dialog box will appear. In the Address field, you can enter the URL for a live Web site or open a local HTML or ASP document on your hard drive or network. Visio will generate a flowchart from the URL or file that you specify. Before you click OK, let's review the other options in this dialog box.

   Click the Settings button to open the Web Site Map Settings dialog box. Here, you will find several tabs where you can control the number of levels, links, extensions, protocols, and attributes you include in your flowchart. You can also set how deep the architecture is searched and represented in your diagram. The layout of your flowchart can be controlled through the Modify Layout button. After you've entered your settings in each tab, click OK to return to the Generate Site Map dialog box. When you click OK in this dialog box, your link will be searched, and your flowchart is built automatically.

To see an example of a basic site architecture, open flowchart.html from the ch03 folder on the *Flash MX Bible* CD-ROM.

When checking an online site's architecture, you will get optimal results by entering a link pointing to the actual filename path as opposed to a general URL. An example of this would be calling for `www.flashsupport.com/default.asp` as opposed to `www.flashsupport.com`.

3. Any broken links or images that are encountered in the site documents will be represented in your flowchart by a large red X placed over the graphic. Using the Filter window, you can add or remove flowchart elements from your document.

4. Save your file as **my_site.vsd**. Refer to Figure 3-13 for an example of what this feature in Visio 2002 will generate. This flowchart is showing three levels of a Web site primarily using HTML with embedded Flash elements (including Flash for navigation within a frameset). A link has been purposefully broken to show how Visio will report any broken images or links it finds within the Web site.

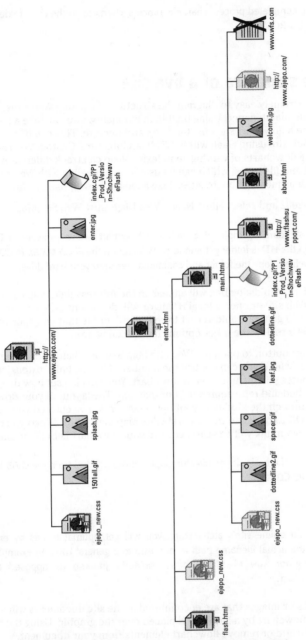

Figure 3-13: Your flowchart shows three levels of the Web site's architecture. You can easily tell if any links are broken; an X is drawn over the graphic.

Caution

If you decide to check out the architecture of a large Web site like www.google.com, you could end up waiting a long time for Visio to produce a result, even if only searching three levels, it may even freeze up your computer.

You can use another feature within Visio to track the development and modification made on your Web site. Modification dates, file size changes, and various other information will be compared to a previous .vsd file when you go to Web ⇨ Reports ⇨ Compare to previous document and select a previous document made using Visio. Then you can save the generated report.

If you aren't concerned about Web sites already produced, you can also create conceptual flowcharts for planning purposes. When you're opening a new document, choose File ⇨ New ⇨ Web Diagram ⇨ Conceptual Web Site. You will be provided with a blank page to construct your flowchart in the same fashion as previous exercises.

On the CD-ROM

MD Dundon's tutorial on "Storyboarding and Planning Interactivity" includes templates for concept presentations and suggestions for improving your workflow and delivering better projects with less production stress. You will find the Bonus_Tutorials.pdf in the Bonus_Tutorials folder on the CD-ROM. The example files for MD Dundon's tutorial are in the et01_dundon subfolder.

Summary

✦ You're clients will rely on you to understand and guide the production process involved with Flash content creation.

✦ Careful planning will help you to create Flash solutions that best meet the goals of your project. The technical issues, such as usability, target audience, and delivery platform should be balanced with the aesthetic aspects of experience design.

✦ To structure the development of Flash projects many Web developers use a two-phase production model that involves six milestones: Business Initiative, Creative Solutions, Approval, Production, QA, and Delivery.

✦ During the production period, it is helpful to keep six key concepts in mind: asset assembly, a master Flash architecture, a local test environment, HTML page layout, a server staging environment, and proper QA testing. After production is finished, you also need to devise a strategy for systematic maintenance.

✦ You can use Visio to create organizational and process flowcharts. After you have developed these flowcharts, you can more easily create the functional specification for your Flash site. You can also create flowcharts of completed Web sites using automated features within Visio.

✦   ✦   ✦

Mastering the Flash Environment

◆   ◆   ◆   ◆

Chapter 4
Interface
Fundamentals

Chapter 5
Drawing in Flash

Chapter 6
Symbols, Instances,
and the Library

Chapter 7
Applying Color

Chapter 8
Working with Text

Chapter 9
Modifying Graphics

◆   ◆   ◆   ◆

When you're ready to jump in and get started on the road to efficient and painless production, this section will give you all the information you need to feel comfortable in the Flash authoring environment. Chapter 4 introduces you to the Flash workspace and gives you tips for customizing the UI. You will learn the difference between a window and a panel and discover some of the timesaving features that have been added to Flash MX. Chapter 5 is where you'll find coverage of all the Flash drawing and selection tools. You'll also learn how to control snapping behavior and how to create and edit groups. In Chapter 6, you'll find out what makes Flash so much more powerful than simple vector graphics programs. Symbols and Symbol instances are the basis for all optimized Flash projects and the Library gives you all the options you'll need to keep your project assets organized. Chapter 7 includes coverage of color issues specific to Web production and explains how to use the Color Swatches and Color Mixer panels to enhance your projects with custom colors, gradients, bitmap fills, and more. Chapter 8 guides you through the various options for creating and editing text in Flash, including Dynamic and Input text and vertical text. You will learn how to control font display and find out how to create and use font symbols. Finally, in Chapter 9 you will be introduced to the more advanced tools for editing graphics and text in Flash, including the Free Transform and Transform Fill tools and the Advanced Color Effects menu.

Interface Fundamentals

◆ ◆ ◆ ◆

In This Chapter

Getting started in
Flash MX

Accessing the learning
resources available
in Flash

Getting to know
the fundamental
Flash interface: What's
new in Flash MX

Controlling windows
and panels

Creating custom
keyboard shortcut sets

Using the Toolbox and
shortcut keys

Using the Zoom control
and View menu
commands

Understanding and
navigating the Timeline

Managing layers and
Layer folders

Understanding the print
settings in Flash

◆ ◆ ◆ ◆

This chapter gives you a tour of the Flash workspace and the various methods for organizing and navigating your documents. Fundamental features of the authoring environment are defined, but in some cases the explanation of more-complex functionality will be deferred to later chapters. This chapter gets new users oriented to the program and introduces experienced users to some of the new MX features.

Getting Started

When you walk into a studio, the first thing you need to know is where to find your tools. Although you might have an idea of where to start looking based on past experience, nothing improves your workflow more than being able to reach for something without hesitation. This kind of familiarity and comfort in a workspace is a prerequisite for the mastery of any craft.

Fortunately, many of the features of the Flash MX interface will look familiar to you if you've worked in other graphics applications. However, there are also many unique features that you will need to understand before you can tackle your Flash projects with the ease of an expert. We begin by introducing the Flash interface and pointing out the tools available for managing and customizing your Flash "studio." We've done our best to keep new terminology consistent with the interface. Where inconsistencies occur, we've tried to choose terms most consistent with other Macromedia products and documentation.

You'll soon notice that there is often more than one way to access an option. As the steps for carrying out a task are described, we include shortcut keys or menu paths listed in brackets. You should feel comfortable and ready to get to work in no time.

Welcome to Flash MX

Whether you've been using Flash since the early days of version 2, or you've just opened the program for the first time, you'll quickly see that this is the most mature interface yet from Macromedia. As Flash has grown and evolved, the interface has also seen a number of variations. With a newly streamlined panel system and the addition of an intuitive Property inspector, Flash MX should make artists and programmers feel equally comfortable, and those multitasking, do-it-all developers should be more efficient than ever.

Tip

Because the Property inspector and the Toolbox now provide access to all tool options (with the exception of some drawing and text attributes that are adjusted in the Preferences window), there are now only three panels that you might need to open separately for additional options while editing graphics on the Stage. These are: Color Mixer, for adding alpha, gradients, and custom colors; Align for accurately arranging elements in relation to each other or to the Stage; and Transform for quickly making exact size or rotation adjustments. Simple, right?

Help menu options

In addition to robust online support, Macromedia has added a series of Help panels in Flash MX to introduce new features and resources. If the Welcome panel (shown in Figure 4-1) doesn't load when you first run Flash, you can open it at any time from the Help menu.

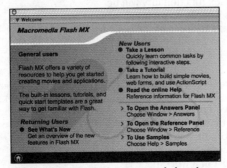

Figure 4-1: The Welcome panel showing resources for General users

The Welcome panel offers options for viewing a custom introduction to program and support features. By choosing the **Designer** or **Developer** option you will be prompted to choose a custom Panel Set and be shown highlights related to these specific uses of the program. The **General users** option will show an overview of all available learning resources.

If you prefer to access support features directly, the Flash Help menu will direct you to two kinds of help: offline and online. Unless you've removed the help files from your Flash installation, a number of offline resources are accessible directly from the Help menu. These resource topics will launch your web browser and load an HTML file (offline Web page). First, with **What's New**, you can get an introduction to the new Flash MX features. Next, new users may benefit from the **Flash Lessons** and **Samples** that also highlight new MX features. The **Tutorials** give an introduction to three specific areas: Flash MX, ActionScript, and Components.

If you're working on your own projects and need to get more specific help, **Using Flash** provides a searchable offline list of help topics for general Flash tasks. The **ActionScript Dictionary** is the first place to look for offline help with your scripting questions. Finally, Macromedia has provided two guided entry points to a vast array of online resources. The **Flash Exchange** is a new online resource created to support use and development of the new Flash MX extensions. The **Flash Support Center** is Macromedia's original online resource, sometimes also referred to as the Designer's or Developer's Resource Center. This is Macromedia's primary vehicle for the distribution of up-to-date information about Flash and Flash-related topics. This is a searchable area with current (and archived) articles on many Flash topics. You can also find links to downloads, documentation, forums, and many other invaluable Flash-related resources and updates.

Here is a summary list of the options available from the Help menu:

✦ **Help ⇨ What's New:** An illustrated panel overview of new MX features.

✦ **Help ⇨ Lessons:** Guided lessons with prebuilt Flash files.

✦ **Help ⇨ Tutorials:** HTML introductions to Flash MX, ActionScript, and Components.

✦ **Help ⇨ Using Flash:** Searchable HTML help for general Flash MX tasks.

✦ **Help ⇨ ActionScript Dictionary:** HTML description of syntax and use of ActionScript, with sample entries and notes on deprecated elements.

✦ **Help ⇨ Flash Exchange:** Macromedia's online resource for extensions. Get or submit extensions and learn how they allow you to add new features to Flash.

✦ **Help ⇨ Manage Extensions:** Loads control panel for managing installed Macromedia extensions.

✦ **Help ⇨ Samples:** HTML list of sample Flash movies that highlight new features with reusable source files available in the Flash 6 Samples folder.

✦ **Help ⇨ Flash Support Center:** Macromedia's central page for troubleshooting. Searchable TechNotes and a Flash Forum for developers of all skill levels.

A new Answers panel replaces the Macromedia Dashboard as a central location for accessing updated resources that can be docked with other panels in your workspace.

The first time you use Flash Help in Windows XP, you may get a prompt to install the Java player — simply follow the onscreen instructions.

The MX interface on Macintosh and Windows

Before discussing the various Flash menu items, panels, and miscellaneous dialog boxes, we can begin with a look at the interface with its default array of toolbars and panels as they appear on Macintosh and on Windows.

The layered panel groupings of Flash 5 have been replaced by a flexible structure of individual panels that can remain free floating or be docked in any order in a vertical stack. The Panels submenu has been retired and all panels are now directly accessible from the main Window menu or invoked by using shortcut keys.

The implementation of panels is consistent across both Mac and Windows. Throughout the book, we discuss each panel in context with the tools and tasks where it is used. As you'll quickly find, there are many ways to arrange these panels for a customized workflow. Your preferred panel layouts for different tasks can be saved as custom Panel Layouts and recalled from the Panel Sets menu.

In addition to the default Panel Set, Macromedia has provided a series of custom Panel Sets, designed to suit the workflow of a designer or a developer and arranged for specific monitor resolution settings. Because the differences between these two sets only make sense when you're familiar with the use of panels, we can begin with the default set (Window ⇨ Panel Sets ⇨ Default Layout). Figure 4-2 shows how this looks on the Mac. Figure 4-3 shows how the default Panel Set looks on Windows.

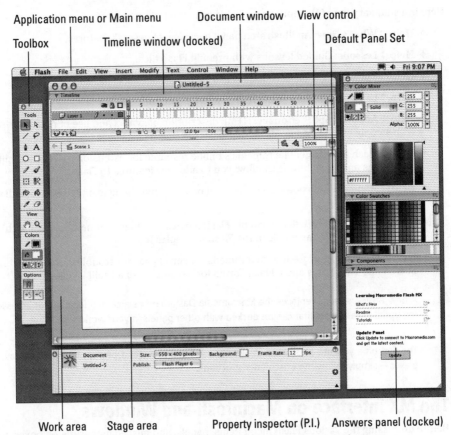

Application menu or Main menu — Document window — View control
Toolbox — Timeline window (docked) — Default Panel Set
Work area — Stage area — Property inspector (P.I.) — Answers panel (docked)

Figure 4-2: The default layout of panels as they appear on Macintosh OS X

Note

Although there are some visible differences between Macintosh and Windows interfaces for Flash MX, these are largely due to differences in the operating systems that are apparent in any application. For the sake of clarity, we've compared the two overall interfaces here before discussing individual items. For the most part, however, we use Macintosh OS X and Windows XP illustrations interchangeably, pointing out differences only when they directly affect workflow.

Two optional features are absent from the Mac version that can be found under Window ⇨ Toolbars in the Windows version of Flash. These are the Main Toolbar and the Status Bar. The Main Toolbar allows quick access to commonly used Toolbox and panel options. The Status Bar provides a brief description of specific tools in the Toolbox or the Main Toolbar as their icons are pointed to with the cursor. The Controller found in the Toolbar menu on Windows has the same function as the Controller found in the main Window menu on the Macintosh. Both are used to control the Playhead on the Timeline.

Toolbox (docked)

Application menu or Main menu   Document window   View control

Timeline window (docked)   Default Panel Set

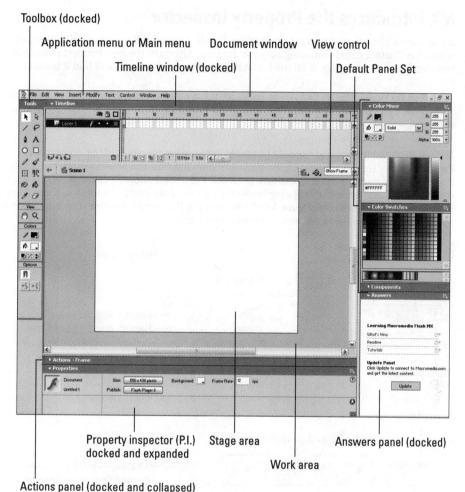

Property inspector (P.I.)   Stage area   Answers panel (docked)
docked and expanded

Work area

Actions panel (docked and collapsed)

Figure 4-3: The default layout of panels as they appear on Windows XP

Tip

Because the Main Toolbar and the Status Bar provide mostly redundant information and take up valuable screen space, they are only useful if they help you to get familiar with the program. These toolbars are disabled by default and most users become experienced without even realizing these extra tools are available.

Another minor way in which the Windows version differs from the Mac version is that the Toolbox and the Controller can be docked (or undocked) to the program window. The Toolbox and Controller can be dragged to the edge of the program window to dock seamlessly in the interface. Note that the Toolbox docks only to the sides, while the Controller can also dock to the top and bottom, as well as mesh with other toolbars. To prevent docking while moving either the Toolbox or Controller, press the Control key while dragging.

MX introduces the Property inspector

If you were a Flash 5 user, you may be looking for the Launcher Bar and wondering why there is another floating panel cluttering up your desktop. Although the new Property inspector takes up a little more space than the Launcher Bar did, we think you will find it invaluable.

Tip   You no longer have to find screen space for these nine nested panels that have been integrated into the Property inspector: Stroke, Fill, Character, Paragraph, Text Options, Instance, Effect, Frame, and Sound.

Instead of launching separate panels to access options for certain tools or objects, the Property inspector has integrated the most common options and allows you to access these and other fundamental features of Flash from one central location. Because most common options are available on the Property inspector you will only need to access separate panels for a few advanced features. Figure 4-4 shows how the Property inspector displays different options depending on which item is currently selected.

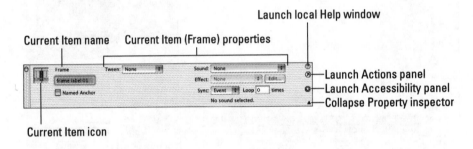

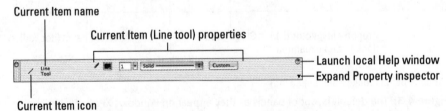

Figure 4-4: The Property inspector, as it appears when a frame is selected (top), and when the Line tool is selected (bottom)

The top figure shows the Property inspector (expanded), as it appears when a frame is selected — displaying Frame properties and options, as well as icons for launching the Help panel, Actions panel, and Accessibility panel (for adding Accessibility features now available in Flash MX). The bottom figure shows the Property inspector (collapsed), as it appears when the Line tool is selected — displaying Line tool properties and options. The launcher icon for the Help panel is still available, but Actions and Accessibility options do not apply to the Line tool, so these launcher icons disappear.

Cross-Reference   The new Accessibility features available in Flash will be explained and applied in Chapter 20, "Making Your First Flash MX Project."

Depending on what is currently selected, the Property inspector will display relevant attributes for a document, frame, symbol, shape, or text box. Pop-up menus and editable value fields make it quick and easy to make changes without hunting through panel sets or the application menu bar. As shown in Figure 4-4, when an element is selected that can have code attached to it, a gray arrow appears on the right edge of the Property inspector. Clicking this icon will launch the Actions panel for editing code on individual frames, Buttons, or Movie Clips.

Managing Windows and Panels

Whether you have chosen one of the Panel sets available from the Window menu or have just opened Flash with the default display, one of the first things you'll want to learn is how to customize the Flash environment to suit your workflow. Whether you're working on an 800x600 laptop screen or on a 1600x1200 dual-monitor setup, panels give you the flexibility to create a layout that fits your screen real estate and production needs.

To save your current panel layout as a custom set that can be accessed from the Panel Sets menu the next time you open Flash, follow these simple steps.

1. Open and arrange any panels that you want to include in your custom layout.

2. Go to Menu ➪ Save Panel Layout.

3. You will be prompted by a dialog box to name your panel layout. Enter a name that will help you remember why you made that panel set, such as "animation" or "scripting."

4. Your custom layout will now appear in the list of available panel sets (Window ➪ Panel Sets).

Note Deleting panel sets is not quite as simple as adding them, but it can be done. On Windows, you will find panel sets saved under C:\documents and settings\(username)\Application Data\Macromedia\Flash MX\Configuration\Panel Sets. On Mac, you will find the same information saved in the users file on your hard drive; under hd:users: (username): Library: Application Support: Macromedia: Flash MX: configuration: Panel Sets. After you find the name of your custom panel set in the folder where it is saved, you can delete it and it will no longer appear in the Flash Panel Sets menu.

All the interface elements have built-in control features (see Figure 4-5 for the controls that you will see on both Mac and Windows panels), but you can also manage what appears in your workspace with the main application menu. Rather than go through a laundry list of all the application menu options, we will note the various features that apply to individual windows and panels as their uses are described.

Tip To make the interface easier to use, Macromedia kindly made the whole title bar of the panels active so that you can expand or collapse a panel by clicking anywhere in the top gray bar, not only on the Expand/Collapse arrow.

For clarity, we have capitalized terms that refer to specific Flash interface features such as Document window, Work area, Timeline, Panel set, Toolbox, and Options area. You may see these words lowercase in other parts of the text, where they are used as general terms, rather than as labels for specific parts of the Flash interface.

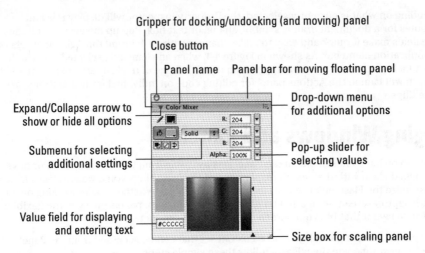

Gripper for docking/undocking (and moving) panel

Close button

Panel name   Panel bar for moving floating panel

Expand/Collapse arrow to show or hide all options

Drop-down menu for additional options

Submenu for selecting additional settings

Pop-up slider for selecting values

Value field for displaying and entering text

Size box for scaling panel

Figure 4-5: The controls noted here on the Macintosh Color Mixer panel, are consistent with the control icons you will see on other panels for both Macintosh and Windows.

The use of the terms *window* and *panel* may also be unclear. For practical purposes, any interface element that can be grouped or nested with other like elements to create a set is considered a panel, while elements that remain independent or can only be docked to the application or document window are referred to as windows. There are some important exceptions (and some nonsensical exceptions) to this order. We have created a list here of elements as we commonly name them in each category, with a note of how they are listed from the Window section of the application (or main) menu.

✦ **Windows**

Document (⇨ New Window or File ⇨ New)

Timeline (⇨ Timeline)

Output (⇨ Output)

✦ **Panels**

Answers (⇨ Answers)

Align (⇨ Align)

Mixer (⇨ Color Mixer)

Swatches (⇨ Color Swatches)

Info (⇨ Info)

Scene (⇨ Scene)

Transform (⇨ Transform)

Actions (⇨ Actions) — best viewed undocked for dual monitors

Debugger (⇨ Debugger)

Movie Explorer (⇨ Movie Explorer)

Reference (⇨ Reference)

Accessibility (⇨ Accessibility)

Components (⇨ Components)

Component Parameters (⇨ Component Parameters)

Library (⇨ Library) — best viewed undocked

Common Libraries (⇨ Common Libraries ⇨ Buttons, ⇨ Learning Interactions, ⇨ Sounds)

Sitespring (⇨ Sitespring) — best viewed undocked.

✦ **Independent Exceptions**

Property inspector (⇨ Properties)

Controller (⇨ Controller)

Toolbox (Window ⇨ Tools)

And that, honestly, is every panel and window and moveable box that you will ever need to use in the Flash authoring environment. Some menu items look a bit like panels, such as the Document and Layer Properties dialog boxes or the Publish Settings dialog box, but these only stay open while the menu item is active. We describe the actual uses and options for most of these various interface elements as we discuss tasks where they are applied. For getting started with Flash, we will be introducing the Property inspector, Toolbox, Document window, Scene panel, Timeline, and Controller, along with the menu items that apply to these. The remainder of the panels and windows will be described as they are used in chapters discussing drawing, animation, interactivity, and other specific production topics.

Contextual menus

As in many other programs, you will find Flash contextual menus pop up in response to a right-click (Control+click for the Mac) on a selected item in the Timeline, Library panel, or on the Stage. Contextual menus duplicate most functions and commands that are accessible either through the application menu, or through the various panels and dialog boxes, which are discussed in this chapter. Because contextual menus show you only those options relevant to the element you have selected, they provide a handy authoring shortcut that can also help you get familiar with Flash.

Focus: Making panels or windows active

Prior to Flash 4, there was only one area of the application that required users to pay attention to focus — when selecting colors for either the stroke or fill — when it was easy to confuse the two. As the interface has grown to include more panels and windows that can be active at different times within the Flash environment, focus has become an important aspect of the program to be conscious of. What is focus? *Focus* is a term used to describe which part of the application is active, or has priority, at a given time. For example, all panels, such as the Actions panel, do not automatically "have focus" — this means that you have to click within the panel to begin working there. Similarly, to return to the Document window or Stage to edit an element, you must click there to return focus to that aspect of the application. The Property inspector is a new feature that can actually give you a reminder of what area or element is active, because it displays the attributes of the currently active item. Otherwise, if a panel or dialog box doesn't seem to respond, just remember to *focus* on what you're doing.

Keyboard shortcuts

Keyboard shortcuts allow you to work more quickly, by avoiding the hassle of clicking through a menu to activate a feature with your mouse. This is a workflow trick that many people use even when working in text-editing applications. Instead of browsing to the Edit menu to find the Copy command, you can just press the key combination Ctrl+C (or ⌘+C on Mac). We have included the default keyboard shortcuts for most tools and features as they are introduced, by listing them in parentheses after the tool or menu item name. When key options are different on Mac and Windows, we list both keys. Thus the convention for showing the keyboard shortcut for Copy in both Windows and Mac would be (Ctrl+C or ⌘+C). A default set of keyboard shortcuts is available without having to change any settings. But if you would like to use different shortcut keys for certain tasks, you can make changes to the default settings in the Keyboard Shortcuts dialog box shown in Figure 4-6.

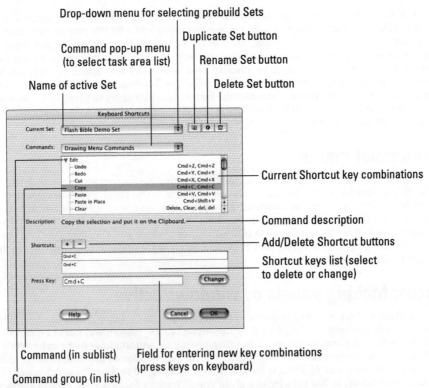

Figure 4-6: The Keyboard Shortcuts dialog box as displayed on Mac OS X. The appearance is slightly different on Windows, but the options available are the same.

As shown in Figure 4-6, the Keyboard Shortcuts dialog box enables you to customize your Flash keyboard shortcuts to maintain consistency with other applications or to suit a personalized workflow. Not only can you choose keyboard shortcuts developed from other applications, you can also save your modifications and custom settings. A full explanation of this dialog box follows.

New Feature
Flash MX has introduced a set of keyboard shortcuts for the Actions panel. This is a boon for coders who may wish to use different shortcuts when editing in the Actions panel than when working in the Document window.

The reason to celebrate this feature is that it accommodates users who have a specific preference or need to access tools differently — for example, drawing tablet with one hand, keyboard with the other. It can also make it possible for developers who have disabilities to work with greater speed and ease. The disadvantage of this feature is that, in a busy studio where artists are swapping seats like musical chairs, irresponsible keyboard changes can lead to team grief. In a studio, keyboard shortcuts must be implemented with regard for others working in the same environment.

Tip
By default, Flash uses built-in keyboard shortcuts designed for the Flash MX application. You can also select a built-in keyboard shortcut set from one of several popular graphics applications, including Macromedia Fireworks, Adobe Illustrator, and Adobe Photoshop. Instead of manually changing a duplicate of the Flash MX set to match your favorite program, simply switch the Current Set using the menu list.

You will find the Keyboard Shortcuts dialog box in the application menu (Edit ➪ Keyboard Shortcuts, or in OS X go to Flash ➪ Keyboard Shortcuts). To create a new keyboard shortcut, you must first duplicate an existing set, from which you can then add or subtract existing shortcuts to form your custom shortcut set. Here's the process:

1. Select a shortcut set from the **Current Set** submenu. This is now the active set.

2. Duplicate the active set by clicking the **Duplicate Set** button. The Duplicate dialog box appears. Enter a new name for this set in the **Duplicate Name** field and click **OK**.

   A similar procedure is employed to rename a shortcut set. Simply click the **Rename Set** button and enter the new name in the ensuing dialog box. (Note that you can rename all the built-in sets that ship with the program, with the exception of the Flash MX set.)

3. Select a commands list from the **Command** pop-up menu (Drawing Menu Commands, Drawing Tools, Test Movie Menu Commands, or Actions panel Commands) either to add a command or to modify it.

4. Next, in the Command list, choose either a grouping or a command from one of the previously chosen commands lists. Note that some lists have sub-lists. Click the plus sign (or small arrow on the Mac) to expand a particular category.

5. Now choose a command that you want to add (or subtract) — a description of the selected command appears in the **Description** area.

6. To delete the existing shortcut, click the minus (–) Shortcut button.

7. To add a shortcut for this command, click the plus (+) Shortcut button, and then enter the shortcut key combination in the **Press Key** entry box. Simply press keys on the keyboard, rather than typing the key names. Click **Change** and then **OK** to close the dialog box.

8. Or, to change an existing command, select the command and click the **Change** button.

9. To delete a shortcut set, click the **Delete Set** button, then select the set to be deleted from the ensuing Delete Set dialog box and click the **Delete** button. (Because you cannot delete the built-in sets that ship with the program, they do not appear in the Delete Set dialog box.)

Tip   Like Panel Set files, Keyboard Shortcut sets are stored in the Keyboard Shortcuts folder — found in the supporting files under Documents and Settings (on Windows), or under Users (Mac). You can navigate to this location on your hard drive and copy, backup, restore, delete, or otherwise manipulate any of these files from this folder. Keyboard Shortcuts are transferable between machines, although we had no success transferring them across platforms.

The Toolbox

The vertical bar titled **Tools** that appears by default on the left side of the interface is referred to as the Toolbox. Although it is sometimes also called the Drawing Toolbox, it is used for much more than just drawing. If you haven't just installed Flash, or if someone else has changed the defaults in Flash, you may not see the Toolbox on your screen. You can find it in the main Window menu (Window ➪ Tools) or invoke it with shortcut keys (Ctrl+F2 or ⌘+F2).

Controlling the Toolbox

The Toolbox cannot be scaled or minimized, but it can be hidden (and unhidden) along with other panels by choosing View ➪ Hide Panels, by pressing the Tab key, or by choosing Window ➪ Tools.

Note   If you're using a Windows machine, don't confuse Tools with the menu item for Toolbars, which refers to a set of optional menus described in the previous section titled, "The MX interface on Macintosh and Windows."

On Macintosh, the Toolbox is always a free-floating panel that can be moved anywhere on the screen. On Windows, the Toolbox can be deployed as either a floating panel, or as a panel that's docked to either edge of the Flash program window. Docking means that a floating panel is dragged to the edge of the program window, where it then melds to the border of the window. It remains "stuck" there until it is moved to another position or closed.

Tip   On Windows, to drag the Toolbox to the edge of the program window, yet prevent it from docking, press the Ctrl key while dragging.

Because the Toolbox doesn't scale or minimize, it isn't technically a panel. The only option for the Toolbox, other than moving it around the screen or docking it (in the Windows interface), is to disable the tooltips that display when tool icons are pointed to in the Toolbox.

If you would rather not see these little text hints every time you go near the Toolbox, you can turn them off in your General Preferences. (In OS X go to: Flash ⇨ , in OS 9 or earlier and in Windows go to: Edit ⇨) Preferences ⇨ General, and under **Selection Options** uncheck **Show Tooltips**.

Reading the Toolbox

The Toolbox is organized in four main sections (see Figure 4-7 for tool icons and shortcut keys). The top section contains all 16 Flash tools, as follows from left to right and top to bottom: Arrow, Subselect, Line, Lasso, Pen, Text, Oval, Rectangle, Pencil, Paintbrush, Free Transform, Transform Fill, Ink Bottle, Paint Bucket, Eyedropper, and Eraser. The second section contains the Flash View tools: the Hand and Zoom. Beneath the View tools is the Color area, with swatches for assigning Stroke color and Fill color, and buttons for Black and White, No Color, and Swap Color (to reverse stroke and fill colors). The last section of the Toolbox is the Options area, where some of the available tool modifiers appear for any active tool.

The application of individual tools and options in the Toolbox will be explained in chapters related to specific production topics that make up the remainder of this section (II).

Using tool options

Depending on the tool selected, the Options area may display some of the options, or properties, that control the functionality of that particular tool, while other controls may appear in the Property inspector or in a panel that launches separately. Of the options that are located in the Options area, some appear as submenus with multiple options, while others are simple buttons that toggle a property on or off. (For example, if the Lasso is selected, the Magic Wand option can be turned on or off by clicking its toggle button in the Options area.) If an option has more than two settings, these are generally available in a submenu.

Many of the options that appear within the Options area of the Toolbox can also be accessed from the Property inspector, from the application menu, or with keyboard shortcuts.

The migration of tool options from the Toolbox to the Property inspector is not entirely consistent in this version. Although we can hope that options will be more fully integrated into the Property inspector with future versions of Flash, for now you sometimes have to look back in the Options area of the Toolbox for modifiers that you might expect to appear in the Property inspector. Conversely, many tool options do not show up in the Toolbox, so even if the Options area appears empty, look in the Property inspector to be sure you haven't missed anything.

All the tools that are accessed from the Toolbox have keyboard equivalents, or shortcuts, that are single keystrokes. For example, to access the Arrow tool — which is the tool with the black arrow icon, located in the upper-left corner of the Toolbox — you can simply press the **V** key when the Stage or Timeline is in focus. Thus, the V key is the keyboard shortcut for the Arrow tool on both the Mac and Windows. This is faster than moving the mouse up to the Toolbox to click the Arrow tool, and it saves mouse miles on repeated tasks. To help you learn and remember shortcuts, throughout this book, when we mention a new tool, the keyboard shortcut for that tool follows in parentheses, like this: Arrow (V).

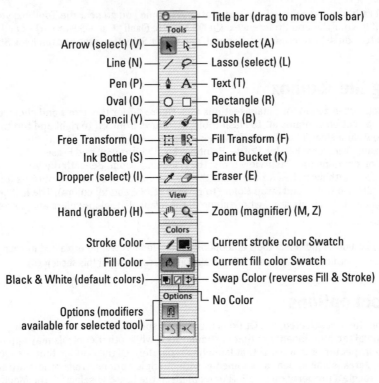

Arrow (select) (V) — Subselect (A)
Line (N) — Lasso (select) (L)
Pen (P) — Text (T)
Oval (O) — Rectangle (R)
Pencil (Y) — Brush (B)
Free Transform (Q) — Fill Transform (F)
Ink Bottle (S) — Paint Bucket (K)
Dropper (select) (I) — Eraser (E)

Hand (grabber) (H) — Zoom (magnifier) (M, Z)

Stroke Color — Current stroke color Swatch
Fill Color — Current fill color Swatch
Black & White (default colors) — Swap Color (reverses Fill & Stroke)
— No Color
Options (modifiers available for selected tool)

Title bar (drag to move Tools bar)

Figure 4-7: The Windows Toolbox is shown here with the keyboard shortcuts for each tool. Aside from system display characteristics and docking behavior, the Toolbox is identical on both Mac and Windows.

The Document Window

The Document window is the work table of your Flash project. This window tells you what document (.fla) is currently active and shows you where you are working in the project. When you open or create a new document, a new Document window automatically appears on the screen. Flash opens a new document whenever the program is launched, but after the program is open, File ➪ New (Ctrl+N or ⌘+N) generates all new documents.

New Feature

Flash MX includes a library of predefined Flash documents that you can use as guides for designing specific kinds of projects. The various styles for these templates are accessible from the File menu (File ➪ New From Template). You can also create your own reusable template from any Flash document by choosing File ➪ Save As Template. Before the template is saved, you are given options for naming, assigning a category, description, and preview icon, making it easy to manage a whole library of custom templates. You will find more coverage of this great feature in the QuickStart: "Flash in a Flash," and in Chapter 14, "Exporting Animation."

Controlling the Document window

Even when you choose to hide all panels, the Document window remains visible and closing the window will close your Flash project. On Macintosh, the Document window is always free floating and can be moved anywhere onscreen by grabbing the top of the panel with your mouse, or scaled by dragging the size box in the lower right corner. By default, on Windows, the Document window is maximized to fill the workspace and it cannot be scaled or moved independently, unless you first click the document **Restore Down** button (between the Minimize button and the Close button) in the top-right corner of the window (below the larger buttons that control the application). This will "free" the Document window from other panels in the program window so that you can move it around and scale it.

The main reason you may want to alter the default placement of the Document window is to organize your panel layouts to suit a dual-monitor workstation. Although you can drastically change the size and location of the Document window, generally you will want it centered in your workspace and scaled to allow you to comfortably work with objects on the Stage. Figure 4-8 shows the Document window on Macintosh as it appears with default settings, and with the Document Properties dialog box open.

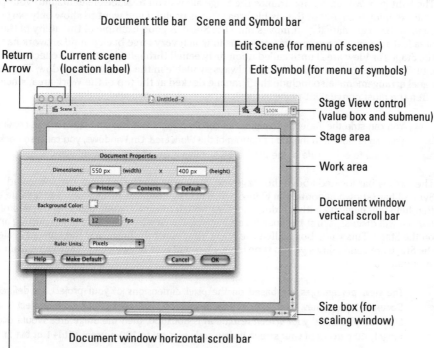

Document window control buttons
(Close/Minimize/Maximize)

Document title bar   Scene and Symbol bar

Edit Scene (for menu of scenes)

Return
Arrow   Current scene
(location label)

Edit Symbol (for menu of symbols)

Stage View control
(value box and submenu)

Stage area

Work area

Document window
vertical scroll bar

Size box (for
scaling window)

Document window horizontal scroll bar

Document Properties menu panel (dialog box)

Figure 4-8: The Document window as it appears with the Documents Properties dialog box open

The default document settings of Flash will automatically create new documents with a size of 550x400 pixels, a white background color, and a frame rate of 12. All of these attributes are displayed in the Property inspector and can be changed at any time. Clicking on the **Size** button in the Property inspector will launch the Document Properties panel which allows you to enter a custom size or use the Match options to automatically create a document that fits your current printer page settings (**Printer**), includes all the elements you have placed into your document (**Contents**), or restores the default size setting (**Default**).

Tip   If you wish to change the default settings for all new documents, invoke the Document Properties panel by clicking the Size button on the Property inspector or choosing Modify ⇨ Document from the main menu. After you have chosen the attributes you would like to assign to new documents, click the Make Default button at the bottom of the panel.

Reading the Document window

The white Stage area is the central part of the Document window that becomes the visible area or "screen" of a published Flash movie (.swf). As noted previously, the color and size of this "background" can be changed at any time, but it is best to establish these settings before you begin creating other elements.

The light gray Work area that frames the Stage allows you to place elements into your project while keeping them out of the visible area. This is useful if you want to show only part of an element or to animate it as it moves onto the Stage. A good example of the utility of the Work area feature can be seen in some cartoons in which very large background artwork hangs off the Stage (or View area) until called upon or tweened through to create the effect of a camera pan. The Stage and the Work area are always available in the Document window. The default panel arrangements also include the Timeline docked at the top of the Work area, since this is often the most convenient place to use it.

Tip   You can strip the Timeline panel out of the Document window and leave it free floating or you can re-dock it to the top or bottom of the Work area. On Windows, you can also dock the Timeline to either side of the Work area, but this is usually an awkward view.

The narrow bar located above the Stage and Work area is referred to as the Scene and Symbol bar (shown in context in Figure 4-8). This bar contains three icons and a value box that help you navigate within a document. Although the scale value box is at the end of the bar, we will discuss it first because it can be useful even when you first begin putting artwork on the Stage. This value box, called the Stage View control, shows you the current scale of the Stage area and allows you to type in new percentages or select a preset value from a submenu.

Note   The view percentages are based on the pixel dimensions of your project, as defined in Document properties, and your screen resolution. For example, if your project size is 500x400 pixels and your screen resolution is 800x600, then the Stage area would occupy roughly 40 percent of your screen if view scale was set to 100 percent (Ctrl+1 or ⌘+1).

The first two settings in the View submenu list are **Show Frame** (Ctrl+2 or ⌘+2), and **Show All** (Ctrl+3 or ⌘+3), these two settings will automatically scale your Stage view to fit your current Document window size. Show Frame sets the Stage view to a scale that fits the Document window without cropping the visible area. Show All sets the Stage view to a scale that includes any elements you have placed in the Work area outside the Stage. You can find these same view options from the application menu (View ⇨ Magnification). There are two additional tools available in the Toolbox (see Figure 4-7), which will also control your view of the Stage and Work area within the Document window.

  The Hand tool (H) allows you to move the Stage area within the Document window by "grabbing" it (clicking and dragging). Double-clicking the Hand icon in the Toolbox quickly gives you the same Stage view as choosing the menu item **Show Frame**. To toggle the Hand tool on while using any other tool, without interrupting your selection, hold down the spacebar.

The Zoom tool, or magnifier (Z, M) does just what the name implies — adjusts the scale of your Stage view. The available magnification range is between 8 percent and 2000 percent. However you can apply this handy tool in a few ways. With the Zoom tool active, clicking consecutively on the Stage will pull in closer to artwork with the *Enlarge* option (Ctrl+(+) or ⌘+(+) key), or move farther away with the *Reduce* option (Ctrl+(–) or ⌘+(–) key). Each click adjusts the Stage view magnification by half. Pressing the Option or Alt key as you click toggles the Zoom tool between *Enlarge* and *Reduce*. Double-clicking the Zoom tool icon in the Toolbox always scales the Stage view to 100 percent (Ctrl+1 or ⌘+1). One last way of applying the Zoom tool while it is active in the Toolbox is to drag a selection box around the area that you want to fill the Document window. Flash will scale the Stage view to the highest magnification (up to 2000 percent), which fills the Document window with the selected area.

Now back to the other icons on the Scene and Symbol bar. The location label on the top left edge of the window shows you the current scene and what part of the project you are editing. The sequence of labels that display in this area, are sometimes referred to as *breadcrumbs*. This is because these labels show the steps, or the path, leading back to the Main Timeline from the location you're editing. When in Symbol Editing mode, you can use the various labels to step your way back to the Main Timeline of the current scene, or click the arrow in front of the labels to return to the Main Timeline of the first scene in your project. To the right is the **Edit Scene** icon, and at the far right is the **Edit Symbols** icon. Click these icons to evoke menus of scenes or symbols in the document that can be opened and edited within the Document window.

 For more about Symbols, and the Symbol Editing mode in particular, refer to Chapter 6, "Symbols, Instances, and the Library."

Using scenes

The Scene panel (Ctrl+U or ⌘+U on Mac or Window ⇨ Scene), allows you to add, name and sequence scenes. By default, when your Flash movie (.swf) is published, the scenes play in the order in which they are listed, as shown in Figure 4-9. Scenes can help to organize a Flash project into logical, manageable parts. However, with the increasingly robust power of ActionScript, there's been a trend among many developers to move away from scene-based architecture. Using individual Flash movies instead of scenes to organize sections of a project results in files that download more efficiently and that are easier to edit due to their modular organization. It's like the difference between one huge ball of all-purpose twine that's the size of a house, and a large drawer filled with manageable spools — sorted neatly according to color and weight.

Dividing logical project parts into separate documents also facilitates efficiency in team environments, where developers can be working on different pieces of a project simultaneously. Scenes can still be useful for organizing certain types of projects, such as simple presentations without a lot of graphics, or for animators who prefer to organize a cartoon in one file before handing it off for integration into a larger site structure.

New Feature Adding named anchor keyframes is a new option in Flash MX. These allow Forward and Back buttons in a Web browser to jump from frame to frame or scene to scene to navigate a Flash movie. Flash automatically makes the first keyframe of each scene a named anchor. For more on how to set and publish named anchor keyframes, refer to Chapter 20, "Making Your First MX Project."

Scene List (default playback
order will be from top to bottom)

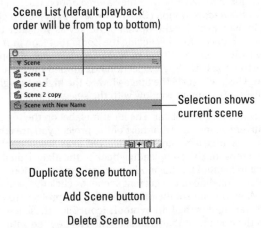

Selection shows
current scene

Duplicate Scene button

Add Scene button

Delete Scene button

Figure 4-9: The Scene panel showing document scenes in the order they will play back by default

To navigate to other scenes from within the Document window:

✦ Click the Edit Scene button on Scene and Symbol bar and then choose the desired scene from the submenu.

✦ Navigate to a specific scene from the application menu with the View ➪ Go To command.

✦ To delete a scene, either use the Scene panel's delete button (to bypass the alert asking if you want to delete the scene use Ctrl+click or ⌘+click), or from the application menu, use the Insert ➪ Remove Scene command.

✦ To add a new scene, either use the Scene panel's Add button or, from the Insert menu, use Insert ➪ Scene. New scenes will continue in the same auto-numbering sequence started with Scene 1. Thus, even if you delete Scene 2, the next added scene will be named Scene 3.

✦ Use the Duplicate button on the Scene panel to make a copy of a scene including all content on the scene's Timeline.

✦ To rename a scene, simply double-click the scene name within the Scene panel and type a new name. Using numbers in scene names will not affect playback order; the scenes will play back from the top to the bottom of the list.

✦ To rearrange scene order, simply click and drag a scene to alter its position in the Scene panel list. You can use actions to direct the movie to access scenes outside the default linear order. For more about actions, refer to Chapter 18, "Understanding Actions and Event Handlers."

Caution

Although scenes give you the visual impression of having a whole new timeline to work on, they are really continuations of the Main Timeline that begins in the first scene of your document. If you're using any Actions to control your movie playback, it's important to avoid duplicate naming on frame labels or named anchors. Thus, even if it seems logical, it isn't a good idea to label the beginning of each new scene "intro," because you won't be able to differentiate these labels as easily for targeting with Actions.

Using Document window options

There are several options available from the application menu that control display or editing in the Document window. These can be helpful when creating or placing elements on the Stage. All of these can be accessed from View on the application menu (notice the shortcut key combinations listed after most commands). The basic function of these various commands are as follows:

✦ **Goto:** Leads to a submenu of scenes in the current movie, including four handy shortcuts to the First, Previous, Next and Last scenes. This menu is also available from the Edit scene icon on the Document window.

✦ **Zoom In:** Increases the scale of the Stage view by 50 percent.

✦ **Zoom Out:** Decreases the scale of the Stage view by 50 percent.

✦ **Magnification:** Leads to the same view options that are available in the Stage View Control on the top right of the Document window. Note that three of these options also have corresponding keyboard shortcuts.

Note

The next four commands: Outlines, Fast, Antialias, and Antialias Text have *no* effect on the way in which Flash exports your movie. Quality decisions are made in the Publish Settings, which are covered in Chapter 21. These settings only affect screen quality and preview speed.

✦ **Outlines:** Simplifies the view of elements on the Stage by showing all shapes as outlines, and all lines as thin lines. This option is helpful when reshaping graphic elements. It also speeds up the display of complex scenes and can assist in getting the general timing and sense of a movie. It is a global equivalent of the outline options available in the Timeline window for layers and frames.

✦ **Fast:** Turns off both anti-aliasing and dithering to speed up display. The default is Off, to create the most accurate screen image and it is only recommended that you turn this option On if you need to reduce demand on your processor.

✦ **Antialias:** Dithers the edges of shapes and lines so that they look smoother onscreen. It can also slow the display, but this is only an issue with older video cards. This is actually a toggle in opposition with the Fast command: turn this On and Fast goes Off.

✦ **Antialias Text:** As with Antialias, this is also a toggle in opposition to the Fast command. It smoothes the edges of text *only* and is most noticeable on large font sizes. You can only have one Antialias option on at a time, so you can make a choice between smoothing text or smoothing shapes, depending on what content you're working with.

✦ **Timeline:** Use this toggle to show or hide the Timeline, even when it is docked in the Document window.

New Feature

All panels now have a Minimize/Maximize triangle icon on the top-left corner. Clicking the icon or anywhere within the title bar of the panel expands or collapses a panel faster than finding the application menu option or the multiple shortcut keys needed to hide it completely. This makes it easy to collapse the Timeline window so that it doesn't take up screen space, while still leaving it available to expand again when you need it.

✦ **Work Area:** Makes the light-gray area that surrounds the Stage available for use. When Work area is visible, your Stage area will display centered in the Document window when you apply Show Frame or Show All. If the Work area has been turned off in the View menu, than the Stage will align to the left side of the Document window.

Caution

Items that are selected and offstage when View ➪ Work area is toggled off can still be deleted, even if they are not visible. So it's best if you don't have anything selected when you choose to hide the Work area.

✦ **Rulers:** Toggles the reference Rulers (which display at the top and left edges of the Work area) on or off — use Modify ➪ Document to change units of measurement. Rulers are a helpful reference for placing guides to align elements in a layout.

✦ **Grid:** Offers three options that control the appearance of the Flash Grid and parameters for snapping behavior.

- **Show Grid:** Toggles visibility of the Grid on or off. This grid does not export with the final Flash movie (.swf), but serves as an authoring reference only.

- **Snap to Grid:** Toggles the Snap to Grid function on or off. Snap to Grid works regardless of whether the Grid has been made visible with View ➪ Grid ➪ Show Grid — if the Grid has not been made visible, elements still snap to the *invisible* Grid.

- **Edit Grid:** Opens the Grid dialog box, where you can change Grid Color, Spacing and the settings for Snap accuracy. Snap accuracy controls how close an item, symbol, or — while drawing — the end of a line must be to a Grid intersection before the item, symbol, or line endpoint snaps to the Grid. Both Show Grid and Snap to Grid check boxes are also included in this dialog box. Edited Grid settings can be saved as the default by clicking the Save Default button, which enables you to have these setting as presets for all subsequent Flash movies.

Note

The default Grid size of 18 pixels is equal to 0.25 inch. Grid units can be changed by entering the appropriate abbreviation for other units of measurement (for example: 25 pt., 0.5", 0.5 in, 2 cm, and so on) in the Grid Spacing entry boxes. Although the specified units *will* be applied to the grid, they will be translated into the current unit of measurement for the Ruler. Thus, if the Ruler is set to pixels, and the Grid units are changed to 0.5 in, then, on reopening the Grid dialog box, the Grid units will be displayed as 36 pix (because pixels are allocated at 72 pix = 1"). Changing Ruler units via Modify ➪ Document also changes Grid units.

✦ **Guides:** When Rulers are turned on, horizontal or vertical Guides can be dragged onto the Stage from respective rulers. These four commands control the parameters of these Guides.

- **Show Guides:** This is a simple toggle to either show or hide Guides that you have dragged out from the rulers.

- **Lock Guides:** This is a toggle that either locks or unlocks all current Guides. This is useful to prevent Guides from accidentally being moved after you have placed them.

- **Snap to Guides:** This is a toggle that extends Snap behavior to Guides. Each Snapping behavior works independently of the others — so, regardless of whether Snap to Grid or Snap to Objects are turned on or off, Snap to Guides can still be active.

- **Edit Guides:** This command invokes the Guides dialog box, where Guide Color and Guide-specific Snap accuracy can be adjusted. Also included are check boxes for the other three Guide commands: Show Guides, Snap to Guides, and Lock Guides. This enables you to establish Guide settings and then click the Save Default button to have these settings as presets for all subsequent Flash movies. To delete all Guides from the stage press the Clear All button.

✦ **Snap to Pixel:** Toggles a new auto-alignment feature of Flash MX on or off. This "magic" feature will only allow X and Y coordinates for an element to be in whole-pixel increments. This is useful for positioning pixel fonts or hairline artwork which can blur if not positioned on an exact pixel.

New Feature

When Snap to Pixel is turned on, a one-pixel grid appears when the Stage view is magnified to 400 percent or higher. This grid is independent of the Show Grid command.

✦ **Snap to Objects:** Due to the specific meaning of *Objects* in ActionScript, it's advisable — for the sake of future clarity — to think of this command as a Snap to Items command. When the Snap modifier is active, and you are moving or manipulating an item from an origin point, the item snaps into alignment with items already placed on the stage.

✦ **Show Shape Hints:** This toggles Shape Hints to make them visible or invisible. It does not disable shape hinting. Shape Hints are used when tweening shapes. For more about Shape tweens (or Shape Morphing) refer to Chapter 11, "Timeline Animation Fundamentals."

✦ **Hide Edges:** Hides selection patterns, so that you can edit items without the visual noise of the selection pixel "highlight." This only applies to currently selected items and allows a clean view without having to lose your selection. Most useful for seeing colors or fine lines that may appear visually distorted by the selection pattern.

✦ **Hide Panels:** Hides/Unhides all visible panels. To return the panels to visibility, you can also select them from the application Window menu or invoke them by pressing F4 or the Tab key (a quick way to hide/unhide panels when you want to see your Document window without any distraction).

Note

The View ➪ Hide Panels command will apply to all panels or windows with the exception of the Document window, while the Window ➪ Close All Panels command does not close the Toolbox, Controller, Timeline, or Document window.

The Timeline Window

The Timeline is like nothing you will find in your analog studio, unless you have a time machine that allows you to move forward and backward in time and up and down between dimensions. This may seem like a rather far-fetched analogy, but understanding the behavior and purpose of a timeline is often the most foreign new concept to grasp if you have not worked in other time-based applications (such as Macromedia Director). A clear understanding of timelines is critical to production in Flash. Even if you know how to use all your other tools, not knowing the Timeline makes working in Flash like trying to work in a studio with no light.

The Timeline window is really composed of two parts: the Layer section where content is "stacked" in depth, and the Timeline/Frames section where content is planned out in frames along the duration of your movie, like on a strip of motion picture film. In the Layer section, you can label or organize your "stacks" of frame rows. You can also lock or hide individual layers or just convert their display to colored outlines on the Stage while you are editing. In the Timeline section, you can control where and for how long content is visible and how it changes over time to animate when the movie plays back. You can also add actions to control how the Playhead moves through the Timeline, making it start and stop or jump to a specific frame.

You can find more on animation techniques in Chapter 11, "Timeline Animation Fundamentals." Actions are introduced in Part V, "Adding Basic Interactivity to Flash Movies."

Controlling the Timeline window

On both Macintosh and Windows, the default position for the Timeline is docked at the top of the Document window, which is often the most logical place to put it. If you don't see the Timeline when you open Flash, go to View ➪ Timeline (Ctrl+Alt+T or ⌘+Option+T) to bring it up on screen. The position, size, and shape of the Timeline can always be adjusted to suit your workflow. The Timeline can be docked to any edge of the Document window, but cannot be grouped with other panels. It can, however, be moved anywhere as a floating window, even exiled to the second monitor — leaving the Document window all for the Stage and Work area.

✦ Move the Timeline by clicking and dragging the bar at the top of the window. If the Timeline is docked, click anywhere in the gray area above the layer stack to undock the Timeline and reposition it.

✦ If undocked, resize the Timeline by dragging any edge (on Windows), or the gripper/size box in the lower-right corner (Mac). If docked, drag the bar at the bottom of the Timeline that separates the layers from the application window, either up or down.

✦ To resize the layer area for name and icon controls (to accommodate longer layer names or to apportion more of the view to frames), click and drag the bar that separates the layer name and icon controls from the Timeline frame area.

To permanently prevent the floating Timeline from docking to the application window, use Edit ➪ Preferences (or Flash ➪ Preferences on OS X) and in the General section, under Timeline Options, check Disable Timeline Docking.

The Controller (Window ➪ Controller on Mac or Window ➪ Toolbars ➪ Controller on Windows) is a small bar of buttons that provides basic control of the Playhead. Access to the Controller can be helpful if you need to pan back and forth along an extended section of the Timeline. You can keep it onscreen as a floating bar, and on Windows you can also dock it anywhere along the top or bottom of the Document window. Some developers prefer using the Controller to using shortcut keys for moving the Playhead. Along with the commands available on the Controller bar, the application Controller menu also lists some more advanced options that are discussed in following chapters as they relate to animation and actions.

Caution Playback speed within the document (.fla) is not as accurate as it is in the movie file (.swf), so the Controller is not intended as a replacement for the Test Movie command (Control ⇨ Test Movie or Ctrl+Enter or ⌘+Return).

As you can see in Figure 4-10, the buttons on the Controller will be familiar to anyone who has used a remote control. The only special function to note is that the Play button will toggle to start and stop without having to use the Stop button.

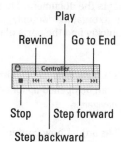

Play

Rewind | Go to End

Stop | Step forward

Step backward

Figure 4-10: The Controller showing callouts for the buttons as they are used to control movement of the Playhead

Tip Using shortcut keys is often the preferred way to move along the Timeline. On both Mac and Windows, pressing the Enter/Return key will work as a toggle to start and stop the Playhead. If you prefer to move along the Timeline frame by frame, pressing the period key (.) moves forward one frame and pressing the comma key (,) moves back one frame. These keys are more intuitively remembered by looking for the less than (<) and greater than (>) symbols.

Reading the Timeline

The Timeline graphically orders Flash content across two dimensions — time and depth — and provides you with some options for how this content is displayed on the Stage and within frames on the Timeline.

Visual display of time

The order of time is displayed by the sequence of frames arranged horizontally, from left to right, as they appear within the duration of your project. Thus, if your movie is set to 20 frames per second, frame 40 occurs at the 2-second point of your animation.

Note Although they say that time and space are without limits, the MX authoring environment supports about 32,000 frames, and the SWF format only officially supports around 1,600 which will actually be so long that you might never find your way from one end of the Timeline to the other. Organizing your work with scenes and movie clips, or even in multiple documents, should avoid ever having to use a Timeline even a tenth of this length.

You can insert, delete, copy, paste and reorder frames as well as convert them to various specific frame types that control how elements will animate. Current frame settings display in the Property inspector when a frame is selected, and you can also add/change a frame name or tween type here. The main controls for editing frames are found in the contextual menu (right-click on Windows or Control+click on Mac) or from the Edit and Insert application menu items.

Tip

As you work with frames you'll find shortcut keys invaluable. These shortcut keys are listed in the application menu following most commands. For a complete list of common Timeline editing tasks and the shortcut keys used for these, refer to Appendix A: "Keyboard Shortcuts."

Visual display of depth

The Timeline layers enable you to separate content onto individual "transparent" work surfaces within the Document window. This allows elements to be animated or edited individually even if they occupy the same timeline (or frame) space as other elements in the document. These layers are arranged vertically, from bottom to top. They enable you to organize content, actions, comments, labels, and sounds so that you will be able to quickly find the parts of the project that you want to edit.

New Feature

Flash MX has added the option of creating Layer folders. This is a huge help to organizing multi-layered documents. With layers moved inside a folder, they can be opened up for editing or hidden away to reduce the number of layers you have to navigate.

You can insert, delete, move or rename layers and folders, as well as adjust how content is displayed in the editing environment. Items placed on layers above can visually obscure other items in layers beneath them, without otherwise affecting each other. With the layer control icons shown at the top of the layer stack, you can set layer visibility (the Eye icon), editability (the Lock icon), and the display mode — regular or outline only (the Square icon). Note, however, that these settings are visible within the editing environment only and do not affect the appearance of the final movie (.swf).

Timeline window features

Figure 4-11 shows the Timeline window, as it appears when it is undocked or floating. The various controls of the window interface are labeled here, but detailed explanation of some of these controls will be deferred to the drawing and animation chapters where they are applied.

As shown in Figure 4-11, the principal parts and uses of the Timeline are

Window features

✦ **Title Bar:** This identifies the Timeline and allows it to be collapsed or expanded by clicking anywhere in the bar.

✦ **Timeline Header:** The Timeline Header is the ruler that shows frame numbers and measures the time of the Timeline — each tick is one frame.

✦ **Playhead or Current Frame Indicator:** The red rectangle with a line extending down through all layers is the Playhead. The Playhead indicates the current Frame. Drag it left or right along the Timeline to move from one area of the Timeline to another. Push it beyond the visible area to force-scroll the Timeline. You can also drag the Playhead at a consistent rate for a preview of your animation; this is called "scrubbing the Timeline."

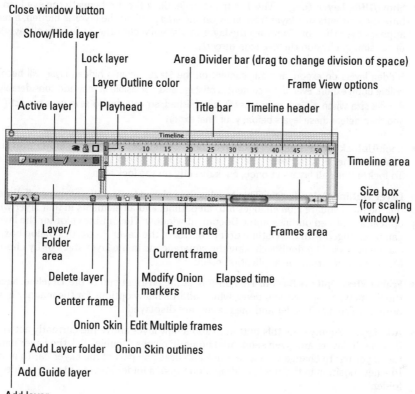

Close window button
Show/Hide layer
Lock layer
Area Divider bar (drag to change division of space)
Layer Outline color
Frame View options
Active layer
Playhead
Title bar
Timeline header
Timeline area
Size box (for scaling window)
Layer/ Folder area
Frame rate
Frames area
Current frame
Delete layer
Modify Onion markers
Elapsed time
Center frame
Onion Skin | Edit Multiple frames
Add Layer folder   Onion Skin outlines
Add Guide layer
Add layer

Figure 4-11: The floating Timeline window with callouts showing the principal parts and control elements

New Feature

On Windows, if you have a mouse with a scroll-wheel, you can now scroll up and down through the layers or by holding down the Shift key while you scroll, you can move the Playhead forward and backward along the Timeline. If all of your layers (or layer folders) are already visible in the Timeline window, than the scroll wheel will just scroll you forward and backward along the Timeline without moving the Playhead.

Layer controls

✦ **Active Layer Toggle:** This is more of an icon, really. To make a layer active, either click the layer's name, or select a frame or group of frames. Then the pencil icon appears, indicating that the layer is now active — that's in addition to this more obvious clue: The Layer bar of the active layer is black, whereas inactive Layer bars are gray. Although you can select multiple layers or content on multiple layers, only one layer will be marked as active at a time. For more about frame selection and editing behaviors, please see the heading "Editing frames and layers," that follows in this section.

✦ **Show/Hide Layer Toggle:** This is a true toggle. Click the dot beneath the eye icon to hide the contents of a layer from view on the stage. When the layer is hidden, a red X appears over the dot. To return the layer to visibility, click the X. To hide all layers at once, simply click on the eye icon directly.

Caution

Hidden layers do export, and any content on the Stage within a hidden layer will become visible upon export. Even if the content is offstage and not visible, it may add considerably to the file size when a Flash movie (.swf) is published, so you should save your project (.fla) and then delete these layers before your final export.

✦ **Lock/Unlock Layer Toggle:** This toggle locks or unlocks the layer to either prevent or enable further editing. When the layer is locked, a padlock icon appears over the dot. To lock/unlock all layers at once, click directly on the lock icon.

✦ **Layer Outline Color Toggle:** This toggles the colored layer outlines on or off. When on, the filled square icon changes into an outline, and all elements in that layer will appear as colored outlines in the Document window. The outline color for the layer can be changed with the Outline Color control of the Layer Properties dialog box, this can be accessed by double-clicking the square icons in the layer stack or by choosing Modify ⇨ Layer from the application menu.

✦ **Frame View Options Button:** This button, at the far-right end of the Timeline, accesses the Frame View options submenu, which affords many options for the manner in which both the Timeline Header and the Frames are displayed.

✦ **Add Layer:** Simply click this button to add a new layer above the currently active layer. By default, layers are given sequential numeric names. Double-click the Layer name in the Layer bar to change the name. Click and drag any part of the Layer bar to move it to a new position in the stack, or drag it on top of a folder layer to place it inside the folder.

✦ **Add Motion Guide Layer:** Motion Guide layers are used to move elements along a path. This button adds a Motion Guide layer directly above (and linked to) the currently active layer. To learn about using Motion Guide layers, refer to Chapter 12, "Applying Layer Types."

✦ **Add Layer Folder:** This new MX feature allows you to create folders for storing groups of layers. New folders will automatically be placed above the currently selected layer and labeled in the same number sequence as layers. They can be renamed or moved in the same way as other layers.

✦ **Delete Layer:** This button deletes the currently active layer, regardless of whether it is locked. Of course, the final layer cannot be deleted.

Note

Since using the delete key on your keyboard does not remove an active layer or folder, but rather removes all of the content from those frames, it can be helpful to get in the habit of right-clicking (Windows) or Control+clicking (Mac) on a layer that you want to remove. You can always click on the trash icon to dump a selected layer or folder, but sometimes the contextual menu click is a work habit you may already have that can easily be applied.

Frame controls

✦ **Center Frame:** Click this button to shift the Timeline so that the current frame is centered in the visible area of the Timeline.

✦ **Onion Skin:** The Onion Skin feature enables you to see several frames of animation simultaneously. Onion skinning is further described in Chapter 11, "Timeline Animation Fundamentals."

✦ **Onion Skin Outlines:** This enables you to see the outlines of several frames of animation simultaneously.

✦ **Edit Multiple Frames:** Normally, onion skinning only permits you to edit the current frame. Click this button to make each frame between the Onion Skin Markers editable.

✦ **Modify Onion Markers:** Click this button to evoke the Modify Onion Markers pop-up. In addition to manual adjustments, the options are used to control the behavior and range of onion skinning.

Timeline status displays

✦ **Current Frame:** This indicates the number of the current frame.

✦ **Frame Rate Indicator:** This indicates the Frame Rate of the movie, measured in fps, or frames per second. The program default is 12 fps, and is usually a good starting point. Ideally, some testing in the final playback environment should be done before deciding on an optimal frame rate. You can double-click the Frame Rate Indicator to invoke the Document Properties dialog box (also Modify ➪ Document or Ctrl+J or ⌘+J), or set the frame rate directly in the Property inspector.

Note

The fps setting is not a constant or absolute—it means maximum frame rate. The actual frame rate is dependent upon a number of variables, including download speed, processor speed, and machine resources—these are variables over which you have no control. However, another factor, over which you do have control, is the intensity of the animation: Complex movement with multiple elements or many layers of transparency is more processor intensive than simple movement. Previewing real-world playback speed at different frame rates—with a little testing on various machines—early on in your development process is *very* important.

✦ **Elapsed Time:** This indicates the total movie time, measured in fps, which would elapse from frame 1 to the current frame—provided that the movie is played back at the optimal speed.

Editing frames and layers

After much heated debate among developers as to whether the frame selection and display behavior was better in Flash 4 or in Flash 5, Flash MX has created the ultimate solution by combining the best of both. This hybrid system offers many useful options, but it may at first result in some confusion for new and experienced users alike. After you learn to recognize the visual conventions of the Timeline and how it displays different types of frames, you will be able to learn a lot about what is happening in an animation just by reading the Timeline. Figure 4-12 illustrates the MX conventions for frame and layer display.

✦ **Keyframe:** A keyframe is any frame in which the contents of the frame may differ from the contents of either the previous or subsequent frames. Filled (black) circles on the Timeline mark keyframes with content.

✦ **Blank Keyframe:** A keyframe that does not contain any content has the same behavior as any keyframe, but it is marked by an empty (white) circle on the Timeline.

✦ **Frame span:** Frame spans are the sections from a keyframe to an endframe (up to, but not including, the next keyframe to the right). Note that these spans can now be selected by double-clicking and dragged as a whole to a different location.

  • **Filled frame(s):** The intermediate frames in a span, following to the right of a keyframe (with content) are shaded gray.

  • **Empty frame(s):** The intermediate frames in a span, following to the right of a blank keyframe are white. A black line also outlines the entire span.

  • **Endframe:** The final frame of a span, marked with a small white rectangle and a vertical line to the right of the rectangle.

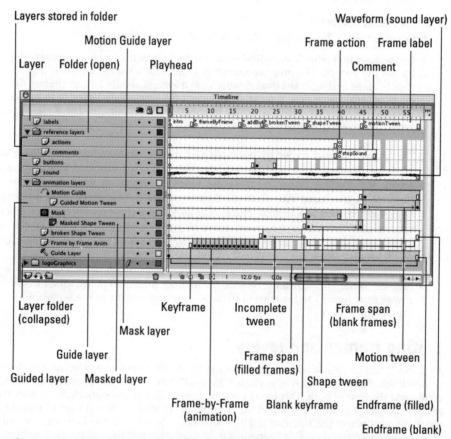

Figure 4-12: Flash MX conventions for naming and display of various frame and layer types

✦ **Frame-by-Frame Animation:** Frame-by-Frame Animation is animation composed entirely of keyframes. In a Frame-by-Frame Animation, the content on every frame is changed manually (rather than tweened).

✦ **Tweened Animation:** Tweened Animation is movement or change in an element interpolated by Flash over a range of frames that extend between two keyframes. An arrow stretching across a colored frame span designates a tween, of which there are two varieties:

• **Motion tweens:** Motion tweens are indicated by a blue tint and can be applied only to groups or symbols.

• **Shape tweens:** Shape tweens are indicated by a green tint and can be applied only to primitive (non-grouped) shapes.

For more on making frame-by-frame animation and using tweens, refer to chapter 11, "Timeline Animation Fundamentals."

✦ **Layer Folder:** These folders are used to organize other layers and they can be named and repositioned in the layer stack the same way as layers. Layer folders do not have individual frame settings and thus show up in the Timeline display as a continuous gray bar. To expand (open) or collapse (close) folders, click the arrow toggle at the left of the folder name or use the contextual menu. Note that dragging a folder inside another folder creates subfolders.

✦ **Motion Guide Layer:** A Motion Guide layer is used to guide an animated item along a path, which can be drawn with either the Pencil or the Line Tool. For more about Motion Guide layers, refer to Chapter 12, "Applying Layer Types."

✦ **Mask Layer:** A Mask layer is a layer that is used to selectively obscure the layers beneath it. For more about Mask layers, refer to Chapter 12, "Applying Layer Types."

✦ **Label:** Labels are used to give frames meaningful names, rather than using frame numbers. The advantage of this is that named keyframes can be moved without breaking ActionScript calls assigned to them. Upon export, labels are included as part of the .swf. Use the field in the Property inspector to add a label to a selected frame. Press Enter/Return after typing a frame label or comment to ensure that the label takes.

✦ **Comment:** Comments are special labels, preceded by a double-slash "//" — Comments do not export, so you can be as descriptive as you need to be without adding to the .swf size. However, you won't be able to read long comments unless you leave a lot of space between keyframes. Add comments in the Property inspector in the same way as labels, just be sure to your text is preceded by two forward slash characters.

✦ **Waveform:** This squiggly blue line in the "sounds" layer is the waveform of a placed sound. This visual reference for your sound makes it easier to synchronize animated elements to a soundtrack.

✦ **Frame Actions:** The small *a*s in frames 1, 20, 40, and 60 of the "actions" layer designate the presence of frame actions (ActionScript).

Frame specifics

Flash users familiar with previous versions may notice that in MX, empty keyframes are now marked with an empty circle (white dot), as they were in Flash 4. The last frame of a span is marked with the empty bar icon that was added in Flash 5. As always, keyframes with content are marked with a filled circle (black dot).

MX offers the option of using either Flash 4 or Flash 5 frame-selection behavior. In Flash 4, individual frames could be selected just by clicking on them, even if they were part of a *span* (a series of frames following a keyframe). With Flash 5, span-based selection was introduced as the default behavior — all the frames in a span would be selected just by clicking one. In Flash MX, the default has gone back to Flash 4 selection style, but double-clicking a frame will select a span. For the option of going back to the Flash 5 selection style, go to Edit ⇨ Preferences (or Flash ⇨ Preferences on OS X) and in the General section, under Timeline Options, select the Span Based Selection check box.

Note Although double-clicking a frame in the default selection style will select a span of frames, if the span is moved, it will automatically extend along the Timeline until it meets another keyframe. This can be helpful or annoying depending on what you are trying to accomplish. With Span Based Selection behavior enabled, when you relocate a span, it does not auto-extend and the original span length is preserved.

To clarify the various frame-editing options available, they are listed here with notes on the ways you can accomplish your intended result. Some of the methods differ depending on whether you have enabled Span Based Selection as described previously. For users of previous versions of Flash, this may take a little getting used to. For new users, deciding on a preference will be a matter of testing out both selection style options. The default methods are listed here first, followed by the methods that differ when Span Based Selection is turned on.

Default MX methods:

✦ **Selecting Frames:** The methods for selecting single frames and spans of frames have been simplified since Flash 5.

- **Frame spans:** To select a span of frames extending between two keyframes, double-click anywhere between the keyframes.

- **Single frames:** To select a single frame within a span, or a keyframe outside of a span, simply click to select it.

- **Multiple frames or spans:** To select multiple frames along the Timeline (within a span or independent of a span), click and drag in any direction until you have selected all the frames you want to include in the selection. You can also use Shift+click to add to a selection of frames.

Note The difference between selecting a frame by dragging over it, and moving a frame by selecting it and then dragging can be hard to differentiate. At first, you may find yourself moving frames that you only wanted to select. The trick is to be sure that you don't release the mouse after you click on a frame before you drag to select other frames. And conversely, if your intention is to move a frame or a series of frames, you have to click and release the mouse to select them first and then click again and drag to move them.

✦ **Moving Frames:** Select the frame(s) that need to be moved and then drag them to the new location.

✦ **Extending the Duration of a Span:** There are two ways to change the duration of a span, which is the same result as inserting frames (F5) or removing frames (Shift+F5) after a keyframe. To change where a span begins, select the keyframe and then drag the keyframe to the position where you want the span to begin. To change where a span ends, Ctrl or ⌘ +click the endframe and drag it to where you want the span to end, or select a blank frame beyond the endframe where you want the span to end and insert a frame (F5) — this automatically extends the span and moves the endframe to the frame you have selected.

Tip

If you're comfortable with Flash 5, you need to know this: If you click and drag any non-keyframe (frame or endframe) without pressing the Ctrl key (or the ⌘ key on Mac), the frame is automatically converted into a keyframe as it is dragged to the new location.

✦ **Copying Frames:** Select the frame(s) that you want to copy. Either Choose Edit ⇨ Copy Frames from the main menu and then Paste Frames into a new location, or press the Alt or Option key while clicking and dragging to copy selected frames to another location in the Timeline.

✦ **Pasting Frames:** Select the frame where you want the copied or cut frames to be inserted (Flash automatically adds frames or layers below and to the right of the selected frame to accommodate the pasted content), and select Edit ⇨ Paste Frames from the menu.

Caution

Edit ⇨ Copy (Ctrl+C or ⌘+C) is not the same as Edit ⇨ Copy Frames (Alt+Ctrl+C or Option+⌘+C). Using Copy will only "remember" and copy the content from a single keyframe, while Copy Frames will "remember" and copy content from multiple keyframes and even from multiple layers. To insert this content correctly in a new location, you have to remember to use the corresponding Paste commands — Paste (Ctrl+V or ⌘+V), or Paste Frames (Alt+Ctrl+V or Option+⌘+V) You may notice that the contextual menu only offers the plural options (Copy Frames or Paste Frames), this is because the plural command will safely work to move content from a single frame or from multiple frames. The singular command is just a simpler shortcut key to use if you know that you only want the content from one keyframe.

✦ **Inserting Frames:** Select the point at which you would like to insert a new frame, and select Insert Frame (F5) from the contextual menu or from the application menu (Insert ⇨ Frame). The visual "clue" that frames have been inserted is that the endframe of a span is moved to the right — this will also push any following keyframes further along the Timeline.

✦ **Inserting Keyframes:** Select the point at which you would like to insert a new keyframe, and select Insert Keyframe (F6) from the contextual menu or from the application menu (Insert ⇨ Keyframe). Note that keyframes can be inserted within a span without extending the span (or pushing the endframe to the right). Thus, inserting a keyframe actually converts an existing frame into a keyframe. So unlike frames, keyframes can be inserted without pushing other frames further down the Timeline.

✦ **Inserting Blank Keyframes:** Select the point at which you would like to insert a new blank keyframe, and select Insert Blank Keyframe (F7) from the contextual menu or from the application menu (Insert ⇨ Blank Keyframe). Inserting a blank keyframe within a span will clear all content along the Timeline until another keyframe is encountered.

Note

If you already have content in the current layer and you insert a keyframe, a new keyframe will be created that duplicates the content of the endframe immediately prior. But if you insert a blank keyframe, the content of the prior endframe will cease and the blank keyframe will, as its name implies, be void of content.

On the CD-ROM

For a hands-on example, refer to the file called "frames_example.fla" in the ch04 folder of the CD-ROM.

✦ **Removing Frames (to shorten a span):** Select the frame(s) that you want to remove, and then choose Remove Frames (Shift+F5) from the contextual menu or from the application menu (Insert ➪ Remove Frames). This does not work for removing keyframes; instead, it will remove a frame from the span to the right of the keyframe, causing all the following frames to move back toward frame 1.

✦ **Clear a Keyframe:** To remove a keyframe and its contents, select the keyframe and choose Clear Keyframe (Shift+F6) from the contextual menu or from the application menu (Insert ➪ Clear Keyframe). When a keyframe is cleared, the span of the previous keyframe is extended to fill all frames until the next keyframe on the Timeline. The same thing will happen if you insert a keyframe in a span and then Undo it (Ctrl+Z or ⌘+Z). Apply Undo (Edit ➪ Undo) twice—the first Undo will deselect the keyframe, and the second Undo will clear it.

✦ **Cutting Frames (leaves blank frames or keyframes):** To replace selected frames in a span with blank frames, while keeping content in the remainder of the span intact, select the frame(s) you want to "blank" and then choose Cut Frames (Alt+Ctrl+X on Windows or Option+⌘+X on Mac) from the contextual menu or from the application menu (Edit ➪ Cut Frames). This "pulls" the content out of only the selected frames, without interrupting content in surrounding frames or shifting any keyframes on the Timeline. The content that you cut can be pasted into another position on the Timeline (as described previously).

Caution   Selecting a frame or keyframe and using the Delete key will remove the content from the entire span, but will not remove the keyframe itself, or change the length of the span. You can delete content from multiple layers this way, but it will leave all the empty frames and keyframes on the Timeline.

✦ **Editing the Contents of a Keyframe:** Select the keyframe where you want to edit content. This moves the Playhead to the selected frame so that its content is visible in the Document window, where it can be edited. Note that if you edit content on a keyframe or frame within a span, the changes will apply to the current frame and the span it is part of.

Cross-Reference   Numerous techniques for editing content are detailed in later chapters of this book that address specific types of content. For the most relevant information, look for chapters that describe the types of content you are working with—vector art, bitmaps, sound, video, and so on.

Span based selection methods:

✦ **Frame spans:** To select a span of frames extending between two keyframes, simply click anywhere between the keyframes.

✦ **Single frames within a span:** To select a single frame within a span, press the Ctrl key (on Windows) or the ⌘ key (on Mac) and click a frame. Keyframes or endframes can usually be selected with a simple click.

✦ **Single frames not within a span:** To select a single frame that is not implicated with a span, simply click to select it.

✦ **Multiple frames or spans:** To select multiple frames along the Timeline (within a span or independent of a span), use Shift+click to add to a selection of the frames.

Figure 4-13 shows a Timeline that illustrates some editing points. The top layer shows the "original" layer, with content starting on a keyframe on frame 1, followed by a span of 19 frames, putting the endframe on frame 20. This layer was copied into all three lower layers, with the result that the initial content of all four layers was the same. When a frame was inserted at frame 10 of the "insert frame" layer, the content was extended, pushing the endframe of the span to frame 21. When a keyframe was inserted at frame 10 of the "insert keyframe" layer, the content was maintained in the new keyframe, but the span was not extended, as indicated by the gray filled frames in the span from frame 10 to frame 20. When a blank keyframe was inserted at frame 10 of the "insert blank keyframe" layer, the content was cleared following the new blank keyframe, as indicated by the white frames extending from frame 10 to frame 20.

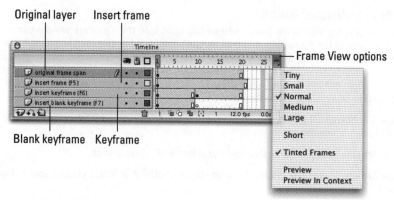

Figure 4-13: Editing on the Timeline

Cross-Reference For more information about how frames are used to author and control animation, refer to Chapter 11, "Timeline Animation Fundamentals."

Layer specifics

Knowing how to work with layers makes all the difference between a well-ordered project and a chaotic mess of elements that you may never be able to sort out if you have to come back to edit later on. The necessity of a logical folder structure and consistent naming conventions is even more crucial in a team environment, where someone else may have to try to find her way around in your document. Like most good production habits, this may seem like extra work at first, but over time it pays off. As your projects get more complex and your archive of Flash documents grows, the few additional steps taken early on will be invaluable down the road.

Being organized doesn't mean you have to always put every layer into a folder, but rather that you just try to find the most efficient way of keeping track of where you've placed different elements. To make it easier to remember what content is on different layers it's a good habit to give your layers meaningful names. It can also be helpful to use consistent abbreviations that help you to recognize what type of content is described by the name (such as "MC" for Movie Clip or "Anim" for animation). To edit a layer name, simply double-click the layer's name on the Layer bar and type into the text field.

Tip With all Flash projects in our studio, we begin the layer structure by creating three layers titled, "actions", "labels," and "functions"—these are always kept at the top of the layer stack. Although these layers don't hold content that is visible on the stage, they make it easy to quickly find any actions placed on the Timeline and to see labels and comments that give an indication of how the movie is structured.

Cross-Reference For detailed methods and suggestions on organizing Flash documents, see Chapter 20, "Making Your First Flash MX Project," and Chapter 32, "Creating a Portfolio site in Flash."

By default, new layers are stacked on top of the currently active layer. To rearrange layers, click in the area between the layer name and the layer toggle icons, and drag the Layer bar to the desired position in the layer stack and release. To move layers into a folder, click and drag the Layer bar onto any layer with a folder icon. To move a layer back out of a folder, drag it to a position above the folder name bar or below all the other layers contained in the folder.

The layers contextual menu

Because many of the controls for layer options are built into the Timeline window, layer properties are one of the few attributes that are not displayed in the Property inspector (frame properties are visible when any layer is selected). The contextual menu (right-click on Windows or Control+click on Mac), provides convenient access to most of the commands you will need when editing layers — including commands otherwise found in the Layer Properties dialog box or in the Insert menu.

✦ **Show All:** Shows all layers. If some layers have had their visibility turned off, this makes them all visible.

✦ **Lock Others:** Unlocks the active layer and locks all other layers.

✦ **Hide Others:** Makes the currently active layer visible, if it is not visible, and hides all others.

✦ **Insert Layer:** Inserts a new layer above the currently active layer with an auto-numbered name that continues the number sequence of existing layers and folders.

✦ **Delete Layer:** Deletes the active layer and all content stored on that layer.

✦ **Guide:** Transforms the current layer into a Guide layer — a reference layer that will only be visible in the authoring environment (.fla).

✦ **Add Motion Guide:** Inserts a new Motion Guide layer directly above the current layer and automatically converts the current layer into a guided layer.

Note A Guide layer differs from a Motion Guide layer. A Motion Guide layer is linked to a guided layer, which usually contains a tweened animation that follows a path drawn on the Motion Guide layer. A Guide layer is not linked to a guided layer and is most often used for placing a bitmap design composition, or other items used for design reference that should not be visible in the final movie (swf). Neither Guide layers nor Motion Guide layers export with the project.

✦ **Mask:** Transforms the current layer into a Mask layer.

✦ **Show Masking:** Use this command on either the Mask or the masked layer to activate the masking effect — essentially, this command locks both layers simultaneously, which enables the masking effect to be visible.

✦ **Insert Folder:** Inserts a new folder above the currently active layer or folder with an auto-numbered name that continues the number sequence of existing layers and folders.

◆ **Delete Folder:** Deletes the currently active folder, along with all the layers stored in that folder.

◆ **Expand Folder:** Opens the current folder to make any layers stored inside visible in the layer stack and on the Timeline.

◆ **Collapse Folder:** Closes the current folder to hide any layers stored in the folder. The elements existing on these stored layers will still be visible in the Document window and in the movie (.swf), but the keyframe rows will not show up along the Timeline.

◆ **Expand All Folders:** Opens all folders to show any stored layers visible in the layer stack and on the Timeline.

◆ **Collapse All Folders:** Closes all folders to hide any layers that have been placed in folders. The elements existing on these stored layers will still be visible in the Document window and in the movie (.swf), but the keyframe rows will not show up along the Timeline.

◆ **Properties:** Invokes the Layer Properties dialog box for the currently active layer. The Layer Properties menu can also be invoked directly by double-clicking the "page" icon or the colored square icon on any layer, and is always available in the application menu (Modify ➪ Layer).

Cross-
Reference

For in-depth coverage of using layer types, refer to Chapter 12, "Applying Layer Types."

Using Frame View options

The main place to find options for controlling the appearance of the Timeline within the window is in the submenu available from the Frame View options button, shown in Figure 4-13. This is sometimes referred to fondly as the "train track button" because the icon looks similar to the symbol used on maps to show railroads.

As noted previously, the Frame View options menu is used to customize the size, color, and style of frames displayed within the Timeline. These features can prove very helpful when you're working with cartoon animation, and want to see each frame previewed. Or, if you're working on an extremely long project with a huge Timeline, it can be helpful to tweak the size of the individual frames, so that you can see more of the Timeline in the Timeline window.

When used in conjunction with the Layer Height option of the Layer Properties dialog box, you can customize your timeline display in several ways to better suit your particular project. Your options include:

◆ **Tiny, Small, Normal, Medium, Large:** These options afford a range of sizes for the width of individual frames. When working on extremely long animations, narrower frames facilitate some operations. Wider frames can make it easier to select individual frames and to read frame labels or comments.

◆ **Short:** This option makes the frames shorter in height, permitting more layers to be visible in the same amount of space. When working with many layers or folders, short layers help speed the process of scrolling through the stack.

✦ **Tinted Frames:** This option toggles tinted frames on or off. With Tinted Frames on, the tints are as follows:

- **White:** Empty or unused frames (for any layer). This is the default. The white color of empty or unused frames is unaffected regardless of whether Tinted Frames is on or off.

- **Gray:** There are two kinds of gray frames: (a) The evenly spaced gray stripes in the default (empty) Timeline are a quick visual reference that indicates every fifth frame, like the tick marks on a ruler. These stripes appear regardless of whether Tinted Frames are enabled. (b) The solid gray color with a black outline, which appears when Tinted Frames are enabled, indicates that a frame contains content, even if it isn't visible on the Stage.

- **Blue:** Indicates a Motion tween span.

- **Green:** Indicates a Shape tween span.

 Regardless of whether Tinted Frames is enabled, Flash displays tween arrows (and keyframe dots) across a tween. However, with Tinted Frames disabled, tweened spans are indicted by colored arrows that also show the type of tween:

- **A red arrow:** Indicates a Motion tween, when Tinted Frames are off.

- **A green arrow:** Indicates a Shape tween, when Tinted Frames are off.

✦ **Preview:** As shown in Figure 4-14, the preview option displays tiny thumbnails that maximize the element in each frame. Thus, the scale of elements is not consistent from frame to frame.

✦ **Preview in Context:** As shown in the lower frame preview of Figure 4-14, when previewed in context, the same animation is seen with accurate scale from frame to frame (because elements are not maximized for each frame).

 The preview in frames option only shows content in keyframes. Thus, if you use this option to view a tweened animation, you will only see images displayed on the Timeline for the first and last frames of the animation.

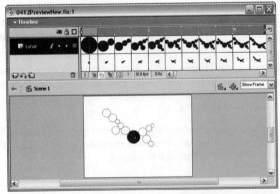

Preview (maximized in frame)

Preview in Context (consistent scale)

Animation (outlined keyframes)

Figure 4-14: In this composite screen shot, the Frames are shown with, Preview option (top) and with Preview in Context option (middle), for the same animation (bottom).

Printing

Although Flash is considered a Web and animation program, it fully supports printed output. The functionality and specific dialog boxes vary slightly from the Mac to the PC — while other variations are subject to which printers and printer drivers are installed on your machine. The File ➪ Page Setup dialog box is the most standard aspect of the program and the choices for paper size, margins, center positioning, and orientation are pretty intuitive.

However, the options available in Layout area of the Page Setup dialog box on Windows or in the Print Margins dialog box on Mac (File ➪ Print Margins), deserve a little more attention. The options here are:

✦ **Frames:** Use this drop-down menu to choose to print either All Frames of the animation or the ecological default, which is to print the First Frame Only.

✦ **Layout:** There are three basic options:

- **Actual Size:** This prints the Frame at full size, subject to the accompanying Scale setting: At what scale do you want to print your frames? Enter a percentage.

- **Fit on One Page:** This automatically reduces or enlarges the Frame so that it fills the maximum printable area, without distortion.

- **Storyboard:** This enables you to print several thumbnails per page in the following arrangements: Boxes, Grid, or Blank. There are accompanying settings for Frames Across, Frame Margin, and Label Frames. This is a great tool for circulating comps and promotional materials.

Tip　When printing Storyboard layouts, use File ➪ Print Preview on Windows (or File ➪ Print ➪ **Preview** on Mac) to ensure optimal results.

✦ **Print Margins (Mac Only):** Note the Disable PostScript check box. When printing single large areas of color surrounded by complex borders, problems may occur on PostScript printers. If you encounter such problems, try using the Disable PostScript check box in the Mac Print Margins dialog box (Edit ➪ Print Margins) or in the PC Preferences dialog box (Edit ➪ Preferences ➪ General ➪ Printing Options). Otherwise, divide the complex area into several simpler areas and use the Modify commands (Modify ➪ Smooth/Straighten/Optimize) to reduce the complexity of these areas (which may, however, drastically alter your artwork — so save first!).

✦ **Print Preview:** On Windows, use the Print Preview command to see an onscreen preview of how the printed output looks, based upon the options you've chosen in the Page Setup dialog box. On Macintosh the Preview button is found in the Print dialog box (File ➪ Print), and will generate a PDF to give a preview of how the final page looks, based upon the options you've chosen in the Print Margins dialog box.

✦ **Print:** Just print it! (This is also where the Mac option for Preview is found.)

✦ **Send (PC only):** This is a new command that invokes the default e-mail client so that you can readily send the Flash file as an attachment.

It is important to note that the Document background color (or Stage color) will not be included on printed output. If you want the background color to appear in your printed output, you must create a filled rectangle of the color that you want in the background and place it on a layer behind the other elements. The printer will then recognize this as artwork and include it in the output.

Summary

✦ Flash MX is the most consistent, cross-platform version yet. Built-in panel sets and robust help features get you started quickly, while the option for saving custom panel sets and custom keyboard shortcut sets allows the workspace to be optimized for specific production needs.

✦ The addition of the Property inspector and the streamlined panel structure make the interface more intuitive than ever before.

✦ The hybrid frame display and selection behavior introduced in Flash MX is more legible and efficient than in past versions.

✦ Layer folders and the expanded frame-editing options make it easy to organize and navigate your document structure.

✦ Although Flash is mainly used to produce Web content, it fully supports printed output.

✦ If you need a quick reminder on any of the fundamental interface elements, this chapter will be your reference.

Now that you know where to find your main tools and how to get comfortable in your workspace, you should be feeling more at home in your Flash MX studio. So it's time to get down to the business of *creating*.

✦   ✦   ✦

Drawing in Flash

This chapter introduces you to the primary tools for creating and manipulating vector graphics in Flash, as well as some of the factors of the Flash environment that affect how elements behave. The primary drawing tools have nearly self-explanatory names: the Line, Oval, Rectangle, Pencil, Paintbrush, and Eraser. However, these tools all have a variety of options and modifiers that make them more sophisticated than they may at first appear. In this chapter, we apply the primary options of these tools to create shapes and line art.

The selection tools — Arrow, Lasso, and Subselection — are found in the top section of the Toolbox and these work more as your hands within the drawing space of Flash, allowing you to select elements or grab and adjust specific parts of a shape or line.

The Pen is a powerful tool that draws lines by laying down editable points. Both the Pen and Subselection tools are used to manipulate those points, and can also be used to select and edit all lines and shapes to manually optimize artwork.

The built-in shape-creation tools of Flash and the adjustable shape-recognition settings make it easy even for people who "can't draw a straight line" to create usable elements for Flash interfaces. In addition to drawing, in this chapter we also apply some of the terrific tools Flash provides to help you organize and align elements as you design.

Cross-Reference If you're already familiar with using the core Flash drawing tools, you may want to refer to Chapter 9, "Modifying Graphics," for a deeper look into the options available for editing artwork, including the powerful new Free Transform tool and the Envelope modifier that allows you to warp and distort shapes.

In This Chapter

Using shape and drawing tools

Setting Paintbrush and Eraser modes

Using selection tools and options

Creating optimized lines and curves

Controlling snap behavior

Choosing fill and stroke styles

Aligning, scaling, and rotating artwork

Using the Primary Drawing Tools

The primary drawing tools — Line, Oval, Rectangle, Pencil, Paintbrush, and Eraser — can be divided into two groups: geometric shapes and freehand lines and strokes. Line, Oval, and Rectangle fall into the first category; Pencil, Paintbrush, and Eraser fall into the second.

Geometric shapes

The pre-built geometric shapes available for creating graphics in Flash are readily found in the Toolbox. The Line, Oval, and Rectangle tools are straightforward but infinitely useful. The multiple stroke styles and the various fill options described later in this chapter can be used with these basic shapes to create nearly any interface element you may need. These shapes are already optimized and can be combined in multiple ways to create more-complex artwork.

Note   In other parts of this book, we use the term *primitive shape* to refer to any shape that is not grouped or converted into a symbol. Creating and using symbols is covered in Chapter 6, "Symbols, Instances, and the Library."

The Line tool

Drawing with the Line tool creates a perfectly straight line that extends from a starting point to an end point, simply by clicking a start position and dragging to the end position before releasing the mouse. You just select the Line tool in the Toolbox and start drawing in the Document window. You can select various Line styles and stroke heights from the Property inspector, as well as set the color with the pop-up Swatches panel accessible from the Stroke color chip on either the Property inspector or the Toolbox. The various options for Line styles and colors are described later in this chapter. Snap settings and Guides can be used to help control where a line is placed and how precisely it connects to other lines. The Line tool will conform to the Snap settings described in the sidebar titled "Simplifying Snap Settings," later in this chapter.

Tip   To restrict the line to 45-degree-angle increments, hold down the Shift key while dragging.

Figure 5-1 shows how a line previews as you drag, and how it appears when the mouse is released and the current line style and stroke height settings are applied.

Figure 5-1: Line tool preview (top) and the final line (bottom) displayed when the mouse button is released

The Oval tool

Drawing with the Oval tool creates a perfectly smooth oval. Ovals are drawn by dragging diagonally from one "corner" of the oval to the other — dragging more vertically will create a taller oval, while dragging more horizontally will create a wider oval.

Tip   Press the Shift key at any time while the shape is being drawn to constrain the shape to a perfect circle.

The Oval tool has no unique options, but it can be filled with any of the fill colors available in the Swatches panel (described in the "Choosing Colors" section later in this chapter) as well as "outlined" with any of the stroke styles or colors. Figure 5-2 shows some of the huge variety of shapes you can create using the Oval tool with different stroke and fill settings.

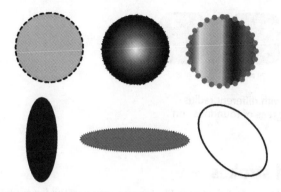

Figure 5-2: Shapes created with the Oval tool, using different stroke and fill settings

The Rectangle tool

The Rectangle tool creates perfect rectangles, which means that all four sides are parallel, regardless of the length or width of the shape. Draw rectangles by clicking to place a starting corner and then dragging toward the opposite corner of your shape until you have the size and shape that you want.

Tip Pressing the Shift key at any time while the shape is being drawn creates a perfect square.

Aside from choosing the stroke and fill to apply to a shape drawn with the Rectangle tool, there is an option on the Toolbox for setting Round Rectangle Radius. This option is set to 0 pt by default, to create rectangles with square or 90 degree corners. The maximum radius setting is 999 pt, but anything higher than 35 pt will actually cause the Rectangle tool to produce the same kind of shape as the Oval tool, unless the shape is drawn very large, or elongated to create the famous "pill button" shape.

Caution The Round Rectangle Radius button is not a toggle, so if you change the radius setting, you have to set it back to 0 to return to drawing standard rectangles.

Choosing a more moderate radius setting will create rounded rectangles or squares with softened corners (see Figure 5-3). You'll want to choose this setting before you create a shape with the Rectangle tool, because the radius cannot be reapplied or easily modified after the shape is drawn.

Tip You can use a handy shortcut while you're dragging out your rectangle shape. Before you release the mouse, you can use the Up arrow key to decrease the radius setting (making the corners more square), or use the Down arrow key to increase the radius setting (making the corners more rounded). This is the best way to get a live preview of the final shape of your rectangle. After you release the mouse, the radius setting will stick and the arrow keys will go back to their usual behavior of moving items up or down on the Stage.

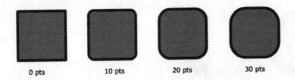

0 pts   10 pts   20 pts   30 pts

Figure 5-3: Rectangles drawn with different radius settings will create different degrees of roundness on the corners.

Freehand lines and strokes

The tools for drawing freehand lines and strokes in Flash come with options for applying different combinations of line processing and shape recognition. So, what does that mean exactly? These are general terms for a class of options that can be set to assist accurate drawing and manipulation of basic shapes. These options can be applied dynamically as you draw with the Pencil or Paintbrush tool, or applied cumulatively to an item selected with the Arrow tool to clean up a shape or line that you've already drawn. These are some of the Flash assistants that can help even a drafting-challenged designer create sharp-looking graphics with ease.

Note   The biggest challenge of drawing in Flash is finding a happy medium between the degree of line variation and complexity required to get the graphic look you want, and the optimization and file size that you need to keep your artwork Web-friendly.

The Pencil tool

The Pencil tool is used to draw lines and shapes. At first glance, it operates much like a real pencil. You can use the Pencil tool with different line styles as you draw a freeform shape. But a deeper examination reveals that, unlike a real pencil, the Flash Pencil tool can be set to straighten lines and smooth curves as you draw. It can also be set to recognize or correct basic geometric shapes. For example, a crude lumpy oval will be automatically recognized and processed into a true, or *perfect,* oval. These shapes and lines can then be further modified after they've been drawn using the Arrow and Subselection tools.

When the Pencil tool is active, one option appears in the Toolbox. This is actually the Pencil Mode pop-up menu, which sets the Pencil tool's current drawing mode. The three modes, or line styles, for the Pencil are: Straighten, Smooth, and Ink. These different settings control the way that line processing occurs as you draw.

RIP   Users of prior versions of Flash may be looking for the Stroke panel, but all line style options now reside in the Property inspector, where they can be selected and modified as described in the section later in this chapter on stroke settings.

Figure 5-4 shows the same freehand drawing done with the different Pencil modes. The drawing on the left was done with the Straighten mode, the drawing in the middle was done with Smooth mode, and the drawing on the right was done with Ink mode. As you can see, each mode is more effective for certain types of lines and shapes. To create a pleasing finished result, you'll most likely use different Pencil modes when working on individual elements of your drawing.

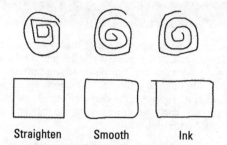

Figure 5-4: Similar sketches made using the three different Pencil modes to show how line processing will effect various shapes: Straighten (left), Smooth (center), and Ink (right)

Straighten

Drawing with the Straighten option processes your drawings while taking into account both line and shape recognition. This means that nearly straight lines are straightened, and wobbly curves are smoothed. Approximate geometric shapes, such as ovals, rectangles, and triangles are recognized and automatically adjusted.

Smooth

Drawing with the Smooth option reduces the zeal with which Flash automatically processes your drawings. With the Smooth option, line straightening and shape recognition are not applied, but curved lines are smoothed. Additionally, a line that ends near another line is joined automatically, if the Connect Lines tolerance is set to *Can be Distant.*

Ink

Drawing with the Ink option turns off all line processing. Lines remain as you've drawn them. Your lines are *not* smoothed, straightened, or joined.

The Paintbrush tool

The Paintbrush tool is used to create smooth or tapered marks and to fill enclosed areas. Unlike the Pencil tool, which creates a single, solid line, the Paintbrush tool actually creates marks using filled shapes. The fills can be solid colors, gradients, or fills derived from bitmaps. Because the Paintbrush paints only with a fill, the Stroke color chip does not apply to the marks drawn with the brush.

Note Painting with the background color (such as white) is not the same as erasing. Although visually it may appear to accomplish something similar to erasing, you are, in fact, creating a filled item that can be selected, moved, edited, deleted, and erased. Even if you can't see it, it will add to your file size. Only erasing erases!

If you have a pressure-sensitive tablet connected to your computer, an extra button option is available to use the pressure on a tablet to vary the thickness of the brush marks. (Use the Pressure button shown in Figure 5-7.) Working on a tablet with this option allows you to create organic-looking strokes that can be made to taper or vary in width as you change the amount of pressure applied to the tablet surface. Figure 5-5 shows a series of tapered marks created with a pressure-sensitive tablet using a single Brush size and a consistent Zoom setting.

Adjusting Drawing Settings

The degree to which shape recognition processes your drawings as you create them with the Pencil may be adjusted with the Drawing Settings found in Edit⇨Preferences⇨Editing (or Flash⇨ Preferences⇨Editing). By default, all the Drawing Settings are Normal. Each option can be adjusted to make it more specific or more general. The optimal setting combinations will depend on the style of drawing that you're trying to achieve, but in general, the default Normal settings for these controls really only need to be adjusted if you find that you aren't getting the look you want using the Straighten, Smooth, or Ink modes with the Pencil tool.

You can also choose to further simplify lines and shapes that have been drawn with the Pencil in Ink mode by using the Arrow tool to select what you've drawn and then using either the Smooth or Straighten options. Or, for maximum control, manually edit extraneous points with either the Pen or the Subselection tool (as described in the Pen and Subselection sections later in this chapter). Here are the various Drawing Settings and options available in Preferences:

✦ **Connect Lines:** The Connect Lines setting will adjust how close lines or points have to be to each other before Flash automatically connects them into a continuous line or shape. This setting also controls how close to horizontal or vertical a line has to be for Flash to set it at an exact angle. The options are: Must be Close, Normal, and Can be Distant. This setting also controls how close elements need to be to be snapped together when Snap to Objects is turned on.

✦ **Smooth Curves:** Smooth Curves will simplify the number of points used to draw a curve when the Pencil is in Straighten or Smooth mode. Smoother curves are easier to reshape and are more optimized, while rougher curves will more closely resemble the original lines drawn. The options are: Off, Rough, Normal, and Smooth.

✦ **Recognize Lines:** This setting controls how precise a line has to be for Flash to recognize it as a straight line and automatically align it. The options are: Off, Strict, Normal, and Tolerant.

✦ **Recognize Shapes:** This setting controls how accurately you have to draw basic geometric shapes and 90-degree or 180-degree arcs for them to be recognized and corrected by Flash. The options are: Off, Strict, Normal, and Tolerant.

✦ **Click Accuracy:** Click accuracy will determine how close to an element the cursor has to be for Flash to recognize it. The settings are: Strict, Normal, and Tolerant.

These drawing settings do not modify the Straighten and Smooth options for the Arrow tool, which will only reduce point complexity with each application to a shape or line that has already been drawn.

The Lock Fill option is common to both the Paintbrush tool and the Paint Bucket tool (which is discussed in Chapter 9). Although similar to Stroke height and style, the Brush size and Brush shape settings are unique to the Paintbrush tool.

In Flash, the size of applied brush marks is always related to the Zoom setting. Therefore, using the same brush diameter will create different sized brush marks depending on what Zoom setting you work with in the Document window (see Figure 5-6). You could paint over your whole stage in one stroke even with a small brush diameter, if your Zoom was at a low setting like 8 percent. Or you could use a large brush diameter to make detailed lines if your Zoom was at a high setting like 1,500 percent.

Figure 5-5: Drawing with the Paintbrush tool using a pressure-sensitive tablet can create elegant, almost calligraphic marks.

25%   50%   100%   200%   400%

Figure 5-6: Marks made using the same brush size applied with the View at different percentages of Zoom

The Brush Shape option, shown in Figure 5-7, is a button for accessing a menu with nine possible brush shapes that are based on the circle, ellipse, square, rectangle, and line shapes. The oval, rectangle, and line shapes are available in several angles. Although no custom brush shapes are available, you can combine these stock brush shapes with the range of brush sizes to generate a variety of nearly custom brush tips. When using shapes other than circles, note that the diameter sizes chosen in the Brush Size menu apply to the broadest area of any brush shape.

The Paintbrush tool includes options for controlling exactly where the fill is applied. The Brush Mode option menu reveals five painting modes that are amazingly useful for a wide range of effects when applying the Paintbrush tool: Paint Normal, Paint Fills, Paint Behind, Paint Selection, and Paint Inside, as shown in Figure 5-7 (right).

The following images depict various ways in which the Brush modes interact with drawn and painted elements. The base image is a solid white rectangle drawn with a black outline. The boat outline is drawn with the Pencil tool in dark gray on top of the rectangle.

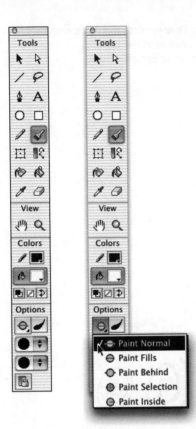

Figure 5-7: The Paintbrush tool and options (left); the Brush mode settings menu (right)

Paint Normal mode

Paint Normal mode, shown in Figure 5-8, applies brush strokes over the top of any lines or fills.

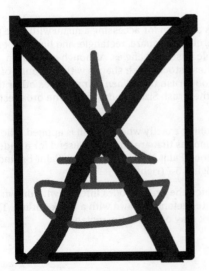

Figure 5-8: In Paint Normal mode, a dark-gray brush mark covers all elements: background, outline, fill, and drawn lines.

Paint Fills mode

Paint Fills mode, shown in Figure 5-9, applies brush strokes to replace any fills, but leaves lines untouched.

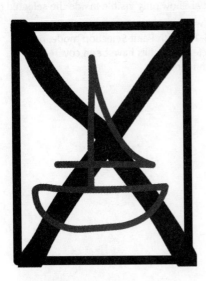

Figure 5-9: In Paint Fills mode, a dark-gray brush mark covers the white background and fill without painting over any of the lines.

Paint Behind mode

Paint Behind mode applies brush strokes only to blank areas and leaves all fills, lines, or other items untouched. As shown in Figure 5-10, the only areas the brush mark covers are those in the background, outside the frame of the picture. Effectively, the brush has gone behind the entire shape. If the stroke had originated within the frame, it would have covered the white fill and gone behind the drawn gray lines and the black outline.

Figure 5-10: In Paint Behind mode, the gray brush mark is only visible on the background outside the frame, because it has gone behind the white fill and the lines.

Paint Selection mode

Paint Selection mode applies brush strokes only to selected fills. In Figure 5-11, a selection was made by shift-clicking both the white fill inside the boat and inside the sail. The same gray brush marks drawn on the previous figure are now only visible inside the selected fills.

Figure 5-11: With Paint Selection mode, only the selected white fills have been covered by the brush marks.

Paint Inside mode

Paint Inside mode, shown in Figure 5-12, applies brush strokes only to the singular fill area where the brush stroke was first initiated. As the name implies, Paint Inside never paints over lines. If you initiate painting from an empty area, the brush strokes won't affect any existing fills or lines, which approximates the same effect as the Paint Behind setting.

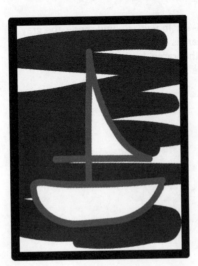

Figure 5-12: With Paint Inside mode, the brush marks only cover the area where the stroke is first started. Lines separate the white fills inside the sail and the boat shape from the background where the stroke was initiated, so those areas are not painted.

For coverage of using the Lock Fill option with the Paintbrush tool and the Paint Bucket tool, refer to Chapter 9.

The Eraser tool

The Eraser tool is used in concert with the Drawing and Painting tools to obtain final, usable art. As the name implies, the Eraser tool is primarily used for rubbing out mistakes. When the Eraser tool is active, three options appear on the Toolbox, as shown in Figure 5-13. The Erase Mode option and the Eraser Shape option are both drop-down menus with multiple options. For Eraser Shape, you can select rectangular or oval erasers in various sizes. The Erase modes are similar to the Brush modes described previously. The third option, the Faucet button, is used to clear enclosed areas of fill. Using the Faucet option is the equivalent of selecting a line or a fill and then deleting it, but the Faucet will accomplish this in one easy step. Select the Eraser tool, choose the Faucet option, and then you will be able to click on any line or fill to instantly erase it. Clicking on any part of a selection with the Faucet will delete all elements in the selection.

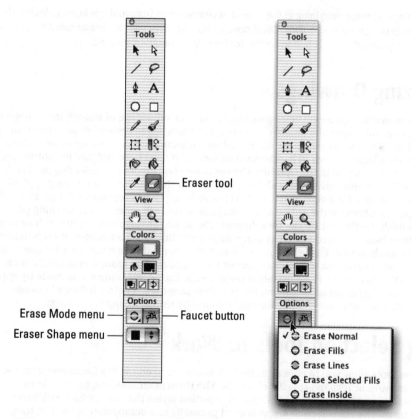

Figure 5-13: The Eraser tool has three options: Erase Mode, Eraser Shape, and Faucet. Both the Mode and Shape options have menus.

The Erase modes and interaction with artwork are consistent with the Paintbrush tool for the most part. The only difference is that, instead of adding a mark to a specified part of a drawing, the Eraser removes marks in a specified part of a drawing. Aside from Erase Normal, Erase Fills, Erase Selected Fills, and Erase Inside, which you will recognize from the previous descriptions of Brush modes, there is a straightforward mode for Erase Lines, that allows you to remove any lines without disrupting your fills.

Note   The Eraser tool only erases lines and fills that are in the current frame of the scene. It won't erase groups, symbols, or text. When you need to erase a part of a group, you have two options: Select the group and choose Edit ➪ Edit Selected from the application menu (or double-click the group), or select the group and choose Modify ➪ Ungroup from the application menu (Ctrl+Shift+G or ⌘+Shift+G).

The only alternative to using the Eraser tool to remove graphic elements or areas of drawings is to select them and then delete them by pressing either the Delete or the Backspace key.

Caution   To quickly erase everything in the current keyframe (even from multiple layers), double-click the Eraser tool in the Toolbox. Don't double-click the Stage with the Eraser selected, but just double-click the Eraser button on the Toolbox. And — poof! — it's erased.

Optimizing Drawings

Aside from making a drawing more geometric, the main advantage of simplifying a shape or line is that it will reduce the number of points that Flash has to remember and thus reduces the final file size. This is especially important for projects such as cartoons or animations that include a large number of hand-drawn shapes. The most powerful tool for optimizing artwork precisely is found in the Optimize Curves dialog box invoked by selecting Modify ➪ Optimize. This feature gives you a slider control to set the amount of smoothing applied between *None* and *Maximum*. You can also choose to apply this repeatedly for greater reduction in points. Checking the option to *Use multiple passes* will repeat the smoothing process until no further optimization can be achieved. The totals message will notify you how many points have been removed and what percentage reduction has been achieved each time you apply the modification. Figure 5-14 shows a sketch drawn with the Pencil in Ink mode, before and after multiple passes of Optimize Curves were applied. The reduction in points is displayed in the dialog box. For illustration purposes, a drastic adjustment was made by applying Optimize Curves set at Maximum. For practical purposes, a better balance between optimization and drawing complexity can be found by testing a range of settings.

Putting Selection Tools to Work

Selection tools allow you to choose items that you want to edit in the Document window, as well as move or reshape specific elements. The three main selection tools — Arrow, Subselection, and Lasso — provide different selection styles that are useful for different editing tasks. The Subselection arrow is used primarily as a companion to the Pen tool, which is covered later in this chapter.

Tip   When you are busy with another tool, you can temporarily toggle to the Arrow tool by pressing the Control or ⌘ key.

The original shapes had 919 curves.

The optimized shape has 404 curves.

This is a 56% reduction.

OK

A: Original shape w/Optimize dialog box   B: Shape after 56% reduction in points

Figure 5-14: Before (left) and after (right), Optimize Curves is used to reduce the complexity of a drawing made with the Pencil tool in Ink mode. The reduction in points translates directly into smaller file size.

The Arrow tool

The Arrow tool is the most common tool used to select and move items — or multiple items — on the Stage. The Arrow tool is also used to reshape lines and shapes, in a way that will be familiar to users who have worked in other vector graphics applications. The Arrow tool's neighbor, which is differentiated by having a white rather than a black arrowhead, is the Subselection tool. The Subselection tool is most useful for moving and editing anchor points created with the Pen tool and adjusting tangents on Bezier curves.

Use the Arrow tool to reshape a line or shape by pulling on the line (or shape) itself, or on its endpoints, curves, or corners. You can also use the Arrow tool to select, move, and edit other Flash graphic elements, including groups, symbols, buttons, and text. When you click a line or item, a mesh pattern appears, to indicate that the line has been selected. If the item is either a Symbol or a Group, a thin colored line (called the *Highlight*) will indicate selection status. This highlight color may be set in the document Preferences dialog box found under Edit ➪ Preferences (or in OS X under Flash ➪ Preferences).

Tip   To temporarily turn off the highlight mesh while editing an element, use Ctrl+H, (or ⌘+H). To toggle it back on, enter the same key shortcut again. Even if you have toggled the highlight off on one element, it will be visible on the next element that you select.

Figure 5-15 shows a shape, a group, and a symbol as they look when unselected (top) and as they appear when selected with the Arrow tool. The mesh pattern on the first circle and outline indicate that these are selected shapes (left), while the thin borders around the circle and outline indicate a group (center) and the thin border with a small crosshair icon indicate a symbol (right). Groups and symbols can be moved but not otherwise edited directly on the Stage with the Arrow tool.

The various ways of using grouped shapes in graphics is explained in Chapter 9, "Modifying Graphics," while a discussion of using and editing symbols is included in Chapter 6, "Symbols, Instances, and the Library."

Figure 5-15: Arrow tool selection highlights (L-R) for a shape, a group, and a symbol

In addition to clicking on a line to select it, you can also select one or more items by dragging a marquee around them when the Arrow tool is active. This operation is called *drag-select.* Additional items can be added to a current selection by pressing the Shift key and clicking the items. When you drag-select to make a selection, previously selected items are deselected and excluded from the selection. In order to include previously selected items, press the Shift key as you drag-select. When a group is selected and you drag to move them on the stage, holding down the Shift key will constrain the movement range of the elements to 45 degrees. This is helpful if you need to move an element up or down while keeping it on the same axis or baseline.

Prior to Flash 4, additional elements were added to a selection simply by clicking them. To use this older selection style, go to Edit ➪ Preferences and under Selection Options, clear the Shift Select check box.

Deselect one or more items by using any of the following methods:

✦ Pressing the Escape key

✦ Choosing Edit ➪ Deselect All

✦ Using the keyboard shortcut Ctrl+Shift+A (or ⌘+Shift+A)

✦ Clicking anywhere outside all the selected items

The Arrow tool can also be used for duplicating items. Simply select an item (or line segment) with the Arrow tool and press the Alt (Option) key while dragging the item to a new location. The original item remains in place, and a new item is deposited at the end of your drag stroke.

Moving multiple elements with the Arrow tool

Text boxes and Groups are selected as single elements and move as a single unit. After you create text in a text box (text features are discussed in Chapter 8, "Working with Text"), Flash treats the text as one block, or group, meaning that all the individual letters move together when the box is selected. Similarly, a group of graphic elements — such as lines, outlines, fills, or shapes — can be grouped and moved or manipulated as a single element. However, when you move an item that is not grouped, only the selected part is moved. This situation can be tricky when you have ungrouped fills and outlines, because selecting one without the other could unintentionally break up your shape. To keep elements (such as a rectangular outline and its colored fill area) together as they are moved, group them first. To group separate elements, first select them all, then group them with Modify ➪ Group (Ctrl+G or ⌘+G). If necessary, they can be ungrouped later using Modify ➪ Ungroup (Ctrl+Shift+G or ⌘+Shift+G). Grouping is further discussed in Chapter 9, "Modifying Graphics."

Tip   Double-clicking a shape that has an outline stroke and a fill will select both. This strategy can also be used on lines with multiple sections. Double-clicking a section will select all the connected parts of a line, rather than just the closest segment.

Using Arrow states to adjust or move drawings

In addition to the actions accomplished by selecting a line (or line section) and clicking an option, three Arrow states — Move Selected Element, Reshape Curve or Line, and Reshape Endpoint or Corner — enable you to reshape and move parts of your drawings. It works like this: As you move the Arrow tool over the Flash Stage, the Arrow tool changes the state of its cursor to indicate what tasks it can perform in context with various items (the line or fill) closest to the Arrow tool's current position.

Tip   When reshaping brush strokes or other filled items with the Arrow tool, make sure that you don't select both the stroke and fill before trying to reshape the outline. If you do, you'll only be able to move the entire brush stroke — you won't be able to reshape it.

Figure 5-16 shows a series of images that demonstrate the various Arrow states as they appear and are applied. On the left, the original shape is shown with the Arrow states displayed as the cursor is moved over the center of the shape (A), over a corner (B) and over a line (C). The center image shows the preview as the Reshape Corner Arrow is used to extend the corner of the square and the Reshape Curve Arrow is used to stretch the curve. The final image on the right shows the resulting changes to the original square.

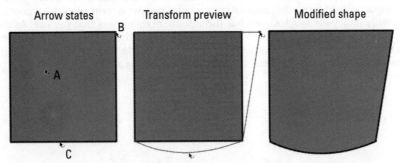

Figure 5-16: Arrow states used to reshape and reposition an element: Move Selected Item Arrow (A), Reshape Corner Arrow (B), Reshape Curve Arrow (C)

Figure 5-17 shows the various Arrow states used to modify a line. The lower images show the Arrow state cursors, the center images show the Arrow states preview as the mouse is dragged, and the top images show the resulting changes to the line when the mouse is released. You will notice that lines have to be selected in order to be moved without changing their shape with the Arrow tool — if the line is not selected, the Arrow will only display Reshape Corner or Reshape Curve states.

Figure 5-17: Using Arrow states to reshape and reposition a line: Move Selected Item (left), Reshape Corner (center), Reshape Curve (right)

Tip Some brush strokes are easier to reshape if you view them as Outlines (as described in Chapter 4).

Knowing your Arrow options

Figure 5-18 shows the three options that appear at the bottom section of the Toolbox when the Arrow tool (A) is selected: Magnet (or Snap to Objects), Smooth, and Straighten. Because the various snap controls can be confusing at first, the Magnet tool is compared with the other snap controls available in Flash in the sidebar titled "Simplifying Snap Settings" later in this chapter.

The Smooth and Straighten options available with the Arrow tool are best used to clean up drawings by smoothing irregular curves or straightening crooked lines. Smoothing or Straightening reduces the number of bumps and variations (or points of transition) in a complex shape or line, by reducing the number of points. The simplest curve or line will only be described by one point at each end.

To simplify a shape or line, click the Arrow tool and select the item you've just sketched, then click the Straighten or Smooth button in the Toolbox (or use Modify ➪ Straighten or Modify ➪ Smooth) to begin shape recognition. For hard-edged items such as a polygon, click the Straighten button repeatedly until your rough sketch reaches the level of angularity that you like. For smooth-edged items that approximate an oval or a waveform, click the Smooth button repeatedly until your rough sketch has the amount of roundness that you like. As shown in Figure 5-19, the simplified shape will usually need some further adjustment to get the result that you want after some of the points have been removed. The tools used for adjusting individual curves and points are the Pen tool and the Subselection arrow.

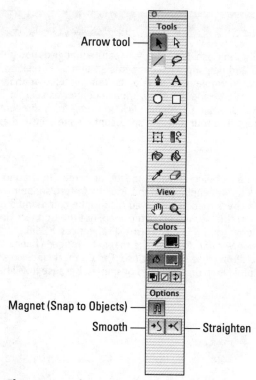

Arrow tool

Magnet (Snap to Objects)

Smooth — Straighten

Figure 5-18: The Arrow tool options available on the Toolbox

original   smooth   straighten

Figure 5-19: The Arrow Smooth and Straighten modifiers applied to simplify a freehand shape

Simplifying Snap Settings

There are now four independent snap settings in Flash. Snapping is a feature that gives you guidance when moving elements on the Stage and helps to align elements accurately in relation to each other, to the drawing grid, to guides, or to whole pixel axis points. You can tell that an item is snapping by the appearance of a small circle beside the Arrow mouse pointer as seen in the first figure shown below. For best control of snapping position, click and drag from the center point or from an outside edge of an element. The four different snap controls are adjusted and applied as follows:

Snap to Object

The Snap to Object is a toggle that causes items being drawn or moved on screen to snap to or align with, other objects on the stage. Click the magnet icon in the Toolbox to turn snapping on or off, or choose View ⇨ Snap to Objects (a check mark is displayed next to the command if it is on). To control the tolerance of the magnet or the "stickiness" of the snap, use the Connect Lines setting found in Edit ⇨ Preferences ⇨ Editing (or in OS X, Flash ⇨ Preferences ⇨ Editing.) By default, the Connect Lines tolerance is set at *Normal.* To make the magnet stronger, change the tolerance to *Can be distant;* to make it less strong, use *Must be close.* The Connect Lines control is the snap behavior you will find most helpful when drawing lines or shapes, because it will help to connect lines cleanly.

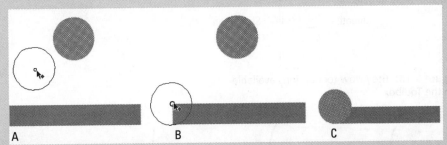

Snapping is apparent, as indicated by the "o" icon next to the mouse pointer as the circle is moved from its original position (left). When the circle is dragged close enough to another element to snap to it, the "o" icon gets slightly larger to let you know to release the mouse. Note that the original position remains visible until the mouse is released and the circle is snapped to its new position (right).

Snap to Grid

Snap to Grid (Ctrl+Shift+' [apostrophe] or ⌘+Shift+' [apostrophe]) is an option available for the Grid item under View ⇨ Grid ⇨ Snap to Grid, which will help to align elements to guides or to the grid as set in the Grid settings dialog box. If Snap to Grid is turned on, elements will show the snap icon by the Arrow cursor when you drag them close to a line in your grid, whether the grid is visible or not. To control the tolerance of this snapping feature, use the settings found under View ⇨ Grid ⇨ Edit Grid (Ctrl+Alt+G or ⌘+Option+G). The first three settings for Snap to Grid are the same as those for Snap to Object, but there is an additional setting, *Always Snap,* which will constrain elements to the grid no matter where you drag them. The following figure shows the default 18 px gray grid as it displays when made visible (View ⇨ Grid ⇨ Show Grid), with the Stage view zoom at 400 percent.

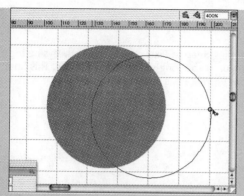

The snap icon as it appears when an element is dragged onto a grid line with Snap to Grid turned on (snapping will work regardless of whether the grid is visible or not).

Snap to Guide

As described in the previous chapter, Guides are vertical or horizontal guidelines that can be dragged onto the Work area or Stage when Rulers are visible, View ➪ Rulers (Ctrl+Alt+Shift+R or ⌘+Option+Shift+R). If Snap to Grid is turned on when you drag guides out, they will be constrained to the grid, otherwise you will be able to place guides anywhere. After guides are set, they will be visible even if you turn Rulers off, to toggle guide visibility use View ➪ Guides ➪ Show Guides (Ctrl+; [semicolon] or ⌘+; [semicolon].) As shown in the figure below, Snap to Guide will allow you to align an element to a guide, even if it is not aligned with the grid.

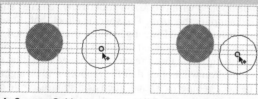

A: Snap to Guide   B: Snap to Grid

The snap icon as it appears when an element is dragged onto a guide with Snap to Guide turned on (A). Note that this guide is not aligned with the grid. Snap to Guide is independent of Snap to Grid, but guides can only be placed outside the Grid when Snap to Grid is turned off.

Snap to Pixel

Snap to Pixel is the only "global" setting that will cause all elements to align with the one pixel grid that is only visible when the View scale is set to 400 percent or greater. This setting does not necessarily help you to align elements with each other, but it does help to keep elements from being placed "between pixels," by constraining X and Y values to whole numbers rather than

Continued

Continued

allowing decimals. There is no shortcut key for turning Snap to Pixel on, but it can always be toggled on and off from the View menu by checking or unchecking View ➪ Snap to Pixel. This final figure shows how the pixel grid displays when the View scale is at 400 percent.

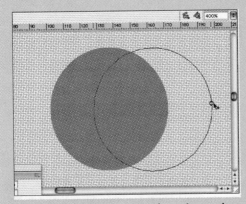

The snap icon as it appears when View scale is at 400 percent or higher with Snap to Pixel turned on. Items will be constrained to whole pixel axis points if they are dragged from the center or from an outside edge.

The Smooth and Straighten options can be applied with the Arrow tool to any selected shape or line to reduce the number of points and simplify the form. The specific effect that these options have on your graphics will be dependent on the Drawing Settings that were used to create the original lines. By minimizing complexity in freehand drawings or shapes, Smooth and Straighten will gradually reduce an erratic graphic into the most simplified form that can be described with the fewest points possible. You will notice that the Smooth and Straighten options won't have a visible effect on a perfect geometric shape, such as a square, circle or triangle — this is because Flash uses shape recognition to determine that these forms are already optimized and cannot be simplified any further.

Although these assistants will nudge a sketch or line style in the direction that you want, they don't add information; so don't be surprised if it takes a few tries to get the right balance between rough drawing and shape recognition.

The Lasso tool

The Lasso (L) is a flexible tool, somewhat like the selection equivalent of the Pen tool crossed with the Pencil tool. The Lasso is primarily used to make freeform selections and to group-select odd or irregular-shaped areas of your drawing. After areas are selected, they can be moved, scaled, rotated, or reshaped as a single unit. The Lasso tool can also be used to split shapes, or select portions of a line or a shape. As shown in Figure 5-20, it has three options in the Toolbox: the Polygon mode button, the Magic Wand, and the Magic Wand properties.

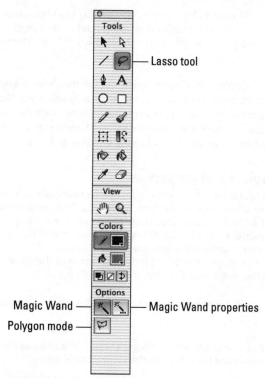

Figure 5-20 labels:
- Lasso tool
- Magic Wand
- Polygon mode
- Magic Wand properties

Figure 5-20: The Lasso tool and options

The Lasso tool works best if you drag a loop around the area you want to select. (Hence, the tool name Lasso!) But if you slip or if you don't end the loop near where you started, Flash closes the loop with a straight line between your starting point and the endpoint. Because you can use the Lasso tool to define an area of any shape—limited only by your ability to draw and use the multiple selection capabilities of Flash—the Lasso tool gives you more control over selections than the Arrow tool.

Tip   To add to a previously selected area, hold down the Shift key before initiating additional selections.

Polygon mode

Polygon mode affords greater precision when making straight-edged selections, or—in mixed mode—selections that combine freeform areas with straight edges. To describe a simple polygon selection, with the Lasso tool active, click the Polygon mode button to toggle on Polygon selection mode. In Polygon mode, selection points are created by a mouse click, causing a straight selection line to extend between mouse clicks. To complete the selection, double-click.

Mixed mode usage, which includes Polygon functionality, is available when the Lasso tool is in Freeform mode. To work in Freeform mode, the Polygon option must be in the off position. While drawing with the Freeform Lasso, press the Alt (Option) key to temporarily invoke

Polygon mode. (Polygon mode continues only as long as the Alt (Option) key is pressed.) As long as the Alt (Option) key is pressed, a straight selection line extends between mouse clicks. To return to Freeform mode, simply release the Alt (or Option) key. Release the mouse to close the selection.

Note Sometimes aberrant selections — selections that seem inside out, or that have a weird, unwanted straight line bisecting the intended selection — result from Lasso selections. That's usually because the point of origination of a Lasso selection is the point to which the Lasso will snap when the selection is closed. It takes a little practice to learn how to plan the point of origin so that the desired selection will be obtained when the selection is closed.

Magic Wand option and Magic Wand properties

The Magic Wand option of the Lasso tool is used to select ranges of a similar color in a bitmap that has been broken apart. After you select areas of the bitmap, you can change their fill color or delete them. Breaking apart a bitmap means that the bitmap image is subsequently seen by Flash as a collection of individual areas of color. (This is not the same as tracing a bitmap, which reduces the vast number of colors in a continuous-tone bitmap to areas of solid color.) After an image is broken apart, you can select individual areas of the image with any of the selection tools, including the Magic Wand option of the Lasso tool.

Cross-Reference To learn more about using and modifying bitmaps in Flash, refer to Chapter 16, "Importing Artwork."

The Magic Wand properties option has two modifiable settings: Threshold and Smoothing. To set them, click the Magic Wand properties button while the Lasso tool is active.

The Threshold setting defines the breadth of adjacent color values that the Magic Wand option includes in a selection. Values for the Threshold setting range from 0 to 200: The higher the setting, the broader the selection of adjacent colors. Conversely, a smaller number results in the Magic Wand making a narrower selection of adjacent colors. A value of zero results in a selection of contiguous pixels that are all the same color as the target pixel.

The Smoothing setting of the Magic Wand option determines to what degree the edge of the selection should be smoothed. This is similar to antialiasing. (Antialiasing dithers the edges of shapes and lines so that they look smoother on screen.) The options are Smooth, Pixels, Rough, and Normal.

The Subselection tool

The Subselection arrow (A) is the companion tool for the Pen and is found in the Toolbox to the right of the Arrow tool. The Subselection tool has two purposes:

✦ To either move or edit individual anchor points and tangents on lines and outlines.

✦ To move individual objects.

When moving the Subselection tool over a line or point, the hollow arrow cursor displays one of two states:

✦ When over a line it displays a small, filled square next to it, indicating that the whole selected shape or line can be moved.

✦ When over a point, it displays a small, hollow square, indicating that the point will be moved to change the shape of the line.

Note If you use the Subselection tool to drag a selection rectangle around two items, you'll find that clicking and dragging from any line of an item will allow you to move only that item, but clicking any point on an item will allow you to move all items in the selection.

Figure 5-21 shows the use of the Subselection tool to move a path (A), to move a single point (B), to select a tangent handle (C), and to modify a curve by adjusting its tangent handle (D). Note that a preview is shown before releasing the handle.

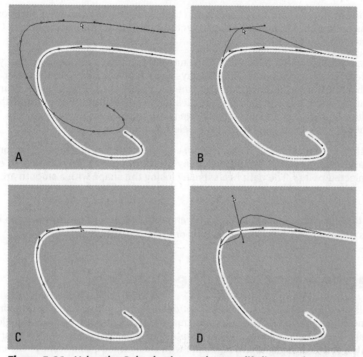

Figure 5-21: Using the Subselection tool to modify lines and curves

The Subselection tool is most useful for modifying and adjusting paths. To display anchor points on a line or shape outline created with the Pencil, Paintbrush, Line, Oval, or Rectangle tools, simply click the line or shape outline with the Subselection tool. This reveals the points that define the line or shape. Click any point to cause its tangent handles to appear. If you have a shape that is all fill, without any stroke, you'll need to position the Subselection tool precisely at the edge of the shape in order to select or move it with the Subselection tool.

To convert a corner point into a curve point, follow these steps:

1. Click to select the point with the Subselection tool.

2. While pressing the Alt (Option) key, click and drag the point.

3. A curve point with tangent handles appears, replacing the original corner point.

Note By holding down the Ctrl (or ⌘) key, the Pen tool can be used to mimic the function of the Subselection tool for moving lines or points, but not for converting a curve point into a corner point.

An important use of the Pen tool/Subselection tool combo is editing lines for optimal file size. The more simple your shapes, the smaller your file size and the faster your movie downloads. Most often, this involves deleting extraneous points. There are a couple of ways to delete points:

✦ Select the line or outline with the Subselection tool, which causes the individual points to appear as hollow circles along the line. Select the point that you wish to delete. Click the delete key.

✦ Select a line or outline with the Pen tool, then move the cursor over the point that you want to delete. The cursor updates and displays a small inverted *v* (^) to the lower right, which is the Corner Point cursor. Click the point with the Corner Point cursor, and continue to hover over the point. After clicking with the Corner Point cursor, the cursor updates and displays a small minus sign (–) to the lower right, which is the Delete Point cursor. Click the point with the Delete Point cursor to delete it.

✦ When deleting more than one point from a closed shape, such as an oval or polygon, use the Subselection tool to drag and select any number of points. Press Delete to eliminate the selected points. The path heals itself, closing the shape with a smooth arc or line.

Tip If you used the Subselection tool to select a path and then Shift+select several points on it, those points can be moved in unison by dragging or by tapping the arrow keys.

Creating Precise Lines with the Pen Tool

The Pen tool (P) is used to draw precision paths that define straight lines and smooth curves. These paths define adjustable line segments, which may be straight or curved — the angle and length of straight segments is completely adjustable, as is the slope and length of curved segments. To draw a series of straight-line segments with the Pen tool, simply move the cursor and click successively: Each subsequent click defines the end point of the line. To draw curved line segments with the Pen tool, simply click and drag: The length and direction of the drag determines the depth and shape of the current segment. Both straight and curved line segments can be modified and edited by adjusting their points. In addition, any lines or shapes that have been created by other Flash drawing tools can also be displayed as paths (points on lines) and edited with either the Pen tool or the Subselection tool.

Creating shapes with the Pen tool takes a little practice, but it will produce the most controlled optimization of artwork. Because no points are auto-created, every line and curve is defined only with the points that you have placed. This saves having to delete points from an overly complex path that may result from drawing with the Pencil or the Paintbrush tool.

Tip If you're working on a background color that is too similar to your Layer Outline Color, the points on your line will be difficult to see and adjust. Remember that you can always change the Layer Outline Color to contrast with the background.

The Preferences for the Pen tool are located in the Pen tool section of the Preferences dialog box. (Choose Edit ➪ Preferences ➪ Editing, or on OS X, Flash ➪ Preferences ➪ Editing.) There are three settings: Pen Preview, Point display, and Cursor style:

✦ **Show Pen Preview:** With this option checked, Flash will display a preview of the next line segment, in response to moving the pointer, prior to clicking to make the next endpoint and complete the line.

✦ **Show Solid Points:** Check this option to display selected anchor points as solid points, and unselected points as hollow points. The default is for selected points to be hollow and for unselected points to be solid.

✦ **Show Precise Cursors:** This option toggles the Pen tool cursor between the default Pen tool icon and a precision crosshair cursor. This can make selecting points much easier and is recommended if you will be doing detailed adjustment on a line.

Tip You can also use a keyboard shortcut to toggle between the two Pen cursor displays: Caps Lock toggles between the precise Crosshair and the Pen icon.

As Figure 5-22 shows, the Pen tool displays a number of different icons to the lower right of the cursor. These are the Pen states, which will tell you at any given time what action the Pen can perform on a line. The Pen states are shown in this composite image, which is a detail of a path describing a white line over a light-gray background, shown at a Zoom setting of 400 percent.

Pen Icons
A: Empty state area (x)
B: Complete to End Point (o)
C: Remove Point (-)
D: Add Point (+)
E: Convert Point (^)

Pen/Subselect Icons
F: Adjust Line
G: Adjust Point

Point Icons
H: Selected (Filled)
I: Unselected (Empty)
J: Single tangent handle
K: Double tangent handle

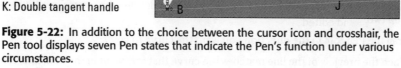

Figure 5-22: In addition to the choice between the cursor icon and crosshair, the Pen tool displays seven Pen states that indicate the Pen's function under various circumstances.

The seven Pen states are as follows:

✦ The Pen displays a small *(x)* when it's simply over the stage (A).

✦ When the Pen is hovered over an endpoint, it displays an *(o)* to indicate that this is an endpoint (B). Click this point to connect a continuation of this path or, when making a closed shape, to close the path.

✦ When the Pen hovers over a corner point, it displays a minus (–) sign to indicate that clicking this corner point will delete it (C).

✦ When the Pen is over a path (a line between two points), it displays a plus (+) sign to indicate that clicking there will add a point to the path (D).

✦ When the Pen hovers over an existing point, it displays a carat (^) to indicate that clicking that point will turn it into a corner point (E).

✦ With the Ctrl (or ⌘) key pressed, the Pen behaves like the Subselection arrow, so it switches to the hollow arrow icon with a filled black box (F) over lines, or a hollow white box (G) over points.

✦ When adjusting a path with either the Pen tool or the Subselection arrow, the default for selected points is a filled circle (H), while unselected points display as hollow squares (I). Note that the unselected points display a single tangent handle (J), bound toward the selected point, which displays two tangent handles (K).

Now that you've toured the various Pen tool icons and Pen states, it's time to start drawing and see how these actually apply as you work. To draw and adjust a straight-line segment with the Pen tool, follow these steps:

1. Click to place the first point of your line (wherever you want the line to start).

2. Then choose the next point and continue to click to create subsequent points and define individual line segments.

3. Each subsequent click creates a corner point on the line that determines the length of individual line segments.

4. To adjust straight segments, press the Ctrl (or ⌘) key and click a point to select it. Continue pressing the Ctrl (⌘) key as you drag and move the point to change the angle or length of the segment.

5. Or, with the Ctrl (⌘) key pressed, click and drag on the tangent handles of the point to adjust the line. Remember that corner points occur on a straight segment or at the juncture of a straight segment and a curved segment.

Tip   When creating straight lines with the Pen tool, press the Shift key to constrain lines to either 45-degree or 90-degree angles.

To draw and adjust a curved line segment with the Pen tool, follow these steps:

1. Click to create the first anchor point and without releasing the mouse, continue to Step two.

2. Drag the Pen tool in the direction you want the curve to go.

3. When the preview of the line matches the curve that you want in the final line, release the mouse and then move to click and place the next point in the segment. Repeat this process to create subsequent curve points for curved segments.

4. Or, simply click elsewhere without dragging to place a point and make the subsequent segment a straight line with a corner point.

5. As with adjusting straight segments, press the Ctrl (⌘) key and click a point to select it, continue pressing the Ctrl (⌘) key as you drag and move the point to change the angle or length of the segment.

6. Or, with the Ctrl (⌘) key pressed, click and drag on the tangent handles of the point to adjust the depth and shape of the curve.

Although both corner points and curve points may be adjusted, they behave differently:

✦ Because a corner point defines a corner, adjusting the tangent handle of a corner point only modifies the curve that occurs on the same side as the tangent handle that is being adjusted.

✦ Because a curve point defines a curve, moving the tangent handle of a curve point modifies the curves on both sides of the point.

✦ To Convert a corner point into a curve point, simply select the point with the Subselection arrow and while pressing the Alt (Option) key, drag the point slightly. A curve point with two tangent handles will appear, replacing the original corner point.

✦ To adjust one tangent handle of a curve point independent of the other handle, hold down the Alt (Option) key while dragging the tangent handle that you want to move.

✦ Endpoints cannot be converted into curve points unless the line is continued or joined with another line. To join two endpoints, simply click on one endpoint with the Pen tool and then move to the point you want to connect it with and click again. A new line segment will be created that joins the two points.

✦ You can also use the arrow keys, located on your keyboard, to nudge selected corner and curve points into position. Press the Shift key to augment the arrow keys and to make them nudge 10 pixels with each click.

Note   You can also reshape any lines or shapes created with the Pen, Pencil, Paintbrush, Line, Oval, or Rectangle tools by dragging with the Arrow tool, or by optimizing their curves with Modify ➪ Optimize.

Choosing Colors

Whenever any of the Flash Drawing or Painting tools is used, the stroke and fill colors are determined by the current settings of the color controls located in the Flash Toolbox and on the Property inspector. The controls on the Toolbox are always visible regardless of which tool is being used. The Property inspector only displays the color controls if they can be applied to the active tool or to a selected element. Thus, if you select the Line tool, both Stroke and Fill color chips will be visible on the Toolbox, but the Property inspector will only display a Stroke color chip. Although these chips indicate the current color, they're really also buttons: Click any color chip to select a new color from the pop-up Swatches panel. The Swatches panel is shown in Figure 5-23 as it pops up from the Toolbox (top) or from the Property inspector (lower).

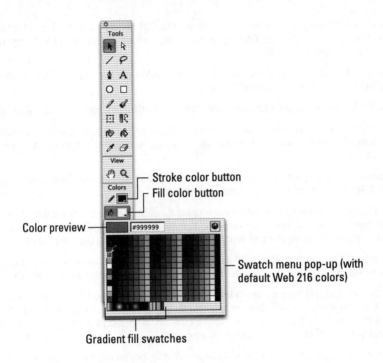

Stroke color button

Fill color button

Color preview

#999999

Swatch menu pop-up (with default Web 216 colors)

Gradient fill swatches

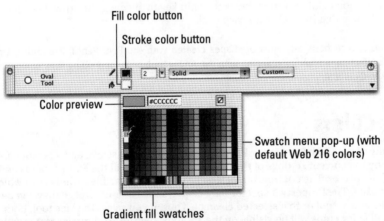

Fill color button

Stroke color button

Color preview

#CCCCCC

Swatch menu pop-up (with default Web 216 colors)

Gradient fill swatches

Figure 5-23: The current Swatches pop-up invoked by clicking the Stroke or Fill color chip in the Toolbox (top), or by clicking an available chip on the Property inspector (bottom)

If you've been working in Flash with any of the built-in Panel sets, you'll notice that this pop-up displays the same color options as the main Color Swatches panel, shown in Figure 5-24 (Shift+F3 or Window ➪ Color Swatches). It includes a Hexadecimal color value box, another iteration of the No Color button (when it applies), and a button that will launch the Color Picker. The Swatches menu evoked with the Fill color chip includes the same solid colors available for stroke, as well as a range of gradient fill styles along the bottom of the panel.

Swatch panel options menu

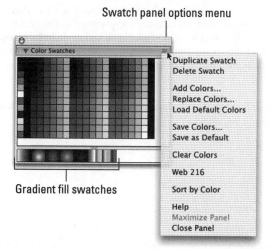

Figure 5-24: The default palette as displayed in the main Color Swatches panel

The custom palette options available in the Color Swatches panel are discussed in detail, along with the Color Mixer panel, and other colorful issues in Chapter 7, "Applying Color."

You can set the fill and stroke colors before you draw something, or select an element on the Stage and adjust it by choosing a new color from the stroke or fill swatches. The Oval, Rectangle, Paintbrush, and Paint Bucket tools all rely upon the fill settings to set or customize the type and color of fill that will be applied to a new shape that is about to be drawn, or when changing the color of a selected shape (or shapes).

The Colors section of the Toolbox includes three buttons, arrayed beneath the Fill color swatch. These are, from left to right, Black and White, No Color, and Swap Colors. The Black and White button sets the stroke to Black and the fill to White. The No Color button sets the active chip to not apply a color. The Swap Colors button swaps the current colors between the Stroke and Fill color chips.

Choosing Line Styles

In Flash MX, for all tools that draw or display a line or outline, the thickness of the line—or *stroke*—is controlled by either dragging the Stroke Height slider or by entering a value in the Stroke Height numeric entry box. These controls are both now available on the Property inspector, as shown in Figure 5-25. The stroke options are only visible when they can be applied—if a drawing tool that creates lines is active in the Toolbox or if an element with a stroke has been selected.

Generally, in Flash, lines that are independent, or not attached to any fill are referred to as *lines,* while lines or outlines on a filled shape are referred to as *strokes.* Lines and strokes are created and edited with the same tools.

Changes to stroke color and style apply to lines or curves drawn with the Pen, Line, Pencil, Oval, and Rectangle tools. For ovals and rectangles, the changes apply only to the outline, not to the fill. As with fill color settings, you can select a stroke thickness and style before you create any artwork (as long as the tool you're going to use is active in the Toolbox), or you can select a line in the Document window with the Arrow tool and change the stroke properties in the Property inspector.

All the options for choosing and modifying strokes that existed in the Stroke panel in Flash 5 have been integrated into the Property inspector.

Figure 5-25: The Property inspector gives you all the controls you will need to select stroke height, color, and style.

When dragging the Stroke height slider, the numeric entry box updates and displays a height readout analogous to the current position of the slider. This also functions as a precise numeric entry field. Simply enter a value to create a stroke with a specific height, or thickness. Permissible values range from 0.1 to 10, with fractions expressed in decimals.

Depending upon the level of zoom, the height difference of some lines may not be visible on screen — even though zooming in closer allows you to see that the stroke height is correct. Lines set to a height of 1 pixel or lower will appear to be the same thickness unless the Stage view is zoomed to 200 percent or closer. However, all line heights will still print correctly on a high-resolution printer and will be visible in your final Flash movie (.swf) to anyone who zooms in close enough.

The Stroke Style drop down available on the Property inspector (as shown in Figure 5-25), offers the choice of Hairline or six standard, variable-width strokes, or line styles, which are: Solid, Dashed, Dotted, Ragged, Stippled, and Hatched. Hairline strokes always have the same 1-pixel thickness, while the other six line styles can be chosen and combined with any stroke height. If these styles do not deliver the line look you need, the Custom button on the Property inspector invokes a Stroke Style dialog box (Figure 5-26), which can be used to generate custom line styles by selecting from a range of properties for each preset line. Basic properties include Stroke Thickness and Sharp Corners. There are other settings that vary depending on what style of stroke is chosen.

Points are the default unit of measurement for determining the length of lines or spaces and Stroke Thickness in the Line Style dialog box.

To closely examine a custom line before you begin drawing with it, click the Zoom 4x check box beneath the preview area of the Line Style dialog box. Note the Sharp Corners check box, which toggles this Line Style feature on or off — select the check box to turn Sharp Corners on.

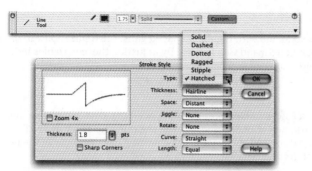

Figure 5-26: The Stroke Style dialog box available from the *Custom* button on the Property inspector. The properties displayed vary depending on the style of line selected for adjustment.

Tip

Although there is no way to save custom line styles within the stroke style dialog box, you can create a separate document (.fla) and save samples of your favorite lines there. This will ease your workflow if you want to reuse custom line styles extensively. You can apply these styles quite easily to other lines by opening the document and using the Eyedropper tool in conjunction with the Ink Bottle tool. For more information, see the sections on the Eyedropper and the Ink Bottle tools in Chapter 9.

Of course, the best way to get an idea of the variety of possible strokes is to experiment with settings and sizes for each style, but the following samples and brief descriptions will give you an overview of the different properties for each of the six standard styles.

Hairline

The Hairline line style provides a consistent line thickness that doesn't visually vary at different zoom levels. This is the best line style to choose if you're creating artwork that you want to scale without losing the original line width. Regardless of whether an object with this stroke is enlarged or reduced in size, the hairline stroke will always display as 1 pixel wide.

Solid

The Solid line style draws a smooth, unbroken line. The customization variables for this style are limited to Thickness and Sharp Corners. These two are variables can also be adjusted on all line styles.

Note

The Solid Line Style is the optimal Line Style for Web viewing because it requires fewer points to describe it and is consequently less file intensive. The smaller file sizes theoretically translate into faster download times when the artwork is transmitted over the Web. This really only becomes an issue if you're making extensive use of complex line styles.

Dashed

The Dashed line style draws a solid line with regularly spaced gaps. Customization variables specific to this style are Dash Length and Gap Length. By adjusting these variables individually, it is possible to get a wide range of line patterns.

Dotted

The Dotted line style draws a row of circles with evenly spaced gaps. At first glance, this style appears to have only one variable—Dot Spacing. Change the numeric entry in this field to control the gaps between the dots, and remember that changing the thickness of the line will change the size of the actual dots.

Ragged

The Ragged line style draws a ragged line with various gaps between uneven strokes. The quality of both the raggedness and the gaps are adjustable. This style has three unique parameters: Pattern, Wave Height, and Wave Length. Each of these has a drop-down menu with options that can be combined to create a range of wild possibilities.

Stippled

The Stippled line style creates a line from a series of small irregular "patches" that goes a long way toward mimicking an artist's hand-stippling technique. The qualities of stippling are adjustable with three variables unique to the nature of stippled lines: Dot Size, Dot Variation, and Density. Each of these variables has a drop-down with multiple settings that can be adjusted to create a wide array of stroke densities and patterns.

Hatched

The Hatched line style draws a textured line of amazing complexity, which can be used to mimic an artist's hand-drawn hatched-line technique. This line style has six parameters unique to hatched lines: Thickness (hatch-specific), Space, Jiggle, Rotate, Curve, and Length.

Note　The Hatched line style thickness settings are different from the point size thickness settings that are available for all lines. The default thickness setting (measured in points) defines the thickness or height of the overall hatched line, while the hatch thickness setting defines the width of the individual vertical strokes that create the density of the hatched line texture.

Designing and Aligning Elements

After you've drawn some lines or shapes, you'll want to organize them in your layout. Flash provides some useful tools to help with moving or modifying elements that will be familiar if you've worked in other graphics programs. Aside from using the Flash Grid and manually placed Guides to control your layout, you can quickly access the Info panel and the Align panel to dynamically change the placement of elements on the stage. The Transform panel is the most accurate way to modify the size, aspect ratio, rotation, and even the vertical or horizontal "slant" of an element.

 Controlling the Flash Grid and placing Guides is introduced in Chapter 4.

The precise alignment possible with these panels is especially helpful if you're working with detailed artwork or multiple shapes that need to be arranged in exact relation to each other.

 If you group elements before modifying them, the Transform panel saves the original size and rotation of the group so that changes can be removed at any time.

Drawing Panels

When drawing in Flash, the drawing panels — Info, Align, and Transform — can be your best friends. Use the Info panel to modify the coordinates and dimensions of an item. Use the Align panel to align, *regularize* (match the sizes of), or distribute several items on Stage either relative to each other or to the Stage area. Or use the Transform panel to scale, rotate, and skew an item.

 The new Free Transform tool is detailed in Chapter 9, "Modifying Graphics." This MX addition to the Toolbox offers powerful options for modifying artwork, including a new Envelope modifier not available from the Transform panel.

You will find the Info panel (Ctrl+I or ⌘+I) and the Align panel (Ctrl+K or ⌘+K) both at the top of the Designer panel set that is available from the Window menu (Window ⇨ Panel Sets ⇨ Designer). To open either of these panels alone, or to open the Transform panel (Ctrl+T or ⌘+T), simply use shortcut keys or find them directly in the Window menu.

The Info panel

Use the Info panel, shown in Figure 5-27, to give precise coordinates and dimensions to your items. Type the values in the fields provided, and by default your item will be transformed relative to its top-left corner. To adjust the transform center point, use the Alignment Grid to choose any side or corner of your selected element as the starting point before applying changes.

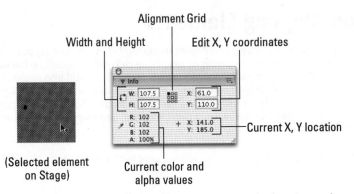

Alignment Grid

Width and Height   Edit X, Y coordinates

—Current X, Y location

(Selected element   Current color and
on Stage)   alpha values

Figure 5-27: Use the Info panel options to change the location and dimensions of an item.

The Info panel has these controls:

✦ **Width:** Use this numeric entry field to alter the width of a selected item.

✦ **Height:** Use this numeric entry field to alter the height of a selected item.

> **Tip**   Units for both Width and Height are measured in the units (pixels, inches, points, and so on) set in Ruler Units option of the Document Properties dialog box (Ctrl+M or ⌘+M). Note, however, that upon changing the unit of measurement, the item must be deselected and then reselected in order for these readouts to refresh and display in the current units.

✦ **Alignment Grid:** The alignment grid is located just to the left of the numeric entry fields that are used for adjusting the X and Y location of any selected item. This alignment grid consists of nine small squares. Together, these squares represent an invisible bounding box that encloses the selected item. Every shape created in Flash, even circles, resides within an imaginary rectangular bounding box that includes the extremities of the shape. The alignment grid enables you to position the selected item relative to either the upper-left corner or to the center of its bounding box. Click either square to define which origin point to use for position or size adjustments.

> **Note**   The X (horizontal) and Y (vertical) coordinates are measured from the upper-left corner of the Flash Stage, which is the origin with coordinates 0,0.

✦ **X:** Use this numeric entry field to either read the X coordinate of the item or to reposition the item numerically, relative to the center point on the X (or horizontal) axis.

✦ **Y:** Use this numeric entry field to either read the Y coordinate of the item or to reposition the item numerically, relative to the center point on the Y (or vertical) axis.

✦ **RGBA:** This sector of the Info panel gives the Red, Green, Blue, and Alpha values for graphic items and groups at the point immediately beneath the cursor. Values for symbols, the background, or interface elements do not register.

✦ **+ X: / + Y:** This sector of the Info panel gives the X and Y coordinates for the point immediately beneath the cursor—including offstage or Work area values. A negative X value is to the left of the Stage, while a negative Y is located above the Stage.

To scale or reposition an item, select the item and then open the Info panel with Window ➪ Info, as shown in Figure 5-27:

✦ First you must choose to scale or reposition the item relative to either the center, or to the upper-left corner. (The selected square turns black to indicate that it is selected.)

  • To work relative to the center, select the center square of the Alignment Grid.

  • Or to scale relative to the upper-left corner, click that square of the Alignment Grid.

✦ To scale the item numerically, enter new values in the Width and Height fields, and then click elsewhere or press Enter to apply the change.

✦ To reposition the item numerically, enter new values in the X and Y fields (located in the *upper* half of the panel), and then either press Enter or click elsewhere, outside the panel, to apply the change.

The Align panel

The Align panel (Ctrl+K or ⌘+K), shown in Figure 5-28, is one of many features for which you'll be grateful every time you use it. It enables you, with pixel-perfect precision, to align or distribute items relative to each other or to the Stage.

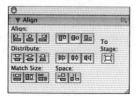

Figure 5-28: Use the Align panel to both size and arrange items with ease.

The Align panel has five controls. The icons on the buttons show visually how the selected items will be arranged:

✦ **Align:** There are six buttons in this first control. The first group of three buttons is for horizontal alignment, and the second group of three is for vertical alignment. These buttons align two or more items (or one or more items with the Stage) horizontally (top, middle, bottom) or vertically (left, middle, right).

✦ **Distribute:** This control also has six buttons, three for horizontal distribution and three for vertical distribution. These buttons are most useful when you have three or more items that you want to space evenly (such as a set of buttons). These buttons distribute items equally, again vertically or horizontally. The different options enable you to distribute from edge to edge, or from item centers.

✦ **Match Size:** This control enables you to force two or more items of different sizes to become equal in size; match items horizontally, vertically, or both.

✦ **Space:** This option enables you to space items evenly, again, vertically or horizontally. You may wonder how this differs from Distribute. Both are similar in concept, and if your items are all the same size, they will have the same effect. The difference becomes more apparent when the items are of different sizes:

- Distribute evenly distributes the items according to a common reference (top, center, or bottom). For example, if one item is larger than the others, it may be separated from the other items by less space, but the distance between its top edge and the next item's top edge will be consistent with all the selected items.

- Space ensures that the spacing between items is the same; for example, each item might have exactly 36 pixels between it and the next.

✦ **To Stage:** On the right, you will also notice a To Stage button. When this button is selected, all adjustments will be made in relation to the full Stage.

To align an item to the exact center of the Stage, do the following:

1. Click to select the item that you want to center.

2. Click To Stage in the Align panel.

3. Click the Align horizontal center button.

4. Click the Align vertical center button.

The Transform panel

The Transform panel (Ctrl+T or ⌘+T), gives precise control over scaling, rotation, and skewing of a shape. With this panel, instead of making adjustments "by eye"—which may be imprecise—numeric values are entered in the appropriate fields and applied directly to the selected shape. As shown in Figure 5-29, the value fields in the Transform panel make it easy to modify the size and position of an element. However, once transformations are applied to an ungrouped shape, these numbers reset when it is deselected.

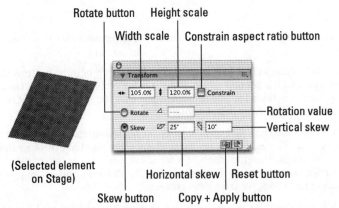

Figure 5-29: Use the Transform panel to scale, rotate, and skew items.

There are some powerful new Transform options available in Flash MX from the Toolbox and from the Transform submenu of the Modify menu. These more-complex editing tools are explained in Chapter 9, "Modifying Graphics." However, the best place to start with transform options is the Transform panel, and these options are applied as follows:

✦ **Scale:** Use this to size the selected item by percentage. Enter a new number in the Scale field and press the Enter key. The shape scales to the specified percentage of its original scale. To constrain the shape to its current proportions, click the Constrain check box. To restore the shape to its original size, press the Reset button. However, once the shape is deselected, it cannot be Reset. The only way to get back to the shape's original size is to immediately use Edit ➪ Undo until it is reset, or close your document without saving changes (in which case you'll probably lose other work as well). You can also get back to the original size mathematically by applying a new scale percentage that compensates for the changes you have previously applied (for example, scale a shape to 200 percent, then to get back to the original size after it has been deselected, scale the shape to 50 percent).

Tip   When using the Transform panel with groups and symbol instances, the original settings can be reset even after the item has been deselected. Making and using symbols is explained in Chapter 6, "Symbols, Instances, and the Library."

✦ **Rotate:** Click the radio button and then specify a rotation for the selected item by entering a number in the Rotate field. Pressing the Return or Enter key will apply the change to the selected item. The item will be rotated clockwise around its center point. To rotate an item counterclockwise enter a negative number in the Rotate field.

✦ **Skew:** Items can be *skewed* (slanted in the horizontal or vertical direction) by clicking the Skew radio button, and then entering values for the horizontal and vertical angles. Click Apply and the item will be skewed to the values entered.

✦ **Copy and Apply Transformation:** Press this button and Flash makes a copy of the selected item (including shapes and lines), with all transform settings applied to it. The copy is pasted in the same location as the original, so select it with the Arrow tool and move it to a new position. Your original will be left unchanged.

✦ **Reset:** This button, at the bottom-right corner of the panel, removes the transformation you just performed on a selected object. However, after the object is deselected, this button does not work. For shapes, this is really an Undo button, rather than a Reset button. However, you can use the Reset button for instances, groups, or type blocks even after they have been deselected (but not after you save your movie).

The Edit menu

Many of the commands in the Edit menu are discussed in Chapter 4, "Interface Fundamentals," but some of these commands can be helpful in creating or modifying graphics and are worth mentioning again here:

✦ **Undo:** When you make a mistake, before you do anything else, apply this command to get back to where you started. The default number for combined Undos that Flash remembers is 100, the maximum number is 200. Because Undo "memory" occupies system memory, you can set this level much lower if you find you don't rely on it. This setting is controlled in the General tab of the Document preferences dialog box.

Note   Flash generates an Undo stack for several different parts of the interface: Each timeline (Main Timeline and Movie Clip timelines) has its own undo stack, as does the ActionScript panel. Furthermore, Undo does not transcend Focus: You cannot Undo work on the Stage from the ActionScript panel — you must first return focus to the Stage to exercise Undo.

✦ **Redo:** The anti-Undo, this redoes what you just undid.

✦ **Cut:** This removes any selected item(s) from the Document window and places it on the clipboard.

✦ **Copy:** This copies any selected item(s) and places it on the clipboard, without removing it from the Document window.

✦ **Paste:** Disabled if nothing has been copied or cut, this pastes items from the clipboard into the currently active frame on the currently active layer. You can also paste text into panel controls.

✦ **Paste in Place:** This is like Paste, except that it pastes the object precisely in the same area of the Stage from which it was copied (but it can be on a new Layer or Keyframe).

✦ **Paste Special (PC only):** This is a Windows only menu that allows some specialized copying of content into Flash. This is not recommended when working in a cross-platform environment because it is platform-specific and will limit how the document can be edited on other platforms.

✦ **Clear:** This removes a selected item(s) from the Stage *without* copying it to the clipboard.

✦ **Duplicate:** This command duplicates a selected item or items, without burdening the clipboard. The duplicated item appears adjacent to the original.

✦ **Select All:** Selects all items in the Document window in the currently active keyframe of the project.

✦ **Deselect All:** Deselects all currently selected items.

✦ **Edit Symbols:** Select an instance of a symbol and choose this command to edit in symbol-editing mode. For more about symbols and editing symbols, refer to Chapter 6, "Symbols, Instances, and the Library."

✦ **Edit Selected:** This is only enabled if a group or symbol is selected on the Stage. It opens a selected group or symbol for editing in a separate *edit space* identified in the location label area of the Document window. This same kind of edit space is invoked for symbols by choosing Edit Symbol.

✦ **Edit in Place:** This command opens a selected group or symbol in a separate tab of the Document window (shown in the location label area of the Document window), and allows you to edit this group or symbol while still seeing the other elements on the Stage dimmed in the background for reference.

✦ **Edit All:** When editing a group, Edit All is used to go back to editing the main Flash scene. You can always do this also by clicking on the Scene location label of the Document window.

Summary

✦ The geometric shapes available from the Toolbox are a quick and accurate way of creating basic elements that can be customized with various fill and stroke styles.

✦ Shape recognition and line processing provide variable levels of correction to hand-drawn shapes and strokes that can make it easier to create "perfect" graphics.

✦ Line styles can be modified in the Property inspector to create a huge variety of textures and widths.

✦ By adjusting and applying the various Snap modifiers, you can control how "auto" alignment behavior will affect elements as you work.

✦ The Pencil, Paintbrush, and Pen tools allow you to draw freeform or Bézier lines that can be edited using the Arrow options and the Subselection tool.

✦ By using specific modes for the Paintbrush and Eraser tools, you can choose exactly what areas of artwork are modified.

✦ Optimizing artwork manually by editing points with the Subselection tool, or automatically by using the Optimize Curves option can greatly reduce file size by simplifying lines and curves.

✦ The Info, Align and Transform panels give you several precise options for arranging and modifying elements on the Stage.

✦　　✦　　✦

Symbols, Instances, and the Library

✦   ✦   ✦   ✦

In This Chapter

Working with libraries
in Flash: Document
library, Common
libraries, and Shared
libraries

Organizing your Library
and resolving conflicts

Defining content types
and managing assets

Understanding symbol
types: Graphic symbols,
Button symbols, and
Movie Clips

Editing symbols

Modifying instance
properties

Building nested symbol
structures to create
animated buttons

Using the Movie
Explorer

✦   ✦   ✦   ✦

Symbols are the key to both the file-size efficiency and the interactive power of Flash. A *symbol* is a reusable element that resides in the current movie's Library, which is accessed with Window ⇨ Library. Each time you place a symbol on the stage or inside of another symbol, you're working with an *instance* of that symbol. Unlike using individual graphic elements, you can use many instances of a given symbol, with little or no addition to the file size.

Using symbols helps reduce the file size of your finished movie because Flash only needs to save the symbol once. Each time that symbol is used in the project, Flash refers to its original profile. Then, to support the variations of an instance, Flash only needs to save information about the differences — such as size, position, proportions, and color effects. If a separate graphic were used for each change, Flash would have to store a complete profile of all the information about that graphic — not just the changes, but also all of the points that specify what the original graphic looks like.

Furthermore, symbols can save you a lot of time and trouble, particularly when it comes to editing your movie. That's because changes made to a symbol are reflected in each instance of that symbol throughout the movie. Let's say that your logo changes halfway through production. Without symbols, it might take hours to find and change each copy of the logo. However, if you've used symbol instances, you need only edit the original symbol — the instances are automatically updated throughout the movie.

In this chapter, you learn to create and edit symbols stored in your Document library. You also learn to use symbol instances, both within the movie and within other symbols, and to modify individual instances of a symbol.

Understanding the Document Library

The Library is the storehouse for all reusable elements, known as *symbols,* which can then be placed as symbol *instances* within a Flash movie. Imported sounds and bitmaps are automatically placed in the Library. Upon creation, Graphic symbols, Button symbols and Movie Clips are also stored in the Library. It's a good practice to convert nearly every main item within a Flash document into a symbol, and to then develop your project from instances derived from these original symbols.

As shown in Figure 6-1, the Library Window (top) — Window ⇨ Library — is separate from the three default asset Libraries (bottom) that are accessed from the application menu at Window ⇨ Common libraries. However, these libraries are related. When you choose Window ⇨ Library (F11), you open a Library specific to the current Flash document (.fla), whereas Common libraries are available whenever Flash is open and provide elements that you can drag into the Document library to use in your own project. All of the Library panels can be docked in a vertical panel stack or accessed individually as floating panels. In Figure 6-1, the document Library is shown in *Wide* state, while the Common libraries are shown in *Narrow* state. All library panels can be toggled between these two view options.

Document library

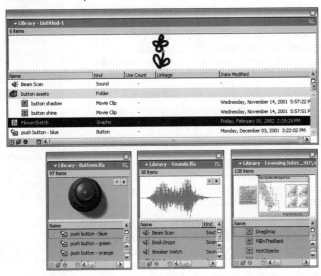

Common libraries

Figure 6-1: The Library window is specific to the current document (.fla), while the other panels, known as the Common libraries, are available whenever Flash is open.

Choose Window ⇨ Common Libraries to open the submenu of Common libraries that ship with Flash. The default Buttons, Sounds, and Learning Interactions libraries contain a selection of pre-built Flash elements that can be reused in any Flash project. These are stored in the Libraries folder of the Flash application folder. To add your own buttons, symbols, or even complete libraries for specific projects, first save them in a Flash document (.fla) with a descriptive name, and then place that Flash file in the Libraries folder within the Flash Program folder on your hard drive.

New Feature

The number of Common libraries in Flash MX has been reduced to three from the six that were available in Flash 5, but the new author-time and runtime Shared libraries feature offers an optimized workflow solution for managing assets. Also, the Smart Clip Library has been replaced by the new Components panel (F11). Using and modifying components is described in Chapter 29, "Using Components."

You can also access elements stored in the Library of any document by choosing File ➪ Open As Library from the application menu (see Figure 6-2). The Library will open next to the Document window of your current project, but it is visually differentiated from your original project Library because it displays with a gray background rather than a white background.

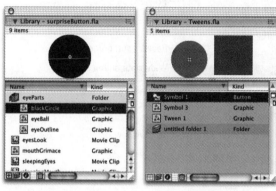

Library for active document
(invoked by using
Window ➪ Library)

Library for an inactive
document (invoked by using
File ➪ Open as Library)

Figure 6-2: The Library for the current document has a white background (left), while other libraries that may be opened will have a gray background color (right).

You can copy assets from a source Library to a current Document library by dragging items from the source Library onto the current document Stage, or directly into the Library. This will also work if you have two documents open, and you want to move assets between the two Libraries. But it is also then possible to drag or copy and paste elements directly from one document Stage onto another, or drag an item from a source document Stage into a current document's Library.

Flash MX introduces a new, Shared library feature that allows assets from a source document (.fla) to be linked to multiple destination documents. This creates a more optimized workflow than making individual copies of Library assets in multiple documents. By linking documents to one central asset Library, it is easier to make updates and to maintain consistency if a project involves more than one document (.fla). You can find more information on the two specific ways of using shared assets in the section, "Working with Shared Assets and Fonts" later in this chapter.

Cross-
Reference   The methods for creating and using Shared libraries is fully explained in Chapter 28, "Sharing and Loading Assets."

Reading the Library

Every Flash document has its own Library, which is used to store and organize symbols, sounds, bitmaps, and other assets such as video files. As shown in Figure 6-3, the item highlighted — or selected — in the *Sort Window* is previewed in the *Preview Window*. Each item in the Library has an icon to the left of the name to indicate the content type. Click any heading to sort the window by Name, Kind (type), Use Count, or Date Modified (all headings shown in Figure 6-1).

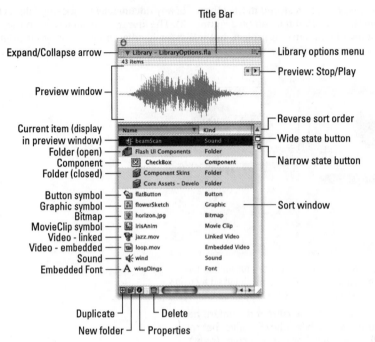

Figure 6-3: The Library window as viewed in Narrow state

If the item selected in the Library is a Button symbol with an Over state, or a Movie Clip or sound file with more than one frame on its timeline, you'll see a controller in the upper-right corner of the Preview window. This Preview Stop/Play controller pops up to facilitate previewing these items. It's almost equivalent to the Play option that's found in the options menu. As shown in Figure 6-4, the Library Options pop-up menu lists a number of features, functions, and controls for organizing and working with items in the Library.

The following commands found in the Library Options menu will help you to add or modify content that is stored in your Document library.

✦ **New Symbol:** Choose this item from the Options menu to create a new symbol. When a new symbol is created, it is stored at the root of the Library Sort window. To create a new symbol in a folder, select the desired folder first — the new symbol will be placed in the selected folder.

✦ **New Folder:** Items in the Library can be organized in folders. The New Folder button simply creates a new folder within the Sort window.

✦ **New Font:** Use this option to invoke the Font Symbol Properties dialog, which is the first step in creating a Font Symbol for use within a Shared Library. For more information about Shared libraries and Font symbols, refer to the section on "Working with Shared Assets and Fonts" in this chapter, as well as to Chapter 28, "Sharing and Loading Assets."

✦ **New Video:** Creates a new empty Video object in the Library. For more on using Video objects with ActionScript, refer to Chapter 28, "Sharing and Loading Assets."

✦ **Rename:** Use the Rename option to rename an item in the Sort window.

Figure 6-4: The Library window and the Options pop-up menu

✦ **Move to New Folder:** Use the Move to New Folder option to open the New Folder dialog.

Note Library items can also be moved between folders by dragging.

✦ **Duplicate, Delete:** Select Duplicate to create a copy of an item and Delete to delete an item in the Sort window.

✦ **Edit:** Choose Edit to access the selected symbol in Symbol Editing mode.

Tip Double-clicking a symbol on the Stage takes you to Edit in Place mode, which is a variant of Symbol Editing mode, that will allow you to see other elements on the Stage dimmed in the background for layout reference.

✦ **Edit With:** Provided that you have appropriate external applications installed, most imported assets (such as sounds, bitmaps, and vectors) will have this command available to jump to the external editing environment of your choice.

✦ **Properties:** Click to invoke the related Properties dialog for the particular symbol type—Sound, Bitmap, Symbol, Component or Video Properties. The Properties dialog is a central control that allows you to rename an element, access Edit mode, or access the Linkages dialog box from one location. This is also where you can define or edit the Source for any element.

✦ **Linkage:** Use this command to invoke the Linkage options menu. Linkage means that you can assign an identifier string to a Movie Clip symbol, a Font symbol, a sound, or a `Video` object so that it can be accessed with ActionScript. This is an aspect of Shared libraries. For more information about Shared libraries and linkage, refer to Chapter 28, "Sharing and Loading Assets."

✦ **Component Definition:** With Flash MX, Movie Clips with customizable behavior previously known as Smart Clips, are now organized in the Component panel. This Library option invokes the Define Component dialog box, which is used to assign variable names and object names to the pre-built movie clips. Each of the new components that ship with Flash, are discussed in Chapter 29, "Using Components."

✦ **Select Unused Items:** Select Unused Items to find any items stored in the Library that have not been used in the current project.

✦ **Update:** Use this option if you've edited items subsequent to importing them into Flash. Items will be updated without the bother of reimporting. This option can also be used to swap in a new element of the same kind to replace an item already used in your project.

✦ **Play (or Stop, if currently playing):** If the selected asset has a timeline or is otherwise playable (such as a sound), click this to preview the asset in the Library Preview window. If the asset is currently playing, this option is updated to Stop — in which case, click to stop playing.

✦ **Expand Folder/Collapse Folder:** Use this command to toggle the currently selected folder in the sort window open or closed.

✦ **Expand All Folders/Collapse All Folders:** Use this command to toggle all folders and subfolders in the sort window open or closed.

✦ **Shared Library Properties:** Use this command to invoke the Shared Properties dialog box, which is another aspect of Shared libraries. For more information about Shared libraries, refer to the section on Working with Shared Assets and Fonts later in this chapter, as well as to Chapter 28, "Sharing and Loading Assets."

✦ **Keep Use Counts Updated:** Use this command to tell Flash to continuously keep track of the usage of each symbol. If you're working with multiple, complex graphics and symbols, this feature can slow down your processor.

✦ **Update Use Counts Now:** Use this option to tell Flash to update the usage of each symbol. This command is a one-time check, and is probably less of a drain on system resources than the previous command, which checks continuously.

Selecting New Symbol, Duplicate, or Properties from the options menu launches the Symbol Properties dialog box, shown in Figure 6-5. Use this dialog box to give the symbol a unique name and assign it a behavior (as a symbol type — Graphic, Button, or Movie Clip). However, if the Properties option is chosen for a sound asset, then the Sound Properties dialog box appears. For more information on Sound Properties, refer to Chapter 15, "Adding Sound."

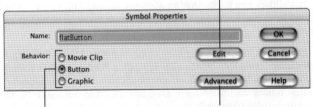

Launch Symbol Editing mode

Assign symbol behavior   Expand panel to show Advanced options

Figure 6-5: The Symbol Properties dialog box. Note the button for Advanced options — this will expand the dialog box to include Linkage and Source information for the selected element.

Organizing the Library

When your movies start to become complex, you'll find that the Library gets crowded, and it can be hard to find symbols. When this happens, you'll appreciate the capability to create and name folders for your symbols. You can organize your Library folders however you like, but here are a few suggestions for greater productivity:

✦ Create a separate folder for each Scene.

✦ Create folders for certain kinds of symbols, such as buttons, sounds, or bitmap imports.

✦ Store all symbols or graphics that relate to a specific element (such as a logo or an animated character) together in one folder.

When you build complex layered structures in your movie—a Movie Clip symbol on the first frame of a Button symbol, with a text symbol on the layer above it, and a sound on the layer above that—the Library doesn't indicate this hierarchy. But you can—just put all the associated symbols in a folder with a name that describes the final element. You can also nest folders within other folders. Working with folders in the Library is almost exactly the same as working with folders in the Layers area of the Timeline window:

✦ To create a folder, click the folder icon at the bottom-left corner of the Library.

✦ To move a file or folder into another folder, simply drag it over the target folder.

✦ To move a folder that's been nested within another folder back to the top level of the Library, drag the folder until it is just above the Library list and over the word Name and release.

Note   Putting symbols in different folders does not affect the links between them and their instances (as opposed to the way moving a graphic file into a new folder breaks an existing link on a Web page). Flash tracks and updates all references to Library items whenever they are renamed or moved into separate folders.

The Movie Explorer is a way of getting a visual overview of the nested relationship of symbols, Movie Clips, and other items within your document. Refer to the end of this chapter for more on the Movie Explorer.

Resolving Conflicts between Library Assets

Importing or copying an asset into your current project Library will occasionally invoke a Resolve Library Conflict alert box asking if you want to Replace Existing Items and Instances. This alert box appears when you are trying to add a new asset to your Library with the same name as an asset already present in your current document. If you choose not to replace the existing item, the newly added items will have the word *copy* added to their file names. For example, if you have an item named *photo* in your current library and attempt to add another item to the Library with the same name, the new item would be given the name *photo copy* in the Library. To rename the added item, simply double-click on the item name in the Library list and type a new name.

If you choose to replace the existing item in your Library, all instances will be replaced with the content of the newly added item. If you choose to cancel the import or copy operation, the selected items will not be added to your current document and the existing items stored in the Library will be preserved.

Caution There is one Library action for which there is neither undo nor escape: Delete. Any item that is deleted from the Library is gone forever, including all instances throughout the current document (.fla).

Working with Shared Assets and Fonts

Flash MX has expanded the functionality of shared assets by now making it possible to create author-time as well as runtime Shared libraries. This allows a development team to maintain consistency during production by having centralized sources for fonts or other assets, in addition to being able to create a Library of assets that can be uploaded to the server and shared with multiple movies (.swfs). These source assets could include any element that is normally created in a Flash movie, as well as assets such as bitmaps, fonts, sounds, or video that are imported and usually embedded in individual project (.fla) files. This production strategy has the benefit of trimming file sizes, because the asset source is not saved with the project file (.fla) that references it.

Updating or replacing symbols using author-time sharing is straightforward and will be familiar to anyone who used the Swap symbol option and the Properties panel in Flash 5 to update and import assets. You can update or replace a symbol in your current project (.fla) with any other symbol accessible on your local network. Any modifications or effects applied to instances of the symbol will be preserved, but the contents of the symbol stored in the library will be replaced with the contents of the new symbol that you select.

To update or replace a symbol with new content:

1. In the current project Library panel select the symbol that you want to replace (Graphic symbol, Button, or Movie Clip).

2. Choose Properties from the contextual menu or from the Library options menu and under Source in the Symbol Properties dialog box, select the Browse button to find the .fla file that contains the symbol you want use.

3. In the Open dialog box, navigate to a symbol that will be used to update or replace the selected symbol in the Library and click Open. Click OK to close the Symbol Properties dialog box.

4. The symbol name will remain the same, but the content in the Library and in all instances used in your project should now contain the updated content.

Cross-Reference For more information about creating and using runtime shared assets and libraries, refer to Chapter 28, "Sharing and Loading Assets."

Defining Content Types

Understanding the behavior of various media types and learning to streamline asset management unlocks the true potential of Flash for combining compelling content with small file sizes. The basic structures for storing, reusing, and modifying content within a Flash project are not complicated, but the reason for using various symbol types does deserve explanation.

Raw data

When you create graphics directly in Flash, by using the shape tools, text tool, or any of the other drawing tools, you produce raw data or primitive shapes. These elements can be copied and pasted into any keyframe on the timeline, but they do not appear in the project Library. Each time the element appears, Flash has to "read" and render all the points, curves, and color information from scratch, because the information is not stored in the Library. Even if the shape looks exactly the same on keyframe 10 as it did on keyframe 1, Flash has to do all the work to "re-create" the shape every time it appears. This will quickly bloat the size of the .swf file. Also, because each element is completely independent, if you decide to make any changes, you'll have to find and edit each appearance of an element manually. This could be a daunting task if your project involves any animation or nested symbols.

Groups

The first step toward making raw data more manageable is to use groups. By grouping a filled shape with its outline stroke, for example, it becomes easier to select both parts of the shape to move around in your layout. If you added a text element that you also wanted to keep aligned with your artwork, you could add this to the group as well. Groups can be inclusive or they can be cumulative, so that you can select multiple elements and create one group (Ctrl+G or ⌘+G) that can be accessed on the same edit level by double-clicking the whole group once. If you add another element (even another group) to the first group, you will find that you have to click in to a deeper level to edit individual elements. In this way groups can grow more and more complicated, which is helpful if you're trying to keep multiple elements in order.

The important thing to remember about groups, however, is that they are *not* symbols. Although groups have a similar selection highlight to symbols, you will notice that they don't have a crosshair icon in the center, and that the group information won't appear in your project Library. No matter how careful you are about reusing the same raw data and grouping elements to keep them organized, when it comes to publishing your movie (.swf) or trying to update any single element, you will be no better off than if you had just placed raw elements wildly into your project. Flash still treats each shape and line as a unique element and the file size will grow exponentially each time you add another keyframe containing any of your raw data, even if it is grouped. The best way to use groups in your project is for managing symbols, or to organize elements that you plan to keep together and convert into one symbol.

Native symbols

Imported sound, video, bitmap, or font symbols will all automatically be stored in the Library to define *instances* of the asset when it is used in the project. In addition, there are three basic *container* symbol types that can be created in the Flash authoring environment. Movie Clip symbols, Graphic symbols, and Button symbols all have timelines that can "hold" images, sounds, text or even other symbols. Although it is always possible to make the behavior of a symbol instance different from the behavior of the original symbol, it is generally best to decide how you will be using a certain element and then assign it the symbol type that is appropriate to both its content and expected use in the project.

To make a decision on what type of symbol to use, it helps to have a clear understanding of the benefits and limitations of each of the symbol types available in Flash. Each symbol type has specific features that are suited to particular kinds of content. Each symbol type is marked with a unique icon in the Library, but what all symbols have in common is that they can be reused within a project as symbol instances, all defined by the original symbol.

A Flash project Library may contain these symbol types created directly in Flash:

 Graphic symbols are used mainly for static images that will be reused in a project. Flash ignores any sounds or actions inside a Graphic symbol. Graphic symbols will not play independently of the Main Timeline and thus require an allocated frame on the Main Timeline for each frame that you want to be visible within the symbol. If you want a Graphic symbol to loop or repeat as the Main Timeline moves along, you have to include another whole series of frames on the Main Timeline to match the length of the Graphic symbol timeline for each "loop."

 Movie Clips are actually like movies within a movie. They're good for animations that run independently of the movie's Main Timeline. They can contain actions, other symbols, and sounds. Movie Clips can also be placed inside of other symbols and are indispensable for creating interactive interface elements such as animated buttons. Movie Clips can continue to play even if the Main Timeline is stopped, thus they only need one frame on the Main Timeline to play back any number of frames on their own timeline. By default, Movie Clips are set to loop, so that as long as there is an instance of the Movie Clip visible on the Main Timeline it can loop or play back the content on its own timeline as many times as you need it to, without needing a matching number of keyframes on the Main Timeline.

 Button symbols are used for creating interactive buttons. Button symbols have a timeline limited to four frames, which are referred to as *states*. These states are related directly to user interaction and are labeled as Up, Over, Down, and Hit. Each of these button states can be defined with graphics, symbols, and sounds. After you create a Button symbol, you can assign independent actions to various instances in the main movie or inside other Movie Clips. Like Movie Clips, Button symbols only require one frame on any other timeline to be able to playback the three visible states (frames) of their own timeline.

 Components are a new feature of Flash MX that is actually derived from the Flash 5 Smart Clip feature. Components are pre-built Movie Clips for interactive Flash elements that can be reused and customized. Each component has its own unique set of ActionScript methods that allow you to set options at runtime. Refer to Chapter 29, "Using Components," for more details.

Imported media elements

A Flash project Library will also store certain types of imported assets, to define instances of the asset when they are used in the movie. You can place these imported assets into native Flash symbol structures by converting a bitmap into a Graphic symbol or placing a Sound inside a Button symbol, for example.

 Bitmaps are handled like symbols, the original image is stored in the Library and anytime the image is used in the project it is actually a copy, or an *instance,* of the original. To use a bitmap asset, drag an instance out of the Library and onto the Stage. Export settings for individual bitmaps are managed from within the Library by choosing Properties from either the contextual menu or the Library options menu. However, you will not be able to apply color or alpha effects to the symbol instance unless you convert it into a native Flash symbol type (Graphic, Button, or Movie Clip symbol). The topic of importing and using bitmaps in Flash is covered in detail in both Chapter 16, "Importing Artwork," and Chapter 37, "Working with Raster Graphics."

Flash MX now offers an option to "Import to Library" that is especially useful for bringing in a series of bitmaps. Instead of having all the images dumped into the Document window, you can load them directly into your Library.

✦ **Vector graphics,** upon import from other applications, arrive on the Flash stage as a group, and unlike bitmaps, may be edited or manipulated just like a normal group drawn in Flash. These elements will not be stored in the Library until they have been converted to a native symbol type. Vectors are discussed in greater detail in Chapter 16, "Importing Artwork," and Chapter 38, "Working with Vector Graphics."

In Flash MX, dragging a primitive shape or group into the Library panel from the Stage will automatically invoke the Convert to Symbol dialog box so that you can name and assign a symbol type to the element before it is added to your Library.

Use care in managing the properties of 8-bit images in the Flash Library. The Smoothing option renders custom predithered hybrid Web colors differently from the original colors.

Sounds are also handled like symbols by the Library, but they can be assigned different playback behavior after they are placed on a timeline. Flash can import (and export) sounds in a range of sound formats. Upon import, these sound files reside in the Library. To use a sound, drag an instance of the sound out of the Library and onto the Stage. Export settings for sound files are managed from within the Library by choosing Properties from either the contextual menu or the Library options menu. Playback behavior and effects can be defined with the Property inspector after a sound is placed on a timeline. Importing and using sounds effectively is a critical topic covered in Chapter 15, "Adding Sound," and Chapter 39, "Working with Audio Applications."

Video Assets like Font symbols, can be embedded or linked. Embedded video assets, like bitmaps, can have Color and Alpha effects applied if they are first converted to a native Flash symbol type. Chapter 17, "Embedding Video," explains the new options for embedding video directly in a Flash movie.

Font symbols are symbols created from font files to make them available for use in Dynamic text fields. Font symbols can also be defined as shared fonts, to make them available to multiple movie files (.swf), without the file size burden of embedding the font into each file individually. Refer to the section, "Working with Shared Assets and Fonts" later in this chapter, as well as to Chapter 28, "Sharing and Loading Assets," for more details.

Graphic Symbols versus Movie Clips, by Robin and Sandy Debreuil

Graphic symbols are a quick and tidy way of placing static information into a timeline, while Movie Clips animate independently on their own timeline. Graphic symbols should be used to hold single frames of raw data, or multiple frames when it is important to preview your work while designing it, as with linear animation. Movie Clips must be used when ActionScript is involved, or when an animation must run regardless of what is happening around it. However, the use of one type of symbol instead of the other may not always involve clear-cut choices, because often, either will work. Consequently, to use symbols effectively, it's important to know the pluses, minuses, and absolutes of both Graphic symbols and Movie Clips. Here are some tips to keep in mind:

✦ Instance properties of Graphic symbols (height, color, rotation, and so on) are frozen at design time, whereas Movie Clips can have their instance properties set on the fly with ActionScript. This makes Movie Clips essential for programmed content such as games.

✦ Scrubbing the Main Timeline (previewing while working) is not possible with Movie Clips, although it is possible with Graphic symbols. This makes Graphic symbols essential for animating cartoons. Eyes open, eyes closed — it's that big of a difference.

✦ Movie Clips can't (easily) be exported to video or other linear mediums. This is only significant if you plan to convert your .swf files to another time-based medium.

✦ A Graphic symbol's instance properties are controlled (modified) at design time, with the options available in the Property inspector. One advantage is that this is simple and sure, because you have an instant preview of what's happening. In addition, this information is embedded right in that particular instance of the Graphic symbol — meaning that, if it is either moved or copied, all of this information comes with it.

✦ A Movie Clip's instance properties can be controlled at design time or set with ActionScript. This gives it great flexibility, although it's a little more abstract to work with ActionScript. One advantage is that the actions do not need to be directly linked to the Movie Clip, which has the concurrent disadvantage that care must to be taken when moving Movie Clips that have visual qualities defined with ActionScript.

✦ Graphic symbols that are animated (have more than one frame) and are nested with other animated graphic symbols may have problems with synchronization. For example, if you have a pair of eyes that blink at the end of a ten-frame Graphic symbol, and you put the graphic symbol containing those eyes within a five-frame Graphic symbol of a head . . . the eyes will never blink. The head Graphic symbol will run from frame 1 to frame 5, and then return to frame 1, only displaying the first 5 frames of the eyes Graphic symbol. Or, if you nest the eyes Graphic symbol into a 15-frame head Graphic symbol, they will blink on frame 10, and then every 15 frames. That's ten frames, then blink, and then they loop back to frame 1; however, when reaching frame 5 this time, the movie they are in loops back to frame 1 (it's a 15-frame movie), and thus resets the eyes to frame 1.

✦ Movie Clips do not have the problem/feature described in the preceding bullet point. They offer consistent, independent timeline playback.

Editing Symbols

Because every instance of a symbol is linked to the original, *any* edit applied to that original is applied to every instance. There are several ways to edit a symbol, covered in the following sections.

Editing a symbol in Symbol Editing mode

Symbol Editing mode will open the stage and timeline of the selected symbol into the Document window, replacing the view of the current keyframe in the Main Timeline with a view of the first keyframe in the symbol's timeline. To edit a symbol in Symbol Editing mode:

✦ Select an instance on the Stage and choose Edit ⇨ Edit Symbols, or Edit Selected from the application menu.

✦ Select an instance on the Stage and right-click (Control+click), then choose Edit from the contextual menu.

Editing a symbol in a new window

This method is useful if you're working on two monitors and want to quickly open a new window to edit in while keeping a view of the Main Timeline open and available. On Macintosh these two windows are always separate, but you can click on either window to switch back and forth. On Windows, you can switch between these windows by choosing from the Window menu. To edit a symbol in a new window, select an instance on the Stage and right-click (Control+click), and then select Edit In New Window from the contextual menu.

Editing a symbol in place

The advantage of Edit In Place is that, instead of opening the symbol in a separate edit space, you can edit your symbol in context with the surrounding movie. Other elements present on the current keyframe are visible but dimmed slightly and protected from any edits you make on the selected symbol. To do this:

✦ Select an instance on the Stage and chose Edit ⇨ Edit in Place from the application menu.

✦ Select an instance on the Stage and right-click (Control+click) and then select Edit In Place from the contextual menu.

✦ Double-click the instance on the Stage.

Editing symbols in the Library

You might not have an instance of your symbol available to select for editing, but you can still edit it. Just edit it from the Library. Open your movie's Library with Window ⇨ Library (⌘+L or Ctrl+L) from the application menu. Select the symbol in the Library that you want to edit and do one of the following:

✦ Double-click the symbol's icon (not its name), in the Library list.

✦ Right-click (Control+click) then select Edit from the contextual pop-up menu.

✦ If you have opened the Symbol Properties dialog box (see Figure 6-4), you can move to Symbol Editing mode by clicking the Edit button.

Returning to the Main Timeline or scene

After you've edited your symbol, you'll want to go back to the scene to make sure that your changes work properly. Just do one of the following:

✦ Select Edit ➪ Edit Document from the application menu or use the shortcut keys — Control+D (or ⌘+D).

✦ Select the scene name in the left corner above the Stage view in the Document window, as shown in Figure 6-6.

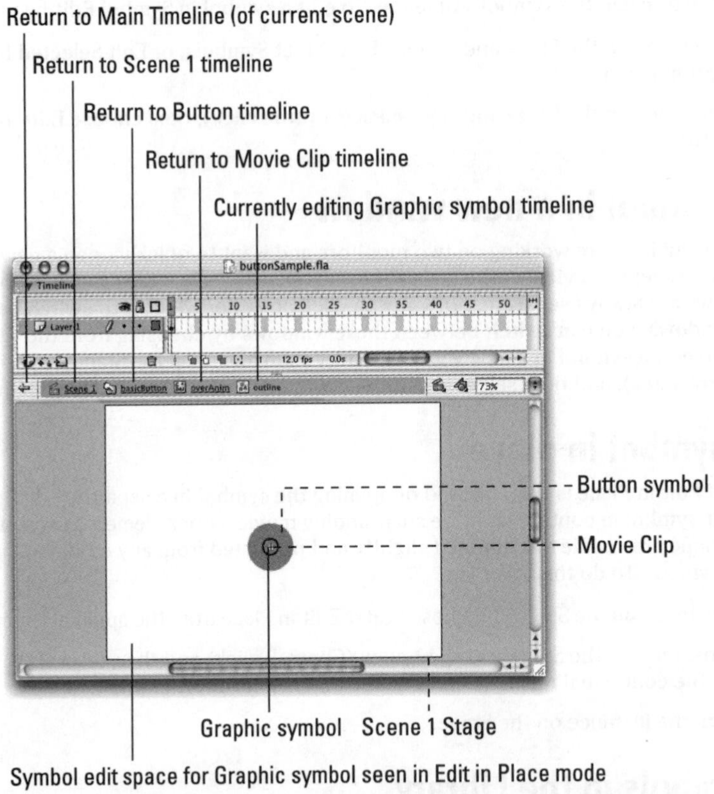

Return to Main Timeline (of current scene)

Return to Scene 1 timeline

Return to Button timeline

Return to Movie Clip timeline

Currently editing Graphic symbol timeline

Button symbol

Movie Clip

Graphic symbol   Scene 1 Stage

Symbol edit space for Graphic symbol seen in Edit in Place mode

Figure 6-6: The location label of the Document window is used to identify the current edit space and to return to the Main Timeline of the current scene.

Editing and Developing

Development in Flash occurs in one of two places: in the Main Timeline and on the Stage, or within a symbol, which has its own edit space and timeline. But how do you know when you are on the Stage or when you are in Symbol Editing mode? Here's one clue: At the upper left of the Document window is the location label area. If you're working on the main Stage, you'll see a single tab with the name of the scene. Unless you name your scenes, this tab should simply say, Scene 1 (or Scene 2). However, in Symbol Editing mode, a second tab appears to the right of the scene name: This tab displays the name and icon of the current group or symbol (Movie Clip, Graphic symbol, or Button symbol). If you have nested symbols, more tabs may appear. In this manner, you have convenient access to the hierarchy of your files, no matter how deeply you nest your symbols.

Symbol Editing mode is much like working on the regular Stage. You can draw with any of the drawing tools; add text, place symbols, import graphics, and sound, and use ActionScript. When you're done working with a symbol, you have an encapsulated element, whether it is a static Graphic, a Movie Clip, or a Button. This element can be placed as many times as needed on your Stage or within other symbols. Each time you place it, the symbol's entire contents and timeline (if it is a Button or a Movie Clip) will be placed as well, identical to the original symbol stored in the Library. Remember that even if you access Symbol Editing mode from an instance on the Stage, all changes that you make will propagate to every other instance derived from the original symbol in the Library. The only color changes that can be made to one instance at a time without affecting the other instances of the same symbol are those applied using the Color menu on the Property inspector, as explained in the following section on Modifying Instance Properties.

The Stage (if it is not Zoomed to fill the screen) is surrounded by a gray area. This is the Work area, which indicates the edges of the movie, as defined in the Document properties. The dimensions of any symbol, however, are not limited to the size of the Stage. If you make your symbols too large, when you place them on the Stage, portions that fall outside of the Stage will not be visible in the final movie (.swf), but they will still be exported and will add to the file size. Remember that it is always possible to scale a symbol instance to make it smaller than the original symbol if necessary.

Modifying Instance Properties

Every instance of a symbol has specific properties that can be modified. These properties only apply to the specific instance—not to the original symbol. Properties such as the brightness, tint, alpha (transparency), and behavior can all be modified. An instance can also be scaled, rotated, and skewed. As previously discussed, any changes made to the original symbol will be updated in each instance—this still holds true even if some of the instances also have properties that are modified individually.

Applying color effects to symbol instances

Each instance of a symbol can have a variety of Color effects applied to it. The basic effects are changes of brightness, tint, and *alpha* (transparency). Tint and alpha changes can also be combined for special effects. To apply color effects to a symbol instance:

1. Select the instance that you want to modify.

2. Select one of the options from the Color drop-down menu in the Property inspector. Figure 6-7 shows the basic color menu drop-down options.

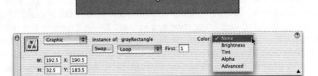

Figure 6-7: The Color menu has basic options to choose from. After a color effect is selected, the controls for that effect are available in the Property inspector.

The options available from the Color menu are as follows:

- **None:** No effect is applied.

- **Brightness:** Adjusts the relative brightness or darkness of the instance. It ranges from 100 percent (white) to –100 percent (black), the default setting is 0 percent (no visible change to instance appearance). Use the slider to change the value or just type a numeric value into the entry field.

- **Tint:** Enables you to shift the color of an instance. Either select a hue with the color picker, or enter the RGB values directly. Then, select the percentage of saturation (Tint Amount) by using the slider or by entering the percentage in the entry field. This number ranges from 0 percent (no saturation) to 100 percent (completely saturated).

- **Alpha:** Enables you to modify the transparency of an instance. Select a percentage by using the slider or by entering a number directly. The alpha percentage (or visibility setting) ranges from 0 percent (completely transparent) to 100 percent (no transparency).

- **Advanced:** When you select the Advanced option from the Color menu, a Settings button appears to the right of the menu. The Settings button invokes the Advanced Effect dialog box that enables you to adjust both the tint and alpha settings of an instance. The controls on the left reduce the tint and alpha values by a specified percentage, while the controls on the right either reduce or increase the tint and alpha values by a constant value. The current values are multiplied by the numbers on the left, and then added to the values on the right.

Cross-Reference

The Advanced option includes a range with negative alpha values. Potential uses for this capability, together with more information about using the Color menu, are detailed in Chapter 9, "Modifying Graphics."

Changing the symbol behavior of an instance

You don't need to limit yourself to the native behavior of a symbol. For example, there may be times when you want a Movie Clip to have the behavior of a Graphic symbol so that you can preview animation on the Main Timeline. You don't have to go through the extra effort of creating a new symbol — just change the behavior of the instance as needed:

1. Select the instance that you want to modify.

2. From the Behavior drop-down in the Property inspector, select the desired behavior. As shown in Figure 6-8, you can select Graphic, Button, or Movie Clip, which is the default behavior.

Figure 6-8: Using the menu on the Property inspector, you can change the behavior of a symbol instance at any time.

The more-complex uses of symbol instances are covered in Parts V, "Adding Basic Interactivity to Flash Movies," and VII, "Approaching ActionScript."

Swapping symbols

There may be times when you need to replace an instance of one symbol with an instance of another symbol stored in your project Library. Luckily, you don't have to go through and re-create your entire animation to do this — just use the Swap Symbol feature, illustrated in Figure 6-9. This feature only switches the instance of the symbol for an instance of another symbol — all other modifications previously applied to the instance will remain the same. Here's how to swap symbols:

1. Select the instance that you want to replace.

2. Click the Swap symbol button on the Property inspector, choose Modify ➪ Swap Symbol from the application menu, or right-click (Control+click) and choose Swap Symbol from the contextual menu.

3. Select the symbol that you want to put into the place of your current instance from the list of available symbols.

4. Click OK to swap the symbols.

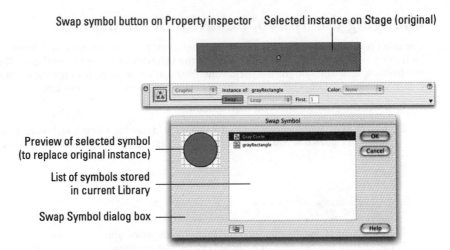

Figure 6-9: With a symbol selected in the Document window, click the Swap symbol button of the Property inspector to invoke this Swap Symbol dialog box.

Building Nested Symbol Structures

Understanding the various symbol types individually is the first step, but the next step is integrating these building blocks to create organized, optimized Flash projects that will be extensible, easy to edit, and fast to build. Although the workflow for different types of Flash projects are covered in depth in other parts of this book, we can synthesize the overview of different symbol types by walking through the steps of creating a Button symbol with some nested animation and Graphic symbols.

To demonstrate building an animated Flash movie from various symbol types, we made a Button symbol called basicButton that uses some raw shapes, some Graphic symbols, and some Movie Clips, all nested inside a Button symbol timeline.

On the CD-ROM

The completed source file (sampleButton.fla) for this series of demonstrations is included on the CD-ROM in the ch06 folder.

Converting a raw shape into a Graphic symbol

The best way to begin creating any graphic element is to first consider the final shape that you need and to try to find the most basic primitive shapes that you can use to build that element. Keep in mind that instances can be scaled, skewed, and adjusted with color effects. Instead of drawing three circles to make a snowman, you would make just one circle and convert that into a symbol so that you could build your snowman from scaled instances of just one symbol stored in the Library. A resourceful animator we know built a Christmas tree by reusing instances of a symbol he had made for a dog's tail in the same animation—a wagging tail and a tree all built from just one Graphic symbol stored in the Library! Raw graphics can be converted into Graphic symbols after they have been drawn, or you can first create a new Graphic symbol and then draw the raw shapes directly inside the Graphic symbol—either way, the end result is a contained visual element that will be stored in the Library to define any instances that you need to place in your movie.

To build the simple graphics used in basicButton, we can begin by converting a primitive shape into a Graphic symbol:

1. Select the Oval tool and set the fill color to green and the stroke color to black with a stroke height of 3.

2. Create an oval on the Stage, and hold down the Shift key while dragging out the shape to create a perfect circle. Double click the fill with the Arrow tool to select the stroke and the fill, and then use the Property inspector to set the width to 75 and the height to 75.

If you open the Library panel—Window➪Library (F11)—you will notice that the shape you've drawn is not visible in the Sort window because raw data is not stored in the Library.

3. While the stroke and the fill are both still selected, press F8 or choose Insert ➪ Convert to Symbol from the application menu.

4. In the Convert to Symbol dialog box, choose Graphic for the behavior and give the symbol the name **plainCircle,** then click OK. You should now see the plainCircle symbol with the Graphic symbol icon next to it in the Library.

Instances of this Graphic symbol can now be reused in your document in as many places as you need it just by dragging an instance onto the Stage from the Library panel. For the basicButton example, we will want to use an instance of plainCircle inside of a new Button symbol rather than on the main Stage, so you can delete the instance of plainCircle that is now on the Main Timeline.

Using Graphic symbols in a button

Button symbols are similar to Movie Clips that have a special timeline structure linked to mouse states. For a Button to take us to a new point on the Main Timeline or to load any other elements, ActionScript needs to be added to the Button instance.

Adding actions to buttons for more advanced interactivity is discussed in Chapter 18, "Understanding Actions and Event Handlers."

In this example the button will simply work as a structure for an animation that reacts to the mouse. Begin by inserting a new Button symbol.

1. Click the **New Symbol** button in the Library panel, choose Insert ➪ New Symbol from the application menu or use the shortcut keys — Control+F8 (⌘+F8).

2. In the Create New Symbol dialog box, choose **Button** as the behavior and for our example, give this symbol the name **basicButton.** Then click **OK.**

3. This Button symbol will now be stored in the Library and you will automatically be in Symbol Editing Mode in the Document window, ready to add some content to the button.

4. You will notice that the timeline shows four keyframes with labels that define the button state by mouse behavior: Up, Over, Down, and Hit. These various keyframes can have multiple layers and contain any visual element or sound that you want. The button states function as follows:

   - **Up:** Any elements placed in the Up keyframe will be associated with the button as it appears on the Stage when it is present but not activated by any mouse interaction.

   - **Over:** Any elements placed in the Over keyframe will be associated with the button when the mouse rolls over it on the stage, but as soon as the mouse rolls off the button it will revert to its Up state.

   - **Down:** Any elements placed in the Down keyframe will be associated with the button only when the mouse is over it and clicked and held down — as soon as the mouse is released, the button will revert to its Over state.

   - **Hit:** The Hit keyframe is actually never visible on Stage, but this instead defines the area of the button that is "sensitive" to the mouse. Whatever shape is present on this frame will be considered part of the button's *hit area*. It is important to note that it is better not to have holes or gaps in the hit area unless it is intended. For example, if you have text as a button, it is best to use a solid rectangle that matches the width and height of the total text area. Using the actual text would result in an irregular button hit area — whenever the mouse rolled into the space between letters the button would revert to its Up state and could not be clicked.

For this example, we will be creating animation to be placed into the various visible states, but the main shape of the button will always be consistent so we can begin by creating a layer to define the main shape of the button.

5. Rename Layer 1, **buttonOutline** and insert two frames (F5) after the first keyframe to create a span of three frames (for Up, Over, and Down).

6. With the Playhead set on the first keyframe, drag an instance of **plainCircle** onto the Button stage and make sure that it is now visible in the Up, Over, and Down states of the Button, but not on the Hit state.

7. Center the instance on the button Stage by using the Align panel (Ctrl+K or ⌘+K). Select the instance of **plainCircle** and copy it to the clipboard (Ctrl+C or ⌘+C).

8. Create a new layer and name it **hitArea.** Insert a blank keyframe (F7) on frame 4 (Hit). To paste the copy of **plainCircle** instance into the center of the blank Hit keyframe, use Paste in Place (Ctrl+Shift+V, or ⌘+Shift+V.) If you have done a straightforward paste instead, make sure that the instance of plainCircle is centered to the button Stage.

9. The timeline of your Button symbol should now look like Figure 6-10.

10. Return to the Main Timeline by using the location label.

11. If you don't see an instance of your basicButton on the stage of the Main Timeline, drag an instance out of the Library and place it on the first frame of the Main Timeline.

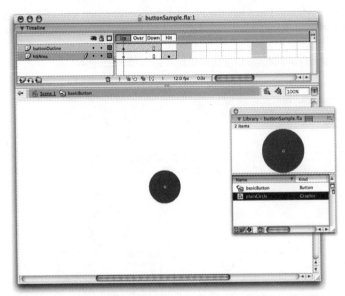

Figure 6-10: The Symbol Editing view of the basicButton timeline, with Up, Over, Down, and Hit states defined with instances of the plainCircle Graphic Symbol

Animating Graphic symbols in a Movie Clip

After you have created some Graphic symbols to define your basicButton, you can now start building some animation to add to it. Animation can be built by placing artwork in keyframes on the Main Timeline, but this limits how the animation can be used, and can make it difficult to add more elements to your project without disturbing the keyframe structure of the animation. If you need animated elements that can be reused, and quickly moved to different parts of the Main Timeline or placed into a Button symbol timeline, it is best to begin by creating a Movie Clip.

1. Click the New Symbol button in the Library panel, choose Insert ➪ New Symbol from the application menu or use shortcut keys Control+F8 (⌘+F8.)

2. In the Symbol Properties dialog box, choose Movie Clip as the behavior and for the basicButton example, give this symbol the name **overAnim.**

3. Create a new circle on the first frame of the Movie Clip timeline with a black stroke and no fill. Select the outline with the Arrow tool and use the Property inspector to set its width and height to 25. Then use the Align panel to center it on the Stage.

4. Convert this raw shape into a Graphic symbol (F8) with the name **outline.**

5. Insert a keyframe (F6) on frame 10 of the Movie Clip timeline so that you have a span of frames from frame 1 to frame 10 with the **outline** Graphic symbol visible.

6. Select the instance of **outline** on keyframe 10 and use the Property inspector to scale it up to 50 high and 50 wide.

7. Now select keyframe 1 and use the Property inspector to set a Motion tween. This will create an animation of the **outline** Graphic symbol scaling up from its original size to the larger size that you gave it in frame 10.

8. The timeline of your Movie Clip should now look like Figure 6-11.

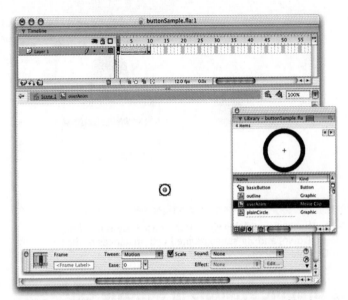

Figure 6-11: The Timeline of the Movie Clip **overAnim**, showing a Motion tween of the Graphic symbol **outline**, from frame 1 to frame 10

Adding a Movie Clip to a Button symbol

The final step in our example is to add the **overAnim** Movie Clip to the **basicButton** symbol. This is the secret to animated Button symbols — by nesting multi-frame Movie Clip animations into the single frames assigned to the Up, Over, and Down states of the Button symbol timeline, you can create different animated "reactions" as the mouse rolls over or clicks the button.

1. To go back inside your button and add animation, double-click the instance of basicButton on the Stage or the symbol in the Library.

2. Create a new layer inside the Button timeline and name it **outlineAnim**. Make sure that this new layer is above the original **buttonOutline** layer.

3. On the **outlineAnim** layer, insert a new keyframe (F6) on frame 2 (Over).

4. Drag an instance of **overAnim** from the Library onto the button Stage in the keyframe you just created, and use the Align panel to center it.

5. To ensure that the animation is only visible on the Over state of the button, make sure that the content on the overAnim layer only occupies one frame on the timeline. If the

overAnim symbol extends into frame 3, either insert a blank keyframe (F7), or remove a frame (Shift+F5) to keep it contained on frame 2.

6. Your Button symbol timeline should now look like Figure 6-12.

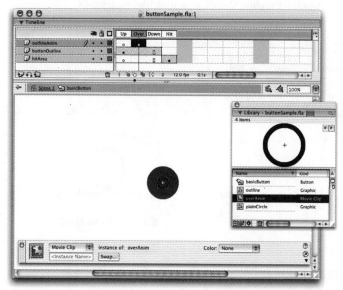

Figure 6-12: The timeline of Button symbol basicButton with the Movie Clip overAnim placed on the Over keyframe of the outlineAnim layer

You can test your Button symbol with this animation added to see how it is working, by pressing Control+Enter (⌘+Return) on the keyboard to view the movie (.swf) in the Test Movie environment. Now when you roll over the green button with your mouse, you should see the outline circles animate. Remember that you still only have one keyframe on your Main Timeline, so this demonstrates how both a Button symbol and a Movie Clip symbol will play back their own timelines even if they are placed into a single frame on another timeline. We still need to add some animation for the Down state of our basicButton, so close the .swf window to go back to the Button timeline.

Modifying a Movie Clip instance

Instead of creating an entirely new animation to display on the Down state of our basicButton, we can reuse the overAnim Movie Clip and change its appearance by adding a color effect to the instance.

1. Add a new layer to the Button symbol and name it **outlineAnimTint**.

2. Insert a blank keyframe on frame 3 (Down).

3. Drag an instance of the **overAnim** Movie Clip from the Library, or just copy the Over frame on the **outlineAnim** layer and paste it into the blank keyframe you just created.

4. Select the instance of the **overAnim** Movie Clip that you placed on the **Down** keyframe and with the Property inspector, select Tint from the Color effect menu. Choose white as the tint color from the Swatches that pop up from the color chip and then enter a tint value of 100 percent by using the slider or by typing into the value box.

5. Your Button symbol timeline should now look like Figure 6-13.

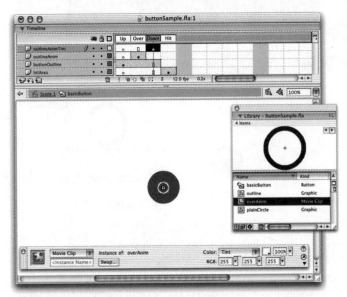

Figure 6-13: The basicButton timeline with an instance of the **overAnim** Movie Clip placed on the Down keyframe and modified with a Color Tint

Test your animated button again (Control+Enter, or ⌘+Return) and you will see that animation now appears when you click on the button. But instead of the original black that appears on the Over state, the animation for the Down (click) state is white. The three visible states of your button should now resemble Figure 6-14.

Up state   Over state   Down state

Figure 6-14: The finished animated button as it appears in the Up, Over, and Down states

You have seen how symbols are created, nested, and modified and you are probably realizing that this basic animated Button symbol was only the beginning.

On the
CD-ROM

If you would like to deconstruct another layered symbol structure, we have included a silly, but slightly more complex animated Button on the CD-ROM. You will find the source file, surpriseButton.fla, in the ch06 folder. Figure 6-15 shows the three visible button states and diagrams the basic symbol nesting.

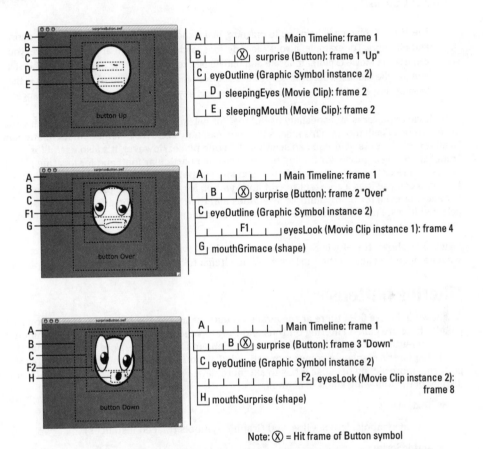

Note: Ⓧ = Hit frame of Button symbol

Figure 6-15: The animation as it appears in the three visible button states, Up, Over, and Down (left), with a diagram of the basic nested elements visible in each state (right)

As your symbol structures get more layered and complex it can be helpful to have some guidance when you are trying to navigate to a specific item in your project, or just trying to remember exactly how you organized things as you were building. Although careful use of layer names, frame labels and symbol names will be indispensable, the Movie Explorer introduced in this next section provides a great assistant for finding your way through the structure of any Flash document.

Using the Movie Explorer

The Movie Explorer panel is a powerful tool for deciphering movies and finding items within them. It can be opened from the application menu by choosing Window ➪ Movie Explorer (Alt+F3 or Option+F3).

Tip
The Movie Explorer will help you to organize, build, and edit your projects with greater clarity and efficiency. For example, if your client decides to change the font at the last minute, you can use the Movie Explorer to locate and update all occurrences of the original font—this still requires the tedious work of selecting the text boxes and manually choosing a new font in the Property inspector, but at least you can find the text in your project that needs to be changed.

The Movie Explorer is an especially useful tool for getting an overview and for analyzing the structure of a Flash movie. This means that you can now see every element in its relationship to all other elements, and you can see this all in one place. However, it's also useful for troubleshooting a movie, for finding occurrences of a particular font, and for locating places where you refer to a certain variable name in any script throughout a movie. As an editing tool, you can use it as a shortcut to edit any symbol, for changing the properties of an instance, or even for doing multiple selections and then changing the attributes of the selected items. Furthermore, the Find function is an incredible timesaver when working on complex project files.

Figure 6-16 shows the Movie Explorer as well as the Movie Explorer Settings dialog box, which you can open by clicking the Customize Which Items to Show button in the Movie Explorer.

Filtering buttons

As shown in Figure 6-16, there are several icon buttons across the top of the Movie Explorer panel. These are called Filtering buttons and they have icons representative of their function. Click any button to toggle the display of those elements in your file. Note, however, that the Movie Explorer's display becomes more crowded as you select more buttons—and that it performs more slowly because it has to sift more data. From left to right, the buttons filter the display of the following kinds of content:

- ✦ Text
- ✦ Button symbols, Movie Clips, and Graphic symbols (placed instances)
- ✦ ActionScript
- ✦ Video, Sounds, and Bitmaps (placed instances)
- ✦ Frames and Layers
- ✦ The Movie Explorer Settings dialog box

Note also the Find field, which enables you to search through all items currently displayed in the Movie Explorer to find specific elements by typing in the name of the symbol, instance, font name, ActionScript string or frame number.

The Display list

Below the icons is a window with the Display list. Much like Windows Explorer, or the Mac Finder, the Movie Explorer displays items hierarchically, either by individual scene or for all scenes. These listings are expandable, so if you have selected the Text button, an arrow (or on Windows, a plus [+] sign), will appear beside the name of any scene that includes text. Clicking the arrow (or plus sign) displays all the selected items included in that scene. At the bottom of the Display list, a status bar displays the full path for the currently selected item.

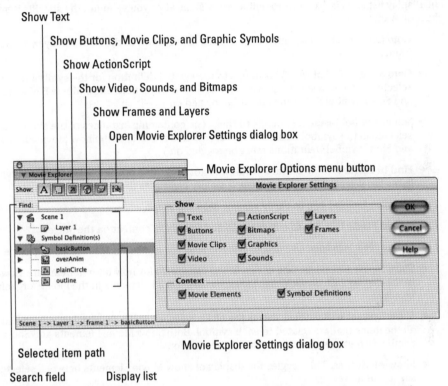

Figure 6-16: The Movie Explorer displaying the file structure for the button example created in the previous section

In Figure 6-17, the Text filter button has been selected. As shown, clicking the arrow sign beside the Text icon in the Display list shows the complete text, including basic font information.

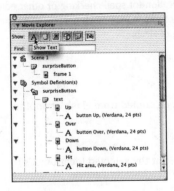

Figure 6-17: The Movie Explorer for the **surpriseButton** example that is included on the CD, with the Text filter button chosen to view text and font information inside the file

The Movie Explorer Options menu

The Options menu is accessed by clicking the options triangle, in the upper-right corner of the Movie Explorer panel. These commands allow you to control how much detail is shown in the Display list and also to perform edits or revisions after you've found the specific items that you want to modify:

✦ **Goto Location:** For a selected item, this transports you to the relevant layer, scene, or frame.

✦ **Goto Symbol Definition:** This jumps to the symbol definition for the symbol that's selected in the Movie Elements area. (For this to work, both Show Movie Elements and Show Symbol Definitions must be toggled on.)

✦ **Select Symbol Instances:** Jumps to the scene containing instances of the symbol that is selected in the Symbol Definitions area. (For this to work, both Show Movie Elements and Show Symbol Definitions must be toggled on.)

✦ **Find in Library:** If the Library Window is not open, this opens the Library and highlights the selected item. Otherwise, it simply highlights the item in the Library.

✦ **Rename:** Enables you to easily rename selected items.

✦ **Edit in Place:** Use this to edit the selected symbol in context on the Stage.

✦ **Edit in New Window:** Use this to edit the selected symbol in Symbol Editing mode.

✦ **Show Movie Elements:** One of two broad categories for how filtered items are viewed in the Display List, Show Movie Elements displays all elements in the movie, organized by scene.

✦ **Show Symbol Definitions:** This is the other category of the Display List, which shows all the items that are related to each symbol. Both Show Movie Elements and Show Symbol Definitions may be displayed simultaneously.

✦ **Show All Scenes:** This toggles the display of Show Movie Elements between selected scenes, or all scenes.

✦ **Copy All Text to Clipboard:** Use this command to copy text to the clipboard. Text may then be pasted into a word processor for editing, spell-checking, and other textual operations not found in Flash.

Unfortunately, getting text back into Flash is not as easy as copying it out to the clipboard. If you copy a large amount of text out to another application for spell-checking or other editing, you will have to manually update individual text blocks in your Flash document to integrate any changes that were made to the text outside of Flash.

✦ **Cut:** Use this command to cut selected text.

✦ **Copy:** Use this command to copy selected text.

✦ **Paste:** Use this command to Paste text that has been copied from Flash or another application.

✦ **Clear:** Use this command to clear selected text.

✦ **Expand Branch:** This expands the hierarchical tree at the selected location; it's the menu equivalent of clicking the tiny plus (+) sign or right-facing arrow.

✦ **Collapse Branch:** This collapses the hierarchical tree at the selected location; it's the menu equivalent of clicking the tiny minus (–) sign or down-facing arrow.

✦ **Collapse Others:** This collapses the hierarchical tree everywhere except at the selected location.

✦ **Print:** The Movie Explorer prints out, with all the content expanded, displaying all types of content selected.

You can also access the commands found in the Movie Explorer options menu via the contextual menu.

The contextual menu

Select an item in Movie Explorer and right-click (Ctrl+click) to invoke the contextual menu related to that particular item. Non-applicable commands are grayed-out, indicating that these are not available in context with the item selected.

Figure 6-18 shows the contextual menu of the Movie Explorer. Among the most useful commands is the Goto Location option at the top. When you can't find an item (because it's on a masked layer or is invisible), this command can be a lifesaver.

When planning or looking for ways to improve a project, the Movie Explorer can provide an excellent map to the structure and function of what you've already accomplished. Whenever relevant, print out the Movie Explorer; this document can function as a project file for finished work, providing a reference of all scripting and Movie Clip placement. As such, it can make it much easier to return to a project months later. It can also facilitate collaboration amongst developers, whether they share the same studio or need to communicate long distance. Finally, for all the reasons listed in this chapter, the Movie Explorer can also be used as a tool for both learning and teaching.

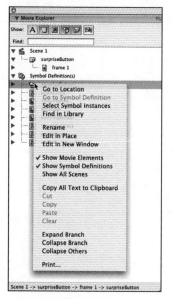

Figure 6-18: The Movie Explorer's contextual menu

Summary

✦ The Library can be organized with folders and symbols, and assets can be rearranged without breaking their linkage to instances deployed within the project.

✦ Symbols are the building blocks of Flash. They save you time, reduce your file size, and add flexibility to your movies. When ActionScript is used to control symbol behavior or display, symbols are considered as objects within an object-oriented authoring environment.

✦ Flash handles imported sounds, bitmaps, and video assets as symbols. They reside in the Library, and instances of these assets are deployed within a Flash project.

✦ In addition to imported assets, there are three other kinds of symbols that can be created within Flash: Graphic symbols, Movie Clips, and Button symbols.

✦ Movie Clip symbols and Button symbols have timelines that play independently from the Main Timeline. Although Graphic symbols also have their own timelines, they are still tied to the Main Timeline and require a frame for every frame of their own timeline that will be visible.

✦ Using symbols within a project is as easy as dragging an asset or symbol from the Library and onto the stage, although it's usually best to have a new layer ready and to have the appropriate keyframe selected.

✦ Symbols can be edited in a number of ways. Any edits to a symbol are reflected by all instances of that symbol throughout the project.

✦ The Property inspector offers a central control for modifying symbol instances. The color and transparency of individual instances of a symbol can be modified, via the color effect controls. Furthermore, symbol types can be reassigned using the behavior drop-down menu, and specific instances can even be replaced with other symbol instances by using the Swap symbol button.

✦ The Movie Explorer is a powerful tool for navigating movies and finding specific items within them.

✦　　✦　　✦

Applying Color

Before we get into the specifics of applying color with Flash, we want to discuss some of the fundamental theory behind working with color that's destined for display on the Web. In the process, we also introduce some cool resources that may be helpful to you, both in concert with Flash and as bona fide Web resources on their own. We explore the options for choosing and modifying your color palette in the Swatches panel and how the Flash tools access color. Then we show you how to work with the new Property inspector menus and the Flash Swatches panel and Mixer panel to select, change, mix, and apply solid colors, gradients, and even bitmap fills.

As some users will remember, the multi-panel interface of Flash 5 made it almost as daunting to explain the advanced color controls, as it was to use them. Fortunately, Flash MX has streamlined the panel system so that editing a gradient fill no longer requires opening three different panels. Color controls are now much more integrated and easy to find.

The new method for specifying bitmap fills in the Mixer panel eliminates the need to place an imported image on the Stage to be broken apart and sampled before it can be used as a fill pattern for other elements.

Flash symbol instances can be tweened so that they will change color over time. Although this involves color, the selection of colors for the original symbol used in the keyframes of the tween is merely a rudimentary application of fill and line color, as described in this chapter. Applying the Color Effect controls available in the Property inspector to symbol instances is discussed in Chapter 9, "Modifying Graphics." Methods for controlling color with ActionScript and the Flash Color Object are covered in Chapter 25, "Controlling Movie Clips."

Introducing Color Basics

Computer monitors display color by using a method called *RGB color*. A monitor screen is a tightly packed array of pixels arranged in a grid, where each pixel has an address. For example, a pixel that's located

✦ ✦ ✦ ✦

In This Chapter

Introducing color basics

Working with
Flash color

Organizing the Color
Swatches panel

Creating and importing
custom color sets

Using the Color Mixer
panel to modify colors

Adding transparency
to strokes and fills

Making and applying
Gradient fills

Selecting bitmap fills

✦ ✦ ✦ ✦

16 rows down from the top and 70 columns over from the left might have an address of 70,16. The computer uses these addresses to send a specific color to each pixel. Because each pixel is composed of a single red, green, and blue dot, the colors that the monitor displays can be "mixed" at each pixel by varying the individual intensities of the red, green, and blue color dots. Each individual dot can vary in intensity over a range of 256 values, starting with 0 (which is *off*) to a maximum value of 255 (which is *on*). Thus, if red is *half-on* (a value of 127), while green is *off* (a value of 0), and blue is fully *on* (a value of 255), the pixel appears reddish-blue or purple.

The preceding paragraph describes unlimited, full color, which is sometimes referred to as *24-bit color*. However, some computer systems are still incapable of displaying full color. Limited color displays are either 16-bit or 8-bit displays. Although a full discussion of bit-depth is beyond the scope of this book, it is important to note several points:

✦ 24-bit color is required to accurately reproduce photographic images and smooth color transitions in gradients.

✦ Because 8-bit and 16-bit systems are color challenged, they can only display a limited number of colors, and they must dither-down anything that exceeds their *gamut,* which is their expanse of possible colors. *Dithering* means that, in order to approximate colors that are missing from the palette, the closest colors available are placed in close proximity to fool the eye into seeing a blended intermediate color. This can result in unwanted pixel patterns.

✦ Some image formats, such as GIF, use a color palette which limits them to 256 colors. This is called *indexed color.* Indexed color is ideally suited for reproducing vector graphics that have solid fills and strokes, but will often create noticeable *banding* (uneven color) when applied to photographic images.

✦ Bitmap images will not accurately translate an indexed color palette, so matching color between GIF images and JPEG images can be unpredictable because the JPEG will expand the original indexed palette of a GIF file to include colors that may not be within the Web-Safe color palette.

✦ Calibration of your monitor is essential for accurate color work. For more information check out www.colorpar.com.

Discussing Web-Safe color issues

Web-Safe color is a complex issue, but what it boils down to is this: The Mac and PC platforms handle their color palettes differently, so browsers don't have the same colors available to them across platforms. This leads to inconsistent, unreliable color—unless you're careful to choose colors for Web design from the Web-Safe palette. The Web-Safe palette is a selection of 216 colors that's consistent on both the Mac and the PC platforms for the Netscape, Explorer, and Mosaic browsers. The Web-Safe palette contains only 216 of 256 possible indexed colors, because 40 colors vary between Macs and PCs. Use the Web-Safe palette to avoid color shifting and to ensure greater design (color) control.

By default, the Swatches panel (Ctrl+F9) loads with Web 216 colors, and if the swatches are modified, this swatch palette can always be reloaded from the options menu at the upper right of the panel. Web 216 restricts the color palette to Web-Safe colors. However, *intermediate colors* (meaning any process or effect that generates new colors from two Web-Safe colors); such as gradients, color tweens, transparent overlays, and alpha transitions; will not be constrained to Web-Safe colors.

But when there are over 16 million possible colors, why settle for a mere 216? If you do settle for 216 colors, remember that the value of color in Web design (or any design or art for that matter) has to do with color perception and design issues, and numbers have little to do with that.

So what's the point? Consider your audience. Choose a color strategy that will enable the majority of your viewers to view your designs as you intend them to appear. For example, if your audience is the public schools, then you must seriously consider limiting your work to the Web-Safe palette. (If you choose this route, then hybrid swatches may enable you to access colors that are technically unavailable, while remaining within the hardware limitations of your audience.) On the other hand, if you're designing an interface for a stock photography firm whose clients are well-equipped art directors, then color limitations are probably not an issue. But in either case, understand that no one will see the exact same colors that you see. The variables of hardware, calibration, ambient light, and environmental decor are insurmountable.

Using hexadecimal values

Any RGB color can be described in hexadecimal (hex) notation. This notation is called hexadecimal because it describes color in base-16 values, rather than in base-10 values like standard RBG color. This color value notation is used because it describes colors in an efficient manner that HTML and scripting languages can digest. Hex notation is limited to defining *flat color,* which is a continuous area of undifferentiated color. In HTML, hexadecimal is used to specify colored text, lines, background, borders, frame cells, and frame borders.

A hexadecimal color number has six places. It allocates two places for each of the three color channels: R, G, and B. So, in the hexadecimal example 00FFCC, 00 signifies the red channel, FF signifies the green channel, and CC signifies the blue channel. The corresponding values between hexadecimal and customary integer values are as follows:

16 integer values: 0 1 2 3 4 5 6 7 8 9 10 11 12 13 14 15

16 hex values: 0 1 2 3 4 5 6 7 8 9 A B C D E F

The Web-Safe values in hexadecimal notation are limited to those colors that can be described using combinations of the pairs 00, 33, 66, 99, and FF. White is described by the combination FFFFFF, or all colors *on* 100 percent. At the other end of the spectrum, Black is described by the combination 000000, all colors on 0 percent, or *off*. A medium gray would be described by the combination 666666, or all colors on 40 percent.

Using custom Web-Safe colors

There are a couple of valuable tools used to create custom-mixed Web-Safe colors. They build patterns composed of Web-Safe colors that fool the eye into seeing a new color. These are essentially blocks of preplanned dithers, built out of the Web-Safe palette, that augment the usable palette while retaining cross-platform, cross-browser color consistency:

✦ **ColorSafe** is an Adobe Photoshop filter plug-in that generates hybrid color swatches with this logic. ColorSafe (Mac and Win) is available directly from BoxTop software at www.boxtopsoft.com. Furthermore, the ColorSafe demo is included in the software folder of the *Flash MX Bible* CD-ROM.

✦ **ColorMix** is an easily used online utility that interactively delivers hybrid color swatches, much like ColorSafe. It is free at www.colormix.com. After you mix a custom dithered swatch, you can download it and save it as a GIF for import into Flash.

After you've created some custom swatches and have saved them to a folder on a local machine, the new Flash MX options of importing directly to your document Library and specifying a bitmap to apply as a fill from the Color Mixer panel makes using any custom color or pattern easier than ever. Figure 7-1 shows the Web-Safe colors used to create a custom-dithered swatch and the mixed custom color as it displays when imported to Flash.

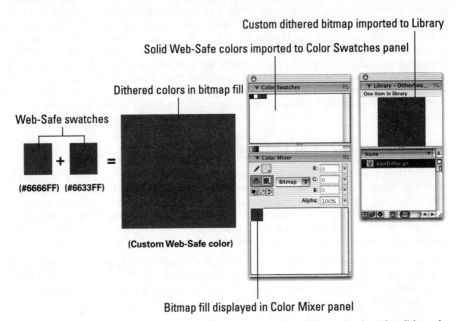

Figure 7-1: Two Web-Safe colors mixed to create a custom dithered color. The dithered GIF file was imported to the Flash Library and the solid colors derived from the GIF were added to the Color Swatches panel.

Note that the dithered GIF color is only displayed in the Mixer panel under the Bitmap fill option, while the solid Web-Safe colors can be added directly to the Swatches panel. The steps for adding colors from a GIF file to the Swatches panel are described in the "Importing custom palettes" section later in this chapter, while the steps for applying a bitmap fill are described in the section on "Selecting bitmap fills" at the end of this chapter.

Using color effectively

According to some developers, the issue of color on the Web has been seriously confused by the misperception that people can set numbers to give them Web-Safe colors, and that — if they do that — they will have *good* color. Have you ever noticed that as soon as someone starts designing onscreen, it's as if he's forgotten anything he may have learned about legibility and design on the printed page? While getting caught up in the excitement of layered patterns and multicolored text, there is a tendency to overlook the obvious problem that the end result is entirely illegible. Although we all want to be creative and unique, there are certain color rules that can actually be more liberating than they are restrictive.

Although unconventional design choices can add an element of surprise, a touch of humor, or just a visual punch that will help your layout stand out from the rest, it is vital that you don't compromise your end goal. When you get noticed, you want to deliver you message successfully—whether that message is "Buy this product" or just "Hey, this is a cool site." If you start to carefully deconstruct the layouts that grab your attention, you will probably find that there are consistencies to the choices that were made in the design, regardless of the content. You'll begin to notice that even the most bizarre or cutting-edge designs share certain features that make them eye-catching and memorable.

Much of the underlying strategy in a design may be transparent, or not *consciously* perceived by the viewer. But don't make the mistake of thinking that individual preference is completely unpredictable. The secret to successful design is leveraging the unconscious visual language that we are physically and culturally conditioned to respond to. Individual viewers may have specific preferences for certain colors or styles, but they will all recognize and understand many of the same visual conventions.

Although learning to apply all these conventions and to integrate them into your own design style can take years of study and practice, there are some fundamental "truths" that will serve you well, no matter how long you've been designing:

✦ **Color is relative.** Humans perceive color relative to the context of other colors in which the color is set. Most art schools offer at least one course about color. They often start with color experiments that are conducted with pieces of colored paper. An early assignment is to make three colors look like more than three colors—by placing small scraps of the same color on larger pieces of different colors. Students are always amazed to learn how much a person's perception of a single color is influenced by placing it on those different-colored backgrounds. Figure 7-2 shows how the same shade of gray can appear lighter or darker depending on the background color. The lesson is that color is *not* an absolute—it never was before computers, and it never will be to the human eye.

Figure 7-2: The same gray circle displayed on different background values will appear to be darker or lighter by comparison.

✦ **Contrast is king.** Only one thing is more important than color: contrast. Contrast is the relative difference in lightness or darkness of items in a composition. Here's a good test: Take a colorful design that you admire and render it to grayscale. Does it still work? Contrast is a major factor in good color composition. Figure 7-3 shows different amounts of contrast created by relative differences in value.

Figure 7-3: Varying levels of color contrast determine legibility and emphasis.

To ensure a strong design, it can be helpful to work on your initial layouts in grayscale. When you have contrast working for you, then you can start to add color with the confidence that the design will not be visually muddy—or hard to read—because of poor contrast. Often, the same color scheme can be a disaster or a huge success, all depending on the contrast created in the design. The concept of contrast also applies to other characteristics of your design—size, texture, even mood. Try to use contrast wherever you want to create emphasis or add drama. But remember: If you make everything huge and flashing red, or extra-small and pale gray, you will no longer have any contrast. The strength of contrast is in variety. Figure 7-4 shows how contrast can be achieved by varying the size and style of your text.

low **MEDIUM** **H I G H**
contrast contrast *contrast*

Figure 7-4: Contrast can also be achieved by adding variety to the size and shape of elements.

✦ **Less is more.** Keep in mind that the power of contrast should always be used in moderation. White text on black backgrounds can be great for headlines, but after more than a few paragraphs, it will make the reader feel as though her retina is actually being burned by the text on the page—one of the best ways to keep someone from actually reading your copy. Also, don't be afraid of empty space; the impact of individual elements is often dependent on having a little room to "breathe." One element in a striking color will be much more effective than a whole page filled with competing colors.

✦ **Start at the beginning.** Visual hierarchy is the best "secret weapon" in any designer's arsenal. Although you may not be sure what the most important element is in your design, if you don't give your reader a place to start, chances are you'll lose his attention. By deciding on the order of importance for elements on your design and then using other design conventions of contrast, size and color to guide the reader through your layout, you'll create motivation for him to actually stick around long enough to absorb your message. Think of your content as the elements of a good story: In order to make the narrative compelling, you have to have a catchy intro, a juicy middle, and a rewarding ending or payoff. You might argue that you want to let readers make their own choice about where to start (like starting at the back of a novel), but if you don't create a visual structure, the reader won't feel empowered to make any choices. Presented with a big muddle of uncertain order, he will most likely move on to a design where he can find the beginning, middle, and end at a glance, before deciding what he wants to read first. Figure 7-5 shows an example of poorly defined visual hierarchy (top) and an example with a few more clues for the reader (bottom). Of course, these examples don't even use color, but as mentioned earlier, it can be best to plan the structure of your layout before adding color to support it.

Here's the bottom line: Color can help a good design look *great,* and when used with strategy it can help to engage the viewer and sell your message. But no amount of color can save a poorly planned design, so consider the underlying structure, contrast and visual hierarchy of your layout before adding color.

Figure 7-5: Giving visual cues to your readers about the order of importance of different elements helps them to quickly get oriented in your layout.

If you need some inspiration or want to take the guesswork out of choosing color schemes, there are some tools that you can use to generate harmonious color families for your designs. There are innumerable books on color theory and design but these online sources can get you started with some ideas:

✦ **Color Schemer** is a handy utility that will generate a palette of harmonious colors for any key color that you want to start with. Although the full version of the software is for Windows only, the online version is equally helpful and can be used regardless of what platform you are working on. It is free at www.colorschemer.com/online.

On the CD-ROM

We have included a 15-day trial version of Color Schemer 2.0 in the software folder of the *Flash MX Bible* CD-ROM.

You can generate lists of RGB or Hexidecimal colors from the Web-Safe palette and also choose to darken or lighten all colors in the palette until you find the exact color set you like. Color Schemer also offers a basic color tutorial that will help you understand how harmonious palettes are generated. You can find it at www.colorschemer.com/tutorial.html.

✦ **Hot Door Harmony** is a powerful color plug-in for Adobe Photoshop that will help you to dynamically create complementary and analogous color schemes using the classic Red Yellow Blue color wheel for Web-Safe, Mac, Windows, or full-color palettes. Swatches can be edited using RGB, CMYK, HSL, HSV, or Lightness color controls. Saved swatches can be exported to Photoshop or Illustrator or exported in Color Table format for direct import into the Flash Swatches panel. The Mac demo version can be downloaded for free from `www.hotdoor.com/harmony`.

Note   At the time of this writing, Hot Door Harmony was not available for OS X.

Working in the Color Swatches Panel

The most commonly used source for selecting colors as you work in Flash is the Color Swatches panel (Ctrl+F9). Although the controls for loading or modifying specific palettes are only available on the main Color Swatches panel, both the Toolbox and the Property inspector give you quick pop-up menus to access whatever colors are currently loaded. The Color Swatches panel is included in all the default Flash panel sets, but if it isn't visible, you can always find it in the application menu under Window ➪ Color Swatches. Figure 7-6 shows the swatches for the default Web 216 colors as they display in the pop-up menu on the Toolbox (A), the Property inspector (B), and in the main Swatches panel (C). The Swatches panel is shown with the options menu that is invoked by clicking on the top-right corner of the panel.

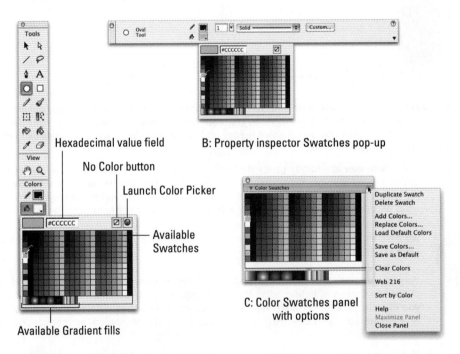

Figure 7-6: The default color palette as it displays on the Toolbox (A) and Property inspector (B) pop-up menus and on the Color Swatches panel (C)

Tools that create lines include the Line tool, Pencil, Ink Bottle, Pen, and — because they draw outlines around the fills — both the Oval and Rectangle tools. Each tool relies upon the Stroke color button, which appears in both the Toolbox and in the Property inspector.

In addition to tools that create lines, there are also tools that create fields of color or fills. The fill tools include the Paintbrush, Paint Bucket, Oval, and Rectangle tools. Each of these tools is accompanied by the Fill color button, which appears in the Toolbox and in the Property inspector. Although the Fill Swatches pop-up is similar to the Stroke pop-up, it has one significant difference: It has another row of swatches at the bottom, which are gradient swatches — click one to fill with a pre-built gradient style.

For all drawing tools, basic color selection is accomplished by clicking either the Stroke or Fill color buttons, and then choosing a color from the Swatches pop-up. This pop-up displays the same Swatch set that is currently loaded in the Color Swatches panel. It also includes a hexadecimal color-entry box — which facilitates keyboard entry, as well as cut-and-paste of hex values. Depending upon the tool selected, the Swatch menu available from the Toolbox may display a No Color button above the solid Swatches as well as a button that launches the Color Picker.

The color chips displayed on the Toolbox will always display the most recently selected stroke and fill colors, while the Property inspector will only display the color chips relevant to the active tool or the currently selected item.

Note　You cannot apply a fill or stroke of None (or No Color) to an item that has already been drawn. Instead, remove the fill or stroke by selecting it and using Edit ➪ Clear or pressing the Backspace (Delete) key.

If the color you want is not available in the current Swatch menu, you may opt to invoke the Color Picker by clicking the Color Picker button. Alternatively, you may also open the Color Mixer panel to create a new color and add it to the currently loaded selection of Swatches. The Color Swatches panel allows you to load, add, delete, and modify various color sets for individual documents. Whatever changes are made to the Swatches panel will be saved with the document (.fla) that is currently active.

Color Swatches panel options

Think of the Color Swatches panel (Figure 7-6) as a way to organize your existing swatches and to manipulate the display of colors that are available in the other panels. Use the Swatches panel to save color sets, import color sets, and reorder or change selected colors. The options menu of the Swatches panel provides controls that are used to manipulate and administrate individual swatches as well as various color sets:

✦ **Duplicate Swatch:** Use this to duplicate a selected swatch. This can be useful when you want to make a range of related color swatches by duplicating and then editing subsequent swatches from the Color Mixer panel.

New Feature　You can now duplicate a selected swatch with just one click — as you move the pointer into the space below the current solid swatches set, the pointer icon changes from a Dropper into a Paint Bucket. Just click and a duplicate of the currently selected swatch will be added to the color set.

✦ **Delete Swatch:** Botched a swatch? Select and delete it here.

✦ **Add Colors:** Opens the Import Color Swatch menu, which is a simple dialog box used to locate, select, and import color sets. Add Colors retains the current color set and appends the imported color set at the bottom of the panel.

Caution

Be careful about creating huge color sets! In some cases, the Swatch color pop-ups may extend beyond the visible screen and you'll have to use the Swatches panel to be able to scroll to choose colors that are hidden off-screen. This can happen if you add colors from a complex GIF image to the default Web 216 set.

✦ **Replace Colors:** Also opens the Import Color Swatch menu. However, Replace Colors replaces the current color set when it loads the selected color set. If the current set has not been saved, it will be lost.

✦ **Load Default Colors:** Clears the current color set and replaces it with the default Web 216 swatch palette. Again, if the current set has not been saved it will be lost. Flash MX allows you to change the specification for your default color palette if you prefer not to use Web 216. (See Save as Default.)

✦ **Save Colors:** Opens the Export Color Swatch Menu, which is used to name and save color sets to a specific location on your hard drive. Color sets may be saved in either the Flash Color Set (.clr), or Color Table (.act) format that can be used with Macromedia Fireworks and Adobe Photoshop. Gradients can only be imported and exported from Flash using the .clr format.

✦ **Save as Default:** Saves the current Swatch set as the default set to be loaded in the Swatch panel for all new Flash documents.

✦ **Clear Colors:** Removes all colors currently loaded in the Swatch panel, leaving only the black and white swatches and a grayscale gradient.

✦ **Web 216:** Loads the Web-Safe palette. This option makes it safe to mess with the swatches in Flash, because no matter what you do, you can always just reload this original default color set.

Tip

You can override the default Web 216 color set by switching the Color Mixer panel to either the RGB or HSB (Hue, Saturation, Brightness) color spaces. You can then mix your own fresh colors, add them to the Swatches, and save that palette as the default. Another alternative is to locate the Photoshop Color Tables on your hard drive (or download a specialty color table from the Web) and replace the default set with a broader gamut.

✦ **Sort by Color:** This organizes the swatches by hue rather than by mathematical number and can visually be a more logical way to find colors in your current set. Note, however, that once you apply this sort there is no way to toggle back to your original swatch order. So it is best to save any custom palette first before sorting so that you have the option of going back to the other display if you prefer it. Figure 7-7 shows the Web 216 palette as it appears sorted numerically (left), and as it appears sorted by hue (right).

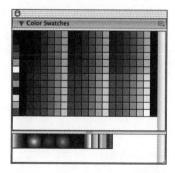 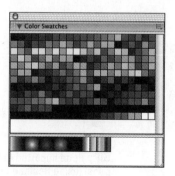

Web 216 swatches in default order   Web 216 swatches sorted by color

Figure 7-7: The default Web 216 palette as it appears sorted by number (left), and as it appears when sorted by hue (right), using the Sort by Color option

Importing custom palettes

The option of loading custom swatches is helpful if you're developing a Flash project that you want to match with a predefined palette—whether this is out of necessity or just for inspiration. For example, you can match your Flash elements to a corporate logo or to the range of hues in a photo that you love. In addition to loading the colors in a specific GIF file, Flash allows you to load RGB color palettes from other graphics applications, which have been saved as Color Tables (in the .act format).

Loading a custom GIF color palette

To simplify your Flash Swatch selection to match the colors in a company logo or other GIF image, follow these steps:

1. Clear the currently loaded color set by choosing Clear Colors in the Color Swatches panel options menu.

2. Choose Add Colors from the Color Swatches panel options menu and, in the Import Color Swatch dialog box, specify the GIF file that you want to define the imported color set.

3. Flash will load the colors from the GIF image into the Color Swatches panel and you can then save the document (.fla) to keep these colors as the loaded set.

4. To organize the loaded color set in the Color Swatches panel by hue, choose the Sort by Color option. You can always add or delete swatches from this new set.

Our sample source GIF image and the resulting imported Swatch palette are shown in Figure 7-8.

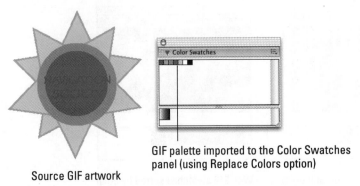

GIF palette imported to the Color Swatches
panel (using Replace Colors option)

Source GIF artwork

Figure 7-8: This is the simple logo GIF file that was specified as the
source for a custom Swatch palette. The resulting swatches match
the logo colors exactly.

Creating and loading a custom Color Table

If you want to load a color palette that will match the hues in a photograph, you can generate
a Color Table in Adobe Photoshop or Macromedia Fireworks.

1. Open a bitmap image (.jpeg, .tif or .psd) in Photoshop and convert the image to
   indexed color (Image ⇨ Mode ⇨ Indexed Color). (Bitmaps saved in .gif format are
   already in indexed color mode.)

2. Next set and save a Color Table by going to Image ⇨ Mode ⇨ Color Table. Leave the
   Table setting in the Color Table dialog box on Custom and select Save.

3. Give the Color Table a name that you will remember ("Sky Colors") and save the .act
   file to a folder where you can find it again. Creating a Custom Palettes folder on your
   system, where you can store and organize any of the Color Tables or source GIFs that
   you may want to use again, is a good idea.

4. Open a Flash document (.fla) and from the Color Swatches panel options menu choose
   Add Colors if you want new colors added to the currently loaded set (or Replace Colors
   if you want to use only your new colors).

5. From the Import Color Swatch dialog box, browse to your Color Table (.act) file and
   select it. Flash will load the new colors into the Swatch panel and you can then sort
   and save this set with your document.

Our sample source bitmap image and the resulting Color Table loaded into the Color
Swatches panel are shown in Figure 7-9.

**On the
CD-ROM**

In our example, we created a Color Table from an image of a cloudy sky. You can find the
source bitmap (.gif) image and the Photoshop Color Table (.act) file, along with a Flash document (.fla) that has the .gif imported and the color palette loaded in the Sky Palette folder
in the ch07 folder on the CD-ROM.

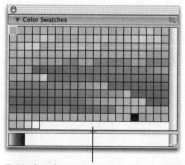

Source bitmap image

Color Table (.act) imported to the Color Swatches
panel (using Replace Colors option)

Figure 7-9: An image used to generate a Color Table (.act) in
Photoshop, and the resulting color set loaded into the Flash
Swatch panel

Refer to the color insert pages to see the Web 216 and sky colors swatch samples discussed
in this section printed in color.

Using the Color Mixer Panel

Think of the Color Mixer panel as the "boss" of the Color Swatches panel. The Swatches panel
handles the color inventory and serves up the available colors, but the Mixer panel has the
power to modify those colors and add the variations to the current set. Flash MX has introduced a nifty new Color Mixer panel that makes choosing and modifying all types of strokes
and fills easier than ever.

In Flash MX, the Fill panel is no longer needed to select a Color style. The new Color style
menu available on the Color Mixer panel allows you to choose the type of color pattern that
you want to work with — including solid colors, linear and radial gradients, and bitmap fills.

As shown in Figures 7-10 through 7-13, the Color Mixer panel enables you to create new
colors, with settings in any of three color spaces — RGB, HSB (Hue, Saturation Brightness),
or hex — using either the condensed Color bar or the expanded "rainbow" Color Selection
field. All colors are handled with four channels, which are RGBA (Red, Green, Blue, Alpha);
these values can be individually adjusted using the Color value fields and slider controls. The
new Tint slider control allows you to dynamically shift your current color darker or lighter.
Whatever fill or stroke color is currently selected in any of the Swatch menus will be displayed in the Mixer panel where it can be modified.

As shown in Figure 7-11, new colors can be added to the current palette loaded in the Color
Swatches panel — just select Add Swatch from the Color Mixer panel options and the color
will be added to the colors currently loaded in the Swatches panel.

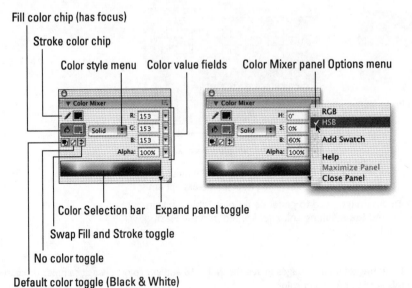

Fill color chip (has focus)

Stroke color chip

Color style menu   Color value fields   Color Mixer panel Options menu

Color Selection bar   Expand panel toggle

Swap Fill and Stroke toggle

No color toggle

Default color toggle (Black & White)

Figure 7-10: The Color Mixer panel and the Options menu

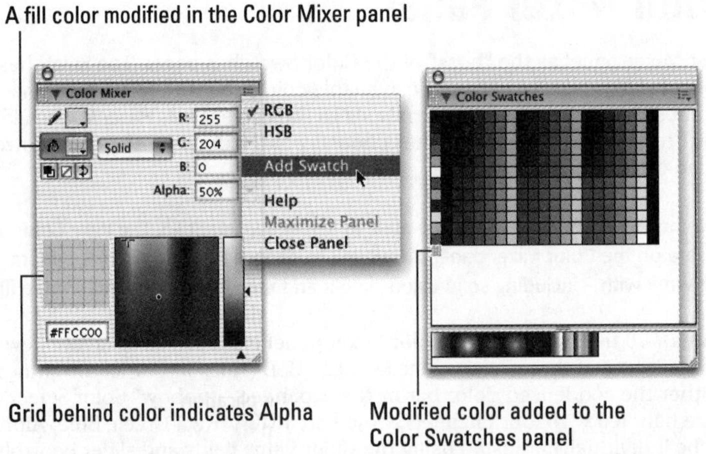

A fill color modified in the Color Mixer panel

Grid behind color indicates Alpha   Modified color added to the
Color Swatches panel

Figure 7-11: Colors modified in the Mixer panel can be added to the
Swatches panel.

Any color swatch selected in the Swatches panel will be loaded into the Mixer panel as a
starting point only—modifications made in the Mixer will not change the original color in the
Swatches panel. The new color or gradient that you create in the Mixer will only be added as
a new swatch when you select Add Swatch from the options menu. You can always edit your
custom color by selecting the new swatch, but the modified version will be treated as a new
color and will also have to be added to the Swatches panel separately.

Caution The colors you create and add to the Swatches panel will be saved with the document (.fla) as long as you do not reload the default set or overwrite the loaded Swatch set. If you want to save your custom mixed colors, remember to save the Flash color set (.clr) to a folder using the Save Colors command in the Swatches panel before you reload the default Web 216 color set or Replace Colors with a new palette.

Expanded Color Mixer panel

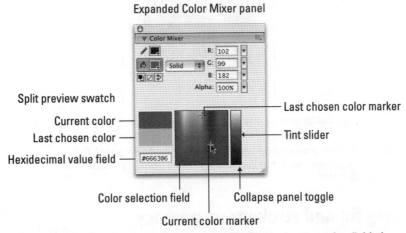

Figure 7-12: The expanded Color Mixer panel showing the Hex value field, the split preview swatch, and the new Tint slider control

When selecting a color from the Swatches pop-up palette in the Mixer panel, the cursor converts to a Dropper tool that allows you to sample color from anywhere in the interface just by dragging the Dropper and clicking the color you want to pick up. You can pluck colors from icons in the Flash application, from any element that you have in the Document window and even from elements on your desktop or in other application windows that are currently open. Figure 7-13 shows the Dropper being used to sample the yellow from the Scene icon on the Flash Document window to be used as a fill color. The same Dropper feature is available from any of the Swatches pop-ups, but the colors you select this way will not be stored in the Swatches panel unless you use the Color Mixer panel option to Add Swatch.

 Caution To pick up colors with the Dropper outside of the Flash application itself, be careful not to release the mouse button while you move the mouse from the Swatches in the Color Mixer panel to the other color that you want to sample. If you release the mouse before moving it to the color you want to sample, you will only be able to pick-up colors from inside the Flash application.

Dropper used to sample color from the Flash scene icon

Document window

Mixer panel

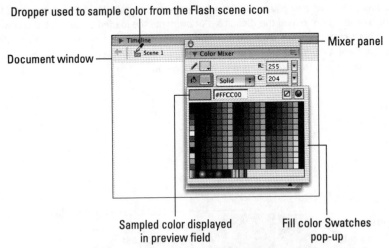

Sampled color displayed
in preview field

Fill color Swatches
pop-up

Figure 7-13: When the Swatches pop-up is selected in the Mixer panel, the cursor converts to a Dropper tool that can pick up colors from any visible element on your desktop.

Adjusting fill and stroke transparency

The Alpha control in the Color Mixer panel is used to adjust the transparency of stroke and fill colors, either to modify a selected shape or to create a new color that can be added to the Color Swatches panel.

> **Note**
>
> The Color Mixer panel alpha control is used only to adjust stroke and fill colors. To dynamically change the transparency of individual symbol instances, the Color effect options in the Property inspector are used as described in Chapter 9, "Modifying Graphics." The color and transparency of Movie Clips can also be controlled with ActionScript using the Color object, as described in Chapter 25, "Controlling Movie Clips."

There are two ways to change the alpha value for a selected color: Either drag the Alpha slider until the preview display looks right, or enter a numeric value directly in the alpha value box. Numeric entry is useful when you already know what level of transparency is required, while the slider is useful for interactive fiddling with transparency to get it just right — as indicated in either the stroke or fill color chip. To see a larger preview of your alpha adjustments, expand the Mixer panel so that you can see the large preview box to the left of the expanded Color Selection field. The larger preview display also gives you a split view that allows you to compare the last chosen setting with the current setting.

In Figure 7-14, a stroke color and a fill color have both been adjusted to 50 percent alpha and then added to the Swatches panel. While the Alpha slider is being dragged to a new setting, the preview displays the original 50 percent alpha value (bottom) as well as the current 25 percent alpha value (top). The rectangle below the panels shows the 50 percent alpha stroke and fill applied to the shape. The Flash Grid has been turned on (View ➪ Grid ➪ Show Grid), so that the alpha is easier to see — on a flat white background, the color just looks lighter rather than transparent.

Alpha value field

Most recently modified fill color

Most recently modified stroke color   Modified colors added to the Swatches panel

Alpha Slider control

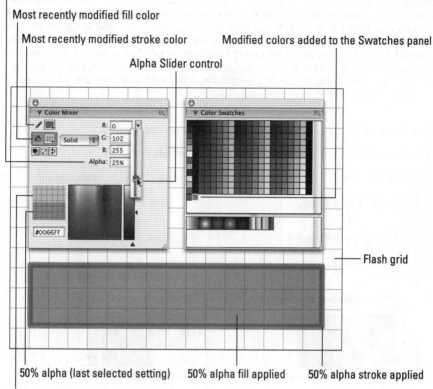

Flash grid

25% alpha preview (current setting)

50% alpha (last selected setting)   50% alpha fill applied   50% alpha stroke applied

Figure 7-14: The Color Mixer panel expanded to show the large preview swatch. The adjusted stroke and fill colors that are added to the Color Swatches panel are shown below the other solid fill colors in the current palette.

Caution   Although transparency can be a seductive effect, use it sparingly because it can cause your movie (.swf) to take a performance hit, especially if there are a lot of overlapping animated transparencies. If you can achieve the effect that you want by using a Tint instead (fading to a solid color), then save the alpha effect for graphics that you need to layer on top of other elements or textured backgrounds.

Working with gradient fills

Gradients are composed either by blending two or more colors together in bands across a plane (linear gradient) or from the center to the edge of an object in concentric circles (radial gradient). These two basic styles of gradient fill can be modified to create virtually unlimited variations. Creating custom gradients in Flash 5 required skillful juggling of three different panels, but Flash MX has centralized the editing tools in the Color Mixer panel, making it so easy that we should soon suffer from a plague of snazzy gradient fill effects.

Figure 7-15 shows the new gradient editing controls in the Mixer panel, with the preview display for a linear gradient (left) and for a radial gradient (right). When working with linear gradients, the position of the Color Pointers on the Edit bar will correspond to control points on the blend from left to right. When used in conjunction with radial gradients the Gradient Edit bar corresponds to the radius, or a slice from the center out to the edge, of the circular gradient. Color Pointers at the left end of the Gradient Edit bar represent the center — or inside — of the radial gradient, while Color Pointers at the right end represent the outside border. The active Color Pointer is identified by a black fill in the pointer, unselected Color Pointers have a white fill in the pointer.

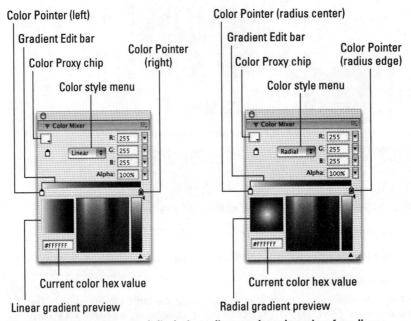

Figure 7-15: The Mixer panel displaying edit controls and preview for a linear gradient (left) and for a radial gradient (right)

The main Swatches panel and any of the fill Swatches pop-ups display the pre-built linear and radial gradients that are included in the default palette. To edit an existing gradient swatch, just select it from the any of the fill Swatches pop-ups or select it from the main Swatches panel, and it will be loaded into the Mixer panel where the relevant controls will be displayed automatically. The other option is to start by choosing a gradient style from the central menu on the Mixer panel to load a basic linear or radial gradient that can be modified. When you create a custom gradient in a document, your settings will appear when you go back to the Mixer panel menu. To start with an unmodified default gradient, just select one from the fill Swatches palette. Figure 7-16 shows the two methods of selecting a gradient style to modify.

Cross-Reference   The Transform Fill tool was previously an option of the Paint Bucket tool, but is now an independent tool used to scale, rotate, and skew gradient or bitmap fills after they have been applied to an item. This tool is introduced in Chapter 9, "Modifying Graphics."

Color style menu

Fill color Swatches pop-up

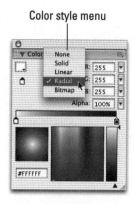
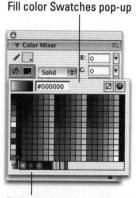

Default gradient swatches

Figure 7-16: The various default gradient styles can be selected from any of the fill Swatches pop-ups, or one of the two basic grayscale gradient styles can be selected from the central Mixer panel menu.

Controlling gradient fill colors

The colors in a gradient and the distribution of blending are adjusted by sliding the Color Pointers along the Gradient Edit bar in the Mixer panel. These pointers are the access points to the key colors that define the gradient. After you click on a pointer to make it active, you can assign the color that will be blended in its range, either by using the Swatches pop-up from the Color Proxy chip or by choosing a color in the Color Selection field. The value fields and the color slider controls can also be used to modify an assigned color in a gradient the same way as any solid color.

You can adjust the pattern of the blend by clicking and dragging any of the Color Pointers to slide them to new positions along the Edit bar. You can add additional Color Pointers to the gradient range by clicking anywhere along the Edit bar. These additional pointers will create new control points in the gradient that can be dragged to new positions or assigned new colors to define the gradient pattern. To remove Control Pointers simply drag them downward away from the Edit bar, they will detach and disappear, taking their assigned color and control point with them. Figure 7-17 shows a basic radial gradient modified with the addition of a new Color Pointer. To save a custom gradient to your Swatches panel, choose Add Swatch from the Mixer panel options menu.

By selecting an element on the stage, you can also apply or dynamically modify its gradient fill using the Mixer panel. When an item is selected in the Document window, you will see the current fill displayed in the fill color chip on the Property inspector. To load the fill into the Mixer panel, select it from the Swatches pop-up preview in the Property inspector. After the selected fill is loaded in the Mixer panel, any changes you make will update on the item dynamically. Remember to select Add Swatch from the options menu if you want to store the new gradient in the Swatches panel. Figure 7-18 shows the display of the Mixer panel when a shape is selected with a solid fill (left). When the fill is loaded in the Mixer panel, any changes made will be applied directly to the selected shape (center and right).

Added Color Pointer

Two point gradient   Three point gradient

Figure 7-17: A radial gradient from gray to black (A),
modified with the addition of a central Color Pointer
assigned a color of white (B)

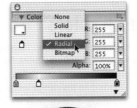

Original Solid Fill   Loading Custom Radial Fill   Modifying Radial fill by adding
                                                          another Color Pointer

Figure 7-18: Selecting a filled shape (left), changing the fill style in the Mixer panel (center),
and dynamically editing the fill (right)

Tip   To make it easier to see how a gradient looks in a selected shape, you can toggle off the
display of the selection mesh by using Shift+Ctrl+E (Shift+⌘+E).

Using alpha settings with gradients

As mentioned previously, all the normal Color sliders and value fields will apply to control points on a gradient. You may have noticed already, that this means you can add alpha to the blend range of any gradient. To create a soft transition between a bitmap or a patterned background and a solid color, you can create a gradient from a 0 percent alpha to a 100 percent alpha of the same solid color. To demonstrate just one application of this feature, we will walk through the steps of adding the appearance of a vignette (or softened edge) to a photograph imported into Flash:

1. Import a bitmap into Flash and place it on the Stage, then lock the bitmap layer.

2. Create a new layer above the Bitmap layer and name it **gradient** (see Figure 7-19).

Figure 7-19: Imported bitmap placed on the Stage with a new layer above it for the gradient

3. Open the Mixer panel and set the gradient style to radial, or select the default grayscale radial gradient from the fill Swatches panel. Set the stroke color to black with a stroke height of 2.

4. Select the Gradient layer and then use the Rectangle tool to drag out a rectangle on the Stage that is the same size as the photograph on the layer below (see Figure 7-20).

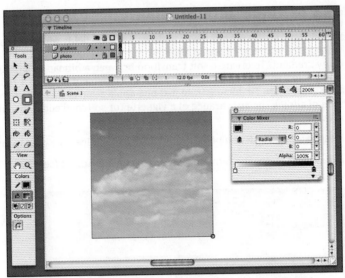

Figure 7-20: Drawing a rectangle with a radial gradient fill and a black stroke of 2; rectangle dragged out to match the size of the photograph on the layer below

5. Select the fill of the rectangle and then select the left (white) Color Pointer on the Edit bar and assign it a color of black and an alpha value of 0 percent (see Figure 7-21).

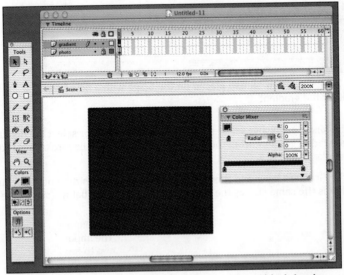

Figure 7-21: Both Color Pointers assigned a color of black for the selected gradient fill

6. Use Shift+Ctrl+E (Shift+⌘+E) to hide the selection mesh and adjust the position of the Color Pointer by sliding it along the Edit bar, until you like the way the blend looks on top of the photo (see Figure 7-22).

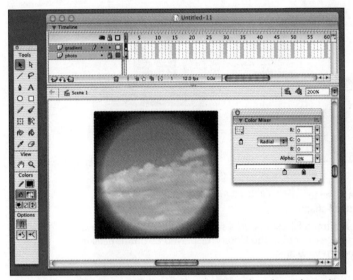

Figure 7-22: The final gradient can be previewed as the Color Pointer is moved to adjust the edge of the alpha blend.

Selecting bitmap fills

The other feature that the Flash MX Color Mixer panel can brag about is the menu option for selecting bitmap fills. Instead of having to import and break apart a bitmap in Flash before it can be sampled to use as a fill, Flash MX allows you to browse to any bitmap in the Library or elsewhere on your system and choose a bitmap that will automatically be tiled at 100 percent scale to fill a selected shape.

To apply a bitmap fill directly to an existing shape:

1. Select the shape fill with the Arrow tool.

2. Open the Mixer panel and choose Bitmap from the central fill style menu.

3. If you have bitmaps stored in your current Document library, they will be available from the Bitmap Preview area of the Mixer panel. Simply click on the thumbnail of the bitmap that you want to apply and it will automatically fill the selected shape.

4. If you do not have any bitmaps available in the current document, selecting Bitmap from the fill style menu in the Mixer panel will launch the Import to Library dialog box, where you can browse your system and specify a bitmap to be imported and applied as a fill.

Figure 7-23 shows a selected shape with a bitmap fill applied, chosen from the available thumbnails in the Mixer panel Preview area.

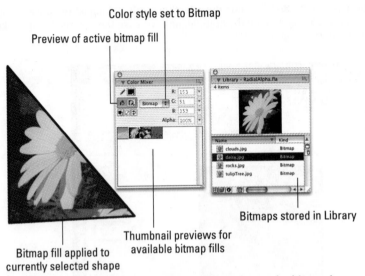

Color style set to Bitmap

Preview of active bitmap fill

Bitmaps stored in Library

Thumbnail previews for available bitmap fills

Bitmap fill applied to currently selected shape

Figure 7-23: A bitmap fill applied to a selected shape. The bitmap is chosen from images stored in the Library, displayed as thumbnails in the Mixer panel Preview area.

Cross-Reference   The Transform Fill tool can be used to scale, rotate, or skew the bitmap fill as described in Chapter 9, "Modifying Graphics."

Working with Droppers, Paint Buckets, and Ink Bottles

So far in this chapter, we've introduced the various ways of controlling your palette and setting stroke and fill colors on items selected with the Arrow tool. There is one other set of tools used for applying colors and fills that will make modifying existing artwork even easier. You have already seen the Dropper tool in action when selecting a color from any of the Swatches pop-ups — where the Arrow pointer automatically converts to the Dropper and allows you to pick up a color from any visible element to be loaded into the active fill or stroke color chip.

This same tool can be summoned at any time by clicking on the Eyedropper tool (I) icon in the Toolbox. You will notice that when the Eyedropper tool is used to pick up a fill color or bitmap, it immediately converts into the Paint Bucket (K). This tool will allow you to dump the selected fill into any other shape just by clicking on it. If you have a fill or stroke selected when you invoke the Eyedropper tool, any other fill or stroke that you pick up with the Dropper will be applied instantly to the selected item.

When you sample a stroke with the Eyedropper tool, it converts into an Ink Bottle (S), which can be used to apply the stroke to any other item. If the item already has a stroke, it will be modified and if the item did not previously have a stroke, the Ink Bottle will add one.

The various options and methods for putting these tools to best use are covered in Chapter 9, "Modifying Graphics," where we also take a close look at the Transform Fill tool and the new Free Transform tool.

Summary

✦ The science of color on the computer is far from accurate. There are many variables involved in the presentation of color over the Web. One variable revolves around the issue of Web-Safe color.

✦ Web-Safe color does not ensure "good color"—there are many strategies that go into applying color skillfully, but contrast can be the defining factor that makes a design either succeed or fail.

✦ Although Flash doesn't directly support color scheme plug-ins, colors can be loaded into the Swatches panel from source GIF files or custom Color Table (.act) files, or they can be sampled with the Dropper tool to load them into the active color chip.

✦ The Swatches pop-up available from the Toolbox or from the Property inspector gives immediate, intuitive access to the currently loaded swatches and all custom colors that have been added to the main Color Swatches panel. It also permits direct insertion of hexadecimal values.

✦ The Color Swatches panel is used to save out color sets, import color sets, and reorder or change selected colors and gradients.

✦ The new MX configuration of the Color Mixer panel allows it to be used to create and modify gradients and select bitmaps to be used as fills, in addition to adjusting the alpha and tint of new or existing colors. New colors can be added to the current swatches, to make them available in any of the Swatches pop-ups.

✦ The Eyedropper, Paint Bucket, and Ink Bottle tools work together to select and apply fill and stroke colors. The options for these tools are discussed along with the new Transform Fill and Free Transform tools in Chapter 9, "Modifying Graphics."

✦ Advanced color capabilities of Flash include color tweening, scriptable color, and negative alpha. These topics are discussed in depth in subsequent chapters.

✦   ✦   ✦

Working with Text

For designers who love fonts, Flash is a dream come true. Even if you never plan to animate anything, you may want to use Flash simply to see your fonts displayed how you want them, wherever and whenever you need them. Of course, there are a few exceptions to this unequivocal freedom, but Flash MX has the options to give you text styles to meet a range of project needs.

Because Flash is a vector program, it enables the integration of most fonts within the movie without any fuss. For most text content, this means that fonts don't have to be rendered into bitmap elements — the .swf files that Flash publishes (or exports) will include all the necessary information for the font to display properly on every browser.

In this chapter, we introduce the various text types available in Flash and explain how and why they are used. We also look into some basic font-management issues and give you strategies for handling fonts in your project files (.fla) as well as in your published movies (.swf).

Flash MX has introduced some brilliant new Static text options for handling vertical and right-to-left reading text. We will look at these new options along with the other character and paragraph controls now available in the Property inspector. This chapter also touches on some special considerations for working with international character sets.

Cross-Reference For coverage of the new TextScroll component used to add a pre-built scroll bar to Dynamic text fields, refer to Chapter 20, "Making Your First Flash MX Project." For a detailed explanation of using the TextField object for controlling editable text with ActionScript, refer to Chapter 31, "Applying HTML and Text Field Formatting."

Considering Typography

Typography is the formal term for the design and use of text. Although Flash offers the capability to deliver finely designed typography to your audience, too many Flash artists are typography challenged. Unfortunately, no matter how well Flash renders text, it can't disguise bad design or make up for a designer's lack of knowledge about working with type. As with color, sound, animation or any other specialized area of production, the amount you can learn about typography is really only limited by your interest.

✦ ✦ ✦ ✦

In This Chapter

Finding resources to help you learn more about typography

Understanding Flash text field types

Creating text boxes and choosing text behavior

Using the Property inspector to specify styles and alignment

Controlling font export and display

Troubleshooting font management

Reshaping and manipulating text characters

✦ ✦ ✦ ✦

Although many people can get by without ever studying typography formally, they are missing the chance to leverage one of the most powerful and complex tools of graphic design. Although computers have changed the way that final designs are created, they have not changed the fundamental principals and uses of typography. The best part about studying typography is that your knowledge will be equally useful no matter what medium or computer application you are working with.

Because type is such an important and long-standing aspect of design, there are innumerable resources available to guide and inspire you. Just wander through the graphic design section of any bookstore or do a search online for *typography,* and you will be able to find something that can introduce you to the basics or help you push your skills further.

In this chapter, we use some common typography terms that are familiar to most people who have designed with text. Although a more detailed explanation of the source and meaning of these terms is beyond the scope of this book, you will be able to follow visually how things like kerning and leading apply to text in Flash.

If you are unfamiliar with typography, here are some excellent resources to get you started:

✦ *The Non-Designer's Type Book* by **Robin Williams.** This is a must-read (and study) for anyone who really wants to take her Flash Web designs to the next level.

✦ *The Elements of Typographic Style* by **Robert Bringhurst.** This is a manual of typography and book design that concludes with "appendices of typographic characters and currently available digitized fonts [and] a glossary of terms."

✦ *Jan Tschichold: A Life in Typography* by **Ruari McLean.** This is an inspiring and informative biography of the life and work of one of the most influential masters of modern typography.

✦ *Type in Use* by **Alex W. White.** This book offers a concise primer on the history of publication design and includes many useful examples of effective strategies for designing pages with type.

✦ *The End of Print* by **Lewis Blackwell and David Carson.** This colorful book charts the creative evolution of one of the most legendary mavericks of contemporary graphic design.

 Jane Nisselson's tutorial on *The Human Interface* provides an eye-opening perspective on how we read and interpret visual information. Through Virtual Beauty, her New York-based studio, Nisselson applies her understanding of the limitations of sensory bandwidth to designing interactive interfaces and motion graphics for broadcast. Nisselson's tutorial is in the Bonus_Tutorials.pdf in the Bonus_Tutorials folder on the CD-ROM.

Text Field Types in Flash

Flash MX allows you to include text in your projects in a variety of ways. Often one Flash project will contain several different text types, each suited to a specific kind of content. The steps for creating text fields and editing type will be described later in this chapter, but we will begin here with an overview of the three main text types used in Flash: Static, Dynamic, and Input.

You will find examples of each style of text field in the textSamples.fla file in the ch8 folder of the CD-ROM.

The Text tool is used to create text boxes and to enter and modify type. When a text box is first created in Flash MX, the default text type is Static, but it can be assigned a different text type or behavior in the Property inspector at any time. Subsequent text fields will automatically be assigned the most recently selected behavior. This makes it quicker to create a series of text fields of the same type, but it means you should double-check the behavior if you need a variety of different text boxes with different behaviors.

Figure 8-1 shows the basic controls that appear in the collapsed Property inspector when the Text tool is selected from the Toolbox.

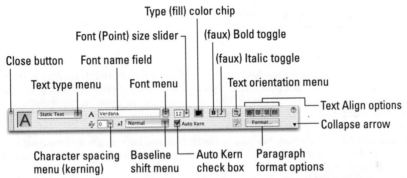

Figure 8-1: The basic text options that appear in the (collapsed) Property inspector when the Text tool is active or a Static text block is selected with the Arrow tool

Static text boxes are used for display type or text content created at author-time (in the .fla), that won't change at runtime (in the .swf). Dynamic text fields are used to hold text content that is generated at runtime from a live data source, or text that will be updated dynamically, such as weather or sports scores. Input text fields are exactly what they sound like, fields created for text that is entered at runtime by users. Input text fields are used whenever we need users to do things like enter passwords or answers to questions.

 For the purpose of brevity we often refer to both Dynamic and Input text fields as *editable text fields,* because both of these text field types can be modified at runtime (unlike Static text blocks, which can be modified only at author-time.)

Static text blocks

Although the term *Static text* sounds limiting, this type of text block actually offers the most design options at author-time. Static text blocks can be scaled, rotated, flipped, or skewed, and they can be assigned a variety of colors or alpha levels while preserving individual editable text characters. Static text can also be animated or layered like any other graphic element in Flash. By default, Flash embeds the outlines for any fonts used in Static text for display on other machines, but you may also choose to specify a generic device font to reduce the size of your final movie or to eliminate anti-aliasing or smoothing on small text.

As described later in this chapter, you can select sections of Static text and enter a URL in the link field to create a text link to a Web page or to an e-mail address in your Flash movie without any additional coding.

By default, Static text boxes are horizontal, and they can be either *expanding* boxes, that allow you to keep typing along one line as it extends to fit the type, or fixed-width boxes that will constrain your text box to a set width and auto-wrap the text to fit. These two types of text fields will look the same when selected by clicking once with the Arrow tool, but by double-clicking you can see the text box handle icon that indicates the current behavior of the box. Figure 8-2 shows the respective icons for expanding or *label* text and for fixed-width or *block* horizontal Static text.

Figure 8-2: The handle icons for expanding (left) and for fixed-width (right), horizontal Static text boxes

Flash MX has also added the option for both left-to-right and right-to-left reading vertical text blocks. Have you ever wanted a line of text characters to stack vertically, but found it tedious to use a hard return between each letter? Thanks to vertical text, you can now easily switch your type alignment from horizontal to vertical, with characters either stacked or rotated. This eliminates the headache of trying to read sideways while editing type—with a simple menu choice you can switch from vertical to horizontal and back again with no hard returns or freehand rotations required. Figure 8-3 illustrates how the vertical text option changes the orientation of Static text.

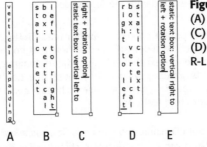

Figure 8-3: Vertical text box orientations:
(A) Vertical expanding, (B) Vertical fixed-height L-R,
(C) Vertical fixed-height L-R with rotate option,
(D) Vertical fixed-height R-L, (E) Vertical fixed-height
R-L with rotate option

Aside from giving developers authoring in English more options for cool layouts, this feature makes Flash much friendlier for developers authoring in language sets that require vertical or right-to-left character flow. As described later in this chapter, the alignment of vertical text can also be modified to anchor it to the top, center, or bottom of the text box.

Although the default orientation for text in Flash is horizontal and left to right, you can modify the Vertical Text settings in the Editing tab of the Flash Preferences dialog box, as shown in Figure 8-4 (File ⇨ Preferences or, in OS X, Flash ⇨ Preferences.) To make all new Static text fields automatically orient vertically, select the Default Text Orientation check box, and to change the default text flow, select the Right to Left Text Flow check box. You also have the option of disabling kerning on vertical text by selecting the No Kerning check box.

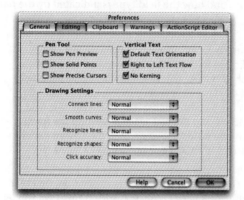

Figure 8-4: Changing the default Vertical Text settings in the Preferences dialog box

Editable text fields: Dynamic and Input

Editable text begins like Static text as a *block,* but when converted to Dynamic or Input behavior, these editable text boxes are referred to as *text fields* — probably because they are often used as empty fields in which users can input text, as with a form or a password entry. Think of an editable text field as an empty window with a name attached to it. When text or data is sent to the Flash movie (swf), it is sent to a specific named text instance, which ensures that it will be displayed in the proper window or editable text field. Dynamic text fields can display information supplied from a database, read from a server-side application, or loaded from another Flash movie (or another part of the same Flash movie).

Because Dynamic text fields are generated or edited on the fly (at runtime), there are limitations on how much you can control the appearance of the text at author-time. You cannot apply special formatting or shape modifications (such as skewing or kerning) directly to Dynamic text fields. However, Dynamic text field instances are recognized by Flash MX in the same way as other Movie Clip instances, so you can assign a name to a Dynamic text field instance and use ActionScript to control its appearance.

Caution

The Flash 5 convention of naming editable text fields using a variable name only has been modified by the introduction of the Flash MX TextField object. In Flash MX, all editable text fields are recognized as nameable instances of the TextField object. It is important to differentiate these two naming conventions. Variable names should only be used to identify editable text fields for backwards compatibility with older versions of the Flash Player, and the variable name or var attribute of a text field should not be the same as its instance name.

For an introduction to ActionScript objects, please refer to Chapter 24, "Knowing the Nuts and Bolts of Code," and for a detailed explanation of using the TextField object, refer to Chapter 31, "Applying HTML and Text Field Formatting."

Dynamic text can be authored horizontally in expanding or fixed-width fields, but they cannot be rotated or modified with the Vertical text option. Figure 8-5 shows how a Dynamic or Input text field will display when unselected (top) and how the field type is indicated by the handle icons when the text is double-clicked.

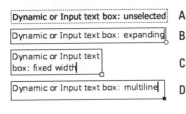

Figure 8-5: An unselected editable text field is indicated in the authoring environment by a dashed outline (A), when double-clicked the field will display either an expanding handle icon (B), or a fixed-width handle icon (C). If the text field is multiline and the text extends beyond the frame of the field (for scrolling), then the square handle changes from white/empty to black/filled (D).

When the Render text as HTML button in the Property inspector is toggled on, rich text formatting such as links and font styles indicated in Dynamic text with HTML tags will be recognized by Flash and applied when the text is rendered in the Flash movie (.swf).

The Text Tool and Property Inspector

Although Flash is neither an illustration program like Freehand, nor a traditional page-layout program like Quark, its text-handling capabilities are robust and easy to use. Although nearly any style of text can be created directly in Flash, you can also import text created in other applications as vector artwork. With applications such as Macromedia Freehand, you can even preserve your type as editable text blocks when it is imported to Flash.

For more information on importing vector graphics, refer to Chapter 16, "Importing Artwork." For coverage of some of the vector graphics applications that can be used to create Flash-friendly artwork, including text, refer to Chapter 38, "Working with Vector Graphics."

The Text tool

The Text tool, shown in Figure 8-6, delivers a broad range of control for generating, positioning, and modifying text. Although the basic Text tool is located in the Flash Toolbox, when the tool is active, the controls for working with text are found in the Property inspector.

The Character, Paragraph, and Text Options panels have been replaced by the intuitive controls centralized in the Property inspector.

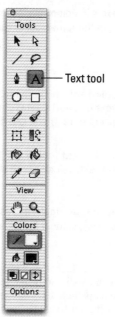

Figure 8-6: The Text tool is used to create all text blocks and text fields in Flash.

— Text tool

Creating Static text blocks

To create text in your current Flash document, click the Text tool in the Toolbox to activate it. You may choose to create new text in your Document window with either of two methods:

✦ **Label text:** To enter text on one extending line click on the Document Stage and begin typing. To control the width of a line of label text, you can either enter hard returns with the Enter or Return key as you type, or you can convert the label text into block text by dragging the round corner handle to a specific width — it will change to a square handle to indicate that the box is now constrained instead of expanding. Refer to Figure 8-2 (left image) for an illustration of the round label text handles.

Tip If your text continues beyond the viewable area of the Document window, you can add some line breaks, click and drag to move the label text box, or select View ➪ Work Area to make the entire text label visible.

✦ **Block text:** To define the width for an area of text that will constrain your type by auto-wrapping as you enter more characters, click on the Document Stage and drag the box to the width that you want. You can change the width of your block text at any time by double-clicking the box to invoke the square corner handle and then dragging the handle to set a new width. Refer to Figure 8-2 (right image) for an illustration of the square box text handles. You can convert a text block into label text by double-clicking on the square corner handle — it will change to a round handle to indicate that the box is now extending instead of constrained.

Tip   The handles on text boxes or fields are only visible when the text is in Edit mode. To return an existing text box to Edit mode, either double-click the item with the Arrow tool or click it once with the Text tool.

Modifying or deleting text

Flash handles text as a group which allows you to use the Text tool to edit the individual letters or words inside a text area at any time by clicking on the text box and then typing or drag-selecting specific characters. To select the whole block or group of text, you can click once anywhere on the text with the Arrow tool.

To delete individual characters, click and drag to select them with the Text tool or use the Backspace key (the Delete key on Mac). To delete a whole group of text, select it with the Arrow tool and then use the Backspace key (or Delete key).

Tip   Double-clicking a text block with the Arrow tool will also activate the Text tool — this allows you to modify the individual characters or to change the text box style, without having to go to the Toolbox.

You can use most common text editing/word processing commands in Flash. Cut, Copy, and Paste will work to move selected text within Flash and also between Flash and other applications that handle type. Although Flash does not include an internal spell-check, you can use the Movie Explorer to copy your text to the clipboard and then paste it into a word processing application for more specialized editing. The Movie Explorer can also make it much easier to find and modify text if you are working with a complex document.

To access this feature, first open the Movie Explorer panel for the document you are editing — either from the application menu (Window ➪ Movie Explorer) or with the F4 shortcut key and then use any of the following options to modify text:

✦ **To see all the text used in your current document:** Set the Movie Explorer to Show Text with the option button at the top of the panel. The contents of each text box will be listed along with the Font and point size that was used.

✦ **To search for a specific item:** enter the Font name, instance name, frame number, or ActionScript string in the Find field of the Movie Explorer panel.

✦ **To edit the contents of individual text blocks:** Double-click any listing in the Movie Explorer panel and then type in the field as you would if you were editing a filename in any other list.

✦ **To specify a new font or font size:** Select any text item listing that you want to change in the Movie Explorer and then simply change the font settings in the Property inspector. Use Shift+select to select multiple items in the Movie Explorer if you want to apply a change to more than one text box at a time.

✦ **To copy text:** Use the Copy command in the Movie Explorer options menu to copy a currently selected line of text to the clipboard. Or to copy all the text in your current document to the clipboard without having to select items individually in the Movie Explorer, use the Copy All Text to the Clipboard command in the Movie Explorer options menu.

Setting text attributes in the Property inspector

The Text tool does not include options in the Toolbox because the extensive text controls are centrally located in the Property inspector. All Flash text is created with the same Text tool in text blocks or boxes, but when a text block is created, it can be assigned specific behavior with the Property inspector.

Although Font style and size menus can always be accessed from the application menu (Text ⇨ Font and Text ⇨ Size), the options for controlling text are not visible in the Property inspector unless the Text tool is active or a text block is selected with the Arrow tool. The options available in the Property inspector will vary slightly, depending on the kind of text selected.

Static text options

When working with Static text, you can modify both the font and paragraph attributes with the following options, shown in Figure 8-7:

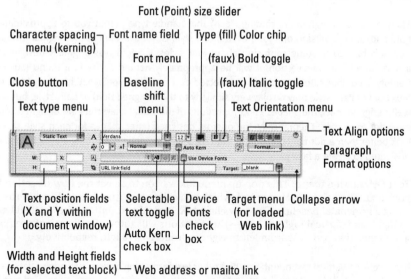

Figure 8-7: The main options available for Static text in the (expanded) Property inspector

✦ **Text type menu:** This drop-down allows you to specify Static, Input, or Dynamic behavior for your text. Set this behavior first to invoke the relevant options in the Property inspector.

✦ **Font field (and menu):** When the Text tool is active, this displays the name of the current font. Click the arrow button to invoke a scrolling menu of available fonts. Choose a font from this scrolling menu to set the font for the next text element that you create. Or, to change the font of existing text in the Document window, first select individual characters with the Text tool or select the whole group with the Arrow tool, and then choose a different font from the scrolling menu. When selecting a font from the Property inspector menu, the currently highlighted font is previewed in the style or typeface that will display.

Tip

The font of existing text can also be changed from the application menu with Text ➪ Font. The advantage of this method is that the list is more expansive and easier to scan. The disadvantage of this list is that it doesn't preview the fonts in their typefaces.

✦ **Font size:** You can select the size of your type with either a pop-up slider or a point size entry field. When the Text tool is active, it displays the current font size in the entry field. You can change the font size by typing a specific point size number in the field. If you click the arrow button to the immediate right of the text entry field, a pop-up slider allows you to select a font size — as you move the slider, the font size number will update in the entry field.

✦ **Type Color chip:** Click this button to invoke the current Swatches, which — in addition to current and temporary swatches — also enables you to acquire a color from anywhere within the interface by sampling with the Dropper arrow.

✦ **Bold and Italic:** The Bold option is a radio button that toggles selected text between either Normal or faux Bold. The Italic option is another radio button. It toggles selected text between Normal and faux Italic.

Note

Many computer programs (including Flash) that handle type permit you to approximate a bold and/or italic version of a font, even if this style is not available in the original installed font; this has led to some confusion about font styles. If a font was originally designed to include a bold or italic version, it will be appropriately named in the font menu (such as Century Schoolbook Bold), and will be selected as a *separate* typeface. With many fonts the faux bold or italic style may display very similarly to the designed Bold or Italic style, but with well-designed fonts, the shapes and proportions of individual characters are designed separately for each style. Theoretically, the original designed letter shapes for each style should look better than a normal letter shape thickened with an outline to create a faux bold style, or slanted to create a faux italic style.

✦ **Text Orientation menu:** This pop-up menu allows you to select the flow direction for your text. The default is Horizontal, which will orient text from Left to Right in rows along a horizontal baseline. The new Flash MX vertical text options are Vertical Left to Right, and Vertical Right to Left — these options will automatically orient the text in columns that progress from left to right or from right to left, respectively.

Note

If you select a Vertical text orientation, the other text formatting options will apply slightly differently than they do to Horizontal text. Please see the section that follows on Vertical text for descriptions of the controls that are relevant to vertically oriented type.

✦ **Text Align options:** The top-right area of the panel displays four buttons for the arrangement of text: Left, Center, Right, and Full Justification. When editing, alignment affects the currently selected paragraph(s) only. When entering text, use these options to predetermine the alignment before text entry, and all subsequent text will be aligned accordingly.

✦ **Character spacing menu:** This value field and slider are used to change the space or kerning between individual letters. The default setting of 0 applies the built-in kerning of the font, while any settings between +1 and +60 will add more space between characters and any setting between –1 and –60 will decrease space between characters (extreme settings will cause the letters to overlap).

✦ **Baseline shift:** There are three options in this drop-down menu. Normal resets text to the baseline. Superscript shifts Horizontal text above the baseline and Vertical text to the right of the baseline. Subscript sets Horizontal text below the baseline and Vertical text to the left of the baseline.

✦ **Auto Kern check box:** If the font includes built-in kerning information, which evens out the spaces between letterforms, check this to activate automatic kerning.

✦ **Paragraph Format options:** The Format button invokes the Paragraph Format options dialog box shown in Figure 8-8, for the following additional text controls:

- **Right Margins:** Use this numeric entry field (or click the arrow button to invoke the interactive slider) to define the space between the text and the right border of the text box. By default, this space is described in pixels.

- **Line Spacing:** Use this numeric entry field or associated slider to adjust line spacing. By default, Line Spacing is described in points. Regardless of settings for individual fonts, the largest font on a line will always determine line spacing for that line. This setting is described in points.

- **Indentation:** Use this numeric entry field or associated slider to adjust the indent, also described by default in pixels, of the first line of a paragraph. The indent is relative to the left margin. This setting is described in pixels.

- **Left Margins:** Use this numeric entry field (or click the arrow button to invoke the interactive slider) to define the space between the text and the left border of the text box. By default, this space is described in pixels.

Note The default units of measurement for both the Margin and Indentation entries of the Paragraph Format options dialog box are determined by the Ruler Units for the movie. Ruler Units can be reset in the Document Properties dialog box, which is accessed from the application menu with Modify ⇨ Document or from the keyboard by pressing Ctrl+J (⌘+J).

Figure 8-8: The Paragraph Format options dialog box for Horizontal text invoked with the Format button in the Property inspector

✦ **Selectable:** Use this toggle button to make selected text, or text that's entered subsequently, selectable when displayed on users' machines. This allows users to copy and paste your text into other text-editing applications or browser windows. Type in Vertical text boxes cannot be made selectable.

✦ **Use Device Fonts:** This little check box is the secret to keeping more control of your font display while taking advantage of device fonts for file size savings. *It is not a substitute for selecting one of the three device fonts that appear at the top of the Font menu.* Rather, it's an innovative way in which Flash enables you to rely on commonly installed fonts without embedding all the font information in your Flash movie (.swf), as described later in this chapter.

✦ **Link entry:** This option is only available for Horizontal Static or Dynamic text. By selecting a text block or an individual word in the Document window, and then entering a URL in this Link entry field, you can add a hyperlink to selected text. The text link will be identified in the authoring environment with a dotted underline — the underline will not be visible in the published .swf file, but the mouse pointer will change to indicate a link when it is over the text.

✦ **Target menu:** This new Flash MX menu will be accessible after you enter a URL in the Link field and it allows you to select a destination for the loaded URL. The options will be familiar to anyone who has worked with HTML page structures. For more information, refer to the description of the getURL() action in Chapter 18, "Understanding Actions and Event Handlers."

Using the application menu commands

Some of the text settings in the Property inspector are also available from the application Text menu:

✦ Under Text ➪ Font, you can select from the same available fonts listed in the Property inspector Font menu, but the list is slightly larger so it can be easier to read.

✦ Under Text ➪ Size, you can select a specific font point size from a list, instead of using the Font size slider in the Property inspector.

✦ Under Text ➪ Style, the commands include:

• **Plain:** Ctrl+Shift+P or ⌘+Shift+P

• **Bold:** Ctrl+Shift+B or ⌘+Shift+B

• **Italic:** Ctrl+Shift+I or ⌘+Shift+I

• **Subscript**

• **Superscript**

✦ Under Text ➪ Align, the commands include:

• **Align Left:** Ctrl+Shift+L or ⌘+Shift+L

• **Align Center:** Ctrl+Shift+C or ⌘+Shift+C

• **Align Right:** Ctrl+Shift+R or ⌘+Shift+R

• **Justify:** Ctrl+Shift+J or ⌘+Shift+J

✦ Under Text ➪ Tracking, you will find a list of options that allow you an alternative way to adjust the space between characters. If you have the Property inspector open as you apply these commands manually, you will see the Character spacing or Tracking value field update. Manual tracking has the advantage that it can be applied either to selected (highlighted) text characters or to the pair of text characters on either side of the cursor:

• **Decrease:** To decrease text character spacing by one half-pixel, press Ctrl+Alt+← (⌘+Option+←). To decrease text character spacing by two pixels, press Shift+Ctrl+Alt+← (Shift+⌘+Option+←).

• **Increase:** To increase text character spacing by one half-pixel, press Ctrl+Alt+→ (⌘+Option+→). To increase text character spacing by two pixels, press Shift+Ctrl+Alt+→ (Shift+⌘+Option+→).

• **Reset:** To reset text character spacing to normal, press Ctrl+Alt+↑ (⌘+Option+↑).

✦ **Scrollable:** The final item in the Text menu, is an option that is only available when an editable text block is selected. When applied to a Dynamic text field, this option makes it possible to enter and scroll through text that extends beyond the frame of the text block (either vertically or horizontally.) This option can be applied by choosing Text ➪ Scrollable from the application menu or from the contextual menu when a Dynamic text block is selected, or by Shift+double-clicking the handle of a Dynamic text block.

Vertical text options

Some of the options that are visible in the Property inspector change slightly when you choose a Vertical orientation for your text box. Figure 8-9 indicates some of the options that are different from those described previously for Horizontal Static text.

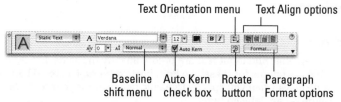

Figure 8-9: The formatting options available in the Property inspector for Vertical text

✦ **Text Align options:** These buttons now function to align the arrangement of text in a vertical text box to Top, Middle, Bottom, and Full Justification. When entering text, use these options to predetermine the alignment before text entry, and all subsequent text will be aligned accordingly.

✦ **Auto Kern check box:** If the font includes built-in kerning information, which evens out the spaces between letterforms, check this to activate automatic kerning. On Vertical text, this setting can be overridden by the Vertical text settings in the Flash Preferences dialog box (refer to Figure 8-4). When No Kerning is selected in Preferences, than the Auto-Kerning toggle in the Property inspector will only apply to Horizontal text.

✦ **Rotate toggle:** This very handy button will flip the characters in your Vertical text box so that the type is turned sideways — or actually resting on the vertical baseline. This is an effective alternative to creating Horizontal text and then using Free Transform to rotate the text box 90 degrees.

✦ **Paragraph Format options:** The Format button invokes the Paragraph Format options dialog box (see Figure 8-10) with the following additional text controls:

  • **Indent:** Use this numeric entry field or associated slider to adjust the space between the top border of the text box and the first character in a column of type. This setting is described in pixels.

  • **Column Spacing:** Use this numeric entry field or associated slider to adjust space between columns of type. By default, Column Spacing is described in points. Regardless of settings for individual characters, the largest character in a column will always determine the calculation of line spacing for that line. This setting is described in points.

- **Top Margin:** Use this numeric entry field or associated slider to adjust the space between the text and the top border of the text box. This setting is described in pixels.

- **Bottom Margin:** Use this numeric entry field (or click the arrow button to invoke the interactive slider) to define the space between the text and the lower border of the text box. This setting is described in pixels.

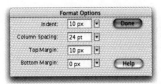

Figure 8-10: The Paragraph Format dialog box for Vertical text invoked with the Format button in the Property inspector

Editable text options

The options available for Dynamic and Input text are predominantly the same, but there are a few important options that are unique for these two Editable text types. Figure 8-11 shows the Property inspector as it displays when you specify Dynamic behavior for your text. Only the options not shown in Figure 8-7 are labeled here.

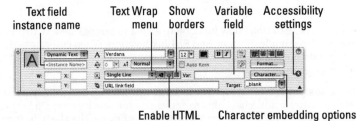

Figure 8-11: The additional options available in the Property inspector when Dynamic text behavior is selected

The following options are common to both Dynamic and Input text:

✦ **Text field instance name:** As described previously, this identifier allows the Flash Player to put your dynamic data in the correct field.

✦ **Text Wrap:** Use this drop-down to choose how your text will be organized in the text field. Choose between Single Line, Multiline (with line breaks), and Multiline with no text wrap.

✦ **Enable HTML:** When this toggle is turned on, Flash preserves rich text styles when displaying Dynamic text. This includes font, font style, hyperlink, paragraph, and other formatting consistent with permissible HTML tags. You can also enable HTML so that the entry field will accept formatting that has been assigned to it in the Actions panel. For more information on this, refer to Chapter 35, "Understanding HTML and Text Field Functions in Flash."

✦ **Show borders:** Use this to draw the text field with a border and a white background that will be visible in your published movie (.swf).

✦ **Variable:** This field is now redundant with the Instance name field, but if used for backwards compatibility it should be assigned a different name than your instance to avoid confusion in Flash MX.

✦ **Character embedding options:** When embedding a font, Flash gives you control over how much of the font information is actually embedded. This button will invoke the Character Options dialog box (shown in Figure 8-12), where you can specify one or more character categories to be embedded — by selecting check boxes for No Characters, All Characters or Only: Uppercase, Lowercase, Numerals, and/or Punctuation. Or, you can simply enter specific characters by typing them into the field at the bottom of the dialog box.

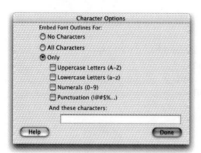

Figure 8-12: The dialog box for specifying characters to include in embedded font information to be exported with your final .swf

The Link and Target value fields are not available in the Property inspector when Input text behavior is selected — this is because you cannot add links to text that users will be entering. The only additional control available in the Property inspector for Input text fields is the Maximum Characters value field. Use the Maximum Characters value field to specify the maximum number of characters that a user can enter in this particular text field. The number of characters can be limited to any number between 0 and 65535. This feature is generally used for controlled content, like passwords.

Font Export and Display

By default, Flash embeds all fonts used in Static text boxes in order to deliver WYSIWYG display in the published movie (.swf.) As long as font outlines are available for text used in your Flash document (.fla), the published movie (.swf) will display consistently, regardless of what fonts the user has installed on his machine.

Note In order to edit a Flash project (.fla) you will need to have the original fonts available, unless you are willing to view the document with a substitute font in the authoring environment. If you select a text block that is displayed with a substitute font, you should still see the name of the original font listed in the Property inspector. As long as this font formatting is not modified, Flash will preserve all the original font information so that when the document (.fla) is opened again on a machine that has the original font, any edits that were made using the default font will be rendered correctly. Although you can make text edits while working with a default font, you will need to have the original font installed in order to publish the final movie (.swf) with the design intact.

This auto-embed font behavior is what endears Flash to type-obsessed designers, but there is a small price to pay: Every embedded font adds to the final file size, and all embedded type is anti-aliased or smoothed. For many projects the additional weight is not an issue. For text at larger sizes, anti-aliasing is usually needed. But if you are trying to keep your files lean and mean and your text crisp at small point sizes, you may want to consider some of the alternatives to default font embedding. Figure 8-13 compares aliased with anti-aliased text.

anti-aliased text (24 pt)
anti-aliased text (8 pt)

aliased text (24 pt)
aliased text (8 pt)

Figure 8-13: Text characters at large point sizes look smoother with Flash's default anti-aliasing applied, but small point sizes can look too blurry with smoothing and will be most legible when aliased (the default for device fonts). This example was zoomed to show the rough edges more clearly on the aliased text.

Caution

If you are working on OS X, you may not notice as much difference between alias and anti-alias text because the system applies automatic smoothing on any screen text, even on application menu lists. Although this feature cannot be turned off completely, the text smoothing menu in your General Preferences panel allows you to specify between the lowest setting (only smoothes text larger than 12 point) and the highest setting (smoothes all text larger than 8 point.) The default setting smoothes any text larger than 9 point.

Specifying device fonts

Device fonts are actually three basic font style designators identified by a preceding underscore in your font menu. These fonts will be familiar to anyone who has worked with HTML text. Although not as exciting as some custom fonts, there are actually whole design styles based on these "generic" fonts — think minimal and unpretentious. You will find the three device font designations: _sans, _serif, and _typewriter, in either the Property inspector font menu or in the application menu under Text ➪ Font. These device font labels will tell the Flash Player to use any equivalent font available on a viewer's system. The formatting that you have applied to the text in your Flash document (.fla), such as bold or italic style and point size, will be preserved and applied to the font selected by the Flash player from the viewer's system to render the text in your Flash movie (.swf).

To give you an idea of how device fonts relate to installed fonts; _sans usually becomes Arial or Helvetica, while _serif usually becomes Times or Times New Roman, and _typewriter becomes Courier. Because these settings utilize the default fonts on the user's machine, this also makes the final movie size smaller, because Flash doesn't have to include their outlines in the exported .swf.

Characteristics of device fonts are that they are always available, always quick to render, but they cannot be rotated and occasionally they will vary slightly in their metrics from player to player. Another important difference between embedded fonts and device fonts is that all embedded fonts will be anti-aliased or smoothed by Flash, while device fonts will be unsmoothed or aliased. This makes device fonts ideal for small type such as image captions or menu items, because when text is smoothed it can make it harder to read at small point sizes.

The Use Device Fonts option

You will notice that even if you have not used one of the device fonts from your font menu, you can still select the Use Device Fonts check box in the Property inspector. This is a terrific "compromise" option if you strive for more specific control over the Flash Player's font choices, but still want to take advantage of the file size savings afforded by device fonts. When the Use Device Fonts option is checked in the Property inspector, the font is not embedded — only the Font Name, Font family/style (serif/sans serif/monospace), and other information are added to specify the font — which adds no more than 10 or 15 bytes to the final .swf file. This information is used so that the Flash player on the user's system will know if the font is installed or not. If the original font is available, it will display exactly as you designed it. If the original font is not present, then the Flash Player will still know whether the substitute font should be serif or sans-serif.

The Use Device Fonts option also works as a toggle to turn off anti-aliasing, this means that even if the user has all the fonts used in your Flash movie installed, Use Device Fonts changes how the type displays:

✦ **When Use Device Fonts is selected,** text will display better at small point sizes. That's because there is no anti-aliasing or smoothing applied to any device font, regardless of its presence on your system.

✦ **When Use Device Fonts is *not* selected,** the font outline is embedded and all characters are smoothed (even if the font is available). Smoothed text can be illegible at small point sizes.

To accurately preview the Use Device Fonts setting on your machine, if you have a font manager (as most Web designers do), then you'll need to make sure you're careful about your font activation settings. Make sure Global activation is turned *off* to limit the number of fonts that the Flash player can find for rendering the movie (.swf).

For best results with this specific Use Device Fonts option, we suggest that you limit your font selection to those that most of your audience is likely to have (all those common fonts that come installed with their machines), or which will translate into one of the default device fonts without wreaking havoc on your design. It is better to be conservative and design your layout using Times, Arial, and Courier than to go wild with custom fonts that will most likely be substituted very differently when the movie is viewed on someone else's machine. Otherwise, for unusual fonts, we suggest that you either embed the characters (Device Font option cleared) or, for limited areas of text (such as headlines), that you break the text apart to create vector shapes, as described later in this chapter.

Troubleshooting font display

Although Flash does an amazing job of displaying fonts consistently and cleanly, even on different platforms, the success of your font export is entirely dependent on the quality and completeness of the font information available when the Flash document is created (.fla). Because Flash can access font information on your system while you are working in the authoring environment, many of the font display problems that can come up during production will only be visible when the Flash movie (.swf) is published.

To display fonts in the published movie (.swf), the Flash Player relies on the font information embedded in the movie, or else on the fonts installed on the user's system. If there are discrepancies between the information available to the Flash Player and the font information that was available to the Flash authoring application when the document was created, you will run into font display problems.

When trouble comes up with fonts (as it almost always does at some point), a good guide to font management is indispensable. We can't describe everything that can go wrong when working with fonts here, and solutions will often vary depending on how you are storing and managing your fonts. Ideally, you should find resources that are specific to the platform and programs you are using.

Tip   A good general guide to some basic font management techniques for Macintosh users is *How to Boss Your Fonts Around* by Robin Williams. Even if you are a Windows user, this book can give you some basic background on how fonts and font management utilities work.

Missing font outlines

TrueType, Type 1 PostScript, and bitmap fonts (Mac only) can be used in Flash. Although Flash exports the system information about the fonts that are used, if the font is damaged or incomplete on your system it may display correctly in the authoring environment (.fla), but when exported the movie (.swf) will appear incorrectly on other systems if the end user doesn't have the font installed. This is due to the fact that although Flash can display the font within the editor by using the screen font, it does not recognize that particular font's outline and can't export information needed to display the text in the .swf. In order to check for this problem in the authoring environment, switch your view to View ➪ Antialias Text. If the text appears jaggy, that's a problem font. These font display problems can be avoided by using device fonts (_sans, _serif, or _typewriter fonts).

Caution   Users running Windows have reported that Adobe TypeManager (ATM) 4.0 or earlier can cause Flash to crash. This problem seems to have been resolved with ATM 4.1. To resolve crashing problems with Flash, either disable ATM or upgrade to a newer version of ATM. Also, Macromedia reccomends using TrueType fonts with Flash, although Postscript Type 1 fonts can be used if ATM is installed and enabled.

Note   At the time of this writing, there was not a version of ATM that would run on OS X, so anyone working on a Mac system who had previously relied on ATM for font management had to either rely entirely on OS X system font managment or find a new utility such as Extensis Suitcase.

Font substitution

Sometimes a project file (.fla) from the Mac will open on a machine running Windows with the Times font displayed in substitution for all of the text! This is actually a helpful feature — at least in terms of how Flash is trying to display the contents of the file when the original font information is not available on your machine. If you do actually have the same font installed on both the Mac and the PC, there may be a slight difference in their names — usually, there's an extra space or an underscore messing up the font sync.

You can also control what fonts are used to substitute in the authoring environment for fonts that are not available on your system — so everything doesn't have to be displayed in the Times font. If Flash cannot find the font information to match what is specified in a file (.fla), you will be notified by the Missing Fonts alert box shown in Figure 8-14, and prompted to select fonts installed on your system to substitute for display.

Figure 8-14: The Missing Fonts alert box used to control font substitution

Note　If you publish or export a document without viewing any of the scenes containing missing fonts, the alert box will only appear when Flash attempts to publish or export the .swf.

The first time that a scene with missing font information is displayed in the authoring environment, you will be prompted by the Missing Fonts alert box to choose one of the following options:

✦ **Choose Substitute Fonts:** To specify individual substitutions from the fonts available on your system for each missing font, click this button to invoke the Font Mapping dialog box shown in Figure 8-15. This dialog box lists all fonts specified in the document that Flash cannot find on your system. To choose a substitute font for a missing font, select the font name in the Font Mapping list and then choose a font installed on your machine from the Substitute Font pop-up menu. Click OK to close the dialog box.

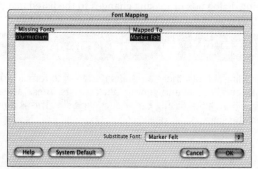

Figure 8-15: The Font Mapping dialog box is used to view missing fonts and to modify mapping of substitute fonts

✦ **Use Default:** This option will substitute all missing fonts with the Flash system default font and dismiss the Missing Fonts alert box.

✦ **Turn Alert off:** To disable the Alert box in the current document, select Don't Show Again for this Document, Always Use Substitute fonts.

Even though the text is displayed in a substitute font, Flash will include the name of the missing font in the Property inspector font menu, as shown in Figure 8-16. Flash will preserve the original font specification when the file is saved so that the text will display correctly when the document (.fla) is opened on a system with the missing fonts installed. You can even apply the missing font to new text by selecting it from the font menu in the Property inspector.

this is type displayed with Marker Felt font
subtituted for missing font BlurMedium

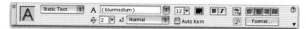

Figure 8-16: The missing font name is displayed in the font menu even when text is displayed in a substitute font in the authoring environment.

Because appearance attributes such as size, leading, and kerning may render differently with a substitute font, any modifications made while viewing text in a substitute font may have to be adjusted when the document is opened on a machine with the missing font available.

Tip　To turn the Missing Fonts alert box off for all documents, clear the Warn on missing fonts check box in the Warnings tab of Flash Preferences (Edit ➪ Preferences or Flash ➪ Preferences for OS X). To turn alerts on again, reselect the check box.

To view all the missing fonts in the currently active document or to reselect font mappings, select Edit ➪ Font Mapping (or in OS X Flash ➪ Font Mapping) from the application menu and repeat the same steps described previously to choose new substitute fonts. To view all the font mapping settings saved on your system or to delete font mappings, close all Flash documents before opening the Font Mapping dialog box or making changes to the listed mapping.

Using Miniml Fonts in Flash MX, by Craig Kroeger

For those of you who are not familiar with Miniml fonts, these are fonts designed to remain crisp (aliased) in Flash and they can be used as an alternative to generic device fonts. These aliased fonts are particularly useful at small sizes, where anti-aliasing can reduce legibility. This is a real concern when designing Flash applications for devices.

ALIASED TEXT
ANTIALIASED TEXT

Crisp aliased text (top) compared to blurry antialiased text (lower)

Author's Note: There are free versions of the Miniml fonts, provided by Craig Kroeger, included on the CD-ROM in the ch8 folder—you may use these to test what you can do with them. Professional versions of these fonts are available at www.miniml.com.

There is also a sample source file (Miniml.fla) on the CD-ROM that shows how the fonts are used in various text field examples. In order for the Miniml fonts to work properly, consider these guidelines:

✦ **Select font:** When the Miniml fonts have been installed on your system, they can be selected from the Font menu in the same way as any other available font. However, the font must be a Miniml font to display properly as aliased text. Other pixel fonts will not work, because they will be anti-aliased.

✦ **Font size:** Miniml fonts must be set to 8 points or any multiple of 8 (16, 24, 32, and so on) The numbers in the font name refer to the font style, *not* what point size it should be set to.

✦ **Vertical Static text:** Miniml fonts can now be used on a vertical axis when they are rotated with the rotate option in Flash MX.

✦ **Spacing Static text:** Only Static text can have adjusted character spacing. When adjusting the character spacing, use whole-pixel values to keep the text aliased. Professional Miniml fonts have versions with increased letter spacing for use with Dynamic or Input text fields.

✦ **Paragraph alignment:** Do not use Center paragraph alignment — only use Left or Right.

✦ **Embed font:** You must embed the Miniml fonts when using Dynamic or Input text fields. In Character Options select the Select All Characters check box to embed the complete font. To reduce overall fill size, only embed the characters you need in your text. Static text is automatically embedded.

✦ **Snap to Pixel:** Use the Snap to Pixel feature under View in the application menu to keep fonts clear. When the fonts are not on whole _x and _y values, the fonts will appear blurry. If you are not using Snap to Pixel, make sure to check your Info panel to set the text box _x and _y values to whole pixels, using the top-left corner as the registration point. To ensure consistent placement of text after you have converted a text box into a symbol, reposition the registration point of the symbol by dragging it from the center to the top left corner of the text box.

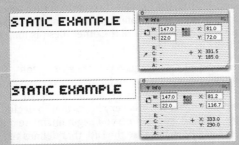

Crisp aliased text (top) compared to blurry antialiased text (lower)

To keep text crisp (aliased), use Snap to Pixel or the Info panel to set X,Y values to whole pixels (top). If text boxes are not aligned to whole X,Y values than the font will be antialiased (bottom).

Continued

Continued

✦ **Using Miniml fonts in motion:** When you are using Miniml fonts in animation, you need to round the _x and _y values to whole values to keep them crisp. Use the following ActionScript to round the numbers down to the closest integer:

```
_x = Math.floor(_x);

_y = Math.floor(_y);
```

✦ **Preview in the Flash Player:** Preview your finished movie in the Flash Player (.swf), to see the aliased text displayed correctly, because it may appear anti-aliased in the authoring environment (.fla).

This may seem like a lot of rules, but I think you will find the results well worth the effort.

Font Symbols and Shared Font Libraries

Using Font symbols and Shared libraries in your Flash authoring workflow offers several benefits that can make it worth the little time it takes to set up. Although you can nest a Static text box inside any other symbol type if you want to reuse a specific text element in your movie, this does not change how the text is published in the Flash document. Using instances of a symbol to place repeated text elements such as logos or taglines offers the same benefits as converting artwork into symbols — you can make changes to the symbol stored in the Library and it will be propagated to every instance in your document, and you can also modify the appearance of individual instances without changing the original symbol.

The difference between text nested in another symbol type and a real Font symbol, is that Font symbols can actually be used to store the display information for an entire font. When placed into a runtime Shared library, Font symbols can be used to link text in one movie to the font display information in a source movie; this allows you to use custom fonts without having to embed the font information in every Flash movie (.swf) individually. This workflow is especially effective on projects that involve multiple .swf files using the same custom fonts and the bonus is that if your client suddenly decides that they prefer "Leonardo script" to "Chickenscratch bold" (or whatever font switcheroo you might come up with), you can make the change in your source Font symbol without even opening any of the other files (as long as the new font is given the same name and it still fits in your layouts).

This all sounds great so far, right? Now for the reality check: Because you are storing font information in a separate file from your layouts, it brings in one more factor that you have to manage. The source font library (.swf) can be in the same directory as your other movie (.swf) files or it can be stored on a completely different server. It is very important to decide on the storage location of your source font files (.fla and .swf) before you begin linking text in your other Flash documents (.fla) to shared Font symbols, because the URL that defines the relative or absolute path is stored in each .fla file and your font links will be broken if you later change the source movie's location.

Note   Runtime shared assets do not need to be available on your local network when you are editing .fla documents that rely on linked assets, but the shared asset .swf must be available at your specified URL in order for the published movies (.swf) to display the linked assets at runtime.

As you can imagine, having your font links fail would be a major disaster, so for this reason many developers don't find it worth the risk of relying on an external font source. On the other hand, there is always an element of uncertainty with Web delivery, so it might not be fair to eliminate what is otherwise an excellent way to optimize font management in your Flash layouts. As with any Web production, just be sure to test early and often as you develop a Flash project that uses shared fonts.

Shared libraries can be used to store other symbol types, but it is best to organize different kinds of assets in separate .fla files. In this chapter, we focus on making Font symbols and creating a source file for a Shared font library.

Cross-Reference For a description of using Shared libraries for other assets as well as an explanation of how to load external .swf files, please refer to Chapter 28, "Sharing and Loading Assets."

Creating a Font symbol

There are two ways that Font symbols can be integrated in your workflow. If you plan to use Font symbols within a Flash document (.fla) simply as a way to make edits faster in that one document, and you don't mind exporting the font information with every .swf, you can create a Font symbol directly in the main Library of your current document and rely on author-time sharing to update instances of the font. However, if you want to save file size by linking to the Font symbol information for runtime sharing, you should open a new Flash document before creating your Font symbols. In either case, the initial steps for creating a Flash Font symbol are the same:

1. Open the Library panel where you want to store the Font symbol.

2. From the Library options panel choose New Font, as shown in Figure 8-17.

Figure 8-17: Choosing to insert a new Font symbol from the Library panel options menu

3. The Font Symbol Properties dialog box appears so that you can enter a name for your Font symbol and select the font you want to embed in the file (see Figure 8-18). The name that you enter shouldn't be the same as the original font name but rather should indicate how the font is being used in your project. For example if you are using Impact font for your titles, instead of naming the Font symbol "Impact" you could name it "myProjectTitle" or some other name that will inform you (and the rest of your team) how the font is being used.

Figure 8-18: Selecting a font to store in the new Font symbol and giving it a reference name.

4. If you also want the option to use faux bold or italic style on text linked to your Font symbol, select the Style check boxes for Bold or Italic to include these characters with the embedded font. This will increase the size of your source .swf only—the additional size will not be passed on to other .swf files that link to the Font symbol for runtime sharing.

Caution

If you create a Font symbol without the Bold or Italic options selected in the Font Symbol Properties dialog box and then try to apply the options in the Property inspector to create faux Bold or Italic style on text that is linked to the symbol, you will encounter one of two problems. If the text you are modifying is in a Static text box, then the applied styles will display, but the additional font information for the modified characters will be exported with your published file—increasing the size of the .swf. If the text you are modifying is in a Dynamic or Input text field, the text will not display in the published .swf file because the font information needed to render the Bold or Italic type on-the-fly will not be found by the Flash Player.

5. Now when you browse the font menu available in the Property inspector or from the application menu (Text ➪ Font) you will see your new font listed with the other fonts installed on your system. Font symbols are also differentiated from regular fonts in the menu with an asterisk (*) following the name it has been given (see Figure 8-19).

Figure 8-19: A Font symbol name followed by an asterisk will be listed with other available fonts in the Property inspector menu (or in the application Text menu).

The next step that you will need to take to use the Font symbol in your project will depend on how you choose to integrate Font symbols into your workflow. As mentioned earlier in this chapter, using symbols for author-time asset sharing can make it easier to propagate changes throughout a document, but any assets used in your document will still be embedded in each movie (.swf) that you publish. Creating a separate library for storing symbols and linking these as runtime shared assets in multiple movies takes a little more work, but it gives you the benefit of both streamlined updates and smaller file sizes. The most appropriate workflow will depend on the scope and content of your particular project and on how willing you are to manage the risks involved with using runtime shared assets.

Author-time update of Font symbols

If you intend to use a Font symbol as an author-time shared asset only, than you can simply leave it in your current Library so that the font will be available in the font menu whenever you want to use it in your project. You will be able to modify any of the text boxes that use your Font symbol in the same way as any other text. There is no limit on the number of colors or sizes that you can use or on what you can type into each text block.

The main reason that this is a more flexible workflow than simply nesting text inside other symbols for reuse is that you can actually change the *characters* used in individual text blocks that reference a Font symbol, while you can only modify the *appearance* of text that is nested in a symbol instance.

The process for updating instances of a Font symbol used within one Flash document (.fla) are much the same as updating any other symbol type or imported asset stored in the Library:

1. Open the current document Library and select the Font symbol that you want to modify.

2. Choose Properties from the Library options menu or from the contextual menu.

3. In the Font Symbol Properties dialog box, simply select a new font from the font menu, but don't change the font name that you had previously chosen. (Now it makes sense why naming your Font symbol with the same name shown in the font menu isn't a good idea, right?)

   You will find that all text that was in your old font will be updated to the new font that you have chosen, while maintaining all other formatting and style attributes.

Tip
If you don't see your text boxes update to the new font immediately after you change it in the Font Symbol Properties dialog, you may need to click on one of the text boxes with the Arrow tool — this will usually prompt Flash to refresh the display.

Using Font symbols in runtime Shared libraries

In order to make your Font symbol available for use in other Flash movies without having to embed the font information in each file, you will need to create links from individual *destination* files to your *source* file or Shared library. This workflow optimizes file sizes by eliminating storage of redundant font information between linked movies. As with HTML files, you have to specify a path in order for the Flash Player to locate font information in one movie (.swf) for text display in another. Because the font information is retrieved from a .swf file by the Flash Player and supplied to another .swf for text display, this is referred to as *runtime* asset sharing.

If you have already followed the steps to create a Font symbol in an otherwise empty Flash document (.fla), the next part of the process is to enter an identifier and a location (path) that will "lead" the Flash Player to your Shared library. As mentioned previously, you will need to know where the published source movie (.swf) will be stored before you can create font links to other documents. The location (or path) can be relative or absolute.

Tip

To keep your linkage intact while preserving source file version numbers as you develop your project, you might want to use the Publish Settings dialog box to give your published source .swf a generic name (such as titleFontSource.swf) while using a more specific naming convention for your source .fla files (such as titleFontSource101.fla). This eliminates the hassle of going back to your destination movies and changing the linkage information if you decide you need to move to a new version name to keep track of modifications to your source file (.fla).

To help clarify how runtime shared fonts are stored and accessed we will walk through the three possible scenarios for Font symbol use and show you how each is displayed in the authoring environment (.fla) and in the published movie (.swf).

On the CD-ROM

The Flash files illustrated in this section are included in the ch8 folder of the CD-ROM. You will find both the fontSource files (shared library file) and the fontLink files (destination document). As long as the files are kept together in the same storage location, the font linkage should remain intact. We have also included a fontEmbed example file with the same text entered on the Stage, but with embedded font information instead of linked font information to demonstrate the significant difference in file size.

The first file you will be working with is a source document, or the Flash document that contains the Font symbols that you want to use as runtime shared assets.

Caution

If you are using the files from the CD-ROM to follow this example, you may need to modify the Font symbol in fontSource.fla to match a font that you have on your system (instead of "Marker Felt") before you can use Test Movie to publish the .swf file (Step 5).

1. Open your source document and select your Font symbol in the Library. If you are looking at the files on the CD-ROM, open "fontSource.fla" and select the Font symbol called "NewFont" in the Library.

2. Open the Linkage properties dialog box (see Figure 8-20), by choosing **Linkage** from the Library options menu or from the contextual menu.

3. Enter an identifier that will help you to remember what this Font symbol is used for in your project (such as "titleFont"). When you enter the identifier, you will see it displayed after the Font symbol name in the Library. In our example file, we used the identifier "fontSource" to make the connection more obvious between the document (fontSource.fla) and the published movie (fontSource.swf). Don't close the Linkage dialog box until you have completed the next step.

Figure 8-20: Setting up Linkage properties for a Font symbol in the Flash source document (.fla)

4. The URL field is where you enter the path to the storage location for the source movie (.swf) that you will publish after you have finished choosing settings in the source document (.fla.) The link can be relative or absolute depending on how you will be storing your project .swfs:

   • If you are planning to keep the source movie (.swf) in the same folder as your individual destination movies (.swf), then all you need to enter in the URL field of the Linkage Properties dialog box is the name of your source .swf file — as in our example: fontSource.swf.

   • If the source .swf file will be stored in a different folder or even on a separate server than the destination (linked) .swf files, then you need to enter an absolute path (Web address) in the URL field to specify the exact storage location of your source .swf file, such as:
   `http://yourserver.com/projectdirectory/sourceName.swf`.

5. Now you can save your source .fla file to the final storage location using File ⇨ Save (Ctrl+S or ⌘+S) and test your source .swf using Control ⇨ Test Movie (Ctrl+Enter or ⌘+Return).(See Figure 8-21.) Although nothing is displayed in the published .swf, if you turn on the Bandwidth Profiler (from the application menu: View ⇨ Bandwidth Profiler or with shortcut keys Ctrl+B or ⌘+B), you will notice that the file size is probably more than 20 KB (our example file was 27 KB). This is the size of the font information for all of the embedded characters included in your Font symbol.

You have successfully created and saved a runtime shared asset. Now you can create another Flash document that will reference the font information stored in fontSource.swf so that you can use your custom font without having to embed the font information.

Figure 8-21: The published source movie (.swf) with embedded font information for our Font symbol to be used in other destination movies as a runtime shared asset

1. Create a new Flash document or open the fontLink.fla file from the CD-ROM, and make sure that you have the Library panel for the current document open.

2. There are two ways of linking another document to the font information in your Shared library:

   • If you have already created a document that uses Font symbols as described in the section on author-time sharing and decide to link to a runtime shared asset instead, you can enter the identifier and the URL of the Shared library movie (.swf)in the Linkage properties for any Font symbol in your Library. To enter linkage information manually, you need to have a Font symbol in the document Library selected so that you can access the Linkage properties dialog box from the options menu or from the contextual menu. Enter the identifier and the URL exactly as they appear in your font source file but instead of Export for Runtime Sharing you will see that Import for Runtime Sharing is selected (see Figure 8-22). You should now find that all instances of the Font symbol in your current document will be updated with the Font information stored in the shared asset movie (.swf) (as long as it is available on your server when you publish the movie (.swf) for your current document).

   • If you are authoring a document (.fla) that does not yet contain any Font symbols and you want to link to your runtime shared asset, you can simply drag the Font symbol from the source library into the current document Library. With your destination document and Library panel open, select Open or Open as Library and browse to the Flash document (.fla) for your shared asset. You can then drag your source Font symbol from the shared asset library and drop it into your destination document Library. If you access Linkage properties for the Font symbol now in your Library, you will see that Flash automatically inserts the identifier and URL for the shared asset. You can now use the font in your new document and it will be linked to the font information stored in the runtime shared asset movie (.swf).

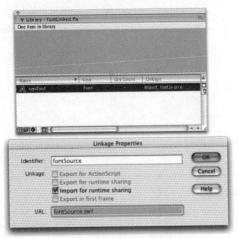

Figure 8-22: Entering link information for a Font symbol in a destination movie in order to use the font information stored in the runtime Shared library

3. When a Font symbol in your Library has the identifier and URL entered in its Linkage properties, you can use the linked font in your document by selecting it from your font menu and using the Text tool as you normally would. When you publish your movie (.swf), you will notice that your file size is much smaller than it would be with embedded font information. For an example of this, compare Figure 8-23 (linked), with Figure 8-24 (embedded).

Figure 8-23: The published .swf file from a document using linked font information from a runtime shared asset

4. If you decide that you want to disable runtime sharing for a Font symbol in a destination document, you can clear the Import for Runtime Sharing check box in the Linkage Properties dialog box. The font information for the characters used in your file will now be exported with the .swf file, so the file size will be larger, but the Flash Player will not require access to the shared asset.

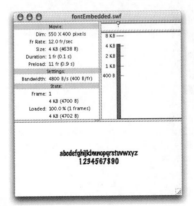

Figure 8-24: The published .swf file from a document using embedded font information

Modifying Text

In addition to all of the powerful text-handling capabilities discussed earlier in this chapter, there are some other ways that you can modify the appearance of text to create custom effects. Flash gives you the ability to reshape and distort Static text to suit your taste (or lack thereof). Figure 8-25 illustrates some of the ways that you can modify text after you have finished editing it with the regular text options.

Figure 8-25: Text boxes can be modified with Free Transform options (top). To create individual characters apply Break apart once (middle), and apply it again to create graphic text (bottom). Graphic text can be modified like any other shape in Flash.

We have included the Flash files for the modified text shown in this section on the CD-ROM. If you want to look at these in the Flash authoring environment, you can open the file called "modifyText.fla" in the ch8 folder.

Because custom text information will add to your file size, it is best to reserve these treatments for special text such as titles or graphics. If you are working with longer sections of text (such as an article or a story), it is better to use common fonts or device fonts to help keep your files smaller and to make the text easier to read.

With long sections of text, you will most likely need to add scrolling, and this is much easier to do if you use Dynamic text. If you use modified Static text or graphic text, it is still possible to add scrolling behavior by creating animation and controls manually, but this is much more time-consuming and will require more information embedded in your final .swf.

When text is nested in a Graphic, Movie Clip, or Button symbol, you can modify its appearance using the Color Effect controls on the Property inspector as described in Chapter 9, "Modifying Graphics."

By selecting a text box with the Arrow tool and activating the Scale option, you can scale your text by dragging the text box handles, but this is not recommended as a way of increasing the size of text unless it has been broken into vector shapes. Because Flash has to interpolate the normal font outlines to scale text this way, it can result in jagged edges when the movie is published. When sizing text, it is much better to simply choose or enter a larger point size in the font menu to ensure a clean outline when the text is exported.

Sampling and sharing text attributes

If you want to use the same font attributes on a variety of text boxes, it is often best to modify one text box so that it has all the qualities you want — including color, size, font, style, and line or character spacing. You then have two options for transferring these attributes to other text boxes using the Eyedropper tool:

✦ **To modify existing text boxes:** You can select other text boxes with the Arrow tool and then activate the Eyedropper tool in the Toolbox and click on your modified text to sample its attributes and transfer them to all the other selected text boxes simultaneously. This is much more efficient and consistent than trying to remember what settings you used and changing them manually on different text boxes.

✦ **To set attributes for new text boxes:** You can load the visual attributes of any text into the Property inspector by activating the Eyedropper tool and clicking on the text to acquire its appearance. The Text tool is automatically activated after text is sampled, so you can immediately begin creating new text with the settings now loaded in the Property inspector.

Converting text into vector shapes

The Break apart command (Ctrl+B or ⌘+B) is used to reduce symbols to grouped shapes, and it can also be used to modify Static text. Applying Break apart once to a text box will break a line of text into individual characters, applying the command again converts the characters into *graphic text* (vector lines and fills). Individual text characters can be grouped or changed to symbols. To make it easier to use individual characters in Motion tweened animation, you can apply the Flash MX Distribute to Layers command to automatically place each character on its own layer.

Breaking apart text and using Distribute to Layers is described in more detail, along with coverage of applying special line and fill effects in Chapter 9, "Modifying Graphics."

Graphic text can be modified using any of the drawing tools, reshaped with the Arrow and Subselect tools or distorted with any of the Free Transform options. You can also select special fills such as bitmaps or gradients to create patterned text, or use the Eraser tool to delete pieces of the letter shapes (as shown in Figure 8-26).

Figure 8-26: Using the Eraser tool to delete
parts of a graphic letter shape

However, after text characters have been converted to lines and fills, they can no longer be edited as text. Even if you regroup the text characters and/or convert the text into a symbol, you can no longer apply font, kerning, or paragraph options. To streamline your workflow, consider how you can combine graphic text with normal text for some effects — rather than converting all text into graphic shapes. Figure 8-27 shows how a graphic version and a character version of the same text can be combined to create an exaggerated drop shadow.

Figure 8-27: Combining versions of the same
text to create a drop shadow (the foreground text
was broken apart once, while the shadow text was
broken apart twice)

There are a few tips and guidelines to remember when converting text to shapes in Flash:

✦ To convert text characters to component lines and fills, the text characters that you want to convert must first be selected, or highlighted. Then choose Modify ➪ Break apart from the application menu. To undo, choose Edit ➪ Undo (Ctrl+Z or ⌘+Z) from the application menu.

✦ Rotation and Break apart can only be applied to fonts with available outline information such as TrueType fonts.

✦ On Macs, PostScript fonts can only be broken apart if a type manager is installed that will handle PostScript fonts.

✦ Bitmap fonts disappear from the screen if you attempt to break them apart.

✦ Test whether a font is a bitmapped font by choosing View ➪ Antialias from the application menu. If the text still appears with ragged edges, it is a bitmapped font and will disappear when broken apart.

As you experiment with graphic text you may want to refer to some of the other chapters that cover working with shapes.

Cross-Reference   For more information on reshaping, and manipulating lines and fills with drawing tools, see Chapter 5, "Drawing in Flash," and for information on animating shapes refer to Part III, "Creating Animation and Effects."

Summary

✦ Flash offers robust and well-organized text editing controls, but you can only make the most of these tools if you are familiar with at least the basic principles of typography.

✦ Studying the history of type in visual communication is one of the most practical and inspiring things you can do to improve your design skills.

✦ Flash MX has centralized type controls in the Property inspector. This makes working with text more streamlined and intuitive than it was in any previous version of Flash.

✦ Although minor issues may come up when working with text in Flash, it is relatively simple to work cross-platform and deliver high-quality presentations to users on many different systems.

✦ Flash offers three text types for various uses in interactive projects: Static text, Dynamic text, and Input text.

✦ Flash requires complete font information to be available on your system in order for text to be exported properly to the final movie (.swf). If you need to open a Flash file (.fla) that includes fonts not available on your system, you can choose temporary substitute fonts without damaging the original font information stored in the file.

✦ To minimize file size and to allow dynamic control of text in published Flash movies (.swf), you may specify generic device fonts that the Flash Player will find on all users' systems.

✦ To use commonly installed fonts without having to embed all of the information required to render font outlines, you can enable the Use Device Fonts option. When the Flash movie (.swf) is exported with this option, only the basic characteristics of the font (name, size, style) are embedded so that the Flash Player can look for an equivalent font on the users machine.

✦ Creating Font symbols and storing them in Shared libraries for either author-time updates or runtime linkage can help you to manage large projects by centralizing font sources and making updates faster and easier.

✦ Lines of type in text boxes can be broken apart into individual characters by applying the Break apart command. When the Break apart command is applied twice to the same text box, the text outline will be converted into vector shapes.

✦　　✦　　✦

Modifying Graphics

After becoming familiar with the Flash authoring environment and learning to use the Drawing tools, you are now ready to move on to the really fun part: messing with the basic shapes and text elements you have made to create your own unique effects!

In this chapter, we revisit some of the core tools to learn new ways of applying them. We also introduce some specialized tools that exist only to transform your artwork. Following a look at how the Eyedropper, Paint Bucket, and Ink Bottle work together to modify strokes and fills, we introduce the newly independent Transform Fill tool.

The Modify Shape submenu offers some special commands we will apply to alter lines and fills, while the Modify Transform submenu introduces the various options available for skewing, stretching, rotating, flipping, and rotating shapes.

Before moving on to explain the Flash stacking order and how to create compound shapes, we introduce the powerful Free Transform tool. Flash MX has added an Envelope modifier that allows you to warp and distort multiple shapes simultaneously. Other MX features worth celebrating include the new stepped Break Apart command on text and the indispensable Distribute to Layers command — these two features combined make animating text infinitely easier than it was in previous versions of Flash.

The final section of this chapter demonstrates how to alter the appearance of individual symbol instances using the Color Effect controls available in the Property inspector.

As various techniques and tools are introduced, we show you how to apply them for modifying artwork and adding the illusion of depth and texture to your 2D graphics.

✦ ✦ ✦ ✦

In This Chapter

Sampling and swapping fills and line styles

Applying the Transform Fill tool to control gradient and bitmap fills

Using Modify Shape options: Lines to Fills, Expand Fill, Soften Edges

Working with the Free Transform tool and new options

Stacking, grouping, and arranging item types

Creating and managing compound shapes

Using Break Apart and Trace Bitmap

Applying Distribute to Layers to auto-separate items

Working with Advanced Effects for color settings on symbol instances

✦ ✦ ✦ ✦

Sampling and Switching Fills and Strokes

The Arrow tool can always be used to select a stroke or fill so that it can be deleted, moved, or modified using any of the Swatches pop-ups or the Stroke Style menu on the Property inspector. But, what do you do if you want to add a stroke or fill to a shape that was not drawn with one? The answer to this dilemma is found in a trio of tools that work nimbly together to provide one of the most unique graphics editing solutions found in Flash. The Eyedropper tool is used to acquire fill and stroke styles or colors and the Paint Bucket and Ink Bottle tools are used to transfer these characteristics to other shapes.

 Note These tools will only apply changes directly to shapes, so to modify an element that has been grouped or converted into a symbol, you must first access the element in Symbol Editing mode.

The Eyedropper tool

As introduced in Chapter 7, "Applying Color," the Dropper that appears when the Arrow tool is used to select colors from any of the pop-up Swatches menus is similar to the Eyedropper tool available in the Toolbox. However, when pulled out of the Toolbox directly, the Eyedropper (I) has slightly different behavior. Although the Eyedropper tool cannot be used to sample colors from elements outside the Document window, it can be used to sample line and fill styles or to simultaneously change the stroke and the fill color chips to the same sampled color.

 Note When used to acquire colors, the Toolbox Eyedropper tool is limited to acquiring colors from the Flash Stage and Work area. However, the Droppers that are accessed from the Swatches pop-ups in the Color Mixer panel, Toolbox, or Property inspector can acquire colors from other visible areas, such as the system background, items on the desktop, or items that are open in other applications. The only "trick" to this is to press and hold the mouse on any of the color chips and only release the mouse when you are hovering over the color that you want to sample. The preview in the Swatches pop-up will change as you roll-over different colors and the color chip will change when you release the mouse to show the color that you have selected.

 Cross-Reference For more information about this feat, refer to Chapter 7, "Applying Color."

The Eyedropper tool doesn't have any options in the Toolbox because they are all built in. As you hover over an item, the Eyedropper displays a small icon to indicate whether it is over a line or a fill that can be sampled by clicking on it. When a line is sampled, the Eyedropper automatically converts to the Ink Bottle tool, and when a fill is sampled, the Eyedropper converts to the Paint Bucket tool.

The composite image shown in Figure 9-1 shows the icons displayed when the Eyedropper is used to sample a fill (A) and apply it to another shape with the Paint Bucket (B), sample a stroke (C), and apply it to another shape with the Ink Bottle (D).

Note

The icons for these different Eyedropper states are more distinct in the Windows version of Flash MX than in the Mac version (shown in Figure 9-1). The paintbrush that indicates a fill and the pencil that indicates a stroke are easier to differentiate, but the function of the tool is the same on both platforms.

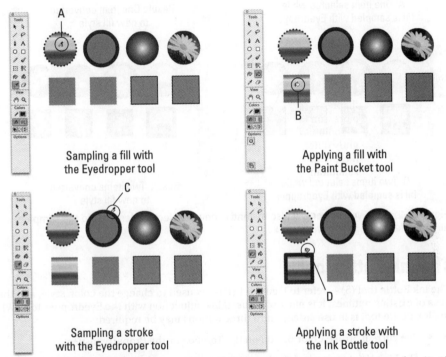

Figure 9-1: The Eyedropper used to sample a fill and apply it with the Paint Bucket (A, B) and to sample a stroke and apply it with the Ink Bottle (C, D)

Any items already selected when the Eyedropper samples a stroke or fill will immediately acquire the applicable stroke or fill style. This is the quickest way to transfer the fill or line styles of one element to a whole group of elements. Figure 9-2 shows the Eyedropper used to sample a fill with one (A) or more (B) elements already selected.

Note

By holding down the Shift key while clicking on a line or a stroke color with the Eyedropper, the Fill and the Stroke color chips will both be converted simultaneously to the new selected color so that it can be applied with any of the other drawing tools.

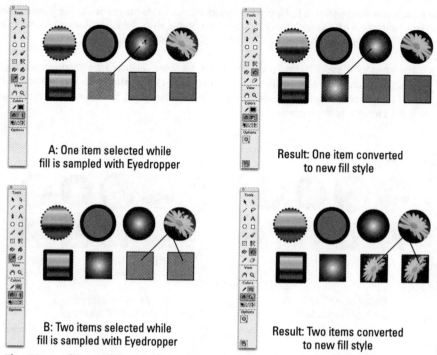

A: One item selected while fill is sampled with Eyedropper

Result: One item converted to new fill style

B: Two items selected while fill is sampled with Eyedropper

Result: Two items converted to new fill style

Figure 9-2: The Eyedropper will also instantly convert selected elements to the sampled fill or stroke style.

The Ink Bottle tool

The Ink Bottle tool (S) — refer to Figure 9-1 (D) — is used to change the color, style, and thickness of existing outlines. It is most often used in conjunction with the Eyedropper tool. When the Ink Bottle tool is in use, attention to three options may be required:

✦ The current Stroke Color option on the Toolbox or the Property inspector

✦ The Line Height option of the Property inspector

✦ The Stroke Style option of the Property inspector

The Ink Bottle will apply the current stroke color and line style, either sampled with the Eyedropper tool or chosen from the pop-up in the Toolbox or the controls in the Property inspector.

Caution When you click a selected line with the Ink Bottle, all other currently *selected* lines are changed simultaneously.

The Ink Bottle is especially useful for applying custom line styles to multiple lines. You can build a collection of custom line styles either off-screen or in a special custom line palette that is saved as a single-frame Flash movie. You can then acquire these line styles whenever you want to reuse them.

Caution   Depending on the level of zoom, some lines may not display accurately on the screen—although they will print correctly on a high-resolution printer. Stroke Height (or thickness) may also be adjusted in the Stroke Style dialog box that is invoked by choosing the **Custom** stroke style option in the Property inspector.

The Paint Bucket tool

The Paint Bucket tool is used to fill enclosed areas with color, gradients, or bitmap fills. Although the Paint Bucket tool is a more robust tool than the Ink Bottle, and can be used independently of the Eyedropper tool, it's often used in conjunction with the Eyedropper tool. That's because, as was discussed earlier in the section on the Eyedropper tool, when the Eyedropper tool is clicked on a fill, it first acquires the attributes of that fill and then automatically converts to the Paint Bucket tool. When the Paint Bucket tool is active, as shown in Figure 9-3, two options are available from the Toolbox: Lock Fill and Gap Size. The Gap Size drop-down, which is shown at the right, offers four settings to control how Flash handles gaps or open spaces in lines when filling with the Paint Bucket tool.

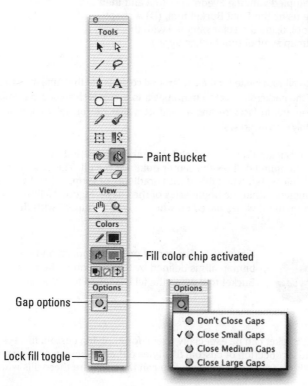

Figure 9-3: The Paint Bucket tool (left) and Gap size options (right)

When the Eyedropper tool is used to acquire a fill that is a broken-apart bitmap, the Eyedropper tool is automatically swapped for the Paint Bucket tool and a thumbnail of the bitmap image appears in place of the fill color chip. This procedure also automatically engages the Paint Bucket Lock Fill Option.

Cross-Reference For more information about working with bitmaps, refer to Chapter 16, "Importing Artwork."

The final appearance of a bitmap fill can vary greatly depending on how it is applied. Figure 9-4 shows a series of shapes all filled with the same bitmap to illustrate the various results achieved from using different steps to define the fill.

A   B   C   D

Figure 9-4: (A) A shape drawn with the Rectangle tool using a bitmap fill selected in the Mixer panel; (B) A bitmap fill applied with Arrow tool selection and Mixer panel fill style menu, after the shape was drawn; (C) A broken apart bitmap sampled with the Eyedropper tool and then applied to the finished shape using the Paint Bucket tool; (D) A shape filled with the Paint Bucket tool, using the color sampled with the Eyedropper tool from the Bitmap symbol (not broken apart)

Caution Using the Paint Bucket to fill with white (or the background color) is not the same as erasing. Painting with white (or the background color) may appear to accomplish something similar to erasing. However, you are, in fact, creating a filled item that can be selected, moved, deleted, or reshaped. Only erasing erases!

Another behavior of the Paint Bucket that can be helpful to recognize is that the exact location where the Paint Bucket is applied defines the center point for the fill. This has no visible effect when filling with solid colors, but when filling with gradients or bitmap fills it will make a difference how the fill is aligned within the boundaries of the shape. Figure 9-5 illustrates how the center point of a gradient fill varies based on where it was "dumped" with the Paint Bucket.

Figure 9-5: The center point of gradient and bitmap fills is defined by the location of the Paint Bucket tool when the fill is applied to a shape.

Like the Ink Bottle, the Paint Bucket can be especially useful for applying custom fill styles to multiple items. You can build a collection of custom fill styles either off-screen or in a special, saved, custom-fills-palette, single-frame Flash movie. You can then acquire these fills whenever necessary.

Caution If you click with the Paint Bucket tool on one of several selected fills, *all* of the selected fills will be simultaneously changed to the new fill.

Using the Paint Bucket Gap Size option

As shown in Figure 9-3, the Gap Size option drop-down offers four settings that control how the Paint Bucket treats gaps when filling. These settings are Don't Close Gaps, Close Small Gaps, Close Medium Gaps, and Close Large Gaps. These tolerance settings enable Flash to fill an outline if the endpoints of the outline aren't completely joined, leaving an open shape. If the gaps are too large, you may have to close them manually. Figure 9-6 illustrates how the Gap size option settings affect the Paint Bucket fill behavior.

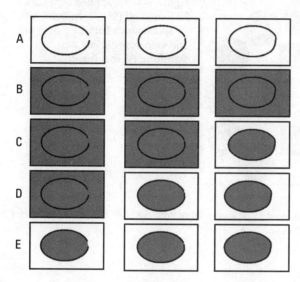

Figure 9-6: Paint Bucket fill applied with various Gap size settings: (A) Original oval outline with decreasing gap sizes, left to right, with no fill; (B) Gray fill applied with Don't Close Gaps; (C) Gray fill applied with Close Small Gaps; (D) Gray fill applied with Close Medium Gaps; (E) Gray fill applied with Close Large Gaps

Note   The level of zoom changes the apparent size of gaps. Although the actual size of gaps is unaffected by zoom, the Paint Bucket's interpretation of the gap is dependent upon the current Zoom setting. When zoomed in very close, the Bucket will find it harder to close gaps; when zoomed out, the Bucket will find it easier to close gaps.

Using the Paint Bucket Lock Fill option

The Paint Bucket's Lock Fill option is the same as the Brush Lock Fill option—it controls how Flash handles areas filled with gradient color or bitmaps. When this button is turned on, all areas (or shapes) that are painted with the same gradient or bitmap will appear to be part of a single, continuous, filled shape. The Lock Fill option locks the angle, size, and point of origin of the current fill to remain constant throughout the selected shapes. Any modifications made to a filled shape will be applied to the other shapes filled using the same Lock Fill option.

Cross-Reference   Working with gradient colors is discussed in Chapter 7, "Applying Color."

To demonstrate the distinction between fills applied with or without the Lock Fill option, as shown in Figure 9-7, on the left, we created five shapes and filled them with a bitmap with Lock Fill off. The image is rendered separately from one shape to the next. On the right, those same shapes were filled with the same bitmap, but with Lock Fill on. Note how the image is now continuous from one shape to the next. Bitmap fills are automatically tiled to fill a shape, so the bitmap fill on the right was also scaled using the Transform Fill tool to make it easier to see the continuation of the image between the various shapes.

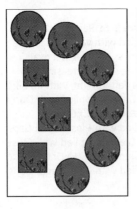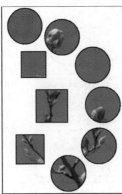

Figure 9-7: Fill applied with Lock fill turned off (left), compared with fill applied with Lock fill turned on and then scaled using the Transform Fill tool (right)

Tip   When the Eyedropper tool is used to pick up a fill or gradient from the scene, the Lock Fill button is automatically toggled on.

Transforming Fills

The Transform Fill tool (F) was originally an option for the Paint Bucket tool, but in Flash MX it now has a home on the main Toolbox, right next to the new Free Transform tool. Transform Fill is used only to modify bitmap or gradient fills and will not apply to simple color fills. The Transform Fill will do many of the same things as the Free Transform tool, but it only modifies the *fill* of a shape without changing the stroke or outline appearance at all. This is a lot like scooting, rotating, or skewing a larger piece of material behind a frame so that a different portion is visible.

The Transform Fill tool, like the Eyedropper tool, does not have any options in the Toolbox, but it does apply differently depending on the type of fill selected. To use the Transform Fill tool, select it in the Toolbox, and then simply click an existing gradient or fill. A set of three or four adjustment handles appears, depending on the type of fill. Three transformations can be performed on a gradient or bitmap fill: adjusting the fill's center point, rotating the fill, and scaling the fill. The extra set of adjustment handles displayed on bitmap fills allows them to be skewed.

Figure 9-8 illustrates the various adjustment handles on three types of fills (top) and the icons that display when the pointer is rolled over each of the handles (bottom).

Transform Fill tool

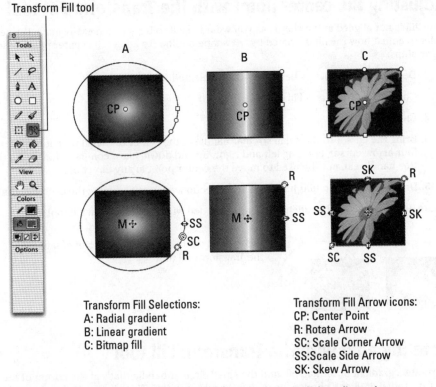

Transform Fill Selections:
A: Radial gradient
B: Linear gradient
C: Bitmap fill

Transform Fill Arrow icons:
CP: Center Point
R: Rotate Arrow
SC: Scale Corner Arrow
SS: Scale Side Arrow
SK: Skew Arrow

Figure 9-8: The Transform Fill tool applied to (top, L-R): Radial gradient, Linear gradient, and bitmap fill. Each handle type displays an icon on rollover to indicate its function (bottom).

These general characteristics may differ if a fill (or bitmap fill) has been variously copied, rotated, or pasted in any number of ways. The fundamental rules are as follows:

✦ The round center handle moves the center point.

✦ The round corner handle rotates.

✦ The round edge handles skew either vertically or horizontally.

✦ The square edge handles scale either vertically or horizontally.

✦ The square corner handle scales symmetrically.

Tip
To see all the handles when transforming a large element or working with an item close to the edge of the Stage, choose View ➪ Work Area from the application menu or use the shortcut keys Shift+Ctrl+W (Shift+⌘+W).

Adjusting the center point with the Transform Fill tool

If the fill is not aligned in the shape, as you would like it to be, you can easily move the center point to adjust how the fill is framed by the shape outline. To adjust the center point, follow these steps:

1. Deselect the fill if it has been previously selected.

2. Choose the Transform Fill tool.

3. Click the fill.

4. Bring the cursor to the small circular handle at the center of the fill until it changes to a four-arrow cursor, pointing left and right, up and down, like a compass, indicating that this handle can now be used to move the center point in any direction.

5. Drag the center circular handle in any direction you want to move the center of the fill.

Figure 9-9 shows a radial gradient (left) repositioned with the Transform Fill tool (right).

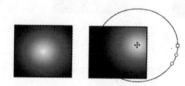

Figure 9-9: Adjusting the center point of a fill with the Transform Fill tool

Rotating a fill with the Transform Fill tool

To rotate a gradient or bitmap fill, find the small circular handle that's at the corner of the fill. (In a radial gradient, choose the middle circular handle.) This circular handle is used for rotating a fill around the center point. Simply click the circular handle with the Rotate cursor and drag clockwise or counterclockwise to rotate the fill. Figure 9-10 shows a bitmap fill (left) as it appears when rotated clockwise (right).

Figure 9-10: Rotating a fill with the Transform Fill tool

Adjusting scale with the Transform Fill tool

To resize a bitmap fill symmetrically (to maintain the aspect ratio), find the small square-corner handle, which is usually located at the lower-left corner of the fill. On rollover, the diagonal arrow icon appears, indicating the direction(s) in which the handle will resize the fill. Click and drag to scale the fill symmetrically. On radial gradients, the center round handle is used to scale with the gradient aspect ratio constrained. Linear gradients only have one handle for scaling, and this handle will always scale in the direction of the gradient banding.

To resize a fill asymmetrically, find a small square handle on either a vertical or a horizontal edge, depending on whether you want to affect the width or height of the fill. On rollover, arrows appear perpendicular to the edge of the shape indicating the direction in which this handle will resize the fill. Click and drag a handle to reshape the fill.

Figure 9-11 shows the three fill types with their respective scale options. Linear gradient fills (left) can only be scaled in the direction of the gradient banding, but they can be rotated to scale vertically (lower) instead of horizontally (upper). Radial gradient fills (center) can be expanded symmetrically (upper) with the circular handle, or asymmetrically (lower) with the square handle. Like Linear gradients, they can be rotated to scale vertically rather than horizontally. Bitmap fills (right) can be scaled by the corner handle to maintain the aspect ratio (upper), or dragged from any side handle to scale asymmetrically (lower).

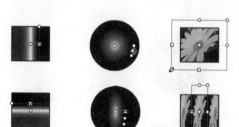

Figure 9-11: Scaling fills symmetrically (top) and asymmetrically (bottom)

Note The right column of Figure 9-11 is a good example of a situation in which scaling a bitmap fill smaller with the Transform Fill tool causes it to tile — or repeat — and fill the space of the original image.

Skewing a bitmap fill with the Transform Fill tool

To skew a bitmap fill horizontally, find the small round handle at the middle of the right-hand border. Click the handle, and arrows appear, parallel to the edge of the fill, indicating the directions in which this handle will skew the fill. Drag to skew the image in either direction. Figure 9-12 shows a bitmap skewed horizontally (left) and vertically (right). Note that the skew procedure is still active after it has been applied, meaning that the skew may be further modified — this behavior is common to all functions of the Transform Fill tool.

Figure 9-12: Skewing a bitmap fill with the Transform Fill tool

Note Gradient fills cannot be skewed; they can only be scaled on the horizontal or vertical axis.

Transform Fill Used for Effects

You will apply the Transform Fill tool most often to get a patterned fill or a gradient aligned and sized within its outline shape. A simple way of adding more depth to shapes is to modify gradient fills so that they appear to reflect light from one consistent source. You can choose to emulate a soft light for a more even illumination, or to emulate a hard, focused light that will emphasize dramatic shadows. As you create a composition on the Stage, you can use the Transform Fill tool to modify individual elements so that they appear to share a common light source. Figure 9-13 illustrates how a default radial gradient (left) can be modified to emulate a soft (center) or hard (right) illumination.

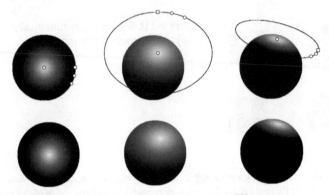

Figure 9-13: Applying Transform Fill to create different illumination effects

To show how these lighting effects can be applied to create the illusion of 3D, we created a little scene using only radial fills that were modified with the Transform Fill tool. Figure 9-14 shows the radial gradients as they appeared when drawn with the default settings (left) and how the scene appeared after the gradients were modified with Transform Fill and some basic shape scaling as described later in this chapter.

On the CD-ROM   If you want to deconstruct this example, we have included the file on the CD-ROM with both the unmodified and the final transformed shapes. You will find the file named SphereLighting.fla in the ch09 folder of the CD-ROM.

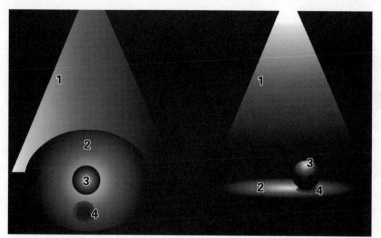

Figure 9-14: The Transform Fill tool used to modify default radial gradient fills (left) to create the illusion of 3D lighting effects (right)

Modify Shape Menu Commands

The three specialized commands found in the application menu (under Modify ➪ Shape), provide modification options that cannot be achieved with any other tools in Flash.

Lines to Fills

Lines to Fills does exactly what its name implies: It converts lines defined by single points into shapes defined by an outline of editable points. To apply the Lines to Fills command simply select any lines that you wish to convert before choosing Modify ➪ Shape ➪ Lines to Fills. After a line has been converted in this way it can be editing like any other filled shape, including adding bitmap or gradient fills or applying the Arrow or Subselect tools to adjust the corners and curves of the outlined shape.

Cross-Reference   The Arrow tool and the Subselect Arrow tool are discussed in Chapter 5, "Drawing in Flash."

Creating scaleable artwork

The Lines to Fills command is especially important, because it provides the one solution for maintaining line to fill ratios when scaling artwork that would require lines to display at smaller than 1 point size. Fills do not have the same display limitation as lines and they will maintain visual consistency as they are scaled larger or smaller. In Figure 9-15, the image on the left was drawn using the pencil tool to make lines around the eyes and on the whiskers of the cat cartoon. When it was scaled, the lines were not visually consistent with the fills. The image on the right was modified using the Lines to Fills command before scaling it down to 25 percent size. In this case, the ratio between the outlines around the eyes and the whiskers was consistent with the other filled shapes in the cartoon.

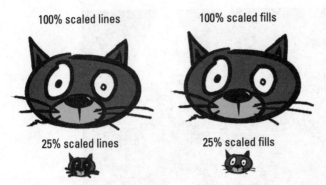

Figure 9-15: Using the Lines to Fills command to ensure consistency when scaling artwork

Note

Remember that in Flash, the smallest line size that can be displayed is 1 point. Lines with a height of less than 1 point will all appear to be the same size on screen when viewed at 100 percent scale. The difference in size will only be visible when the View is scaled larger or zoomed in. However, the lines will print correctly on a high-resolution printer.

Correcting rounded corners and lines

Another important task that the Lines to Fills command will accomplish is creating true square corners on angled shapes. As you have probably noticed by now, one of the quirks of the Flash drawing tools is that lines over 1 point in thickness have rounded ends and soft corners by default. By converting lines to fills, you can apply the Straighten modifier or edit individual points in the shape to create true sharp corners and squared ends on lines.

Figure 9-16 illustrates the difference between a default rectangle with a 2-point stroke (A), the same rectangle converted with Modify ⇨ Shape ⇨ Lines to Fills (B), and then modified using the Modify ⇨ Straighten command (C).

Figure 9-16: Using the Lines to Fills and Straighten commands to create true square corners

Figure 9-17 illustrates the slightly different process to create squared ends on a line. The original 2-point line (A), is converted using Modify ⇨ Shape ⇨ Lines to Fills (B), and then because the Straighten command can be unpredictable on multiple curved lines, the extra points in the line are instead removed manually using the Subselect tool (C). After the extra points along the curve of the line are deleted, be certain to convert the final two points that define the end of the line into corner points by Option (Alt)+clicking them with the Subselect tool to ensure a perfectly flat end.

Figure 9-17: After converting a line to a fill, it is possible to manually edit the points that define the end of the shape to eliminate the curve and create a clean, flat edge.

Expand Fill

The Expand Fill command has two options that are used to size fills up or down evenly on all sides of a shape. To apply the command, select the fill(s) that you want to modify. Then choose Modify ⇨ Shape ⇨ Expand Fill. The Expand Fills dialog box appears, where you can choose to expand or inset (shrink) the fill by a specific pixel value. Keep in mind that this command applies differently than a normal scale modification. Because the fill expands or shrinks from all sides evenly, an extreme modification can cause a shape to bloat to the extent that unfilled areas are obscured, or conversely can cause a shape to shrink to the point that some of the areas are no longer visible. When applied moderately, the Expand Fill command can be very helpful for adjusting multiple filled shapes consistently, without scaling lines in the same area of the artwork.

Figure 9-18 includes a rectangle, a cartoon cat, and a sketch of some grapes. The original shapes are shown on the left, the expanded fills in the center, and the inset fills on the left. As you can see, expanding fills will often obscure the strokes surrounding a shape, while choosing to inset a fill will leave space between the fill and any surrounding stroke.

Figure 9-18: Modifying an original shape (left) with the Expand Fill command using the expand option (center) or the inset option (right), will respectively bloat or shrink a fill by a specified pixel amount.

The Expand Fill command can also be used to create custom text forms. Figure 9-19 shows how the original text shape (left) can be modified using either the expand or inset option. To create bloated balloon-like text (center), or shrunken, eroded text (right), you first have to apply the Modify ⇨ Break Apart command (Ctrl+B or ⌘+B) twice to reduce the text to simple filled shapes. By selecting all of the letter shapes before applying the Expand Fill command, you can modify the whole word at the same time.

Figure 9-19: Text broken apart into letter shapes (A) can be expanded (B), or inset (C) to create custom text effects.

Other text-editing options are discussed in Chapter 8, "Working with Text."

Soften Fill Edges

The Soften Fill Edges command is the closest thing to a blur filter available in Flash. This command, like the Expand Fill command, can only be applied to fills and gives you the option to expand or inset the shape by a specific number of pixels.

Caution   Flash MX will allow you to select a line and choose the Soften Edges command from the Modify ⇨ Shape menu, but once the command is applied, the line will just disappear from the Stage — surprise! If you make this mistake, you can recover your line by immediately choosing Edit ⇨ Undo (Ctrl+Z or ⌘+Z).

The unique effect of Soften Fill Edges is created by a series of banded fills around the original fill that decrease in opacity toward the outermost band. You can control the number and width of these bands by entering values in the Soften Fill Edges dialog box (shown in Figure 9-20) to create a variety of effects, from a very subtle blurred effect to a dramatic stepped appearance around the edges of the fill.

Figure 9-20: The Soften Fill Edges dialog box with settings for controlling the edge effect

The Soften Fill Edges dialog box controls the following features of the fill modification:

✦ **Distance:** Defines the number of pixels the original shape will expand or shrink

✦ **Number of Steps:** Sets the number of bands that will appear around the outside edge of the fill

✦ **Expand or Inset:** Controls whether the bands will be added to the outside edge of the fill (expand) or stacked on the inside edge of the shape (inset)

Figure 9-21 shows how the original fill (left) appears after Soften Fill Edges is applied with the Expand option (center), or with the Inset option (right).

Figure 9-21: Applying Soften Fill Edges with the Expand option and with the Inset option

The width of the individual bands is equal to the total number of pixels set in Distance divided by the Number of Steps. When the edge of the shape is magnified, the individual bands can clearly be seen. Figure 9-22 shows a series of eight bands, each 1 pixel wide, created by using a Distance setting of 8 with a Number of Steps setting of 8.

Figure 9-22: A magnified view of the banded edge of a fill created by applying Soften Fill Edges

As with the Expand Fill command, Soften Fill Edges can create interesting text effects when applied to broken-apart letter shapes. Figure 9-23 shows an effect created by combining the original white text with a "shadow" made by applying the Soften Fill Edges command to a broken apart copy of the text that was filled with dark gray.

Soften Fill Edges

Figure 9-23: A shadow effect created by layering the original text over a copy that was broken apart, filled with dark gray and modified using Soften Fill Edges

On the CD-ROM

The Soften Fill Edges examples shown in Figure 9-21 and Figure 9-23 are included on the CD-ROM in the ch09 folder. The file is named "SoftenEdges.fla."

Free Transform Commands and Options

The commands we have looked at so far in this chapter are generally used for localized modification of lines or fills. In this section, we will introduce some commands that are applied to create more dramatic change of whole items or even groups of items.

The basic transform commands can be applied to primitive shapes or to symbols, groups, and text blocks, but it is important to know that any transformations applied to symbols, groups, or text blocks are saved in the Info panel even if they are unselected and then reselected later on. This allows these items to easily be reverted to their original appearance. The transform settings for primitive shapes, on the other hand, are reset to the default values in the Info panel as soon as they are deselected. This means that while a primitive shape is actively being modified, you can revert to the original appearance, but as soon as you apply a change and deselect the shape, its modified appearance will be considered original the next time it is selected.

As shown in Figure 9-24, there are various ways to access the transform commands available in Flash.

The Transform panel

The Transform panel (Ctrl+T or ⌘+T) includes value fields for horizontal and vertical scale percentages, degrees of rotation and degrees of vertical and horizontal skew. These fields can be used as visual reference or as a way to enter precise transform values. The Transform panel also includes two important buttons.

The **Copy and apply transform** button is used to duplicate the selected item with all transformations included. When you select this button, you may not notice that anything has happened to your selected item — this is because Flash places the duplicate exactly on top of the original. To see both the original and the duplicate, drag the duplicate to a new position in the Document window.

The **Reset** button will revert a transformed symbol, group, or text field to its original appearance and return all values in the Transform panel to the default settings. This can also be achieved by selecting Modify ➪ Transform ➪ Remove Transform. If you only want to remove the most recently applied modification, use Edit ➪ Undo (Ctrl+Z or ⌘+Z).

The Modify Transform menu

The commands found in the application menu under Modify ➪ Transform, reflect the new features available with the Free Transform tool. In addition, the commands in the application menu allow you to choose specific combinations of transform options as well as a couple of "shortcuts" for commonly needed modifications. Because these shortcuts are unique to the application menu, they deserve a brief description, although they are nearly self-explanatory.

✦ **Rotate 90 degrees CW or Rotate 90 degrees CCW:** Used to rotate any selected items by a half-turn in the chosen direction around the central axis point of the selection.

Tip   You can also use shortcut keys to rotate any selected item in 90-degree increments. To rotate an item 90 degrees clockwise, use Ctrl+9 or ⌘+9. To rotate an item 90 degrees counterclockwise, use Ctrl+7 or ⌘+7.

✦ **Flip Vertical or Flip Horizontal:** Used to place the item in a mirrored position either on the vertical axis (calendar flip) or the horizontal axis (book flip).

Free Transform tool

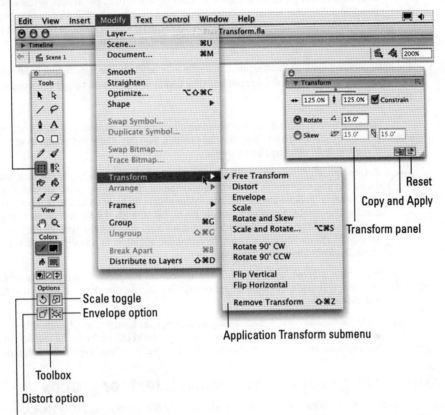

Scale toggle
Envelope option

Toolbox

Distort option

Rotate & Skew toggle

Figure 9-24: The various ways to access transform commands in Flash. The Free Transform tool (left), the Application Transform submenu (center), and the Transform panel (right)

The Free Transform tool

The Free Transform tool (Q) available directly from the Toolbox, allows you to apply transform commands dynamically with various arrow icons. These icons appear as the pointer is moved over the control points or handles of the selected item. Various transform states can also be invoked from the contextual menu. Although the position of these arrow icons can vary with the position of the pointer, they provide consistent indication of what transformation will be applied from the closest available handle. To finish any transformation, simply deselect the item by clicking outside of the current selection area.

 Move arrow: This familiar arrow indicates that all currently selected items can be dragged together to a new location in the Document window.

Axis point or transformation point: By default, this circle marks the center of an item as the axis for most transformations or animation. By dragging the center point to a different location, you can define a new axis or transformation point for modifications applied to the item. To return the axis point to its default location at the center of the item, double-click the axis point icon.

 Note The scale of shapes will always originate from the side opposite the handle that is selected, while the scale of symbols will originate from the center unless the axis point is moved to a side or a corner.

 Skew arrow: Generally available on any side of an item between transformation points. By clicking and dragging the outline, you can skew the shape in either direction indicated by the arrows.

 Rotate arrow: Generally available near any corner of an item. By clicking and dragging, you can rotate the item clockwise or counterclockwise around the transform axis. Note that if you move the arrow directly over the closest corner handle, the rotate arrow will usually be replaced with the Scale Corner arrow. To rotate around the opposite corner point without moving the axis point, press the Alt (Option) key while dragging. To constrain rotation to 45-degree increments, press the Shift key while dragging.

 Scale Side arrow: Available from any handle on the side of an item. Clicking and dragging will scale the item larger or smaller, in one direction only relative to the transform axis.

 Scale Corner arrow: Appears only on the corner handles of an item and is used to evenly scale the item larger or smaller, in all directions from the transform axis. To constrain the aspect ratio of the shape, press the Shift key while dragging.

Transforming shapes and symbols, text, or groups

Figure 9-25 shows how a symbol and a shape will display differently once they have been modified and deselected, than reselected with the Free Transform tool. The symbol (left) displays transform handles that are aligned with the originally modified item and the values of the transformation settings are preserved in the Transform panel. The shape (right), however, displays transform handles that are aligned to default values unrelated to the original modifications and the values in the Transform panel are also reset to default.

Free Transform limit options

The first two options in the Toolbox for the Free Transform tool are actually just toggles to limit the modifications that can be applied to a selected item. It can sometimes be easier to use the Free Transform tool with more specific behavior. When the Rotate and Skew button or the Scale button are toggled on, they will exclude all other modifications.

 The Rotate and Skew toggle protects the selected item from being scaled accidentally while you're rotating or skewing it. This Toolbox option is equivalent to selecting Modify ➪ Transform ➪ Rotate and Skew from the application menu or from the contextual menu.

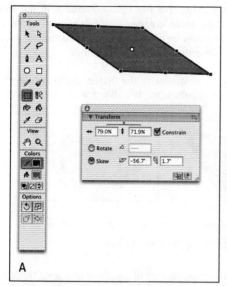
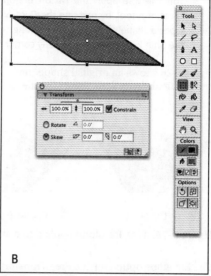

Figure 9-25: The Free Transform handles and Transform panel settings displayed for a symbol (left), and for a shape (right) that have been reselected after an initial modification

The Scale toggle protects the selected item from all other transformations while it is being sized larger or smaller. This Toolbox option is equivalent to selecting Modify ➪ Transform ➪ Scale from the application menu or from the contextual menu.

Tip   If you want the scale of a symbol to originate from a corner rather than from the center, remember that you can move the axis point by dragging it to a new position.

Free Transform special shape options

As seen in Figure 9-24, the last two options in the Toolbox for the Free Transform tool — **Distort** and **Envelope** — are not available for symbols, groups, or text fields. However, when transforming primitive shapes, these two options can be used to create complex modifications not easily achieved using other Flash tools.

Note   Remember that you can access the primitive shapes in a group or symbol by entering Symbol Editing mode. It is also possible to convert text fields into primitive shapes by applying the Break Apart command (twice).

Distort works by widening or narrowing the sides of the item, or stretching out the corners. This transform option does not bend or warp the shape; it allows sides of the shape to be scaled individually. To apply Distort, first select a shape with the Free Transform tool in the Toolbox, and turn on the Distort toggle in the Options area of the Toolbox. You will then be able to click and drag handles on the sides or corners of the item to stretch or compress individual sides. This is equivalent to selecting a shape with the Arrow tool and choosing Modify ➪ Transform ➪ Distort from the application menu or selecting Distort from the contextual menu.

Tip   You can also apply the Distort option to a shape that has been selected with the Free Transform tool, by pressing the Control (⌘) key while dragging a side or corner handle. To taper a shape or move two adjoining corner points an equal distance simultaneously, press the Shift key while dragging any corner handle with the Free Transform tool.

Figure 9-26 shows an original shape (left), being modified with the Distort option (center), and the final shape with distort handles as they appear when the shape is reselected (right).

Deselect   Distort Transform   New Distort Transform

Figure 9-26: Free Transform applied to a shape using the Distort option

The Envelope option for the Free Transform tool may be one of the most engaging transform methods available in Flash. Once you try it, you may be stretching, squashing, bending, and warping for hours. On the other hand, as you get used to working with this nifty little option, you will find it faster than ever to create unique shapes.

The Envelope option allows you to work with control points and handles much the same way you would when editing lines or shapes using the Subselect tool. The powerful difference is that the Envelope can wrap around the outside of multiple items so that the control points and handles will curve, scale, stretch, or warp all of the lines and shapes that are contained within the Envelope selection.

To apply the Envelope, first select a shape or multiple shapes with the Free Transform tool and then toggle on the Envelope option in the Toolbox. The Envelope will offer a series of control points and tangent handles. The square points are used to scale and skew the shape(s), while the round points are actually handles used to control the curve and warp of the shape(s). The Envelope option can also be accessed by selecting the shapes you want to transform and choosing Modify ➪ Transform ➪ Envelope from the application menu, or selecting Envelope from the contextual menu.

Figure 9-27 shows an original shape (left), being modified with the Envelope option (center), and the final shape with Envelope handles, as they appear when the shape is reselected (right).

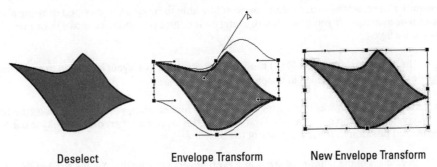

Deselect   Envelope Transform   New Envelope Transform

Figure 9-27: Free Transform applied to a shape using the Envelope option

Modifying Item Types

In previous chapters, we have focused on the features of the timeline and how your Flash projects are ordered in time from left to right. Now we are going to look at the arrangement of items from the front to the back of the Stage, or the stacking order of elements in Flash, how multiple items can be moved together, and how the Break Apart and Trace Bitmap commands are applied to change item types.

Stacking order

Within a single layer, Flash stacks items of the same type in the same order they are placed or created, with the most recent item on top, subject to the *kind* of item. The rules that control the stacking order of various kinds of items are simple:

✦ Within a layer, ungrouped primitive shapes or lines are always at the *bottom* level, with the most recently drawn shape or line at the top of that layer's stack. Furthermore, unless you take precautions, drawn items either compound with, or cut into, the drawing beneath them.

✦ Groups and symbols (including bitmaps) stack above lines and shapes in the *overlay* level. To change the stacking order of several drawings, it's often advisable to group them first, as described in the next section of this chapter.

To change the stacking order within a layer, first select the item that you want to move. Then, do one of the following:

✦ **To move the item to the top of the stacking order,** select Modify ⇨ Arrange ⇨ Bring to Front (Alt+Shift+↑ or Option+Shift+↑).

✦ **To move an item to the bottom of the stacking order,** select Modify ⇨ Arrange ⇨ Send to Back (Alt+Shift+↓ or Option+Shift+↓).

✦ **To move the item up one position in the stacking order,** select Modify ⇨ Arrange ⇨ Bring Forward (Ctrl+↑ or ⌘+↑).

✦ **To move the item down one position in the stacking order,** select Modify ⇨ Arrange ⇨ Send Backward (Ctrl+↓ or ⌘+↓).

Remember the stacking order rules: You won't be able to bring an ungrouped drawing above a group or symbol — if you need that drawing on top, group it and then move it, or place it on a separate layer.

The Align panel (Ctrl+K or ⌘+K) used to distribute items in a layout in relation to each other or to the Stage is detailed in Chapter 5, "Drawing in Flash."

To stack an item in a lower layer above an item in a higher layer, you simply change the order of the layer among the other layers: First activate the layer, and then drag the Layer bar to the desired position in the layer stack of the timeline.

Regardless of the number of layers in a Flash project (.fla), neither the file size nor the performance of the final movie (.swf) will be adversely impacted because Flash flattens movies upon export.

Grouping

As discussed in Chapter 5, "Drawing in Flash," grouping shapes or lines makes them easier to handle. Rather than manipulating a single item, group several items to work with them as a single unit. Grouping also prevents shapes from being merged with or cropped by other shapes. In addition, the stacking of groups is more easily controlled than ungrouped drawings. Here's how to create groups:

1. Use Shift+click to select multiple items or drag a selection box around everything that you want to group. This can include any combination of items: shapes, lines, and symbols — even other groups.

2. Select Modify ➪ Group (Ctrl+G or ⌘+G). The selected elements are now grouped.

3. To ungroup everything, select the group then use Modify ➪ Ungroup (Ctrl+Shift+G or ⌘+Shift+G). Ungrouping will only separate grouped items, it will not break apart bitmaps, symbol instances, or text as the Break Apart command does.

Be careful when ungrouping. Your newly ungrouped drawings may alter or eliminate drawings below in the same layer.

To edit a group:

1. Either select the group and then choose Edit ➪ Edit Selected, or double-click the group. Everything on stage — except for the parts of the group — is dimmed, indicating that only the group is editable.

2. Make the changes in the same way you would edit individual primitive shapes or symbols, if there are other groups or symbols included in a larger group, you'll have to click-in deeper to edit those items. You can keep double-clicking on compound groups to gradually move inside to the deepest level or primitive shape available for editing. You can use the location labels to move back out level by level, (or double-click an empty area of the Stage), or go to Step 3 to return to the Main Timeline.

3. To stop editing the group, choose Edit ➪ Edit All, or use the location labels to return to the main scene. Other items on stage return to normal color.

Applying Break Apart

The Modify ➪ Break Apart command (Ctrl+B or ⌘+B), is rather like an Undo command for groups and symbols as well as a deconstruction tool for text and bitmaps. To use Break Apart, simply select an item and then apply the command. Occasionally the Break Apart command will need to be applied more than once to reduce a compound group to its core primitive shapes. When applied to a symbol instance, Break Apart will reduce the instance to primitive shapes that will no longer be linked to the original symbol stored in the Library.

Caution Breaking apart is not entirely reversible and when applied to an animated symbol instance, it will discard all but the current frame of the symbol instance timeline.

Breaking apart text

When text is reduced to shapes using Break Apart, it can be filled with gradients and bitmaps and also modified with the shape Transform options. Specific examples of using the Break apart command are shown in Chapter 8, "Working with Text," and in Chapter 16, "Importing Artwork."

New Feature When applied to text fields, Break Apart now works in two stages. The text is first separated into individual letters that can then be edited as individual text items or broken apart a second time to reduce them to primitive shapes.

Figure 9-28 illustrates how text is broken apart in two stages, so that the original block (left) is first separated into individual letters (center), and then when broken apart a second time, reduced to shapes (right).

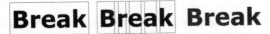

Figure 9-28: A text field (left) broken apart once (center) and then once again (right)

Caution It is not recommended to break apart symbols or groups that are included in a Tweened animation, because the results may be unpredictable and not easy to undo. Breaking apart complex symbols or large text blocks can also add to the file size of your final movie.

Creating Metallic Type

To demonstrate how text characters can be modified after they've been converted to shapes, we have applied some gradient fills to create the illusion of shiny metal letters. The file for this effect is titled "metalType.fla" and is included in the ch09 folder of the CD-ROM. Start with a document that has a dark gray background.

1. First type a word or words on the Stage to create a text block. This effect will work best if applied to a bold, sans serif font at a fairly large point size. We used Verdana bold set at 50pt.

2. Select the text block and apply the Break Apart command (Ctrl+B or ⌘+B), once to break the text block into individual letters, and then a second time to convert the letters into shapes.

3. With the letter shapes still selected, load a default grayscale linear gradient into the Color Mixer panel and then adjust it so the gradient is dark at each end with a highlight in the center. Set the left and far right Color pointers to black and then add a new Color pointer in the center of the Edit bar and set it to white, as shown in Figure 9-29.

Figure 9-29: Text shapes selected and filled with a custom linear gradient created in the Mixer panel

4. Next use the Transform Fill tool to rotate the gradient fill clockwise to a 45-degree angle in each letter shape. You may also scale each fill slightly or adjust individual center points to align the highlight on each letter, as shown in Figure 9-30.

Figure 9-30: Linear gradients aligned in each letter shape with the Transform Fill tool

5. Now to create a more three-dimensional look, make a copy of all the letter shapes in a new layer below the current layer. Use the copy (Ctrl+C or ⌘+C) and paste (Ctrl+V or ⌘+V) commands. Turn the visibility of the original layer off (click the Eye icon) for now, so you can see only the copied letter shapes.

6. Select all the copied letter shapes and using the Color Mixer panel, reverse the gradient fill colors. Set the center Color pointer to black and both end Color pointers to white, as shown in Figure 9-31.

Figure 9-31: Copied letter shapes on a new
layer with reversed gradient fill applied

7. Next, use the Modify ⇨ Shape ⇨ Expand Fill command to expand the fill in all the
selected letters by 2 pixels.

8. If you turn the visibility of both layers back on, you should see that you now have two
opposing gradient fills and the copied letter shapes are slightly larger than the original
letter shapes. Figure 9-32 compares the letters with the original gradient and the
letters with the modified gradient.

Figure 9-32: Original letter
shapes with gradient fill (top)
and copied letter shapes with
reversed and expanded gradient
fill (bottom)

9. Select all the copied letter shapes on the lower layer and drag them behind the
original letter shapes so that they're aligned just slightly above and to the right of
the original shapes. This will create the illusion of a metallic beveled edge on the
original letter shapes, as shown in Figure 9-33.

Figure 9-33: Copied letter shapes
aligned behind the original letter
shapes to create the illusion of a
beveled metallic edge

Breaking apart bitmaps

When applied to bitmaps placed in the Document window, Break Apart will make it possible to select the bitmap image with the Eyedropper tool to apply as a fill to other shapes. This is not the same as tracing a bitmap, which reduces the vast number of colors in a bitmap to areas of solid color and converts it to vector format, as described in the section that follows. Figure 9-34 shows an imported bitmap placed on the Stage and sampled with the Eyedropper tool to create a colored fill in the rectangle below (left) compared to the same bitmap broken apart and sampled with the Eyedropper tool to create an image fill in the rectangle below (right).

Figure 9-34: A bitmap and the fill that results from sampling it with the Eyedropper tool when it is intact (left) and when it has been broken apart (right)

It isn't necessary to break apart bitmaps to use as fills, because they can be specified with the Mixer panel, as described in Chapter 7, "Applying Color." But breaking apart bitmaps allows them to be selectively edited and also allows the visible area of the bitmap to be modified with the shape Transform options.

Caution   Although the Distort and Envelope modifiers of the Free Transform tool can be applied to a bitmap after it has been broken apart, they may not have the result you expect. Instead of distorting or warping the actual bitmap image, you'll find that these modifiers reveal how Flash "sees" bitmap fills. The visible area of the bitmap is not really treated as a shape, but rather as a mask, or shaped window that allows a certain part of the bitmap to be visible. You can distort or warp the viewable area, but the bitmap itself will not be modified, as it is when you apply the Rotate or Skew modifiers.

Figure 9-35 illustrates a bitmap that has been broken apart (left) so that colored areas in the background of the image can be selected with the Magic Wand option of the Lasso tool (center) and then deleted to leave the flower floating on the white Stage (right). Any stray areas of unwanted color can be cleaned up using the Lasso tool or the Eraser tool.

Figure 9-35: A bitmap broken apart and selectively deleted using the Magic Wand option of the Lasso tool

About the Magic Wand option

The Magic Wand option of the Lasso tool is used to select ranges of a similar color in either a bitmap fill or a bitmap that's been broken apart. After you select areas of the bitmap, you can change their fill color or delete them, without affecting the Bitmap Swatch in the Mixer panel. Click the Magic Wand option in the Toolbox to invoke the Magic Wand Settings dialog box.

Cross-Reference

For more information about the Lasso tool, refer to Chapter 5, "Drawing in Flash."

Magic Wand Threshold setting

The Threshold setting defines the breadth of adjacent color values that the Magic Wand will include in a selection. Values for the Threshold setting range from 0 to 200 — the higher the setting, the broader the selection of adjacent colors. Conversely, a smaller number results in the Magic Wand making a narrower selection of adjacent colors.

A value of zero results in a selection of contiguous pixels that are all the same color as the target pixel. With a value of 20, clicking a red target pixel with a value of 55 will select all contiguous pixels in a range of values extending from red 35 to red 75. (If you're familiar with Photoshop, it's important to note that the Flash Threshold is unlike Photoshop, in which a Threshold setting of 20 will select all contiguous pixels in a range of values extending from red 45 to red 65.)

Magic Wand Smoothing setting

The Smoothing setting of the Magic Wand option determines to what degree the edge of the selection should be smoothed. This is similar to antialiasing. (Antialiasing dithers the edges of shapes and lines so that they look smoother on screen.) The options are Pixels, Rough, Normal, and Smooth. Assuming that the Threshold setting remains constant, the Smoothing settings will differ as follows:

✦ **Pixels:** Clings to the rectangular edges of each pixel bordering similar colors.

✦ **Rough:** With this setting, the edges of the selection are even more angular than with Pixels.

✦ **Normal:** Results in a selection that's somewhere between Rough and Smooth.

✦ **Smooth:** Delivers a selection with more rounded edges.

Tracing bitmaps

The Trace Bitmap command is used to convert an imported image from a bitmap to a native Flash vector graphic with discrete, editable areas of color. This unlinks the image from the original symbol in the Library (and also from the Bitmap Swatch in the Color Mixer panel). It is possible to create interesting bitmap-based art with this command. However, if your intention is to preserve the look of the original bitmap with maximum fidelity, you will have to work with the settings — and you will most likely find that the original bitmap is actually smaller in file size than the traced vector image. Figure 9-36 includes a selected bitmap image on the left, and the final vector image that resulted from the settings shown in the Trace Bitmap dialog box.

Figure 9-36: Selecting a bitmap (left) and choosing settings in the Trace Bitmap dialog box to define the final vector image (right)

To trace a bitmap, follow these steps:

1. Use the Arrow tool to select the bitmap that you want to trace — it can be in Symbol Editing mode, or directly on the Stage.

2. Use Modify ➪ Trace Bitmap to invoke the Trace Bitmap dialog box and set the options according to your needs:

- **Color Threshold:** This option controls the number of colors in your traced bitmap. It limits the number of colors by averaging the colors based on the criteria chosen in Color Threshold and Minimum Area. Color Threshold compares RGB color values of adjacent pixels to the value entered. If the difference is lower than the value entered, then adjacent pixels are considered the same color. By making this computation for each pixel within the bitmap, Flash averages the colors. A lower Color Threshold delivers more colors in the final vector graphic derived from the traced bitmap. The range is between 0 and 500, with the default setting being 100.

- **Minimum Area:** This value is the radius, measured in pixels, that Color Threshold uses to describe adjacent pixels when comparing pixels to determine what color to assign to the center pixel. The range is between 1 and 1,000, with the default setting being 8.

- **Curve Fit:** This value determines how smoothly outlines are drawn. Select Very Tight if the shapes in the bitmap are complex and angular. If the curves are smooth, select Very Smooth.

- **Corner Threshold:** This setting determines how sharp edges are handled, choose Many Corners to retain edges and Few Corners to smooth the edges.

3. Click **OK**. Flash traces the bitmap, and the original pixel information is converted to vector shapes. If the bitmap is complex, this may take a while. Depending on the settings you have chosen, the final look of the traced graphic can vary between being very close to the original or very abstracted.

Tip If your objective is for your traced bitmap to closely resemble the original bitmap, then set a low Color Threshold and a low Minimum Area. You'll also want to set the Curve Fit to Pixels and the Corner Threshold to Many Corners. Be aware that using these settings may drastically slow the tracing process for complex bitmaps and result in larger file sizes. If animated, such bitmaps may also retard the frame rate dramatically.

As shown in Figure 9-37, the traced bitmap can vary in how closely it resembles the original bitmap (A). The image in the center (B) was traced with lower settings to achieve a more detailed image: Color Threshold of 25, Minimum Area of 2 pixels, Curve Fit of Pixels, and Corner Threshold of Many Corners. The image on the right (C) was traced with higher settings to create a more abstract graphic image: Color Threshold of 100, Minimum Area of 25 pixels, Curve Fit of Very Smooth, and Corner Threshold of Few Corners.

A   B   C

Figure 9-37: Bitmap images (A) can be traced to create different styles of vector graphics by using low settings (B) or high settings (C).

Caution   If you drag a bitmap from the Library onto the Stage and then attempt to acquire the bitmap fill by first tracing the bitmap and then clicking with the Eyedropper tool, be careful of how selection effects the results. If the traced bitmap is still selected, clicking with the Eyedropper acquires the nearest color and replaces the entire traced bitmap with a solid fill of the acquired color. If the traced bitmap is not selected, the Eyedropper simply acquires the nearest solid color and loads it into the fill color chip.

Using Distribute to Layers

This new MX feature is a marvelous timesaver if you're managing multiple elements that need to be moved to animate on their own layers. If you've imported several items to the Document window, or you've created a complex graphic that you decide needs to be split up on different layers, you can use this command to do most of the work for you. Instead of having to manually create new layers and copy and paste items one by one, you can select a number of individual items in the Document window and apply Distribute to Layers to have Flash automatically create a layer for each selected item.

To apply Distribute to Layers, select the items that you want to have moved to discrete layers — these items can be symbols, groups, shapes, text blocks, and even bitmaps or video objects. Strokes and fills for an individual shape will be kept together on the same layer, as will items in a group or a multi-part symbol. The items you select can be on different source layers, but they must all be on the same frame of the timeline. When items have been distributed to new layers, you can delete any old layers that have been left empty.

The auto-created layers will be stacked from top to bottom below the currently selected layer in the order that the selected items were created. So the most recently created item should be placed on a layer at the bottom of the stack, just above the layer that was formerly below the selected layer, while the item that was created before the others in the selection will be placed at the top of the stack, just below the currently selected layer. If you are completely disoriented by now, have a look at Figure 9-38 to see a file with the layer order before applying Distribute to Layers to the selected items, and look at Figure 9-39 to see how the new layers were stacked and named.

Characters from a broken apart text block will be stacked in layers in the same order that the text block was created (from left to right, right to left, or top to bottom). Flash will name auto-created layers with the following conventions:

✦ A new layer made for any asset stored in the Library (a symbol, bitmap, or video clip) will be given the same name as the asset.

✦ A new layer made for a character from a broken-apart text block is named with the text character or letter.

Caution When applying Distribute to Layers to text blocks that have not been broken apart, new layers will be named with the entire text string. It is best to rename these layers since they will usually be difficult to read and may even exceed the 64 character limit for layer names.

✦ A new layer made for a shape (which is not stored in the Library) will be named in the same numeric sequence as other layers in the current document (Layer 1, Layer 2, and so on).

✦ A new layer made for a named symbol instance will be given the instance name instead of the stored symbol name.

Any layer can always be renamed after it has been created.

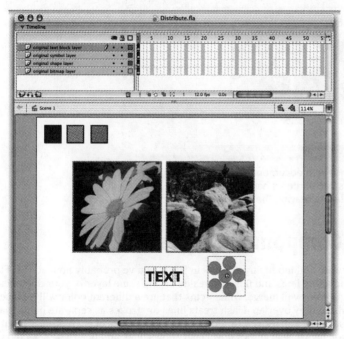

Figure 9-38: A Flash document with the original layer structure for some bitmaps, symbols, shapes, and a broken-apart text block to be distributed to layers

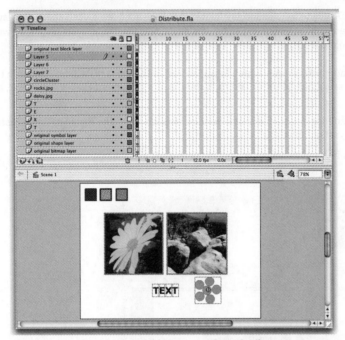

Figure 9-39: The same Flash document after Distribute to Layers has been applied. All selected items have been moved to newly created, auto-named layers, leaving the original layers empty.

Working with Compound Shapes

As you have been drawing and modifying artwork in Flash, you've probably noticed that Flash has a unique way of handling lines and fills that reside on the same layer of your document. Items that are the same color will merge, while items that are a different color will replace or cut out other items where they overlap. Flash treats lines or strokes as separate items than fills, so these can be selected and moved or modified independently of each other, even if they are the same color. Figure 9-40 shows how Flash allows lines and fills to be selected individually, even if they are the same color.

Figure 9-40: A black oval fill with a black stroke may not appear to have a discrete outline, but Flash allows these two elements to be selected separately.

Tip

By double-clicking an element you can select all the related segments. This works for selecting the stroke and fill of a shape or for selecting connected sections of a segmented line (such as the four sides of a rectangle).

Both lines and fills are divided into segments at points of intersection. Figure 9-41 shows a fill split into two independent shapes by drawing a line on top of it (top), or expanded by merging with another fill of the same color (bottom).

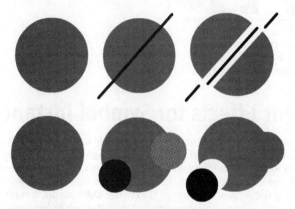

Figure 9-41: A fill split by an overlapping line drawn on the same layer (top). Two fills of the same color merge into a compound shape when they intersect on the same layer (bottom).

These behaviors can be destructive or helpful to your artwork, depending on how you manage individual elements. The key point to remember is that primitive shapes cannot be overlapped on the same layer while deselected without affecting each other. If items are grouped or converted into symbols, they remain independent and will not be compounded or deleted by intersection with other items. Items on layers are also autonomous and will not merge with or erase items that exist on other layers.

Lines or fills can be moved over other primitive shapes without affecting them, as long as they remain selected — as soon as they are deselected they will intersect or merge with adjacent primitive shapes on the same layer. Figure 9-42 illustrates the process of moving a selected shape over and then off of another shape while keeping the two shapes independent (top). The result if the shape is deselected while it is overlapping another shape, before being reselected and moved, to create a compound shape (bottom).

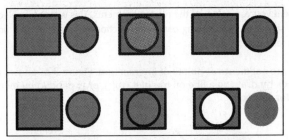

Figure 9-42: A shape moved across another shape while being continuously selected (top), compared to a shape that is deselected while on top of another shape, and then reselected and moved (bottom)

Using Advanced Color Effects for Symbol Instances

Many of the effects discussed in this chapter have only been applicable to shapes, but as introduced in Chapter 6, "Symbols, Instances, and the Library," the Color menu in the Property inspector provides some options for modifying the appearance of symbol instances without changing the original symbol stored in the Library. The individual color settings are useful and fairly straightforward, but by using the Advanced Effect option in the Color menu, it is possible to combine more than one effect for more precise control of an instance's appearance.

Cross-Reference   Because these examples are not very helpful illustrated in black and white, we have included the relevant graphics in the color insert of the book.

The Advanced Effect dialog box shown in Figure 9-43 shows the two columns of settings for Red, Green, and Blue color channels, plus the setting for Alpha. This dialog box is invoked when a symbol instance is selected on the Stage, by selecting **Advanced** from the Color drop-down menu on the Property inspector, and then clicking on the **Settings** button. Although these columns may seem redundant at first, they actually provide very different options for controlling the appearance of instance color. The important difference between these two types of controls is that the first column creates *relative* changes by applying percentage-based adjustment, while the second column creates *absolute* change by adding or subtracting integer values.

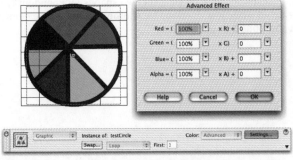

Figure 9-43: The Advanced Effect dialog box shown with the symbol instance "testCircle," with no effect applied

Other than playing with these settings, the easiest way to understand what some of the possible combinations will produce is to dig out your calculator and find a chart of RGB color swatches (that list decimal values rather than hex values). By taking the RGB values in your original instance, multiplying them by the percentage entered in the relative value field, and than adding the value shown in the absolute color field you will arrive at the new RGB value that will appear in the symbol instance when the effect is applied.

Relative color control

The first column of values will adjust the color of the instance relative to the percentages of color (or alpha), present in the original with a range of –100 percent to 100 percent. The default or "no effect" setting is 100 percent. With these controls, 100 percent red does not change everything to pure red or 255 red, but rather it displays 100 percent of the current percentage of red in the existing colors. For example, yellow (255, 255, 0) cannot be made more orange by increasing the amount of red since 255×100 percent is still 255 — the maximum amount of red — however, by reducing the percentage of green to 45 percent of the original value, the ratio of red will be increased making the visible color shift to orange (255, [255×45 percent], 0 or 255, 102, 0).

This process of reducing the amount of the opposite (or *complementary*) color to alter the ratio of colors is called subtractive color adjustment and it can be helpful to remember some basic color theory to predict how it will alter the appearance of your symbol instance. Because the color value changes that you make are applied to all the colors in your symbol, the overall effect can be more complex than just shifting one color in your palette. As shown in our second example of the testCircle instance (printed in the color insert), *reducing* the percentage of red and green to 0, made the gray and white areas shift to blue, while the red and green areas shifted to black and the originally black areas were unaltered.

Because the maximum value for relative alpha is also 100 percent, this control cannot be used to increase the alpha setting of an instance. For example, a symbol that has an alpha fill of 50 percent cannot be made to appear more solid since 100 percent of 50 percent is still only 50 percent alpha.

Absolute color control

The settings in the right column are referred to as absolute color controls because they add or subtract color in concrete amounts regardless of the color values in the symbol instance. The scale of absolute color is from 255 to –255 and the default or "no effect" setting is 0. When absolute color is applied to a symbol instance, it is possible to make more drastic global color changes.

The effect of absolute color value changes made in the Advanced Effect dialog box is similar to the effect of using the Tint option of the Color menu. What makes these controls more advanced is that not only can you add a tint by increasing the value of certain colors, but you can also add an *inverse* tint by using negative values. So, for example, you could add a blue tint to all the colors present in the symbol instance shown in Figure 9-43, with the exception of white and pure blue (which already contain 255 blue), by entering a value of 255 Blue, or you could add a yellow tint to all colors containing blue by entering a value of –255 Blue, this would make pure blue (0, 0, 255), turn to black (0, 0, 0) and white (255, 255, 255), turn to pure yellow (255, 255, 0).

Cross-Reference You can see the original testCircle symbol instance and the three modified examples described in this section, printed in the color insert.

Perhaps one of the most valuable feats that the absolute values can perform is to make a symbol instance that contains alpha fills or strokes appear less transparent. Because the alpha settings are absolute, it is possible to shift an item with an original alpha setting of less than 100 percent, to any opacity level between invisible (–255) and completely solid (255).

If you've entered negative values in the relative alpha setting, it is even possible to make an area with an alpha fill visible while solid areas are made invisible. Consider a shape that has an area of solid fill (100 percent or 255 alpha) and an area of transparent color (40 percent or 102 alpha). If this shape is converted into a symbol and then modified using the Advanced Effect options, you could enter a relative alpha value of –100 percent and then enter an absolute alpha value of 255. When these effect settings were applied, the solid fill in the symbol instance would be invisible with 0 percent alpha (255 × –100 percent + 255 = 0), while the originally transparent fill would be visible with 60 percent alpha (102 × –100 percent + 255 = 153).

The confusion that these settings sometimes cause has created debate about whether negative alpha settings can really be applied. As long as you can remember that outside of the absolute settings in the Advanced Effect dialog box, 0 percent alpha is invisible, while inside the Advanced Effect dialog box, a 0 alpha setting is equal to no effect, you will be able to prove as we just did, that negative alpha effects can be used to invert alpha values, similar to the way that negative color effects can be used to invert color values.

On the CD-ROM   Expert illustrator Dorian Nisinson walks you through the process of applying gradient fills to create the illusion of depth in her tutorial on "Creating Faux 3D." To see the finished image that is described in the tutorial, refer to the color insert pages.

Summary

✦ After you've mastered the basic drawing tools in Flash, there are innumerable methods for modifying artwork to create custom effects.

✦ The Eyedropper, Ink Bottle, and Paint Bucket tools work together to select and apply fill and stroke styles to multiple items or to swap styles between items.

✦ The Transform Fill tool is no longer an option of the Paint Bucket tool and can be accessed directly on the Toolbox to modify gradient fills and bitmap fills for precise alignment and appearance inside individual shapes.

✦ The commands available in the Modify ➪ Shape menu can be applied to convert lines into fills and to modify fills with unique parameters.

✦ The Free Transform tool now has two powerful options that can be applied to shapes only, as well as two options that restrict the Free Transform behavior to make it easier to achieve specific tasks.

✦ Flash organizes artwork with specific parameters and the Modify ➪ Arrange commands can be used to help define the stacking order when you're working with similar items on the same layer.

✦ The Break Apart command can be used to convert bitmaps and text so that they can be edited like shapes to create special effects.

✦ Trace Bitmap is used to convert imported bitmaps into vector graphics with varying degrees of detail.

✦ Distribute to Layers is a timesaving new command that can be very helpful when preparing artwork for animation on separate layers.

✦ The Advanced Effect dialog box for color settings on symbol instances allows you to make dramatic changes to the appearance of individual instances without modifying the original symbol. The absolute value fields make it possible to invert or override both color and alpha settings of an instance without editing the original symbol.

✦   ✦   ✦

Creating Animation and Effects

P A R T

✦   ✦   ✦   ✦

In This Part

Chapter 10
Science of Motion

Chapter 11
Timeline Animation
Fundamentals

Chapter 12
Applying Layer Types

Chapter 13
Character Animation
Techniques

Chapter 14
Exporting Animation

✦   ✦   ✦   ✦

Now that you're comfortable with the Flash tools and making static Graphic symbols and groups, it's time to move on to creating animated elements and dynamic effects. Chapter 10 introduces some of the fundamental production and planning issues that you need to consider when designing animated elements. Chapter 11 will give you all the information you need to start working with time-based content. Learn to create frame-by-frame and tweened animation and how to use Movie Clips to control the display of content on multiple timelines. Chapter 12 introduces the various layer tools that will make your production easier and allow you to add more advanced effects. If you are interested in character animation, Chapter 13 provides comprehensive coverage of character animation and the tricks that professional animators use to create engaging and optimized cartoons. When you're ready to transfer your Flash content to the Web or to a tape format, Chapter 14 will help you to tailor your content to specific viewing environments and will walk you through the steps for exporting final content from the Flash authoring environment.

Science of Motion

In This Chapter

Designing compelling animation

The elements of illusion: reality versus perception

Creating and breaking the "laws" of nature

Applying Newton's Laws in animation

Have you ever wondered what makes some animation so compelling and other animation so dull? Regardless of the content of a site, or even the style or quality of the graphics, some animation is engaging, while other animation is just annoying or even pathetic — we've all seen it, limping or flashing across our screens at one time or another.

Of course, your response to animation is partly determined by what you're expecting from an interface (sometimes you want diversion, and other times you just want to find information — fast!) Most designers are aware of the issues of usability and relevance that should be considered when adding animation to an interface (whether they decide to ignore them or not). But, what happens after you've done all your audience research and content planning and you decide that some animation would be appropriate?

The next step should be fun, right? Unfortunately, unless you have the privilege of working with a skilled animator, you're actually entering one of the most complex and challenging areas of visual design. Although most people recognize "good" animation when they see it, the leap from *appreciating* motion to *designing* motion is difficult, even for people who have natural aptitude.

You possess an innate understanding of physics, even if you've never taken a science class in your life — you know what to expect when you bounce a ball — but do you know how to interpret what happens so that it can be re-created frame-by-frame in an animation? The challenge of designing motion is translating daily experience into a time-based, 2D environment. Your eyes and brain will tell you if something isn't right, but how do you know what can be done to correct it? The ability to analyze perceptions that we normally take for granted is the true skill of animation and motion graphics design.

With experience, animators can intuitively finesse the many visual factors that effectively communicate motion — even bending the rules to suit their personal animation styles or to convey specific atmospheres and characters. But, the first step toward making better animation is becoming familiar with some of the fundamental concepts and laws that govern matter in the real world.

Establishing Ground Rules

No matter what the style or purpose your animation ultimately has, you'll need to establish guidelines for yourself if you want to create an engaging and convincing experience for the user. This may seem limiting at first, but these self-imposed ground rules make content more meaningful to your audience. The most commonly recognized example of structured, shared expression is music. Even the wildest music is based on an underlying structure of notes and timing (or else it isn't exactly music).

Structure is also one of the key characteristics that shape great books or even movies. Consider the difference between a private journal and a well-crafted story, or the difference between a home movie and an engrossing film. This doesn't mean that you're stuck repeating the same old narrative over and over again, or that you have to follow someone else's rules. But if you have free license to create any experience for your audience, it's even more important to decide on the rules that will guide your designs so that all the elements and animations support your idea.

Artists who prefer not to follow the most commonly used conventions must work even harder to establish their own signature style — or to create content defined by the consistent choices they make. As in music, the possible choices for the basic aspects of animation are practically infinite — a little faster, a little slower, spinning or bouncing or wiggling or jumping or fading or . . . you get the idea. The guidelines that you establish for each project will help you to make the right decisions. There isn't an exact formula for "good animation," the variables are too broad, but once you create some rules for yourself, you'll be able to make the choices that best support your goals for a specific animation.

Defining Variables

To establish guidelines that will support your design process, you first have to analyze the choices that are relevant to the content. Is the tone of the project peaceful, quiet, fast, slick, funny, scary? Try to be as specific as you can about the approach that will best suit your content. Then try to make consistent choices that will support that description. Some of the questions that may help you to frame the basic elements of your project include:

What kind of motion suits the style of the project or personality of a character?

How does color communicate your theme or idea?

How does sound support the atmosphere or character?

If you try to make a design that is "all of the above," it will end up being too vague and confusing to keep anyone interested. One of the hardest things to learn as a designer (and to communicate to clients) is that if you try to make a site that is a little bit of everything in an attempt to suit all audiences, you'll only weaken your message and your branding and/or dilute the experience for everyone. The very best designs are consistent enough that they allow anyone to understand them (or at least get what they're about), and specific enough in style that they have a memorable personality and attitude.

Of course, there are some things that do appeal to many people — humor or surprise, well-executed visual complexity, engaging and functional navigation — but even these elements can be too generic. They need to be added to your design with a specific (and hopefully original) style. After you've decided what style is appropriate for the project, you can begin to plan the elements that will create the experience for the audience.

Although it may seem like "over-thinking" to consider these kinds of factors for every project, try to see how often you can apply at least some of the questions outlined in the following sections to really focus your design strategy.

The environment

What planet are you on? As you begin to plan and build a virtual environment, even in a 2D space, thinking of it as a real "place" can be helpful. Decide what kind of place you want it to be and what characteristics will help the audience to understand where they are.

Is this a soft, fuzzy world where everything floats gently as it moves, or is this a hard metallic world where things are heavy and make abrupt/fast movements, or maybe even a liquid world where things are very smooth and quiet, with organic movement? These are extreme examples; obviously, the possibilities are endless. Try to include all the factors that define an environment as you experience it visually:

How light or dark is it?

Is everything very distinct or blurred and layered?

How crowded or open is the space?

How quickly can things move?

How much does gravity affect objects?

Is space (depth) limited or endless?

The main thing to keep in mind is that all the elements and movement that you add to the design should help the audience to "locate" themselves in the environment that you want. Aside from natural environmental analogies, try to consider historical and cultural context, too. Is this meant to have a retro feel or a post-modern feel? Is it an environment influenced by multicultural elements, or is it defined only by a very specific subculture?

If you find yourself thinking, "Well, all I really want is to make a cool site that the audience will like," then remember the point made previously: The more specific you can be about the kind of environment you want to create, the better chance you will have of making a design that the audience will be interested in. Most people are pretty jaded viewers by now, and something that looks "trendy" or like a jumble of many other things they've seen before is not likely to hold their attention very long.

The materials

As you consider the overall environment that you want to create, you also have to decide on the smaller details that will be consistent with your idea. Even if you're working purely with Flash strokes and fills, trying to imagine the kinds of materials that would be most appropriate for your graphic elements can be helpful. Do you want elements to be jagged and hard or fuzzy or squishy? How much volume do shapes or graphic elements have? Are any of the items transparent? Considering these questions will help you to make decisions about line styles and perhaps even colors, but most importantly these decisions will help you to design motion that will be convincing and appropriate for each item.

If your materials are soft, motion will include a lot of stretching and squashing and maybe even jiggling. If you want materials to seem hard, motion will probably include more sliding and crashing or "clicking." If objects are heavy, they will have a lot more inertia. If objects are very light, they will need to move in a way that conveys "weightlessness." Some of these types of motion are hard to describe, but if you can visualize them clearly (or even better, find examples in real life), you'll have an easier time planning and making your animation.

Even if you decide that your "materials" are actually best kept very flat and graphic (like construction paper or felt cutouts), than you can still focus on that kind of look and avoid throwing in gradient fills or shiny highlights. The most important thing is to simply have a clear concept in mind that will allow you to make (and explain) the design choices that best support your content.

The motion

Choosing to add animation to an item can be a quick decision, but finding the right kind of motion to add can take a lot more time. If you've made some of the decisions suggested so far in this chapter, then you will have a much easier time narrowing down the style of motion that you want to add.

Flash MX provides some great options for controlling the speed and pattern of motion, but until you have a clear "flight path" mapped out, you won't be able to use these tools effectively. There are few things worse than spending a lot of time creating an animation, only to realize that the motion lacks personality or seems meaningless. Most ineffective animation is the result of poor planning. This is one area of design where endless options can work against you. It can be fun, and helpful for learning, to just play with different kinds of movement in Flash MX, but this is not the best way to develop a project, unless you're already an experienced animator. "Designing" animation by simply throwing some random tweens and easing together, is the visual equivalent of whistling tunelessly or absent-mindedly strumming a guitar — entertaining for the person doing it, very annoying for everyone else.

Although experienced animators develop an intuitive sense of timing and rhythm, designers who are just starting to experiment with motion will have a better chance of success if they have a very specific example to refer to. Reference for animation (or styles of movement) can be found almost anywhere in the real world — you just have to observe carefully, and if possible document the motion with video or a sequence of stills. Often documentation of motion will surprise you. It wasn't until cameras were used to photograph horses running that artists realized there were moments during the horse's "run cycle" that all four feet were tucked under their stomachs. Before this motion was captured on film, it had become a convention to illustrate running horses with their legs stretched out forwards and backwards, like a rocking horse.

These are some resources that we have found inspiring as motion references:

✦ **Eadweard Muybridge:** A photographer who did some of the first "stop-motion" images ever made. His classic photographic sequences can be found in books published in the Pictorial Archive series by Dover Publications.

✦ **Lawrence Jordan:** Lawrence Jordan created strange and wonderful animated films using cut-out graphics and stop-frame animation. In his 40-year career, he produced a body of work that has been influential for many artists working in new media. Learn more about him in an essay in the Bright Lights Film Journal at www.brightlightsfilm.com/30/lawrencejordan.html.

✦ **Bruce Conner:** Bruce Conner is a visionary and groundbreaking artist who works in a variety of mediums. He was honored with an exhibit at the Walker Art Center in 1999/2000, and they have produced the most comprehensive catalogue on his work to date. Find out more about Bruce Conner on the Walker Art Center Web site at www.walkerart.org/programs/vaexhibconner.html.

Of course, you probably also have examples in mind of animation that you've seen and admired. This can be a great way to analyze "how it's done," but you should always aspire to develop a unique style rather than to copy someone else's directly. The history of animation is rich and full of many examples of diverse styles that have been effective. By looking back at the work done by great animators and filmmakers, you'll likely find something that will inspire you and offer new possibilities for the ways that images and motion can be rendered on a 2D screen.

Adding Personality

As many great animations have shown, any object can be given its own personality. There is really no medium quite as effective as animation for allowing you to give life to the characters that would otherwise stay in your imagination. Even if you don't aspire to be a character animator in the strictest sense, any element that is animated within your Flash projects should have some recognizable "personality." You don't have to add eyes and a mouth to an object in order for it to be expressive. In fact, the main expression of any animated element should be conveyed by the way it moves, even more strongly than by the exact composition of the graphic.

You can add personality to a line or a letter as easily as you can add personality to a cartoon character. A common exercise done in art schools to help students realize the expressive power of abstract lines and shapes is to give the students a list of atmospheres or emotions that they have to interpret and communicate with purely abstract lines and forms. The most surprising thing about this exercise is how similar most people's drawings turn out to be. Although the drawings do not include any concrete symbols or signs, students realize how concise their shared visual language really is (even if they aren't always conscious of it).

As an animator, you can draw on the common visual vocabulary to communicate a great deal to your audience without having to "spell it out." Most people would probably recognize "angry" movement or "joyous" movement if they saw it. There certainly are some personal and cultural variations in interpretation, but the basic recognition is usually very consistent. As with some of the other topics described so far in this chapter, this is an aspect of motion design that may not at first seem relevant to every project. However, if you take the time to consider how you want to connect with your audience, you'll probably be able to pin down a fairly specific emotional tone or personality that you want your animation to have.

Keeping Ideas Fresh

Some of the greatest modern works of art and music are based on the concept of permutation — the process of exploring all the possibilities within a specific, usually limited, group of elements. Permutation of a limited set of options can yield more surprising or unique results than unlimited options, because forcing yourself to work within defined boundaries allows the content of your work to influence the final result in ways that you may not have previously considered.

For example, if you allow yourself to choose any colors from a full palette, this may seem very liberating. But the truth is you'll probably choose colors (or at least color combinations) that are familiar or "comfortable" for you, without even giving some new options a real chance. A much more inventive use of color can be achieved by forcing yourself to work with a truly random selection of colors (or to create an effective design with a more limited palette), you may be surprised by how well pink and brown go together, or by how much you can do with just a few colors. At the very least, experimenting with randomness or intentional limitation in a design can help open up new possibilities to keep your work from getting stale.

The next step is to observe and experiment to find the kinds of motions that best represent the personality or tone that you want the audience to recognize. Some of the factors that you can consider in designing expressive motion include the following:

✦ **Speed:** How fast or how slow does an object move? Does it accelerate or decelerate?

✦ **Timing and rhythm:** How does the object's movement loop or change over time. Finding music to help with the timing and pace of an animation is often helpful.

✦ **Consistency or irregularity:** How much variety is there in an object's movement? Does it follow a repeated pattern, or a random path of motion?

✦ **Anticipation or surprise:** Does the object give some visual "foreshadowing" as it moves, or does it make sudden, unexpected movements?

✦ **Freedom or constraint:** How "large" or "small" are the movements that the object can make? Does it move all around your composition or stay in a very restricted area? How much of the object moves at any one time?

The "meaning" of these various kinds of movement may be debated as much as the "meaning" of various colors. However, it is safe to assume that overall there will be enough consistency between viewers on the meaning of certain kinds of motion for this to be an effective way of communicating the character of an object. If you're not sure how a certain motion will be "read" by your audience, just test it out on a few people—show them what you're working on, and then ask them what emotion or personality *they* think the object has. If enough people recognize the "mood" that you want your animation to have, you've succeeded! If most people are confused or have very different responses, than you probably need to simplify and clarify what you're trying to communicate. It's not likely that most people "read" that an object has slightly low self-esteem but is feeling fairly optimistic. However, most people will recognize movement consistent with extreme shyness or joy (or any other simple and exaggerated emotion).

Exaggeration is the foundation of the art of animation. Define the kind of movement that may communicate a particular emotion to your audience, and then see how far you can push it. In some cases you may want very overt movements, and in other cases you may want more conservative or subtle movements, but by pushing the boundaries you can assess your options and find the right balance for a particular character or object.

Manipulating Perception and Illusion

As you spend time analyzing motion in the real world and motion in more-stylized animations, you will become more aware of some of the tricks that your eyes can play on you. Animators, like magicians, know how to take advantage of people's often- unreliable perception to create illusions. By understanding how the audience's eyes and minds put visual information together to "see" things, clever performers and designers are able to convince the audience that they're seeing something that may not actually be happening.

Another interesting phenomenon that makes an animator's job a little easier is referred to as *suspension of disbelief.* This is something you participate in whenever you really *want to believe* you're seeing something—children are often the best at this. When you push doubt aside, your eyes can be very forgiving as your brain works even harder to compensate for any gaps that may spoil the illusion or the spectacle that you want to believe in.

Some visual "tricks" in animation have been used so consistently that people now expect them as conventions, instead of seeing them as poorly rendered versions of a real-life motion. Most people recognize that a swirling cyclone of lines, with hands and feet or other objects occasionally popping out of it, is usually "a fight." An oval blur or circular scribble at the bottom of a character's legs is not a cloud, but is, in fact, their feet spinning extra fast. Lines radiating from an object don't mean that it is spiky, but can instead mean that it is shiny or hot. (Our favorite cartoon convention is the light bulb appearing over a character's head when they've suddenly gotten an idea.) Figure 10-1 shows a sequence by animator Richard Bazley that uses the simple but effective technique of blurred lines to simulate motion that is "faster than the eye can see." This classic device can be modified to show rockets blasting off or wind rushing by or any object moving so quickly that it becomes a blur.

© 2002 Richard Bazley

Figure 10-1: Blurred lines effectively communicate the idea of wind or fast-moving elements "rushing by" in an animation.

We have included SWF files for most of the examples discussed in this chapter. Because the figures only show a few frames from an animation, you can get a better idea of how a motion plays by reviewing the files in the ch10 folder of the CD-ROM. We thank animators Richard Bazley, Tom Winkler, and Sandro Corsaro for kindly sharing some of their expert examples with us.

There are innumerable examples of cartoon tricks, but the main thing to keep in mind is that you don't have to draw every detail of a movement to make it convincing. Instead, it's better to find ways that you can exaggerate the motion to make it more *expressive*. A well-executed illusion will save you time drawing and will also make your animation more fun to watch.

Several examples of cartoon motion "tricks" that you may be familiar with are discussed in Chapter 13, "Character Animation Techniques."

Viewpoint, framing, and depth

By thinking of the Flash Stage area as a camera viewfinder rather than as a sketch pad, you'll be able to start crafting the various scenes in your animation to have some of the same expressive qualities as shots from a well-edited film. The ability to manipulate view-point is one of the strongest storytelling devices available to filmmakers and animators alike. Audiences have come to accept (and expect) seeing things from new angles and perspectives. Screen images have evolved from the basic wide-angle, theater-audience perspective of early film to the spinning, time-defying 360-degree *Matrix* views of action—don't be afraid to push your "camera" beyond the limits of normal human perception. Choosing how you will frame animation can have as much effect on your audience as the actual content in each scene. The traditional "bird's-eye" or "mouse's-eye" reconsideration of viewpoint is as effective in a digital design as it is in sketches or drawings. Try to use your content to inspire a framing strategy that adds both interest and meaning to your designs.

Depth is another key element to consider when composing a scene and choosing a viewpoint. Traditional animators are cautious to avoid awkward line intersections caused by overlapping elements. When the lines from two different elements "bump" into each other unintentionally, it can make a drawing look flat—this is known as a *tangent.* Tangents interrupt the illusion of depth created by scaling and layering elements in a composition. The main thing to avoid is an overly busy layout that may confuse the viewer's understanding of the picture plane. Try to keep elements that are meant to be behind or in front of other elements from looking as though they are joined or existing uncomfortably in the same space. Add a little more separation between elements that don't have enough visual clarity.

With careful planning, overlapping elements will add depth to your designs. Notice in Figure 10-2 that the overlapping of the larger figure on the right with the border helps it jump into the foreground, while the overlapping of the smaller figure on the left makes it hard to tell which element is supposed to be in front.

Figure 10-2: Overlapping should be planned (right) to avoid tangents that may flatten out the depth of the composition (left).

Another common device used to add depth to a scene is to choose a viewpoint that allows you to add a natural frame or border around the image. By giving the viewer a reference point for where they are located in the plane of the image, you can exaggerate the feeling of depth. In drawing or painting, windows are often used to frame a view in the distance, but in anima-tion you can find more original "frames" by choosing unique viewpoints. In a scene from Richard Bazley's animated film *The Journal of Edwin Carp,* he uses the view from the back of a police van to add depth to a simple composition of two characters talking. Imagine how much flatter and less interesting the scene shown in Figure 10-3 would be if the characters were not framed by the outline of the van.

Figure 10-3: By using a clever but logical framing device, Richard Bazley has added a great deal of depth to this animated scene.

In another scene, Bazley uses the convention of a character running into the camera to enhance the feeling of panic as Edwin Carp's mother runs down a hallway. As shown in Figure 10-4, by using an extreme viewpoint, Bazley makes a simple scene more humorous and dramatic while still being very efficient with his artwork.

Figure 10-4: By using an extreme viewpoint, an otherwise simple Motion tween can add drama and humor to a scene.

Anticipation

This is one of the primary techniques used to give animation personality and life. If you haven't spent much time studying animation, it's easy to overlook, but animation without anticipation appears robotic. Anticipation communicates the organic tension that exists in "real life" motion. Visualize a baseball pitcher winding up before he throws a fastball. If the ball just flew out of his hand without his body first coiling back to gather force, you wouldn't have the visual information to understand that the force was transferred from the pitcher's body to the ball. It would appear that the ball just suddenly had the ability to fly on its own. Figure 10-5 shows a classic example of anticipation as a character gathers force before launching into a run.

Figure 10-5: By "winding up" before taking off in a run, a character communicates the urgency and force behind his movement.

The principle of anticipation can be used to add extra life to almost any motion. Picture how an element would "gather force" before jumping into the main movement and then add a drawing or two to exaggerate that movement in your animation. Generally, anticipation can be communicated by reversing the main motion for a few frames before and after a tween (or frame-by-frame sequence). For example, if an item is going to move to the left, have it back up a little to the right first, and then after it stops moving to the left, have it stagger back a little to the right before reaching its final resting point. If an item is going to suddenly get larger, have it shrink just a little first before popping up to the larger size, and then allow the item to grow just a little beyond the final size so that it can appear to "settle" into the final size at the end of the animation. These inverted motions at the beginning and ending of an animated sequence are also referred to as *bounces,* because they can be compared to the motion of a ball bouncing. Depending on the effect you're trying to achieve, bounces can be very small and subtle or extremely exaggerated. Figure 10-6 illustrates how a small bounce can be added to give antici-pation and follow-through to an animated head turn. This same kind of bounce works equally well on eye blinks and on almost any other small movement that needs a little extra life.

character designs © **www.sandrocorsaro.com**

Figure 10-6: Subtle bounces add anticipation and follow-through to head turns and other movements.

Although you may not at first be conscious of these "extra" movements when you watch a cartoon, it is one of the conventions that an audience associates with polished, professional animation. If you start to watch carefully for anticipation and follow-through motions, you'll see them on nearly every movement in well-crafted animations.

Secondary motion

Of course, some items don't need to bounce like a ball, but instead should flap or float as they move. It's still helpful to keep the pattern of a bounce in mind, but the modified patterns that you apply to items to visually show the forces of acceleration or gravity in motion is called *overlapping action.* A single object or character can have multiple overlapping actions — overlapping action added to smaller details of an item are sometimes called *secondary motion.* After you've planned the basic motion pattern of your main element, consider how you may add life and detail to your animation with overlapping action and secondary motion.

Figure 10-7 shows an example of an animation with overlapping action added to a character's belly as he runs. Secondary motion has been added by also animating the character's hat with overlapping action as he runs. The combination of these smaller motion patterns with the pattern of the basic run cycle makes the animation dynamic and gives the character personality.

On the CD-ROM Expert animator Richard Bazley, provides some of his suggestions for efficient and engaging animation in a tutorial that you will find in the Bonus_Tutorials folder on the *Flash MX Bible* CD-ROM — one of the things you will notice about his work is that he often adds frame-by-frame secondary motion to make simple tweened animation more dynamic and lifelike.

Figure 10-7: Overlapping action and secondary motion add life and personality to animation.

Understanding the Laws of Nature

Depending on your learning style, you may find it easier to simply observe and copy patterns of movement or to analyze the underlying principles of force that cause these patterns. Either approach can be effective. Even if you're more of a visual person than a theory-oriented person (as many animators are), an overview of some of the basic principles of physics can help to give you a framework for understanding the limitless variations of animated motion. The stylized interpretations of movement found in motion graphics and cartoons often deny the "laws of nature"—that's what makes them so entertaining. However, if you don't know the basic physics that dictate motion in reality, it can be more difficult to extrapolate convincing motion to fantastic lengths.

Advanced interactive motion can be designed using physics formulas to define the behavior of objects controlled with ActionScript. Although the math may look a little bit intimidating at first, it's often easier to understand when you can get visual feedback on how the numbers directly affect motion patterns. In fact, more than a few top designers claim to be "math-impaired," but the beauty of motion controlled by numbers has given them the incentive to learn (or relearn) some of those scary calculus and physics equations. Spending a little time polishing up your math skills can allow you to efficiently script realistic, organic motion that would be insanely time-consuming or even impossible to render manually. Even if you never intend to use ActionScript to define the patterns of motion in your animations, a basic under-standing of how physics and math can be used to calculate motion makes it much easier to plot movement and plan your drawings. Math and physics, like color and type are a powerful part of the "vocabulary" of motion graphics. Regardless of how you choose to apply them, these principles can be helpful for planning and modifying animation.

Almost all animated motion can be analyzed or designed using Newton's Laws. If you sat through science class in high school, these scientific descriptions of how objects interact with force will sound familiar. Of course, in animation you aren't required to obey these laws. In fact, you'll probably create more interesting animations by pushing these laws to the limits or even by inverting them to create objects with unexpected behavior.

Law #1: Inertia

Objects that are at rest will stay at rest and objects in motion will stay in motion unless acted upon by an unbalanced force. In animation terms, objects should show a change in force if they're going to have a change in motion. This is communicated visually with anticipation and with overlapping actions, as described earlier in this chapter. Most animation will seem much more lifelike with forgiving transitions. Allow objects to ease in and out of motion and to settle into new positions in your composition. Unless you want them to appear robotic, objects don't just change behavior suddenly without showing some anticipation and delayed secondary animation. You can add an element of surprise to an object's movement by intentionally dis-regarding inertia. For example, if an object stops cold without any visual indication of a change in force, it will appear jarring and hard, or if a very small object takes a long time to accelerate it will seem "hesitant."

Law #2: Acceleration

The acceleration of an object as produced by a net force is directly proportional to the magni-tude of the net force, in the same direction as the net force, and inversely proportional to the mass of the object. In animation terms, speed is dependent on a combination of mass and force; increasing force will increase speed, while increasing mass will decrease speed. An important related concept is *terminal velocity*. Although most people have heard this term, not everyone can explain what it means. Basically, once an item is falling fast enough for air resistance to be strong enough to prevent gravity from increasing the speed, then it has reached terminal velocity or the maximum speed of its fall. Objects with greater mass take longer to reach terminal velocity so they accelerate for longer, generally hitting the ground while still accelerating. An object with less mass will quickly reach terminal velocity and appear to float to the ground, since it doesn't gain any more speed. Figure 10-8 shows an animation of the classic acceleration "test"—two objects dropped from the same height.

By modifying the principles of acceleration, you can create whimsical environments where can-non balls might float and feathers crash to the ground (or any other variation you can think of).

Figure 10-8: Acceleration is determined by mass, and objects with more mass will take longer to reach terminal velocity.

Law #3: Action/reaction force pairs

This is the most commonly quoted of Newton's Laws: "For every action there is an equal and opposite reaction." Although this law is often used as a metaphor for human behavior, it was originally intended to explain how forces interact and affect objects. This is the law that will explain how far backwards a character may fall when pulling on a rope that breaks. The force is directed along the rope and acts equally on objects at either end of the rope—the end result is that a character literally pushes himself backwards by pulling on the rope, as shown in Figure 10-9.

This is also the law that explains why a ball bounces back up into the air when it strikes the ground. If there weren't any gravity or friction acting on the ball, it would bounce back to the exact height that it originally fell from. The actual result is that the ball reaches only a percentage of its original height with each bounce; this percentage will depend on how hard the surface is and how heavy and/or "bouncy" the ball is. You can plan a realistic series of bounces by using a consistent percentage to calculate the descending height of each bounce. The bounce shown in Figure 10-10 was calculated by using a multiple of 0.5 (or ½) for the distance traveled in each bounce.

This bounce will be much improved by adding some Easing to make the acceleration more realistic. To see the final result animated, open the "bounce50percent.swf" in the ch10 folder of the CD-ROM. Ideally, a convincing bounce will also include some *stretch 'n squash*—one of the most widely used animation "tricks" used to make motion look more realistic. This is discussed in more detail in Chapter 13, "Character Animation Techniques."

Figure 10-9: The force of pulling on a rope causes the character to fly backward when the rope breaks.

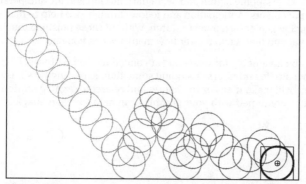

Figure 10-10: A starting pattern for a bounce can be plotted using a consistent multiple to calculate the height of each bounce.

If you're interested in exploring the formulas for more advanced motion patterns, any basic physics textbook will help you get started. Two useful sources that we recommend for motion designers are:

✦ *Physics for Game Developers,* by David M. Bourg

✦ Jack's Page, a Web site created by physics teacher Jack Orb to provide information on basic physics and optics for computer-rendered graphics (with sample JavaScript), `www.kw.igs.net/~jackord/j6.html#p1`

Summary

✦ To engage an audience, it's important for motion to have meaning. Meaning is derived when an animation includes visual cues that are part of our common "vocabulary."

✦ Motion should support the underlying concept and content of your project. If motion is simply added as decoration without having some connection to the ideas in the content, it will distract from your design instead of enhancing it.

✦ Motion can communicate mood, emotion, and personality as effectively as text or color. Although the meaning of certain styles of motion can have a different personal or cultural impact, the way that core emotions are linked to styles of motion is remarkably similar for most people.

✦ To convey a strong message or establish a convincing mood, you must first evaluate the variables and then make consistent design choices to support your original concept.

✦ Careful observation and documentation of motion in daily life will help you to build a "reference library" to draw from when creating animation. Exaggeration and interpretation are crucial for developing a personal style. However, your animation will not be convincing unless you can build on a core understanding of motion in the real world.

✦ There are many useful "tricks" or conventions that you can learn to give your animation a more professional look. Overlapping action and secondary motion add life and personality to basic animated movements. Anticipation and follow-through also help to make an animation more convincing and entertaining to watch. Without these finishing touches, animation will appear flat and lifeless no matter how many tweens you use.

✦ Physics equations can be invaluable for designing advanced motion patterns. Even if you don't have a propensity for numbers, spending some time exploring how basic equations explain force will make it easier to analyze and re-create organic motion. A little math and science combined with your graphics can help to create magic.

✦   ✦   ✦

Timeline Animation Fundamentals

✦   ✦   ✦   ✦

In This Chapter

Animating frame-
by-frame

Editing multiple
frames and using
onion skinning

Working with
Shape tweens

Adding Shape hints

Applying Motion tweens

Using Easing to
enhance animation

Optimizing and
integrating multiple
sequences

✦   ✦   ✦   ✦

In this chapter, we discuss the basic methods and tools used to create animations in Flash. Animation is the process of creating the illusion of movement or change over time. Animation can be the movement of an item from one place to another, or it can be a change of color over a period of time. The change can also be a morph, or change in shape, from one shape to another. Any change of either position or appearance that occurs over time is animation. In Flash, changing the contents of successive frames (over a period of time) creates animation. This can include any or all of the changes mentioned previously, in any combination.

Basic Methods of Flash Animation

In Flash, there are three basic methods of animation:

✦ **Frame-by-frame animation** is achieved by manually changing the individual contents of each of any number of successive keyframes.

✦ **Tweened animation** is achieved by defining the contents of the start and end points of an animation, and then allowing Flash to interpolate the contents of the frames inbetween. As discussed previously, this is often referred to as tweening. There are two kinds of tweening in Flash:

  • Shape tweening

  • Motion tweening

Most projects will require you to use a combination of all three methods. There's a growing trend among advanced Flash developers to animate almost exclusively by controlling Movie Clips with ActionScript. Although this might seem intimidating to illustrators or animators who are more comfortable using analog tools, this programmatic approach to creating motion (and even artwork) dynamically makes sense. After all, computer animation is the art of orchestrating items according to various properties over time — and in the digital realm numbers describe all properties, even color.

Flash MX Components make it easier than ever for beginning programmers to integrate ActionScripted elements into Flash projects.

Before you jump into scripting, however, it helps to know how to animate on the Main Timeline with simple groups and graphics.

Cross-Reference

If you need to review the features of Flash MX timelines, please refer to Chapter 4, "Interface Fundamentals." The characteristics and uses of the various symbol types in Flash MX are described in Chapter 6, "Symbols, Instances, and the Library."

Frame-by-Frame Animation

The most basic form of animation is frame-by-frame animation. Because frame-by-frame animation employs unique drawings in each frame, it's ideal for complex animations that require subtle changes — for example, facial expression. However, frame-by-frame animation also has its drawbacks. It can be very tedious and time-consuming to draw unique art for each frame of the animation. Moreover, all those unique drawings contribute to a larger file size. In Flash, a frame with unique art is called a *keyframe*. As shown in Figure 11-1, frame-by-frame animation requires a unique drawing for every movement or change, which makes nearly every frame a keyframe.

Figure 11-1: When you use keyframes to gradually add to the artwork, the text appears to be written out letter by letter in the final animation.

The example that is shown in Figure 11-1 (keyframeText.swf) was created by inserting keyframes (F6) with the same text repeated in every frame and then erasing the letters in sequential keyframes so that the text appears letter by letter until the whole word is written out in keyframe 10. This process of modifying your original artwork to create a sequence is one use of frame-by-frame animation. Another approach is to create completely unique artwork in a series of blank keyframes (F7).

As shown in Figure 11-2, the changes in the lines from frame to frame can add a lot more motion to the final animation. If you are a skilled illustrator you will be able to keep enough consistency from keyframe to keyframe that it will seem to be the same shape or figure moving to a new position. If you are an aspiring illustrator (like this author), you will end up with a lot more variation between your drawings. As long as you are not trying to get a very precise sequence, this variation can actually be a lot of fun to watch — every line will dance and move in your final animation. Keep in mind that you are not restricted to just one series of frames; you can keep adding elements with their own keyframe sequences on separate layers.

On the CD-ROM

The source files for the examples in this section are included on the CD-ROM — they're in the Keyframe folder of the ch11 folder.

The images shown in Figure 11-2 are from the file named faceFramebyFrame.fla. The roughness of the individual drawings can add more life to the final animation if you're working in a loose style.

Figure 11-2: A loosely sketched sequence can be paced by adding more "repeater" frames between the unique keyframe images.

Adding keyframes

To add a keyframe to the timeline, select the frame that you would like to convert into a keyframe. Then, do one of the following:

✦ Convert a frame into a keyframe:

- Right-click (or Control+click on Mac) the frame and select **Insert Keyframe** from the contextual menu.

- Select Insert ⇨ Keyframe from the application menu.

- Press F6 on the keyboard.

✦ Convert a frame into a *blank* keyframe:

- Right-click (or Control+click on Mac) the frame and select **Insert Blank Keyframe** from the contextual menu.

- Select Insert ⇨ Blank Keyframe from the application menu.

- Press F7 on the keyboard.

Note   If you select a frame in a span, the selected frame will be converted to a keyframe without adding to the length of the span. If you insert a keyframe at the end of a span, the keyframe will be add to the length of the sequence. If you convert a frame in a span to a blank keyframe, all content will be cleared from the keyframe and the following frames of the span.

Tip   If you need to make a sequence of keyframes, but you would rather not have to press F6 or F7 repeatedly to create individual keyframes, you can select a range of frames and use the Modify ⇨ Frames ⇨ Convert to Keyframes (F6) or Modify ⇨ Frames ⇨ Convert to Blank Keyframes (F7) command to quickly convert all selected frames to keyframes or blank keyframes.

Creating frame-by-frame animation

The basic steps for creating a frame-by-frame animation are as follows:

1. Start by selecting the frame in which you'd like your frame-by-frame animation to begin.

2. If it's not already a keyframe, use Insert ➪ Keyframe (F6) to convert it.

3. Then, either draw or import the first image for your sequence into this keyframe. Wherever possible, use symbols and flip, rotate, or otherwise manipulate them for reuse to economize on file size.

4. Select the next frame and either make the artwork from the previous keyframe available for modification, by adding a keyframe (F6) — make any changes or additions that you want — or if you want to create a completely new image from scratch or place an imported image, make the next keyframe a blank keyframe (F7).

5. Continue to add keyframes and change the contents of each keyframe until you've completed the animation. Finally, playback your animation by returning to the first keyframe and then selecting Control ➪ Play from the application menu (Enter or Return key), or preview the animation in the test movie environment by choosing Control ➪ Test Movie (Ctrl+Enter or ⌘+Return).

Modifying Multi-Frame Sequences

To control the pacing of your animation, you can add more frames (F5) between the keyframes, or add more keyframed (F7) images to the sequence to extend its length. Adding more frames between keyframes will "hold" or pause the animation, until the Playhead hits the next keyframe with changed content. In the example shown in Figure 11-2, the face holds on some frames while the butterfly continues to move in keyframed drawings on its own layer. To speed up (or shorten) animation you can remove frames (Shift+F5) or keyframes (Shift+F6) to shorten the sequence. You can make changes in the length of a span by selecting a frame in the span that you want to modify and using the application menu commands (or shortcut keys), or you can simply drag the endframe of the span to change its position on the Timeline.

Tip   If you drag the endframe of a span to a new position, Flash will automatically insert a new keyframe in the endframe's original location. If you want to change the length of a span without adding more keyframes, hold down the Ctrl or ⌘ key while clicking and dragging the endframe to a new position.

Cross-Reference   For a review of the methods used to edit frames and keyframes, refer to Chapter 4, "Interface Fundamentals."

Inserting more frames does work to slow down an animated sequence, but generally if you insert more than two frames between keyframes the movement will be interrupted and the animation will start to look too choppy. Try adding more keyframes to the sequence with very subtle change to the content in each keyframe if you want to create a slower, smoother animation.

By default Flash will loop the content on your timeline, so if you want a sequence to be repeated, you don't need to draw it over and over again. If you notice that your animation disappears before it loops to play again, check to make sure that there are no extra empty frames at the end of the sequence, or that the endframe of one of your sequences is not further down the timeline than the endframe of the element that disappears. Although you won't see anything on the Stage in these frames, Flash will still play those frames if they exist on the timeline. Obviously, blank frames can be used in an animation whenever you want to empty the Stage — either as a pause between sequences or to create the illusion that your artwork has disappeared.

To illustrate how blank frames playback in an animation we've created a silly example with a pair of eyes that appear and disappear while a solid rectangle remains visible on the layer above it (see Figure 11-3).

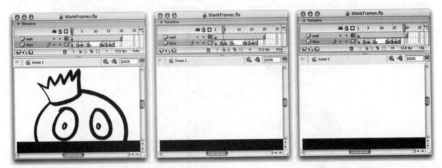

Figure 11-3: You can insert blank keyframes to clear artwork from the Stage. Remember that the Playhead will continue along the timeline if there are frames on any one of the layers, even if the artwork on other layers is no longer present.

Editing multiple frames

One of the drawbacks of manually creating unique artwork on every frame is that changes can be very time-consuming. If you decide to change the color of an element or perhaps edit out a feature of your artwork, repeating this edit on every frame of a sequence will be tedious and labor-intensive. Fortunately, Flash provides a shortcut that can make repeated edits on multiple frames much more efficient. **Edit Multiple Frames** allows you to see and select items on multiple frames for simultaneous modification. As shown in Figure 11-4, the Edit Multiple Frames option is turned on with the toggle button at the top of the Document window. When this feature is active you can use any of the selection methods (Arrow tool, Lasso, application menu, or shortcut keys) to select the parts of your artwork that you wish to move, modify or delete. This feature is especially helpful for edits that need to be consistent from frame to frame, such as moving all of your artwork to a new position in your layout.

The frames visible and available for selection are marked by a gray span on the timeline with start and end handles. The number of frames included in the span can be adjusted with the Arrow tool by clicking and dragging the round handles on the timeline to a new position.

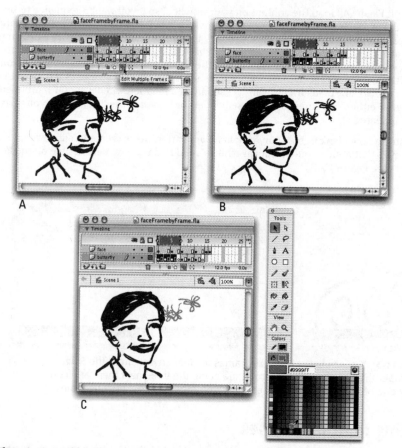

Figure 11-4: With Edit Multiple Frames toggled on (A), you can select elements on various frames in a sequence (B) to be modified simultaneously (C).

Onion skinning

Traditional animators are able to work on layers of transparent cels using a light table. This allows them to create consistent drawings and to plan the pacing of movement in a sequence of cels. As you move from keyframe to keyframe in Flash, you might feel that you are working blind, since you can only see the artwork on the current frame. If you are creating artwork for a sequence of related keyframes, it is crucial to have some visual indication or "map" of the changes from frame to frame. Fortunately Flash has an effective digital version of the traditional light table. This handy feature is called onion skinning because onion skins are multi-layered and thin enough to see light through. In Flash, onion skinning allows you to see several frames of your artwork displayed at one time. The onion markers on the timeline determine the number of frames that are visible. Onion skinning can be turned on or off whenever you need it using the toggle buttons on the top of the Document window. As shown in Figure 11-5, there are actually two options for onion skinning: **Onion Skin** or **Onion Skin Outlines.**

Figure 11-5: Onion Skin will show grayed-out or ghosted artwork on multiple frames, while Onion Skin Outlines will show colored outlines of the artwork on multiple frames.

The current frame (indicated by the position of the Playhead) is displayed at 100 percent opacity, while the other frames in the sequence are displayed at a slightly reduced opacity or as outlines, depending on the Onion Skin button you have selected.

Tip   Layers that are locked will not be visible when onion skinning is active.

The number of frames that are included in the onion skin display can be controlled either by choosing a setting from the **Modify Onion Markers** menu (shown in Figure 11-6), or by selecting the round marker handles with the Arrow tool and sliding them to a new position on the timeline. The number of frames that you select from the Modify menu will be shown before and after the current frame—so in our example with **Onion 2** selected, the onion skin markers actually span five frames (the current frame, plus two frames on each side.)

Figure 11-6: You can control the number of frames visible when onion skinning is turned on with the Modify Onion Markers menu, or by dragging the round handles of the onion skin markers to a new position on the timeline with the Arrow tool.

Tweening

Tweening is one of the most powerful Flash animation features. Whether you are creating character animation or motion graphics, or even the most basic button effect, you will find tweening indispensable. Once you have planned your animation and created the initial artwork, you can use Flash tweening to generate the transitional images between one keyframe and another. This is the tool that makes it possible for an artist to quickly generate smooth, precise animation — without spending half their life manually filling in unique graphics on every frame. Instead, you can establish a beginning point and an endpoint, and only make drawings, or key art, for each of those points. Then you let Flash interpolate and render, or *tween*, the changes between the keyframes. Tweening can be used to render changes in size, shape, color, position, and rotation.

Tweening also minimizes file size because you don't have to include unique information on each frame in the animation. Because you define the contents of the frames at the beginning and end point, Flash only has to save those graphics, plus the values needed to make the *changes* on the frames in between. Basically, Flash only has to store the difference between the beginning frame and the endframe so that the images on the frames in between can be calculated and rendered.

The other significant benefit of using tweens to generate an animated sequence is that if you want to make a change, you only need to modify the beginning or end point and Flash will instantly update the images in between. Two kinds of tweens can be created in Flash — Shape tweens and Motion tweens — each applied for specific purposes. Both tween types are represented on the timeline by a colored fill with a continuous arrow on the span between the start keyframe and the end keyframe of the animation. Shape tweens are represented by a green fill and Motion tweens by a blue fill. If a tween is incomplete, either because the wrong tween type has been applied or because information on one of the defining keyframes is missing, the continuous arrow will be replaced with a dashed line.

The type of tween that you want to apply is selected from the Tween menu in the Property inspector. As shown in Figure 11-7, the options available for controlling the playback of the final tween depend on the type of tween selected.

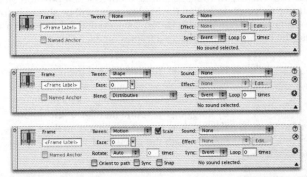

Figure 11-7: When you specify a tween type in the Property inspector, the relevant options for controlling the tween will also be available.

Shape tweening

Shape tweening is useful for morphing basic shapes — for example turning a square into a circle, or animating the drawing of a line by tweening from a dot to a finished line. Flash can only Shape tween primitive *shapes,* so don't even try to Shape tween a group, symbol, or editable text — it won't work. You can tween multiple shapes on one layer, but for the sake of organization and animation control, it's best to put each shape on its own layer. This allows you to adjust the speed and length of shape tweens individually, and also makes it much easier to figure out what's going on if you need to edit the file later on.

The source files for the examples in this section are located on the CD-ROM, in the Shape Tweening folder of the ch11 folder.

Figure 11-8 shows an animated "smile" created by interpolating the graphics between a dot and a curved stroke with a Shape tween. Flash nimbly handles this simple transition, rendering a gradually extending line on the frames between the dot of the pursed mouth and the final curve of the smile.

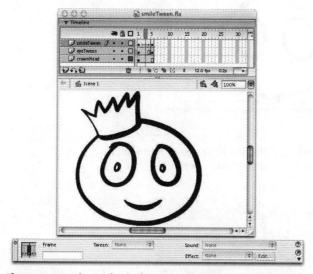

Figure 11-8: After a dot is drawn on keyframe 1 and an arc is drawn on keyframe 5, a Shape tween is applied to render the shapes on the frames in the span between — creating an animation.

Here are the steps for creating a Shape tween:

1. Select the frame in which you'd like to start the animation. If it's not already a keyframe, convert it into one.

2. Then draw your starting image on the Stage (see Figure 11-9). Always remember that shape tweening only works with *shapes* — not groups, symbols, or editable text. To shape tween these items, you first need to break them apart into shapes (Modify ➪ Break Apart).

3. Next, insert a keyframe (F6) on the timeline where you want the animation to end and modify the artwork to define the end point of the animation (see Figure 11-10). If you want to create the artwork in the final frame from scratch, then insert a blank keyframe (F7) instead of a keyframe that includes the artwork from the first keyframe.

4. Select the keyframe at the beginning of the span that you want to interpolate with a Shape tween. Remember that results will be easiest to control and modify if you only tween one shape per layer.

Figure 11-9: The contents of the first keyframe in your span will define the starting point for the Shape tween.

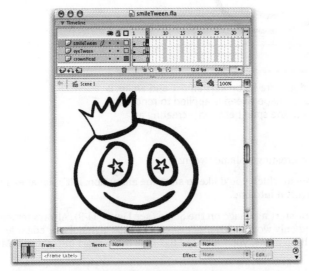

Figure 11-10: The contents of the final keyframe after your span will define the ending point for the Shape tween.

5. Open the Property inspector if it is not already available by selecting Window ➪ Properties from the application menu (Ctrl+F3 or ⌘+F3), as shown in Figure 11-11.

6. Choose **Shape** from the **Tween** drop-down menu. The span between the start keyframe and the end keyframe of your animation will now display with a green fill and an arrow to indicate that a Shape tween has been applied.

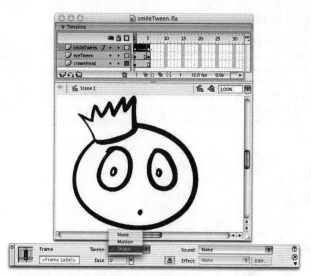

Figure 11-11: Specify Shape as the tween type with the Property inspector Tween menu.

7. As shown previously in Figure 11-7, the Property inspector panel updates to present two options for modifying the Shape tween:

- Set the **Ease** slider if you want to vary the rate or speed of the animation. This is useful if you want to create the effect of acceleration or deceleration. If you want your animation to start slowly and progressively speed up, push the slider down to add an Ease In. This will cause **In** to display adjacent to the slider and will update the value field with a negative number (between –1 and –100). For an animation that starts fast and progressively slows, push the slider up to add an Ease Out. The word **Out** will appear and a positive number (between 1 and 100) will display in the value field. If you want the rate of your animation to stay constant, leave the slider in the middle (0). You can also type any number between -100 and 100 directly into the Ease value field.

- Select a **Blend** type: **Distributive** blending creates smoother interpolated shapes, whereas **Angular** blending creates interpolated shapes that preserve corners and straight lines. If your end points contain shapes with corners and lines, select Angular blending. Otherwise, use the default Distributive blending.

8. Preview the animation by selecting Control ➪ Play (Enter) from the application menu, or use Control ➪ Test Movie (Ctrl+Enter or ⌘+Return) to publish a .swf file.

Note   If you accidentally assign the wrong tween type to the start keyframe of your animation or if you delete the artwork on the start or the end keyframes, you will notice that the arrow icon on the timeline is replaced with a dashed line. This indicates that the tween is broken or incomplete. To restore the tween, it is usually best to select the first keyframe and choose None from the Tween menu in the Property inspector. Then check your timeline and your artwork to make sure that you have shapes on both a beginning and an end keyframe for Flash to interpolate. When you think all the elements are in place, select the first keyframe and chose Shape from the Tween menu in the Property inspector to reapply the tween.

Adding Shape Hints

Because Flash will calculate the simplest way to interpolate from one shape to another, you will occasionally get unexpected results if the shapes are complex or extremely different from one another. Shape tweening becomes less reliable the more points there are to be calculated between the defined keyframes. In our example we have added a keyframe at the end of the span with the eyes of the character changed from circles to stars. We want the animation to be a smooth transition from the rough circle to the star shape in each eye. As shown in Figure 11-12, a basic Shape tween results in some odd in-between shapes.

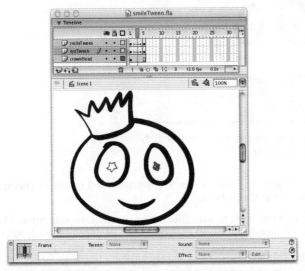

Figure 11-12: When a Shape tween is added to create an animation from the round eye to the star shape, the transition artwork that Flash generates is not the shape we want it to be.

One way of making the in between artwork more precise is to insert keyframes in the middle of the Shape tween so that you can manually adjust the shapes that Flash has generated. Another option that allows you to control a tween without modifying any artwork is to add *Shape Hints* for Flash to follow when rendering the in between shapes. Shape Hints allow you to specify points on a starting shape that should match with specified points on the final shape. This helps Flash to "understand" how the shapes are related and how the transitional images should be rendered. Compare Figure 11-12 with Figure 11-13 to see the improvement that Shape Hints can make in the precision of in between shapes.

Caution   When copying and pasting a span of frames into a new timeline — such as in Movie Clip — Flash drops the shape hints. When pasting is confined to the Main Timeline, hints are retained.

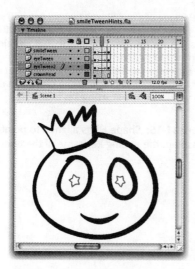

Figure 11-13: Placing shapes on individual layers and adding Shape Hints to control the way that Flash renders in between shapes can greatly improve the precision of Shape tweens.

Shape Hints can only be added to artwork on keyframes that define the beginning and ending points of a Shape tween. To add Shape Hints to the artwork in a Shape tween, follow these steps after you have created a basic Shape tween:

1. Begin by selecting a shape on the starting keyframe and choosing Modify ⇨ Shape ⇨ Add Shape Hint from the application menu (Shift+Ctrl+H or Shift+⌘+H).

2. Flash places a small red circle, labeled with a letter, onto the Stage — this is your first Shape Hint. Additional Hints can be added and they will also be identified alphabetically.

3. To specify a point on your starting shape, use the Arrow tool to select and move the first Hint (a) — position it on an area of the shape (for example, a corner or a curve) that you want to match up with an area on the final shape, as shown in Figure 11-14.

Figure 11-14: Shape Hints positioned on a shape in the starting keyframe for a Shape tween

4. When you move the Playhead to the final keyframe of your Shape tween, you will see a lettered Hint that matches the one that was placed on the starting keyframe. Position this Hint with the Arrow key so that it marks the area of the final shape that should match up with the area specified on the starting shape. The Hint will only be recognized by Flash if it attaches correctly to the artwork. You will know that your Hints are positioned properly when their fill color changes from red to green on the final keyframe (see Figure 11-15) and from red to yellow on the starting keyframe.

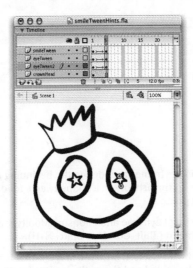

Figure 11-15: Shape Hints aligned to points on a shape in the ending keyframe of the tween

5. Preview the new in between shapes by *scrubbing* the timeline (dragging the Playhead with the Arrow tool to review frames in the tweened sequence).

6. Continue to add or reposition Hints until Flash renders the inbetween shapes correctly.

7. To remove an individual Hint, drag it off the Stage with the Arrow tool. To remove all Hints from an active keyframe, select Modify ⇨ Shape ⇨ Remove All Hints from the application menu. A shortcut is to Right-click (Ctrl-click on Mac) any of the Hints to invoke the contextual menu, as shown in Figure 11-16, for these and other options as you are working.

Figure 11-16: The contextual menu offers some options for working with Shape Hints.

Tip

If the Shape Hints are not visible after you have placed them, make sure that the Show All Hints option in the contextual menu is toggled on, or use the application menu to select View ➪ Show Shape Hints (Alt+Ctrl+H or Option+⌘+H) — this option is only available if the layer and keyframe that contain the Hints is currently active.

Motion tweening

Motion tweening is useful for animating groups, symbols, and editable text; however, it cannot be used to animate primitive shapes. As the name suggests, Motion tweening is applied to move an item from one place to another, but it's capable of much more. Motion tweening can also be used to animate the scale, skew, or rotation of items; as well as the color and transparency of a symbol.

Note

Motion tweening can only be applied to one item per layer — use multiple layers to Motion tween multiple items in the same span of the timeline.

The pacing of a Motion tweened sequence can be modified at any point — simply insert a keyframe for each phase of the animation. In addition to the scale and color effect settings applied to the actual symbol instance, the settings in the Property inspector that control Easing and Rotation can be adjusted on each keyframe of a Motion tween. So, if you use a tween to move a symbol from frame 1 to frame 10 and stop the tween on frame 11, you can have the symbol sit still for 10 frames (no tween), and then start a new tween (of this same symbol on the same layer) with rotation or an alpha fade from frames 20 to 30. The possibilities are almost endless.

Like a Shape tween, a Motion tween is more efficient than frame-by-frame animation because it doesn't require unique content for each frame of animation. Yet it is *not* appropriate for all effects — sometimes you'll need to use either frame-by-frame animation or Shape tweening to create the kind of in betweens you need in a sequence.

Here's how to create a Motion tween:

1. Select the frame in which you'd like to start your animation. If it's not already a keyframe, make it one by selecting Insert ➪ Keyframe (F6).

2. Draw or import the image that you want to tween. Just remember that you can only motion tween groups, symbols (including imported bitmaps — which are, by default, symbols), and editable text (a text block).

   • If you are using an image, group it or turn it into a symbol, as shown in Figure 11-17.

Cross-Reference

Refer to Chapter 6, "Symbols, Instances, and the Library," for a review of creating symbols.

   • If you already have the element as a symbol in your current Library, you can just drag it from the Library onto the Stage.

   • If you are using editable text, you don't have to do anything — it's already an element that can be Motion tweened.

3. Select the frame where you want the tween to end and make it a keyframe by selecting Insert ➪ Keyframe (F6).

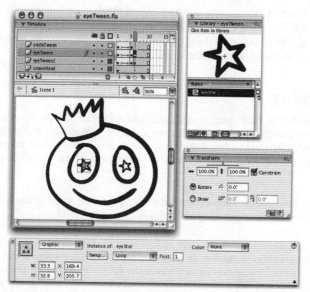

Figure 11-17: The artwork on the first keyframe of the span you want to Motion tween should be a text box, a group, or a symbol.

4. Make any modifications to the symbols that you want animated on the beginning and end keyframes, as shown in Figure 11-18. Remember that you can move tweened elements, as well as scale, skew, and rotate them. If your end point images are symbols, you can also use the Color Effect menu to modify Tint, Alpha, and Brightness.

Refer to Chapter 9, "Modifying Graphics," for a review of color effects and other possible symbol modifications.

Alpha effects in Motion tweens will slow most fps settings. The only way to make sure that the fps is honored, no matter what, is to use a stream sync sound that loops over the course of any critical fps playback. For more on the relationship between streaming sounds and fps rate, see Chapter 15, "Adding Sound."

5. There are three different ways that you can apply a basic Motion tween to a span between two keyframes:

• Select the beginning keyframe, then open the Property inspector (Window ➪ Properties) and use the Tween menu to specify a Motion tween.

• Right-click (Control+click on Mac) any frame between the two keyframes and select Create Motion Tween from the contextual menu.

• Select the beginning keyframe or any frame in the span and choose Insert ➪ Create Motion Tween from the application menu.

Read This Before Using Create Motion Tween

If you have not converted your artwork into symbols before using the Create Motion Tween command, Flash automatically converts any item in the selected keyframe into a symbol with the generic name of Tween followed by a number (i.e. Tween1, Tween2) Although this might seem like a handy shortcut, it actually creates a mess that you will need to clean up later.

Since the symbols are auto-created and named, you will not have the same control over how your Library is organized and how your artwork is optimized. It is much better to analyze the most efficient way to convert your artwork into symbols and to reuse those symbols as much as possible than to allow Flash to make generic symbols that may be redundant. As with all elements in your Flash project, it is also much more useful to assign meaningful names to your symbols that will help you navigate the project when you need to make edits.

Manually creating and naming your own symbols before assigning a tween to specific keyframes helps avoid redundant or confusing items being added to your document (.fla) Library. If you make a habit of using the Property inspector to assign tweens, you will always be reminded if you haven't converted an element into a symbol.

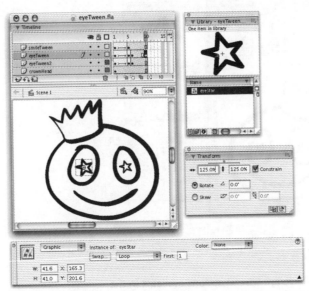

Figure 11-18: Modify the features of the symbol on the end keyframe that you want to interpolate with a Motion tween.

6. Select the first keyframe of your Motion tween and use the options in the Property inspector to add more control to the final tween, as shown in Figure 11-19.

- **Rotate:** You can rotate tweened items using this option. Select a rotation type from the drop-down menu and then type the number of rotations in the value field. Automatic rotation rotates your item in the direction that requires the least amount of motion, while Clockwise and Counterclockwise rotate your item in the indicated direction. In both cases, the rotation will be completed as many times as you specify in the value field. If you type 0 in the entry field, or select None from the drop-down menu, no rotation will occur (other than rotation that has been applied to the symbol with the Transform panel.)

- **Orient to path:** When your item follows a path (or Motion guide), turning this selection on forces the item to orient its movement to that path. We discuss paths in the next chapter.

- **Sync:** This same feature can be accessed from the application menu using Modify ➪ Frames ➪ Synchronize Symbols. When this setting is activated on a tween, you can replace the symbol in the first keyframe and it will automatically be updated in the remaining frames and in any other synchronized keyframes that follow. This setting is also important if your animation is contained within a Graphic symbol. Flash will recalculate the number of frames in a tween on a Graphic symbol's timeline so that it will match the number of frames available on the Main Timeline. Sync ensures that your animation loops properly when the animated symbol is placed in the Main Timeline, even if the frame sequence in the Graphic symbol is not an even multiple of the number of frames assigned to the symbol in the Main Timeline.

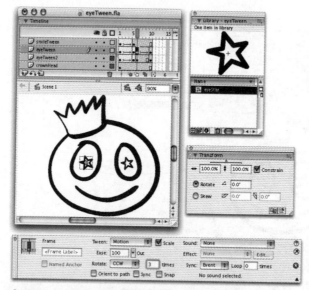

Figure 11-19: There are several options available in the Property inspector that apply to Motion tweens.

Tip   You can tell if a tweened sequence is synchronized because the vertical lines separating the keyframes from the span are not visible when this setting is applied.

- **Snap:** This option snaps your animated item into alignment with a Motion guide. Motion guides are discussed in the next chapter.

7. Other elements can be Motion tweened on the same span of the timeline, as long as they are on separate layers (see Figure 11-20). You can interpolate different features on each tween and also apply any control settings that you wish—Flash will read and render the Motion tween on each layer independently.

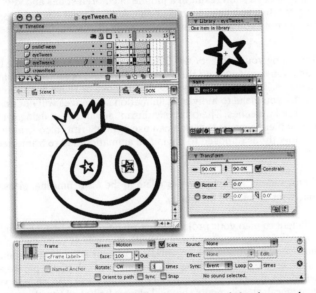

Figure 11-20: Multiple items can be animated simultaneously using separate settings by Motion tweening on individual layers.

Tweened zooms (where an item starts at a reduced scale and is tweened to full-scale or larger) and tweened alpha effects can be both CPU and bandwidth intensive—not only can they result in larger files that take longer to download, but they also require more computing horsepower on the user's machine. These cautions also apply to multiple tweens rendered within the same span of the timeline. Our advice: Use complex effects and multiple tweens judiciously.

As with Shape tweens, the arrow icon on the timeline span of your Motion tween will be replaced with a dashed line if the tween is broken or incomplete. A common mistake with Motion tweens is to try and animate multiple elements on the same layer. To restore the tween, it is usually best to select the first keyframe and choose None from the Tween menu in the Property inspector. Then check your timeline and your artwork to make sure that you have only a single group or symbol (not a shape) on a layer with both a beginning and an end keyframe for Flash to interpolate. When you think all the elements are in place, select the first keyframe and chose Motion from the Tween menu in the Property inspector to re-apply the tween.

Integrating Multiple Animation Sequences

So far in this chapter, we've looked at creating different types of animation on the Main Timeline. As you can tell, even with the simple examples that we've used, adding multiple tweens to the Main Timeline can soon result in a jumble of colored spans and keyframes that might be hard to navigate when you need to make edits. Authoring all animation sequences on the Main Timeline also puts you at risk of unintentionally displacing multiple sequences as you make edits.

The best solution for keeping your project (.fla) files manageable as you continue to add animation is to move animation sequences off the Main Timeline and organize them instead on individual symbol timelines. This makes it much easier to move or reuse animation and will also ensure that any edits you make to individual animation sequences will not disrupt sequences on other symbol timelines. The other significant advantage of using symbols to organize multiple animated elements is that you can use ActionScript to control the playback of each symbol independently, as opposed to having all animation tied to frame sequences on the same (Main) timeline.

 Cross-Reference   For a review of how various symbol timelines relate to the Main Timeline, please refer to Chapter 6, "Symbols, Instances, and the Library."

Although it is more efficient to plan your project structure before you begin adding animation—so that you can integrate the animation with symbols as you create it—Flash is flexible enough to allow you to optimize the organization of your animation sequences even after you have built them on the Main Timeline. The extent to which you separate and nest animated elements will depend on the complexity of the project and also on how you intend to reuse animation. In general, any elements that will always be linked together on playback can be stored in the same symbol. If you want to have the option of altering playback speed or placement of certain elements independently, than these should be stored in discrete symbols. For example, if you have an animated logo that may be used in a project separately from an animated title, than these two elements should be in individual symbols. On the other hand, if the logo always appears in the same way with the title, than these two elements can be stored in a single symbol (on separate layers, if necessary).

Moving tweens onto symbol timelines

As discussed in Chapter 6, all symbols have their own timelines, so you could just as easily store an animation in a Graphic symbol as in a Movie Clip. The important difference to remember is that a Graphic symbol timeline must still be tied to frames on the Main Timeline, while a Movie Clip timeline will playback independently, regardless of how many frames it is assigned on the Main Timeline. The only benefit of using a Graphic symbol to store an animated sequence is that it can be previewed frame-by-frame directly in the authoring environment, even if it is nested. Nested Movie Clip timelines only play in the Test Movie environment or in the final movie (.swf)—the animation can still be previewed in the authoring environment if you are in Symbol Editing mode, but you will not be able to see how the animation on the Movie Clip timeline syncs with animation on other symbol timelines or with the Main Timeline. Despite these limitations, it is still best to use Graphic symbols to store static elements and Movie Clip symbols to store any animated sequences.

To illustrate how tweens are moved from the Main Timeline to a Movie Clip timeline we will modify our tween example created in the last section. To reorganize a file (.fla) that has animation built on the Main Timeline, follow these steps:

1. Analyze the Main Timeline carefully to see how the various animated sequences need to relate to each other in the final movie (.swf) Decide which frame spans you need to keep tied together and which should be independent.

2. Pay close attention to how the transitions between different animated sequences are handled on the Main Timeline. If two different phases of a tween share a common keyframe (for example if you have scaled an element in one tween and then rotated the same element in another tween that continues from the final keyframe of the first tween), you must keep these tweens together or else insert an additional keyframe before you separate them in order to keep both tweens intact, as shown in Figure 11-21.

Tip To be certain that linked sequential tweens can be separated without getting messed up, it can be helpful to remove the tween from the end keyframe of the first tweened sequence after inserting another keyframe (F6) to maintain the beginning of the tween that follows. This ensures that there is no interpolation between the end keyframe of the first tween and the start keyframe of the second tween.

Figure 11-21: Removing the tween from the end keyframe between two sequences that will be separated can help to avoid broken tweens.

3. Double-click the span or Shift-select the beginning and end keyframes of the sequence that you want to move off the Main Timeline.

4. With all frames in the sequence selected, choose **Copy Frames** from the contextual menu (see Figure 11-22), or Edit ➪ Copy Frames from the application menu (Alt+Ctrl+C or Option+⌘+C).

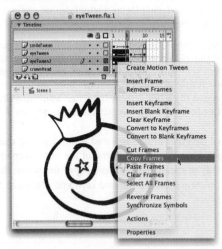

Figure 11-22: Be sure to use **Copy Frames** rather than simply **Copy** to move a sequence of frames to the clipboard.

5. Create a new symbol by selecting Insert ➪ Create Symbol from the application menu (Ctrl+F8 or ⌘+F8.) Assign the symbol **Movie Clip** behavior and give it a name that will be useful for identifying the animation, as shown in Figure 11-23.

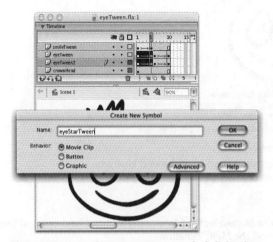

Figure 11-23: In the Create New Symbol dialog box, assign Movie Clip behavior and enter a meaningful name for your new symbol.

6. Select the first frame of the symbol timeline and choose **Paste Frames** from the contextual menu or Edit ⇨ Paste Frames from the application menu (Alt+Ctrl+V or Option+⌘+V). Flash will automatically insert enough layers and frames to accommodate the content you paste into the symbol timeline (see Figure 11-24). Your animation sequence is now stored inside the symbol, and can easily be accessed from the Library for reuse or editing.

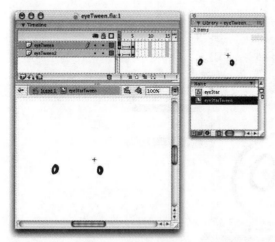

Figure 11-24: When you use Paste Frames to place the content from the clipboard into your symbol, you will keep the layers and keyframes intact.

New Feature   Flash MX now preserves the original layer names when content is pasted into a new timeline.

Create as many new symbols as you need to hold all of the individual animation sequences that you want to work with in your project. When you are finished, you should have a set of named Movie Clip symbols in your Library that are easy to identify, containing animated elements that will now be efficient to edit or reuse.

Organizing Symbol Instances on the Main Timeline

You may have noticed in the last section that we suggested copying your animation sequences from the Main Timeline to be pasted into Movie Clips — even though this results in redundant content. The rationale for leaving the original sequences on the Main Timeline as you copy them into separate symbols, is that they provide a useful reference for where the symbol instances should be placed on the Stage and how they should be arranged on the Main Timeline. The simplest way to "rebuild" your animation, using the Movie Clips you have created, is to insert a new layer for each symbol on the Main Timeline directly above the original sequence that was copied. As you drag each symbol instance onto the Stage, you will be able to align the artwork with the original sequence on the Stage and also to determine how many frames the symbol should occupy on the Main Timeline.

Using the example from the previous section, we will proceed to replace the tweened sequences on the Main Timeline with our Movie Clip instances.

1. Insert a new layer on the Main Timeline directly above the original tweened sequence (see Figure 11-25) by selecting the original layer and using the New Layer button in the Timeline window or choosing Insert ➪ Layer from the application menu (or the contextual menu).

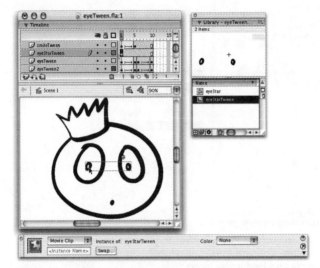

Figure 11-25: The original animation sequences can help you to place and align the symbol instances as you rebuild your project with Movie Clips.

2. After you finish placing a symbol instance on a new layer in the Main Timeline, you can delete the layer containing the original tweened sequence. You will quickly see how much cleaner and easier to modify the Timeline becomes when the tweened and frame-by-frame sequences are replaced with Movie Clip symbol instances, as shown in Figure 11-26.

Because the Movie Clip timelines will loop automatically, you can repeat an animation sequence as many times as you like, either by holding on a single frame of the Main Timeline, or by extending the span of the Movie Clip so that it remains visible as the Main Timeline continues to play. You can quickly change the order of your animation by moving the Movie Clips to new positions on the Main Timeline—without having to worry about disrupting any tweens.

On the CD-ROM

You can compare the original file with the final rebuilt file by opening the "eyeTween" example file in the Motion tween folder and comparing it to the "eyeSymbol" example in the Integrate folder. These folders, as well as some others relevant to this chapter, are located in the ch11 folder of the CD-ROM.

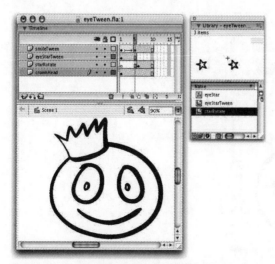

Figure 11-26: The Main Timeline will get easier to manage as you replace the tweened and frame-by-frame sequences with Movie Clip instances.

Reusing and Modifying Symbol Instances

Although you won't be able to preview the animation in your Movie Clip instances by scrubbing the Main Timeline, you can now easily move or reuse your animated elements. In our example, we have placed additional instances of the starRotate Movie Clip on new layers to create some animated background elements (see Figure 11-27).

Now that your animation is stored on symbol timelines, you can use ActionScript to control the playback of each element independently of the Main Timeline. For example, rather than stopping the Main Timeline, you can place a stop action on the Movie Clip timeline to hold the animation of one element while the other elements continue to play, as shown in Figure 11-28.

Cross-Reference For an introduction to using ActionScript to control timelines, refer to Chapter 18, "Understanding Actions and Event Handlers."

As discussed in previous chapters, the appearance of symbol instances can be modified without having to edit the contents of the original symbol. This can be helpful when working with static elements, but it really becomes indispensable when working with animated elements. Imagine the time it would take to copy and paste a series of tweens or a frame-by-frame sequence on the Main Timeline and then to edit the artwork on each keyframe just to change the scale or the color of your animated element each time you want to use it. Now be very happy that the little extra time spent moving your animated sequences off the Main Timeline and into Movie Clips makes it possible to drag and drop your animated elements and then to scale, rotate or apply color effects to get endless variations without ever having to edit the original keyframe artwork.

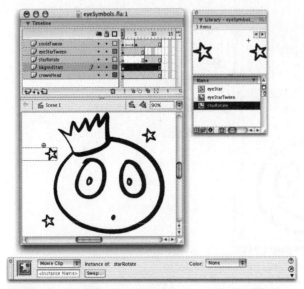

Figure 11-27: Movie Clips make it easy to place multiple instances of your animated elements.

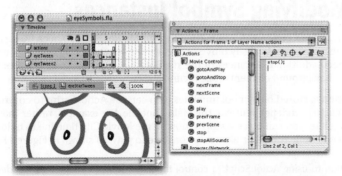

Figure 11-28: ActionScript can be added to Movie Clip timelines to control the playback of animated elements, independent of the Main Timeline.

In our example (see Figure 11-29), we have modified the appearance of some of the animated stars by transforming instances of the original starRotate Movie Clip.

Cross-Reference   For a review of the options for modifying symbol instances, refer to Chapter 9, "Modifying Graphics."

The beauty of Movie Clips is that you always have the option to modify the appearance of individual symbol instances or to make global changes by modifying the artwork in your original symbol. If you decide that an element should be changed every place that it appears, it will be much quicker to edit the original symbol than it would be to modify all of the symbol instances individually.

Figure 11-29: By transforming symbol instances, you can add almost endless variation to the appearance of your animated sequences without having to modify any keyframe artwork.

If you decide that you want to keep the artwork, but not the animation for some of the Movie Clip instances you have placed on the Main Timeline, you can use Modify ➪ Break Apart (Ctrl+B or ⌘+B) to remove the link to the animated Movie Clip, while keeping an instance of the original static symbol on the Stage.

On the CD-ROM We have included different versions of our example file so that you can see how the structure of the file was altered with the steps explained in this section. The files are located in the Modify folder in the ch11 folder of the CD-ROM.

A feature that comes in handy when creating animation loops, is the option to reverse a sequence of frames. You can reverse a tween or a frame-by-frame sequence as long as there is a keyframe at each end of the sequence that you select. One of the most common ways to use this feature is to copy a sequence of frames for an animation, place it on the timeline immediately following the original sequence and then apply the Modify ➪ Reverse Frames command to create a seamless loop. When the timeline is played back, instead of completing one sequence and then jumping directly back to the starting keyframe, you will now have a second sequence that smoothes the transition from the final artwork, back to the original artwork on the starting keyframe of the sequence. In our example, we decided to create a loop of the smile.

1. The first step is to copy and paste the frames for the smile animation (you can place them on the same layer, but for clarity we have placed them on a layer directly above the original smile).

   You can select all the frames in the sequence and use the Copy Frames command, or hold down the Option (Alt) key while dragging the selected span to a new layer (or position on the timeline). Make sure that the copied sequence is placed immediately following the original sequence (either on the same layer or on a new layer), as shown in Figure 11-30.

Figure 11-30: Place the copied sequence immediately following the original sequence on the timeline.

2. With all of the frames (and keyframes) of the copied sequence selected, choose Modify ⇨ Reverse Frames from the application menu or from the contextual menu. Flash will automatically rearrange the order of the selected frames so that the animation is reversed, as shown in Figure 11-31. You can also make adjustments to the length of the sequence or apply different tween settings (for example, you may want to change Easing from In to Out).

Figure 11-31: After the sequence is reversed, you can make adjustments to polish the loop.

We could fill an entire book with illustrations of the various ways that you can move, edit, and recombine your animated sequences, but the basic principals are always the same. Use symbols to keep your files optimized and your options open. Nest symbols to keep your project organized. Try to keep your Main Timeline uncluttered and easy to modify by putting frame-by-frame animation and tweens on Movie Clip timelines. Let Flash do as much work for you as possible, but don't be afraid to manually tweak animated sequences by inserting keyframes or modifying artwork. Use layers to keep elements organized and when you need to animate multiple items on the same span of the timeline. Plan and design your animation in logical sections rather than in complex groups — complexity can be added by nesting multiple symbols. Avoid redundant work and keep your files small and easy to manage by reusing artwork and animation whenever possible.

Summary

✦ The Flash MX authoring environment includes several features that have been adapted from tools that are used for creating traditional animation. Onion skinning, keyframes and tweens are the digital equivalents of layered transparent cels, key art, and manual in betweens.

✦ There are three basic ways in which you can create animated effects, including frame-by-frame animation and two types of interpolated animation, Shape and Motion tweens. Most projects will require a combination of all three types of animation.

✦ You can use Shape tweens only to interpolate primitive shapes (including broken apart text), and you can use Motion tweens only to interpolate editable text, symbols, or groups. Bitmaps can also be Motion tweened because they are recognized and stored in the Library in the same way as symbols.

✦ Tweens add less to file size than frame-by-frame animation because Flash calculates the difference between the keyframes rather than having to store unique artwork for every frame in a sequence. However, tweens can be very processor intensive if complex transitions or alpha layers need to be interpolated and rendered.

✦ You can create frame-by-frame animation by inserting keyframes (F6) and modifying the artwork in each frame, or by inserting blank keyframes (F7) and creating completely new artwork in each frame.

✦ You can modify the pace of frame-by-frame animation by inserting or deleting frames; however, in order to keep the motion smooth, you may also need to modify keyframes.

✦ You can modify the pace of tweened animation by extending or shortening the span of the tween and also by adjusting the Easing settings to create acceleration or deceleration in a sequence.

✦ Symbols are an integral part of creating optimized Flash animation. Primitive shapes or artwork must be converted into symbols before they can be Motion tweened and most animation should be organized in Movie Clip symbols instead of on the Main Timeline.

✦ By temporarily converting a symbol instance's behavior from Movie Clip to Graphic symbol, it is possible for you to preview animation that would otherwise not be visible when scrubbing the Main Timeline.

✦ By nesting artwork and animation in symbols, you can create sophisticated and complex animated effects while keeping your project structure easy to modify and your Main Timeline uncluttered. The Main Timeline should not be considered a space to author animation, but rather as a place to integrate all of the elements that you have created and stored in the Library as symbols.

✦　　✦　　✦

Applying Layer Types

✦ ✦ ✦ ✦

In This Chapter

Using Guide layers
for reference

Creating Motion Guides
to control animation

Applying Mask layers
for special effects

Masking animation
and creating nested
animated masks

✦ ✦ ✦ ✦

Besides storing and organizing the contents of your project (.fla), Flash layers offer some special features that will help you to create more advanced animation. Standard layers can be locked, hidden, or displayed as outlines, but they can also be converted into Guide layers, Motion Guides, or Mask layers. Each of these layer types can be used to accomplish specific authoring tasks.

Cross-Reference
ActionScript can also be used to guide or control animation and to apply dynamic masking. For an introduction to these more advanced alternatives to Mask layers and Motion Guides, refer to Chapter 27, "Interacting with Movie Clips."

Flash MX gives you the flexibility to quickly change the behavior of layers at any time in the authoring environment, so that you can take advantage of the special characteristics of each of these layer types as needed.

With the layer buttons at the lower-left corner of the Timeline window, you have the option of creating standard layers, Motion Guide layers, and Folder layers. If you have already created a standard layer, it can be converted into any of the special layer types by using the contextual menu (invoked by right-clicking or Ctrl+clicking the layer bar), or by changing settings in the Layer Properties dialog box (invoked by double-clicking the layer icon or by choosing Modify ➪ Layers from the application menu).

Flash MX will automatically convert layers if they are dragged into specific positions in the stacking order with other layer types — although this sounds a bit cryptic, it will make sense as you read about each layer type and how they affect other layers.

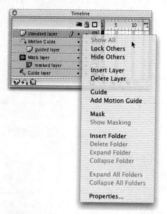

Figure 12-1: A unique icon in the layer stack identifies each of the layer types. The behavior of a layer can quickly be assigned or changed using the contextual menu.

Guide Layers

Guide layers are the only type of layer that is not exported with your final Flash MX movie (.swf). Guide layers are used primarily when you need to use an element as a reference in the authoring environment (.fla), but you don't want it to be part of the finished movie (.swf). To convert an existing layer into a Guide layer, you can use the contextual menu and select Guide. Alternatively, you can invoke the Layer Properties dialog box (shown in Figure 12-2) by double-clicking the layer icon (or choosing Modify➪Layers from the application menu) and then selecting the Guide check box.

Figure 12-2: The Layer Properties dialog box can be used to convert a standard layer into a Guide layer, Mask layer, or even a Layer folder.

Tip   As you are developing a project, it can be helpful to "turn off" certain layers while you're testing content on other layers. For example, by temporarily turning a layer that contains a large background graphic into a Guide layer, the movie (.swf) will render more quickly for preview in the test movie environment—just remember to turn all layers that you want exported back into Normal layers before publishing your final movie (.swf)—either by unchecking Guide in the contextual menu or selecting the Normal check box in the Layer Properties dialog box.

Bitmaps and video sequences can be placed in Guide layers if you want to use them as reference for drawings or animated sequences that are drawn in Flash—think of it like working with tracing paper to "redraw" images. The content on a Guide layer will add to the file size of the Flash document (.fla), but it will not be included with or add to the file size of the exported movie (.swf). Guide layers are also helpful when organizing layouts in Flash that require special alignment, such as a circular or diagonal arrangement of multiple elements.

To create a Guide layer that will serve as a reference for aligning a custom layout follow these steps:

1. Add a new layer to your Flash document (.fla) and make it a Guide layer. You have a couple of options for adding a Guide layer:

    • Use the contextual menu or the Layer properties dialog box to convert a standard layer into a Guide layer.

    • Use the Add Motion Guide Layer button to insert a Motion Guide layer and then drag the guided layer above the Motion Guide layer in the stacking order to revert the Motion Guide to a (static) Guide layer.

> **Note** Guide layers are actually just Motion Guide layers that don't have any guided layers nested below them.

2. Drag the Guide layer below your Art layers in the stacking order, or add a new layer above the Guide layer if you need a fresh layer for arranging artwork.

3. Place an imported image on the Guide layer for reference, or use the Flash drawing tools to create any guide image needed (such as a circle or a diagonal line).

4. Make sure that Snap to Objects is active by toggling on the Magnet option in the Toolbox or checking View⊅Snap to Objects in the application menu.

5. Use the Arrow tool to drag elements on the Art layers into alignment with the reference on the Guide layer (see Figure 12-3).

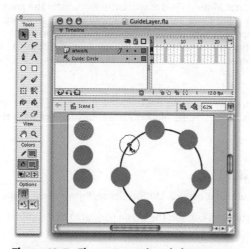

Figure 12-3: The center point of elements on your Art layers can be snapped to align with the reference on your Guide layer if it is recognized as a Flash shape or line.

6. When you test your movie (Ctrl+Enter or ⌘+Return), you won't see the content of the Guide layer displayed in the .swf (see Figure 12-4).

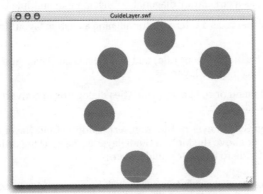

Figure 12-4: When the movie is viewed in the test movie environment, the content of the Guide layer will not be visible.

7. You can add to or modify the reference content on the original Guide layer or add additional Guide layers if needed. Use the Visibility toggle button (Eye icon) to control which layers display as you're working on different elements.

Motion Guides

The graphics on Motion Guide layers, as on Guide layers, will not be exported with the .swf file, but the important difference is that Motion Guides will actually control the path of movement for an animated element on another layer, rather than simply serving as a visual reference for static content. A Guide layer is automatically converted to a Motion Guide layer if another layer is nested below it to become a *guided* layer. To describe it simply, Guide layers only suggest what can be done, whereas Motion Guide layers dictate what something on another layer will do.

The files shown in these Motion Guide examples are included on the CD-ROM for your reference. You will find the source .fla files in the motionGuide subfolder located in the ch12 folder.

Applying a Motion Guide

To define the path for an animated element using a Motion Guide, follow these steps:

1. Define a Motion Guide layer that will contain the guide (or path) and a guided Art layer that will contain your animated element(s):

   • Select the layer that contains your animated elements and then use the Add Motion Guide button to insert a Motion Guide layer above your Art layer. You can also use the contextual menu or select Insert ➪ Motion Guide from the application menu to add a Motion Guide layer.

- If a Guide layer is already present and you want to convert it into a Motion Guide layer, simply drag your Art layer below the Guide layer in the stacking order (see Figure 12-5).

- If you have added a Motion Guide layer, but your Art layer is not nested below it as a guided layer, simply rearrange your layer stack by moving layers until the Art layer is indented below the Motion Guide layer indicating that it will be guided.

Note   Dragging a *Guide* layer *above* a Normal layer will not convert it into a Motion Guide layer, but dragging a *Normal* layer *below* a Guide layer will convert the Normal layer into a guided layer and the Guide layer into a Motion Guide.

2. Create a stroke that will define the path of the animation. You can use the shape tools or any of the other drawing tools. Although you can snap your animated elements to the edge of a filled shape, paths are usually defined by a stroke only.

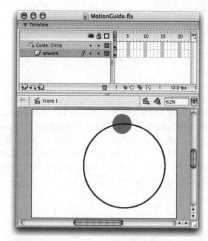

Figure 12-5: One or more Art layers can be *guided* simultaneously when nested below a Motion Guide layer.

3. Create a Motion tween on your Art layer. Make sure that Snap to Objects is active and use the Arrow tool to snap the registration point of the animated element to the path on both the beginning and end keyframes of the tween.

Tip   Flash will always chose the most efficient path to animate tweened elements, meaning it will interpolate the shortest route from the position defined in the starting keyframe to the position defined in the end keyframe. Occasionally, you may want to override this default efficiency. To force Flash to animate an element the "long way around" a closed path, it is necessary to add a gap to the stroke, as shown in Figure 12-6. The gap can be very, very small, but it should cut the stroke that defines your path, creating a space between the starting point and the ending point of your animation—because Flash will not jump gaps in a motion path, it will instead tween your animated element the long way around the shape.

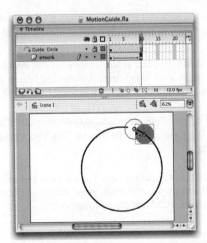

Figure 12-6: The registration point of the animated item must be snapped to the Motion Guide on both the beginning and end keyframe of the tween.

4. Scrub the timeline to preview the animated element; it should now follow the path defined in the Motion Guide. You can reposition your artwork in the beginning or end keyframes to adjust where the animation starts and stops on the path. The path can be adjusted by modifying the stroke on your Motion Guide layer. Use the Lock layer toggle to protect other layers as you make adjustments to specific elements. You can also apply easing and rotation to the artwork on your Motion tween layer and preview the interpolation by turning on onion skinning (see Figure 12-7).

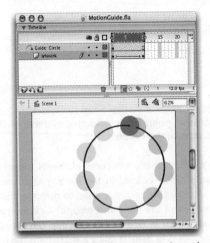

Figure 12-7: Guided tween previewed with onion skinning turned on

5. When the movie (.swf) is published, the stroke on the Motion Guide layer will not be exported, but the animation will still be rendered to tween along the path that was defined in the authoring environment (.fla).

Adding control to animation along a path

Even after you have succeeded in getting your tweened animation to follow the path defined in your Motion Guide layer, you may find that the movement of the animated element is not exactly as you would like. Fortunately, there are a few different ways that you can modify how a tweened element will follow a Motion Guide.

Using Orient to path

The first control to consider is found in the Property inspector when the first keyframe of your Motion tween is selected — the Orient to path check box (shown in Figure 12-8) will force an item to rotate as it follows a curved path so that it stays aligned or "headed" along the path. When Orient to path is not active, an animated item will maintain the same orientation throughout the tween, with no relation to the curves or loops in its Motion Guide.

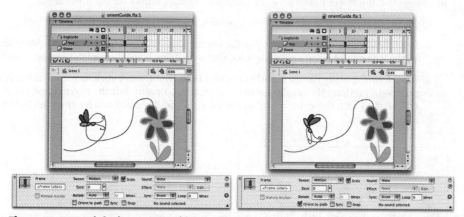

Figure 12-8: By default, a tweened item will maintain the same orientation as it tweens along a curved path (left). Orient to path will keep an animated item headed along the curves or loops in a Motion Guide (right).

Registration and center point alignment

The second important factor that determines how an animated element will move along a Motion Guide is where the registration point of the symbol is located. By default, the registration point is generally at the center of the symbol, but this may not be the point of the item that you want to snap to the Motion Guide. To modify the alignment of a guided symbol, you have two options: You can modify the registration point of the symbol (refer to Figure 12-9) or change the alignment of the artwork in Symbol Editing mode (refer to Figure 12-10).

To modify the registration point of the symbol, follow these steps:

1. Select the symbol on the first keyframe of the tween by clicking it with the Arrow tool on the Stage.

2. Activate the Free Transform tool in the Toolbox and drag the registration point to a new location.

3. Use the Arrow tool to snap the newly positioned registration point to the Motion Guide.

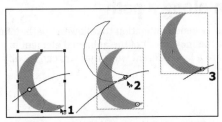

Figure 12-9: When Free Transform is active, you can modify the registration point of a symbol without changing the alignment of the artwork in relation to the center point.

To change the alignment of the artwork in Symbol Editing mode, follow these steps:

1. On the first keyframe of the tween, double-click the symbol with the Arrow tool.

2. Reposition the artwork in relation to the center point of the Stage in Symbol Editing mode so that the center point crosshair is located where you want the registration point to be.

3. Return to the Main Timeline and you should see that the artwork in your symbol is now positioned differently in relation to the registration point, but the registration point is still aligned with the centerpoint of the symbol and it should still be snapped to the Motion Guide.

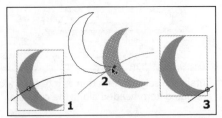

Figure 12-10: By changing the position of artwork in Symbol Editing mode, you can alter its alignment relative to the center point and the registration point.

Mask Layers

In the real world, a mask is used to selectively obscure items beneath it. In Flash, a Mask layer is used to define the visible area of layers nested beneath it. Multiple layers can be nested as *masked* layers beneath a single Mask layer. As with Motion Guide layers, the content on Mask layers is not visible in the final .swf because it is intended only to modify how content in nested masked layers is rendered.

The various examples discussed in this section can be found in the mask subfolder of the ch12 folder. You may find it helpful to examine the structure of these files to understand the many ways that Mask layers can be applied.

Almost any symbol or filled shape (excluding strokes) may be used to create a mask. However, Flash will ignore bitmaps, gradients, transparency, colors, and line styles in a Mask layer. Masks may be animated or static. The only other limitations are that you cannot apply a mask to content in another Mask layer, and Mask layers cannot be placed within Button symbol timelines.

Although groups, text boxes, and Movie Clips or Graphic symbols can all be used to define a mask, only one such item will be recognized on a single Mask layer. Multiple primitive shapes can be used to define a mask, but they will override all other items existing on the same Mask layer.

Masking with a filled shape

Here's how to create the simplest form of mask:

1. To begin with, the content that will be visible through the mask should be in place on its own layer, with visibility turned on. This will become the masked layer.

2. Create a new layer stacked above the masked layer. This will become the Mask layer.

3. In the Mask layer, create the "aperture" through which the contents of the masked layer will be viewed. This aperture can be any filled item, text, or a placed instance of a symbol that includes a filled item. (Of course, lines *can* be used as masks if they are first converted to fills with the Modify ⇨ Shapes ⇨ Convert Lines to Fills command.)

4. Now, position your mask content over the content on the masked layer (refer to Figure 12-11), so that it covers the area that you will want to be visible through the mask.

Figure 12-11: The content on the upper layer will define what is visible in the lower layer(s).

5. Right-click (or Ctrl+click) the layer bar of the Mask layer to invoke the contextual menu (refer to Figure 12-12), and choose Mask from the menu (or use the Layer Properties dialog box to change the layer behavior from Normal to Mask).

Figure 12-12: Convert the upper layer into a Mask layer by selecting Mask from the contextual menu.

6. The layer icons will change to indicate that the masked layer is now subordinate to the Mask layer and both layers will automatically be locked to activate the mask. The contents of the masked layer are now visible only through the filled portion(s) of the Mask layer, as shown in Figure 12-13.

Figure 12-13: When the mask is active, the content on the Mask layer will no longer be visible, but it will define the visible area of the content on the masked layer underneath.

7. To reposition, or otherwise modify, the Mask layer, temporarily unlock it (refer to Figure 12-14).

Figure 12-14: If the Mask layer is unlocked, the contents will be visible and can be edited.

8. To reactivate masking, lock the Mask layer again (and confirm that the masked layer is also locked).

Caution

When you first start working with Mask layers it is easy to forget to lock both the Mask layer and the masked layer to make the mask effect visible. If you are ever having trouble editing or viewing your masked effect, just remember that when the layers are unlocked the mask art is visible and editable and when the layers are locked the final masked effect is "turned on."

Masking with a group

Grouped filled shapes can also be used as a mask, as long as the Mask layer doesn't also contain primitive ungrouped shapes. If a mask is composed of multiple items, using a group makes it easier to position the mask, as shown in Figure 12-15.

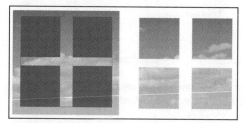

Figure 12-15: Grouped filled shapes can make it easier to position more complex masks.

Masking with a symbol instance

As you are reminded in nearly every chapter of this book, working with symbols is working smart because doing so helps to reduce file size. Because symbols comprised of filled shapes can be used as masks, there's no reason *not* to use a symbol from your Library to make a mask. (If you've already made a shape on your Mask layer, go ahead and convert it into a symbol so that you can use it again without adding to the final file size.) Reusing symbol instances to define masks is especially logical if you are making multiple masks that all have the same basic shape—for example, if you need a mask that is rectangular or oval, you will often find a symbol in your library that was created to define the active area of a button or some other basic element, and it will be smarter to modify an instance of that symbol so that it works as a mask than to add redundant elements that will add to file size.

Note Although in theory you can use a Button symbol instance as mask artwork, it is important to note that a Button symbol instance placed into a Mask layer will no longer function as a button. The result of this workflow is similar to selecting a Button symbol instance and assigning it Graphic symbol behavior in the Property inspector.

To illustrate the way that symbols can be reused as both graphic content and as mask elements, we have used the same symbol as static content on a masked layer and then Motion tweened the same symbol on a Mask layer to create an animated oval reveal. Because a single animated circle could be made more simply by just tweening the circle on the Art layer, we have added some other instances of the circle symbol to the Art layer so that the Mask layer will actually have a purpose. Figure 12-16 shows (A) the tweened symbol on the Mask layer (unlocked so that the symbol is visible), and (B) the resulting animated Mask (locked so that the tweened symbol masks the symbol instances on the Art layer).

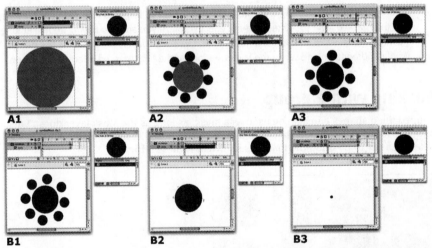

Figure 12-16: Symbol instance tweened on a Mask layer (A) to create an animated mask for symbol instances on the Art layer—when both layers are locked to apply masking (B)

If the example shown in Figure 12-16 appears confusing in the printed graphic, try opening the example file symbolMask.fla from the mask folder inside the ch12 folder on the CD-ROM.

Masking text

Not only can text be masked, it can also be used to mask other graphics. To mask text, simply set up your Mask and Art layers as described in the previous section, with the text to be masked on the lower layer, and the filled item that you'll use for your aperture on the Mask layer, as shown in Figure 12-17.

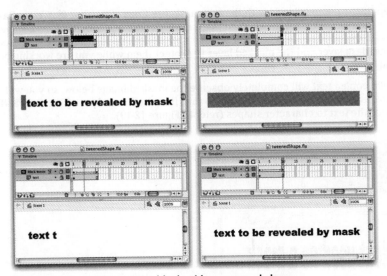

Figure 12-17: Masking a text block with a tweened shape

To use text as a mask, the layers should be set up as described previously. In this situation, the text (which goes on the Mask layer) will look as though it were filled by whatever is placed on the lower layer. For this to be effective, a larger point size and fuller, bold letterforms are best, as shown in Figure 12-18.

Figure 12-18: Using text as a mask for another image

Caution

Although you can type as much text as you like in a single text box to apply as a mask, you can only have one text box per Mask layer. To use multiple text boxes as mask elements, you will need to add separate Mask layers for each text box.

Since the edges of mask letterforms may be hard to discern if the image underneath is not a solid color, it can be helpful to add an outline to make the mask letters more legible. Since a stroke added to the text on the Mask layer would not be visible, it is necessary to copy the text onto a Normal layer stacked above the Mask layer:

1. To keep the text copy aligned with the text mask, use Copy (Ctrl+C or ⌘+C) and Paste in Place (Shift+Ctrl+V or Shift+⌘+V) to place a copy of the text into the Normal layer exactly on top of the mask text. After you have copied the text in the Mask layer, lock both the Mask layer and the masked layer to protect them while you are working on the Normal layer.

2. The solid copied text will completely obscure the masked image below, so you will need to create an outline of the text. To do this, first use Break Apart (Ctrl+B or ⌘+B) to reduce the text to character shapes (refer to Figure 12-19).

Figure 12-19: Apply the Break Apart command twice to reduce the copied text block to primitive letter shapes.

3. Use the Ink Bottle tool to add a 1- or 2-pixel stroke to each letter shape, as shown in Figure 12-20. Remember to add a stroke to the counter spaces of any letters with internal openings (such as *O*s or *B*s).

Figure 12-20: Use the Ink Bottle tool to add a thin stroke to the edges of all the letter shapes.

4. Next use the Arrow tool to select and delete the fills in each letter shape, leaving only the outline stroke, as shown in Figure 12-21.

Figure 12-21: Use the Arrow tool to delete the fills in each letter shape.

5. When you are finished, and the visibility is toggled back on for all layers, the text should show the image through the mask letters but now also have an outline that makes the text easier to read. (Refer to Figure 12-22.) You can use the Ink Bottle tool to modify the outline on the Normal layer at any time by applying a different color, style, or thickness of stroke.

Figure 12-22: The final letter shape outlines help to make the Mask text more legible over the art on the masked layer.

Motion Guides and Movie Clip Masks

As you have seen in examples so far, you can Shape tween primitive shapes or Motion tween symbol instances directly on the Main Timeline in Mask layers to create animated masks. But what if you want to add more control to the movement of a mask? Unfortunately, one of the limitations of Mask layers is that they can't be nested below Motion Guide layers to become guided elements. However, by using a Movie Clip symbol instance as the content of your Mask layer, you have the option of adding a Motion Guide to the Movie Clip timeline to control the movement of the element that defines your mask.

To create a mask that contains an element controlled by a Motion Guide, follow these steps:

1. Set up an Art layer and a Mask layer on the Main Timeline as in previous examples. Because the animation of your mask will exist on a Movie Clip timeline, you only need one frame on each layer.

2. Unlock the Mask layer and, on the first keyframe of the Main Timeline, insert a new symbol (Ctrl+F8 or ⌘+F8). In the Symbol Properties dialog box, specify Movie Clip behavior and name the symbol ("circleAnim"), as shown in Figure 12-23.

Figure 12-23: Insert a Movie Clip symbol that will contain the Motion Guide to control the animated mask content.

3. After you click OK in the Symbol Properties dialog box, Flash automatically opens the symbol timeline in the Document window.

4. Add a Motion Guide layer that contains the path for the animation and a guided layer that contains a Motion tween of the symbol that you want to define the final mask, as shown in Figure 12-24.

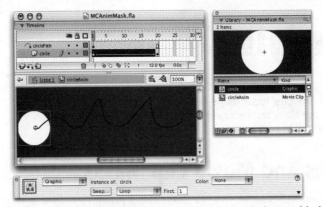

Figure 12-24: A Motion Guide and a Motion tween layer added to the Movie Clip timeline

5. When you return to the Main Timeline, you will see only the first frame of the animation that you just created in the Movie Clip (as shown in Figure 12-25). You can select the Movie Clip instance on the Mask layer to alter its position on the Stage.

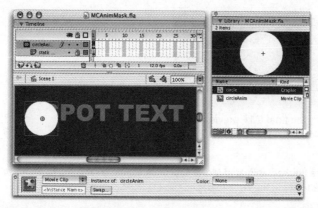

Figure 12-25: The first frame of the Movie Clip animation visible on the Mask layer in the Main Timeline

6. If you want to see how the whole Motion Guide aligns with the content on the masked layer, double-click the Movie Clip symbol instance on the Mask layer to enter Edit-in-place mode (refer to Figure 12-26). You will now be able to scrub the Movie Clip time-line and see how the animation lines up with (the dimmed out) content on the Main Timeline. You can make adjustments as needed to the Motion Guide layer or to the tweened symbol that will define the mask.

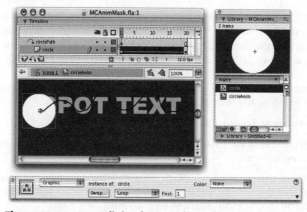

Figure 12-26: Use Edit-in-place mode to align the Motion Guide on the Movie Clip timeline with the content on the masked layer of the Main Timeline.

7. After you have all the elements aligned and edited as you want, lock both the Mask layer and the masked layer and test the movie (Ctrl+Enter or ⌘+Return) to see how the guided animation in the Movie Clip on the Mask layer reveals the content on the masked layer. Figure 12-27 shows one frame of the Motion tween in our example as it displays in the final .swf.

Figure 12-27: The final SWF previewed in the Test Movie environment

On the CD-ROM

To see how the finished animated Movie Clip mask example looks, open MCAnimMask.swf from the mask folder in the ch12 folder on the CD-ROM.

Of course, content on masked layers can also be animated separately from the content on Mask layers. The endless possibilities for layering Masks and masked content can start to get confusing when the additional variable of animation is thrown in. To make the best use of these features, take the extra time to carefully consider the most efficient way to achieve the final effect that you want. First consider what you would like to see on the Stage and then plan any animation of visible elements. The next step should be adding a Mask if needed, and finally adding animation to the Mask itself. Try to create your effects with the fewest possible animated elements — you will waste less production time and end up with a more optimized file.

Tip

When working on multiple nested layers, it can be visually confusing to work on animation while all layers are displayed. Use the "Eye" toggle to hide or show specific layers so that you can concentrate on only the elements that you are currently editing. Also, to avoid accidentally changing the wrong items, lock all layers that you are not currently modifying.

Keeping some basic principles in mind as you are working with multiple masks and animated elements will help you to follow the logic of masking in Flash:

✦ The mask always goes above the item that is revealed by it.

✦ Filled items on Mask layers work like "windows" that reveal content on the masked layers nested beneath them.

✦ The content on Mask layers is only visible in the authoring environment if the Mask layer is unlocked. For the applied mask to preview properly in the authoring environment, both the Mask layer and the masked layer(s) must be locked.

✦ Mask layers will only apply to layers that are nested below them as masked layers. Normal layers or Guide layers that may be lower in the layer stack (but not nested with the Mask layer) won't be affected by the mask.

✦ Multiple layers can be nested below a single Mask layer, but masks cannot be applied to other Mask layers, and each Mask layer can only contain one masking item (with the exception of multiple primitive shapes).

✦ Content on Mask layers is not visible in the final movie (.swf).

Summary

✦ The four layer types available in the Flash authoring environment are Normal, Mask, and Guide or Motion Guide. Mask layers apply to nested *masked* layers and Motion Guide layers apply to nested *guided* layers. A unique layer icon identifies each layer type.

✦ Layer types can be assigned or modified in the Layer Properties dialog box, invoked by double-clicking any layer icon.

✦ Guide layers are used to hold content that is only needed for reference in the authoring environment, or to speed up movie testing as you develop a project — by temporarily keeping the content on specific layers from being exported with the .swf.

✦ To move a tweened element along a specific path, you can add a Motion Guide layer to control the animation.

✦ Motion Guide layers are actually Guide layers that have another layer nested below them as a guided layer.

✦ Any content that you create in a Flash document can be masked with a static or animated Mask layer.

✦ Filled shapes, text, and symbol instances can be used to define the mask area (or window) on a Mask layer, but this content will not be visible in the final movie (.swf).

✦ You can animate the content of a Mask layer by creating a Motion tween or a Shape tween directly on the Main Timeline, but Motion Guides cannot be applied to Mask layers. To control the animation of a mask with a Motion Guide, it is necessary to use a Movie Clip instance to define the area of the mask. The Motion tween and the Motion Guide layer can then be created on the Movie Clip timeline.

✦ The linkage between various layers can be modified at any time by rearranging the order of the layer stack.

✦　　✦　　✦

Character Animation Techniques

F lash is a powerful tool capable of creating high-quality cartoons much like those you might see on Nickelodeon, Cartoon Network, and so on. This is due to Flash's unique drawing tools, file format, and scalability. By "scalability," we mean that a Flash cartoon can be scaled up to the size and quality of the finest video or even film resolution cartoons. Because the subject of creating broadcast cartoons can be extremely complex (and could even fill a book of it's own) we focus on some fundamental techniques and tricks that will start you on the way to becoming the next Tex Avery.

Although there are specific tips and tricks for working in Flash, most of the basic principals of animation will apply regardless of the authoring environment or production process that is being used. You can often learn more about animation principals by watching classic animated films than by looking at material that is currently available online — at least those examples created by "animators" who have mastered the art of motion tweening but have not spent any time learning techniques for effective character animation.

There is great potential for Flash to produce animated content that rivals the best classic material, but sadly there are not many animators with traditional animation skills who have made the transition to working directly in Flash, nor are there many Flash experts who have taken the time to study animation. Those few individuals who are able to combine knowledge of animation principals with technical aptitude in Flash will have the best of both worlds.

Working with Large File Sizes

Because Flash output is usually intended for the Web, Flash file size is often a dominant concern. But when creating cartoons for broadcast output, this concern is thrown to the wind. In cartoon land, you create for digital video output via QuickTime or AVI and these file sizes can be huge. It's common for such projects to expand into the gigabytes, so it's important to have the equipment to handle this kind of work. This means large, fast hard drives and plenty of RAM.

The extensive use of bitmaps and full-fidelity 16-bit 44 kHz stereo audio tracks means that Flash itself will require a great deal of RAM. Your machine should have at least 256 MB of RAM with a minimum of

✦ ✦ ✦ ✦

In This Chapter

An introduction to cartoon animation

The importance of the storyboard

Cartoon sound

Expressing motion and emotion

Anticipation, weight, and overlapping actions

Walk cycles and coloring tricks

Lip-syncing

Syncing with music and sound effects

Using Flash tweening for cartoons

Cartoon backgrounds and scenery

Character animation

✦ ✦ ✦ ✦

128 MB available to Flash. Even with this configuration, however, you may — like some nefarious cartoon character — paint yourself into a corner and find that you need more RAM in order to render (export raster video) your scene. In addition, the time required to perform a render can often exceed 45 minutes. This may cause you to think that the machine has crashed. . . . Sometimes it has, sometimes it has not.

When rendering complex scenes that take a long, long time, it may seem that all is proceeding just fine, but then Flash may hiccup and report that there isn't enough memory to finish. That's when patience is required. Remember that, although some amazing cartoon animations can be created in Flash, it was engineered to create small, compact files for the Web; our cartoon use is pushing it far beyond its calling. Keeping this in mind may save a brick from going through your monitor.

Caution   You'll spend many hours working on your animation, so back it up as much and as often as you can! The project file is precious. Make a habit of keeping incremental backups on various hard drive volumes or on removable storage, such as Zip or Jaz disks so that you won't lose everything when disaster strikes (it will). A good plan is to make a new copy on a different hard drive volume or removable disk after each major change, rotating through two or three different storage locations. This way if Flash eats your project file or a disk or drive fails, you can always go back to the version you saved an hour ago (which should be on a different disk) without losing much time.

JibJab.com's Collage Animation Workflow, by Gregg Spiridellis

Like everything else in the world, there are a number of different ways to go about creating collage animation with Flash; no one way is wrong or right. This tutorial is meant to explain the way that JibJab.com creates low-bandwidth animation experiences using photo-collage. We've spent a lot of time honing our craft and working out hidden kinks, and now it's time for us to share what we've learned.

Cross-Reference   To see screen grabs from one of JibJab's unique collage animations, refer to the color insert pages.

Our biggest concern whenever we start any project (collage or otherwise) is always file size. Those two little words never leave our minds from the time we start a project until the moment it's posted on the site. Someday we'll live in a perfect world in which everyone has super-broadband connections, but the sad reality is that today most of the online world is still dialing in. You could use Flash to create the next Sistine Ceiling, but if it's 10MB most people won't hang around to see it! When working with photos in Flash it is especially easy to get carried away. However, it's important to remember, "File size is everything."

Preproduction

Like any type of production, it all starts with the idea. Before you dive into cutting up and animating photos, we recommend spending a good amount of time developing characters and thinking about what it is you're trying to say or do. Once all that is in place the real fun — storyboarding — begins.

This is where you must assess (and minimize) your needs. Keeping your file small requires constantly reusing the same elements. Flash allows you to scale, twist, flip, rotate, and skew any symbol in your library, so part of the art of collage animation lies in coming up with new ways to reuse existing elements. If you were to create a marionette-type character, for example, there is no reason why an arm symbol, with a little stretching and pulling, couldn't also serve as a leg. Or maybe two characters in your story just *happen* to be wearing the same thing. As you sit down to storyboard, it's crucial that you keep the idea of reusing symbols in mind.

Production

Once the storyboards (and soundtrack) are in place, we're almost ready to begin animating. First, however, we must prepare the images for importing.

Step 1: Reduce the image

In order to keep the final file size down, we reduce all of our images in Photoshop and ImageReady before importing them to Flash. For example, if we want to import a photo of a head that is originally 600x600 at 300 dpi, we would first reduce the image size to 72 dpi. Next we would look at our storyboards to find the largest usage of the photo. If the head never takes up more than half of the frame and our movie size is 550x400, we would further reduce the photo to 275x275 at 72 dpi. It's a rough estimate, but it guarantees that we won't waste a lot of bandwidth.

After all of our images are reduced in size, we further reduce them by using ImageReady. This allows us to choose how much we want to compress the different elements. We might reduce key photos such as faces as little as 10–20 percent while we might reduce less important elements such as hands or feet as much as 80–90 percent. This is a personal call and everything depends on what you're willing to sacrifice. Remember, every little bit counts and the goal is to have a small, fast-loading file.

Step 2: Trim the image

When all the images are reduced in size and compressed, the next step involves trimming the unwanted image area. There are two ways to go about this. In Photoshop 6 you can create a layered file, erase whatever you do not want, save it as a .png file, and import the file into Flash. Or you can do it the old fashion way: Save your picture as a .jpg file and import that file. If you go the .jpg route, you will need to do your trimming in Flash:

1. Select File ➪ Import and choose the .jpg you want to import.

2. Once the photo is on the stage, select it with the Arrow tool and then select Modify ➪ Break Apart.

3. After the photo is "broken apart," you can use the Eraser tool to get rid of any unwanted image areas.

4. When you are finished erasing extra parts of the picture, make sure you optimize the points by applying the "smooth" option while the image is selected with the Arrow tool.

Tip

Keeping curves clean is another way to reduce file size.

Step 3: Make symbols

No matter what technique you use to trim your photos, the next step is the same: You *must* convert the photos to symbols to make them part of your library.

Step 4: Animate the image

The last (and most time consuming) step of the production process is animating. There aren't too many tricks for this part of the process, but the same rule applies . . . reuse, reuse, and reuse. Try to do as much as you can with as little as you can by using the symbols in your Library. Wherever you can create reusable actions, they should be saved as Movie Clips. Whether it's a walk cycle, a dance cycle, or a crude, chop-jawed, talking head, if an action occurs more than once in your file, save it as a Movie Clip.

Post-Production

When your animation is complete (and all your hard work is done), there are just a few more steps that you need to take before posting your file. The first step is to test your movie in order to find out exactly how big (or small) it is. At this point you can gauge by how much you still need to reduce the size of your movie.

First, check to see if there are any elements that you can remove from your file. In your Library window, select Options, then select Update Use Counts Now. Flash will tell how many times each of the elements in your library have been used. If you have five different hand symbols and one of them was used only one time, it might make sense to delete that symbol and replace it with another hand. It hurts to add all that extra file size for a piece that you've only used once. If that one hand is crucial to your animation, you might choose to keep it — it's your call.

The final step for reducing the size of your file is to once again adjust the compression. The default Quality setting in Flash is 50 percent jpeg compression. You can double-click the bitmap icons (the "green trees") for the JPEGs in your library to open the Bitmap Properties dialog box. At the bottom of the window, deselect the checkbox for Use imported JPEG data and change the Quality setting to whatever you see fit. For less-important elements, we sometimes reduce it to 15 percent. Go through your file with a fine-toothed comb to figure out exactly which of the images you can change the quality on, then test your movie again to see how much size you shaved off.

And there you have it! You're now ready to send your movie out into the world, confident in the fact that you have not scared off our 56k dial-up friends.

The Storyboard

Let's assume that you already have characters and a story (why else would you want to create a cartoon show?) and that you want to build a cartoon based on that small beginning. In this section, we touch on some of the tips that you need to think about in the storyboard phase. Although it's okay to play around, never start a serious cartoon project without a storyboard. The storyboard is your roadmap, your plan, your menu of things needed, and your best friend when your project gets complicated — without it, you're lost.

On the CD-ROM

You'll find a storyboard template on the CD-ROM, in the ch13 folder. It's an EPS (storyboardMAC.eps or storybPC.eps) template form that includes all the essentials of a basic storyboard. Print it out as is, or import it into FreeHand, Illustrator, or Flash, and modify it to suit your needs.

First, break up the story into workable cartoon scenes. In creating a broadcast cartoon, we use the terminology a bit differently. Long before Flash, cartoonists used the terminology of a scene to describe something quite different than a Flash Scene. By "scenes," we mean a cartoon scene, which is much like a movie or TV scene — not a Flash Scene. Remember that cartoons are fast-paced adventures. Most cartoon scenes last less than 30 seconds. A cartoon scene is usually a section of dialog or action that tells a part of the story. Generally, a cartoon scene can stand-alone, but it needs other scenes to complete the story. Because of the length of time required for most cartoon scenes, it would become unruly if we were to rely solely upon Flash's Scene function. You'd scroll through the timeline forever, just trying to cover a 45-second scene. But as you'll learn in this section, there's still use for the Flash Scene function.

After your cartoon scenes are established, break each of these scenes into shots. A shot is a break in the camera focus. For example, a soap opera (they are famous for this) will have a scene of dialog, but the camera will cut back and forth to whoever is talking at the time — which means that one scene may have many shots. Although the art of cinematography is beyond the scope of this book, that is what's involved when deciding shots in a cartoon scene.

Never create an entire cartoon in one Flash project file (.fla)! Even trying to load the huge files created can cause problems for Flash. Instead, use Flash's Scene function for shots. (This may seem confusing at first, but the utility of this method will become clear as you work on your masterpiece.) Make a separate Flash file for each storyboard scene of your cartoon; then, within each of these Flash files, assign a Flash Scene for each of the shots within a storyboard scene. Think of it this way: The Flash project file is the Storyboard Scene, and nested within that project file is the Flash Scene, or shot. Although this may seem contrary to the way in which you usually work with Flash, we are trying to reconcile the traditional terminology of cartoon animation with the recent terminology of the Flash program. Besides, the creation of broadcast cartoons isn't an advertised use of Flash.

The single most important work you'll do in your cartoon is not the drawing but the voices of your characters; the voices are what make the character. Obtaining a voice can be as simple as your speaking into a microphone or as complex as having a highly paid professional acting into a microphone. The key here is not the voice, but the emotion put into it. The right mix of unique voice and emotion can be taken into a sound program, such as Sound Forge or Acid, and tweaked with the proper plug-ins to render the cartoon sound that you're looking for. Voice effects can always be added digitally, human emotion cannot. Some online voice resources are

✦ www.voicecasting.com

✦ www.voicetraxwest.com

✦ www.world-voices.com

Another important part of the cartoon is the use of sound effects. Try to imagine Tom and Jerry or Road Runner without them. There's nothing like a good CLANK, followed by the tweeting of birds, when the old anvil hits Wile E. Coyote's head. Many good sound effects collections are available on CD-ROM and online. These collections, used primarily by radio stations, come on CD-ROM and can be imported into the digital realm easily. One resource for such collections is www.radio-mall.com, which has a range of effects at a broad range of prices; furthermore, most of their collections have RealAudio links, which means that you can audition them online.

Sometimes, though, you just can't buy the sound you need. So, when you need that special CLANK, it's time to set up the microphone and start tossing anvils at unsuspecting heads. Really, though, it's not difficult to set up your own little Foley stage or sound effects recording area. A good shotgun microphone (highly directional for aiming at sound) and DAT recorder are ideal, although you can get by with less.

Tip   If you have to scrimp, don't pinch pennies on the microphone. A good microphone can make an average capture device sound better.

The capture device (audio tape, DAT, miniDV, MD, and so on) should be portable not only in order to get it away from the whirring sound of hard drives and fans but also to enable you to take it on location when needed. Another advantage of a battery-powered portable device is that static from power line voltage won't be a problem. After you get started and begin playing around, you'll be surprised at the sounds that you can create with ordinary household objects. Be creative — innovate! Sound effects are an art form unto itself. Although your dinner guests may think you've gone mad as they regard your meditative squeezing of the dish soap bottle, don't worry about it. You know you are right! When amplified, it will make a nice whoosh. Great for fast limb movement of that character doing a karate chop.

Cross-Reference   For coverage of importing and editing sound in Flash, please refer to Chapter 15, "Adding Sound." For coverage of other sound applications including Sound Forge and Acid, refer to Chapter 39, "Working with Audio Applications." There are also many great resources available online for further study of sound and sound effects — one tutorial that we found useful was through the webmonkey site at `http://hotwired.lycos.com/webmonkey/98/33/index0a.html`.

Some Cartoon Animation Basics

In the world of film, movies are shot at 24 fps (frames per second), while in video and 3D animation 30 fps is the norm. But for cartoons 12 to 15 fps is all that's needed. The cartoon language of motion that we've all learned since childhood has taught our minds to expect this slightly jumpy quality of motion in a cartoon. As an animator, this is good for you, because 15 fps means half the amount of hand drawing work that 30 fps requires. It also means that you can get your cartoon done within your lifetime and maybe take a day off here and there. Actually, there are a lot of scenes in which as few as three drawings per second will suffice — depending on how well you can express motion with your art or drawing. The rule of motion here is that things that move quickly require fewer frames (drawings), while things that move slowly require more frames. This is the main reason you'll hardly ever see slow-motion sequences in cartoons. Broadcast cartoons have lots of fast-paced motion. Fewer drawings are produced more quickly and are less costly. These are very significant factors when battling budgets and deadlines.

Expressing motion and emotion

The hardest part of animation is expressing motion and emotion. Learning to do this well will save you time and make your work stand out above the rest. One of the best exercises you can do in this respect is to simply watch the world around you as though your eyes were a camera, clicking off frames. Videotaping cartoons and advancing through them at single-frame speed is also a revealing practice. (If you have digitizing capabilities, there's nothing better than capturing a cartoon to your hard drive and then analyzing the results, as you get a more stable frame this way.) If you employ Flash's capability to import raster video you can use actual video as your guide and even practice drawing on top of it. While this is good for getting the mechanics of motion down, it's really just a start.

Exaggerate everything! After all, this is what makes it a cartoon. Tex Avery, whom we mentioned earlier, created cartoons that revolutionized animation with overblown and hilarious motion. You can read about him at www.brightlightsfilm.com/22/texavery.html.

Anticipation

Anticipation is a technique that is used when characters are about to do something, like take off running. Before lunging into the sprint, characters slowly back up, loading all their motion into their feet until their motion reverses and sends them blasting off in the other direction. In a more subtle form, this is shown in Figure 13-1, when Weber the pelican takes flight from his perch on the pier.

Figure 13-1: Anticipation is used to accentuate Weber's take off.

Weight

Keep the weight of objects in mind. This helps to make your cartoon believable. A feather falls more slowly than an anvil. The feather also eases out (slows down) before landing gently on the ground, while the anvil slams the ground with such force as to make a gashing dent in it. Humor can play a role here by giving extreme weight to things that do not have it (or vice versa) thereby causing a surprise in the viewer's preconceived notion of what should happen — and this is the seed of humor.

Overlapping actions

Visualize a jogging Santa Claus, belly bouncing up and down with each step. Because of its weight, the belly is still on a downward motion when the rest of the body is being pushed upward by the thrust of the push-off leg. This opposing motion is known as overlapping actions. Another good example of overlapping actions is the scene in which the muscle-man bully catches Weber and wrings his neck, as shown in Figure 13-2. Note that, as the bully thrusts forward, Weber's body reacts in the opposite direction . . . only to catch up just in time for the thrust to reverse and go the other way.

Figure 13-2: Overlapping actions are often used to accentuate movement.

Blurring to simulate motion

Blurring is a technique or device that animators use to signify a motion that's moving faster than the frame rate can physically show. In film, this manifests itself as a blurred out of focus subject (due to the subject moving faster than the camera's shutter can capture). You may have already employed this effect in Photoshop, with the motion blur filter. In cartoon animation, blurring is often (and easily) described with blur lines. Blur lines are an approximation of the moving subject utilizing line or brush strokes that trail off in the direction that the subject is coming from. When used properly, this great device can save hours of tedious drawing. A good example of animated motion blur can be seen in Figure 13-3, which shows the opening sequence in which the word *Weber* turns into Weber the pelican.

Figure 13-3: Blur lines simulate the effect of motion that is "faster than the eye can see."

To see some other animated examples of the blurred line effect, look in the blur lines folder of the R_Bazley folder inside the ch13 folder on the CD-ROM. Richard Bazley has used blur lines effectively to create a collapsing ceiling and a rush of wind.

Animator's Keys and Inbetweening

In Chapter 11, "Timeline Animation Fundamentals," you learned about two Flash animation methods: frame-by-frame and tweening. This section focuses on traditional cartoonist frame-by-frame techniques together with traditional cartoonist's keys and in between methods to accomplish frame-by-frame animation. Despite the similarity of terminology, this topic heading does not refer to a menu item in Flash. Instead, it should be noted that animation programs such as Flash have derived some of their terminology (and methods) from the vintage world of hand-drawn cell animation. Vintage animators used the methods of keys and inbetweening to determine what action a character will take in a given shot. It's akin to sketching, but with motion in mind. In this sense, keys are the high points, or ultimate positions, in a given sequence of motion. Thus, in vintage animation:

✦ Keys are the pivotal drawings or highlights that determine how the motion will play out.

✦ Inbetweens are the fill-in drawings that smooth out the motion.

In Flash, the usual workflow is to set keyframes for a symbol and then to tween the intervening frames, which harnesses the power of the computer to fill the inbetweens. Although this is fine for many things, it is inadequate for many others. For example, a walk sequence is too subtle and complex to be created simply by Shape or Motion tweening the same figure — each key pose in the walk requires a unique drawing. So, let's take a look at the traditional use of keys and inbetweens for generating a simple walk sequence that starts and ends according to a natural pace, yet will also generate a walk loop.

Walk cycles (or walk loops)

Humans are incredibly difficult to animate convincingly. Why? Because computers are too perfect — too stiff. Human movement is delightfully sloppy — and we are keenly aware of this quality of human movement, both on a conscious and a subconscious level. (Another term for this is body language.) Experienced animators create walk cycles with life not by using perfectly repeating patterns, but rather by using the dynamic quality of hand-drawn lines to add just the right amount of variation to basic movements.

The most difficult part to creating a walk cycle is giving the final walk distinctive qualities that support the role that the character plays. This again is something that only gets easier with practice. There is no substitute for drawing skill and time spent studying human movement, but to get started it can be helpful to study a basic walk pattern.

On the CD-ROM

The three walk cycle examples shown in this section are included on the CD-ROM for you to open and analyze. The frame-by-frame pattern of the different walks can be a good starting point for designing your own walk cycle. You will find the files in the "Walks" folder inside the ch13 folder of the CD-ROM.

Many 3D programs have pre-built walk cycles that you can modify. We started with a basic walk made in Poser (a popular 3D character animation program from Curious Labs) and output it as an image sequence that could be traced in Flash. As seen in Figure 13-4, this walk cycle was composed of 10 different poses, but the final result is fairly generic.

Figure 13-4: A traced sequence from a basic walk cycle that was created in Poser

Notice that the main pivot points of the figure create a balanced pattern that can be used as a basis for many other kinds of figures. Also notice that as the figure moves through the cycle, there is a slight up and down movement that creates a gentle wave pattern along the line of the shoulder. This wave motion is what will keep your figure from looking too mechanical. It is important to remember that the final pose in the cycle is not identical to the first pose in the cycle — this is crucial for creating a smooth loop. Although it might seem logical to create a full cycle of two strides and then loop them, you will get a stutter in the walk if the first and last frames are the same. Whatever pose you *begin* the cycle with should be the next logical "step" after the final pose in your cycle, so that the pattern will loop seamlessly.

Although the figures are shown here with the poses spaced horizontally, you will actually draw your poses on individual frames (best done on a Movie Clip timeline), but align the drawings on top of each other so that the figure "walks in place" as if on a treadmill. Once you have established your walk cycle, the horizontal movement is added by tweening the walk cycle Movie Clip. As shown in Figure 13-5, by using a Motion tween to scale the walk cycle Movie Clip and move it from one corner of the Stage to another, you can create the illusion that the figure is walking toward the viewer.

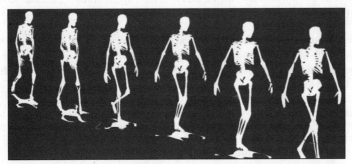

Figure 13-5: A series of angled poses in a walk cycle work well to create the illusion that the figure is walking toward the viewer if the final Movie Clip is scaled as it is Motion tweened from the far corner to the near corner of the Stage.

The speed of the Motion tween has to match the speed of the walk cycle. If the tween is too slow (too little distance or too many frames), the figure will seem to be walking in place. If the tween is too fast (too much distance or too few frames), the figure will seem to be sliding over the ground. Play with the ratio of your Motion tween, and if the figure needs to walk faster or slower, than make adjustments to the walk cycle itself rather than just "pushing" or "dragging" the figure with your Motion tween. Also keep in mind that a figure should seem to walk more quickly as it gets closer to the viewer. In the skeleton walk example, the Motion tween is eased-in so that as the figure gets closer (larger), the walk appears to cover more ground.

Achieving realistic human walk cycles can take hours of work and require very complex walk cycles (often 30 or more poses.) Fortunately, many cartoons actually have more personality if they use a simplified or stylized walk cycle that suites the way they are drawn. Figure 13-6 shows a walk cycle that only required three drawings to create a serious but child-like stride for an outlined character.

Notice that the legs, arms, torso and head of the character are all animated on separate layers. This allows you to reuse the same drawings for both sides of the body — by simply offsetting the pattern so that the legs swing in opposition to each other, with the leg on the far side layered underneath the leg on the near side. This economy of effort is helpful not only because it is faster, but also because it makes it easier to maintain the symmetry of your character if you are trying to keep the motion simple and stylized.

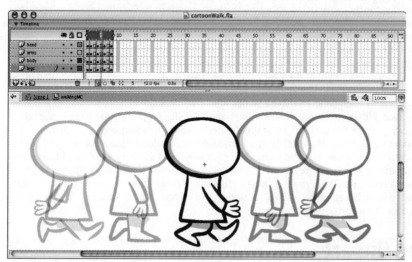

Figure 13-6: A stylized walk cycle created by flipping and reusing the same three drawings for both legs of an outlined character

Repeaters

You may notice there are some blank, nonkeyed frames (repeaters) in the timeline for the cartoon walk. These were used to economize drawing time and to slow the walk of the character. If a speedier walk were called for, we would simply delete these repeater frames. A good basic rule about repeaters is to add no more than one repeater frame between keys; adding more causes the smoothness of motion to fall apart. If the motion must proceed more slowly, then you have to draw more inbetweens.

Fortunately, with Flash onion skinning (the capability to see before and after the current time in a dimmed graphic), which is discussed in Chapter 11, "Timeline Animation Fundamentals," the addition of a few more inbetweens is not an enormous task. In fact, onion skinning is indispensable for doing inbetweens, and even for setting keys. One pitfall of onion skinning is the tendency to trace what you're seeing. It takes practice to ignore the onion lines and use them only as a guide. You need to remember that the objective is to draw frames that have slight, but meaningful differences between them. Although it can mean a lot more drawing, it's well worth it. Because you'll use your walk (and running) cycles over and over during the course of your cartoon, do them well.

Tip One real timesaver in creating a walk cycle is to isolate the head and animate it separately via layers or grouping. This trick helps to prevent undesirable quivering facial movements that often result from imperfectly traced copies. Similarly, an accessory like a hat or brief case can be isolated on a separate layer. Finally, if the character will be talking while walking, make a copy of the symbol and eliminate the mouth. Later, the mouth will be added back as a separate animation. We cover this later in the section on lip-syncing.

Types of walks

So far, we've covered the mechanics of a walk cycle. But for animators, the great thing about walking—in all its forms—is what it can communicate about the character. We read this body language constantly every day without really thinking about it. We often make judgments about people's mood, mission, and character based on the way that they carry themselves. Picture the young man, head held high, confidently striding briskly with direction and purpose: He is in control of the situation and will accomplish the task set before him. But if we throw in a little wristwatch checking and awkward arm movements, then that same walk becomes a stressful "I'm late." This late gait suggests a very different story of the person who didn't plan ahead. Or, witness the poor shlub—back hunched, arms dangling at his sides. He moves along, dragging his feet as if they each weigh a thousand pounds. That tells the sad story of a person who's a basket case. Finally, what about a random pace, feet slipping from side to side, sometimes crisscrossing, other times colliding, while the body moves in a stop-and-start fashion as if it were just going along for the ride? Is that someone who couldn't figure out when to leave the bar? Of course, these are extreme examples. Walks are actually very subtle and there are limitless variations on the basic forms. But if you begin to observe and analyze these details as they occur in everyday life, then you'll be able to instill a higher order in your animations. Simply take time to look. It's all there waiting for you to use in your next animation. Then remember that because it's a cartoon, *exaggerate!*

Coloring the art

Now, to color in the character between the inked lines—in traditional animation, this was the most tedious and time-consuming job of all: endless thousands of cels to be hand painted and dried. Most often, armies of low-paid workers in far away lands did it. But with Flash it's a snap! That's because of Flash's wonderful (and sometimes mysterious) gap-jumping fill tool, the Paint Bucket. With Flash, you never run out of paint, and it dries instantly—a real time-saver to be sure!

The model sheet

Here's a coloring time-saver that you can use for yourself within Flash: Use a fully colored model of your character at the start of a cycle or scene. This will serve as a color model and will be discarded when the cycle or shot is finished. It's very important to keep a model sheet, which is an archive of color models—finished, fully colored characters—to maintain consistent color across the span of the project. (It's also quite useful at the start of future projects.) "Why," you may ask, "is this necessary now that Flash has color sets?"

Although Flash has the ability to save color sets, it's still difficult to remember which yellow was used on a certain area of the character, especially when there are ten different yellows in the palette. Making such a color mistake—even a slight shade off—will cause unsightly flicker on playback. The Eyedropper tool makes no mistakes. So, to develop good animation habits, start a model sheet. When you begin a scene, copy the appropriate color model and paste it into the cycle, setting it off to the side of the active art in the first frame (if needed, ungroup it). Acquire the color that you need with the Eyedropper tool and then set about the business of filling.

When filling, we've found that the most efficient method is to go through the entire cycle with one color, filling all objects of that color. Then go back to the beginning and sweep through again, doing the next color. This method saves you the tedium of constantly having to change the Paint Bucket's color, and also minimizes the possibility of mistakes. If some places fill while others don't, you'll probably need to adjust the Paint Bucket Gap size modifier.

Gap problems

There are, however, times when you can't find the gaps and the Paint Bucket just won't work. In this case, keep looking because the gaps are there. But if it just doesn't work, no matter how much you zoom in and click with the Paint Bucket, then you may need to zoom in and use the Arrow tool to close the gap by adjusting a stroke. In a situation in which it's not aesthetically pleasing to do that, use the Brush tool (set to the same fill color and to paint fills only) to fill the gaps manually. Perhaps this would be the case on a head and neck that you don't want connected to the body (remember earlier about the advantages of animating the head separately). You would use the Brush tool to paint a stroke of fill connecting the inked lines and then fill the larger areas with the Paint Bucket. This is a great tool, a little mysterious at times, but it's a huge time-saver.

 For a review of working with the Paint Bucket and using the Gap size modifier, refer to Chapter 9, "Modifying Graphics."

Speed coloring

A good way to speed up the coloring process is to allocate one of the mouse buttons (if you have a programmable mouse) to perform the keyboard shortcut for step forward advancing (which is the > key). If you have a pressure-sensitive graphics tablet, then you can allocate a button on the pen to do the same. With a setup like this, you can leave the cursor in pretty much the same place and click-fill, click-advance; click-fill, click-advance . . . and so on.

 The process for creating custom shortcut keys is discussed in Chapter 4, "Interface Fundamentals."

Temporary backgrounds

Another problem that's easily solved is the process of filling areas with white. If you're like most people, you've accepted the default background color of white — which makes it impossible to distinguish when filling white areas. In this case, it's monstrously helpful to create a very light color that you don't plan to use in the final art, something like a light pink. While coloring, temporarily change the background color in the Property inspector or in the Movie Properties dialog box (Modify ⇨ Document) to the substitute color for the background of the entire movie. This makes it much easier to see what you're doing when using white as a fill color for objects such as eyeballs, teeth, and clouds. Then, when you're done coloring, you can set the background color back to white.

Flash Character Design Strategies, *by Sandro Corsaro*

Flash offers a cheaper, faster, and more malleable approach to creating animation than anything that has been seen in the history of animation. While traditional animation production can be unforgiving, the Flash authoring environment offers animators a variety of starting points in fulfilling their visions. Many creative types who are experienced with Flash can delve into projects with simple thumbnail sketches or even with just concepts in their heads. Purists, and developers working with larger teams, generally prefer the traditional storyboard route. Whether it is intended for Web or broadcast, creating an efficient Flash animation begins and ends with the strategy of your initial design. That design can be on paper, in Flash or even in your head. What is crucial is that on some level, there is a clear and concise plan in the design. For the purposes of this tutorial, we will look at two simple examples involving design strategy.

By now you should be are familiar with the concept of breaking elements into reusable parts or pieces. For Web purposes, this keeps the file small and saves the artist production time. This systemized approach to animation is the evolution of *limited animation* — the cut-out system that has changed since it was first applied by Hanna-Barbera for television shows like *The Flintstones* and *Scooby Doo*. When Fred would talk, his mouth would be on one layer, while his head and body would be on another. If Fred tilted his head during a rant, his mouth and head would tilt during the animation, while his upper body would be held. Why do you think all those great Hanna-Barbera characters always had some sort of accessory (like a tie or necklace) around their necks? This design strategy was effective even with a constrained budget, because it allowed for maximum animation with minimal artwork.

Today, Flash has the potential to revolutionize the production process by building on the animation techniques used in the past. Just like the traditional cel method, inactive Flash layers can be "held" while action layers continue with additional frames of movement. The newest feature of this evolution is that symbols, unlike old-school painted cels, can be flipped, stretched, and squashed without having to redraw the artwork. A traditional painted animation cel of a left arm could not be reused for the right arm. On the simplest level, appendages can be flipped, rotated and scaled to complete character designs. The model sheet created in Flash of Da Boss, (shown in Figure 13-7) is an example of effective reuse of artwork.

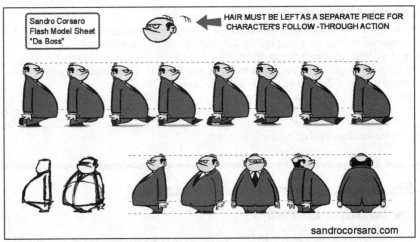

Figure 13-7: By designing the character in reusable pieces, you can simplify your workflow while increasing the options for how the character can be animated.

To see the animated Flash version of the model sheet for Da Boss, open the modelSheet.swf from the S_Corsaro folder in the ch13 folder on the CD-ROM.

The script called for this character to be constantly pacing his office. When I designed the character, I broke him into three distinct parts, each with their own animation. The first part was the combed-over hair—I kept it as a separate piece from the head, so it could undulate up and down as he paced. This provides a nice secondary action to his walk. Although the hair is a small detail, without the initial planning, attempting to add it later in the animation process would have proven frustrating and time-consuming. The second animation was the inertia of the heavy upper body. As Da Boss walked, his body needed to convey a sense of weight and power. Utilizing the animation principle of stretch and squash, the symbol of his upper body cycles through various shapes in conjunction with his walk.

The final and most dynamic component of the character's movement is the leg cycle taking place on the layer underneath his upper body. Only one leg has actually been drawn—the other is offset and placed on a lower layer to create a looped walk. As the legs move into each keyframe, the first two elements described above are adjusted to create the secondary animation. On the low points of the walk, his weight squashes down, while his hair holds (or pauses) for a momentary beat. A progression of movement follows in the next few keyframes to get to the inverse position of this low point.

Besides the basic model movement, a turnaround was also needed for the animators to work with this character. Obviously some of the views can be flipped, but what about the front and back? Copy and paste your front view to create your back view. Build on your finished artwork to create the new artwork. Figure 13-8 illustrates how the front view of the Da Boss was modified to create the back view. Unlike the traditional animation process, which travels in distinct and separate stages from point A to B to C, think of Flash animation as a more integrated progression as point A *becomes* B which *transforms* into C. Always try to build on your work, rather than starting from scratch each time you need a new movement or character.

Figure 13-8: With small modifications, the same artwork can be used for the front and back of the character.

Perhaps the most convincing example of the benefits of strategizing your design can be understood by referring to Figure 13-9. These were three different characters intended to be tweed for broadcast purposes, but the actual animation only had to be created once.

On the CD-ROM

To see how the motion is actually reused in the example shown in Figure 13-9, open reuseWalk.swf from the S_Corsaro folder in the ch13 folder on the CD-ROM.

Figure 13-9: When a character is designed strategically, you can reuse your animation as well as your artwork to quickly create other characters.

Because of the strategy involved in the original character design I was able to transform him into the other two characters, reusing both his graphic symbols and the actual animation. By tweaking the timing of one leg on the run cycle, and obviously making some other artistic changes, the skateboarder character was created from the same artwork as the character running to catch a bus.

Flash is a very sophisticated authoring environment for animation, but nonetheless there is no substitute for knowledge of motion. To create truly compelling and intriguing animation in any genre, you must understand the scientific fundamentals of this art. The best place to learn about the principles of animation is in the daily environment around you. Observe the way things move and then strategize how to translate that movement efficiently using the tools available in Flash.

Flash Tweening

You can use Flash tweening to help your cartooning. Now that you've created some symbols, such as the walk cycle, here's where you can save a great deal of time making them slink and prance across the view without drawing every tedious frame. The hard manual drawing work is done, now you'll choreograph the character. Once you've built a library of various walks, runs, turnarounds, and stand stills (a piece of walk cycle that ends with the character just standing still), you can use computer power to help you tell a story. Remember that you can always create more symbols of the character as needed — in fact, you can steal from other symbols to create new ones.

Panning

Use the techniques discussed earlier in this chapter to get your walking symbol looping, stationary in the middle of the view. Then move the background elements to give the illusion of the camera following alongside the walking character, a sort of dolly. The trick for creating extra long pans are described later in this chapter. It usually requires a little experimentation to get the motion of the background to match the stride of the step. If the timing isn't correct, you'll notice that the feet will seem to skate across the ground. To fix this, adjust the speed of the background by either increasing or decreasing the number of frames in the tween of the background. Another trick is to set the walking symbol to start at one end of the view and proceed to the other by tweening the symbol itself. What's really cool is to use a mixture of both. Again, to get it just right, experiment.

Instance swapping

There comes a time when the star of your show must stop walking (or running, or whatever he's doing) and reach into his pocket to pull out a hot rod car and make his getaway. This is where instance swapping comes in. At the end of the tween, create a keyframe on the next frame (the frame immediately following the last keyframe in the tween), and then turn off Motion tweening for that keyframe in the Property inspector. This causes the symbol to stop at whichever frame the cycle ended on in the timeline. To swap the symbol, follow these steps:

1. Click the symbol to select it on the Stage.

2. Open the Property inspector.

3. Click the Swap Symbol button.

4. In the Swap Symbol dialog box, select the symbol that you want to replace it with (in this case, the one where he reaches into his pocket).

5. Click OK.

If you loop the play of the symbol, you can also choose the frame on which the symbol's cycle will start. Other choices are limiting the symbol to play once and playing just a single frame (still).

Caution   When you change a symbol instance on a Motion tween, if the Synchronize box is checked, the old symbol instance will not be replaced with the new one — which is Swap Symbol failure. If you turn off tweening on the frame where you Swap the symbol, synchronization is not an issue.

Finally, unless you've drawn all your symbols to perfect scale with each other, this new symbol may not fit exactly. No problem! To fix this, simply enable onion skinning from the Main Timeline, and set it to show the previous frame (the frame the tween ended on). Now you can align and scale the new symbol to match the ghosted image. We can't begin to tell you how much you'll use this simple instance-swapping function when you create your cartoon. This is one of the unique functions that sets Flash apart from all other cel-type animation programs. After you have a modest library of pre-drawn actions, the possibilities for combining them are endless.

Motion guides

Although not terribly useful for tweening a walking character, the Flash Motion Guide feature is tops for moving inanimate objects. If your character needs to throw a brick, a straight tween between points and some blur lines will do fine. If he needs to lob that brick over a fence to clang a pesky neighbor, then the use of Motion Guides is the ticket. Here's how:

1. Turn the brick into a graphic symbol if you haven't already. This makes it easier to make changes to the brick later.

2. Create a Motion Guide layer.

3. Draw an arc from start to destination. This is best done by drawing a line with the Line tool and then retouching it with the Arrow tool until you have bent it into the desired arc. This method keeps the motion smooth. (Using the Pencil tool to draw the motion guide would create too many points and can cause stuttering in the motion.)

Although your brick is flying smoothly, something's wrong. Again, the computer made things too darned smooth. You could insert a few keyframes in the tween and rotate slightly here and there to give it some wobble. But that's still not convincing. You want this brick to mean business! Here's what to do: Because the brick is already a symbol, go back to the brick symbol and edit it, adding a few more frames. Don't add more than three or four frames, otherwise this will slow it down. At each of these new frames, mess up the brick a little here and there; differ the perspectives a little from one frame to another. Then, when you go back to your Main Timeline, the brick should be twitching with vengeance as it sails toward its target.

Cross-Reference   For more information on creating and using Motion Guides, refer to Chapter 12, "Applying Layer Types."

Lip-Syncing

Now, here's the part we've all been waiting for . . . a word from our character. If done properly, lip-syncing is where a character can really spring to life. This is accomplished by drawing the various mouth positions that are formed for individual *phonemes,* which are the basic units of sound that make up a spoken word. Then these phonemes are melded together into *morphemes,* which are distinct units of a word, like a syllable. Morphemes are then strung together over the course of a sentence to present the illusion of a talking, animated character. Huh? Phonemes? Morphemes? What the devil are we talking about? Well, it's really not as complicated as all that, but it's important to know how a spoken word is made. Most languages, although populated with thousands of words, are really made up from around 30 to 60 distinct sounds, or phonemes. For cartooning, these phonemes can be reduced to about 10 basic mouth positions. Some of these positions can be repeated for more than one sound because many sounds share roughly the same mouth positions. Although there are more subtleties in the real world, for cartoons, reliance upon transitions between mouth positions is convincing enough.

Earlier, we suggested that the face in an action (walk) cycle should be drawn without a mouth. That's because this method facilitates the use of layers (in the timeline) for the addition of lip-syncing. To do this, create a layer above the character so that you can freely draw in the mouth positions needed to add lip-syncing. It's also very helpful to put the voice track on another separate layer directly above the Mouth layer. This makes it easy to see the waveform of the sound while you draw, giving important clues to where and when the sound occurs visually.

Since Flash 4, Flash has had the capability to scrub the Timeline, which means that you can drag the Playhead, or current frame indicator, and hear the sound as you drag. This functionality is limited to streaming sounds, which means that the sounds have their Sync option in the Property inspector set to Streaming. The capability to hear the sound and see the animation in real time is an important tool for lip-syncing. This real-time feedback is critical for getting the timing just right. There's nothing worse than being plagued with O.G.M.S. (Old Godzilla Movie Syndrome), in which the mouth doesn't match the sounds coming from it. To scrub most effectively, here's a hint: If you've been following this chapter's advice, then you've probably loaded a ton of moving bitmaps into your scene, which can be a serious hindrance to playback within the Flash authoring environment. To overcome this drag and to get real-time playback at the full-frame rate, simply hide all layers except the mouth layers and turn off anti-aliasing.

Shape morphing is not for lip-syncing

You may be asking, "What about using shape morphing to save time in lip-syncing?" Well, shape morphing is a wonderful tool, but, for lip-syncing, it's more hassle than it's worth. Your mouth drawings will become very complicated because they consist of lips, tongue, teeth, and facial features. Furthermore, because shape morphing only seems to work predictably on the simplest of shapes out of the box, shape hinting is required. Thus, by the time you've set all hinting (and even hinting heavily still leaves you with a mess at times), you might have had an easier time and obtained a better result (with greater control) if you had drawn it by hand.

Expression and lip-syncing

With regards to control and expression, it's important to remember to use the full range of expression when drawing the talking mouths. Happy, sad, or confused — these give life to your character. Furthermore, always emphasize mouth movements on those syllables that correspond with spikes of emotion in the voice track. These sections usually have a spike in the waveform that's easily recognized in the voice track. This device helps to convince the viewer that proper sync is happening.

Lip-sync tricks

There are a few more tricks to help ease the load. When characters talk, they do not always have to be looking you square in the face. Try lip-syncing the first few words to establish that the character is speaking, and then obscure the character's mouth in some natural way. (Refer to Figure 13-10.) The head and body of a character can move with the words being said, but the mouth can be hidden by changing the angle of the head, or with a prop such as a microphone, or even with a moustache — think about this when designing your character's features. A bit of design savvy can save a bunch of time without detracting from a character's purpose in the story line.

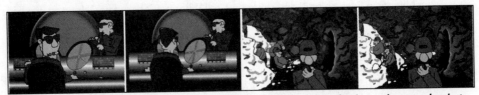

Figure 13-10: Lip-syncing tricks include economy of effort, such as having a character begin to speak and then turn away naturally (left). Appropriate props and even moustaches can also be used to hide mouths (right).

Many animators use a mirror placed nearby and mouth (act out) the words they're trying to draw. This is extremely helpful when learning to do lip-sync. It is also of great help in mastering facial expressions. Just try not to get too wrapped up in drawing every nuance you see. Sometimes less is more. After you get over feeling a bit foolish about talking to yourself in the mirror, you'll be on your way to animating good expressive lip-synced sequences. Another trick that you can use to ease the load is to reuse lip-sync. Do this by copying frames from previous stretches of mouth movements to new locations where the words are the same, and then tweak the copied parts to fit the new dialog. Still, there is no magic lip-sync button. Even with all these tricks, effective lip-syncing is hard work. It's also one of the more tedious tasks in animation, as it demands a great deal of practice to get it right.

Syncing with music and sound effects

Because our brain works to create connections between sound and visual input, it is relatively easy to make movement in your animation match up with audio elements in your soundtrack. Even a few carefully considered links between your sound and visuals can really help to gel things because when the action on screen syncs to the sound (music or effect), it helps to draw in the viewer. If you've already succeeded with lip-syncing work, then this type of syncing is easy. All that's required is a bit of instance swapping set to the beat of the music. If you study your music waveform for visual clues and then scrub it for the sound, you're sure to find the exact section where the change in action (instance swap) needs to go. You don't have to make your sync tight to every note. To keep the shot engaging, sync to the highlights, or hard beats.

Adding sound effects is really the fun part. It's easy and highly effective. Either working from your storyboard, or as you're animating, you'll know where you want to insert a sound effect. For example, when the anvil hits the head, a CLANK is needed there. If the effect you need is on hand, great! Just make sure it has the necessary duration, and then plug it in at the frame where it should start. For broadcast animation you'll set the sound sync to Streaming for the soundtrack exclusively. In addition to using separate layers for each voice track, it's wise to confine your sound effects to a layer or two. This leads to less confusion; yet using two layers enables more than one sound effect to occur at a time.

On the CD-ROM　For the following Expert Tutorial, we've supplied a short track for your use, lip_track.wav or lip_track.aif, which you'll find in the B_Turner folder inside the ch13 folder of the CD-ROM. These tracks include the major sounds used in the English language.

Lip-Syncing Cartoons, *by Bill Turner*

These days, there's an abundance of Flash-authored cartoons on the Internet, so it's hard not to get caught up in the spirit and try one yourself — after all, cartooning is easy . . . just scribble some lines, color it, and there-you-go! Whoops — not so fast. "Houston, we have a *problem*." Too much of this animation looks like junk — like a foreign film that's been dubbed, except worse, because all the actors' lips were numbed with Novocain.

For animated characters to really come alive, you need to know how to do lip-sync. To get quality lip-sync effects, you either need to draw them yourself or hire someone else to do it for you. Although this tutorial can't possibly cover every circumstance known to human communication, it can get you started on the road to lip service. There are some prequalifications: (a) you must be able to draw in Flash, which usually means drawing with a tablet, preferably a pressure-sensitive graphics tablet (such as a Wacom tablet), and (b) you need to have a recorded voice track on its own layer in Flash.

Because lip-sync can't be described in a simple a, b, c routine tutorial, you'll be required to improvise — in your style of drawing. I can't tell you how to do that. Style comes from years of practice and experimentation. But if you do know how to draw and you do have a style, then the intention here is to provide a context in which you might discover the basic trick of lip-sync.

The major sounds, known as phonemes, are less numerous than you might think. It's how these sounds meld together to become words and sentences that add an aura of complexity. Although one might surmise, from the alphabet, that there are 26 sounds, there aren't nearly that many. That's because many letters have the same basic mouth shape, movement, and pronunciation. And because we're now in the land of cartoons, we can simplify even further — the really great cartoons are often the simple ones built of tireless simple reinterpretation.

In this tutorial, to keep it simple, we'll deal with the two dominant views of talking heads: profile and face forward. A face forward talking head is probably the easiest to animate in Flash because the mouth can be animated on a layer that's situated in the layer stack above a drawing of a mouthless head. A talking head in profile is more difficult because of the need to redraw the portion of the face that extends down from the nose, to and including the chin, for *every* frame. Of course, including nose-to-chin movements can also enhance the animation of a face forward talker, and doing so would make for a more expressive animation. But we want to move quickly here.

In Figure 13-11, you see a mouthless head (provided on the CD-ROM in the B_Turner folder for both demonstration and practice) in both of the basic orientations: face forward and profile. Note the playback head is at frame #12, at the beginning of the word *Meyers*.

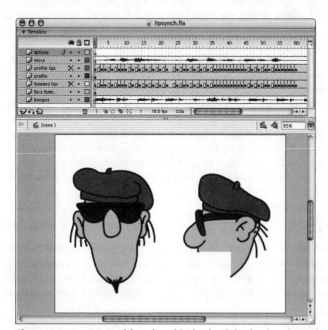

Figure 13-11: A mouthless head in both of the basic orientations: face forward and profile

To help get you started, Bill Turner has supplied a fully functional FLA file for you to work on, with the base character already drawn (lipsynch.fla.) The spoken test line reads, "Zinkle Meyers is very talented on the bongo drums. Flip Flap beats his hands on the smooooth skins. Dig the rhythm. Excellent!" Creating lip-sync for this line requires a number of mouth positions. To demonstrate the concepts, the first sentence of this test line is supplied, already drawn to lip-sync. It is your task to draw the mouth positions for the remainder of the spoken text.

The Sync option

If you were setting this file up from scratch, you'd want to start by placing the voice sound track on its own layer on the timeline. You'd rename this layer with a meaningful name, such as voice, and then, in the Property inspector, you'd set the Sync option to Stream.

Never use Event as the Sync option for any sound that must sync to the Flash timeline. Otherwise, the timing of the voice will not be locked to the frame rate, meaning that the mouth drawings may not appear simultaneously with their appropriate sounds, thus losing sync.

Cross-Reference
For a full explanation of the Streaming versus Event sound settings, refer to Chapter 15, "Adding Sound."

Getting into sync

The best way to understand lip-sync is to have the sample file open. Note that there is a visible waveform (the little squiggly stuff) that shows where the peaks and valleys of the sound occur across the timeline. Note, too, that the voice is brought in as a separate asset. It's on it's own layer, separate from background sounds or music. Otherwise, it would be impossible to see the voice within the waveform if it were premixed with other sounds before bringing it into Flash. If you're producing a cartoon show, it's best to have each character recorded separately, particularly in cases in which they may talk over each other simultaneously. This separation gives you more control when animating. In fact, the entire animation is broken into layers for ease of editing. There's at least one layer for each major element. You might also note that the bongo sound track is set to event. This is useful while authoring because it mutes the track when scrubbing the timeline to listen for timings in the voice track. If both were set to streaming, it would be more difficult to concentrate on the voice alone. (You must remember to reset this option to Stream when syncing is completed, or you could just delete that layer until after you are done animating the mouth.)

The phonemes

Now for the phonemes, there are several standard mouth positions for most of the major sounds, as shown in Figure 13-12. Although this is not a rigid rule, it does provide a good basis from which to expand into greater mastery of lip-sync. First, you'll note that the word *Meyers* begins on frame 12 of the animation. The mmmm sound is best represented with the bottom lip tucked slightly under the top lip. Try saying mmmm to see for yourself. In the word *Meyers*, this mmmm sound lasts two frames and is then followed by the long *I* sound. Notice that we didn't sync the word as it is spelled, e-y-e, because that's more complicated than it needs to be. The word Meyers is usually pronounced M-I-ER-Z, with the *ER* being just an *ease-out* (mouth holds shape but gets slightly smaller as phoneme trails off) of the long *I* sound. The word ends with the Z phoneme, which is simply drawn with the mouth slightly open, and the tongue at the top of the mouth.

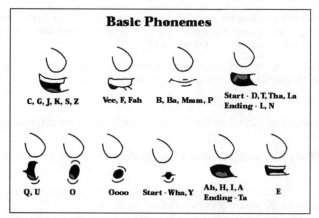

Figure 13-12: You can combine a few basic phonemes to create lip-synced speech.

In the next section of speech, the "very talented" part is a fast-moving set of syllables, so every available frame is needed to represent it. Here, you'll notice that most of the movement occurs when the tongue engages the roof of the mouth for both the *T* and *L* phoneme. Now, because the *T* and *L* are nearly the same mouth position, you can use the luxury of duplicating frames. Similarly, the *V* sound requires the same basic mouth formation as the *M* sound, so you could copy this one as well from the Meyers word. Although the *B* sound, in *bongos*, uses nearly the same mouth as M and V, we don't copy that one. Here, we draw a new mouth to add a bit of chaos because we don't want the mouth to look like a machine. The logic behind deciding which part to copy and which part to make new drawings for is a large part of the art of lip-sync. In short, it's all about balancing how much new artwork you really want to do, while avoiding obvious repetition.

Now that I've given you an insight into how this is done, I've left the rest of the phrase for you to complete. To accomplish this, you'll probably want to reuse many of the supplied mouth positions to sync the remaining voice. Remember that timing is the most crucial part. You can determine where a new mouth position is needed, or where the mouth needs work, by slowly scrubbing the timeline. Then, if you need new mouths, simply draw them in. We highly recommend doing this drawing yourself, because this practice will start you on your way to becoming a master of lip-sync.

Backgrounds and Scenery

As you have learned in previous chapters, in Flash you work in an area that is called the Stage (or Movie) area. For broadcast animation (or any other kind, for that matter) it is better to think of it as the viewfinder of a camera. The main difference between this camera and the traditional kind, or even those used in 3D animation, is this: *You can't move it*. So, to give the illusion of camera movement, everything within the view must move. This is not as hard as it might seem with Flash's capability to use animated graphic symbols. A good example is in Richard Bazley's animated short, *The Journal of Edwin Carp*.

In a scene where the view seems to pan up from Edwin's bed to show a crack in the ceiling, all of the elements on the Stage have to move to create the illusion of a camera move. Here are the steps for creating this effect, as shown in Figure 13-13:

1. A graphic symbol of the entire scene of animation that was larger than the camera's view was made (so that white space wouldn't show at the edges),

2. The symbol was placed in the Main Timeline.

3. The symbol was scaled and placed on the first keyframe to frame the medium view of Edwin in his bed.

4. The symbol was then scaled and placed on a later keyframe to frame the view of the cracked ceiling.

5. By tweening between these two keyframed views, the illusion of a camera zoom out and pan up is created as the whole scene moves on the Stage.

Figure 13-13: A few shots from the bedroom scene in
The Journal of Edwin Carp

On the CD-ROM This scene and several others from *The Journal of Edwin Carp*, an animated feature film that was done entirely in Flash are included on the CD-ROM in the R_Bazley folder inside the ch13 folder. Richard Bazley also describes some of his other clever animation techniques in his tutorial on "2D Character Animation" in the Bonus_Tutorials.pdf on the CD-ROM.

Bitmaps

As mentioned previously, when designing with Flash for the Web, the use of raster (bitmap) images should be kept to an absolute minimum. But for broadcast output, there's no limit. Not only can you use as many images as you'd like (within system constraints), but doing so will make a richer, far more attractive finished product. And, unlike the SWF format, when output as raster video, even animations built with a lot of bitmaps will play at the proper frame rate. So move, animate, scale, and rotate them — even play sequences of them. The sky and RAM are the only limits.

QuickTime limitations

Beginning with Flash 4, Flash expanded its import capabilities to include raster video — QuickTime and AVI. When using video output for broadcast you can export to these formats too, and video that has been embedded in a Flash MX project file (.fla) will show up when output to SWF format. Unfortunately, Flash does not recognize alpha channels embedded in the QuickTime 32-bit animation codec (which supports traveling mattes, or alphas). However, you can use Mask layers on the video in Flash. Remember that you also have the option to link the video file rather than saving it within the Flash project file (thank goodness) — it makes a pointer to it instead. This will keep your file sizes much more manageable. The only drawback to linking video instead of embedding it is that it won't show up when output to the SWF format.

The option of combining video with vector animation has brought tremendous functionality to Flash because animations can be keyed (composited) over (or behind) live video without having to recomposite in After Effects. To take advantage of this, keep your live video at the same frame rate as the Flash project. Note, however, that Flash will only export the audio from the video clip in some formats, so you may need to reapply sound in a video-editing application. An alternate solution is to bring the video and audio tracks into Flash separately and to synchronize them there before exporting to your chosen format.

 Cross-Reference For more detailed information about the various options for exporting animation and audio, refer to Chapter 14, "Exporting Animation."

Building layered backgrounds in Photoshop

By using layers in Photoshop to create artwork, multiplane shots are easily accomplished in Flash. Using layers is very important to the organization of the animation. It is not uncommon for a single shot to require more than 20 layers to keep things where they need to be in the visual stacking order. When designing backgrounds (or *scenery,* to be more precise) remember that, at some point, background elements may need to be foreground elements. For instance, the sky will always be in the background, so it is on a layer furthest down in the stack. Other background elements, however, may sometimes need to be in the foreground to facilitate movement of the character either in front of or behind them. To allow flexibility in how your various elements interact, they should be kept on separate layers.

When creating layered backgrounds, use of Photoshop and alpha channels delivers the most versatility. When using Photoshop for scenery elements, it's mandatory to work in layers and to save a master file with all layers intact. Elements can then be exported to individual files (with alpha channels) as needed. (Retaining the master layered Photoshop file gives you maximum options later, if edits or changes occur. It can also be used as a resource for subsequent animations, so don't flatten or discard your master layered Photoshop file. Instead, number and archive it!) Why the alpha channels? When translating the Photoshop elements into Flash vector scenery, they automatically mask themselves — so a little preplanning in Photoshop can save lots of time later.

For guidelines on importing raster artwork to Flash, refer to Chapter 16, "Importing Artwork." More suggestions for preparing raster artwork in Photoshop are included in Chapter 37, "Working with Raster Graphics."

Flash Mask layers

Whoops! You got to a point where you didn't use layers and now you need a mask. Some situations may be either too complicated or else unforeseeable in the original design. Flash Mask layers can come to the rescue. Here's the good news: You can mask (and animate the mask) interactively with the other elements while in Flash. The bad news is that it may be more difficult to create a precise mask in Flash than it would have been to export an alpha channel from the original Photoshop file. A classic example of masking used in character animation is the black circle that closes in on a scene at the end of an animated episode — this simple animated shape mask is easy to add in Flash.

For detailed explanation of creating various mask types in Flash, refer to Chapter 12, "Applying Layer Types."

Long pans

Long pans are a standard device of animated cartoons, as when Fred Flintstone runs through the house and furniture keeps zipping past (that must be one looooong living room). This can be done in a couple of ways in Flash. For landscape backgrounds, it's usually best to first create a very wide bitmap of the landscape and then to Motion tween it horizontally, with keyframes for stopping and starting as needed within the tween. If something is either falling or ascending, use a tall bitmap and Motion tween vertically. Another solid technique is to create art of the objects that will pan (such as clouds) and then loop them as the background layer, across the view. To get smooth results when using looping, don't use easing in or out with the tween setup. Also, to maintain constant speed, maintain the exact number of frames between the keyframes. Then, copy the tween by Alt (Option) dragging the selected tween frames to the desired area in the timeline. Repeat copying until you've covered the time needed.

For Web animation, it is best to use Movie Clips for looping animation, but if you are planning to output your animation to video, all animation has to be laid out in keyframes on the Main Timeline (or in Graphic symbols.) When exported to video, only the first frame of any Movie Clips will display, unless you use After Effects to translate the .swf before final output.

For more information on exporting animation, refer to Chapter 14, "Exporting Animation."

In the Weber cartoon scene of a chase along the beach, a camera pan was created by tweening a symbol of the whole beach scene horizontally. As shown in Figure 13-14, the "camera view" reveals only a small area of the larger background scene.

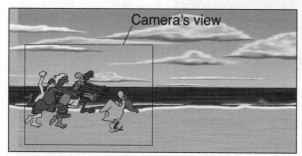

Figure 13-14: The chase scene from the Weber cartoon is created with a looping pan.

Multiplane pans

To provide 3D-motion depth during the pan, keep this rule in mind: An object that is further away appears to move slower (than a nearer object) as it moves across the view. This takes some experimenting to get it right, but once mastered, this will add a professional touch to your animations. For example, in a 100-frame pan:

✦ The sky moves very slowly at 100 pixels total.

✦ The water moves more quickly at 125 pixels total.

✦ The character on the beach moves more quickly than the water at 150 pixels total.

✦ A parked car in the immediate foreground moves most rapidly at 250 pixels total.

Blurring to simulate depth

The multiplane camera was used in early Disney films to give a feeling of depth in the animation of flat artwork. There was physical space between the individual cels when photographed. By using a short depth of field lens, the artwork that was further away from the lens lost focus slightly. (You may have noticed this in still photography yourself.) If you set up your scenery using bitmaps, you can recreate this effect. A good example of this is the pier scene from the Weber cartoon, which is shown in Figure 13-15. In Photoshop, it's a simple case of using incrementally higher doses of Gaussian blur on the layers of your scenery that are further way. The further the object is, the more blur that is applied — just be sure that the blur is applied to the alpha channel that Flash will use in compositing. Photographers use this technique to bring attention to the element in the shot that is in focus. Using it in animation tends to generate the illusion of depth. However, using it in the foreground can also portray various elements such as fog.

Figure 13-15: The opening pier scene from the Weber cartoon has a feeling of depth that was created by using Photoshop blur on the background layers.

Finishing Up

When you have a shot done, it's often helpful to see it play at full speed. Unfortunately, Flash is unable keep up with all of the sounds, bitmaps, and complicated vectors that go into broadcast-quality animation. Plus, it's impossible — even with the most macho of processors — to play the shot at full speed, without hiding a bunch of elements. But, hey, you're the director of this masterpiece, it's time for dailies, and you need to see it all.

The best way to do this and to cut down on file size is to export a raster video at 320×240 pixels, using the standard QuickTime Video codec (Mac) or the Microsoft Video 1 codec. These codecs are for draft purposes only, so it may have banding and artifacts from compression, but the point is to generate something that even a machine that's ill-equipped for high-end video output can display easily at full frame-rate speed. This method will be of great help in revealing those areas of the animation that still need further tweaking and work before going out to the final published version. The general movement and pace of the shot will make itself known. Look for errors such as unintended jumpiness in frames, and color shifts or inconsistencies between views. Furthermore, your lip-syncing efforts will either be a glory to behold or a disaster in need of medical attention. Other things, such as sound clipping (pops in high volume sound) also become apparent here. To put it bluntly, if the preview makes you cringe, then it needs work — if not, you're ready for final output.

Final output

Now, after checking endlessly you're ready for the final video file of the shot to be rendered. Back it up one more time. Then, when you've safely archived your final project file, it's time to choose the codec that your playback equipment can use and render one out for the tube. Then, when you have rendered all your shots at full screen, you can take them into Premiere or After Effects for more detailed editing and tweaking, utilizing all the power that these applications offer. For example, you might want music to play gently in the background across all of your scenes. Although this would be impossible to piece together with separate Flash project files, it's a snap in Premiere. Again, the possibilities are endless. Some suggested workflows for output of character animation are described in detail in Chapter 14, "Exporting Animation."

Summary

✦ Flash can be a powerful tool for the creation of broadcast-quality cartoons. In such cases, many of the usual file-size concerns related to Flash development are set aside because the final output will not have to be Web friendly.

✦ The task of a cartoon animator is to express motion and emotion. Anticipation and overlapping actions are basic tools used by cartoon animators to add drama to a character's movement.

✦ Coloring the art is critical to the final quality of the cartoon—the model sheet, speed coloring, and the use of temporary backgrounds ease the task and lead to greater consistency.

✦ Flash tweening, including instance swapping and motion guides, is one of the most useful aspects of Flash as a cartoonist's tool.

✦ Lip-syncing, which is critical to fine cartoon animation, is not a push-button task—even with Flash, an animator must understand the relationship between expression and lip-sync, and have a working knowledge phonemes, and syncing with music and sound effects.

✦ There are many ways to create effective backgrounds and scenery. These techniques include the use of bitmaps, layers, multiplane pans, blurring to simulate depth, and innumerable combinations of these basic techniques.

✦ Sandro Corsaro has honed the skill of reusing both artwork and animation in Flash to optimize production. By sketching directly in Flash and reusing artwork, Sandro is able to keep the spontaneity of hand-drawn strokes, while saving hours of redundant work.

✦ After a cartoon is created in Flash, final output may include using either Premiere or After Effects for the final polish.

✦ Veteran animator Richard Bazley has compiled a number of insightful tricks from his use of Flash to create his animated short, *The Journal of Edwin Carp*. These include the judicious reuse of drawings, knowing when and where to "cheat," the advantages of simplicity, the power of layers, and the process of making a stagger. In his tutorial on "2D Character Animation" in the Bonus_Tutorials folder on the CD-ROM, he also shared some thoughts about the relevance of performance and acting to animation, timing, diagramming dialog, and animation business.

✦ The key point of this entire chapter is this: Artists animate, but computers can only save time.

✦ ✦ ✦

Exporting Animation

✦ ✦ ✦ ✦

In This Chapter

A history of
digital video

Preparing Flash movies
for video output

Using Flash MX
Broadcast templates

Exporting audio from
a Flash document

Using Flash image
sequences in video
applications

✦ ✦ ✦ ✦

Flash isn't just a vector graphics tool for the Web. Using Flash, you can create amazing video effects for your home videos or professional productions. This chapter explains how to use digital video with Flash. It also shows you how to export high-quality material from Flash to use in your video-editing applications.

As more developers learn how flexible and powerful the Flash MX authoring environment is, Flash graphics will be seen on screens in every possible context. With a little bit of tweaking, animations originally designed for the Web can be repurposed for stand-alone presentations, broadcast, high-resolution digital projection, or even for transfer to film.

In this chapter we go over the main factors that need to be considered when preparing Flash MX content for output to various linear formats.

High-Quality Video Output from Flash

While Flash is primarily used to create interactive animations and presentations on the Web, you can also generate high-quality output for other media uses. Macromedia began as a company called MacroMind, specializing in frame-by-frame video animation tools for desktop computers. Their flagship product, VideoWorks, eventually became Director, which was the first widely used Macromedia authoring product. Like Director, Flash also has some "hidden" video animation capabilities. You can use Flash to create spinning logos for your own corporate, creative, or home videos. Or, you could export those shape morphs — so difficult to create elsewhere — to layer over other video content. As detailed in Chapter 41, "Working with QuickTime," Flash can output the content of a .fla as a QuickTime multimedia file. Flash can also generate numbered still sequences for use in other video-editing applications.

In previous Mac versions of Flash, 100 percent video-based (a.k.a. raster-based) QuickTime (QT) files could be directly rendered via the Export Movie command. Macromedia has added a more robust solution — based on QuickTime 4 — that exports Flash MX material directly to a Flash track for use in conjunction with video and audio tracks from other sources. This is wonderful if you want to create QTs for QuickTime 4-enabled applications.

Note All references to QuickTime 4 can also be applied to QuickTime 5 or 6 — QuickTime 4 is just the earliest version that is integrated with Flash.

Most Mac and PC applications that use the QuickTime architecture — such as Adobe Premiere and Adobe After Effects — will import QuickTime Flash movies. Some DV-only NLE (nonlinear editing) software, such as Discreet, cinestream, will not allow you to import QuickTime Flash movies. For the best video results, you will want to export still image sequences from Flash instead of using QuickTime Flash files, or export traditional QuickTime Video files (available only on the Macintosh version of Flash) or AVI files (available only on the PC version of Flash).

Note Because the export process for sequences uses generic vector or raster formats, you lose all interactivity that you have created in Flash. But that's perfectly fine because we're transferring our Flash movie to a linear viewing environment like video — we're simply making something to watch on a television or on a computer monitor without any involvement from the audience.

Flash artwork is completely scalable and flexible for just about any media use. Combined with the QuickTime architecture, Flash artwork can be output to DV tape or motion picture film. If you think your project looks good in Flash, you should be able to repurpose that hard work into another format very easily.

A Quick Video Primer

If you're a neophyte to digital video, then you need to know some basic terms and procedures involved with digital video. The following section will be useful if you've never used digital video or used it without really knowing what you were doing.

A brief history of digital video

In the past, viewing or editing digital video on a desktop computer was almost impossible. It required expensive hardware such as super-fast processors, huge hard drives, video-capture boards, and professional-quality video decks and cameras. Beginning at $15,000, such systems were out of reach for most users. But like most technology after it has been around for a while, digital video equipment has become much more affordable for the average user. Although digital video still requires fast and efficient computers to work well, it isn't nearly as expensive as it was in the past. You can get 120GB hard drives for under $200! Since the advent of the DV (Digital Video) format (a.k.a. DVCAM or miniDV), consumer-level video cameras and decks are catching up to the quality of their professional-level counterparts.

The need for space

Why does digital video require so many resources? To begin with, digital video is entirely *raster-based*. This means that, unlike Flash and other vector file formats, each frame of digital video requires almost every pixel on the screen to be remembered and stored individually. *Vector* formats, on the other hand, use mathematical descriptions of objects on the screen and compute any differences or movement from frame to frame very efficiently. The resolution of an average television set is roughly equivalent to a 640×480 resolution at 24-bit color depth on your computer monitor. Mathematically speaking, one frame of digital video at this resolution is nearly 1MB!

$$640 \times 480 \times 3^* = 921{,}600 \text{ bytes} = 900\text{KB} = 0.88\text{MB}$$

---

*Each byte has 8 bits. Therefore, 24 bits is equivalent to 3 bytes.

If that isn't bad enough, consider that 1 second of video contains 30 frames. That's 26MB for just 1 second of video! Only the fastest systems and hard drives on the market could deliver such performance. One solution to this performance bottleneck was to compress the data. Thus, most digital video now employs some form of compression (for storage) and decompression (for playback). The short form of this expression is *codec* (*co*mpression and *dec*ompression). You may have already heard of many codecs in use today, but what you probably don't know is that there are three kinds of codecs: Software, hardware, and hybrid.

Note

Cinepak, Indeo, RealVideo, and Sorenson are all software-based codecs, meaning that the computer processor has to decompress each frame of compressed video. These differ from hardware-based codecs, such as MJPEG (Motion JPEG, based on the Joint Photographic Experts Group compression scheme), which need video-capture cards to compress and decompress each frame of video.

The latest breed of codecs today are hybrids, both software and hardware based, such as the MPEG (Moving Picture Experts Group) and DV codecs. MPEG currently has two versions, MPEG-1 and MPEG-2. Originally, MPEG-1 and MPEG-2 video needed special hardware to playback, but as computer processors got faster, software-based players could handle the decompression tasks. Today, MPEG-2 is standard for DVD.

DVD, or digital versatile/video disc, is a new storage medium that can handle feature-length movies in a snap. DVD should not be confused with DV. DV refers to true Digital Video, in which the source video originates as binary (zeros and ones) data. Furthermore, the general term *digital video* should not be confused with *DV*. *Digital video* usually refers to the any video that has been stored as binary data, although it most likely originated from an analog source such as a regular VHS or BetaCam video camera. *DV* refers to video that originated from a digital (a.k.a. *binary*) source and that remains digital through any number of edits on a digital system. With the current implementation of DV, using IEEE-1394 (a.k.a. *FireWire* or *iLINK*) technology, video is transferred from digital tape to your computer hard drive with no loss of quality. The DV footage is not recompressed unless the image in the footage is changed during editing by adding effects or transitions. But like any digital video, DV still requires a lot of hard drive space—about 2GB for every 9 minutes.

Note

Older operating systems have a maximum file size limit of 2GB. This means that you cannot have more than 9 minutes of DV-compressed footage in one QuickTime or AVI file. However, you can string many movies together during playback for continuous recording. New versions of the Mac OS (version 9.0.4 or higher) and of the Windows OS support files that are larger than 2GB. Even so, some applications may not be capable of using these larger files unless they've been updated to do so.

Codec, frame size, and frame rate: The keys to manageable video

Before you begin any digital video project you should have a clear understanding of codecs. Most software-based codecs are intended for computer playback and distribution, while hardware-based codecs are intended for capturing and editing original footage to be used for television broadcast or feature films. You can repurpose hardware-based codec video by compressing it with a software-based codec. Most video developers take high-quality video and shrink it, in both frame and file size, to fit onto multimedia CD-ROMs or the Web.

Three variables can be applied to digital video to make it more manageable for most consumer computer systems: frame size, frame rate, and compression. Developers often use all three variables to shrink huge 9GB video projects down to 3–5MB, which may lead to undesirable results.

First, let's talk about frame size. Although most professional video uses a 640×480 or greater frame size, you may have noticed that most video on multimedia CD-ROMs only takes up a quarter or less of your entire computer monitor. Most video on the Web or CD-ROMs is rendered at 320×240 resolution, half the resolution of broadcast video. Actually, this is only slightly less than the horizontal-line resolution of your VHS recordings.

What about frame rate? You may have also noticed that video on multimedia CD-ROMs often looks a little jerky or choppy. Although this may be due to a slow processor, it's more likely that — in order to cut the file size — the frame rate of the video was reduced. It's not un-common to find CD-ROM frame rates as low as 12 or 15 fps (frames per second) — about half of the original frame rate of broadcast video. This slower frame rate is also the default frame rate of a new Flash movie, to ensure consistent playback on slower machines. Despite the drop in video quality, the lower frame rates result in much smaller file sizes with fewer frames for the processor to play within each second, which delivers better CD-ROM performance.

Finally, how does compression affect video? You've probably noticed that Web and multimedia CD-ROM video is often blocky looking. This is due to the software-based compression that has been used on the video. Codecs look for areas of the frame that stay consistent over many frames, and then log those areas and drop them from subsequent frames. The result is that no unnecessary repetition of data exists that needs to be continually decompressed. But, depend-ing on the level of compression used, the properties of the codec itself, and the settings used in running that codec, the video varies in quality.

Keeping with the trend of better and faster, digital video continues to improve dramatically. This is well illustrated by the fact that many popular Web sites, such as Apple's QuickTime Web site (`www.apple.com/quicktime`), now enable visitors to download larger, higher-quality videos (upwards of 15MB) for playback on newer, faster systems.

Playback bottlenecks

Digital video needs to be kept small for two reasons: storage and playback. So far, we have largely discussed storage issues. But playback (or transfer rate) further complicates the creation of digital video. Despite the relatively large capacity of CD-ROMs (650MB), most CD-ROM readers have limited transfer rates of about 600KB/second. It's important to note that each second of video cannot exceed the transfer rate, otherwise the video will drop frames to keep up with the audio. So if the video is distributed via CD-ROM, this factor results in serious limitations.

Let's look at some of the math involved under ideal (choppy) playback conditions: If you use 15 fps for compressed video, you are limited to a maximum of roughly 40KB per frame. (Remember, though, that the playback stream usually includes an audio track as well, which means that less than 40KB is available for the video component of each individual frame.)

 Cross-Reference   For more information on audio formatting and compression, see Chapter 15, "Adding Sound."

Unfortunately, the Web still affords less than ideal playback conditions for video. On the Web, transfer rates can be as slow as 500 bytes/second. On average, a 56KB modem downloads around 4KB/second. The ideal Web video should stream to the user while loading the page. If you intend to stream video quickly, you have to keep this very small transfer rate in mind. Large videos simply will not stream! This is why most Web sites offer larger videos as a download file. But you do have an alternative. Later in this section, you can learn how to extract a minimal number of frames in order to simulate digital video motion with Flash, yet keep your Flash files streaming quickly. As modem technologies get faster, though, we'll most likely see bigger and better video delivered across the Web. The ADSL (Asymmetrical Digital Subscriber Line) modem was developed with the MPEG-1 and -2 standards in mind.

Adjusting Flash Movies for Video Output

By default, Flash MX uses a frame rate of 12 fps for all new movies. Unless you have changed this setting with the Modify ➪ Document command (Ctrl+J or ⌘+J), this is the setting for any Flash document you have created so far. As mentioned earlier in this chapter, broadcast (NTSC) video needs 30 fps (29.97 fps to be exact) for motion to be smooth and fluid. It may be necessary for you to add more blank frames between each of your tweened keyframes to accommodate a faster frame rate. Your 5-second intro to your Web site may have been possible with 70 or fewer frames, but now you need 300 frames for the same amount of time in full-motion video. Flash doesn't support interlacing (or field-ordering) with any export method (see the "What Is Interlacing?" sidebar for an explanation of interlacing). As a result, you need twice the number of frames (double the frame rate) used for every second of NTSC video — 59.94 fps to be exact — to properly render full-motion video from Flash. It's easier to use 60 fps in Flash and then conform the rendered sequence to 59.94 fps in the video-editing application.

However, 60 fps may be an unrealistic frame rate to time your animation. Several hundreds (if not thousands) of frames are necessary for this frame rate. As you will see later in this chapter, you can achieve high-quality video using 30 fps for your Flash documents. If you have the flexibility and skill to animate at 60 fps, you may want to do so.

Caution   If you are using the PAL or SECAM video systems, which are video systems used outside of North America, then you need to use different frame sizes and frame rates to accurately render Flash content. Use the same methods described here, but adjust any values to fit within PAL or SECAM specifications.

If possible, restrict your Flash movie to one scene for video-editing purposes. Flash exports all scenes within a Flash movie into a sequence or QT/AVI movie, which may complicate the editing process later. It's easier to make more Flash movies and render them independently of each other.

Frames stored in Movie Clips do not export with sequences. Make sure that you have either removed any Movie Clip symbols or that you have replaced them with the actual frames contained within the Movie Clip.

To replace a Movie Clip symbol with the actual frames contained within it:

1. Open the Movie Clip in the Library, and select the frames in the timeline.

2. Copy the frames with the Copy Frames command (Ctrl+Alt+C or ⌘+Option+C) in the Edit menu.

3. Go back to the Scene and paste the frames with the Paste Frames command (Ctrl+Alt+V or ⌘+Option+V). Paste the frames on their own layer, so that they won't conflict with any tweens or settings in other layers.

Caution   Remember that, unlike regular Flash movies, the exported sequence will not have any interactivity. The sequence is simply a collection of still images that will be compiled later in your video-editing application. (So don't mistakenly overwrite or delete your original Flash document!)

You may also need to adjust your Flash document's pixel width and height. Depending on the type of video-editing software and hardware you are using, this setting needs to be 640×480, 640×486, 720×534 (DV), 720×540 (D1) or something else. Again, use the Modify ➪ Document command to adjust the size of your Flash document. You can notice that adjusting pixel sizes of the Flash document doesn't have the same effect as changing pixel heights or widths of raster-based images. Usually, adjusting pixel sizes will distort or change the shape of elements. With Flash, the document's pixel size is independent of the pixel sizes of any elements it may contain. You're simply adding or subtracting space to the area of the Stage. If you intend to bring the sequence into another video-editing application such as Adobe Premiere and you are outputting with the DV format, a movie size of 720×534 should be used. Why? The DV format uses non-square pixels delivering the same 4:3 aspect ratio with 720×480 as other video formats do with only 640×480 square pixels. By using 720×534 movie sizes, the frame can be stretched to fit a 720×480 DV workspace without losing any resolution quality. It's better to adjust the size before you export any material intended for broadcast video delivery (or for transfer to any NTSC recording media), especially with raster formats. Not only does this ensure optimal quality, it could easily lessen the video rendering time needed in other applications.

Note   The movie sizes just listed should work equally well for MJPEG video hardware and DV hardware. If you use these baseline settings, you can then accommodate either MJPEG or DV specifications in your video-editing application.

Not only do you need to have the proper frame size for high-quality video output, but you also need to be aware of overscanning. TV sets overscan video images, which means that information near the edges of the frame may be cropped and not visible. Because the amount of overscan is inconsistent from TV to TV, some general guidelines have been developed to make sure vital information in the frame is not lost. The crux of the guidelines is simple: Don't put anything important (such as text) near the edges of the frame. Video has two safe zones: title-safe and action-safe. To see these zones on a sample document in Flash, refer to Figure 14-1.

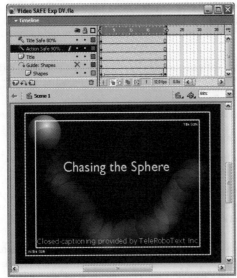

Figure 14-1: While designing for broadcast content in Flash MX, you should always be aware of the safe-zone boundaries for NTSC video playback.

What Is Interlacing?

Most computer monitors are non-interlaced, which means that each "frame" of video is fully displayed with each screen refresh. Most TV sets, though, are interlaced displays, which means that each frame of video consists of two fields, one upper and one lower, and each screen refresh shows one field then the other. Therefore, each second of video contains 60 fields, or 30 frames. Because Flash doesn't export field-ordered sequences, you have to compensate for the lack of individual fields by using two Flash frames for every regular frame of video.

The action-safe zone is approximately 90 percent of the 720×534 (or 640×480) frame size we're using in Flash, which calculates into 648×480 (or 576×432). All of your Flash artwork should be contained within the limits of the action-safe zone. The title-safe zone is about 80 percent of the total frame size. For a 720×534 frame size, any text on the Flash stage should fall within the borders of a 576×427 centered frame. With a 640×480 frame size, this centered frame size would be 512×384.

Finally, you may need to adjust the colors and artwork you used in your Flash document. NTSC video, while technically 24-bit, doesn't display some colors very well. In general, bright and saturated RGB colors tend to bleed on regular TV sets. Here are some guidelines for using broadcast (and WebTV)-safe color:

✦ Avoid one-pixel-wide horizontal lines. Because NTSC is interlaced, this line flickers constantly. If you need to use thin lines, try blurring a one-pixel line or simply never use anything less than a two-pixel stroke width.

Tip

You can convert a one-pixel or hairline stroke to a fill by choosing Modify ➪ Shape ➪ Convert Lines to Fills. Use Modify ➪ Shape ➪ Soften Fill Edges on the converted line to blur it.

✦ Do not use very fine textures as they may flicker and bleed at the edges. Because most NTSC monitors have low-quality resolutions, the fine details are lost anyway.

✦ Avoid using any color that uses a color channel's maximum intensity. Use a NTSC color filter on any bitmap art, such as the NTSC Colors filter in Adobe Photoshop.

• Full red (R: 255, G: 000, B: 000) displays horribly on TV sets. Replace a full red with R: 181, G: 000, B: 000.

• Pure white backgrounds should also be avoided and replaced with R: 235, G: 235, B: 235. Like red, pure white can cause annoying screen flicker, especially if high contrast objects are placed against the white.

• As a rule of thumb, keep your RGB values within the 16 to 235 range, instead of 0 to 255. Although Photoshop's NTSC Colors filter actually allows certain 255 values to be used, you should *only* use these values if they do not occupy large solid areas in the Flash movie.

✦ Use the NTSC & Web Safe color set (ntsc_web_179.act file) on the *Flash MX Bible* CD-ROM (see Chapter 7, "Applying Color," for more information on importing or switching color sets). Of the 216 Web-safe color palettes, only 179 of them are NTSC/WebTV safe. NTSC TV sets are capable of displaying more colors than that, but if you're used to working with Web color palettes, then you may find this optimized palette handy. There's another color set file, ntsc_213_colors.act, on the CD-ROM that you can use if you're just taking Flash content to video, which has 213 NTSC-safe colors, converted from the 216 Web-safe colors. Because 35 colors in this set are outside of the Web-safe colors, you should not use this palette for Web and broadcast work.

✦ If you're using video-editing software that allows both color and levels corrections on imported clips, then you can avoid making time-consuming adjustments to your original Flash movie. After you've generated a Flash sequence and imported the sequence into your video-editing application, restrict the gamut of the sequence clip using the values in the preceding tips.

Tip

In After Effects, use the Broadcast Colors filter to perform NTSC color adjustments on imported sequences or movies. This filter can adjust either luminance or saturation values to bring out-of-gamut colors into the NTSC color gamut. Use caution, however, as reducing the luminance may cause artifacts from MJPEG or DV compression to become more obvious. Reducing saturation is the preferred method for using the Broadcast Colors.

Using Flash MX Broadcast Templates

Flash MX makes it easier to design content intended for specific viewing environments by including templates, which are prebuilt "starter" files that include size guidelines for various project types.

To start a new document in the Broadcast template (or copy elements from an existing document into a new properly sized document), choose File ➪ New From Template. In the New Document dialog box (shown below), choose Broadcast in the Category list. Then, in the Category Items list, choose BroadcastExport. Click the Create button.

Flash MX will make a new document with instructional guides, as shown in the figure below. The Broadcast template has red frame lines that indicate the screen zones relevant to designs intended for television.

A document created with the Broadcast template will have the Work area turned off. As a result, the Stage will be positioned in the top left corner of the Document window and any elements offstage will not be seen. If you need to position elements offstage, toggle the Work area on in the View menu.

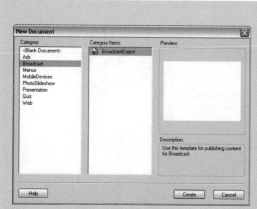

The New Document dialog box

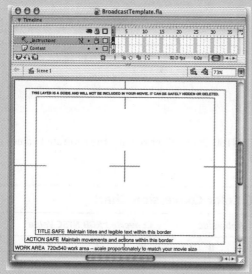

The guide frames of the Broadcast template

Note that the Broadcast template creates a document with a 720×540 frame size. This size is intended for output to D1 video. If you intend to output to DV video, use the custom template we have provided on the *Flash MX Bible* CD-ROM. We have also included a sample title screen document, BroadcastTemplate.fla, in the ch14 folder of the CD-ROM.

Continued

Continued

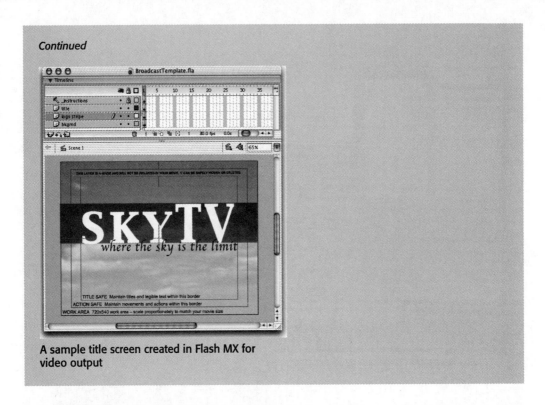

A sample title screen created in Flash MX for
video output

Refer to Table 14-1 to see how Photoshop's NTSC Colors filter remaps the saturated values of
the Web-safe color palette.

Table 14-1: NTSC Color Conversion Chart

Original Web HEX Value	Original RGB Web Value			Converted RGB NTSC Value		
	R	G	B	R	G	B
FF0033	255	000	051	227	000	045
CC6699	204	051	153	204	102	153
FF00FF	255	000	255	210	000	210
FF00CC	255	000	204	219	000	175
FF0099	255	000	153	226	000	136
FF0066	255	000	102	230	000	092
CC00FF	204	000	255	199	000	248
00CCCC	000	204	204	000	170	170
00FFFF	000	255	255	000	170	170

Original Web HEX Value	Original RGB Web Value			Converted RGB NTSC Value		
	R	G	B	R	G	B
33FFFF	051	255	255	045	225	225
66FFFF	102	255	255	101	253	253
00CCFF	000	204	255	000	160	201
0099FF	000	153	255	000	147	245
00FFCC	000	255	204	000	178	143
33FFCC	051	255	204	047	237	190
00FF99	000	255	153	000	188	113
33FF99	051	255	153	050	249	150
00CC66	000	204	102	000	193	096
00FF00	000	255	000	000	210	000
00FF33	000	255	051	000	210	042
00FF66	000	255	102	000	198	079
33FF00	051	255	000	047	234	000
66FF00	102	255	000	088	220	000
99FF00	153	255	000	122	203	000
99CC00	153	204	000	142	190	000
FFFF66	255	255	102	252	252	101
CCCC00	204	204	000	170	170	000
CCFF00	204	255	000	148	185	000
FFCC00	255	204	000	191	153	000
CC9900	204	153	000	197	148	000
FF9900	255	153	000	216	130	000
FF6600	255	102	000	248	099	000
FF0000	255	000	000	181	000	000
CC0000	204	000	000	181	000	000

Creating Sequences from Flash Movies

A *sequence* is a series of still images that simulate full-motion video when played back continuously. Think of a sequence as a regular QuickTime or AVI broken down into individual frames. Another analogy would be that of a flipbook made of individual sketches that animate when you thumb through the pages quickly. Flash MX can export a scene or movie as a series of still images as well, with quite a bit of flexibility.

Because Flash artwork is vector-based, it supports all the major vector formats used in other applications: EPS 3.0 (or higher), Illustrator, and DXF formats. On the Windows version of

Flash, you can also export metafile sequences in the WMF and EMF formats. Generally, all of these vector formats will retain the scalable quality that Flash offers for the Web; that is, you can shrink or expand the size of vector formats, displaying equal smoothness and quality at all sizes. Most vector formats can also embed raster content, and any raster content will have a finite resolution capacity. You will notice degradation on any embedded raster elements if you scale the entire vector graphic beyond its original fixed pixel size.

You can also export a still sequence in raster-based formats such as PICT (Mac only), BMP (PC only), GIF, JPEG, or PNG. We can review the benefits of each format and the particular uses each can have, but first, we should look at how the exporting of individual frames is accomplished in Flash.

On the CD-ROM

For a complete list and description of the various file formats that can be imported or exported from Flash MX, please refer to Bonus Appendix A, "Flash Compatible Media Formats." You will find the Bonus_Appendix.pdf on the CD-ROM.

Export process in Flash

After you have opened a Flash document that you wish to export, make sure that your document falls within the guidelines described in the last section. All of these settings are critical for flawless video playback: 30 or 60 frames per second, 640×480 (or greater) movie dimensions, integration of scenes and Movie Clips, and color gamut restrictions. When you're all ready to go, the actual export process is quite simple. You will export your Flash document as a series of still images that can later be compiled by a video application.

On the CD-ROM

You can use the characterAnim.fla document from the ch14 folder of the *Flash MX Bible* CD-ROM. Sandro Corsaro (www.sandrocorsaro.com) provided this excellent sample of his Flash animation.

1. Open your Flash document and select File ➪ Export Movie.

2. Browse to (or create) the folder where you want to store the sequence. Choose an empty folder — you don't want to have several files from the sequence mixed with other files. See Figure 14-2.

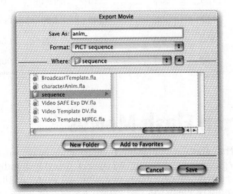

Figure 14-2: The Export Movie dialog box in the Mac version of Flash MX

3. In the Format menu (Mac) or Save as type menu (Windows), choose the type of file you want Flash to create. If you're using the sample Flash document on the book's CD-ROM, use the PICT format if you're using the Macintosh version of Flash MX (see Figure 14-3 for specific settings). Use the BMP format if you're using the Windows version (see Figure 14-4 for specific settings). Later, you can use the exported PICT or BMP sequence in the Adobe After Effects section.

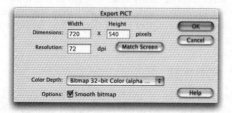

Figure 14-3: The Export PICT dialog box on the Mac

Figure 14-4: The Export Bitmap dialog box on Windows

4. Specify a filename and click Save. Flash MX will automatically append a series of numbers to the end of the file names, such as anim_0001, anim_0002, and so on. Flash generates a still image for each frame in the Flash timeline. This process can be quite lengthy if you have several hundreds of frames on the timeline. When you browse the directory where the files were saved, you should see a listing similar to that of Figure 14-5.

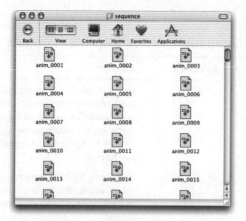

Figure 14-5: When you export a Flash movie as a sequence, Flash generates a still image (that is, one file) for each frame in the Flash movie.

For the highest quality video rendering, use a vector file format for export. The next section details each file type and its particular uses. However, if you export a raster image at the full size of the video frame (such as 720×540), you will not experience any resolution loss as long as you don't scale the exported artwork in the video application.

If you want to jump right into After Effects to output this footage to DV video, then proceed to the "Importing Image Sequences into After Effects" section at the end of this chapter. If you need to export an accompanying Stream sound (or series of sounds in a soundtrack on the Main Timeline), then jump to the section of this chapter titled "Exporting Audio from Flash Documents."

Uses of each sequence format

Flash can export in a variety of file formats, and each one has a particular purpose. While vector formats allow the most scalability, some Flash artwork does not display properly when converted from vector to raster. Raster formats usually maintain the highest fidelity to original Flash artwork, but the file sizes can be rather large.

Vector sequence formats

Use a vector format type for your sequences when you want the highest quality image translation in applications such as Adobe After Effects or Premiere (see Table 14-2 for a list of formats that can be exported from Flash). Flash exports vector sequences very quickly, but these files may take longer to re-render in your video-editing application than raster formats. Once you see the smooth edges of vector-rendered sequences, though, you can see that it is worth the extra time. Vector formats automatically matte out the Flash background color, making it quick and easy to superimpose Flash graphics with other content.

You may want to test a single EPS or AI file export (using File ⇨ Export Image) from Flash MX in your target video application. The EPS format natively uses CMYK (Cyan, Magenta, Yellow and blacK) color space. Flash artwork uses RGB (Red, Green and Blue) color space. If the RGB colors are converted to the CMYK color space during the export, you may notice extreme color shifts with your Flash artwork when you view it in your video application.

Table 14-2: Flash-Compatible Vector Sequence Formats

Export Format	Extension	Description
EPS (6.0 or earlier); Encapsulated PostScript	.eps	Universal vector format recognized by most editing or design applications. This is the preferred format for high-quality vector export. However, any gradients created in Flash will not export well with this format.
Illustrator; Adobe Illustrator	.ai	Proprietary file format mainly used by Adobe applications. Any gradients created in Flash will not export well with this format.

Export Format	Extension	Description
DXF; Drawing eXchange Format	.dxf	AutoCAD 2D/3D file format. Because this format does not support fills, it is mainly used for drafting plans or schematic drawings. This format is used by most CAD, 3D, and modeling programs for transferring drawings to other programs.
WMF/EMF; Windows Meta File/ Enhanced Meta File	.wmf, .emf	There's no reason to use these formats over the other vector formats. While some non-Microsoft applications support them, they aren't widely used on either Mac or PC systems.

Caution   Mask layers (and the artwork that they mask) will not export properly in EPS sequences. The artwork in the Mask layer will show up in the exported EPS file(s). If you use Mask layers in your Flash document, export raster image sequences instead of vector.

Raster formats

All raster formats can export at variable pixel widths, heights, and resolutions. As long as your Flash movie (.fla) is in the proper aspect ratio for video (usually 4:3), you can scale up your Flash movie on export (see Table 14-3 for a list of raster formats that Flash supports). This will save time during the re-rendering process in the video-editing application. Not all raster file formats support alpha channels, which are necessary if you intend to super-impose exported Flash graphics on top of other video content.

Cross-Reference   Refer to Chapter 37, "Working with Raster Graphics," for more detailed information on the options associated with each raster file format.

Table 14-3: Flash-Compatible Raster Sequence Formats

Flash Export Format	File Extension	Description
PICT (Mac only); Picture	.pct (or .pict)	Can be used with many PC and all Mac programs. Variable bit-depths and compression settings with support for alpha channels. Allows for lossless compression.
BMP (PC only); Windows Bitmap	.bmp	Can be used with all PC and some Mac programs. Variable bit-depths and compression settings with support for alpha channels. Allows for lossless compression.
GIF; Graphics Interchange File	.gif	Limited to a 256-color palette. Not recommended for full-motion NTSC video.

Continued

Table 14-3: *(continued)*

Flash Export Format	File Extension	Description
JPEG; Joint Photographic Experts Group	.jpg (or .jpeg)	Only supports 24-bit RGB color. No alpha channel support. Recommended for full-motion NTSC video, but this format does throw out color information due to its lossy compression method.
PNG; Portable Network Graphic	.png	Supports variable bit-depth and compression settings with alpha channels. Lossless compression schemes make it ideal for projects intended for NTSC video output.

Creating AVI Files on Windows

If you want a quick-and-dirty 100-percent raster-based video version of your Flash document, and you use the PC version of Flash, then you can export your Flash document as a Video for Windows (.avi) file. If you want the best video quality for output to videotape, you shouldn't use this method for rendering video. Flash doesn't support interlaced video and won't create the smoothest possible video content directly. This export file format is used primarily for digital video intended for computer playback, not NTSC playback.

Note   You can render a Flash movie at twice the frame rate of NTSC video (29.97×2 = 59.94 fps) using the necessary codec for your video hardware. If you want to play the AVI through your IEEE-1394 (a.k.a. *FireWire, iLink*) hardware, you need to resize the 720×534 AVI movie to 720×480 in a video-editing application or by using the Dimensions property of the Export AVI Settings dialog box. Do not change the properties of the original Flash project (.fla) via Modify ➪ Document! DV uses non-square pixels, and shapes will be stretched if you use a 720×480 movie size in Flash.

Choose **Export Movie** from the File menu. Select a folder (or create one) to store the AVI file, type the filename, and click **Save**. You will then see the Export Windows AVI dialog box with the following options (see Figure 14-6).

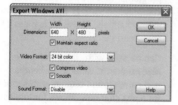

Figure 14-6: Adjust the values of the Windows AVI settings to accommodate your playback needs.

Dimensions

This property enables you to scale your AVI movie. If you wish to scale the movie's width separate from the height, clear the **Maintain Aspect Ratio** check box for this property. This may be necessary if you have to accommodate non-square pixel formats such as DV or D1.

Video format

The drop-down menu associated with this property enables you to choose a bit-depth for the AVI movie. For serious video work, you'll want to choose 24-bit color or greater.

✦ **8-bit color:** Limits the rendered movie to 256 colors that are determined on the fly by Flash.

✦ **16-bit color:** Limits the movie to 65,536 colors; also known as High Color in Windows or Thousands of Colors on the Mac.

✦ **24-bit color:** Enables the movie to use full RGB color (16.7 million colors); also known as True Color on the PC or Millions of Colors on the Mac.

✦ **32-bit color w/ alpha:** Enables the movie to use full RGB color and store an alpha channel for compositing effects. Not all video codecs can store alpha channel information.

✦ **Compress video:** If this option is checked, you are given the option to select a video compressor (codec) after you click **OK** on the Export Windows AVI dialog box. If you don't select this check box, Flash generates uncompressed video frames, which can take over 1MB of file space per frame. In general, you don't want to use uncompressed video, because it takes a lot more time to re-render uncompressed video into the hardware codec used by your video setup.

Even if you want to use uncompressed video, we recommend that you select the Compress video option and choose None for the compressor.

✦ **Smooth:** Using the smooth option anti-aliases the Flash graphics. This adds more time to the export process, but your AVI file looks much more polished. If you just want faster exporting, and you only need a rough AVI movie, then clear the **Smooth** check box.

Sound format

This drop-down list enables you to specify the audio sampling settings. If you didn't use any audio in your Flash movie, then choose **Disable**. For a description of each of the sampling rates and bit-depths, refer to Appendix B: "Digital Sound Basics."

Video compression

When you've chosen the options you need, click **OK**. If you specified **Compress Video**, you'll see the dialog box shown in Figure 14-7.

Figure 14-7: Choose the proper video codec for your video output hardware, or select a software-based codec for computer playback and distribution.

In the Video Compression dialog box, you can select a software- or hardware-based codec to use for the AVI movie. By default, Flash chooses **Full Frames** (Uncompressed). This option is the same as deselecting **Compress Video**, which forces Flash to render full-frame video. Because you probably want manageable file sizes, choose the codec that will be compatible with your video hardware. If you want to simply review your Flash work as an AVI movie, use Cinepak or Indeo codecs. Adjust the codec settings as necessary for your needs. Smaller files and lower quality will result from using compression qualities less than 100 percent, exporting selective keyframes, and limiting data rates. For high-quality rendering using hardware-based codecs, make sure that the hardware codec (such as MJPEG or DV) is set to 100 percent compression quality with no keyframes or data-rate limiting. When you have chosen all the appropriate settings, click **OK**.

Flash then exports an AVI movie file to the folder you specified. Depending on the length of your Flash movie and the video codec used, the export process could take less than a minute or many hours. Unfortunately, Flash doesn't give you an estimated time for completion like Adobe Premiere or After Effects does. When Flash has finished exporting the file, you can view the video with Windows Media Player or with the software that your video hardware uses.

Exporting Audio from a Flash Document

If you created a Flash animation with Stream sounds that are synchronized to the animation of the artwork, you may want to export the audio as a separate file to combine with exported image sequences in a video application such as Adobe After Effects. If you created QuickTime Video or Windows AVI files, then you can export audio directly in the export options of these file formats. This section describes how to export audio separately from the animation within a Flash document.

On the CD-ROM

Open the characterAnim.fla document from the ch14 folder of the *Flash MX Bible* CD-ROM. You can export the audio track of this document to use with the matching image sequence that was exported earlier in this chapter.

1. Open the Flash document. Make sure any and all sounds that you want to include in the exported audio file are located on the Main Timeline (that is, Scene 1). Each sound on a keyframe should be set to the Stream sync option in the Property inspector.

2. Choose File ➪ Export Movie. On Windows, choose **WAV audio** in the Save as file type menu, and specify **soundtrack.wav** as the filename. See Figure 14-8 for the WAV settings that follow the Export Movie dialog box. On the Mac, choose **QuickTime Video** in the Format menu, and specify **soundtrack.mov** as the file name. With the Mac version of Flash MX, you can not export a sound file — you can, however, export a QuickTime Video and simply disregard the video track when you import the .mov file into your video-editing application. See Figure 14-9 for the QuickTime Video settings that follow the Export Movie dialog box.

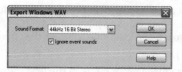

Figure 14-8: The Export Windows WAV dialog box

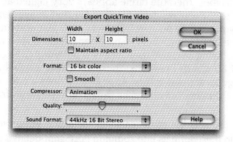

Figure 14-9: The Export QuickTime Video dialog box

Caution Though you can export Event sounds with the WAV file format on the Windows version of Flash MX, we recommend that you only use Stream sounds for exact synchronization of sound and image in your Flash animations.

Once you have exported the sound from the Flash document, you're ready to combine the exported image sequence with the sound file. In the next section, you learn how to combine these sources in Adobe After Effects 5.5.

Importing Image Sequences into After Effects

Now that you've created an image sequence (and supporting audio track, if necessary) with Flash MX's Export Movie command, you can bring the newly generated material into most video-editing applications. Not all video-editing applications will accept still image sequences and will automatically treat them as one video clip (as Adobe After Effects or Premiere do). In this section, you see how to prepare an image sequence for video output.

Adobe After Effects is the video production equivalent of Photoshop. After Effects allows you to modify moving images in ways similar to how you modify still images in Adobe Photoshop. With powerful native tools and filters, as well as a vast array of custom effects plug-ins, After Effects is a program with enough depth to keep many motion graphics designers happy for years. Although After Effects is a complex program with innumerable settings, you can certainly use it for simple tasks as well.

Note At the time of this writing, Adobe After Effects 5.5 was the latest version of the product. You can download a trial version of this software at www.adobe.com/products/aftereffects/tryreg.html

Using After Effects, you can achieve the highest quality video from your Flash-generated image sequence. That's because After Effects offers subtle controls for video clip and composition settings that deliver crisp, interlaced, frame-accurate video.

After Effects can continuously rasterize any vector content, meaning that After Effects can re-render each vector frame into a raster frame. Most video applications, such as Adobe Premiere, rasterize the first frame of a vector image and continue to reuse that first rasterized version for the entire render process.

What does that mean? Simply put, if you have a small vector circle in the first frame of a project that grows larger in subsequent frames, then the circle appears very jagged at the larger sizes. Although both Premiere and After Effects render a Flash-generated image sequence at the same quality, please note that if you want to do special effects with just one frame (or still) from a Flash movie (not an entire image sequence), then After Effects does a much better job. Also note that this can be confusing because there are two potential uses of material imported from Flash into either After Effects or Premiere. These are either single-frame imports or multiframe imports. The general point is this: After Effects does a consistent high-quality job with both types, whereas Premiere only handles the latter type (multiframe) well.

 Caution While EPS and AI image sequences offer the most scalability for digital video production, Flash poorly translates gradients in these formats into common PostScript-defined colors. As a result, gradients appear as solid color fills in After Effects. If you're using gradients in your Flash artwork, it's best to export the movie as a raster sequence. After Effects can import a PNG, BMP, or PICT sequence, which has less degrading compression than JPEG.

The following steps show you how to import a sequence into After Effects 5.5. If you exported an image sequence from the exercise earlier in this chapter, then use that sequence for this exercise.

1. Open an existing After Effects project file (.aep) or create a new project (Ctrl+Alt+N or ⌘+Option+N).

2. Double-click in the Project window to import the image sequence. In the Import File dialog box, browse to the folder containing the image sequence. Select the first file of the sequence (for example, anim_0001) and select the appropriate **Sequence** check box (such as PICT Sequence, JPEG Sequence, EPS Sequence, and so forth), as shown in Figure 14-10. Click **Import**.

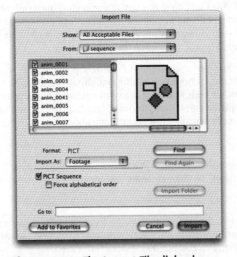

Figure 14-10: The Import File dialog box

3. If After Effects detects an alpha channel in the imported file(s), then an Interpret Footage dialog box opens, as shown in Figure 14-11. You must tell After Effects how to treat the alpha channel. For any image (or image sequence) with an alpha channel imported from Flash, use the **Straight—Unmatted** setting.

Figure 14-11: After Effects automatically detects the presence of an alpha channel in imported file(s). For alpha channels that Flash creates, use the Straight—Unmatted setting.

4. Select the imported sequence (now shown as one footage item) in the Project window and choose File ➪ Interpret Footage ➪ Main. This time, the Interpret Footage dialog box (see Figure 14-12) displays the complete settings for the selected footage file. In the Frame Rate section, enter the correct frame rate in the **Assume this frame rate** field. If you followed the guidelines given earlier in this chapter, then you used a 30 or 60 fps for your Flash document. Enter that value here. Also, make sure **Square Pixels** is selected for the Pixel Aspect Ratio setting. If you are using the image sequence from the earlier exercise, then use a frame rate of **30 fps**.

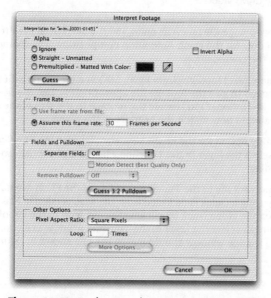

Figure 14-12: In the complete Interpret Footage dialog, you can set the frame rate and pixel aspect ratio for the Flash image sequence.

5. Import any supporting audio file for the image sequence. For our sample image sequence, you can import the soundtrack.wav or soundtrack.mov file you created in an earlier section. You should use the Interpret Footage command on this file as well — make sure it has the same frame rate as the image sequence.

6. Create a new composition via the Composition ➪ New Composition command (Ctrl+N or ⌘+N). Name the composition **Flash Animation**. Depending on your video hardware, the settings for a new composition will vary. For the **Duration** section, enter a value greater than or equal to the length of the imported Flash sequence. See Figure 14-13 for a DV-specific composition. For the sample image sequence, use a duration of 4 seconds and 25 frames (0;00;04;25), as shown in Figure 14-13.

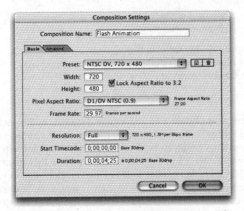

Figure 14-13: Composition settings for DV-format (for example, MiniDV, DVCAM) video

7. Drag the Flash sequence footage file (such as anim_[0001-0145]) from the Project window to the Timeline window for the Flash Animation composition. The footage will automatically center in the composition.

8. Since you are using square pixel footage (from Flash MX) in a DV composition using non-square pixels, you need to size the footage file appropriately. Use the fit-to-comp shortcut (Ctrl+Alt+F or ⌘+Option+F) to rescale the footage to the size of the comp. The borders of the footage should now match the borders of the comp.

9. Check the **Frame Blending** option for the image sequence layer in the Timeline window. Alternatively, you can select the layer in the Timeline window and choose Layer ➪ Switches ➪ Frame Blending.

10. Drag the imported soundtrack file to the Timeline window of the Flash Animation composition. If you are using a QuickTime Video from the Mac version of Flash MX as your soundtrack, turn off the video track by clicking the eye icon to the left of the layer name. Alternatively, you can select the layer in the Timeline window and choose Layer ➪ Switches ➪ Video. The Timeline window should match the one shown in Figure 14-14.

Figure 14-14: The After Effects Timeline window with the two imported Flash assets

11. Change the background color of the composition by choosing Composition ⇨ Background Color. For this example, try a legal NTSC white value, with an RGB value of 235, 235, 235. When you're finished, your composition window should look like Figure 14-15.

Figure 14-15: The Flash Animation composition window

12. Save your project as **flashAnimation.aep**.

13. Now, you're ready to render the composition to a final DV file. With the Flash Animation composition selected in the Project window, choose Composition ⇨ Add to Render Queue. The Render Queue window will appear, as shown in Figure 14-16.

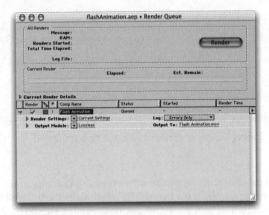

Figure 14-16: The After Effects Render Queue window

14. Click the **Current Settings** text to the right of the Render Settings option in the Render Queue window. In the Render Settings dialog box, choose the settings shown in Figure 14-17 for DV-formatted output. Click **OK** when you are finished.

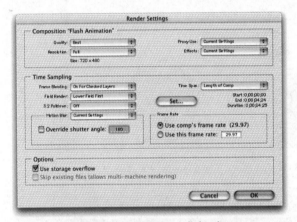

Figure 14-17: The Render Settings dialog box

15. Click the **Lossless** text to the right of the Output Module option in the Render Queue window. This will open the Output Module Settings dialog box, shown in Figure 14-18. Choose **QuickTime Movie** in the Format menu. In the Video Output section, click the **Format Options** button. This will open the Compression Settings dialog box, shown in Figure 14-19. Choose **DV — NTSC** for the Compressor, and click **OK**. Select the **Audio Output** check box of the Output Module Settings dialog box, and make sure the audio is set to 44.100 kHz at 16 Bit Stereo. Click **OK** to close the dialog box.

16. Click the file name text to the right of the Output To option in the Render Queue window. Choose a location to store the QuickTime movie, and specify a file name, such as **flashAnimation.mov**.

17. Finally, click the **Render** button in the Render Queue window. After Effects examines the composition and creates a DV-formatted file.

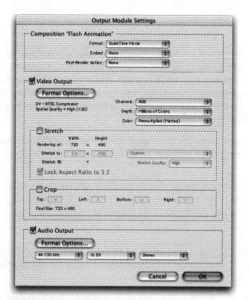

Figure 14-18: The Output Module Settings dialog box

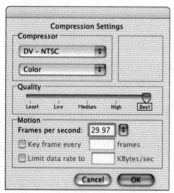

Figure 14-19: The Compression Settings dialog box

You can output the DV file to your DV camcorder or deck using another video application like Adobe Premiere or Apple Final Cut Pro. Or, you can use the DV file in another project file in After Effects or your preferred video-editing application.

Tip   Try using the Broadcast Colors filter on the image sequence layer in the Flash Animation composition. This filter can replace illegal NTSC colors with less saturated versions of the offending colors.

Summary

✦ You can use Flash to export animations as high-quality image sequences. An image sequence is a series of numbered still images. Certain video-editing applications, such as Adobe Premiere and After Effects, can import both raster and vector sequences. These sequences can be composited with other video tracks and output to film or to the video format of your choice — which opens up a whole new realm of motion techniques for content generated in Flash!

✦ You can use Flash also to export high-quality raster-based AVI and QuickTime movies. It should be noted, however, that these movie files will not contain any Flash inter-activity or Flash tracks.

✦ Desktop digital video systems have become more affordable with the advent of the DV format, used by MiniDV and DVCAM camcorders and decks. Because DV material is binary from start to finish, there is virtually no loss of video quality during the editing process.

✦ Because Flash is designed for optimal playback on the Web, Flash movie properties (frame size, frame rate, and the number of total frames) need to be adjusted to work with high-quality digital video.

✦ NTSC television sets and WebTVs have color signal limitations. Avoid using highly saturated colors and thin lines in Flash movies intended for interlaced video delivery.

✦　✦　✦

Integrating Media Files with Flash

In This Part

Chapter 15
Adding Sound

Chapter 16
Importing Artwork

Chapter 17
Embedding Video

You can create a wide range of graphic elements directly in Flash, but most projects will also require imported assets. This section covers the three main media types that you can use to enhance your Flash projects. Chapter 15 will introduce you to the process for importing and controlling sound in Flash. This chapter also covers various compression options and how to edit and export sound from Flash. You will learn techniques that help you to get the most bang per byte in your final Flash movies. Chapter 16 addresses the specific workflow and optimization issues related to importing vector and bitmap artwork (and text) from other programs to the Flash authoring environment. Find out how to maintain color consistency and how to preserve layers and vector outlines when moving graphics from other programs, including Adobe Illustrator, Macromedia FreeHand, Fireworks, and Adobe Photoshop. Flash MX offers a whole range of new possibilities for video content. Chapter 17 focuses on the process for embedding video directly in Flash movies.

Adding Sound

✦ ✦ ✦ ✦

In This Chapter

Working with
audio formats

The new Speech codec

Importing sounds
into Flash

Adding sounds to
buttons and frames

Understanding
Sync options

Compression in the
Publish Settings

Customizing
compression in
the Library panel

VBR MP3

Export tips

✦ ✦ ✦ ✦

One of the most neglected (or perhaps understated) aspects of multimedia development is sound. Because the majority of people who use Flash (or create multimedia) come from graphic-arts backgrounds, it's no surprise that sound is often applied as the last effect to a visually stunning presentation — there may be little or no consideration for the soundtrack in early stages of development. Moreover, it's the one element that is usually taken from a stock source, rather than being original work by the Flash designer. (Exceptions exist, of course, as many Flash designers have demonstrated time and time again.)

You can use sound in Flash movies to enhance interactive design with navigation elements such as buttons, to layer the visitor's experience with a background soundtrack, to add narrative, or for more experimental uses. This chapter focuses on the fundamentals of importing and integrating sound files into your Flash project. We also discuss the intricacies of controlling audio output, with particular attention to MP3 bit rates. You'll learn how to use the Publish Settings dialog box and compare that with the enhanced control that is available for customizing compression from within the Sound Properties dialog box of the Library. This chapter will guide you through the use of audio within a Flash document and suggest tips for getting the most bang per byte in the final Flash movie (.swf file).

Cross-Reference In this edition of the book, we have moved the discussion of "Basics of Sampling and Quality" to Appendix B, "Digital Sound Basics."

Sound File Import Formats

You have the ability to import most file formats in either the Windows or Macintosh version of Flash. All major sound file types, like MP3 and WAV, are compatible on both versions. Once a sound file is imported into a Flash document, the resulting .fla file can be edited on either platform.

Flash MX can import the following sound file formats:

✦ **MP3 (MPEG-1 Audio Layer 3):** Among the many advantages of MP3 sound files for Flash MX users, the most obvious is that they are cross-platform. Flash MX can import MP3 files on either the PC or the Mac. This single advantage improves Flash workflow in cross-platform environment. Other advantages are the efficiency of MP3 compression, the increasing availability of MP3 files, as well as the ease of creating MP3 files with common players like Windows Media Player or Apple iTunes. For more information about MP3s, please see the sidebar at the end of the section.

✦ **WAV (Windows Wave):** Until the relatively recent support for MP3, WAV files reigned for nearly a decade as the standard for digital audio on Windows PCs. Still, the WAV format remains the primary acquisition sound format (that is, the format in which you record sound from a microphone or other sound source on your computer). Flash can import WAV files created in sound applications and editors such as SoundForge, Mixman, or ACID. The imported WAV files can be either stereo or mono and can support varying bit and frequency rates. Unassisted, Flash MX for Macintosh cannot import this file format. But with QuickTime 4 or later installed, WAV files can be directly imported into Flash MX on a Mac.

✦ **AIFF or AIF (Audio Interchange File format):** Much like WAV on the PC, the AIF format is the most commonly used digital audio format for sound acquisition on the Mac. Flash can import AIFF sounds created in sound applications and editors such as Peak, DECK II, or SoundEdit. Like WAV, AIFF supports stereo and mono, in addition to variable bit depths and frequency rates. Unassisted, Flash MX for Windows cannot import this file format. But with QuickTime 4 or later installed, AIFF files can be imported into Flash MX on Windows. The Windows version of Flash MX recognizes, properly opens, and can edit Flash documents created on the Mac that contain AIFF sounds.

✦ **Sun AU:** This sound format (.au file) was developed by Sun Microsystems and Next, and it is the native sound format on many Solaris and UNIX systems, just as WAV and AIF are native to Windows and Macintosh, respectively. The Sun AU format is frequently used with sound-enabled Java applets on Web pages.

✦ **QuickTime:** QuickTime audio files (.qta or .mov files) can be imported directly into Flash MX, provided that you have QuickTime 4 or later installed. Once a QuickTime audio file is imported into a Flash document, the sound file appears in the Library just as any other sound would.

✦ **Sound Designer II:** This proprietary audio file format created by Digidesign is used with its signature professional audio suite, Pro Tools. Sounds saved in this file format can only be imported into the Macintosh version of Flash MX. If you need to use a Sound Designer II file (.sd2 file extension) with the Windows version of Flash MX, you can import the file directly if you have QuickTime 4 or later installed.

Tip

If you're working in a cross-platform environment, take a few precautions to ensure that the sound files used in your Flash documents will be editable on both platforms. Don't rely upon the imported sound that's embedded in the Flash document (.fla file) as your master sound file. Do make sure that the master sound is retained as both WAV and AIF files, and that both sound sources are distributed with the Flash document. Of course, if you have QuickTime 4 or later installed on all of your machines, you only need to keep one master sound file, as either a WAV or AIF file.

These sound file types are structural or "architecture" based, meaning that they simply indicate the wrapper used to encode digital audio. Each of them can use a variety of compression techniques or a variety of audio *codecs*. A codec is a *compression* and *decompression* module

MP3s Demystified

MP3 is a noteworthy technology as well as a file format. It excels at the compression of a sound sequence — MP3-compressed files can be reduced to nearly a twelfth of their original size without destroying sound quality. MP3 was developed under the sponsorship of the Motion Picture Experts Group (MPEG) using the following logic: CD-quality sound is typically sampled at a bit depth of 16 (16-bit) at sample rate 44.1 kHz, which generates approximately 1.4 million bits of data for each second of sound — but that second of sound includes a lot of data for sounds that most humans cannot hear! By devising a compression algorithm that reduces the data linked to imperceptible sounds, the developers of MP3 made it possible to deliver high-quality audio over the Internet without excessive latency (the delay between playing a sound and hearing it back). Another way of describing this is to say that MP3 uses perceptual encoding techniques that reduce the amount of overlapping and redundant information that describe sound. As implemented by Flash MX, MP3 has the added advantage that it can stream longer sounds, which means that the sound begins to play in the Flash movie before the sound file has been received in its entirety. Shockwave Audio, the default audio compression scheme for Macromedia Director–based Shockwave movies, is actually MP3 in disguise.

for digital media. Sound and video is encoded (compressed) with a specific technique by an application or device. After it is encoded, it can be played back (decompressed) by a media player that has access to the codec module. In order for a sound file to play on your computer, you must have the audio codec used in that file installed on your system. MP3 files, for example, can be compressed in a variety of bit rates and frequencies, as can WAV and AIF files. Once Flash MX imports a sound file, the wrapper type (AIF, WAV, AU, and so on) is stripped. Flash simply stores the sound file as generic PCM (Pulse Code Modulation) digital audio. Moreover, Flash MX will convert any imported 8-bit sound file into a 16-bit sound file. For this reason, it's best not to use any precompression on your sound files before you bring them into Flash MX.

Note   Individual MP3 sound files in the Flash document's Library can be adjusted to retain their original compression. This is the sole exception to the rule we just mentioned in the preceding paragraph. As we'll see later in this chapter, however, Flash MX may need to recompress all sound files in a Flash movie, depending on their use in the movie's timeline.

Sound Export Formats

You can decide which sound format (or codec) to use for audio when publishing Flash document files to Flash movies (.swf files). Although the default Publish Settings in Flash MX is to export all audio with the MP3 format, sound can also be exported in several other audio formats. The benefits and drawbacks of each format are noted in the list that follows.

New
Feature   Flash MX features a Speech codec, which is ideally suited to compress voice-only sound files.

Regardless of the format that you choose for exporting your sounds, you can individually specify a compression scheme for each sound in the Flash document's library. Furthermore, each format has specific options and settings that we'll examine later in this chapter.

✦ **ADPCM (Adaptive Differential Pulse-Code Modulation):** ADPCM is an audio compression scheme that converts sound into binary information. It is primarily used for voice technologies, such as fiber-optic telephone lines, because the audio signal is compressed, enabling it to carry textual information as well. ADPCM works well, because it records only the difference between samples and adjusts the encoding accordingly, keeping file size low. ADPCM was the default setting for older versions of Flash, such as Flash 2 and 3. It isn't as efficient as MP3 encoding but is the best choice for situations in which compatibility is required with *all* older Flash Players.

✦ **MP3 (MPEG-1 Audio Layer 3):** Over the last three years, MP3 has become the standard for digital audio distributed on the Internet. Although MP3 compression delivers excellent audio quality with small files, it's much more processor-intensive than other compressors. This means that slower computers may gasp when they encounter a high-bit-rate MP3 audio while simultaneously processing complex animations. As always, it's wise to know your audience, and, when in doubt, to test your Flash movie with MP3 audio on slower computers. The Flash Player supports MP3 only at versions 4 and above. Note that Flash Player 4 for the Pocket PC does *not* support MP3 sound, and it's likely that forthcoming Flash Players for other devices with slow processors may not support MP3 playback.

✦ **Raw (Raw PCM):** Flash MX can export sound to .swf files in a raw audio format. If you use this setting, Flash won't compress any audio. However, uncompressed sound makes very large files that would be useless for Internet-based distribution. As uncompressed sound, audio in the imported sound file retains its original fidelity. We recommend that you use the Raw format only for Flash movies that you intend to distribute on fixed media, like CD-ROM or DVD-ROM.

✦ **Speech (Nellymoser):** This new audio codec in Flash MX is specifically designed for audio sources that contain mostly human speech, like narrative or instructional content. Macromedia licensed audio technology from Nellymoser, Inc., which specializes in the development of voice-only audio codecs. All sounds that use the Speech codec will be converted to mono sounds. The real powerplay for this codec will likely be seen in Flash server-side applications, as this codec is incredibly efficient and a fast encoder with a low computer processor overhead. For example, if you want to use the new Camera and Video object to stream live video from a web cam, the Speech codec will optimize the audio information very efficiently. If you save a Flash MX document (.fla file) as a Flash 5 document (.fla file) using the new Save as Flash 5 feature in File ⇨ Save As, any sounds set to use Speech will be changed to ADPCM. Flash Player 6 must be used to play back sounds encoded with this format. Note that Flash 5 and MX documents use the same file extension, .fla.

Cross-Reference   We'll examine the specific export options for each audio format later in this chapter. This section will help you determine which format you should use for your specific needs.

Table 15-1 shows the compatibility of Flash's audio export formats with various platforms.

Table 15-1: Audio Export Formats for Flash Players

Export Format	Flash 3 or earlier	Flash 4 and 5	Flash 6	Comments
ADPCM	Yes	Yes	Yes	Good encoding scheme; compatible with all Flash players, and works well for short sound effects like button clicks.
MP3	No	Yes	Yes	Best general use encoding scheme, and ideal for music tracks.
*Not compatible with Flash Player 4 for the Pocket PC.				
Raw	Yes	Yes	Yes	No compression, lossless, large file sizes.
Speech	No	No	Yes	Excellent compression for human speech; avoids "tinny" sounds for voices; Ideally suited for real-time compression with Flash server-side applications.

Importing Sounds into Flash

In the preceding section, we discussed the various sound formats that Flash MX can import and export. In addition to our discussion of the merits of the MP3 and new Speech codecs, we also explained the uses of platform specific AIF (Mac) and WAV (Windows) audio files. But we didn't delve into the process of importing sound into Flash MX. So, let's get started.

Note   When working with sound, you may encounter some interchangeable terminology. Generally, these terms — *sound file, sound clip,* or *audio file* — all refer to the same thing, a single digital file in one of several formats, which contains a digitally encoded sound.

Unlike other imported assets, such as bitmaps or vector art, Flash doesn't automatically insert an imported sound file into the frames of the active layer on the timeline. In fact, you don't have to select a specific layer or frame before you import a sound file. That's because all sounds are sent directly to the Library immediately upon import. At this point, the sound becomes part of the Flash document (.fla file), which may make the file size balloon significantly if the sound file is large. The sound does not become part of the Flash movie (.swf file), however, nor will it add to the size of the Flash movie unless it is assigned to a keyframe, as an instance of that sound, or it is set to export for use in ActionScript.

New Feature   Flash MX now allows you to directly load MP3 files into Flash movies from the Flash Player. Previously, Macromedia Generator (or an equivalent server-side application) was necessary to transform sound files into Flash movies (.swf files) on the fly. We'll show you how to load and attach sounds with ActionScript in Chapter 28, "Sharing and Loading Assets."

Although this may seem peculiar, it does serve a useful purpose: It helps to ensure that instances of the sound will be employed within your project, rather than duplicates of the same large sound file, which helps minimize the byte size of the Flash movie (.swf file). So, to use an imported sound within Flash you must first import the sound, and then assign an instance of that sound to a specific layer and keyframe.

To import a sound file into the Flash MX authoring environment:

1. Choose File ➪ Import (Ctrl+R or ⌘+R), or File ➪ Import to Library. For sound assets, these commands work identically.

2. From the Files of type list (Windows) or Show list (Mac) in the Import dialog box, select All Sound Formats.

Caution On the Mac OS X version of Flash MX, you may need to choose All Files in the Show menu in order to select an appropriate sound file.

3. Browse to the sound file that you want to import.

4. Click Open.

The selected sound file is imported into your Flash document (.fla file) and arrives in the document's library with its filename intact. If the Library panel is closed, you can open it by choosing Window ➪ Library, or by using the keyboard shortcut (Ctrl+L or ⌘+L). With the Library panel open, locate the sound, and click it to highlight the name of the sound file where it appears in the Library list. The waveform appears in the Library preview pane, as shown in Figure 15-1. Click the Play button above the waveform to audition the sound.

Figure 15-1: This is a stereo sound in the movie's library.

Cross-Reference Refer to the "Fine-tuning Sound Settings in the Library" section later in this chapter for an explanation of how unique compression settings can be specified for each sound in a document's library.

Sounds may also be loaded from a shared library. Refer to Chapter 28, "Sharing and Loading Assets," to learn more about shared libraries. Chapter 28 also shows you how to preload a MP3 file into a Flash movie (.swf file). To learn how to assign a linkage identifier string to an asset, such as a sound file, refer to Chapter 27, "Interacting with Movie Clips."

How Sound Is Stored in a Flash Movie

Earlier in this chapter, we mentioned that when you import a sound file into a Flash MX document (.fla file), an entire copy of the sound file is stored within the document. However, when you place a sound on a timeline, then a reference is made to the sound in the library. Just as symbol instances refer to a master or parent symbol in the library, sound "instances" refer to the master sound resource in the library. Throughout this chapter, we use the term "instance" for sound assets with this understanding in mind. When the Flash document is published as a Flash movie, the master sound in the library is compressed and stored *once* in the final movie (.swf file), even though there may be several instances of that sound used through the movie (for example, in multiple frames on multiple timelines). This type of efficient storage, however, applies to Event sounds only. Whenever you use Stream sounds, the sound file is stored in the Flash movie each time you refer to the sound in a timeline. For example, if you compressed a sound to export from Flash as a 3 KB sound asset in the final movie (.swf file), you could reuse that sound as an Event sound several times without adding significant bytes to the file size. However, that same compressed sound (at 3 KB) would occupy 12 KB in the final movie if it were placed four times as a Stream sound on keyframes within the movie. We'll discuss Event and Stream sounds later in this chapter, so you may want to refer back to this sidebar at a later point.

It is also worth mentioning that Flash MX must have enough available RAM on the computer system to accommodate imported sound files. For example, if you import a 30 MB WAV file into a Flash MX document, then you must have an additional 30 MB of RAM available to the application. On 32-bit Windows operating systems and Mac OS X, you will not likely experience problems with memory usage, where virtual memory exists alongside the physical RAM within the computer. On Mac OS 9.x or earlier, though, you may want to increase the available RAM to the Flash MX application file if you import large sound files into Flash documents. Otherwise, you may experience frequent crashes and/or out of memory (or low memory) error messages.

You can also import sound files into a Flash document by dragging the sound file from the desktop to the Timeline window or the Library panel. On the Macintosh, you can drag the sound file to the Stage as well. This method can be especially useful when you have searched for a sound file using the operating system's search tool (Start ⇨ Search in Windows, or Sherlock in the Mac OS), and want to quickly bring the found file into Flash MX.

 Caution   When you import a sound file using this method on the Windows version of Flash MX, the sound file will be placed in its own Flash document (.fla file). If you want to use another document, then drag it from the new document's Library panel to the other document's Library panel. Remember, Windows users can not drag sound files to the Document window (or Stage area) — doing so may result in an OLE error dialog box instructing you to use File ⇨ Import instead.

Assigning a Sound to a Button

The interactive experience can be enhanced by the addition of subtle effects. The addition of sounds to correspond with the various states of a button is perhaps the most obvious example. Although this effect can be abused, it's hard to overuse an effect that delivers such meaningful user feedback. Here, we show how different sounds can be added to both the Over (rollOver) and the Down (press) states of a button. For more general information about creating the buttons themselves, see Chapter 6, "Symbols, Instances, and the Library," and see Chapter 18, "Understanding Actions and Event Handlers," to learn how to add code to buttons. Because buttons are stored in the Library, and because only instances of a Button symbol are deployed within the Flash movie, sounds that are assigned to a button work for all instances of that Button symbol. However, if different sounds are required for different buttons, a new Button symbol must be created. You can create a new Button symbol from the same Graphic symbols as the previous button (provided it was built out of symbols) or duplicate it in the Library panel using the Duplicate command in the Library's options menu.

 As you'll see shortly, there is no longer a Sound panel in the Flash authoring environment. If you used Flash 5, look to the Property inspector for the options that were formerly in the Sound panel.

To add a sound to the Down state of a Button symbol:

1. From the Buttons Library (Window ➪ Common Libraries ➪ Buttons), choose a button to which you want to add sound effects. Drag an instance of the button from the Buttons Library to the Stage. Edit the Button symbol by double-clicking it on the Stage, or by choosing Edit from the Library options menu. Both methods invoke the Symbol Editing mode.

2. Add a new layer to the button's timeline, label the new layer sound, and then add keyframes to this layer in the Over and Down columns. Your timeline should look similar to Figure 15-2.

Figure 15-2: The timeline for your button should resemble this timeline.

3. Next, select the frame of the button state where you want to add a sound for interactive feedback (such as a clicking sound for the down state), and then access the Property inspector by doing one of the following: (a) right-click/Control+click the selected frame, choose Properties from the contextual menu; or (b) choose Window ➪ Properties. An alternative method (with the frame selected) is to simply drag the sound from the Library panel onto the Stage.

You should now have the new Flash MX Property inspector open, as shown in Figure 15-3. Click the arrow in the lower-right corner of the Property inspector to see all of the options. For more information about the new Flash MX interface, refer to Chapter 4, "Interface Fundamentals."

Sound attributes

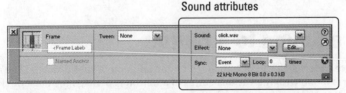

Figure 15-3: The new Property inspector houses the options for sound usage.

4. Choose the sound clip that you want to use from the Sound menu. This menu lists all of the sounds that have been imported and that are available in the library of the current movie. In this example, we used the click.wav sound found in the ch15 folder of the book's CD-ROM.

5. The next step is to use the Sync menu to choose *how* you want the sound to play. For this lesson, simply use the default, which is the Event option. We'll defer our exploration of the other options in the Sync menu for a later section.

You have now added a sound to your button state. Remember, you're still in Symbol Editing mode, so to test the button, return to the Scene 1 timeline (that is, the Main Timeline) either by clicking the Scene 1 location label at the upper-left corner of the Document window, or by pressing Ctrl+E (⌘+E). Then, choose Control ➪ Enable Simple Buttons, or Control ➪ Test Movie.

To add a sound to the Over state of a Button symbol, simply retrace the preceding steps, referencing the Over state of the button wherever appropriate. Remember that different sounds can be assigned to the Up, Over, and Down states of a Button symbol. A sound that is added to the Up state will play whenever the mouse rolls out of a button's hit area.

For a completed example of this button, refer to the Flash movie **button_sound_100.fla** located in the ch15 folder of the *Flash MX Bible* CD-ROM. This movie has a button with sounds attached and was made with the same technique described in this section.

Adding Sound to the Timeline

In addition to the use of sounds to enhance the interactivity of buttons, another popular use of sound in Flash is to provide a background score. The simplest way to achieve this is to place the sound within its own layer in the Main Timeline (Scene 1), at the precise frame in which you want the sound to begin. To do this, you must first import the sound (as described earlier in this chapter) and also create a new layer for it.

If you don't have access to sounds, you can use the sample sound **atmospheres_1** to practice. This sound is in the ch15 folder of the *Flash MX Bible* CD-ROM. It is available in both WAV and AIF formats.

Adding sound files to the timeline is similar to assigning sound to a button. To add sounds to a timeline, follow these steps:

1. Add a new layer to the timeline and label the layer with the name of the sound. We also tend to name sound layers as **sound** or **background track**.

2. Create a keyframe on the sound layer at the frame where you want the sound to begin.

3. With that keyframe selected, open the Properties inspector. Make sure you have expanded the view to show all of the sound attributes.

4. If you remembered to import the sound that you want to use, you can now choose that sound clip from the Sound drop-down menu. If you find yourself stuck at this point, review the preceding steps and/or retrace your steps through the methodology for adding sound to a button.

5. From the Effect menu, choose how the sound should be handled by Flash. The Effect menu offers several preset fading and panning treatments, plus custom, which invokes the Edit Envelope dialog box. For no special effect, choose None. For more about the Effect presets and the Edit Envelope dialog box, refer to the subsequent section, "Applying effects from the Effect menu of the Property inspector."

6. From the Sync menu, choose one of four options — Event, Start, Stop, or Stream — to control how you want to the sound to be synchronized. (See the next section for a detailed explanation of Sync options.)

7. Specify how many times you want the sound to loop. To loop the sound for an extended period of time (for example, as a background track), enter a high number, such as 999. For specific information about looping stream sounds, refer to the next section.

8. Perform any last-minute editing or finessing of the sound file (see "Editing Audio in Flash" later in this chapter). Then return to the Main Timeline and save your work.

Your sound is now part of the timeline. Its waveform is visible on the layer to which it was added. Test your sound by pressing the Enter key on your keyboard, which plays the timeline. Or, for sound with a Sync setting of Stream, manually "scrub" the sound by dragging the Playhead across the timeline. To perform the most accurate test of the sound, use either Control ⇨ Test Scene or Control ⇨ Test Movie to see and hear it as a Flash movie (.swf file).

Tip   If you sync a sound to the timeline using the Stream feature, you should test your Flash movie (.swf file) on various platforms and machines with different processor speeds. What looks and sounds good on the latest PowerMac G4 might be less impressive on an underpowered legacy machine, like a first-generation Pentium machine.

Organizing Sounds on the Timeline

There is no technical limit to the number of sound layers; each layer functions like a separate sound channel, and Flash mixes them on playback. (This capability of Flash might be considered an onboard, economy sound mixer.) There is, however, a practical limit, because each sound layer potentially increases the movie's file size, while the mix of multiple sounds may burden the computer it's being run on.

Tip   If you can't recall the *name* of a particular sound in the timeline, remember that with tooltips enabled from the Preferences dialog box (Edit ⇨ Preferences in Windows and Mac OS 9 or earlier, Flash ⇨ Preferences in Mac OS X), the filename of the sound will pop-up whenever the mouse pointer is over the waveform.

Enhanced viewing of sound layers

Because sound is different from other types of Flash content, some users find that increasing the layer height of the sound layers eases working with multiple sounds in the timeline. That's because a taller layer height provides a better visual cue due to the unique waveforms of each sound. To increase the layer height for individual layers:

1. Right-click/Control+click the layer in the Timeline window, and then choose Properties from the contextual menu.

2. At the bottom of the ensuing Layer Properties dialog box, change the layer height from the default 100 percent to either 200 or 300 percent.

3. Note that these percentages are relative to the settings chosen in the Frame View options menu. For more information on the intricacies of the Timeline window, see Chapter 4, "Interface Fundamentals." For an actual example of this enhanced viewing, open the file titled **enhanced_view.fla**, located in the ch15 folder on the CD-ROM.

Tip   Your movie's frame rate, as specified in the Document Properties dialog box (Modify ⇨ Document), affects the expanse (or number) of frames that a sound occupies on the timeline. For example, at Flash's default setting of 12 frames per seconds (fps), a 30-second sound clip extends across 360 frames of the timeline. At 18 fps, the same 30-second clip expands to 540 frames — but in either case, the time length of the sound is unchanged.

Organizing sound layers with a layer folder

Flash MX introduces a new organization tool for layers in any timeline: Layer folders. We discuss layer folders in Chapter 4, "Interface Fundamentals." To nest sound layers in a layer folder, create a new layer folder and then drag each of the sound layers to the folder. As you drop each layer on the folder, it will nest within the folder.

Synchronizing Audio to Animations

In film editor's lingo, to *synchronize*, or *sync*, means to precisely match picture to sound. In Flash, sound can be synchronized to the visual content of the timeline. Flash sync affords several options for the manner in which the audio clip is related to graphics or animation on the timeline. Each of these sync options is appropriate for particular uses, which the following sections discuss.

The Sync options in the sound area of the Property inspector control the behavior of sound in Flash movies, relative to the timeline in which the sound is placed. The Sync option you choose will depend on whether your sound is intended to add dimension to a complex multimedia presentation or to add interactivity in the form of button-triggered sound, or whether it is intended to be the closely timed sound track of an animated cartoon.

Event

Event is the default Sync option for all sounds in Flash, so unless you change this default to one of the other options, the sound will automatically behave as an Event sound. Event sounds begin contemporaneously with the keyframe in which they occur and then play independently of the timeline. If an Event sound is longer than the timeline, it will continue to play even though playback on the timeline has stopped. If an Event sound requires considerable time to load, the movie will pause at that keyframe until the sound has loaded completely. Event sounds are the easiest to implement and are useful for background soundtracks and other sounds that don't need to be synced. Again, Event is the default Sync setting in the Sound menu of the Property inspector.

Caution   Event sounds can degrade into a disturbing inharmonious round of out-of-tune sound loops. If the timeline holding the Event sound loops before the sound has completed, the sound will begin again — over the top of the initial sound that has not finished playing. After several loops, this can become intolerable. To avoid this effect, use the Start Sync option.

Start

The Start Sync option is similar to an Event sound, but with one crucial difference: If any instance of that sound is already playing, then no other instance of that sound can play. In other words, the Start Sync tells the sound to begin playing only if other instances have finished playing or if it's the first instance of that sound to play. This option is useful when to avoid the layering problem discussed in the previous caution note for Event sounds.

Note Start sounds are actually a type of Event sound. Later in this chapter, when we refer to Audio Stream and Audio Event settings in the Publish Settings dialog box, realize that Start sounds belong to the Audio Event category.

Stop

The Stop Sync option is similar to the Start Sync option, except that any and all instances of the selected sound will stop playing when the Stop Sync occurs. This option comes in handy when you want to mute a specific sound in a crowd of others. For example, if you created a sound mixer with an arrangement of Button instances, you could assign the Stop Sync to a mute button for each of the sounds in the mixer.

Stream

Stream sounds are similar to a traditional track in a video-editing application. A Stream sound locks to the timeline and has priority over visual content. When Stream sound is chosen, the Flash Player attempts to pace the animation in sync with the sound. However, when animations either get too complex or are run on slower machines, the Flash Player will skip — or drop — the frames as needed to stay in sync with the Stream sound. A Stream sound will stop once the animation ends (at the end of the timeline) or, more specifically, when the Playhead reaches the last frame that includes the waveform of the Stream sound. A Stream sound can be *scrubbed*; by dragging the Playhead along the layer's frames in the Timeline window, the Stream sound will play in direct relationship to the content as it appears, frame by frame. This is especially useful for lip-sync and coordinating the perfect timing of sound effects with visual events.

Cross-Reference See Chapter 13, "Character Animation Techniques," for more information on lip-sync.

To use sound effectively, it's important to understand how Stream sounds work. When a Flash document is published as a Flash movie (.swf file) and the Sync option for a sound is set to Stream, Flash breaks the sound into chunks that are tied to the timeline. Although this is transparent to you, it is nearly the equivalent of breaking a single sound file into many separate files and adding them to the timeline as individual pieces — but that would be a lot of work. Luckily, Flash does this for you.

Tip When adding sounds to the timeline, no matter how many times you tell a Stream sound to loop, a Stream sound will stop playing wherever the visual waveform in the Timeline window ends. To extend a Stream sound's looping capacity, add as many frames as necessary to a Stream sound's layer.

Stopping Sounds

The default behavior of Event sounds is for them to play through to the end, regardless of the length of the timeline on which they exist. However, you can stop any sound, including Event sounds. Place another instance of the same sound at the keyframe where the sound should stop and assign this instance as a Stop sync option. This Stop setting can be on any layer, and it will stop all instances of the specific sound. Let's give this a try.

Stopping an Event sound

In this section, we'll show you how to stop an Event sound using two different methods. The first method will use a Stop sound on a keyframe in the Main Timeline (Scene 1). The second method will use a Button instance with a Stop sound on its Down state.

1. Create a Flash document that has an Event sound placed on the first keyframe and has enough frames on the timeline to display the entire waveform of the sound. You can use the enhanced_view.fla file from the book's CD-ROM as a practice file.

2. Create a new layer in the Timeline window, and name this layer **stop sound**.

3. On the Stop sound layer, pick a frame that's about five seconds into the sound displayed on the original layer. Create a keyframe on this frame in the Stop sound layer.

4. With this keyframe selected, open the Property inspector. In the Sound menu, chose the same sound file that was used in the original Sound layer.

5. In the Sync menu of the Property inspector, choose **Stop**. As a Stop sound, this setting will tell the Flash Player to stop any and all instances of the sound that is specified in the Sound menu.

6. Save your Flash document, and test it (Control ➪ Test Movie). When the Playhead reaches the keyframe with the Stop sound, you should no longer hear the Event sound.

Now, we'll show you how to play and mute an Event sound by clicking buttons. We'll place an Event sound on one Button symbol instance, and then a Stop sound on another Button symbol instance.

1. In a new Flash document, create a copy of the Play and Stop buttons from the Circle Buttons folder in the Buttons Library (Window ➪ Common Libraries ➪ Buttons). To do this, drag each of the buttons from the Buttons Library panel to your document's Stage. Close the Buttons Library when you are done. Rename Layer 1 to **buttons**. Your document's Stage should resemble Figure 15-4.

2. Import a sound file to use as your Event sound. You can use the atmospheres_1 sound from the book's CD-ROM.

3. In the document's Library panel, double-click the Play button to edit the symbol. In the Timeline window, create a new layer and name it **sound**.

4. Insert a keyframe on the Down state of the Sound layer.

5. Select the keyframe made in Step 4, and open the Property inspector. Select the imported sound's name in the Sound menu, and leave the Sync menu at the default Event setting. When you are finished, your document should resemble Figure 15-5.

Figure 15-4: The Play and Stop buttons on the Stage

Figure 15-5: This sound will play when the Play button is clicked.

6. Now, double-click the Stop button in the Library panel. Repeat Steps 3 through 5. This time, however, choose Stop in the Sync menu for the atmospheres_1 sound.

7. Save your document and test it (Control ➪ Test Movie). In Test Movie mode, click the Play button. You should hear the imported sound begin to play. When you click the Stop button, the sound should stop playing.

You may have noticed that, if you click the Play button repeatedly, new instances of the sound will begin to play, overlapping with the original playing sound instance. Regardless, the Stop Sync will stop all of them. If you want to prevent the Play button from enabling this type of overlap, go back to the sound keyframe on the Play button and change its Sync option to Start.

On the CD-ROM   You can find a completed example of the Play and Stop buttons exercise as **stop_sound_100.fla**, located in the ch15 folder of the book's CD-ROM.

Stopping a single instance of a Stream sound

A single instance of a Stream sound can also be stopped. To do this, simply place an empty keyframe in the Sound layer at the point where the sound should stop.

1. Open the enhanced_view.fla file, located in the ch15 folder of the book's CD-ROM.

2. Switch the layer view of the atmospheres_1 layer back to 100% in the Layer Properties dialog box.

3. Select the first frame of the atmospheres_1 layer. In the Property inspector, switch the Sync option to Stream.

4. Select frame 60 of the atmospheres_1 layer, and insert a blank keyframe (F7). This is the point where the Stream sound will stop playing.

5. Save your Flash document, and test it (Control ➪ Test Movie). Notice that the sound stops playing at frame 60. You can open your Bandwidth Profiler (View ➪ Bandwidth Profiler) in the Test Movie mode to see the Playhead move as the movie plays.

The Bandwidth Profiler also reveals a fact we touched upon earlier: Stream sounds export only the actual portion of the sound that's used in the timeline. In our example, 60 frames' worth of the atmospheres_1 sound was about 12 KB (at default MP3 compression).

Stopping all sounds

You can stop the sounds that are playing in all timelines (including Movie Clips) at any point by doing the following:

1. If there isn't already an Actions layer on your timeline, add a new layer, label it **actions**, and then select the frame that occurs at the point where you want all sounds to stop. Make this frame into a keyframe.

2. With the keyframe selected, open the Actions panel by pressing the F9 key, or by navigating to Window ➪ Actions. The title bar of the Actions panel should read Actions — Frame.

3. Make sure your Actions panel is in Normal mode. In the options menu of the panel, Normal mode should be checked. If it isn't, select this choice in the menu. Click the Actions booklet in the left pane of the panel, and then click the Movie Control booklet. Double-click the stopAllSounds action. The following ActionScript code,

```
stopAllSounds ();
```

appears in the Script pane of the Actions panel, as shown in Figure 15-6.

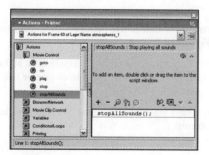

Figure 15-6: Any sound that's currently playing stops when the movie reaches a keyframe with a stopAllSounds action

4. Save your Flash document, and then test it with Control ➪ Test Movie. When the movie's Playhead reaches the frame with the `stopAllSounds` action, every sound that is currently playing will stop.

The `stopAllSounds` action stops only sounds that were playing at the time the action is executed. It will not permanently mute the sound for the duration of the movie. You can proceed to re-initialize any sounds any time after the `stopAllSounds` action has executed. If you want to stop playback again, you will have to enable another `stopAllSounds` action or use a Stop sound.

Editing Audio in Flash

Although Flash was never intended to perform as a full-featured sound editor, it does a remarkable job with basic sound editing. If you plan to make extensive use of sound in Flash, we recommend that you consider investing in a more robust sound editor. You'll have fewer limitations and greater control over your work.

In Chapter 39, "Working with Audio Applications," we discuss several popular sound editors that are commonly used in concert with Flash.

Sound-editing controls

Flash MX has basic sound-editing controls in the Edit Envelope dialog box, which is accessed by clicking the Edit button in the Property inspector. (As you may recall from previous sections, you must first select the keyframe containing the sound, and then open the Property inspector.) The Time In control and the Time Out control, or Control Bars, in Edit Envelope enable you to change the In (start) and Out (end) points of a sound. The envelope handles are used to create custom Fade In and Fade Out effects. The Edit Envelope dialog box also allows you to edit each sound channel separately if you are working with a stereo (two-channel) sound.

Edits applied to a sound file in the Edit Envelope dialog box affect only the specific instance that has been assigned to a keyframe. The original file that resides in the Flash document's library is neither changed nor re-saved.

A sound's In point is where the sound starts playing, and a sound's Out point is where the sound finishes. The Time In control and the Time Out control are used for setting or changing a sound's In and Out points. Here's how to do this:

1. Start by selecting the keyframe of the sound you want to edit, and then access the Property inspector.

2. Click the Edit button in the sound attributes area of the Property inspector to open the Edit Envelope dialog box, shown in Figure 15-7.

3. Drag the Time In control and Time Out control (located in the horizontal strip between the two channels) onto the timeline of the sound's waveform to define or restrict which section will play.

4. Use the envelope handles to edit the sound volume by adding handles and dragging them up or down to modulate the volume.

5. Click the Play button to hear the sound as edited before returning to the authoring environment. Then, rework the sound if necessary. When you've finessed the points and are satisfied with the sound, click OK to return to the Property inspector. Then save your Flash document.

Property inspector   Click the Edit button to open the Edit Envelope dialog box

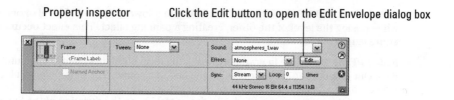

Left channel   Envelope handles

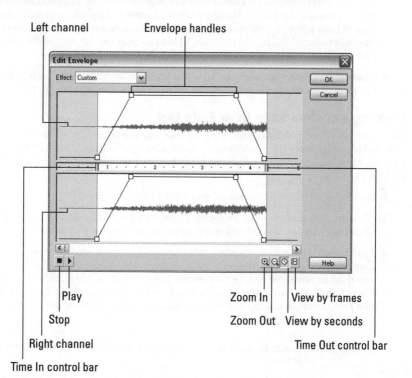

Play   Zoom In   View by frames

Stop   Zoom Out   View by seconds

Right channel   Time Out control bar

Time In control bar

Figure 15-7: The sound-editing tools and options of the Edit Envelope, which is accessed from the new Property inspector

Applying effects from the Effect menu of the Property inspector

You can apply a handful of preset fades and other effects to a sound by selecting the effect from the Effect menu located in the sound attributes area of the Property inspector. For many uses, the Flash presets will be more than sufficient, but if you find yourself feeling limited, remember that more subtle effects can be created in an external sound editor. Flash's preset effects are described in detail here:

✦ **None:** No effect is applied to either of the sound channels.

✦ **Left Channel/Right Channel:** Plays only the right or left channel of a stereo sound.

✦ **Fade Left to Right/Fade Right to Left:** This effect lowers the sound level of one channel while raising the level of the other, creating a panning effect. This effect occurs over the entire length of the sound.

✦ **Fade In/Fade Out:** Fade In gradually raises the level of the beginning of a sound clip. Fade Out gradually lowers the level at the end of a sound. The default length for either effect is approximately 25 percent of the length of the clip. We've noticed that even if the size of the selection is edited with the control bars, the duration of the Fade In/Fade Out will remain the same. (Thus, a 35-second sound clip with an original default Fade In time of nine seconds, still has a 9-second Fade In time even when the selection's length is reduced to, say, 12 seconds.) This problem can be resolved by creating a Custom Fade.

✦ **Custom:** Any time you manually alter the levels or audio handles within the Edit Envelope dialog box, Flash MX automatically resets the Effect menu to Custom.

Creating a custom Fade In or Fade Out

For maximum sound-editing control within Flash, use the envelope handles to create a custom fade or to lower the audio levels (or amplitude) of a sound. In addition to creating custom fades, the levels can be lowered creatively to create subtle, low-volume background sounds. Here's how:

1. Select the keyframe of the sound you want to edit.

2. Click the Edit button of the Property inspector to open the Edit Envelope dialog box. Click the envelope lines at any point to create new envelope handles.

3. After handles have been created, you can drag them around to create your desired volume and fading effects. The lines indicate the relative volume level of the sound. When you drag an envelope handle downward, the line slopes down, indicating a decrease in the volume level, while dragging an envelope handle upward has the opposite effect. The Edit Envelope control is limited to eight envelope handles per channel (eight for left and eight for right).

Tip   Envelope handles may be removed by dragging them outside the Edit Envelope dialog box.

Other controls in the Edit Envelope control

Other useful tools in the Edit Envelope dialog box warrant mention. See Figure 15-7 for their locations.

✦ **Zoom In/Zoom Out:** These tools either enlarge or shrink the view of the waveform, and they are particularly helpful when altering the In or Out points or envelope handles.

✦ **Seconds/Frames:** The default for viewing sound files is to represent time in seconds. But viewing time in frames is advantageous for syncing Stream sound. Toggle between viewing modes by clicking either the Seconds or Frames button at the lower right of the Edit Envelope dialog box.

The Loop option

This option appears in the Property inspector, yet a measure of its functionality occurs in conjunction with the Edit Envelope dialog box. The Loop field is used to set the number of times that a sound file will loop (or repeat). A small looping selection, such as a break beat or jazz riff, can be used for a background soundtrack. A short ambient noise can also be looped for an interesting effect. To test the quality of a looping selection, click the Edit button, which takes you to the Edit Envelope dialog box, where you can click the Play button for a preview of your loop. If the loop isn't perfect or has hiccups, use the In and Out control bars and envelope handles to trim or taper off a blank or adversely repeating section.

In Chapter 39, "Working with Audio Applications," we discuss the creation of precise loops with Sonic Foundry's ACID Pro and Propellerhead's Rebirth.

Flash links looped sounds and handles them as one long sound file (although it's really one little sound file played repeatedly). Because this linkage is maintained within the editing environment, the entire expanse of a looped sound can be given a custom effect in the Edit Envelope. For example, a simple repeating two-measure loop can be diminished over 30 loops. This is a subtle effect that performs well, yet is economical as regards file size. Note, however, that this applies only to Event sounds. See the "How Sound Is Stored in a Flash Movie" sidebar earlier in this chapter.

Sound Optimization Overview

There are several considerations to be aware of when preparing Flash sound for export. For Web-based delivery, the primary concern is to find an acceptable middle ground between file size and audio quality. But the concept of acceptability is not absolute; it is always relative to the application. Consider, for example, a Flash Web site for a record company. In this example, sound quality is likely to be more important than file size because the audience for a record company will expect quality sound. In any case, consideration of both your audience and your method of delivery will help you to determine the export settings you choose. Luckily, Flash MX has capabilities that enhance the user's experience both by optimizing sounds more efficiently and by providing improved programming features to make download delays less problematic.

We'll talk more about Flash MX's new MP3 loading features in Chapter 28, "Sharing and Loading Assets."

There are two ways of optimizing your sound for export. The quickest, simplest way is to use the Publish Settings dialog box and apply a one-setting-optimizes-all approach. This can work well if all of your sound files are from the same source. For example, if all of your sound material is speech-based, then you may be able to use global settings to encode all of your Flash sound. However, if you have a variety of sound sources in your movie, like a combination of musical scores along with narrative tracks, then the Publish Setting dialog box may not deliver the highest possible level of optimization.

If you demand that your Flash movie has the smallest possible file size, or if your Flash project includes audio from disparate sources, or uses a combination of audio types — such as button sounds, background music, speech — it's better to fine-tune the audio settings for each sound in the Library. This method gives you much better control over output.

Cross-Reference This chapter discusses the Publish features of Flash MX, which is explained in greater detail in Chapter 21, "Publishing Flash Movies."

Publish Settings for Audio

Choose File ➪ Publish Settings (Ctrl+Shift+F12 or Shift+⌘+F12) to access the Publish Settings dialog box, in order to take a global approach to the control of audio output quality. Then choose the Flash tab of the Publish Settings dialog box, shown in Figure 15-8. This tab has three areas where the audio quality of an entire Flash movie can be controlled *globally*.

New Feature You can also access the Flash tab of Publish Settings using the Property inspector. Click the document's Stage or Work area, and in the Property inspector click the Flash Player button to the right of the Publish.

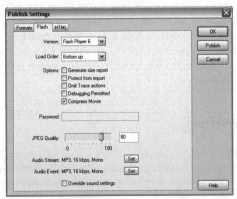

Figure 15-8: The Flash tab of the Publish Settings dialog box has five options to control audio quality.

The Flash tab of the Publish Settings dialog box has three options for controlling audio quality:

✦ **Audio Stream:** Controls the export quality of Stream sounds. To customize, click Set. This gives you a number of options, which are described in the section that follows. Flash MX supports MP3, which is the optimal streaming format, as well as a new Speech codec.

✦ **Audio Event:** Controls the export quality of Event sounds. To customize, click Set. This gives you the same number of options as the Set button for Audio Stream. These options are described in the section that follows.

✦ **Override Sound Settings:** If this box is checked, Flash uses the Publish Settings, rather than the individual audio settings that are fine-tuned in the Library panel for the current document. For more information, see the section "Fine-Tuning Sound Settings in the Library," later in this chapter.

The Set options

Audio Stream and Audio Event have individual compression settings, which can be specified by their respective Set button options. If you click either Set button on the Flash Tab, the same Sound Settings dialog box appears — it is identical for both Audio Stream and Audio Event, which means that the same options are offered for both types of sound. The Sound Settings dialog box, shown in various permutations in Figure 15-9, displays numerous settings related to the control of audio quality and audio file size. The type of compression chosen governs the specific group of settings that appear.

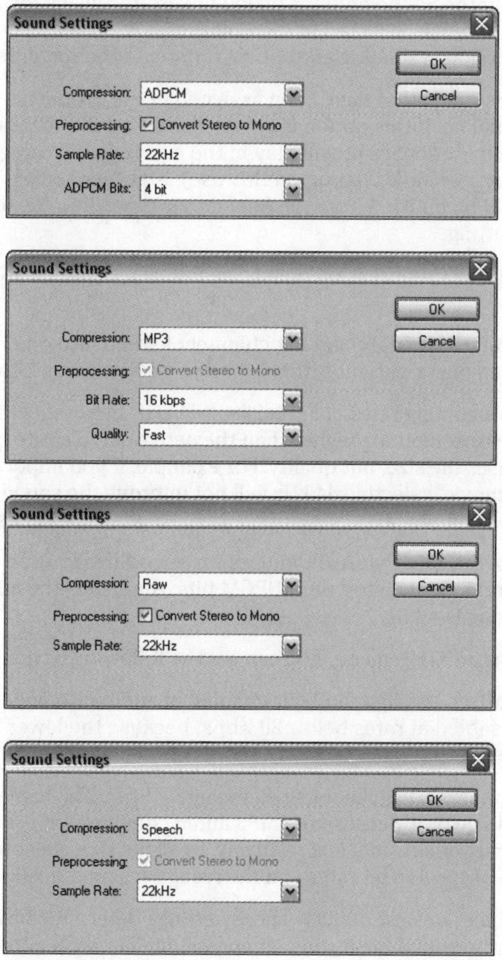

Figure 15-9: The various options in the Sound Settings dialog box

Note   The impact of individual sound settings may be overridden by another setting. For example, a Bit Rate setting of 160 Kbps may not result in good sound if the Quality is set to Fast. Optimal results require attention to *all* of the settings. This is like a set of interlinked teeter-totters: A little experimentation will reveal the cumulative or acquired impact of each setting on the others. However, the need to experiment here is hobbled by the lack of a preview mechanism. By contrast, tuning a sound in the Library is much more serviceable, because there's a sound preview button adjacent to the settings controls. For more about this work-flow, refer to the following section of this chapter, "Fine-Tuning Sound Settings in the Library."

The specific options that are available in the Sound Settings dialog boxes are always related to the compression, or audio-encoding scheme, selected in the Compression drop-down menu. That's because different compression technologies support different functionalities:

✦ **Disable:** This option turns off all sounds that have been assigned in the Property inspector to keyframes in any timeline. If this option is selected, only sound that has been linked and attached for use in ActionScript will play in the movie (see Chapter 27, "Interacting with Movie Clips," for more information on this use). All other sound sources assigned in the movie will be omitted from the final movie (.swf file). No additional options accompany this setting.

✦ **ADPCM:** With ADPCM selected in the Compression menu, the following options are available:

- **Convert Stereo to Mono:** Mixes the right and left channel of audio into one (mono) channel. In sound engineer parlance, this is known as "bouncing down."

- **Sample Rate:** Choose from sampling rates of 5, 11, 22, or 44 kHz. Increasing the sample rate of an audio file to something higher than the native sample rate of the imported file simply increases file size, not quality. For example, if you import 22 kHz sounds into the Flash movie, selecting 44 kHz will not improve the sound quality. For more information on sample rates, see Appendix B, "Digital Sound Basics."

- **ADPCM Bits:** Set the number of bits that ADPCM uses for encoding. You can choose a rate between 2 and 5. The higher the ADPCM bits, the better the audio quality. Flash's default setting is 4 bits.

✦ **MP3:** If you select MP3 in the Compression menu, you can set the following options:

- **Convert Stereo to Mono:** Mixes the right and left channel of audio into one (mono) channel. This is disabled at rates below 20 Kbps, because the lower bit rates don't allow stereo sound.

- **Bit Rate:** MP3 measures compression in kilobits per second (Kbps). The higher the bit rate, the better the audio quality. Because the MP3 audio compression scheme is very efficient, a high bit rate still results in a relatively small file size. Refer to Table 15-2 for a breakdown of specific bit rates and the resulting sound quality.

- **Quality:** Choose Fast, Medium, or Best quality. These settings determine how well Flash MX will analyze the sound file during compression. Fast will optimize the audio file in the shortest amount of time, but usually with less quality. Medium will analyze the sound waveform better than the Fast setting, but takes longer to compress. Best is the highest quality setting, taking the longest time to compress the sound file. Note that the file size of the final compressed sound will not be affected by any Quality setting—it simply instructs Flash how well it should analyze the sound during compression. The longer Flash takes to analyze a sound, the more likely the final compressed sound will capture the high highs and the low lows. If you have a fast computer processor, then we recommend you use the Best setting during your final Flash movie publish. During development and testing, you may want to use Fast to avoid long waits.

✦ **Raw:** When Raw (also known as Raw PCM audio) is selected in the Compression menu, there are two options:

  • **Convert Stereo to Mono:** Mixes the right and left channel of audio into one (mono) channel.

  • **Sample Rate:** This option specifies the sampling rate for the Audio Stream or Audio Events sounds. For more information on sample rate, please refer to Appendix B, "Digital Sound Basics."

✦ **Speech:** When the new Speech codec is selected in the Compression menu, there is only one option available: Sample Rate. Any sound compressed with the Speech codec will be converted to mono (one-channel) sound. Even though the Speech codec licensed from Nellymoser was designed for 8 kHz, Flash MX "upsamples" this codec to those frequencies supported by the Flash Player. See Table 15-3 for an overview of these sampling rates and how they affect sound quality.

Table 15-2: MP3 Bit Rate Quality

Bit Rate	Sound Quality	Good For
8 Kbps	Very bad	Best for simulated moonwalk transmissions. Don't use this unless you want horribly unrecognizable sound.
16 Kbps	Barely acceptable	Extended audio files where quality isn't important, or simple button sounds.
20, 24, 32 Kbps	Acceptable	Speech or voice.
48, 56 Kbps	Acceptable	Large music files; complex button sounds.
64 Kbps	Good	Large music files where good audio quality is required.
112–128 Kbps	Excellent	Near-CD quality.
160 Kbps	Best	Near-CD quality.

Table 15-3: Speech Sampling Quality

Sample Rate	Sound Quality	Good For
5 kHz	Acceptable	Sound playback over extremely limited data connections, like 19.2 Kbps wireless Internet modems used by mobile devices.
11 kHz	Good	Standard telephone-quality voice audio.
22 kHz	Excellent	Not recommended for general Internet use. While this setting produces higher fidelity to the original sound, it consumes too much bandwidth. For comparable sound, we recommend using a mid-range MP3 bit rate.
44 kHz	Best	See description for 22 kHz.

Tip

As a general rule, if you use the Publish Settings to control audio export globally, we recommend choosing MP3 at 20 or 24 Kbps. This will result in moderate to good sound quality (suitable for most Flash projects), and the ratio of file size-to-quality will give reasonable performance.

Supporting audio and MP3 playback

Although this is becoming less of an issue with the release of Flash MX and Flash Player 6, it may still be important to consider that MP3 is not supported by Flash Player 3 (or earlier), as well as some device players, like Flash Player 4 for the Pocket PC. There may be a number of users in your audience that haven't upgraded their Flash Player plug-in to version 4, much less to versions 5 or 6. Although it would be nice to assume that your audience will eventually upgrade, it's more realistic and advisable to consider implementing a transitional solution. For example, you could provide both a Flash 3 movie with ADPCM-encoded audio and a Flash 6 movie with MP3-encoded audio. Include information on the splash page about the benefits of Flash Player 6: reduced download time and increased audio quality. This is an incentive for users to upgrade. You'll also want to provide a link to Macromedia to download the new plug-in. Another, more "invisible" solution is to add intelligence to your splash page with a plug-in detection script that automatically serves users the movie that corresponds to the version of the Flash Player they have installed.

Cross-Reference

To add plug-in detection to your Flash movies, use one of the HTML templates installed with Flash MX. HTML templates are discussed in the "Using the HTML settings" section of Chapter 21, "Publishing Flash Movies." For custom plug-in detection solutions, refer to Chapter 22, "Integrating Flash Content with HTML," and Chapter 42, "Working with Dreamweaver MX."

In addition, you can use some new MX features in the ActionScript language to check the capabilities of the Flash Player installed on a user's system. Using the System.capabilities object, you can check to see whether an MP3 decoder is installed. The specific property is

```
System.capabilities.hasMP3
```

More importantly, though, you can script your movies to check whether the Flash Player has access to general audio output. Some devices with the Flash Player may not have any audio output. This property is

```
System.capabilities.hasAudio
```

Caution

These new additions to the ActionScript language are only available in Flash Player 6. Earlier versions of the Flash Player will not recognize these objects or properties.

Cross-Reference

You can find more detailed coverage of the System and Capabilities objects in the *Macromedia Flash* MX *ActionScript Bible*, by Robert Reinhardt and Joey Lott.

Fine-Tuning Sound Settings in the Library

The Publish Settings dialog box is convenient because it permits you to tweak a minimal set of sound adjustments, whereupon Flash exports all of your "noncustomized" Stream sounds or Event sounds at the same rate and compression. However, if you have many sounds and you are seriously concerned about obtaining the ideal balance of both optimal sound quality and minimum file size, you will need to export them at different rates and compressions. Consequently, for the fullest level of control over the way in which Flash compresses sound for delivery, we recommend that each sound be optimized, individually, in the Library panel. In fact, it would be impossible for us to overemphasize this bit of sound advice: *We recommend that each sound be optimized, individually, in the Library.*

Tip   As you become more advanced with Flash MX, particularly with ActionScript, you will likely want to store sound files in separate Flash movies (.swf files) that are individually loaded into a master Flash movie on your Web site. Also, Flash MX allows you to load MP3 files directly into movies, as they play in the Web browser. We'll discuss these features in Chapter 28, "Sharing and Loading Assets."

Settings for audio in the Library

Audio settings in the Library panel are similar to those discussed previously for the Publish Settings dialog box. These settings appear in the Sound Properties dialog box, shown in Figure 15-10. To access these settings, either (a) double-click the icon of the sound in the Library, or (b) select the sound as it appears in the Library and (i) click the Properties button, or (ii) choose Properties from the Library panel's options menu.

New Feature   Flash MX also allows you access the compression settings alone for a sound file by right-clicking (or Control+clicking on the Mac) the sound file in the Library panel. Choose Export Settings from the contextual menu, and the Sound Settings dialog box will appear. These are the same compression settings that we'll be discussing in this section.

Figure 15-10: The Sound Properties dialog box enables you to control the compression settings and to precisely balance all other related settings for each individual sound in the Library.

The top half of the Sound Properties dialog box displays status information about the sound file: To the far left is a window with the waveform of the selected audio; to the right of the waveform is an area that displays the name of the file together with its location, date, sample rate, channels, bit depth, duration, and file size.

Note The file location will indicate the full absolute path to the sound file (for example, C:\Inetpub\ wwwroot\mysound.mp3) if you save your Flash document (.fla file) in a volume or hard drive that is different than the location of the sound file.

The lower half of the dialog box is titled Export Settings. The first setting is a menu that is used to select the Compression scheme. The Compression options, and the subsequent compression-related options that appear in the other settings, are exactly the same as the sound options of the Publish Settings dialog box, discussed earlier in this chapter.

Beneath the Export Settings is where estimated results are displayed. Here, the estimated final file size (after compression) of the clip is displayed, together with the compression percentage. This is an extremely important tool that is easily overlooked.

Caution The estimated final file size is just that, an estimate. In our tests, the file size reported in the Sound Properties was consistently different from the actual file size reported by the size report generated during publishing. You can generate a text file containing detailed information about your final movie by enabling Generate size report in the Flash tab of the Publish Settings. Once enabled, you can view the size report in the Output window in Test Movie mode.

The buttons to the right of the Sound Properties dialog box offer the following options:

✦ **Update:** Click this button to have Flash check for an update of the audio file, if the original MP3, WAV, or AIFF file has been modified, and update it accordingly. Generally, this works only on the machine on which the audio file was originally imported. If you stored your files on a network server, then all the members of your Flash production should be able to use this feature.

✦ **Import:** This enables you to import another audio file into the Flash environment. The imported audio file will overwrite the existing sound displayed in the Sound Properties dialog box, but will retain the original sound's name. This feature is useful if you originally imported a placeholder or low-quality sound and need to specify a new file to be used in its place.

✦ **Test:** This excellent feature enables you to audition the export quality of the sound based on the options that you've selected from the Compression menu (and supporting options in the Export Settings).

✦ **Stop:** Click this button to stop (silence) the sound that has been auditioned using the Test button.

✦ **Help:** This launches the Flash Help system within your default Web browser.

Fine-tuning your audio in the Sound Properties dialog box of the Library panel has three benefits. Foremost of these benefits is the ability to set specific compressions and optimizations for each individual sound. Another benefit is the Test button — this is an excellent way to audition your audio file and to know what it will sound like when it is exported with different compression schemes and bit rates; hearing is believing. Finally, the estimated results, which display how each setting will affect the compressed file size, is a powerful tool that helps to obtain the desired balance of quality and file size. In contrast, optimizing sounds with the Publish Settings is more of a blind process — it is not only more global; it's also more of a painful trial-and-error method.

Combining methods for controlling sounds

One of the coolest things about Flash audio is that you can combine the two methods of controlling sounds, using both the Publish Settings and the Library panel's Sound Properties dialog box to streamline your work flow while still maintaining a relatively high degree of control over sound quality. (This method works best if you already have some experience with sound behavior in Flash.)

For example, let's assume that you have three different Event sounds in your Flash project. Two of these are simple button sounds. You decide that you won't require specialized compression for the sound used with the buttons. So, based on your prior experience of sound behavior in Flash, you go directly to the Publish Settings and set Event sounds to publish as MP3 at 48 Kbps with Best Quality.

Note   We assume that you have left the sounds used for the buttons untouched in the Library panel, leaving the Compression setting in the Sound Settings dialog box at Default. The Default option tells Flash to handle the compression for these sounds with the Publish Settings.

But the third sound is a loop of background jazz music that you want to be heard at near-CD quality. For this sound, you access the Sound Properties dialog box and try a number of combinations — and test each one — until you find a balance between file size and audio quality that pleases your ears. For example, you may decide to assign this sound to export as an MP3, stereo at 64 Kbps, with Quality set to Best.

Final Sound Advice and Pointers

Here are a few final notes about sound and some pointers to more complex sound-related topics that may help your work with sound files in Flash MX.

VBR (Variable Bit Rate) MP3

Macromedia has licensed the Fraunhofer MP3 codec, which supports streaming MP3 with a constant bit rate. However, neither Flash MX nor any Flash Player supports Variable Bit Rate (VBR), or VBR MP3, encoding for Stream sounds. VBR MP3 is a variant of MP3 that utilizes specialized algorithms to vary the bit rate according to the kind of sound that is being compressed. For example, a soprano solo would be accorded a higher bit rate than a crashing drum sequence, resulting in a superior ratio of quality to file size. There are a number of sound applications, such as the Apple iTunes, MusicMatch Jukebox, and the MP3 creation packs available for Windows XP Media Player, that export VBR MP3. If you have access to a sound application that exports VBR MP3, you'll be happy to know that you can import your VBR MP3 sound files, which are (theoretically) optimized for file size and quality beyond the compression capabilities of Flash MX, and that the compression of such files can be maintained by doing the following:

✦ In the Flash tab of the Publish Settings, leave the option to Override Sound Settings unchecked.

✦ In the Sound Properties (or Export Settings) dialog box, which is accessed from the Library panel, choose Default for the Compression option in Export Settings.

✦ The Sync option (located in the Property inspector) for the sound cannot be set to Stream.

If you choose to use VBR MP3 files in your Flash documents, you may need to test the following options of VBR compression in your MP3 creation software:

✦ **Bit rate:** Test the minimum bit rate that VBR will use for the MP3 file. Regular MP3 files use CBR, or Constant Bit Rate, which keeps the sound's bit rate steady through the entire sound file. With VBR, the bit rate can vary in ranges that you specify. Some higher bit rates like 320 Kbps may not import well into the Flash MX authoring tool.

✦ **Quality:** Most VBR-enabled MP3 software allows you to also pick an arbitrary quality setting for VBR MP3 files. Using terminology like Lowest, Medium Low, and High (and several in between) or percentages (1-100%), you can alter the quality of the bit rate. Note that this "quality" is not necessarily used in the same manner that Flash MX refers to quality for MP3 compression.

You may find that Flash MX will give you an import error for some VBR- (and CBR-) encoded MP3 files. If a particular setting created a MP3 file that couldn't import into Flash MX, then try another bit rate and/or quality combination. However, we have found that Flash MX has strange inconsistent behavior when it comes to importing MP3 files. For example, you may find that one VBR setting/combination does not work for a particular sound file, but that it works fine for others. Even more strangely, the now-defunct Macromedia Generator server software seemed to acknowledge a wider range of MP3 files than Flash 5's import feature did.

Cross-Reference

You can find more information about VBR encoding at the following URL:

`www.fezguys.com/columns/057.shtml`

We also recommend reading the "null sound" Flash tutorial at:

`www.vrprofessionals.com/html/whitepaper/nullsound.htm`

This tutorial shows you how to use a Stream sound to kick other Event sounds into streaming mode. Robert Reinhardt contributed a chapter to August de los Reyes's *Flash Design for Mobile Devices* (Hungry Minds, 2002) covering this technique.

Optimizing sounds for bandwidth usage

It goes without saying that every Internet developer strives to make every file and data transaction as small and efficient as possible to accommodate the majority of slow network connections in use today. As a Flash developer incorporating sound into your projects, you'll want to properly plan sound usage in an effort to avoid 1MB .swf file downloads.

Table 15-4 explores many of the available network bandwidths that are in use on the Internet. However, as you've likely experienced, it's highly unusual to actually get the full download (or upload) speed out of your network connection. Variables like network congestion, server load and phone line conditions affect the quality of your network speed. Using the same "formula" that Macromedia uses to determine approximate download speeds in the Bandwidth Profiler (within Test Movie mode), we calculated estimated bandwidth speeds for the connection speeds shown in Table 15-4. Since Flash MX displays compressed sound information in Kbps units, we converted these connection speeds into Kbps bit rates. More importantly, though, we also provided a 50-percent portion of this bit rate, as you'll likely need to save room for other Flash material, like vector artwork, bitmap graphics, and animations.

Using Table 15-4 as a guide, try to plan your Flash project for your target audience. Actually, you may have more than one target audience. As such, you may need to develop several versions of your sound assets, with each version targeted to a specific connection speed. File sizes in Tables 15-6 and 15-7 are listed in bytes with the size in rounded kilobytes listed below in parentheses.

Table 15-4: Bit Rates for Flash Movies

Hardware Support	Theoretical Bandwidth	Estimated Bandwidth	Percent of Theoretical	100% Bit Rate	50% Bit Rate
14.4 Kbps	1.8 KB/s	1.2 KB/s	67	9.6 Kbps	4.8 Kbps
19.2 Kbps	2.4 KB/s	1.6 KB/s	67	12.8 Kbps	6.4 Kbps
28.8 Kbps	3.6 KB/s	2.3 KB/s	64	18.4 Kbps	9.2 Kbps
33.6 Kbps	4.2 KB/s	2.8 KB/s	67	22.5 Kbps	11.2 Kbps
56 Kbps	7 KB/s	4.7 KB/s	67	37.6 Kbps	18.8 Kbps
64 Kbps	8 KB/s	5.4 KB/s	67	43.2 Kbps	21.6 Kbps
128 Kbps	16 KB/s	10.7 KB/s	67	85.6 Kbps	42.8 Kbps
256 Kbps	32 KB/s	21 KB/s	67	168 Kbps	84 Kbps
384 Kbps	48 KB/s	32 KB/s	67	256 Kbps	128 Kbps
768 Kbps	96 KB/s	64 KB/s	67	512 Kbps	256 Kbps
1.5 Mbps	192 KB/s	129 KB/s	67	1032 Kbps	516 Kbps
11 Mbps	1408 KB/s	943 KB/s	67	7544 Kbps	3772 Kbps

Once you've decided your target audience(s), you can determine the maximum Kbps that your sound files should use. Table 15-5 shows you the bit rates of Raw, Speech, and ADPCM mono sounds. We don't include MP3 bit rates here because they're already calculated (and available) for you in the Compression menu of the Sound Properties dialog box: 8, 16, 20, 24, 32, 48, 56, 64, 80, 112, 128, and 160 Kbps. In Table 15-5, bit rates that are suitable for analog modem connections (14.4, 28.8, 33.6, and 56 Kbps) are shown in bold.

Note   If you'd like to see the actual sample rate used by Flash MX's MP3 compression options, see Table 15-7.

Table 15-5: Mono Bit Rates for Streaming Sound

Sampling Rate	Raw	Speech	ADPCM 2-bit	ADPCM 3-bit	ADPCM 4-bit	ADPCM 5-bit
5 kHz	80 Kbps	**10 Kbps**	**10 Kbps**	**15 Kbps**	**20 Kbps**	**25 Kbps**
11 kHz	176 Kbps	**22 Kbps**	**22 Kbps**	**33 Kbps**	44 Kbps	55 Kbps
22 kHz	352 Kbps	44 Kbps	44 Kbps	66 Kbps	88 Kbps	110 Kbps
44 kHz	704 Kbps	88 Kbps	88 Kbps	132 Kbps	176 Kbps	220 Kbps

In Tables 15-6 and 15-7, we calculate the file sizes that one second of mono (one-channel) sound occupies in a Flash movie (.swf file). Use the values in these tables as multipliers for your sound file's actual length. For example, if you know that you have a 30-second sound-track file, the final Flash movie file size (containing just the audio) would be about 60 KB with ADPCM 3-bit, 5 kHz compression. Regardless of the actual content of the digital audio, these encodings will produce consistent file sizes based on length and resolution.

Table 15-6: File Sizes in Bytes (KB) for One Second of Mono Audio

Sample Rate	Raw	Speech	ADPCM 2-bit	ADPCM 3-bit	ADPCM 4-bit	ADPCM 5-bit
5 kHz	11037 (10.8)	1421 (1.4)	1397 (1.4)	2085 (2.0)	2774 (2.7)	3463 (3.4)
11 kHz	22061 (21.5)	2829 (2.8)	2777 (2.7)	4115 (4.0)	5532 (5.4)	6910 (6.8)
22 kHz	44109 (43.1)	5581 (5.5)	5541 (5.5)	8296 (8.1)	11051 (10.8)	13806 (13.5)
44 kHz	88205 (86.1)	11085 (10.8)	11065 (10.8)	16576 (16.2)	22086 (21.6)	27597 (27.0)

Table 15-7: File Sizes in Bytes (KB) for One Second of Mono MP3 Audio

Bit Rate	Size	Output Sample Rate	Bit Rate	Size	Output Sample Rate
8 Kbps	1263 (1.2)	11 kHz	56 Kbps	5605 (5.5)	22 kHz
16 Kbps	2511 (2.5)	11 kHz	64 Kbps	8543 (8.3)	44 kHz
20 Kbps	3135 (3.1)	11 kHz	80 Kbps	10716 (10.5)	44 kHz
24 Kbps	3369 (3.3)	22 kHz	112 Kbps	14980 (14.6)	44 kHz
32 Kbps	4487 (4.4)	22 kHz	128 Kbps	17112 (16.7)	44 kHz
48 Kbps	5605 (5.5)	22 kHz	160 Kbps	17112 (16.7)	44 kHz

Note   You may notice that some bit rate settings in Table 15-7 create the same file size for the MP3 compression. This is a known bug of Macromedia Flash MX. You may also find that the Convert Stereo to Mono option for MP3 compression does not affect the outcome of some settings.

Extracting a sound from a FLA editor file

Sometime you may be handed a Flash document (.fla file) that has sound embedded within it and told that the original sounds have either been lost or are no longer available. Here's how to extract a sound from such a file:

1. Back up the file. If the original file is named sound.fla, you might resave it as sound_extraction.fla. If you want to start with an exercise file, save a copy of the enhanced_view.fla file on the book's CD-ROM. You can skip Steps 2 through 4 if you are using this file.

2. Add a new layer in the timeline, at the top of the layer stack. Label this layer **sound extraction**. With the first frame of this layer selected, open the Property inspector. In the Sound menu, specify the sound file from the library that you wish to export.

3. Add enough frames to the Sound extraction layer so that you can see the entire wave-form of the sound file.

4. Delete all other layers.

5. Open the Library panel and locate the sound that needs to be extracted from the file. In the example file, the sound is named atmospheres_1.wav. Note that any other assets within this file are irrelevant to this process. That's because Flash will utilize only Library items that have been actually used within the movie.

6. Double-click the sound icon for atmospheres_1.wav in the Library panel to invoke the Sound Properties dialog box. Set the Compression to Raw. This ensures that the sound will be exported as uncompressed audio. Select a sample rate that matches the one listed to the right of the waveform display, near the top of the Sound Properties dialog box. If the sound is specified as a Stereo sound, make sure the Convert Stereo to Mono option is unchecked.

7. Access the Flash tab of the Publish Settings dialog box, and make sure that the Override Sound Settings check box is *not* checked.

8. Now we're ready to extract the sound file from the Flash document (.fla file). We've created a movie that will ignore all other assets in the library except this sound, and we've told Flash to export the sound with the original sample rate of the sound, as uncompressed (Raw) audio. Choose File ⇨ Export Movie, and specify a file location, name, and file type. If you're using the Windows version of Flash MX, choose WAV Audio as the file type. If you're on a Mac, choose QuickTime Video.

9. For Windows users, the Export Windows WAV dialog box appears with those sound specifications. In the Sound Format menu, make sure the audio specifications match those of your audio source in the Library panel and then click OK.

   For Mac users, the Export QuickTime Video dialog box appears. Ignore all of the options except Sound Format. In this menu, select the sound setting that matches the specifications of the sound file. For our example, this setting should be 44 kHz 16 Bit Stereo. Click OK.

10. For Windows users, the process is complete. You now have a WAV copy of your Flash movie sound asset. For Mac users, we still have a couple of steps to complete:

    1. Open the exported QuickTime movie in the QuickTime Pro Player. You must have the Pro version installed.

    2. Choose File ⇨ Export.

3. Select Sound to AIFF in the Export menu.

4. Click the Options button, and in the Sound Settings dialog box, set the Compressor to None and choose a sample rate, bit depth, and channel type that match the sound from the Flash document. For our example sound, this should be 44.1 kHz, 16 bit, and Stereo. Click OK.

5. Finally, specify a filename and location for the exported file, and click Save.

Cross-Reference

Several sound-related topics must be deferred until after our discussion of Flash MX's enhanced ActionScripting capabilities. Work your way forward to Chapter 27, "Interacting with Movie Clips," and Chapter 28, "Sharing and Loading Assets."

Summary

✦ Flash movies (.swf files) can use four types of audio compression: ADPCM, MP3, Raw, and Speech. ADPCM is compatible with all versions of the Flash Player. MP3 is compatible with most versions of Flash Player 4, 5, and 6. The Speech codec is compatible only with Flash Player 6.

✦ When sound is imported to a Flash document, it's added and displayed in the Library panel. You can assign sounds from the Library panel to a keyframe on a timeline. You can also use sounds with ActionScript.

✦ Sounds can be assigned to the Up, Over, and Down states of a Button symbol.

✦ The Sync options control how a sound will play in relation to the rest of the timeline.

✦ Use the Loop setting in the Property inspector to multiply the length of the original sound.

✦ Stream sounds force the Flash Player to keep playback of the timeline in pace with the sound.

✦ Use a `stopAllSounds` action to stop all sounds that are currently playing in the movie.

✦ The Effect menu in the Property inspector contains useful presets for sound channel playback. You can perform custom edits with the Edit Envelope dialog box.

✦ Global audio compression is controlled in the Flash tab of the Publish Settings dialog box.

✦ Use the Sound Properties dialog box in the Library panel to customize the audio compression schemes of individual sounds.

✦ The Sound Properties dialog box enables you to test different compression settings and to hear the results. Useful file size information is also provided in the Export Settings section of this dialog box.

✦ Variable Bit Rate (VBR) MP3 sound files can be brought into Flash and exported without degrading the encoding; however, Flash itself cannot encode using VBR.

✦ ✦ ✦

Importing Artwork

Although Flash gives you powerful options for creating and modifying a variety of graphics, you don't have to limit yourself to the Flash authoring environment. That's because Flash also has the capability of importing artwork from a wide range of sources. You can import both vector and raster graphics, and you can use both types in a variety of ways.

In this chapter, we discuss the differences between vector graphics and raster or bitmap images. We also show you how to import external artwork so that it can be used in a Flash movie, as well as tell you about the Flash features that can be used to handle imported bitmap images and vector graphics.

We define all the formats that Flash supports and go over some of the issues to consider when preparing artwork for import from various programs. We also introduce some new MX features that are helpful for managing imported assets and give some insight into optimizing your final file size.

Cross-Reference

This chapter focuses on importing bitmap and vector artwork. For information on creating and exporting Flash-friendly artwork in other applications, refer to Part IX, "Expanding Flash."

Defining Vectors and Bitmaps

In addition to various sound and video formats, Flash supports two types of image formats: vector and bitmap. *Vector* graphic files consist of an equation that describes the placement of points and the qualities of the lines between those points. Using this basic logic, vector graphics tell the computer how to display the lines and shapes, as well as what colors to use, where to put them on the Stage, and at what scale.

Flash is a vector program. Thus, anything that you create with the Flash drawing tools will be described in vector format. Vector graphics have some important benefits: They're small in file size and they scale accurately without distortion. However, they also have a couple of drawbacks: Highly complex vector graphics may result in very large file sizes, and vectors aren't really suitable for creating continuous tones, photographs, or artistic brushwork.

✦ ✦ ✦ ✦

In This Chapter

Defining rasters and vectors

Knowing the file formats for import to Flash

Preparing bitmaps

Importing and copying bitmaps

Importing sequences

Setting bitmap properties

Converting rasters to vectors

Using external vector graphics

Importing and copying vector artwork

Optimizing complex vector artwork

✦ ✦ ✦ ✦

Bitmap (sometimes also referred to as *raster*) files are described by an arrangement of individual pixels, which are mapped in a grid like a piece of graph paper with tiny squares. Each square represents a single pixel, and each of these pixels has specific color values assigned to it. So, as the name implies, a bitmap image maps out the placement and color of each pixel on the screen. A line is "drawn" by filling each unique pixel, rather than simply using a mathematical formula to connect two points as is done with vectors.

Note Do not be confused by the name *bitmap.* You might already be familiar with the bitmap format used by Windows, which has the file extension .bmp. Although *bitmap* may refer to that particular image format, it's frequently applied to raster images in general, such as GIF, JPEG, PICT, and TIFF files, as well as many others.

Although bitmap images aren't created in Flash, they can be used within Flash projects. To do this, you need to use an external bitmap-editing application and then import the bitmaps into Flash. Figure 16-1 shows a vector image and a bitmap image of the same logo, scaled at 100 percent.

Figure 16-1: A vector image drawn in Flash (left), and the same image imported as a bitmapped GIF graphic (right)

Although these vector and bitmap images are of similar quality when at their original size, the difference becomes more apparent when the same images are scaled to a larger size. Unlike vector graphics, bitmap images become more pixilated as they are scaled larger, because there is a finite amount of information in the image and Flash has to spread this information over more pixels. As explained later in this chapter, Flash is able to interpolate the pixel information by using Smoothing to reduce the jagged appearance of the scaled pixel pattern, but this can also cause the image to look blurred. Figure 16-2 shows the difference between vector and bitmap graphics when scaled in Flash with Smoothing turned off.

Figure 16-2: The same vector (left) and bitmap (right) image scaled to 200 percent in Flash to illustrate the difference in image quality

Simple bitmap images are often larger in file size than simple vector graphics, but very complex bitmap images (for example, a photograph) can be smaller and display better quality than vector graphics of equal complexity. Figure 16-3 shows a bitmap image, compared to a vector image of equal complexity (created by tracing the bitmap). The original bitmap is a smaller file and better suited for reproducing the photographic image.

Original bitmap 16KB   Traced vector image 198KB

Figure 16-3: File size comparison of an imported bitmap image (left), and a traced vector image of equivalent complexity (right)

The general rule of thumb is to use scalable, bandwidth-efficient vector graphics as much as possible within Flash projects, except for situations in which photographs — or photographic-quality, continuous-tone images — are necessary for special content.

Tip   Most 8-bit raster images are GIFs, and they are most frequently used for images with large areas of solid color, such as logos and text. Rather than use this image type in Flash, consider re-creating or tracing this artwork with Flash drawing tools. The final Flash movie (.swf) will not only be smaller, it will also look cleaner and be scalable.

Knowing the File Formats for Import to Flash

You can import a variety of assets (in compatible formats) directly into your Flash project library, or you can import or copy and paste from another application into the Flash Document window. Assets can also be dragged from one Flash Document window or library to another. Files must be a minimum size of 2 pixels by 2 pixels for import into Flash.

Caution   Copying and pasting bitmap images into Flash from other applications does not always transfer transparency settings, so it may not be the best workflow for some assets. Using the Import dialog box and specifying that the artwork be imported as an editable object will preserve transparency settings from Macromedia Fireworks.

Cross-Reference   For a complete listing of all media formats supported by Flash MX, refer to Bonus Appendix A, "Flash-Compatible Media Formats," on the CD-ROM. For a full discussion of importing and handling sound assets, refer to Chapter 15, "Adding Sound." For coverage of other bitmap and vector applications, refer to Chapter 37, "Working with Raster Graphics," and Chapter 38, "Working with Vector Graphics," respectively.

For now, we will focus strictly on image formats for Flash import, as shown in Table 16-1.

Table 16-1: Image Formats for Flash Import

File Type	Extension	Description	Platform
Adobe Illustrator/	.ai, .eps	Adobe Illustrator files are imported into Flash as vector graphics (unless they contain bitmap images).	Windows Macintosh
AutoCAD DXF	.dxf	Drawing eXchange format is the original inter-program format for AutoCAD drafting software. Because this format does not support fills, it is mainly used for drafting plans or schematic drawings. This format is used by most CAD, 3D, and modeling programs for transferring drawings to other programs.	Windows Macintosh
Bitmap	.bmp, .dib	Bitmap is a Windows format for bitmap images. Don't be confused by the format name—not all bitmap images are Windows Bitmaps. Can be used with all Win and some Mac applications. Allows variable bit depths and compression settings with support of alpha channels. Supports lossless compression. Ideal for high-quality graphics work.	Windows Macintosh (only with QuickTime4 or later)
Enhanced Metafile	.emf	Enhanced Metafile is a proprietary Windows format that supports vectors and bitmaps internally. This format is occasionally used to import vector graphics, but for most professional graphics work this is not a recommended format.	Windows
Flash Player	.swf, .spl	Flash Player files are exported Flash movies. The movie is flattened into a single layer and scene, and all animation is converted to frame-by-frame animation.	Windows Macintosh
FreeHand	.fh7, .fh8, .fh9, fh10	This is the vector-based format of Macromedia's FreeHand 7, 8, 9, or 10.	Windows Macintosh
GIF image or animated GIF	.gif	Graphic Interchange Format (GIF), was developed by Compuserve as a bitmap image type that uses lossless compression. Limited to a 256-color (or less) palette. Not recommended as a high-quality Flash export format, even for Web use.	Windows Macintosh
JPEG image	.jpg	Joint Photographic Experts Group (JPEG) images are a bitmap type that uses lossy compression. Supports 24-bit RGB color. Recommended for Web-friendly compression of photographic images. Because of small file size, JPEG is often the native format for digital still cameras. No support for alpha channels.	Windows Macintosh
MacPaint image	.pntg	This is a legacy format for the old Mac Paint program.	Windows (with QT4) Macintosh (with QT4)

File Type	Extension	Description	Platform
PICT image	.pct, .pict	Compatible with many Win and all Mac applications. Allows variable bit depths and compression settings with support of alpha channels (when saved with no compression at 32 bits). Supports lossless compression. Can contain vector or raster graphics. Ideal for high-quality graphics work.	Windows (with QT4) Macintosh
PNG image	.png	The Portable Network Graphic (PNG) format is another type of bitmap image that supports variable bit depth (PNG-8 and PNG-24) and compression settings with alpha channels. PNG files imported to Flash from Macromedia Fireworks as editable objects (unflattened), will preserve artwork in vector format. Lossless compression schemes make it ideal for high-quality graphics work. The recommended media type for imported images with alpha channels.	Windows Macintosh
Photoshop image (2.5 or higher)	.psd	This is the layered format for most versions of Photoshop—from version 2.5 through version 6. Although it is possible to import PSD files, it's not the best alternative. If you have the PSD, open it in Photoshop, optimize it for use in Flash, and then export it as either a JPEG or a PNG for ideal import into Flash.	Windows (with QT4) Macintosh (with QT4)
QuickTime image	.qtif	This is the static raster image format created by QuickTime. Not commonly used.	Windows (with QT4) Macintosh (with QT4)
QuickTime movie	.mov	QuickTime is a video format created by Apple Computers. Flash MX now supports embedded QuickTime video as well as linked QuickTime video.	Windows (with QT4) Macintosh (with QT4)
Silicon Graphics image	.sgi	This is an image format specific to SGI machines.	Windows (with QT4) Macintosh (with QT4)
TGA image	.tga	The TGA, or Targa, format is a 32-bit format that includes an 8-bit alpha channel. It was developed to overlay computer graphics and live video.	Windows (with QT4) Macintosh (with QT4)
TIFF image	.tif or .tiff	TIFF is a lossless, cross-platform image type used widely for high-resolution photography and printing.	Windows (with QT4) Macintosh (with QT4)
Windows Metafile	.wmf	Windows Metafile is a proprietary Windows format that supports vectors and bitmaps internally. This format is generally used to import vector graphics.	Windows

Continued

Table 16-1: *(continued)*

File Type	Extension	Description	Platform
Toon Boom Studio file	.tbp	Vector format for files created with Toon Boom Technologies proprietary animation software. Preserves layers/scenes/sound etc. Imported with support from the Toon Boom Studio Importer plug-in (TBSi) shipped with Flash MX.	Macintosh (with TBSi) Windows (with TBSi)

Caution   Although you can export to the GIF format from Flash, this should be considered as an option for raw information transfer only—and not as a means for creating final GIF art. For optimal quality and control, GIFs exported from Flash should be brought into Fireworks for fine-tuning and optimization. A preferable workflow is to export a PNG sequence from Flash that can be brought into Fireworks for fine-tuning and final GIF output.

Preparing Bitmaps

Flash is a vector-based application, but that shouldn't stop you from using bitmaps when you *need* to use a bitmap. There are many situations in which either the designs or the nature of the content require that photographic images be included in a Flash project. You can import a wide variety of bitmap image types, including JPEG, GIF, BMP, and PICT using the methods described in the next section.

Considering that it's a vector-based program, Flash supports bitmap graphics extraordinarily well. However, because the most common use of Flash movies is for Web presentations, you always need to keep file size in mind. Here's what you can do to limit the impact of bitmap images on Flash playback performance:

✦ Limit the number of bitmaps used in any one frame of a Flash movie.

✦ Remember that, regardless of how many times the bitmap is placed on the Stage, the actual bitmap (or its compressed version in the .swf file) is downloaded before the first occurrence of the bitmap (or its symbol instance).

✦ Try spreading out bitmap usage, or hide a symbol instance of the bitmap in an earlier frame before it is actually visible, so that it will be loaded when you need it.

Tip   If you need to include several high-resolution bitmap images in your Flash movie, consider using an ActionScript preloader or try breaking up the Flash movie into several linked Flash movies.

Cross-Reference   For an example of an optimized Flash movie structure that uses an ActionScript preloader and multiple .swf files, see Chapter 32, "Creating a Portfolio Site in Flash."

When you want to bring raster images into Flash documents, you should know what portion of the Flash Stage the image will occupy. Let's assume that you're working with the default Flash document size of 550×400 pixels. If you want to use a bitmap as a background image, it won't need to be any larger than 550×400 (as long as your movie will not be scaleable.) So, assuming that you're starting with a high-resolution image, you would downscale the image to the largest size at which it will appear in the Flash movie *before* you import it into Flash; for our example, that would be 550×400.

Use an image-editing program such as Macromedia Fireworks or Adobe Photoshop to down-size the pixel width and height of your original image if necessary.

Raster Images: Resolution, Dimensions, and Bit Depth

Resolution refers to the amount of information within a given unit of measurement. Greater res-olutions mean better quality (or more image information). With respect to raster images, resolu-tion is usually measured in pixels per inch (when viewed on a monitor) or dots per inch (when output on film or paper).

What is resolution?

The resolution of an original image changes whenever the scale of the image is changed, while the pixel dimensions remain fixed. Thus, if an original photograph is scanned at 300 pixels per inch (ppi) with dimensions of 2"×2", subsequently changing the dimensions to 4"×4" will result in a resolution of 150 ppi. Although a 4"×4" image at 300 ppi could be interpolated from the original image, true resolution will be *lost* as an image is scaled larger. When an image is digitally enlarged, the graphics application simply doubles existing pixel information, which can create a softened or blurred image. Reducing the scale of an image has few undesirable side effects — although a much smaller version of an original may lose some fine details.

Because all raster images consist of pixels, and because resolution simply describes how many pixels will be arranged in a given area, the most accurate way of referencing raster images is by using the absolute pixel width and height of an image. For example, a 4000×5000 pixel image could be printed or displayed at any size with variable resolutions. This image could be 4"×5" at 1000 ppi, or it could be 8"×10" at 500 ppi — without any loss of information. Remember that res-olution simply describes how much information is shown per unit. When you reduce the pixel width and height of an image, the resolution is lowered accordingly and after any pixels are thrown out, discarded, or interpolated, they're gone for good.

Raster images: Bit depth

Bit depth is an important factor that influences image quality and file size. *Bit depth* refers to the amount of information stored for each pixel of an image. The most common bit depths for images are 8-bit and 24-bit, although many others exist. An 8-bit image contains up to 256 colors, while a 24-bit image may contain 16.7 million color values. Depending on their file format, some images can also use an 8-bit alpha channel, which is a multilevel transparency layer. Each addition to an image's bit-depth is reflected in a considerable file size increase: A 24-bit image contains three times the information per pixel as an 8-bit image. Mathematically, you can calculate the file size (in bytes) of an image with the following formula (all measurements are in pixels):

```
width×height×(bit depth ÷ 8) = file size
```

Note: You divide bit depth by 8 because there are 8 bits per byte.

When importing 8-bit images in formats such as GIF, BMP, and PICT, it is preferable to use the default Lossless (PNG/GIF) compression setting in Bitmap Properties to avoid adding Flash's default Publish Settings Quality 24-bit JPEG compression. 8-bit images that use Web-Safe color palettes will ensure greater display predictability for people viewing your Flash artwork on older systems with 8-bit video cards.

If you mask bitmaps with a Mask layer in the Flash timeline, the entire bitmap is still exported. Consequently, before import you should closely crop all images that will be masked in Flash. For example, if all you need to show is a face, crop the image so that it shows the face with as little extraneous background information as possible.

Be aware that Flash doesn't resize (or resample) an image to its viewed or placed size when the Flash movie (.swf) is created. To illustrate how the size of an imported bitmap can impact the size of a final Flash movie (.swf), we compared two different image resolutions used in identical layouts. Using the same source image, we sized the JPEG at two different pixel dimensions, and then placed it in two identical Flash documents (.fla). The first version of the image had a 400×600 pixel dimension, while the second version had a 200×300 pixel dimension — exactly half the size of the first. In both Flash documents, the final image was displayed at 200×300 pixels.

In one Flash document (we'll call it Movie A), the larger JPEG was imported and resized by 50 percent (using the Info panel) to match the smaller image. In the other Flash document (Movie B), the smaller JPEG was imported and placed at its original size, occupying the same portion of the Flash Stage as the image in Movie A. Although both Flash movies contained a bitmap of the same display size on the Flash Stage, the resulting .swf files (using the same level of JPEG compression on export) had drastically different file sizes. Movie A was 44.1KB, whereas Movie B was 14.8KB! Movie A is nearly three times larger than Movie B. The difference in image resolution could be seen when a view magnification greater than 100 percent was used within the Flash Player, the larger JPEG in Movie A was much less pixilated than the smaller JPEG in Movie B.

Preserving Bitmap Quality

When you choose to use bitmap images, remember that they won't scale as well as vector drawings. Furthermore, bitmaps will become degraded if the viewer scales your movie so that the bitmap is displayed larger than its original size. Here are a few points to consider so that you can avoid this, or at least minimize the effects:

✦ Know your audience and design for the largest screen (at the highest resolution) that your audience may have. Or, if you deviate from this, remember that audience members with optimal equipment will see a low-quality version of your work. If you're using ActionScript to load image assets, consider having low-res and high-res versions of the images available.

✦ Measure your largest hypothetical image dimensions in pixels. One way to determine these dimensions is to use the Flash Info panel to read the size of a placed image or a place-holder shape. Another way is to take a screen capture of your mock-up, and then measure the intended image area in Photoshop.

✦ Create or resize your bitmap image to the maximum hypothetical dimensions. If there are any rotations or skews required, it is better to do these within your image-editing application — prior to importing bitmaps into Flash.

✦ Import images into Flash at the maximum required size, and then scale them down to fit into your layout.

The advantage of using this approach is that the movie can be scaled for larger monitors without causing the bitmap image to degrade. The disadvantage is that it requires sending the same large bitmap to all users. A more sophisticated solution is to use JavaScript to detect browser dimensions and then send the appropriately scaled bitmaps to each user.

Other workaround solutions that may help preserve the quality of your final presentation include the following:

✦ Restrict scaling capability of your published movie. This can be done using HTML options in the Publish Settings or using ActionScript.

For coverage of Publish Settings refer to Chapter 21, "Publishing Flash Movies." For coverage of advanced options for controlling Flash movies including the Stage object, refer to the *Macromedia Flash MX ActionScript Bible* by Robert Reinhardt and Joey Lott.

✦ Set the bitmap's compression to Lossless (GIF/PNG) if it is already optimized in GIF format.

✦ Trace the bitmap to convert it to a vector graphic (covered later in this chapter).

✦ Never apply double JPEG compression to your images. If you have compressed and saved images in JPEG format outside of Flash, be certain to select the **Use imported JPEG data** check box when importing the images to Flash.

Before sizing and importing bitmaps, you need to consider how you will set the dimensions for the Flash movie (.swf) in the HTML tab of the Publish Settings dialog box. You also need to know whether the bitmap is to be scaled in a motion tween. If the Flash movie scales beyond its original pixel width and height (or if the bitmap is scaled larger in a tween), then bitmap images will appear at a lower resolution with a consequent degradation of image quality.

Scaling of Flash movies is discussed in Chapter 21, "Publishing Flash Movies," and Chapter 22, "Integrating Flash Content with HTML."

If you're uncertain of the final size that you need for a bitmap in Flash, it may be best to import a temporary low-resolution version of the image—being careful to store your original high-resolution version where you can find it later. Convert the imported low-resolution bitmap into a Graphic symbol in Flash. Whenever you need to place the bitmap, drag an instance of the symbol onto the Flash Stage. Then, during final production and testing, after you've determined what pixel size is required for the maximum scale of the final bitmap, create and import a higher-resolution image, as follows:

1. Double-click the icon of the original low-resolution bitmap in the Flash Library to access the bitmap's properties.

2. In the Bitmap Properties dialog box, click the **Import** button and select the new, higher-resolution version of the bitmap.

3. Upon re-import, all symbols and symbol instances will update automatically, with all the scaling, animation, and placement of the image maintained.

Importing and Copying Bitmaps

When importing bitmaps, Flash supports all the formats that QuickTime supports—as long as QT4 or later is installed (refer to Table 16-1). However, the implementation of this reliance upon QuickTime can be confusing the first time you try it. If you attempt to import any previously unsupported format, the dialog box shown in Figure 16-4 appears. If you click **Yes**, the image is imported as a bitmap. According to Macromedia, you will always get this warning so you'll be aware when QuickTime is used to complete the import, and there are no adverse consequences to importing files in this manner.

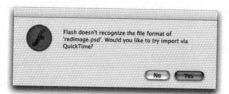

Figure 16-4: This warning dialog box appears when a file format that requires QuickTime support is imported to Flash.

Importing a bitmap file into Flash

Flash MX has added the option to import directly to the document Library in addition to the standard option of importing to the Document Stage. When a bitmap file is imported to the Stage, it will still be listed in the Library as well. To import a bitmap into Flash, follow these steps:

1. If you want to import an item to the Document Stage, make sure that there's an active, unlocked layer. If no layer is available for placement of the imported item, the Import command is dimmed and you will only be able to use the Import to Library option.

2. Select File ➪ Import (Ctrl+R or ⌘+R) or File ➪ Import to Library.

3. The Import (or the Import to Library) dialog box opens. Navigate to the file that you'd like to import, select it, and click the **Open** button.

The Import dialog box, shown in Figure 16-5, and the Import to Library dialog box are identical, except that Import to Library will place the asset directly into the document Library without placing an instance on the Stage. Remember that any file that requires QuickTime support will invoke the dialog shown in Figure 16-4 — in that case, it's okay to click **Yes**; the file should import correctly.

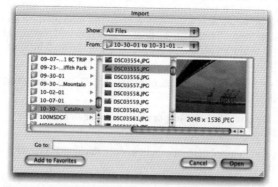

Figure 16-5: The Import dialog box as it appears on Mac. Multiple files can be imported in the same batch by selecting them from the file list in the Import Browser window.

Because Flash offers full support for the PNG image format (including lossless compression and multilevel transparency), PNG is an ideal format for images that you intend to import into Flash. The PNG format has two types, PNG-8 and PNG-24. Generally, only PNG-24 images support 24-bit color and an alpha channel, but the file sizes can often be prohibitive. Macromedia Fireworks makes it possible to create PNG-8 files with transparency for import to Flash.

The PNG format is discussed in depth in Chapter 37, "Working with Raster Graphics."

When using bitmap images with transparent areas, display problems can occasionally occur with certain color settings and file types. For troubleshooting assistance, refer to the Macromedia TechNote on "Transparency Support in Flash" at: www.macromedia.com/support/flash/ts/documents/transparent_bitmaps.htm.

Importing sequences

When using the Import dialog box, if you have a series of images in the same storage location that include sequential numbers at the end of their filenames, Flash prompts you to import the files as a sequence. If that's what you want to do, select **Yes** from the dialog box to have Flash import all the files and place them into numeric sequence in successive keyframes on the current timeline. Otherwise, select **No**, and only the single file that you've selected will be imported.

If you are importing a series of stills to be used sequentially to create animation (stills from a video sequence for example), this feature can save a lot of time spent placing and ordering images manually. The most efficient workflow is to create a Movie Clip symbol before importing the images, so that the sequence can be imported directly to the Movie Clip timeline. This method creates an animated element that can easily be placed anywhere in your Flash project. If you have already imported a sequence to the Main Timeline and decide that it would be more easily managed as a symbol, simply create a Movie Clip, then cut the images from the Main Timeline and paste them into the Movie Clip timeline.

For more coverage on how to create bitmap sequences from QuickTime video, refer to Chapter 41, "Working with QuickTime."

Although sequential import is not an option when using Import to Library, it is possible to manually select multiple images for import while using either of the Import dialog boxes. In order to bring more than one file into Flash in the same batch, Shift+click to select multiple items in sequence or use Ctrl+click (or ⌘+click) to select multiple non-sequential items in the file list window of the Import dialog box.

Copying and pasting a bitmap into Flash

Here's how to use the clipboard to import a bitmap into Flash:

1. Copy the bitmap from your image-editing application.

2. Return to Flash and make sure that you have an active, unlocked layer that you can paste the bitmap into, this can be on the Main Timeline or on any symbol timeline.

3. Paste the bitmap onto the stage by selecting Edit ➪ Paste from the menu (Ctrl+V or ⌘+V).

When pasting a selected area from Photoshop, any transparency (alpha channel) is ignored.

Setting Bitmap Properties

The Bitmap Properties dialog box, shown in Figure 16-6, has several options that are used to control the quality of your imported bitmaps. Settings in the Bitmap Properties dialog box will override the default JPEG compression setting for the document that is controlled in the Flash tab of the Publish Settings dialog box (File ➪ Publish Settings).

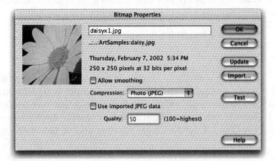

Figure 16-6: The Bitmap Properties dialog box controls the compression settings applied to bitmaps imported into Flash.

Follow these steps to use the Bitmap Properties dialog box:

1. Open the document's Library panel with Window ➪ Library to access bitmaps in your current project (.fla).

2. Double-click one of the bitmap's icons, or use the contextual menu to open the Bitmap Properties dialog box. You can also select Properties from the Library options menu or, with the bitmap highlighted, click the Properties button. Now, set the properties of your bitmap as needed:

    • **Preview Window:** This displays the bitmap according to the current settings.

Tip   Although the preview window in the Bitmap Properties dialog box may only show a small portion of your image, you can move the picture around within the preview window by clicking and dragging the image to view different areas.

    • **Name:** This is the name of the bitmap, as indicated in the Library. To rename the bitmap, highlight the name and enter a new one.

    • **Image Path, Date, Dimensions:** Beneath the filename, Flash lists the local path, dimensions, and date information for the source of the imported image (not available if you pasted the image from the clipboard).

    • **Update:** This feature enables you to re-import a bitmap if it's been altered outside of Flash. Flash tracks the original location of the imported bitmap and will look for the original file in that location when the Update button is clicked.

    • **Import:** This opens the Import Bitmap dialog box. When using this button, the new imported bitmap will replace the current bitmap (and all instances, if any), while retaining the original bitmap's name and all modifications that have been applied to the bitmap in Flash.

- **Test:** This button updates the file compression information, which appears at the bottom of the Bitmap Properties dialog box and the image in the Preview window. Use this information to compare the compressed file size to the original file size after you have selected new settings.

- **Compression Type drop-down:** The compression setting enables you to set the bitmap's compression to either Photo (JPEG) or Lossless (PNG/GIF). Photo is good for very complex bitmap images (photographs for example); Lossless is better for graphic bitmap images with simple shapes and fewer colors. Play around with these settings to see which works best to give you a balance between file size and image fidelity for each particular image. Figure 16-7 shows a comparison of these two settings applied to an imported GIF file (top) and applied to an imported JPEG image (bottom). The GIF with default lossless compression is only 4.7KB. Applying a reduced JPEG Quality compression of 50 results in a larger file size (7KB) for a worse-looking image. Conversely, the JPEG with a Quality of 50 is only 9KB, while the JPEG forced to lossless compression is 145.6KB, without a huge difference in display quality.

Figure 16-7: *Top:* A GIF file imported to Flash using PNG/GIF (Lossless) compression (left) and imported with forced JPEG (Lossy) compression (right); *Bottom:* A JPEG file imported to Flash using JPEG (Lossy) compression (left) and imported with forced PNG/GIF (Lossless) compression (right)

- **Use imported JPEG data/Use Document default quality:** If the imported image is a JPEG, the first option will appear—select this check box to avoid double-JPEG compression. If the image is not a JPEG, the second option will appear—select this check box to apply the global JPEG Quality setting defined in the Publish Settings dialog box for your current document. To select a new compression setting for an image, clear the check box beside Use imported JPEG data or Use Document default quality and enter a new setting between 1 and 100 in the Quality value field. This is not recommended for imported JPEGs because it will result in double JPEG compression. On uncompressed source files, higher Quality settings will produce better quality images but also larger file sizes. Figure 16-8 includes a JPEG published with imported data and a JPEG published with a reduced Quality setting (double JPEG compression).

- **Allow Smoothing (anti-aliasing):** Select this check box to enable Flash to anti-alias, or smooth, the edges of an image. Results may vary according to the image. Generally, this is not recommended because it blurs an image. However, Smoothing can be beneficial for reducing jagged edges on low-res images scaled in an animation. Figure 16-9 shows the effect of smoothing applied to a GIF image (top), and smoothing applied to a JPEG image (bottom).

3. Click **OK**. All copies of this bitmap used in Flash are updated to the new settings.

For specific bitmap compression recommendations for different types of source files, please refer to the section on Bitmap compression guidelines that follows later in this chapter.

Document (.fla)

Movie (.swf)

Use imported JPEG data   JPEG quality 50

Figure 16-8: The same bitmap image as it displays (A) in the Flash document (.fla), and (B) in the published Flash move (.swf) using imported JPEG data (left) and using a reduced Quality setting of 25 (right)

Being Prepared for Common Problems

Flash retains existing JPEG compression levels on any imported JPEG image, but, if specified in the Bitmap Properties dialog box, it applies additional JPEG compression (set in the Quality field) when the movie is published or exported. Recompressing an image that has already been compressed usually leads to serious image degradation, due to the introduction of further compression artifacts. When importing JPEGs, you'll note that the Use imported JPEG data check box is selected by default in the Bitmap Properties dialog box. This is the preferred setting because Flash has a relatively generic JPEG compression engine, which is usually less effective than Fireworks or Photoshop, and because recompressing a JPEG is generally detrimental to image quality.

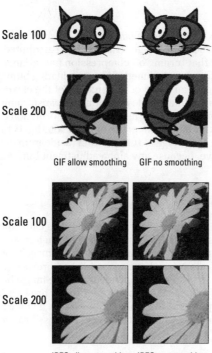

Scale 100

Scale 200

GIF allow smoothing   GIF no smoothing

Scale 100

Scale 200

JPEG allow smoothing   JPEG no smoothing

Figure 16-9: Compare the images with Flash smoothing (left) to the images with no smoothing (right).

Tip

If you import JPEG images, make sure that you either test the results of further JPEG compression or else select the Use imported JPEG data check box in the Bitmap Properties dialog box, which is accessible from the Flash Library.

You can apply compression settings to each individual bitmap in the Library with the Flash Bitmap Properties dialog box to determine the quality that you need before you use the general JPEG settings in the Export Movie or Publish Settings dialog box. Any Quality defined in the Bitmap Properties dialog box will override the JPEG Quality in Publish Settings. To apply the Publish Settings compression to an image, you must select the Use document default check box in the Bitmap Properties dialog box.

Note

Flash JPEG compression is not displayed in your authoring view (.fla). To see how additional compression is affecting an imported image, you either have to refer to the preview image in the Bitmap Properties dialog box, or test your movie (.swf) to see how the final image displays after Flash compression is applied.

Cross-Reference

You'll find JPEG export settings for Flash movies (.swf files) discussed in greater detail in Chapter 21, "Publishing Flash Movies."

Bitmap shift

There is a known problem in Flash that's referred to as *bitmap shift,* in which colors may shift slightly from one instance to another of the same image. This has been attributed to several causes. Some developers have reported that turning off compression has, at times, eliminated problems with bitmap shift. Another reported method for eliminating bitmap shift is to make the image a symbol, and then assign it an alpha of 99 percent. Yet the clearest explanation and fix are as follows: Flash renders a bitmap while animating or transforming it, and then re-renders the bitmap as a static image when the motion or transformation ceases. Often, the two don't quite match. From this perspective, the optimal solution is to set the final bitmap's scaling to 99 percent. The advantage of this solution (aside from the fact that it works) is that it's less processor intensive, because any alpha adjustment burdens the processor with additional computations.

Cross-browser consistency

We've received more than a few queries about image formats and Flash's capability to transcend issues of browser inconsistency, so here's the answer. Many image formats, such as .png, are not supported across all browsers. When you import such an image format into Flash and publish or export to the .swf format, you have accomplished browser independence — because the Flash movie (.swf) is browser independent and the image has been encapsulated within the .swf format. (The image is not being sent to the browser in the imported format and then magically empowered to display.) Conversely, if you export any Flash document (.fla) to .png or to any other format that's subject to cross-browser inconsistency, browser independence is lost.

JPEG rotation

This is perhaps the trickiest problem to analyze. When animation that includes a bitmap is resolved and the image is displayed at an angle, it can be distorted — regardless of whether it was rotated in Photoshop and imported with the angle. Or if it was imported into Flash on the square and subsequently rotated, the manner of the distortion changes, but not the perception of distortion!

✦ When rotated in Flash, hard edges, such as text, may appear choppy — as if they had been cut out with pinking shears. Yet, when zoomed, this effect is less problematic.

✦ When rotated in Photoshop, prior to import into Flash, hard edges are less choppy. Although the file will increase (to accommodate the larger overall shape), the background will become a fixed color, and a certain flutter may occur along the edges of the transition between the background and the image. Yet, other straight lines and text will appear smoother and more acceptable. However, at 200 percent zoom, text looks worse than the same image rotated in Flash.

Before rotating a bitmap in Flash, you should perform a few tests to see how your specific bitmap will be affected by the combination of compression, zoom, smoothing, and rotation (either in or out of Flash). Your choices and your decision will vary, subject to the nature of the bitmap and the manner in which it will be used within Flash.

Using the Bitmap Buttons in the Property Inspector

When a bitmap is selected in the Document window, the new Flash MX Property inspector displays the bitmap's name, symbol type, current size, and X, Y location. In addition to these basic bitmap properties, the Property inspector offers two useful options — the Swap button and the Edit button.

Swap

The Swap button invokes the Swap Bitmap dialog box, allowing you to specify a different bitmap from the current project Library to replace the bitmap selected in the Document window. This can be considered a localized equivalent of the Import option of the Bitmap Properties dialog box. Rather than replacing the original bitmap symbol in the Library and all instances of the image, the Swap button will simply replace the currently selected bitmap instance without altering the symbols in the Library or any of the other instances of the bitmap that may occur in your project.

Edit

The Edit button of the Property inspector will open the selected bitmap for editing outside of Flash, either in your default image editing application or the application that was used to save the bitmap file, if it is installed on your system. After you edit the image and choose Save, it will automatically be updated in the Flash document. If you prefer to select a specific application for editing a bitmap, select the bitmap in the Library before choosing Edit With from the options menu or the contextual menu. The Edit With menu item launches the Select External Editor dialog box that allows you to browse or search for a specific application installed on your system (or network). When you have selected the application of your choice, it will be launched and the bitmap is opened for editing.

Note   Bitmaps imported from Fireworks as PNG files specified as editable objects cannot be edited in an external image editor.

Making Sense of Bitmap Compression

Although we did some sample testing to try to show you all the possible image-compression combinations and the final results, the truth is that the optimal settings are entirely dependent on the quality of the original image and the final appearance needed in the context of your design. The main goal when testing various compression strategies should always be to find a balance between image quality and file size. The ideal balance will vary depending on the purpose the image serves in your presentation. For example, when using bitmap images in animation sequences, you may find that you can get away with using higher compression settings because the detail in the image may not be as important as it would be if the image was used in a catalogue or some other presentation where the detail and color would be more critical.

The following compression workflows are intended to serve only as general guidelines. You will have to experiment with the specific value settings in each case to find the best results for your particular content and project needs.

24-bit or 32-bit lossless source files

If you have 24-bit (or 32-bit including an alpha channel), high-resolution source images saved without compression in PNG-24, PICT, or TIFF format, you have two workflow options.

✦ **Set JPEG compression in Bitmap Properties dialog box:** If you want to control the compression applied to each imported image individually, clear the Use document default quality check box in the Bitmap Properties dialog box and choose a JPEG compression setting that achieves the best balance of image quality and file size for each imported image in your Library. This approach gives you the option of applying more compression to some images than to others.

✦ **Set JPEG compression in Publish Settings dialog box:** If your source images have similar color and content, as well as consistent resolution, you may find it more efficient to use the compression settings in the Publish Settings dialog box to apply the same JPEG compression to all of your images. This makes it faster to test different compression settings on all the images in your project at once. If this is the workflow that you choose, make sure that the Use document default quality check box is selected in the Bitmap Properties dialog box for each imported image—this will ensure that the Quality settings in the Publish Settings dialog will be applied when the Flash movie (.swf) is published.

The main benefit to importing uncompressed source files is that you will not be tied to a specific resolution and thus will maintain the option of changing compression settings at any time in the development process. The main drawback is that your project files (.fla) will be much larger, and each time you test your movie (.swf), you will have to wait for Flash to apply JPEG compression on the images. This might not seem important at first, but the cumulative time loss over the course of developing a project does add up.

Tip　As mentioned previously, it can be helpful to work with lower resolution placeholder images as you develop a project. You can use the Import option in the Bitmap Properties dialog box to load your high-resolution images in the final stages of the project.

The image formats PNG-24, PICT, and TIFF also support alpha channels when saved with 32-bit color. Alpha channels allow import of complex masks that might otherwise be difficult to create in Flash. The surprising thing you'll notice is that even after you apply Flash JPEG compression to an imported PNG, PICT, or TIFF image, the transparency will be maintained. You might say that Flash lets you have your alpha and eats the file size too.

Cross-Reference　The process for creating alpha channels in PICT and TIFF files is slightly different than that used for PNG files. For more information on creating alpha channels in source bitmaps, refer to Chapter 37, "Working with Raster Graphics."

Special Considerations for Fireworks PNG Files

Macromedia Fireworks offers one of the most flexible file formats for import into Flash. Fireworks PNG files can contain bitmap and vector artwork, as well as text, layers, guides, and even frames. Fireworks PNG files can be imported into Flash as either flattened images or as editable objects, with various options for handling the contents of the file. When importing images exported from Fireworks into Flash, you will be prompted by the Fireworks PNG Import Settings dialog box to make selections for the following import options:

✦ **To import the PNG as one bitmap image to the current layer or to the Library, select Import as Single Flattened Image.** This option rasterizes all vector artwork. When this option is selected, all other options will be unavailable. If you choose this option, you may want to apply Flash JPEG compression to the bitmap image either in Bitmap Properties or in Publish Settings. To edit a flattened image, you can launch Fireworks from inside Flash and edit the original PNG file (including any vector data or text).

✦ **To import more complex files, select one of the following File Structures:**

 • **Import as Movie Clip and Retain Layers** to import the PNG file as a Movie Clip with all frames and layers intact inside a Movie Clip symbol.

 • **Import into New Layer in Current Scene** to import the PNG file into a single new layer in the current Flash document at the top of the stacking order. All Fireworks layers will be flattened, but not rasterized unless specified, and any frames in the Fireworks file will be included on the new layer.

✦ **For Objects select either Rasterize if Necessary to Maintain Appearance to rasterize Fireworks fills, strokes, and effects in Flash as part of a bitmap image, or select Keep All Paths Editable to preserve vector paths in Flash.** Some Fireworks fills, strokes, and effects may be lost on import.

✦ **For Text the same options can be chosen as those listed for Objects.**

As with most files created in external applications, you will find that rasterized and flattened Fireworks vector artwork and text will import more consistently to Flash, but you also lose all the benefits of having editable vector art and text. Although the option for launching Fireworks at any time to edit the original PNG file does make rasterized Fireworks images less limiting than other bitmaps, it is usually worth the little extra time you might need to spend simplifying your artwork to get it to import to Flash with vectors and editable text intact.

8-bit lossless source files

Source files in 8-bit formats are restricted to 256 (or fewer) colors and will generally be optimized to a file size that is Web-friendly. These files are usually saved in GIF or PNG-8 format and are best suited for graphics that have simple shapes and limited colors, such as logos or line drawings. PNG-8 and GIF files can still support an alpha channel, but unlike 24-bit images, you will not want to apply any JPEG compression to these files when they're brought into Flash.

Caution To avoid display problems, when exporting GIF files with transparency for use in Flash, the index color and the transparency color should be set to the same RGB values. If these settings are not correct, transparent areas in the imported GIF may display as solid colors in Flash. For more information on this issue, refer to the Macromedia TechNote on Transparency support in Flash at: `www.macromedia.com/support/flash/ts/documents/transparent_bitmaps.htm`.

Applying JPEG compression to 8-bit files will usually result in larger file sizes and degraded image quality (refer to Figure 16-7). To preserve the clean graphic quality of 8-bit images, follow these steps:

1. In the Bitmap Properties dialog box, make sure that **Lossless** (PNG/GIF) compression is selected. This is the default for imported 8-bit images, but it never hurts to double-check to ensure that it hasn't been changed by mistake.

2. Decide whether to leave the default setting for **Allow Smoothing** in Bitmap Properties. The image will have sharper edges if this option is unchecked, so it is best to make a decision on this setting depending on whether you prefer smoothed edges when the image is scaled larger.

Remember that the JPEG Quality specified in Publish Settings will not apply to imported images that have been set to **Lossless** compression in the Bitmap Properties dialog box.

Source files with lossy compression

Although JPEG is the native bitmap compression format in Flash, it is generally advisable to use an alternative application for optimal JPEG compression on images. In our experience, JPEG compression from either Macromedia Fireworks or Adobe Photoshop produces smaller file sizes and more consistent image quality than JPEG compression applied in Flash. If you have created an optimized Web-ready JPEG using your preferred lossy compression method, you will want to avoid adding additional compression to the image when it is imported to Flash.

Caution JPEG images saved with the option for progressive download selected will not allow Flash to use imported JPEG data when the image is imported. Because this is a popular option for Web images used in HTML sites, it is important to advise anyone providing you with images for a Flash project to be certain that this option is turned off when the JPEGs are created. If you must use JPEGs saved with progressive download, the only option is to choose a higher quality JPEG setting to try to minimize the effect of double-JPEGing — unfortunately this also results in larger file sizes.

If you find that a JPEG file size is not reduced enough to fit the parameters of a particular project, it is better to go back to the uncompressed source file to redo the JPEG compression than it is to apply additional compression in Flash. As in all media production, double JPEGing images in Flash produces diminishing returns — by the time you get the file down to a size that you want, it will have so many compression artifacts that it will probably be unusable. By going back to the uncompressed source file and adjusting your compression settings to produce a new JPEG file, you will end up with a cleaner image and a smaller file size than you would by compounding the JPEG compression in Flash.

For optimal results when importing JPEG images to Flash projects, the main settings to consider are the **Use imported JPEG data** and the **Allow Smoothing** check boxes in the Bitmap Properties dialog box.

✦ To maintain the original JPEG compression of your imported image simply select the check box to Use imported JPEG data from the Bitmap Properties dialog box. When this check box is selected, the original compression will be preserved and the JPEG Quality specified in Publish Settings will not be added to your imported JPEG image.

✦ Smoothing is only advised if you will be scaling the JPEG image in Flash and you want to minimize the jagged edges with aliasing. The compromise of Smoothing is that the image will also appear slightly blurred — this may or may not be desirable depending on the detail in the original image.

Although you can clear the Use imported JPEG data check box and choose a setting in the Quality field, remember that this compression will be added to the compression on the original image and will cause inferior results.

Converting Rasters to Vectors

Have you ever wanted to take a scan of a "real" pen-and-ink drawing that you made and turn it into a vector graphic? It's not incredibly hard to do, and the results are usually pretty close to the original (see Figure 16-10). You can also turn continuous tone or photographic images into vector art, but the converted version will not likely bear much resemblance to the original. However, this can be useful for aesthetic effects.

Figure 16-10: Compare the raster version (left) of the sketch to its traced vector version (right).

As described in Chapter 9, "Modifying Graphics," bitmap images can be traced in Flash to convert them to vector shapes. Figure 16-3 illustrated why this is not recommended for complex photographic images — the file size will be huge and the image quality will not be as satisfactory as the original JPEG. However, converting rasters to vectors allows you to create some unique visual effects in Flash. After an image has been traced, you can use any of the Flash tools available for shapes, including the Distort and Envelop options of the Free Transform tool. You can also select parts of the image individually to modify colors, or even add custom gradient or bitmap fills.

Trace Bitmap is different from using the Break Apart command on a bitmap. When an image is broken apart, it is perceived by Flash as areas of color that can be modified or sampled for use as a fill in other shapes. Break Apart actually duplicates the automatic conversion handled by the Mixer panel to show bitmaps from the Library in the bitmap fill menu. Although images that are broken apart can be modified with the drawing and painting tools, you cannot select individual parts of the image with the Arrow tool or apply the Optimization command, Smooth/Straighten options or Distort and Envelop modifiers as you can with a traced vector image.

 Cross-Reference For more information on using the Break Apart command, refer to Chapter 9, "Modifying Graphics."

To apply Trace Bitmap, select a bitmap image that has been imported to Flash (ideally with lossless compression and no Smoothing) and placed in the Document window then select Modify ➪ Trace bitmap from the application menu to invoke the Trace Bitmap dialog box as shown in Figure 16-11.

Figure 16-11: Use the Trace Bitmap dialog box to select settings for converting a raster image into vector shapes.

The settings for the Trace Bitmap command are detailed in Chapter 9, but the default settings can be a good place to start. Higher Color Threshold and Minimum Area values reduce the complexity of the resulting Flash artwork, which means smaller file sizes. This process is most effective when applied to simple images with strong contrast. In these cases tracing a bitmap graphic can actually reduce the file size and improve the appearance of the image. The settings shown in Figure 16-11 were used to trace the GIF image shown in Figure 16-12. When viewed at a scale of 175 percent, the difference in image quality can clearly be seen, and this difference will be exaggerated the more the images are scaled—the vector image will remain smooth, while the bitmap will break apart and look increasingly jagged.

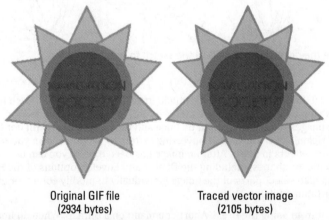

Original GIF file
(2934 bytes)

Traced vector image
(2105 bytes)

Figure 16-12: Images with simple shapes and limited colors can be cleaner and more scaleable when converted from bitmap (left) to vector art (right) using the Trace Bitmap command.

In order to get the best results from using Trace Bitmap, we advise reducing the number of colors in the original image before importing it to Flash. Figure 16-13 shows an imported image that was converted to indexed color and reduced to four colors in Photoshop before saving as a GIF image for import to Flash. After the image is traced, you can simplify the shapes further by applying the Optimize command (Modify ➪ Optimize), which will clean up the image and reduce the final file size. You can also use any of the drawing tools to further modify the image.

Imported 4 Color GIF image   Traced and Optimized vector image

Figure 16-13: A reduced-color GIF image (left) can be traced and then simplified using the Optimize command (right).

Using External Vector Graphics

All artwork drawn in Flash is vector based and, as shown in Table 16-1, Flash also offers robust support for external vector formats, including Macromedia FreeHand and Adobe Illustrator. However, not all vector graphics are created the same. Some vector graphics may be simple objects and fills, while others may include complex blending or paths that add significant weight to a Flash movie. Although most vector graphics are by nature much smaller than raster graphic equivalents, don't assume that they're optimized for Flash use.

Importing vector graphics from other applications is fairly simple and straightforward. However, because most vector graphics applications are geared for print production (for example, publishing documents intended for press), you need to keep some principles in mind when creating artwork for Flash in external graphics applications:

✦ **Limit or reduce the number of points describing complex paths.**

✦ **Limit the number of embedded typefaces (or fonts).** Multiple fonts add to the final movie's (.swf) file size. As described later in this chapter, converting fonts to outlines is one way to avoid adding extra fonts to your Flash file.

✦ **To ensure color consistency between applications, use only RGB colors (and color pickers) for artwork.** Flash can only use RGB color values, and automatically converts any CMYK colors to RGB colors when artwork is imported. Color conversions can produce unwanted color shifts.

Note   When Flash imports a vector file with any placed grayscale images, the images will be converted to RGB color, which will also increase the file size.

✦ **Unless you're using Macromedia FreeHand, you may need to replace externally
created gradients with Flash gradients, or accept the file size addition to the Flash
movie.** Gradients created in other drawing applications are not converted to Flash gradients when the file is imported. This chapter shows you how to redraw gradients in
Flash.

✦ **Preserve layers where possible to help keep imported artwork organized**. Some vector formats use layers, and Flash can recognize these layers if the graphic file format is
correctly specified. Layers keep graphic elements separate from one another and can
make it easier to organize items for use in animation.

✦ **If the artwork you are importing includes large areas of solid color, such as a plain
background, consider excluding those parts of the graphic from import.** They can
easily be replaced in Flash after the more complex parts of the artwork are brought in.

**Cross-
Reference**   For coverage of using other applications to create vector artwork for Flash refer to Chapter 38, "Working with Vector Graphics."

Importing Vector Artwork

Vector graphics from other applications can be imported into Flash with relative ease using
the Import dialog box, as shown in Figure 16-14. These graphics are imported as groups, and
can be used just like a normal group drawn in Flash. You can also copy and paste or even
drag and drop artwork from external applications, but this gives you less control over how
the vector information will be translated in Flash — for example, transparency or special fill
types may be lost and any layers will be flattened into the currently selected Flash layer.

Figure 16-14: The Import dialog box used for selecting
files for import to Flash

Most vector graphics are imported as grouped items on a single layer. Because Flash recognizes vector artwork as grouped shapes, unlike bitmaps, imported vector graphics will not
appear in the Library until converted into symbols. Some programs also offer the option of
preserving layered artwork and importing it either to separate Flash layers or to keyframes.

Various import options for different source files are described in the "Importing Groups and Layers" section, later in this chapter. For basic import of a vector graphic to Flash, simply follow these steps:

1. To import a file to the Stage of your Flash document, make sure that you have an empty, unlocked layer selected and chose File ➪ Import.

2. In the Import dialog box, choose a file format to browse using the Files of Type (Win) or Show (Mac) menu.

3. Find the vector file that you wish to import and select it from the file list, then choose **Open**.

In Mac OS 9.x or earlier, click **Add** to add a selected file to the import list, then click Import to bring the selected file(s) into Flash.

4. If the application you are importing from includes options for how the artwork will be placed in Flash, you will be prompted to make choices from an application-specific dialog box. Depending on your options, the artwork will be imported to a single layer or to multiple layers or keyframes in your Flash document after you click **OK**.

If you choose to rasterize the vector artwork into a bitmap image when importing to Flash, remember to apply JPEG compression using the Quality setting in the Bitmap Properties dialog box, or if the Use document default quality check box is selected, set JPEG Quality in the Publish Settings dialog box before exporting your Flash movie (.swf).

5. To edit the imported graphic with Flash shape tools, ungroup the elements (Shift+Ctrl+G or Shift+⌘+G) or double-click parts of the group until you are able to select strokes and fills in Symbol Editing mode. To store elements in the Library so they are reusable, convert them to Graphic symbols. If you have imported a layered sequence into multiple Flash keyframes, consider cutting and pasting the frames into a new Movie Clip symbol.

For more information on working with grouped artwork in Flash refer to Chapter 9, "Modifying Graphics." For more information on using symbols refer to Chapter 6, "Symbols, Instances, and the Library."

Here's how to use the clipboard to import a vector image into Flash:

1. Select all vector elements that you wish to include. Copy the selected items from your vector drawing application.

2. Return to Flash and make sure that you have an active, unlocked layer that you can paste the vectors into, this can be on the Main Timeline or on any symbol timeline.

3. Paste the graphics onto the stage by selecting Edit ➪ Paste from the menu (Ctrl+V or ⌘+V).

4. You may want to group or move parts of the pasted graphic onto new layers in your Flash document for better organization and for animation.

If you import a Fireworks PNG file by cutting and pasting into Flash, all vector elements will be rasterized into a flattened bitmap image.

Importing Groups and Layers

Macromedia Fireworks, FreeHand, and Adobe Illustrator will give you the option of flattening or rasterizing your vector graphics when importing to Flash, but it is often preferable to preserve layers as well as editable text and vector artwork. Because generic numbered layer names, such as Layer 1, may be redundant with layers already present in your Flash document, it is important to give layers meaningful names in the external application before importing to Flash. To avoid unexpected color shifts, it is recommended that you convert your color space to RGB in any external application before saving files that will be imported to Flash.

Importing Macromedia Fireworks files

As described in the section on importing bitmap files, Fireworks PNG files can preserve graphics in vector format if they are imported to Flash as *editable objects*. If a Fireworks file is flattened and rasterized on import, the vector artwork will be converted to bitmap format, but by launching Fireworks from inside Flash you will still have the option of editing the original vector artwork or text in the source PNG file. For a description of the import options for Fireworks files please refer to the sidebar, "Special Considerations for Fireworks PNG Files" in the previous section on "Making Sense of Bitmap Compression."

Caution If you import a Fireworks PNG file by cutting and pasting into Flash, all vector elements will be rasterized into a flattened bitmap image.

Importing Macromedia FreeHand files

FreeHand is one of the most compatible applications for transferring vector artwork into Flash. When importing FreeHand files, you can preserve library symbols and pages in addition to layers and text blocks. You may also choose a specific page range to import. Figure 16-15 shows the options available from the FreeHand Import dialog box that is invoked when importing files with the FreeHand (.fh) extension into Flash. Although FreeHand can export a variety of file formats, including .swf and .eps, the native .fh format will give you the most editing options for files imported to Flash.

Cross-Reference For more information on working with FreeHand files, refer to Chapter 38, "Working with Vector Graphics." You will also find some sample FreeHand files in the ch38 folder on the CD-ROM.

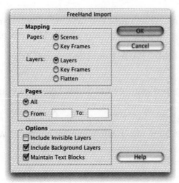

Figure 16-15: The FreeHand Import dialog box used to specify how the vector file will be handled when placed into Flash

Remember to convert your FreeHand file to RGB color mode. If the file is in CMYK, it will be converted automatically on import to Flash and this may cause unexpected color shifts. There are some other special considerations when importing FreeHand artwork. To ensure seamless translation of FreeHand elements imported into Flash observe the following guidelines:

✦ Any placed grayscale elements in FreeHand will be converted to RBG color when imported to Flash, which may increase file size.

✦ EPS files placed in FreeHand will not be viewable when imported to Flash, unless you select the Convert Editable EPS when Imported option in FreeHand Import Preferences before you place an EPS into FreeHand. Regardless of the settings used, Flash will not display information for any placed EPS imported from FreeHand.

✦ Strokes with square caps will be converted into rounded caps in Flash.

✦ Be cautious with compound shapes: When importing overlapping elements that you want to keep intact in Flash, place them on separate layers in FreeHand and import the layers into Flash. If items on a single layer are overlapping when imported, they will be divided or merged at intersection points in the same way as primitive shapes created in Flash.

✦ Flash will only support up to eight colors in an imported gradient fill. If a gradient created in FreeHand contains more than eight colors, Flash will use clipping paths to interpret the gradient. Clipping paths will increase file size. To work around this issue, use gradients that contain eight or fewer colors in FreeHand or replace the imported gradient with a Flash gradient fill as described later in this chapter.

✦ Imported FreeHand blends will also increase Flash file size because Flash interprets each step in a blend as a separate path.

As shown in Figure 16-16, Flash will recognize text and limited-color gradient fills imported from FreeHand, making it easy to edit these elements directly in Flash.

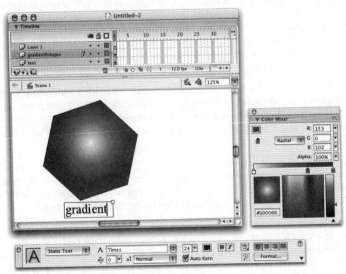

Figure 16-16: FreeHand files can be edited directly in Flash, but shapes and text elements will still need to be converted into symbols before being stored in the Library for reuse.

Importing Adobe Illustrator files

Flash MX supports direct import of Adobe Illustrator (.ai) and Adobe Illustrator EPS (.eps) files saved as version 8.0 or earlier. Even if you are working with a newer version of Illustrator, when using **Save As** you have the option of saving your file as an earlier version.

Caution Adobe Illustrator 6.0 is the only version that can import to Flash with placed bitmap images, but this is not an ideal workflow because early versions of Illustrator cannot save artwork color values in RGB space. You must specify Illustrator 7 or 8 in the Illustrator document options when saving to ensure color consistency for artwork imported to Flash. If you choose Illustrator 6 or lower format, then RGB values will not be saved and color shifts may result.

You will be given the same options when importing an Illustrator file in .ai or .eps format — as shown in Figure 16-17, you may select to transfer Illustrator layers to equivalent Flash layers or to keyframes or to flatten all layers and import the artwork as grouped shapes on a single layer.

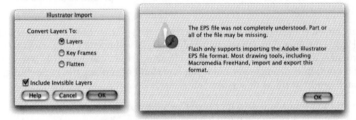

Figure 16-17: The Illustrator Import options dialog box for EPS or AI files and the often-seen EPS warning box

After selecting your import options and clicking OK, you may see the EPS warning box shown in Figure 16-17. Although this warning is intended to display only if the file was incorrectly saved, we've found that it appears on nearly any type of Illustrator file imported to Flash — simply click **OK** and the file should import correctly. As shown in Figure 16-18, the artwork will be imported as grouped elements and they will not be stored in the Library because they are perceived by Flash as grouped shapes.

Although you can scale, move, or rotate the grouped elements, to modify individual parts of the graphic you must either ungroup the elements or click in to Symbol Editing mode until you are able to select the strokes and fills of a particular element. Figure 16-19 shows how the grouped items appear when selected (top) and how they appear when selected after being ungrouped (bottom).

Any small inconsistencies in fill style are easy to fix once the elements are ungrouped in Flash. Remember that you can delete fills, add strokes, scale, or otherwise modify the imported artwork with any of the Flash tools. Figure 16-20 illustrates how the artwork appears when first imported (to layers) and how it appears at various stages in Symbol Editing mode.

To make the artwork efficient to reuse and update, it is best to convert the whole graphic into a symbol. If you intend to animate parts of the graphic individually, then convert these into discrete symbols and place them on separate layers. Figure 16-21 shows the original artwork from Figure 16-18 after various parts of the graphic have been converted to Graphic symbols (now shown stored in the Library).

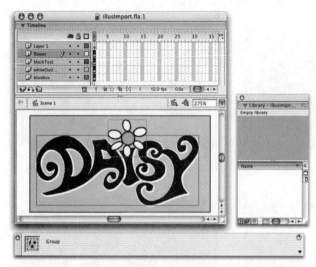

Figure 16-18: Illustrator artwork imported to Flash layers as grouped elements

Figure 16-19: Ungrouping imported vector artwork to allow selection of strokes and fills

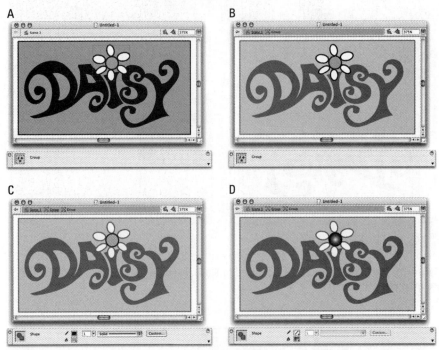

Figure 16-20: Double-clicking a grouped item (A) takes you into Symbol Editing mode, but if the item is in a compound group, you may have to continue double-clicking until you are able to isolate the stroke and fill of one part of the group for modification (D).

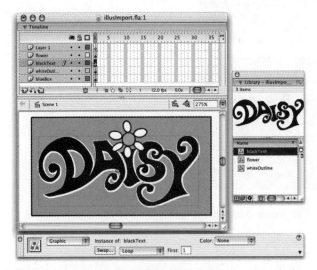

Figure 16-21: Illustrator artwork imported to layers in Flash and converted to Graphic symbols

Animating Imported Vector Graphics

A handy feature of many popular illustration programs is support for layers. Just like layers in a Flash document (.fla), layers in illustration programs enable you to keep individual groups of graphics separate from one another. A simple technique with animating vector graphic files is to animate or tween each layer separately in the Flash authoring environment.

A quick example of an easily converted illustration movie is a logo. If you have created artwork in FreeHand or Illustrator and have kept the elements separated by layers, then you can quickly create an interactive Flash graphic.

For this exercise you can use the sample logo, daisyLogo.ai or daisyLogo.eps, in the ch16 folder of the CD-ROM.

1. Create a layered graphic in FreeHand or Illustrator. Before each part of the element is created, make a new layer for it.

2. If you use extensive text controls (such as kerning, leading, tracking, and so on), then convert the text to outlines (or paths).

3. Save the layout as a FreeHand file, an EPS file, or an Illustrator AI file. Flash MX now supports direct import of either Illustrator or FreeHand files.

CMYK colors shift when imported into the RGB color space of Flash. Moreover, some masking and cropping information (for bleeds) may not be interpreted correctly by Flash. To see the color difference between CMYK import and RGB import for the logo used in this example, refer to the color insert.

4. Import the FreeHand, EPS, or AI file into Flash, being certain to select the option to preserve your artwork in layers and vector format. You may want to create a new scene or symbol to contain the imported graphic(s). Otherwise, the layers from the imported file will be stacked with your current layers. See Figure 16-21 for reference.

5. You may convert the layered elements into symbols for reuse or easier modification later. You will need to make button symbols for any element that you want to use interactively (such as the flower animation triggered by the mouse). Repeat this step for every layer.

6. Now add any Flash tweens or actions to the groups or symbols in each layer. At this point, you could continue creating a full Flash project with other components, or export a Flash movie (.swf).

As you can see, in just six straightforward steps, you can create an animated logo and many other quick translations of vector graphics into interactive presentations that can be included in other projects or in an e-mail. Whenever you're developing complicated layered work in an illustration application such as FreeHand or Illustrator, you can take advantage of those layers in Flash.

Check out the completed interactive logo, daisyAnim.fla or daisyAnim.swf, located in the ch16 folder of the CD-ROM.

Optimizing Vectors

All vector graphics are made up of paths in one shape or another. A path can be as simple as a straight line with two points, a curved line with two points, or 500 or more points along an irregular shape or fill. This is why vector graphics are best suited for graphic images such as logos, architectural drawings, and clip art that do not include continuous tones. Fonts are also made up of paths. As you've seen with Flash-drawn graphics, you can scale them to any size without any loss of resolution, unlike raster (bitmap) artwork, which cannot scale larger than its original size without loss of resolution.

Note

Vector graphics are eventually *rasterized,* so to speak. The vector formatting for drawn shapes and text is more of a simplified storage structure that contains a mathematical description (that is, smaller than a bit-for-bit description) of an object or set of objects. When the vector graphic is displayed, especially with anti-aliasing, the video card needs to render the edges in pixels. Likewise, the PostScript RIP (Raster Image Processor) of a laser printer needs to convert the vector information, or an EPS (Encapsulated PostScript) file, into printer "dots."

When you use imported vector graphics in Flash movies, you should minimize the number of points describing curved lines or intricate outlined graphics (for example, "traced" raster images). A big problem with creating cool graphics in vector-based applications such as Illustrator, FreeHand, and 3ds Studio Max is the number of points used to describe lines. When these graphics are imported into Flash, animations are slower and harder to redraw (or refresh) on the computer screen. In addition, the file size of the Flash movie grows considerably. Most vector applications include features that will allow you to optimize or simplify artwork before importing it to Flash.

Cross-Reference

For tips on optimizing vector artwork in other applications, including Adobe Illustrator, Streamline, and Macromedia FreeHand, as well as coverage of export options refer to Chapter 38, "Working with Vector Graphics."

There are also a number of ways that you can simplify artwork after it has been imported to Flash. Many of these Flash features have been discussed in previous chapters, but we will briefly summarize them here.

Tracing complex vector artwork

Many graphics programs, such as Discreet's 3ds Studio Max and Adobe Dimensions can create some astonishing vector-based graphics. However, when you import EPS versions of those graphics into Flash, they either fall apart (display horribly) or add unrealistic byte chunks to your Flash movie. But, this doesn't mean that you can't use these intricate graphics in your Flash movies. You can try several different procedures with intricate vector artwork, including smoothing as described previously, to make intricate graphics more Flash-friendly.

Depending on the specific use of the artwork, you may also be able to output small raster equivalents that won't consume nearly as much space as highly detailed vector graphics. However, there are some instances when the best solution is a bit more labor-intensive. To get just the right "translation" of a complex vector graphic in your Flash movie, you may need to try redrawing the artwork in Flash. Sound crazy and time-consuming? Well, it's a bit of both, but some Flash designers spend hour after hour getting incredibly small file sizes from "hand-tracing" vector designs in Flash.

For example, if you made a highly detailed technical drawing of a light bulb, and wanted to bring into Flash, you could import the original EPS version of the drawing into Flash, place it on a locked layer, and use Flash drawing tools to re-create a simplified version of the object (see Figure 16-22).

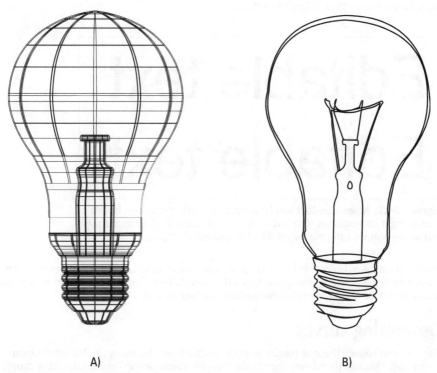

A)   B)

Figure 16-22: Compare the original imported vector artwork of the light bulb (left) with the simplified version drawn in Flash (right).

Cross-Reference

There are many Flash SWF tools that can help to speed up the work of optimizing vector artwork. One example is Electric Rain's Swift 3D, which can simplify 3D models and output SWF files. We take a closer look at Swift 3D in Chapter 40, "Working with 3D Graphics."

Converting text to outlines

Another aspect of vector graphics that you need to keep in mind — especially when working with other designers — is font linking and embedding. With most vector file formats, such as Illustrator, FreeHand, or EPS, you can link to fonts that are located on your system. However, if you give those files to someone who doesn't have those fonts installed, then he won't be able to see or use the fonts. Some formats enable you to embed fonts into the document file, which circumvents this problem. However, whether the fonts are linked or embedded, you may be unnecessarily bloating the size of the vector graphic.

You can break apart imported text in Flash by using the Modify ➪ Break Apart command (Ctrl+B or ⌘+B). In Flash MX you have to first break the text into letters and then break them apart a second time to get basic shapes.

You can also convert any text into outlines (or *paths*) in most drawing or illustration programs (see Figure 16-23). In FreeHand 10, select the text as a text block (with the Arrow tool, not the Text tool) and choose Text ⇨ Convert to Paths. In Illustrator 10, select the text as an object and choose Type ⇨ Create Outlines.

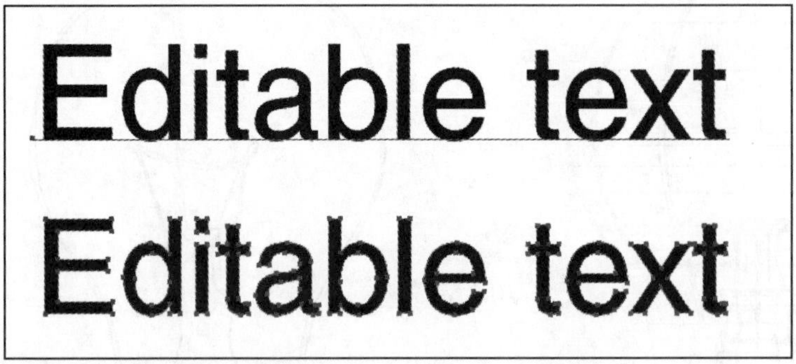

Editable text
Editable text

Figure 16-23: Make sure that you have finished editing your text before converting it into outlines. The text at the top can be edited, whereas the text at the bottom can only be modified as individual shapes.

If you have a lot of body text in the graphic, you may want to copy the text directly into a Flash text box and use a _sans, _serif, or other device font. These fonts do not require additional file information (as embedded fonts do) when used in a Flash movie.

Optimizing curves

You can also reduce the complexity of paths within Flash, by using the Modify ⇨ Optimize command. This has the same effect as the Simplify command in FreeHand, with a couple of extra options. When working with bitmaps or symbols, be sure to use the Modify ⇨ Break Apart command, and if you are working with a group, ungroup it (Modify ⇨ Ungroup) before you use the Optimize command — you can't optimize groups or symbols. Figure 16-24 shows the effect of maximum smoothing on a complex seashell graphic.

Figure 16-24: The Optimize Curves dialog enables you to specify multiple passes, which means that Flash will optimize the graphic at a given setting as much as it possibly can.

Cross-Reference For a more detailed description of the Optimize Curves options, refer to Chapter 5, "Drawing in Flash."

Replacing blends with gradient fills

If you're using a drawing application that doesn't support SWF export, then you can still work around EPS blends in Flash. Replacing externally rendered "blends" with Flash gradients, an old trick among 3D Flash designers, drastically cuts down on Flash movie (.swf) file sizes. Unless you're using a program that supports Flash gradients in SWF export, gradients or blends created in drawing, illustration, or 3D programs will not be converted to Flash gradients when the graphic(s) are imported into Flash.

On the CD-ROM Use the 3Dgraphic.eps file, located in the ch16 folder of the CD-ROM, if you need a sample image for the following steps.

Because many graphics applications do not render Flash-style gradients, it's up to you to decide to accept the file size "weight gains" of shaded blends or to re-create the blends with Flash gradients after the artwork has been imported into the Flash authoring environment. The extra work of replacing a gradient is necessary even when importing Flash-compatible gradients if you have imported a gradient that goes beyond Flash's blend range of eight colors. Here's the general process for replacing externally created blends in Flash:

1. After the artwork has been rendered as an EPS or AI file, open Flash. Create a new graphic symbol and open this symbol in the Symbol Editing stage. Import the EPS graphic into the first frame of the symbol.

2. Break apart (Ctrl+B or ⌘+B) or ungroup the imported vector artwork to the point where you isolate the blend separately from the rest of the graphic. If you break apart the imported vector graphic, then it should be reduced to "symbol" parts and groups in one step, as shown in Figure 16-25. Note that Flash will convert EPS blends to symbols (accessible from the Flash Library). These symbols will contain a mask layer and a blend layer.

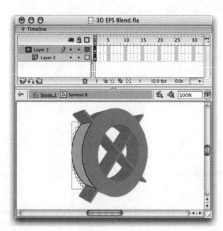

Figure 16-25: When the Break Apart command is applied to the imported graphic, you can access individual groups within the graphic, including the EPS blends.

3. Access the timeline of each symbol that contains a blend, and delete the "blend" graphics. Keep the original Mask Layer intact, but replace the Blend Layer contents with a Flash gradient. You may need to make a three- or four-color gradient, and use the Transform Fill tool to modify the direction and size of the gradient.

Refer to Figures 16-26 and 16-27 for more details.

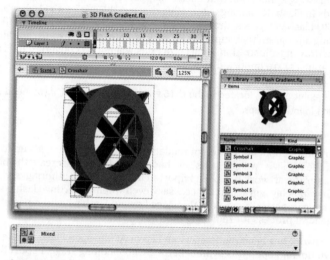

Figure 16-26: Double-click a selected symbol to enter Symbol Editing mode. Replace the blend in the lower layer of the symbol with a Flash gradient.

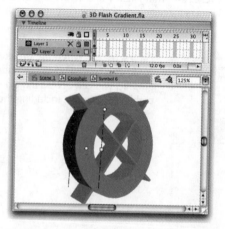

Figure 16-27: The Flash version of the blended EPS graphic

When you are done replacing each blend's symbol with a Flash gradient, you'll have a cleaner (and slightly smaller) Flash movie. If you are working with multiple imported vector graphics that have blends, you'll end up with much smaller Flash movies (.swf) — which means Web visitors will spend less time waiting to see your movies.

Tip

Remember that gradients created in Macromedia FreeHand or Adobe Illustrator can be directly exported to SWF format as Flash gradients. However, if the gradient contains more than eight colors, Flash will add clipping paths when it is imported. Also, remember that FreeHand blends will always be interpreted by Flash as a series of paths, which can increase file size and sometimes add banding to the blend.

Summary

✦ Flash can use a variety of external media, which allows you to select the most effective format for various types of content.

✦ Bitmaps are best suited for photographic images, or images that contain detailed shading and/or complex color blends.

✦ Bitmaps can be optimized or compressed in your image-editing application or in Flash, but it is important to follow a workflow that will avoid double JPGing on any artwork.

✦ Bitmaps can be converted to vector artwork in a variety of ways. This process works best on simplified bitmap images or when used to create special image effects.

✦ Vector graphics are most often used for logos, line drawings, and other artwork that does not include complex patterns and blends.

✦ Flash supports import of layers and editable text and gradients from some graphics applications including Macromedia FreeHand, Fireworks, and Adobe Illustrator. Some care is needed in preparing files to get the best results, but being able to reuse your file structure and editable elements created in other applications can save a lot of time.

✦ Although the native file format of Flash is vector and this format is very efficient by design, often vector graphics still need to be optimized.

✦ Most graphics applications include their own options for reducing the complexity of vector art. However, using Flash's various tools for optimizing vector artwork can also be an effective way to reduce your final file size.

✦ ✦ ✦

Embedding Video

In This Chapter

Shooting clean video

Prepping video for compression

Compressing video in Flash MX

Using Sorenson Squeeze

Understanding Sorenson Spark Pro edition

Knowing FLV and SWF output

Comparing Spark compression to other video codecs

One of the most exciting new features of Flash MX is the power to add digital video footage in Flash movies (.swf files), playable within Flash Player 6! Designers and developers alike have long awaited this feature. Now, video can be played without relying upon additional plug-ins like Apple QuickTime or Real Systems RealOne player. In this chapter, we'll show you how to embed a video file into a Flash MX document, specify import quality of the video, and control playback of the video within the Flash movie.

Preparing a Video File

Before you consider importing digital video footage into Flash MX, you need to plan how the video will be used within the Flash movie (or Web site). Will you be using several video clips for product demonstrations, interviews, or pre-recorded events? Will you be using video for special effects such as a time-lapse effect of moving clouds or the sun setting? The more footage you plan to use, the more important it will be to make sure you're acquiring the footage properly — you wouldn't want to redo all your footage after you've seen the results in the Flash movie! In this section, we provide tips for making sure you have the best possible video quality for your Flash presentations.

Note
If you already have some video that you want to bring into Flash MX, then jump to the section titled "Importing the Video" later in this chapter.

Garbage in, garbage out

You may have heard this phrase before, which means that you can't get something from nothing. Ever tried making a soup with bad ingredients and thought it would still taste good? The same principle holds true for video production. Four primary factors influence the quality of your video footage: source format, image quality, sound quality, and subject matter.

Source format

The source format is the container in which the video is stored, whether it's a digital recording encoded on miniDV or DVCAM tape, an analog recording on VHS or Hi8 tape, or a direct MPEG file recorded on your digital camera. Each recording medium has inherent resolution limitations — some formats can store more information than others.

The more information that the medium stores, the higher quality the recording will be. The following list outlines the resolution capacities of common recording mediums. For the purposes of our discussion, we'll restrict this list to video formats and exclude film formats, such as 35mm or 16mm motion picture film. These formats are compared by line resolution, which is the number of horizontal scan lines the format can capture. Line resolution is not the definitive attribute for video quality, but it does measure the capacity of potential visual information captured by the camera or recording device. The most important factor to remember when comparing line resolutions is that video is primarily targeted at television screens that, in North America, display 525 lines of resolution.

Practically speaking, television sets display a maximum of 483 lines of visible resolution — the remaining lines convey other information such as the sync pulse. Although HDTV (High Definition TV) is capable of displaying 1080 lines of resolution, most multimedia producers will not be using HD cameras to record video.

✦ **VHS, VHS-C or 8mm video tape:** These tape formats, especially VHS, are the most common video formats in use by consumers today. The average household VCR records video in VHS format. These tape formats can record about 240 lines of resolution. This resolution is less than half of the potential scan lines that can be shown on a TV screen, which is why the VHS recordings of your favorite TV shows don't exactly match the live broadcasts. These tape formats are analog in nature — the signal they record is not digital and can deteriorate from copy to copy. You need to capture this source with an analog video capture card.

✦ **S-VHS or Hi8 video tape:** S-VHS and Hi8 video use the same tape sizes as their VHS and 8mm equivalents, but they capture up to 400 lines of resolution. This resolution capacity comes very close to the 525 lines of resolution that a television can display. You probably won't encounter many S-VHS camcorders anymore, but Hi8 video camcorders are still very popular and in wide use today. While the video quality is a noticeable improvement, the video signal is still analog, so like with VHS, you must capture it with an analog video capture card.

✦ **miniDV, Digital8, or DVCAM tape:** The new breed of video recording devices for consumer, prosumer, and professional use is the DV (Digital Video) format. DV formats use the DV codec to digitally record video, while storing audio at near-CD or CD-quality sampling rates. The native resolution for the DV format is 525 lines, but the actual resolution a DV camcorder will record will vary from model to model. Most high-end DV camcorders are considered broadcast quality, meaning the video image is good enough to use on a television show such as the evening news. Many computer systems today ship with an IEEE 1394 (also known as FireWire or iLink) port to capture digital video from DV recording devices. When video is transferred digitally from a camera to a computer over an IEEE 1394 connection, there is no loss of quality.

✦ **Betacam SP, Digital Betacam:** These tape formats are for serious video professionals who work in the television industry. Betacam SP has been the industry standard for network television for over 30 years. While Betacam SP is an analog format, Digital Betacam (also known as DigiBeta) records video with a proprietary Sony codec. Both formats capture 550 or more lines of resolution.

✦ **MPEG file recording:** Many digital cameras can also record MPEG video at various sizes and resolutions. Most digital cameras use the MPEG-1 codec, which was used in the original Video CD (or VCD) format. Sony has recently introduced a new Micro MV format, which records video in the MPEG-2 format used by DVD Video discs, at similar line resolutions to DVD Video (525 lines). Most MPEG recording devices capture at line resolutions equal to or less than VHS quality.

As a general guideline, we recommend using a miniDV camcorder to record video that you intend to use for multimedia presentations within a Flash movie. Several factors beyond the recording format affect the quality of any recording. In the next two sections, we discuss variables that influence the visual and audio portions of a recording.

Tip   If you're a beginner videographer and want to know more about video resolution, check out the following links:

```
http://www.bealecorner.com/trv900/respat/
http://hometown.aol.com/ajaynejr/vidres.htm
http://www.elitevideo.com/new2.htm
```

Image quality

Regardless of the source format that you use for your video recording, the recording device may have other limitations. The recorded resolution of your camera may be significantly lower than the upper limit of your recording format's line resolution. For example, the DV format is capable of storing 525 lines of resolution. However, your specific DV camcorder may have an effective resolution of 490 lines. The following variables can affect the quality of the picture that is recorded by the camera. Note that this list is by no means exhaustive for the professional videographer — we chose these topics as a general summary to guide you in your video production.

✦ **Optics:** The characteristics of the lens (or lens system) that your camera uses are known as the optics. The optical quality of video camcorders can vary wildly. Many camcorders boast Carl Zeiss lenses, which have been known for their precision and accuracy. Some lenses are constructed of plastic, while others are glass. Neither lens type is necessarily better than the other, but the only way to accurately judge the optical system of your camera is to conduct extensive testing with a resolution target.

✦ **CCD:** The CCD, or charged-coupled device, is the electronic plate that captures the image being rendered by the camera's lens. You can think of the CCD as the digital film that's being exposed to the light coming through the lens. CCDs come in a variety of sizes, ranging from ¼ inch to 1 inch. While these sizes may sound incredibly small, even ¼ inch CCDs can capture amazing detail. The larger a CCD is, however, the more information it can capture. Most cameras only have one CCD, but some cameras have three CCDs — one for each color of the RGB (red, green, and blue) spectrum. These are known as 3-chip or 3-CCD cameras, and they have better color fidelity than single-chip CCD cameras. Color fidelity, simply put, is the measure of how closely the recorded color of an image matches the original colors of the subject.

✦ **Tape quality:** The quality of the tape on which you record the video can also affect the quality of the overall image. Each tape brand has unique characteristics, such as the type of metal particles that are magnetized onto the tape. Some brands (or stocks) are more durable and can withstand the rigors of repeated recordings. In general, you should always record on a fresh tape — and preferably one listed as premium or high quality.

✦ **Shutter mechanism:** The shutter mechanism is the device that controls how quickly the CCD samples the image rendered by the lens. Most camcorders have shutters that record interlaced video, which records two inter-woven fields (or separate halves of a picture) to create one frame of video. Have you ever noticed how the image on your TV flickers when you pause a VHS recording? You're seeing the two fields of the frame alternating. Computer monitors do not display interlaced video. Rather, they use progressive scanning, to minimize a flicker effect. Some higher-end camcorders have progressive scan shutters, which record the image with higher apparent resolution. We'll discuss de-interlacing video later in this chapter.

✦ **Exposure**: You should make every effort to properly shoot your video footage with the correct exposure. Exposure refers to the amount of light captured by the CCD and the shutter mechanism. Some camcorders do not allow you to control the exposure — it's all automatic. The biggest pitfall for most videographers is underexposing your video footage or shooting in low light. When you try to record a poorly lit subject, you tend to see noise in the darkest areas of the image. Video noise is a random pattern of dots that show up on the image. Finally, make every effort to properly white balance your shot — some camcorders allow you to control the color temperature. You'll notice the effects of color temperature in the video samples on the CD-ROM.

So what do all these variables boil down to? In a nutshell, we recommend that whenever possible, you should shoot video with a camcorder that has a superior optical system with 3 CCDs, using high-quality tapes and properly controlling your exposure. Avoid shooting in low light, unless you are shooting with a particular effect in mind, such as infrared lighting.

Sound quality

Every videographer should consider how audio is recorded during production. Most video camcorders have a decent built-in stereo microphone, but professional videographers equip themselves with accessories beyond those that ship with the camera. Review the following guidelines for capturing sound with your video recording:

✦ **External microphones:** To achieve the best possible audio recording, put an external microphone as close as possible to the source of the sound. If you want to record a person talking, an external microphone, such as a wireless lavaliere mic that's pinned to the person's shirt, collar, or tie, will produce a much cleaner recording than the microphone on the camera.

✦ **Balanced versus unbalanced audio:** Most microphones you will find at electronics stores use a stereo or mono 3.5mm mini adapter that plugs into the microphone jack on your camcorder. These microphones are considered "unbalanced" audio sources, due to the nature of their internal wiring. For many video shoots this may not pose a problem. However, professional audio engineers use balanced audio for all sound sources. The cabling for balanced audio tends to be a heavier gauge than that of the consumer variety. Many balanced microphones have a 3-pin XLR connector, and most camcorders require an XLR adapter to connect these sources to the mini microphone jack. Many professional video cameras have built-in XLR jacks.

✦ **Sampling rate and bit-depth:** Unless you're using a DV format camcorder, it's likely that you will have little or no control over the specific sampling rate and bit-depth used to record audio on the camera. DV camcorders allow you to record with either 32 kHz or 48 kHz. 32 kHz audio is recorded at 12-bit, which is suitable for recording dialog and live action. 48 kHz is recorded at 16-bit, which is suitable for recording live musical performances or any other scene requiring high fidelity.

✦ **Audio levels:** One of the most overlooked aspects of video production is monitoring the audio levels of your source while recording. Most camcorders only record audio with AGC, or Automatic Gain Control. This "feature" allows the camcorder to determine how much an audio signal should be boosted or minimized during recording.

Professional audio engineers prefer to manually monitor and adjust sound levels while the recording is taking place. Undesirable side effects of using AGC include amplified background noise during silent periods, audio distortion, and sudden jumps or drops in audio levels. Whenever possible, listen to your audio source through headphones connected to the camera.

✦ **Unwanted noise:** Do your best to minimize any background noise when you are recording. The microphone(s) connected to your camera will pick up more noise than you may realize. Each microphone has a different "pick-up" pattern, determining the range and direction of sound that it will receive.

In summary, we recommend that you record audio as close as possible to the source, using balanced microphones and monitoring the audio feed with headphones connected to the camera. For most video recording, either the 32 kHz or 48 kHz sampling rates will yield superior audio reproduction.

Subject matter

Last, but by no means least, the type of subject matter you are shooting can influence the results of video compression in Flash MX. When it comes to video compression, the most important factor to remember is variability from frame to frame. Simply put, how much and how often does your subject matter change? Are you recording the Indy 500, panning fast race cars accelerating at incredibly fast speeds? Or, are you recording a time lapse of a flower blooming? In general, you will achieve the best results with video compression if the subject matter does not move randomly and wildly. Here are some general guidelines when choosing and shooting your subject matter:

✦ **Use a tripod:** One of the most common mistakes amateur videographers make is to hand-hold the video camcorder. Unless you need to freely move with your camera or intentionally want to introduce shakiness to your video image, always mount your camera on a tripod.

✦ **Avoid quick and jerky movements:** If you need to follow your subject matter by panning the head on the tripod, practice the movement a few times before recording. Try to be as slow and fluid as possible. The quicker you pan a video camera while recording, the more likely you'll see compression artifacts show up in your final video in the Flash movie.

✦ **Avoid zooming:** While it may be tempting, do not zoom the lens while recording your subject matter. It's better to use the zoom to frame the shot before you record. Of course, you may intentionally want to using wild zooming effects to recreate the next "Blair Witch" mockumentary, but be aware that any rapid movement from zooming the lens will likely compress very poorly in the Flash movie.

✦ **Lock focus:** All camcorders can auto-focus the lens. If you plan to record a stationary object, you may want to switch to manual focus. If your subject matter moves away from the focus "spot" used by the camera, it may refocus on areas behind the subject matter. This type of focus drifting may yield very unpleasant compression artifacts in the Flash video.

Another factor to consider is the area of the video composition that changes from frame to frame. In a previous example, we mentioned panning a race car. In that example, the entire picture changes in every frame. Compression works best on video footage with the least amount of movement per pixel in the frame. For example, if you mount your camera on a tripod and keep the camera motionless, you can record the motion of a single subject, such as the flight of a bee between flowers. In such an example, the video compression in Flash MX is much more effective than it would be in the example of the race car.

Comparing Video Sources

On the *Flash MX Bible* CD-ROM, you will find three video samples in the ch17 folder. You can use these examples to test compression settings in Flash MX and Sorenson Squeeze. Each sample was recorded with a different camera.

✦ **sample_low.mpg:** This video file was recorded with a Sony DSC-S70 Cybershot camera. While this camera is designed to shoot stills, it can also record MPEG-1 video files. This file was recorded in high quality mode at 320 × 240, 15 frames per second. The microphone on this camera is mono (single-channel).

sample_low.mpg was recorded with a digital still camera.

✦ **sample_mid.avi:** This video file was recorded with a Sony DCR-PC100 miniDV camcorder. This camcorder has a stereo built-in microphone and a single CCD. The quality captured by this camera is average for most DV camcorders. Compare the color temperature of this recording to that of the sample_high.avi.

sample_mid.avi was recorded with an average miniDV camcorder.

✦ **sample_high.avi:** This video file was recorded with a Sony DSR-PD150 miniDVCAM camcorder. This professional camera has superior exposure and color temperature control. Among other differences with the previous samples, the audio was recorded with a wireless Shure microphone and an UP4 receiver, which uses a 3-pin XLR output. The PD150 can accept this XLR output.

sample_high.avi was recorded with a high-end DVCAM camcorder and a wireless XLR microphone.

When you open these files in a video viewer such as Windows Media Player or Apple QuickTime Player, notice that the files recorded by the DV camcorders appear stretched horizontally. The DV format uses non-square pixels, while most display devices like computer monitors use square pixels. Unless the video viewer compensates for non-square pixels, the video image will appear stretched. Flash MX will not compensate for non-square pixel footage, so you should either convert the footage to square pixels in a video application such as Adobe Premiere or QuickTime Player Pro edition. Alternatively, you can import the footage "as is" into Flash MX and transform the width to correctly render the picture. This latter method, however, will still import the extra pixels used in the non-square footage, making your Flash movie's file size (as a .swf file) larger than necessary.

We offer you these samples so that you may experiment with them in Flash MX. You will find that cleaner video (such as that shot with the high-end video camcorder) will exhibit less video noise in the Spark-compressed version within the Flash MX document.

Editing footage

Once you have recorded the video with your camcorder, it's time to start editing the footage in a digital video editor like Adobe Premiere or Apple Final Cut Pro.

Tip   Don't try editing video clips in Flash MX — you don't want to waste space in either the Flash MX document or the Flash movie (.swf file). You should only bring finished video clips into Flash MX.

It's beyond the scope of this book to fully explain the process of editing video footage, but we offer the following pointers to maximize the compression benefits of the Spark codec that Flash MX uses for video:

✦ **Watch transitions and filter effects:** Keep the general rule in mind that we mentioned previously — refrain from global changes to the entire frame. Some effects and transitions, such as cross-fades and slow dissolves, introduce rapid changes to successive frames of video. These changes will require more keyframes to retain quality, and these keyframes will add significant weight to the file size of the compressed video in Flash MX. Otherwise, if you don't want the extra weight, you'll have to accept less quality in the overall image.

✦ **Minimize duration:** The shorter you make your finished video clip, the smaller the file size of your Flash movie (.swf file). While you can stream video content just like any Flash content, you should keep in mind the data rate of your target audience.

✦ **Enable necessary tracks:** Use video and audio tracks only if you need both in your final Flash movie. While you can disable the audio in the Flash document's Publish Settings, you can prevent major headaches by importing only the essential material you require.

When you finish editing your video, make a master version that can serve for other purposes beyond your Flash movie presentation. You may even want to output a final version of the edited footage to DV tape. In the next section, we discuss what output format to use for your edited footage. Later, this output format will be compressed and embedded in the Flash MX document.

Cross-Reference We look at data rates of Flash video in the "Publishing Flash Movies with Video" and "Using Sorenson Squeeze for Flash Video" sections later in this chapter.

Choosing an import format

After you complete the editing phase for your video footage, you're ready to output a final version of your video project that you can import into a Flash MX document. The following checklist should help you determine how to get the most effective use out of Flash MX's video codec, Sorenson Spark. Just like you don't want to re-JPEG a JPEG (that is, save a JPEG file again with more JPEG compression), you will find that it's best to retain as much original quality from the video as possible before you bring it into Flash MX.

✦ **Frame size:** Most video sources are captured and edited at full frame NTSC sizes, such as 640 × 480 and 720 × 480. It's unlikely that you'll want to expend the bandwidth required to display this full frame size. A starting frame size should be 320 × 240; work your way down from there. If you are targeting Web users with dial-up connection speeds such as 28.8 or 56 Kbps, you may want to consider a frame size of 160 × 120. Remember, when you scale down a bitmap-based element in Flash MX, you don't actually throw away any pixels — the full size of the graphic is retained in the final Flash movie (.swf file).

✦ **Frame rate:** When you capture video from your camcorder to your desktop video editing application, the video has a frame rate of 29.97 fps (NTSC) or 25 fps (PAL). This frame rate, like regular video frame sizes, will consume massive amounts of bandwidth in a Flash movie. As a general rule, keep your video frame rate as close as possible (or lower than) the frame rate of your Flash movie, as defined in the Document Properties dialog box (Modify ➪ Document). Most video on the Internet has a frame rate of 12 or 15 fps.

✦ **Video compression:** Keep your final video file in the codec in which it was originally captured. For example, if you captured and edited the video with the DV codec, use the DV codec for the video file you create to import into Flash MX. You can also use the Uncompressed option when you save your final video file, available in Apple QuickTime Player Pro or any video editing application such as Adobe Premiere or Apple Final Cut Pro.

✦ **Audio compression:** Follow the same guidelines for video compression. DV-formatted video stores audio uncompressed. Flash MX will recompress audio in a video file that has been imported. As such, it's not ideal to apply any compression to the audio track before you bring into Flash MX.

✦ **De-interlacing:** We mentioned earlier in this chapter that video recorded by camcorders is interlaced. However, computer monitors (and the graphics displayed on them) are progressively scanned and do not require interlacing. (You may notice how "soft" your DV footage appears in most desktop video editing applications; this is due to the even and odd "interlaces" being multiplied to accommodate the progressive scanning of computer video.) The general rule of thumb is to use a de-interlace filter (or export option) on any video footage that you intend to use for computer playback. However, if you resize your video to 320×240 or smaller and decrease the frame rate from its original rate, you effectively de-interlace the video footage. Usually, you will not see any difference enabling a de-interlace filter on top of these reductions.

After you have gone through this checklist for your video footage, export a final video file that you can import into Flash MX. Most video applications (including Apple QuickTime Player Pro) can re-save a finished video file with a new frame size, frame rate, video and audio compressions, and other options such as de-interlacing. Flash MX can import a variety of video file formats, listed in Table 17-1.

Table 17-1: Video Import Formats for Flash MX

Format	Platform	Required Drivers	Description
AVI (.avi) Audio Video Interleaved	Windows Macintosh	DirectX 7 or higher, or QuickTime 4 or higher	Standard Windows video format; usually the format in which video is captured on Windows; can use any combination of video and audio codecs.
DV (.dv) Digital Video stream	Windows Macintosh	QuickTime 4 or higher	Format saved from applications such as Adobe Premiere or Apple QuickTime Player Pro; uses the DV codec for video and uncompressed audio.
MPEG (.mpg, .mpeg) Motion Picture Experts Group	Windows Macintosh	DirectX 7 or higher, or QuickTime 4 or higher	Pre-compressed video in the MPEG-1 or MPEG-2 codec; a format used by many digital cameras that save to media format such as Compact Flash (CF) and Memory Stick.

Continued

Table 17-1: *(continued)*

Format	Platform	Required Drivers	Description
QT (.mov) Apple QuickTime	Windows Macintosh	QuickTime 4 or higher	Standard video format on the Mac; usually the format in which video is captured on the Mac; can use any combination of video and audio codecs.
WMV (.wmv, .asf) Windows Media files	Windows	DirectX 7 or higher	Precompressed video in a modified MPEG-4 codec developed by Microsoft to use with the Windows Media Player.

Of the formats listed in Table 17-1, we recommend that you import formats that don't apply any recompression to the original source format of your video. If you can avoid using compressed video like Windows Media and MPEG files, you can prevent further artifacts from being introduced into the video by Flash's video compressor. Compression artifacts are areas in the video frame where detail is lost. The process of compressing a file already using compression is known as recompression.

Caution   If you try to import MPEG files into the Macintosh version of Flash MX, you will not be able to use the audio track in the Flash MX document (or Flash movie). Only Windows' DirectX driver will successfully convert both the video and audio tracks in a MPEG file to a format usable in the Flash MX document. To import a MPEG via QuickTime on the Mac, you will need to use an application like Discreet Cleaner 5.1 (or higher) to convert the MPEG to a QuickTime movie that uses another codec.

Importing the Video

After you create a video file in the desired import format, you're ready to bring it into Flash MX. This section will introduce you to the Sorenson Spark codec options available in Flash MX. In the latter half of this section, we walk you through the process of importing one of the sample files on the *Flash MX Bible* CD-ROM.

Linked versus embedded video

Starting with Flash MX, there are now two methods in which Flash content can interact with video content. When Flash 4 was released, QuickTime movies could be imported into the Flash authoring environment. There, you could animate and develop Flash content that interacted with the QuickTime movie. However, in Flash 4 and 5, you could only export QuickTime Flash movies (.mov files) that required the Apple QuickTime 4 (or higher) Player to view. The QuickTime video files were linked to the Flash document (.fla file), which meant that the Flash document didn't store the actual video content. You can still use linked video files in Flash MX to create QuickTime Flash movies.

For more information on QuickTime Flash movies, read Chapter 41, "Working with QuickTime."

The second method that you can use to view video in Flash Player 6 is to embed the video file in the Flash document (.fla file) as well as the Flash movie (.swf file). This new method allows Flash MX to encode your video with the new Sorenson Spark codec (discussed in the next section). It's important to understand this new codec does not require any additional plug-ins for playback—the Web user needs only to have Flash Player 6 installed on her/his browser. Spark does not use any system-level video codecs; the Spark codec is built into Flash Player 6.

If you select a QuickTime movie to import into either the Windows or Macintosh version of Flash MX, you will see the dialog box shown in Figure 17-1. To use the QuickTime video file as an embedded video playable by Flash Player 6, choose the first option. To use the video file for a QuickTime Flash movie, choose the second option.

Figure 17-1: The Import Video dialog box will appear when you import a QuickTime video file into Flash MX.

This chapter deals explicitly with the new embedding video features of Flash MX. In the next section, we explore the compression options available for the Sorenson Spark codec in Flash MX.

Spark compression options

Flash MX ships with the Sorenson Spark Basic edition video codec. Quite honestly, this codec is among the best codecs we have ever used. In this section, we discuss the options of the Spark Basic edition. Before we do that, we offer a quick review of video compression schemes.

Video codecs can compress image data in two different ways—temporally and spatially. A temporal compression algorithm, or interframe compressor, compares the data between each frame and stores only the differences between the two. A spatial compression algorithm, also known as intraframe compression, will compress the data in each frame, just as the JPEG format compresses data in a still image. Most video codecs designed for Web playback, including Sorenson Spark, do not use a lossless compression technique with either temporal or spatial algorithms. Rather, some color and detail information is thrown out in an effort to minimize the amount of data that is saved with each frame. For example, if the original video source recorded a sunset with 80 shades of orange, the compressed version of the sunset may only include 50 or fewer shades of orange. You may have noticed the extremes of lossy compression in Web videos where a person's face is hardly distinguishable, looking more blocky than human.

Historically speaking, most new codecs developed in the last few years rely upon the ever-increasing computer processor speeds to efficiently decompress each frame of video on playback. For this reason, you may want to test video playback on a number of machines and devices that support the Flash Player 6 and video decoding.

Sorenson Spark uses interframe (temporal) compression, but it also uses intraframe compression when making keyframes. (You see how tricky keyframes can be in just a moment.) A keyframe in video footage is similar to a keyframe in a Flash Timeline. A keyframe defines a moment in time where a significant change occurs. For example, if a section of video has three hard cuts from one scene to another to another, the compressed version of that video should have a keyframe at the start of each scene. A keyframe then becomes the reference for subsequent frames in the video. When the following frame(s) are compared to the keyframe, only the differences are remembered (or stored) in the video file. As soon as the scene changes beyond a certain percentage, a new keyframe will be made in the video. Video keyframes are created while the movie is being compressed (or imported) into Flash MX.

Caution Video keyframes are the reason you should be careful with special effects or filter use in transitions from scene to scene in your video. The more frequently your video changes from frame to frame, the more keyframes your video file will need. Keyframes take up more file size than interframes between the keyframes.

Now that you have had an introduction to compression concepts, let's look at the options available in the Basic edition of the Sorenson Spark codec. Create a new Flash document in the Flash MX authoring environment, and use File ⇨ Import to select a video file. For this example, you can use the sample_high_import.mov file from the *Flash MX Bible* CD-ROM. When you select this QuickTime file for import, select the Embed video in Macromedia Flash document option in the Import Video dialog box. When you click OK, you'll see the Import Video Settings dialog box shown in Figure 17-2.

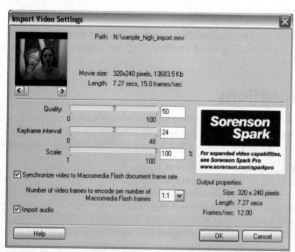

Figure 17-2: The Import Video Settings dialog box controls the compression options for the Sorenson Spark codec.

✦ **Source movie properties:** To the right of the movie preview icon, you will find information about your source import movie. The movie's frame size (that is, width and height dimensions), file size, duration, and frame rate will be displayed. Note that any source movies with sizes larger than 360×240 (or 320×240) will be displayed as 360×240 (or 320×240).

✦ **Quality:** This slider and text field allow you to enter a value from 0 to 100. This scale is similar to JPEG quality, where 100 is maximum quality and 0 is least quality. For most video, you will find that 60 is the minimum acceptable quality. Anything lower than this may be too compressed and appear blocky.

✦ **Keyframe interval:** This slider and text field control how often the Spark codec will create keyframes in the video. A value of 0 will insert no keyframes. Lower values (except 0) insert more keyframes, while higher values insert fewer keyframes. One sample file set to use 0 as a keyframe interval (with all other settings equal) compressed to 42 KB, while the same file set to use 1 as a keyframe interval compressed to 219 KB. The same file set to use 48 as a keyframe interval compressed to 45 KB.

On the CD-ROM

Compare the visual quality of the sample_0kf_50qu.swf, sample_1kf_50qu.swf, and sample_48kf_50qu.swf files, located in the ch17 folder of the book's CD-ROM. In this case, fewer keyframes (0 keyframe interval or 48 keyframe interval) produce a cleaner video image – the background behind Robert does not display as much video noise. Each sample used a Quality value of 50.

✦ **Scale:** This slider and text field control the frame size of the imported video file as it appears on the Flash Stage. As you change the Scale value, the Output properties in the lower right will show the new size of the video frame. You can use the Scale control to effectively resize larger full-frame video files (that is, with frame sizes of 640×480 or larger) to more web-friendly sizes such as 320×240 or 160×120. Unfortunately, you can not independently resize the width from the height to correct the pixel aspect ratio of DV format video files.

✦ **Synchronize video to Macromedia Flash document frame rate:** When this check box is selected, Flash MX will adjust the source video file's frame rate to match the frame rate of the current Flash document. For example, if a source file has a frame rate of 15 fps and the Flash document has a rate of 12 fps, this selected option will drop three frames from each second of the imported video. If you clear this option, Flash MX will assign each frame of video to one frame of the Flash timeline. As such, the video may play slower than real time because it's keeping the same number of frames but being played back at a slower frame rate. You can see this "delay" effect by watching the Length value change in the Output properties area as you clear the check box and/or select it.

✦ **Number of video frames to encode per number of Macromedia Flash frames:** This menu controls the ratio of video frames to Flash frames. This option works hand-in-hand with the Synchronize option to reduce the number of frames that are actually imported into the Flash document. By default, a 1:1 ratio is selected, which preserves the original frame rate of the source video. You can use this control to reduce the frame rate of your source video by choosing an appropriate ratio. Whenever possible, we recommend that your final video frame rate be at least 12 fps for smooth video playback.

✦ **Import audio:** With this check box, you can choose to either import (selected check box) or ignore (cleared check box) the audio track of the source video.

✦ **Output properties:** The lower right corner of this dialog box will update to reflect the current values of the options previously discussed. Note that you can not directly change any values in this area.

Now that you're familiar with the options within the Import Video Settings dialog box, the next section will walk you through the steps of using them with one of the sample files on the book's CD-ROM.

This section covered the settings available for the Basic edition of the Sorenson Spark codec. Later in this chapter, we explore the extended options offered by the Pro edition of the Spark codec, available in Sorenson Squeeze. Squeeze is a separate encoding application that offers superior compression over the native encoding found in Flash MX.

Unfortunately, the Import Video Settings dialog box does not provide estimated bandwidth or data rates for the selected options. We discuss data rate and bandwidth concerns in the "Publishing Flash Movies with Video" section later in this chapter.

Adjusting audio compression

As strange as it may sound, the audio track of a digital video file is imported and retained in its original source format. Flash MX uses the global audio settings found in the Publish Settings dialog box to control the compression applied to your imported video's audio track. Most importantly, audio linked to an embedded video is treated as Stream sound so that it will be properly synched to the playback of the video. Therefore, you must specify the video's audio compression in the Audio Stream options of the Publish Settings dialog box.

For more information on audio compression, read Chapter 15, "Adding Sound." Flash MX now features a Speech codec that can also be used for the audio track of a video clip.

Compressing video with Flash MX

In this section, we show you how to go through the process of selecting a video file and embedding it in a Flash MX document. Remember, embedded video can be played only with Flash Player 6.

For this example, make a copy of the sample_high_import.mov to a local folder or your desktop.

1. Open a new Flash document (File ⇨ New).

2. Open the Document Properties (Modify ⇨ Document), and set the frame rate to 12 fps. Alternatively, you can change the frame rate in the Property inspector. Click any empty area of the Stage or Work area to show the document properties in the Property inspector.

3. Using File ⇨ Import (Ctrl+R or ⌘+R), browse to the sample_high_import.mov file that you copied to your system. With the filename selected, click Open in the Import dialog box.

4. In the Import Video dialog box, make sure Embed video in Macromedia Flash document is selected. Click OK.

5. In the Import Video Settings dialog box, specify a Quality of 75 and a Keyframe interval of 24, as shown in Figure 17-3. Also synchronize the video frame rate to the Flash document's frame rate. Click OK when you are finished adjusting the settings.

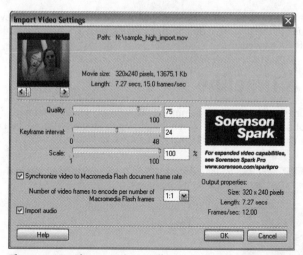

Figure 17-3: These settings will compress the video with acceptable quality.

6. When the Import progress bar is finished, Flash MX will display the dialog box shown in Figure 17-4. One feature of video import in Flash MX is that it will automatically expand a timeline (if necessary) to accommodate the length of the video file. Since video is a streaming asset (like Stream sound), the timeline that holds the video needs to be as long as the video clip. In this example, Flash MX needs 87 frames to display the entire clip. Click Yes in this dialog box.

Figure 17-4: Flash MX will ask you if you want to add more frames to the timeline to display the full video clip.

7. The video clip appears on the Main Timeline of the current Flash document. Flash MX automatically centers the video clip as well. Save your Flash document as sampleVideo_100.fla, and test it (Ctrl+Enter or ⌘+Enter). The Flash movie (.swf file) is only 72 KB. Not bad for seven seconds of web video! That's roughly a data rate of 10 KB/s, or 80 Kbps.

8. You can further modify the quality of the video clip's audio track by adjusting the Audio Stream settings in the Publish Settings. By default, Flash MX will use MP3 compression at 16 Kbps, mono, with Fast quality. Open the Publish Settings dialog box (File ⇨ Publish Settings), and click the Flash tab. Click the Set button for the Audio Stream option, and choose a new codec. For example, you can choose MP3 compression at 20 Kbps, mono, with Best quality. This will produce a slightly larger file size with better audio quality than the default. Close the Publish Settings dialog box, and retest your movie.

You may want to repeat this exercise, experimenting with different Quality and Keyframe interval, and Scale values in the Import Video Settings dialog box. Try other sample video files on the book's CD-ROM as well.

Using Video in a Timeline

In the preceding section, you learned how to import video into a Flash document. Now, we'll get into practical use of the Video objects. When you embed video into your Flash document, you add an Embedded Video object to the Library, as shown in Figure 17-5.

Figure 17-5: An Embedded Video in the Library panel

As with other symbols in the Library, you can reuse the same Embedded Video object as several instances throughout the Flash document with no significant file size gains. Keep in mind, though, that video on a Flash timeline is treated just like Stream sound — only the frames of video that you can view within the Timeline window will be exported with your Flash movie.

Tip   You can effectively trim your video by removing frames at the tail of the clip.

Controlling playback of video

You can control the playback of your Embedded Video object by controlling the playback of the timeline in which it is contained. In the following steps, you add play and stop buttons to the Main Timeline to control the video.

Cross-Reference   To learn more about basic actions and Button instances, read Chapter 18, "Understanding Actions and Event Handlers."

For this example, open the sampleVideo_100.fla file from the ch17 folder of this book's CD-ROM. Alternatively, you can start a new file and embed a new video file into the Flash document. You should have an Embedded Video object on a layer in the Main Timeline (that is, Scene 1) before we proceed with the steps.

1. Add a new layer, and rename it buttons.

2. Open the Buttons library (Window ➪ Common Libraries ➪ Buttons). From this library's Circle Buttons folder, drag instances of the Play and Stop buttons to the Stage. Position them under the video, as shown in Figure 17-6.

Figure 17-6: The Play and Stop buttons positioned under the video

3. Select the Play button, and open the Actions panel (F9). In the panel's options menu, switch to Expert mode and type the following actions into the Script pane:

```
on (release){
    play();
}
```

4. Select the Stop button, and open the Actions panel (F9). In Expert mode, type the following actions into the Script pane:

```
on (release) {
    stop();
}
```

5. Save your Flash document as sampleVideo_200.fla, and test it (Ctrl+Enter or ⌘+Enter). Click the Stop button to stop the video, and click the Play button to resume play.

6. Now, let's stop the video from playing at the beginning at the movie. Create a new layer named actions, and select frame 1 of this layer. Open the Actions panel, and type the following action in the Script pane:

```
stop();
```

7. Open the Buttons library once again, and select the Buttons layer in the Timeline window. Drag instances of the Rewind, Step Ahead, and Step Back buttons onto the Stage. Position these instances below the video, as shown in Figure 17-7.

Figure 17-7: These buttons will add more playback control to the video clip.

8. With the Rewind instance selected, open the Actions panel (F9) and type the following actions into the Script pane:

```
on (release){
    gotoAndStop(1);
}
```

9. With the Step Back instance selected, type the following actions into the Script pane of the Actions panel:

```
on (release){
    prevFrame();
}
```

10. With the Step Ahead instance selected, type the following actions into the Script pane of the Actions panel:

```
on (release){
    nextFrame();
}
```

11. Save your Flash document again, and test it (Ctrl+Enter or ⌘+Enter). Try out each of your control buttons. If one didn't work, go back and check its code in the Actions panel.

On the CD-ROM

You can view the completed Flash document, sampleVideo_200.fla, located in the ch17 folder of the book's CD-ROM. This document also has additional background graphics.

Placing and controlling video within a Movie Clip

While you can place Embedded Video objects on the Main Timeline of a Flash movie, you may find it useful to place video within a Movie Clip symbol, and re-use instances of that Movie Clip throughout the document. In the following steps, you change the structure of the sampleVideo_200.fla to make a control bar Movie Clip object, as well as a video Movie Clip object. For this example, open the sampleVideo_200.fla file from the ch17 folder of this book's CD-ROM.

1. In the Timeline window, expand the contents of the backgrounds folder. Lock the following layers: sampleVideo, videoFrame, and videoBackground. Then, select all of the Button instances and remaining background element by choosing Edit ➪ Select All (Ctrl+A or ⌘+A). Your document should resemble Figure 17-8.

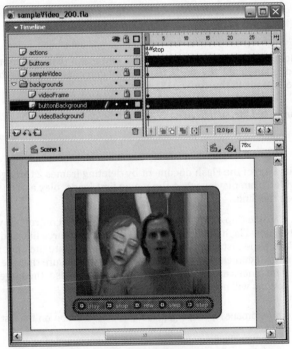

Figure 17-8: Select all of the Button instances and the artwork behind them.

2. With these items selected, choose Insert ➪ Convert to Symbol (F8). In the Symbol Properties dialog box, type the name **controlBar**. Select the Movie Clip behavior as well, and click OK.

3. With this new Movie Clip object selected on the Stage, open the Property inspector and assign the instance name **controlBar**. Rename the Buttons layer to controlBar, and delete the empty buttonBackground layer.

4. Unlock the sampleVideo layer, and select the sampleVideo object on the Stage. Press the F8 key to convert this object to a Movie Clip object. In the Symbol Properties dialog box, name this symbol **myVideo**. When you click OK, you see a message asking if you want to assign more frames to the symbol's timeline. Choose Yes on this dialog box.

5. With the new symbol selected on the Stage, open the Property inspector and give the instance the name **myVideo**. Now that the instance is named, you can target this Movie Clip instance with ActionScript. Rename the sampleVideo layer to myVideo as well.

6. Now you need to update the ActionScript code on each of the Button instances within the controlBar instance. Double-click the controlBar instance on the Stage to edit the symbol in place.

7. For each of the buttons, insert the path _parent.myVideo. in front of each navigation action. For example, for the Play button, the code in the Script pane should be changed to:

```
on (release){
    _parent.myVideo.play();
}
```

8. Save your Flash document as sampleVideo_300.fla, and test it (Ctrl+Enter or ⌘+Enter). Notice that the video automatically starts to play. You can control the playback of the video by using the buttons in the controlBar instance.

On the CD-ROM You can find the completed file, sampleVideo_300.fla, in the ch17 folder of the *Flash MX Bible* CD-ROM.

You can tidy the Main Timeline of the Flash document by deleting frames 2 through 89. Also, if you want to stop the video from playing when the movie first loads, play a stop(); action on frame 1 of the myVideo timeline.

By placing your video in a Movie Clip, you can more easily re-use this control bar with other video clips. Simply create a new Flash document, import the video source file, and nest it in a Movie Clip symbol. Name the instance myVideo, and copy and paste the controlBar instance from this exercise's document to your new document. Make sure that the controlBar and myVideo instances are on the same timeline; otherwise, the target path assigned in the Buttons' actions will not work.

Tip To stop the video from automatically looping, place a stop(); action on the last frame of the myVideo timeline.

Publishing Flash Movies with Video

When you use Embedded Video objects in a Flash movie, you're making the decision to use rather large file sizes on the Web. One of Flash's original claims to fame is the ability to stream lightweight animation, graphics, and sound over the Web. While it may seem contrary to use video for lightweight graphics, video can be streamed into Flash Player 6. Careful attention must be given to the data rate of the Flash movie containing the video. Use the following guidelines for matching a target data rate to a specific video frame size:

✦ **Dial-up modem:** This connection speed includes 28.8, 33.6, and 56 Kbps modems. For these data rates, we recommend that you use video at 160×120 (or smaller), at 12 fps or slower.

✦ **Broadband or LAN connection:** If your target audience has a fast Internet connection such as DSL, cable, high-speed wireless, T1, or T3, you have much more flexibility with your data rate options for Flash video. A common video size for this connection type is 320×240, with a frame rate of 15 fps or higher. However, because the video frame rate is tied to the frame rate of the Flash movie, you may want to stick with 12 fps. 12 fps is the default frame rate for documents in Flash MX.

 Sorenson Squeeze offers several output settings for Flash video, to use with various connection speeds. We discuss Squeeze in the last section of this chapter.

In truth, Macromedia Flash movies do not stream into the Flash Player — they download progressively. Video streaming, as it is referred to by QuickTime, RealOne, and Windows Media Players, means that the video file is never downloaded as one single file to the end user. Rather, a streaming video server delivers the video in realtime, sending the video frame by frame to the player. A progressive download, on the other hand, is downloaded to the player. However, the term progressive means that the video can start playback as soon as a certain percent of the video has downloaded into the player. So, while a 5 MB file size may sound large for the Web, the user may not have to wait for the entire 5 MB to download in order to begin his/her viewing of the video. Macromedia's offers the following formula to determine the average wait time for a given video clip:

```
wait time = total download time - clip duration + 10% of clip duration
```

So, if you have a Flash movie that's 300 KB with a duration of 20 seconds, a user with a 56 Kbps modem with an average download rate of 4.7 KB/s will wait an estimated 64 seconds for the entire file to download (300 KB ÷ 4.7 KB/s = 63.8 seconds). However, using the formula, you can calculate how long the user must wait before the movie begins playback:

```
64 seconds - 20 seconds + 2 seconds = 46 seconds
```

During longer wait times, you may want to offer some interim activity while the user waits, such as some important news to read, a simple game, or an interesting animation.

Many dial-up users are willing to wait for larger high-quality digital video files. Therefore, you may want to offer visitors the choice to select which video file they want to download.

 We show you how to build preloaders for Flash movies and assets in Chapter 28, "Sharing and Loading Assets."

Storing video in a separate Flash movie

Anytime you have a very large asset (in file size) that you want to use in a Flash movie on the Web, your best bet is to make it its own Flash movie (.swf file) that loads into your "master" Flash movie for the Web site (or page). This idea holds true for sound files, video files, and bitmap graphics. In this section, we show you how to put an Embedded Video object into a timeline, make it a Flash movie (.swf file), and load it into another Flash movie.

On the CD-ROM For this example, make a copy of the sampleVideo_300.fla file, located in the ch17 folder of the *Flash MX Bible* CD-ROM.

1. Open the sampleVideo_300.fla file, and double-click the myVideo instance on the Stage. Inside of this symbol, select the Embedded Video object and delete it. You should have nothing in the myVideo symbol.

2. Delete frames 2 through 87 of the myVideo timeline.

3. Go back to the Main Timeline (that is, Scene 1). You will now see a small white dot in the middle of the Stage, representing the myVideo instance. Place this dot at the top-left corner of the videoFrame artwork, as shown in Figure 17-9. The X and Y coordinates of this position are 115, 80, respectively. In later steps, we will load the video file (as another .swf file) into this empty instance.

Figure 17-9: The empty Movie Clip will hold the external video .swf file.

4. Now, create a new Flash document while leaving the sampleVideo_300.fla open. Open the Library for the sampleVideo_300.fla document, and drag the sampleVideo Embedded Video object to the Stage of the new document. When the message box appears asking if you want to add 87 frames to the timeline, click Yes.

5. Save the new Flash document as **video.fla.**

6. Change the width and height of the video.fla document to match the dimensions of the Embedded Video object. In this example, the width of the video is 320 pixels, and the height is 240. Choose Modify ➪ Document to change these dimensions.

7. Center the Embedded Video object on the Stage, using the Align panel. Alternatively, you can use the new Flash MX shortcut, Ctrl+Alt+2 or ⌘+Option+2 to center vertically, and Ctrl+Alt+5 or ⌘+Option+5 to center horizontally.

8. Resave the video.fla document, and test it (Ctrl+Enter or ⌘+Enter). Close the Test Movie window after you've verified that the Embedded Video plays.

9. Close the video.fla document, and go back to the sampleVideo_300.fla. In the next few steps, you add the ActionScript to load the video.swf file you created in Step 8. The `myVideo` instance will be the target of a `loadMovie` action.

10. On the Main Timeline of the sample_300.fla document, create a new layer and name it **myText.** This layer will contain a Dynamic text field, and the text "Load movie" will appear in the field. You will add a link to this text to initiate a `loadMovie` action into the `myVideo` instance, using the video.swf as the movie to be loaded.

11. Select the Text tool, and click once on the Stage. Make sure you create this text on the myText layer. In the field, type **Load video.**

12. With the text field selected, open the Property inspector. Give this field an instance name of `myText`, and enable the HTML button. (If you are unfamiliar with text fields, read Chapter 8, "Working with Text.")

13. Select the Load video text in the text field, and in the Property inspector, type the following ActionScript code in the URL field. This code uses the `asfunction` available for HTML text fields in Flash movies. We discuss the `asfunction` in Chapter 31, "Applying HTML and Text Field Formatting." This code will link the **Load video** text to execute the `loadMovie` action with the `myVideo` instance, specifying the `video.swf` file to load into the `myVideo` instance. When you are finished, your document will resemble Figure 17-10.

```
asfunction:myVideo.loadMovie,video.swf
```

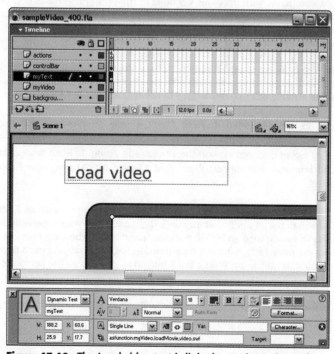

Figure 17-10: The Load video text is linked to ActionScript code.

14. Save your Flash document as sampleVideo_400.fla, and test it (Ctrl+Enter or ⌘+Enter). Click the Load video text, and the video.swf will load into the myVideo instance and begin to play.

You can find the completed Flash document, sampleVideo_400.fla, in the ch17 folder of the *Flash MX Bible* CD-ROM.

With this workflow, you can create several video documents and publish them as individual Flash movies (.swf files). Then, change the URL for the Load video text to point to the new file, replacing the existing filename.

In Chapter 28, "Sharing and Loading Assets," you will learn how to display a loading progress bar for assets like video and sound files.

Using named anchors with video timelines

Flash MX introduces a new Web browser feature: named anchors. A named anchor is a special frame label on the Main Timeline of a Flash movie that registers in the browser's history. The history remembers all of the Web pages that a user has visited during the current browser session. (Depending on the browser preferences, the histories can store months of Web page URLs.) One major complaint with previous versions of the Flash Player was that pressing the Back button on the Web browser would take the user to a different Web page instead of a prior scene or frame label in the Flash movie. For example, if a Web visitor came to your all-Flash site and clicked one menu, and then went somewhere else in the movie, he/she would have no way of pressing the Back button on the browser to get to that last "place" seen in the Flash movie; the Web browser would simply refresh to the very beginning of the Flash movie, or go to the last HTML page visited. You can now also bookmark specific sections of a Flash movie — the named anchor will append a label to the end of the file's URL.

Named anchors are supported in Flash Player 6 only on browsers that support the `fscommand` with JavaScript, such as Internet Explorer for Windows or Netscape 3.x to 4.x. Netscape 6 or higher does not support the `fscommand` action. To learn more about named anchors and browsers that support them, read Chapter 20, "Making Your First Flash MX Project."

In this section, you learn how to add named anchors to a Flash movie with an Embedded Video object. You will make an anchor at any defining moment in your video clip. Then, you will publish the Flash movie with an HTML document and watch the video play in Internet Explorer for Windows or Netscape 3.x–4.x on either Mac or Windows. As each named anchor plays, you will be able to hit the browser's Back button to go back to the previous named anchor.

Open the video_anchors_starter.fla file, located in the ch17 folder of the *Flash MX Bible* CD-ROM.

1. Create a new layer in the starter document, and name the layer **labels.**

2. Insert a keyframe on frame 2 of the Labels layer. In the Property inspector, assign the frame label marker_1 to this keyframe, and select the Named Anchor check box. See Figure 17-11.

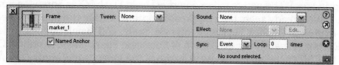

Figure 17-11: Frame labels can also be named anchors.

3. Place more keyframes and named anchors along the Main Timeline. Place them wherever you'd like to tag an area of the video. For example, you can add frame labels marker_2, marker_3, marker_4, and marker_5 at frames 130, 210, 280, and 435, respectively. Again, make sure you select the Named Anchor check box for each label.

4. Create a new layer, and name it **actions.** On frame 1 of the Actions layer, add a stop(); action in the Actions panel. Also add a stop(); action to frame 435 of the Actions layer. These are the first and last keyframes of the movie, respectively.

5. Save your Flash document as video_anchors.fla. Open the Publish Settings (File ⇨ Publish Settings) and click the HTML tab. In the Template menu, choose **Flash with Named Anchors.** This template inserts a JavaScript function into the HTML document that will catch the named anchors as they play in the browser.

6. Preview the Flash movie within an HTML document by choosing File ⇨ Publish Preview ⇨ HTML. When the Flash movie loads into the Web browser, the video clip will be paused. Click the Play button, and the video will play. As the video plays, the URL of the HTML document will change. For example, when the marker_1 frame plays, you'll see the document URL change to video_anchors.html#marker_1. When you reach the end of the movie, press the browser's Back button. If the last anchor that played was marker_5, pressing the Back button will take you to the marker_4 label.

On the CD-ROM

You can find the finished example file, video_anchors.fla, in the ch17 folder of the *Flash MX Bible* CD-ROM. This file includes an additional action on frame 1 to keep the Stage of the Flash movie from scaling in the browser: Stage.scaleMode = "noScale";. The HTML tab of the Publish Settings is also set to use 100 percent of the width and height of the browser window. Combined, these two changes allow the movie to appear centered in the browser window without scaling.

You can go back to the Flash document and adjust the placement of your named anchors. You can also use named anchors to create bookmarks. When you view a specific anchor that you'd like to go to straight away, create a bookmark. Named anchors work only with the Main Timeline (that is, Scene Timelines) of the current movie loaded in the browser. This means you can not make named anchors inside of Movie Clip timelines or in timelines of movies loaded into Level 1 or higher of the Flash Player.

Note

If you access a bookmarked Flash movie (or HTML page) in the browser, you need to wait for all prior frames of the Flash movie to load into the browser. The browser can not request an individual portion of a .swf file to download.

Using Sorenson Squeeze for Flash Video

Needless to say, the plain fact Macromedia Flash MX can import and embed video files playable by Flash Player 6 is truly remarkable. Just when you thought you've seen everything with Flash MX though, we need to tell you your journey with Flash video doesn't end with the Flash MX authoring tool. The native video compressor in Flash MX is Sorenson Spark Basic edition. As you have already seen, the compressor options within the Import Video Settings dialog box are limited to Quality, Keyframe interval, Scale, and Synch options. What you can't see in this dialog box is that the Basic edition of Sorenson Spark encodes only in CBR, or constant bit rate. CBR encoding means each frame of the video is uniformly compressed, consuming the same (or constant) data rate throughout the entirety of the clip. If you're familiar with MP3 sound, you may already be aware of CBR encoding with music. The same principle applies to video compression as well.

We all know, however, that each frame of video may not require the same amount of data to describe. For example, a solid field of blue (such as a big blue sky) may not need as much data as a field of multi-colored flowers, where several pixels in the frame have a different color. If your video footage contains a mixture of compositions and subject matter, it could benefit from another type of encoding known as VBR, or variable bit rate. VBR encoding allows the compressor to change the rate of compression applied to each frame of video. Therefore, one frame may need only 200 bytes, while another may need as many as 400 bytes. In practice, just about all video footage can benefit from VBR encoding. One of the drawbacks to encoding with VBR is that it takes longer to compress a video clip than it does with CBR encoding.

Unfortunately, Flash MX does not allow you to apply VBR encoding to imported files. Fortunately, Macromedia teamed up with Sorenson to offer an application that does: Sorenson Squeeze. This application, which is sold separately from Flash MX, comes in three editions:

✦ **QuickTime only:** This version of Squeeze can output QuickTime movies that use the Sorenson Video 3 codec. It includes a license for the Sorenson Video 3 Pro edition, enabling Sorenson Video 3 Pro options in other video applications (such as Adobe Premiere and Discreet Cleaner) as well.

✦ **Flash MX only:** This version of Squeeze creates Flash .flv and .swf files using the Sorenson Spark Pro codec, which we describe later in this section.

✦ **Combined:** This version can make QuickTime video movies (.mov files), Flash Video files (.flv files), and Flash movies (.swf files). For the purposes of our coverage, we discuss this version in the remainder of the chapter.

Sorenson Squeeze allows you to compress video files with Sorenson Spark Pro, which uses 2-pass VBR encoding. 2-pass VBR means that Squeeze will carefully examine each frame of video—twice. On the first pass, Squeeze analyzes the content of each frame. On the second pass, Squeeze performs the actual encoding, using the information it gathered from the first pass. The following list describes the added functionality Sorenson Squeeze offers beyond the native capabilities of Flash MX:

✦ **Superior encoding control:** Sorenson Squeeze can use either CBR or 2-pass VBR compression with your digital video. You can adjust audio and video data rates independently, and specify other codec options not available in Flash MX. We discuss these options in a later section.

✦ **Batch processing:** You can create several output versions of your digital video files with Sorenson Squeeze. Using the compression presets (discussed later), you can make a variety of low- and high-bandwidth movies all in one go.

✦ **DV capture:** Sorenson Squeeze can capture video directly from a DV source, over an IEEE 1394 (also known as FireWire or iLink) connection. Just connect your DV camcorder or deck to the computer and capture a live feed from the camera.

✦ **Multiple output formats:** Sorenson Squeeze can open several file formats and output either QuickTime Sorenson Video 3.0, Flash movie (.swf file), or Flash video (.flv file) formats. As such, you can make different movie formats for all of your Web video needs. You can use the Flash movie or Flash video formats with your Flash-based Web material and use the QuickTime movies for non-Flash Web pages.

✦ **Filter settings:** You can adjust the contrast, brightness, gamma, white restore, and black restore of the video image. Squeeze can also de-interlace your video footage, reduce video noise, crop the video frame, and fade the footage in and/or out. You can even normalize the audio track of the video file.

✦ **Compression presets:** Perhaps the most useful feature of Sorenson Squeeze is the ability to use bandwidth presets for your video compression. Squeeze has predefined compression options for the following connection speeds: Modem, ISDN, Broadband Low, Broadband, Broadband High, LAN CD, and CD High Quality. You can adjust the compression settings of each preset, but you can not add your own custom presets.

You can install a demo version of Sorenson Squeeze from the *Flash MX Bible* CD-ROM. You can find it in the software folder.

Choosing a Flash output file type

After you install the demo version of Sorenson Squeeze, go ahead and launch the application. The Sorenson Squeeze interface is shown in Figure 17-12. The output formats are represented as three file icons in the application's toolbar.

For any given video file, you can enable one or more of these formats to be exported in a batch.

Flash video

Sorenson Squeeze introduces a new video file format that can be imported into Flash MX: Macromedia Flash video (.flv file). A Flash video is a video file that has been compressed with the Sorenson Spark codec. As such, it can be quickly imported into a Flash MX document — no further encoding is necessary. Just like regular video files (such as .avi or .mov files), Flash video files have a frame rate, frame size (dimensions), and an optional audio track. Once you import the Flash video file into your Flash MX document, you can add further interactivity to it with ActionScript. We show you how to import a Flash Video file later in this chapter.

Make sure your Flash video file uses the same frame rate as the Flash movie that will be hosting it. If your Flash movie's frame rate is slower than the Flash Video's frame rate, the video will play at the slower frame rate and lose sync with its audio track. Alternatively, you can match the frame rate of your Flash movie to that of the Flash video file.

QuickTime output

Flash SWF output

Flash FLV output

Figure 17-12: You can choose one of three output formats in Sorenson Squeeze.

Flash movie

Squeeze can also create fully functional Flash movies (.swf files) from your digital video files. If you don't need to add anything to your video in Flash MX, you can simply choose your digital file and specify a compression setting for the Flash movie (.swf file) to be output from Squeeze. Voila! You have an instant Flash movie that can be loaded into an existing Flash movie with the `loadMovie` action, or viewed independently in a separate HTML document.

Tip   You can create Flash movies (.swf files) containing video with frame rates different from Flash movies that load them. This means that you can create a 15 fps Flash movie from Sorenson Squeeze and load it into a slower playing 12 fps Flash movie. As soon as the Flash movie with video starts to play, both movies will play at the speed of the Flash movie with video. Video content is treated just like Stream sound in the Flash Player—it will govern the Player's frame rate.

QuickTime Sorenson video

Finally, Squeeze can output QuickTime video files by using the Sorenson Video 3 codec. The Spark codec can be used only by Flash Player 6 at this time. Unlike other video codecs that have system-level files that can be used by all video applications, the Spark codec is built into Flash Player 6, Flash MX, and the Squeeze authoring tools. Because of this limitation, you may want to offer video files in other player formats, such as QuickTime, RealOne, or Windows Media, in addition to your video-enabled Flash movies.

Even though Spark Pro offers amazing compression and quality, you may be able to achieve better video quality at smaller file sizes with QuickTime movies and various video codecs. We examine video formats and codecs in the "Comparing Video Compression" section in the Bonus_Tutorials.pdf located on the book's CD-ROM.

Choosing a compression setting

Each output format can use a range of preset compression settings in Sorenson Squeeze, as shown in Figure 17-13. Each compression setting targets a specific data rate for the output file. When you choose a compression setting, Squeeze will add a new file to the Output File queue for each format you have enabled. For example, if you pressed the Flash FLV Output and Flash SWF Output buttons in the Squeeze toolbar, pressing the Broadband compression setting would add two files to the Output File queue: one Broadband Flash Video file (.flv file), and one Broadband Flash movie (.swf file).

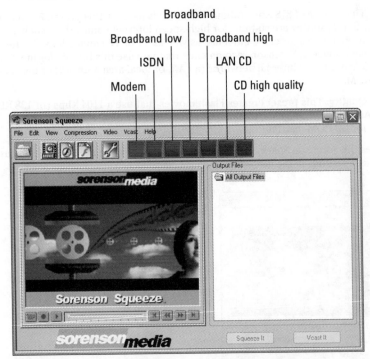

Figure 17-13: Sorenson Squeeze has seven compression presets.

The following list is a brief description of each preset as applied to Flash SWF output. Refer to Table 17-2 for more detailed technical information for each preset. Keep in mind that these presets are designed to stream movies at the appropriate bit rate, meaning that the Web visitor won't experience long delays in viewing the content.

✦ **Modem:** Squeeze targets users with dial-up modems by using a 39 Kbps bit rate on Flash movies (.swf files). This bit rate is roughly 4.9 KB/s, which works well for 56 Kbps modems. People with slower modems will notice delays with the video while it preloads into Flash Player 6.

✦ **ISDN:** For this preset, the target bit rate is 94 Kbps (about 11.8 KB/s) for Flash movies (.swf files). Dual ISDN connections are capable of speeds up to 128 Kbps, so this data rate falls well within this limit.

✦ **Broadband Low:** This preset has a target bit rate of 196 Kbps, which is 24.5 KB/s. Flash movies created with this bit rate are suitable for most ADSL or cable modem connections, as well as T1 or T3 connections.

✦ **Broadband:** This preset targets a bit rate of 298 Kbps, which is about 37 KB/s. This setting will work for users with the same connections mentioned in Broadband Low.

✦ **Broadband High:** This preset uses a bit rate of 415 Kbps, or 52 KB/s. This bit rate approaches the upper practical limit of most ADSL and cable modem connections

✦ **LAN CD:** The bit rate of 878 Kbps (about 110 KB/s) is used by this preset. Flash movies created with this setting are suitable for high-speed Internet connections such as 1 Mbps (or higher) DSL or cable modems, as well as T1 or T3 connections. As the preset's name suggest, Sorenson recommends that you use this bit rate for movies that are delivered over internal networks (a LAN, or local-area network) or distributed on a CD-ROM.

✦ **CD High Quality:** This preset creates Flash movies that use a 1104 Kbps (or 138 KB/s) bit rate. As the name suggests, this output setting will create high quality video, intended for CD-ROM distribution.

Each preset uses the Sorenson Spark Pro codec settings shown in Figure 17-14. We discuss the details of these settings in the next section.

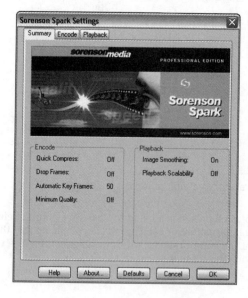

Figure 17-14: The Sorenson Spark Settings dialog box allows you to view the codec settings.

Table 17-2: Compression Settings in Sorenson Squeeze

Preset	Format	Video	Frames	Video Bit Rate	Audio Sample	Audio Bit Rate
Modem	Flash SWF	160 × 120	6 fps	31 Kbps	11.025 kHz Mono	8 Kbps
	Flash FLV	160 × 120	6 fps	31 Kbps	11.025 kHz Mono	352 Kbps
ISDN	Flash SWF	240 × 180	1:3	78 Kbps	22.050 kHz Mono	16 Kbps
	Flash FLV	240 × 180	1:3	78 Kbps	22.050 kHz Mono	352 Kbps
Broadband Low	Flash SWF	240 × 180	1:2	164 Kbps	22.050 kHz Mono	32 Kbps
	Flash FLV	240 × 180	1:2	164 Kbps	22.050 kHz Mono	705 Kbps
Broadband	Flash SWF	320 × 240	1:2	250 Kbps	44.100 kHz Stereo	48 Kbps
	Flash FLV	320 × 240	1:2	250 Kbps	44.100 kHz Stereo	705 Kbps
Broadband High	Flash SWF	320 × 240	1:2	351 Kbps	44.100 kHz Stereo	64 Kbps
	Flash FLV	320 × 240	1:2	351 Kbps	44.100 kHz Stereo	1411 Kbps
LAN CD	Flash SWF	480 × 360	1:1	750 Kbps	44.100 kHz Stereo	128 Kbps
	Flash FLV	480 × 360	1:1	750 Kbps	44.100 kHz Stereo	1411 Kbps
CD High Quality	Flash SWF	480 × 360	1:1	976 Kbps	44.100 kHz Stereo	128 Kbps
	Flash FLV	480 × 360	1:1	976 Kbps	44.100 kHz Stereo	1411 Kbps

Audio for all FLV output presets use Raw audio, meaning it's uncompression. FLV files are imported into Flash MX documents, where the audio compression is controlled via the Publish Settings. Audio for all SWF output presets use Fraunhofer MP3, which is the same MP3 codec used by Flash Player 6.

Note that Sorenson Squeeze often uses ratios for frame rates, as shown in Table 17-2. These ratios applied to the native source file's frame rate. For example, a ratio of 1:2 means that Squeeze will create 1 frame from every 2 frames in the source video, effectively halving the frame rate of the video. If a source video was 30 fps (rounded up from the 29.97 fps of NTSC vide), Squeeze creates a 15 fps Flash movie or Flash Video file. We strongly recommend that you use absolute frame rates instead of frame ratios. Flash movies and Flash video files created from Squeeze should play at the same rate as the Flash movie that will use them. However, if you are playing a Flash movie with video in its own browser window, frame rate synchronization may not be a problem.

Tip

You can load a Flash movie with video (or Stream sound) that uses a frame rate different from the Flash movie that is hosting it. The Flash movie with the video or Stream sound will take over the frame rate of Flash Player 6. For example, if a Flash movie containing video with a frame rate of 15 fps were loaded into a Flash movie with a frame rate of 6 fps, Flash Player 6 would play both Flash movies at 15 fps. We have provided two files, loadVideo.swf and video.swf, located in the fps folder of the ch17 folder on the *Flash MX Bible* CD-ROM. On a final note, in truth, it's actually the Stream sound used for the audio track of an Embedded Video object in a Flash movie that forces the frame rate playback. If you create a Flash movie or Flash Video file without an audio track, the video will play at the frame rate of the hosting movie.

Customizing a compression setting

While you can't create you own compression presets in Sorenson Squeeze, you can adjust the existing presets discussed in the last section. To adjust a compression setting, choose Edit ⇨ Compression Settings. From that menu, choose the preset you want to change. When you select the preset, you see the Compression Settings dialog box, shown in Figure 17-15.

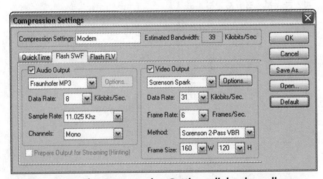

Figure 17-15: The Compression Settings dialog box allows you to change a preset.

✦ **Audio Output:** The options in this portion of the dialog box control how the audio track will be compressed. If you do not want to include the audio portion of the original source video file, clear this check box. You may want to read Appendix B, "Digital Sound Basics" for more information on digital audio.

- **Codec:** For Flash SWF output, you can choose only the Fraunhofer MP3 codec. For Flash FLV output, you can choose either Fraunhofer MP3 or Raw. Fraunhofer MP3 encoding is the same MP3 compression available in Flash MX. Raw is uncompressed PCM (Pulse Code Modulation) audio, and retains the original quality of your source video at the expense of increased data rate.

- **Data Rate:** This menu is enabled only if Fraunhofer MP3 is selected in the Codec menu. Here, you can select a bit rate in the range of 8 to 192 Kbps. Note that Flash MX can compress audio in only the 8 to 160 Kbps range for MP3 audio.

- **Sample Rate:** Squeeze allows you to choose 8, 11.025, 22.050 or 44.100 kHz for the compressed audio. Higher sample rates yield better quality but consume more bandwidth.

- **Channels:** You can choose to encode the audio as Mono (one channel) or Stereo (two channel). Stereo audio requires twice as much bandwidth as mono audio.

✦ **Video Output:** The options in this portion of the dialog box control how the video track will be compressed. If you want to export only the audio portion of your original source video file, clear this check box.

- **Codec:** For Flash SWF and FLV output, you can choose only the Sorenson Spark codec.

- **Data Rate:** You have greater flexibility with the video data rate then you do with the audio data rate. Not only can you choose from the options in the menu (48-1600 Kbps), but you can also type a custom value into the field. Unless you enable other codec options discussed in the next section, this will be the maximum data rate that the video can use.

- **Frame Rate:** You can choose any of the values in this menu for the frame rate of the Flash SWF or FLV output. Make sure this value matches the frame rate you will be using for other Flash movies in your Web site. You can choose a frame rate or ratio, but we recommend that you use a fixed frame rate. Common Internet video frame rates are 12 and 15 fps. You can also type a custom value into this field as well if the value you want is not in the menu.

- **Method:** This is where the power of Sorenson Squeeze comes to play. By default, Sorenson 2-pass VBR (discussed earlier in this chapter) is selected. You can also choose CBR, or constant bit rate. This is the encoding method that Flash MX uses, but it does not produce the same high quality and low file sizes that 2-pass VBR does. If you need a quick draft version of the file, you can use CBR — it's much faster than VBR, at the expense of quality and file size.

- **Frame Size:** You can specify the width and height of the video with these two menus. Frame sizes can be selected from the menus, or typed into the fields directly.

✦ **Save As:** Use this option to save your custom preset to a Sorenson Settings file (.xss file). You can rename preset names by specifying a new name in the Compression Settings field before you click the Save As button.

✦ **Open:** This option allows you to access a previously saved settings file and load its settings into the current Compression Setting.

✦ **Default:** This option loads the original specifications of the Compression Setting you currently have open. If you've accidentally changed a value and can't remember what the original value was, click this button to restore all values in the Compression Setting.

Cross-Reference

To accurately adjust these settings for your target audience's bit rate, we recommend that you review Table 15-4, "Bit Rates for Flash Movies," in Chapter 15.

You can also specify custom settings for the Spark Codec in Squeeze by clicking the Options button next to the Video codec menu. When you click this button, you see the Sorenson Spark Settings dialog box, shown in Figure 17-14 with the Summary tab displayed. When you click the Encode tab, you see the options shown in Figure 17-16.

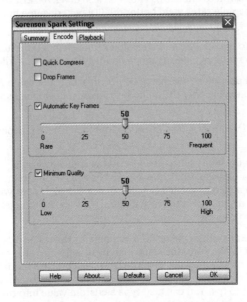

Figure 17-16: The Encode tab contains the settings that control video key frames and image quality.

✦ **Quick Compress:** This option will shave about 20 percent off the total encoding process with minimal difference in quality. According to Sorenson's documentation, one second of video takes about 1.2 seconds to encode *without* this option enabled.

✦ **Drop Frames:** This option works hand in hand with the Automatic Key Frames and Minimum Quality options. If you use these options with values that exceed the video data rate you specified in the Compression Settings, Squeeze will drop frames from the output video file to maintain the data rate you entered in the Compression Setting dialog box. For example, if you choose a minimum quality of 75 and the data rate of the video for that quality exceeds the data rate you specified, Squeeze will drop frames from the video to keep the data rate.

✦ **Automatic Key Frames:** This setting specifies a threshold value to determine when a new video key frame is created. Values closer to 0 need a greater difference between frames to create a video key frame, while values closer to 100 need less difference.

Smaller values will create fewer key frames. Sorenson recommends that you use values between 35 and 65. You may need to create a few versions of the video to find the optimum setting. We recommend that you use the default 50 value.

✦ **Minimum Quality:** This option controls the image quality of the video. When you select this check box, you can choose a value in the range of 0 to 100. These values mirror the Quality setting in Spark Basic edition. In general, you'll find that values below 50 are unacceptable. We recommend trying values in the range of 60 to 80. If you do not have the Drop Frames option selected, Squeeze will increase the video data rate to accommodate the value of Minimum Quality. For example, if you specify a video data rate of 160 Kbps, set Minimum Quality to 75, and disable Drop Frames, Squeeze will increase the data rate beyond 160 Kbps for any frames when necessary.

When you click the Playback tab of the Sorenson Spark Settings dialog box, you see the options shown in Figure 17-17.

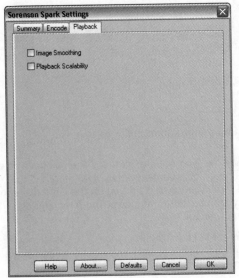

Figure 17-17: The Playback tab contains options that can optimize video playback on slower machines.

✦ **Image Smoothing:** This option works much like Flash's bitmap smoothing feature. For any blocky or pixelated areas of the video frame, the Spark Pro codec will smooth the edges of the affected area. Sorenson recommends this option only for low quality (or low video data rates) delivered to dial-up modem connections.

✦ **Playback Scalability:** This option is worth considering for any video that you intend to deliver to target audiences with slower computers. When enabled, this option will encode the video frames in such a way that only slower machines will drop frames evenly. For example, a 30 fps movie may be too fast for a slower computer to decompress while playing. A movie with Playback Scalability encoding will drop even frames, playing the 30 fps movie at 15 fps.

Applying Filters to Video in Sorenson Squeeze

You can use Sorenson Squeeze to adjust the image quality of your video, as well as polish the volume (or levels) of your video's audio track. When you click the Filters button on the toolbar (or choose Edit ➪ Filter Settings), the Filter Settings dialog box appears.

Filter Settings can adjust the quality of your video image and sound.

In the following list, we briefly describe each of the filter options. Not all video will need to use these filters, but you can save yourself some time and trouble in other video applications. You may notice that capture video looks dull and lackluster when displayed on the computer monitor. Television screens display color differently than computer monitors. The filter controls allow you to translate the video image to a computer monitor.

✦ **Contrast and Brightness:** These sliders control the lightness range of the image. Contrast will adjust the difference in lightness between light and dark areas of the image, while Brightness will control the overall lightness of the entire image.

✦ **Gamma:** This slider can also adjust the interaction of light and dark areas in the image. You may find it easier to control the contrast and brightness of the image by using the Gamma slider alone.

✦ **White Restore:** This slider controls the white point of the image. As its value is increased, the greater the range of white in the image.

✦ **Black Restore:** This slider controls the black point of the image. As its value is increased, more dark colors will be converted to black.

✦ **Deinterlace:** This menu allows you to de-interlace captured video. Each frame of NTSC video is made of two interlaced fields, but computer monitors are progressively scanned. For most captured video, you will want to use the Auto Remove Interlacing. You can force Squeeze to remove interlacing of either Even or Odd dominant frames — you should consult your video hardware documentation to see which field is dominant. All DV format video is lower field (or Even) dominant. If you have a video file that used 3:2 pulldown for footage that was transferred from film, you should choose one of the Remove Telecine options.

- ✦ **Video Noise Reduction:** Sorenson recommends that you use this control to remove video noise, which is best described as "speckled" video, where shadow or highlight detail may appear dirty. Use the Light option for video captured by low-end DV camcorders. You will not see a difference in the video image with this option, but it will improve the efficiency of the encoding process, potentially resulting in a slightly smaller file size. Use the Heavy option for video captured from low quality sources, such as VHS or 8mm video. You will see a difference in the visual quality of the image — some areas may appear slightly blurry or unnaturally smooth.

- ✦ **Fade In:** When this check box is selected, you can fade into your video footage. Choose either Black or White as the starting color of the fade, and specify a duration in seconds.

- ✦ **Fade Out:** When this check box is selected, you can fade out the tail of your video footage. Choose either Black or White as the ending color of the fade, and specify a duration in seconds.

- ✦ **Cropping:** When this check box is selected, you can trim the borders of your video image by dragging the bounding box in the preview window, or typing values in the L (left), T (top), R (right), or B (bottom) fields. You can also choose from sizes in the menu. If you transferred video from VHS or broadcast television to DV tape, you may need to crop the black borders of the video capture.

- ✦ **Normalize Audio:** When this check box is selected, Squeeze will adjust the audio track of the video source. If the original level (or volume) of the video track was rather quiet, use this option to boost the levels to a full range of loudness. Note that normalizing may produce a hiss sound in periods of silence.

Compressing video with Sorenson Spark Pro

In this section of the chapter, we walk you through the process of encoding video with Sorenson Spark and using either Flash FLV or SWF output in other Flash presentations. While you will create one Flash FLV file and one Flash movie (.swf file), you do not need to create both file types to incorporate video into your Flash project. FLV files can be imported into existing Flash MX documents, while Flash movies can be loaded directly into Flash Player 6.

Make a copy of the sample_high.avi file, located in the ch17 folder of the *Flash MX Bible* CD-ROM.

1. Open Sorenson Squeeze, and choose File ➪ Open. Browse to the sample_high.avi file that you copied from the book's CD-ROM.

2. Press the Flash FLV Output and Flash SWF Output buttons on the Squeeze toolbar.

3. Now press the Filter Settings button on the toolbar. Select the Contrast check box, and drag the slider to the first tick mark left of the center. Check the Normalize Audio option as well, as shown in Figure 17-18. Click OK.

Figure 17-18: Boosting the contrast of the image will improve this video's appearance on computer monitors.

4. Click the Broadband compression button on the toolbar. This will add two files to the Output Files queue, as shown in Figure 17-19. These files will be saved in the same folder as the original source video file.

Figure 17-19: The Output Files queue lists the files that are waiting to be encoded.

5. Squeeze is ready to encode the Flash Video file (.flv file) and Flash movie (.swf file) from the original source video. Press the Squeeze It button in the lower right corner of the application window. Squeeze starts the encoding process for the output files. You can preview the compression by clicking the Preview On button in the Squeezing dialog box. When the compression is finished, click the Close button and quit the Squeeze application.

6. Now you will import the Flash Video file (.flv file) into a new Flash MX document. Open Flash MX, and create a new document.

7. Choose File ➪ Import, and browse to the folder where the sample_high_Broadband.flv file was saved by Sorenson Squeeze. Select the file and import it into the document.

8. When the video imports, you see a message indicating the video will require 109 frames to display. Click Yes to this dialog box.

9. The frame rate of the Flash document needs to match the frame rate of the FLV file that was created from Squeeze. Our original source video was 30 fps (rounded up from the NTSC 29.97 fps frame rate), and Squeeze used a 1:2 ratio for the output frame rate. This means that the video from the FLV file has a frame rate of 15 fps. Choose Modify ➪ Document, and enter 15 in the Frame Rate field. Click OK to close the Document Properties dialog box.

10. Now you must decide what audio compression you wish to use for the audio track of the video. Open the Publish Settings (File ➪ Publish Settings), and click the Flash tab. Press the Set button for the Audio Stream option, and choose an audio codec and compression setting. For this example, you can try MP3 with a 20 Kbps bit rate. Choose Best in the Quality menu, and leave the Convert Stereo to Mono check box selected.

11. Save your Flash document as sampleVideo_squeeze.fla, and test it (Ctrl+Enter or ⌘+Enter). As you watch the video, pay attention to the quality of the audio track. You may want to go back to the Publish Settings to try out a new bit rate.

You can find the sampleVideo_Broadband.flv and .swf files in the ch17 folder of the *Flash MX Bible* CD-ROM. The Flash document sampleVideo_squeeze.fla and .swf are also located here.

Compare the quality of the Flash movie created from the FLV file to the original Flash movie (.swf file) that Squeeze created. Squeeze used a higher bit rate for the audio of this .swf file. Remember, one of the reasons for using FLV files is that you can add ActionScript and other Flash elements to the structure of the Flash movie containing the video.

For more information on video compression, read Jen deHaan's tutorial, "Comparing Video Compression," in the Bonus_Tutorials.pdf located in the Bonus_Tutorials folder of the *Flash MX Bible* CD-ROM. The tutorial examines the quality of video compression from Macromedia Flash MX, Wildform Flix 2.1, Sorenson Squeeze, Adobe After Effects 5.5, and Apple QuickTime Pro.

Summary

✦ Everything from tape format to camera lens can affect the quality of your original source video. Higher quality video footage will compress better in low bit rates for Internet delivery.

✦ The type of subject matter recorded in your video footage will affect the efficiency of any video compression or format. Footage with less movement will always compress smaller than footage with constantly changing content.

✦ You may need to create an in-between video source file before you import your video into Flash MX. For example, you may want to reduce 720×480 video footage to 320×240 and/or remove interlacing before you import the video.

✦ Flash MX can import a wide variety of video file formats, including .mov, .avi, .dv, .wmv, .asf, and .mpg files.

✦ Flash MX encodes video with the Sorenson Spark Basic edition codec, which uses CBR (constant bit rate) encoding. You have limited control over the compression options in Flash MX.

✦ The Sorenson Spark codec is built into Flash Player 6. Web users will not need to download any additional software to view video in Flash 6 movies.

✦ Sorenson Squeeze can compress Flash Video files (.flv files) or Flash movies (.swf files) with the Sorenson Spark Pro edition codec. This codec produces higher quality video with smaller file sizes than the Basic edition, due to the 2-pass VBR encoding used by the Pro edition. Squeeze is a separate application that is not included with the Flash MX installation.

✦ Pay attention to the frame rate you use for Flash Video and Flash movie output from Sorenson Squeeze. Whenever possible, try to use one universal frame rate across all of your Flash movies for any given project.

✦   ✦   ✦

Adding Basic Interactivity to Flash Movies

So far you've been learning how to make *things* — drawing shapes, creating symbols and working with frames and adding special assets. In the next three chapters you will learn how to integrate these various elements and how to make things *happen*. Chapter 18 introduces the concepts you need to understand when adding interactivity to presentations. Chapter 18 also gives you an orientation in the Flash MX Actions panel, where you will find some significant changes from Flash 5. Chapter 19 will give you the skills needed to control playback of multiple timelines. You will see how easy it is to use ActionScript to control display of internal elements in your Flash movies, including nested Movie Clips. If you want to see how these concepts and techniques are applied to real Flash production, Chapter 20 has just what you need — a step-by-step explanation of how to build a basic Flash presentation with a non-linear interface. The project will also introduce you to some important new Flash MX features such as components, named anchor keyframes, and accessibility options.

P A R T

V

◆ ◆ ◆ ◆

In This Part

Chapter 18
Understanding
Actions and Event
Handlers

Chapter 19
Navigating Flash
Timelines

Chapter 20
Making Your First
Flash MX Project

◆ ◆ ◆ ◆

Understanding Actions and Event Handlers

In This Chapter

Knowing events and event handlers

Understanding Flash actions

Using the Actions panel

Learning your first five Flash actions

Executing actions with event handlers

Using getURL

Making invisible buttons

Interactivity in a Flash movie can broadly be thought of as the elements that react and respond to a user's activity or input. A user has many ways to give input to a Flash movie, and Flash has even more ways to react. But how does interactivity actually work? It all starts with actions and event handlers.

Actions and Event Handlers

Even the most complex interactivity in Flash is fundamentally composed of two basic parts: the *behavior* (what happens), and the *cause* of the behavior (what makes it happen). Here's a simple example: Suppose you have a looping soundtrack in a movie and a button that, when clicked, turns the soundtrack off. The *behavior* is the sound turning off, and the *cause* of the behavior is the mouse clicking the button. Another example is stopping an animation when it reaches a certain frame on its timeline. When the last keyframe of the animation is played (the *cause*), an action on that keyframe stops the animation (the *behavior*). In Flash, behaviors are referred to as *actions*. The first step in learning how to make interactive movies is becoming familiar with the list of possible actions. However, actions can't act without being told to act *by* something. That something is often the mouse coming in contact with a button, but it can also be a keystroke, or simply a command issued from a keyframe. We refer to any occurrence that can cause an action to happen (such as the button click in the preceding example) as an *event*. The mechanism we use to tell Flash what action to perform when an event occurs is known as an event handler. This cause-and-effect relationship seems obvious, but it is an extremely important concept. For the purposes of creating basic interactivity, the difference between an action and the cause of an action is merely a practical detail. As the set of Flash actions continues to grow with each release of the Flash authoring tool (and therefore the scripting capabilities that they provide), understanding the relationship between actions and the things that cause them can be the key to adding more sophisticated behavior to your movies with traditional programming techniques. Every interactive framework, whether it is Macromedia Flash or Macromedia Director or Apple DVD Studio Pro, has unique handlers for specific events. Table 18-1 relates interactive events with Flash handlers.

Table 18-1: Events and Flash Handlers

Event	Type	Event handler	Example
Playback	Time-based	Keyframes MovieClip object	Timeline plays until it reaches a certain frame; a Movie Clip instance monitors the amount of time that has passed in a movie.
Mouse	User input	Button object MovieClip object	Visitor clicks a button; Mouse movement detected over a Movie Clip instance.
Key press	User input	Button object MovieClip object	User presses the Enter key to submit a form; an alert appears if the Caps Lock key is enabled.
Data	System-based	MovieClip object data objects	Search results will display in the Flash movie when the results have fully loaded.

Don't worry, we're taking it one step at a time. First, we will set up the Actions panel, whose look-and-feel has changed from previous versions of Flash. Then we'll look at actions that control movie playback. Later in this chapter, you'll learn how to call these actions in various ways with three kinds of event handlers: button states, keyframes, and keystrokes.

What is ActionScript?

Every interactive authoring system uses a language (or code) that enables elements within the system to communicate. Just as there are several languages that people use to speak to one another around the globe, there are hundreds of programming languages in use today. In an effort to make Flash more usable to computer programmers, Flash's scripting language, called ActionScript, changed much of its formatting in Flash 5 to mirror JavaScript, a fundamental component for DHTML and HTML Web pages. Right now, we focus on using the most basic Flash ActionScript.

Cross-Reference   If you're interested in learning the fundamental building blocks of ActionScript programming, check out our advanced coverage of ActionScript in Chapters 24 through 33. The three chapters of Part V are intended to provide a starting point for Flash designers and developers who are new to Flash actions and interactive concepts. Exhaustive coverage of the ActionScript language can be found in the *Macromedia Flash MX ActionScript Bible,* by Robert Reinhardt and Joey Lott.

Setting up the Actions panel

Flash MX has a specific interface element that allows you to add interactive commands to Flash movies — the Actions panel. As with Flash 5, you don't have to use menus to select actions — you can type them by hand in or out of Flash! You can open the Actions panel in a number of ways:

✦ Go to Windows ➪ Actions

✦ Press the F9 key

✦ Alt+double-click (or Option+double-click) a keyframe in the Timeline window

If you have a keyframe selected in the Timeline window, the Actions panel will be titled **Actions - Frame** (see Figure 18-1). If you have a Movie Clip symbol instance selected on the Stage, you'll see the name **Actions - Movie Clip**. Finally, if you have a Button instance selected on the Stage, the Actions panel will be titled **Actions - Button**.

New Feature
> The Actions panel in Flash MX now differentiates between Button and Movie Clip "object" actions. In Flash 5, both Movie Clip and Button instances were called Object Actions.

Don't be confused—there is only one Actions panel. Flash MX simply lets you know the object to which you are assigning actions.

Normal versus Expert mode

Flash MX has two authoring modes for actions: Normal and Expert. By default, Flash MX uses the Normal mode. In this mode, most actions have user-definable parameters that can be set in the gray area above the Script pane of the Actions panel. You can hide the Actions pane of the Actions panel by clicking the arrow on the divider line between the left and right panes. Figure 18-1 shows a breakdown of the new Actions panel in Flash MX.

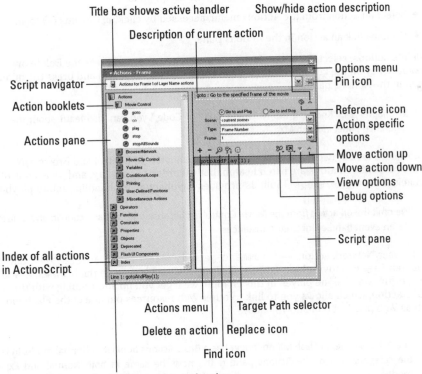

Figure 18-1: The Actions panel enables you to instantly add, delete, or change Flash interactive commands. This Actions panel is in Normal mode.

You can choose the authoring mode for the Actions panel in three ways:

✦ Choose Normal or Expert mode in the panel's options menu.

✦ Press Ctrl+Shift+N or ⌘+Shift+N on the keyboard to enter Normal mode, or Ctrl+Shift+E or ⌘+Shift+E on the keyboard to enter Expert mode. Make sure you have clicked somewhere within the Actions panel before you try to use this shortcut (in other words, make sure the panel has "focus").

✦ In the View options, choose Normal or Expert mode.

New Feature

Flash MX has introduced a highlighted outline or bar to indicate which area of the authoring environment has focus. When the Actions panel (in Expert mode) has focus, a highlighted bar will show up on the left side of the Script pane.

For this chapter, we work entirely within the Movie Control booklet, located within the Actions booklet in the Actions pane. In Expert mode, Flash enables you to type, copy, cut, and paste code at will into the Script pane.

You can add actions to the Script pane in one of three ways:

✦ Drag an action from the Actions pane to the Script pane.

✦ Select an action from the Actions menu, accessed by clicking the plus (+) icon.

✦ Double-click an action in the Actions pane.

To delete actions, select the action line(s) in the Script pane, and press the Delete or Backspace key on the keyboard. Or, you can select the action line(s) and press the minus (–) button in the Actions panel.

Cross-Reference

In Chapter 24, "Knowing the Nuts and Bolts of Code," you can also learn about the new Reference panel in Flash MX.

For now, let's look at two booklets in the Actions pane: Movie Control and Browser/Network. The Movie Control actions are listed in alphabetical order. goto, play, and stop control the playback of the movie. stopAllSounds provides a global tool for handling sound playback.

Note

We omit the on action from the Movie Control list because on is not an action in and of itself—it's an event handler for Button instances.

The Browser/Network actions — fscommand, getURL, loadMovie, loadVariables, and unloadMovie — let movies load external files and communicate with the browser, a Web server, or the stand-alone player. In this chapter, we'll get you up and running with the getURL action, which allows you to link to other Web resources outside of the Flash movie (such as Web pages and file downloads).

RIP

The Actions panel in Flash MX no longer has a Basic Actions booklet in Normal mode. In fact, the categorization of the Actions pane is the now the same in both Normal and Expert modes.

The remaining Action booklets primarily offer extended ActionScript programming capabilities. We discuss their use in later chapters.

Deprecated and Incompatible Actions: What Are They?

As the ActionScript language of Flash continues to expand and encompass new functionality, older actions will coexist with newer and better actions (or methods, properties, event handlers, and functions, which we discuss later). While Flash Player 6 will continue to support Flash 5 and earlier actions, it's better not to use older actions if the newest version of Flash has a new way of accomplishing the same task. Older actions that have been replaced with a new action (or new way to perform the same task) are called deprecated actions. The Actions panel in Flash MX now houses all deprecated actions in the Deprecated booklet of the Actions pane. Why shouldn't you use these actions? As we see in more advanced scripting, Flash MX has specific syntax to target Movie Clips and determine whether certain frames have loaded, among other features of the ActionScript "dot syntax" language. The following figure shows the actions within the Actions booklet inside of the Deprecated booklet. Note that there are other groups of deprecated actions inside the Deprecated booklet as well.

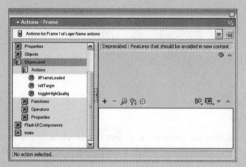

Actions that are highlighted in the Deprecated booklet should be avoided if possible. However, Flash Player 6 will support these older actions.

Flash MX will also let you know if certain actions are not supported with the Player version that is selected in the Flash format's Publish Settings. Note that you can also find this setting in the Property inspector when you click an empty area of the Stage or the Work area. If an action is not supported by the version you have selected, the action will be highlighted in yellow. The following figure shows this type of highlighting in the Actions panel for Mac OS X. You will notice that the tooltip (or rollover description) indicates which version of the Flash Player supports the action.

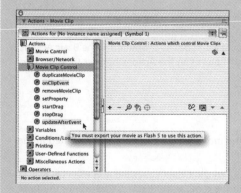

Flash Player 4 (or earlier) will not support the onClipEvent or updateAfterEvent actions (among others), as these actions were introduced in Flash 5.

Continued

Continued

Finally, Flash tells you if you have added conflicting actions to one keyframe or object. For example, if you have several `goto` actions on one frame or button, Flash MX highlights the offending action(s) in red, as shown in the following figure. The red highlighting appears only in Normal Mode. The Status bar of the Actions panel also provides further information about the conflict.

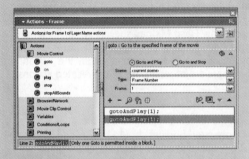

Red-highlighted actions are in conflict with previously added actions. You must remove or correct the parameters if you want your movie to behave correctly.

Your First Five Actions

Now that you have a general picture of what actions do, let's look at five common actions in detail. At this point, we're describing only the functionality of each action, not how to add an action to your movie. Information on adding an action is covered in the next section, "Making Actions Happen with Event Handlers."

You will find coverage of further actions (and full-blown ActionScript) in later chapters. For exhaustive coverage of the ActionScript language, be sure to read the *ActionScript Bible* by Robert Reinhardt and Joey Lott.

As they appear in the Flash interface, the actions are coincidentally sorted from top to bottom roughly according to their complexity. Let's take it from the top.

In an attempt to get everyone — designers and coders alike — familiar with ActionScript syntax, Flash MX no longer refers to actions differently in Normal mode than in Expert mode. Flash 5's Actions panel (in Normal mode) would list Stop All Sounds in the Basic Actions booklet (no longer in MX) as well as stopAllSounds in the Actions booklet (now located in the Movie Control booklet in MX).

goto

The `goto` action changes the current frame of the movie to the target frame specified in the `goto` settings. The `goto` action has two variations:

> ✦ **Go to and Stop:** Changes the current frame to the frame specified and then halts playback. Go to and Stop is often used to produce toolbar-style interfaces where the user clicks buttons to view different areas of content in a movie.

✦ **Go to and Play:** Changes the current frame to the frame specified, and then executes a `play` action. Like Go to and Stop, Go to and Play can be used to create toolbar interfaces, but it provides the capability to show animated intro sequences as preludes to individual content areas. Go to and Play also gets frequent use in choose-your-own-adventure style animations, in which the user guides an animated character through different paths in a narrative. Note that Go to and Stop is the default type of Go To action. To create a Go to and Play action, you must first add a `goto` action, and then check the Go to and Play option in the Parameters area of the Actions panel.

Each `goto` action enables you to jump to certain areas of the Flash movie. The parameters of the `goto` actions start with the largest time unit, the Scene, and end with the smallest one, the Frame.

You can specify frames in other scenes as the target of `goto` actions with the Scene parameter. In the Scene drop-down menu, you can find a list of all the scenes in your movie, as well as built-in references to <current scene>, <next scene>, and <previous scene>, as shown in Figure 18-2. The Scene drop-down can be used together with the Type and Frame parameters to target a frame in any Scene in a movie.

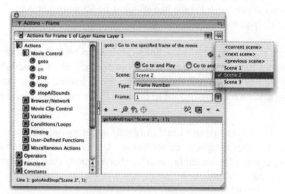

Figure 18-2: Setting the goto action that targets a specific Scene (shown in the Mac version of Flash MX)

Caution   While we haven't looked at actions specifically for use in Movie Clip instances, make a note that you can not use a goto action specifying a Scene within a Movie Clip instance. In this case, you should target the Main Timeline to go to and stop (or play) the keyframe label in the desired scene, omitting the Scene's name. For example, `_root.gotoAndStop("products");` executed from a Movie Clip timeline would tell the Main Timeline to go to and stop on the frame label `products`, which would be located in a different scene.

There are five methods of specifying the frame to which the movie should go when it receives a `goto` action. You set the method by selecting the appropriate Type and Frame parameters. After you've chosen the method to refer to your target frame, select or enter the frame's name or number under that setting's options (see Figure 18-3).

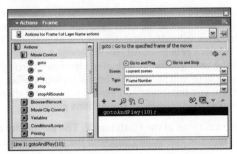

Figure 18-3: Setting the goto action with a frame number

The methods for specifying the frame are

✦ **Number:** Specify the target frame as a number. Frame 1 is the beginning of the movie or scene. Number spans scenes, so if you have a movie with two scenes, each containing 25 frames, and you add a Go to action with Frame Number set to 50, your action advances the movie to the 25th frame of the second scene.

Caution

Using frame numbers to specify the targets of `goto` actions can lead to serious scalability problems in Flash movies. Adding frames at the beginning or in the middle of a movie's timeline causes the following frames to be renumbered. When those frames are renumbered, all `goto` Frame Number actions must be revised to point to the correct new number of their target frames.

In the vast majority of cases, `goto` actions that use Label to specify target frames are preferable to `goto` actions that use Number to specify target frames. Unlike numbered frame targets, `goto` actions with labeled frame targets continue to function properly even if the targeted frame changes position on the timeline.

✦ **Label:** Individual keyframes can be given names via the Label field in the Property inspector. Once a frame is labeled, a `goto` action can target it by name. To specify a label as the target of a `goto` action, select Frame Label in the Type drop-down menu. Then either type the name of the frame into the Frame text field, or select it from the automatically generated list of frame labels in the Frame drop-down menu as seen in Figure 18-4.

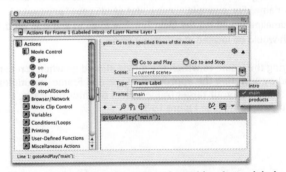

Figure 18-4: Setting the goto action with a frame label

Note The automatically generated list of labels that appears in the Label menu can include labels from other scenes, but not labels that are inside Movie Clips. To target a label in a Movie Clip instance, you should use the dot syntax and object reference notation that was introduced to ActionScript in Flash 5. For more information, see Chapter 19, "Navigating Flash Timelines."

✦ **Expression:** Specify the target frame as an interpreted ActionScript code segment. Expressions are used to dynamically assign targets of goto actions. Expressions are covered in Chapter 21.

✦ **Next Frame:** Specify the frame after the current frame as the target frame and stop playback. Next Frame can be used in conjunction with Previous Frame to quickly set up a slide-show-style walk-through of content, where each of a series of contiguous keyframes contains the content of one "slide." Note that this option actually changes the syntax of a goto action to nextFrame().

✦ **Previous Frame:** Specify the frame before the current frame as the target frame and stop playback. This option will change the syntax of a goto action to prevFrame().

play

This simple action is one of the true foundations of Flash. play sets a movie or a Movie Clip in motion. When a play action is executed, Flash starts the sequential display of each frame's contents along the current timeline. The rate at which the frames are displayed is measured as frames per second, or fps. The fps rate can be set from 0.01 to 120 (meaning that the play action can cause the display of as little as 1 frame every 100 seconds to as many as 120 frames in 1 second, subject to the limitations of the computer's processing speed). The default fps is 12. Once play has started, frames continue to be displayed one after the other, until another action interrupts the flow, or the end of the movie or Movie Clip's timeline is reached. If the end of a movie's timeline is reached, the movie either loops (begins playing again at frame 1, Scene 1), or stops on the last frame.

Cross-Reference Whether a movie loops automatically depends on the Publish settings described in Chapter 21, "Publishing Flash Movies."

Once the end of the Movie Clip's timeline is reached, playback loops back to the beginning of the clip, and the clip continues playing. To prevent looping, add a stop action to the last frame of your Movie Clip.

Note A single play action affects only a single timeline, whether that timeline is the main movie timeline or the timeline of a Movie Clip instance. For example, a play action executed inside a Movie Clip does not cause the Main Timeline to begin playing. Likewise, any goto action on the Main Timeline doesn't migrate to the Movie Clips that reside there. A timeline must be specifically targeted to control playback along that timeline. If there is no specified target, the action is referring to its own timeline. However, this is not the case for animations within Graphic symbol instances. An animation in a Graphic symbol is controlled by actions on the timeline in which the symbol instance is present — Flash ignores actions on a Graphic symbol's timeline.

stop

stop, as you may have guessed, halts the progression of a movie or Movie Clip that is in a play state. stop is often used with buttons for user-controlled playback of a movie, or on frames to end an animated sequence.

Tip Movie Clip instances placed on any timeline will begin to play automatically. Remember to add a stop action on the first frame of a Movie Clip if you don't want it to play right away.

stopAllSounds

A simple but powerful action that mutes any sounds playing in the movie at the time the action is executed, stopAllSounds does not disable sounds permanently—it simply cancels any sounds that happen to be currently playing. It is sometimes used as a quick-and-dirty method of making buttons that shut off background looping soundtracks. stopAllSounds is not appropriate for controlling whether individual (or specific) sounds are played or muted. For information on more accurate control over sounds, please see Chapter 15, "Adding Sound," and Chapter 27, "Interacting with Movie Clips."

getURL

Want to link to a Web page from a Flash movie? No problem. That's what getURL is for. You can find the getURL action in the Browser/Network booklet in the Actions pane. getURL is simply Flash's method of making a conventional hypertext link. It's nearly the equivalent of an anchor tag in HTML (i.e. <A HREF="...">), except that Flash's getURL also allows for form submission. getURL can be used to link to a standard Web page, an FTP site, another Flash movie, an executable, a CGI script, or anything that exists on the Internet or on an accessible local file system.

getURL has three parameters that are familiar to Web builders (the first one, URL, is required for this action to work):

✦ **URL:** This is the network address of the page, file, script, or resource to which you are linking. Any value is permitted (including ActionScript expressions), but the linked item can be displayed only if the reference to it is correct. URL is directly analogous to the HREF attribute of an HTML anchor tag. You can use a relative or absolute URL as well. Examples:

```
http://www.yoursite.com/
ftp://ftp.yoursite.com/pub/documents.zip
menu.html
/cgi-bin/processform.cgi
```

Since Flash 4, getURL can now link to documents on the Web from the stand-alone Flash Player. Execution of a getURL action in the standalone Player causes the default Web browser to launch and load the requested URL (see Figure 18-5).

Tip You can specify secure domain URLs by using the https protocol for SSL (Secure Socket Layer) connections.

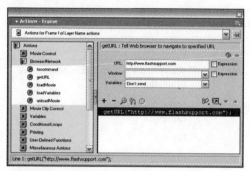

Figure 18-5: Setting the URL of a getURL action

✦ **Window:** This is the name of the frame or window in which you wish to load the resource specified in the URL setting. Window is directly analogous to the TARGET attribute of an HTML anchor tag. In addition to enabling the entry of custom frame and window names, the Window setting provides four presets in a drop-down menu:

- **_self:** Loads the URL into the same frame or window as the current movie. If you do not select an option in the Window menu, this behavior will be the default.

- **_blank:** Creates a new browser window and loads the URL into it.

- **_parent:** Removes the current frameset and loads the URL in its place. Use this option if you have multiple nested framesets, and you want your linked URL to replace only the frameset in which your movie resides.

- **_top:** Loads the URL into the current browser and removes all framesets in the process. Use this option if your movie is in a frame, but you want your linked URL to be loaded normally into the browser, outside the confines of any frames.

Note Frame windows and/or JavaScript windows can be assigned names. You can target these names by manually typing the name in the Window field. For example, if you had a frame defined as <FRAME NAME="main". . .>, you could load specific URLs into a frame named main from a Flash movie.

✦ **Variables:** This option enables getURL to function like an HTML form submission. For normal links, the Variables setting should be left at its default value, Don't Send. But in order to submit values to a server-side script, one of the submission methods (Send Using GET or Send Using POST) must be selected. For a complete discussion on submitting data to a server from a Flash movie (using the new LoadVars object), see Chapter 30, "Sending Data In and Out of Flash."

Tip getURL functions in the Test Movie environment. Both the Flash stand-alone player and the Test Movie command give you access to external and/or local URLs.

Although this chapter focuses on using actions in Normal mode, you should start familiarizing yourself with the ActionScript notation that Flash uses for each action (see Table 18-2). As you use Flash for more advanced interactivity, you'll need to have a firm grasp of code notation. Part VII, "Approaching ActionScript," teaches you how to start building code from the ground up.

Table 18-2: Common Actions and ActionScript Notation

Action	ActionScript Notation	Arguments
Go to and Stop	`gotoAndStop(arguments);`	Scene Name (Frame Label, Number, or Expression)
Go to and Play	`gotoAndPlay(arguments);`	Scene Name (Frame Label, Number, or Expression)
Next Frame	`nextFrame();`	None
Previous Frame	`prevFrame();`	None
Next Scene	`nextScene();`	None
Previous Scene	`prevScene();`	None
play	`play();`	None
stop	`stop();`	None
stopAllSounds	`stopAllSounds();`	None
getURL	`getURL(arguments);`	URL, Target frame or window, Variable send method

Making Actions Happen with Event Handlers

The first five common actions — `goto`, `play`, `stop`, `stopAllSounds`, and `getURL` — provide many of the behaviors that you need to make an interesting interactive Flash movie. But those five actions can't make your movies interactive on their own. They need to be told when to happen. To tell a Flash movie when an action should occur, you need event handlers. Event handlers specify the condition(s) under which an action can be made to happen. For instance, you might want to mouse-click a button to initiate a `play` action, or you might want a movie to stop when a certain keyframe in the timeline is reached. Creating interactivity in your movies is simply a matter of deciding what event you want to detect (mouse click, keystroke, and so on), adding the appropriate event handler to detect it, and specifying the action(s) that should be performed when it happens.

Before we describe each event handler in detail, let's see an example of exactly how an event handler merges with an action to form a functioning interactive button.

Combining an action with an event handler to make a functioning button

Imagine that you have a short, endlessly looping movie in which a wire-frame cube rotates. Now imagine that you want to add a button to your movie that, when clicked, stops the cube from rotating by stopping the playback of the looping movie. Here's what you need to do.

On the CD-ROM

For this exercise, you can use the **rotatingCube.fla** file located in the ch18 folder on the *Flash MX Bible* CD-ROM. The finished file is named **rotatingCube_complete.fla**.

1. Open the example Flash document (.fla file), and make a new layer called **button.**

2. Place a button on the button layer. You can use Flash MX's sample Stop button found in the Circle Buttons folder of the Buttons library (Window ➪ Common Libraries ➪ Buttons). See Figure 18-6 to see this button's placement on the Stage.

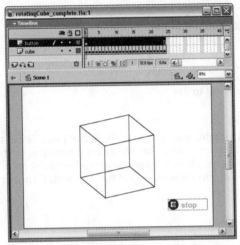

Figure 18-6: The Stop button on the Stage

Tip

Selecting buttons and editing button properties can sometimes be tricky if buttons are enabled in the Flash authoring environment. For easier button manipulation, disable buttons by unchecking Enable Simple Buttons under the Control menu.

3. With the Stop Button instance selected, open the Actions panel (F9), and then open the Actions ➪ Movie Control booklet in the Actions pane.

4. Double-click the on event handler in the Movie Control booklet, or drag it to the Script pane. A list of parameters for on appears in the top right portion of the Actions panel. This area contains all the event handlers for Button instances.

5. By default, the Release option of the Event setting (shown in Figure 18-7) is already checked. The Release event is one of two kinds of mouse-click events (the other is Press; both are described later in this chapter in the section titled "The Flash event handlers"). Notice that the Script pane indicates the events that are selected. You've now told Flash that you want something to happen when the mouse clicks the button. All that's left is to tell it what should happen. In other words, you need to nest another action within the on (release){} code.

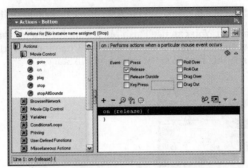

Figure 18-7: Adding a Release event to the on handler

6. Now we'll try another method for adding an action to the Script pane. Select the top line on (release){ in the Script pane. Then, click the plus (+) button in the toolbar of the Actions panel. From the menu, choose Actions ➪ Movie Control ➪ stop. A stop action will be placed between the curly braces ({}) of the on handler. The Script pane should now read as follows:

```
on (release){
  stop();
}
```

The stop action, represented by the code stop(); is contained by the curly braces { and } that mark the beginning and end of the list of actions that are executed when the release event occurs (there could be any number of actions in this list). Each action line (handlers excluded) must end with the semicolon (;) character.

7. We now have a button in our Flash movie that stops the movie's playback when it is clicked. Save your Flash document (.fla file), and test the movie using Control ➪ Test Movie. When you click the button, the rotating cube animation should stop.

Tip

In this example we selected the event handler before adding our action. This helped illustrate the individual role that each of those elements plays. During real production, however, you may simply drag or add any action to the right pane without first specifying an event handler—Flash automatically adds an on handler with a release event to actions that are added to Button instances.

To make any interactivity in your movies, you simply have to apply the basic principles we used to make the stop button: Decide which action (or actions) you want to happen, and then indicate when you want that action to happen with an event handler.

In the first part of this chapter, we explored six actions. Let's look now at the list of Event Handlers you can use to make those actions happen.

The Flash event handlers

Three primary event handlers exist in Flash: those that detect mouse activity on Button instances (button manipulation), those that recognize when a key is pressed on the keyboard (key presses), and those that respond to the progression of the timeline (keyframes).

Flash MX builds upon the event model introduced in Flash 5. As a Flash developer, you now have an inordinate amount of control over events and event handlers with ActionScript. We'll look at this new event model in Chapter 25, "Controlling Movie Clips."

Working with mouse events and buttons

Event handlers that occur based on the user's interaction with a button rely entirely on the location and movement of the mouse pointer. If the mouse pointer comes in contact with a Button symbol's Hit area, it changes from an arrow to a hand symbol. At that time the mouse is described as "over" the button. If the mouse pointer is not over a button, it is said to be *out* or *outside* of the button. General movement of the mouse *without* the mouse button depressed is referred to as *rolling*. General movement of the mouse *with* the mouse button pressed is referred to as *dragging*.

Event handlers and actions on buttons must be placed only on Button instances on the Stage, not on the four frames in the timeline of the original Button symbol. Flash MX will not allow you to place actions on any event handlers in the Button symbol timeline.

Here are the mouse-based events for Flash buttons. In this edition of the book, we list the event's Normal mode name first, as in Press, followed by its formatting displayed by the Script pane, as in press.

Press (press)

A single mouse click can actually be divided into two separate components: the downstroke (the *press*) and the upstroke (the *release*). A Press event occurs when the mouse pointer is over the Hit area of a button *and* the downstroke of a mouse click is detected. Press is best used for control panel-style buttons, especially toggle switches.

Typically, developers should program irreversible decisions or primary navigation so that users can abort their click by rolling the cursor away from the Hit area before releasing the mouse. For example, a user might click a button for more information, then decide she would rather not get that information. We do not recommend Press for important user moves such as these because it does not give users an opportunity to abort their move.

Release (release)

A Release event occurs when the mouse pointer is over the Hit area of a button *and* both the downstroke and the upstroke of a mouse click are detected. Release is the standard button click Event Handler.

If you use the Track as Menu Item behavior for a Button instance in the Property inspector, a button will respond to a Release event over its Hit state even if the mouse was pressed outside of the button's Hit area.

Release Outside (releaseOutside)

A Release Outside event occurs in response to the following series of mouse movements: The mouse pointer moves over a button's Hit area; the mouse button is pressed; the mouse pointer is moved off the button's Hit area; and the mouse button is released. Release Outside can be used to react to an aborted button click.

Roll Over (rollOver)

A Roll Over event occurs when the mouse pointer moves onto the Hit area of a button without the mouse button depressed.

Note To perform standard rollover button effects, such as graphic art changes or sound events, you can insert graphics and sound on to the Over state of the Button symbol timeline. It's common practice, however, to create invisible buttons over Movie Clip instances that have specialized rollover effects.

Roll Out (rollOut)

A Roll Out event occurs when the mouse pointer moves off of the Hit area of a button without the mouse button depressed.

Drag Over (dragOver)

A Drag Over event occurs in response to the following series of mouse movements: The mouse button is pressed while the mouse pointer is outside the Hit area of a button *and* the mouse pointer moves over the Hit area while the mouse button is still depressed. Drag Over is rather obscure, but could be used for special cases of interactivity such as revealing an Easter egg in a game (for example, when the mouse button is held down and mouse movement occurs over a specific area, ActionScript can detect the coordinates of the mouse movement and reveal a Movie Clip instance that is otherwise invisible on the Stage).

Drag Out (dragOut)

A Drag Out event occurs in response to the following series of mouse movements: The mouse button is pressed while the mouse pointer is over the Hit area of a button *and* the mouse pointer moves outside the Hit area with the mouse button still depressed.

Capturing keyboard input

You can also trigger event handlers with events that occur on the user's keyboard. You can enable your Flash movies to "capture" a key press (also known as a keystroke) initiated by the user. The Key Press event lets you execute an action (or series of actions) when the user presses a key on the keyboard. The implementation method for a Key Press event handler may be confusing: To add a Key Press event handler, you must first place a button onstage at the frame where you want the keyboard to be active. You then attach the Key Press event to the Button instance's on handler.

Tip If you are using the button only as a container for your keystroke event handler and you do not want the button to appear on Stage, you should make sure that (in Symbol Editing mode) all the frames of the Button symbol timeline are blank.

The Key Press event, which was introduced with Flash 4, opens up many possibilities for Flash. Movies can have keyboard-based navigation, buttons can have keyboard shortcuts for convenience and accessibility, and games can have keyboard-controlled objects (such as ships and animated characters). But watch out for some potential "gotchas" to keyboard usage, *specifically with* on *handlers.* If you're planning ambitious keyboard-based projects, you may want to check this list of potential issues first:

✦ The Esc key does not work as a key press.

✦ Multiple key combinations are not supported. This rules out diagonals as two-key combinations in the classic four-key game control setup. It also means shortcuts such as

Ctrl+S are not available. You can, however, use the Shift key in combination with another key to specify an uppercase letter or symbol. (See the case-sensitive note later in this list.)

✦ If presented in a browser, the Flash movie must have "focus" before keystrokes can be recognized. To "focus" the movie, the user must click anywhere in the space it occupies within the browser window. Keyboard-based movies should include instructions that prompt the user to perform this initial mouse click.

Tip

You can use the JavaScript `focus()` method in HTML documents to automatically draw attention to a Flash movie contained within the page. You can use the `onLoad` event to initiate a JavaScript function that includes the `focus()` method to enable this behavior as soon as the page loads into the browser.

✦ Because the Enter, less-than (<), and greater-than (>) keys are used as authoring short-cuts in the Test Movie environment, you may want to avoid using them as control keys in your movies. If you need to use those keys in your movies, make sure that you test the movies in a browser.

✦ Key Press events are case-sensitive. For example, an uppercase letter "S" and a lowercase letter "s" can trigger two different actions. No case-insensitive keystroke event (that is, one that would enable both cases of a letter to trigger the same action) exists for Button instances and the `on` handler. Achieving case-insensitivity would require two separate `on` handlers (and their contained actions), one for each case of the letter, on the same Button instance. For example, the following code would stop the current timeline when either the s key or Shift+s key (or the s key with Caps Lock enabled) was pressed:

```
on (keyPress "s"){
    stop();
}
on (keyPress "S"){
    stop();
}
```

Note

ActionScript's Key object, its methods, and its properties enable you to do much more with Key Press events than the `on` handler does. The Key object is discussed in greater detail in the *Macromedia Flash MX ActionScript Bible* by Robert Reinhardt and Joey Lott.

Capturing time events with keyframes

The keyframe event handler depends on the playback of the movie itself, not on the user. Any action (except the `on` handler) can be attached to any keyframe on the timeline. An action attached to a keyframe is executed when the playhead enters the keyframe, whether it enters naturally during the linear playback of the movie or as the result of a `goto` action. So, for instance, you may place a `stop` action on a keyframe to pause the movie at the end of an animation sequence.

In some multimedia applications, keyframe event handlers can differentiate between the playhead *entering* a keyframe and *exiting* a keyframe. Flash has only one kind of keyframe event handler (essentially, on enter). Hence, as a developer, you do not need to add keyframe event handlers explicitly — they are a presumed element of any action placed on a keyframe. As mentioned in an earlier note, ActionScript in Flash MX has a new event model, as well as the `onClipEvent` handler introduced in Flash 5, that allows you to work more explicitly with an `enterFrame` event. We look at the different event models in Chapter 25, "Controlling Movie Clips."

Tip
Complex movies can have dozens, or even hundreds, of actions attached to keyframes. To prevent conflicts between uses of keyframes for animation and uses of keyframes as action containers, it is highly advisable to create an entire layer solely for action keyframes. Name the layer **actions** and keep it on top of all your layers for easy access. Remember not to place any symbol instances, text, or artwork on your actions layer. You can also create a labels layer to hold — you guessed it — frame labels.

Creating Invisible Buttons and Using getURL

In this section, we'll show you how to create an "invisible button," and practice the use of getURL actions. An invisible button is essentially a Button symbol that has only a Hit state defined, with empty Up, Over, and Down states. Once you have created an invisible button, you can use it to convert any type of Flash element into a button. By dragging an instance of the invisible button on top of another piece of artwork or Symbol instance on the Stage, you can add interactivity to that element.

On the CD-ROM
Make a copy of the themakers_ad_starter.fla file, located in the ch18 folder of the book's CD-ROM. This file contains a sample layout of graphics and text for a mock Flash ad, sized for display on a Pocket PC screen. This document uses a Flash 3 version setting in the Publish Settings, which is why some actions will be highlighted in yellow in the Actions panel.

With the starter .fla file open in Flash MX, quickly familiarize yourself with the existing content. There are four layers on the Main Timeline (Scene 1). The Comments layer indicates what the Flash document is, the Border layer contains a black box with no fill, the Graphics layer contains a Graphic symbol of branding artwork, and the animText layer contains a Movie Clip instance featuring a tweened animation. Go ahead and test this movie to see how these elements currently play. When the animation finishes, you should see the artwork displayed in Figure 18-8.

Figure 18-8: The artwork of the Flash ad

In this exercise, you're going to add two invisible buttons to this movie. One will be an oval-shaped button that fits over the thumbprint graphic, and another will be a rectangular-shaped button that fits over the company's name. The thumbprint button, when clicked, will open the e-mail client to send an e-mail to the company. When the user clicks the name button, a new browser window will open displaying the company's Web page.

1. In the starter Flash document, create a new layer named **actions**. Place this layer just underneath the Comments layer.

2. Select the first frame of this layer and open the Actions panel (F9) in Normal mode. In the plus (+) menu, choose Actions ➪ Movie Control ➪ stop. This will add a **stop( );** action to the keyframe. Currently, there is more than one frame on the Main Timeline, and if this Flash movie were to be developed further, we wouldn't want the Playhead going past the first frame without some input from the user.

3. With this first frame of the actions layer still selected, open the Property inspector and in the <Frame Label> field, type **//stop.** This will add a frame comment of //stop to the layer in the Timeline window. This comment provides a quick visual cue about the behavior of this keyframe.

4. Now, we're going to make our first invisible button. Choose Insert ➪ New Symbol (Ctrl+F8 or ⌘+F8) and make a new Button symbol named **invisibleButton_rect.** This button will be the rectangular button that is placed over the company's name. Flash will take you right inside the symbol's workspace as soon as you press the OK button in the Create New Symbol dialog box.

5. Rename Layer 1 to **hit area graphic.** On this layer of the Button symbol's timeline, create a keyframe for the Hit state. Move the Playhead in the Timeline window to this new keyframe.

6. Select the Rectangle tool, and draw a uniform square on the symbol's Stage. The square can be any color, although we prefer red for invisible buttons. If you drew the shape with a stroke, delete the stroke. Select the square, and in the Property inspector, give the square a width and height of **50** pixels. Then, using the Align panel, center the square on the Stage. Your Button symbol and timeline should now resemble Figure 18-9.

Figure 18-9: The square will act as the active area of the Button symbol.

7. Now, go back to Scene 1 (the Main Timeline), and create new layer. Rename this layer **linkButton,** and place it above the Graphics layer.

8. Open the Library panel (F11), and drag an instance of the invisibleButton_rect symbol to the Stage. Place this instance over the company's name. Using the Free Tranform tool, size the instance to fit the size of the text, without overlapping other elements on the Stage. You'll notice that your Button instance has a transparent aqua blue tint that overlays the underlying elements (as shown in Figure 18-10). This is Flash MX's way of letting you select and manipulate an invisible button. You will not see this color effect for the button when the document is published as a Flash movie (.swf file).

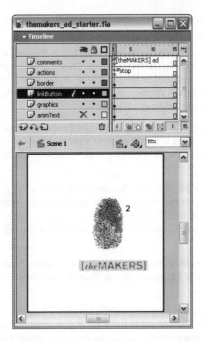

Figure 18-10: The aqua blue tint of the Button instance indicates the presence of a button that has only a Hit state.

9. With the Arrow tool, select the Button instance on the Stage, and open the Actions panel (F9). Your Action panel title bar should read **Actions - Button**. Using the booklets in the Actions pane, add an on handler from the Actions ➪ Movie Control booklet. Inside the on handler, add a getURL action from the Actions ➪ Browser/Network booklet.

10. With the getURL action highlighted in the Script pane, type a Web page URL in the URL field of the action's settings in the top right portion of the Actions panel. For this example, we used the URL http://www.theMakers.com. When you link to domain names, make sure you specify the transfer protocol (such as http://, ftp://, and so on). If you are linking to relative URLs, specify the name of the HTML document (or other resource) that you want to access. Then, choose **_blank** in the Window menu. This will make the link open in a new browser window. When you are finished, your Actions panel should contain similar settings to those shown in Figure 18-11.

11. Save your Flash document as **themakers_ad_100.fla,** and test it using Publish Preview ➪ HTML (Ctrl+F12 or ⌘+F12). In the browser window, roll over the company's name in the Flash movie. You'll notice that this area is an active button. When you click the button, a new browser window will open, displaying the company's Web page.

12. Now, let's go back to the Flash document and add another invisible button. We'll use a different procedure this time. On the Scene 1 timeline, create a new layer and name it **emailButton.** Place this layer above the linkButton layer.

13. On the first frame of the emailButton layer, select the Oval tool, and draw a perfect circle anywhere on the Stage. Again, you can use any fill color you wish. If the circle has a stroke, delete the stroke. With this circle selected, open the Property inspector and give the circle a width and height of **50** pixels.

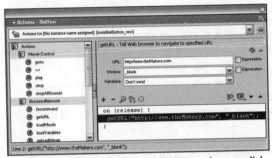

Figure 18-11: These settings will direct a button click on this instance to [theMAKERS] Web site, in a new browser window.

14. With the circle selected, choose Insert ⇨ Convert to Symbol (F8). In the Convert to Symbol dialog box, make a Button symbol named **invisibleButton_oval** and click OK.

15. Now, edit the new symbol, either by double-clicking the instance on the Stage, or by double-clicking its listing in the Library panel. On this symbol's timeline, rename Layer 1 to **hit area graphic**. Now, select the keyframe for the Up state, and drag it to the Hit state. Note that you may need to click, then click and drag the keyframe for this method to work properly. When you are finished, your circle shape should be on only the Hit area of the button's timeline.

16. Go back to the Main Timeline (Scene I), and you'll notice that our circle button is now an invisible button, just like our rectangular one. Move the circular invisible button over the thumbprint graphic, and use the Free Transform tool to shape the circle as an oval that closely matches the shape of the thumbprint, as shown in Figure 18-12.

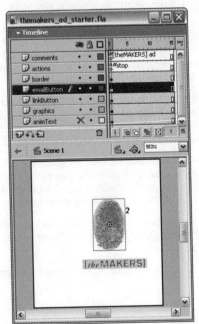

Figure 18-12: The thumbprint graphic now has an invisible button on top of it.

17. With the oval invisible button selected, open the Actions panel. Repeat Steps 9 and 10 of this exercise. This time, however, we'll use a mailto: URL, as in mailto:info@ theMakers.com. Type this value into the URL field of a getURL action for this Button instance. For this getURL action, however, you do not need to specify a Window setting.

18. Save your Flash movie once again, and preview it in a browser. When you click the active area over the thumbprint graphic, the default e-mail client on your system should open, displaying a new message window with the To: field predefined to the URL you typed in Step 17.

Tip

You can specify subject lines and body text in mailto: URLs as well, just as you can with HTML documents. For example, the following code will open a new e-mail message window addressed to info@theMakers.com, a subject line of "Web Feedback" and body text of "Here are my comments".

```
getURL("mailto:info@theMakers.com?subject=Web%20Feedback&body=H
ere%20are%20my%20comments%3A");
```

Now you know how to make invisible buttons and add getURL actions to them. In your own work, you may come to realize the true benefit of invisible buttons: You can quickly drag several instances of either invisible button shape (oval or rectangle) to the Stage to create active areas. This offers two benefits: First, you don't have to make Button symbols from regular graphics that don't need four button states, and second, you can make "hidden" areas in interactive puzzles or games.

Summary

✦ ActionScript is Flash's interactive language. It is a set of actions that enables Flash to communicate with internal elements (timelines, symbols, sounds, and so on) and external Web pages and scripts.

✦ Flash interactivity is based on a relatively simple structure: An event handler waits for something to happen (a playback point being reached or the user providing input), and when that something does happen, it executes one or more actions (which alter the movie's playback, behavior, or properties; loads a file; or executes a script).

✦ There are two authoring modes for adding actions in Flash: Normal and Expert. Normal mode enables you to add interactivity easily by clicking action names and using pre-configured option boxes to set parameters. Expert mode enables experienced Flash users to type actions directly and to copy text from other applications into Flash.

✦ The Movie Control booklet contains the fundamental actions for navigating Flash playback through multiple scenes and keyframes, as well as controlling soundtracks. The Browser/Network booklet contains the getURL action, which can direct the browser window to external Web resources such as HTML pages and ftp downloads.

✦ All actions need an event handler to activate them. Event handlers include keyframes on a timeline, button clicks, mouse movements, and key presses. More advanced event handlers are discussed in later chapters.

✦ Invisible buttons allow you to create interactive areas on top of other Flash artwork or symbols.

✦ ✦ ✦

Navigating Flash Timelines

In This Chapter

Working with
Movie Clips

Using targets and paths

Exploring absolute
and relative paths

Using Dots notation

Introducing the
evaluate action

Creating a
sound library

Unlike most multimedia authoring applications, Flash has the ability to use multiple simultaneous timelines in its movies. So far, most of the examples in this book have only one timeline or have used only one scene. You've seen how to add basic actions to your movies to make them interactive. Now, we begin exploring the world of multiple movie timelines using the Movie Clip symbol.

Movie Clips: The Key to Self-Contained Playback

A powerful addition to the Flash format was the Movie Clip symbol, which was introduced in version 3. Movie Clips enabled Flash developers to create complex behaviors by nesting self-contained sequences of animation or interactivity inside each other. These sequences could then be placed as discreet, self-playing modules on the Main Timeline (for example, Scene 1). Initially, the key to the power of Movie Clips was their ability to communicate with and control each other via the tellTarget action.

In Flash 4, the role of Movie Clips was expanded—they could be used with ActionScript. That capability put Movie Clips at the foundation of advanced interactivity in Flash. In Flash 5, when ActionScript matured into a full-blown scripting language that mirrored JavaScript, Movie Clips become the central object of programming. Now, in Flash MX, Movie Clips continue to play a vital role in the organization of a Flash movie's content and interactivity. In this chapter, we'll look at several key features of the Movie Clip symbol.

Cross-Reference

We'll discuss Movie Clip symbols as the MovieClip object in Part VII, "Approaching ActionScript," where we'll also explore the object's methods and properties.

How Movie Clips interact within a Flash movie

Previous chapters dealt with Flash movies as a single sequence of frames arranged along a single timeline. Whether the playback along that timeline was linear (traditional animation) or non-linear (where the Playhead jumps arbitrarily to any frame), our example movies have normally comprised only the frames of a single timeline. Ostensibly, a single timeline may seem to provide everything you'd need to create any Flash behavior, but as you get more inventive or ambitious, you'll soon find yourself conceiving ideas for animated and interactive segments that are thwarted by the limits of a single timeline.

Suppose you want to create a looping animation of a dog with its tail wagging. You decide that the tail should wag every five seconds and the dog should bark every 15 seconds. On a single timeline, you'd need a loop of 180 frames to accommodate the timing of the bark (assuming a frame rate of 12 frames per second), and repeating keyframes for the wagging tail artwork every 60 frames. Although animating a dog in that manner would be a bit cumbersome, it wouldn't be impossible — until your dog had to move around the screen as an integrated whole. Making the bark and the wagging tail loop while the whole dog moved around complex paths for extended periods of time would quickly become impractical, especially if the dog were only one part of a larger environment.

Now imagine that you could make the dog by creating two whole separate movies, one for the tail and one for the barking mouth (and sound). Could you then place those movies as self-contained, animated objects on the Main Timeline, just like a graphic or a button? Well, you can — that's what Movie Clips are all about. Movie Clips are independent sequences of frames (timelines) that can be defined outside the context of the Main Timeline and then placed onto it as objects on a single frame. You create Movie Clips the same way you create a Graphic symbol (in the Symbol Editing mode). Unlike a Graphic symbol, a Movie Clip (as the name implies) acts in most cases just like a fully functional Flash movie (.swf file), meaning, for instance, that frame actions in Movie Clip timelines are functional. After you have created a Movie Clip as a symbol, you drop instances of it into any keyframe of the Main Timeline or any other Movie Clip timeline. The following are some general Movie Clip principles:

✦ During playback as a Flash movie (.swf file), a Movie Clip instance placed on a timeline begins to play as soon as the frame on which it occurs is reached, whether or not the Main Timeline (or the clip's parent timeline) is playing.

✦ A Movie Clip plays back autonomously, meaning that as long as it is present on the Stage it is not governed by the playing or stopping of the Main Timeline.

✦ Movie Clips can play when the Main Timeline is stopped, or stay halted when the Main Timeline plays.

✦ Like a Graphic or a Button symbol, Movie Clips can be manipulated on the Stage — you can size them, skew them, rotate them, place effects such as alpha blending on them, or tween them, all while the animation within them continues to play.

✦ All timelines play at the frame rate specified by the Document Properties dialog box (Modify ⇨ Document) or the new Property inspector (when the Document window is focused). However, it is possible to modify playback behavior of a timeline with ActionScript routines.

In our dog wagging and barking example, the tail and head of the dog could be looping Movie Clips, and then those movie clips could be nested inside another Movie Clip symbol (representing the entire dog). This "whole" dog clip could then be tweened around the Stage on the Main Timeline to make the dog move. You could use the same principle to move a Movie Clip of a butterfly with flapping wings along a motion path.

One movie, several timelines

Because a Flash movie can have more than one timeline existing in the same space and time, there must be a way of organizing Movie Clips within the Main Timeline (Scene 1) of your Flash document. Just like artwork can be placed inside of any symbol, symbol instances can be nested within other symbols. If you change the contents of the nested symbol, the parent symbol (the symbol containing the other symbol) will be updated as well. Although this may not seem special, it's of extreme importance to Movie Clips and Flash interactivity. Because the playback of each Movie Clip timeline is independent from any other timeline, you need to know how to tell Flash which Movie Clip you want to control.

The Flash movie diagram in Figure 19-1 illustrates multiple timelines. This Flash movie has two layers on the Main Timeline, Layer 1 and Layer 2. Layer 1 has a Movie Clip (instance "A") that exists for 19 frames on the Main Timeline. Layer 2 has a Movie Clip (instance "B") that exists for 10 frames on the Main Timeline, but it also contains a nested Movie Clip (instance "C").

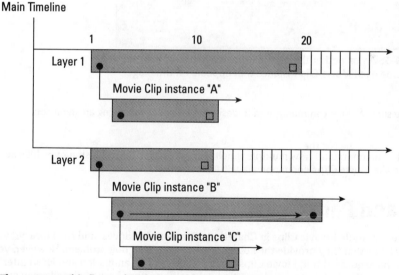

Figure 19-1: This figure shows one method of diagramming Flash timelines.

In Figure 19-1, if the Main Timeline has a `stop` action on the first frame, then all three Movie Clips will continue to play unless there are `stop` actions on their first frames or they are told to stop by actions targeted to them. If the Main Timeline plays to frame 20, instance "A" will no longer be on the Stage, regardless of how many frames it may have on its timeline. Figure 19-2 shows a more practical diagram of a timeline hierarchy.

Main Timeline

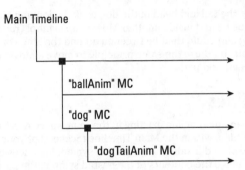

"ballAnim" MC

"dog" MC

"dogTailAnim" MC

Figure 19-2: Flash movies can be flow-charted in this fashion. This diagram is similar to the Movie Explorer's method of displaying Flash movie information.

In Figure 19-2, you can see three Movie Clips. Two of them, `ballAnim` and `dog`, occupy space on the Main Timeline. The other one, `dogTailAnim`, is nested within the `dog` Movie Clip. Each Movie Clip instance on any given timeline needs to have a unique name — you can't have two or more Movie Clip instances on the same timeline with the same name. The instance name is specified in the Property inspector, shown in Figure 19-3. To see the settings for a particular instance, you must have the instance selected on the Stage before referencing the Property inspector.

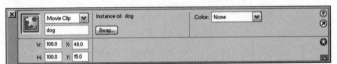

Figure 19-3: Among other things, the Property inspector enables you to name each Movie Clip instance that appears on the Stage.

Note   The suffix `Anim` is commonly used to designate a symbol containing an animation.

Now that you understand how multiple timelines can exist within a Flash movie, let's see how you can make Movie Clips communicate with one another.

Targets and Paths Explained

If you already studied Movie Clips in Chapter 6, "Symbols, Instances, and the Library," you probably know that they provide the solution to our animated dog problem. However, you might not have guessed that Movie Clips can also add logic to animation and Flash interfaces. Let's take our animated dog example a little further: When dogs bark, their tails may stop wagging. Our hypothetical dog may look strange if it is barking and wagging at the same time. Suppose we wanted to stop the tail wagging during every bark. We'd have to have some way for the barking head Movie Clip to control the tail Movie Clip so that we could tell the tail to stop wagging when the dog barks, and then tell the tail to return to its wagging loop again when the bark's over.

Well, you have a few ways to control the tail Movie Clip from the barking head Movie Clip. In Flash 3 and 4, the `tellTarget` action was used to let actions on any timeline (including Movie Clip timelines and the Main Timeline) control what happens on any other timeline. How? `tellTarget` simply provided a mechanism for extending basic actions such as `play` and `stop`, enabling them to specify (or *target*) the timeline upon which they should be executed. Targets are any Movie Clip instances that are available at the current "state" of a Flash movie—you can't target a Movie Clip that isn't displayed (or existing) on the Stage. For example, suppose you had two Movie Clips, one on frame 1 and another on frame 10 of the Main Timeline. If the Main Timeline was stopped on frame 1, you couldn't target the Movie Clip on frame 10 because the instance is not on the current frame.

Since Flash 5, developers have been able to direct actions to specific timelines by attaching the same actions as *methods* to the `Movie Clip` object (we define methods in the following sidebar). As such, the `tellTarget` action is a deprecated action; it's still supported in the Flash Player 5 and 6, but it's been replaced with more versatile actions and syntax that make its use outdated. For an overview of deprecated actions, see the sidebar on deprecated actions in the preceding chapter. In this chapter, you work exclusively with the preferred ActionScript dot syntax to control Movie Clip instances. First, however, you need to understand how targeting works in Flash movies.

Note   If you're new to scripting, please read the "The New and Improved ActionScript" sidebar.

Paths: Absolute and relative modes

Earlier in this chapter, you learned how multiple Movie Clip timelines appear on the Stage. It's entirely possible to nest several Movie Clips within another Movie Clip. To understand how Movie Clips communicate with one another by using actions, you need to have a firm grasp of Movie Clip paths. A path is simply that—the route to a destination, an address *per se*. If you have a Movie Clip instance named `tailAnim` inside a `dog` Movie Clip instance, how is Flash supposed to know? What if there was more than one `tailAnim` in the entire movie, with others nested in other Movie Clips besides the `dog` instance? You can specify a Movie Clip's path in an absolute or a relative mode.

An *absolute path* is the full location (or target) information for a given Movie Clip instance from any other location (or target). Just like your postal address has a street name and number and a ZIP code so that people can find you on a map, all Movie Clips have a point of origin: the Main Timeline (that is, Scene 1). In Flash MX, you can use either the Slashes or *Dots* notation with absolute paths. See the sidebar titled "Paths in Flash 4 or Earlier Movies" for an explanation of the Slashes notation.

Note   Dots notation and dot syntax are synonymous terms, and are used interchangeably through this book.

The Dots notation follows the ActionScript language conventions. With Dots notation, the Main Timeline becomes

```
_root
```

The New and Improved ActionScript

Flash 5 introduced a new method of writing all ActionScript called *dot syntax*. Earlier versions of Flash used a natural-language scripting environment that was menu-based, in which actions could be read and understood easily and accessed via pop-up menus and dialog boxes. While most people prefer easy-to-use scripting environments, the production demands of complex interactive projects are often compromised by such menu-driven scripting environments. Computer programmers prefer to create, edit, and debug scripting with a language that can be accessed and modified easily. Consequently, we see the best of both worlds with Flash MX.

ActionScript adheres closely to the ECMA-262 specification that is based on JavaScript, the universal scripting language used by most browsers for interactive HTML and DHTML documents. Therefore, Flash ActionScript uses a dot syntax. What does that mean? It means that all actions are written within a standard formula that is common with object-oriented programming (OOP) languages:

```
Object.property = value;
```

or

```
Object.method();
```

The examples beg four things to be defined: objects, properties, methods, and values. An *object* is any element in a program (in this case, the Flash movie) that has changeable and accessible characteristics. Objects can be user-defined (in other words, you create and name them) or predefined by the programming language. Flash has several predefined objects, meaning that they're already built into the ActionScript language. We look at object types in more detail in later chapters. An important object (and perhaps the easiest to conceptualize) is the MovieClip object. Any Movie Clip instance on the Stage is an object, such as ballAnim or dogTailAnim. An object has characteristics, or *properties*, that can be updated or changed throughout the movie. An example of a Movie Clip property is scale, which is referred to as _xscale and _yscale. We look at Movie Clip properties in Chapter 25, "Controlling Movie Clips." Properties always have some data accompanying them. This data is called the property's *value*. Using the previous example, at full size, a Movie Clip's _xscale is 100 (the scale property uses percent as the unit of measure). For a Movie Clip instance named ballAnim, this would be represented in ActionScript syntax as:

```
ballAnim._xscale = 100;
```

Finally, objects can be enacted upon by procedures that do something to or with the object. These procedures are called *methods*. One method for the MovieClip object is the gotoAndPlay() method, which we used as a basic action in the previous chapter. In Flash 5 or higher movies, methods can be created for your own objects or predefined for existing Flash objects. Any basic action can be attached as a method to any Movie Clip instance, as in:

```
ballAnim.gotoAndPlay("start");
```

The preceding example tells the ballAnim Movie Clip to direct its Playhead to the frame label start on its timeline. This chapter helps you understand how to use the gotoAndPlay() method for Movie Clips.

A Movie Clip instance named `dog` on the Main Timeline (or _root) would have an absolute path of

    _root.dog

And, following in suit, a Movie Clip instance named `tailAnim` that is nested within the `dog` Movie Clip would have the absolute path of

    _root.dog.tailAnim

A *relative path* is a contextual path to one timeline from another. From a conceptual point of view, think of a relative path as the relationship between the location of your pillow to the rest of your bed. Unless you have an odd sleeping habit, the pillow is located at the head of the bed. You may change the location of the bed within your room or the rooms of a house, but the relationship between the pillow and the bed remains the same.

With Flash, relative Movie Clip paths are useful within Movie Clips that contain several nested Movie Clips. That way, you can move the container (or parent) Movie Clip from one timeline to another and expect the inner targeting of the nested Movie Clips to work. As with absolute paths, there are two methods of displaying relative paths: Slashes and Dots notations. To refer to a timeline that is above the current timeline in Dots notation, use

    _parent

You can use relative Dots notation to refer up and down the hierarchy at the same time. For example, if you have two nested Movie Clips, such as `tailAnim` and `barkingAnim`, within a larger Movie Clip named `dog`, you may want to target `tailAnim` from `barkingAnim`. The relative Dots path for this is

    _parent.tailAnim

This path tells Flash to go up one timeline from the current timeline, `barkingAnim`, to its parent timeline (the `dog` timeline), and then look for the instance named `tailAnim` from there.

You can also use successive _parent references to travel up in the timeline hierarchy multiple times, such as

    _parent._parent

Using the `dog` instance example again, if you wanted to control the Main Timeline (which is the parent timeline of the dog instance) from the tailAnim instance, you could use `_parent._parent` in the target path of an action executed from the `tailAnim` timeline.

Note   You can directly control the Main Timeline using the reference _root. However, as we'll see later in this chapter, you may load entire .swf files into Movie Clip instances of other .swf files, thereby changing the reference to _root.

As with absolute paths, we recommend that you become familiar with using the Dots notation for relative paths.

Okay, that's enough theory. Now, you're going to practice nesting Movie Clips inside of other Movie Clips, as well as target actions at specific instances using Dots notation.

Targeting Movie Clips in Flash MX

In this section, you'll see how to make Movie Clips interact with one another by using Dots notation and ActionScript. Specifically, you're going to create our barking and wagging dog example. You will begin this exercise with a starter .fla file located on the book's CD-ROM.

On the CD-ROM   Open the stella_starter.fla file found in the ch19 folder of this book's CD-ROM.

With the starter file open in Flash MX, test the movie using Control ⇨ Test Movie. You'll see that our dog, Stella, is wagging her tail. At timed intervals, she will bark. Right now, her tail keeps wagging as she barks. In this exercise, we'll show you how to stop the tail from wagging while Stella's barking. Close the Test Movie window and take a look at the Library panel. You'll find the following assets listed:

✦ **bark.wav:** This is the sound file used for Stella's bark. You will find this sound on the bark layer of the barkAnim timeline.

✦ **barkAnim:** This Movie Clip symbol contains the animation for Stella's barking head. If you double-click this symbol in the Library panel, you'll see that the timeline has two layers, one for the sound and another for the head animation. This symbol is used in the stella Movie Clip symbol.

✦ **body:** This Graphic symbol is artwork of Stella's body and legs. This is no animation on its timeline. The body symbol is used in the stella Movie Clip symbol.

✦ **head:** This Graphic symbol is artwork of Stella's head. You'll find a couple of instances of this symbol in the barkAnim symbol.

✦ **stella:** This Movie Clip timeline contains instances of the barkAnim, body, and tailAnim symbols.

✦ **tail:** This Graphic symbol contains the artwork for Stella's tail.

✦ **tailAnim:** This Movie Clip symbol contains two instances of the tail symbol. Each instance is rotated differently to create the wagging effect.

Now, you're going to add some behaviors to the movie. First, you'll need to name the instances in the movie. ActionScript can find a Movie Clip instance only by its name. Using the Property inspector, we'll add instance names to all of the Movie Clip instances. Each instance will be named with a _mc suffix, as in tailAnim_mc, in order to work with Flash MX's new code hinting feature.

New Feature   Flash MX has introduced code hinting to the Actions panel. We'll take more about code hints in Chapter 24, "Knowing the Nuts and Bolts of Code." Code hints show you related actions to specific objects (such as Movie Clip instances) in the Script pane of the Actions panel. In this exercise, we'll begin to see how code hints work.

Once the instances are named, we can then target the instances with ActionScript. In this example, we'll target the tailAnim_mc instance from the barkAnim_mc. When the keyframe containing the barking mouth inside of barkAnim_mc is reached, the movie will tell the tailAnim_mc to go to and stop on a specific frame. When the barking is over, tailAnim_mc will be told to continue playing.

1. With stella_starter.fla open in Flash MX, select the instance of the Stella symbol on the Stage, on the Main Timeline. Open the Property inspector, and name the instance stella_mc in the <Instance Name> field, as shown in Figure 19-4.

Figure 19-4: You can name Movie Clip instances in the Property inspector.

2. Double-click the stella_mc instance on the Stage to edit the Stella symbol in the Library. Select the barkAnim symbol instance, and again, using the Property inspector, name this instance barkAnim_mc in the <Instance Name> field.

3. Select the tailAnim symbol instance located on the tailAnim layer. Name the instance in the Property inspector, using the name tailAnim_mc in the <Instance Name> field.

4. With all of our instances named, we can now target actions to specific timelines. Your first goal is to stop the wagging tail while Stella barks. Double-click the barkAnim_mc instance to edit the symbol's timeline.

5. On the barkAnim_mc timeline, create a new layer and rename it **actions**. On frame 14 of this new layer, insert an empty keyframe (F7). Frame 14 is the frame just before the Stream sound on the bark layer begins. On frame 14, you want to tell the tailAnim_mc instance to stop playing. So, let's give this keyframe a frame comment that indicates this behavior. With the keyframe selected, open the Property inspector and, in the <Frame Label> field, type **//stop wagging**, as shown in Figure 19-5.

Figure 19-5: Frame comments can be used to describe the actions on a keyframe.

6. After you have assigned a comment on the frame, you're ready to write the ActionScript to perform the described behavior. With frame 14 selected on the Actions layer, open the Actions panel (F9). To keep this exercise within the scope of Normal mode in the Actions panel, we'll show you how to use the `evaluate` action to write Dots notation in ActionScript. In the Actions pane, open the Actions ➪ Miscellaneous Actions booklet. Double-click the `evaluate` action found there.

Caution   The `evaluate` action will not appear in the Actions ➪ Miscellaneous Actions booklet if the Actions panel is in Expert mode.

7. When `evaluate` is added to the Script pane, all you will see is a semicolon character, ; . However, in the top right portion of the panel, you'll find an Expression field. Click once inside this field. Then click the Target Path selector icon (see Figure 18-1 for its location). The Insert Target Path dialog box will open, as shown in Figure 19-6. Make sure Dots is selected in the Notation setting and Absolute is selected in the Mode setting. Click the plus icon (+) next to the `stella_mc` instance to reveal the nested instances, `barkAnim_mc` and `tailAnim_mc`. Finally, select the `tailAnim_mc` instance, since it contains the wagging animation that you want to stop.

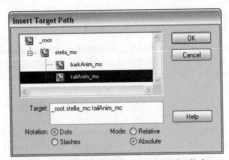

Figure 19-6: The Insert Target Path dialog box can help you build the path to a Movie Clip instance.

8. With the cursor still within the Expression field, type a single dot, or period (.). Almost immediately, you'll see the code hints menu appear next to your text. Because you named your instances with a _mc suffix, Flash MX knows that the code hinting should show actions (or methods and properties) relevant only to Movie Clip instances. In the menu, choose stop( ). When you are finished, your Actions panel should resemble Figure 19-7.

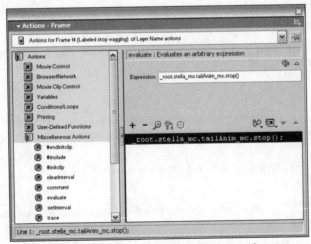

Figure 19-7: This action will tell the tailAnim_mc instance to stop playing.

9. Use this same technique to tell the tailAnim_mc instance to start playing again once the bark has ended. In the barkAnim symbol timeline, create yet another actions layers (you can make more than one to prevent overlap of your frame comments). Place these new Actions layers beneath the original Actions layer. On frame 20 of this second Actions layer, insert an empty keyframe (F7). Assign a frame comment of //**start wagging** in the <Frame Label> field of the Property inspector for this keyframe.

10. Repeat Steps 6 through 8 for the action on this keyframe. This time, however, choose a play() action from the code hints menu in the Actions panel.

11. Now you're ready to test your movie. Save the Flash document as **stella_absolute.fla**. You'll use the suffix _absolute to let you know that you used absolute target paths in this example. After you have saved the file, use Control ➪ Test Movie to view your movie. When Stella barks, her tail should stop wagging. When the bark is over, the tail should resume wagging.

This example has shown you how to target Movie Clip instances using absolute paths, built with the Insert Target Path dialog box and the evaluate action in Normal mode of the Actions panel. However, you can also try using relative paths to target the instances. In the ch19 folder of the book's CD-ROM, open the **stella_relative.fla** file to see an example of relative path addressing. Note that this example also uses a gotoAndPlay(2) action on the //stop wagging keyframe to make sure Stella's tail is pointed down during the bark. You can also find a completed example file for the exercise you just completed, **stella_absolute.fla**.

Paths in Flash 4 or Earlier Movies

Before Flash 5, the Main Timeline was represented in a Movie Clip path as a starting forward slash (/) character. The absolute path of a Movie Clip instance named dog on the Main Timeline is

    /dog

Any nested Movie Clips inside of the dog instance would be referenced after that starting path. For example, the absolute path to tailAnim, an instance inside the dog Movie Clip instance would be

    /dog/tailAnim

Another / character was put between the two instance names. Think of the / as a substitute for the period or dot (.) in ActionScript target paths. Use of the / character in Movie Clip paths is known as the *Slashes* notation.

The equivalent to _parent in Slashes notation is a double-dot, as in

    ../

The two dots here work just like directory references for files on Web servers; use a pair of .. for each timeline in the hierarchy.

Just like tellTarget is considered a deprecated action in Flash MX, the Slashes notation is deprecated syntax. It will still work with the Flash 5 and 6 Players, but subsequent versions of the Flash authoring program will be built upon the Dots notation.

Using Movie Clips to Create Sound Libraries

Chapter 15 discussed the ins and outs of sound import and use in Flash documents. In this chapter, we show you how to create sound Movie Clips that are nested within a larger sound "library" Movie Clip. With sound library Movie Clips, you can transport sets of sounds easily between timelines and other Flash movies. In this section, you learn the importance of the following items:

✦ Consistent timeline structure

✦ Naming conventions for Movie Clip instances

✦ Nested Movie Clip instances

✦ Streamlining Movie Clip production

These production principles are rather straightforward and relatively simple to learn. Flash MX has introduced new ways to load and play sounds on the fly using ActionScript. We'll look at these features in Part VII, "Approaching ActionScript."

On the CD-ROM

You'll find sound files (.WAV and .AIFF) in the ch19 folder of the *Flash MX Bible* CD-ROM. Make a copy of the pianoKeys_starter.fla file for this exercise.

Overview of the pianoKeys Movie Clip

Open the pianoKeys_starter.fla file. A `pianoKeys_mc` Movie Clip instance is already on the Stage of the Main Timeline. Double-click the `pianoKeys_mc` instance to enter the Symbol Editing mode, as shown in Figure 19-8. Note that the Timeline is docked to the left side of the Document window.

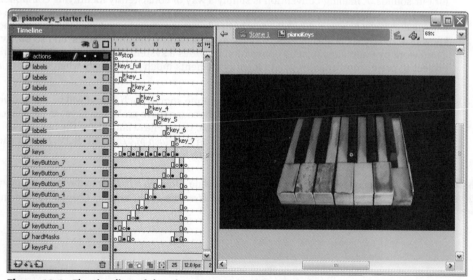

Figure 19-8: The timeline of the pianoKeys Movie Clip symbol

The timeline for the pianoKeys symbol has several layers for individual Button instances and labels. If you test this movie using Control ⇨ Test Movie (Ctrl+Enter or ⌘+Enter), you'll see that the Button instances over each piano key will tell the Playhead of the pianoKeys timeline to go to that key's frame label. For the first key on the left, the button on layer keyButton_1 has the following action list:

```
on (press, keyPress "a") {
    gotoAndStop ("key_1");
}
on (rollOver) {
    gotoAndStop ("keys_full");
}
```

These actions don't use any Dots notation—they are simple navigation actions that you learned in the last chapter. When the keyButton_1 instance is clicked with the mouse, the Playhead moves to the key_1 label on the current timeline, which is the pianoKeys timeline. Unless targeting is used, all actions on a Button instance will target the timeline on which the Button exists.

When the timeline goes to the key_1 frame label, a new PNG bitmap of a "pressed" piano key (key_01.png on the keys layer) appears on top of the pianoKeys_full.png bitmap that is placed on the bottom keysFull layer. Note that the pianoKeys_full.png bitmap is present throughout the entire pianoKeys timeline. Each Button instance in the pianoKeys Movie Clip sends the Playhead to the appropriate piano key frame label.

Now that you have an understanding of what's happening in this Movie Clip, let's create some sound Movie Clips that the pianoKeys instance can target.

Making sound Movie Clips

Before we start making new Movie Clip symbols, you need to establish *a naming convention* for our sounds. A naming convention is simply a way of consistently identifying components in any project, in or out of Flash. To a member of a Web production team, the importance of naming conventions can not be overemphasized—everyone involved with the project should know how to give names to images, sounds, symbol names, instance names, and so on. Even if you work by yourself, a naming convention provides a system of integrating elements from project to project and enables you to identify elements much more easily when you open old files.

1. For each key on the piano, we'll make a unique sound. Each sound will be on its own timeline where it can be targeted to play. Because there are seven keys on the piano, you need to import seven sounds into Flash. Using File ⇨ Import (or the new File ⇨ Import to Library), locate the ch19 folder on the *Flash MX Bible* CD-ROM. Import each of the key sounds (AIF or WAV files) into your Flash document.

Cross-Reference

Imported sounds do not show up on the timeline—they go straight into the movie's Library. If you need to know how to import sound files into Flash, refer to Chapter 15, "Adding Sound."

2. Create a new Movie Clip symbol (Insert ➪ New Symbol) and give it the name **sound_1**, as shown in Figure 19-9. This Movie Clip's timeline will be dedicated to the key_1 sound that you imported in the Step 1.

Figure 19-9: The Symbol Properties dialog box with the Movie Clip behavior selected

3. Flash will automatically move you into the Symbol Editing mode for the sound_1 Movie Clip symbol. Rename Layer 1 to **labels** and make a new layer called **sound**. Position the sound layer below the Labels layer. On frame 30 of both layers, press the F5 key to add more frames to the timeline.

4. On the Labels layer, you need to establish three "states" or positions for the sound: no sound, initiate sound, and mute sound. Why? Remember that all Movie Clips will try to play as soon as they appear on a timeline. So, you need to make sure there's nothing on the first frame (no sound state). For the remaining two states, add two frame labels: one called **start** on frame 3 of the Labels layer, and another called **mute** on frame 15 of the Labels layer (see Figure 19-10). Make sure that you add these labels to unique keyframes — if you try to add a label to a regular frame, the label will be attached to an earlier keyframe.

Note   You won't be using the mute state of this timeline in this exercise, but we'll explain how it can be used at the end of the chapter.

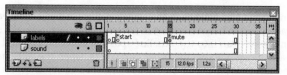

Figure 19-10: Each sound will use the same structure as the sound_1 Movie Clip: an empty first frame and two labels for starting a sound and stopping a sound.

5. Add an empty keyframe (F7) on frame 3 of the Sound layer. With that frame selected, open the Property inspector, and select the key_1.wav (or key_1.aif) sound from the Sound menu. Make sure you are viewing the expanded settings of the Property inspector by clicking the arrow at the lower-right corner of the inspector. Leave the Sync setting at Event so that multiple instances of the key_1 sound can overlap (play on top of one another). See Figure 19-11 for reference.

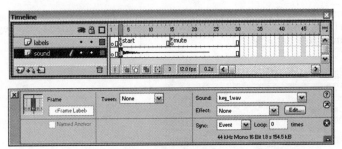

Figure 19-11: When the start label is played on the sound_1 timeline, the key_1 sound will play.

6. Repeat Step 5 for frame 15 on the Sound layer. This time, however, change the Sync setting to Stop, as shown in Figure 19-12. When this keyframe is played, all instances of the key_1 sound will stop playing.

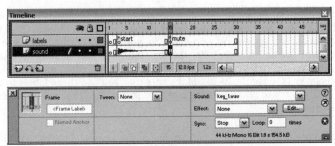

Figure 19-12: Whenever the Stop Sync setting is selected, the sound waveform on the timeline will appear as a short blue line.

7. Now you need to add some stop actions to the timeline. Because you want each sound Movie Clip to play each time its respective key is pressed, you need to make sure playback from one action doesn't run into the timeline space of other labels. Add a new layer called **actions** and move it above the other two layers. Open the Actions panel (F9), and select frame 1 of the Actions layer. Choose the stop action from the Actions ⇨ Movie Control booklet, and drag it to the Script pane of the Actions Panel, as shown in Figure 19-13. In the Property inspector, give this action keyframe a comment of **//stop** in the <Frame Label> field.

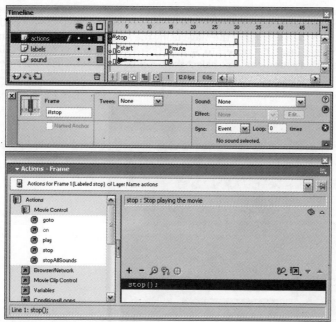

Figure 19-13: This stop action will prevent the sound's timeline from playing when the Flash movie first loads.

8. Copy the `stop` keyframe on frame 1 by selecting the keyframe and pressing Ctrl+Alt+C (⌘+Option+C). You can also right-click (Control+click on the Mac) the keyframe and select Copy Frames from the contextual menu. Then, select frame 10 of the Actions layer and press Ctrl+Alt+V (or ⌘+Option+V) to paste the `stop` keyframe. Repeat for frame 20. The placement of these stop actions is a bit arbitrary — you only need to stop the Playhead from playing into labels that occur later in the timeline. When you're finished with this step, your timeline should resemble the one shown in Figure 19-14.

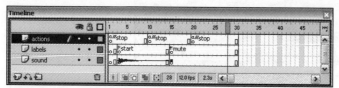

Figure 19-14: These stop actions will keep each area of the timeline from playing into the others.

9. Next, you add an icon to this Movie Clip so an instance of the symbol can be seen on the Stage. Make a new layer and name it **icon**. Place this new layer beneath the other layers in the Timeline window.

10. On the first frame of the Icon layer, draw a white rectangle. Then, use the Text tool to add the text **Sound** (with a black fill color) on top of the rectangle. Select both items and align them to the center of the Stage using the Align panel. With both items still selected, choose Insert ➪ Convert to Symbol (F8). In the Symbol Properties dialog box, name the symbol **soundIcon**, and select the **Graphic** Behavior. Click OK. When you're finished, your sound_1 timeline should resemble Figure 19-15.

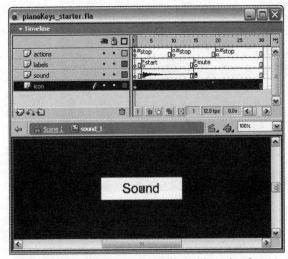

Figure 19-15: The soundIcon will provide a visual representation for this sound on the Stage.

11. Add keyframes for the soundIcon instance on frames 3, 10, 15, and 20 of the Icon layer, as shown in Figure 19-16.

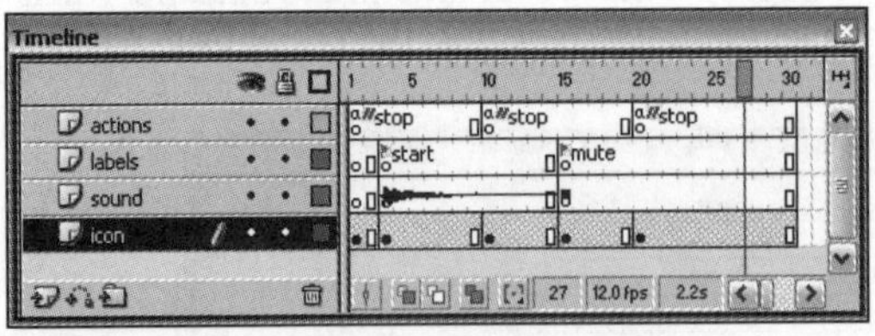

Figure 19-16: The soundIcon needs to have dedicated instances for each state of the sound_1 timeline.

12. Select the instance of soundIcon on frame 3, and open the Property inspector. Choose the Advanced option in the Color menu, and then click the Settings button. In the Advanced Effect dialog box, type **255** in the second column text field for the **Green** color channel (see Figure 19-17).

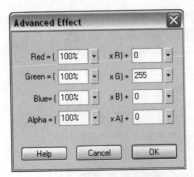

Figure 19-17: When the sound_1 timeline reaches the start label, the soundIcon will turn green.

13. Repeat Step 12 for the instance of soundIcon on frame 15. This time, however, type **255** in the second column text field for the **Red** color channel (see Figure 19-18). This step completes the first sound Movie Clip.

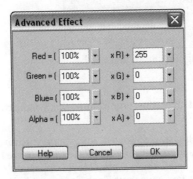

Figure 19-18: When the sound_1 timeline reaches the mute label, the soundIcon will turn red.

Now, you need to repeat this process for key sounds 2 through 7 — but don't worry! Because you created a coherent structure for the sound_1 timeline, creating the other Movie Clips will be relatively painless.

14. Open the document's Library panel (Ctrl+L or ⌘+L). Right-click (Control+click on the Mac) the sound_1 Movie Clip and choose Duplicate from the contextual menu.

15. Name the new Movie Clip copy **sound_2**, and make sure that the Movie Clip behavior is selected. Click OK.

16. Double-click the sound_2 Movie Clip in the Library to edit this symbol's timeline. *Remember that you're no longer working on the sound_1 timeline.*

17. Select frame 3 of the Sound layer, and open the Property inspector. Choose key_2.wav (or key_2.aif) from the Sound menu, as shown in Figure 19-19. Leave all other settings the same.

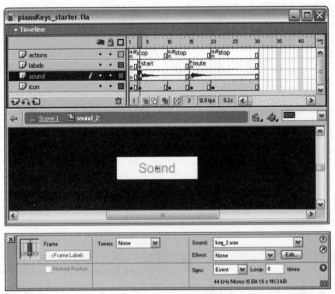

Figure 19-19: In Step 16, you're changing the sound that will be played back on the sound_2 timeline.

18. Repeat Step 17 for frame 15 of the Sound layer. However, change the Sync setting to Stop for this keyframe.

That's it! You can now easily create the remaining sound Movie Clips (sound_3 through sound_7) by repeating Steps 14 through 18 and incrementing the Movie Clip's name by one number each time. When you've finished creating all seven sound Movie Clips, you're ready to create a sound library Movie Clip. Make sure you save your Flash document before you proceed to the next section of this exercise.

On the CD-ROM

You can refer to the **pianoKeys_starter_sounds.fla** file located in the ch19 folder of the *Flash MX Bible* CD-ROM. This file has the seven sound Movie Clips in the Library panel, sorted in the keySounds folder.

Nesting sounds into a sound library Movie Clip

You have seven sound Movie Clips all ready to go, but we need somewhere to put them on the Stage. It's feasible to place each sound Movie Clip on the Main Timeline's Stage, but your Stage will start to get cluttered if many Symbols populate that space. So, you'll make a Movie Clip container for all those sounds. We refer to a container for sounds as a sound library, or soundLib for short.

1. Create a new Symbol by choosing Insert ➪ New Symbol (Ctrl+F8 or ⌘+F8). Name the symbol **soundLib** and give it a Movie Clip behavior. Click OK. The Stage switches to Symbol Editing mode for the soundLib Movie Clip timeline.

2. Rename the Layer 1 to **sounds** and drag an instance of the sound_1 Movie Clip from the Library panel to the Stage. Open the Property inspector and give the name sound_1_mc to the instance in the <Instance Name> field.

3. Drag an instance of each remaining sound Movie Clip (sound_2 through sound_7) onto the Sounds layer. Make sure that you name each instance after its symbol in the Library, adding the suffix _mc, just as you did in Step 2. Place each instance on the Stage from top to bottom, with the sound_1_mc instance at the top. Use the Align panel to center the instances horizontally and to space them evenly. When you are finished, your Stage should resemble Figure 19-20.

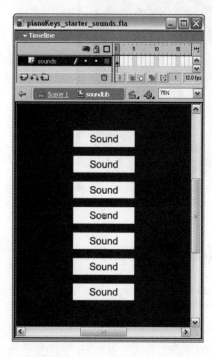

Figure 19-20: The soundLib timeline contains all seven sounds as individual instances.

4. Go to the Scene 1 timeline (the Main Timeline). Create a new layer called **soundLib_mc**, and place the layer above the pianoKeys_mc layer. Place an instance of the soundLib Movie Clip on frame 1 of the soundLib layer. Give the instance the name **soundLib_mc** in the Property inspector. You may need to resize the soundLib_mc instance so that it fits on the left side of the Stage, as shown in Figure 19-21.

Our sound library is now complete. All that remains is to add actions to your pianoKeys Movie Clip to target the sounds in the correct order.

On the CD-ROM You can compare your working Flash movie to the finished sound library in the **pianoKeys_starter_soundLib.fla** file, located in the ch19 folder of the *Flash MX Bible*.

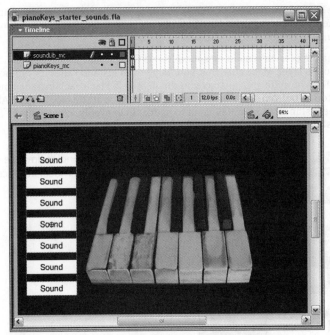

Figure 19-21: The sound Movie Clips will be accessed from the soundLib_mc instance on the Main Timeline.

Targeting sounds with ActionScript syntax

Now you have a Movie Clip instance called soundLib_mc along with the instance pianoKeys_mc, both located on the Main Timeline. The remainder of this exercise shows you how to add ActionScript to the pianoKeys timeline that will target the sound instances in the soundLib_mc instance.

> **Note**
>
> There will be more than one Actions layer in this timeline. The Actions layer in Step 1 is a new layer in addition to the existing actions layer (with the //stop comment).

1. Enter the Symbol Editing mode by double-clicking the pianoKeys_mc instance in Scene 1. On the pianoKeys timeline, add a new layer and name it **actions**. Move this new Actions layer underneath the layer that contains the key_1 frame label, as shown in Figure 19-22.

2. On frame 3 of the new Actions layer, you need to add actions that will play the first sound in our sound library. Remember that the Button instances on the pianoKeys timeline already move the playhead to each key's label. Insert a blank keyframe (F7) on frame 3.

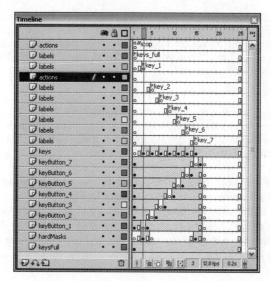

Figure 19-22: Don't be afraid to keep information separated on Actions and Labels layers. Separating the information will make it much easier for you to access the appropriate sections of your timelines.

3. With the keyframe selected, open the Actions panel (F9). In the panel's options menu (located in the right corner), make sure Normal mode is enabled. Double-click the `evaluate` action in the Actions ➪ Miscellaneous Actions booklet. You should now see a single semicolon (;) in the Script pane, along with an Expression field in the upper-right portion of the panel.

4. Click once in the Expression field, and click the Target Path selector icon (see Figure 18-1 for the location of this icon). In the Insert Target Path dialog box, chose Dots in the Notation setting, and Absolute in the Mode setting. Then, expand the listing for the `soundLib_mc` instance. Select the `sound_1_mc` instance, as shown in Figure 19-23. Click OK.

Figure 19-23: The Insert Target Path dialog box will show you all of the Movie Clip instances in your Flash document.

5. Now, type a dot, or period (.) after the absolute path in the Expression field of the Actions panel. Immediately, the code hints menu will pop up after the dot. In the menu, double-click the `gotoAndPlay` action. Finally, complete the expression by typing **"start"** in the Expression field. When you are finished, you should see the following line of code in the Expression field:

```
_root.soundLib_mc.sound_1.mc.gotoAndPlay("start")
```

This code looks at the Main Timeline (`_root`) and then looks for a Movie Clip instance named `soundLib_mc`. Then, it tells the timeline of `sound_1_mc` instance inside of `soundLib_mc` to move the Playhead from the stopped first frame to the `start` label keyframe. You can also refer to Figure 19-24 to see this code.

Note   For the sound to play more than once, we use the `gotoAndPlay()` action instead of the `gotoAndStop()` action. If a timeline goes to and stops on a keyframe, any other actions that tell the timeline to go to the same keyframe won't work. Why? Because the Playhead is already on that frame; it doesn't need to go anywhere. By using `gotoAndPlay()`, the Playhead on the sound_1 timeline will go to the frame label and continue playing until it reaches the `stop` keyframe just after the frame label.

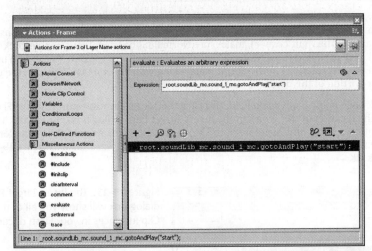

Figure 19-24: This ActionScript targets sound_1_mc and tells it to play the "start" frame.

6. Now, open the Property inspector. With frame 3 of the second Actions layer selected, type **//play sound** into the <Frame Label> field. Your Timeline window should resemble Figure 19-25.

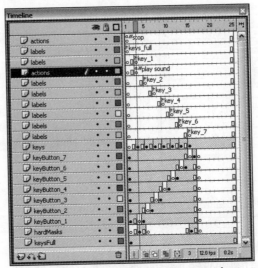

Figure 19-25: The //play sound comment lets you know what the actions on this keyframe do.

At this point, you will want to test your movie to see if the action is finding the target and playing the sound. Save your document, and use Control ⇨ Test Movie to create a Flash movie (.swf file). Make sure that the action on the keyframe works by clicking the first key on the piano keyboard (from the left), and that you hear a sound. Notice that you'll also see the soundIcon instance change to green when you click the first key.

7. Now, you need to enable all the other sounds in the soundLib_mc instance. Create a new layer and name it **actions**. Place the new layer underneath the Label layer that contains the key_2 frame label. Copy the //play sound keyframe from the previous Actions layer, using the method described in Step 8 of the "Making sound Movie Clips" section. Then, paste the copied keyframe to the new Actions layer, on frame 5.

8. Select the new //play sound keyframe in the Actions layer underneath the key_2 frame Label layer. Open the Actions panel (F9). You need to change the sound's target to sound_2 in the Expression field:

```
_root.soundLib_mc.sound_2_mc.gotoAndPlay("start")
```

See Figure 19-26 for reference.

9. Repeat Steps 7 and 8 for each key and sound. Each key_ frame label should have its own Actions layer with a //play sound keyframe. Test your movie each time you add a new keyframe with ActionScript. If a particular key doesn't work, check two things: the target's name in the ActionScript and the instance name of the sound in the soundLib_mc Movie Clip. Most errors occur as a result of not naming a Movie Clip instance.

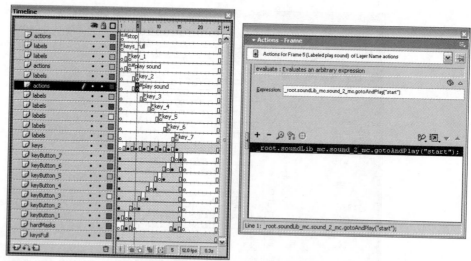

Figure 19-26: This timeline has enabled two sounds from the sound library.

When you've finished adding frame actions for every key, save the document and test it. After all's been said and done, you should have a functional Flash piano (well, at least 7 keys' worth!) that plays a sound whenever you click a piano key. If you want to change the sounds, you can either update the sound file in the Library or import new ones.

You can refer to the complete exercise file, **pianoKeys_complete.fla**, located in the ch19 folder of the book's CD-ROM.

Using other features of the sound library

You may be wondering why the `mute` frame label from the sound Movie Clip instances never made a debut in the ActionScript of this example. To be honest, we couldn't very easily create a damper pedal for our Flash piano, which could, we imagine, be used to mute a playing sound. However, it's more important that you understand the fundamental nature of building reusable elements in your Flash projects. Most developers need to plan for a bit of uncertainty in projects they take on, so it can be useful to build around likely scenarios. In the case of your sound library, it's likely that if you need to play a sound, then you'll probably need to shut it off too. We encourage you to build your own exercise around the following steps:

1. Open a new Flash document, and open the pianoKeys_complete.fla document as well. You can also choose to open the Library of this document by using File ➪ Open as Library.

2. Drag the soundLib Movie Clip symbol from the pianoKeys_complete.fla Library panel to the Library panel of the new Flash document.

3. Name the instance of the Movie Clip symbol `soundLib_mc`.

Now, it's up to you. For starters, create two Button instances: one that targets a sound's start label and another that targets its mute label. The code for the first button would look like this:

```
on (release){
    _root.soundLib_mc.sound_1_mc.gotoAndPlay("start");
}
```

The code for the second button would be this:

```
on (release){
    _root.soundLib_mc.sound_1_mc.gotoAndPlay("mute");
}
```

As you can probably tell, we've just created two buttons that will play and stop the sound in the sound_1_mc instance, located in the soundLib_mc instance. In this fashion, you can create sound mixers that turn specific sounds on or off.

Cross-Reference We'll discuss more sound-related ActionScript (and new MX sound features) in Chapter 27, "Interacting with Movie Clips," and Chapter 28, "Sharing and Loading Assets."

Summary

✦ Movie Clips are the key to Flash interactivity. Each Movie Clip has its own independent timeline and playback.

✦ Each Movie Clip instance needs a unique name on any given timeline. You cannot reuse the same name on other Movie Clips on a timeline. You can, however, use the same instance name on different timelines.

✦ There are two types of target paths for Movie Clips: absolute and relative. Absolute paths start from the Main Timeline and end with the targeted instance name. Relative paths start from the timeline that's issuing the action(s) and end with the targeted instance name.

✦ The Slashes and Dots notations are formats for writing either absolute or relative paths. The Slashes notation is considered deprecated, and should be avoided unless you are authoring for Flash 4 or earlier players. The Dots notation was introduced in Flash 5 and has a more complete syntax for programming in ActionScript.

✦ All Movie Clips and Flash movie elements should adhere to a naming convention.

✦ Together with the Insert Target Path dialog box, the evaluate action provides an easy transition to the world of Dots notation ActionScript.

✦ The use of a sound library Movie Clip enables you to store sounds in one area, and target them from others. Sounds used in a sound library can be updated easily and reused in other Flash movies.

✦   ✦   ✦

Making Your First Flash MX Project

✦   ✦   ✦   ✦

In This Chapter

Creating a Main
Timeline layout

Making an image
slide show

Adding navigation
elements to a
presentation

Using the ScrollBar
component

Creating an effect
with a custom fade
component

Inserting named
anchors into your
Flash movie

Adding accessibility
information to movie
elements

✦   ✦   ✦   ✦

Now that you've learned the basic principles behind Flash actions, you probably want to start creating a presentation to put on a Web site. For this edition of the *Flash Bible*, we integrated several basic production principles into one chapter. This chapter teaches you how to make a simple interactive Flash movie that has basic navigation and text functionality, before you get into the nitty gritty of ActionScript in Part VII of the book.

The Main Timeline as the Site Layout

Before you can start creating a Flash project, you need to know what you're communicating — what is the basic concept of the experience? Is this an all-Flash Web site? Is this a Flash animation that introduces some other type of content (HTML, Shockwave Director movies, and so on)? For the purposes of this chapter, you create a Flash movie for a basic all-Flash presentation. In a sense, this project will be the Flash equivalent of a Microsoft PowerPoint presentation. Let's look at the completed project (shown in Figure 20-1) that you will create in this chapter.

On the CD-ROM   In a Web browser, open the **main.html** document, located in the ch20 folder of the *Flash MX Bible* CD-ROM. This movie contains two completed sections of the presentation.

When you load the main.html file into a Web browser with the Flash Player 6 installed, you see the presentation's title, Digital Video Production, along with four navigation buttons that take you to each section of the presentation. The opening section, Introduction, has a Dynamic text field featuring the new ScrollBar component. When you click the Video Equipment button in the navigation bar, a Movie Clip featuring five video items is displayed along with another Dynamic text field with the ScrollBar component. The Next and Previous buttons allow you to browse the video items. Each video item uses a custom component that fades the item onto the Stage.

Figure 20-1: The completed presentation

Cross-Reference   In this book, we show you how to use pre-built or custom components. Read Chapter 29, "Using Components," for more information on the pre-built components shipped with Flash MX. To learn how to build a custom component like the Fade component used in this chapter, read the *Macromedia Flash MX ActionScript Bible* by Robert Reinhardt and Joey Lott.

You will also notice that when you click each navigation button that the browser history will update. You can click the Back button of the Web browser to go directly to the previous section of the presentation. In this chapter, we show you how to create named anchors in the Flash document.

If you have a screen reader installed and are using the Windows operating system, you will hear each item in the Introduction section described by the screen reader. A screen reader is an application that assists visually impaired computer users by speaking text aloud. The Flash Player 6 ActiveX control will only work with screen readers that adhere to the MSAA (Microsoft Active Accessibility) specification built into Windows operating systems. As of this writing, only the Window-Eyes screen reader by GW Micro adheres to MSAA. In this chapter, you learn how to add accessibility information to elements in your Flash document.

Creating a plan

Once you know what goals you want to achieve with your Flash content, you should map the ideas on paper (or with your preferred project planning or flowchart software). We create a basic presentation for digital video production that has four areas: introduction, video equipment, audio equipment, and editing software. Our organizational chart for this site has four discrete areas, as shown in Figure 20-2.

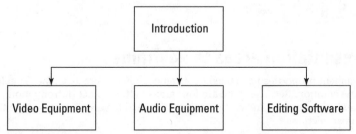

Figure 20-2: Our organizational chart will help us plan our Flash movie architecture

In this chapter, you will create the first two sections: introduction and video equipment. If you prefer, you can continue to develop the presentation with your own graphics.

Cross-Reference

Flowchart creation and project planning are discussed with greater detail in Chapter 3, "Planning Flash Projects."

Determining Flash movie properties

After you've made your organizational chart, you'll want to determine the frame rate, size, and color of the Flash document. We've skipped much of the "real-life" planning involved with Flash Web sites, which is discussed in Chapter 3, "Planning Flash Projects." For this example, we have made a starter Flash document for you to use, containing all of the elements necessary to complete the chapter. This document contains some of the basic graphic elements already positioned on the Stage.

On the CD-ROM

Make a copy of the **main_starter.fla** document, located in the ch20 folder of the *Flash MX Bible* CD-ROM. Before you open this file, you should install the Miniml font files from the ch08 folder.

Open the starter document in Flash MX. This document uses a frame size of 640×480 (to maintain the aspect ratio of a computer monitor), a standard frame rate of 12 fps, and a white background color. These are set in the Document Properties dialog box, shown in Figure 20-3, which is accessed by Modify ➪ Document (Ctrl+J or ⌘+J).

Figure 20-3: The Flash document properties

Mapping presentation areas to keyframes

Once the Flash document properties have been determined, you can create a Main Timeline structure for the presentation. Because there are four areas in the project (introduction, video equipment, audio equipment, and editing software), you'll have keyframes on the timeline that indicate those sections.

1. Create a new layer, and name it labels. Place this layer at the top of the layer stack in the Timeline window.

2. With the Arrow tool, select frame 10 of the Labels layer, and press the F6 key. This creates a keyframe on frame 10.

Tip   Always leave some empty frame space in front of your "real" Flash content. You can later use these empty frames to add a preloader, as discussed in Chapter 28, "Sharing and Loading Assets."

3. With the keyframe selected, open the Property inspector. In the Label field, type **intro**. After you have typed the text, press the Tab (or Enter) key to make the name "stick."

4. Repeat Steps 2 and 3 with frames 20, 30, and 40, with the frame labels **video**, **audio**, and **software**, respectively.

5. Select frame 50 of the Labels layer, and press the F5 key. This will enable you to read the very last label, software. Your Timeline window should resemble Figure 20-4.

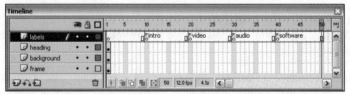

Figure 20-4: Frame labels will be used to differentiate each section of the site.

6. Select frame 50 on all other layers in the Timeline window, and press the F5 key to extend the content on these layers across the entire timeline, as shown in Figure 20-5.

Figure 20-5: The content in the heading, background, and frame layers will be present throughout the entire movie.

7. Save your Flash document as **main_100.fla**.

8. Make a new layer, and rename it **actions**. Place this layer below the Labels layer. Add a keyframe on frame 10 of the Actions layer, and open the Actions panel (F9). Make sure the Actions panel is in Normal mode by clicking the options menu in the top-right corner of the panel and selecting Normal mode.

9. Click the Actions booklet (located in the left-hand column of the Actions panel) to expand the actions contained there. Then, click the Movie Control booklet. Double-click the stop action. This adds the following code to the Script pane in the right-column of the Actions panel:

```
stop();
```

10. Close the Actions panel, and open the Property inspector. Make sure frame 10 of the Actions layer is selected. In the <Frame Label> field, type //**stop**. The // characters assign a frame comment instead of a frame label. Although this step isn't necessary for the functionality of the movie, frame comments can provide quick and easy access to the designer's or programmer's notes. Your Timeline window should now look like Figure 20-6.

Figure 20-6: Unlike labels, frame comments cannot be used in ActionScript. Comments can provide quick visual references for ActionScript code.

11. Save the Flash document again.

At this point, the Flash document has a skeleton architecture (a blueprint) for our interactive functionality. Now, let's add some content to each section of the movie.

On the CD-ROM   You can find the **main_100.fla** document in the ch20 folder of this book's CD-ROM.

Creating content for each area

In this section, you create navigation artwork for each area of the presentation. You also build some content for the video section.

1. In the starter document, create a new layer named **menu**. Place this layer beneath the Actions layer. Insert a keyframe on frame 10 of the Menu layer.

2. On frame 10 of the Menu layer, use the Text tool to add a Static text block with the text **Introduction**. For this example, use the Miniml font hooge 05_53 at 12 points with bold formatting. Use the Property inspector to set these options. Place the text near the left edge of the Stage below the heading, as shown in Figure 20-7.

 On the CD-ROM If you don't have this font installed, copy the Miniml font files from the ch08 folder of the *Flash MX Bible* CD-ROM.

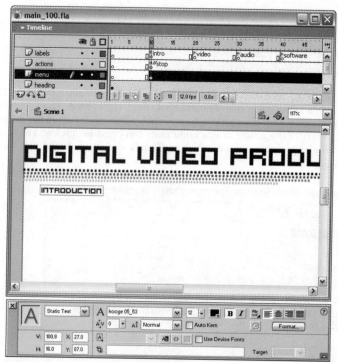

Figure 20-7: Use the Text tool to add the Introduction text to the Stage.

3. Repeat Step 2 for the text **Video Equipment**, **Audio Equipment**, and **Editing Software**. Space these text blocks across the Stage beneath the heading, as shown in Figure 20-8. Again, all of these text blocks should be on frame 10 of the Menu layer. Later, you will convert each of these text blocks to a Button symbol.

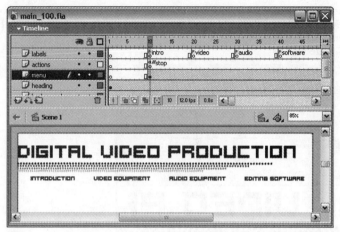

Figure 20-8: Add text that describes each section of the presentation.

Now, you add a graphic that let's you know which section is currently active. To do this, a black square will appear next to the appropriate text block. When the presentation starts, the black square will be next to the Introduction text. When the user navigates to the Video Equipment section, the black square will appear next to the Video Equipment section. Open the Library panel, and expand the graphics folder. There, you will find a Graphic symbol named marker. You will use this symbol in a moment.

4. Create a new layer on your Main Timeline (that is, Scene 1), and name it **marker**. Place this layer underneath the Menu layer.

5. On frame 10 of the Marker layer, insert a keyframe. Drag the Marker symbol from the Library to the Stage. Position the instance of the marker to the left of the Introduction text, as shown in Figure 20-9.

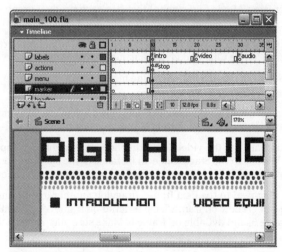

Figure 20-9: This marker designates the active section.

6. Insert another keyframe on frame 20 of the Marker layer — make sure you do not insert empty keyframes. Move the instance of the marker at frame 20 to the left of the Video Equipment text, as shown in Figure 20-10.

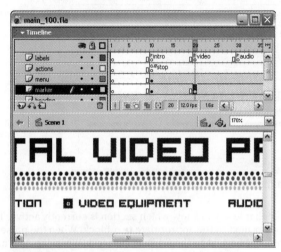

Figure 20-10: When the user goes to the Video Equipment section, the marker will appear next to the Video Equipment text.

7. Repeat Step 6 from frames 30 and 40 of the Marker layer, moving the marker instance to the left of the Audio Equipment and Editing Software text, respectively. You now have the marker changing its position for all sections of the timeline.

   Now let's add a slide show of the video equipment that can be used for digital video production. This slide show will appear in the Video Equipment section of the presentation. For this, you create a Movie Clip symbol that has each product graphic on a separate keyframe.

8. Create a new symbol using Insert ⇨ New Symbol (Ctrl+F8 or ⌘+F8). Make sure the Behavior option is set to Movie Clip, and give it a name of **videoEquip**.

9. Flash MX automatically switches to Symbol Editing mode, on the videoEquip timeline. Rename Layer 1 to **items**.

10. Add keyframes to frames 2, 3, 4, 5, and 6 of the Items layer. There are six items in the videoItems folder of the Library, and each item is put on its own keyframe.

11. Move the Playhead to frame 1 of the videoEquip timeline, and drag the dvTape Movie Clip symbol from the Library to the Stage. Once an instance of the symbol is on the Stage, name the instance **dvTape** in the <Instance Name> field of the Property inspector.

12. Continue moving the Playhead to the next frame, dragging another item to the Stage for each frame. Place cameraLow on frame 2, cameraMid on frame 3, cameraHigh on frame 4, dvDeck on frame 5, and dvCable on frame 6. Make sure you name each instance

in the Property inspector, using the same name as the symbol in the Library. When you're finished, press the < and > keys to review your frames. Check Figure 20-11 to compare your work. You may want to center each graphic on the Stage using the Align panel (Ctrl+K or ⌘+K). As you progress with this exercise, you can adjust the exact placement of each item. Before you proceed to the next step, check that each instance is named in the Property inspector.

Figure 20-11: You should have six filled keyframes on the item layers of the videoEquipment timeline.

13. Now you need to insert an Actions layer for this Movie Clip symbol. Create a new layer, and rename it **actions**. Select frame 1 of the Actions layer, and open the Actions panel. Add a stop action to make sure the items don't automatically loop when the movie loads:

```
stop();
```

14. Return to the Main Timeline (Scene 1) by clicking the Scene 1 tab in the upper-left corner of the Document window.

15. Create a new layer, and rename it **content**. Place this layer underneath the marker layer. Insert a new keyframe on frame 20 of the Content layer.

16. Open the Library panel, and drag the **videoEquip** symbol from the Library to the Stage. Place it just left of the center of the Stage, as shown in Figure 20-12. In the Property inspector, name this instance **videoEquip** as well.

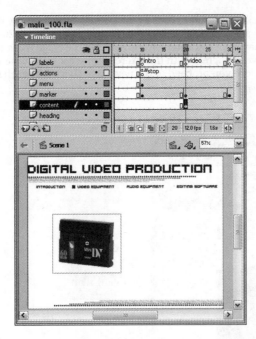

Figure 20-12: The videoEquip instance will only be present in the video section of the timeline.

17. Select frame 30 of the Content layer, and press the F7 key. This inserts a blank keyframe. Now, the `videoEquip` instance will only show in the Video Equipment area of the timeline.

18. Save your Flash document as **main_200.fla**.

Now you have some content in the Flash document. In the next section, you add navigation controls to the videoEquip symbol.

You can find the **main_200.fla** document in the ch20 folder of this book's CD-ROM.

Main Timeline versus Scene Structure

Arguably, you might be wondering why you are using keyframes to delineate each section, instead of new scenes. There are two reasons to use one scene (in other words, one Main Timeline):

✦ You can see the entire layout of our site very easily on one timeline.

✦ You can blend interstitials (transitions between each area of the site) over two sections more easily. It's much easier to have one Movie Clip instance span the area between two section keyframes on the Main Timeline.

Ultimately, the decision is yours. Make sure that you determine your Flash architecture well before you start production within the Flash MX authoring environment. It's not a simple task to re-architect the layout once production has begun.

Adding Navigation Elements to the Main Timeline

In the last section, you created a timeline for a digital video production presentation. You inserted content placeholders for the intro, video, audio, and software sections of the timeline, and you made a Movie Clip with video item graphics to place in the video section. However, you had no way of actually getting to any section except the intro frame. In this section, you convert the text blocks in the menu to Button instances, whose actions will control the position of the Playhead on the Main Timeline.

Creating text buttons for a menu

In this part of the exercise, you make menu buttons that will enable the user to navigate to the different areas of the Flash movie.

1. On the Main Timeline of your main_200.fla document, select frame 10 of the Menu layer.

2. With the Arrow tool, select the Introduction text block. Press the F8 key to convert this text into a symbol. In the Convert to Symbol dialog box, name the symbol **introButton**. Assign it a Button behavior.

3. Now we need to add a Hit state to the introButton timeline. By default, Flash MX will use the last frame of a Button symbol timeline for the Hit state, unless content is added to the Hit state keyframe. Double-click the introButton instance on the Stage to switch to Symbol Editing mode.

5. Select the Hit frame of Layer 1 on the introButton timeline, and press the F7 key to insert an empty keyframe.

6. Click the Onion Skin Outlines button in the Timeline window toolbar. This enables you to view the previous frames of the introButton timeline, as shown in Figure 20-13.

Figure 20-13: Onion skinning enables you to align the contents of several keyframes accurately.

7. Select the Rectangle tool, and draw a filled rectangle that covers the same area of the Introduction text block. You can use any fill color because the user never sees the Hit state. Make sure you turn off the stroke, or delete the stroke after the shape is drawn. Your button's timeline should resemble the one shown in Figure 20-14.

Figure 20-14: The Hit state defines the "active" area of the Button instance in the movie. When the user's mouse pointer enters this area, the Over frame of the Button is displayed.

8. Select the shape you drew in Step 7, and press the F8 key to convert it to a Graphic symbol named **hitArea**. You will reuse this shape for the other buttons in this section.

9. Next you add an Over state to the introButton, so that the user has a visual indication that it's an active button. Select the Over frame of Layer 1, and press the F6 key. This copies the contents of the previous keyframe into the new one. Select the Introduction text block with the Arrow tool, and change the fill color to a shade of blue such as #0099CC in the Toolbox or the Property inspector. You can also turn off Onion Skin Outlines at this point.

10. Return to the Main Timeline (that is, Scene 1) of your document, and save your Flash document. Select Control ➪ Test Movie to test the states of the introButton.

You can also use Control ➪ Enable Simple Buttons to preview the graphical states of a Button instance directly on the Stage.

11. Now you put an action on the introButton instance. Select the introButton instance on the Stage, and open the Actions panel (F9). In Normal Mode, double-click the goto action in the Action ➪ Movie Control booklet. Flash MX automatically adds the on(release){} code to hold the goto action in the Script pane. In the parameter area of the Actions panel, select the **Go to and Stop** option. In the Type drop-down menu, select **Frame Label**. In the Frame drop-down menu (located at the end of the field), select **intro**. Your Actions panel should resemble Figure 20-15.

12. If you test our movie at this point, the introButton won't do anything — the Playhead is already on the intro frame label. Add a button for each section on the site. Repeat Steps 2 to 9 for each section name in your movie. Note that you should reuse the hitArea Graphic symbol from Step 8 for the remaining buttons — use the Free Transform tool to size each new instance of hitArea to match the size of the text block in the Button symbol. You should end up with four buttons: introButton, videoButton, audioButton, and softwareButton.

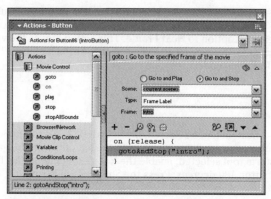

Figure 20-15: With these actions, the introButton instance will move the Main Timeline Playhead to the intro frame label.

13. Repeat Step 11 for each new Button instance. For each button instance, change the Frame drop-down menu selection to match the name of the button's area (for example, gotoAndStop("video"); on the videoButton).

14. Save your Flash document as **main_300.fla**, and test it (Ctrl+Enter or ⌘+Enter).

You can find the **main_300.fla** document in the ch20 folder of this book's CD-ROM.

When you test your Flash movie, you should be able to click each button to go to each area of the movie. If a button isn't functioning, double-check the code on the instance. Make sure that each Button instance has a Button behavior in the Property inspector. In the next section, you add buttons to the videoEquip Movie Clip symbol, so that the user can browse the pictures of the video items.

Browsing the video items

In this section, you go inside the videoEquip symbol and add some navigation buttons for the video items.

1. From the Main Timeline of our main_300.fla, double-click the videoEquip instance on frame 20 of the Content layer. Flash MX switches to Symbol Editing mode.

2. Make a new layer on the videoEquip timeline, and rename the layer to **buttons**.

3. Open the Buttons Library (Window ➪ Common Libraries ➪ Buttons). In the Buttons Library panel, double-click the Circle Buttons folder. Drag the **circle button — next** Button symbol to the Stage. Place the Button instance below and to the right of the dvTape instance.

4. With the circle button—next instance selected, open the Actions panel. Double-click the `goto` action to add this action to the Script pane. In the parameters area of the panel, change the Type menu option to **Next Frame**. This action moves the videoEquip Playhead one frame forward with each mouse click on the Button instance. The Script pane should show the following code:

```
on (release){
    nextFrame();
}
```

5. With the circle button—next instance selected, press Ctrl+D (⌘+D) to duplicate the instance on the Stage. Move the duplicate instance to the left of the original arrow button. With the Transform tool selected, enable the Rotate modifier in the Toolbox. Rotate the duplicated button 180 degrees. Press the Shift key while rotating, to lock in 45-degree steps.

6. Select both arrow buttons, and align them horizontally to each other by using the Align panel. Insert some descriptive text next to the instances, as shown in Figure 20-16.

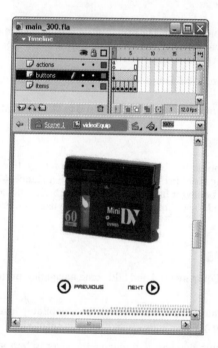

Figure 20-16: Add text to the buttons to describe their functionality.

7. Select the left arrow, and open the Actions panel. Select the `nextFrame();` action in the Actions list. In the parameter area, change the `goto` action's Type menu option to Previous Frame. The Script pane should show the following code:

```
on (release){
    prevFrame();
}
```

8. Save your Flash document as **main_400.fla**, and test it. Click the Video Equipment button, and try the new navigation arrows for your video items catalog.

You can further enhance your presentation by adding more information in the videoEquip Movie Clip symbol. In the next section, we add a scrolling text window that displays descriptions of the video items.

On the CD-ROM   You can find the **main_400.fla** document in the ch20 folder of this book's CD-ROM.

The topic of Flash usability has received a lot of press lately, particularly because many Flash interfaces are considered experimental or non-intuitive to the average Web user. In December 2000, Macromedia released a new section to their Web site — Macromedia Flash Usability. You can read their usability tips and view examples of interface design at `www.macromedia.com/ software/flash/productinfo/usability`.

Closely related to usability is accessibility: How easily can someone with a disability access the content within your Flash movie? We look at the new Flash MX accessibility options in the last section of this chapter.

Text Scrolling with the ScrollBar Component

Continuing from your previous Flash movie example with the video items, we demonstrate basic scrolling text using Dynamic text fields and the new ScrollBar component in Flash MX. Unlike previous versions of Macromedia Flash, you do not need to concern yourself with developing the ActionScript and interface artwork for a simple scrolling text field. We demonstrate this technique for one item in the videoEquip symbol to get you started.

Cross-Reference   If you haven't used text fields yet, read Chapter 8, "Working with Text." We explore ActionScript features of text fields in Part VII, "Approaching ActionScript." We discuss components in Chapter 29, "Using Components."

1. In the Flash document you created from the previous section, double-click the videoEquip instance on the Stage, at frame 10 of the Content layer. Flash MX switches to Symbol Editing mode.

2. Add a new layer, and rename it **description**. Move this layer beneath the Buttons layer. On frame 1 of the Description layer, select the Text tool and create a Dynamic text field. This field should accommodate several lines of text, as shown in Figure 20-17. The size of the text field should match the size of the text area you wish to display in the scrolling text window. Specify Verdana as the font, at 12 pt. Give the field an instance name of **item_1**, set the Line type menu to Multiline, and select the Selectable, Enable HTML, and Show border options. Do *not* assign a Var name to this text field.

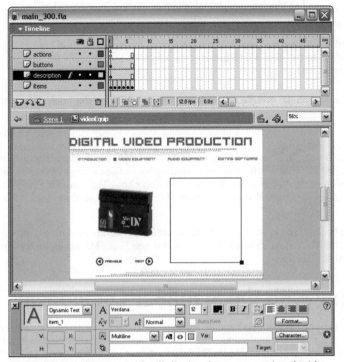

Figure 20-17: This text field will display the text associated with the first video item.

3. Now, some text needs to be inserted into the item_1 field. Open the **item_1.rtf** document in a text editor such as WordPad or TextEdit. This file is located in the ch20 folder of the *Flash MX Bible* CD-ROM. Select the contents of this text document, and copy it (Ctrl+C or ⌘+C). Go back to Flash MX, double-click the text field, and paste the text into the field by pressing Ctrl+V or ⌘+V. The item_1 text field should not expand in size to hold the text, as shown in Figure 20-18.

New Feature

Flash MX will allow you to copy text into a text field, even if it exceeds the visible capacity of the field. Instead of expanding the text field to accommodate all the text, the field control handle in the lower-right corner will turn into a filled black square, indicating that there's more text in the field.

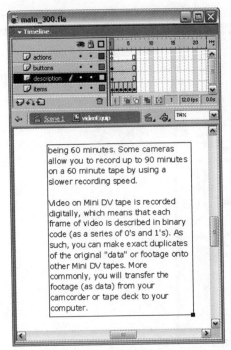

Figure 20-18: The item_1 field with the description text, showing the bottom portion

4. In order to scroll the text in the item_1 field, you need to add a ScrollBar component to the text field. Make sure frame 1 of the Description layer is selected. Open the Component panel (Window ⇨ Components), and drag the ScrollBar component from the panel to the text field's right edge. When you release the mouse button, the ScrollBar component should auto-expand to the height of the text field, as shown in Figure 20-19. If it doesn't, click and drag to the right edge until it expands. We find that dragging the component just inside the right edge works consistently.

5. Save the Flash document as **main_500.fla**, and test it (Ctrl+Enter or ⌘+Enter). Click the Video Equipment navigation button, and try the ScrollBar component. If the text in the item_1 text field is not scrolling, go back to the authoring environment and make sure the text field was named item_1. Do not proceed with any further steps until the ScrollBar component is functioning properly.

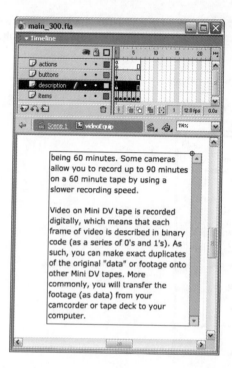

Figure 20-19: The ScrollBar component allows you to add scrolling to text fields easily.

6. Open the Property inspector, and select the ScrollBar component instance. Components are a special type of Movie Clip symbol that have custom properties and values that can be easily changed in the Property inspector. Components replace Smart Clips from Flash 5. Of special interest with the ScrollBar component is the Target Textfield value in the Property inspector, as shown in Figure 20-20. This value tells the ScrollBar instance which text field it should control. In the next few steps, you create more text field and ScrollBar component instances. You will manually change the Target Textfield value for these new instances.

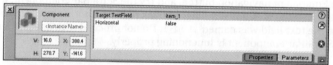

Figure 20-20: Components have custom properties and values that are accessed in the Property inspector.

7. Insert a keyframe on frame 2 of the Description layer. This creates a new instance of the Dynamic text field and ScrollBar component.

8. Select the Dynamic text field on frame 2 of the Description layer, and make sure the ScrollBar instance is deselected. Open the Property inspector, and change the instance name of the Dynamic text field to **item_2**.

9. Double-click the item_2 text field, and select the contents of the field by pressing Ctrl+A or ⌘+A. Then, delete the text by pressing the Backspace or Delete key.

10. Deselect the text field, and select the ScrollBar component instance on frame 2 of the Description layer. In the Property inspector, change the Target Textfield value to **item_2**.

11. In your preferred text editor, open the **item_2.rtf** file from the ch20 folder of the *Flash MX Bible* CD-ROM. Copy the text from this document and paste it into the item_2 text field in Flash MX.

12. Repeat Steps 7 through 11 for frames 3, 4, 5, and 6 of the Description layer. When you are finished you should have six separate Dynamic text fields, one per keyframe. Each ScrollBar component instance should target the text field on the given frame.

13. Save your Flash document again, and test it (Ctrl+Enter or ⌘+Enter). When you go to the Video Equipment section, you should be able to click the Next button to reach each video item's description field, and the field should be scrollable.

The next step in real production would be to finesse the artwork, and to add transitional effects between each video item. In the next section, you can add a custom Fade component that we created for use in this exercise.

You can find the completed document, **main_500.fla**, in the ch20 folder of the *Flash MX Bible* CD-ROM.

Using the Custom Fade Component

So far, much of the material and artwork used in this presentation could have been accomplished with a traditional HTML page layout in Macromedia Dreamweaver with GIF or JPEG graphics. In this section, you will add a fade effect to each of the video items in the videoEquip symbol. We created a custom component that can be snapped to any Movie Clip instance on the Stage. This component will fade in or out a Movie Clip instance, based on settings in the Property inspector. To see this fade effect in action, open the main.swf file from the ch20 folder in Flash Player 6. When you go to the Video Equipment section, each item will fade in. In other words, the alpha of the each Movie Clip instance animates from 0 to 100 percent.

To learn how to build your own custom components, read the component coverage in the *Macromedia Flash MX ActionScript Bible*, by Robert Reinhardt and Joey Lott.

The Fade component snaps to Movie Clip instances just like the ScrollBar component snaps to text fields. Since we built the Fade component for you, you won't find the Fade component in the Component panel along with the Flash MX components. The Fade component is located in the starter document's Library, and has been saved in each version of the main_ document that you've created in previous sections. Let's add the Fade component to the video items in the videoEquip symbol.

1. Open your saved Flash document from the previous section. On frame 20 of the Content layer, double-click the videoEquip instance on the Stage to edit the symbol.

2. Open the Library panel, and drag the Fade component to the dvTape instance on the stage. When you release the mouse button, the Fade component should snap to the top-left corner of the dvTape instance, as shown in Figure 20-21. We made a custom icon for this Fade component: a little gradient box with a capital F. This icon will not show up in the actual Flash movie (.swf file) — it is only displayed in the authoring environment.

Figure 20-21: The Fade component snaps to the top-left corner of the Movie Clip instance.

3. The default settings for the Fade component instance can be viewed in the Property inspector. Select the Fade component instance at the top-left corner of the dvTape instance, and open the Property inspector. This component has three options, as shown in Figure 20-22: direction (in to fade in the targeted instance, out to fade out the targeted instance), increment (how much should the alpha change per frame execution), and _targetInstanceName (the Movie Clip instance that the Fade component instance has snapped to).

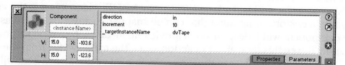

Figure 20-22: This custom component has three settings.

4. Save the Flash document as **main_600.fla**, and test it (Ctrl+Enter or ⌘+Enter). When you click the Video Equipment button, the first video item will fade into the Stage.

5. Repeat Step 2 for the other instances on frames 2, 3, 4, 5, and 6 of the videoEquip timeline.

6. Save the Flash document again, and test it. After you click the Video Equipment button, click the Next button. Each video item will fade into the Stage.

If you want to use the Fade component in other Flash documents, simply drag the Fade component from one Library to another document's Library. Alternatively, you can copy and paste the Fade component instance from one document to another. Try different increment values for the Fade component (in the Property inspector) to see how the fade animation is affected in the Flash movie.

On the CD-ROM You can find the completed document, **main_600.fla**, in the ch20 folder of the *Flash MX Bible* CD-ROM.

Adding Named Anchors

Flash Player 6 gives Flash movies extended functionality in some Web browsers, allowing the Back and Forward buttons of the browser to navigate to areas *within* the Flash movie. In earlier versions of the Flash Player, the Web browser's Back button would reset the position of the Flash movie to the first frame every time the movie reloaded into the browser. Now, you can add named anchors to Flash movies. Named anchors, when played, alert the browser's history to the location of the current anchor within the Flash movie. When another anchor is played, you can click the browser's Back button to go back to the previous named anchor.

Caution Named anchors are only supported in Web browsers that support `fscommand` and JavaScript interactivity. Currently, Internet Explorer 4 (or higher) on Windows or Netscape 3.x to 4.x on Windows or Macintosh supports the named anchor feature of Flash Player 6. Netscape 6.0 or higher (on any platform) or Internet Explorer on Mac (any version) does not support named anchors.

You can add named anchors to Flash 6 movies in two ways:

✦ Enable the Named Anchor on Scene option in the Preferences dialog box. On Windows or Mac OS 9.x (or earlier), you can access the preferences by choosing Edit ➪ Preferences. On Mac OS X, choose Flash ➪ Preferences. You will find the Named Anchor on Scene option in the General tab of the Preferences dialog box.

✦ Check the Named Anchor option in the Property inspector. Select a frame in the Timeline window, assign a frame label, and select the Named Anchor check box.

Note If you save your Flash MX document as a Flash 5 document, any frame labels that were also named anchors will not retain the named anchor setting.

In the presentation you're building in this chapter, we do not use any scenes. Therefore, we will add named anchors to all of the frame labels you created in previous sections.

1. Open the last Flash document you created from the previous section. Select frame 10 of the Labels layer, and open the Property inspector. Select the Named Anchor option, underneath the Frame Label field.

2. Repeat Step 1 for frames 20, 30, and 40 of the Labels layer.

3. Open the Publish Settings (File ➪ Publish Settings). Click the HTML tab, and choose the **Flash with Named Anchors** option in the Template menu. Click OK to close the Publish Settings dialog box.

4. Save the Flash document as **main_700.fla**, and preview the presentation by choosing File ➪ Publish Preview ➪ HTML. Flash MX creates the Flash movie (.swf file) and HTML file, and opens the default Web browser. If you have a supported Web browser, you can click on each navigation button (that is, Introduction, Video Equipment, etc.) and see the browser's history update. After you have clicked into one section, you can visit the previous section by clicking the browser's Back button.

You can find the **main_700.fla** document in the ch20 folder of this book's CD-ROM.

In Chapter 17, "Embedding Video," we show you how to use named anchors for embedded video in a Flash movie.

Making the Movie Accessible

This final section of the chapter will show you how to add accessibility information to your Flash presentation. As we mentioned earlier in this chapter, screen readers on the Windows operating system, working in concert with the Flash Player 6 ActiveX control, can read content inside of Flash movies. Window-Eyes 4.2 from GW Micro was engineered to work with Flash Player 6 through the use of MSAA (Microsoft Active Accessibility) technology. As of this writing, it is the only screen reader capable of accessing Flash content.

You can download a demo version of Window-Eyes for the Windows operating system at www.gwmicro.com. This version will only work for 30-minute durations—you will need to restart your computer to initiate a new session.

We recommend that you review the Accessibility information in the Using Flash MX guide that ships with Flash MX, which can also be viewed through the HTML guide installed with Flash MX. Choose Help ⇨ Using Flash command in the Flash MX application. We provide a quick overview of the Accessibility features of Flash MX in this section.

Screen readers will access information within the Flash movie differently, depending on the features of the specific screen reader. Here we discuss Accessibility options as they relate to Window-Eyes 4.2. You will add some content to the Introduction section of the presentation that can be read aloud by Window-Eyes.

1. In the last Flash document you created in the previous section, insert an empty keyframe at frame 10 of the Content layer on the Main Timeline (that is, Scene 1).

2. Create a Dynamic text field with an instance name of **description**. Use the same options for this text field that were used in the text fields for the videoEquip symbol. Make sure the text field can accommodate several lines of text, as shown in Figure 20-23.

3. Open the **introduction.rtf** document in the ch20 folder of the *Flash MX Bible* CD-ROM. Copy the text in this document, and paste it into the Dynamic text field, as you did in previous sections.

4. Open the Library panel, and double-click the Flash UI Components folder. Flash MX creates this folder whenever you add components to a Flash document. Drag the ScrollBar component from the Library to the right edge of the description text field on the Stage. The ScrollBar instance will snap and expand to the size of the text field, as shown in Figure 20-23.

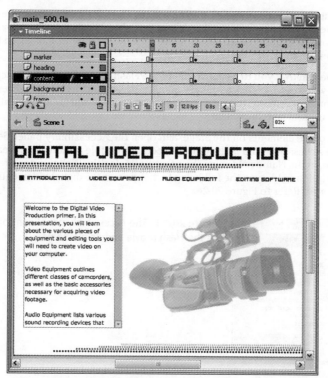

Figure 20-23: The screen reader can read this text field's contents.

5. With frame 10 of the Content layer active, drag an instance of the cameraHigh Movie Clip symbol (located in the videoItems folder) from the Library panel to the Stage. In the Property inspector, change the alpha of this instance to **30** percent. Name the instance **cameraHigh** as well.

Now you will use the Accessibility panel to add information to specific elements in the Introduction section of the presentation. You can open the Accessibility panel in two ways: a) select the Movie Clip, Button, or text field instance and click the Accessibility icon in the Property inspector, or b) choose Window ⇨ Accessibility.

You can add general information about your Flash movie by deselecting all elements on the Stage (you can press the Escape key to do this quickly) and opening the Accessibility panel.

The Make Movie Accessible option allows the screen reader to see elements inside of the Flash movie. If this option is cleared, the screen reader will not be able to read any elements of the Flash movie.

The Make Child Objects Accessible option allows elements other than the current Name and Description in the Accessibility panel to be accessed by the screen reader.

Clear the Auto Label option. Auto Labeling will tell Flash Player 6 to describe buttons and other elements by associating the closest text object to the element. For example, if you had some text underneath a Button instance, Auto Label would assign this text to the Button instance for the screen reader.

The Name field allows you to assign a title to the Flash movie, while the Description field allows you to add a quick summary about the Flash movie. Window-Eyes will read the Name contents, but not the Description contents. Let's add some general information to the current Flash document.

6. Deselect all of the elements on the Stage, and open the Accessibility panel. Select the Make Movie Accesssible and Make Child Objects Accessible options, and clear the Auto Label option. In the Name field, type the presentation's title, Digital Video Presentation. In the Description field, type the following text: A primer for digital video equipment and accessories. Refer to Figure 20-24.

Figure 20-24: The Accessibility panel controls options for the Flash movie and its elements.

7. Now select the Introduction button on frame 10 of the Menu layer. In the Accessibility option, enter the options shown in Figure 20-25. Note that you will not assign a keyboard shortcut description for this example. The Name and Description for this button will be read after the general information you added in the previous step. Window-Eyes will say the word "button" before it reads the name. For this example, Window-Eyes will say, "Button. Introduction. Access the introduction section of the presentation."

Note If you do want to have a keyboard shortcut read by the screen reader, then you should type out the text for any modifier key or combination including the + character, such as Ctrl+E. You will also need to add ActionScript to the Button (or Movie Clip) instance to make the movie respond to the key press that you described in the Accessibility panel.

8. Repeat Step 7 for each Button instance in the Menu layer.

9. Select the `description` text field on frame 10 of the Content layer, and make sure the Make Object Accessible check box is selected in the Accessibility panel. It is not necessary to add a description to this text field — the text inside of the field will be read automatically by the screen reader.

10. Select the `cameraHigh` instance on frame 10 of the Content layer, and clear the Make Object Accessible option in the Accessibility panel. Not all elements need to be read by the screen reader, and this graphic does not need to be revealed to visually impaired users.

Figure 20-25: The Name and Description contents for buttons can be read by Window-Eyes.

11. Save your Flash document as **main_800.fla**, and preview it in Internet Explorer for Windows. Make sure the Window-Eyes application is active. As soon as the movie loads into the browser, Window-Eyes reads the information for the movie, then reads the name and descriptions of the buttons. Then it will read the text inside of the description text field. After Window-Eyes reads the last Flash element, it speaks the word "bottom," indicating the end of the Web page has been reached. If you added body text to the HTML document, Window-Eyes would read that text as well.

You can find the completed Flash presentation, **main_800.fla**, in the ch20 folder of the *Flash MX Bible* CD-ROM. This document contains the first two sections of the presentations – on your own, try adding your content to the remaining sections using techniques you learned in this chapter.

You can continue to add more accessibility information to other elements in the Flash document. You can even add information to elements within Movie Clip symbols. Try adding descriptions to the buttons inside of the videoEquip symbol.

Screen reader technology can only interface with Flash movies played by the Flash Player 6 ActiveX control. Screen readers cannot access Flash movies played by the stand-alone Flash Player 6.

You can learn more about ActionScript and accessibility from the *Macromedia Flash MX ActionScript Bible*, by Robert Reinhardt and Joey Lott.

Summary

✦ Before you can start to create an interface in Flash, you need to have a plan for your Flash movie timeline. Create an organizational chart outlining the sections of the presentation.

✦ Determine your Flash movie properties (frame size, frame rate, and background color) before you undergo production in Flash.

✦ If you don't have final art for a Flash production, you can still create a functional prototype of the presentation using placeholder graphics. When the final artwork is ready, replace the placeholder graphics with the final artwork.

✦ You can create simple slide shows or product catalogs using sequential keyframes and buttons with `nextFrame()` and `prevFrame()` actions.

✦ The Hit area of a text-based Button symbol should always be defined with a solid shape.

✦ You can achieve basic text scrolling by snapping the new Flash MX ScrollBar component to a Dynamic or Input text field.

✦ You can apply time-based alpha effects to artwork with the custom Fade component.

✦ You can add accessibility information to Flash 6 movies. Windows-based screen readers designed to work with Flash Player 6, such as GW Micro's Window-Eyes 4.2, can read this information.

✦   ✦   ✦

Distributing Flash Movies

◆ ◆ ◆ ◆

In This Part

Chapter 21
Publishing Flash
Movies

Chapter 22
Integrating Flash
Content with HTML

Chapter 23
Using the Flash
Player and Projector

◆ ◆ ◆ ◆

When you finally have your project assembled in the Flash authoring environment and you're ready to prepare it for final presentation, this section will explain all the options available for delivering Flash content to your audience. Chapter 21 details every option and setting in the Publish Settings of Flash MX that will control your final file size and format. This chapter also includes tips for optimizing your file sizes for faster downloads and better performance. Chapter 22 covers all the HTML techniques relevant to integrating Flash content on Web pages. You can learn to load Flash movies into framesets and how to create plug-in detection systems for your Flash movies. If you are planning to distribute Flash content offline or you want to avoid plug-in problems, Chapter 23 will walk you through the various methods for creating Flash stand-alone projectors and using the Flash stand-alone player.

Publishing Flash Movies

✦ ✦ ✦ ✦

In This Chapter

Using the Bandwidth Profiler

Generating a size report

Understanding Flash movie publish options

Using HTML templates with your Flash movies

Creating bitmap image alternates for your Flash movie

✦ ✦ ✦ ✦

If you have read the entire book to this point, you're probably more than ready to get your Flash movies uploaded to your Web server to share with your visitors. This chapter shows you how to create Flash movies (.swf files) from Flash MX so that your Flash movies can be played with the Flash Player plug-in or ActiveX Control for Web browsers. We'll show you how to test your Flash movies, prepare Flash movie options, and adjust other output formats from Flash MX, such as HTML documents and image formats.

Testing Flash Movies

You have four ways to test your Flash documents: in the Timeline window using the Play command, in the authoring environment using the Test Movie and Scene commands, in a browser using the Publish Preview command, or in the standalone Flash Player using Flash movies (.swf files) made with the Export Movie command. There are several reasons why you should test your Flash movie (.swf file) before you transfer Flash movies to your Web server (or to the intended delivery medium):

- ✦ Flash documents (.fla files) have much larger file sizes than their Flash movie (.swf file) counterparts. To accurately foretell the network bandwidth that a Flash movie requires, you need to know how large the final Flash movie will be. If the download demand is too overwhelming for your desired Internet connection speed (for example, a 28.8 Kbps modem), you can go back and optimize your Flash document.

- ✦ The Control ➪ Play command in the Flash authoring environment does not provide any streaming information. When you use the Test Movie or Scene command, you can view the byte size of each frame, and how long it will take to download the Flash movie (.swf) from the Web server.

- ✦ Movie Clip animations and actions targeting Movie Clip instances cannot be previewed using the standard Control ➪ Play command (or the Play button on the Controller) in the Flash authoring environment.

Tip

You can temporarily preview Movie Clip symbol instances within the Flash authoring environment (for example, the Timeline window) by changing the Symbol instance behavior to Graphic instead of Movie Clip. Do this by selecting the instance, opening the Instance Panel, and choosing Graphic in the Behavior drop-down menu. However, when you switch the behavior back to Movie Clip, you will have lost the original instance name of the Movie Clip.

✦ Most scripting done with Flash actions, such as `loadMovie()`, `loadVariables()`, and `startDrag()`, cannot be previewed with the Play command. Enabling Simple Frame Actions or Simple Buttons in the Control menu has no effect with new scripting actions. You need to use Test Movie to try out most interactive functions in a Flash movie.

Tip

Any actions that require the use of remote CGI (Common Gateway Interface) scripts to load variables, movies, or XML data, will now work in the Test Movie environment. You do not need to view your .swf files in a browser to test these actions.

✦ Accurate frame rates cannot be previewed with the Play command (Control ➪ Play) in the authoring environment. Most complex animations appear jerky, pausing or skipping frames when the Play command is used.

Using the Test Scene or Movie command

You can test your Flash movies directly within the Flash MX interface by using the Control ➪ Test Movie or Test Scene command. When you choose one of these commands, Flash MX opens your Flash document in a new window *as a Flash movie (.swf file)*. Even though you are only "testing" a Flash movie, a new .swf file is actually created and stored in the same location as the Flash document (.fla file). For this reason, it is a good idea to always save your Flash document before you begin testing it.

Caution

If your movie is currently titled Untitled1, Untitled2, and so on in the application title bar, it has not yet been saved. Make sure you give your Flash movie a distinct name before testing it.

Before you use the Test Scene or Movie command, you need to specify the settings of the resulting Flash .swf file. The Test Scene or Movie command uses the specifications outlined in the Publish Settings dialog box to generate .swf files. The Publish Settings dialog box is discussed later in this chapter. For the time being, we can use the Flash MX default settings to explore the Test Scene and Movie commands.

Test Movie

When you choose Control ➪ Test Movie (Ctrl+Enter or ⌘+Enter), Flash MX generates a .swf file of the entire Flash document that is currently open. If you have more than one Flash movie open, Flash MX creates a .swf file for the one that is currently in the foreground and that has "focus."

The New Look of Test Movie in Flash MX

By default, Flash MX now sizes a tested movie at its actual pixel size. In previous versions of Flash, the tested movie would scale to the size of the Test Movie window. In the Windows version of Flash MX, the Test Movie environment will be in the same window mode as the Flash document environment. Meaning, if the Flash document window is maximized, the Test Movie window will be maximized. The scale of the Flash movie is 100 percent, regardless of the window's size. To size the Flash movie in an actual-size window, click the Restore Down button (the middle button in the far-right corner of the menu bar) and make sure View ➪ Show All is unchecked, as shown in the following figure.

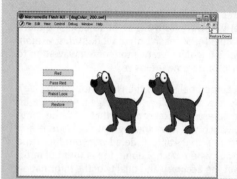 

Click the Restore Down button (left) to see the true size of the Flash movie (right).

If you enable View ➪ Show All, the Flash movie will scale to fit the size of the Test Movie window.

On the Macintosh, the default Test Movie window will always be the size of the actual Flash movie. The pixel width and height of a Flash movie is determined in the Document Properties dialog box (Modify ➪ Document).

Test Scene

If you are working on a lengthy Flash document with multiple scenes, you may want to test your scenes individually. You can do this by using Control ➪ Test Scene (Ctrl+Alt+Enter or ⌘+Option+Enter). The process of exporting large movies via Test Movie may require many minutes to complete, whereas exporting one scene will require a significantly smaller amount of time. Movies that require compression for several bitmaps and MP3 sounds usually take the most amount of time to test. As is shown in the next section, you can analyze each tested scene (or movie) with the Bandwidth Profiler.

Tip   You can use the Test Scene command while you are in Symbol Editing mode to export a .swf file that contains the current symbol timeline. The movie will not contain anything else from your Flash document. Note that the symbol's center point will become the top-left corner of the playback stage.

One Reason to Use Imported MP3 Files

If you have imported raw audio files (.WAV or .AIF files) into your Flash document, you may notice lengthy wait times to use the Test Movie or Publish commands in Flash MX. Why? The default MP3 encoding process consumes much of the computer processor's power and time.

Flash MX has three MP3 compression qualities: Fast, Medium, or Best. Fast is the default MP3 quality setting—this is by far the fastest method of encoding MP3 sound. Because MP3 uses perceptual encoding, it compares a range of samples to determine how best to compress the sound. Fast compares a smaller range of samples than either Medium or Best. As you increase quality, the sampling range increases.

This process is similar to building 256-color palettes for video files; it's best to look at all the frames of the video (instead of just the first frame) when you're trying to build a palette that's representative of all the colors used in the video. While MP3 doesn't quite work in this fashion, the analogy is appropriate. So, at Best quality, the MP3 encoding scans more of the waveform to look for similarities and differences. However, it's also more time intensive.

As strange as it may seem, the quality does not affect the final size of the Flash movie (.swf file). The bit rate of the MP3 sound is the same regardless of the quality setting. Again, we'll use an analogy—consider the file sizes generated by three different digital cameras that have the same number of pixels in the pictures. The best camera, which will have the highest quality lens and recording mechanism, produces better-looking pictures that capture detail *and* produces the same file size as the others. This is one of the few times where it's not about the amount of information stored in the compressed file—it's a matter of the accuracy and quality of the information within that quantity.

If you want to avoid the wait for Flash MX to publish Flash movies that use MP3 compression, we recommend that you compress your source audio files to the MP3 format (including support for VBR—Variable Bit Rate—compression) and import those MP3 files into Flash MX. Unless the MP3 sound file is used for Stream Sync audio, Flash MX will export the audio in its original MP3 compressed format.

For more information on sound in Flash movies, read Chapter 15, "Adding Sound."

How to use the Bandwidth Profiler

Do you want to know how long it will take for a 28.8 Kbps modem to download your Flash movie or scene? How about a 36.6 Kbps modem? Or a 56 Kbps modem? Or a cable modem? The Bandwidth Profiler enables you to simulate any download speed.

On the CD-ROM

In the ch21 folder of the *Flash MX Bible* CD-ROM is a Flash document called **bandwidth.fla**. You can use that Flash movie for this section.

To use the Bandwidth Profiler, you first need to create a movie or scene to test. When you create a Flash movie with the Control ⇨ Test Movie or Scene commands, Flash opens the .swf file in its own window.

View menu

The Test Movie or Scene viewing environment changes the application menu bar in Flash MX, specifically the View and Control menus. The first four commands in the View menu are the same as those of the Flash Player plug-in viewing controls:

✦ **Zoom In:** Selecting this option enlarges the Flash movie.

✦ **Zoom Out:** Selecting this option shrinks the Flash movie.

✦ **Magnification:** This submenu enables you to change the zoom factor of the movie. The Flash movie is displayed at the original pixel size specified in the Modify ⇨ Document dialog box when 100 percent (Ctrl+1 or ⌘+1) is the setting. For example, if the movie size is 500×300 pixels, it takes up 500×300 pixels on your monitor. If you change the size of the viewing window, the movie may be cropped. The lower section of this submenu enables you to change the viewable area of the Flash movie. Show Frame (Ctrl+2 or ⌘+2) will show only the frame boundary area in the Player window. Show All (Ctrl+3 or ⌘+3) shrinks or enlarges the Flash movie so that you can view all the artwork in the Flash movie, including elements off stage.

✦ **Bandwidth Profiler:** To view the Bandwidth Profiler in this new window, use View ⇨ Bandwidth Profiler (Ctrl+B or ⌘+B). The viewing window will expand to accommodate the Bandwidth Profiler.

   • The left side of the profiler displays three sections: Movie, Settings, and State. Movie indicates the dimensions, frame rate, size (in KB and bytes), duration, and preload (in number of frames and seconds). Settings displays the current selected connection speed (which is set in the Debug menu). State shows you the current frame playing and its byte requirements, as well as the percent of the movie that has loaded.

   • The larger right section of the profiler shows the timeline header and graph. The lower red line beneath the timeline header indicates whether a given frame streams in real-time with the current modem speed specified in the Control menu. For a 28.8 Kbps modem, any frame above 200 bytes may cause delays in streaming for a 12 fps movie. Note that the byte limit for each frame is dependent on frame rate. For example, a 24 fps movie has a limit of 120 bytes per frame (for a 28.8 Kbps modem connection).

   • When the Bandwidth Profiler is enabled, two other commands are available in the View menu: Streaming Graph (Ctrl+G or ⌘+G) and Frame By Frame Graph (Ctrl+F or ⌘+F).

✦ **Show Streaming:** When Show Streaming is enabled, the Bandwidth Profiler emulates the chosen modem speed (in the Control menu) when playing the Flash movie. The Bandwidth Profiler counts the bytes downloaded (displayed in the Loaded subsection of the State heading), and shows the download/play progress via a green bar in the timeline header.

✦ **Streaming Graph:** By default, Flash opens the Bandwidth Profiler in Streaming Graph mode. This mode indicates how the Flash movie streams into a browser (see Figure 21-1). Alternating light and dark gray blocks represent each frame. The size of each block indicates its relative byte size. For our bandwidth.swf example, all the frames will have loaded by the time our playhead reaches frame 13 when the movie is played over a 56 Kbps connection.

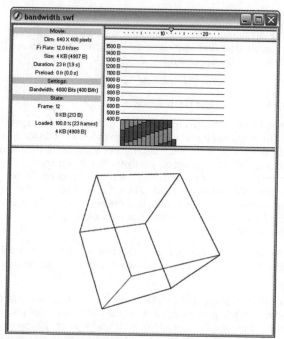

Figure 21-1: The Streaming Graph indicates how a movie will download over a given modem connection. Shown here is our bandwidth.swf as it would download over a 56 Kbps modem.

✦ **Frame By Frame Graph:** This second mode available to the Bandwidth Profiler lays each frame side by side under the timeline header (see Figure 21-2). Although the Streaming Graph enables you to see the real-time performance of a Flash movie, the Frame By Frame Graph enables you to more easily detect which frames are contributing to streaming delays. If any frame block goes beyond the red line of the graph (for a given connection speed), then the Flash Player halts playback until the entire frame downloads. In the bandwidth.swf example, frame 1 is the only frame that may cause a very slight delay in streaming when the movie is played over a 28.8 Kbps connection. The remaining frames are right around 200 bytes each—right at the threshold of 200 bytes per frame for a 28.8 Kbps modem connection playing a 12 fps Flash movie.

Control menu

Use the Control menu to play (Enter key) or rewind (Ctrl+Alt+R or ⌘+Option+R) the test movie. Rewinding pauses the bandwidth.swf movie on the first frame. Use the Step Forward (. or > key) and Step Backward (, or < key) commands to view the Flash movie frame by frame. If a Flash movie doesn't have a `stop()` action on the last frame, the Loop command forces the player to infinitely repeat the Flash movie.

Cross-Reference

We'll discuss the new Flash MX debugging features of the Control menu in Chapter 36, "Solving Problems in Your Movies."

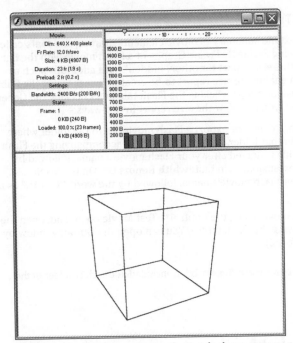

Figure 21-2: The Frame By Frame Graph shows you the byte demand of each frame in the Flash movie.

Debug menu

The Debug menu also features commands that work in tandem with the Streaming and Frame By Frame Graphs:

✦ **14.4, 28.8, 56K:** These settings determine what speed the Bandwidth Profiler uses to calculate estimated download times and frame byte limitations. Notice that these settings use more practical expectations of these modem speeds. For example, a 28.8 modem can theoretically download 3.5 kilobytes per second (KB/s), but a more realistic download rate for this modem speed is 2.3 KB/s.

✦ **User Settings 4, 5, and 6:** These are user-definable speed settings. By default, they are all 2.3 KB/s.

✦ **Customize:** To change the settings for any of the modem speeds listed previously, use the Customize command to input the new value(s).

Cross-Reference

The Control menu also contains List Objects and List Variables commands. List Objects can be used to show the names of Movie Clip instances or ActionScript Objects in the Output window, while the List Variables command displays the names and values of any currently loaded variables, ActionScript Objects, and XML Data. We'll discuss how these features can be used in Chapter 36, "Solving Problems in Your Movies."

Using the size report

Flash MX also lets you view a text file summary of movie elements, frames, and fonts called a size report. In addition to viewing Frame By Frame Graphs of a Flash movie with the Bandwidth Profiler, you can inspect this size report for other "hidden" byte additions such as font character outlines. You can enable the size report to be created by accessing the Publish Settings dialog box (File ➪ Publish Settings), clicking the Flash tab, and checking the Generate size report option. Once enabled, you can view the size report in two ways:

1. After you publish, publish preview, or export a Flash movie, go to the folder where the .swf file was created. In that folder, you'll find a text file accompanying the Flash movie. On Windows, this file is named after your Flash movie's name, followed by "Report" and the .txt file extension, as in **bandwidth Report.txt**. On the Macintosh, this file is named after your Flash movie's name, followed by the word "Report," as in **bandwidth.swf Report**.

2. When you test your Flash movie using the Control ➪ Test Movie command, open the Output window while viewing the Flash movie. You can open the Output window by going to Window ➪ Output (F2).

A sample size report, called **bandwidth Report.txt**, is included in the ch21 folder of the *Flash MX Bible* CD-ROM.

Publishing Your Flash Movies

After you've made a dazzling Flash movie complete with Motion Tweens, 3D simulations, and ActionScripted interactivity, you need to make the Flash movie usable for the intended delivery medium — the Web, a CD-ROM (or floppy disk), or a QuickTime Flash movie, to name a few. As we mentioned in the introduction to this book, you need the Flash MX application to open .fla files. Because the majority of your intended audience won't have the full Flash MX application, you need to export or publish your Flash document (.fla) in a format that your audience can use. More importantly, Flash documents are authoring documents, while Flash movies are optimized for the shortest delivery times and maximum playback performance.

You can convert your Flash document (.fla files) to Flash movies (.swf files) by using either the File ➪ Export Movie or File ➪ Publish/Publish Settings commands. The latter command is Flash's Publish feature. You can specify just about all file format properties in one step using the File ➪ Publish Settings command. After you've entered the settings, the File ➪ Publish command exports any and all file formats with your specified parameters in one step — all from the Flash MX application.

The Export Movie command is discussed throughout the book. For more information on exporting still images in raster/bitmap formats, see Chapter 37, "Working with Raster Graphics." To export vector formats, see Chapter 38, "Working with Vector Graphics." To export QuickTime or AVI files, see Chapter 41, "Working with QuickTime," and Chapter 14, "Exporting Animation."

Three commands are available with the Publish feature: Publish Settings, Publish Preview, and Publish. Each of these commands is discussed in the following sections.

A Word about the Export Movie Command

Even though Flash MX streamlines the process of creating Flash movies with the Publish commands (discussed in the next section), it is worth mentioning that the File ➪ Export Movie command provides another route to creating a .swf file. Although the Publish command is the quickest way to create HTML-ready Flash movies, the Export Movie command can be used to create updated .swf files that have already been placed in HTML documents, or Flash movies that you intend to import into Macromedia Director movies (see Chapter 43, "Working with Director").

Publish Settings

The Publish Settings command (File ➪ Publish Settings) is used to determine which file formats are exported when the File ➪ Publish command is invoked. By default, Flash MX ships with Publish Settings that will export a Flash movie (.swf file) and an HTML file with the proper markup tags to utilize the Flash Player 6 plug-in or ActiveX Control. If you want to customize the settings of the exported file types, you should familiarize yourself with the Publish Settings before you attempt to use the Publish command.

Selecting formats

Select File ➪ Publish Settings to access the Publish Settings dialog box, which is nearly identical for both the Windows and Macintosh versions of Flash MX. The dialog box opens to the Formats tab, which has check boxes to select the formats in which your Flash document will be published (see Figure 21-3). For each Type that is checked, a tab appears in the Publish Settings dialog box. Click each type's tab to specify settings to control the particulars of the movie or file that will be generated in that format.

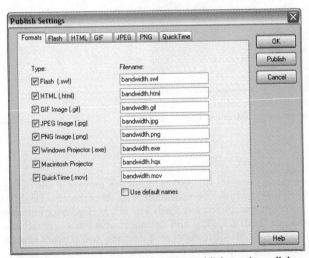

Figure 21-3: The Formats tab of the Publish Settings dialog box enables you to select the published file formats and to use default or custom names for these published files.

The Use default names check box either enables or disables default names (disabled means that the Filename fields are unavailable or grayed out). For example, if your movie is named intro.fla, then, if Use default names is selected, this is the base from which the names are generated in publishing. Thus, intro.swf, intro.html, intro.gif, and so on would result.

> **Tip**
>
> By deselecting Use default names, you can enter non-version-specific filenames for Flash documents that you incrementally save as you work. For example, if you have a Flash document named main_100.fla, deselect Use default names and set the Flash movie filename to main.swf, then every new Flash document version you save (for example, main_101.fla, main_102.fla, and so on) will still produce a main.swf file. This way, you can consistently refer to one Flash movie (.swf file) in your HTML code and incrementally save your Flash documents.

Using the Flash settings

The primary and default publishing format of Flash MX movies is the Flash movie (.swf) format. Only Flash movies retain full support for Flash actions and animations.

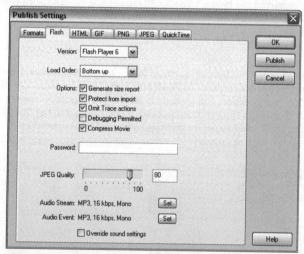

Figure 21-4: The Flash tab of the Publish Settings dialog box controls the settings for a movie published in the Flash format.

Here are your options in the Flash tab (see Figure 21-4):

✦ **Version:** This drop-down menu provides the option to publish movies in any of the Flash movie formats. To ensure complete compatibility with all of the new Flash MX features, select Flash 6. If you haven't used any Flash 5 or MX ActionScript commands or Dots notation, you can use Flash 4. Flash 1 and 2 support only basic animation and interactive functions. Flash 3 supports just about all animation and artwork created in Flash MX, but it doesn't recognize any actions introduced with either Flash 4 or 5, editable text fields (such as form elements), or MP3 audio. If in doubt, you should test your choice of version in that version's Flash Player.

Tip

You can download older versions of the Flash Player from the Macromedia site at www.macromedia.com/support/flash/ts/documents/oldplayers.htm.

✦ **Load Order:** This option determines how the Flash Player will draw the first frame of the Flash movie as it is downloaded to the plug-in or player. When Bottom up (the default) is chosen, the layers load in ascending order: The lowest layer displays first, then the second lowest, and so on, until all of the layers for the first frame have been displayed. When Top down is selected, the layers load in descending order: the top-most layer displays first, then the layer underneath it, and so on. Again, this option affects the display of only the first frame of a Flash movie. If the content of the first frame is downloaded or streamed quickly, you probably won't notice the Load Order's effect.

Note

Load Order does not affect the order of actions spread across layers for the same frame. ActionScript will always execute in a top-down fashion; the actions on the top-most layers will execute before actions on lower layers.

✦ **Generate size report:** As discussed earlier in this chapter, the size report for a Flash movie can be very useful in pinpointing problematic bandwidth-intensive elements, such as font characters. When this option is checked, the Publish command exports a text (.txt) file on Windows or a SimpleText file on the Macintosh. You can view this document separately in a text-editor application like Notepad or BBEdit.

✦ **Protect from import:** This option safeguards your Flash movies on the Internet. When enabled, the .swf file cannot be imported back into the Flash MX authoring environment, or altered in any way.

Caution

The Protect from import option will *not* prevent a web browser from caching your .swf files. Also, Macromedia Director can import and use protected Flash movies. Flash utilities like SWF-Browser from www.swifftools.com can break into any .swf file and extract artwork, symbols, and sounds. There's even an application called Action Script Viewer from www.buraks.com/asv that can extract ActionScript from your .swf files! Even Notepad can open Flash movies and see variable names and values. For this reason, you should always use server-side scripts to verify password entries in Flash movies, rather than internal ActionScripted password checking with if/else conditions. Don't store sensitive information such as passwords in your source files!

✦ **Omit Trace actions:** When this option is selected, Flash MX will remove any trace() actions used in your Flash document's ActionScript code. trace() actions will open the Output window in Test Movie mode for debugging purposes. In general, if you used trace() actions, you will want to omit them from the final Flash movie — they can't be viewed in the Flash Player anyway.

Cross-Reference

We discuss the use of trace() actions in Chapter 36, "Solving Problems in Your Movies."

✦ **Debugging Permitted:** If this option is checked, then you can access the Debugger panel from in the Debug Movie environment, or from a Web browser that is using the Flash Debug Player 6 plug-in or ActiveX control. To install the Flash Debug Player plug-in or ActiveX control, go to the Players folder in your Macromedia Flash MX application folder. There, you will find a Debug folder. With your browser applications closed, run one (or more) of the following files:

- **Install Flash Player 6 AX.exe** to install the ActiveX control for Internet Explorer on Windows 95/98/ME/NT/2000/XP.

- **Install Flash Player 6.exe** to install the plug-in for Netscape on Windows 95/98/ME/NT/2000/XP.

- **Install Flash 6 Player** to install the plug-in for Netscape and/or Internet Explorer for Macs running OS 9.x or earlier.

- **Install Flash Player 6 OSX** to install the plug-in for Netscape and/or Internet Explorer for Macs running OS X 10.1 or greater.

Flash MX creates a .swd file along with the .swf file when the Debugging Permitted option is checked. You must upload both the .swd and .swf files to your web server for remote debugging to function. We discuss remote debugging in Chapter 36, "Solving Problems in Your Movies."

✦ **Compress Movie:** This new option available in Flash MX allows you to enable compression in Flash 6 movies only. When enabled, this compression feature will greatly reduce the size of text or ActionScript-heavy Flash movies. However, you will see little or no size difference on other Flash elements, like artwork and sounds. Compression works only with Flash Player 6 and cannot be used on Flash 5 or earlier movies.

✦ **Password:** If you checked the Debugging Permitted option, you can enter a password to access the Debugger panel. Because you can now debug movies over a live Internet connection, you should always enter a password here if you intend to debug a remote Flash movie. If you leave this field empty and check the Debugging Permitted option, Flash MX will still ask you for a password when you attempt to access the Debugger panel remotely. Simply press the Enter key if you left this field blank.

✦ **JPEG Quality:** This slider and text-field option specifies the level of JPEG compression applied to bitmapped artwork in the Flash movie. The value can be any value between (and including) 0 to 100. Higher values apply less compression and preserve more information of the original bitmap, whereas lower values apply more compression and keep less information. The value entered here applies to all bitmaps that enable the Use document default quality option, found in the Bitmap Properties dialog box for each bitmap in the document's Library. Unlike the audio settings discussed in a moment, no "override" option exists to disregard settings in the Library.

✦ **Audio Stream:** This option displays the current audio compression scheme for Stream audio. By clicking the Set button (see Figure 21-4), you can control the compression applied to any sounds that use the Stream Sync setting in the Sound area of the Property inspector (when a sound keyframe has focus). Like the JPEG Quality option discussed previously, this compression value is applied to any Stream sounds that use the Default compression in the Export Settings section of each audio file's Sound Properties dialog box in the document's Library. See Chapter 15, "Adding Sound," for more information on using Stream sounds and audio compression schemes.

✦ **Audio Event:** This setting behaves exactly the same as the Audio Stream option, except that this compression setting applies to Default compression-enabled Event sounds. See Chapter 15, "Adding Sound," for more information on Event sounds.

Tip   Flash MX supports imported MP3 audio that uses VBR (Variable Bit Rate) compression. However, Flash MX cannot compress native sounds in VBR. If you use any imported MP3 audio for Stream Sync audio, Flash will recompress the MP3 audio on export.

✦ **Override sound settings:** If you want the settings for Audio Stream and Audio Event to apply to all Stream and Event sounds, respectively, and to disregard any unique compression schemes specified in the document's Library, check this option. This is useful for creating multiple .swf file versions of the Flash movie (hi-fi, lo-fi, and so on) and enabling the web visitor to decide which one to download.

When you are finished entering the settings for the Flash movie, you can proceed to other file type settings in the Publish Settings dialog box. Or, you can click OK to return to the authoring environment of Flash MX so that you can use the newly entered settings in the Test Movie or Scene environment. You can also export a Flash movie (and other file formats currently selected in Publish Settings) by clicking the Publish button in the Publish Settings dialog box.

Using the HTML settings

HTML is the language in which the layout of most Web pages is written. The HTML tab of the Publish Settings dialog box (see Figure 21-5) has a number of settings that control the way in which Flash MX will publish a movie into a complete Web page with HTML tags specifying the Flash Player.

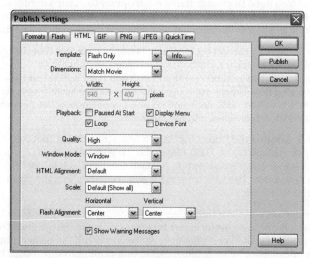

Figure 21-5: The HTML tab controls flexible Flash movie options—you can change these options without permanently affecting the Flash movie.

The settings available in the HTML tab include:

✦ **Template:** Perhaps the most important (and versatile) feature of all Publish Settings, the Template setting enables you to select a predefined set of HTML tags to display your Flash movies. To view the description of each template, click the Info button to the right of the drop-down list (shown in Figure 21-5). All templates use the same options listed in the HTML tab—the template simply places the values of those settings into HTML tags scripted in the template. You can also create your own custom templates for your own unique implementation of Flash movies.

You can view the "source" of each template in the HTML folder found inside of the FirstRun folder of the Flash MX application folder. Although these template files have .html extensions, use Macromedia Dreamweaver MX, Notepad (Windows) or SimpleText (Mac) to view the files. All of the preinstalled templates include HTML tags to create an entire Web page, complete with ⟨HEAD⟩, ⟨TITLE⟩, and ⟨BODY⟩ tags.

Note The Template option in this HTML tab has nothing to do with the New from Template command (File ➪ New from Template) introduced with Flash MX. For more information on Flash MX templates, please read the QuickStart, "Flash in a Flash."

- **Detect for Flash 3:** With this template, Flash creates an HTML document that checks for Flash Player 3 (or higher) plug-in or ActiveX control. If JavaScript or VBScript detects the plug-in, the Flash movie will be served. If there is no Flash Player (or the user has an earlier Flash Player), a GIF or JPEG will be loaded into the page. You must choose either the GIF or JPEG option in the Format tab of the Publish Settings dialog box. This template is useful for serving Flash ad banners to a wide target audience. Make sure that you have selected Flash 3 as the version in the Flash tab.

- **Detect for Flash 4:** Same as the Detect for Flash 3 template, except that the JavaScript and VBScript check for Flash Player 4 (or higher) plug-in orActiveX control. You need to change the Version option to Flash 4 in the Flash tab of the Publish Settings. Use this template only if you are using Flash 4-specific ActionScripts, such as variable declarations or loadVariable() actions.

- **Detect for Flash 5:** Same as the Detect for Flash 3 template, except that the JavaScript and VBScript check for Flash Player 5 (or higher) plug-in or ActiveX control. Change the Version option to Flash 5 in the Flash tab of the Publish Settings dialog box. Unless your Flash documents use Flash 5-specific ActionScripts (Dots notation, XML data, and so on), choose one of the previous templates and corresponding version in the Flash tab.

- **Detect for Flash 6:** Same as the Detect for Flash 3 template, except that the JavaScript and VBScript check for Flash Player 6 (or higher) plug-in or ActiveX control. Change the Version option to Flash 6 in the Flash tab of the Publish Settings dialog box. Use this template if you are publishing the Flash document as a Flash 6 movie.

- **Flash Only:** This default template simply inserts the ⟨OBJECT⟩ and ⟨EMBED⟩ tags for a Flash 6 movie. It does not perform any browser or plug-in detection. If the user does not have the Flash Player plug-in or ActiveX control, the browser may produce an error message, a missing plug-in icon, or a prompt to download the latest plug-in or ActiveX control, depending on the browser configuration. The HTML produced by this template may allow an earlier Flash Player (such as Flash Player 4) to attempt playback of your newer Flash movie. Keep in mind that any version of the Flash Player will try to render any Flash movie file. However, you may get unpredictable results when a newer-version Flash movie loads into an older player.

- **Flash w/AICC Tracking:** Use this template if you are creating Flash movies that incorporate components from the Learning Interactions Library (Window ➪ Common Libraries ➪ Learning Interactions). Use this template if you want the components in the Flash movie to be compliant with the AICC (Aviation Industry CBT Committee) training guidelines. The template will create JavaScript/VBScript functions that can work with the ActionScript of the learning components. For more information on AICC guidelines, see www.aicc.org. Note that this template will function only in web browsers that support the fscommand from Flash movies.

- **Flash w/SCORM Tracking:** This template will create the HTML and JavaScript/VBScript functions to enable communication between Flash movies that use the components from the Learning Interactions Library and the HTML page. SCORM, which stands for Shareable Content Object Reference Model, is a set of guidelines for learning systems created by the U.S. Department of Defense Advanced Distributed Learning (ADL) Initiative. Both SCORM and AICC guidelines aim to promote interoperability among learning and training systems. Note that this template will only function in Web browsers that support the fscommand() from Flash movies.

- **Flash with FSCommand:** Use this template if you are using the fscommand() action in your Flash movies to communicate with JavaScript in the HTML page. The fscommand() is discussed in Chapter 22, "Integrating Flash Content with HTML." The necessary <OBJECT> and <EMBED> tags from the Flash Only (Default) template are also included.

- **Flash with Named Anchors:** If you are using the new named anchors feature of Flash MX, you will want to use this template for your published HTML document. This template creates the necessary JavaScript to enable the Back button on your Web browser with named anchors within your Flash movie. Named anchors allow you to designate specific keyframes (and scenes) that register in the browser's history when played.

For an example of named anchors in action, read Chapter 20, "Making Your First Flash MX Project."

- **Image Map:** This template does not use or display any Flash movie. Instead, it uses a GIF, JPEG, or PNG image (as specified in the Publish Settings' Format tab) as a client-side image map, via an <IMG> tag with a USEMAP attribute. Use a frame label of #map in the Flash document (.fla file) to designate which frame is used as the map image. See "Using the GIF settings" later in this chapter for more details.

- **Pocket PC 2002:** This template will create the necessary <OBJECT> tag to enable the Flash Player ActiveX control on the Pocket PC 2002 operating system. The Pocket PC is the new breed of PDA (personal data assistant) device that can play Flash movies in Pocket Internet Explorer.

If you are designing Flash movies for the Pocket PC, be sure to check out the new Pocket PC document template (File ➪ New from Template). We explore the world of Flash and Pocket PC development in Chapter 45, "Making Movies for the Pocket PC."

- **QuickTime:** This template creates both the <OBJECT> and <EMBED> tags to display QuickTime Flash movies. You need to enable the QuickTime file type in the Publish Settings' Format tab. A QuickTime Flash movie is a special type of QuickTime movie, playable with QuickTime 4 or higher. QuickTime 4 can recognize Flash 3 features only, while QuickTime 5 can play Flash 4 movies with ActionScript specific to that version of the Flash Player. You must choose Flash 3 or Flash 4 as the Version option in the Flash tab. Depending on the options selected in the QuickTime tab of Publish Settings, the Flash movie may or may not be stored within the QuickTime movie file. See Chapter 41, "Working with QuickTime," for more information.

You may have noticed that the Java and Generator templates are no longer available in Flash MX. With the release of Flash MX, Macromedia no longer supports Generator development in the Flash authoring development. You will need to use the Flash 5 authoring tool to continue development with Macromedia Generator.

✦ **Dimensions:** This setting controls the WIDTH and HEIGHT values of the <OBJECT> and <EMBED> tags. The dimension settings here do not change the original Flash movie; they simply create the area through which your Flash movie is viewed on the Web page. The way that the Flash movie "fits" into this viewing area is determined with the Scale option (discussed later). Three input areas exist: a drop-down menu and two text fields for width and height.

- **Match Movie:** If you want to keep the same width and height that you specified in the Document Properties dialog box (Modify ⇨ Document), then use this option in the drop-down menu.

- **Pixels:** You can change the viewing size (in pixel units) of the Flash movie window by selecting this option and entering new values in the Width and Height text fields.

- **Percent:** By far one of the most popular options with Flash movies, Percent scales the movie to the size of the browser window—or a portion of it. Using a value of 100 on both Width and Height expands the Flash movie to fit the entire browser window. If Percent is used with the proper Scale setting (see the description of the Scale setting later in this chapter), the aspect ratio of your Flash movie will not be distorted.

The new Stage object and its supporting methods allow you to disable or override automatic scaling of the Flash movie. For example, the following action added to frame 1 of your Flash movie will disable scaling:

```
Stage.scaleMode = "noScale";
```

- **Width and Height:** Enter the values for the Flash movie width and height here. If Match Movie is selected, you shouldn't be able to enter any values. The unit of measurement is determined by selecting either Pixels or Percent from the drop-down menu.

✦ **Playback:** These options control how the Flash movie plays when it is downloaded to the browser. Each of these options has an <OBJECT> and <EMBED> attribute if you want to control them outside of Publish Settings. Note that these attributes are not viewable within the Publish Settings dialog box—you need to load the published HTML document into a text editor to see the attributes.

- **Paused at Start:** This is equivalent to adding a stop() action on the first frame of the first scene in the Flash movie. By default, this option is off—movies play as soon as they stream into the player. A button with a play() action can start the movie, or the Play command can be executed from the Flash Player shortcut menu (by right-clicking or Control+clicking the movie). Attribute: PLAY=true or false. If PLAY=true, the movie will play as soon as it is loaded.

- **Loop:** This option causes the Flash movie to repeat an infinite number of times. By default, this option is on. If it is not checked, the Flash movie stops on the last frame unless some other ActionScripted event is initiated on the last frame. Attribute: LOOP=true or false.

- **Display Menu:** This option controls whether the person viewing the Flash movie in the Flash Player environment can access the shortcut menu via a right-click (Windows) or Control+click (Mac) anywhere within the movie area. If this option is checked, the visitor can select Zoom In/Out, 100 percent, Show All, High Quality, Play, Loop, Rewind, Forward, and Back from the menu. If this option is not checked, the visitor can only select About Flash Player from the menu. Attribute: `MENU=true` or `false`.

- **Device Font:** This option applies to Flash movies played only in the Windows version of the Flash Player. When enabled, this option replaces fonts that are not installed on the Player's system with antialiased system fonts. Attribute: `DEVICEFONT=true` or `false`.

✦ **Quality:** This menu determines how the Flash artwork in a movie will render. While it would be ideal to play all Flash movies at high quality, slower processors may not be able to redraw anti-aliased artwork and keep up with the frame rate.

- **Low:** This setting forces the Flash Player to turn off anti-aliasing (smooth edges) completely. On slower processors, this may improve playback performance. Attribute: `QUALITY=LOW`.

- **Auto Low:** This setting starts in Low quality mode (no anti-aliasing) but will switch to High quality if the computer's processor can handle the playback speed. Attribute: `QUALITY=AUTOLOW`.

- **Auto High:** This setting is the opposite of Auto Low. The Flash Player starts playing the movie in High quality mode, but if the processor cannot handle the playback demands, it switches to Low quality mode. For most web sites, this is the optimal setting to use because it favors higher quality first. Attribute: `QUALITY=AUTOHIGH`.

- **Medium:** This quality produces anti-aliased vector graphics on a 2×2 grid (in other words, it will smooth edges over a 4-pixel square area), but it does not smooth bitmap images. Artwork will appear slightly better than the Low quality, but not as smooth as the High setting. Attribute: `QUALITY=MEDIUM`. This quality setting will only work with the Flash 5 or higher Player.

- **High:** When this setting is used, the Flash Player dedicates more of the computer's processor to rendering graphics (instead of playback). All vector artwork is anti-aliased on a 4×4 grid (16-pixel square area). Bitmaps are smoothed unless they are contained within an animation sequence such as a Motion Tween. By default, this setting is selected in the HTML tab of the Publish Settings dialog. Attribute: `QUALITY=HIGH`.

- **Best:** This mode does everything that High quality does, with the addition of smoothing all bitmaps — regardless of whether they are in Motion Tweens. This mode is the most processor-intensive. Attribute: `QUALITY=BEST`.

✦ **Window Mode:** The Window Mode setting works only with the Flash ActiveX control on Internet Explorer for Windows 95/98/ME/NT/2000/XP. Therefore, it applies only to 32-bit Windows versions of Internet Explorer. If you intend to deliver to this browser, you can animate Flash content on top of DHTML content. Attribute: `WMODE=WINDOW`, or `OPAQUE`, or `TRANSPARENT`.

✦ **HTML Alignment:** This setting works much like the `ALIGN` attribute of `<IMG>` tags in HTML documents, but it's used with the `ALIGN` attribute of the `<OBJECT>` and `<EMBED>`

tags for the Flash movie. Note that these settings may not have any effect when used within a table cell (`<TD>` tag) or a DHTML layer (`<DIV>` or `<LAYER>` tag).

- **Default:** This option horizontally or vertically centers the Flash movie in the browser window. If the browser window is smaller than a Flash movie that uses a Pixel or Match Movie dimensions setting (see Dimensions setting earlier in this section), the Flash movie will be cropped.

- **Left, Right, Top, and Bottom:** These options align the Flash movie along the left, right, top, or bottom edge of the browser window, respectively.

✦ **Scale:** This setting works in tandem with the Dimensions setting discussed earlier in this section, and it determines how the Flash movie displays on the HTML page. Just as big-screen movies must be cropped to fit the aspect ratio of a TV screen, Flash movies may need to be modified to fit the area prescribed by the Dimensions setting.

- **Default (Show all):** This option fits the entire Flash movie into the area defined by the Dimensions setting without distorting the original aspect ratio of the Flash movie. However, borders may appear on two sides of the Flash movie. For example, if a 300×300-pixel window is specified in Dimensions and the Flash movie has an aspect ratio of 1.33:1 (for example, 400×300 pixels), then a border fills the remaining areas on top of and below the Flash movie. This is similar to the "letterbox" effect on wide-screen video rentals. Attribute: `SCALE=SHOWALL`.

- **No Border:** This option forces the Flash movie to fill the area defined by the Dimensions setting without leaving borders. The Flash movie's aspect ratio is not distorted or stretched. However, this may crop two sides of the Flash movie. Using the same example from Show All, the left and right sides of the Flash movie are cropped when No Border is selected. Attribute: `SCALE=NOBORDER`.

- **Exact Fit:** This option stretches a Flash movie to fill the entire area defined by the Dimensions setting. Using the same example from Show All, the 400×300 Flash movie is scrunched to fit a 300×300 window. If the original movie showed a perfect circle, it now appears as an oval. Attribute: `SCALE=EXACTFIT`.

- **No Scale:** This option prevents the Flash movie from scaling beyond its original size as defined in the Document Properties dialog box (Modify ➪ Document). The Flash Player window size (or the web browser window size) has no effect on the size of the Flash movie. Attribute: `SCALE=NOSCALE`.

✦ **Flash Alignment:** This setting adjusts the `SALIGN` attribute of the `<OBJECT>` and `<EMBED>` tags for the Flash movie. In contrast to the HTML Alignment setting, Flash Alignment works in conjunction with the Scale and Dimensions settings, and determines how a Flash movie is aligned within the Player window.

- **Horizontal:** These options — Left, Center, and Right — determine whether the Flash movie is horizontally aligned to the left, center, or right of the Dimensions area, respectively. Using the same example from the Scale setting, a 400×300-pixel Flash movie (fit into a 300×300 Dimension window with `SCALE=NOBORDER`) with a Flash Horizontal Alignment setting of Left crops only the right side of the Flash movie.

- **Vertical:** These options — Top, Center, and Bottom — determine whether the Flash movie is vertically aligned to the top, center, or bottom of the Dimensions area, respectively. If the preceding example used a Show All Scale setting and had a Flash Vertical Alignment setting of Top, the border would occur only below the bottom edge of the Flash movie.

✦ **Show Warning Messages:** This useful feature alerts you to errors during the actual Publish process. For example, if you selected the Image Map template and didn't specify a static GIF, JPEG, or PNG file in the Formats tab, Flash returns an error. By default, this option is enabled. If it is disabled, Flash suppresses any warnings during the Publish process.

Using the GIF settings

The GIF (Graphics Interchange File) format, developed by CompuServe, defined the first generation of Web graphics and is still quite popular today, despite its 256-color limitation. In the context of the Publish Settings of Flash MX, the GIF format is used to export a static or animated image that can be used in place of the Flash movie if the Flash Player or plug-in is not installed. Although the Flash and HTML tabs are specific to Flash movie display and playback, the settings of the GIF tab (see Figure 21-6) control the characteristics of a GIF animation (or still image) that Flash MX will publish.

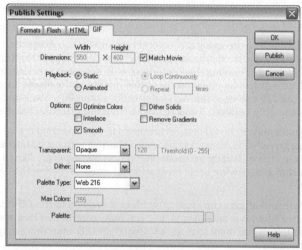

Figure 21-6: Every subtle aspect of a GIF animation or still image can be finessed with these settings of the GIF tab of the Publish Settings dialog box.

The settings in the GIF tab include the following:

✦ **Dimensions:** This setting has three options: Width, Height, and Match Movie. As you might surmise, Width and Height control the dimensions of the GIF image. These fields are enabled only when the Match Movie check box is unchecked. With Match Movie checked, the dimensions of the GIF match those of the Flash Movie that is being published.

✦ **Playback:** These radio buttons control what type of GIF image is created and how it plays (if Animated is chosen).

• **Static:** If this button is selected, then Flash exports the first frame of the Flash movie as a single still image in the GIF format. If you want to use a frame other than the first frame, use a frame label of #Static on the desired frame. Alternatively, you could use the File ➪ Export Image command to export a GIF image from whatever frame the Current Frame Indicator is positioned over.

• **Animated:** If this button is selected, Flash exports the entire Flash movie as an animated GIF file (in the GIF89a format). If you don't want to export the entire movie as an animated GIF (indeed, a GIF file for a Flash movie with over 100 frames would be most likely too large to download easily over the Web), you can designate a range of frames to export. Use a frame label of #First on the beginning frame of a given range of frames. Next, add a frame label of #Last to the ending frame of the desired sequence of frames. Flash actually is pretty good at optimizing animated GIFs by saving only areas that change over time in each frame—instead of the entire frame.

- **Loop Continuously:** When the Animated radio button is selected, you can specify that the animated GIF repeats an infinite number of times by selecting the Loop Continuously radio button.

- **Repeat __ times:** This option can be used to set up an animated GIF that repeats a given number of times. If you don't want the animated GIF to repeat continuously, enter the number of repetitions here.

✦ **Options:** The options in the Options settings control the creation of the GIF's color table and how the browser displays the GIF.

- **Optimize Colors:** When you are using any palette type other than Adaptive, this option removes any colors preexisting in the Web 216 or custom palettes that are not used by the GIF image. Enabling this option can only save you precious bytes used in file overhead—it has no effect on the actual quality of the image. Most images do not use all 216 colors of the Web palette. For example, a black-and-white picture can use only between 3 and 10 colors from the 216-color palette.

- **Interlace:** This option makes the GIF image download in incrementing resolutions. As the image downloads, the image becomes sharper with each successive "scan." Use of this option is usually personal preference. Some people like to use it for image maps that can provide basic navigation information before the entire image downloads.

- **Smooth:** This option anti-aliases the Flash artwork as it exports to the GIF image. Text may look better when it is anti-aliased, but you may want to test this option for your particular use. If you need to make a transparent GIF, smoothing may produce unsightly edges.

- **Dither Solids:** This option determines whether solid areas of color (such as fills) are dithered. In this context, this type of dithering would create a two-color pattern to mimic a solid color that doesn't occur in the GIF's color palette. See the discussion of dithering later in this section.

- **Remove Gradients:** Flash gradients do not translate or display very well in 256 or fewer colors. Use this option to convert all Flash gradients to solid colors. The solid color is determined by the first color prescribed in the gradient. Unless you developed your gradients with this effect in mind, this option may produce undesirable results.

✦ **Transparent:** This setting controls the appearance of the Flash movie background, as well as any Flash artwork that uses alpha settings. Because GIF images support only one level of transparency (that is, the transparent area cannot be anti-aliased), exercise caution when using this setting. The Threshold option is available only if Alpha is selected.

- **Opaque:** This option produces a GIF image with a solid background. The image has a rectangular shape.

- **Transparent:** This option makes the Flash movie background appear transparent. If the Smooth option in the Options setting is enabled, Flash artwork may display halos over the background HTML color.

- **Alpha and Threshold:** When the Alpha option is selected in the drop-down menu, you can control at what alpha level Flash artwork becomes transparent by entering a value in the Threshold text field. For example, if you enter 128, all alphas at 50 percent become completely transparent. If you are considering an animated GIF that has Flash artwork fading in or out, you probably want to use the Opaque transparent option. If Alpha and Threshold were used, the fade effect would be lost.

✦ **Dither:** Dithering is the process of emulating a color by juxtaposing two colors in a pattern arrangement. Because GIF images are limited to 256 colors (or fewer), dithering can often produce better-looking images for continuous tone artwork such as gradients. However, Flash's dithering seems to work best with the Web 216 palette. Dithering can increase the file size of a GIF image.

  - **None:** This option does not apply any dithering to the GIF image.

  - **Ordered:** This option applies an intermediate level of dithering with minimal file size overhead.

  - **Diffusion:** This option applies the best level of dithering to the GIF image, but with larger file size overhead. Diffusion dithering only has a noticeable effect when the Web 216 palette is chosen in Palette Type.

✦ **Palette Type:** As mentioned earlier in this section, GIF images are limited to 256 or less colors. However, this grouping of 256 is arbitrary: Any set of 256 (or fewer) colors can be used for a given GIF image. This setting enables you to select predefined sets of colors to use on the GIF image. See Chapter 7, "Applying Color," for more information on the Web color palette.

  - **Web 216:** When this option is selected, the GIF image uses colors only from the limited 216 Web color palette. For most Flash artwork, this should produce acceptable results. However, it may not render Flash gradients or photographic bitmaps very well.

  - **Adaptive:** With this option selected, Flash creates a unique set of 256 colors (or fewer, if specified in the Max Colors setting) for the GIF image. However, these adapted colors fall outside of the Web color palette. File sizes for adaptive GIFs are larger than Web 216 GIFs, unless few colors are chosen in the Max Colors setting. Adaptive GIFs look much better than Web 216 GIFs, but they may not display very well with 8-bit video cards and monitors.

  - **Web Snap Adaptive:** This option tries to give the GIF image the best of both worlds. Flash converts any colors close to the 216 Web palette to Web-Safe colors and uses adaptive colors for the rest. This palette produces better results than the Adaptive palette for older display systems that used 8-bit video cards.

  - **Custom:** When this option is selected, you can specify a palette that uses the .act file format to be used as the GIF image's palette. Macromedia Fireworks and Adobe Photoshop can export color palettes (or color look-up tables) as .act files.

✦ **Max Colors:** With this setting, you can specify exactly how many colors are in the GIF's color table. This numeric entry field is enabled only when Adaptive or Web Snap Adaptive is selected in the Palette Type drop-down menu.

✦ **Palette:** This text field and the "..." browse button are enabled only when Custom is selected in the Palette Type drop-down menu. When enabled, this dialog box is used to locate and load a palette file from the hard drive.

Using the JPEG settings

The JPEG (Joint Photographic Experts Group) format is just as popular as the GIF format on the Web. Unlike GIF images, though, JPEG images can use much more than 256 colors. In fact, JPEG files must be 24-bit color (or full-color RGB) images. Although GIF files use lossless compression (within the actual file itself), JPEG images use lossy compression, which means that color information is discarded in order to save file space. However, JPEG compression is very good. Even at its lowest quality settings, JPEG images can preserve quite a bit of detail in photographic images.

Another significant difference between GIF and JPEG is that GIF images do not require nearly as much memory (for equivalent image dimensions) as JPEG images do. You need to remember that JPEG images "uncompress" when they are downloaded to your computer. While the file sizes may be small initially, they still open as full-color images in the computer's memory. For example, even though you may get the file size of a 400×300-pixel JPEG image down to 10KB, it still requires nearly 352KB in memory when it is opened or displayed.

Flash publishes the first frame of the Flash movie as the JPEG image, unless a #Static frame label is given to another frame in the Flash movie. The limited settings of the JPEG tab of the Publish Settings dialog (see Figure 21-7) control the few variables of this still photo-quality image format:

✦ **Dimensions:** This setting behaves the same as the GIF Dimensions setting. Width and Height control the dimensions of the movie. But these fields are enabled only when the Match Movie check box is unchecked. With Match Movie checked, the dimensions of the JPEG match those of the Flash Movie.

✦ **Quality:** This slider and text field work exactly the same way as the JPEG Quality setting in the Flash tab of Publish Settings. Higher values apply less compression and result in better quality, but they create images with larger file sizes.

✦ **Progressive:** This option is similar to the Interlaced option for GIF images. When enabled, the JPEG image loads in successive scans, becoming sharper with each pass.

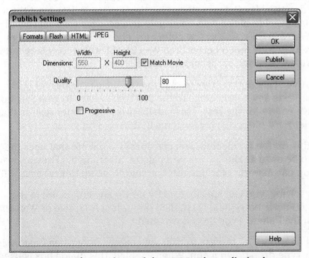

Figure 21-7: The settings of the JPEG tab are limited because JPEGs are still images with relatively few variables to be addressed.

Using the PNG settings

The PNG (Portable Network Graphic) format is another still-image format. The PNG specification was developed in 1996 by the W3C (World Wide Web Consortium), and the format is an improvement over both the GIF and JPEG formats in several ways. Much like JPEG, it is excellent for transmission of photographic quality images. The primary advantages of PNG are variable bit-depths (images can be 256 colors or millions of colors), multilevel transparency, and lossless compression. However, most browsers do not offer full support for all PNG options without some kind of additional plug-in. When in doubt, test your PNG images in your preferred browser.

The settings of the PNG tab (see Figure 21-8) control the characteristics of the PNG image that Flash will publish.

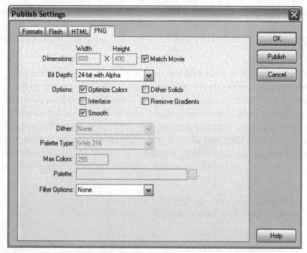

Figure 21-8: The settings found on the PNG tab closely resemble those on the GIF tab. The PNG was engineered to have many of the advantages of both the GIF and JPEG formats.

The PNG tab options are

✦ **Dimensions:** This setting works just like the GIF and JPEG equivalents. When Match Movie is checked, you cannot alter the Width and Height of the PNG image.

✦ **Bit Depth:** This setting controls how many colors are created in the PNG image:

• **8-bit:** In this mode, the PNG image has a maximum color palette of 256 colors, similar to the palette function of GIF images. When this option is selected, the Options, Dither, Palette Type, Max Colors, and Palette settings can be altered.

• **24-bit:** When this option is selected, the PNG image can display any of the 16.7 million RGB colors. This option produces larger files than 8-bit PNG images, but it renders the Flash artwork most faithfully.

- **24-bit with Alpha:** This option adds another 8-bit channel to the 24-bit PNG image for multilevel transparency support. This means that Flash will treat the Flash movie background as a transparent area, so that information behind the PNG image (such as HTML background colors) shows through. Note that, with proper browser support, PNG can render anti-aliased edges on top of other elements, such as HTML background images!

Note Flash MX's PNG export or publish settings do not reflect the full range of PNG options available. PNG can support transparency in both 8-bit and 24-bit flavors, but Flash enables transparency only in 24-bit with Alpha images.

✦ **Options:** These options behave the same as the equivalent GIF Publish Settings.

✦ **Dither, Palette Type, Max Colors,** and **Palette:** These settings work the same as the equivalent GIF Publish Settings. Because PNG images can be either 8- or 24-bit, these options apply only to 8-bit PNG images. If anything other than 8-bit is selected in the Bit Depth setting, these options are disabled. Please refer to the previous section for more information.

✦ **Filter Options:** This drop-down menu controls what type of compression sampling or algorithm the PNG image uses. Note that this does not apply an art or graphic "filter effect" like the filters in Adobe Photoshop do, nor does it throw away any image information — all filters are lossless. It simply enables you to be the judge of what kind of compression to use on the image. You need to experiment with each of these filters on your Flash movie image to find the best filter-to-file size combination. Technically, the filters do not actually look at the pixel data. Rather, they look at the byte data of each pixel. Results vary depending on the image content, but here are some guidelines to keep in mind:

  - **None:** When this option is selected, no filtering is applied to the image. When no filter is applied, you usually have unnecessarily large file sizes.

  - **Sub:** This filter works best on images that have repeated information along the horizontal axis. For example, the stripes of a horizontal American flag filter nicely with the sub filter.

  - **Up:** The opposite of the sub filter, this filter works by looking for repeated information along the vertical axis. The stripes of a vertical American flag filter well with the up filter.

  - **Average:** Use this option when a mixture of vertical and horizontal information exists. When in doubt, try this filter first.

  - **Paeth:** This filter works like an advanced average filter. When in doubt, try this filter after you have experimented with the average filter.

  - **Adaptive:** This filter provides the most thorough analysis of the image's color and creates the most accurate color palette for the image. However, it usually provides the largest file sizes for the PNG format.

Creating Windows and Macintosh projectors

To export a Mac stand-alone projector, check the Macintosh Projector option in the Formats tab. To publish a Windows stand-alone projector, check the Windows Projector option in the Formats tab.

 The Mac projector published by Flash MX is carbonized for playback on both Mac OS X or Mac OS 9.x (or earlier) systems.

 The process of creating and using Flash stand-alone projectors is described in Chapter 23, "Using the Flash Player and Projector."

Using the QuickTime settings

Now that Apple QuickTime 4 or higher includes built-in support for Flash tracks and .swf files, you may want to publish QuickTime movies (.mov files) in addition to your Flash movies (.swf files). If you want to enable QuickTime movie output via the Publish command, make sure that it is selected in the Formats tab of the Publish Settings dialog box.

 The QuickTime publish settings are discussed at length in Chapter 41, "Working with QuickTime."

 Flash MX no longer supports RealPlayer publishing. If you would like to read our coverage of RealPlayer from the Flash 5 Bible, check the book's Web site (flashmxbible.com) or flashsupport.com for more information.

Publish Preview and Publish Commands

After you have entered the file format types and specifications for each in the Publish Settings dialog, you can proceed to preview and publish the file types you selected.

Using Publish Preview

The Publish Preview submenu (accessible from File ⇨ Publish Preview) lists all of the file types currently enabled in the Publish Settings. By default, HTML is the first file type available for preview. In general, the first item enabled in the Formats tab of Publish Settings is the first item in the submenu and can be executed by pressing Ctrl+F12 or ⌘+F12. Selecting a file type in the Publish Preview menu launches your default browser and inserts the selected file type(s) into the browser window.

 When you use Publish Preview, Flash MX actually creates real files in the same location as the saved Flash document (.fla file). In a sense, previewing is the same as running the Publish command, except that Publish Preview will save you the steps of opening the browser (or player) and loading the files manually.

Using Publish

When you want Flash to export the file type(s) selected in the Publish Settings, choose File ➪ Publish (Shift+F12). Flash creates the new files wherever the Flash movie was last saved. If you have selected an HTML template in the HTML tab of Publish Settings, you may receive a warning or error message if any other necessary files were not specified. That's it! After you've tested the files for the delivery browser and/or platforms of your choice, you can upload the files to your Web server.

Tip   We highly recommend using Macromedia Dreamweaver MX for managing file uploads to your web server. Dreamweaver MX has a new cloaking feature that can hide specific file extensions (such as .fla) from site file lists—preventing them being accidentally uploaded to your Web server.

Summary

✦ To minimize your wait time during publishing or testing Flash movies, you may want to use MP3 files for all of your Event Sync sounds.

✦ Test your Flash movies and scenes within the Flash authoring environment. The Bandwidth Profiler can provide vital information about frame byte requirements and can help you find problematic streaming areas of the Flash movie.

✦ The size report that can be generated from the Export Movie or Publish commands for Flash movies lists detailed information regarding any and all Flash elements, such as audio, fonts, and frame byte size.

✦ The Publish Settings dialog box enables you to pick any number of file formats to export at one time. You can control just about every setting imaginable for each file type and use HTML templates to automate the insertion of Flash movies into your Web pages.

✦ Publish Preview will automatically launch your preferred browser and load the selected publish file(s) into the browser window.

✦   ✦   ✦

Integrating Flash Content with HTML

✦   ✦   ✦   ✦

In This Chapter

Defining HTML tags
and attributes for the
Flash Player

Filling the entire browser
window with a Flash
movie

Detecting the Flash
Player plug-in or
ActiveX control

Sending commands to
JavaScript from a Flash
movie

✦   ✦   ✦   ✦

If you're not one for automated HTML production using templates, this chapter is for you. This chapter teaches you the ins and outs of the `<OBJECT>` and `<EMBED>` tags, as well as some secrets to using `<FRAMESET>` tags to display Flash movies. At the end of this chapter, we examine how Flash movies can interact with JavaScript and DHTML by using `fscommand` actions from Flash.

Writing Markup for Flash Movies

In Chapter 21, you learned how to use the Publish feature, which included automated HTML templates. These templates created the necessary HTML tags to display Flash movies on Web pages. This section discusses the use of Flash movies in your handwritten HTML documents. You can also use this knowledge to alter HTML documents created by the Publish feature.

Note

In the following code examples, we use an asterisk (*) when displaying optional parameters that are not in the default options that are enabled in the Flash Only HTML template. We also use the term plug-in to mean both the Netscape plug-in and the ActiveX control for Flash Player 6.

You can use two tags to place Flash movies on a Web page (such as an HTML document): `<OBJECT>` and `<EMBED>`. You need to include both of these plug-in tags in HTML documents, as each tag is specific to a browser: `<OBJECT>` for Internet Explorer on Windows, and `<EMBED>` for Netscape on Windows and Mac (and Internet Explorer on Mac). Each tag works similarly to the other, with some slight differences in attribute names and organization. Remember that if both sets of tags are included with the HTML, only one set of tags is actually read by the browser, depending on which browser is used to view the Web page. Without these tags, the browser cannot display Flash movies with other HTML elements such as images and text.

Tip   You can, however, directly link to Flash movies (.swf files) as an alternative method for displaying Flash content. That method, however, precludes the use of parameters to control the look and playback of the Flash movie—it would be the same as loading the Flash movie straight into the stand-alone Flash Player. For more information on direct linking, see Colin Moock's tutorial, "Filling the Browser Windows Using the <FRAMESET> Tag," in the **Bonus_Tutorials.pdf** in the Bonus_Tutorials folder of the *Flash MX Bible* CD-ROM.

Using the <OBJECT> tag

Microsoft Internet Explorer for Windows uses this tag exclusively to enable the Flash Player ActiveX control. When the Flash Only HTML template is used in Publish Settings, the HTML document that is published uses the <OBJECT> tag in the following way. Some of these options (marked with an asterisk) are created only if you enable/disable specific options in the HTML tab of the Publish Settings dialog box.

New Feature   Flash MX ActionScript has introduced a new Stage object that allows you to control or override many of the same properties that the Player HTML tags specify. For more details on the Stage object, refer to the *Macromedia Flash MX ActionScript Bible* by Robert Reinhardt and Joey Lott.

```
A.  <OBJECT
B.      classid="clsid:D27CDB6E-AE6D-11cf-96B8-
        444553540000"
C.      codebase="http://download.macromedia.com/pub/
        shockwave/cabs/flash/swflash.cab#version=6,0,0,0"
D.      WIDTH="550" HEIGHT="400"
E.      ID="home"
F.      ALIGN="">
G.      <PARAM NAME=movie VALUE="home.swf">
H.*     <PARAM NAME=play VALUE=false>
I.*     <PARAM NAME=loop VALUE=false>
J.*     <PARAM NAME=menu VALUE=false>
K.      <PARAM NAME=quality VALUE=high>
L.*     <PARAM NAME=scale VALUE=noborder>
M.*     <PARAM NAME=salign VALUE=LT>
N.*     <PARAM NAME=wmode VALUE="transparent">
O.*     <PARAM NAME=devicefont VALUE=true>
P.      <PARAM NAME=bgcolor VALUE=#FFFFFF>
Q.*     <PARAM NAME=flashvars VALUE="title=My%20Flash%Movie">
R.  </OBJECT>
```

A. <OBJECT: This is the opening tag containing the ID code and locations of the ActiveX control for the Flash Player. Note that this opening tag includes the attributes lettered B through F.

B. classid: This lengthy string is the unique ActiveX identification code. If you are inserting the <OBJECT> tag by hand in a text editor, make sure that you copy this ID string exactly.

C. codebase: Like the codebase attribute of Java <APPLET> tags, this attribute of the <OBJECT> tag specifies the location of the ActiveX control installer (.cab file) as a URL. Notice that the #version=6,0,0,0 portion of the URL indicates that the Flash Player version 6 should be used. You can also specify specific minor releases, such as

#version=5,0,29,0, which would install the Flash 5.0 r29 ActiveX control. If the visitor doesn't have the ActiveX control already installed, Internet Explorer automatically downloads the control from this URL.

D. WIDTH **and** HEIGHT: These attributes control the actual width and height of the Flash movie as it appears on the Web page. If no unit of measurement is specified, these values are in pixels. If the % character is added to the end of each value, the attribute adjusts the Flash movie to the corresponding percent of the browser window. For example, if 100 percent was the value for both WIDTH and HEIGHT, the Flash movie fills the entire browser, except for the browser gutter. See Colin Moock's tutorial on the CD-ROM to learn how to minimize this gutter thickness.

E. ID: This attribute of the <OBJECT> tag assigns a JavaScript/VBScript identifier to the Flash movie, so that it can be controlled by HTML JavaScript/VBScript functions. By default, this attribute's value is the name of the actual .swf file, without the .swf extension. Each element on an HTML page should have a unique ID or NAME attribute. The NAME attribute is discussed in the next section.

F. ALIGN: This attribute of the <OBJECT> tag determines how the Flash movie will align on the HTML document. The acceptable values for this attribute are LEFT, RIGHT, TOP, or BOTTOM. As with <IMG> tags in HTML, the ALIGN attribute gives very loose layout control. It's likely that you'll want to rely on the ALIGN attribute of table cell tags such as <TD> to position a Flash movie with other HTML elements.

G. <PARAM NAME=movie VALUE="home.swf">: This is the first set of <PARAM> subtags within the <OBJECT></OBJECT> tags. Each parameter tag has a unique NAME= setting, not to be confused with JavaScript NAMEs or IDs. This parameter's NAME setting movie specifies the filename of the Flash movie as the VALUE attribute. Note that you can pass Flash variables to the movie directly by specifying them in the filename. For example, home.swf?firstName=Joe will pass a variable named firstName with a string value of Joe to the _root timeline (that is, _level0). You can also use the new Flash MX flashvars (item Q) HTML attribute to do this type of data transfer as well.

H. <PARAM NAME=play VALUE=false>: This optional parameter tells the Flash Player whether it should start playing the Flash movie as it downloads. If the VALUE equals false, the Flash movie loads in a "paused" state, just as if a stop action was placed on the first frame. If the VALUE equals true, the Flash Player starts playing the movie as soon as it starts to stream into the browser. If this tag is omitted, the Flash Player will behave as if play equals true.

 I. <PARAM NAME=loop VALUE=false>: This optional setting tells the Flash Player whether the Main Timeline (any scene timeline, for instance) should repeat when the Playhead reaches the last frame. If VALUE equals false, the playhead will not loop. If VALUE equals true, the Playhead will loop. If this parameter tag is omitted, the Flash Player by default will loop playback of the Main Timeline.

J. <PARAM NAME=menu VALUE=false>: This setting controls the display of the Flash Player menu that can be invoked by right-clicking (Windows) or Control+clicking (Mac) the Flash movie in the Web browser. If you set this option to false, the menu will display the options shown in Figure 22-1. If you set this option to true, all of the options will be available to the end user, as shown in Figure 22-2. When the menu is enabled, the user has quite a bit of playback control over the Main Timeline of the Flash movie. Usually, you will not want to offer this unrestricted control to people viewing the movie. Note that only the developer version of the Flash Player will show the Debugger option in this menu. Also, the player's Settings option is available in both modes of the menu.

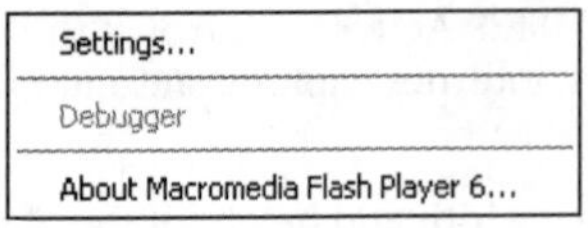

Figure 22-1: The Flash Player menu with control options disabled

Figure 22-2: The Flash Player menu with control options enabled

K. `<PARAM NAME=quality VALUE=high>`: This parameter has a `NAME` attribute-setting quality that controls how the Flash movie's artwork renders within the browser window. `VALUE` can be `low`, `autolow`, `autohigh`, `high`, or `best`. Most Flash movies on the Web use the `autohigh` value, as this forces the Flash Player to try rendering the movie elements anti-aliased. If the processor of the machine can't keep up with the Flash movie using anti-aliased elements, it turns off anti-aliasing by switching to a `low` quality. For a full description of each of the `quality` settings, please refer to the section "Using the HTML settings" in Chapter 21, "Publishing Flash Movies."

L. `<PARAM NAME=scale VALUE=noborder>`: This optional parameter controls how the Flash movie scales in the window defined by the `WIDTH` and `HEIGHT` attributes of the opening `<OBJECT>` tag. Its value can be `showall`, `noborder`, `exactfit`, or `noscale`. If this entire subtag is omitted, the Flash Player treats the movie as if the `showall` default setting was specified. The `showall` setting fits the Flash movie within the boundaries of the `WIDTH` and `HEIGHT` dimensions without any distortion to the original aspect ratio of the Flash movie. Again, refer to "Using the HTML settings" section of Chapter 21 for a complete description of the `scale` settings and how they work within the dimensions of a Flash movie.

M. `<PARAM NAME=salign VALUE=LT>`: This parameter controls the alignment of the Flash movie within the space allocated to the viewing area of the movie within the browser. For example, if you size your Flash movie to use 100 percent of the width and height of the browser window, a `VALUE` of `LT` would align the Flash movie to the left and top of the browser window. The acceptable values for this parameter are `L` (left edge), `R` (right edge), `T` (top edge), `B` (bottom edge), `LT` (left and top edge), `RT` (right and top edge), `LB` (left and bottom edge), or `RB` (right and bottom edge). For more information, please see our coverage in Chapter 21.

N. `<PARAM NAME=wmode VALUE=transparent>`: This Player option works only with Internet Explorer (version 3 or higher) for Windows. If you are only targeting an audience that uses this browser, you can control how the Flash movie's background color appears on top of the HTML or DHTML elements on the Web page. There are three acceptable values:

- `window`: This value is the default appearance of movies playing in the Flash Player on Web pages. With this value, movies play within the area specified by the `WIDTH` and `HEIGHT` attributes (discussed in item D), and the background color of the Flash movie's stage (as defined by Document Properties or item P later in this section) displays.

- `opaque`: This value provides the same visual appearance of the movie's Stage as `window` does. However, if you want to animate other DHTML objects in front of or behind a layer containing the Flash movie, it is recommended that you use the `opaque` value.

- `transparent`: This value allows the Stage of the Flash movie to act like an alpha channel. When enabled, the Flash movie appears to float on the HTML page, without any background color to reveal the corners of the Flash movie's Stage. Again, while this feature is somewhat extraordinary, it will function only within Internet Explorer on Windows. Also, since the browser must anti-alias the Flash artwork on top of other HTML elements, playback of Flash animations may suffer.

O. `<PARAM NAME=devicefont VALUE=true>`: This feature controls how Flash text appears in the browser window and works only on the Windows operating system. Like the device fonts with the Flash MX authoring environment (_sans, _serif, and _typewriter), this option can display any and all embedded text to system fonts such as Times and Arial. To do this, set `VALUE` to true. To disable device font rendering in this fashion, set `VALUE` to `false`. If this tag is omitted from the HTML, the value will default to false. Finally, the rules of Flash device fonts apply to system device fonts as well. For example, device or system fonts cannot be masked, rotated, or manipulated with the Tranform panel or the Property inspector.

Note

This seldom-used setting does not work predictably from use to use. In our tests, we could not get `devicefont` to work consistently from movie to movie, nor could we propose any reasonable use for it. It's likely that this is a legacy setting, meaning that it was made available for machines that had slow video or computing performance when the Flash Player was first introduced to the market.

P. `<PARAM NAME=bgcolor VALUE=#FFFFFF>`: This last parameter name, `bgcolor`, controls the background color of the Flash movie. If you published an HTML document via the Publish command, the `VALUE` is automatically set to the background color specified by the Modify ⇨ Movie command in Flash. However, you can override the Movie setting by entering a different value in this parameter tag. Note that this parameter, like all HTML tags and attributes concerning color, uses hexadecimal code to describe the color. For more information on color, see Chapter 7, "Applying Color."

Q. `<PARAM NAME=flashvars VALUE="title=My%20Flash%Movie">`: This new Flash Player movie attribute allows you to declare variables within the Flash movie when it loads into the Web browser. `flashvars` literally stands for "Flash Variables." This new feature allows you to circumvent the browser URL length limitation for declaring variables in the Flash movie's filename. For example, you can use client-side (e.g. JavaScript) or server-side (e.g. ASP, PHP) scripting to dynamically write the VALUE for this tag in your HTML, passing information from databases into the Flash movie at load time.

R. </OBJECT>: This is the closing tag for the starting <OBJECT> tag. As is shown later in this chapter, you can put other HTML tags between the last <PARAM> tag and the closing </OBJECT> tag for non-ActiveX–enabled browsers, such as Netscape. Because Internet Explorer for Windows is the only browser that currently recognizes <OBJECT> tags, other browsers simply skip the <OBJECT> tag (as well as its <PARAM> tags) and only read the tags between the last <PARAM> and </OBJECT> tags.

Tip

While the Flash MX HTML publishing templates do not reflect the usage of quotes around parameter names or values, we recommend that you consistently apply quotes around names and values, such as <PARAM NAME="bgcolor" VALUE="#FFFFFF">. This syntax is especially important for the new flashvars attribute.

Using the <EMBED> tag

Netscape uses the <EMBED> tag to display non-browser native file formats that require a plug-in, such as Macromedia Flash and Shockwave Director or Apple QuickTime. Following is a sample listing of attributes and values for the <EMBED> tag. Again, attributes with an asterisk are generally optional for most Flash movie playback.

```
A.  <EMBED
B.       src="home.swf"
C.*      play=false
D.*      loop=false
E.       quality=high
F.*      scale=noborder
G.*      salign=LT
H.*      wmode=transparent
I.*      devicefont=true
J.       bgcolor=#FFFFFF
K.       WIDTH=550 HEIGHT=400
L.*      swLiveConnect=false
M.*      NAME="home"
N.*      ALIGN="left"
O.       TYPE="application/x-shockwave-flash"
P.       PLUGINSPAGE="http://www.macromedia.com/shockwave/
         download/index.cgi?P1_Prod_Version=ShockwaveFlash">
Q.  </EMBED>
```

A. <EMBED: This is the opening <EMBED> tag. Note that lines B through H are attributes of the opening <EMBED> tag, which is why you won't see the > character at the end of line A.

B. src: This stands for "source," and it indicates the filename of the Flash movie. This attribute of <EMBED> works exactly like the <PARAM NAME=movie VALUE="home.swf"> subtag of the <OBJECT> tag.

C. play: This attribute behaves in the same manner as the play parameter of the <OBJECT> tag. If you omit this attribute in your HTML, the Flash Player will assume that it should automatically play the Flash movie.

D. loop: This attribute controls the same behavior as the loop parameter of the <OBJECT> tag. If you omit this attribute in your HTML, the Flash Player will automatically loop playback of the movie's Main Timeline.

E. quality: This attribute controls how the Flash movie's artwork will display in the browser window. Like the equivalent <PARAM NAME=quality> subtag of the <OBJECT> tag, its value can be low, autolow, autohigh, high, or best.

F. scale: This attribute of <EMBED> controls how the Flash movie fits within the browser window and/or the dimensions specified by WIDTH and HEIGHT (item K). Its value can be showall (default if attribute is omitted), noborder, exactfit, or noscale.

G. salign: This attribute controls the internal alignment of the Flash movie within the viewing area of the movie's dimensions. See the description for the salign parameter of the <OBJECT> tag for more information.

H. wmode: This attribute controls the opacity of the Flash movie's background color and works only on Internet Explorer for Windows. We can only assume that this attribute was included with the Flash HTML publishing templates to allow for backward compatibility with older Internet Explorer browsers on Windows that could read <EMBED> tags if <OBJECT> tags were not present.

I. devicefont: This attribute controls the visual appearance of any text within a Flash movie, and only functions correctly on the Windows operating system. See the description for devicefont in the <OBJECT> tag section.

J. bgcolor: This setting controls the Flash movie's background color. Again, this attribute behaves identically to the equivalent <PARAM> subtag of the <OBJECT> tag. See that tag's description in the preceding section.

K. WIDTH and HEIGHT: These attributes control the dimensions of the Flash movie as it appears on the Web page. Refer to the WIDTH and HEIGHT descriptions of the <OBJECT> tag for more information.

L. swLiveConnect: This is one attribute that you can't find in the <OBJECT> tag. This unique tag enables Netscape's LiveConnect feature, which enables plug-ins and Java applets to communicate with JavaScript. By default, this attribute is set to false. If it is enabled (for example, the attribute is set to true), the Web page may experience a short delay during loading. The latest versions of Netscape don't start the Java engine during a browsing session until a Web page containing a Java applet (or a Java-enabled plug-in such as the Flash Player) is loaded. Unless you use fscommand actions in your Flash movies, it's best to leave this attribute set to false.

Caution Currently, Netscape 6.2 does not support LiveConnect features with the Flash 6 Player. Based on our research, the JVM (Java Virtual Machine) and/or the Flash Player will need to be updated to support fscommand actions to and from Flash movies in Netscape 6.2 (or higher). Some previous versions of Netscape (all 3.0 and 4.0 versions, for example) support fscommand actions when LiveConnect is enabled.

M. NAME: This attribute works in tandem with the swLiveConnect attribute, allowing the Flash movie to be identified in JavaScript. The value given to the NAME attribute will be the Flash movie object name that can be used within your JavaScript programming.

N. ALIGN: This attribute behaves exactly the same as the ALIGN parameter for the <OBJECT>. See its description in the preceding section for more information.

O. `TYPE="application/x-shockwave-flash"`: This attribute tells Netscape what MIME (Multipurpose Internet Mail Extension) content-type the embedded file is. Each file type (TIF, JPEG, GIF, PDF, and so on) has a unique MIME content-type header, describing what its content is. For Flash movies, the content-type is `application/x-shockwave-flash`. Any program (or operating system) that uses files over the Internet handles MIME content-types according to a reference chart that links each MIME content-type to its appropriate parent application or plug-in. Without this attribute, Netscape may not understand what type of file the Flash movie is. As a result, it may display the broken plug-in icon when the Flash movie downloads to the browser.

P. `PLUGINSPAGE`: Literally "plug-in's page," this attribute tells Netscape where to go to find the appropriate plug-in installer if it doesn't have the Flash plug-in already installed. This is not equivalent to a JavaScript-enabled autoinstaller. It simply redirects the browser to the URL of the Web page where the appropriate software can be downloaded.

Q. `</EMBED>`: This is the closing tag for the original `<EMBED>` tag in line A. Some older or text-based browsers such as Lynx are incapable of displaying `<EMBED>` tags. You can insert alternate HTML (such as a static or animated .GIF with the `<IMG>` tag) between the `<EMBED>` `</EMBED>` tags for these browsers.

Caution

You may be surprised to learn that all versions of Internet Explorer (IE) for the Macintosh cannot read `<OBJECT>` tags. Rather, IE for Mac uses a Netscape plug-in emulator to read `<EMBED>` tags. However, this emulator does not interpret all `<EMBED>` tags with the same level of support as Netscape. As a result, the `swLiveConnect` attribute does not function on IE for Mac browsers. This means that the `fscommand` action is not supported on these browsers.

On the CD-ROM

You can find Colin Moock's tutorial, "Filling the Browser Window by Using the `<FRAMESET>` Tag," in the **Bonus_Tutorials.pdf** in the Bonus_Tutorials folder of the *Flash MX Bible* CD-ROM. This tutorial shows you how to scale Flash movies to the full width and height of a browser window.

Detecting the Flash Player

What good is an awesome Flash experience if no one can see your Flash movies? Because most Flash content is viewed with a Web browser, it's extremely important to make sure that your HTML pages check for the existence of the Flash Player plug-in before you start pushing Flash content to the browser. There are a variety of ways to check for the Flash Player, and this section provides an overview of the available methods.

Plug-in versus ActiveX: Forcing content without a check

The Flash Player is available for Web browsers in two forms: the Flash Player plug-in (as a Netscape-compatible plug-in) and the Flash Player ActiveX control (for use only with Microsoft Internet Explorer on Windows 95/98/ME/NT/2000/XP).

If you directly insert a Flash movie into a Web page with the `<EMBED>` tag (for Netscape browsers), one of two scenarios will happen:

1. The browser has the Flash Player plug-in and will load the Flash movie.

2. The browser does not have the Flash Player plug-in and displays a broken plug-in icon.

If scenario 2 occurs and the `PLUGINSPAGE` attribute of the `<EMBED>` tag is defined, the user can click the broken plug-in icon and go to the Macromedia site to download the Flash Player plug-in. If no `PLUGINSPAGE` attribute is specified, clicking the broken plug-in icon will take you to a generic Netscape plug-in page.

If you insert a Flash movie into an HTML document with the `<OBJECT>` tag (for Internet Explorer on Windows only), one of two scenarios will happen:

1. The browser has the Flash Player ActiveX control and will load the Flash movie.

2. The browser does not have the Flash Player ActiveX control and will autodownload and install the ActiveX control file from the Macromedia site.

The ActiveX control will autodownload and install only if the `classid` and `codebase` attributes of the Flash movie's `<OBJECT>` tag are correctly specified. Depending on the user's security settings, the user needs to grant permission to a Security Warning dialog box (shown in Figure 22-3) to commence the download and install process.

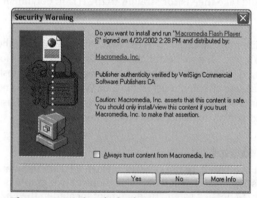

Figure 22-3: The Flash Player 6 ActiveX control will automatically download if Microsoft Internet Explorer for Windows encounters an HTML page with Flash content.

Although using the `<OBJECT>` and `<EMBED>` tags by themselves is by far the simplest method for integrating Flash content into a Web page, it's not the most user-friendly method of ensuring that the majority of your Web visitors can view the Flash content. The most common way to detect Flash movies is by using JavaScript and VBScript, as we see in the next section.

JavaScript and VBScript player detection

The use of scripts written into an HTML document is very popular for Flash Player detection. If you're getting familiar with Flash MX's ActionScript syntax, you'll find that JavaScript detection code isn't all that complex. JavaScript is a universal scripting language that most 3.0 or higher Web browsers can employ to some capacity. Microsoft's implementation of JavaScript, called JScript, isn't exactly the same as Netscape's JavaScript. For this reason, you can translate some JavaScript functionality into Microsoft's proprietary Web-scripting language, VBScript.

You'll find the HTML, Flash documents, movies, and GIF files for this section in the ch22 folder of the *Flash MX Bible* CD-ROM.

In this section, we look at how to create an HTML document that checks for the presence of the Flash Player plug-in with JavaScript, and the Flash ActiveX control with VBScript. We use two images of a traffic light — one Flash movie with a green light animating on and off, and one GIF image with a red light on — to display the results of our plug-in and ActiveX detection. Many Web sites employ a similar mechanism: Before an HTML page with Flash content can be accessed, the visitor will be presented with a splash screen telling them whether they have the Flash Player installed. If they don't have it, they can click a link to get the plug-in or ActiveX control. As a backup, many splash pages also include a link to bypass the detection in case the detection fails. This link would take the visitor straight to the HTML document that contains the Flash content.

The Flash Player can be detected with most JavaScript-enabled Web browsers by using the JavaScript array `navigator.mimeTypes`. The value for this array is always empty for Internet Explorer browsers, including IE 4.5 on Macintosh. IE 5.0 (or higher) for Macintosh now supports this array. While we can use VBScript to detect for IE on Windows, there is no script plug-in detection available for IE 4.5 on Macintosh. You can however, use the Flash Sniffer method, discussed in the next section, to detect Flash on IE 4.5 on Macintosh.

Detecting the plug-in with JavaScript

By rearranging the JavaScript code that is created by the Detect for Flash 6 HTML template in the Publish Settings, we can set up a testing mechanism that delivers one of two graphics to the visitor's Web browser. Copy the `scriptDetection.html` document located in the ch22 folder of the *Flash MX Bible* CD-ROM and open it in your preferred text editor (SimpleText, Notepad, BBEdit, and so on), or, even better, in Macromedia Dreamweaver. Look at lines 10 to 15 in the following listing.

The ⊃ indicates a continuation of the same line of code. It should not be written in the actual JavaScript code in the HTML document.

```
10. var plugin = 0;
11. var activeX = 0;
12. var plugin = (navigator.mimeTypes && ⊃
     navigator.mimeTypes["application/x-shockwave-flash"]) ⊃
     ? navigator.mimeTypes["application/x-shockwave- ⊃
     flash"].enabledPlugin : 0;
13. if ( plugin ) {
14.    plugin = parseInt(plugin.description.substring ⊃
     (plugin.description.indexOf(".")-1)) >= 6;
15. }
```

Line 10 initializes a variable `plugin` to save a value that indicates the presence of the Flash Player 6 plug-in on Netscape (or IE 5.0 Mac). Line 11 initializes a variable called `activeX` to save a value that indicates the presence of the FlashPlayer 6 ActiveX control. At this point, we create them with a value of 0, meaning that the plug-in and ActiveX Control are not installed. This is used for worst-case scenarios in which the user may be using a version of JavaScript that doesn't interpret the detection code correctly.

Line 12 is borrowed from the Detect Flash 6 HTML template output. It uses the `mimeTypes` **array** of the `navigator` JavaScript object to determine whether the Flash Player (in any version) is installed. If the Flash Player plug-in is installed, the variable `plugin` is now equal to the value `[object Plugin]`. If this is `true`, lines 13 and 14 will execute. Using the `description` property of the `Plugin` object, we can determine whether the Flash Player is the correct version. In this example, we check whether it's greater than or equal to 6. Notice that we can use a comparison as the value of the `plugin` variable. If Flash Player 6 (or higher) is installed, `plugin` will equal `true` (or 1); if a lower version is installed, `plugin` will equal `false` (or 0).

Creating a test object in VBScript

At this point, if the visitor is using Netscape (on any operating system) or Internet Explorer on the Macintosh, the variable `plugin` will have a value of either 0 or 1. However, we still need to check for the ActiveX control, if the visitor is using Internet Explorer for Windows. Line 11 already initialized a variable called `activeX`. Lines 16-21 check to see if VBScript can create a Flash object in the document:

Note   The ⊃ indicates a continuation of the same line of code. It should not be written in the actual JavaScript code in the HTML document.

```
16. else if (navigator.userAgent && ⊃
        navigator.userAgent.indexOf("MSIE")>=0 && ⊃
        navigator.userAgent.indexOf("Windows")>=0){
17.     document.write('<SCRIPT LANGUAGE=VBScript\> \n');
18.     document.write('on error resume next \n');
19.     document.write('activeX = ( IsObject(CreateObject ⊃
        ("ShockwaveFlash.ShockwaveFlash.6")))\n');
20.     document.write('<' + '/SCRIPT>');
21. }
```

Line 16 determines whether the visitor is using Internet Explorer on Windows. If that's the browser the visitor is using, lines 17 to 21 will execute. These lines of code create the VBScript that is necessary to check for the existence of the Flash 6 Player ActiveX control. Using the `IsObject` and `CreateObject` methods, VBScript can determine whether the ActiveX Control is installed. If it is installed, the variable `activeX` will equal `true` (or 1). Note that this variable is available to both JavaScript and VBScript.

Inserting the graphics

After the variables `plugin` and `activeX` have been set appropriately, we can use these variables to either display a Flash movie (.swf file) or a GIF image graphic. In the body of the HTML document, we can reuse the `plugin` and `activeX` variables to insert either the Flash or GIF graphics. Lines 31 to 36 of the HTML document will write the tags to display the Flash movie or the GIF image for Netscape (on any platform) or IE on the Mac.

Note   The ⊃ indicates a continuation of the same line of code. It should not be written in the actual JavaScript code in the HTML document.

```
31. if ( plugin ) {
32.    document.write('<EMBED SRC="trafficLightGreen.swf"
         WIDTH="105" HEIGHT="185" SWLIVECONNECT="FALSE"
         QUALITY="HIGH"></EMBED><BR><FONT
         FACE="Verdana,Arial,Geneva" SIZE=2>Flash
         Player 6<BR>Plug-in detected.</FONT>');
33. } else if (!(navigator.appName &&
       navigator.appName.indexOf("Netscape")>=0 &&
       navigator.appVersion.indexOf("2.")>=0)){
34.      document.write('<A HREF="http://www.macromedia.com
           /shockwave/download/index.cgi
           P1_Prod_Version=ShockwaveFlash">');
35.      document.write('<IMG SRC="trafficLightRed.gif"
           WIDTH="105" HEIGHT="185" BORDER="0"></A><BR>
           <FONT FACE="Verdana,Arial,Geneva" SIZE=2>Flash
           6 Player<BR>Plug-in not installed.</FONT>');
36. }
```

If the `plugin` variable is not equal to `false` (line 31), line 32 will execute. Line 32 uses the `<EMBED>` tag to insert a Flash movie (.swf file), depicting a green light that animates to a full green color, and the HTML text "Flash Player 6 Plug-in detected." If the `plugin` variable is equal to `false` and the browser is Netscape 2.0 or higher (line 33), then lines 34 and 35 will create `<A HREF>` and `<IMG>` tags, depicting a static GIF image of a red traffic light that links to the Macromedia download area. Then, JavaScript will create the HTML text "Flash Player 6 Plug-in not installed."

Lines 43 to 52 perform the same functionality for Internet Explorer for Windows. If the `activeX` variable is `true`, then an `<OBJECT>` tag is written and a green traffic light will animate on. If it's not installed, then a static GIF image of a red traffic light will be displayed.

Finally, we should do two more things:

1. Tell IE 4.5 (or earlier) Mac users that we can't detect the Flash 6 Player plug-in.

2. Tell other users that they can either proceed to the main Flash site, or click the appropriate traffic light to download the plug-in or ActiveX control.

Lines 59 to 62 tell IE 4.5 (or earlier) Mac users that we can't detect their plug-in settings. We can either leave it to them to decide whether they should download the plug-in, or we could direct them to a sniffer movie (discussed in the next section) to determine whether the plug-in is installed.

Lines 63 to 65 check whether either the plug-in or the ActiveX control is installed. If it is, we tell the visitor to proceed to the main Flash site. Note that you would want to insert more JavaScript code here that includes a link to your Flash content.

Lines 66 to 74 check whether the plug-in and the ActiveX control are both absent. If neither is installed, we tell them which traffic light (lines 67 to 74) to click.

Although you'll most likely want to spruce up the look and feel of this page to suit your particular site, you can use this scripting layout to inform your visitors about their plug-in or ActiveX control installations.

Using a Flash sniffer movie

If you would prefer to avoid JavaScript and VBScript, you can also use small Flash movies known as *sniffers* to detect the Flash Player. Sniffers are virtually hidden from the visitor, and they direct the HTML page to a new location (using a `getURL` action) where the real Flash content (or site) exists. If the Player is not installed, the movie won't be able to play and direct the HTML page to a new location. If this happens, a special `<META>` tag in the `<HEAD>` of the HTML document will direct the browser location to a screen that informs the visitor to download the plug-in or ActiveX control.

Making the sniffer movie

The sniffer movie is a small Flash movie that has the same background color as the HTML document. We do not need any artwork or symbols in this movie.

1. Open Flash MX, and in a new Flash movie document (.fla file), rename Layer 1 to **actions**.

2. Add a keyframe on frame 2 of the Actions layer. With this keyframe selected, open the Actions panel (F2).

3. In the Actions panel, we create some ActionScript that checks for Flash 3 (or earlier). If Flash Player 3 is detected, then the movie will stop here and launch a URL for Flash 3 movies. If a later version of the player is detected, a separate keyframe labeled `checkPlayer` will be called. We can direct each version of the Player to a unique URL. The basic principle of this ActionScript is to use Flash version-specific actions to determine which Player is displaying the movie:

```
// create a Flash variable, whose value is equal to the
// $version environment variable in Flash Player 4, 5,
// or 6. This action line will not be read by Flash
// Player 3(or earlier).

player = eval("$version");

// The $version value will be in the format:
//
// abc 1,2,3,4
//
// where abc is the operating system (e.g. WIN, MAC)
// and 1 and 2 are the major version designations
// (e.g. 4.0, 5.0, etc.) and 3 and 4 are the minor and
// sub-minor version designations (e.g. r20, r27, etc.)
//
// By default, Flash 6 ships with a Player version equal
// to WIN 6,0,0,0 or MAC 6,0,0,0. However, the Flash
// Player is available on other platforms like UNIX and
// POCKETPC as well.
//
// We just need the major version designation at
// placeholder 1. Using a while loop and substring(), we
// can extract this number, searching for the space (" ")
// between the platform text and the version numbers. The
// major version starts just after the space (" "). The
// Flash Player 3 will disregard this section of code.

playerLength = length(player);

i=1;
```

```
while (i<=playerLength) {
  currentChar = substring(player, i, 1);
  if (currentChar eq " ") {
    platform = substring(player, 1, i-1);
    majorVersion = substring(player, i+1, 1);
    break;
  }
  i = i+1;
}

// This code will check the value of majorVersion.
// Flash Player 3 will not be able to execute the
// call() action, but Flash Player 4 or higher will.

if (majorVersion == " ") {
  // Flash Player 3 will execute this code
  // automatically, because it will not interpret
  // the if action.
  getURL("flash3.html");
} else {
  call("checkPlayer");
}

// We will prevent the movie from accidentally looping.

stop ();
```

4. Now you need to create a keyframe with actions that will be executed by Flash Player 4, 5, or 6. Add a keyframe on frame 5, and in the Property inspector assign a label of **checkPlayer** in the <Frame Label> field. Press the F5 key on frame 20 to add more empty frames to the layer so that you can read the frame label.

5. Select frame 5, and open the Actions panel (F9). In Expert mode, type the following code into the Script pane. This code checks to see if the Flash Player is version 4, 5, or 6 (or higher):

```
// majorVersion will be equal to either 4, 5, or 6 in
// Flash Player 4, 5, or 6, respectively.

if (Number(majorVersion) == 4) {
  // Flash Player 4 will execute this code.
  getURL("flash4.html");
} else if (Number(majorVersion) == 5) {
  // Flash Player 5 will execute this code.
  getURL("flash5.html");
} else if (Number(majorVersion)>=6) {
  // Flash Player 6 or higher will execute this code.
  getURL("flash6.html");
}
```

6. Change the size of the movie frame to **18** pixels × **18** pixels, in the Document Properties dialog box (Modify ➪ Document). This is the smallest size a Flash movie can have. Change the background color of the movie to match the background color of the HTML document. Click OK.

7. Save the Flash movie as **sniffer.fla**.

8. Open the Publish Settings dialog box (File ⇨ Publish Settings). Check the Flash and HTML options in the Formats tab. Uncheck the Use default names option, and rename the HTML file to **sniffer_start.html**.

9. In the Flash tab, select Flash 4 in the Version drop-down menu.

Note We are using the Flash 4 format because the Flash 3 Player will ignore all Flash 4 or higher actions, and the Flash 4 Player will recognize the formatting of the variable and ActionScript structures. Flash 5 SWF files restructure variables and ActionScript (even Flash 4-compatible code) in a manner that doesn't work consistently in the Flash 4 Player.

10. In the HTML tab, select the Flash Only template. Click the Publish button located on the right side of the Publish Settings dialog box.

11. When the files have been published, click OK to close the Publish Settings dialog box. Save your movie again.

You now have sniffer_start.html and sniffer.swf files in the same folder as your sniffer.fla file. In the next section, we add some additional HTML tags to the sniffer.html document.

Integrating the sniffer movie into an HTML document

After you have made the sniffer.swf and the sniffer.html files, you can modify the HTML document to guide the browser to a unique URL where plug-in information and a download screen will be shown. Remember that the ⮎ indicates a continuation of the same line of code. Do not insert this character into your HTML document.

1. Open the sniffer_start.html file in your preferred HTML document editor. Macromedia Dreamweaver, Notepad (Windows), SimpleText (Mac), or BBEdit (Mac) will do just fine.

2. Somewhere between the `<HEAD>` `</HEAD>` tags, insert the following HTML `<META>` tag:

```
<META http-equiv="Refresh" content="15; ⮎
URL=download.html">
```

This `<META>` tag has two attributes, `http-equiv` and `content`. The `http-equiv` attribute instructs the hosting Web server to add the value of `http-equiv` as a discrete name in the MIME header of the HTML document. The value of the `content` attribute becomes the value of the MIME entry. Here, the Web browser will interpret the META tag as

```
Refresh: 15; URL=download.html
```

in the MIME header. This name/value pair tells the browser to reload the browser window in 15 seconds with the file `download.html`. After testing, you may decide to increase the time the browser waits before reloading a new URL. On slower connections (or during peak Internet hours), you may find that 15 seconds is not long enough for the initial HTML and Flash movie to load into the browser.

Caution Some older browsers may require an absolute URL in the content attribute. This means that you may need to insert a full path to your HTML document, such as `http://www.yourserver.com/download.html`, as the URL in the content attribute.

3. You may want to create some text on this HTML document that indicates its purpose. If the user does not have the plug-in installed, he or she will be staring at a blank white page until the refresh is activated. For the purposes of this example, create an HTML table that centers the text "Checking for Flash Player..." on the page.

4. Save the HTML file as **sniffer.html**. If you want this to be the default page for your Web site, you may need to rename this file to index.html or default.asp. At this point, you need to create a download.html file. As a temporary measure, you can use the scriptDetection.html file discussed in the preceding detection method. You also need to create flash3.html, flash4.html, and flash5.html files for the getURL actions in the sniffer.swf movie.

We have included sample sniffer.html, download.html, flash3.html, flash4.html, flash5.html, and flash6.html files on the *Flash MX Bible* CD-ROM. The Flash movie placeholder documents (for example, flash3.html, flash4.html, and so on) do not contain any Flash movie URLs.

When you have your HTML documents ready, you can load the sniffer.html document into a browser. If the Flash Player is not installed, then the META tag should transport the browser location to the download.html URL. If the Flash Player is installed, then the Flash ActionScript will direct the browser to the appropriate page.

You can find an extended discussion of Flash Player detection in Sascha Wolter's tutorial, "Scriptless Flash Player Detection," in the **Bonus_Tutorials.pdf** located in the Bonus_Tutorials folder of the Flash MX Bible CD-ROM.

Using Flash Movies with JavaScript and DHTML

The ActionScripting features of Flash MX have once again increased the range of interactive and dynamic possibilities for Flash movies on the Web. Prior to Flash 4, Flash movies could interact with external HTML or scripts only through the fscommand action. This meant mapping commands and variables to JavaScript, which, in turn, passed information to the document object model of DHTML, Java applets, or CGI (Common Gateway Interface) scripts. Now that Flash movies can directly send and receive data to server-side CGI scripts, just about anything can be done within the Flash movie. However, if you want to directly communicate with the Web browser or the HTML document, you need to use fscommand actions or getURL actions with javascript: statements. Because all JavaScript-capable browsers do not support these methods, we're limiting our discussion to fscommand actions and JavaScript-controllable Flash movie properties.

A word of caution to Web developers

This section covers fscommand actions, which, when used in Flash movies on Web pages, are supported by only a handful of browsers. Currently, not one version of Internet Explorer for Macintosh (up to version 5.1) can interpret fscommand actions directed to JavaScript functions (see the Caution note in "Using the <EMBED> Tag" section earlier in this chapter). Only Netscape browsers versions 3.0 through 4.x offer cross-platform support for fscommand actions. Internet Explorer 3 and higher for Windows 95/98/ME/NT/2000/XP also supports fscommand actions. Our coverage of the fscommand actions assumes that you have basic knowledge of JavaScript and Flash ActionScript. If you don't know how to add actions to frames or buttons, please read Chapter 18, "Understanding Actions and Event Handlers." If you don't know JavaScript, you can still follow the steps to the tutorials and create a fully functional Flash-JavaScript movie. However, because this isn't a book on JavaScript, we don't explain how JavaScript syntax or functions work.

Cross-Reference

We'll gladly refer you to the *JavaScript Bible* by Danny Goodman for more information on the JavaScript language.

How Flash movies work with JavaScript

As mentioned earlier, Flash MX has an action called `fscommand`. `fscommand` actions are used to send a command (and an optional argument string) from a Flash movie to its hosting environment (such as a Web browser or standalone Flash Player). What does this mean for interactivity? The `fscommand` offers the capability to have any Flash event handler (Button instance, `onClipEvent`, frame actions, and so on) initiate an event handler in JavaScript. Although this may not sound too exciting, you can use `fscommand` actions to trigger anything that you would have used JavaScript alone to do in the past, such as updating HTML-form text fields, changing the visibility of HTML elements, or switching HTML background colors on the fly. Most Flash-to-JavaScript interactivity works best with dynamic HTML (DHTML) browsers such as Netscape 4 or higher and Internet Explorer 4 or higher. We look at these effects in the next section.

Caution

Currently, Netscape 6 and 6.2 do not support `fscommand` interactivity from Flash movies with JavaScript.

Flash movie communication with JavaScript is not a one-way street. You can also monitor and control Flash movies with JavaScript. Just as JavaScript treats an HTML document as an object and its elements as properties of that object, JavaScript treats a Flash movie as it would any other element on a Web page. Therefore, you can use JavaScript functions and HTML hyperlinks (`<A HREF>` tags) to control Flash movie playback.

Note

For JavaScript to receive Flash `fscommand` actions, you need to make sure that the attribute `swLiveConnect` for the `<EMBED>` tag is set to `true`. By default, most Flash HTML templates have this setting omitted or set to `false`.

Changing HTML attributes

In this section, we show you how to dynamically change the `BGCOLOR` attribute of the `<BODY>` tag with a `fscommand` action from a Flash movie while it is playing in the browser window. In fact, we change the background color a few times. Then, after that has been accomplished, we show you how to update the text field of a `<FORM>` tag to display what percent of the Flash movie has been loaded.

On the CD-ROM

Open the Flash movie countdown.fla located in the ch22/PercentLoaded folder of the *Flash MX Bible* CD-ROM. This is quite a large Flash document (over 14MB) as it uses many imported bitmap images and sounds to demonstrate slow-loading movies. If you are using the Mac OS 9.x or earlier version of Flash MX, you may want to increase the memory allocation for the Flash MX application file to 64MB or higher.

Adding fscommands to a Flash movie

Open a copy of the countdown.fla Flash movie from the *Flash MX Bible* CD-ROM, and use Control ➪ Test Movie to play the Flash .SWF version. You should notice that the filmstrip countdown fades to white, and then to near-black, and then back to its original gray color.

This countdown continues to loop until the entire first scene has loaded into the Flash Player. When the first scene has loaded, playback will skip to a Movie Clip of two dogs (in "negative") and a title sequence. There's more to the Flash movie, but for now, that's all we need to deal with.

Our goal for this section of the tutorial is to add `fscommand` actions to specific keyframes in the countdown.fla document. When the Flash Player plays the frame with the `fscommand` action, the Player sends a command and argument string to JavaScript. JavaScript then calls a function that changes the background color to the value specified in the argument string of the `fscommand` action (see Figure 22-4). To be more exact, you add an `fscommand` action to the frames where the color fades to white, black, and gray. When the Flash movie changes to these colors, so will the HTML background colors.

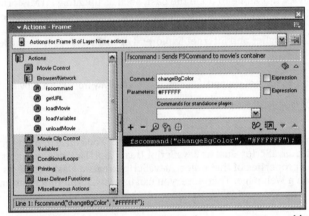

Figure 22-4: Frame 16: `fscommand` of `changeBgColor` with an argument of `#FFFFFF` (the hexadecimal code for the color white)

Here's the process:

1. On frame 16 of the Introduction scene, add a keyframe on the Actions layer. With the keyframe selected, open the Actions panel (F9). Make sure the panel is in Normal mode. Add an `fscommand` action from the Actions ➪ Browser/Network booklet. In the Command field, type **changeBgColor**. In the Parameters field, type **#FFFFFF**. The command `changeBgColor` is mapped to a JavaScript function called `changeBgColor` later in this tutorial. The argument string `#FFFFFF` is passed to that function, changing the HTML background color to white.

2. On frame 20, add another `fscommand` action to the corresponding keyframe on the Actions layer. Again, insert **changeBgColor** in the Command text box. In the Parameters field, type **#333333**. This argument changes the HTML background color to a dark gray.

3. On frame 21 of the Actions layer, follow the same instructions as you did for Step 2, except use **#9E9E9E** for the argument string. This changes the HTML background color to the same color as the Flash movie countdown graphic.

4. On frame 66 of the Actions layer, add another `fscommand` action with a `changeBgColor` command. This time, use an argument string of **#000000**, which changes the HTML background color to black.

5. Now that we've added several `fscommand` actions, let's try them out in the browser. Save the document as **countdown_100.fla**, and open the Publish Settings dialog box (for more information on Publish Settings, refer to Chapter 21, "Publishing Flash Movies"). In the Formats tab, uncheck Use default names, and type **countdown.swf** as the SWF filename, and **countdown_100.html** as the HTML filename. In the HTML tab, select the template **Flash with FSCommand**. Click OK to close the Publish Settings dialog box. Select the File ➪ Publish command to export the Flash movie and HTML document.

Next, we look at the automated JavaScript code that the HTML template created. While the basic code structure has been set up, we need to make some alterations and additions to the JavaScript for our `fscommand` actions to work.

Enabling JavaScript for Flash movies

Although the Flash with FSCommand template does a lot of the JavaScripting for you, it doesn't automatically map out the commands and arguments (args) to JavaScript-defined functions. In this section, we add the necessary JavaScript to make the `fscommand` actions work in the browser. What follows is the JavaScript code that Flash MX generates, along with the custom function `changeBgColor` that we wrote.

Note   Any numbered line of code marked with an asterisk (*) is custom JavaScript code that Flash MX does not create. Also, remember that the ⤵ indicates a continuation of the same line of code. Do not insert this character into your HTML document.

```
1.   <SCRIPT LANGUAGE=JavaScript>
2.   <!--
3.   var InternetExplorer = ⤵
     navigator.appName.indexOf("Microsoft") != -1;
4.*  var stringFlash = "";
5.   // Handle all the FSCommand messages in a Flash movie
6.       function countdown_DoFSCommand(command,args){
7.           var countdownObj = InternetExplorer ⤵
               ? countdown : document.countdown;
8.*          stringFlash = stringFlash + args;
9.*          if(command=="changeBgColor"){
               changeBgColor();
             }
         }
10.*     function changeBgColor(){
11.*         document.bgColor = stringFlash;
12.*         stringFlash = "";
         }
13.  // Hook for Internet Explorer
         if (navigator.appName && ⤵
           navigator.appName.indexOf("Microsoft") != -1 ⤵
           && navigator.userAgent.indexOf("Windows") != -1 ⤵
           && navigator.userAgent.indexOf("Windows 3.1") ⤵
           == -1){
         document.write('<SCRIPT LANGUAGE=VBScript\> \n');
         document.write('on error resume next \n');
         document.write('Sub countdown_FSCommand(ByVal ⤵
           command, ByVal args)\n');
         document.write('  call ⤵
```

```
                    countdown_DoFSCommand(command,ù args)\n');
                document.write('end sub\n');
                document.write('</SCRIPT\> \n');
            }
        //-->
14.  </SCRIPT>
```

The following is a line-by-line explanation of the code:

1. This HTML tag initializes the JavaScript code.

2. This string of characters is standard HTML comment code. By adding this after the opening `<SCRIPT>` tag, non-JavaScript browsers ignore the code. If this string wasn't included, text-based browsers such as Lynx might display JavaScript code as HTML text.

3. This variable simply condenses the JavaScript code that detects Internet Explorer into a single term, `InternetExplorer`.

4. *We added this line of code to declare a variable called `stringFlash`. Its value is set to nothing by putting two straight quote characters together. This variable is necessary for `fscommand` arguments to pass cleanly into JavaScript functions on both Netscape and Internet Explorer.

5. This is comment code added by the Macromedia team to let us know that the following JavaScript code is designed to catch the `fscommand` actions from a Flash movie.

6. This is the initial JavaScript function that works exclusively with Flash `fsommand` actions. The function's name is the value of the `NAME` attribute of the `<EMBED>` tag (or the value of the `ID` attribute of the `<OBJECT>` tag) followed by an underscore and `DoFSCommand(command,args){`. In this example, the Flash movie `NAME` is `countdown`. Notice that the command and arguments that were specified in Flash are passed to this function as `(command,args)`, respectively.

7. This is a handy optional variable that the Flash with FSCommand template created. Strangely, it is not necessary unless you need to refer to the differing document object models between Internet Explorer and Netscape. Instead of testing for either browser, you can insert the `countdownObj` variable in your own JavaScript code. For this example, though, it is not needed.

8. *This code makes the `stringFlash` variable called in line 4 equal to the argument string (`args`) from the Flash `fscommand` action. Because `stringFlash` was equal to nothing (`""`), `stringFlash` is now the same as the original argument string. This isn't necessary for Internet Explorer, but some earlier versions of Netscape don't recognize arguments straight from the Flash Player without it.

9. *This compares the passed command string from the Flash `fscommand` action to the string `changeBgColor`. If they're the same, JavaScript executes the code contained within the `if` statement. Because we made only one unique command in Flash for this sample, we only have to map the Flash `fscommand` of `changeBgColor` to the JavaScript function `changeBgColor()`.

10. *This is where the function `changeBgColor()` is defined. Remember that line 9 maps the Flash `fscommand` of `changeBgColor` to this JavaScript function.

11. *This line of code passes the variable `stringFlash` to the `document.bgColor` property, which controls the HTML background color. When the Flash `fscommand` action sends the command `changeBgColor`, the JavaScript `changeBgcolor()` function is invoked, which passes the argument string from the Flash `fscommand` action to `document.bgColor`.

12. *This resets the variable `stringFlash` back to nothing (`""`), so that future invocations of the `fscommand action` don't use the same argument from the previous execution.

13. This section of code detects the presence of Internet Explorer for Windows and maps the JavaScript functions to VBScript (which is used exclusively by Windows-only versions of Internet Explorer).

14. The closing `</SCRIPT>` tag ends this portion of JavaScript code.

That's it! We also added `<CENTER>` tags around the `<OBJECT>` and `<EMBED>` tags to center the Flash movie on the HTML page. Once you've manually added the custom lines of JavaScript code, you can load the HTML document into either Internet Explorer or Netscape (see the caveats mentioned at the beginning of this section). When the Flash Player comes to the frames with FSCommands, the HTML background should change along with the Flash movie. Next, we add a `<FORM>` element that displays the percentage of the Flash movie that has loaded into the browser window.

You can find the completed version of the countdown.fla movie on the *Flash MX Bible* CD-ROM. It is called countdown_100.fla and is located in the ch22 folder. You will also find countdown.swf and a fully JavaScripted HTML document called countdown_100.html.

Using the PercentLoaded() method

JavaScript can control several Flash movie properties. It's beyond the scope of this book to describe each JavaScript method for Flash movies. If you want to see a complete list of Flash JavaScript methods, see the Macromedia Flash tech support page (The ⤵ indicates a continuation in the URL. Do not type this character into the browser location field.):

```
http://www.macromedia.com/support/flash/ts/documents/⤵
tn4160.html
```

In this section, we use the `PercentLoaded()` method to display the Flash movie's loading progress update as a text field of a `<FORM>` element. First, we add the necessary `fscommand` action to the Flash movie, then HTML `<FORM>` elements, and then we add the appropriate JavaScript.

1. Open the countdown_100.fla movie that you modified in the previous section. There should already be an empty keyframe present on frame 1 of the Actions layer. Add an `fscommand` action to this keyframe. Type **PercentLoaded** in the Command field. This command has no arguments, so leave the Parameters field empty. Add the same `fscommand` action to the keyframes on frames 10, 20, 30, 40, 50, 60, and 67 of the Actions layer.

2. Save your Flash movie as **countdown_200.fla**, and open the Publish Settings dialog box. In the Formats tab, uncheck the HTML file format, and leave the SWF filename as **countdown.swf**. Then, publish your Flash movie.

3. In a text editor such as Notepad or SimpleText, open the countdown_100.html document from the previous section. Immediately resave this document as **countdown_200.html**.

4. Add the following HTML after the `<OBJECT>` and `<EMBED>` tags:

```
<FORM METHOD="post" ACTION="" NAME="flashPercent"
STYLE="display:show">
  <INPUT TYPE="text" NAME="textfield" SIZE="5" STYLE =
"display:show">
</FORM>
```

The code in Step 4 uses two `NAME` attributes so that JavaScript can recognize them. Also, the DHTML `STYLE` attribute assigns a `display:show` value to both the `<FORM>` and `<INPUT>` tags.

Caution

Netscape 4's implementation of the document object model (DOM) doesn't allow styles to be updated on the fly unless the page is reformatted (for example, the user resizes the window). It could be possible to write more JavaScript code that would insert JavaScript styles for the `<FORM>` elements, but that's beyond the scope of this section.

5. Now we need to map the `PercentLoaded` command from the Flash `fscommand` action to a JavaScript function. Add the following `if(command=="PercentLoaded")` statement to the `function countdown_DoFSCommand` of the HTML document:

```
function countdown_DoFSCommand(command, args) {
    var countdownObj = InternetExplorer ? countdown : ⊃
      document.countdown;
    stringFlash = stringFlash + args;
    if(command=="changeBgColor"){
       changeBgColor();
    }
    if(command=="PercentLoaded"){
       moviePercentLoaded();
    }
}
```

6. Add the following JavaScript after the `function changeBgColor()` section. The following `moviePercentLoaded` function tells the browser to update the `<FORM>` text field with the percent of the Flash movie currently loaded. When the value is greater than or equal to 99, then the text field reads 100 percent and disappears after two seconds. As mentioned earlier, Netscape is unable to change the `style` of the `<FORM>` elements on the fly. (The ⊃ indicates a continuation in the URL. Do not type this character into the browser location field.)

```
function moviePercentLoaded(){
    var m = InternetExplorer ? countdown : ⊃
      document.countdown;
    var Percent = m.percentLoaded();
    var temp = 0;
    if(Percent >= 99 ){
      document.flashPercent.textfield.value="100 %";
      if (navigator.appName.indexOf("Microsoft") != -1){
        setTimeout("document.flashPercent.⊃
          textfield.style.display = 'none'",2000);
```

```
        setTimeout("document.flashPercent.style.⊃
          display = 'none'",2000);
          }
      }
    else {
        temp = Percent;
        document.flashPercent.textfield.value = temp⊃
          + " %" ;
      }
  }
```

7. Save the HTML document and load it into a browser. If you run into errors, check your JavaScript syntax carefully. A misplaced ; or } can set off the entire script. Also, the function names specified in the Flash fscommand actions and the JavaScript code are case-sensitive and must be exactly the same. If you continue to run into errors, compare your document to the countdown_200.html document on the *Flash MX Bible* CD-ROM. We also recommend that you test the preloading functionality from a remote Web server. If you test the file locally, the Flash movie will load 100 percent instantaneously.

Caution   Remember, this type of interactivity won't work on Netscape 6 or 6.2. If you want to test with a Netscape browser, use Netscape versions 3 through 4.x.

Okay, that wasn't the easiest task in the world, and, admittedly, the effects might not have been as spectacular as you may have thought. Now that you know the basics of Flash and JavaScript interactivity, however, you can take your Flash movie interactivity one step further.

Summary

✦ You can customize many Flash movie attributes by adjusting the attributes of the <OBJECT> and <EMBED> tags in an HTML document. Scaling, size, quality, and back-ground color are just a few of the Flash movie properties that can be changed within HTML without altering the original .swf file.

✦ Even though you can set the WIDTH and HEIGHT attributes of a Flash movie to 100 percent, the browser window will still show a small border around the Flash movie. To minimize this border effect, place the Flash movie in a single frame within the <FRAMESET> tag.

✦ You can detect the Flash Player plug-in or ActiveX control in a variety of ways: by using the <OBJECT> and <EMBED> tags alone, by using JavaScript and VBScript to check for the presence of the plug-in or the ActiveX Control, or by inserting a Flash sniffer movie into an HTML document with a special <META> tag.

✦ Flash movies can interact with JavaScript and DHTML elements on a Web page. This type of interactivity, however, is limited to the 3.0 or higher versions of Internet Explorer (on 32-bit Windows versions) and Netscape (on Windows and Macintosh). Currently, Netscape 6.0 and higher do not support Flash and JavaScript interactivity.

✦ Flash movies can send commands to JavaScript with the Flash action, fscommand. An fscommand action consists of a user-defined command and argument (or parameter) string.

✦ Although the Flash with FSCommand HTML template will set up the initial JavaScript to enable support for `fscommand` actions, it won't find the `fscommand` actions you specified in the Flash movie and map them to JavaScript functions. You have to do this manually.

✦ `fscommand` actions can be used to change HTML document attributes or styles.

✦ The Flash Player plug-in has JavaScript-specific methods that can be used to send or receive information to a Flash movie. For example, JavaScript can query a Flash movie to determine how much of it has downloaded to the browser.

✦   ✦   ✦

Using the Flash Player and Projector

◆ ◆ ◆ ◆

In This Chapter

Creating a Flash projector

Controlling a stand-alone with `fscommand` actions

Distributing the Flash Player

Third-party utilities for Flash stand-alones

◆ ◆ ◆ ◆

This chapter, the last in Part VI, explores alternative means of distributing your Flash movies, as self-contained executable applications for CD-ROMs or floppy disks. We also look at the broad support available for the Flash Player plug-in for Web browsers.

The Stand-Alone Flash Player and Projector

The stand-alone Flash Player and projector let you take your Flash right off the Web and onto the desktop without having to worry whether users have the plug-in. In fact, you don't even need to worry about them having browsers! Stand-alone players and projectors have similar properties and limitations, although they're slightly different.

   ✦ **Stand-alone player:** This is an executable player that comes with Flash MX. You can open any .swf file in this player. The stand-alone player can be found in the Macromedia/ Flash MX/Players folder (Windows) or the Macromedia Flash MX:Players folder (Mac) on the volume where you installed Flash MX.

   ✦ **Projector:** A projector is an executable copy of your movie that doesn't need an additional player or plug-in to be viewed. It's essentially a movie contained within the stand-alone player. The projector is ideal for distribution of Flash applications on floppy disks or CD-ROMs. Figure 23-1 shows a Flash movie played as a projector.

For the sake of simplicity, we refer to both projectors and movies played in the stand-alone Flash Player as *stand-alones* in this discussion. Because both the projector and stand-alone player have the same properties and limitations, you can apply everything discussed here to either one you choose to use.

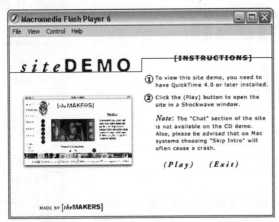

Figure 23-1: This movie is being played as a projector.

> **Note** Due to the differences in operating systems, Flash stand-alones on the Mac have the application menu listed in the system bar at the top of the Macintosh desktop area. On Windows, the application menu bar is part of the stand-alone window, as shown in Figure 23-1.

Creating a projector

When you have finished producing a Flash movie, it's fairly simple to turn it into a projector. You have two ways to create a self-contained projector. Turning your Flash movies into self-contained projectors typically adds 800K (Windows projectors) or 1MB (Mac projectors) to the final file size. If you create a Mac projector from the Windows version of Flash MX, the projector will add about 1.4MB to the size of the .hqx file.

> **Note** As each new version of Flash is released, the projector size will likely increase. Flash 4 projectors added 280K to a movie's file size (Windows projector), or 316K to the file size (Mac projector), while Flash 5 added 368K (500K Mac) to the file size. As the Flash Player's features are expanded, we'll likely see the size of the player continue to increase with each release of Flash.

Method 1: Using the Publish command

The simplest way to make a Flash projector file is to use the Publish feature of Flash MX. In three short steps, you can have a stand-alone Flash movie presentation:

1. Select File ➪ Publish Settings from the application menu.

2. When the Publish Settings dialog box opens, select the Formats tab and then check the projector formats. Publish both Windows and Macintosh projectors using this method. Figure 23-2 shows the Publish Settings dialog box with the appropriate formats selected.

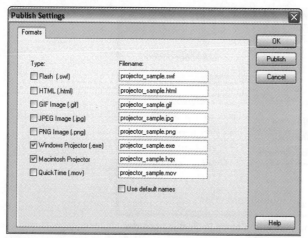

Figure 23-2: Select the projector formats in the Publish Settings dialog box.

3. Click the Publish button in the Publish Settings dialog box, and your Flash movie will be published in all of the formats (for example, SWF, GIF, JPEG, and projector formats) specified with Publish Settings.

Method 2: Using the stand-alone Flash Player

You can also create a Flash projector file using the stand-alone Flash Player executable file that ships with Flash MX. You can find the stand-alone Flash Player in the Players folder of the Flash MX application folder.

Note   If you use this method to create a projector, you can only make a projector for the current platform. Meaning, if you are using the Windows version of the stand-alone Flash Player, then you can only create a Windows projector.

1. Export your Flash movie as a .swf file using File ⇨ Export Movie. Alternatively, you can use the Publish feature to create the .swf file.

2. Open the exported Flash movie (.swf file) in the stand-alone Flash Player.

3. Choose File ⇨ Create Projector from the stand-alone player's application menu, as shown in Figure 23-3.

4. When the Save As dialog box opens, name the projector and save it.

Tip   If your movie is set to play at full screen (see fscommand coverage later in this chapter), press the Esc key to make the stand-alone player menu bar appear. If the Flash movie is set to play without the application menu, you should use the Publish method to create a projector.

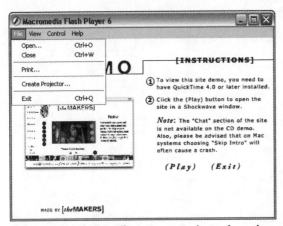

Figure 23-3: Choose File ➪ Create Projector from the stand-alone player menu.

Distribution and licensing

Distribution of stand-alone projectors or the Flash Player is free; you don't have to buy a license to distribute either the stand-alone Flash Player or projector. However, according to Macromedia, you need to follow specific guidelines for distributed Flash Players and projectors. The runtime license agreement and Macromedia logos can be downloaded from the Macromedia Web site. For more information, check out `www.macromedia.com/support/shockwave/info/licensing/`.

Distribution on CD-ROM or floppy disk

Flash has become increasingly popular for use on multimedia CD-ROMs, especially as embedded .swf files in larger Macromedia Director projectors. Stand-alones can be used as front-ends for installations, splash screens for other programs, or even as complete applications. When you combine the good looks of a Flash interface with a few `fscommand` actions (see the next section for more information), some simple scripting (BAT files and AppleScript), and put them together on a CD-ROM that's programmed to start automatically on insertion, you have a first-class product.

Because Flash movies can be very small (even when packaged as a projector), you can fit interactive multimedia presentations on 3.5-inch 1.44 MB floppy disks! This is truly revolutionary, as floppy disks can be copied very easily on any system with a floppy drive — you don't need a CD recorder to distribute your Flash movies in promotional mailers to clients. Arguably, though, floppy disks (and drives) are becoming more obsolete. Most new Macintoshes (from the tower G3 models or later) do not have floppy drives. Whenever possible, you may want to distribute Flash content on recordable CDs.

fscommand actions

`fscommand` actions can be used to provide greater functionality to your stand-alones. These actions can turn a simple Flash movie into something spectacular! When combined with additional scripting and executables, you can make fully functional applications. Table 23-1 lists `fscommand` actions for stand-alones.

Table 23-1: fscommand Actions for Stand-Alones

FSCommand	Arguments	Function
"fullscreen"	"true" or "false"	"true" sets the stand-alone to full-screen mode, without a menu. "false" sets it to the size specified by the movie properties.
"allowscale"	"true" or "false"	Allows for scaling of the movie. "false" sets the movie to the size specified by the Document Properties dialog box (Modify ⇨ Document). This doesn't actually keep the stand-alone from being resized, it only keeps the movie inside of it from being scaled.
"showmenu"	"true or "false"	Toggles the menu bar and the right-click/Control-click menu. "true" enables them; "false" turns them both off.
"trapallkeys"	"true" or "false"	Captures all key presses, including those that would normally control the player. If you have turned off the menu with the showmenu command, you will need to manually create a quit command to exit the player or projector.
"exec"	Path to executable (BAT, COM, EXE, and so on)	Opens an executable from within the stand-alone player. The application opens in front of the projector.
"quit"	No argument	Closes the stand-alone.

When an fscommand action is added in the Actions panel (set in Normal mode), you can access stand-alone–specific commands from a drop-down menu (see Figure 23-4). Refer to Chapter 18, "Understanding Actions and Event Handlers," for more information on adding actions to Flash frames or buttons.

Flash 5 offered an undocumented Save command for use in fscommand actions. This command allowed a Windows projector to save variables from the Flash movie to a text (.txt) file on the end user's system. While Flash MX no longer offers this feature, you can combine Flash movies with Director projectors and the FileIO Xtra to write text files on either Mac or Windows systems. Even better, Flash MX ActionScript now contains a SharedObject object that enables local storage of information from Flash movies. We demonstrate the SharedObject object in Chapter 33, "Creating a Game in Flash." Both SharedObject objects and the FileIO Xtra methods are discussed in the *Macromedia Flash MX ActionScript Bible* by Robert Reinhardt and Joey Lott.

Make sure you list the commands and arguments for fscommand actions as strings, not as expressions (unless you purposely want to refer to an ActionScript variable). If you do not encapsulate the command and argument in quotes, as in fscommand ("allowscale","true");, it may not be interpreted by the stand-alone.

You can also open HTML documents (even ones stored on a distributed CD-ROM) in the system's default Web browser by using the getURL() action. The following getURL() action will open a file named start.html that's in the same location as the stand-alone movie:

```
getURL("start.html");
```

Or, alternatively, you can display remote content in the Web browser by specifying absolute URLs, such as:

```
getURL("http://theMakers.com/index.html");
```

While `fscommand` actions are relatively simple to use, Flash MX ActionScript has introduced a new `Stage` object that allows you to control many of the same features of the Flash Player. Refer to the coverage of the `Stage` object in the *Macromedia Flash MX ActionScript Bible* by Robert Reinhardt and Joey Lott.

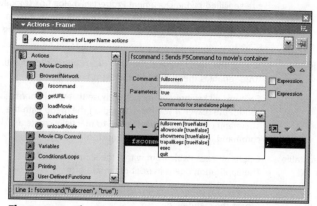

Figure 23-4: The Actions panel sports a convenient drop-down menu for `fscommand` actions, specific to the stand-alone Flash Player or projector.

Stand-Alone Limitations and Solutions

When you distribute your Flash movies as stand-alones, you may think that you won't have to worry about streaming and download. As a consequence, stand-alones are often made considerably larger than a typical Flash movie—which can be a mistake! Very large movies (1MB or more) may not play well on slower computers. Remember that Flash movies require the computer processor to compute all of those vector calculations, especially for rich animation. When you try to give a slower computer 1MB of Flash at once, it may not be able to handle it.

Tip   One way to get around this limitation is to break your movies into several smaller movies. You can use the `loadMovie`/`unloadMovie` actions to open and close other movies within the original movie. You should use these actions in your stand-alones.

You should also test your movies on a variety of computers, especially if you plan to put a lot of development time and money into distributing them on CD-ROM. Some processors handle the movies better than others, and you often have to decide which processor you want to target as the lowest common denominator.

Using the Flash Player Plug-In for Web Browsers

Flash movies can be played only in Web browsers that have the Flash Player plug-in or ActiveX control installed. Macromedia has made huge strides in making the plug-in prepackaged with newer Web browsers and operating system installation programs, eliminating the need for users to manually download and install the plug-in themselves. Unfortunately, the Flash 6 version of the plug-in will likely only be included in future releases of Web browsers and operating systems. Remember that Flash Player 3, 4, and 5 plug-ins can *try* to play Flash 6 movies; however, new features in Flash 6 movies (such as new ActionScript syntax and features) will not be available.

Note   For up-to-date information on the Flash Player plug-in, see Macromedia's download page at www.macromedia.com/shockwave/download/alternates.

Supported operating systems

Since Flash 3, Macromedia has greatly expanded its platform support for the Flash Player plug-in. At the time of this writing, you can download Flash Players for Windows 95/98/ME/NT/2000/XP and for Mac Power PCs. By the time this book is published, version 6 players should be available for Sun Solaris and Linux *x*86. At conferences worldwide, Macromedia has demonstrated that Flash graphics can be ported to a variety of GUIs (graphical user interfaces) and operating systems. We've also heard reports of Flash graphics showing up in add-on applications for the Sega Dreamcast and set top boxes from Motorola.

Supported browsers

The Flash Player plug-in works best with Netscape and Internet Explorer browsers. Any browser that is compliant with Netscape Navigator 2.0's plug-in specification or Internet Explorer's ActiveX technology can support the Flash Player plug-in or ActiveX control, respectively. Note that Mac versions of Internet Explorer use a Netscape plug-in emulator to use the Flash Player plug-in rather than an ActiveX control.

For AOL subscribers, any version of AOL's 3.0 through 7.0 browsers (except for the earliest 3.0 release that used a non-Microsoft Internet Explorer shell) will support Macromedia plug-ins.

Caution   The Flash action fscommand, when used to communicate with JavaScript, will work only with certain browser versions. Currently, no versions of Internet Explorer on the Macintosh (up to version 5.1) support the fscommand action. Netscape 3.01 through 4.x (on both Macintosh and Windows) or Internet Explorer 3.0 or greater for Windows 95/98/NT/2000/XP is necessary for fscommand implementation. Netscape 6.0 or higher does not support fscommand interactivity with JavaScript.

For a comprehensive list of supported browsers (and Flash compatibility), please see the Macromedia tech note at www.macromedia.com/support/flash/ts/documents/browser_support_matrix.htm

The Flash Player on the Pocket PC and Other Devices

The development for the Flash Player is so demanding that Macromedia dedicates an entire department's worth of resources to the job. The Flash Player has been made available for Pocket PC devices using the Pocket PC 2002 operating system from Microsoft. Computer hardware manufacturers such as Compaq, Hewlett-Packard, and Casio currently manufacture a wide range of PDAs (Personal Data Assistants) that can use the Flash Player via the Pocket Internet Explorer Web browser. At the time of this writing, Flash Player 5 was available for most Pocket PCs. As the computer processing power of Palm, Handspring, and Sony devices (that implement the Palm OS) become faster, we'll likely see Flash Players support extended to these devices. Nokia has released phones in Japan that can play full-color Flash animations as well!

It's no surprise that the Flash Player is being adopted so widely by computer and device manufacturers. The SWF format allows rich media such as animation, sound, and video to be transmitted over incredibly slow (or congested) networks. Until high-speed wireless access becomes more available, we'll likely need to keep wireless connection speeds such as 19.2 Kbps in mind while we develop Flash movies that can be accessed by a universal audience.

Plug-in and Flash movie distribution on the Web

Anyone can download the Flash Player plug-in for free from the Macromedia Web site. You can direct visitors at your Web sites to Macromedia's Flash Player download page, `www.macromedia.com/shockwave/download/index.cgi?P1_Prod_Version=ShockwaveFl ash`. In fact, according to Macromedia's licensing agreement, if you're publishing Flash movies on your Web site, you need to display the "Get Shockwave Player" logo or "Get Flash Player" logo on your Web site. This logo should link to Macromedia's download page, just listed. However, you need to license the right to distribute any Shockwave plug-in installer from Macromedia. For more details on licensing, see `www.macromedia.com/support/shockwave/info/licensing/`.

You can find the official Macromedia button graphics at `www.macromedia.com/support/programs/mwm/swb.html`.

Plug-in installation

In Chapter 21, "Publishing Flash Movies," we discuss the Publish feature of Flash MX and the use of preformatted HTML templates to deliver your Flash movies to your Web site. The template and/or handwritten HTML that you use for your Flash-enabled Web pages determines the degree of difficulty your visitors will have upon loading a Flash movie.

Cross-Reference

We devote an entire section on plug-in detection to the *Flash MX Bible*. See Chapter 22, "Integrating Flash Content with HTML," for more information. For instructions on how to use Dreamweaver MX to create detection pages for Flash movies, see Chapter 42, "Working with Dreamweaver MX."

Because Web browsers vary dramatically between operating systems (for example, Internet Explorer for the Mac behaves very differently from Internet Explorer for Windows), you should make the plug-in process as invisible as possible. The following HTML templates offer satisfactory Flash Player detection:

✦ **Detect Flash 3:** This template inserts an `<OBJECT>` tag for Internet Explorer (just as the Flash Only template will) and JavaScript detection code for the presence of the Netscape plug-in. When a Netscape browser loads the HTML page, JavaScript checks for version 3 of the Flash Player plug-in. If the plug-in is installed, JavaScript writes the proper `<EMBED>` tag and attributes for the Flash movie. If the plug-in is not installed, JavaScript writes HTML code for a static GIF or JPEG image, depending on which image format is enabled in the Formats tab of the Publish Settings.

✦ **Detect Flash 4:** This template works in the same way as the Detect Flash 3 template, except that it checks for Flash Player 4 plug-in or ActiveX control. Note that the Flash 4 format should be selected in the Flash tab of the Publish Settings, as well as a static image format in the Formats tab.

✦ **Detect Flash 5:** This template uses the same HTML and JavaScript code as the Detect Flash 3 template, except that it checks for version 5 of the Flash Player plug-in. Note that the Flash 5 format should be selected in the Flash tab of the Publish Settings, as well as a static image format in the Formats tab.

✦ **Detect Flash 6:** Again, this template offers the same HTML and JavaScript code as the previously mentioned templates, except that the code checks for version 6 of the Flash Player plug-in. Flash 6 should be selected in the Version menu of the Flash tab of the Publish Settings, as well as a static image format in the Formats tab.

While the Flash Only template doesn't use any JavaScript detection for the Flash Player plug-in, the `CODEBASE` attribute of `<OBJECT>` will direct Internet Explorer for Windows to the download location of the Flash Player ActiveX control. This process should be relatively straightforward for Windows users. For visitors using Netscape 3.0 or greater (on any platform), the `PLUGINSPAGE` attribute of `<EMBED>` provides the browser with the plug-in location and prompts the visitor to go there. This same minimal level of detection is available in all of the other HTML templates in the Publish Settings dialog box as well.

Cross-Reference   For information on other templates, please refer to Chapter 21, "Publishing Flash Movies."

Unfortunately, you can never predict with any certainty how visitors will encounter a Flash plug-in installation. Most of the automated HTML coding from earlier versions of Flash (3.0 and earlier) and/or Aftershock may make an "upgrade" installation very difficult for Web visitors. For example, if an HTML document uses JavaScript to detect the Flash Player version 3 plug-in and the visitor's browser is using the version 4 or 5 plug-in, the browser may return a false value for the plug-in and direct the visitor to a non-Flash page. The older JavaScript code doesn't know that the Flash Player 4 or 5 plug-in is perfectly capable of playing older Flash movies. If you have created Web pages and Flash movies with Flash 3.0 or earlier, see Macromedia's tech note at `www.macromedia.com/support/flash/ts/documents/flash4_detection.htm` for more information on updating JavaScript code to detect Flash Player version 4 or higher.

Alternative Flash-Content Players

Macromedia has teamed up with RealSystems and Apple to enable Flash content in the RealOne Player and the QuickTime Player, respectively. By enabling Flash content in other players, Macromedia is promoting the acceptance of Flash as the de facto vector standard for Web graphics. Moreover, with so many alternatives for Flash playback, it is more likely that your Web visitors can see your Flash content.

 The Java Player HTML template and supporting JAR files are no longer shipped with Flash MX. As the Java Player had limited Flash 2 support, it's not surprising that Macromedia no longer supports its development.

RealOne Player with Flash playback

With a little effort, you can repackage your Flash movies as RealFlash presentations over the Web. Web visitors can use the RealPlayer G2, RealPlayer 8, or the new RealOne Player to play Flash, RealAudio, or RealVideo (among a long list of RealMedia types) content. RealPlayer movies stream from a RealServer (special server software running concurrently with Web server software) into the RealPlayer plug-in (Netscape) or ActiveX control (Internet Explorer).

 Flash MX no longer includes built-in support for publisihing Flash movies tuned for RealPlayer. You can find more information about Flash and RealPlayer at `service.real.com/help/library/guides/production8/realpgd.htm`.

QuickTime Player

Apple introduced playback support for Flash movies with QuickTime 4. Better yet, Macromedia has included QuickTime Flash export options with Flash 4, 5, and MX. A QuickTime Flash movie (.mov file) is essentially a Flash movie (.swf file) packaged as a QuickTime media type.

 The QuickTime architecture and QuickTime Flash format are discussed at length in Chapter 41, "Working with QuickTime."

You can use the QuickTime HTML template in Publish Settings to create an instant Web page that uses the QuickTime Player plug-in. It uses the `<OBJECT>` and `<EMBED>` tags to prescribe the name, width, height, and plug-in download location.

QuickTime 4 can support only Flash 3 graphics and actions, while QuickTime 5 can support Flash 4 SWF format features, including `loadVariables` actions. Flash movies can act as a timeline navigator for other QuickTime media, such as video or audio.

 At the time of this writing, there was not an upgrade to the QuickTime Player that supported Flash 5 or 6 SWF features.

For interactive Flash content, you should limit yourself to Flash 4-compatible actions, which we discuss in Chapter 41, "Working with QuickTime."

Tip

For a demo of QuickTime Flash, check out Apple's QuickTime Sprites overview page at www.apple.com/quicktime/overview/sprites.html.

Shockwave Player

Since Director 6.5, you can include Flash movies (.swf files) in your Director movies, either as stand-alone Director projectors or as part of Shockwave movies (.dcr files) on the Web. The Flash Asset Xtra is automatically installed as part of the default Shockwave plug-in installation process. Among other benefits, Shockwave movies enable you to integrate Flash movies with QuickTime video and use Flash assets with Macromedia's Multiuser Server (which is part of the Director Internet Studio software package).

Cross-Reference

For more information on Director and Flash interactivity, please read Chapter 43, "Working with Director."

Player Utilities

You can also reformat and modify stand-alones for both Windows and Macintosh. A few software companies create applications specifically designed to modify Flash movies and stand-alones:

✦ www.flashjester.com

✦ www.swifftools.com

✦ www.screentime.com

✦ www.alienzone.com/screensaver_features.htm

✦ www.screenweaver.com

✦ www.goldshell.com/flashforge

Some of these companies offer more than just one utility for Flash movie development, such as the JTools of FlashJester. For updates to this list, check out the book's Web site, listed in the preface of the book.

Tip

You can find directories of Flash utilities at www.flashmagazine.com and graphicssoft.about.com/cs/flashtools.

One of our favorite utilities is Versiown, created by Goldshell Digital Media. This handy utility allows you to modify the properties of a Flash (or Director) projector file, specifically .exe versions for Windows. With Versiown, you can:

✦ Add or modify the version information that shows up in the Properties dialog box, accessible by right-clicking the .exe file and choosing Properties.

✦ Add a custom icon for the .exe file of the projector. Together with an icon utility like IconBuilder from Iconfactory (which is a filter plug-in for Adobe Photoshop), you can make custom .ico files to be used as icons for your Flash projectors.

You can download trial versions of Versiown at www.goldshell.com/versiown. A trial of IconBuilder is available at www.iconfactory.com/ib_home.asp.

Future Players, Future Features

Who can predict where Flash content will show up next? While the Flash Player plug-in has made its way into browser installations all over the world, there are still other possible avenues for Flash content. Currently, there is no SVG output from the Flash authoring environment — nor are there any conversion utilities to translate SWF files into SVG files (at the time of this writing). Or, maybe you would like to see Flash content supported in some other authoring application as an additional asset. If you have feature requests or general comments regarding the Flash authoring application or the Flash SWF format, you can send feedback to Macromedia at `wish-flash@macromedia.com`.

Note   You can use the Get Info dialog box (Mac OS 9.x or earlier) or the Show Info dialog box (Mac OS X) on Mac files to easily replace the icon image for Flash projector files on the Mac. Open the .ico file made from IconBuilder in an image editor such as Adobe Photoshop, use Edit ⇨ Select All to select the entire image, copy it to the clipboard (Edit ⇨ Copy) and paste it into the picture area of the Get (or Show) Info dialog box.

Summary

✦ Flash movies can be viewed in Web pages with the Flash Player plug-in or ActiveX control. You can also play Flash movies (.swf files) with the stand-alone Flash Player included with the Flash MX application, or you can publish a Macintosh or Windows projector that packages the stand-alone Flash Player and .swf file into one executable file.

✦ You can freely distribute a Flash movie projector or stand-alone Flash Player as long as you adhere to the guidelines outlined at Macromedia's Web site.

✦ Flash movies can be distributed with other multimedia presentations such as Macromedia Director projectors. Your Flash movies may be small enough to distribute on a 1.44MB floppy disk.

✦ The Actions panel of Flash MX has a stand-alone-specific submenu for the `fscommand` action. `fscommand` actions can control playback and execute external applications from a stand-alone.

✦ Flash movies can be viewed best with the Macromedia Flash Player plug-in or ActiveX control. However, you can also view Flash movies with third-party products, such as the RealOne Player or the Apple QuickTime Player.

✦ You can enhance your Flash movies with third-party tools such as FlashJester's JTools for Flash.

✦   ✦   ✦

Approaching Actionscript

♦ ♦ ♦ ♦

In This Part

Chapter 24
Knowing the Nuts
and Bolts of Code

Chapter 25
Controlling
Movie Clips

Chapter 26
Using Functions
and Arrays

Chapter 27
Interacting with
Movie Clips

Chapter 28
Sharing and
Loading Assets

Chapter 29
Using Components

Chapter 30
Sending Data In
and Out of Flash

Chapter 31
Applying HTML and
Text Field Formatting

Chapter 32
Creating a Portfolio
Site in Flash MX

Chapter 33
Creating a Game
in Flash

♦ ♦ ♦ ♦

Chapter 24 introduces the basic syntax of ActionScript code so that you will understand why all those brackets, dots, and quote marks are used. In Chapter 25 you learn how to control methods and properties of MovieClip objects. If you thought animating Movie Clips was fun, wait until you start to apply more sophisticated control to multiple elements with ActionScript! Chapter 26 covers using functions and arrays, two of the most crucial techniques for organizing and controlling dynamic data. Chapter 27 takes you to the next level of Movie Clip control with an overview of how to detect collisions and how to use the Color and Sound objects to control dynamic movie elements. Flash MX has introduced some terrific new features for dynamic data loading. Chapter 28 will introduce you to MP3 and JPEG loading and will also discuss how to share and load assets between multiple SWF files. Flash 5 Smart Clips have evolved into Flash MX components, and Chapter 29 will get you starting using the pre-built components that ship with Flash.

If you've made it this far, you will be surprised to find in Chapter 30 how easy it is to create dynamic forms that send data with the new LoadVars object and to integrate XML data with your Flash movies. Chapter 31 gives you the tools you need to take control of text fields using HTML tags and the new TextFormat object. The final two chapters in this section give you an opportunity to work through complete Flash projects. You can apply your new ActionScript know-how to build a portfolio site in Chapter 32 and an interactive game in Chapter 33.

Note: If you're hungry for more ActionScript, you will find everything you need for more advanced code in the *Macromedia Flash MX ActionScript Bible* by Robert Reinhardt and Joey Lott.

The new Flash MX interface for Mac OS X

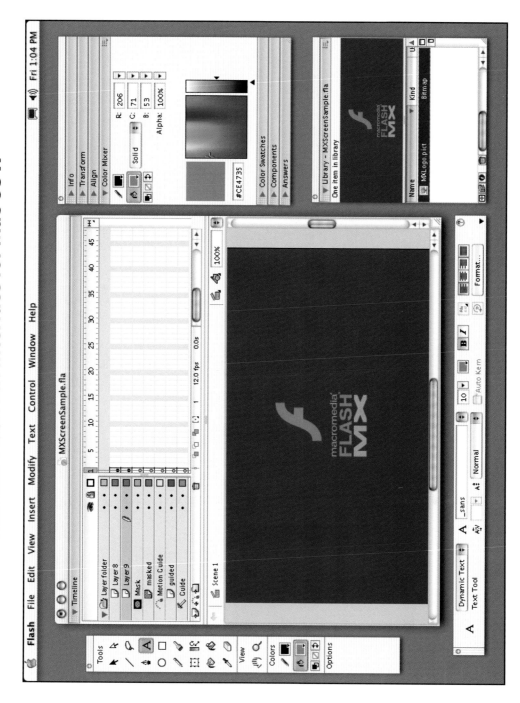

Learn to customize your Flash MX work space in Chapter 4

The new Flash MX interface for Windows XP

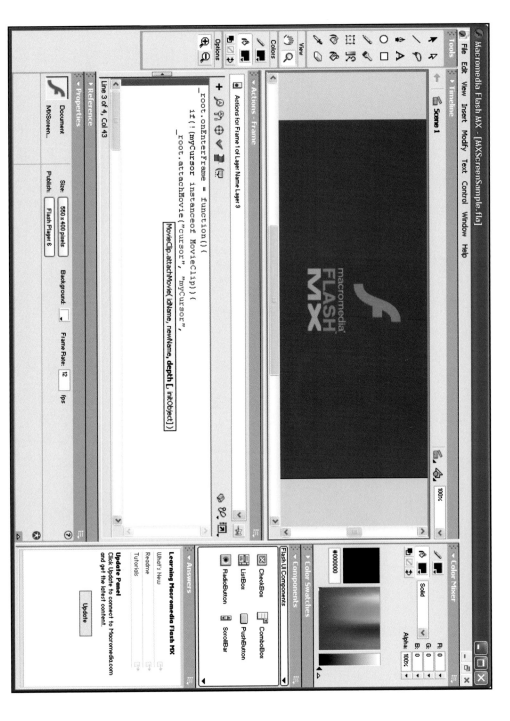

Learn to customize your Flash MX work space in Chapter 4

Planning Flash MX projects

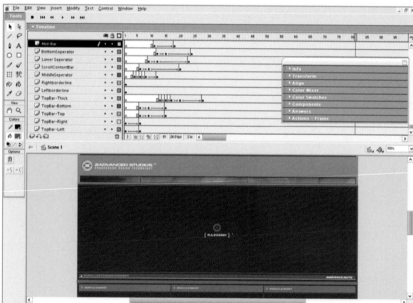

Eric Jordan takes you under the hood of 2advanced.com in Chapter 3

Working with color

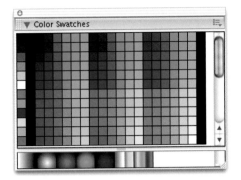

Default Web 216 swatches

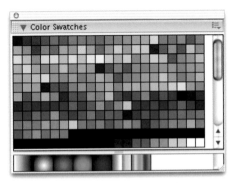

Web 216 Sort by Color

Source GIF image for loaded colors

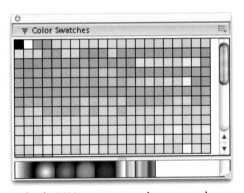

Flash MX custom color swatches

Learn to customize your Flash MX Color Swatches panel in Chapter 7

Importing vector artwork

Original vector artwork in Adobe Illustrator

EPS v7.0
(Illustrator RGB)

EPS v7.0
(Illustrator CMYK)

EPS files with different color spaces imported to Flash MX

For guidelines on importing vector artwork refer to Chapter 16

Relative color adjustment with Advanced Effect settings

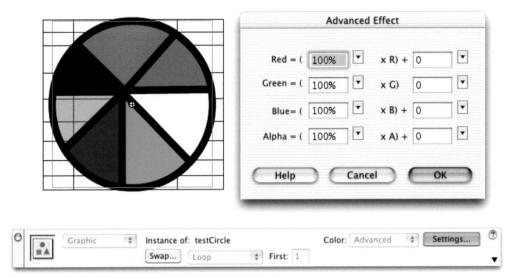

Original color symbol: 100 percent Red, Green, Blue, Alpha

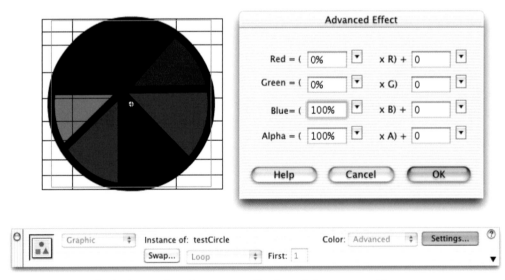

Relative color: 0 percent Red and 0 percent Green

Learn to modify symbol instances with Advanced Color Effects in Chapter 9

Absolute color adjustment with Advanced Effect settings

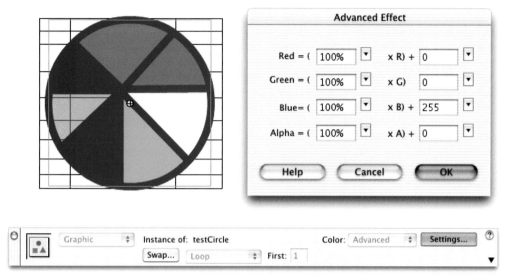

Absolute color: +255 Blue

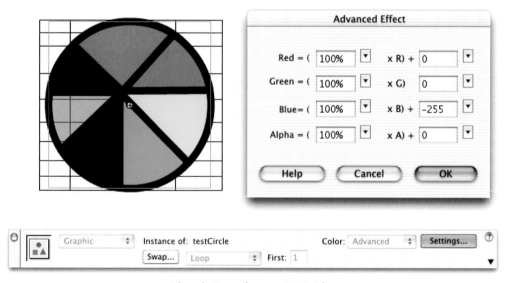

Absolute color: +–255 Blue

Learn to modify symbol instances with Advanced Color Effects in Chapter 9

Creating artwork with Flash drawing and effects tools

Dorian Nisinson

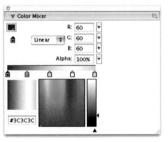

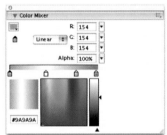

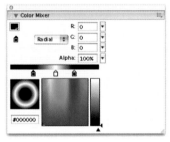

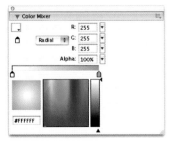

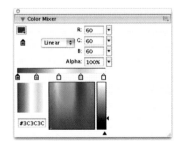

Create and modify custom gradients for faux 3D effects in Chapter 9

Use Corel Painter to create artwork for Flash animation

Arena Reed illustrates a technique for "Painted" animation in Chapter 37

Animation fundamentals and character animation techniques

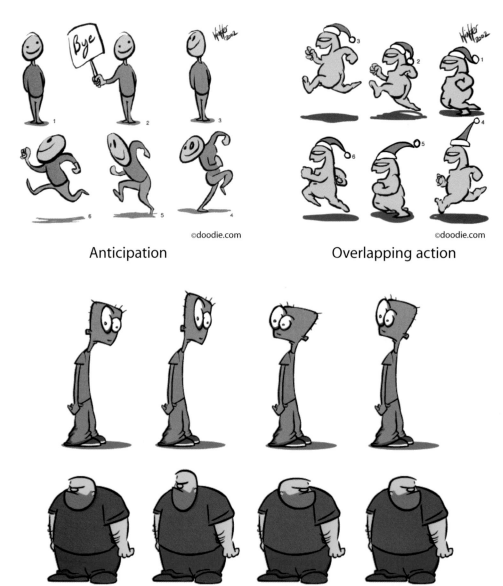

©doodie.com

Anticipation

©doodie.com

Overlapping action

character designs © **www.sandrocorsaro.com**

Bounces for head turns

Learn from examples by expert animators in Part III

Advanced animation strategies and special effects

Richard Bazley's illustrative animation drawn directly in Flash

JibJab.com's optimized collage animation

Learn from examples by expert animators in Part III

Comparing video sources

Low-quality sample:
from a digital still camera

Mid-quality sample:
from a DV camcorder

High-quality sample:
from a DVCAM camcorder

Integrate media files with Flash in Part IV

Comparing GIF compression settings

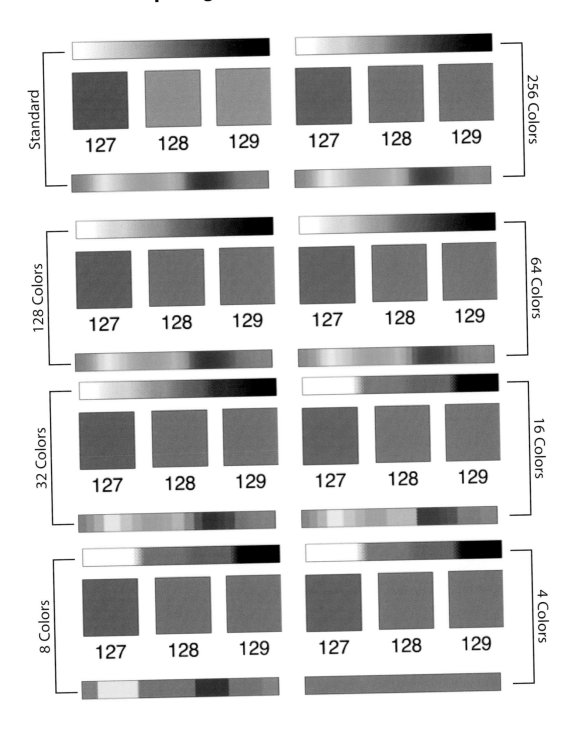

Optimize Raster images for Flash in Chapter 37

Build complete Flash MX projects

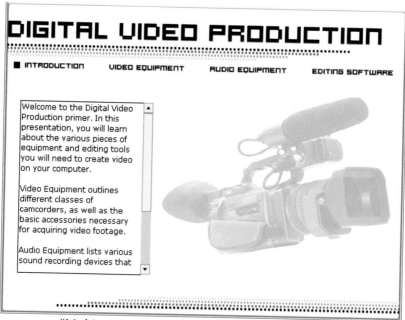

"Making Your First MX Project" in Chapter 20

"Creating Printable Paper Airplanes" in Chapter 25

Flash MX project examples apply to real-world work flow

Build complete Flash MX projects

"Creating a Portfolio Site in Flash" in Chapter 32

"Creating a Game in Flash" in Chapter 33

Flash MX project examples apply concepts to real-world work flow

Optimize artwork from other applications for Flash projects

3ds max™ artwork re-rendered for Flash

"Working with 3D Graphics" in Chapter 40

Knowing the Nuts and Bolts of Code

In This Chapter

Describing interactive problems

Speaking the ActionScript language

Understanding the value of variables

Working with conditionals

For many serious Web developers, Flash 5's enhanced programming capabilities were the single most important new feature of the product. Now, more than ever, elements inside Flash MX movies can be dynamic, have machine-calculated properties, and respond to user input. Movies can communicate with server-side applications and scripts by sending and receiving processed and raw data. What does this mean for your movies? It means you have the capability to produce truly advanced movies (such as Flash asteroids, a multiplayer role-playing adventure game, or a navigational interface with a memory of the user's moves). It also means that Flash can be used to produce many complex Web applications (such as database-driven e-commerce product catalogs) without the need for Macromedia Generator.

Macromedia Generator templates cannot be created with Flash MX. If you need Generator functionality, you will need to use the Macromedia Flash 5 or earlier version.

While the core ActionScript language has not changed in Flash MX, the Actions panel has been reorganized and improved to facilitate faster and more efficient coding. The addition of components, which are an enhanced version of Flash 5's Smart Clips, makes it simpler for you to add interface elements to your Flash projects. Flash MX has been designed to allow developers to build rich media applications — far beyond the scope of motion tweens and animations. This chapter introduces you to the programming structure of ActionScript and explains how to start using code within your Flash movies.

If you are new to scripting, we highly recommend that you review Part V, "Adding Basic Interactivity to Flash Movies," before you begin this chapter.

Breaking Down the Interactive Process

Before you can become an ActionScript code warrior, you need to realize that this isn't just a weekend activity — if you want to excel at Flash ActionScripting, you'll need to commit the time and energy necessary for the proper revelations to occur. It's not likely that you'll understand programming simply by reading this chapter (or the whole book). You need to create some trials for yourself, to test your textbook knowledge and to apply problem-solving techniques.

You might be thinking, "Oh no, you mean it's like geometry, where I'm given a problem, and I have to use theorems and postulates to create a proof?" Not exactly, but programming, like geometry, requires strong reasoning and justification skills. You need to be able to understand how values (for example, the height of a Movie Clip instance) are determined, what type of changes you can perform on those values, and how changes to one value might affect another value. Confused? Don't worry, we take this one step at a time.

See Chapter 3, "Planning Flash Projects," for more detailed information regarding project planning and management.

Define your problems

Regardless of what interactive authoring tool you use (Macromedia Dreamweaver MX, Macromedia Flash MX, Macromedia Director, and so on), you can't begin any production work until you have a clear idea of the product. What is it that you are setting out to do? At this point in the process, you should use natural language to describe your problems; that is, define your objective (or problem) in a way that you understand it. For example, let's say that you want to make a quiz. You'll have to run through a list of goals for that interactive product:

✦ Is it a true/false test?

✦ Or will it be multiple choice?

✦ Or fill-in-the-blank?

✦ An essay test?

✦ How many questions will be in the quiz?

✦ Will there be a time limit for each question?

✦ Will you notify the person of wrong answers?

✦ How many chances does the person get to answer correctly?

There are other questions, of course, that could help define what your product will encompass. Don't try to start Flash production without setting some project parameters for yourself.

Clarify the solution

After you have defined the boundaries for the project, you can start to map the process with which your product will operate. This step involves the procedure of the experience (in other words, how the person will use the product you are creating). With our quiz example, you might clarify the solution as:

1. The user starts the movie and types his or her name.

2. After submitting the name, the user will be told that he or she has 10 minutes to complete a 25-question quiz that's a combination of true/false and multiple-choice questions.

3. Upon acknowledging the instructions (by pressing a key or clicking a button), the timer starts and the user is presented with the first question.

4. The timer is visible to the user.

5. The first question is a true/false question, and the correct answer is false.

6. If the user enters a true response, a red light graphic will appear and the sound of a buzzer will play. The user will be asked to continue with the next question.

7. If the user enters a false response, a green light graphic will appear and the sound of applause will play. The user will be asked to continue with the next question.

8. This process repeats until the last question is answered, at which point the score is tallied and presented to the user.

The preceding eight steps are very close to a process flowchart, as discussed in Chapter 3, "Planning Flash Projects." In real-life production, you would want to clarify Step 8 for each question in the same amount of detail as Steps 5 to 7 did. As you can see, once you start to map the interactive experience, you'll have a much better starting point for your scripting work. Notice that we're already using logic, with our if statements in Steps 6 and 7. We're also determining object properties such as _visible in Step 4. While we may not know all the ActionScript involved with starting a timer, we know that we have to learn how time can be measured in a Flash movie.

Note   We use the terms scripting, programming, and coding interchangeably through this chapter and other parts of the book.

Translate the solution into the interactive language

After you have created a process for the movie to follow, you can start to convert each step into a format that Flash can use. This step will consume much of your time as you look up concepts and keywords in this book, the *Macromedia Flash MX ActionScript Bible*, or Macromedia's *ActionScript Dictionary* (now a PDF file) that ships with Flash MX. It's likely that you won't be able to find a prebuilt Flash movie example to use as a guide, or if you do, that you'll need to customize it to suit the particular needs of your project. For our quiz example, we could start to translate the solution as:

1. Frame 1: Movie stops. User types name into a text field.

2. (a) Frame 1: User clicks a submit Button symbol instance to initiate the quiz. The instructions are located on frame 2. Therefore, the Button action uses a gotoAndStop(2) action to move the playhead to the next frame.

2. (b) Frame 2: Static text will be shown, indicating the guidelines for the quiz.

3. Frame 2: User clicks a start quiz Button symbol instance. An action on the Button instance starts a timer and moves the playhead to frame 3.

4. Frame 3: The current time of the timer is displayed in a text field, in the upper-right corner of the Stage.

5. Frame 3: The first question is presented in the center of the Stage. A button with the text True and a button with the text False are located just beneath the question. The correct answer for the question is hidden in a variable name/value. The variable's name is answer, and its value is false. This variable declaration appears as a frame action on frame 3. A variable, called score, will also be declared to keep track of the correct answer count. Its starting value will be 0.

6. (a) Frame 3: If the user clicks the True button, an if/else action will check whether answer's value is equal to true. If it is, an action will set the _visible of a greenLight Movie Clip instance to true, and initiate and play a new Sound object for the applause.wav file in our Library. Also, the value of score will increase by 1. If the value of answer is not true, then an action will set the _visible of a redLight Movie Clip instance to true, and initiate and play a new Sound object for the error.wav file in our Library. The value of score will be left as is.

6. (b) Frame 3: A Button instance will appear, and when clicked, take the user to frame 4.

7. (a) Frame 3: If the user clicks the False button, an if/else action will check whether answer's value is equal to true. If it is, an action will set the _visible of a greenLight Movie Clip instance to true, and initiate and play a new Sound object for the applause.wav file in our Library. Also, the value of score will be increased by 1. If the value of answer is not true, an action will set the _visible of a redLight Movie Clip instance to true and initiate and play a new Sound object for the error.wav file in our Library. The value of score will be left as is.

7. (b) Frame 3: A Button instance will appear, and when clicked, it will take the user to frame 4.

While there is more than one way we could have translated this into ActionScript-like syntax, you'll notice that a few key concepts are presented in the translation: where events occur (frames or buttons), and what elements (for example, Button symbols or Movie Clip instances) are involved.

Most importantly, you'll notice that we used the same procedure for both the True and the False buttons. Even though we could hardwire the answer directly in the Button actions, we would have to change our Button actions for each question. By placing the same logic within each Button instance, we only have to change the value of the answer variable from frame to frame (or from question to question).

Granted, this example was already translated for you, and 90 percent of your scripting woes will be in the translation process — before you even have a testable Flash movie. You need to learn the basic terminology and syntax of the ActionScript language before you can start to write the scripting necessary for Steps 1 to 7. And that's exactly what the rest of this chapter (and the rest of Part VII of the book) will do.

Because the vocabulary of the ActionScript language has become so immense, Robert Reinhardt and Joey Lott have created a separate book, the *Macromedia Flash MX ActionScript Bible*, to thoroughly address the syntax of ActionScript. If you are new to scripting and programming, we recommend that you start with our coverage of ActionScript here before reading the *Macromedia Flash MX ActionScript Bible*.

You can find the ActionScriptDictionary.pdf file for the Macromedia *ActionScript Dictionary* PDF file in the Goodies ➪ Macromedia ➪ Documentation folder of the Flash MX installation CD-ROM. The trial version of Flash MX does not include this PDF file. If you only have the trial version of Flash MX, you can search the online ActionScript Dictionary at www.macromedia.com/support/flash/documentation.html.

The Basic Context for Programming in Flash

With the enhanced Actions panel (also known as the ActionScript editor) in Flash MX, you can program interactivity in two ways: by using a drag-and-drop menu-based set of actions (Normal mode), or by writing interactive commands directly into the Script pane of the Actions panel (Expert mode).

See our explanation of the Actions panel in Chapter 18, "Understanding Actions and Event Handlers".

Flash MX has a new Reference panel that allows you to look up ActionScript terms, with definitions, usage, and code examples. We'll show you the Reference panel later in this section.

Normal mode

This mode consists primarily of attaching actions to keyframes and buttons, selecting parameters for those commands from drop-down menus (or Action booklets), and/or entering parameters by hand into option fields. Although this method of programming can feel unnatural to traditional programmers, the resulting ActionScript looks and reads the same as the code produced with Expert mode.

Expert mode

In Expert mode, you can type your code from scratch, as well as insert your code with the help of Action booklets. Syntactically, ActionScript looks and feels very much like JavaScript. Macromedia has gone to great lengths to make ActionScript compatible with ECMA-262 (the standard programming guidelines derived from JavaScript). And like other object-oriented languages, ActionScript is composed of many familiar building blocks: variables, operators, conditionals, loops, expressions, built-in properties, subroutines, and native functions.

Using Esc Shortcut Keys for Actions

In Flash MX, you can choose to show or hide shortcut keys in the Actions panel. In the options menu of the Actions panel, choose View Esc Shortcut Keys (if it's not already checked). Now, click the plus (+) menu of the Actions panel to access ActionScript commands. You'll notice that shortcut keys are defined after the name of the command. You can use these shortcuts in either Normal or Expert mode. For example, `loadMovie()`, in the Actions ➪ Browser/Network menu, has a keyboard shortcut of Esc+l+m. If you give the Actions panel focus and press the Esc key, then the l key, then the m key, the `loadMovie` action will appear in the actions list of the Script pane, complete with placeholders for arguments. The shortcut will not work if you try to press the keys simultaneously — you must press the keys in sequence, as described in the previous example. Each key must be pressed and released before you type the following key(s) in the shortcut.

Accessing ActionScript commands

All of the ActionScript commands are found easily in the Flash interface in the Action booklets or plus (+) button menu in the Actions panel. However, the assembly of actions with one another is not something Flash MX automatically performs. Although it is beyond the scope of this chapter to fully explain fundamental programming principles, we can give a sense of the whole of ActionScript by providing you with an organized reference to each of its parts.

Actions list organization in the Actions panel

In Normal mode, you can add a line of code below any existing statement by highlighting the existing statement in the Actions list and then adding your action. If you accidentally add your code in the wrong place, or if you want to move code around, simply select the lines that you want to move and drag them with the mouse. You can also cut, copy, and paste code within the actions list or from one list to another using Ctrl+X (⌘+X), Ctrl+C (⌘+C), and Ctrl+V (⌘+V), respectively.

In Expert mode, the highlighting mechanism for selected actions changes. You are free to select partial or entire lines of code, and modify the code in any way you want. With Flash MX, you can even edit your code in your preferred text editor! If you want to create your own programming macros in other programming applications, you can write your scripts outside of the Flash authoring environment and copy the final code into the Actions panel when you're done.

Tip   To make sure that you don't have any syntax errors after reorganizing code in Expert mode, click the Check Syntax button in the Actions panel toolbar. Flash will alert you if there are scripting errors by placing messages in the Output window and won't let you enter Normal mode until the error(s) has been fixed.

The Reference panel

Are you sick of opening the PDF file for the Macromedia *ActionScript Dictionary* every time you need to look up a specific action? Or maybe you don't want to drag this book everywhere you go, especially while traveling. Well, Flash MX has added a new Reference panel that contains all the syntax of the ActionScript language. You can access the Reference in a few ways:

✦ Choose Window ➪ Reference.

✦ Click the Reference icon in the Actions panel.

✦ Right-click (or Control+click on Mac) an action in the left hand Actions pane of the Actions panel and choose View Reference in the contextual menu.

Let's quickly show you how to use the new Reference panel in an actual Flash document.

1. Open a new document (File ➪ New).

2. Select frame 1 of Layer 1, and open the Actions panel by pressing the F9 key.

3. Make sure the Actions panel is in Normal mode by choosing the mode from the options menu of the panel. Open the Actions booklet and click the Browser/Network booklet. Double-click the loadMovie action. The action will appear in the Script pane, as shown in Figure 24-1. By default, Flash MX assigns the loadMovieNum() action, which loads a Flash movie into a level of the Flash Player.

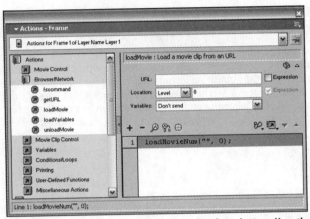

Figure 24-1: The Actions panel with a loadMovieNum() action in the Script pane

4. With the `loadMovieNum()` action selected in the Script pane, click the Reference icon (that is, the blue book with the question mark) at the top right of the Actions panel. The Reference will open, displaying the definition for the `loadMovie()` action, as shown in Figure 24-2.

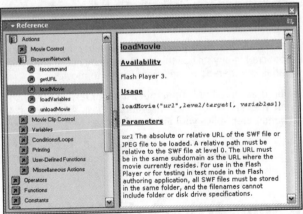

Figure 24-2: The Reference panel with the definition for loadMovie

You can select other actions from the Actions pane of the Reference panel and view their descriptions.

Tip

You can also print descriptions from the Reference panel by choosing Print from the options menu at the top-right corner of the panel.

Using the #include Action

ActionScript has an action that enables you to insert external text files (with an .as file extension). Now, you can write ActionScript in any text or script editor and save that text separately from the Flash document (.fla file). When you publish a Flash movie (.swf file) from the Flash document, Flash MX will retrieve the .as file and insert the actions to the action list where the #include action was issued. For example, the following code could be written in a contact.as file, which, as the name implies, contains a person's contact information for the Flash movie:

```
contactName = "Joseph Farnsworth";
contactStreet = "675 Locust Street";
contactCity = "Chicago";
contactState = "IL";
contactPhone = "312-555-1342";
contactEmail = "jfarnsworth@mycompany.com";
```

In a Flash document, you could insert this code into a keyframe of the Main Timeline (or a Movie Clip timeline) by using the #include action. You can use the #include action within any Flash event handler including keyframe, Button instance, onClipEvent, and so on:

```
#include "contact.as"
```

Make sure you do *not* insert a semicolon at the end of the #include line. Think of the #include action as a special tag for Flash MX, letting it know that it should replace the #include line of code with all the code within the referred file. The following code will result in a "malformed" error in the Output window, upon testing or publishing the Flash document:

```
#include "contact.as";
```

Why is the #include action useful? For experienced programmers, the #include command allows freedom to write ActionScript in any text editor. You can define entire code libraries of custom functions. These .as libraries can then be reused from movie to movie.

Note that the #include action is executed only upon publishing or testing the Flash movie. You cannot upload .as files to your Web server for "live" insertion of Flash ActionScript. Anytime you change the .as file, you will need to republish your Flash movie (.swf file).

You can find more information on the #include action in Chapter 35, "Getting Your Code under Control." We use the #include action extensively in Chapter 32, "Creating a Portfolio Site in Flash."

One Part of the Sum: ActionScript Variables

In any scripting or programming language, you will need some type of "memory" device—something that can remember the values and properties of objects or significant data. This type of memory device is referred to as a *variable*.

Variables are named storage places for changeable pieces of data (numbers and letters). One of the first obstacles for designers learning a scripting language to overcome is the concept that variable names in and of themselves have no meaning or value to the computer. Remember that the computer can't perform anything unless you tell it to. Even though any given scripting language has a certain set of built-in properties and functions, variables can simplify your scripting workload by creating shortcuts or aliases to other elements of the ActionScript language. One prime example of a "shortcut" variable is the pathname to a deeply nested Movie Clip instance, such as:

```
_root.birdAnim.birdHouse.birdNest.birdEgg
```

truncated to a variable named `pathToEgg` as:

```
pathToEgg = _root.birdAnim.birdHouse.birdNest.birdEgg;
```

Once `pathToEgg` is declared and given a value, then we can reuse it without referring to the lengthy path name, as in:

```
with(pathToEgg){
    gotoAndPlay("start");
}
```

The important concept here is that you could just as easily have given `pathToEgg` a different name, such as `myPath`, or `robPath`, or whatever word(s) you'd like to use. As long as the syntax and formatting of the expression is correct, you have nothing to worry about.

Another example of a variable that stores path information is the URL to a Web resource, such as a CGI script. Oftentimes, you may have different server URLs for testing and deployment. Instead of changing the URL in every action of the Flash document, you can use a variable name. That way, you only need to change your variable's value once. In the following sample code, we set a `serverURL` variable to the actual URL we want to access. We then refer to that `serverURL` name in other actions, such as `getURL()`.

```
serverURL = "http://www.theMakers.com/?section=rbase";
getURL(serverURL);
```

Note Variables in ActionScript are "typed," meaning that their value is explicitly set to be either a string, number, Boolean, or object. When working with variables, you must therefore know what data type the value is. We discuss data typing in Chapter 26, "Using Functions and Arrays."

Variables in ActionScript are attached to the timeline of the movie or Movie Clip instance on which they are created. If you create a variable x on the Main Timeline, that variable is available for other scripting actions on that timeline. However, from other Movie Clip timelines, the variable is not directly accessible. To access the value of a variable on another timeline (such as a Movie Clip instance), enter the target path to the clip instance in which the variable resides, a dot (`.`), and then enter the variable name. For instance, this statement sets the variable `foo` to be equal to the value of the variable `bar` in Movie Clip instance named `ball`:

```
foo = _root.ball.bar;
```

Whereas this statement sets the variable `bar` to be equal to the value of the variable `foo` on the Main Timeline:

```
bar = _root.foo;
```

Tip Variables in ActionScript are not case-sensitive and cannot start with a number.

Flash MX ActionScript introduces a new location to store variables, independent of any timeline: `_global`. You can access global variables from any object or timeline in the Flash movie—hence the name global. You only need to specify the `_global` path to assign a value to the global variable. To read a global variable, you simply specify the name. For example, on frame 1 of the Main Timeline, you can specify the following ActionScript in the Actions panel:

```
_global.firstName = "George";
```

Then, if you wanted to use the firstName variable within a Movie Clip instance's timeline, you simply refer to the variable firstName. The following code will insert the firstName variable into a TextField object named user. This code would be placed inside of a Movie Clip symbol containing the TextField object:

```
user.text = firstName;
```

Even though the _global path is not specified, Flash MX will look for a variable named firstName on the current timeline. If a variable by that name does not exist on the current timeline, Flash Player 6 will look in _global for the variable and return any value for that variable.

Caution   You need to publish your Flash documents as Flash 6 movies to use the _global path.

String literals

In programmer speak, a string is any combination of alphanumeric characters. By themselves, they have no meaning. It is up to you to assign something meaningful to them. For example, giving a variable the name firstName doesn't mean much. We need to assign a value to the variable firstName to make it meaningful, and we can do something with it. For example, if firstName = "Susan", we could make something specific to "Susan" happen.

You can also use much simpler name/value pairs, such as i = 0, to keep track of counts. If you want a specific Movie Clip animation to loop only three times, you can increment the value of i by 1 (for example, i = i + 1, i += 1, and i ++ all do the same thing) each time the animation loops back to the start. Then, you can stop the animation when it reaches the value of 3.

Expressions

Flash uses the term *expression* to refer to two separate kinds of code fragments in ActionScript. An expression is either (a) a phrase of code used to compare values in a Conditional or a Loop (these are known as *conditional expressions*), or (b) a snippet of code that is interpreted at runtime (these are known as *numeric expressions* and *string expressions*). We discuss conditional expressions later in this chapter.

Numeric and string expressions are essentially just segments of ActionScript code that are dynamically converted to their calculated values when a movie runs. For instance, suppose you have a variable, y, set to a value of 3. In the statement x = y + 1, the y + 1 on the right side of the equal sign is an expression. Hence, when the movie runs, the statement x = y + 1 actually becomes x = 4, because the value of y (which is 3) is retrieved (or "interpreted") and the calculation 3 + 1 is performed. Numeric and string expressions are an extremely potent part of ActionScript because they permit nearly any of the options for actions to be set based on mathematical calculations and external variables rather than requiring fixed information. Consider these two examples:

✦ The Type option of a goto action could be set as an expression that returns a random number in a certain range, sending the movie to a random frame.

✦ The URL option in a getURL action could be made up of a variable that indicates a server name and a literal string, which is the file path.

As we mentioned in an earlier section, to change all the URLs in your movie from a staging server to a live server you'd just have to change the value of the server variable. Anywhere that you see the word *expression* in any action options, you can use an interpreted ActionScript expression to specify the value of the option. Just enter the code, and then check the Expression option.

To use a string inside an expression, simply add quotation marks around it. Anything surrounded by quotation marks is taken as a literal string. For example, the conditional: if (status == ready) wrongly checks whether the value of the variable status is the same as the value of the nonexistent variable ready. The correct conditional would check whether the value of status is the same as the string "ready" by quoting it, as in: if (status == "ready").

You can even have expressions that indirectly refer to previously established variables. In ActionScript, you can use the dot syntax (and array access operators) to indirectly refer to variables, or you can use Flash 4's eval() function (to maintain backward compatibility).

We like to use the phrase "setting and getting" to help beginners understand how equations and expressions work in ActionScript code. An equation is any line of code that sets an object or variable to a new value. The order of syntax terms can be confusing to designers and developers new to code writing. Do you specify a value first? How do you know where to insert the = sign? If you remember the phrase "setting and getting", you'll know how to write basic equations. The variable you want to set (or assign a new value) is always on the left side of the equation, while the new value is always on the right.

```
what you want to set = the value you want to get
```

For example, if you wanted to set a variable named currentTime to the amount of time that has elapsed since the Flash movie started playing in the Flash Player, then you would place currentTime on the left side of the equation, and the actual value of the time on the right side:

```
current time in the movie = the number of milliseconds that have elapsed
```

Translated into actual code, this would be

```
currentTime = getTimer();
```

Again, another important aspect of variables to remember is that the name of a variable is quite arbitrary. What we called currentTime could just as well be named myTime, movieTime, elapsedTime—or whatever you want to call it. As long as you consistently refer to your variable's name in subsequent ActionScript code, everything will work as expected.

Array access operators

If you have a variable called name_1, you can write the expression _root["name_" + "1"] to refer to the value of name_1. How is this useful? If you have more than one variable, but their prefixes are the same (for example, name_1, name_2, name_3, and so on), you can write an expression with two variables as a generic statement to refer to any one of the previously established variables: _root["name" + i], where i can be any predefined number.

eval() function and Flash 4's Set Variable

If you want to use old-fashioned ActionScript to indirectly refer to variable names and values, you have two ways to go about it:

✦ Use the `Set Variable` action, specifying the variable name as a Slash-notated expression:

```
set("/name_" add i, "Robert Reinhardt");
```

✦ Use the `eval()` function, specifying the variable as an expression:

```
eval("_root.name_" add i) = "Robert Reinhardt";
```

Variables as declarations

In most scripting languages, you usually don't have to declare a variable without its value; that is, you don't need to say variable `firstName` and then address it again with a value. In Flash ActionScript, you don't need to pre-establish a variable in order to invoke it. If you want to create a variable on the fly from a Movie Clip to the Main Timeline, you can. Most variables that you use in Flash will be declared in a timeline's keyframes. Let's create a couple of simple variables in a Flash document.

1. Open a new Flash document (File ➪ New).

2. Rename Layer 1 to **actions**.

3. Select frame 1 in the Timeline window, and open the Actions panel by pressing the F9 key. In the panel's options menu, switch to Expert mode. Type the following action in the Script pane. See Figure 24-3.

```
firstName = "Franklin";
```

Figure 24-3: A variable declaration in the Actions panel.

4. Save your Flash document as **variable_frame.fla**, and test it (Ctrl+Enter or ⌘+Enter). Choose Debug ➪ List Variables. In the Output window, you will see the following line of text:

```
Variable _level0.firstName = "Franklin"
```

As you can see in this example, the `firstName` variable is shown at `_level0`, which is the `_root` of the current Flash movie. All variables belong to a specific timeline or object.

Variables as text fields

Since Flash 4, text could be specified as *text fields*. A text field can be used as a dynamic text container whose content can be updated via ActionScript and/or the intervention of a server-side script (known in Flash MX as *Dynamic text*), or it can accept input from the user (known in Flash MX as *Input text*).

You can access a text field's properties by selecting the text field and opening the Property inspector. In the inspector, you can define the parameters of the text object, including its Var (for Variable) name and instance name.

New Feature

Text fields in Flash MX are now `TextField` objects. The instance name of a `TextField` object should be different than the Var name. In fact, we recommend that you do not specify a Var name for text fields in Flash 6-compatible movies — some components such as the ScrollBar will not work if you target the Var name of text field.

An Input text field is editable when the Flash movie is played in the Flash Player; the user can type text into the text field. This newly typed text becomes the value of the text field's Var name, or the new Text property of the text field. On a login screen, you can create an Input text field with an instance name `login`, where the user enters his/her name, such as Joe. In ActionScript, this would be received as `login.text = "Joe"`. Any text that you type into a text field during the authoring process will be that property's initial value.

To review this process of text fields and variable names, let's create a simple example.

1. Create a new Flash document (File ➪ New). Rename Layer 1 to **textfield**.

2. Open the Property inspector (Window ➪ Properties). Choose the Text tool, and click once on the Stage. Extend the text field to accommodate at least five characters. In the Property inspector, choose **Input Text** in the drop-down menu located at the top-left corner of the inspector. Click the **Show border** button in the inspector. In the <Instance Name> field, assign the instance name **firstName**. In the Var field, assign the name **firstName_var**. Refer to Figure 24-4.

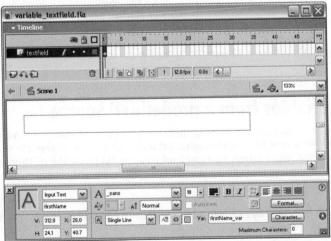

Figure 24-4: The Property inspector settings for the Input Text field

3. Save your Flash document as **variable_textfield.fla**, and test it (Ctrl+Enter or ⌘+Enter). In the Test Movie window, type your name into the `firstName` text field. Then, choose Debug ➪ List Variables. Among other information, you will see the following lines of text:

```
Variable _level0.firstName_var = "Holly"
Edit Text: Target="_level0.firstName"
    variable = "firstName_var",
    text = "Holly",
```

Note that this sample assumes that the name Holly was typed into the text field.

This simple exercise demonstrates how the Var assignment of a `TextField` object differs from the instance name assignment. The actual text displayed in the `TextField` object can be accessed in two ways: 1) as a variable called `firstName_var`, or 2) as a property of the `TextField` object, `firstName.text`. Dynamic text fields behave in the same manner as well.

Cross-Reference

For an introduction to all of the different types of text fields, read Chapter 8, "Working with Text." We will explore more ActionScript-related aspects of text fields in Chapter 31, "Applying HTML and Text Field Formatting."

Declaring Variables in ActionScript

There are several ways to establish, or declare, variables in a Flash movie. You can create them directly with ActionScript (or with `TextField` objects, as shown in the last section), load them from a text file or server-side script, or include them in HTML tags.

Using actions to define variables

The most common way to create a variable is to type the variable's name and value in the Script pane of the Actions panel, on a specific timeline's keyframe. Most basic variables will have values that are string literals.

If you are using Normal mode in the Actions panel, a `var` action has one option: variables. Note that the `var` action can be used for local variables that only exist for the duration of a function execution.

Cross-Reference

We discuss local variables in Chapter 26, "Using Functions and Arrays."

Loading variables from a predefined source

You can also establish variables by loading them from an external source, such as a text file located on your Web server or even through a database query or a server-side script. By using the `loadVariables()` action, you can load variables in this fashion. There are three primary options for the `loadVariables` action: URL, Location, and Variables. See Figure 24-5 for the Normal mode view of `loadVariables()`.

Note

There's more than one way to load data into Flash 6-compatible movies. See the cross-reference note at the end of this section.

URL specifies the source of the variables to be loaded. This can be a relative link to the variable source (you don't need to enter the full path of the resource). You can specify whether this URL value is a literal value (`"http://www.theMakers.com/cgi-bin/search.pl"`) or an expression that uses a variable or a combination of variables (`serverURL + scriptPath + scriptApp`). If you want to point to a specific file, type its relative path and name here. If you want to access a database that returns dynamic data, insert the path to the script, such as `"http://www.domain.com/cgi-bin/search.pl"`.

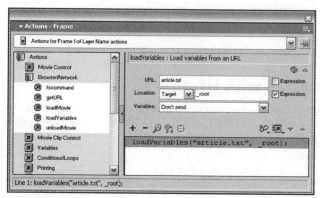

Figure 24-5: The options of the loadVariables action

The Location option determines where the variables are to be loaded. You can send the name/value pairs to a level or a timeline target. If you want the variables to be available on the Main Timeline, use `_root` or `_level0`. You can also specify a Movie Clip target using a relative or absolute address. To load to the current Movie Clip (the one initiating the `loadVariables` action), use the target `this`.

The last option is Variables, and this drop-down menu specifies whether you are sending and loading (in other words, receiving) variables. If you want to load variables from a static source, like a text file, you should choose Don't Send. If you are sending a query to a database-driven engine, then you will need to choose either GET or POST. Note that the use of `loadVariables` in the GET or POST method means that you are sending variables declared on the active time-line to the specified URL, which, in turn, will send name/value pairs back to the Flash movie.

The formatting of name/value pairs is standard URL-encoded text. If you want to encode name/values in a text file (or a database), you need to use the following format:

```
variable=value&variable=value...
```

Basically, in URL-encoded text, name/value pairs are joined by an ampersand (&). To join multiple terms in a value, use the plus (+) symbol, as in:

```
name1=Joe+Smith&name2=Susan+Deboury
```

New Feature There are several ways to load data into a Flash movie. Flash MX introduces the new `LoadVars` object, which gives you more control over dynamic data. The `LoadVars` object is discussed in Chapter 30, "Sending Data In and Out of Flash."

Sending variables to URLs

You can also send variables to a URL by using the `getURL` action. Any name/value pairs that are declared on the active timeline will be sent along with the `getURL` action, if a variable send method is defined (GET or POST). Note that `getURL` is only used to send variables out of a Flash movie—it will not retrieve or load any subsequent name/value pairs. If you use a `getURL` action on a Movie Clip timeline as follows:

```
firstName = "Robert";
getURL("/cgi-bin/form.cgi", "_blank", "GET");
```

the Flash movie will send the following request to your server:

```
http://www.server.com/cgi-bin/form.cgi?firstName=Robert;
```

The output of the `form.cgi` script would be opened in a new browser window (`"_blank"`).

Establishing variables with HTML

You can also send variables to Flash movies in the `<EMBED>` and `<OBJECT>` tags that call the Flash movie. In the SRC attribute of `<EMBED>` or the `PARAM NAME=movie` subtag of the `<OBJECT>` tag, attach the name/value pairs to the end of the Flash movie filename, separated by a question mark (?).

```
<OBJECT...>
<PARAM NAME=movie VALUE="flash.swf?name=Rob">
<EMBED SRC="flash.swf?name=Rob">
```

This method will work with Flash 4, 5, and 6 movies. However, Flash Player 6 can recognize a new HTML attribute, FLASHVARS. Now, you can specify longer strings of name/value pairs that will be declared in the Flash movie as soon as it loads into the Flash Player. The previous method that we showed is limited to strings that are about 1024 characters long (depending on the Web browser), which include the movie's full URL. With this new FLASHVARS attribute, you don't need to rely on the URL of the movie. Here's an example of declaring a few variables with the FLASHVARS attribute:

```
<OBJECT...>
<PARAM NAME=movie NAME="flash.swf">
<PARAM NAME=flashvars
NAME="firstName=Gregory&lastName=Smith&address=1234+Hollywood+Way">
<EMBED SRC="flash.swf"
FLASHVARS="firstName=Greg&lastName=Smith&street=1234+Broadway">
```

In practical use, you would not hard code the name/value pairs directly into the HTML document. You can use client-side JavaScript or server-side scripting (like ASP or ColdFusion) to dynamically "write" the name/value pairs into the HTML document before it is served to the user's Web browser.

Creating Expressions in ActionScript

You can write expressions either by manually typing in the primary option fields of ActionScript commands, or by dragging and dropping actions from action booklets in the Actions panel. There are no scripting wizards in Flash; Flash MX will not automatically script anything for you. However, it will provide you with booklets of operators, objects, and functions available in the ActionScript language.

New Feature In a sense, components perform many features for you automatically. Components contain built-in ActionScript to perform their tasks.

Operators

Operators perform combinations, mathematical equations, and value comparisons. See Table 24-1 for a list of common operators in the ActionScript language.

General and numeric operators

These operators are used for common mathematical operations of adding, subtracting, multiplying, and dividing. You can also use these operators to compare numeric values, such as > or <.

```
if (results > 1)
name = "Robert";
_root["name_" + i] = newName;
```

String operators

The Flash 4–specific operator add joins one value with another value or expression. If you want to concatenate two variables to create a new variable, use the add string operator. Again, this syntax should only be used for Flash 4 movies.

```
set ("fullName", firstName add " " add lastName);
```

Logical operators

These operators join several expressions to create conditions. We discuss these further in the "Checking conditions: If. . .Else actions" section of this chapter.

```
// Flash 5 syntax below

if (results > 1 && newResults < 10){
   // do something...
}

// Flash 4 syntax below

if (results > Number("1") and newResults < Number("10")){
   // do something...
}
```

Table 24-1 describes the ActionScript operators available in Flash 4 and higher syntax.

Table 24-1: ActionScript Operators

Flash 5+	Flash 4	Definition
+	+	Adds number values and joins (concatenates) strings in Flash 5
-	-	Subtracts number values
*	*	Multiplies number values
/	/	Divides number values
=	=	Equals; used for assignment of variables, properties, methods, and so on in Flash 5; can be used for comparison in Flash 4

Continued

Table 24-1: *(continued)*

Flash 5+	Flash 4	Definition
==	=	Equals; used for comparison in `if/else . . . if` conditions
!=	<>	Does not equal
<	<	Less than
>	>	Greater than
<=	<=	Less than or equal to
>=	>=	Greater than or equal to
( )	( )	Group operations together, as in `x = (x+y) * 3;`
" "	" "	Indicate that the enclosed value should be interpreted as a string, not as an expression
==	eq	Is equal to; for example, `if (name == "derek")` or `if (name eq "derek")`
=== (F6)	N/A	Strict equality operator; both of the compared values must be the same data type and value. This operator is compatible only with Flash Player 6.
!=	ne	Is not equal to
!== (F6)	N/A	Strict inequality operator; both of the compared values must have different values and data types. This operator is compatible only with Flash Player 6.
<	lt	Alphabetically before; if the strings compared have multiple characters, the first character determines the alphabetical position
>	gt	Alphabetically after
<=	le	Alphabetically before or the same as
>=	ge	Alphabetically after or the same as
+	add	Join two strings together or add a string to a variable
&&	and	Logical comparison; requires that two or more conditions be met in a single comparison
||	or	Logical comparison; requires that one of two or more conditions be met in a single comparison
!	not	Logical comparison; requires that the opposite of a condition to be met in a single comparison

Checking conditions: if. . .else actions

Conditions lie at the heart of logic. To create an intelligent machine (or application), we need to create a testing mechanism. This mechanism (called a conditional) needs to operate on rather simple terms as well. Remember the true/false tests that you took in grade school? `if/else` statements work on a similar principle: If the condition is true, execute a set of actions. If the condition is false, disregard the enclosed actions and continue to the next condition or action.

You can simply create isolated `if` statements that do not employ an `else` (or `then`) statement. Solitary `if` statements are simply ignored if the condition is false. `else` statements are used as a default measure in case the tested condition proves false. `else if` statements continue to test conditions if the previous `if` (or `else if`) was false. Refer to following examples for more insight:

✦ **Basic `if` statement:** The code between the curly braces is ignored if the condition is false.

```
if (condition is true){
      then execute this code
}
```

✦ **Extended `if`/`else if`/`else` statement:** If the first condition is true, code immediately after the first condition is executed and the remaining `else if` and `else` statements are disregarded. However, if the first condition is not true, the second condition is tested. If the second condition is true, its code executes and all other statements in the `if` group are ignored. If all conditions prove false, then the code between the curly braces of the final `else` is executed.

```
if ( first condition is true){
    then execute this code
} else if (second condition is true){
    then execute this code
} else {
    otherwise, execute this code
}
```

In production, you could have an `if`/`else` structure that assigned the value of one variable based on the value of another, such as:

```
if (x == 1){
  name = "Margaret";
} else if (x == 2){
  name = "Michael";
} else {
  name = "none";
}
```

Caution

Do not use a single = sign in a condition, as this will actually set the variable's value. For example, if you wrote `if (x = 1){}`, then ActionScript will actually set x = 1, and not check whether x's value is equal to 1. Moreover, the condition would always evaluate to `true`. In our experience, many beginners make this common mistake in their ActionScript code. We can't emphasize enough the importance of making sure you use an == operator in `if` and `else if` expressions for "is equal to" comparisons.

In Normal mode, you can add an `if` statement in ActionScript by choosing the `if` action from the plus (+) button in the top-left corner of the Actions panel, or by selecting it from the Actions ➪ Conditions/Loops booklet. In the Condition text field, enter the expression that identifies what circumstance must exist for the statements in your conditional to be executed. Remember that, in your expression, literal strings must be quoted, and the == operator must be used for string or numeric comparisons. To add an `else` clause, select the first line of the `if` statement, and then double-click the `else` or `else if` action in the Actions ➪ Conditions/Loops booklet.

You can join two conditions using logical compound operators such as and (&&), or (||), or not (!), as in:

```
if (results >1 && newResults < 10){
    gotoAndPlay ("end");
} else if (results > 1 ! newResults < 10) {
    gotoAndPlay ("try_again");
}
```

In this sample code, the first if statement has two expressions — both need to be true in order for the gotoAndPlay("end"); code to execute. If both are not true, the else if condition executes. If the first condition is true and the second condition is not true, the gotoAndPlay("try_again"); code will execute. If neither the if nor the else if conditions are true, then no code will be executed.

We'll take a look at a step-by-step example of if statements in the exercise at the end of this chapter.

Branching conditions with switch() and case

In Flash MX ActionScript, you can now use switch() and case statements. switch() and case can replace extended if and else if actions. Instead of declaring a true/false expression (as is done with if statements), switch() uses an expression that can return any value — you are not limited to true and false conditions with switch(). In pseudo-code, a switch() code structure would look like this:

```
test a value
    if the value equals this expression
        then execute this code
    if the value equals this expression
        then execute this code
    if none of the expressions match the value
        then execute this code
end test
```

In the previous code example, one or more "if" statements (called case clauses) could execute. Meaning, the tested value could execute more than one segment of code nested within the clauses. You could translate the previous pseudo-code into the following ActionScript code:

```
currentFrame = _root._currentframe;
switch(currentFrame){
    case 10:
        helpBox.gotoAndStop("products");
    case 20:
        helpBox.gotoAndStop("services");
    case 30:
        helpBox.gotoAndStop("contact");
    default:
        helpBox._x = _root._xmouse;
        helpBox._y = _root._ymouse;
}
```

In the previous code example, while it's only possible for currentFrame to equal one value, the default clause will also execute — regardless of the value of currentFrame. However, you may not want to execute the default clause (or multiple case clauses). In this situation, you need to use the break action to "escape" the switch() action. The break action prevents subsequent clauses from being evaluated.

In the "Loops" section later in this chapter, the `break` action is discussed in more detail.

In the following code, only one clause can execute:

```
currentFrame = _root._currentframe;
switch(currentFrame){
    case 10:
        helpBox.gotoAndStop("products");
        break;
    case 20:
        helpBox.gotoAndStop("services");
        break;
    case 30:
        helpBox.gotoAndStop("contact");
        break;
    default:
        helpBox._x = _root._xmouse;
        helpBox._y = _root._ymouse;
}
```

You can use `switch()` actions for many other situations. If you wanted to make a card game in Flash, you could use a `switch()` expression to pick a card suit based on a random number:

```
1.  suitNum = Math.round(Math.random()*3);
2.  switch(suitNum){
3.      case 0:
4.          suit = "diamonds";
5.          break;
6.      case 1:
7.          suit = "spades";
8.          break;
9.      case 2:
10.         suit = "hearts";
11.         break;
12.     case 3:
13.         suit = "clubs";
14.         break;
15. }
16. cardFace.gotoAndStop(suit);
```

In this code, a random number is picked (line 1), and used as an expression in the `switch()` action (line 2). The random number (represented as a variable named `suitNum`) will then be matched to a `case` clause. The matching clause will set a variable named `suit` to equal a specific card suit and exit the `switch()` action (lines 3 through 15). A Movie Clip instance named `cardFace` will go to and stop on a frame named after one of the card suits (line 16).

In a working example of a card game, the `switch()` code for the suit matching would occur within a function. We discuss functions in Chapter 26, "Using Functions and Arrays."

Note The switch(), case, and default actions can be used in Flash 4, 5, and 6 movies. Even though the switch() syntax was only introduced in Flash MX, the ActionScript will be compiled to be compatible with Flash Player 4 or 5 if you choose these versions in the Version menu of the Publish Settings' Flash tab.

Loops

A loop is a container for a statement or series of statements that are repeated as long as a specified condition is exists. A basic loop has three parts: the condition, the list of statements to be repeated, and a counter update. There are four types of loops in ActionScript:

✦ while

✦ do . . . while

✦ for

✦ for . . . in

Each of these loop types has a specific use. Depending on the repetitive actions you wish to loop, you need to decide how best to accommodate your code with loop actions.

while(*condition*){ *actions* }

In this loop type, the condition of the loop is evaluated first, and, if it is true, the actions within the curly braces will be executed. The actions will loop indefinitely (causing a script error) unless there is a way out of the loop — a counter update. A counter update will increment (or decrement) the variable used in the while condition. Here you see a breakdown of a typical while loop. Note that a variable used in the condition is usually set just before the while action is executed.

```
count = 1;  // Initial variable
while (count <= 10){  // Condition
  _root["clip_" + count]._xscale = 100/count; // Statements to be repeated
  count = count + 1; // Counter update
}   // Termination of loop
```

In this example, a variable named count starts with a value of 1. The first time the while action executes, count's value is less than (or equal to) 10. Therefore, the actions within the curly braces are executed. The first action in the loop uses the count value to form the name of a Movie Clip instance, clip_1, and alter its X Scale property by a value of 100/1 (which is equal to 100). Then, the count variable is incremented by 1, giving it a new value of 2. The while condition is then re-evaluated.

The second time the while action is executed, count's value, 2, is still less than (or equal to) 10. Therefore, the actions within the curly braces are executed again. This time, though, the first action in the loop will address the clip_2 instance's X Scale property, and make that property's value 50 (100/2 = 50). Then, count will be incremented by 1, giving it a new value of 3. Again, the while condition is re-evaluated.

The while condition will continue to execute its nested actions until count exceeds a value of 10. Therefore, clip_1 through clip_10 will show a decrease in X Scale.

Note This type of loop was called the Loop While action in Flash 4.

do{ *actions* } while (*condition*);

This type of loop is very similar to the `while` loop discussed previously, with one important exception: The actions in the `do{}` nesting will always be executed at least once. In a `do . . . while` loop, the condition is evaluated after the actions in the loop are executed. If the `while` condition is `true`, the actions in the `do{}` nesting will be executed again. If the `while` condition is `false`, the loop will no longer execute.

```
count = 1; // Initial variable
do{ // do loop
  _root["clip_" + count]._xscale = 100/count; // Statements to be repeated
  count = count + 1; // Counter update
} while (count <= 1); // Condition
```

In this example, the actions within the `do{}` nesting will execute automatically without checking any condition. Therefore, the X Scale of `clip_1` will be set to 100, and the `count` value will increase by 1, giving it a new value of 2. After the actions execute once, the condition is checked. Because the value of `count` is not less than (or equal to) 1, the loop does not continue to execute.

for(*initialize; condition; next*){ *actions* }

The `for` loop is a supercondensed `while` loop. Instead of assigning, checking, and reassigning a variable action in three different actions, a `for` loop enables you to define, check, and reassign the value of a counter variable.

```
for(i = 1; i <= 10; i++){ // Initial variable value, condition, and update
  _root["clip_" + i]._xscale = 100/i; // Statements to be repeated
} // Termination of loop
```

This `for` loop does exactly the same as the `while` loop example we used earlier. When the loop is started, the variable i is given a starting value of 1. A condition for the loop is specified next, i <= 10. In this case, we want the loop to repeat the nested actions until the value of i exceeds 10. The third parameter of the `for` loop, i++, indicates that i's value should be increased by 1 with each pass of the loop. Note that this parameter can use ++ (to increase by 1) or -- (to decrease by 1) operators. You can also use expressions like i = i*2 for the update.

for(*variableIterant* in *object*){ *actions* }

The final type of loop, `for . . . in`, is the most complex looping mechanism. A `for . . . in` loop does not need a condition statement. Rather, this loop works with a find-and-replace keyword mechanism. Basically, a *variableIterant* is declared, which is simply a placeholder for a property or position index within an object or array, respectively. For every occurrence of the variableIterant, the actions within the `for . . . in {}` nesting will be executed. The `for . . . in` loop can only be used with objects and arrays, and even then, not all properties of this elements can be enumerated.

```
for(name in _root){ // Placeholder and object
  _root[name]._xscale = 50; // Statements to be repeated
} // Termination of loop
```

In the preceding code example, the term `name` is used to designate a property of the `_root` timeline. In this case, we want to change all Movie Clip instances on the Main Timeline to a 50 percent X Scale value. We don't need to specify the actual target paths of each individual instance — the `for . . . in` loop will search for all instances on the Main Timeline, apply the change, and exit the loop.

Although this might look a bit confusing, it can be more helpful than you can imagine. Have you ever had a bunch of nested Movie Clip instances that all need to play at the same time? In Flash 4, you would have had to use several `tellTarget(){}` actions, each one specifying the target path. You could use a while loop to shorten the lengthy code, but, even still, you would need to list the specific parts of the each Movie Clip path, as in:

```
count = 1;
while(count <= 10){
    path = eval("_root.clip_" + count);
    tellTarget(path){
        play();
    }
    count++;
}
```

In Flash 4, the preceding code block would tell `clip_1` through `clip_10` to start playing. But what if you didn't know (or care to remember) all the paths to several differently named Movie Clip instances? For example, if you had a Movie Clip instance named `nestAnim` with several nested Movie Clip instances with different names (for example, `squareAnim`, `triangleAnim`, and `circleAnim`), you would have to specifically name these instances as targets. In Flash 5 or MX, the `for . . . in` loop would let you control any and all nested Movie Clip instances simultaneously:

```
for(name in nestAnim){
    nestAnim[name].play();
}
```

With just three lines of code, all Movie Clip instances in the `nestAnim` Movie Clip instance will start to play. How? Remember that the variableIterant `name` is simply a placeholder for a property of the `nestAnim` Movie Clip object. The `for . . . in` loop will find every occurrence of an instance inside of `nestAnim`. And the word `name` has no significance. We could use a variableIterant `myName`, and everything would still work fine. Think of the variableIterant as a wildcard in file searches or directory listings in MS-DOS or UNIX:

```
nestAnim[*].play();
```

Although this syntax won't work with ActionScript, it does illustrate the processing of a `for . . . in` loop. Everything and anything that is playable on the `nestAnim` timeline will play.

On the CD-ROM Check out the mcPlay.fla and forInLoop.fla files, located in the ch24 folder of the *Flash MX Bible* CD-ROM.

break

The `break` action is not a type of loop — it is an action that enables you to quickly exit a loop if a subordinate condition exists. Suppose you wanted to loop an action that hides, at most, `clip_1` through `clip_10` (out of a possible 20 Movie Clip instances), but you want to have a variable control the overall limit of the loop, as `upperLimit` does in the following code block. `upperLimit`'s value could change at different parts of the presentation, but at no point do we want to hide more than `clip_1` through `clip_10`. We could use a `break` action in a nested `if` action to catch this:

```
count = 1;
while(count <= upperLimit){
```

```
    if(count > 10){
       break;
    }
    _root["clip_" + count]._visible = false;
    count++;
}
```

Tip

You can use break statements to catch errors in your loops (such as during a debug pro-cess) . However, you may want to check out Flash MX's new breakpoint feature in the Actions and Debugger panels. For more information on this feature, read Chapter 36, "Solving Problems in Your Movies" on the *Flash MX Bible CD-ROM.*

continue

Like the break action, continue enables you to exit the execution of actions within a loop. However, a continue action won't exit the loop action. It simply restarts the loop (and con-tinues evaluating the current condition). Usually, you will place a continue action with an if nest — otherwise, it will always interrupt the actions within the loop action. For example, if you wanted to omit a particular value from going through the loop actions, you could use the continue action to bypass that value. In the following code block, we will hide clip_1 through clip_10, except for clip_5:

```
count = 1;
while(count <= 10){
  if(count == 5){
    count++;
    continue;
  }
_root["clip_" + count]._visible = false;}
```

Adding a loop to your actions list

To create a loop, add one of the loop-type actions in the Actions panel, using the plus (+) button in the top-left corner of the panel (or selecting it from the Actions booklet). In the Condition text field, enter an expression that describes the conditions under which the loop should continue repeating. Before the end of the loop, be sure to update whatever the loop relies on in order to continue, usually a counter. If you forget to update a counter, you will be stuck forever in the loop, and Flash will imperiously stop the script from continuing.

Loops in ActionScript are not appropriate for running background processes that listen for conditions to become true elsewhere in the movie. While a loop is in progress, the screen is not updated and no mouse events are captured, so most Flash actions are effectively not exe-cutable from within a loop. Loop actions are best suited to abstract operations such as string handling (for example, to check each letter of a word to see whether it contains an @ symbol) and dynamic variable assignment.

Loops to execute repetitive actions, which affect tangible objects in the movie, should be created as repeating frames in Movie Clips. To create a permanently running process, make a Movie Clip with two keyframes. On the first frame, call the subroutine or add the statements that you want to execute; on the second frame use a gotoAndPlay(1); action to return to the first frame. Alternatively, you can use the onClipEvent(enterFrame) or onEnterFrame handler to execute repetitive actions.

Cross-Reference   The `onClipEvent` and `onEnterFrame` handler are discussed in the next chapter, "Controlling Movie Clips."

Properties

Properties are characteristics (such as width and height) of movies and Movie Clips that can be retrieved and set. You can use variables to store the current value of a given property, such as:

```
xPos = _root._xmouse;
```

which will store the current X position of the mouse pointer (relative to the Stage coordinates of the Main Timeline) in the variable `xPos`.

Cross-Reference   See Chapter 25, "Controlling Movie Clips," for more information on Movie Clip (and movie) properties.

Built-in functions

ActionScript contains a number of native programming commands known as *functions*. Among others, these functions include `getTimer`, `getVersion`, `parseFloat`, `parseInt`, `int`, `string`, `substring`, `escape`, and `unescape`. It's beyond the scope of this chapter (and this book) to discuss the practical use of every new function and ActionScript element in Flash MX. We do, however, discuss many built-in functions throughout this part of the *Flash MX Bible*.

Cross-Reference   Because ActionScript has expanded so much over the last two versions of the Flash authoring tool, Robert Reinhardt and Joey Lott created a companion book, the *Macromedia Flash MX ActionScript Bible*, to specifically address all the terms of the ActionScript language.

Creating and calling subroutines

Whether they're called functions or subroutines, most programming languages provide a mechanism for programmers to create self-contained code modules that can be executed from anywhere in a program. ActionScript supports subroutines by using the ActionScript `function` constructor. You can create functions on any timeline, and, just like Movie Clip instances, functions have absolute or relative paths that must be used to invoke them. For example, if you have the following function on a Movie Clip named `Functions`, located on the Main Timeline:

```
function makeDuplicate(target, limit){
    for(i=1;i<=limit;i++){
        _root[target].duplicateMoviecClip(target+"_"+i, i);
    }
}
```

then to invoke it from another timeline, you would execute it as follows:

```
_root.Functions.makeDuplicate("clip",5);
```

Executing it would create five duplicates of the Movie Clip instance named `clip`, naming the duplicates `clip_1`, `clip_2`, `clip_3`, `clip_4`, and `clip_5`.

Cross-Reference   We discuss functions in greater detail in the Chapter 26, "Using Functions and Arrays."

Subroutines in Flash 4 Movies

To create a subroutine in Flash 4-compatible movies, first attach an action or series of actions to a keyframe. Next, give that keyframe a label. That's it, you have a subroutine. To call your subroutine from any other keyframe or button, simply add a `call` action, and then enter the name of the subroutine into the Frame text field using the following syntax: Start with the target path to the timeline on which the subroutine keyframe resides, enter a colon (:), and then enter the subroutine name (for example: `call ("/bouncingball:getRandom")`). When you call a subroutine, all the actions on the specified keyframe are executed. The subroutine must be present on the movie timeline (either as a keyframe or an embedded Movie Clip instance) for it to work.

Subroutines in Flash 4 movies do not accept passed parameters, nor do they return any values. To simulate passing and receiving variable values, set the necessary variable values in the action list that calls the subroutine before it is called, and then have the subroutine set other variables that can be retrieved afterward by any other actions.

Make a Login Sequence with Variables

In this section, we show you how to use variables to create an interactive form in Flash that accepts or rejects user input. You will create two Input text fields into which Web visitors will type a username and password. Using ActionScript, we will check the values of the entered data with predefined name/value pairs.

Caution Do not use the following example for secure information over the Web. You could use a login sequence like this in a Flash adventure game, or modify it to work in a Flash quiz. The login information is not secure within the confines of a Flash movie (.swf file).

1. Open a new Flash document.

2. Create two text fields on one layer called **text fields**. Make each text field long enough to accommodate a single first name and/or password. For demonstration purposes, make the text in the text fields large — around 24 points. Make sure that you use a non-white fill color for the text.

3. Access the properties for each text field by selecting the text field (with the Arrow tool) and opening the Property inspector, shown in Figure 24-6. In the Text Type drop-down menu, select the **Input Text** option for both fields. For the top text field, assign the instance name **userEnter**. For the other text field, assign the Instance name **passwordEnter**, enable the Password option, and restrict the text length to 8 characters. Do not assign a Var name to either text field.

Figure 24-6: The passwordEnter variable will be an Input Text field with the Password option enabled and a restricted character length of 8 characters.

4. Create a new layer and name it **static text**. Create text blocks that describe the two text fields, as shown in Figure 24-7. For example, make a text block with the word **Login:** and another one with the word **Password:**. Align these text blocks to the left of the text fields. Note that these text blocks do not need the Input Text behavior; they should be **Static text** blocks.

Login: ☐
Password: ☐

Figure 24-7: Here we have four text areas: two Static text blocks on the left and two Input text fields on the right. The Static text cannot be altered and/or "read" by ActionScript.

5. Create a new Movie Clip symbol (Ctrl+F8 or ⌘+F8), called **errorMessage**, that displays an error message, such as INVALID or LOGIN ERROR. Rename Layer 1 of its timeline to **actions**. On that layer, the first frame of the Movie Clip should be blank with a stop(); frame action.

6. Create another layer called **labels**. On frame 2 of this layer, make a keyframe and assign it the label **start** in the <Frame Label> field of the Property inspector.

7. Then, create a new layer called **anim** and move it underneath the Actions layer. On this layer, create a tweening animation of your message fading in and out (or scaling up and down, and so on). Start the Motion Tween on frame 2 of the anim layer, underneath the start label of the Actions layer. You'll need to make the message a Graphic symbol of its own in order to tween the alpha state. Add enough frames and keyframes to cycle this message animation twice. The very last frame of the animation should have a frame action (on the Actions layer) gotoAndStop(1);. When you are finished with this step, your Movie Clip timeline should resemble the one shown in Figure 24-8.

8. In the main movie timeline (Scene 1), create a new layer called **errorMessage**. Drag the Movie Clip symbol from the Library on to the Stage. Position it underneath the user and password text fields. Select the Movie Clip instance on the Stage and access its settings in the Property inspector. Assign the instance name of errorMessage.

9. Create another layer named **labels**. Assign a frame label of start to frame 1 of the Labels layer. Add a keyframe to the frame 10 of the Labels layer, and label it **success**. Make sure all other layers on frame 10 have empty keyframes.

10. Extend all the layers to frame 20 by selecting frame 20 across all of the layers and pressing the F5 key.

11. Make a new layer called **success** and place a text block and/or other graphics suitable for a successful login entry. It should only appear on frame 10, so if necessary, move its initial keyframe to that frame. When you're finished with the step, your Stage and Main Timeline should resemble Figure 24-9.

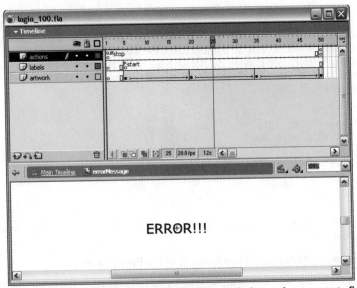

Figure 24-8: The errorMessage Movie Clip symbol contains an empty first frame and an animation that begins on the start label. This animation will play only if the user enters an incorrect login.

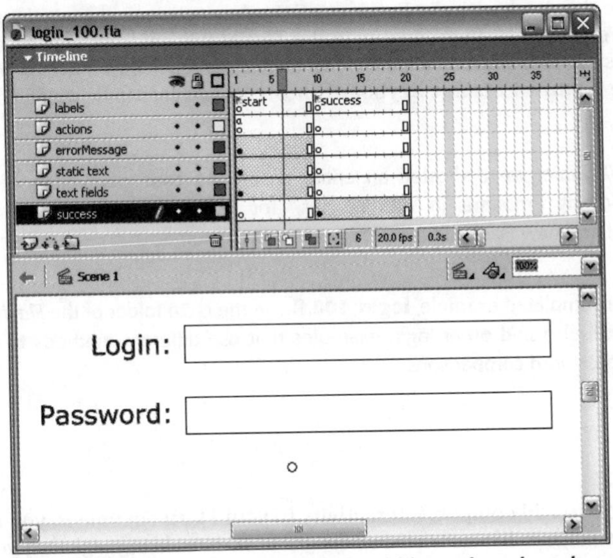

Figure 24-9: Your Main Timeline should have three key elements: a login frame, an error message Movie Clip, and a success frame.

12. Create a new layer on the Main Timeline called **button**, and make a Button symbol on it. You can make one of your own, or use one from Flash MX's Button library (Window ⇨ Common Libraries ⇨ Buttons). Place it to the right of or underneath the user and password fields. Select the Button symbol instance, and open the Actions panel. Add the following ActionScript code in the Script pane (note that the ⊃ character indicates a continuation of the same line of code; do not type or insert this character into your actual code):

```
on (release){
  if (userEnter.text == "Sandra" && ⊃
    passwordEnter.text == "colorall"){
      _root.gotoAndStop ("success");
  } else {
      _root.errorMessage.gotoAndPlay("start");
  }
}
```

You can change the userEnter.text and passwordEnter.text values to whatever string you desire.

13. Add an empty keyframe (F7) on frame 10 of the Button layer.

14. On the Main Timeline, create an **actions** layer, and place it at the top of the layer order. On the first frame, add a stop(); frame action.

15. Save the Flash document as **login_100.fla**. Test the movie's functionality with the Test Movie command (Control ⇨ Test Movie).

Most login forms like this work with the Return or Enter key active to submit the information. However, this key press also has functionality in the Test Movie environment, so assign a key press to the Button symbol instance only *after* you have tested the initial ActionScript code. You can also choose Control ⇨ Disable Keyboard Shortcuts in Test Movie mode to avoid any key press conflicts.

In the *Flash MX Bible*, we dedicated an entire chapter to code debugging. Please read Chapter 36, "Solving Problems in Your Movies," for more information about using the Debugger panel and new Flash MX features, such as breakpoints.

You can find the completed example, **login_100.fla**, in the ch24 folder of the *Flash MX Bible* CD-ROM. You will also find other login examples that use different methods to make the username and password comparisons.

Summary

✦ Before you begin to add complex interactivity to your Flash document, you need to break down the steps in the interactive process in a natural language that you can understand.

✦ After you know what you want your presentation to do, you can start to clarify the interactive steps and translate those steps into Flash-compatible actions.

✦ You can add ActionScript to your Flash document with the Actions panel. The Actions panel operates in two modes: Normal and Expert. If you want to see the options of each action in fields and drop-down menus, add actions with Normal mode. If you want the most flexibility with editing your code, use Expert mode.

✦ Variables are a programming device that enable you to store property values, strings, paths, or expressions in order to reduce the redundancy of code and to simplify the process of computing information.

✦ Variables can be declared with actions, Input or Dynamic text fields, or by loading them from an external data source, such as a CGI script, text document, or HTML query.

✦ Expressions are equations that refer to a mathematical operation, a string concatenation, or an existing code object (another variable or object value).

✦ You can use `if/else if/else` actions to add intelligence to your interactive actions. These actions test a condition and execute a certain set of actions if the condition is true.

✦ Loop actions execute a given set of actions repeatedly until a loop condition is no longer true.

✦   ✦   ✦

Controlling Movie Clips

In This Chapter

Understanding the `MovieClip` object

Working with properties of the `MovieClip` object

Creating Mouse Drag behaviors

Explaining the new MX event model

Making sliders that dynamically change properties

In Chapter 19, "Navigating Flash Timelines," we established the key role that Movie Clips have within the Flash movie structure. By having a timeline that plays separately from other timelines, Movie Clips enable multiple events to occur — independently or as part of an interaction with other Movie Clips. This chapter explores how to manipulate movie clips beyond navigation actions such as `gotoAndPlay` or `stop`.

Movie Clips: The Object Overview

Since Flash 5, the implementation of ActionScript mirrors true object-oriented programming languages. Much like JavaScript, each element in a Flash movie has a data type. A data type is simply a category to which an element belongs. In the current version of ActionScript, there are six data types available: `boolean`, `number`, `string`, `object`, `function`, and `movieclip`. For our purposes, a Movie Clip instance *is* an object, and we'll refer to it as such throughout Part VII of this book. An object is any element in Flash MX that has changeable and accessible characteristics *through ActionScript*. Objects can be user-defined (you create and name them) or predefined by the programming language. The `MovieClip` object is a predefined object, meaning that all of its characteristics are already described in the ActionScript language.

Cross-Reference

For a brief overview of object-oriented programming concepts, please review the sidebar titled *The New and Improved ActionScript* located in Chapter 19, "Navigating Flash Timelines." For more information on data types, please read Chapter 26, "Using Functions and Arrays."

A `MovieClip` object is the same Movie Clip instance we've seen in previous chapters. Any instance of a Movie Clip is a unique object in ActionScript. However, we haven't treated it like an object in our scripting. Before we can proceed with a discussion of Movie Clips as Flash movie assets, you need to understand what predefined characteristics are available in the `MovieClip` object. See Figure 25-1 for more information.

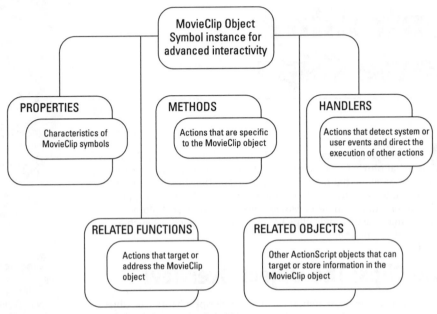

Figure 25-1: An overview of the MovieClip object

Movie Clip properties

Each Movie Clip instance has definable properties, or attributes, that control its appearance, size, and position. For example, you can move a Movie Clip instance to a new position on the Stage by changing the value of its X or Y coordinate. This property in ActionScript is denoted as _x or _y, respectively. Some properties have values that are read-only, meaning that these values can't be altered. One read-only property is _url, the value of which indicates the download location of the Movie Clip (or .swf file) such as http://www.yourserver.com/swf/background.swf. Figure 25-2 is a summary of the properties of the MovieClip object. For more information on each property, please refer to Table 25-1.

All properties are preceded by the underscore (_) character. In Table 25-1, each property has an R (as in *read*) and/or W (as in *write*) designation. All properties can be read, which means that you can retrieve that property's current value. The values of some properties can also be changed, through ActionScript. The table represents these properties with the W designation.

In Flash 4 ActionScript, these properties were retrieved by using the getProperty action. Properties are altered using the setProperty action. For Flash 5 or 6 movies, you should avoid using these actions.

Use the propInspector Movie Clip in the Library of the property_inspector.fla file, located in the ch25 folder of the *Flash MX Bible* CD-ROM to see the values of Movie Clip or Movie properties.

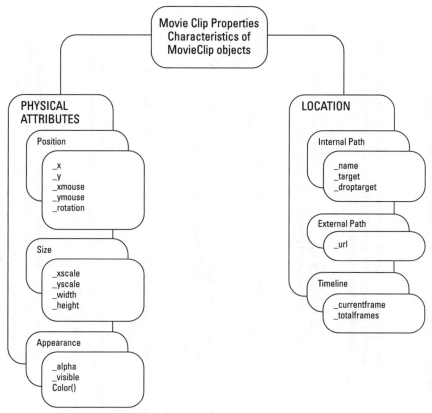

Figure 25-2: Properties of the MovieClip object

Movie Clip methods

Although the name might sound intimidating, don't be scared. Methods are simply actions that are attached to objects. As you now know, Movie Clips qualify as objects in Flash. A method looks like a regular action except that it doesn't (and in most cases, can't) operate without a dot syntax reference to a target or an object:

Action: `gotoAndPlay("start");`

becomes

Method: `_root.gotoAndPlay("start");`

As actions, interactive commands are executed from the timeline on which they are written. As methods, interactive commands are tied to specific (or dynamic) targets. Figure 25-3 lists the methods and Table 25-2 reviews every method associated with the `MovieClip` object. Some methods can be used with Movie Clip instances and with the entire Flash movie (`_root`, `_level0`, and so on), while others can be used only with Movie Clip instances. The "Flash 4" column indicates whether the method (when used as an action) is compatible in Flash Player 4. Some commands need to be written in dot syntax, as a method (designated as "M" in the table) of a timeline or `MovieClip` object. Other commands can be used as actions (designated as "A" in the table), meaning that the `MovieClip` object name need not precede the command.

Table 25-1: Flash Movie and Movie Clip Properties

Category	Property	Timeline	Flash 4	Flash 5+	Definition
Position	_x	MC	RW	RW	The horizontal distance between a Movie Clip's center point and the top-left corner of the stage upon which it resides. Increases as the clip moves to the right. Measured in pixels.
		Movie	RW	RW	
	_y	MC	RW	RW	The vertical distance between a Movie Clip's center point and the top-left corner of the stage upon which it resides. Increases as the clip moves downward. Measured in pixels.
		Movie	RW	RW	
	_xmouse	MC	N/A	R	The horizontal distance (in pixels) between the zero point of a Movie Clip (or the movie) and the current position of the mouse pointer.
		Movie	RW	R	
	_ymouse	MC	N/A	R	The vertical distance (in pixels) between the zero point of a Movie Clip (or the movie) and the current position of the mouse pointer.
		Movie	RW	R	
	_rotation	MC	RW	RW	The amount (in degrees) that a Movie Clip is rotated off plumb. Returns values set both by the Transform panel (or Transform tool) and by ActionScript.
		Movie	RW	RW	
	_xscale	MC	RW	RW	The width of a Movie Clip instance (or Movie) as a percentage of the parent symbol's actual size.
		Movie	RW	RW	
Size	_yscale	MC	RW	RW	The height of a Movie Clip instance (or movie) as a percentage of the parent symbol's actual size.
		Movie	RW	RW	
	_width	MC	R	RW	The width (in pixels) of a Movie Clip or the main Movie Stage. Determined not by the width of the canvas but by the width of the space occupied by elements on the Stage (meaning it can be less or greater than the canvas width set in movie properties).
		Movie	R	R	

Category	Property	Timeline	Flash 4	Flash 5+	Definition
	`_height`	MC	R	RW	The height (in pixels) of a Movie Clip or the main Movie Stage. Determined not by the height of the canvas but by the height of the space occupied by elements on the Stage.
		Movie	R	R	
Appearance	`_alpha`	MC	RW	RW	The amount of transparency of a Movie Clip or movie. Measured as a percentage: 100 percent is completely opaque, 0 percent is completely transparent.
		Movie	RW		
	`_visible`	MC	RW	RW	A Boolean value that indicates whether a Movie Clip instance is shown or hidden. Set to 1 (or `true`) to show; 0 (or `false`) to hide. Buttons in "hidden" movies are not active.
		Movie	RW	RW	
	`Color()`	MC	N/A	RW	`Color()` is a ActionScript object, not a property of the `MovieClip` object. Because Movie Clips can be specified as the target of the `Color` object, color values of a Movie Clip can be treated as a user-definable property. We discuss the `Color` object in Chapter 27.
		Movie	N/A	RR	
Internal Path	`_name`	MC	RW	RW	Returns or reassigns the Movie Clip instance's name (as listed in the Property inspector).
		Movie	R	R	
	`_target`	MC	R	R	Returns the exact string in Slashes notation that you'd use to refer to the Movie Clip instance. To retrieve the dot syntax path, use `eval(_target)`.
		Movie	R	R	
	`_droptarget`	MC	R	R	Returns the name (in Slashes notation) of the last Movie Clip upon which a draggable Movie Clip was dropped. To retrieve the dot syntax path, use `eval(_droptarget)`. For usage, see "Creating Draggable Movie Clips" in this chapter.
		Movie	R	R	

Continued

Table 25-1: (continued)

Category	Property	Timeline	Flash 4	Flash 5+	Definition
External Path	_url	MC	R	R	Returns the complete path to the Flash movie (.swf file) in which the action is executed, including the name of the Flash movie (.swf file) itself. Could be used to prevent a movie from being viewed if not on a particular server.
		Movie	R	R	
Timeline	_currentframe	MC	R	R	Returns the number of the current frame (for example, the frame on which the playhead currently resides) of the Movie or a Movie Clip instance.
		Movie	R	R	
	_totalframes	MC	R	R	Returns the number of total frames in a Movie or Movie Clip instance's timeline.
		Movie	R	R	
	_framesloaded	MC	R	R	Returns the number of frames that have downloaded over the network.
		Movie	R	R	
Global	_quality	Movie	N/A	RW	The visual quality of the movie. The value is a string equal to: "LOW" (no antialiasing, no bitmap smoothing), "MEDIUM" (anti-aliasing on a 2×2 grid, no bitmap smoothing), "HIGH" (anti-aliasing on a 4×4 grid, bitmap smoothing on static frames), "BEST" (anti-aliasing on a 4×4 grid, bitmap smoothing on all frames).
	_focusrect	Movie	RW	RW	A Boolean value that indicates whether a yellow rectangle is shown around buttons when accessed via the Tab key. Default is to show. When set to 0, the Up state of the button is shown instead of the yellow rectangle.
	_soundbuftime	Movie	RW	RW	The number of seconds a sound should preload before it begins playing. Default is 5 seconds.

MC = Movie Clip; R = Read property (cannot be modified); W = Write property (can be modified)

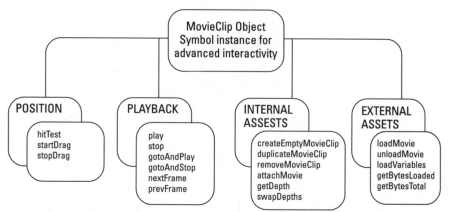

Figure 25-3: Common methods of the MovieClip object

onClipEvent: The original Movie Clip handler

In Flash 5, the onClipEvent handler was added to the ActionScript language. In Flash 4 or earlier, your only event handlers were keyframes and Button instances. In Flash 5 or higher movies, you can add actions to the wrapper of a Movie Clip instance—meaning that these actions are not added to keyframes on the Movie Clip's timeline. Nine events can be used with the onClipEvent handler. Refer to Table 25-3 for a summary of these events.

Cross-
Reference

If you would like to read a review of events and event handlers, see Chapter 18, "Understanding Actions and Event Handlers."

Let's create a simple example of onClipEvent() in action.

1. Open a new Flash MX document (File ⇨ New).

2. Draw any artwork you wish, and make the artwork a Movie Clip symbol.

3. Select the Movie Clip instance on the Stage. In the Property inspector, name the instance **tracker**.

4. With the tracker instance selected on the Stage, open the Actions panel (F9). In Expert mode, type the following code into the Script pane:

```
onClipEvent (mouseMove){
  this._x = _root._xmouse;
  this._y = _root._ymouse;
  updateAfterEvent();
}
```

This code uses onClipEvent() to track the position of the user's mouse and apply that position to the MovieClip object—effectively moving the MovieClip object with the mouse pointer. The code is executed every time the user's mouse moves. The updateAfterEvent() action will tell the Flash Player to refresh the video display each time a mouse move is detected, resulting in a smoother movement of the object.

5. Save your Flash document as **tracker_oce.fla**, and test it (Ctrl+Enter or ⌘+Enter). As you move the mouse, the artwork will follow the mouse.

Table 25-2: Common Movie and Movie Clip Methods

Category	Method	Flash 4	Definition	Usage

Position	startDrag
	M, A
		Yes	Enables the user to move a Movie Clip instance on the Stage. The Movie Clip moves (or drags) in tandem with the movements of the mouse. You can specify whether the mouse pointer locks to the center of the Movie Clip instance and if the drag area is constrained to a range of X and Y coordinates (in the parent symbol or timeline space). Constraining the drag area is useful for slider controls.	`timeline.startDrag(lock, min X, min Y, max X, max Y);`
				
				`myMC.startDrag(false, 200,0,200,200);`

	stopDrag M, A	Yes	Stops any startDrag action currently in progress. No target needs to be specified with this action.	`timeline.stopDrag();` `myMC.stopDrag();`

Playback	play
	M, A
		Yes	Starts playback from the current position of the Playhead on a specified timeline.	`timeline.play();`
				`_root.play(); // plays the Main Timeline`
				`_root.myMC.play(); // plays myMC`

	stop
	M, A
		Yes	Stops playback on a specified timeline.	`timeline.stop();`
				`_root.stop(); // stops the Main Timeline`
				`_root.myMC.stop(); // stops myMC`

	gotoAndPlay
	M, A
		Yes	Jumps the Playhead of a specified timeline to a label, frame number, or expression, and starts playing from there.	`timeline.gotoAndPlay(position);`
				`_root.myMC.gotoAndPlay("start");`
				`// plays from the "start" label of the myMC timeline`

	gotoAndStop
	M, A
		Yes	Jumps the Playhead of a specified timeline to a label, frame number, or expression, and stops playback.	`timeline.gotoAndStop(position);`
				`_root.myMC.gotoAndStop("mute");`
				`// stops playback on the "mute" label of myMC`

	nextFrame M, A	Yes	Moves the Playhead of the specified timeline to the next frame.	`timeline.nextFrame();` `_root.myMC.nextFrame();`
	prevFrame M, A	Yes	Moves the Playhead of the specified timeline to the previous frame.	`timeline.prevFrame();` `_root.myMC.prevFrame();`

Category	Method	Flash 4	Definition	Usage

Internal Assets	createEmpty MovieClip
	M
		No	Makes a blank (empty) Movie Clip instance on the Stage (or nested in another Movie Clip instance). The new instance is placed directly above the parent instance, at a specified depth. Higher depth numbers appear above lower depth numbers (for example, a Movie Clip at depth 2 is stacked above a Movie Clip at depth 1).
			
			This method works only in Flash 6 movies played in Flash Player 6.
				timeline.createEmptyMovieClip(new name, depth);*
				_root.createEmptyMovieClip("myMC", 1);
				myMC._x = 50;
				*You should not specify a new path for the copy. It will be located from the same root as the parent MC instance.

	duplicate MovieClip
	
	M, A
		Yes	Makes a copy of an existing Movie Clip instance on the Stage (or nested in another Movie Clip). The new copy is placed directly above the parent instance, at a specified depth. Higher depth numbers appear above lower depth numbers (for example, a Movie Clip at depth 2 is stacked above a Movie Clip at depth 1).	*timeline.duplicateMovieClip(new name*, depth);*
				myMC.duplicateMovieClip("myMC_2", 20);
				myMC_2._x = 200;
				*You should not specify a new path for the copy. It will be located from the same root as the parent MC instance.

	remove MovieClip M, A	Yes	Deletes a previously duplicated Movie Clip instance. When used as a method, you do not need to specify a target. You cannot remove a Movie Clip instance that is manually inserted on any timeline frame from the Library.	*timeline.removeMovieClip();* myMC_2.removeMovieClip();
	attachMovie M	No	Places an instance of a Movie Clip symbol from the Library into the specified timeline. Each attached instance requires a unique name and depth. Attached Movie Clip instances can be deleted with removeMovieClip.	*timeline.attachMovie(ID*, new name, depth);* _root.attachMovie("eye", "eye_1", 1); *You need to specify a unique identifier to attached MC symbols in the Library, using the Linkage Properties.

Continued

Table 25-2: *(continued)*

Category	Method	Flash 4	Definition	Usage

	`getDepth`
	M
		No	Returns the current depth of a duplicated (or attached) `MovieClip` object. If you attempt to retrieve the depth of a Movie Clip instance that you manually placed on the Stage, ActionScript will return -16383 as the value of `getDepth()`.
			
			This method works only in Flash 6 movies played in Flash Player 6.
				timeline.getDepth();
				`_root.attachMovie("eye", "eye_1", 1);`
				`trace(eye_1.getDepth());`

	`swapDepths`
	M
		No	Switches the depth placement of two duplicated or attached Movie Clips. This method is useful for placing one Movie Clip instance in front of (or behind) another instance.	*timeline.swapDepths(depth);*
				timeline.swapDepths(target);
				`eye_1.swapDepths(10); // depth`
				`eye_1.swapDepths(eye_2); // target`

External Assets	`loadMovie`
	M, A
		Yes	Loads an external movie (.swf file) or JPEG file into the main movie. As one of the most powerful features of Flash, this method enables you to break up your Flash movie into several smaller components, and load them as needed. This method can load movies (.swf files) or JPEG images (.jpg files) into Movie Clip targets.
			
			Note: You can only load JPEG images with `loadMovie()` if you are publishing Flash 6 movies for use in Flash Player 6. We discuss the use of JPEG files with `loadMovie()` in Chapter 28.
				timeline.loadMovie(path, send variables*);
				`myMC.loadMovie("menu.swf");`
				OR
				`myMC.loadMovie("image.jpg");`
				*You can also send Flash variables to the newly loaded .SWF file with an optional `"GET"` or `"POST"` parameter. This is discussed in Chapter 24.

	`unloadMovie` M, A	Yes	Removes an externally loaded movie (.swf file) from the main movie. This method enables you to dump movie assets when they are no longer needed. Use this method for assets loaded into Movie Clip targets.	*timeline.unloadMovie();* `myMC.unloadMovie();`

Category	Method	Flash 4	Definition	Usage
	loadVariables M, A	Yes	Loads external text-based data into the movie. This method enables you to access data (in the form of variable name/value pairs) from server-side scripts or text files, and place it in a Movie Clip target.	*timeline.loadVariables(path, send variables*)* myMC.loadVariables("info.txt"); *See note in loadMovie. We discuss loadVariables() and the new LoadVars object in Chapter 30.
	getBytesLoaded M	No	Returns the number of bytes that have streamed into the Flash Player for a specified Movie Clip (or movie).	*timeline.getBytesLoaded();* loadBytes = myMC.getBytesLoaded();

	getBytesTotal
	M
		No	Returns the total file size (in bytes) for a loading movie or Movie Clip. Combined with getBytesLoaded(), you can use this method to calculate the movie's loaded percentage.	*timeline.getBytesTotal();*
				totalBytes = myMC.getBytesTotal();
				loadBytes = myMC.getBytesLoaded();
				newPercent = (loadBytes/totalBytes)*100;

M = Method, A = Action

On the CD-ROM You can find a completed version of the file **tracker_oce.fla** in the ch25 folder of the *Flash MX Bible* CD-ROM.

Event methods: The MX Movie Clip handler

In Flash MX, event handlers for MovieClip objects can now be written and executed from any other event handler. This means that you can code the same event handlers used for onClipEvent() in keyframe or Button instance actions. While this may not seem like a monumental leap forward, this new event model allows you to create event handlers that are not directly attached to physical instances of a Movie Clip on the Stage. For a summary of common event methods, see Table 25-3.

Cross-Reference It is beyond the scope of this book to discuss all of the event methods introduced in Flash MX. Please refer to the *Macromedia Flash MX ActionScript Bible* by Robert Reinhardt and Joey Lott for more information.

To get a better idea how this event model works, let's create a simple example.

1. Create a new Flash MX document.

2. Draw some artwork, and make it a Movie Clip symbol.

3. Select the new instance on the Stage. Name the instance **tracker** in the Property inspector.

4. Create a new layer on the Main Timeline (that is, Scene 1). Name the layer **actions**.

5. Select frame 1 of the Actions layer, and open the Actions panel (F9). In Expert mode, type the following code into the Script pane:

```
tracker.onMouseMove = function (){
    this._x = _root._xmouse;
    this._y = _root._ymouse;
    updateAfterEvent();
};
```

This code adds an onMouseMove() method to the tracker instance. Each time the user's mouse moves, the function written for the method will execute. We discuss funtions in the next chapter.

6. Save your Flash document as **tracker_eventmodel.fla** and test it (Ctrl+Enter or ⌘+Enter). The artwork will follow your mouse pointer as you move it on the Stage.

On the CD-ROM You can find the completed document, **tracker_eventmodel.fla**, in the ch25 folder of the *Flash MX Bible* CD-ROM. In this folder you will also find another document that uses multiple event handlers, **tracker_eventmodel_adv.fla**.

You can continue to add more event methods to the tracker instance, for the instance to respond to mouse clicks, time elapsing, and so on.

Caution The new event model for Flash MX movies works only in Flash Player 6. If you need to use events with Movie Clips that are compatible with Flash Player 5, use onClipEvent() handlers.

Table 25-3: Common onClipEvent and MX Event Handlers

Category	onClipEvent	MX Event Handler	Definition	Usage

Playback	load	onLoad	This event is triggered when (a) a Movie Clip instance first appears on the Stage; (b) a new instance is added with `attachMovie` or `duplicateMovieClip`; or (c) an external Flash movie (.swf file) is loaded into a Movie Clip target.
			
			Note: The `onLoad` method does not function properly on individual instances. When a Flash movie (.swf file) loads into a level or a Movie Clip target, any existing methods will be overwritten, including `onLoad`. See the Usage example to see how `onLoad` can be used.
				```onClipEvent(load){```
				 ``` trace(_name + " has loaded.");```
				 ```}```
				 OR
				 ```movieclip.prototype.onLoad = function(){```
				 ``` trace("A movie or Movie Clip has loaded.");```
				 ```};```

	unload	onUnload	This event occurs when (a) a Movie Clip instance exits the Stage (just after the last frame has played on the Main Timeline), or (b) an external Flash movie (.swf file) is unloaded from a Movie Clip target. Actions within this handler type will be executed *before* any actions in the keyframe immediately after the Movie Clip's departure keyframe.	```onClipEvent(unload){```
				 ``` trace(_name + " has unloaded.");```
				 ```}```
				 OR
				 ```_root.holder.onUnload = function(){```
				 ``` trace(this._name + " has unloaded.");```
				 ```};```

	enterFrame	onEnterFrame	This event executes when each frame on a Movie Clip instance's timeline is played. The actions within this event handler will be processed *after* any actions that exist on the keyframes of the Movie Clip timeline. Note that `enterFrame` events will execute repeatedly (at the same rate as the movie's frame rate), regardless of whether any timelines within the movie are actually playing frames.	```onClipEvent(enterFrame){```
				 ``` trace(_name + " is playing.");```
				 ```}```
				 OR
				 ```_root.holder.onEnterFrame = function(){```
				 ``` trace(_name + " is playing.");```
				 ```};```

Continued

Table 25-3: *(continued)*

Category	onClipEvent	MX Event Handler	Definition	Usage

User Input	mouseMove	onMouseMove	This event is triggered each time the mouse moves, anywhere on the Stage. All Movie Clip instances with this event handler defined receive this event. Combined with the hitTest method, this event can be used to detect mouse movements over Movie Clip instances.	```onClipEvent(mouseMove){```
				 ``` myX = _root._xmouse;```
				 ``` myY = _root._ymouse;```
				 ``` if(this.hitTest(myX, myY, true) == true){```
				 ``` trace("Mouse move over MC.");```
				 ``` }```
				 ```}```
				 OR
				 ```_root.holder.onMouseMove = function(){```
				 ``` var myX = _root._xmouse;```
				 ``` var myY = _root._ymouse;```
				 ``` if(this.hitTest(myX, myY, true)){```
				 ``` trace("Mouse move over " + this._name);```
				 ``` }```
				 ``` updateAfterEvent();```
				 ```};```

	mouseDown	onMouseDown	This event occurs each time the left mouse button is pressed (or down) anywhere on the Stage. All Movie Clip instances with this event handler receive this event.	```onClipEvent(mouseDown){```
				 ``` myX = _root._xmouse;```
				 ``` myY = _root._ymouse;```
				 ``` if(this.hitTest(myX, myY, true)){```
				 ``` trace("Mouse press on MC.");```
				 ``` }```
				 ```}```
				 OR
				 ```_root.holder.onMouseDown = function(){```
				 ``` var myX = _root._xmouse;```
				 ``` var myY = _root._ymouse;```
				 ``` if(this.hitTest(myX, myY, true)){```
				 ``` trace("Mouse press on " + this._name);```
				 ``` }```
				 ```};```

Category	onClipEvent	MX Event Handler	Definition	Usage

	mouseUp	onMouseUp	Each time the left mouse button is released (when the user lets up on the mouse button), this event is triggered. All Movie Clip instances with this handler receive this event.	`onClipEvent(mouseUp){`
				`    myX = _root._xmouse;`
				`    myY = _root._ymouse;`
				`    if(this.hitTest(myX, myY, true)){`
				`        trace("Mouse release on MC.");`
				`    }`
				`}`
				
				OR
				
				`_root.holder.onMouseUp = function(){`
				`    var myX = _root._xmouse;`
				`    var myY = _root._ymouse;`
				`    if(this.hitTest(myX, myY, true)){`
				`        trace("Mouse release on " + this._name);`
				`    }`
				`};`

	keyDown	onKeyDown	When the user presses a key, this event occurs. Combined with the Key.getCode method, you can use this event handler to detect unique key presses.
			
			Note: As of this writing, onKeyDown does not function in the current release of Flash Player 6. Use Key.addListener() with a listener object to detect key down events. This advanced use of the Key object is discussed in the *Macromedia Flash MX ActionScript Bible*.
				`onClipEvent(keyDown){`
				`    newKey = Key.getCode();`
				`    myKey = Key.UP;`
				`    if(newKey == myKey){`
				`        trace("UP arrow is pressed.");`
				`    }`
				`}`

	keyUp	onKeyUp	This event happens when the user releases a key (when the finger leaves the key). Same functionality as the keyDown event.
			
			(**Note:** As of this writing, onKeyUp has strict conditions for its use in the current release of Flash Player 6. Use Key.addListener() with a listener object to detect key down events. This advanced use of the Key object is discussed in the *Macromedia Flash MX ActionScript Bible*.)
				`onClipEvent(keyUp){`
				`    newKey = Key.getCode();`
				`    myKey = Key.LEFT;`
				`    if(newKey == myKey)`
				`        trace("LEFT arrow released.");`
				`}`

Continued

Table 25-3: *(continued)*

Category	onClipEvent	MX Event Handler	Definition	Usage

External Input	data	onData	This event is triggered when (a) the `loadMovie` action retrieves an external Flash movie (.swf file) and puts it in a Movie Clip target, or (b) the data from a file or script with the `loadVariables` action (targeted at a Movie Clip instance) is finished loading.	`onClipEvent(data){`
				`    trace("New data received.");`
				`}`
				OR
				`_root.holder.onData = function(){`
				`    trace("New data received.");`
				`}`

Other objects and functions that use the MovieClip object

Movie Clips can be used with other ActionScript objects to control appearance and sounds and to manipulate data.

We will discuss the `Color`, `Sound`, and `Mouse` objects and the `print()` function in Chapter 27, "Interacting with Movie Clips."

Color object

This object requires a Movie Clip as a target. After a new object is created with the `Color()` constructor, you can control the color effects of the targeted Movie Clip.

Sound object

With this object, you can create virtual sound instances on a Movie Clip timeline and target them for later use.

If you are publishing Flash 6 movies, you can now load MP3 files directly into `Sound` objects. We'll discuss this feature in Chapter 28, "Sharing and Loading Assets."

Mouse object

This object controls the appearance of the mouse pointer within the Flash movie Stage. After the `Mouse` object is hidden, you can attach a `MovieClip` object to the X and Y coordinates of the mouse pointer.

print() function

This function prints a frame (or series of frames) in the targeted timeline. Each frame prints to one piece of paper. Use this function to print high-quality artwork. Note that alpha and color effects applied to `MovieClip` objects do not print reliably with this method — use the `printAsBitmap()` function instead.

tellTarget() action

This Flash 4-compatible action can direct actions to a specific Movie Clip timeline. To be compatible with Flash 4, you need to use Slash notation for the target path. We strongly discourage you from using `tellTarget()` actions if you are designing Flash 5 or higher movies.

with() action

This action enables you to avoid needless replication of object references and paths. By specifying a target for the `with()` action, you can omit the path from nested actions. We will demonstrate the `with()` action in the next section.

Working with Movie Clip Properties

Now that you have a sense of what a Movie Clip can do (or be told to do), let's get some practical experience with the Movie Clip properties. This section shows you how to access Movie Clip appearance properties that control position, scale, and rotation.

Note   The following exercises use Button symbols from the prebuilt Common Libraries that ship with Flash MX. To access buttons from the Common Libraries, choose Window ⇨ Common Libraries ⇨ Buttons to open the Flash library file and drag an instance of any button into your Flash document.

Positioning Movie Clips

You can change the location of Movie Clip instances on-the-fly with position properties such as _x and _y. How is this useful? If you want to create multiple Movie Clip instances that move randomly (or predictively) across the Stage, you can save yourself the trouble of manually tweening them by writing a few lines of ActionScript code on the object instance:

1. Create a new movie file (Ctrl+N or ⌘+N).

2. Draw a simple shape such as a circle. Select the shape and press F8 to convert it into a symbol. Choose the Movie Clip behavior in the Symbol Properties dialog box and give the new Movie Clip symbol a unique name such as **circle**.

3. Create a new layer on the Main Timeline (that is, Scene 1) and name the layer **actions**.

4. Select frame 1of the Actions layer, and open the Actions panel (F9). Turn on Expert mode and type the following code into the Script pane:

```
circle.onEnterFrame = function(){
    this._x += 5;}
```

5. Save your document as **movieclip_x.fla**, and test the movie (Ctrl+Enter or ⌘+Enter). The Movie Clip instance moves across the Stage.

How does this code work? In Step 4, you specified that the onEnterFrame event method should be assigned to the Movie Clip instance circle. Regardless of the number of frames on any playing timeline, the enterFrame event is triggered continuously. Therefore, any actions nested within the handler will be executed repeatedly.

Our nest contains one action: this._x += 5. On the left side of the action, this refers to the object instance to which this handler and code has been applied. In our case, this refers to our circle Movie Clip instance. Immediately after this is the property for X position, _x. By adding the property _x to the object this, Flash knows that we want to change the value of this property.

On the right side of the action are the operators += and the value 5. By combining the + and = operators, we've created a shortcut to adding the value of 5 to the current X position of the circle Movie Clip instance. Each time the enterFrame event occurs, the circle object moves 5 pixels to the right.

Cross-Reference   We dissect operators and expressions in Chapter 24, "Knowing the Nuts and Bolts of Code."

To show how quickly you can replicate this action on multiple Movie Clips, select the circle instance on the Stage and duplicate it (Ctrl+D or ⌘+D) as many times as you wish. Name each new instance with a different name in the Property inspector, such as circle_2, circle_3, and so on. For each instance you create, you can duplicate the code on frame 1, specifying the same actions. For example, for two objects, `circle_1` and `circle_2`, you could write the following code on frame 1:

```
circle_1.onEnterFrame = function(){
    this._x += 5;}
circle_2.onEnterFrame = function(){
    this._x += 5;}
```

When you test your movie, each instance moves independently across the Stage.

Tip   To move the instance diagonally across the Stage, add the action `this._y += 5` to the `onEnterFrame` function. This moves the instance down 5 pixels each time the handler is processed. Also, we'll show you how to consolidate duplicated actions in Chapter 26, "Using Functions and Arrays."

Scaling Movie Clips

In the last example, you learned how to access the _x and _y properties of the `MovieClip` object. The next example shows you how to use a Button symbol to enlarge or reduce the size of a Movie Clip on the Stage.

1. Create a new movie file (Ctrl+N or ⌘+N).

2. Draw a shape (or multiple shapes), select the shape(s), and press F8 to convert the artwork into a symbol. Give the Movie Clip symbol a distinct name to identify it in the Library.

3. Select the instance of the Movie Clip on the Stage, and open the Property inspector. Give the Movie Clip a unique name. In this example, we've named the instance **circle**.

4. From the Button library, drag an instance of a button onto the Stage.

5. Now we create an ActionScript that will enlarge our `circle` Movie Clip instance. Select the Button instance on the Stage and open the Actions panel. In Expert mode, type the following code into the Script pane:

```
on (release){
  with (circle){
    _xscale += 10;
    _yscale += 10;
  }
}
```

This code uses the `with()` action to target the `circle` instance with a nested group of actions. In this case, we've increased the values of the _xscale and _yscale properties by 10 percent. With each release event on the Button symbol, the scale properties of the `circle` instance will be changed.

6. Save your document as **movieclip_scale.fla** and test the movie (Ctrl+Enter or ⌘+Enter). Each time you click the Button instance, your `circle` instance enlarges by 10 percent.

7. Duplicate the Button instance (Ctrl+D or ⌘+D). With the new copy of the Button instance selected, change the code in the Actions panel so that it reads:

```
on (release){
  with (circle){
    _xscale -= 10;
    _yscale -= 10;
  }
}
```

By changing the += operator to -=, each click on this Button instance will reduce (shrink) the `circle` instance by 10 percent.

8. Resave your Flash file and test the movie again. Make sure that each Button instance behaves appropriately. If one doesn't work (or works in an unexpected manner), go back to the Flash document and check the code on both Button instances.

Caution

In this simple exercise, we haven't placed any limits on how much the Movie Clip can be reduced or enlarged. If you click the reduce button enough times, the Movie Clip instance will actually start enlarging again. We discussed creating conditions and logic for Movie Clips in Chapter 24, "Knowing the Nuts and Bolts of Code."

Rotating Movie Clips

Let's move along to the rotation property, `_rotation`, which is used to control the angle at which our Movie Clip is shown. In this sample, we'll use the same Flash document that we created in the preceding section.

Note

If you drew a perfect circle in past exercises for the `MovieClip` object, you will want to edit your Movie Clip symbol to include some additional artwork that provides an indication of orientation and rotation. If you try to rotate a perfect circle, you won't see any visual difference on the Stage. Because the value of the rotation property is determined from the center point of the Movie Clip, you can also move the contents of the Movie Clip (in Symbol Editing mode) off-center to see updates in the `_rotation` value.

1. Select the Button instance you used to enlarge the `circle` Movie Clip instance. Change the button's ActionScript in the Actions panel to:

```
on (release){
  circle._rotation += 10;
}
```

2. Now, select the Button instance you used to shrink the `circle` Movie Clip instance. Change the button's ActionScript in the Actions Panel to:

```
on (release){
  circle._rotation -= 10;
}
```

3. Save your document as **movieclip_rotation.fla** and test the movie. Each button should rotate the `circle` Movie Clip instance accordingly.

At this point, you should have a general knowledge of how to access a Movie Clip's properties. Repeat these examples using other properties that can be modified, such as _width and _height. Try combining all the properties into one Button instance, or one event method or onClipEvent() handler.

Creating Draggable Movie Clips

Flash 4 introduced the drag-and-drop feature, which enables the user to pick up objects with the mouse pointer and move them around the movie stage. Flash 5 added some other ways to use the drag-and-drop feature with the onClipEvent Movie Clip handler. As we briefly discussed, Flash MX ActionScript can use a new event model for MovieClip objects. The drag-and-drop action in Flash is based entirely on Movie Clips. The only objects that can be moved with the mouse are Movie Clip instances. So, if you want a drawing of a triangle to be moveable by the user, you have to first put that triangle into a Movie Clip, and then place a named instance of that clip onto the Stage. Flash's drag-and-drop support is fairly broad, but more-complex drag-and-drop behaviors require some ActionScript knowledge.

Drag-and-drop basics

In mouse-based computer interfaces, the most common form of drag-and-drop goes like this: A user points to an element with the mouse pointer, clicks the element to begin moving it, and then releases the mouse button to stop moving it. One method of adding drag-and-drop functionality is the use of a nested Button instance in a Movie Clip symbol. A startDrag() action is added to an on() handler for that Button instance. Let's try out this technique:

1. Start a new Flash document.

2. Create a circle with the Oval tool. Select the artwork and press the F8 key. In the Convert to Symbol dialog box, select the Button behavior. Name the symbol **dragButton**.

3. Now, you will nest the Button instance inside of a Movie Clip symbol. With the dragButton instance selected on the Stage, press the F8 key again. In this Convert to Symbol dialog box, select the Movie Clip behavior. Name the symbol **dragObject**.

4. With the new Movie Clip instance selected, open the Property inspector. Give the instance the name **dragObject_mc**. This name can be used with the startDrag() method.

5. Double-click the dragObject_mc instance to edit the symbol. With the nested Button instance selected on the Stage, open the Actions panel. Make sure Expert mode is selected in the options menu of the panel and type the following code into the Script pane:

```
on (press){
  this.startDrag();
}
```

Even though your startDrag() action will be applied to the same Movie Clip that houses our button, a startDrag action can target any Movie Clip from any button, or from any keyframe.

6. At this point, your button, when clicked, causes the dragObject_mc Movie Clip instance to start following the mouse pointer. Now you have to tell the Movie Clip to stop following the pointer when the mouse button is released. After the last curly brace (}) highlighted in the actions list of the Script pane, type the following code:

```
on (release){
  this.stopDrag();
}
```

 Caution It is possible to use a button that is not contained in the draggable Movie Clip to stop the dragging action. If you use a button like that, remember that when your only event handler is on (release), your action will not be executed if the mouse button is released when it is no longer over the button (which is likely to happen when the user is dragging things around). You should also add an on (releaseOutside) event handler to capture all release events.

7. Save your Flash document as **movieclip_drag.fla**. Test your movie with Control ➪ Test Movie (Ctrl+Enter or ⌘+Enter). Click the circle and drag it around the Stage. To stop dragging, release the mouse button.

Did it work? Great! Now we can tell you about the other basic settings for the startDrag() action. Next, we'll look at additional features of the startDrag() action. You may want to select an existing startDrag() action in the Script pane of the Actions panel and switch to Normal mode to more clearly see these options.

Lock mouse to center

This setting, which is the first option specified in the parentheses of the startDrag() method, controls how the Movie Clip instance will position itself relative to the position of the mouse pointer. There are two values for this option: true or false. When set to true, this option makes the dragged Movie Clip instance center itself under the mouse pointer for the duration of the drag movement. If the dragged Movie Clip instance is not already under the mouse pointer when the startDrag() action occurs, the instance will automatically be moved under the pointer, providing that the pointer is not outside the region defined by Constrain to Rectangle (discussed in the next section). The following code will "snap" the center of the Movie Clip instance dragObj_mc to the mouse pointer:

```
_root.dragObj_mc.startDrag(true);
```

When this option is set to false, the Movie Clip instance will move with the mouse pointer from the point at which it was clicked. For example, if you click the draggable object on its left edge, that's where the object will "snap" the mouse pointer:

```
_root.dragObj_mc.startDrag(false);
```

Constrain to rectangle

To specify the limits of the rectangular region within which a draggable Movie Clip instance can be dragged, you can add additional parameters to the startDrag() method. First, determine the pixel locations of the four corners of the rectangle. The pixel coordinates are set relative to the top-left corner of the Stage upon which the draggable Movie Clip instance resides. For example, the following code would constrain the draggable Movie Clip instance named dragObject_mc to a 300-pixel square region in the top-left corner of the Main Timeline's Stage:

```
_root.dragObject_mc.startDrag(false, 0, 0, 300, 300);
```

Note If the draggable Movie Clip instance is located outside of the defined drag region when the `startDrag()` action occurs, the instance is automatically moved into the closest portion of the drag region.

Detecting the drop position: Using _droptarget

In the "Drag-and-drop basics" section, we showed you how to make Movie Clip instances that the user can move around. But what if we wanted to force the user to move a `MovieClip` object into a certain location before we let him or her drop it? For instance, consider a child's shape-matching game in which a small circle, square, and triangle should be dragged onto corresponding larger shapes. If the child drops the small circle onto the large square or large triangle, the circle returns to its original location. If, on the other hand, the child drops the small circle onto the large circle, the small circle should stay where it is dropped, and the child should receive a "Correct!" message. That kind of game is quite possible in Flash, but it requires some understanding of Movie Clip properties. Here's how it works — we'll use the circle as an example.

New Feature In the following steps, we'll show you new methods of the `MovieClip` object that were introduced with Flash MX. These methods allow you to assign Button behaviors to Movie Clip instances, without nesting a physical Button instance within the Movie Clip.

1. Open a new Flash document (File ⇨ New).

2. With the Oval tool, draw a circle that is 100×100 pixels. Convert the artwork to a Movie Clip symbol and name the instance **circle_mc**. Scale the artwork to 25 percent in the Transform panel. Position this instance along the bottom left of the Stage, as shown in Figure 25-4.

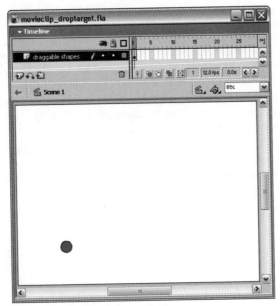

Figure 25-4: The circle_mc instance

3. Duplicate the circle_mc instance by selecting it on the Stage and choosing Edit ➪ Duplicate (Ctrl+D or ⌘+D). Place the new copy above the original instance, as shown in Figure 25-5. Scale the artwork to 125 percent in the Transform panel and name the instance **circleBig_mc** in the Property inspector.

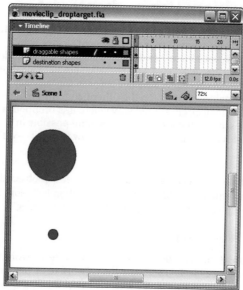

Figure 25-5: The circleBig_mc instance

4. Create a new Movie Clip symbol from scratch by choosing Insert ➪ New Symbol (Ctrl+F8 or ⌘+F8). Name the symbol **statusMessage**. Inside of this symbol, create a short animation displaying the text "Correct!" Leave the first frame of the symbol empty, and create the text (and supporting tweens, if desired) on frame 2 and higher. Create a frame label named **correct** on frame 2 of a new layer named labels, as shown in Figure 25-6. Also, place a stop(); action on frame 1 of an Actions layer in the timeline.

5. Go back to the Main Timeline (that is, Scene 1) and place an instance of statusMessage along the bottom of the Stage, centered. With the instance selected, open the Property inspector and name the instance **status_mc**.

6. Now, we will make the circle_mc instance draggable by adding some frame actions — we won't use a Button instance as we did earlier in this chapter. On the Main Timeline, create a new layer named **actions**. Select frame 1 of this layer, and in the Actions panel type the following code into the Script pane:

```
circle_mc.onPress = function(){
  this.startDrag();
};
```

Here, the new `onPress()` method of the `MovieClip` object is used to assign a press Button behavior to the instance. In this code, we tell the `circle_mc` instance to start dragging when it is clicked on the Stage. Note that, as soon as a Movie Clip instance has a Button event assigned to it, the mouse pointer will switch to a finger icon when it rolls over the area of the `MovieClip` object.

Figure 25-6: The statusMessage symbol timeline

7. Next, we need to tell the `circle_mc` to stop dragging when the mouse button releases. Underneath the last line of the code from Step 4, type the following code:

```
circle_mc.onRelease = function(){
  this.stopDrag();
  if (this._droptarget == "/circleBig_mc") {
    _root.status.gotoAndPlay ("correct");
  } else {
    this._x = 112;
    this._y = 316;
  }
};
```

This code uses the new `onRelease()` method. The code for this method will be executed when the mouse button is released after a mouse click on the `circle_mc` instance. The instance is told to stop dragging, and then ActionScript evaluates if the current instance (this) is dropped on top of `"/circleBig_mc"`. When the user drops any Movie Clip instance, the instance's _droptarget property is updated. The _droptarget property specifies the name of the Movie Clip instance upon which the dragged Movie Clip instance was last dropped. If no instance is underneath the dragged instance, _droptarget will return nothing (that is, an empty string). If the _droptarget is the large circle ("/circleBig_mc"), the dragged instance will stay where it was dropped and the status_mc Movie Clip instance will play its "Correct!" animation. Otherwise, the dragged instance (circle_mc) will return to the X and Y coordinates of its starting point (112, 316).

8. Save your Flash document as **movieclip_droptarget.fla** and test it (Ctrl+Enter or ⌘+Enter). Click and drag the circle_mc instance on top of the circleBig_mc instance. The dragged instance will stay put on top of the larger circle, and the "Correct!" message will animate. Click and drag the circle_mc instance off the circleBig_mc instance, and release the drag outside of the larger circle. The smaller circle will snap back to its original starting point.

You can continue this example with other shapes, using the same methodology. Create a separate onPress() and onRelease() method for each new drag interaction.

For further study, we've included this basic child's drag-and-drop game as a sample document called **movieclip_droptarget.fla** on the *Flash MX Bible* CD-ROM in the ch25 folder.

Making alpha and scale sliders

A compelling use of a draggable Movie Clip is a slider that can alter the properties of another object. By checking the position of a Movie Clip, you can use the position's X or Y coordinate value to alter the value of another Movie Clip. In this section, we create two sliders (one for alpha and another for scale) that will dynamically change the transparency and size of a Movie Clip instance on the Stage. Many thanks to Sandro Corsaro (www.sandrocorsaro.com) for supplying the artwork of our dog Stella and the park sign.

You need to copy the **slider_basic_starter.fla** file from the ch25 folder of the *Flash MX Bible* CD-ROM. You'll use premade artwork to understand the functionality of startDrag, stopDrag, and duplicateMovieClip.

Assembling the parts

In this section, we set up the basic composition of the Stage, using elements from the slider_basic_starter.fla Library. You will add artwork of a dog and a park sign to the movie. The dog artwork will be duplicated using the duplicateMovieClip method, and the duplicate instance will be manipulated by the sliders that we create in the next section. The park sign will be used to remove the duplicate instance using the _droptarget property and the removeMovieClip method.

1. Open your copy of the slider_basic_starter.fla. Rename Layer 1 to **dog_1**.

2. Access the document's Library by pressing Ctrl+L or ⌘+L. Open the dogElements folder, and drag the dog Movie Clip symbol onto the Stage. Place the instance in the upper-left corner of the Stage.

3. With the dog instance selected, open the Property inspector. In the <Instance Name> field, type **dog_1**, as shown in Figure 25-7.

4. Using the Text tool, add the words **Original Dog** under the dog_1 instance. You don't need to make a new layer for this artwork.

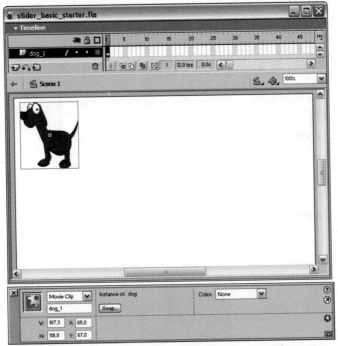

Figure 25-7: The dog_1 instance will be used as our reference MovieClip object. The scale and transparency of this dog instance will not be changed.

5. Create a new layer and name it **parkSign**. Move this layer below the dog_1 layer. Drag the parkSign Movie Clip symbol, located in the parkSignElements folder in the Library, to the lower-right corner of the Stage. In the Property inspector, assign the instance the name **parkSign**. In the Transform panel, reduce the size of the parkSign instance to 50%, as shown in Figure 25-8.

6. Create a new layer called **actions**, and place it above all the other layers. Select the first keyframe of this layer. In the Actions panel (in Expert mode), add the following actions:

```
dog_1.duplicateMovieClip("dog_2", 1, {_x: 350,_y:175});
```

This line of code duplicates the instance dog_1, names the new instance dog_2, and places it on the first depth layer of the current timeline (_root). However, Flash MX ActionScript allows us to do a little more with the duplicateMovieClip() method. You can now assign an initObject parameter that is passed to the duplicated instance. In this example, we create an object with _x and _y properties that are passed to the dog_2 instance. This argument positions the dog_2 instance at the X coordinate of 350 (350 pixels from the left corner of the Main Timeline Stage) and the Y coordinate of 175 (175 pixels down from the left corner).

7. Save your document as **slider_basic_100.fla**, and test the movie (Ctrl+Enter or ⌘+Enter). You should see a new instance of the dog_1 Movie Clip appear on the right side of the Stage (see Figure 25-9).

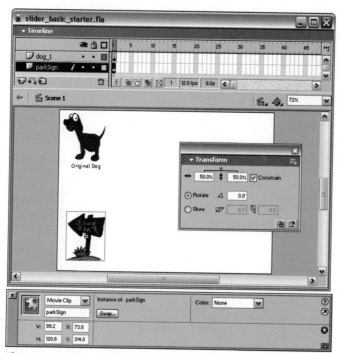

Figure 25-8: The parkSign instance will be used to remove duplicates of the dog_1 Movie Clip instance.

Figure 25-9: The duplicateMovieClip() method creates a new instance of a MovieClip object. Unless you alter the new instance's X and Y position, it will appear directly above the parent instance.

Now that we have some artwork on the Stage, we can manipulate the duplicated Movie Clip with a pair of dynamic sliders.

Building the sliders

In this section, you'll create two sliders: one for scale and one for transparency. We'll only need to make one slider Movie Clip symbol, and we'll use a new instance for each slider. The basic "problems" of a dynamic slider are to (a) retrieve the position value of an object on the slider (we'll call this the *slider bar*) and (b) set the value of another object equal to (or some factor of) the position value of the slider bar. Finding the position of a slider bar is relatively straightforward. The difficulty lies in creating the value scale for the slider.

Because we have already determined the properties that will be altered (scale and transparency) we need to establish a range of values that each property can use. Luckily, both scale (as _xscale and _yscale in ActionScript) and transparency (as _alpha) use percentage units. However, scale can be any value that's greater than 0 percent and less than 3,200 percent. Alpha has a range of 0 to 100 percent. If we want to use the same parent slider for each property slider, we need to manipulate the position values of the slider bar differently for each property. Let's start with building the basic slider.

On the CD-ROM

Resume using the same file you finished in the previous section. Otherwise, you can open a copy of **slider_basic_100.fla**, located in the ch25 folder of the *Flash MX Bible* CD-ROM.

1. Create a new Movie Clip symbol (Ctrl+F8 or ⌘+F8) and name it **slider**. In Symbol Editing mode, rename the first layer **sliderRule**. On this layer, drag an instance of the sliderRule Graphic symbol (located in the sliderElements folder of the Library) onto the Movie Clip Stage.

Note

The sliderRule artwork contains a line that is 200 pixels long, bound with a circle on each end. The length of this line determines the position range for the slider bar. Therefore, our absolute range is between 0 and 200.

2. With the sliderRule Graphic selected, open the Info panel. On the right side of the Info panel (on the diagram of the square bounding box), make sure that the registration point is set to the top-left corner of the selection's bounding box. Then enter the values **−28.4** for the X coordinate and **−12.4** for the Y coordinate, as shown in Figure 25-10.

3. Create another layer for the slider Movie Clip and name it **position**. Drag an instance of the sliderBar Movie Clip (located in the sliderElements folder of the Library) to the slider Movie Clip Stage.

4. With the sliderBar instance selected, open the Transform panel. Type **90** in the Rotate field and press Enter. In the Info panel, click the center registration point in the bounding box diagram and enter **100** for the X coordinate and **−0.3** for the Y coordinate.

5. To see the position of the sliderBar instance, we need to assign a unique instance name. Select the sliderBar instance and type **position** in the <Instance Name> field of the Property inspector, as shown in Figure 25-11.

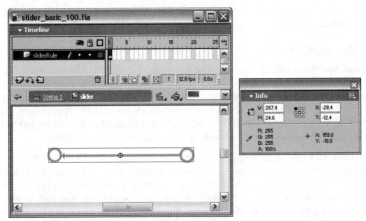

Figure 25-10: The sliderRule's starting point (just to the right of the first left-hand circle) needs to be at the slider Movie Clip's zero X coordinate.

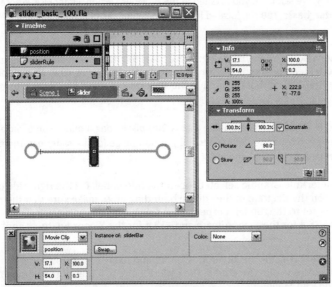

Figure 25-11: The starting X coordinate for the position Movie Clip instance is set to 100. When the Flash movie starts, this value will be applied to the scale and alpha properties of the dog_2 instance on the Main Timeline.

6. Now we need to make the `position` Movie Clip instance draggable. In earlier sections of this chapter, you saw how to embed a button in the draggable Movie Clip to receive `mouseDown` and `mouseUp` events. In this example, we're going to make a button-free draggable Movie Clip instance, using the new `onPress` and `onRelease` methods for

`MovieClip` objects. Create a new layer in the slider symbol, name it **actions**, and move it above the position layer. Open the Actions panel. Type the following code in the Script pane:

```
position.onPress = function(){
  this.startDrag (true, 10, 0, 200, 0);
  _global.state = "down";
};
```

To make the position instance draggable, we need to detect a mouse press event on the position instance. When a mouse click occurs on the instance, the actions nested within the `onPress` function will be executed.

The second line of code enables the dragging behavior of the `position` instance by using the `startDrag()` method on `this`. Because it's used as a method and not as an action, we don't need to specify a target instance in the arguments. The arguments prescribed here lock the mouse to the center of the object and constrain the draggable region to a bounding box defined by 10, 0 and 200, 0. This effectively keeps the `position` instance confined to the line of our sliderRule Graphic.

Note

We've limited the left end of the `startDrag` to the X coordinate of 10. This keeps the scale properties from going below 10 percent. If you try to assign a value of 0 or less to the scale properties, Flash will start scaling the instance back up to positive values in an unpredictable manner.

The third line of code sets a variable called `state` in the `_global` namespace to the value of `"down"`. Because we'll be using two instances of the slider Movie Clip symbol, we need to know whether any instance has received the a mouse press event. We'll see why we need this code in later steps.

7. Now we need to be able to stop dragging the `position` object when the mouse button is released. We'll use the `onRelease` handler to define our actions. Open the Actions panel for frame 1 of the Actions layer. Type the following code after the last curly brace of the `onPress` function:

```
position.onRelease = function() {
  this.stopDrag ();
  _global.state = "up";
}
```

This block of code performs in the same manner that our code in step 6 did. Once a mouse release event (the act of releasing the left mouse button) is detected (line 1), we stop the dragging of the position instance initiated in step 6 (line 3). Finally, we set the `state` variable in the `_global` namespace to `"up"`.

Next, we'll create two instances of the slider Movie Clip symbol on the Main Timeline Stage: one for scale and one for alpha.

8. Exit the Symbol Editing mode and return to the Scene 1 timeline (the Main Timeline). Create a new layer called **scaleSlider**. Open the Library and drag an instance of the slider Movie Clip to the Stage. Name this instance `scaleSlider` in the Property inspector.

9. Move the `scaleSlider` instance to the lower right of the Stage.

10. Create another layer called **alphaSlider**. Drag another instance of the slider Movie Clip onto the Stage, and name the instance `alphaSlider`. Rotate this instance –90°. Place the instance near the right edge of the Stage, as shown in Figure 25-12.

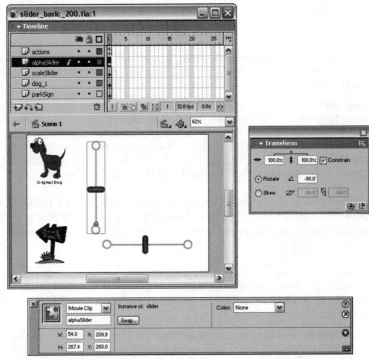

Figure 25-12: At this point, your Flash document's Stage should contain the dog and parkSign artwork as well as two instances of the slider Movie Clip symbol.

11. Save your Flash document as **slider_basic_200.fla** and test it. You should be able to drag the position instances on both sliders.

Checking the positions of the sliders

Once we have a slider bar that is draggable, we need to access the new values of the `position` instance and apply the values to the properties of the `dog_2` instance. To do this, we need to have an event handler whose sole job is to check the X coordinate of the `position` instance. In this section, you'll learn how to make an `onEnterFrame` handler on the `_root` timeline.

On the CD-ROM   Resume using the Flash document that you created in the last section. If you didn't complete that section, make a copy of the **slider_basic_200.fla** file located in the ch25 folder of the *Flash MX Bible* CD-ROM.

1. Select frame 1 of the Actions layer in the Main Timeline (that is, Scene 1). Open the Actions panel. In the Script pane, after the `duplicateMovieClip()` action, type the following code:

```
_root.onEnterFrame = function(){
  with(dog_2){
    _xscale = scaleSlider.position._x;
    _yscale = scaleSlider.position._x;
    _alpha = alphaSlider.position._x;
  }
};
```

Because the event method `onEnterFrame` is specified for the `_root` timeline, this block of code will execute continuously in our Flash movie. Why? Any timeline will continuously enter a frame for playback, even if a `stop()` action is applied to all timelines. The speed at which the `onEnterFrame` event occurs is determined by the frame rate of the Flash movie (as defined by the Modify ➪ Document dialog box). The frame rate of 12 fps was already set in the sample file before you opened it. Therefore, this block will execute 12 times each second.

2. What happens on each execution of the `onEnterFrame` event? The second line of code uses the `with()` action to target the `dog_2` object with the remaining nested actions. The third and fourth lines of code set the X and Y scale properties of the `dog_2` instance to the value returned by the current X coordinate of the `position` instance (relative to the coordinates within the slider Movie Clip symbol). Notice that the target path for the `position` instance is the `scaleSlider` instance in lines 3 and 4. The fifth line sets the alpha property of the `dog_2` instance equal to the X coordinate of the `position` instance within the `alphaSlider` instance.

3. Save your Flash document as **slider_basic_300.fla** and test it. When you drag the bar on the bottom scale slider, notice how the *size* of the `dog_2` instance increases as you drag it to the right. When you drag the bar down on the left alpha slider, you'll see that the *opacity* of the `dog_2` instance decreases.

Note

You may be wondering why the X coordinate of the `position` instance is used for the `alphaSlider` instance, instead of the Y coordinate. Indeed, you do drag the bar on a vertical axis instead of a horizontal one. However, the `position` instance exists within the space of the slider Movie Clip symbol, which has a horizontal orientation in Symbol Editing mode. The X coordinate is derived from the Stage of Symbol Editing mode, regardless of the instance's orientation.

Okay, we have the sliders changing the size and opacity of the `dog_2` instance. However, nothing happens as we drag the bar on the `alphaSlider` instance toward its upper limit. Because the X coordinate of the `position` instance starts at 100, we won't see any visual effect to the alpha property as it increases beyond 100 percent. The lower limit of the alpha slider is 10 percent—it's prevented from going below that value by the coordinate arguments of the `startDrag` method. Therefore, it would be better to have the `alphaScale` slider convert the X coordinate of the `position` instance to a true 0 to 100 range of values.

To do this, we need to develop an equation that will do the work of automatically remapping values to a 0–100 scale. We know that the lowest X coordinate of the position instance is 10 and the highest X coordinate is 200. If we want the highest position of the bar to provide 100 percent opacity, we need to divide 200 by a number that will give us 100. Dividing 200 by 2 gives us 100. How does that work for the low end? If the X coordinate returns the lowest value of 10, our lowest opacity value will be 5.

4. With frame 1 of the Actions layer of the Main Timeline selected, open the Actions panel and modify the fifth line of the onEnterFrame function to read:

```
_alpha = (alphaSlider.position._x)/2;
```

5. Save your Flash document and test it. Now, as you drag up with the bar for the alphaSlider, the opacity increases. As you drag down, it decreases.

So far, so good. However, it would be useful if the alphaSlider's position instance started with an X coordinate of 200. This would initialize the dog_2 instance with an opacity of 100 percent. We could physically move the position instance within the slider symbol to an X coordinate of 200, but that would increase the scale of the dog_2 instance to 200 percent at the start. To change only the position instance of alphaSlider at the start of the movie, we'll add another line of code to frame 1 of the Actions layer on the Main Timeline.

6. Select frame 1 of the Actions layer and open the Actions panel and add the following code to the Script pane, just after the closing line (} ;) of the onEnterFrame() handler:

```
alphaSlider.position._x = 200;
```

This block of code will execute once, when the position instance (a MovieClip object) first appears (or loads) on the Stage.

7. Save the Flash document and test it. This time, the alphaSlider's bar (its position instance) will immediately start at the upper limit.

Removing Movie Clips

At this point in the chapter, you have two sliders that dynamically control the scale and alpha of the dog_2 Movie Clip instance on the Stage. What if you wanted to get rid the dog_2 instance? How would you delete it? The only way to remove a duplicated Movie Clip instance is to use the removeMovieClip() method or action. In this section, we show you how to use the _droptarget property and the removeMovieClip() method of the MovieClip object.

On the CD-ROM

Resume using the same document, slider_basic_300.fla, that you created in the last section. Alternatively, you can open the **slider_basic_300.fla** file located in the ch25 folder of the *Flash MX Bible* CD-ROM.

1. Select the frame 1 of the Actions layer on the Main Timeline and open the Actions panel. Type the following code after the last line of ActionScript currently in the Script pane:

```
dog_2.onPress = function(){
  this.startDrag (true, 0, 0, 550, 400);
};
dog_2.onRelease = function(){
```

```
    this.stopDrag ();
    if(eval(this._droptarget) == parkSign){
      this.removeMovieClip();
      _root.onEnterFrame = null;
    }
};
```

Most of this code is already familiar to you. Here we want to make only our duplicate dog instance (dog_2) draggable.

When a mouse press event is detected on the dog_2 instance, the function declared within the onPress() method for dog_2 will execute. The startDrag() method of the current dog instance (this) will be enabled and constrained to the dimensions of the Flash movie Stage.

When a mouse release event is detected over the dog_2 instance, the stopDrag() method will be executed. The last if statement checks whether the _droptarget property of the current dog instance is equal to the target path of the parkSign instance. If the dog_2 instance is over the parkSign instance on the Stage when the dragging stops, the current dog instance is removed.

Finally, if the dog_2 instance is removed, you must reset the onEnterFrame() method assigned to _root—otherwise, the onEnterFrame() method will generate errors in the Output window. By assigning a value of null to _root.onEnterFrame, the function established earlier will be deleted.

Note   We use the eval() action on the _droptarget property because _droptarget returns the path of the target in Slashes notation (for Flash 4 compatibility). If we use eval() on the _droptarget property, Flash will return the target path in dot syntax.

2. Save your Flash document as **slider_basic_400.fla** and test it. When you drag the dog_2 instance over the parkSign instance, the dog_2 instance disappears.

On the CD-ROM   You can find a completed version of **slider_basic_400.fla** in the ch25 folder of the *Flash MX Bible* CD-ROM.

In the next chapter, you'll learn how to expand your knowledge of ActionScript code by using functions and arrays. These code devices allow you to organize code and data much more efficiently with ActionScript.

Summary

✦ The MovieClip object has unique properties, methods, and handlers. Using dot syntax, you can access these characteristics of the MovieClip object.

✦ You can change a Movie Clip instance's position, scale, and rotation using ActionScript. Most physical attributes are accessed by specifying the Movie Clip's path followed by the property name, as in _root.myInstance._rotation.

✦ You can create draggable Movie Clips in Flash MX ActionScript without the use of any Button instances, by using the onPress() and onRelease() methods of the MovieClip object.

✦ The `_droptarget` property of Movie Clip instance (instance A) indicates the path of the Movie Clip instance (instance B) upon which a Movie Clip instance (instance A) is dropped.

✦ As the sliders example demonstrated, you can use the values of one Movie Clip instance's properties to change the property values of another Movie Clip instance.

✦   ✦   ✦

Using Functions and Arrays

In This Chapter

Data typing in
ActionScript

Using functions
in ActionScript

Adding arrays to
manage data

Creating dynamic
menus

Now that you've had some practice applying ActionScript to MovieClip objects, you can start to explore the programming concepts behind subroutines and arrays. This chapter introduces you to data types, subroutines, arrays, and complex uses of functions.

In previous chapters, you may have found yourself repeating the same actions (or type of actions) in several event handlers within a movie. *Functions* allow you to group actions into code blocks, referred to by custom names. *Arrays* are a different kind of grouping mechanism — instead of grouping actions, an array groups multiple items of data. Before we can discuss functions and arrays, though, you need to understand the types of data that are available in ActionScript.

What Are Data Types?

Simply put, ActionScript has several types of data that can be declared (or loaded) into the Flash movie. So far, you have worked primarily with three types of data in previous chapters: strings, numbers, and MovieClip objects. In this section, we define each data type available in Flash MX ActionScript.

Understanding data types is rather straightforward. The most difficult aspect of working with data types is knowing which data types work correctly with the operation you want to perform in ActionScript. We will work with examples throughout this chapter to help you understand how data types are used.

string

We've seen string data types throughout the *Flash MX Bible* already. Any time you have a value in quotes, it is typed as a string. If you have an expression that refers to string data types, its data type will be a string as well. All of the following examples have a string data type:

```
firstName = "Frank";
lastName = "Houston";
fullName = firstName + lastName;
pathSuffix = "1";
```

Tip

All text contained with Input and Dynamic text fields have a data type of `string`. If you need to perform numeric operations with text field values, make sure you convert the `string` data to `number` data by using the `Number()` function. We discuss the `number` data type in the next heading.

Note

Feel free to try out the following code examples in new Flash document files. Create a new file, and rename layer 1 to **actions**. Using the Actions panel, add the code examples to frame 1 of the actions layer. After you type each code block, test the movie to see the output from the `trace()` actions appear in the Output window.

If a variable has a `string` data type, any of the `String` object methods can be used with that data. For example, if you want to convert the case of all characters in the value of `firstName` to uppercase (turn "Frank" into "FRANK"), you could do the following operation:

```
firstName = "Frank";
firstName = firstName.toUpperCase();
trace("firstName = " + firstName);
```

Here, the `String` object method `toUpperCase()` converts any lowercase characters in a string value to uppercase characters. Likewise, you can extract specific information from a string. For example, if you wanted to find where a space occurs within a string and return the value of the string from the point in the value to the end of the value, you could use the following code:

```
myVersion = "Netscape 4.71";
startChar = myVersion.indexOf(" ") + 1;
myVersion = myVersion.slice(startChar, -1);
trace("myVersion = " + myVersion);
```

In the preceding code, the `indexOf()` method searches for the first occurrence of a space (" ") within the string value for `myVersion`. `indexOf(" ")` for `myVersion` will return the position (as a number, counting from left to right) of the space character. For this example, `indexOf(" ")` will return a 9. Then, we add 1 to this value to the character position after the space. In our example, the tenth position of `myVersion`'s value is a "4." Then, by using the `slice()` method, we can extract the rest of the string from the `startChar` value of 10. The -1 option tells Flash to continue all the way to the end of the string's value from the starting point of `startChar`. Note that in this example, the final value of `myVersion` is a string value of "4.71."

Cross-Reference

For more information on methods that can be performed upon `String` objects and string values, see the `String` object coverage in the *Macromedia Flash MX ActionScript Bible*. You can also look up the `String` object in the Reference panel.

number

A *number data type* is any value (or expression value) that refers to a discrete numeric value in ActionScript. A value must be typed as a number for it to work properly in mathematical operations.

```
myAge = "27";
futureYears = "5";
myAge = myAge + futureYears;
trace("I will be " + myAge + " years old in " + futureYears + " years.");
```

If this code was added to frame 1 of your Flash document and tested, the following `trace()` information would appear in the Output window:

```
I will be 275 years old in 5 years.
```

Obviously, this isn't the answer we were looking for. Because `myAge` and `futureYears` were specified as string values (with quotes), ActionScript simply *concatenated* (joined) the two string values as "27" + "5", which is "275". To see these values as numbers, we need to change the code to the following:

```
myAge = 27;
futureYears = 5;
myAge = myAge + futureYears;
trace("I will be " + myAge + " years old in " + futureYears + " years.");
```

Now, the values of `myAge` and `futureYears` appear as real numbers to ActionScript, and the mathematical operation will add the values of `myAge` and `futureYears` correctly. The `trace()` output will now read:

```
I will be 32 years old in 5 years.
```

You can convert `string` data values to `number` data values by using the `Number()` function. In the string example from the last section, you could convert the `myVersion` string value to a number value by adding this line of code:

```
myVersion = Number(myVersion);
```

So we can now perform mathematical operations on the "4.71" value of `myVersion`, which is now simply 4.71.

boolean

There will be times when you will designate a variable's value as either `true` or `false`. Variables that use `true` or `false` are said to have a *Boolean value*. Boolean values are useful for either/or situations, or when you need a toggle switch — just like a light switch, which is on or off. In the following code, a variable named `isLoading` is initialized with a `true` value but later switched to a `false` value when loading is complete:

```
onClipEvent(load){
    _root.isLoading = true;
    trace("isLoading's type = " + typeof(_root.isLoading));
}
onClipEvent(enterFrame){
    if(this._framesloaded >= this._totalframes){
        _root.isLoading = false;
    }
}
```

This code could be placed on a Movie Clip instance. When the Movie Clip instance appears on the Stage, the `load` event will occur, and the Output window will display:

```
isLoading's type = boolean
```

You can check the data types of declared variables and objects with the `typeof` operator.

movieclip

As the data type name implies, Movie Clip instances on the Stage have a data type of movieclip. ActionScript distinguishes MovieClip objects from other code-based objects so that you can more easily detect MovieClip objects in your code. The following variable value will be typed as movieclip:

```
path = _root.ballAnim;
```

As long as a physical Movie Clip instance named ballAnim exists on the Main Timeline (_root), path's data type will be movieclip. If ballAnim did not exist, path's data type would be undefined. Since path is classified as a movieclip, methods of the MovieClip object can then be applied to it. In the following code, the gotoAndStop(1) method will be passed along to _root.ballAnim:

```
path.gotoAndStop(1);
```

object

This data type refers to any code-based objects that you create with ActionScript. For example, in the next chapter, we will use the Color and Sound objects to enhance interactive presentations. Each of the following variables would be typed as object:

```
myColor = new Color(_root.ballAnim);
mySound = new Sound();
myList = new Array();
myObject = new Object();
```

If you used this code in your Flash movie, you would see object types in the Output window when Debug ⇨ List Variables is used in the Test Movie environment:

```
Variable _level0.myColor = [object #1, class 'Color'] {}
Variable _level0.mySound = [object #2, class 'Sound'] {}
Variable _level0.myList = [object #3, class 'Array'] []
Variable _level0.myObject = [object #4, class 'Object'] {}
```

Cross-Reference

We discuss the new instanceof operator introduced with Flash MX later in this section. You can now test the class of objects in ActionScript.

function

In ActionScript, you can define your own subroutines of ActionScript code. We discuss subroutines and constructor functions later in this chapter. The function data type will be assigned to any ActionScript code that begins with the function action, such as:

```
function myGoto(label){
    gotoAndStop(label);
}
```

undefined

If you check for the data type of a non-existent code element, ActionScript will return a data type of undefined. For example, if you tried to create a variable that stored a reference to a MovieClip object that was not currently present on the Stage, a data type of undefined will be returned. Create a new Flash document with no elements on the Stage in any frame. With the first frame of the document selected, type the following code into the Script pane of the Actions panel:

```
myMovieClip = _root.ballAnim;
trace("the data of myMovieClip is " + typeof(myMovieClip));
```

Test your Flash movie (Ctrl+Enter or ⌘+Return). The Output window will report:

```
the data of myMovieClip is undefined
```

Checking data types with typeof

Now that you know the various data types in ActionScript, you'll want to know how to check the data type of a given piece of information. Using the `typeof` operator, you can determine the data type of an ActionScript element. The `typeof` operator accepts only one option: the name of the ActionScript element that you wish to test. For example, you can trace a variable (or object) type in the Output window:

```
firstName = "Robert";
trace("firstName has a data type of " + typeof(firstName));
```

When this movie is tested, the Output window will display:

```
firstName has a data type of string
```

You can use `typeof` in `for . . . in` loops, so that actions will be executed with specific data types. The following ActionScript code will take any `string` variables on the Main Timeline and move them to the `_global` namespace:

```
for(name in _root){
  if(typeof(_root[name])=="string" && _root[name] != _root["$version"]){
    _global[name] = _root[name];
    delete _root[name];
  }
}
```

The preceding code block will move all variables except the native `$version` variable to the new `_global` namespace.

On the CD-ROM
You can see the returned values of the `typeof` operator in the **typeof_simple.fla**, **typeof_advanced.fla**, and **moveVariables.fla** files, located in the ch26 folder of the *Flash MX Bible* CD-ROM.

Checking class type with instanceof

Flash MX introduces a new operator to ActionScript: `instanceof`. With this operator, you can check the class type of a specific object in ActionScript. A class is similar to a data type but a little more detailed. As you saw in the object data discussion, several different objects returned `object` as their data type. However, these objects belong to different classes. In fact, you probably noticed the class type showing up in the Output window when you chose Debug ➪ List Variables.

Let's take a look at an example that compares `typeof` to `instanceof`. Create a new Flash document and select frame 1 of the default layer. In the Actions panel, type the following code into the Script pane:

```
currentDate = new Date();
trace("the data type of currentDate is " + typeof(currentDate));
```

After you've written this code, test the Flash movie (Ctrl+Enter or ⌘+Enter). The Output window will display the following text:

```
the data type of currentDate is object
```

Now, let's use the typeof operator in an if statement. After the last line of code that you typed, enter the following code:

```
if(typeof(currentDate) == "object"){
  trace("currentDate has a data type of object");
}
```

When you save and test this movie, the last line of the Output window will be:

```
currentDate has a data type of object
```

However, if you wanted to check what kind of object currentDate was, the typeof operator would not be able to help us out. Enter the instanceof operator. Add the following code to the actions list for frame 1:

```
if(currentDate instanceof Date){
  trace("currentDate is a Date object");
}
```

When you test the movie, you will see the following text display in the Output window:

```
currentDate is a Date object
```

Now, let's try an if . . . else statement that compares currentDate to a different class, such as Sound. Add the following code into the Actions panel for frame 1:

```
if(currentDate instanceof Sound){
  trace("currentDate is a Sound object");
} else {
  trace("currentDate is not a Sound object");
}
```

When you test your movie, you will see the following text displayed in the Output window:

```
currentDate is not a Sound object
```

While these are simple tests, you can start to see how instanceof allows you to check the class types of your data.

Overview of Functions as Procedures

A primary building block of any scripting or programming language is a procedure. A *procedure* is any set of code that you wish to reserve for a specific task. A procedure is useful for code that you wish to reuse in multiple event handlers (for example, Button instances and keyframes). In Flash ActionScript, procedures are called *functions* and are created with the function action.

What functions do

A *function* (or *procedure*) sets aside a block of code that can be executed with just one line of code. Functions can execute several actions and pass options (called *arguments*) to those actions. All functions must have a unique name, so that you know what to reference in later lines of code. In a way, functions are equivalent to your own custom additions to the Flash ActionScript language. In Flash MX, you can define a function on a specific timeline and refer to its path and name to execute it.

Note In Flash 4 movies, use the `call` action to execute code blocks located on other keyframes in the Flash movie.

When to create a function

For people new to scripting, perhaps the most confusing aspect of functions is knowing when to create them in a Flash movie. Use the following guidelines to help you determine when a function should be created:

✦ If you find yourself reusing the same lines of code on several Button instances, `MovieClip` objects, or keyframes, you should consider moving the actions to a function. In general, you should not pile up ActionScript on any single Button instance or keyframe.

✦ If you need to perform the same operation throughout a Flash movie, such as hiding specific Movie Clip instances on the Stage, you should consider defining a function to take care of the work for you.

✦ When you need to perform complex mathematical operations to determine a value, you should move the operations to a function.

How to define a function

When you add a function to a keyframe on the Main Timeline or a Movie Clip timeline, you are defining the function. All functions have a target path, just like other objects in ActionScript. All functions need a name followed by opening and closing parentheses, but arguments (options to pass to the function) inside the parentheses are optional.

Tip Functions are usually defined at the very beginning of a Flash movie (or within a Movie Clip instance that loads within the first frames of Flash movie). We recommend only placing functions on timeline keyframes — you can, however, execute functions from any event handler in a Flash movie.

As a simple example, let's say you wanted to create a function that has one `gotoAndStop()` action. This function will have a shorter name than `gotoAndStop()`, and it will be faster to type and use in our ActionScript code. You can place this on the first keyframe of your document's Main Timeline.

```
function gts(){
    _root.gotoAndStop("start");
}
```

This function, when evoked, will send the Main Timeline Playhead to the `start` label. We could further expand the functionality of `gts()` by adding an argument, which we'll call `frameLabel`:

```
function gts(frameLabel){
    _root.gotoAndStop(frameLabel);
}
```

In this version of the gts() function, instead of hard-coding a frame label (such as start) into the actual gotoAndStop() action, you specify an argument with the name frameLabel. Just like variable names, the names of your function and its arguments are entirely up to you—the name frameLabel has no significance. ActionScript simply knows that if you pass an argument to the gts() function, it should place that argument where the frameLabel term occurs in your actions. An argument acts as a placeholder for information that will be supplied to the function on a per-use basis; that is, you can specify a different value for frameLabel each time you evoke the gts() function.

Caution   Beware of naming your functions (and arguments) after already existing ActionScript terms. If in doubt, you should probably choose a word that does not resemble any JavaScript syntax (with later upgrades to ActionScript in mind). You'll see many examples in tutorials or books in which programmers always prefix names with my, as in myColor or myLabel, to avoid any potential naming conflicts.

How to execute a function

After you have defined a function on a timeline's keyframe, you can create actions that refer to the function's actions. The standard method for executing a function is

```
path to function.functionName(arguments);
```

At the end of the preceding section, we defined a function named gts() on the Main Timeline. If we added a Button instance to our movie, we could then execute the function from the Button instance with the following code:

```
on(release){
    _root.gts("start");
}
```

When this Button instance is clicked, the function gts() on the _root timeline (the Main Timeline) is executed. The function is passed the argument "start". In our function gts(), we defined frameLabel as an argument that occurs in the gotoAndStop() action. Therefore, the Main Timeline will go to and stop on the "start" frame label.

Later in this chapter, you use functions to create a dynamic reusable menu system in a Flash movie.

Caution   A function cannot be executed unless it was previously defined and recognized by the Flash Player. The keyframe containing the function declaration needs to be "played" before the function is available for use. For example, if you define a function on frame 10 of a Movie Clip instance that has stopped on frame 1 (and never played to frame 10), Flash will not have registered the function in memory.

Managing Related Data: The Array Object

Have you ever had a bunch of variables that have a lot in common? For example, do you have variables such as name_1, name_2, name_3, name_4, and so on? These variables look like lists of common information, such as:

```
name_1 = "John";
name_2 = "Vanessa";
name_3 = "Jennifer";
name_4 = "Frank";
```

In programming languages, an *array* is a list of values that can be addressed by their position in the list. An array is created by using the Array constructor:

```
visitors = new Array();
```

The preceding code object simply creates the array container for data. You create an array with information already specified, such as:

```
visitors = new Array("John","Vanessa","Jennifer","Frank");
```

or

```
visitors = ["John", "Vanessa","Jennifer","Frank"];
```

To access an item in `visitors`, you would use the array access operators with an array index number. To access the first position's data, you would use the following code:

```
message = "Hello " + visitors[0] + ", and welcome.";
```

Here, `visitors[0]` will return the value "John". If you traced the `message` variable, it would read:

```
Hello John, and welcome.
```

In most programming languages, the first index value (the starting position) is 0, not 1. In the following table, you'll see how the index number increases with our sample `visitors` array.

Index Position	0	1	2	3
Index Value	John	Vanessa	Jennifer	Frank

You can set and get the values within an array using the array access operators. You can replace existing array values by setting the index position to a new value, and you add values to the array by increasing the index number, as in:

```
visitors = new Array("John","Vanessa","Jennifer","Frank");
visitors[3] = "Nicole";
visitors[4] = "Candice";
```

In the example, "Nicole" replaces "Frank", and "Candice" is added to the end of the array. You can also add elements to the array using the push method of the `Array` object, as in:

```
visitors = new Array("John", "Vanessa","Jennifer","Frank");
newLength = visitors.push("Nicole","Candice");
```

This code will add "Nicole" and "Candice" after "Frank" and set the variable `newLength` equal to the `length` of the `visitors` array. `length` is an `Array` property that returns the number of elements in the array. In the preceding example, `newLength` is equal to 6, because there are now 6 names in the array.

You can read more about methods of the `Array` object in the *Macromedia Flash MX ActionScript Bible*.

You look at arrays in a function example later in this chapter.

Emulating Arrays in Flash 4 Movies

In Flash 4, you could only emulate arrays, using expressions for variable names. In our array examples for Flash 5 ActionScript, you could create an array-like structure for a Flash 4 movie by using the following code:

```
name_1 = "John";
name_2 = "Vanessa";
name_3 = "Jennifer";
name_4 = "Frank";
```

Then, you could use another variable, i, to indirectly refer to different name_ variables, as in:

```
i = 2;
currentName = eval("name_" add i);
message = "Hello " add currentName add ", and welcome!";
```

For Flash 4 compatibility, the add operator (instead of the + operator) and the eval() function are used to return the current value of the name_ variable we want to insert. If you traced the message variable, the Output window would display:

```
Hello Vanessa, and welcome!
```

We mention array emulation in this section only because many Flash developers may encounter clients who wish to have Flash movies (or sites) that will work with the Flash Player 4 plug-in, because that plug-in version is likely to be installed on more computers.

Creating a Dynamic Reusable Flash Menu

In this section, you use arrays to create a dynamic code-built menu that you can adjust for any Flash movie. You create a Main Timeline with six sections for a photographer's site and a menu that navigates to those four sections. While that sounds simple enough, we create the menu entirely from ActionScript code.

1. Create a new Flash document (Ctrl+N or ⌘+N).

2. Rename Layer 1 to **labels**. Create new keyframes (press the F6 key) on frames 2, 10, 20, 30, 40, and 50. Select frame 60 and press the F5 key.

3. Starting on frame 2 of the Labels layer, assign the following label names to the keyframes you created in Step 2: **about**, **interiors**, **exteriors**, **landscapes**, **portraits**, and **editorial**.

4. Add a new layer, and name it **actions**. Add a keyframe on frame 2 of the Actions layer. With that keyframe selected, open the Actions panel and add a stop(); action. In the Property inspector, type **//stop** in the <Frame Label> field. This will create a frame comment of stop. The stop(); action on frame 2 will prevent the Main Timeline from playing past our about section when the movie first loads.

5. Create another layer called **heading**. Add keyframes on this layer, matching the keyframes in the Labels layer. Insert some graphics in each keyframe for each section. As a starting point, you can simply add text headings to each section (for example, About the Company, Interior Photography, and so on). You need this Heading layer so that you have some indication that the Playhead on the Main Timeline actually moves when an item in the menu is clicked.

6. Create another layer called **background**. Place this layer at the bottom of the layer stack. Draw a filled rectangle that spans the top of the document, as shown in Figure 26-1.

7. Now you create an array that contains the names of each of your frame labels. Add a new layer to the Main Timeline and name it **menu actions**. Select the first keyframe on the menu Actions layer. Open the Actions panel (F9) and add the following code (note that the ⊃ indicates a continuation of the same line of code; do not insert this character into your actual code):

```
sectionNames = new Array("about", "interiors", ⊃
  "exteriors", "landscapes", "portraits", "editorial");
```

This line of ActionScript will create an array object named `sectionNames`. We can now refer to each section of our timeline using array syntax, such as `sectionNames[0]`, `sectionNames[1]`, and so on. We use this array to build the actual button text in our menu.

8. In the same block of code, add the following line to the Script pane for frame 1 of the menu Actions layer:

```
sectionCount = sectionNames.length;
```

This code creates a new variable named `sectionCount`. The `length` property of an array will return the current number of elements inside of the array. Therefore, because we put six elements into the array (in Step 7), `sectionCount` will be equal to 6. You may be wondering why you just didn't manually insert the value 6 here. The point to using an array is that we can change the elements of the array at any point, and the rest of your code will update automatically to reflect the changes. In this way, we are building a dynamic menu system.

9. Save your Flash document as **menuArray_100.fla**. At this point, your Flash document should resemble Figure 26-1.

10. Now you need to create some menu elements that you can use to build a dynamic menu from ActionScript. First, you need to make a Movie Clip "container" for the menu items. This container will be a Movie Clip instance on the Stage. Press Ctrl+F8 (⌘+F8) to create a new symbol. Name this symbol **menu** and choose the Movie Clip behavior. Flash MX automatically switches to Symbol Editing mode.

11. Within the timeline of the menu symbol, rename Layer 1 to **menuItem**. This layer will hold a template Movie Clip instance for the menu item(s). Again, create a new Movie Clip symbol by pressing Ctrl+F8 (⌘+F8). Name this symbol **menuItem**, and choose the Movie Clip behavior.

12. Within the timeline of the menuItem symbol, rename Layer 1 to **button**. On this layer, create or add a Button symbol. In this example, we used the Oval buttons — blue button from the Ovals folder of the Buttons library (Window ➪ Common Libraries ➪ Buttons). This will be the actual button that appears in the menu. Center your Button instance on the Stage, using the Align panel.

13. Add a new layer to the menuItem symbol, and name it **textField**. On this layer, create a Dynamic text field that can accommodate the longest name you specified in the `sectionNames` array. In the Property inspector, give this Dynamic text field the instance name `label`. Use whatever font face you prefer. Place the text field to the right of the button, as shown in Figure 26-2.

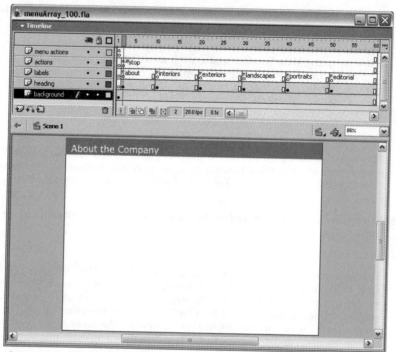

Figure 26-1: The Main Timeline has frame labels and artwork for each section of the presentation.

14. Add another layer to the menuItem symbol and rename it **actions**. Select frame 1 of this layer, and in the Actions panel, add the following code:

```
label.text = labelName;
stop();
```

This code will put the value of the labelName variable into the label text field. You will see how labelName is declared in Step 19.

15. Select the Button instance that you added in Step 12. Open the Actions panel, and type the following code in the Script pane:

```
on(release){
    _root.gotoAndStop(labelName);
}
```

This code will use the value of a labelName variable as the frame label for the gotoAndStop() action. Notice that you will control the Main Timeline's Playhead by indicating _root. Shortly, you will assign each instance of menuItem a unique labelName value.

16. Open the menu Movie Clip symbol by double-clicking it in the Library. Drag an instance of menuItem from the Library to the menuItem layer on the menu timeline. With this instance selected, open the Property inspector and assign a name of **menuItem**, as shown in Figure 26-3. You will use this instance as a prototype for the real buttons in the menu symbol. Align this instance to the center of the Stage.

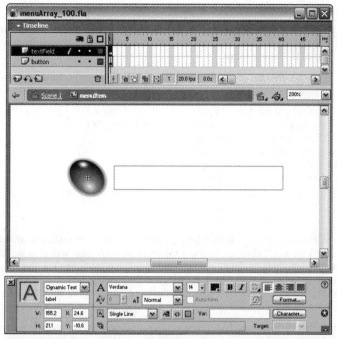

Figure 26-2: The menuItem instance will be used to create each button in the dynamic menu. Using ActionScript, the label text field will be filled with the appropriate section name.

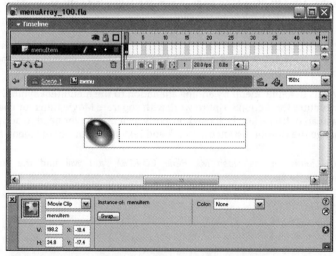

Figure 26-3: We will duplicate the menuItem instance in ActionScript to build each button in the menu symbol.

17. Save your Flash document.

18. Go back to the Main Timeline and create a new layer named **menu**. On this layer, place an instance of the menu Movie Clip symbol from the Library. In the Property inspector, give this symbol the name **menu**.

19. Open the Actions panel for frame 1 of the menu Actions layer. Add the following ActionScript to the Actions list:

```
for(i=0;i<sectionCount;i++){
  menu.menuItem.duplicateMovieClip("menuItem_"+i, i);
  currentItem = menu["menuItem_"+i];
  currentItem.labelName = sectionNames[i];
  if(i != 0){
    prevItem = menu["menuItem_"+(i-1)];
    currentItem._y = prevItem._y + prevItem._height;
  }
}
```

This code inserts a `for` loop that will duplicate the `menuItem` instance (inside of the `menu` instance) for each element in the `sectionNames` array. It will also set the value of `labelName` in each duplicated `menuItem` instance (`currentItem`) to the name of the appropriate section name. Notice that you specify `i` for the index number of the `sectionNames` array because the position index of every array starts at 0 — your `menuItem` numbering will also start at 0.

After an instance is duplicated for the section name, you then reposition the `menuItem` instance below the previous one (`prevItem`). You need to perform this operation only for instances greater than 1 because the starting instance does not need to be moved down.

20. Before you can test the movie, you need to hide the original `menuItem` instance in the `menu` instance. After the `for` loop code, insert the following action:

```
menu.menuItem._visible = false;
```

21. Save your Flash document again and test it (Ctrl+Enter or ⌘+Return). Unless you had a syntax error in your ActionScript or forgot to name a Movie Clip instance, you will see a dynamic menu built by ActionScript (as shown in Figure 26-4).

You can enhance this dynamic menu by adding animation to the menuItem symbol timeline. You can also restructure the ActionScript to work with separate Movie Clips for each `sectionName`, instead of frame labels. If used properly, you may never need to script a menu again! Simply change the Button instance artwork and text styles for unique menu interfaces.

In the ch26 folder of the *Flash MX Bible* CD-ROM, you will find the completed **menuArray_100.fla** file.

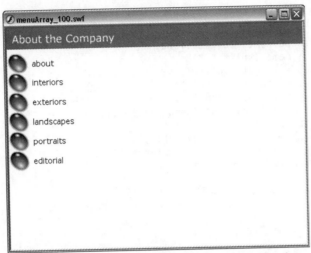

Figure 26-4: The ActionScript code in the menu Actions layer duplicates the menuItem instance in the menu instance. Each duplicated instance has a unique labelName value, which is used in the gotoAndStop() action by each Button instance.

Functions as Methods of Objects

We've already discussed functions as procedure mechanisms in Flash movies. Functions can be used to define a set of actions that are later executed when the function is invoked. In ActionScript, you can also use functions as methods of other code objects. *Methods* are actions mapped to other objects. Unlike properties and values, methods carry out a task with that object. In this section, we deconstruct a Flash document (.fla file) that uses a function to create a menu completely from ActionScript.

On the CD-ROM Make a copy of the **createMenu_100.fla** file, located in the ch26 folder of the *Flash MX Bible* CD-ROM.

Open a local copy of the createMenu_100.fla file in Flash MX. You'll notice that the Main Timeline has a setup similar to the menuArray_100.fla file that was discussed in the last section. We have a series of labels, indicating sections of the Flash movie. Test this Flash movie, and you'll see a dynamic menu display. Clicking each button takes you to the corresponding section of the Flash movie.

Unlike the previous menuArray_100.fla example, though, notice that we have different text on the menu buttons than the text used in the frame labels. For example, the Our Products menu button takes you to the `products` label on the Main Timeline. For this Flash movie, a function with multiple arguments enables you to specify the text of the menu buttons separately from the targeted labels (and timelines).

Select the first frame of the Functions layer. In the Actions panel, you'll see this function appear in the Script pane:

```
function createMenu(names,targets,labels){
  var itemName = names.split(",");
  var itemTarget = targets.split(",");
  var frameLabel = labels.split(",");
  for(var i=0;i<itemName.length;i++){
    this.attachMovie("menuItem","menuItem_"+i,i);
    var currentItem = this["menuItem_"+i];
    currentItem.label.text = itemName[i];
    currentItem.itemTarget = eval(itemTarget[i]);
    currentItem.labelName = frameLabel[i];
    if(i>0){
      var prevItem = this["menuItem_"+(i-1)];
      currentItem._y = prevItem._y + prevItem._height;
    }
  }
}
```

The `createMenu()` function has three arguments: `names`, `targets`, and `labels`. The value for these arguments will be supplied as a method of a Movie Clip instance when the function is executed. Similar to our previous menuArray_100.fla example, we will use arrays to store the values of our frame labels (and section names). However, we'll also create an argument (and array) to store the button text that will appear on the menu buttons. In this way, you can create ActionScript that correctly uses frame labels in other `goto` actions without worrying about the text that is actually used as a button item. The `targets` argument is used to create an array of timeline targets for each button item.

The function also uses the `attachMovie()` method (instead of `duplicateMovieClip()`) to use the `menuItem` Movie Clip symbol in the instance timeline executing the function. In our example, a menu Movie Clip instance is created on the Stage with code outside of the `createMenu()` function, using the new `createEmptyMovieClip()` method. This empty Movie Clip instance is assigned the `createMenu()` function as a method, just as `duplicateMovieClip()` or `attachMovie()` is a method of the `MovieClip` object:

```
menu.createMenu = createMenu;
```

This line of code creates a new method called `createMenu`, specifically for the `menu` instance (object) on the Stage. It also sets this method to use the function `createMenu` as its value. Therefore, whenever we evoke the `createMenu` method of the `menu` object, the actions within the `createMenu` function will run.

Caution

The act of creating and assigning a method name for an object does not actually execute the method or the function. We're simply defining a method for the object, so that it can be evoked later. Do not use parentheses for method (and function) assignment—doing so will actually execute the function upon assignment.

Note that you can use any method name you prefer—it need not match the name of the function as our example does. So, you could write:

```
menu.customMenu = createMenu;
```

The function `createMenu` also uses the `this` syntax to make the function work in relation to the object that is executing it. `this` will equal `_root.menu` for the method assignment, `menu.createMenu = createMenu`. However, if we had another menu instance, such as `menu_2`, that used the `createMenu` function as a method, `this` would refer to its path for its method. Herein lies the power of a function as a method of an object — you can assign the same function (and arguments) to unique objects (or Movie Clip instances) on the Stage.

To execute the method `createMenu` for the `menu` instance, you need to specify the method and any arguments you will supply the method. In our example, the following line (note that the ⊃ indicates a continuation of the same line of code; this character does not appear in the actual code) executes the `createMenu` method for the menu instance:

```
menu.createMenu("Home,Our Products,Our ⊃
    Services","_root,_root,_root","main,products,services");
```

In this line of code, the following arguments are passed to the `createMenu` function arguments:

```
names = "Home,Our Products,Our Services"
targets = "_root,_root,_root"
labels = "main,products,services"
```

When the `createMenu` method is evoked, the `createMenu` function parses these arguments into the actions contained with the function. The `split()` method for `String` objects takes the values of `names`, `targets`, and `labels` and makes each comma-delimited item (that is, an item separated by a comma) into a separate array element. While you do not see the code structure of an array specified in the function, ActionScript will create the following array from the `split()` method for the `names` argument:

```
itemName[0] = "Home"
itemName[1] = "Our Products"
itemName[2] = "Our Services"
```

You will, however, see references to these array items in the function:

```
itemName[i]
```

This reference is used to take each `itemName` element and put it on the proper `menuItem` Movie Clip instance in the `menu` object.

The `itemTarget` array is used to let each `menuItem` instance know which timeline target it should address with its `gotoAndStop()` action (contained on the Button instance within the menuItem symbol in the Library). The `frameLabel` array assigns the proper frame label for the `gotoAndStop()` action for the Button instance.

This movie also uses a `clearMenu` function (and method) to delete the `menuItem` instances and arrays.

To show you how function methods can speed your workflow, let's create a duplicate menu on a different object.

1. Open the createMenu_100.fla file.

2. Create a new layer and name it **rect**.

3. On frame 1 of the rect layer, draw a rounded rectangle with the Oval tool. In this example, size the rectangle to 175x105 using the Property inspector.

4. With the rectangle selected, press the F8 key to convert the artwork into a symbol. Choose the Movie Clip behavior, name the symbol **rect**, and choose the top left registration point, as shown in Figure 26-5.

Figure 26-5: Make sure you choose the top-left corner registration point, so that the menuItem instances will start from this position.

5. With the instance selected on the Stage, open the Property inspector and name the instance **rect**. Position the `rect` instance in the lower-left corner of the Stage, as shown in Figure 26-6.

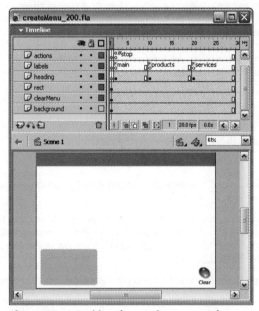

Figure 26-6: Position the rect instance at the lower-left corner of the Stage.

6. Select frame 1 of the Functions layer and open the Actions panel. After the last line of code already in the Script pane, type the following actions. Do not insert the ⊃ symbol in your actual code. This character indicates a continuation of the same line of code:

```
rect.createMenu = createMenu;
rect.clearMenu = clearMenu;
rect.createMenu("Home,Our Products,Our ⊃
  Services","_root,_root,_root","main,products,services");
```

This code performs the same ActionScript as our earlier method for the menu instance. This time, however, the menu will be created on the rect instance.

7. Save your Flash document as **createMenu_200.fla**, and test it (Ctrl+Enter or ⌘+Return). Menu items will now appear on the rect instance as well as the menu instance.

You can refer to the completed version of this exercise, **createMenu_200.fla**, located in the ch26 folder of the *Flash MX Bible* CD-ROM.

Functions as Constructors for Objects

Functions can also be used with the new constructor to create objects with properties and methods assigned by the function. This means that you can use a function to create unique objects, based on parameters that you pass as arguments to the function upon invocation. In this section, we deconstruct another function example that creates an entire sound library with ActionScript, without using any Movie Clip instances.

Make a local copy of the **soundObjects.fla** file, located in the ch26 folder of the *Flash MX Bible* CD-ROM.

You will learn about ActionScript for Sound objects in the next chapter.

Open your copy of the soundObjects.fla file in Flash MX. You'll notice that there aren't any Movie Clips and/or physical elements on the Stage. Select the first (and only) frame on the Actions layer. Open the Actions panel and you'll see the following code:

```
function createLib(start,end){
  for(i=start;i<=end;i++){
    if(i==start){
      this.snd = new Array();
    }
    _root.createEmptyMovieClip("sndStorage_" + i, i);
    var target = _root["sndStorage_"+i];
    this.snd[i] = new Sound(target);
    this.snd[i].attachSound("sound_"+i);
  }
}
soundLib = new createLib(1,7);
soundLib.snd[1].start();
soundLib.snd[2].start();
```

There are three sections to this code: the function definition; the object creation and assignment; and the method execution of the Sound objects.

Function definition

The `createLib()` function has two arguments: `start` and `end`. Again, these are user-defined function names and arguments. You could rename the function and arguments to your own preferred terms. The `for` loop in the `createLib()` function will create a `snd` array object within the calling object (`this`). This array will contain `Sound` objects that use the AIF sound files in the Library. Note that each of the sounds in the Library has been set to export with the Flash movie (.swf file), as defined by the Linkage Properties for each sound.

Cross-Reference   See Chapters 28, "Sharing and Loading Assets," for more information on symbol linkage.

Object creation and assignment

After the `createLib()` function is defined, we can use it for new objects. In our example, a new object named `soundLib` is created after the function definition:

```
soundLib = new createLib(1,7);
```

First, the object is declared as being on the current timeline (`this` or `_root`). By not specifying `_root` directly, you can load this Flash movie into `MovieClip` objects in other Flash movies and retain proper targeting paths for the `createLib()` function. If you test this movie on its own, `soundLib` will be declared on `_root` or `_level0`. Using the `new` constructor, we create the `snd` array and `Sound` objects relative to the `soundLib` object. We are creating a unique object with specific properties and values. This enables you to make as many objects as you desire, all from one function:

```
soundLib_1 = new createLib(1,3);
soundLib_2 = new createLib(4,7);
```

These actions (not used in our example) would create two separate `soundLib` objects, each using a specific range of `Sound` objects from the Library.

The numbers specified in the parentheses indicate the sounds to use from the Library. Remember that in our function `createLib()`, the `start` and `end` arguments are used to form the linkage identifiers

```
"sound_"+i
```

where `i` is defined by the `start` argument and incremented until the `end` argument value is reached.

Sound object method execution

Finally, after the `Sound` objects are created within the `soundLib` object, we can play the sounds with the built-in ActionScript `start` method for `Sound` objects:

```
this.soundLib.snd[1].start();
this.soundLib.snd[2].start();
```

These lines of code tell the `Sound` objects located in the 1 and 2 index positions of the `snd` array (in this example, `sound_1` and `sound_2` from the Library) to play.

This is just one way of using functions to create new objects. You can use functions to create other types of data-based objects for record storage and retrieval as well as to create unique `Color` objects to reference with more than one Movie Clip target.

Caution

During further testing, we discovered that the `setVolume` method of the Sound Object controls all Sound Object instances on a given timeline. This means that you should create one Sound Object instance *per timeline*. For example, if you want to separately control the volume of five individual sounds, make sure you create each of those Sound Object instances on a separate Movie Clip instance. To safeguard for this condition, we used the new `createEmptyMovieClip()` method in our example to assign each sound to a separate timeline, designated by `target` in the `createLib()` function.

Summary

✦ ActionScript has six data types: `boolean`, `function`, `movieclip`, `number`, `object`, and `string`.

✦ The data type of an ActionScript element can be checked using the `typeof` operator.

✦ The most common use of a function is as a procedure, which is a set of actions that execute when the function's name is evoked.

✦ A procedure should be created when the same actions are repeated within a Flash movie or when you want to avoid storing long action lists within Button instances.

✦ A function is defined with the `function` action, in the format `function name(arguments){actions}`.

✦ A function can be executed when the name of the function is evoked. The format of a function call is `targetPath.functionName(arguments);` as in `_root.createLib(1,7)`.

✦ Arrays can manage related information, such as lists. An array is initiated with the `Array` constructor, as in `myArray = new Array();`.

✦ Array elements have an index number, indicating their position in the array. Array index numbers start with 0 and increment by 1 with each new element.

✦ To access an item in an array, use the array access operators (`[ ]`) with an array index number.

✦ Functions can be used as methods of ActionScript objects. A method is prescribed by creating a unique method name after the object and setting the method's value equal to a function name (for example, `_root.menu.createMenu = createMenu;`). Parentheses and arguments are omitted from the method assignment.

✦ Objects can be created with the function constructor. Functions intended for this use describe properties and methods for objects using the `this` target path. A new object is created by specifying an object name and setting its value equal to a new instance of the function name, as in `myObject = new createLib(1,7);`.

✦   ✦   ✦

Interacting with Movie Clips

♦ ♦ ♦ ♦

In This Chapter

Defining collisions

Using the hitTest()
method

Using the Color object

Accessing the
Sound object

Controlling the volume
and balance of a sound

Printing Flash
movie frames

♦ ♦ ♦ ♦

This chapter continues your exploration of the MovieClip object in ActionScript. You will explore the ins and outs of collision detection for MovieClip objects and learn how to control the visibility of the mouse pointer or attach a custom cursor to the mouse pointer. We'll look at other ActionScript elements such as Color and Sound objects that work with MovieClip objects to create visual and audio effects, respectively. You will also learn how to print individual frames of a Flash movie, creating high-quality output for hard copy artwork.

Movie Clip Collision Detection

Have you ever wanted to detect the intersection of two elements in a Flash movie? If two Movie Clip instances overlap on the Stage, how would you know? How would you tell ActionScript to look for an overlap? In ActionScript, there are two primary types of intersections (or collisions):

♦ **User-initiated collisions:** This type of intersection occurs when you click and drag an object (a MovieClip object) and overlap another MovieClip object as you drag or release. You can also consider the mouse pointer an "object" that can intersect with another object. For example, if you move the mouse pointer over a MovieClip object, you can detect when the mouse pointer enters the space of the MovieClip object.

♦ **Script- or time-based collisions:** This type of intersection between objects happens when randomly moving objects collide with one another, such as balls bouncing around the Stage, detecting the edges of the frame and responding to other boundaries or objects.

In this section, you'll look at examples in each of these categories. Let's begin with a quick review of the _droptarget property of the MovieClip object.

Using _droptarget

A collision between two MovieClip objects can occur if the user drags one Movie Clip instance to the location of another Movie Clip instance. We first examined the startDrag() action and method in Chapter 25, "Controlling Movie Clips." In the dog movie, we used the _droptarget property of a MovieClip object to detect whether the area of one `MovieClip` object occupied the area of another Movie Clip object. To recap, you can test the intersection of two Movie Clips with the following code:

```
on(press){
 this.startDrag(true);
}

on(release){
 if(eval(this._droptarget) == _root.mcInstance2){
  trace("this MC instance overlaps mcInstance2");
 } else {
  trace("this MC instance does not overlap mcInstance2");
 }
 this.stopDrag();
}
```

This code could occur on a Button instance within the first Movie Clip instance. When the user clicks the Button instance, the Movie Clip `startDrag()` method is invoked, and the user can drag the Movie Clip instance on the Stage. When the user releases the mouse, the `_droptarget` property (which returns target paths in Slashes notation) is evaluated to convert the target path to dot syntax. If the `_droptarget` property returns the path to another instance, the `if` condition will see whether the path matches `_root.mcInstance2`. If the paths match, the `trace()` action indicating an overlap is executed. Otherwise, a separate trace action will notify us that the instance is not on top of `mcInstance2`.

Cross-Reference   To see a fully functional example of the `_droptarget` property in action, please review the section "Detecting the drop position: Using _droptarget" in Chapter 25, "Controlling Movie Clips."

Collision detection with hitTest()

You can also perform more advanced collision detection using the `hitTest()` method of the `MovieClip` object. `hitTest()` will do exactly what it says — it will test to see whether a "hit" occurred between two elements. `hitTest` has two formats:

```
mcInstance.hitTest(anotherInstance);
```

or

```
mcInstance.hitTest(x coordinate, y coordinate, shapeFlag);
```

With this method, you can determine whether the X and Y coordinates are within the space occupied by the Movie Clip instance. You can use `onClipEvents` such as `mouseMove` or new event handlers like `onMouseMove()`to constantly check for a hit occurrence:

```
onClipEvent(mouseMove){
 if(this.hitTest(_root._xmouse, _root._ymouse, true)){
  trace("A hit has occurred");
 }
}
```

or

```
myMC.onMouseMove = function(){
 if(this.hitTest(_root._xmouse, _root._ymouse, true)){
  trace("A hit has occurred");
 }
};
```

This code will report a trace() action anytime the mouse pointer is moved within the artwork of the Movie Clip instance to which the onClipEvent or onMouseMove() handler is attached. The shape flag attribute of hitTest() defines the actual test area for the hit. If the shape flag is set to true, a hit occurs only if the X and Y coordinates occur within the actual artwork of the Movie Clip instance. If the shape flag is set to false, a hit will occur whenever the X and Y coordinates occur within the bounding box of the Movie Clip instance. In Figure 27-1, if the left circle uses a shape flag of true, a hit is reported whenever the X and Y coordinates occur within the shape of the circle (not within the bounding box). If the right circle uses a shape of false, a hit is reported when the X and Y coordinates occur within the bounding box.

Figure 27-1: The shape flag determines the boundary of the Movie Clip instance for the hitTest() method.

You can see a working example of shape flags and the hitTest() method in the **hitTest_xy.fla** file, located in the ch27 folder of the *Flash MX Bible* CD-ROM. Open this Flash document, and test the movie. As you move your mouse within the space of each object, you will notice that the hit area is different for each object. You will create your own Flash movie that uses hitTest() in our coverage of the Mouse object in this chapter.

The other format for the hitTest() method is to simply specify a target path to compare for a hit occurrence. With this syntax, you cannot use a shape flag option; if any area of the bounding box for a Movie Clip instance touches the bounding box of the tested instance, a hit occurs. For example, you can modify the ActionScript used earlier to indicate a hit between instances, instead of X and Y coordinates:

```
onClipEvent(mouseMove){
 if(this.hitTest(_root.mcInstance2)){
  trace("A hit has occurred.");
 }
}
```

or

```
myMC.onMouseMove = function(){
 if(this.hitTest(_root.mcInstance2)){
  trace("A hit has occurred.");
 }
};
```

This code assumes that other actions are actually initiating a startDrag() action. Also, we have omitted the other half of the if condition in both this example and the previous example. If you omit a condition operator and test condition, ActionScript assumes that you are testing for a true result (as a Boolean value). The following if conditions are exactly the same:

```
myMouseClick = true;
if(myMouseClick){
 trace("myMouseClick is true.");
}
if(myMouseClick == true){
 trace("myMouseClick is true.");
}
```

Therefore, to test for a `true` value with any `if` statement, specify the variable (or method) that has a Boolean value. The `hitTest()` method will yield either a `true` (a hit has occurred) or a `false` (no hit has occurred) result. Note that, with scripting languages, it is more common to use the former example for testing `true` conditions.

You can see a working example of targets and the `hitTest()` method in the **hitTest_target. fla** file, located in the ch27 folder of the *Flash MX Bible* CD-ROM. You will create a Flash movie that uses this type of `hitTest()` method in our coverage of the `Sound` object later in this chapter.

Using the Mouse Object

With ActionScript, you can emulate new mouse pointers (that is, the graphic shown for the mouse pointer) by using the `startDrag()` behavior (with lock to center `true`) on Movie Clips containing icon graphics. However, this technique does not hide the original mouse pointer — it would appear directly above the dragged Movie Clip instance. ActionScript features a static `Mouse` object, which has two simple methods:

✦ `show()`: This method reveals the mouse pointer. By default, the mouse pointer will appear at the start of a movie.

✦ `hide()`: This method turns off the mouse pointer's visibility. To reveal the mouse pointer again, execute the `show()` method.

Once the `Mouse` object (that is, the mouse pointer) is hidden, you can lock a `MovieClip` object containing a new icon graphic to the position of the mouse pointer. In this section, you will create a Flash movie with a large circle `MovieClip` object. When the mouse pointer moves into the area of this object, you will attach a smaller circle to the mouse pointer's position. The `hitTest()` method will be used to determine when the mouse pointer movies into the area of the large circle, and the `attachMovie()` method of the `MovieClip` object will affix the small circle to the mouse pointer's position.

1. Create a new Flash document (Ctrl+N or ⌘+N). Rename Layer 1 to **circle**.

2. Select the Oval tool, and draw a circle. In the Property inspector, set the circle's size to 25×25.

3. With the circle artwork selected, press the F8 key to convert the artwork into a Movie Clip symbol. Name the symbol **circle**.

4. Name the instance on the Stage **circleLarge_mc** in the <Instance Name> field of the Property inspector. Increase the size of this particular instance to 200×200, and apply a Tint effect to fill the instance with a different solid color. Center the instance on the Stage using the Align panel.

5. Now, have to link the circle symbol in the Library to the exported Flash movie (.swf file). Right-click (Control+click on the Mac) the circle symbol, and choose Linkage. Select the Export for ActionScript check box, and type **circle** in the Identifier field, as shown in Figure 27-2.

Figure 27-2: The circle symbol is now linked to the Flash movie.

Once the circle symbol is linked, you can dynamically insert the symbol into the Flash movie with ActionScript. Remember, you want to attach the circle to the mouse pointer when it enters the space of the circleLarge_mc instance.

6. On the Main Timeline (that is, Scene 1), create a new layer and name it **actions**. Select frame 1 of this layer, and open the Actions panel. In Expert mode, type the following code in the Script pane:

```
1. circleLarge_mc.onMouseMove = function() {
2.  if(this.hitTest(_root._xmouse,_root._ymouse, true)){
3.   if (!(circleSmall_mc instanceof MovieClip)) {
4.    _root.attachMovie("circle","circleSmall_mc",1);
5.   }
6.   circleSmall_mc._x = _root._xmouse;
7.   circleSmall_mc._y = _root._ymouse;
8.   Mouse.hide();
9.   updateAfterEvent();
10.  } else {
11.   if(circleSmall_mc instanceof MovieClip){
12.    circleSmall_mc.removeMovieClip();
13.   }
14.   Mouse.show();
15.  }
16. };
```

Here, you use the new event handler onMouseMove() for MovieClip objects introduced in Flash MX ActionScript. This handler is assigned to the circleLarge_mc in line 1. When the mouse moves in the Flash movie, the function(){} code will execute.

If the X and Y position of the mouse pointer intersects with the circleLarge_mc instance, the if condition in line 2 will execute. Line 3 checks to see if the new graphic (that is, the circle symbol in the Library) exists in the movie. If it doesn't, the symbol is attached to the Main Timeline (_root) in line 4. The new instance is named circleSmall_mc.

Lines 6 and 7 position the X and Y coordinates of the circleSmall_mc instance by referencing the current position of the mouse pointer (_root._xmouse and _root._ymouse). Line 8 hides the mouse pointer icon, while Line 9 uses the updateAfterEvent() function to force a video refresh of the Flash movie. This allows the circleSmall_mc to move very smoothly across the Stage.

Lines 10–15 will execute if the mouse pointer is not within the space of the `circleLarge_mc` instance. Line 11 checks to see if `circleSmall_mc` exists in the movie—if it does, it will be removed (line 12). The mouse pointer will also reappear when the mouse moves outside of the `circleLarge_mc` instance (line 14).

7. Save your Flash document as **mouse_hitTest.fla**, and test it (Ctrl+Enter or ⌘+Enter). In the Test Movie window, move the mouse pointer into the space of the large circle. When the mouse enters this area, the small circle from the Library will attach itself to the position of the mouse cursor and hide the original pointer. When you move the mouse out of the large circle, the small circle disappears and the original mouse pointer returns. See Figure 27-3 for these comparisons.

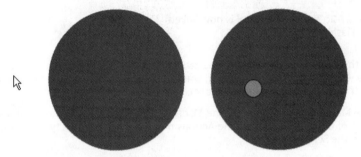

Figure 27-3: The left image shows the mouse outside the large circle, while the right image shows the mouse inside the large circle with the small circle attached.

That might have seemed like a lot of work to hide a mouse pointer, but in the process, you learned how to attach your own icons to the mouse pointer. You can use this same methodology to add any custom graphic to the mouse pointer. Simply add a different linked symbol to the Library, and change the linkage ID in the `attachMovie()` method.

On the CD-ROM

You can find the completed example, **mouse_hitTest.fla**, in the ch27 folder of the *Flash MX Bible* CD-ROM.

On the CD-ROM

To continue learning about the `hitTest()` method, check out James Robertson's tutorial, "Complex Hit Detection on the Z Axis," in the **Bonus_Tutorials.pdf** located in the Bonus_Tutorials folder of the *Flash MX Bible* CD-ROM.

Manipulating Color Attributes

The `Color` object in ActionScript gives you unprecedented control of the appearance of your `MovieClip` objects. By controlling the color (and transparency) of your artwork with ActionScript's `Color` object, you can

✦ Create on-the-fly color schemes or "skins" for Flash interfaces.

✦ Enable users to select and view color preferences for showcased products on an e-commerce site.

✦ Instantly change the color attributes of a Flash design-in-progress for a client.

Because color is controlled through the Color object, we'll quickly review the unique methods available to this object. Refer to Table 27-1 for more information. Note that this table is organized by order of practical use.

Table 27-1: Methods for the Color Object

Method	Definition	Options
setRGB	Changes the RGB offset for the specified Color object (and targeted Movie Clip). This method changes all colors in the targeted instance to one solid RGB color.	*colorReference.setRGB(0xRRGGBB);* where: *colorReference* is the name of the Color object. We'll discuss the creation of Color objects in this section. *RR, GG,* and *BB* are the offset values (in hexadecimal) for the Red, Green, and Blue channels, respectively.
getRGB	Retrieves the values established with the last setRGB execution. If you want to reapply RGB offsets to a new Color object, use this method. You can also retrieve RGB numeric values of any Movie Clip instance on the Stage that has a Tint effect applied to it.	*colorReference.getRGB();* No options or arguments for this method.
setTransform	Changes the RGB offset and percentage values for the specified Color object (and targeted Movie Clip). This method produces visual results that resemble both left- and right-hand color controls in the Advanced Effect dialog box for the Advanced option in the Color menu of the Property inspector.	*colorReference.setTransform(colorTransformObject);* where: *colorTransformObject* is the name of a Object that has percentage and offset properties for Red, Green, Blue, and Alpha channels. We'll discuss the intricacies of these properties in the following sections.
getTransform	Retrieves the values established with the last setTransform execution. Use this method to reapply color transforms to new Color objects. You can also use this method to retrieve the color values of Movie Clip instances that have an Advanced Effect applied in the Property inspector.	*colorReference.getTransform();* No options or arguments for this method.

Creating a Color object

To manipulate the color attributes of a Movie Clip instance, you need to create a new `Color` object that references the Movie Clip instance. In the following steps, you learn to use the constructor for the `Color` object. Let's work out the steps required to take control of color properties.

On the CD-ROM For the exercises with the `Color` object, make a copy of the **dogColor_starter.fla** document in the ch27 folder of the *Flash MX Bible* CD-ROM. Thank you, Sandro Corsaro of `www.sandrocorsaro.com`, for supplying the artwork of the dog!

1. Select the instance of the dog graphic on the Stage. Open the Property inspector and name this Movie Clip instance **dog_1**.

2. Create a new layer on the Main Timeline, and name the layer **buttons**.

3. Open the Components panel and drag an instance of the PushButton component onto the Stage. Place the instance near the left corner of the Stage. We will discuss components in more detail in Chapter 29, "Using Components." For now, we'll guide you through the use of this component for the purposes of this exercise.

4. Select the `PushBar` instance on the Stage, and open the Property inspector. Make sure the Parameters tab is selected in the lower-right corner of the inspector. Name this instance **redButton**. Type the text **Red** in the Label field. In the Change Handler field, type **changeColor**. Refer to settings shown in Figure 27-4.

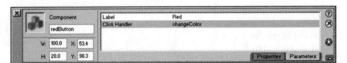

Figure 27-4: The parameters for this instance of the PushButton component

5. Now you need to specify a `changeColor()` function in the movie. This function will be executed by the `redButton` instance when it is clicked. Create a new layer on the Main Timeline and name it **actions**. Select frame 1 of the Actions layer, and open the Actions panel (F9). In Expert mode, type the following code into the Script pane:

```
function changeColor(obj){
 var label = obj.getLabel().toLowerCase();
 if(label == "red"){
  dogFill_1 = new Color(_root.dog_1);
  dogFill_1.setRGB(0xFF0000);
 }
}
```

In this function, the `obj` argument represents the PushButton instance that is executing the function. When the `redButton` instance is clicked, `obj` will equal `redButton`. (You'll be adding more instances in short order.) Line 2 of this function establishes a variable named `label` that returns the Label text inside of the `obj` instance and converts the `label` text to lowercase. If `label` equals "red" in line 3, lines 4 and 5 will execute. Line 4 creates a new `Color` object called `dogFill_1`, which refers to the _root.dog_1 Movie Clip instance you made in Step 1. Once the dogFill_1 object is initiated, you can access methods of the Color object, such as setRGB(). In line 5, you changed the color of the Movie Clip instance to pure red, designated by 0xFF0000 in hexadecimal.

New Feature

Choose View Line Numbers in the options menu of the Actions panel to see line numbers next to your ActionScript code. The options menu is located at the top right corner of the panel.

6. Save the Flash document as **dogColor_100.fla**, and test the movie. Click the redButton instance on the Stage. The color of the dog_1 Movie Clip should change to bright red. Close the Flash movie, and return to the Flash MX authoring environment.

7. To see the getRGB() method in action, let's create some trace() messages for the Output window. Go back to the changeColor() function on frame 1. Add the following line of code just before the closing curly brace (}) of the if() action. Type this as one line of code:

```
trace("dogFill_1's RGB numeric value = " + ⮠
  dogFill_1.getRGB());
```

8. Save the document and test the movie. When you click the redButton instance, the Output window will open and display the following text:

```
dogFill_1's RGB numeric value = 16711680
```

9. To change this value back to the hexadecimal value that you entered in the setRGB() method, you need to convert the value to base 16. Add the following action after the last trace() action from Step 6:

```
trace("dogFill_1's RGB hex value = " + ⮠
  dogFill_1.getRGB().toString(16));
```

10. Save the document and test the movie. When you click the redButton instance, the Output window should open and display the new value:

```
dogFill_1's RGB numeric value = 16711680
dogFill_1's RGB hex value = ff0000
```

However, you won't need to convert getRGB()'s native return value to set another Color object equal to a previous setRGB() value. In the following steps, you will create another dog and Color object team.

11. Duplicate the dog_1 Movie Clip instance on the Stage (Edit ⇨ Duplicate), and name the new instance **dog_2** in the Property inspector. Position the dog_2 instance to the right of dog_1.

12. Duplicate the Red PushButton instance on the Stage, and position the new instance below the original one. In the Property inspector, change its instance name to **passRedButton**. Change its Label value to **Pass Red**. Leave the Click Handler set to changeColor.

13. Select frame 1 of the Actions layer, and open the Actions panel. On the closing curly brace line of the existing if() code in the changeColor() function, add the following code:

```
else if (label == "pass red"){
   dogFill_2 = new Color(_root.dog_2);
   dogFill_2.setRGB(dogFill_1.getRGB());
}
```

14. Save the Flash document and test the movie. When you click the redButton instance, the dog_1 Movie Clip instance turns red. When you click the passRedButton instance, the dog_2 Movie Clip instance turns red.

Note If you click the second PushButton instance first, the dog_2 Movie Clip instance will turn black. Why? Because the first button's actions were not executed, and there was no previous setRGB() method execution for the getRGB() method to refer to. Moreover, there was no dogFill_1 object either. Consequently, ActionScript returns a zero or null value for the getRGB() method. In hexadecimal color, zero is equivalent to black.

Now that you've had some experience with the Color object's setRGB() and getRGB() methods, let's move on to the more complex colorTransformObject. We'll use the Flash document from this exercise, so keep the dogs on the Stage!

On the CD-ROM You can find the completed Flash document, **dogColor_100.fla**, in the ch27 folder of the *Flash MX Bible* CD-ROM.

Creating a Transform object

The two remaining methods of the Color object, setTransform() and getTransform(), require a more thorough understanding of RGB color space. Before the setTransform() method can be used with a Color object, you need to create a generic object using the Object constructor. This generic object will become a colorTransformObject once you have assigned color properties to the generic object.

The properties of the colorTransformObject are:

✦ **ra**—the Red channel percentage

✦ **rb**—the Red channel offset

✦ **ga**—the Green channel percentage

✦ **gb**—the Green channel offset

✦ **ba**—the Blue channel percentage

✦ **bb**—the Blue channel offset

✦ **aa**—the Alpha channel percentage

✦ **ab**—the Alpha channel offset

The *a* properties are percentage-based, ranging in value from –100 to 100. The *b* properties are offset-based, ranging from –255 to 255 (derived from 24-bit RGB color space, in which each 8-bit color channel can have a range of 256 values).

While these properties and values may seem complex, refer to the Advanced options of the Color menu for symbol instances in the Property inspector for guidance. With the Advanced option chosen in the Color menu, the left-hand color controls are percentage-based, while the right-hand controls are offset-based. Admittedly, color is difficult to visualize from numbers. To accurately predict the color changes with setTransform(), you'll use the Advanced Effect dialog box to help you out.

Make a copy of the **dogColor_100**.fla if you didn't complete the previous section's exercise. This document is located in the ch27 folder of the *Flash MX Bible* CD-ROM.

1. Using the same Flash document (.fla file) from the previous exercise, select the original dog_1 Movie Clip instance on the Stage. Open the Property inspector, and choose the Advanced option in the Color menu. Press the Settings button to the right of the menu. In the Advanced Effect dialog box, enter the following value on the left-hand side: **–100% Blue**. On the right-hand side, enter these values: **37 G** and **255 B**. Refer to Figure 27-5. Click OK to close the dialog box. With these values, the dog_1 instance should be a monochrome blue with yellow eyes. Normally, you would want to write these values down so that you had them to use later. Because you have them printed here in this book, erase them by choosing None from the Color menu in the Property inspector. The dog_1 instance should now appear in its original state.

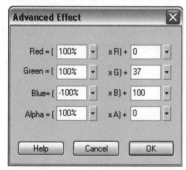

Figure 27-5: These settings will change the color of the dog_1 instance.

2. Duplicate one of the existing PushButton instances on the Stage. Place the duplicated instance underneath the last PushButton instance. Name the name instance **rabidButton**. Change the Label value to **Rabid**. Leave the Click Handler set to changeColor.

   With this new instance, you will create some code that will initiate a new Color object, and a new colorTransformObject. The colorTransformObject will be given properties that have the same values as those determined in Step 1. Then, you'll execute the setTransform() method for the Color object, using the colorTransformObject's data for the color change.

3. Select frame 1 of the Actions layer and open the Actions panel (F9). Starting on the line containing the last curly brace of the else if() action within the changeColor() function, add the following code:

```
else if (label == "rabid"){
    dogColor = new Color(_root.dog_1);
    rabidLook = new Object();
    rabidLook.ba = -100;
    rabidLook.bb = 255;
    rabidLook.gb = 37;
    dogColor.setTransform(rabidLook);
}
```

In the preceding code, you created two objects: `dogColor` and `rabidLook`. `rapidLook` is assigned the `ba`, `bb`, and `gb` `colorTransformObject` properties. Each of these properties is given the values you determined in Step 1. Then, you specified that the `rabidLook` object be used as the target for `dogColor`'s `setTransform` method.

4. Save the Flash document as **dogColor_200.fla**, and test the movie. Click the new PushButton instance that you added in Step 2. The colors of the dog_1 Movie Clip instance should change to match those you saw in Step 1. Close the Test Movie window, and return to the Flash MX authoring environment.

Now you will create a button that restores the original look of the dog_1 Movie Clip instance. The code structure will resemble that of Step 3, but we use a different syntax to assign color properties to the `colorTransformObject`.

5. Duplicate one of the PushButton instances, and place the new instance underneath the last PushButton instance. In the Property inspector, name this component instance **restoreButton**. Change the Label value to **Restore**, and leave the Click Handler set to `changeColor`.

6. Select frame 1 of the Actions layer, and open the Actions panel (F9). Add the following `else if()` action after the last `else if()` action in the `changeColor()` function:

```
else if (label == "restore"){
    dogColor = new Color(_root.dog_1);
    restoreLook = {
        ra: '100',
        rb: '0',
        ga: '100',
        gb: '0',
        ba: '100',
        bb: '0',
        aa: '100',
        ab: '0'
    };
    dogColor.setTransform(restoreLook);
}
```

In the `restoreLook` object, you defined all the default properties using name/value pairs separated by the colon character (:). Notice that all the properties of the `restoreLook` object can be declared and given values within a {} nesting.

Caution   Do not insert a comma after the very last property assignment when you are using this syntax. Doing so will result in an ActionScript error.

7. Save the Flash document again, and test the movie. Click the `rabidButton` instance you created in Step 2. After the dog_1 Movie Clip instance changes color, click the `restoreButton` instance you created in Step 5. Voila! The dog_1 Movie Clip instance reverts to its original color. Click the `redButton` instance that you created in the previous section. This button (which uses the `setRGB()` method) changes the appearance of the dog_1 Movie Clip instance to a solid red color. Now click the `restoreButton` instance—the dog_1 Movie Clip instance reverts to its original look!

While the setRGB() method can alter basic color properties of MovieClip objects, the setTransform() method is the color-control powerhouse. Any look that you can accomplish with the Advanced Effect dialog box, you can reproduce with the setTransform() method and the colorTransformObject.

Tip

Just as the getRGB() method can retrieve the values of a past setRGB() method, you can transfer past setTransform() values using the getTransform() method. You can also use getRGB() to retrieve manually set Tint values applied to Movie Clip instances and getTransform() to retrieve Advanced settings applied to Movie Clip instances with the Property inspector.

Enabling Sound with ActionScript

Flash MX ActionScript offers many object types, and one of the most exciting objects to use is the Sound object. Like most objects, the Sound object has predefined methods that you can use to control each new Sound object. Table 27-2 provides an overview of the Sound object and its common methods.

Table 27-2: Common Methods for the soundObject

Method	Definition	Options
attachSound	Creates a new instance of a sound file (AIF or WAV) available in the Library. The new instance becomes a part of the Sound object and can be targeted with Sound object methods. Unlike attached Movie Clips, attached sounds do not require a depth number.	soundObject.attachSound(libraryID); where: soundObject refers to the sound Object's name libraryID is the name of the sound in the Symbol Linkage properties (available in the Library)
loadSound	Loads a separate MP3 audio source (.mp3 file) into a Sound object. You can begin playback of the MP3 sound as soon as enough bytes have downloaded, or wait until the entire file has downloaded. We will show you how to use this new method in Chapter 28, "Sharing and Loading Assets."	soundObject.loadSound(URL, isStreaming); where: URL is the location of the MP3 file. This location can a relative or absolute path. isStreaming determines if the loading sound will begin playback as soon as enough bytes have downloaded (true), or if the entire sound must download before playback can begin (false).
start	Plays the targeted Sound object. A sound must be attached to the Sound object before it can play.	soundObject.start(inPoint, loopFactor); where: inPoint is the time (in seconds) in the sound where playback should begin. loopFactor is the number of times the sound should be repeated. Both of these parameters are optional and can be omitted.

Continued

Table 27-2: *(continued)*

Method	Definition	Options
stop	Stops playback of the targeted Sound object. If no target is specified, all sounds will be stopped. Note that this is not equivalent to pausing a sound. If a stopped sound is played later, it will start at the beginning (or at the *inPoint*).	*soundObject.stop(libraryID);* where: *libraryID* is the name of the sound in the Linkage properties (available in the Library)
setVolume	Changes the overall volume of method the specified Sound object. This accepts values between 0 and100 (in percentage units). You can enter percentages greater than 100 percent to increase sound output beyond its original recording level, but you may notice digital distortion of the sound.	*soundObject.setVolume(volume);* where: *volume* is a number between 0 and 100
getVolume	Retrieves the current volume of the Sound object.	*soundObject.getVolume();* No options or arguments for this method.
setPan	Changes the offset of sound output from both the left and right channels.	*soundObject.setPan(panValue);* where: *panValue* is a value between −100 (full left-speaker output) and 100 (full right-speaker output). Use a value of 0 to balance sound output evenly.
getPan	Retrieves the values created with a previous setPan execution. Use this method to apply Pan settings consistently to multiple objects, or to store a Pan setting.	*soundObject.getPan();* No options or arguments for this method.
setTransform	Changes the volume for each channel of the specified Sound object. This method also enables you to play the right channel in the left channel and vice versa.	*soundObject.setTransform(soundTransformObject);* where: *soundTransformObject* is the name of an object that has percentage properties for left and right output for the left channel, and left and right output for the right channels.
getTransform	Retrieves the values established with the last setTransform execution. Use this method to reapply sound transforms to new Sounds objects, or to store setTransform values.	*soundObject.getTransform();* No options or arguments for this method.

In Flash MX, ActionScript has added two new properties, `duration` and `position`, and two methods, `getBytesLoaded()` and `getBytesTotal()`, for Sound objects. We will look at the new methods in Chapter 28, "Sharing and Loading Assets." For more detailed information on Sound objects, refer to the Sound object coverage in the *Macromedia Flash MX ActionScript Bible* by Robert Reinhardt and Joey Lott.

The following list of Sound object features offers reasons for using Sound objects over traditional sound Movie Clips or keyframe sounds:

✦ Dynamic event sounds that play in a random or user-defined order

✦ Precise control over volume and panning

✦ The ability to dump (or erase) a Sound object when the sound is no longer needed

All Sound objects are treated as Event sounds. You cannot use Sound objects to control the playback or frame rate like Stream sounds can. However, Flash MX ActionScript does allow you to load MP3 files on the fly and stream their playback — these types of sounds, however, cannot control playback or frame rate synchronization. For more information on Synch modes for sound, please refer to Chapter 15, "Adding Sound."

The Sound object uses sounds directly from the movie's library. You cannot use the Sound object to control sounds that are specified in the Property inspector for any given keyframes.

You can, however, control Stream sounds attached to keyframes on a given timeline by controlling an empty Sound object. Any methods applied to the Sound object will be passed along to the Stream sound.

The next section shows you how to create Sound objects, using the object constructor with the `attachSound()` and `start()` methods.

Creating sound libraries with ActionScript

In the Chapter 19, "Navigating Flash Timelines," you learned how to create a sound library Movie Clip that stored several individual sound Movie Clip instances. You learned how to target these sounds in order to play them (or mute them). From a conceptual point of view, manually creating each sound Movie Clip enabled you to see and work with each sound "object" on the Stage very easily. However, we can produce the sounds for a sound library much more quickly using ActionScript.

In this section, we start with the soundLib Movie Clip that was created in Chapter 19. Make a copy of the **pianoKeys_complete.fla** file from the ch19 folder of the *Flash MX Bible* CD-ROM.

1. Using the Open as Library command in the File menu, select your copy of the pianoKeys_complete.fla file. Opening a Flash document as a Library enables you to access symbols and media in that file.

2. If you don't have a new untitled Flash document open, create a new Flash file (Ctrl+N or ⌘+N). Change the background color of the document to black in the Document Properties dialog box (Modify ➪ Document).

3. Rename Layer 1 to **soundLib_mc**.

4. Drag the soundLib Movie Clip from the pianoKeys Library panel onto the Stage of your new document. If you open the Library for your new document, you'll see that all the elements contained within the soundLib Movie Clip have been imported into your new movie.

5. Close the pianoKeys_complete Library panel, and save your new Flash document as **soundLib_ActionScript.fla**.

6. Select the soundLib instance on the Stage, and open the Property inspector. Give the instance the name **soundLib_mc**.

7. Double-click the soundLib_mc instance on the Stage. In Symbol Editing mode, create a new blank layer and delete the sounds layer. (You always need to have at least one layer in a Movie Clip.) On the empty layer, draw an icon representing the soundLib Movie Clip. In this example, you made a white-filled rounded rectangle with soundLib black text. Center the icon elements to the Movie Clip Stage using the Align panel.

8. Go back to the Main Timeline (click the Scene 1 tab in the upper-left corner of the Document window, or choose Edit ➪ Movie).

   Before you can attach sounds to the soundLib_mc instance, each sound in the Library needs to be given a unique ID name in order for ActionScript to see it.

9. Open the Library panel (Ctrl+L or ⌘+L), and select key_1.wav (or key_1.aif). Right-click (or Control+click on the Mac) the highlighted item, and choose Linkage in the contextual menu. In the Linkage Properties dialog box, select the Export for ActionScript check box and type **sound_1** in the Identifier text field, as shown in Figure 27-6. Click OK.

Figure 27-6: The attachSound() method can only use sounds that have been set to export with the Flash movie (.swf file).

10. Repeat the naming routine from Step 9 on each sound in the Library. Increase the number that you append to the end of sound_ for each new sound (for example, **sound_2** for key_2.wav, **sound_3** for key_3.wav, and so on). When you are finished, each sound should be linked. You can expand the Library panel horizontally to view the ID names in the Linkage column, as shown in Figure 27-7.

11. Now, you need to add the ActionScript code that will create our Sound objects. You will construct a function that, when executed will form a list of sound instances. On the Main Timeline (that is, Scene 1), create a new layer named actions. Alt+double-click (or Option+double-click on the Mac) frame 1 of this layer. This will open the Actions panel. With Expert mode turned on, type the following code:

```
function createLib(num){
  for(var i=1;i<=num;i++){
```

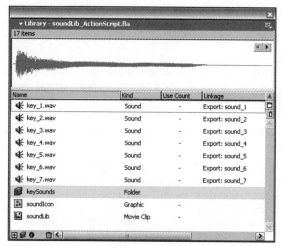

Figure 27-7: Flash MX allows you to view the ID names for linked assets directly in the Library panel.

These first line establishes the name of our function, createLib(). We will want to dynamically change the number of sounds we create with this function. Therefore, we assign an optional parameter (called an argument) num that will be passed to the nested actions within the function.

The second line starts a for loop that cycles its nested actions until the condition i<=num is no longer true. i starts (or initializes) with a value of 1, and the syntax i++ tells i to increase by 1 with each pass of the for loop.

In the next step, we want the for loop to (a) create an array to store a reference to each sound instance; (b) create a new instance of the Sound object for each sound in the Library; and (c) attach each sound in the Library to its new instance.

 Cross-Reference We do not discuss the overall structure and purpose of functions, arrays, and logic in this exercise. Refer to Chapter 26, "Using Functions and Arrays," for more information.

12. In the Actions panel, add the following ActionScript to the code from Step 11:

```
if(i==1){
 this.snd = new Array();
}
this.createEmptyMovieClip("sndStorage_" + i, i);
var target = this["sndStorage_"+i];
this.snd[i] = new Sound(target);
this.snd[i].attachSound("sound_"+i);
 }
}
```

The first line of code in Step 12 checks whether i's current value is 1. During the first pass in the for loop, this will be true. So, the contents of the if nest will be executed.

The second line of code occurs within the if nest. This line creates a new Array object named snd on the current timeline (_root). This line will only be executed once, while the value of i is 1. When i's value increases in subsequent passes of the for loop, this line will be ignored.

The fourth line creates a new Movie Clip instance, whose name starts with sndStorage_. With each pass of the loop, a new instance will be created (for example, sndStorage_1, sndStorage_2, and so on). Each instance will be used to store the attached sound later in the for loop.

The fifth line creates a temporary variable named target that references the newly created sndStorage_ instance.

The sixth line makes a new element in the snd array. The new element is a new Sound object that points to the timeline referenced by the target variable. Ultimately, our Sound objects will be tied to instances nested within the soundLib_mc Movie Clip instance, which you'll see later. Each element in an array has a number indicating its position in the array. Because the value of i increases with each pass of the for loop, each Sound object will have a unique position within the snd array.

The seventh line uses the attachSound() method to take a sound element in the Library and attach it to the Sound object in the snd array. The target for the attachSound() method is specified as "sound_" + i. On each pass of the for loop, this expression will return "sound_1", "sound_2", and so on until our limit prescribed by the num argument is reached.

The complete block of code on the first keyframe of the actions layer should look like this:

```
function createLib(num) {
 for (var i=1; i<=num; i++) {
  if (i == 1) {
   this.snd = new Array();
  }
  this.createEmptyMovieClip("sndStorage_"+i, i);
  var target = this["sndStorage_"+i];
  this.snd[i] = new Sound(target);
  this.snd[i].attachSound("sound_"+i);
 }
}
```

13. Now that we have a function defined to create all the Sound objects on a this object (or timeline), we need to have an object for this to refer to. This object should use the createLib() function to create new Sound objects. With the code for frame 1 of the actions layer displayed in the Actions panel, type the following code after the createLib() function:

```
soundLib_mc.createLib = createLib;
soundLib_mc.createLib(7);
```

The first line of code defines a *method* called createLib that used the function createLib as a value. Because createLib is a function, the createLib() method of soundLib_mc will execute the createLib() function whenever the method is invoked.

The second line of code invokes the `createLib()` method—the use of `()` after the method name indicates that the method is being executed, *not* defined. In addition to executing the `createLib()` method, we're also sending the function the number 7 as the num argument. Therefore, seven Sound objects will be created.

14. Save the Flash document and test it (Ctrl+Enter or ⌘+Enter). While you won't hear or see anything special happen, choose Debug ➪ List Variables in the Test Movie environment. The Output window will open and display the Sound objects, among other variables and objects:

```
Variable _level0.soundLib_mc.snd = [object #2, class 'Array'] [
  1:[object #3, class 'Sound'] {
  duration:[getter/setter] 1752,
  position:[getter/setter] 0
  },
  2:[object #4, class 'Sound'] {
  duration:[getter/setter] 1602,
  position:[getter/setter] 0
  },
  3:[object #5, class 'Sound'] {
  duration:[getter/setter] 1822,
  position:[getter/setter] 0
  },
  4:[object #6, class 'Sound'] {
  duration:[getter/setter] 1672,
  position:[getter/setter] 0
  },
  5:[object #7, class 'Sound'] {
  duration:[getter/setter] 1660,
  position:[getter/setter] 0
  },
  6:[object #8, class 'Sound'] {
  duration:[getter/setter] 1728,
  position:[getter/setter] 0
  },
  7:[object #9, class 'Sound'] {
  duration:[getter/setter] 1785,
  position:[getter/setter] 0
  }
  ]
```

15. Close the Test Movie window and return to the Flash MX authoring environment. Select frame 1 of the actions layer, and add this last bit of code to the Script pane:

```
soundLib_mc.snd[1].start();
soundLib_mc.snd[2].start();
```

The first line of code targets the first declared element, 1, of the snd array, and tells it to begin playback with the start method. Remember that element 1 in the array is a Sound object, which references the sound_1 ID in the Library.

The second line of code targets the second declared element, 2, of the snd array, and tells it to start.

16. Save the Flash document and test it. Both lines of code will execute simultaneously. So, you will hear sound_1 (key_1.wav or key_1.aif) and sound_2 (key_2.wav or key_2.aif) play together.

Now you should practice targeting these Sound objects with Button instances and other keyframes. To access a different sound, simply change the number in the array brackets. In the next chapter, you'll learn how to load a Flash movie (.swf file) into another Flash movie, as well as how to load MP3 files directly into the movie.

You can view the completed sound library movie, **soundLib_ActionScript.fla**, located in the ch27 folder of the *Flash MX Bible* CD-ROM.

During our testing of Sound object methods, we learned that you should attach only one sound per timeline (or Movie Clip instance). While you can create more than one Sound object instance on a timeline, you cannot use the setVolume to control each individual sound—the volume will be set for all Sound object instances on the targeted timeline.

Creating a soundTransformObject

The two remaining methods of the Sound object, setTransform and getTransform, work in the same manner as the transform methods of the Color object. You need to create a generic object using the object constructor before the setTransform method can be used with a Sound object. This generic object will become a soundTransformObject once we have assigned sound channel properties to the generic Object.

Luckily, the soundTransformObject doesn't have as many properties as the colorTransformObject, and they're much simpler to predict with trial and error testing. The properties of the soundTransformObject are

> ✦ **ll**—the percentage of left channel output in the left speaker
>
> ✦ **lr**—the percentage of right channel output in the left speaker
>
> ✦ **rr**—the percentage of right channel output in the right speaker
>
> ✦ **rl**—the percentage of left channel output in the right speaker

The first letter of each property determines which physical speaker is being affected. The second letter determines which channel's output (or its volume) is played in that speaker. Each property can have a value between –100 and 100.

While –100 to 100 is the suggested range of values, you can use values well beyond this range. The Flash Player will do its best to amplify sounds that use values higher than 100. Be warned—you will likely notice severe digital distortion of the sound for extreme values.

The steps to produce and incorporate a soundTransformObject are nearly the same as the colorTransformObject. The only difference is that you specify paths to Sound objects rather than MovieClip objects for the setTransform( ) and getTransform( ) methods. Refer to the steps described earlier in this chapter for colorTransform objects.

Tip

Use the `soundTransformObject` to vary the output of the sounds in the soundLib example you created in this section. Just like the `setTransform()` example for the `Color` object, create buttons that create and execute unique transform settings.

Creating volume and balance sliders for sounds

In this section, you will learn how to control the volume and balance output from a `Sound` object using the slider mechanism from Chapter 25, "Controlling Movie Clips." The slider mechanism works by taking the X position value of the slider's bar and applying it a property of another object. In Chapter 25, you applied the position value of the bar to Movie Clip properties such as `_xscale`, `_yscale`, and `_alpha`. In this exercise, you will apply the position values to the `setVolume()` and `setPan()` methods of the `Sound` object to control the volume and balance output, respectively.

On the CD-ROM

In this section, you'll need to use the **slider_basic_400.fla** file, located in the ch25 folder of the *Flash MX Bible* CD-ROM. If you want to learn how this slider was built, read Chapter 25, "Controlling Movie Clips."

The first part of this exercise will show you how to add the slider to a new document, import a sound, and control the volume of the sound with the slider. In the last steps, you'll apply the same methodology to the balance slider.

1. Open your copy of the slider_basic_400.fla file via the File ➪ Open as Library command.

2. Create a new Flash document (File ➪ New). Rename Layer 1 to **volumeSlider**.

3. Drag the slider Movie Clip symbol from the slider_basic_400.fla Library to the new document's Stage. When you have finished, close the slider_basic_400.fla Library panel.

4. With the slider instance selected on the Stage, open the Property inspector. Name the instance **volumeSlider**. In the Transform panel, rotate the instance –90 degrees. (You can also use the Transform tool to rotate the instance.)

5. Now you need to create a `Sound` object. Import a sound file into the Flash document. Use a sound file that is at least 20 seconds long. You can import the atmospheres_1.wav (or .aif) file located in ch15 folder of the *Flash MX Bible* CD-ROM.

6. Once you have imported a sound file, select the sound in the Library panel. Right-click (Control+click on Mac) the sound file and choose Linkage in the contextual menu. In the Linkage Properties dialog box, select the Export for ActionScript check box and type **sound_1** in the Identifier field. Click OK to close the dialog box.

7. Create a new layer on the Main Timeline (that is, Scene 1), and name the layer **actions**.

8. Select frame 1 of the Actions layer and open the Actions panel (F9). In the Script pane, type the following code:

```
soundtrack = new Sound();
soundtrack.attachSound("sound_1");
soundtrack.start(0,999);
```

This code creates the `Sound` object that the `volumeSlider` instance will control. Line 1 uses the `new Sound()` constructor to establish a `Sound` object name `soundtrack`. Line 2 links the sound_1 asset (that is, the sound file in the Library) to the `soundtrack` object. Line 3 plays the sound, starting at the beginning of the sound (0), and looping it 999 times for indefinite playback.

9. Save your Flash document as **soundSlider_100.fla**. Test the movie (Ctrl+Enter or ⌘+Enter). You will hear the sound attached to the `soundtrack` object begin to play. However, if you click and drag the bar on the slider, you will not hear any volume change with the sound.

   To change the volume of the `soundtrack` object, you need to take the position of the bar in the slider and apply its value to the `setVolume()` method of the `Sound` object. You'll use Flash MX's new event handlers to accomplish this.

10. Select frame 1 of the Actions layer on the Main Timeline. Open the Actions panel, and insert the following code after the last action in the Script pane:

```
volumeSlider.onMouseMove = function(){
 var currentVolume = this.position._x/2;
 soundtrack.setVolume(currentVolume);
};
```

   This code declares an `onMouseMove()` handler for the `volumeSlider` instance. Each time a mouse move is detected, the function defined for this handler will execute. The first line of the function will retrieve the current `_x` value of the `position` instance inside of `volumeSlider`, and divide it by 2. (See our coverage of the slider in Chapter 25 to learn more about this operation.) This value, declared as `currentVolume`, is then applied to the `setVolume()` method of the `soundtrack` object.

11. Save your Flash document again, and test it. Click and drag the bar on the slider. As you move it up, the sound will increase in volume. As you move it down, the volume will decrease.

   Creating a slider that controls the balance output is almost identical to the process of creating the `volumeSlider`. You will make another instance of the slider symbol, and add a new `onMouseMove()` handler for the new instance.

12. Create a new layer on the Main Timeline, and name it **balanceSlider**.

13. Drag an instance of the slider symbol from the Library to the Stage. Place the instance to the right of the `volumeSlider` instance. In the Property inspector, name the instance **balanceSlider**.

14. Select frame 1 of the actions layer, and open the Actions panel. After the last line of code in the Script pane, type the following code:

```
balanceSlider.onMouseMove = function(){
 var currentPan = this.position._x - 100;
 soundtrack.setPan(currentPan);
};
```

   This code declares an `onMouseMove()` handler for the `balanceSlider` instance. When the mouse moves within the Flash movie, the function for the `onMouseMove()` handler will execute. In this function, though, we need to translate the `_x` property of the `position` instance differently. Since pan values are within a range of –100 to 100, we need to map the 0 to 200 range of the slider accordingly. In order for the lowest value (0) to equal –100 and the highest value (200) to equal 100, you simply subtract 100 from the current `_x` property value returned by the position instance. You then apply this value to the `setPan()` method of the `soundtrack` object.

15. Save your Flash document and test it. As you drag the bar on the `balanceSlider` to the right, you should hear the sound play in the right speaker. As you drag the bar to the left, you should hear the sound play in the left speaker.

You may have noticed with both the `volumeSlider` and `balanceSlider` instances that the lowest value of `_x` for the `position` instance is not 0 — it's 10. This low range restriction was added for the scale slider in Chapter 25. If you desire, you can modify the `startDrag()` method found on the Button instance inside of the `position` instance to use 0 instead of 10 for the left drag limit value.

You can find the completed **soundSlider_100.fla** file in the ch27 folder of the *Flash MX Bible* CD-ROM.

For more discussion of sound scripting in Flash movies, read Brock deChristopher's tutorial, "Dynamic Sound Design," in the **Bonus_Tutorials.pdf** file located in the Bonus_Tutorials folder of the *Flash MX Bible* CD-ROM.

Printing with ActionScript

Using the `print` and `printAsBitmap` functions, you can enable your Flash movies to output Flash artwork, text, and bitmaps. With these actions, you can do the following:

✦ **Create Flash ads that have printable specifications for e-commerce merchandise.** Imagine if the next car ad you saw on your favorite Web site automatically printed dealer locations and maps without having to go to the car manufacturer's Web site?

✦ **Make Flash coupons.** You could design printable coupons for e-tailers on the Web that can be printed and redeemed at their brick-and-mortar stores.

✦ **Automate dynamic Web-generated invoices and receipts at e-commerce sites.** With ActionScript, you can format ordered items and add dynamic data to printable sheets.

✦ **Print rich vector illustrations or photorealistic bitmaps from a Web site.** Design Flash portfolio sites that print samples of stock images, or create personalized vector artwork that can be print unique images for each visitor.

✦ **E-mail printable Flash artwork to clients.** The next time you have proof of concepts or finished artwork that needs final approval, you can e-mail your clients the Flash artwork in a standalone projector or .SWF file.

✦ **Design custom contact information pages.** Sick of HTML tables that won't print your nice row-and-column–formatted pages of information consistently from browser to browser? Printable Flash frames will print beautifully each time. You could even add a visitor's contact information to a dynamic database and print it.

Although we can't describe how to do all these tasks in the space of this chapter, we will show you how to get started with the last idea. The following Expert Tutorial by Mike Richards shows you how to add `print` and `printAsBitmap` functions to his cool Flash paper airplane creator.

Table 27-3 summarizes the printing functions of ActionScript.

Because Flash natively uses vector artwork, it translates best when output to a PostScript printer. Nevertheless, both `print` and `printAsBitmap` actions will produce high-quality output to both PostScript and non-PostScript printers.

Table 27-3: Printing Functions in ActionScript

Function	Definition	Options

`print()`
`printNum()`
	This action prints a frame (or series of frames) in the targeted timeline. The `printNum` function is used when targeting Levels. Each frame prints to one piece of paper. Use this function to print high-quality artwork. Note that alpha and color effects do not print reliably with this method. We discuss this function later in the chapter.	*print(target, ["bmovie"," bmax", or "bframe"]);* where:
		   target is the path to Movie Clip instance. Each frame of the Movie Clip is printed unless you designate printable frames with a #p frame label.
		and one of the following options:
		   `"bMovie"` assigns a cropping area for printing, by placing artwork sized to the printable area on a keyframe with the label #b
		   `"bmax"` uses the frame with the largest-sized artwork to determine the printable area.
		   `"bframe"` prints each frame at its largest size to fill the paper width.

`printAsBitmp()` `printAsBitmapNum()`	Same functionality as the `print()` function. Use this action to print artwork that employs alpha or color instance settings. We discuss this function later in the chapter.	*print(target, ["bmovie","bmax", or "bframe"]);* See the `print()` function earlier in this table for descriptions of options.

Creating Printable Paper Airplanes
by Mike Richards

Mike's tutorial provides a great example of distributing interesting printable content on the Web. Instead of formatting and printing text and standard layouts, this tutorial shows you how to print Mike's paper planes.

On the CD-ROM

Mike Richards has already prepared a **paperplane_starter.fla** file that you can find in the ch27 folder of the *Flash MX Bible* CD-ROM. We invite you to review this file's contents and timeline structure, and to copy the file to your hard drive before you start this tutorial.

This tutorial focuses on printing using the `print()` and `printAsBitmap()` actions, which can print frames in any timeline within the Flash movie. These actions become a powerful tool for creating printable content for the Web.

Note Make sure you have your Actions panel set to Normal mode for this tutorial.

Using the print() action to print content in the Main Timeline

When completed, this first section will demonstrate how to print content located on the Main Timeline using the basic print() action. Additionally, this will control the printable area using the Flash movie's bounding box option in conjunction with the frame labels #b and #p.

1. First set the printing boundary box for the paper wing folding instructions. To do this, open your copy of paperplane_starter.fla and select frame 54 on the layer print content.

2. With frame 54 of the print content layer selected, enter **#b** in the <Frame Label> field of the Property inspector. Drag the Graphic symbol named bounding box from the Library to the Stage.

3. Next, specify the frame to be printed. With frame 55 of the layer print content selected, enter **#p** for its label in the Property inspector. Drag the paper wing symbol to the Stage. It is important to note that all frames on the Main Timeline will print if #p is not used to designate printable content.

4. Because a bounding box will be used to define the printable area, it is necessary to horizontally and vertically center the two symbol instances. At the bottom of the timeline window, click the Edit Multiple Frames icon and select the two symbols that were previously placed on the Stage. With both symbols selected, align the horizontal and vertical centers to the Stage using the Align panel. When finished aligning to center, be certain to click the Edit Multiple Frames icon to disable its function.

5. Now we are ready to add the print() action to the button in our movie. Move the playhead on the timeline to frame 65 and select the printer button in the lower-right corner of the Stage. Choose Window ⇨ Actions to add actions to the Button instance. With the Actions panel open, click the Actions booklet, then the Printing booklet, on the left-hand side of the panel. In the Printing booklet, double-click print to place the print() action in the actions list on the right side, as shown in the Figure 27-8. Because there are no alpha effects to preserve in the printed material, choose As vectors in the Print drop-down menu. Because the content resides on the Main Timeline, select Target for the Location option and enter **_root** in the field. Finally, due to specifying a bounding box on the Main Timeline, select Movie for the Bounding box option.

6. Save your Flash document file and select Control ⇨ Test Movie to view the results. In Test Movie mode, select standard wing and click the printer icon in the lower-right corner to print the one page of wing folding instructions.

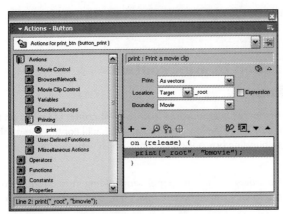

Figure 27-8: The Actions panel with the print() action

Using the printAsBitmap() action with content in a Movie Clip instance

This next section demonstrates how to print content residing in a Movie Clip using the printAsBitmap() action. The print area is controlled by using the Frame bounding box option. The Frame bounding box option scales the print area for each frame of content, ensuring that every page is printed at its maximum printable size. Note that Movie Clip instances can use either print or printAsBitmap() actions, depending on the contents of the Movie Clip symbol. For demonstration purposes, use the printAsBitmap() action.

1. With frame 27 of the layer print content selected, drag the Movie Clip symbol named shuttlePaper from the Library to the work area located to the right of the Stage. With the instance still selected, enter **shuttlePaper_mc** in the <Instance Name> field of the Property inspector. It is not necessary to designate printable frames with #p in the Movie Clip Symbol timeline because the intention is to print all frames within this timeline.

2. Actions for our print button are now ready to be assigned. Move the playhead on the Main Timeline to frame 27 and select the printer button in the lower-right corner of the Stage. With the Actions panel open, click the Actions booklet, then the Printing booklet, at the left side. In the Printing booklet, double-click print to place the print() action in the actions list on the right side. For the Print option, choose As bitmap because the Movie Clip symbol contains alpha effects on the second frame artwork. For the Location option, choose Target. The printable content resides in the shuttle instance on the Main Timeline. Therefore, enter **_root.shuttlePaper_mc** to correctly target the movie, as shown in the Figure 27-9. Finally, choose Frame for the Bounding box option, which allows each page of printable content to be scaled to its maximum size.

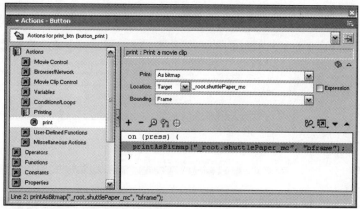

Figure 27-9: The Actions panel for the printAsBitmap() action

Printing a loaded Flash movie

This last example provides a walk through the basics of printing Flash content that is loaded into a target. This method is optimal if the content that you intend to print is significant in size. The *Flash MX Bible* discusses loading Flash movies (.swf files) in Chapter 28, "Sharing and Loading Assets."

1. Move the playhead on the Main Timeline to frame 47 and select the printer button in the lower-right corner of the Stage. Choose Window ⇨ Actions to view the actions list for the Button instance. In this example, the loadMovie() action is used to load a two-frame Flash movie (.swf file), classic_instructions.swf.

2. Next, with the Actions panel open, select the word Placeholder, which is located just outside the top-right corner of the Stage. The onClipEvent(load) handler, along with this._visible = 0, is used to make the content invisible during playback. Even though it is hidden, this Movie Clip instance is still printable. Because content needs to be completely loaded to print, the clip event data is used in conjunction with the methods getBytesTotal() and getBytesLoaded() to confirm the completion of load before printing. For the Print option, As vectors was chosen because the printable content does not contain alpha effects. For Location, Target was chosen. The printable content will load into this Movie Clip with an instance name of classic_placeholder_mc. Therefore, _root.classic_placeholder_mc was entered to correctly target the movie, as shown in Figure 27-10. Finally, the Bounding box option of Frame was chosen to scale each page to its maximum printable size.

3. Save your Flash document and select Control ⇨ Test Movie to view the results. In Test Movie mode, select the first plane and customize the paper plane with art and text. To print the plane and instructions, press the printer icon in the lower-right corner of the Stage.

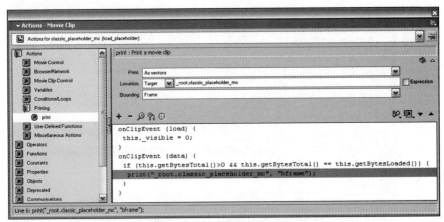

Figure 27-10: The Actions panel showing the actions for Step 2

4. Save the Flash movie and select Control ➪ Test Movie to view the results. In Test Movie mode, select the center plane and customize the paper plane with art and text. Press the printer icon in the lower-right corner of the Stage to print the plane and instructions.

On the CD-ROM

This chapter has introduced many techniques for working with MovieClip objects. You can continue your exploration of ActionScript code for Movie Clips by reading Darrel Plant's tutorial, "Animation on Bézier Curves," in the **Bonus_Tutorials.pdf** file located in the Bonus_Tutorials folder of the *Flash MX Bible* CD-ROM.

Summary

✦ Collisions occur when two or more elements in a Flash movie touch each other. Whenever the space by one Movie Clip instance occupies the space of another, a collision, or "hit," has occurred.

✦ You can detect simple user-initiated collisions by using the startDrag() method and _droptarget property of the MovieClip object.

✦ Using the hitTest() method of the MovieClip object, you can detect the intersection of X and Y coordinates with a specified Movie Clip instance. You can also use hitTest in a similar fashion to _droptarget, where the overlap of two specific Movie Clip instances is detected.

✦ The Color object can store new color values and apply them to Movie Clip instances using the setRGB() and setTransform() methods.

✦ Sound libraries can be created in less time by using ActionScript and the Sound object. Sound objects are created by using Linkage identifiers for sound files in the movie's Library.

✦ ActionScript enables you to change the volume and pan values of any Sound object in your Flash movie.

✦ By using the print() and printAsBitmap() functions, you can output high-quality artwork to a PostScript or non-PostScript printer.

✦   ✦   ✦

Sharing and Loading Assets

✦   ✦   ✦   ✦

In This Chapter

Creating a preloader for your Flash movie

Loading Flash movies into other Flash movies

Loading JPEG images into Flash movies

Loading MP3 audio into Flash movies

Using a preloader for external media files

Centralizing assets with Shared Libraries

✦   ✦   ✦   ✦

Because most Flash movies are downloaded and viewed over the Web, ActionScript has a number of advanced actions that are dedicated solely to controlling the download and display of movies and Library assets. Actions that check the loaded bytes of a Flash movie (SWF file) or media file let developers prevent a movie from playing before a specified portion of it has finished loading. The `loadMovie()` and `unloadMovie()` actions enable movies to be broken into small pieces or assets that are downloaded only if required by user choice.

New Feature

Flash MX ActionScript now allows you to load JPEG and MP3 files directly into Flash movies. These actions require the use of Flash Player 6. We will show you how to load these media files in this chapter.

Managing Smooth Movie Download and Display

When Flash movies are played back over the Internet, they *stream*, meaning that the Flash Player plug-in shows as much of the movie as it can during download, even if the whole file has not been transferred to the user's system or browser cache. The benefit of this feature is that users start seeing content without having to wait for the entire movie to finish downloading.

Note

Technically, a Flash movie file is not a streaming file format, but a progressive download file format, similar to an original Apple QuickTime 3 video movie. A progressive download is one that can be viewed before the entire file has been received by the browser. Streaming file formats are never saved as actual files in the browser cache. You can't save a streaming file, but you can typically save a shortcut or link to the file's location on the Web.

Nevertheless, streaming has potential drawbacks. First, during streamed playback, the movie may unexpectedly halt at arbitrary points on the timeline because a required portion of the movie has not yet downloaded. Second, ActionScript code is ignored when it refers to segments of the movie that have not downloaded. These drawbacks can lead to unpredictable and often undesired playback results.

Thankfully, there's a solution. You can regulate the playback of the movie by using ActionScript code to prevent the movie from playing until a specified portion of it has downloaded. This technique is often referred to as *preloading*. A common preload sequence, or *preloader,* involves displaying only a short message, such as "Loading . . . Please Wait," while the movie loads. Once the appropriate amount of the movie has been retrieved, the movie is allowed to play. ActionScript provides basic and advanced methods of producing a preloader. This section of the chapter shows you how to use three different actions (or methods) to check the download status of a Flash movie:

✦ `ifFrameLoaded`: This action has been around since Flash 3, and it enables you to check whether a specified frame label in the Flash movie has been downloaded by the plug-in. This is the simplest action to use to check a movie's download progress. If you are designing Flash 5 or later movies, this action is considered deprecated.

✦ `_framesloaded` **and** `_totalFrames`: Introduced with Flash 4, these properties can be checked on a Movie Clip timeline or the Main Movie timeline (Scene 1, Scene 2, and so on). `_framesLoaded` returns the current number of frames that have downloaded into the plug-in, while `_totalframes` returns the number of frames that exist on the specified target timeline.

✦ `getBytesLoaded()` **and** `getBytesTotal()`: These methods were introduced in Flash 5 ActionScript. The most accurate way to check the progress of a Flash movie download is to use these methods with other ActionScript code. You can use these methods for the following objects in ActionScript for Flash 6 movies: MovieClip (including loaded movies [SWF files] or JPEG images) and `Sound` objects that load MP3 files.

In this edition of the book, we will show you how to use the `getBytesLoaded()` and `getBytesTotal()` methods in ActionScript to check the download progress of movie assets.

Cross-Reference   You can find our coverage of Flash 3 and 4 movie preloaders (as discussed in the *Flash 5 Bible*) on the book's Web site, `www.flashmxbible.com`.

Preloading a Flash Movie

In this section, you will learn how to preload a Flash movie whose assets are all internal. You will construct a movie timeline containing a preload section. This section will contain two consecutive frames that loop until the entire movie has loaded into the Flash Player. While the movie is loading, a loader graphic will update to display the progress of the download.

On the CD-ROM   Make a copy of the **preloader_starter.fla** file, located in the ch28 folder of the *Flash MX Bible* CD-ROM.

1. With the starter file open in Flash MX, rename Layer 1 to **content**.

2. Create an empty keyframe (F7) on frame 10 of the Content layer. Drag an instance of the pilonsImage Graphic symbol to the Stage on this keyframe. Center the instance on the Stage. Select frame 20 of the Content layer and press the F5 key to extend the layer to this frame.

3. Create a new layer and rename it to **labels**. Place this layer at the top of the layer stack.

4. Add a keyframe on frame 2 of the Labels layer. In the Property inspector, assign this frame a label of **preload**.

5. Add a keyframe on frame 10 of the Labels layer and label this frame **main** in the Property inspector. Your document should now resemble Figure 28-1.

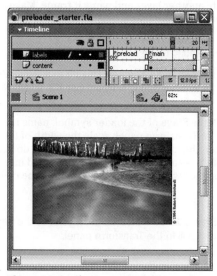

Figure 28-1: The content of this movie starts on the main label.

6. Create a new layer and name it **loader**. Place this layer underneath the Labels layer.

7. With frame 1 of the Loader layer highlighted, select the Rectangle tool. Make sure that you have a stroke and fill color specified in the Toolbox. Draw a rectangle on the Stage. In the Property inspector, size both the stroke and fill of the rectangle to 300 × 10. This rectangle will be the progress bar that will grow as the movie's bytes load into the Flash Player.

8. With the stroke and fill of the rectangle selected, press the F8 key. In the Convert to Symbol dialog box, choose the Movie Clip behavior. Name the symbol **loader** and click the middle-left registration point, as shown in Figure 28-2. Click OK.

Figure 28-2: The rectangle artwork will be part of the loader symbol.

9. With the new instance selected on the Stage of the Main Timeline, name the instance `loader` in the Property inspector.

10. Double-click the `loader` instance on the Stage. In Symbol Editing mode, rename Layer 1 of the loader symbol to **bar**. Create another layer and name it **frame**. Make sure the Frame layer is above the Bar layer.

11. Select the stroke of the rectangle and cut it (Ctrl+X or ⌘+X). Select frame 1 of the Frame layer and paste the stroke in place (Edit ➪ Paste in Place, or Ctrl+Shift+V or ⌘+Shift+V).

12. On the Bar layer, select the fill of rectangle. Convert this fill to a Movie Clip symbol named **bar**. Again, in the Convert to Symbol dialog box, choose the middle-left registration point.

13. With the new instance selected on the Stage of the loader symbol, name the instance **bar** in the Property inspector. In the Transform panel, scale the width of the instance to 1.0%, as shown in Figure 28-3. When the movie first starts to load, you do not want the `bar` instance scaled at full size (100%) — as the bytes of the movie load into the Flash Player, the `_xscale` of the `bar` instance will increase. (We will insert the code to do this later.)

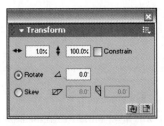

Figure 28-3: Decrease the X scale of the bar instance to 1.0% in the Transform panel.

14. Create another layer and name it **textfield**. Place this layer at the bottom of the layer stack.

15. Select the Text tool and create a Dynamic Text field on frame 1 of the text layer. Place the text field underneath the bar instance, as shown in Figure 28-4. In the <Instance Name> field of the Property inspector, name the text field **percent**. You will use this text field to display the current percent loaded of the Flash movie. You do not need to enable the Show Border (or other options) for this text field.

16. Go back to the Main Timeline (that is, Scene 1). Select the loader instance on the Stage and center it using the Align panel. Select frame 4 of the loader layer and insert an empty keyframe (F7). You only need the loader instance to appear as the movie is preloading.

17. Create a new layer and name it **actions**. Place this layer underneath the Labels layer.

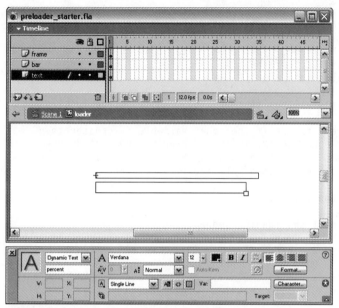

Figure 28-4: The percent field will display the current percent loaded of the movie.

18. Select frame 3 of the Actions layer and insert an empty keyframe (F7). With this frame selected, open the Actions panel. In Expert mode, insert the following code. Do not type the ⊃ character in your actual code. This symbol indicates a continuation of the same line of code. Each line of code is explained in comments within the code.

```
// lBytes stores the current bytes that have loaded

lBytes = _root.getBytesLoaded();

// tBytes stores the total bytes of the movie

tBytes = _root.getBytesTotal();

// percentLoaded calculates the percent of the movie that
// has loaded into the Flash Player.

percentLoaded = Math.floor((lBytes/tBytes)*100);

// Apply the percentLoaded value to the X scale of the
// bar instance within the loader instance

loader.bar._xscale = percentLoaded;

// Fill the percent text field within the loader instance
// with the percentLoaded value followed by the text
// "% of " and the total kilobytes of the movie. For
// example, when half of a 64K movie has loaded, the text
// field will display "50% of 64K loaded."
```

```
loader.percent.text = percentLoaded + "% of " ⊃
  + Math.floor(tBytes/1024) + "K loaded.";

// If the loaded bytes are greater than or equal to the
// total bytes of the movie and the total bytes are
// greater than 0

if (lBytes>=tBytes && tBytes>0) {

  // Check to see if the count variable is greater than
  // or equal to 12. If it is, execute the nested code.
  // This if/else code pauses the movie once 100% of the
  // movie has loaded into the Flash Player.

  if (count>=12) {

    // exit the loading sequence

    gotoAndStop("main");

    // otherwise, if the movie has completely loaded and
    // count is less than 12.

  } else {

    // add 1 to the count variable
    count++;

    // continue to loop the loading sequence
    gotoAndPlay("preload");
  }

  // if the movie hasn't finished loading into the Flash
  // Player then execute this code

} else {

  // loop back to the "preload" frame label
  gotoAndPlay("preload");
}
```

19. Save your Flash document as **preloader_100.fla** and test it (Ctrl+Enter or ⌘+Return). When you enter Test Movie mode, choose View ⇨ Show Streaming or press Ctrl+Enter or ⌘+Return again. As shown in Figure 28-5, you will see the movie's download progress reflected in the _xscale property of the bar instance as well as an updating percent value and total file size in the percent field. When the movie is fully loaded, the loader will pause for about a second and go to the main label.

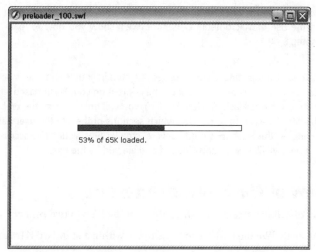

Figure 28-5: The progress bar will grow as the movie loads into the Flash Player.

On the CD-ROM   You can find the completed file, **preloader_100.fla**, in the ch28 folder of the *Flash MX Bible* CD-ROM.

Loading Flash Movies

Long sequences of animation in Flash naturally require the preloading described in the preceding section to guarantee smooth playback. But traditional information-based Web sites done in Flash require a different kind of download management. Suppose you're building a Web site with three sections: products, staff, and company history. Each section is roughly 100 KB in size. In a normal Flash movie, you'd place those sections in a sequential order on the Main Timeline or create a scene for each of them. The last section you place on the timeline would, of course, be the last section to download. Might sound fine so far, but here's the problem: What if the section that appears last on the timeline happens to be the first and only section the users want to see? They'd have to wait for the other two sections to download before they could view the one they want — but they don't even want to see the other two sections, so really they're waiting for nothing. The solution to this problem is the loadMovie() action.

loadMovie() provides a means of inserting one or more external SWF files into a Flash movie (whether that movie resides in a browser or on its own in the stand-alone player). loadMovie() can be used to replace the current movie with a different movie or to display multiple movies simultaneously. It can also be used, as in our company Web site example, to enable a parent movie to retrieve and display content kept in independent SWF files on a need-to-retrieve basis (similar to the way a frame in an HTML frameset can call external pages into different frames).

New Feature You can now use the `loadMovie()` action to load JPEG images directly into your Flash MX movies without the use of Macromedia Generator. We'll show you how to load JPEG files later in this chapter.

Tip If you are concerned about getting accurate usage statistics in your Web server's access logs, you will want to use `loadMovie()` to break up the content on your Flash-based site. If all of your content is stored in one Flash movie (SWF file), you will only see that the Web user has downloaded the site file—you have no idea which sections of the site the user has actually visited. By breaking up the Flash movie into several smaller files, your site's access logs will show which section SWF files were downloaded and viewed by the user.

Basic overview of Flash site architecture

You can produce and distribute straight Flash content on the Web in two primary ways:

✦ Create several small SWF files, with each one living within a standard HTML page on a Web site.

✦ Create one HTML page that hosts one main SWF file that loads additional content through the Flash Player plug-in.

Figure 28-6 illustrates these alternatives.

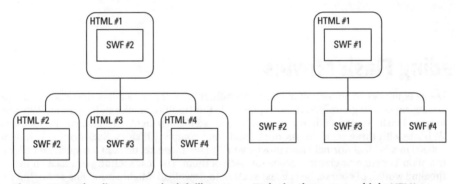

Figure 28-6: The diagram on the left illustrates a Web site that uses multiple HTML pages, each with an individual SWF file. The diagram on the right shows a Web site that uses one HTML page (or frameset) that has one primary SWF file, which loads other SWF files as needed.

If you decide to break up your Flash movies across several HTML pages, your Web visitors will experience:

✦ Short download times for each page

✦ Easier bookmarking of discrete sections of your Web site

✦ Abrupt transitions between each section of the Web site

However, if you use one primary Flash movie in one HTML page (or frameset), your visitors will benefit from

✦ Short download times for each SWF file (Download times vary with file size.)

✦ Seamless integration of new Flash content

✦ Controllable transitions between SWF asset changes

Which method should you use for your Flash projects? The answer depends on the specifics of each Web project. You may decide to use a combination of both methods, especially for larger sites that use several Web technologies (Apple QuickTime, Macromedia Flash and Shockwave, Real Systems RealOne, Microsoft Windows Media, and so on). In either scenario, you can use the loadMovie() action to manage Flash content more easily.

Tip   Now that Flash Player 6 allows you to download JPEG, MP3, and Flash movies with embedded video, you may not need to rely on other plug-in technologies for the Web sites you design and develop.

Storing multiple movies

You may already be wondering how these newly loaded movies are managed relative to the original movie. Macromedia Flash uses the metaphor of *levels* to describe where the movies are kept. Levels are something like drawers in a cabinet; they are stacked on top of each other and can contain things. You can place things in any drawer you like, but once a drawer is full, you have to take its contents out before you can put anything else in. Initially, the bottom level, referred to in ActionScript as _level0 ("Level 0"), contains the original movie, the first movie that loads into the Flash Player. All movies subsequently loaded into the Flash Player must be placed explicitly into a target level. If a movie is loaded into Level 1 or higher, it appears visually on top of the original movie in the Player. If a movie is loaded into Level 0, it replaces the original movie, removing all movies stored on levels above it in the process. When a loaded movie replaces the original movie, it does not change the frame rate, movie dimensions, or movie background color of the original Flash stage. Those properties are permanently determined by the original movie and cannot be changed, unless you load a new HTML document into the Web browser. You can also use a getURL() action to load a new SWF file into the browser to "reset" the Flash Player.

Tip   You can effectively change the background color of the Stage when you load a new movie by creating a rectangle shape of your desired color on the lowest layer of the movie you are loading.

Loading an external SWF file into a movie

A new movie is imported into the Flash Player when a loadMovie() action is executed. In the following steps, you'll learn how to make a button click load an external movie named video_anchors.swf.

On the CD-ROM   Before you begin these steps, make a copy the **video_anchors.swf** file from the ch17 folder of the *Flash MX Bible* CD-ROM. Copy the file to the location on your hard drive where you will save the new Flash document in the forthcoming exercise.

1. Create a new Flash document (File ⇨ New). Save this document as **loadMovie_100.fla** in the same location as your copy of the video_anchors.swf file.

2. Rename Layer 1 to **loadButton**.

3. Drag an instance of the PushButton component from the Component panel to your document's Stage. Place the instance in the lower-left corner of the Stage. In the Property inspector, name the component **loadButton**. In the Parameters tab, select the Label field and type **Load Movie**. In the Click Handler field, type **loadSWF**. Refer to Figure 28-7 to see these settings.

 Cross-Reference We discuss components more thoroughly in Chapter 29, "Using Components."

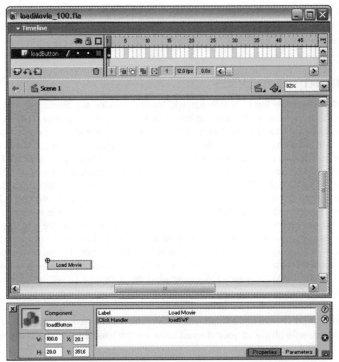

Figure 28-7: When clicked, the loadButton instance will execute a function named loadSWF.

4. Create a new layer and rename it **actions**.

5. Select frame 1 of the Actions layer and open the Actions panel (F9). In the panel's Option menu (located at the top-right corner), make sure Normal Mode is selected. In the Actions pane, click the Actions booklet and then expand the User-Defined Functions booklet. Double-click the `function` action. A `function(){}` action will be inserted into the Script pane. In the parameters area of the Actions panel, type **loadSWF** into the Name field for the `function` action. See Figure 28-8.

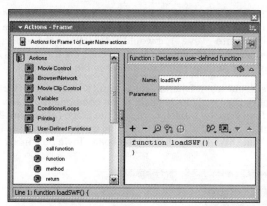

Figure 28-8: The loadSWF() function will be executed when the loadButton instance is clicked.

6. Now, expand the Browser/Network booklet in the Actions pane. In this booklet, double-click the `loadMovie` action. This will insert a `loadMovieNum()` action within the `loadSWF()` function, as shown in Figure 28-9.

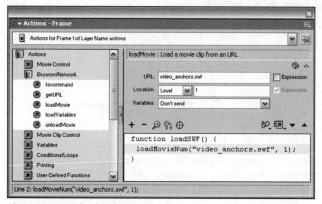

Figure 28-9: The loadMovieNum() action loads the SWF file into a level.

7. Type **video_anchors.swf** into the URL text field. The URL text field contains the network path to the movie file that you want to load. That path must be specified relative to the location of the page that contains your main movie, not relative to the location of the movie itself. Refer to Figure 28-9 to see this setting.

Caution

If you are designing a Web site for early browsers, pay attention to the URL path. Internet Explorer 4.5 (or earlier) for the Macintosh does not resolve paths correctly. For more information, please see Macromedia's tech note at:

www.macromedia.com/support/flash/ts/documents/mac_ie_issues.htm

8. Select the Level option in the Location menu and type **1** into the Location text field. This instructs ActionScript to load video_anchors.swf into _level1. If there had already been a movie loaded into _level1, it would automatically have been replaced by video_anchors.swf. When you are finished entering the options for the loadMovieNum() action, your Actions panel should resemble Figure 28-9.

9. Save your Flash document and test it by choosing Control ➪ Test Movie (Ctrl+Enter or ⌘+Return). When you click the Load Movie PushButton component instance, the video_anchors.swf will load into the top-left corner of the Stage (see Figure 28-10). You can control the playback of the loaded SWF file by using the buttons within its control bar. You can reload the same SWF file by clicking the Load Movie button again.

Figure 28-10: The video_anchors.swf loads into the top-left corner of the Stage.

You can apply this technique to any SWF file that you wish to load into another Flash movie. You can make a series of buttons, each one loading a different SWF file. You can modify the loadSWF() function to switch the URL of the loaded movie, depending on which button is pressed.

On the CD-ROM

You can find the completed example file, **loadMovie_100.fla**, in the ch28 folder of the *Flash MX Bible* CD-ROM. Note that you cannot run the **loadMovie_100.swf** file directly from the CD-ROM — to test this SWF file, you need to copy it and the **video_anchors.swf** file from the ch17 folder to the same location on your hard drive. You can also find a modified version, **loadMovie_101.fla**, that has a series of PushButton components that load different SWF files. This file requires you to enter your own URL paths to SWF files.

When a movie is loaded above any other movie (including the main movie), the Buttons and Movie Clips in the movies on lower levels will continue to be active, even though they may not be visible. To prevent this undesired behavior, you need to send movies on lower levels to an idle or blank frame where no buttons are present. Do that by adding a goto action before your loadMovie() action that sends the current movie to the idle frame. This technique is known as "parking" the movie. If you have to park multiple movies, you'll need to know how to communicate between movies on different levels. This will be discussed shortly.

_level0 or _root: What's the Difference?

Until now, we have referred to the Main Timeline as _root in ActionScript. If you don't employ levels in a Flash movie, _root will always refer to the Main Timeline of the Flash movie that is loaded into a browser. However, if you start to use levels to load external SWF files, _root will be relative to the level that's executing actions.

For example, if the main movie uses a _root reference in an action, such as

```
_root.gotoAndStop(10);
```

then the Main Timeline Playhead will go to frame 10 and stop.

If a loaded movie has the same action within its timeline, it will go to frame 10 on its timeline and stop.

While this works with movies that are loaded into level locations, it will not work with Movie Clip instance targets. As you'll see in the following sections, a movie that is loaded into a Movie Clip target becomes an instance located within the level that the Movie Clip target resides. Therefore, _root will still refer to a different timeline than that of the loaded SWF file.

How Flash handles loaded movies of differing dimensions

A movie loaded onto Level 1 or higher that is smaller in width and height than the Level 0 movie is positioned in the top-left corner of the Stage. We saw this occur with the example in the last section. In this situation, it is possible to have elements that are off-stage within the loaded SWF file. However, when you load a smaller SWF file Stage into a larger SWF file Stage, these off-stage elements are displayed on the Stage of the larger SWF file. To prevent objects from being displayed, you would have to create a curtain layer or a Mask layer above all the other layers in the Level 1 movie that covers up the *work area* (the space outside the movie's Stage).

Movies loaded onto Level 0 that are smaller than the original Level 0 movie are automatically centered and scaled up to fit the size of the original movie. (The manner in which they are scaled depends on the Scale setting in the Publish settings.)

Movies loaded onto Level 0 that are larger than the original Level 0 movie are cropped at the right and bottom boundaries defined by the original movie dimensions.

Placing, scaling, and rotating externally loaded Flash movies

Especially when your movies have different width and height dimensions, it's not very convenient to have newly loaded movies dropped ingloriously in the top-left corner of the Stage. To give you more flexibility with the placement, rotation, and scale of your loaded movies, ActionScript provides the capability to load a Flash movie (SWF file) into a Movie Clip instance. So far, this may not make a whole lot of sense. Loading a movie into a Movie Clip instance seems like a strange feature at first, until you find out what it can do — then it seems indispensable. The easiest way to understand what happens when you load a movie into a Movie Clip is to think of the loadMovie() action as a "Convert Loaded Movie to Movie Clip" action.

When a movie is loaded into a Movie Clip instance, many attributes of the original Movie Clip instance are applied to the newly loaded movie:

✦ The timeline of the loaded movie completely replaces the original instance's timeline. Nothing inside the original Movie Clip (including actions on keyframes) remains.

✦ The loaded movie assumes the following properties from the original Movie Clip instance:

- Instance name

- Scale percentage

- Color effects, including alpha

- Rotation degree

- Placement (X and Y position)

- Visibility (with respect to the _visible property)

✦ Any onClipEvent() handlers (and actions within them) that are written for the original Movie Clip instance will still be available (and executing) on the loaded movie.

✦ Any event handlers such as onMouseMove() or onEnterFrame() or variables assigned to the original Movie Clip instance will be erased once an external SWF file is loaded into the instance.

We like to refer to Movie Clips that are used to load other movies as Movie Clip holders. Usually, you will load movies into empty Movie Clips that don't have any artwork or actions. However, because you'll need a physical reference to the actual area your loaded movie will occupy on the Stage, it's useful to create temporary guides or artwork that indicate this area.

New Feature

In Flash MX ActionScript, you can create empty MovieClip objects dynamically, using the new createEmptyMovieClip() method. You can then load external SWF files into this empty MovieClip object using the loadMovie() method.

The following steps show you how to create a Movie Clip holder and how to load an external SWF file into it. You will use the same file you created in the previous section.

On the CD-ROM

If you didn't complete the example in the last section, make a copy of the **loadMovie_100.fla** file located in the ch28 folder of the *Flash MX Bible* CD-ROM. You will also need to copy the **video_anchors.swf** file from the ch17 folder.

1. Open the loadMovie_100.fla document.

2. Create a new layer on the Main Timeline and rename the layer to **holder**. Place this layer below the Actions layer.

3. Select the Rectangle tool and draw a rectangle on frame 1 of the holder layer. The shape should have the same dimensions as the external Flash movie's Stage, as defined in its Document Properties dialog box. For our example, size the rectangle to 320×240 using the Property inspector.

4. With the rectangle selected, choose Insert ➪ Convert to Symbol or press the F8 key to convert the artwork into a symbol. In the Convert to Symbol dialog box, name the symbol **holder** and choose the Movie Clip behavior. In the Registration grid, click the top-left corner point, as shown in Figure 28-11. Movies loaded into Movie Clip instances load from the top-left corner of the original target Movie Clip.

Figure 28-11: The holder instance will hold the loaded SWF file.

5. With the new instance on the Stage selected, name the instance `holder` in the <Instance Name> field of the Property inspector. Position the instance on the Stage, where you want the external SWF movie to appear. At this point, you can also tween, scale, or apply any color effect to the instance as well. For our example, apply a 50 percent alpha to the instance in the Property inspector.

Now, you need to modify the `loadSWF()` function called by the `loadButton` component instance (already on the document's Stage). This function needs to target the `holder` instance.

6. Select frame 1 of the Actions layer on the Main Timeline. Open the Actions panel (F9). Make sure Normal Mode is enabled in the panel's options menu. Choose the `loadMovieNum()` action in the Script pane. Change the Location menu option to Target and type **holder** in the Location text field. Refer to Figure 28-12 for these settings.

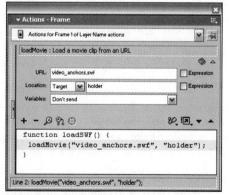

Figure 28-12: The loadMovie() action will load the SWF file into the holder instance.

Note   The instance must be resident on Stage at the time the `loadMovie()` action occurs. Any instance can either be manually placed on the timeline or created with ActionScript code, such as the `duplicateMovieClip()`, `attachMovie()`, and `createEmptyMovieClip()` methods. If any specification of the `loadMovie()` action is incorrect, then the movie will fail to load. The Flash Player will *not* start a request for an external SWF file if the Movie Clip instance target is invalid.

7. Save the Flash document as **loadMovie_200.fla** and test it (Ctrl+Enter or ⌘+Return). When you click the Load Movie component button, the video_anchors.swf will load into the top-left corner of the holder instance. The 50 percent alpha applied to the holder instance will also be applied to the loaded movie, as shown in Figure 28-13.

Figure 28-13: The SWF file loads into the holder instance when the component button is clicked.

To avoid seeing the rectangle artwork in your final Flash movie, go into the Movie Clip symbol for holder and turn the layer containing the rectangle artwork into a Guide layer. Guide layers will not export with the SWF file.

Caution   If you do not have any artwork in your target Movie Clip instance (or have converted the art-work to a Guide layer), you will not be able to scale the instance using the Transform tool or panel. You can, however, transform the instance before you remove the artwork (or convert it to a Guide layer) — the setting will "stick" even after you remove the artwork.

If you need to add functionality to the loaded movie, use ActionScript to control the new loaded movie instance. The next section shows you how to communicate with loaded movies.

On the CD-ROM   You can view the completed file, **loadMovie_200.fla**, in the ch28 folder of the *Flash MX Bible* CD-ROM. For further study, we've also included a `loadMovie()` example as a group of files on the *Flash MX Bible* CD-ROM in the loadTargets folder. Open movie1.html in a browser to view these files in action.

loadMovie() versus loadMovieNum()

You may have noticed that a `loadMovie()` action will be shown as `loadMovieNum()` when a Level location is chosen. Because you can specify variables (that point to dynamic targets) as a Location value, ActionScript needs a way to distinguish a numeric Level location from a Movie Clip instance.

Consequently, if you choose a Level location for a `loadMovie` action (in Normal mode), then the action will show as

```
loadMovieNum("external_1.swf", 1);
```

which specifies that the file `external_1.swf` be loaded into Level 1.

If you specify the Movie Clip target as `holder` for the `loadMovie()` action, the action will appear as

```
loadMovie ("external_1.swf", holder);
```

If you want the `loadMovie()` action to be compatible with Flash Player 4 (or earlier), you will need to specify the Movie Clip target name as a string (that is, enclosed in quotes).

Communicating between multiple movies on different levels

After a movie or two are loaded onto different levels, you may want each timeline to control the other, just as Movie Clips can control each other. To communicate between different levels, you simply need to address actions to the proper level. The method for addressing a level that controls a timeline on a different level is identical to the method for addressing a Movie Clip target that controls the timeline of another Movie Clip instance, except for one small change. You have to indicate the name of the level you want to target rather than the name of the Movie Clip. Level names are constructed like this: First, there's an underscore (_), then there's the word *level*, and then there's the number of the level that you want your action to occur on.

This tells the movie loaded onto Level 1 to go to frame 50:

```
_level1.gotoAndStop(50);
```

This tells the Main Movie timeline to go to frame 50:

```
_level0.gotoAndStop(50);
```

You can also target Movie Clips that reside on the timelines of movies on other levels. Here's an example:

```
_level3.products.play();
```

This sends a `play()` action to the Movie Clip named `products` on the timeline of the movie loaded onto Level 3.

Unloading movies

To lighten the memory required by your Flash movies in the Flash Player or to clear the loaded movie from the Stage, you can explicitly unload movies in any level or Movie Clip target by using the `unloadMovie()` action. The only option for `unloadMovie` is the path to the desired location (for example, `_level1`, `_root.instanceName`).

You can see an example of an `unloadMovie()` action in the **loadMovie_201.fla** file located in the ch28 folder of the *Flash MX Bible* CD-ROM. Here, an `unloadSWF()` function is executed by the `unloadButton` component instance to clear the loaded movie.

If you want to replace an existing loaded movie with another external file, you do not need to unload the movie before loading the new one. A `loadMovie()` action implicitly unloads the existing content in the specified location. We have actually seen problems occur in Flash movies where `unloadMovie()` and `loadMovie()` actions are executed consecutively.

loadMovie() as a method for Movie Clip targets

Both `loadMovie()` and `unloadMovie()` can be used as either an ActionScript method or action for Movie Clip targets. What does this mean? You can apply actions in Flash MX in two ways: as methods of a `MovieClip` object (or some other ActionScript object, as we have discussed in previous chapters) or as a stand-alone action.

As an action, `loadMovie()` and `unloadMovie()` start the ActionScript line of code. When you use actions in this manner, the target of the action is specified as an argument (option) within the action. In the following example, the file external_1.swf is loaded into the `holder` instance:

```
loadMovie("external_1.swf", "holder");
```

As a method, actions are written as an extension of the object using the action. Therefore, the target is already specified before the action is typed. The same example shown previously could be rewritten as a method of the `holder` MovieClip object:

```
holder.loadMovie("external_1.swf");
```

or

```
_root.holder.loadMovie("external_1.swf");
```

Because we have specifically referenced the holder instance as an object, the `loadMovie()` action (now a method) knows where to direct the loading of external_1.swf.

When you use `unloadMovie()` as a method of the `MovieClip` object, you do not need to specify any arguments for the method. For example, `holder.unloadMovie();` will unload any movie in the `holder` instance.

You can see this syntax of the `loadMovie()` method in the **loadMovie_202.fla** file, located in the ch28 folder of the *Flash MX Bible* CD-ROM.

Loading External Files through Proxy Servers

If you are creating Flash movies that will be loaded through proxy servers set up by large Internet service providers (ISPs) on the Internet, you may need to know how to trick them into loading "fresh" SWF files every time a user visits your site. What is a proxy server? With the growth of high-speed Internet connections, such as DSL and cable, many ISPs will process all outgoing HTTP requests through a go-between computer that caches previous requests to the same URL. Anytime you type a Web site URL into a browser, you're making an HTTP request. If that computer, called a *proxy server*, sees a request that was made previously (within a certain time frame), then it will serve its cached content to the end user instead of downloading the actual content from the remote server.

Why do you need to be concerned about caching? If you (or your client) needs accurate usage statistics for a Web site, you will likely want to know which portions of the site your users are actively using (that is, downloading into their browsers). Your Web server will not log a request it never receives — if a proxy server delivers the content to the end user, you will not even know a user is looking at your content.

When a Flash movie makes an HTTP request with a `loadMovie()` action, a proxy server may serve the cached SWF file instead of the one that actually exists on your server. Why is this a problem? If you are updating that SWF file frequently or if you want precise Web usage statistics for your Flash movies and content, then you'll want users to download the actual SWF file on your server each time a request is made.

The question remains: How do you trick a proxy server into serving the real SWF file instead of its cached one? The proxy server knows what's in its cache by the URL for each cached item. So, if you change the name of the loaded Flash movie each time you make a request for it, the proxy server won't ever see an identical match with its cached content.

To change the name of a loaded Flash movie, simply add a random number to the end of the movie's name in the `loadMovie()` action. This random number won't actually be part of the movie's filename. Rather, it will appear as a query at the end of the filename. Place the following actions on the event handler that initiates a `loadMovie()` action:

```
randomNum = Math.round(Math.random()*9999999999);
loadMovie("external_1.swf?" + randomNum, "holder");
```

In the preceding example, a variable called `randomNum` is established and given a random value, a number in the range of 0 to 9999999998. Each time the event handler calling these actions is executed, a different number is appended to the filename of the loaded movie. The proxy server will think that each request is a different and route the request to your Web server.

Not only does this method prevent a proxy server from serving a cached Flash movie file, but it also prevents most browsers from caching the loaded movie in the user's local cache folder.

Loading JPEG Images into Flash Movies

Flash MX ActionScript has added the exciting new capability to load JPEG images into Flash movies — while the movie is playing in a Web browser! In previous versions of the Flash Player, all externally loaded content needed to be in the SWF format. However, starting with Flash Player 6, the doors have opened to download specific media formats directly into Flash movies.

You cannot load JPEG images directly into Flash movies playing in Flash Player 5 or earlier. The user must have Flash Player 6 to use this feature.

There are some basic rules for using JPEG images that are loaded into Flash movies:

✦ Use only standard JPEG files. You can not load progressive JPEG images into Flash movies playing in Flash Player 6.

✦ Watch the file size of JPEG files. Unless your JPEG files are extremely small and/or within a reasonable limit of your target audience's data rate, you will likely want to build a preloader for your JPEG files.

✦ All JPEG images that are loaded dynamically will be smoothed in Flash Player 6. Smoothed bitmaps may have an adverse effect on playback performance. You can control the global rendering of bitmaps and all artwork by using the `_quality` property of the `MovieClip` object. For example, `_quality = "LOW";` will turn off smoothing for all artwork. Use this property with care—most vector artwork and text looks unsightly with low-quality rendering.

✦ Control the physical characteristics of the JPEG image (X and Y coordinates, X and Y scale, rotation, and so on) by controlling those properties of the `MovieClip` object holding the image.

✦ Check the user's version of the Flash Player with ActionScript or JavaScript. The user must have Flash Player 6 installed to load JPEG images directly into Flash movies. We discuss Flash Player detection in Chapter 22, "Integrating Flash Content with HTML."

Keep in mind general issues for bitmap usage in Flash movies. Read our coverage of using bitmap images in Chapter 16, "Importing Artwork," and Chapter 37, "Working with Raster Graphics."

If you are doubt, test the specific JPEG images with your Flash movies. If you encounter problems with loading the JPEG, check the following:

✦ **URL:** Make sure you have the correct path and filename specified in the `loadMovie()` action.

✦ **Location:** Does the target exist into which you want to load? Check the path to the level or `MovieClip` object that will contain the image.

✦ **Format:** Is the JPEG image a standard format? Or does it use progressive encoding? Progressive JPEGs cannot be loaded into Flash Player 6.

Without further ado, let's create a Flash movie that dynamically loads a JPEG image. In this example, we will load a JPEG file located in the same directory as the Flash movie (SWF file). In ActionScript, the loadMovie() action is used to load JPEG images, using the following syntax:

```
instanceName.loadMovie(URL);
```

where *instanceName* is the `MovieClip` object that will hold the JPEG image and *URL* is the relative or absolute path to the JPEG file. In the following code, a JPEG file named cat.jpg will be loaded into a `MovieClip` object named `holder`:

```
holder.loadMovie("cat.jpg");
```

or

```
holder.loadMovie("http://mydomain.com/cat.jpg");
```

For this exercise, we will use the **loadMovie_202.fla** document that you created in a previous section of this chapter. You can also make a copy of this completed file from the ch28 folder of the *Flash MX Bible* before you begin this exercise. You will need to copy the **beach.jpg** file in this location to your local folder as well.

1. Open a copy of the **loadMovie_202.fla** document. Create a new layer named **textfield**. Place the Holder layer at the bottom of the layer stack.

2. Save the Flash document as **loadMovie_300.fla**.

3. On frame 1 of the Textfield layer, select the Text tool and create an Input Text field underneath the `holder` instance artwork. With the text field selected, open the Property inspector and type **imageURL** in the <Instance Name> field. Enable the Show Border option as well. When you are finished, your document's Stage should resemble Figure 28-14.

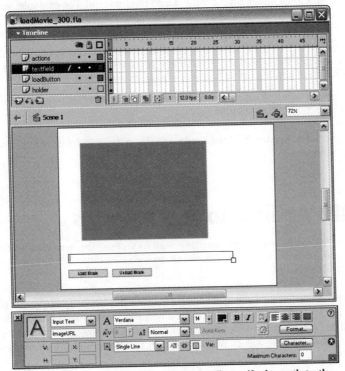

Figure 28-14: The imageURL text field will specify the path to the JPEG image.

4. Select the Load Movie component button on the Stage. In the Property inspector, change the Label value to **Load JPEG**.

5. Select the Unload Movie component button on the Stage. In the Property inspector, change the Label value to **Unload JPEG**.

6. Select frame 1 of the Actions layer and open the Actions panel. In the panel's options menu, make sure Expert mode is enabled. In the Script pane, change the `loadSWF()` function to the following code:

```
function loadSWF() {
   holder.loadMovie(imageURL.text);
}
```

Here, you retrieve the current text in the `imageURL` text field and use it as the URL of the `loadMovie()` method of the holder instance. When the `loadButton` component instance is clicked, the `loadSWF()` function will execute and load the JPEG file specified in the `imageURL` text field into the holder instance.

7. Save your Flash document and test it (Ctrl+Enter or ⌘+Return). In the Test Movie window, type **beach.jpg** into the text field. When you click the Load JPEG button, the beach.jpg image will load into the `holder` instance.

Try typing in other known image URL locations into the text field. For example, you can download the same image from the following location. Be sure to type the full URL, including the `http://` protocol: `http://www.theMakers.com/beach.jpg`

You may want to go back to the Flash document and move the location of the holder instance to better accommodate the size of the JPEG image you are loading. Remember, we still have a 50 percent alpha effect applied to the holder instance as well.

You will learn how to build a loading graphic for JPEG files in the "Using a Preloader for External Assets" section of this chapter.

You can find the completed file, **loadMovie_300.fla**, in the ch28 folder of the *Flash MX Bible* CD-ROM.

Loading MP3 Audio into Flash Movies

If you thought JPEG image loading was exciting, wait to you see the new support for MP3 audio loading into Flash 6 movies. You can now load MP3 files directly into Sound objects that you create with ActionScript.

If you don't know how to use Sound objects, read our coverage of Sound objects in Chapter 27, "Interacting with Movie Clips." You may also want to read Chapter 15, "Adding Sound," if you are unfamiliar with general sound use in Flash movies. You can find expanded and more advanced coverage of Sound objects in the *Macromedia Flash MX ActionScript Bible*.

Here are a few tips for using MP3 files that will be loaded into Flash 6 movies:

✦ Watch file size. MP3 files, especially those of full-length songs, can be very large in file size, easily exceeding 3MB. Make sure your target audience can accommodate the file sizes you are loading.

✦ Test your specific MP3 encoding method(s) before you use the same encoding on several files that you intend to use with Flash 6 movies. In our tests, we have not encountered problems with any MP3 files that we loaded into the Flash Player. However, there are several variations of CBR (Constant Bit Rate) and VBR (Variable Bit Rate) encoding methods available in several audio applications.

✦ MP3 files do not cache on the user's hard drive. All MP3 files loaded through the Sound object in ActionScript are stored in the computer's virtual memory. Be careful with the number of MP3 files downloaded and kept in memory simultaneously.

Review the troubleshooting tips we listed for loadMovie() and JPEG images in the last section. The same principles apply to MP3 files.

Flash MX ActionScript has added a new method to the Sound object: loadSound(). With this method, you can specify a path to an MP3 file just like you did for JPEG images with the loadMovie() method. However, the loadSound() method has an additional argument, isStreaming. We'll discuss this in a moment. The syntax for using the loadSound() method is

```
soundObject.loadSound(URL, isStreaming);
```

where *soundObject* indicates the name of a Sound object created previously in ActionScript and *URL* is the relative or absolute path to the MP3 file. *isStreaming* is a Boolean value (true or false) that determines whether the MP3 file will automatically begin playback as soon as enough bytes have loaded into Flash Player 6 (true) or whether the MP3 file must fully download before playback can begin (false).

In the remainder of this section, you will learn how to load an MP3 file into a Sound object.

Before you begin the following exercise, make a copy of the **loadMovie_300.fla** located in the ch28 folder of the *Flash MX Bible* CD-ROM. You will modify the existing structure of the document that you built in earlier sections of this chapter. You will also need an MP3 file copied to the same location on your hard drive. You can use the **atmospheres_1.mp3** file located in the ch28 folder as well.

1. Open the **loadMovie_300.fla** document.

2. Select the Load JPEG component instance on the Stage. In the Property inspector, change the Label value to **Load MP3** and change the Click Handler value to **loadMP3**.

3. Select the Unload JPEG component instance on the Stage. In the Property inspector, change the Label value to **Unload MP3** and change the Click Handler value to **unloadMP3**.

4. Select the Input Text field on the Stage and change the instance's name to **soundURL** in the Property inspector.

5. Now you need to change the ActionScript in the document to use the Sound object and the loadSound() method. Select frame 1 of the Actions layer and open the Actions panel (F9). Change the loadSWF() and unloadSWF() functions to the following code:

```
function loadMP3() {
  sound_1 = new Sound();
  sound_1.loadSound(soundURL.text, true);
}
function unloadMP3() {
  sound_1.stop();
  delete sound_1;
}
```

In the loadMP3() function (which is executed by the Load MP3 component instance), a new Sound object named sound_1 is created. Then, the loadSound() method of the object is then executed, using the URL specified in the soundURL text field. The isStreaming argument is set to true so that the MP3 will automatically begin to play as soon as enough of the sound file has downloaded into Flash Player 6.

The unloadMP3() function (which is executed by the Unload MP3 component instance) stops the sound playing in the sound_1 object and deletes the object from the movie.

6. Save your Flash document as **loadSound_100.fla**, and test it (Ctrl+Enter or ⌘+Return). In the Test Movie window, type **atmospheres_1.mp3** into the soundURL text field. Click the Load MP3 button, and the MP3 will begin to play. When you click the Unload MP3 button, the sound will stop playing.

Try using other URLs of MP3 files, either locally or remotely. You can specify the following URL to stream the same MP3 file from our Web server:

```
http://www.theMakers.com/sounds/atmospheres_1.mp3
```

You can continue modifying the Sound object into which the MP3 file loads. For example, you can apply the same volume and balance output control from the examples in Chapter 27 to the Sound object in this Flash movie.

We will show you how to monitor the download progress of an MP3 file (and other external files) in the next section.

On the CD-ROM   You can see the completed Flash document, **loadSound_100.fla**, in the ch28 folder of the *Flash MX Bible* CD-ROM.

Using a Preloader for External Assets

In this section, you will learn how to add a preloader that monitors the download progress of any external asset, whether it is a SWF, JPEG, or MP3 file. This preloader combines the same methodology employed by the original **preloader_100.fla** document you built earlier in this chapter. We've already taken the same loader Movie Clip symbol from that exercise and added ActionScript to its timeline. Let's take a quick look at what we've done.

Open the **loader_100.fla** located in the ch28 folder of the *Flash MX Bible* CD-ROM. Open the Library panel and double-click the loader symbol. Inside of this symbol, select frame 1 of the Actions layer. Open the Actions panel, and you will see the following code in the Script pane. Note the ⮐ character indicates a continuation of the same line of code.

```
function checkLoad(obj) {
  var lBytes = target.getBytesLoaded();
  var tBytes = target.getBytesTotal();
  var percentLoaded = Math.floor((lBytes/tBytes)*100);
  bar._xscale = percentLoaded;
  percent.text = Math.floor(percentLoaded) + "% of ⮐
    " + Math.floor(tBytes/1024) + "KB loaded.";
  if (lBytes>=tBytes && tBytes>0) {
    if (count>=12) {
      clearInterval(checkProgress);
      _parent[loadExit]();
```

```
        obj.removeMovieClip();
      } else {
        count++;
      }
    }
    updateAfterEvent();
  }
  checkProgress = setInterval(checkLoad, 100, this);
  stop();
```

While this may seem a bit overwhelming, it's nearly identical to the code you built on the Main Timeline of the preloader_100.fla document. The primary differences are

✦ The code is contained within a function named checkLoad().

✦ Instead of a frame loop, the new setInterval() function is used to repeatedly execute the checkLoad() function. When the loading is finished, the clearInterval() function is called to stop the looping.

✦ The loader instance is dynamically placed in the movie to monitor the download progress of a specific asset — it does not monitor the load progress of the main movie SWF file.

New Feature The setInterval() and clearInterval() functions are new to Flash MX ActionScript. These actions work only in Flash 6 movies.

But that's not all of the code we'll need to get an asset preloader working. Even though we have code with a loader symbol that will continually check the loading progress of an asset, we need some code that will provide some input for the loader symbol, such as what type of file is loading (SWF, JPEG, or MP3) and where the file is loading (a MovieClip object or a Sound object).

Let's take a look at one more chunk of code. Open the loadfile.as file located in the ch28 folder of the *Flash MX Bible* CD-ROM. You can use Macromedia Dreamweaver MX or any other text editor to view the code. Here's what you'll see in the file:

```
function loadFile(){
  var fileExtension = fileURL.text.substr(-3);
  _root.createEmptyMovieClip("holder",1);
  if(fileExtension == "swf" || fileExtension == "jpg"){
    holder.loadMovie(fileURL.text);
    var loadObj = holder;
  } else if(fileExtension == "mp3"){
    sound_1 = new Sound(holder);
    sound_1.loadSound(fileURL.text, true);
    var loadObj = sound_1;
  }
  var initObject = {
    _x: fileURL._x,
    _y: fileURL._y - 40,
    target: loadObj,
    loadExit: null
  };
  _root.attachMovie("loader","loader",2, initObject);
}
```

```
function unloadFile(){
  if(typeof(holder) != undefined){
    holder.removeMovieClip();
  }
  if(typeof(sound_1) != undefined){
    sound_1.stop();
    delete sound_1;
  }
}
```

The loadFile() function takes a URL specified in a fileURL text field (fileURL.text) and loads it into a proper container. If the URL ends with "swf" or "jpg", the function will load the URL into a new Movie Clip instance named holder. If the URL ends with "mp3", the function will load the URL into a new Sound object. The initObject contains the information that the loader symbol will need to work. The X and Y position of the loader instance will be based on the position of the fileURL text field. The target variable (which is specified in the checkLoad() function you saw earlier within the loader symbol) is set to either holder or sound_1, depending on what type of media file is being loaded. Finally, the attachMovie() method attaches the loader symbol from the movie's library to the Main Timeline (_root), passing it the properties of the initObject.

New Feature The ability to pass an initObject to the attachMovie() method is a new feature of Flash MX ActionScript.

Note For this example, the loadExit variable in the checkLoad() function is not used.

The unloadFile() function deletes the objects created by the loadFile() function. If either a holder or sound_1 instance exists, it will be deleted or removed from the movie.

In the following steps, we'll combine the loader symbol from the loader_100.fla with the load-file.as file that we just examined. You will integrate these elements into a new version of the **loadSound_100.fla** that you created in the previous section.

On the CD-ROM Make a copy of the **loader_100.fla, loadfile.as**, and **loadSound_100.fla** files, located in the ch28 folder of the *Flash MX Bible* CD-ROM.

1. Open the loadSound_100.fla document. Save this document as preloader_200.fla.

2. Choose File ➪ Open as Library, and choose the loader_100.fla document.

3. Drag the loader symbol from the loader_100.fla Library panel to the Stage of the preloader_200.fla document. All of the symbols associated with the loader symbol will be transferred to the preloader_200.fla document. Close the loader_100.fla Library panel.

4. Delete the loader instance from the Stage of the preloader_200.fla document. This symbol is linked in the Library of this document and will be attached to the Stage via ActionScript.

5. Delete the Holder layer in the Main Timeline. You will not need a physical Movie Clip instance on the Stage in which to load assets. The code within the loadFile() function creates a holder instance on the fly.

6. Select the Load MP3 component instance on the Stage. In the Property inspector, change the Label value to **Load File**. Change the Click Handler to **loadFile**.

7. Select the Unload MP3 component instance on the Stage. In the Property inspector, change the Label value to **Unload File**. Change the Click Handler to **unloadFile**.

8. Select the Input Text field on the Stage and open the Property inspector. Change the instance name of the field to fileURL. At runtime, the text that is typed into this field will be used by the loadFile() function, which is executed when the Load File component instance is clicked.

9. Select frame 1 of the Actions layer. Open the Actions panel (F9), and delete the existing code in the Script pane. Make sure Expert mode is selected in the panel's options menu and type the following code into the Script pane:

```
#include "loadfile.as"
```

The #include directive will fetch the contents of the loadfile.as file when you publish or test the movie and insert the code into the Flash movie on this keyframe.

10. Save the Flash document, and test it (Ctrl+Enter or ⌘+Return). Type a URL into the Input Text field. You can use the following test URL:

```
http://themakers.com/images/beach.jpg
```

Alternatively, you can type the name of a file in the same location as the tested movie on your hard drive. Click the Load File button, and the loader instance will appear above the Input Text field, indicating the progress of the file's download. See Figure 28-15. When you click the Unload File button, the media will unload from the Flash movie.

Figure 28-15: The loader instance will appear when you click the Load File button.

Try a URL for each of the media formats that Flash Player 6 can load dynamically. If a file fails to load, check the same URL in a Web browser.

On the CD-ROM You can find the completed document, **preloader_200.fla**, in the ch28 folder of the *Flash MX Bible* CD-ROM.

Accessing Items in Shared Libraries

Flash 5 added an exciting new feature to asset management in Flash movies: the capability to link the symbols, sounds, bitmaps, and font symbols within external SWF files to other Flash movies that you use on your Web site. These external SWF files, called *Shared Libraries,* are different than loaded SWF files. Flash MX continues to expand the potential of Shared libraries and has improved the interface and dialog boxes used to create shared items.

New Feature   Flash MX allows you to more easily update shared assets in the Flash documents (FLA files) that use them. Flash MX refers to shared assets as *runtime sharing*. We'll take a look at this feature in just a moment.

The primary benefit of using a Shared library SWF file is that it needs to be downloaded only once, even though several other Flash movies may need to access the same element. For example, if you want to use Blur Medium as an embedded font in several Flash movies (SWF files), you would need to embed the font into each movie. A font can easily consume over 30K in each movie. Multiply that by 10 or 20 files in your Web site that use the font, and you may be eating up a lot of bytes just for the font usage. Instead, if you added a Font symbol to one Shared library SWF file and used that shared asset in all of the Flash movies, you would need to download the font only once, even though it's used by several movies.

A Shared library SWF file doesn't load into a Level or a Movie Clip instance location. Instead, you set up the Library of a Flash document (FLA file) with assets that you want to use in other Flash movies. This document is the basis of the Shared library SWF file. After you assign an identifier to each asset in the Library, you save the Flash document, publish a Flash movie (SWF file) from it, and close the Flash document. Then, you open another Flash document (FLA file) and, using File ➪ Open as Shared library, you open the Shared library Flash document (FLA file). Its Library window will open (in a dimmed gray state), and you can drag and drop assets to your new Flash movie file.

Note   Even though the assets are linked to the external Shared library SWF file, the Flash document (FLA file) will actually store copies of the assets. However, they will not be exported with the Flash movie that is published.

After you have established a Shared library file, any changes to the actual contents of the Shared library Flash document (FLA file) and movie (SWF file) will propagate to any Flash movie that uses the shared assets. In the following sections, you learn how to create a Shared library file and use it with other Flash movies.

Caution   It is recommended that you use only small (low byte size) elements in your Shared libraries to ensure that they are downloaded and available for Flash movies that use them. As with any Web production, make sure that you test early and often before you develop an entire project.

Setting up a Shared library file

To share assets among several Flash movies, you need to establish a Shared library file (or files) that is available to other Flash movie files. To create a Shared library file, follow these steps:

1. Create a new Flash document (Ctrl+N or ⌘+N).

2. To place Flash artwork into the Library, draw the shapes and other elements (text, lines, gradients, and so on). Select the artwork and choose Insert ➪ Convert to Symbol

(F8). In the Convert to Symbol dialog box, choose a symbol type (for example, Graphic, Button, or Movie Clip) that best suits the nature of your artwork.

Flash MX also allows you to define export parameters directly in this dialog box. Click the Advanced button; and in the extended options, check the Export for runtime sharing. Specify a linkage identifier name, and type the relative or absolute URL for the shared SWF file in the URL field. This URL should simply be the path to this Flash movie on the Web server, such as `http://mydomain.com/files/sharedLib.swf`. Alternatively, if you know all of your Flash movies will be stored in the same directory on the Web server, you can simply type the name of the SWF file, as shown in Figure 28-16.

Figure 28-16: Flash MX allows you to add runtime-sharing information directly in the Convert to Symbol dialog box.

3. To place bitmaps and sounds into the Library, import the source files as you normally would, using File ⇨ Import (Ctrl+R or ⌘+R) or File ⇨ Import to Library.

4. Delete all artwork that you have placed on the Stage. Every asset that you want to share should be in the Library.

5. To place an entire font (or typeface) into the Library, open the Library panel and choose New Font from the options menu located at the top-right corner of the Library panel. In the Font Symbol Properties dialog box, type a reference name for the font, choose the font face from the Font menu, and select a faux font style (Bold or Italic) to be applied (optional). See Figure 28-17.

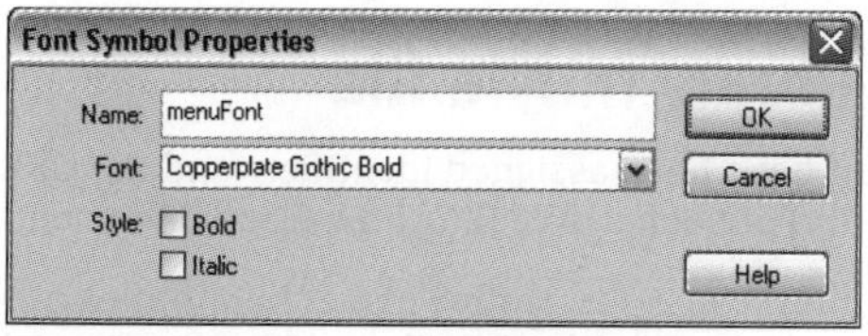

Figure 28-17: Give each embedded font face a descriptive name that indicates its functionality within the Flash movie.

Assigning names to assets

After you have placed each asset into the Library of your starter Flash document (FLA file), you'll need to assign a unique identifier to each asset.

1. Select the symbol, bitmap, sound, and font in the Library. Right-click (or Control+click on Mac) the selected asset and choose Linkage. Alternatively, you can select the item and choose Linkage from the Library's options menu.

2. In the Linkage Properties dialog box, shown in Figure 28-18, choose Export for runtime sharing for the Linkage option. This forces the asset to export with the published SWF file. Then, type a unique name in the Identifier field. In the URL field, enter the intended final location of the SWF file that you will publish from this Flash document. We will discuss this option in more detail in the next section. Click OK to close the dialog box.

Figure 28-18: Each asset in the Library of the Shared library document needs a unique name.

3. Repeat Steps 1 and 2 for each asset in the Library.

Specifying the Shared library's location

A required setting for each asset of the Shared library document is the relative or absolute path (as a URL) to the Shared library SWF on your Web server. To change the URL for all of the assets with the current Shared library document, follow these steps:

1. In the options menu in the Library panel, choose Shared library Properties.

2. In the URL field, type the location of the Shared library SWF file (or where you intend to publish it on the Web). This location will be appended to each shared asset's identifier in the movies that use the assets.

Caution   Make sure that you specify this URL before you start using the Shared library document (FLA file) with other Flash documents (FLA files). The URL location is stored within each document that uses the Shared library SWF file, and it will not update if you decide to change the URL later in the Shared library FLA file.

Publishing the Shared library movie file

After the assets of the Flash document have been assigned identifiers and the URL of the Shared library has been set, you need to publish a SWF file of the Flash document.

1. Save the Flash document (FLA file). Use a descriptive name that notifies other members of your Web production team that this is a Shared library file, such as sharedLib.fla.

2. Publish the Flash movie as a SWF file. No other publish formats are necessary. In the Publish Settings (File ➪ Publish Settings), select only the Flash format in the Format tab. Click OK. Choose File ➪ Publish to create a SWF file from your document.

3. Close the Flash document.

Linking to assets from other movies

After the Shared library SWF file is published, you can use the shared assets in other Flash movies.

1. Create a new Flash document or open an existing one.

2. Using the File ➪ Open as Library command, browse to the folder where your Shared library Flash document (FLA file) was saved. For testing purposes, you should keep this document in the same folder as the other Flash documents that share it. Select the Shared library FLA file and click Open. A separate grayed-out Library panel for the Shared library FLA file will open in the Flash MX authoring environment.

3. Drag the asset(s) that you wish to use into the new Flash document's Library or onto its Stage. Even though Flash MX will copy the contents of each shared asset, the asset will load from the separate Shared library SWF file.

4. To see whether an asset is native to the Flash movie or from a Shared library SWF file, right-click (or Control+click on Mac) the symbol or asset in the Library. Select Linkage from the contextual menu. The Linkage Properties dialog box, shown in Figure 28-19, will indicate whether the symbol (or asset) will be imported from an external Shared library SWF file.

Figure 28-19: If a Shared library asset is used in another movie, the Linkage Properties will indicate the name (and path) of the Shared library SWF file.

When you are done dragging the assets from the Shared library file, close its Library panel. When you publish the new Flash movie(s) that use the Shared library SWF file, make sure you put all of the files on your Web server for live testing. If you used relative URL locations for the Shared library SWF file(s), make sure the files are stored in the proper directories on your Web server.

You can find a Shared library document and Flash document that uses the shared assets in the sharedLib folder of the ch28 folder of the *Flash MX Bible* CD-ROM.

Updating shared assets

Flash MX has added an update feature to assets that have been imported from a Shared library document. To see which assets in your current document are imported, expand the width of the Library panel to view the Linkage column, as shown in Figure 28-20.

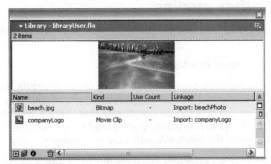

Figure 28-20: The new Flash MX Library panel allows you to quickly view the Linkage settings for each item.

If you have changed the contents of an asset in a Shared library document (FLA file) and published the new SWF file, you can choose to update the reference assets in other Flash documents that use the shared assets. Let's walk through the complete process of updating a Shared library asset.

1. Open the Shared library document (FLA file).

2. Open the Library panel and edit the shared asset you wish to update. For example, if you need to change the artwork with a Movie Clip symbol, double-click the symbol and edit the symbol's content.

3. When you're done editing the asset, save the Flash document and publish a Flash movie. Close the Shared library document.

4. Open a Flash document that uses an asset from the Shared library.

5. Open the Library panel for the document. You'll notice that any changed elements will still appear as they did before the update occurred. Select the asset that was changed in the Shared library document and choose Update from the options menu. Or right-click (Control+click on Mac) the asset and choose Update from the contextual menu. The Update Library Items dialog box will appear, as shown in Figure 28-21. Select the check box next to the asset's name you wish to update and then click the Update button.

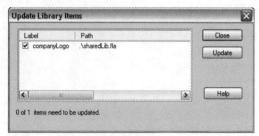

Figure 28-21: You can update shared assets in other Flash documents that use them.

You can also select multiple items in the Library panel and chose Update in the Options menu to update several items at once.

Summary

✦ If you want to make sure that your larger Flash movies don't pause during playback over the Web, you may want to make a preloader for each Flash movie you make.

✦ Preloaders can use three different ways to test the download progress of the Flash movie SWF file: `ifFrameLoaded`, `_framesLoaded/_totalFrames`, and `getBytesLoaded()/getBytesTotal`. The most accurate mechanism uses the `getBytesLoaded()/getBytesTotal()` methods.

✦ You can break up large Flash projects into several smaller Flash movie components that are loaded into a primary Flash movie when they're needed.

✦ The `loadMovie()` action enables you to download SWF files into Level or Movie Clip instance locations.

✦ You can load JPEG images with the `loadMovie()` action in Flash 6 movies.

✦ MP3 files can be downloaded directly into Flash 6 movies using the `loadSound()` method of the `Sound` object.

✦ You can share Flash assets with the Shared library feature. Assets are stored in one or more Shared library SWF files and referenced by other Flash movies.

✦   ✦   ✦

Using Components

A major new feature of Flash MX is the addition of components to the authoring environment. Components offer an easy way to reuse complicated elements within your movie without having to know or write ActionScript. They are the Flash MX equivalent of the Flash 5 program's Smart Clips. Components greatly expand upon the capabilities of Smart Clips. You probably have already noticed a panel including several built-in components that ship with Flash MX. The Macromedia Exchange has many additional components you can add to this. Although it's beyond the scope of this book, you can also build your own custom components. In this chapter, we will take a look at what components are, their parameters, and how to work with the ones included with Flash MX.

In This Chapter

Understanding components

Using components in Flash MX

Using components in your movie

Skinning and modifying

Using style properties

Embedding fonts

Using custom components

Exchanging and acquiring components

While you can make simple components that work exactly like Smart Clips, Macromedia no longer uses the term *Smart Clips.*

What Are Components?

Components are complex Movie Clips with parameters defined during the authoring process. They are essentially a container, holding many assets, which work together to add enhanced interactivity, productivity, or effects to your movies. Components can be used to control your movie, such as moving from one frame to another, or to perform more-complex tasks, such as sending data to and from a server.

Components are one of the ways Macromedia is phasing out the use of Generator. For instance, the ScrollPane component included with Flash MX can be used to dynamically load images into your movie, which in the past was a function performed only by Generator or by complex workarounds using server-side scripting languages, such as PHP. This is great news from a financial standpoint, considering the added expense of purchasing Generator.

Additional components can be downloaded from the Internet to add to those already bundled with Flash MX. Many of the most useful and regularly used elements are already included with the program, such as buttons, scroll bars, and panes. We will look at each one of these components in this chapter.

We will step through each component bundled in Flash MX in the "Components in Flash MX" section, later in this chapter.

Different from Smart Clips

You may already be familiar with the creation and/or usage of Smart Clips, which were introduced in Flash 5. Components are different from Smart Clips, expanding upon this format of definable and reusable Movie Clips. Components are much more extensive, powerful, and robust than Smart Clips.

You are also able to create components in Flash MX and then save them in the Flash 5 format. However, not all features you find in components will be supported by earlier versions of Flash.

Not all Smart Clips will transfer automatically to Flash MX without problems. It depends on how the clips were built, namely their architecture (such as parent-child relationships). Some remodeling and testing may need to occur before they work well in the Flash MX authoring environment.

Why Use Components?

Just as Smart Clips were exchanged with Flash 5, custom components are already being sold, traded, or freely passed around online. Components make it easy for you to share your work with other Flash developers in the community. Similarly, the ability to profit from a job well done is also quite appealing, as illustrated in the past with the sale of ColdFusion components.

While we will focus on the components bundled with the release of Flash MX, this knowledge will also help you use the components you may download from the Web. Components you download sometimes come in *sets,* which may include many similar small applications. A current example of this is a component set made by Macromedia comprised of several graphing utilities, which you could use in conjunction with XML to dynamically set values and have them displayed in a graph at runtime. These sets are essentially a Flash document (FLA file) stored on your computer, although you will need the Extension Manager to install them into Flash MX.

 Cross-Reference For more information on exchanging and downloading components, please see the section "Exchanging and acquiring components" at the end of this chapter.

One of the arguments against using components is the additional file size they will add to your productions. Even though this may be the case, there are several reasons to use components apart from the ease of dragging them to your Stage and modifying the parameters.

First of all, usability is an integral part of effective interface design. Components are an extremely effective way of ensuring that your end user will understand how to use certain elements of your site. A predictable interface does not have to be boring or a cliché. Furthermore, because components can be skinned, they can look completely different from one site to the next. The components shipped with Flash MX are also extremely reliable, given they were built, developed, and tested by professionals. This is not to say that the same level of construction cannot be achieved by thousands of others, but the time and effort spent in complicated coding and testing has already been done for you. And because components are a quick solution to common interface requirements, you will have more time to spend on more-complicated and interesting creative tasks instead of repetitive authoring.

Caution Exercise care with third-party components—even those that you can download from the Macromedia Exchange. Not all components have been thoroughly tested, and some are specifically developed for one particular use in mind. Be sure to test your implementation of a component throughout the development process.

What makes up a component

A component is made up of assets. Once you drag and drop a component onto your Stage, open your Library panel (F11) and take a look at the new addition. A new folder has been added to the Library, containing a series of component instances, folders, and (inside them) Movie Clips containing graphics and a lot of ActionScript. You may notice some of the Movie Clips only contain code. For example, if you have added a Flash UI Component (the components discussed in this chapter), a Global Skins folder within the Flash UI Components folder contains assets used by all UI components. However, some components have their own Skins folder. Within the Skins folder, you will find graphically based Movie Clips defining the way your components appear on the Stage. If you plan on making modifications or deleting some of these assets, it is important to understand the structure and contents of these folders. We will cover this in later sections of this chapter.

How to add a component

You can add a component to your Stage in the following ways:

1. Open the Component panel by going to Window ➪ Components or by pressing Ctrl+F7 or ⌘+F7.

2. Add a component to the Stage by:

    • **Double-clicking:** You can double-click a component, and it will be added to the center of your Stage.

    • **Dragging:** You can add an instance by clicking the component icon and dragging it onto the Stage.

After your component is on the Stage, you can modify the parameters, properties, and graphics manually in various panels, the Library, or by using ActionScript code on objects or frames in a timeline.

Note You can add additional instances of your component to your movie by dragging it from your Library onto the Stage instead of from the Component panel.

You can also add a component to your movie by using the `MovieClip.attachMovie()` method in ActionScript after the instance is added to your library. An example of adding a RadioButton component to the Stage and setting a few properties using ActionScript is as follows:

```
_root.attachMovie("FPushButtonSymbol", "pushbutton1", 10);
_root.pushbutton1.setSize(85, 35);
_root.pushbutton1.setLabel("music");
_root.pushbutton1.setStyleProperty("face", 0x99ccff);
```

This creates an instance of a push button on the stage, which is 85 px wide by 35 px tall, labeled with "music," and has a light blue face color.

Cross-Reference For more information on using the `MovieClip` object and `attachMovie()`, refer to Chapter 25, "Controlling Movie Clips."

Note If you try to add a second component with the same name, you will be prompted by an alert box to `Resolve Component Conflict`. You can choose to use the existing component (default), replace it with the new component (you cannot undo this action), or cancel.

Where to Find Components, Assets, and Parameters

There are many areas of the Flash interface in which you can find, control, and edit your components. Understanding each area where you can alter the content and functionality of your components will help you add custom features to your productions.

✦ **Component panel:** You can find this panel by going to Window ⇨ Components or by using the Ctrl+F7 or ⌘+F7 shortcut. This panel includes all of the components shipping with Flash MX. If you add components or component sets downloaded from somewhere, such as the Macromedia Exchange, you will be able to access the sets from this panel by clicking the drop-down menu.

This is the Component panel, including the drop-down menu where you can access additional component sets.

✦ **Component Definition dialog box:** You can open this dialog box by right-clicking (or Control+clicking on Mac) the component in the Library or using the Library's options menu. This dialog box allows you to add or remove parameters from pre-built or custom components. You are also able to customize or alter the functionality of the component. Other options in this dialog box include setting the Custom UI, Live Preview, and Description. This dialog box is generally intended for advanced component users or authors.

✦ **Component Parameters panel:** You can find this panel by going to Window ⇨ Component Parameters or by using the Alt+F7 or Option+F7 shortcut. Using this panel, you can set values for each parameter of a component instance. Usually, you can set the same values in the Property inspector. This panel can also be used to display custom user interface movies (SWF files) for components.

The Component Definition dialog box allows you to add and remove parameters and functions of components.

✦ **Property inspector:** The Property inspector includes two tabs when you have a component selected. The Parameters tab includes an area similar to the Component Parameters panel, where you can change the values of each parameter depending on how you need to use the component. The Properties tab allows you to add color effects, such as Brightness, Tint, Alpha, or a combination of these attributes. You can also swap the instance from this tab.

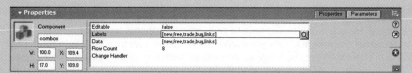

The Property inspector includes tabs where you can change the look of components as well as their parameter values.

✦ **Library:** After dragging components to the Stage, you will notice a new folder added to your Library. For the standard components that ship with Flash MX, this folder is named Flash UI Components. This folder contains components, their graphics, and the assets associated with their construction. Inside the main folder is an instance of each type of component, along with folders for their Skins and Core Assets. Some downloaded components may only add a component instance to the root level of your Library.

✦ **ActionScript:** Not only is there ActionScript in the component assets, but you can also write ActionScript to control components or modify their appearance. The built-in components that ship with Flash MX have several methods and properties that you can use to customize their functionality in frame, Button, or Movie Clip actions.

Modifying component color properties and parameters

There are several ways you can easily modify the appearance and functionality of your components. In pre-built components you found in Flash MX, you can customize the face color of each instance with little effort. Let's look at how this is accomplished.

First of all, open the Property inspector. As you have already seen, the Parameters and Properties tabs contain information on the attributes of your component. This is possibly the easiest and quickest way to change the appearance of your component. Simply by selecting the Properties tab and then the Color menu, you can alter the Brightness, Tint, Alpha, or a combination of these elements by choosing Advanced. You can see the changes made to the face of your component after publishing or previewing your movie.

The Parameters tab allows you to change the built-in component parameters to ones better matching your site or the usage of your component. For example, on a ScrollPane instance, you can change the horizontal and vertical scroll attributes (visibility) in this area by clicking the value area and selecting an option from the list. The Component Parameter panel and the Component Definition dialog box are other areas that allow you to modify or customize the functionality of your components. The Component Definition dialog box enables you to add or remove parameters from your component and assign values to them, thus controlling the actual functionality of the application.

Cross-Reference   For more information on changing the look of components please refer to the section later in this chapter called "Modifying Components."

Removing components from your movie

It is important to understand how to properly remove components from your movie. Removing items from the Library can be an arduous task if attempted manually, particularly if you are already using several components in your movie. Some components share assets, such as the scroll bar. Therefore, care must be taken when removing assets from the Library. It is recommended you have a solid understanding of component structure and asset usage if you attempt to manually remove items from the Flash UI Component folder in the Library.

Thankfully, there is a much easier way to remove components from your movie. The safest way to remove components from your movie is by using a feature built into Flash MX. First, remove all instances from the Stage as you would with any other symbol. Then, go to the Flash UI Component folder, open it, and find the instance of the particular component and delete it. At this point you will be prompted by a dialog box asking whether you want to delete symbol instances. You may wish to stop after completing this step. However, after you have finished all movie editing, you may wish to check for unused symbols by choosing Select Unused Items in the Library's options menu. Look at the unused items and decide if you want to keep or delete them. As always, proceed with caution.

Components in Flash MX

Flash MX includes several components, which provide interface elements and functionality frequently used by developers. You should be able to find a use for some or all of these components at one time or another. Let's take a look at what each of these components does and how to use them in your movies. After dragging any component instance to your Stage, open up the Property inspector and select the Parameters tab to view the parameters discussed in this section.

CheckBox component

The CheckBox component allows you to easily return a `true` or `false` value to your movie without having to write much ActionScript. If the box is checked, it returns a `true` value; if not, it returns a `false` value.

Parameters

CheckBox parameters can be changed to customize the default label text and its placement in relation to the check box graphic. You can also set the initial state and have the option of setting a function, executing as soon as the button state changes.

   ✦ **Label:** This is the name appearing next to the check box. The default value is set to "Check Box."

   ✦ **Initial Value:** Assigning a true value will check the box initially, although the default value for this is set to `false` (unchecked).

   ✦ **Label Placement:** This parameter sets the label to the left or right (default) of the check box.

   ✦ **Change Handler:** This parameter is assigned only if you want to immediately change something on the Stage when the value of the check box changes. Enter the name of the function controlling the change.

Note   When using the Change Handler setting in the Property inspector for all components, the function must be on the same Timeline as the component instance.

Cross-Reference   Refer to the exercise, later in this chapter, called "Using components in your movie" for an example of how to use a Change Handler function with a ComboBox.

How it works

The CheckBox component has a hit area that encompasses the check box itself, as well as the label next to it. The width of a CheckBox instance can be transformed to accommodate more text. Added functionality using ActionScript is possible by using the `FCheckBox` methods.

ComboBox component

The ComboBox component is similar to any standard HTML drop-down list and can be navigated by using the up-arrow, down-arrow, Page Up, Page Down, Home, and End keys. This component is very useful and essentially has two different functionalities. First of all, you can make it "editable," which allows your users to enter text into the top field, which will then cause the box to jump to that item automatically.

Parameters

ComboBox parameters can be changed to set labels and data for each item in the drop-down box, set the top of the pull-down to be a text input box, and customize how many items are viewable when the arrow is selected.

   ✦ **Editable:** This parameter is set to define whether the ComboBox instance can have text entered into the top of the list to search for list items. This value can be passed as data to the movie using the `getValue` method.

   ✦ **Labels:** This array of values composes the text seen by the user when viewing the drop-down box, which you enter in the Values panel.

✦ **Data:** This array is composed of associated values to the labels entered in the array in the Labels parameter.

✦ **Row Count:** The number entered here is how many labels are seen on the drop-down before a scroll bar appears. The default value is set to 8.

✦ **Change Handler:** This is a text string that specifies a function entered into the input field. The instance name of the ComboBox can be accepted. This optional handler will be activated when the user either selects an item in the drop-down or enters a string and hits the Enter key.

How it works

This time when clicking each value in the Property inspector, you will notice a magnifying glass icon next to the drop-down area (refer to the previous sidebar, "Where to Find Components, Assets, and Parameters"). This button brings up a Values panel where you can enter the array of values for the ComboBox Labels and Data parameters using the + or – buttons. A zero-based index system is used, which means the first item in your array is listed as [0]. Functionality can be added using ActionScript, and the FComboBox methods are used for this component.

Note   When you add a ComboBox component instance to a document, the ScrollBar component is automatically added to the Library as well — it is part of the ComboBox component.

ListBox component

The ListBox component also allows you to create lists, although in this case, the values are visible. This component allows selection of multiple listings at once or single selections if desired. As with the ComboBox component, keyboard navigation is allowed, and a zero-based index system is used.

Parameters

The ListBox component parameters include an additional option to select multiple values. Other settings in this tab are similar in function to components mentioned earlier.

✦ **Labels:** Values entered into this area will be the labels on each list button.

✦ **Data:** This parameter is an array of data associated with the labels set in the Labels parameter.

✦ **Select Multiple:** Set to either true or false. A true value allows end users to select multiple values at once when holding down the Ctrl or ⌘ key, and the default value of false allows only one selection at a time.

✦ **Change Handler:** This parameter is optional, and a function name is entered into this area if you want something to happen immediately upon selection.

How it works

This component's functionality is very similar to that of the ComboBox. The main difference in a ListBox component is the visibility of the labels and the ability to select multiple values. If you wish to add functionality using ActionScript, the FListBox functions are used for this component.

Note   When you add a ListBox component to the Stage, a ScrollBar component is automatically added to the Library, too.

PushButton component

This component is essentially a standard button with several different states. The PushButton component is very easy to use and can aid in quick development of mockups or modified to suit more aesthetically inclined productions.

Parameters

The PushButton parameters are perhaps some of the easiest to manage. As with earlier components, you can enter text for the button's label and set a function to execute when the button is pressed.

- ✦ **Label:** This is the text appearing on the button face.

- ✦ **Change Handler:** If you want an event to occur immediately upon pressing the button, enter a function name.

How it works

An instance of a PushButton can have regular, disabled, or active states, which can be customized graphically. It is a very quick way to add interactivity to your movie. For additional functionality of the button, you will need to write ActionScript using the `FPushButton` methods.

RadioButton component

The RadioButton component is similar to those found in HTML documents. It can be used to return `true` or `false` values or immediately change the movie.

Parameters

The RadioButton component has the unique attribute for setting a Group name, which will associate the instance with others on the Stage. Other parameters we have seen in earlier components.

- ✦ **Label:** This is the text you see alongside the RadioButton instance.

- ✦ **Initial State:** This parameter sets the initial state of the button to be `true` or `false` (default). A `false` selection is clear. All buttons having the same group name will allow only one radio button to be selected at one time. If you set more than one RadioButton instance in the same group to initially have a `true` value, the last instance will be selected when you publish your movie.

- ✦ **Group Name:** The value of this parameter specifies which group of RadioButton instances on the Stage the particular instance is associated with. Therefore, only one radio dot appears in this group at one time.

- ✦ **Data:** What value you enter here is associated with the label of the RadioButton instance.

- ✦ **Label Placement:** By default, the label placement is set to the right of the radio button. This is where you can change it to the left.

- ✦ **Change Handler:** This is the name of a function to be immediately executed by the movie.

How it works

The `groupName` parameter is important to understand. Groups of buttons can be added to your document, and in each group, only one button can be selected at one time. Only the width can be resized using the Free Transform tool. The hit area of the RadioButton instance surrounds both the button and the label area. Added functionality can be controlled using the `FRadioButton` methods in ActionScript.

Note   It is important to consider the interactive design of your movie when you add radio buttons or check boxes to your movies. Your decision should not be based on the "look" of a radio button versus a check box. Radio buttons should only be used when you need *one* selection to be made from several choices, and a radio button should never exist outside of a group (that is, you shouldn't have a single radio button appearing on its own). Check boxes should be used when you need to allow *one or more* selections to be made from several choices. You can also use a check box for a single option (for example, a form may have a check box asking if you want to receive promotional e-mails for a product). We recommend that you carefully consider how these elements are designed for use in applications, because this will enhance the usability of your production.

ScrollBar component

The ScrollBar component can be used with Input or Dynamic text fields, enabling the user to scroll through larger amounts of text. This can be very useful if you do not know how much text may need to be dynamically loaded into your movie or input by your users. You cannot use this component with Static text fields.

Cross-Reference   Refer to Chapter 20, "Making Your First Flash MX Project," for an example that uses the ScrollBar component.

Parameters

Consideration of both parameter settings is necessary when working with the ScrollBar component. The Target TextField setting is integral to connect your scroll bar to a Dynamic or Input text field.

✦ **Target TextField:** The instance name of your text field attached to the ScrollBar component is entered into this field.

✦ **Horizontal:** A value of `true` will set this component as a horizontal scroll bar, and a `false` value will set it as vertical.

How it works

When you have a Dynamic or Input text field on your Stage, simply drag the ScrollBar component from the Component panel or your Library onto the text field. It will snap to the side of your text field, which should then display a small black box graphic on the lower-right-hand corner. Once it has snapped to your text field, the instance name of the text field will be automatically entered into the component instance's Target TextField area in the Property inspector. These two items will *not* automatically be grouped together.

Tip   If you have problems snapping your ScrollBar component to the text field, try dragging it right across the selected field from left to right. It should snap much easier this way.

Make sure that correct matching instance and Target TextField names have been applied to your text field and ScrollBar instance, respectively. If you change the text field's instance name, remember to change the value of the Target TextField value of the ScrollBar instance. Or if you change the Target TextField value of the ScrollBar instance, change the instance name of the text field as well.

If you resize your text field, you will need to detach and rejoin the ScrollBar instance for it to resize. The FScrollBar methods in ActionScript provide additional functionality for this component.

ScrollPane component

The ScrollPane component is potentially a very powerful and diverse tool. It adds a window with vertical and horizontal scroll bars on either side and is used to display Movie Clips on the Stage. Because of the scroll bars, you are able to show a lot of content on the Stage without using much space.

Parameters

Parameters for the ScrollPane component will link it to a Movie Clip or image source and also control how your end user will be able to manipulate the ScrollPane content. You can also control scroll bar positioning and visibility with these parameters.

✦ **Scroll Content:** Enter a text string to set to the Linkage ID of the Movie Clip you want to appear in the ScrollPane instance.

✦ **Horizontal Scroll:** The default setting of auto means a horizontal scroll bar will only appear if necessary. A value of true will ensure it is always visible, and a false value turns it off.

✦ **Vertical Scroll:** This parameter functions the same way as the horizontal scroll bar.

✦ **Drag Content:** Setting this parameter to true will allow your users to drag the area within the instance window in order to view the content. A setting of false (default) will require scroll bars to be used instead.

How it works

The ScrollPane component only displays Movie Clips, so you will need to convert any JPEGs (or other bitmap images) to Movie Clips for the images to display. Linkage IDs must be set between the Movie Clip and the scroll content parameter. The Movie Clip simply has to be in the Library and have the Export for ActionScript setting checked in the Linkage properties. An exciting use of the ScrollPane component is using it to display JPEG images loaded from a server. For this to occur, specify the content by employing the FScrollPane. loadScrollContent() method.

Note   When you add a ScrollPane component to a document, the ScrollBar component (which is part of the ScrollPane component) is automatically added to your document's Library.

Using components in your movie

In the following exercise, we will use various components in a movie to activate and deactivate a series of elements. It will provide an example of how you may use components in your movie to create interactivity.

**On the
CD-ROM**

The source file for this exercise called **component_start.fla** is located in the ch29 folder on the *Flash MX Bible* CD-ROM. You will notice several components have been added to the Stage and have been given instance names.

1. Open the component_start.fla and locate the ScrollBar instance and Dynamic text field, which have been grouped on the Stage. Inside this group, the text field has been given an instance name of component_txt. We are dynamically loading a text file named component_txt.txt into the movie at runtime, which is plain text with component_txt= placed at the beginning of the file. Add this code to frame 1 of the Actions layer in this file:

```
loadtext = new LoadVars();
loadtext.onLoad = function(){
    component_txt.text = this.component_txt;
};
loadtext.load("component_txt.txt");
```

**Cross-
Reference**

For more information on the LoadVars object, refer to Chapter 30, "Sending Data In and Out of Flash."

2. Select the ScrollBar instance on the Stage. (You may need to double-click twice as it is grouped.) Open the Property inspector and select the Properties tab. Enter **component_txt** into the Target TextField value and then Publish your movie. Because the text file named component_txt.txt is in the same folder, it will load into our movie at this time. You will notice a scroll bar appears as well. If you encounter problems, make sure the text file is in the same folder as your Flash document (FLA file).

3. Now that our ScrollBar instances and Dynamic text elements are working together, we will group the two RadioButton instances on our Stage so they cannot be selected at the same time. Go back to the Main Timeline by clicking the Scene 1 tab in the Document window. Then select each instance of the RadioButton components and enter the same text string into the Group Name parameters on each button. Let's give the radio buttons a group name of **newsletter**, which best describes our form. This will place both buttons in the same group.

4. Give each instance a different value in the Data field in the Property inspector Parameter tab. This data will be what is returned to the movie indicating the selection. Give the first RadioButton a value of **digest** and the second a data value of **normal** in the Data field for each instance.

5. It is also a good practice to have one radio button already selected by default. In the parameter tab for our "Digest" radio button instance, set the Initial State to **true**. This will immediately update the Stage to show the radio button as selected.

6. Now we are ready to put it all together, and this is the code we enter on the PushButton instance below our form:

```
on (release) {
  if (_root.newsletter.getData() == "digest") {
    _root.gotoAndStop("digest");
  } else if (_root.newsletter.getData() == "normal"){
    _root.gotoAndStop("normal");
  }
}
```

With this code, we are controlling what happens when a user selects an option from your radio button list.

7. Let's activate the ComboBox so users who select an item from the list are automatically taken to a certain area of our movie. This is very similar to what we have accomplished with the RadioButton instances, although we will instead use a different method this time. The instance name of the ComboBox has already been set to `combox`. The values for the combo box's labels and data have already been entered for you into the Label and Data fields, respectively. We can activate the instance of the ComboBox in two different ways. Because our data and labels are the same names, we could simply create a PushButton instance and enter the following code onto the button:

```
on (release) {
  _root.gotoAndStop(_root.combox.getValue());
}
```

However, if you are not using the same data and frame label names, you will need to do something a bit more complex, which can easily be applied to many different components. To avoid putting a lot of code on a button, and to make our drop-down box automatically take our user to a new area, we will start by making a function in frame 1 of the Actions layer called `dropdown`. Add the following code into the Actions panel with frame 1 selected:

```
function dropdown() {
  switch (_root.combox.getValue()) {
    case "new" :
      _root.gotoAndStop("new");
      break;
    case "free" :
      _root.gotoAndStop("free");
      break;
    case "trade" :
      _root.gotoAndStop("trade");
      break;
    case "buy" :
      _root.gotoAndStop("buy");
      break;
    case "links" :
      _root.gotoAndStop("links");
      break;
    default :
      trace("no action matched");
  }
  return true;
}
```

The `switch()` action is much like using `if . . . else`, although is much cleaner. Either way will work to accomplish this. Select the ComboBox instance and enter the function name `dropdown` for the Click Handler, located in the Parameters tab of the Property inspector. Publish your movie, and your drop-down box will go to each area when a label is selected.

Cross-Reference

For more information on the `switch()` action, read Chapter 24, "Knowing the Nuts and Bolts of Code."

8. Now we will add a ScrollPane instance to our movie, which allows us to add Movie Clips to a scrollable window. Drag an instance of the ScrollPane component onto the Stage from the Library, which is located in the Flash UI Components folder. You may wish to move to another frame (such as frame 15) where there is less clutter on the Stage. Open the Library panel, select the file named bg.png, and drag it to the Stage. Convert it to a Movie Clip symbol by pressing the F8 key. You can now delete it from the Stage. Go to the Library panel, right-click (or Control+click on Mac) this new Movie Clip, and select Linkage in the contextual menu. Select the Export for ActionScript check box (which also selects the Export in first frame check box). Set the Linkage ID to **picture**.

9. Select the instance of the ScrollPane on your Stage. Open the Property inspector and select the Parameters tab. For the Scroll Content parameter, enter the string picture that you set as your Linkage ID. Now you can publish your movie, and you will see the image within the ScrollPane window. If you want to be able to drag the picture with the mouse, go back to the Parameters tab in the Property inspector and change Drag Content to **true**. At this point, your movie will appear similar to Figure 29-1.

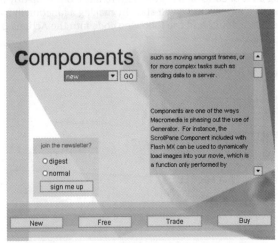

Figure 29-1: The finished movie has fully functional components, which pull data from an external text file and navigate the Timeline based on user input.

Modifying Components

We have already discussed how to alter the color, alpha, or brightness of your component, allowing you to match it to the content on your production. It is a little bit more complicated, but not difficult, to change the graphics. In this section, we will explore how to change the look of your components in several different ways.

Note   Your changes will not be visible in the authoring environment as they are built on the fly when you preview your movie. You will need to publish or preview your movie to see the changes or use a Live Preview.

Changing graphics and fonts

Changing the graphics and fonts of your component instances can vastly improve the overall look of your movie. We have already covered how to change the color properties of your components. Let's look at how we can change the actual graphics of your components.

Located in the Flash UI Components folder in your Library is another folder containing the component skins. Within this folder is another folder for Global Skins and then individual folders for each component type you have on your Stage. When you change the graphics in these folders, it is important to remember that some are shared with other component types. Any changes made to these particular Movie Clips (such as up- or down-arrow graphics) will be applied to all instances of the components you have on the Stage sharing these elements. For example, changing the down arrows will affect the ComboBox, ScrollBar, ScrollPane, and ListBox because they share the same assets.

Something to consider before you use this method is what effect you want to achieve. Changing the colors alone of instances within each Movie Clip in the skins folder can also be accomplished using ActionScript, which we will cover later in this chapter. Using code can be much easier than manually going through each instance to change colors, because remembering each color to maintain consistency can be confusing. If you are considering altering more than just colors, you will need to change instances manually. It is recommended you explore what ActionScript is able to do with style properties and possibly use a combination of the two.

Let's go ahead and change the arrows on several components in a Flash movie. In a later exercise, we will use ActionScript to change the colors. Open the **graphics_start.fla** document, located in the ch29 folder of the *Flash MX Bible* CD-ROM. In this movie, there are already several instances of ComboBox, ScrollBar, RadioButton, and PushButton components on the Stage. As you noticed in our earlier exercise, our components are not matched well to the rest of our interface, as shown earlier in Figure 29-1.

Let's start with modifications of the arrows. Open the Library panel and find the FScrollBar Skins folder. Inside this folder are several Movie Clips consisting of graphics for the various states of each arrow. In this exercise, we will change the shape of the arrow buttons, although any other instances can be customized. When working with the following Movie Clips, take care not to change any ActionScript applied to the buttons.

1. We will first change the regular and disabled states of the down arrows. Find the Movie Clip named fsb_downArrow and open it by double-clicking the Movie Clip icon. Zoom in as necessary. Freely change the shape and/or color of the arrow after double-clicking the instance a second time. (You can see all alterations in the graphics_finish.fla document on the CD-ROM.) When you are finished, check the X and Y coordinates of your arrow instance in each Movie Clip in the Property inspector. Copy the raster graphics from your arrow and paste them into the arrow instance of the fsb_downArrow_ disabled Movie Clip. This button state is used when a button is not active or clickable. Usually, these buttons appear to be faded out. You will want to make sure your X and Y coordinates of this instance are the same as the ones you had in the first Movie Clip. An easy way to do so is by using Edit ⇨ Paste in Place. You do not need to change the colors at this time; we will do this later using ActionScript.

Note

Do not try to copy and paste instances from one Movie Clip to another, because the instance names are copied, and this will cause both to change when you alter the graphics. Be sure to only copy and paste raster graphics into each instance.

2. Repeat this process for each of the arrow buttons, rotating your graphics for the up-arrow buttons. Use the Property inspector to ensure your arrow placements are correct. Also remember to offset the arrow in the _press states. The default settings add 0.5 to each coordinate, although, depending on your graphics, this may be too much. The press states are active when you click each button, and it slightly shifts to represent the button being depressed. You may also want to try changing the shape of some of the other instance graphics at this time.

3. Remember that you must publish your movie before you can see the changes you have made. You should notice at this time that several of components on the Stage now share the new graphics you have just created.

4. It is possible to change the font face of our movie with one line of ActionScript, which is covered in the "Changing button or label fonts" section. In the Expert Tutorial, Jen deHaan will discuss how to embed fonts and change the existing font faces of our components. Making either of these modifications will make a dramatic difference to the overall look of the movie.

Changing component size

If you are planning to change the size of your component to accommodate the size of a label, you should use the `setSize()` or the `setWidth()` methods or the Transform tool for each individual component instance. If you try to use the `_width` or `_height` properties, the layout remains the same, while the actual component is altered, which results in distortion on playback.

 Cross-Reference For more information on using these methods, please refer to the *Macromedia Flash MX ActionScript Bible* by Robert Reinhardt and Joey Lott (Wiley).

Style formats

As you have probably already noticed, you can use ActionScript to change the look of your components. Using ActionScript to change properties is often much easier than doing so manually or making your own graphics. If you completed the preceding task, you may have noticed how time-consuming it can be to go through each Movie Clip and change the colors of your buttons. Luckily, you can globally change attributes using ActionScript. Obviously, the changes you can make will be limited to colors, alignment, and text. If you want to use style formats on your components, you may need to refer to the *ActionScript Dictionary* for the property summaries of each element you wish to change.

To make a new style format, you need to use a constructor and `addListener()` to your style. To set properties of single instances, however, you can use the `setStyleProperty()` method without using an instance of the `FStyleMethod` object. You can also use this method to override style formats. Refer to the `FStyleMethod` property list explanations of the `setStyleProperty()` for each component in the *ActionScript Dictionary* or the *Macromedia Flash MX ActionScript Bible* for how to set each style.

An example of how you would use this to make the text on a PushButton and the label on a RadioButton bold is as follows, with `boldPush` and `boldRadio` instance names:

```
boldPush.setStyleProperty ("textBold", true);
boldRadio.setStyleProperty ("textBold", true);
```

The globalStyleFormat is an instance of the FStyleFormat object, defining the color properties and text of components. Setting a globalStyleFormat will change all instances across the movie. Let's reopen our graphics_start.fla document and change the colors of our components to match the rest of the movie. We will use the globalStyleFormat instance because we want *all* of our elements to be the same color across *all* components. We will enter the following code onto frame 1 of our Main Timeline, in the Actions layer.

On the CD-ROM

This ActionScript is in the finished version of the exercise, called **graphics_finish.fla** located in the ch29 folder on the *Flash MX Bible* CD-ROM.

Tip

You may want to first look at the default settings of the arrow buttons and what color schemes have been used to achieve the look of a button being pressed. Useful descriptions of each method have been provided in the new Flash MX Reference panel, summarizing which term applies to which graphic.

```
globalStyleFormat.arrow = 0xBF8080;
globalStyleFormat.backgroundDisabled = 0xE8D0D0;
globalStyleFormat.background = 0xE2C7C7;
globalStyleFormat.darkshadow = 0x7B3E3E;
globalStyleFormat.face = 0xEDDCDC;
globalStyleFormat.foregroundDisabled = 0xCA9595;
globalStyleFormat.highlight = 0x7B3E3E;
globalStyleFormat.highlight3D = 0xE8D0D0;
globalStyleFormat.radioDot = 0x743A3A;
globalStyleFormat.scrollTrack = 0xE8D0D0;
globalStyleFormat.selection = 0xBD7B7B;
globalStyleFormat.selectionDisabled = 0xD6ADAD;
globalStyleFormat.selectionUnfocused = 0xD6ADAD;
globalStyleFormat.shadow = 0xD6ADAD;
globalStyleFormat.textDisabled = 0xE7CDCD;
globalStyleFormat.textSize = 11;
// this line is required in order to apply the
// changes to our instances
globalStyleFormat.applyChanges();
```

This ActionScript sets various shades of red to each component element, creating a unified look across the movie. You will find it is much easier than manually changing the color of each component in the Library.

Changing button or label fonts

It is relatively easy to change the font color and face on your PushButton component instances (or any labels) now that you understand style formats. You can accomplish this task by using single lines of ActionScript. Because this code will use fonts in the system, it is important to remember that a default system font will be displayed if your end user does not have the particular font installed on his or her system.

Cross-Reference

Using custom font faces and embedded fonts with buttons is covered in the tutorial, "Using Embedded Fonts with Components," later in this section.

1. Open the graphics_start.fla file we used earlier in the chapter to change the graphics associated with several components.

2. To change the font face on the buttons in this file, select any instance of the PushButton. Make sure you have given it an instance name: In this case we are using an instance name of pButton.

3. Make a new **Actions** layer, and on frame 1, enter the following lines of code:

```
pButton.setStyleProperty ("textFont", "Arial Black");
pButton.setStyleProperty ("textColor", "0x333333");
```

This will set your button font face as Arial Black, and the second line of ActionScript makes it dark gray. Repeat this step for the other push buttons as well as the RadioButton labels if you want each one to have different fonts. Otherwise, you can delete the preceding code and set a global style property. If you want all text on all components to appear as Arial Narrow, enter the following lines of code onto frame 1 of the Actions layer. If you have already added the other globalStyleFormat instances in the above exercise, simply add the first line:

```
globalStyleFormat.text = "Arial Narrow";
globalStyleFormat.applyChanges();
```

It is important to remember all text (including ComboBox instances) will now use the Arial Narrow font to display text, as shown in Figure 29-2. More importantly, Arial Narrow will appear in the end user's movie only if this font is installed on his or her computer. Please refer to the Expert Tutorial later in this chapter to learn how to embed fonts to avoid this potential problem.

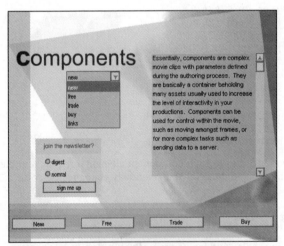

Figure 29-2: Making changes to the font face of our components makes a significant difference to the overall look of the movie. Compare the appearance of the new interface to our earlier interface in Figure 29-1.

On the
CD-ROM

In the ch29 folder of the *Flash MX Bible* CD-ROM, you can find the completed file, **graphics_finish.fla**.

Using Embedded Fonts with Components, *by Jen deHaan*

In this section, we will explore how to use custom fonts on your PushButton and ScrollPane components. There are two ways to accomplish this, and both involve some ActionScript. First of all, let's look at the easier of the two methods.

After adding a PushButton component, give it an instance name of **buttonOne** and a Label of **myButton.** Let's say we want to change the font of myButton to the Arial Narrow font. Simply create a new layer on the Main Timeline and enter the following ActionScript onto frame 1:

```
buttonOne.setStyleProperty ("textFont", "Arial Narrow");
```

Note It is recommended that all code-controlling components be entered on a layer separate from the layer containing the component instance(s).

Just as we can change the font, we can also change the color of the button text in the same way. To do this, add the following code after the ActionScript we wrote in the preceding step. Notice there is a 0x before your color code.

```
buttonOne.setStyleProperty ("textColor", "0x99ccff");
```

You can repeat this step for different elements of the button, as we saw in the earlier section, using the FStyleFormat object. The main problem with using this method for text is the font Arial Narrow will appear only if the end user has this particular font installed on his or her machine. In this case, a default font will be used for the button text. Luckily, there is a way to embed a font in our movie and link the button to this font to ensure a desired result. Let's look at this method now.

On the CD-ROM In the ch29/jen_dehaan folder on the *Flash MX Bible* CD-ROM, you will find files associated with this exercise. You may wish to use the **font_start.fla** document to walk through the next exercise.

To embed a font

First of all, you will need to have a Font symbol in your document, which the button will reference when published.

Cross-Reference Font usage and linking is also covered in Chapter 8, "Working with Text."

Open the font_start.fla from the CD-ROM, which will already have this step completed. You will need to know the Linkage identifier you have given your Font symbol and have selected the check boxes to export the font for ActionScript and in the first frame. The names you have provided are not important. In our file, the identifier and name are both arialN for our Font symbol containing the Arial Narrow font.

To make your font link to buttons

In our file, we have an instance of a PushButton on the Stage and then two more instances pulled from the Library. Our buttons have been given instance names of button1, button2, and button3. The first thing we want to try is changing the fonts of all the buttons on the Stage. On frame 1 of our Actions layer, we need to add the following code:

```
globalStyleFormat.embedFonts = true;
globalStyleFormat.textFont = "arialN";
globalStyleFormat.applyChanges();
```

Publish your movie after adding this ActionScript. Although not a drastic change, you should notice the font on all three of your buttons has changed from the standard font to your embedded font. If you add more components onto the Stage, they will all share this font. Of course, you may not want to have Arial Narrow on everything on the Stage. Let's change button2 and button3 to different fonts.

You will notice two more fonts in the library which have been given Linkage identifier names of gara and sym. Go to frame 1 on the Actions layer and delete or comment out the second line of ActionScript:

```
// globalStyleFormat.textFont = "arialN";
```

Now you will need to add the following lines of code. The first two should already be present from the previous step.

```
globalStyleFormat.embedFonts = true;
globalStyleFormat.applyChanges();
button1.setStyleProperty ("textFont", "arialN");
button2.setStyleProperty ("textFont", "gara");
button3.setStyleProperty ("textFont", "sym");
```

You will notice your three buttons have different fonts now.

Naturally, you can also add color formatting to these buttons within this same block of code. Simply add the code, like we saw earlier in this section

```
button1.setStyleProperty ("textColor", "0x99ccff");
```

anywhere in this list. This will make the Arial Narrow text on button1 a light blue color.

In the same tutorial folder for this chapter, you will find the completed file called **font_finish.fla**.

Custom Components

One of the most exciting aspects of components in Flash MX is being able to make your own creations for distribution or reuse. Custom components usually require a significant amount of ActionScript or at least a solid understanding of the language in order to modify an established component. If you learn how to make your own components to suit common requirements, you will inevitably save a lot of valuable development time. Components (and Smart Clips for that matter) were created to be easily reused amongst projects, and they also allow simple modifications without having to alter the ActionScript code in the component. Given the robust nature of components, you should be able to develop complex applications, detailed right down to custom icons for the library. You can even create your own component sets by dragging all your components into a single FLA file (which is what component sets are essentially saved as). While we will not go into detail on how to create custom components in this chapter due to their complexity, many resources are available to you for learning more about this subject, including the *Macromedia Flash MX ActionScript Bible*.

Live Preview

If you are creating custom components, a Live Preview can be extremely useful. This feature allows you to create an updated view of your component in the authoring environment, so you do not have to publish your movie to view the current state of your component. Creating a Live Preview requires a number of steps to set up your movie structure properly and also ActionScript to activate. It is definitely worth it if you are spending a lot of time creating your own components.

This feature is beyond the scope of this chapter. However, more information on creating a Live Preview can be found in the Support center at the Macromedia Web site: www.macromedia.com/support/flash/.

Exchanging and acquiring components

After you have made your own components, you may be interested in distributing them. Or you may also be looking for a place to find new pre-built elements for your Web site. Luckily, there are many extensive resources online where you can find components for download or for submission. A good place to start searching is at Macromedia:

www.macromedia.com/exchange/flash

To install components, you will need to download the free Extension Manager 1.4 (or higher), which is the first version to be compatible with Flash MX. There is also a specific method for making your components ready for exchange. You will need to package it into an MXI file, which will be readable by this Manager. The file will tell the Manager information regarding the file and the creator. Information about making your components ready for the Extension Manager is available from the same section of the Web site, which includes help and FAQ links.

Summary

✦ Components are a fast and easy way to add interactivity to a movie. They save time and increase usability through consistency, intuitiveness, and solid ActionScript. Components take over where Smart Clips left off, and they are much more powerful. They also assume some of the functionality that Generator provided developers.

✦ Understanding component architecture will help you add and remove them from your movie. After adding a component, further instances should be added from the Library. Remembering that some components share their assets with other components is important when deleting them from your movie.

✦ Some of the most useful elements are already built into Flash MX, including scroll bars, radio buttons, push buttons, drop-down boxes, and window panes. Using these will add user recognition, because they emulate features commonly used across the Internet and on many desktop applications.

✦ You can change the graphics of your components manually in the Library. You should consider your desired outcome, for it may be easier to use ActionScript to change the look of your components. You can change certain assets one by one or globally across your movie.

✦ If you are changing the fonts on your components, you will probably want to embed them to avoid problems if your end user does not have the font you are calling for.

✦ Advanced users of Flash may want to create their own custom components. Custom components can be reused from movie to movie, exchanged, or sold on the Internet. You can download additional components to add to your own movie from online resources, such as the Macromedia Exchange.

✦   ✦   ✦

Sending Data In and Out of Flash

✦ ✦ ✦ ✦

In This Chapter

Understanding TextField objects

Using data in text fields

Managing data acquisition in Flash movies

Loading XML data into Flash movies

Using XMLSocket to communicate with a server

✦ ✦ ✦ ✦

A powerful feature of ActionScript is the extraordinary control of data acquisition and management it provides within a Flash movie. You can load external text data into Flash movies, making it possible to include fresh dynamic content every time a Flash movie is viewed over the Web. In this chapter, you will learn how to access text data stored in a variety of formats that are separate from the actual Flash movie.

Using Text Fields to Store and Display Data

Before we can discuss sending and receiving data with Flash movies, you need to know the basic mechanisms of input and output. Most of the time, your data in Flash will be text based, which means that you will gather information from the user and display new and updated information with text. In ActionScript, Input text fields gather data from the user, while Dynamic text fields can be used to display live and updated text to the user.

Input text fields

Input text fields are created with the Text tool. In the Property inspector, the top-left drop-down menu must be set to Input text for the selected text field. In Flash MX, a text field can be an actual object with an instance name. However, an Input text field has a variable name (designated by Var in the Property inspector) to remain backward-compatible with Flash 5 or 4 movies. The text that is typed inside of an Input text field is the value of that variable (specified by the Var name), and it is the value of the `text` property of the text field's instance name. For example, if you create an Input text field and assign it the Var name `visitorInput`, anything that is typed into that text field during runtime will become the value of `visitorInput`. If you assigned an instance name of `visitor` to the text field, you would access the contents of the text field with the `text` property. To test this, let's create a simple Input text field.

Caution   If you are developing Flash MX movies (that is, Flash 6 is the version listed in the Flash tab of the Publish Settings), we strongly recommend that you use the instance name of the text field to access the contents of the field. Components that work with text fields, such as ScrollBar, do not work correctly if you use the Var name of a text field.

1. Using the Text tool, create a text field on the Main Timeline of a Flash document. Make the box long enough to hold 20 characters. You can type a temporary word or phrase into the text field, but delete these characters before proceeding to the next step.

2. In the Property inspector, select Input Text in the top-left menu. In the <Instance Name> field, type **visitor**. In the Var field, enter the text **visitorInput**. Click the Show Border option as well. Refer to Figure 30-1 for these settings.

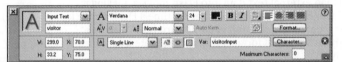

Figure 30-1: The Property inspector controls the settings for text fields.

3. Save your Flash document as **inputText.fla** and test the movie (Ctrl+Enter or ⌘+Return). In the Test Movie window, click the text field and type your first name into the field.

4. Choose Debug ➪ List Variables, and the `visitorInput` variable will display the value you typed in Step 3. In addition, you will see the visitor text field object display along with several properties of the `TextField` object. In our example, we entered the name **Charlie**. Therefore, the Output window displays (among other text):

```
Variable _level0.visitorInput = "Charlie"
Edit Text: Target="_level0.visitor"
    variable = "visitorInput",
    text = "Charlie",
```

Note   The List Variables command always shows the `$version` variable and value, indicating the Flash Player version currently playing the movie.

5. If you change the text in the `visitor` text field, the value will automatically update for the `visitor.text` value or the `visitorInput` variable. You need to choose List Variables from the Debug menu to see the updated value.

   Input text fields not only accept input from the user, but they can also be set to an initial value or updated with a new value with ActionScript code. You can test this with the preceding Flash movie example.

6. If you are viewing the inputText.swf from Step 5, close the Test Movie window to return to the Flash MX authoring environment. Create a new layer, and rename it **actions**. Select the first frame of the Actions layer and press the F9 key to open the Actions panel. In Expert mode, add the following code to the Script pane:

```
visitor.text = "enter your name here";
```

7. Save your Flash document and test it. You should see the text "enter your name here" in the `visitor` text field.

As you can see, Input text fields can accept text input from the user, just like an HTML form. Later in this chapter, we use Input text fields to create a fully functional Flash form that can send and receive information for a CGI (Common Gateway Interface) script.

While you should use the Var name attribute of text fields for Flash movies that require compatibility with Flash Player 5 or 4, we strongly recommend that you leave the Var name blank in the Property inspector for any Flash MX movies.

Dynamic text fields

If you want to display text information to people viewing Flash movies, you have two options: (a) create Static text blocks whose contents can not be updated with ActionScript or (b) create Dynamic text fields that can be filled with internal Flash data or external text data.

Caution Do not use Input or Dynamic text fields unless you need to accept or display live data to the user. Static text is perfectly fine for text used for graphical purposes, where the text does not need to be changed during the presentation.

Dynamic text fields are also objects with instance names, just as Input text fields. The only difference between Input and Dynamic text fields is that you can type into Input text fields. Dynamic text fields are most useful for display of text information that will be changed by the movie (via ActionScript), rather than the user. Using Dynamic text fields, you can display news articles that change on a daily (or hourly) basis, a player's score during a Flash game, and the system time and date, just to name a few.

Tip Both Input and Dynamic text fields use HTML text formatting tags to change the display of text. We discuss HTML use within text fields in Chapter 31, "Applying HTML and Text Field Formatting."

In the following steps, we create a Dynamic text field that is updated with an ActionScript variable action. You can also load external variables for use in Dynamic text fields, which we discuss in the next section. To insert text into a Dynamic text field:

1. Using the Text tool, create a text field on the Main Timeline of a Flash document. Make a field large enough to accommodate multiple lines of text, as shown in Figure 30-2. Choose a normal font size, such as 12.

2. In the Property inspector, select Dynamic Text in the top-left menu. Select Multiline from the Line type menu. In the <Instance Name> field, enter the text **output**. Click the Selectable and Show Border options. Refer to Figure 30-2 for these settings.

3. Add a new layer and name it **actions**. Select the first keyframe of the Actions layer and press the F9 key to open the Actions Panel. Enter the following code on one single line in the Script pane:

```
output.text = "WANTED: Flash Input & Output\r\rA start-up
   Dot com company is looking for a qualified Web
   technology that will present text input and output to
   Web visitors in a more compelling animated and visually
   stunning environment than that possible with HTML.
   Please call:\r\r1-800-555-CODE";
```

In this code, we specify string values (denoted with quotes) for the actual text we want to insert into the `output` Dynamic text field instance. To insert a carriage return in the text, the `\r` character entity is inserted between string values.

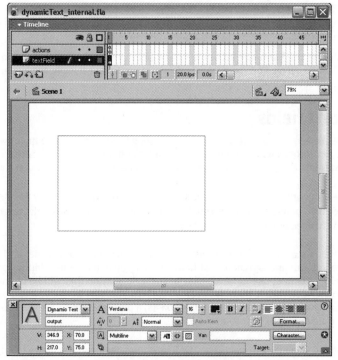

Figure 30-2: The Dynamic text field settings in the Property inspector

4. Save the Flash document as **dynamicText_internal.fla.**

5. Test the movie (Ctrl+Enter or ⌘+Return). The output Dynamic text field updates with the value assigned to the text property of the output instance in ActionScript.

You can also load text data into Input and Dynamic text fields. This data can be returned from a simple text file (TXT file) or from an application that resides on your Web server.

Defining a Data Process with States

When you manipulate text fields with internal ActionScript properties of the TextField object, the data for the text fields is available for use immediately. Meaning, if you declare a variable and a value for that variable, any text field can be given that value as well. When you want to load external data into a Flash movie, you need to create the appropriate steps, or *states,* in your movie to make sure that the data is available for use in the Flash movie. For example, suppose you want to retrieve a news article from a Web server, and the text for that article is contained within a variable named article_1. You can't use or assign the value of article_1 to any other Flash element *unless* the article has fully downloaded to the Flash movie.

So, how do you know when data is available in a Flash movie? Any Flash movie that relies on data exchange between the Flash movie and the Web server should contain four separate states:

✦ An *input* state to gather the information from the user or the movie

✦ A *send* state in which a Flash action sends the data out of the movie

✦ A *wait* state during which the data downloads to the movie

✦ The *output* state in which the data can be used by the Flash movie in text fields and other ActionScript code

Input state

The first step for data exchange requires that you have something to send out of the Flash movie. The input can be a Flash form into which a user types text. The data could be environment variables, such as the time of the day, or the Flash Player version. There could be various substeps in the input state, such as multiple forms or the completion of a quiz to calculate a test score that will be sent to the Web server.

Note   Not all data transactions require input. For example, if you need to retrieve the latest stock quotes or news article from a Web server application, you may simply need to send a request for that data without providing any additional information to the Web server application.

Send state

After the input data has been set or retrieved in the Flash movie, you're ready to send the data to another host, such as an application or script on your Web server. The following actions or object methods can be used to send data out of the Flash movie:

✦ `getURL()`

✦ `loadVariables()` or `MovieClip.loadVariables()`

✦ `loadMovie()` or `MovieClip.loadMovie()`

✦ `LoadVars.load()`

✦ `LoadVars.send()` or `LoadVars.sendAndLoad()`

✦ `XML.load()`

✦ `XML.send()` or `XML.sendAndLoad()`

✦ `XMLSocket.send()`

Of these actions, `getURL()`, `LoadVars.send()`, and `XML.send()` are restricted to a one-way data path; that is, you can only send data out with these actions — you cannot receive external data with them. `getURL()` must target the sought URL to the current browser (or frame) or a new browser window. In many situations, you may only need to send data out of the Flash movie without needing to receive any further data. To send information with the user's e-mail client, you can use a simple `mailto:` URL in a `getURL()` action on a Button instance. Note that the ⊃ character indicates a continuation of the same line of code:

```
on(release){
  email = "admin@server.com";
  subject = escape("Visitor Feedback");
  body = escape("Please let us know how you feel.");
  getURL("mailto:" + email + "?subject=" + subject + ⤴
    "&body=" + body);
}
```

In the preceding code block, the variables `email`, `subject`, and `body` are inserted into the `getURL()` action. Note that you can automatically set subject and body text for the e-mail message as well. To add specific variables to a URL string, you should use the `escape()` function in ActionScript, which converts illegal URL characters such as spaces and ? into URL form-encoded text (for example, a space is converted into %20).

Wait state

If you are sending data from the Flash movie with `loadVariables()`, `loadMovie()`, or any of the object `load()` or `sendAndLoad()` methods, you need to know when the requested data is received by the script or application running on your Web server. The most common way to detect the download state of data into the Flash movie is to use a terminal tag—a name/value pair in the downloaded data that indicates the end of the data string. For example, if the value of the `text` property for the `output` instance that you used in the last section was converted to a name/value pair in a TXT file (as URL form-encoded text), the value would appear as the following (URL-converted characters are shown in bold, and the terminal tag is underlined):

```
article=WANTED%3A%20Flash%20Input%20%26%20Output%0AA%20start%2Dup%20Dot
%20com%20company%20is%20looking%20for%20a%20qualified%20web%20technolog
y%20that%20will%20present%20text%20input%20and%20output%20to%20web%20vi
sitors%20in%20a%20more%20compelling%20animated%20and%20visually%20stunn
ing%20environment%20than%20that%20possible%20with%20HTML%2E%20Please%20
call%3A%0A%0A1%2D800%2D555%2DCODE&success=1
```

At the end of this line of text (or at the very end of a long line of variables), you have inserted a terminal tag `success=1`. With this variable in place, you can set up a frame loop within your Flash movie to detect the existence (loading) of the terminal tag variable. After the terminal tag is loaded, the Flash movie will be directed to the appropriate output state.

Note   You can use GET or POST to send Flash variables to the URL for the SWF file.

All wait states should have a timeout condition: If the data fails to load within a certain time frame, you will assume the Web server (or script) is not functioning correctly. If the timeout condition proves `true`, the Flash movie will go to the appropriate output state. We create a wait state for your Flash form in the next section.

New Feature   You can now avoid the use of terminal tags with the new `LoadVars` object in Flash MX ActionScript. You can also use the Movie Clip `data` event, which is specified with the `onClipEvent()` action. We present the `LoadVars` object in the "Creating a Flash Form" section in this chapter.

Output state

The final step in a data exchange is the actual display of any received data in the Flash movie. However, as indicated in the last state, there are two separate output states: a success display or an error display. If the data was properly received during the wait state, the Flash movie will display the success output state. If the server failed to return any data to the Flash movie, the movie will display an error output state, indicating that there was a problem with the server.

Creating a Flash Form

In this section, we create a Flash form that submits user-entered information to a server-side ASP script that e-mails the data to an e-mail address that we specify with a Flash variable. By accessing a remote ASP script, you make a Flash movie with five data exchange states: input, send, wait, output, and error. You learn how to submit name/value pairs from Flash to remote URLs and learn how to check the receipt of variables from the ASP script using the new LoadVars object. The LoadVars object detects the loading of the external variable data.

You can find the ASP script (**sendmail.asp**) and supporting Flash documents for this section in the ch30 folder of the *Flash MX Bible* CD-ROM. Note that you need an ASP-capable Web server, such as Microsoft IIS or Apache with Chilisoft ASP, to configure and use the **sendmail.asp** script. We have also included the **sendmail.cgi** script written in Perl 5 that was included with the *Flash 5 Bible* CD-ROM.

The ASP script requires the installation of the free w3 JMail Personal ASP component available at

http://tech.dimac.net/websites/dimac/website/products/w3JMail

Flash forms are user data entry forms (just like HTML forms) that are created in Flash MX using Input text fields. When a user types information in these text fields, the information is stored as a property of the text field instance (text). The values of these properties are assigned to variable names and are then sent to a specified Web server using standard GET or POST communication. These same variables are available to the Web server and can be processed there by a server-side program or script. Server-side programs can be written to e-mail this information, manipulate it, store it in a database, or perform many other applications. The same server-side script can also return values to the Flash movie—these can then be displayed or used by the originating Flash movie.

In this exercise, our Flash form solicits feedback from visitors, giving them an opportunity to submit comments, report bugs, or make suggestions for improvement. As each form is submitted, it's e-mailed directly to the e-mail address you specify in the Flash movie.

1. Open a new Flash document (Ctrl+N or ⌘+N).

2. Rename Layer 1 to **labels**. Create keyframes (F6) on frames 5, 15, 25, and 35. Give these keyframes the labels **input**, **wait**, **output**, and **error**, respectively. (Do not give frame 1 a label.) Select frame 45 and press the F5 key to insert more empty frames at the end of the layer.

3. Create a new layer and name it **actions**. On frame 5 of the Actions layer, insert a keyframe (F6) and select it. Open the Actions panel and add a **stop()**; action. In the Property inspector, add a comment of //**stop** in the <Frame Label> field.

4. Create a new layer, and name it **text fields**. Insert keyframes on frames 5, 15, 25, and 35.

5. On frame 5 of the Text fields layer, insert three separate Input text fields. From top to bottom, assign the following instance names to the Input text fields (in the Property inspector): fromName, fromEmail, and comments. The fromName and fromEmail text fields should accommodate one line of text, while the comment field should be set to Multiline in order to hold multiple lines of text. All of the Input text fields should have the Show Border option selected, unless you plan to create your own background graphics. Make each text field long enough to accommodate about 45 characters of text. The comments field should be able to show between five and ten lines of text. (See Figure 30-3.)

6. Create a new layer, and name it **static text**. Insert keyframes on frames 5, 15, 25, and 35. On frame 5, add Static text blocks to the left of the text fields, indicating the purpose of each field, as shown in Figure 30-3.

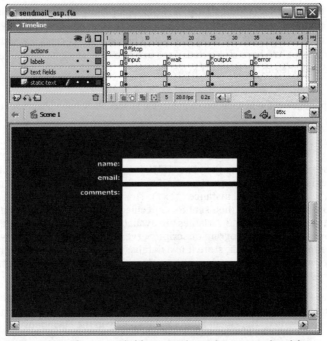

Figure 30-3: These text fields accept input from your site visitors.

7. On frame 15 of the Static text layer (underneath the wait label), insert a Static text block indicating that the information is being sent to the server and that we're waiting for confirmation. In our example, we used the text "Checking the server. . . ."

8. On frame 25 of the Static text layer (underneath the output label), insert a Static text block containing a successful receipt of the visitor's information. In our example, we used the text "Thank you. Your feedback was received at:."

9. You can see that we are setting up the output state to display the time that the server received the data (Figure 30-4). The ASP script returns the time and date of the receipt to the Flash movie Main Timeline. On frame 25 of the text fields layer, create a Dynamic text field with an instance name of **serverTime** and place it underneath the Static text you just made.

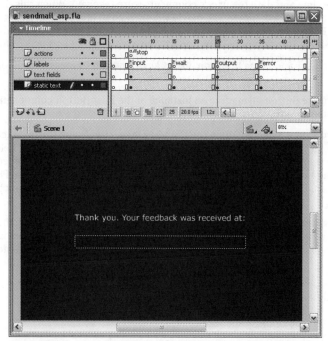

Figure 30-4: The serverTime field will display the time that the server received the Flash form data.

10. On frame 35 of the Static text layer (underneath the `error` label), insert Static text that indicates the data was not successfully received. In our example, we used the text "Sorry, the server is down."

11. Save your Flash document as **sendMail_asp.fla.**

Now, we have all our states defined with placeholder artwork. You can go back later and refine the text and graphics to suit your particular needs. Next, we need to add the interactive elements to the Flash movie:

- A `LoadVars` object to store the data typed in the text fields. This data will be sent off to the ASP script on the Web server.

- A function to transfer the data from the text fields to the `LoadVars` object and send the data to the Web server. This function will also define the e-mail address of the site administrator (or your own e-mail address). This e-mail address will receive the output from the Flash movie.

These actions need to put on the appropriate Flash event handlers. You start by defining a LoadVars object named userComments as well as an onLoad() handler for this LoadVars object. Then you will create a function named sendComments() that establishes the ASP script variables. These variables are then sent to the ASP script using the sendAndLoad() method of the LoadVars object. When the data is received by the ASP script, the Web server will return some confirmation data to the Flash movie, including the time and date the user's comments were received. When this data loads completely into the Flash movie, the movie will then go to and stop on the output frame label. Before we define these functions, though, let's add a PushButton component to the Stage. This component button will initiate the sendComments() function.

12. Create a new layer and name it **button**. Insert keyframes on frames 5 and 15 of this layer.

13. On frame 5 of the Button layer, drag an instance of the PushButton component from the Component panel to the document's Stage.

14. With the component selected, open the Property inspector. Name the instance sendButton. In the Label field, type **Send Comments**. In the Click Handler field, type sendComments. You may need to stretch the width of the PushButton instance to accommodate the Label text. When this component button is clicked in the Flash movie, the sendComments() function will be executed. You'll define this function in the next steps.

15. Create a new layer on the Main Timeline, and rename it to **functions**. Place this layer at the top of the layer stack. Select frame 1 of this layer, and open the Actions panel (F9). In the Script pane, define a LoadVars object named userComments with the following code:

```
1.   userComments = new LoadVars();
2.   userComments.onLoad = function(success){
3.     if (success) {
4.       _root.gotoAndStop("output");
5.     } else {
6.       _root.gotoAndStop("error");
7.     }
8.   };
```

This code creates a new LoadVars object named userComments (line 1). Line 2 defines an onLoad() handler for the new object. Here, a function will be executed when the userComments object receives any external data from the Web server script. In this example, if the data was successfully received (line 3), the Main Timeline (_root) will go to and stop on the output frame label (line 4). If the data was not received or there was an error in sending the data (line 5), the Main Timeline will go to and stop on the error frame label (line 6).

Now you will create the sendComments() function that will be executed when the user clicks the Send Comments button you created in Step 14.

16. After the last line of code in the Actions panel for frame 1 of the Actions layer, type the following code:

```
1.   function sendComments() {
2.     var scriptURL = "http://flaction.com/sendmail.asp";
3.     var obj = userComments;
4.     obj.fromEmail = fromEmail.text;
5.     obj.fromName = fromName.text;
```

```
6.     obj.toEmail = "you@yourdomain.com";
7.     obj.toName = "Your Name";
8.     obj.subject = "Flash Movie Feedback";
9.     obj.body = comments.text;
10.    obj.sendAndLoad(scriptURL, obj, "POST");
11.    _root.gotoAndStop("wait");
12. }
```

This function establishes all of the data that the sendmail.asp requires for successful operation. Line 1 declares the function and its name, `sendComments`.

Line 2 declares a local variable named `scriptURL` that stores the path to the ASP script. If you have installed the ASP script on your Web server, change the path of this variable to reflect the new location.

Line 3 creates a reference to the `userComments` object created in Step 15. This reference is named `obj`. Anywhere you see the term `obj` in subsequent code, know that it refers to the `userComments` object.

Lines 4–9 establish the variables that the ASP script expects to see in the data transmission: `fromEmail`, `fromName`, `toEmail`, `toName`, `subject` and `body`. Change the value of `obj.toEmail` to the recipient's e-mail address (your e-mail address) and the value of `obj.toName` to the recipient's name (your name). If you desire, change the subject of the email in the `obj.subject` declaration (line 8).

Line 10 executes the `sendAndLoad()` method of the `userComments` object (designated as `obj`) that sends the `fromEmail`, `fromName`, `toEmail`, `toName`, `subject` and `body` variables to the `sendmail.asp` script on our Web server. The second `obj` reference indicates that any output from the `sendmail.asp` script should be directed to the `userComments` object. Depending on the browsers of your target audience, you may want to use the GET method for `sendAndLoad()`, as Internet Explorer 4.5 (or earlier) on the Mac does not support the POST method from any browser plug-ins.

After the `sendAndLoad()` method is executed, the Main Timeline will jump to the `wait` frame label (line 11).

17. Finally, add a keyframe to frame 25 of the Actions layer. With this keyframe selected, open the Actions panel and add the following action:

```
serverTime.text = userComments.timeDate;
```

This action takes the server's returned variable, `timeDate`, and uses its value for the `text` property of the `serverTime` text field instance.

18. Save your Flash document again and test it (Ctrl+Enter or ⌘+Return). Type some information into the text fields and click the Send Comments button. If the server script is available, you should see the output state display the time/date receipt from the server.

The server script supports either GET or POST methods. Remember, every data exchange with a Flash movie should use input, wait, output, and error states.

On the CD-ROM

Use the sendmail.asp script on `flaction.com` only for development and/or testing purposes. Do not try to use the script for demanding, high-volume Web sites. The same ASP script is available on the *Flash MX Bible* CD-ROM, in the ch30 folder. You can find the completed version of the Flash document, **sendmail_asp.fla**, in the ch30 folder. We have modified this file to work with the sendmail.cgi Perl script from the *Flash 5 Bible* as well — the Flash document for that script is named **sendmail_perl.fla**.

Using XML Data in Flash Movies

Flash 5 or 6 movies can load (and send) external XML data. This is a very powerful feature, as XML has quickly become a standard data structure for e-commerce purposes and for news services, as well as for easier control over HTML formatting (and style sheets) in the Web browser. You can organize external data with simple XML formatting and use the XML data for text fields and ActionScript code in your Flash movies.

Note   It is beyond the scope of this book to give a thorough explanation of XML. We examine the basic structure of XML and show you how to use XML data in a Flash movie. We recommend that you read the *XML Bible* by Elliotte Rusty Harold for more information on XML. You can also find more detailed ActionScript coverage of XML objects in the *Macromedia Flash MX ActionScript Bible* by Robert Reinhardt and Joey Lott.

Understanding XML

XML is an acronym for eXtensible Markup Language. "Extensible," in this case, means that you can create your own markup tag names and attributes. While there are a few additional rules with XML, its structure very much resembles traditional HTML:

```
<tag name opener>Information here</tag name closer>
```

For basic XML-Flash usage, your XML document needs one "container" tag in which all other subordinate tags will be nested. Each opener and closer tag set is called a node. In the following XML example, the <section> tag is the primary container tag, and the <article> tags are nodes of the <section> tag:

```
<section>
    <article>First article node</article>
    <article>Second article node</article>
</section>
```

You can create as many *child* nodes as you need. In the preceding example, the <section> tag has two child nodes: the first occurrence of <article> . . . </article> and the second occurrence of <article> . . . </article>. In the following example, the first <article> node has two child nodes:

```
<section>
    <article>
        <title>WANTED: New Computer</title>
        <description>Insert description here
        </description>
    </article>
    <article>Second article node</article>
</section>
```

<title>...</title> is the first child node of the first <article>...</article> node. The value of <title> is also considered a child of <title>. In the previous example, "WANTED: New Computer" is the child of <title>.

Caution   Early releases of Flash Player 5 do not ignore white space in XML documents. For this reason, you should not format your XML documents with indented tags or carriage returns between tags. Otherwise, you will need to create an ActionScript routine that removes the white space.

Loading an XML document into a Flash movie

Once you have an XML document structured to use in a Flash movie, you can use the XML document tree in the Flash movie. When an XML document is loaded into a Flash movie, the structure and relationship of all nodes are retained within the Flash Player.

The XML object

Before you can load an XML document into Flash, you need to make an object that will hold the XML data. To do this, use the XML() constructor function, as in

```
myXML = new XML();
```

Just as we created new objects for the Color and Sound objects in ActionScript, you can create as many new instances of the XML object as you need for your movie. You can also use an XML object to store Flash-created XML structures and send them to a server for further processing.

The load method of the XML object

After you have established an object, like the myXML variable in the previous heading, you can invoke built-in methods of the XML object. The load method enables you to specify an external source (as a URL or filename) that holds the XML data. If you had an XML document called articles.xml in the same directory as your SWF file, you could load it by writing the following code:

```
myXML = new XML("articles.xml");
```

or

```
myXML = new XML();
myXML.load("articles.xml");
```

The onLoad() method of the XML object

After the document is loaded into the Flash movie, you can specify another function (or action) to occur, using the onLoad method of the XML object. The onLoad() method simply defines a function to be executed when the XML document is finished loading—it does not actually execute the function (or actions) when the onLoad() is first processed. In the following example, a function named loadArticles() is executed when the XML document, articles.xml, is finished loading:

```
myXML = new XML();
myXML.load("articles.xml");
myXML.onLoad = loadArticles;

function loadArticles(success){
    if(success){
        //perform more XML methods upon the XML data
    } else {
        // indicate that the XML document (or data)
      // did not load.
    }
}
```

In this code example, the loadArticles() function has one argument, success. The onLoad() method returns a Boolean value of true or false. Therefore, our function loadArticles() receives that value, too. If the previous load method successfully loaded the articles.xml document, the onLoad() method will be executed and will return a true value. This true value is passed to the loadArticles() function and inserted into the if condition. If success is equal to true, the nested if actions will be executed. Otherwise, the else actions will be executed.

Check out the XML document load examples on the *Flash MX Bible* CD-ROM in the ch30 folder. These examples demonstrate how XML node values can be manipulated with Flash arrays. You may want to review Chapter 26's coverage of the Array object before looking at these examples.

Introduction to XML and Flash, *by Chris Honselaar*

The source Flash document (FLA file) for Christian's tutorial, along with related assets, can be found in the **ch30/chris_honselaar** folder of the *Flash MX Bible* CD-ROM.

XML is rapidly being added to a wide range of development and client/server applications — and for good reasons. The ability to read and write any XML document in Flash means that you now have a robust and scalable way of exchanging data between Flash and the world.

The support for XML may be one of the best things that has happened since Flash 5. That's because this feature is more or less the missing link between Flash and the rest of the Internet. For those unfamiliar with XML, www.xml.com is a fine place to get started (and to stay up to date, for that matter).

Even if this is your first experience with XML, don't sweat it. This tutorial demonstrates the power of XML in a simple application. You learn how to use Flash to make a template for a little poem book that is linked to an XML file that fills in the actual details.

Starting with Flash MX, use the Text tool to create two text fields to hold the poem title and the poem itself. With the first text field selected, open the Property inspector for this first text field. From the Text type menu, select Dynamic Text. Then, in the <Instance Name> field, enter **title.** Do the same for the second text field, but in the <Instance Name> field, enter **poem.** Also, for the second text field, select Multiline from the Line type menu of the Property inspector.

For more information about working with text and text fields, refer to Chapter 8, "Working with Text," and Chapter 31, "Applying HTML and Text Field Formatting."

To keep things simple, we create an interface with one button that will skip to the next poem. For this example, I used the playback — play button located in the Playback folder of the Buttons Library, which is accessible from Window ➪ Common Libraries ➪ Buttons. Create a new layer in the Main Timeline, name it **Button,** and position your button anywhere that makes sense to you. Now, right-click (Control+click) the Button instance and select Actions from the pop-up menu. Enter the following code in the Actions panel:

```
on (release) {
  displayNextPoem();
}
```

Next, to spark your imagination about exotic ways to use XML, we'll add a Movie Clip that will play behind the poem, controlled by XML! To accomplish this, create another new layer, name it **Movie Clip,** and then, to ensure that the Movie Clips play below the text, move this Movie Clip layer to the bottom of the layer stack.

Now, to create an empty Movie Clip, choose Insert ➪ New Symbol from the main menu. In the Symbol Properties dialog box, choose the Movie Clip behavior and give the Movie Clip a meaningful name, such as **Background Placeholder,** and click OK. This procedure lands you in Edit Symbol mode, but because this is supposed to be an empty Movie Clip, simply exit Edit Symbol mode via Edit ➪ Edit Movie.

Next, create an instance of `Background Placeholder` in the top-left corner of the Stage by dragging this symbol from the library (Window ➪ Library). Use the Property inspector to name the instance `placeholder`.

Great! Our PUI (Poem User Interface) is complete. Now let's have a look at the XML document that drives the content to fill the text fields and placeholder. As noted previously, this XML document (poems.xml) and related assets (poemclip1.swf and poemclip2.swf) for this tutorial are located in the ch30/chris_honselaar folder of the CD-ROM. You can edit it with a plain text editor, such as Notepad (for Windows users), or any other text editor that saves to the TXT format. You may also choose to produce an entirely new XML document. But first, I explain the basic XML layout. Here's the text (the white space between tags was omitted because Flash handles white space in a nonstandard way):

```
<poems>
<poem title="Kahlil Gibran" clip="poemclip2.swf">
Work is love made visible.
And if you cannot work with love but only with distaste, it is better
that you should leave your work and sit at the gate of the temple and
take alms of those who work with joy.
</poem>
<poem title="unix haiku" clip="poemclip1.swf">
wind catches lily
scatt'ring petals to the wind
segmentation fault
</poem>
</poems>
```

Even if you've never used XML, the terms *tag* and *attribute* may be familiar from the HTML world, where they serve equivalent functions. There are two tags here: <poems> . . . </poems> is our root tag. Every XML document should have one pair of tags in which all other tags are nested. Contained within the root are the tags <poem> . . . </poem>, and you can have as many of these as you want. The <poem> tags are nodes within the greater root tags.

Cross-Reference   For more information on XML tag structures, refer to the XML coverage earlier in the chapter.

The <poem> tags have two attributes:

1. title="Kahlil Gibran" indicates that the first poem is called "Kahlil Gibran."

2. clip="poemclip2.swf" means that this poem should be displayed with the Movie Clip poemclip2.swf — thus, this Movie Clip appears in the empty Movie Clip, whose instance was named placeholder.

Note that the actual poem text is contained within the <poem> opening tag and </poem> closing tag.

Now this is how we instruct the Flash movie to load the title, poem text, and Movie Clip from each <poem> tag: Return to the movie, add another layer at the top of the layer stack, label it **actions,** and then double-click the first frame to bring up the Frame Actions Panel. Insert the following script in the right pane:

```
poems = new XML();
poems.onLoad = poemsLoaded;
poems.load("poems.xml");

function poemsLoaded () {
  currentPoem = poems.firstChild.firstChild;
}

function displayNextPoem () {
  title.text = currentPoem.attributes.title;
  placeholder.loadMovie (currentPoem.attributes.clip);
  poem.Text = currentPoem.firstChild.toString();
  currentPoem = currentPoem.nextSibling;
}
```

The first three lines of this script tell ActionScript to find, load, and parse the XML document. It also assigns it to the variable poems.

The next two lines tell Flash to call the function poemsLoaded. In turn, poemsLoaded initializes the variable currentPoem, which is a pointer to the part of the XML document currently showing.

The purpose of the next function, which begins with function displayNextPoem, is to extract the title, text, and associated clip of the current poem and to advance to the next poem.

Flash interprets this XML document by using a DOM, or Document Object Model. This means that the XML is represented as an object, with every tag a subobject, or child, which may also contain subobjects extending to any depth. Attributes are represented as properties of tag objects.

To cycle through all poems, the variable `currentPoem` is created. Initially, it points to the first child (the initial poem) of the first child (the poem's root) of the document. A simple logic of inheritance follows. Finally, `toString()` and `nextSibling` deliver the next object in a child list and all the XML text within that child, respectively. The script may be tiny, but it covers a lot of material.

To complete this tutorial, you need access to the SWF files to which the XML file refers. These files need to be located within the same folder as the Flash document (FLA) and the XMLs. Although you can produce your own, just be sure to give them the same names as those listed in the XML file or edit the file names in the XML code. For testing purposes, you can use the SWF files provided with the tutorial, located in the ch30/chris_honselaar folder of the *Flash MX Bible* CD-ROM.

Using XMLSockets with a Flash Movie, *by Shane Elliott*

In this tutorial, you learn to employ XMLSockets in a Flash movie. You will find all of the associated files on the *Flash MX Bible* CD-ROM. Be aware that this example utilizes a Java server, which requires the Java SDK in order to run and work with the Flash movie interactions.

You can find Shane's files in the ch30/shane_elliott folder of the *Flash MX Bible* CD-ROM.

ActionScript in Flash 5 introduced the capabilities of opening a socket that connects to a back-end database or server and keeping an open line of communication between the Flash movie and the server. Previously, if we wanted to send data back and forth between a server and Flash, we would use the `loadVariables()` action and connect to a back-end program, such as a Perl script, Java servlet, or some other middleware solution. With this older system, name/value pairs would be sent to and from the Flash movies to get a dynamic data flow, allowing data to be served on the fly. Feedback could be initiated by the user or by some system event (such as a timer or upon completion of a set of tasks). With XMLSockets in ActionScript, not only can we open a direct flow of data between our movie and the server, but we can receive the data as nicely formatted XML. This information structure is easier to handle and much more organized. Even though they're called XMLSockets in Flash, they don't require you to send your data as XML to the server, nor do you have to receive it as such. And although the `XMLSocket` object and methods are set up to handle XML elements, you have the option of sending String data as well, providing greater flexibility for database connectivity.

You might ask, "When do I need to use these sockets, and, more important, how do I use them?" Even though you can still use loadVariables() in ActionScript, you must make a request from within the Flash movie to be able to receive data from the server. With XMLSockets, you have a constant open connection. You can tell Flash to do a certain set of actions any time it detects data across this open socket. It's very useful for low-latency client-server applications, such as a chat room, where you want your messages to be sent immediately, or, in the case I describe next, for a Flash login movie. Now, instead of requiring a user to log in to my site or online resource using a standard form and CGI script, I can give the user a much better looking, and possibly more consistent, uninterrupted experience by allowing login through my Flash movie.

Before starting, you need certain graphic elements to be present on your Stage. I created a very simple login page that is focused completely on functionality — an aesthetically pleasing interface would follow this example in a real-world production environment. You need two Input text fields: one for the username and one for the password. Name these input fields **userid** and **password** in the <Instance Name> field of the Property inspector. Include some Static text to label these fields for the user. You also need a Dynamic text field instance named **fromServer** to display the server response. Again, add some Static text to identify the Dynamic text field on the Stage. Last, but not least, you need a login button. I just grabbed one out of the Common Libraries (Window ⇨ Common Libraries ⇨ Buttons), but you can create one of your own if you prefer. You can put all of these graphic elements on one layer, or separate the graphics across multiple layers. When you're finished adding the graphic elements to the Stage, create a new layer for your actions. In our example, the Actions layer is named **action script.**

At this point, there should be only one frame in the Main Timeline (for example, Scene 1). Now, go to the first frame of your Actions layer, select that frame, and open the Actions panel (Window ⇨ Actions). On this frame, we define our socket and tell Flash how to handle the events regarding it.

The following code goes in the Actions panel:

```
function myOnConnect(success) {
  if (success)
    fromServer.text += newline + "Connected...";
  else
    fromServer.text += newline + "Unable to Connect...";
}
function myOnXML(doc) {
  var e = doc.firstChild;
  if(e!=null && e.nodeName == "MESSAGE") {
    fromServer += newline + e.attributes.response;
    // Code here to take you into the protected area
  }
  else {
    fromServer += newline + e.attributes.response;
    // Code here to take you to an exit screen etc...
  }
}

myXML = new XML();
loginTag = myXML.createElement("login");
```

```
loginSocket = new XMLSocket();
loginSocket.onConnect = myOnConnect;
loginSocket.onXML = myOnXML;
loginSocket.connect("localhost",8080);
```

Now let's take a look at each line and go over what it's doing. Skip the function definitions for now and jump down to the following lines:

```
myXML = new XML();
loginTag = myXML.createElement("login");
```

The first line in the preceding code creates a new XML element on the Main Timeline. We will be sending the login information (username and password) in XML format to the Java server. The second line creates a new XML element named login, which is the equivalent to XML that looks like the following:

```
<login />
```

Now, we need to create a socket for communication with the server. That's where the following line of code comes in:

```
loginSocket = new XMLSocket();
```

When you create a new XMLSocket object, the constructor doesn't accept arguments. They're not needed at this point anyway. We don't define any of its options until we actually connect to the server. At this point, we have our XMLSocket object created, and we're ready to move on to the next step. We need to define some of the callback functions that are built into the Flash ActionScript language.

Flash ActionScript recognizes three event handler methods for the XMLSocket object. The Flash movie calls these functions at an internally known time or after a certain event whether you define them or not, but without indicating the event occurrence to you. If we don't define a set of actions to occur for these events, these functions don't do anything in our Flash movie. They're simply there so that you can define (and, in a sense, override) them. Table 30-1 describes the three methods.

Table 30-1: Common Methods of the XMLSocket Object

Method	Description
onConnect(success)	Executed when a connection request initiated through the XMLSocket.connect method either succeeds or fails. (The success variable indicates true or false to tell you whether the connection was a success or not.)
onXML(object)	Called when the specified XML object containing an XML document arrives over your XMLSocket connection. The object is an instance of the XML object containing the XML document received from the server.
onClose()	Initiated when an open connection is closed by the server.

Note Just as we use `on(release)` as an event handler for mouse events on Button instances, other objects have predefined event handlers and events. With data objects and methods, these events tend to occur when data is sent or received by the Flash movie.

The only two we use in this example are `onConnect` and `onXML`. Although Flash knows when to call these methods, there's nothing innately performed by them. Therefore, we must define our own methods to give them customized functionality.

```
loginSocket.onConnect = myOnConnect;
loginSocket.onXML = myOnXML;
```

These two lines simply assign these event handler methods to our customized versions of these methods. The `myOnConnect` and `myOnXML` functions tell our movie exactly what to do when a connection either succeeds or fails (`onConnect`), and what to do when data is received from the server through our socket (`onXML`), respectively.

Now let's go back to the two function definitions in the Flash movie. In frame 1 of the Main Timeline, we defined `myOnConnect` to execute some commands based on the status of the attempted connection. Flash sends the `myOnConnect` function a `success` argument, as a Boolean value (`true` or `false`), so that it knows whether a connection has been established. Then, we add an `if . . . else` statement to handle either case. The function sends a notification to the user by setting the `fromServer` variable (which we defined at the beginning of the movie) to give the user updates on the status of his/her login. You could add more lines of code here if you wanted to jump to another Movie Clip or perform some other action specifically designed for your application.

The `myOnXML` function is a bit more complex. This function is basically looking for data from the server in XML format, and when it detects that data (which has been sent to the Flash socket), it assigns it to `doc` or whatever argument you put into your custom version of `onXML`. In this example, I used `doc` for document. Whatever you choose, just know that it will be used as an `XML` object that's received from the server. Therefore, it must be treated as one throughout your function. You can convert it to a `String` object or parse it like I did in the `myOnXML` function. Once `e` is set to be the `doc.firstChild`, I can access that node's elements and name, as you learned when using XML objects earlier in this chapter.

It's important at this stage of your development that you know the formatting of the XML data the server application will be sending you. If you're not writing the server application yourself, make sure you stay in close contact with the XML developer.

The reason I know to look for the `nodeName` of `MESSAGE` is that I wrote my own Java server application to interact with my Flash movie. Again, I have an `if` statement that performs actions based on the server response. You could add more here as well.

Now, let's look at the last line of code, which is the most important line so far because it actually attempts to make the connection (open the socket) between our Flash movie and our server.

```
loginSocket.connect("localhost",8080);
```

To do that, I use the `connect(host, port)` method. The `connect` method takes two arguments: the `host` and the `port`. The `host` argument refers to one of the following:

✦ A fully qualified DNS name, such as `http://www.flashmxbible.com`

✦ An IP address, such as 205.94.288.213

✦ A computer's name on a LAN, such as Zeus or Atlas

✦ `null`, which means to connect to the host server on which the movie resides

I use `localhost` for the host argument because that (like `null`) also refers to the machine that my Flash movie is running on, which happens to also be where my Java server is residing. Whatever you choose here, just remember the `host` must be the location of the server with which you'll be communicating.

The next argument is the `port`, which refers to the TCP port number on the host used to establish the connection. For security reasons, this number cannot be below 1024. I chose 8080 because I know my computer isn't using that port for anything significant. Some examples of commonly used ports for TCP connections are:

FTP Transfers = 21

HTTP = 80

Telnet = 23

POP3 = 110

Whatever you choose, remember the previous rules and try to make sure nothing else on your computer is using that port number. Now, that last line of code automatically connects the Flash movie to my server when playback begins. Now that we have everything set up graphically and our code is ready to react to our socket events, we need to give some functionality to the login button so that our users can log in to the server. That code looks like this:

```
on (release, keyPress "<Enter>") {
  loginTag.attributes.username = userid.text;
  loginTag.attributes.password = password.text;
  myXML.appendChild(loginTag);
  loginSocket.send(myXML);
}
```

With the preceding code, we are detecting when the user clicks the button or presses the Enter key on the keyboard. When either event is detected, the username and password are sent to the server for verification. With those events detected, let's look at the nested code in the `on` handler.

Remember the `loginTag` XML element we made earlier? Here, we are giving that node some attributes and assigning those attributes to be the `userid` and `password` that the user has entered into our Input text fields. Then, `loginTag` is appended as a child to the `myXML` object. The entire XML object is sent through the `XMLSocket` object named `loginSocket`.

When we use the `send` method, we don't necessarily have to have an XML object as its argument. In this case, we do (`myXML`), but we could just as easily put a string value in its place. As long as the server knows what to expect, we can use any data type or structure. If it's looking for an XML-formatted string and we send it something similar to `"hello"`, the server might become confused. Either way, the `send` method is taking whatever it has as its argument, converting it to a string, and then sending it. So, suppose I, as a user, enter `shane` as my username and `flash` as my password and submit that information as my login. My server receives the following string value from the Flash movie:

```
<login password="flash" username="shane" />
```

I can choose to parse that string and compare the values in my server code, but now that it has left Flash, I'm no longer responsible for what happens to it until the server sends back a response. When the server does send back a response, we have our `myOnXML` function set up to handle it and tell our user whether he/she got in or not.

You can see the final FLA file of my Flash work on the *Flash MX Bible* CD-ROM, in a file called XML_SignIn.fla, located in the ch30/shane_elliott folder. To try the login example, you need to run the Java program name flashlogin.jar and then run the Flash movie that you created. There is also a text file named data.txt on the CD-ROM that contains the usernames and passwords that the server recognizes as valid. If you'd like to modify this file so that you can try your own login info, feel free to do so. Just remember to put a semi-colon at the end of every name/value pair.

Caution

When the XML `send` method is used, it sends a `u\0000` termination character at the end of its string value to let you know when the data is completely sent. You must send this character back to Flash to get the `onXML()` function to recognize that it has received data. Without this termination character, you'll find yourself facing a few problems!

Unifying the Web, *by Colin Moock*

In Flash 5, Macromedia added the XMLSocket class, which can be used to create multiplayer applications, such as games, chat, and shared whiteboards. Initially, few XMLSocket-based multiuser applications were developed for Flash due to both Flash Player 5's slow XML parsing and the need for custom server development. However, with the release of Flash Player 6, XML parsing speed has greatly improved, and over the past year, a good cross-section of multiuser servers have become available both commercially and for free. Creating multiuser applications for Flash has become plausible and approachable, even for less experienced developers.

The canonical example of a multiuser application is a chat room, where two or more users type text that is sent to each other. To create a chat room in Flash, you need some client-side code that creates the connection and sends and receives text. You also need a server-side application that receives and sends messages between the connected Flash clients.

At the skeletal level, the code for a Flash chat client looks something like this:

```
// Create the socket object.
mySocket = new XMLSocket();
// Assign callbacks to respond to connection events and incoming XML.
mySocket.onConnect = handleConnect;
mySocket.onClose = handleClose;
mySocket.onXML = handleIncoming;
```

```
// Connect to the socket server.
mySocket.connect("www.someserver.org", 2001);

// *** Event handler to respond to the completion of a connection attempt.
function handleConnect (succeeded) {
  // If handleConnect's succeeded argument is true, the connection has been
  established.
  if (succeeded) {
    incoming += "Connection established.\n";
  } else {
    incoming += "Connection failed.\n";
  }
}


// *** Event handler called when server kills the connection.
function handleClose () {
  // Tell the user that the connection was lost.
  incoming += ("The server has terminated the connection.\n");
}


// *** Event handler to receive and display incoming messages.
function handleIncoming (messageObj) {
    // Add the message to the chat window
    incoming += ("New message: " + messageObj.toString + "\n");
}


// *** Sends a new XML object to the server
function sendMessage() {
  // Create the message to send as an XML source fragment.
  var message = '<MESSAGE><USER> ' + userID + '</USER>'
                      + '<TEXT>' + outgoing + '</TEXT>'
                      + ' </MESSAGE>';
  mySocket.send(message);
}
```

Of course, as the chat room becomes more complex, the code expands. The most challenging aspect of developing a multiuser application is formulating and responding to custom XML messages. For example, even in a simple tick-tack-toe game, messages must be created to manage player moves, to tell each user when the game has started and ended, and to allow users to start and exit games. On both the server side and the Flash client, logic must be created to respond to these messages.

In my own multiuser application development, I quickly reached the point where I needed a generic codebase to use both on the server side and the Flash side. In March 2002, this generic codebase was launched as a commercial product called Unity. If you are embarking on a new XMLSocket application, I invite you to visit: www.moock.org/unity/. The Unity site includes a great deal of instructive material and sample code that is free for use even without the purchase of a server. In particular, see the Unity Push demo for a walkthrough of the XMLSocket application development process: www.moock.org/unity/clients/unityPush.html. Note that the Unity server itself is also free for academic, artistic, and noncommercial use, or for applications with fewer than 11 simultaneous users.

For further reading on multiuser application development in Flash, see Jon Williams's article, "The Tao of Pong," at

```
hotwired.lycos.com/webmonkey/multimedia/shockwave_flash/tutorials/
tutorial9.html
```

Other commercial and noncommercial socket servers are available at the following sites:

moock commServer, `www.moock.org/chat/moockComm.zip`

Branden Hall's AquaServer, `www.figleaf.com/development/flash5/` `aquaserver.zip`

Jon Williams's MultiServer, `www.shovemedia.com/multiserver/`

Xadra's Fortress, `www.xadra.com/products/main.html`

NowMedia's FlashNow, `www.nowcentral.com/`

On the CD-ROM

If you want to learn more about using Miva with Flash movies, check out Timothy Lo's tutorial, "Interfacing Miva with Flash Movies," in the **Bonus_Tutorials.pdf** file located in the Bonus_Tutorials folder of the *Flash MX Bible* CD-ROM. Miva is a scripting language that can integrate databases with your Web sites. It is XML-based and commonly used for e-commerce solutions.

Summary

✦ Input text fields can accept text data from anyone viewing the Flash movie (SWF file) with Flash Player 4, 5, or 6. Input text fields are treated as ActionScript variables if you access them via their Var name. If you use instance names with text fields, the Flash movie will work only in Flash Player 6.

✦ Dynamic text fields can display any string values retrieved with ActionScript in the Flash movie.

✦ Any data exchange between Flash and a remote application or server-side script should use four steps, or states: input, send, wait, and output.

✦ A Flash form can be used to gather feedback from your site's visitors. The form's data can be sent to a properly configured CGI script for further data processing, such as sending the data in an e-mail to the site administrator.

✦ The LoadVars object can send and load text data to a Web server script or application.

✦ XML data structures are quickly becoming an interbusiness standard for data exchange over the Web. Now Flash can use XML data structures to send and receive data from your Web server.

✦   ✦   ✦

Applying HTML and Text Field Formatting

◆ ◆ ◆ ◆

In This Chapter

Using HTML tags
in text fields

Creating URL links
within Flash text

Controlling text fields
with the TextFormat
object

Accessing functions
within HTML tags

Selecting text in text
fields with ActionScript

◆ ◆ ◆ ◆

This chapter shows you how to control text field formatting and focus using internal HTML tags and ActionScript. Flash MX has greatly enhanced the amount of control you have with text field formatting by using the new TextFormat object with TextField objects (that is, Input and Dynamic text fields). You will also learn how to highlight text within text fields by using the Selection object.

Exploring HTML Usage in Text Fields

As you have been using Flash MX, you may have noticed the HTML button in the Property inspector for text fields. Even though one of the primary advantages of using Flash movies is that you can avoid the fuss of HTML page layout, you can use HTML formatting tags within Input and Dynamic text fields. With Flash MX, you can use <FONT> tags to specify multiple typefaces, colors, styles, and sizes within one text field. You can also use <A HREF> tags to link to internal ActionScript functions or external URLs!

Note

In Flash 4 movies, you cannot specify more than one set of formatting specifications for any text field. For example, if you created a text field that used black-colored Verdana text at 18 points in faux bold, then you could not insert any other typeface, color, or size in that text field.

Supported HTML tags

You can use the following HTML tags to format your Flash text fields. You can insert these tags into ActionScript variable values, or you can apply them (without knowing or writing the syntax) using the Property inspector. As you already know, text fields in Flash MX ActionScript are now real objects with instance names. As such, you need to address specific properties of the TextField object to insert HTML text. In previous chapters, you've used the following syntax to assign text to a text field instance:

```
instanceName.text = "Enter your last name here";
```

You cannot assign HTML tags in the `text` property of a `TextField` object. You must use the `htmlText` property to assign HTML formatted text, such as:

```
instanceName.htmlText = "Enter your <b>last</b> name here.";
```

Here, the `<B>` tag is used to bold the text "last" in the text field instance. In a moment, you will create your own examples that use the `htmlText` property. Let's review the HTML tags that are available to use in ActionScript:

Font and paragraph styles

The basic `<FONT>` and physical "faux" styles for text (bold, italic, and underline) can be applied to Flash text.

✦ **`<B>`:** Placing `<B></B>` tags around Flash text in string values for text field variables applies **bold** formatting to the enclosed text.

✦ **`<I>`:** Placing `<I></I>` tags around Flash string values *italicizes* the enclosed text.

✦ **`<U>`:** The `<U></U>` tags <u>underline</u> the enclosed text.

✦ **`<P>`:** The `<P>` tag inserts a paragraph break between lines of text. You can use the `ALIGN` attribute to specify `LEFT`, `RIGHT`, `CENTER`, or `JUSTIFY`, to apply the respective justifications to the Flash text.

✦ **`<BR>`:** The `<BR>` tag inserts a carriage return at the point of insertion. This is equivalent to the `newline` operator in ActionScript.

✦ **`<FONT COLOR='#HEX CODE'>`:** The `<FONT>` tag with the `COLOR` attribute can change the color of your Flash text. This color is specified in hexadecimal values, just like regular HTML. For example, `"<FONT COLOR='#FF0000>This is red text.</FONT>"` uses full red for the text color.

✦ **`<FONT FACE>`:** The `<FONT>` tag with the `FACE` attribute enables you to specify a specific typeface to the enclosed text. You can specify Flash device fonts for the `FACE` value, such as `<FONT FACE='_sans'>` to use the Sans Serif device font.

✦ **`<FONT SIZE>`:** The `SIZE` attribute of the `<FONT>` tag enables you to specify the point size of Flash text. You can use absolute values (in pt sizes), such as `<FONT SIZE='18'>`, or relative values, such as `<FONT SIZE='+1'>`, to change the size of text.

✦ **`<TEXTFORMAT>`:** This tag is a Flash-specific formatting tag that you won't find in traditional HTML. `<TEXTFORMAT>` has four attributes: `INDENT`, `LEADING`, `LEFTMARGIN`, and `RIGHTMARGIN`, that control the margin and line spacing of text within the text field. Each of these attributes uses pixels as the unit of measurement. To get a feel for how these attributes work, create a Static text with a paragraph of text, click the Format button in the Property inspector for the selected text field, and change the settings in the Format Options dialog box.

New Feature

The `<TEXTFORMAT>` tag is new to Flash MX. You can only use this HTML tag within text fields for Flash MX movies. Make sure the Version menu in the Flash tab of the Publish Settings (File ➪ Publish Settings) is set to Flash 6.

URL and ActionScript linking

You can use the `<A>` tag with the `HREF` attribute to apply URL links within Flash text fields. For example, you can insert the following HTML into a string value for the `htmlText` property of a text field instance, to link the text [*the*MAKERS] Web site to the appropriate URL:

```
<A HREF='http://www.theMakers.com'>the Makers Web site</A>
```

You can also specify a `TARGET` attribute for the `<A>` tag. The `TARGET` attribute determines which browser window or frame will display the URL link in the `HREF` attribute. As with regular HTML, you can use the default `_top`, `_parent`, `_self`, or `_blank` values, as described for the `getURL()` action. Later in this section, we show you how you can also execute internal ActionScript functions from `<A HEF>` tags.

Caution You cannot type HTML tags directly into any text block or field—the actual tags will show up in the text field as the Flash movie runs in the Flash Player. The formatting tags are specified in ActionScript code or are "hidden" in Static text. (The Property inspector applies the formatting.)

Formatting text with the Property inspector

You don't necessarily need to write out HTML tags to apply them to your Flash text. You can use the Property inspector to assign HTML formatting to all Text types (that is, Static, Input, and Dynamic). For Input and Dynamic text fields, you will need to enable HTML formatting by pressing the Render text as HTML button in the Property inspector. In this section, we demonstrate the use of HTML formatting within Static and Dynamic text fields.

1. Open a new Flash document (Ctrl+N or ⌘+N). If the background color of your document is a nonwhite color, then set the background color to white in the Document Properties dialog box (Ctrl+J or ⌘+J). Save your Flash document as **htmlText.fla**.

2. Select the Text tool and open the Property inspector. Make sure the Text type menu (in the top-left corner of the inspector) is set to static text. Click once on the Stage and type the following text (with carriage returns) in the text block, using Verdana at 18 points:

```
Flash MX Bible
by Robert Reinhardt & Snow Dowd
```

3. With the text block still active, select the Flash MX Bible text and, in the Property inspector, change the point size to 24 and click the B (for bold) option, as shown in Figure 31-1. Enter the following URL in the URL field of the Property inspector and choose _blank in the Target menu.

```
http://www.amazon.com/exec/obidos/ASIN/0764536567
```

New Feature The Property inspector in Flash MX allows you to assign a target window for URL-linked text.

4. With the text block still active, select the Robert Reinhardt text and, in the Property inspector, enter the following text for the URL field:

```
mailto:robert@theMakers.com
```

Figure 31-1: You can selectively change text within one text block or field.

5. Now, select the Snow Dowd text and enter the following text in the URL field of the Property inspector:

```
mailto:snow@theMakers.com
```

See Figure 31-2 for an example of how the URL-linked text will appear.

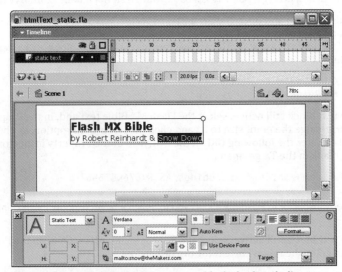

Figure 31-2: URL-linked text appears with dashed underlines. You will not see this dashed underline in the actual Flash movie (SWF file).

6. Save the Flash document, and test the Flash movie (SWF file) in your Web browser by choosing File ➪ Publish Preview ➪ HTML. When you click the Flash MX Bible text, the browser loads the Amazon.com page for the *Flash MX Bible* in a new window. When you click either author's name, your e-mail client opens a new message window.

On the CD-ROM

You will find the completed **htmlText_static.fla** document in the ch31 folder of the *Flash MX Bible* CD-ROM.

Try making another example with your own text and URL links. You can even add `javascript:` commands to URL links.

Cross-Reference

If you want to learn how to send an e-mail message from a Flash movie without relying on an e-mail client and the `mailto:` method, read Chapter 30, "Sending Data In and Out of Flash."

Inserting HTML tags into text fields with ActionScript

In this section, we continue with the previous example that you created in the last section. We convert the Static text block into a Dynamic text field and manipulate the formatting with ActionScript.

1. Resave your Flash document from the last section as **htmlText_dynamic.fla**. We will convert this Static text into a Dynamic text field, so you'll want to keep your original Static text example for future reference.

2. Select the text block and open the Property inspector. Change the text type to Dynamic text and make sure the HTML option is enabled. In the `<Instance Name>` field, type the name **book**. Now, this text field can be updated with ActionScript directed at the `book` instance. You can also disable the Show Border option if you don't want to see a bounding box around your text.

3. Save the Flash document and test it (Ctrl+Enter or ⌘+Return). While the Flash movie is playing in the Test Movie window, choose Debug ➪ List Variables. You should see the HTML formatting tags displayed in the Output window. The `book` object has several properties and values. The `htmlText` property reads as one continuous line displaying the following markup:

```
htmlText = "<TEXTFORMAT LEADING=\"2\"><P ALIGN=\"LEFT\"><FONT
FACE=\"verdana\" SIZE=\"24\" COLOR=\"#000000\"><A
HREF=\"http://www.amazon.com/exec/obidos/ASIN/0764536567\"
TARGET=\"\"><B>Flash MX
Bible</B></A></FONT></P></TEXTFORMAT><TEXTFORMAT LEADING=\"2\"><P
ALIGN=\"LEFT\"><FONT FACE=\"verdana\" SIZE=\"18\"
COLOR=\"#000000\">by <A HREF=\"mailto:robert@theMakers.com\"
TARGET=\"\">Robert Reinhardt</A> &amp; <A
HREF=\"mailto:snow@theMakers.com\" TARGET=\"\">Snow
Dowd</A></FONT></P></TEXTFORMAT>",
```

You can observe the proper ActionScript syntax for HTML formatting in the Output window. Note that any quotes around values of tag attributes are preceded by a back-slash, as in `<FONT FACE=\"verdana\">`. Because the value of `htmlText` is already a string data type surrounded by quotes, any internal quotes need to be declared with a backslash character.

4. Close the Test Movie window and go back to the Main Timeline of your Flash document. Create a new Dynamic text field, and in the Property inspector, enable the HTML option. Make sure the text field is set to Multiline. In the `<Instance Name>` field, type the name **book_2**. The text field should be somewhat wider than the previous text field.

5. Add a new layer, and name it **actions**. Select the first frame of the Actions layer and open the Actions panel (F9). Make sure the panel is in Expert mode by choosing this mode in the options menu. In the Script pane, specify an HTML-formatted string value for the `htmlText` property of the `book_2` instance, such as the following code:

```
book_2.htmlText = "<FONT FACE=\"Verdana\" SIZE=\"24\"
COLOR=\"#0000FF\"><B><A
HREF=\"http://www.amazon.com/exec/obidos/ASIN/0764536141\">Flash MX
ActionScript Bible</A></B></FONT><BR><FONT SIZE=\"18\"
COLOR=\"#000000\">by <A HREF=\"mailto:robert@theMakers.com\">Robert
Reinhardt</A> & <A HREF=\"mailto:joey@person13.com\">Joey Lott</A>";
```

Note This code should appear as one line of code in the Script pane of the Actions panel.

6. Save the Flash document and test it. The `book_2` text field will display the HTML-formatted value that you specified in the Actions layer.

You can also use variables in expressions for HTML-formatted text fields, such as the following (note that the `bookURL` variable and value should appear on one line of code):

```
bookURL = "http://www.amazon.com/exec/obidos/ASIN/0764536141";
bookName = "Flash MX ActionScript Bible";
book_2.htmlText = "<A HREF=\"" + bookURL + "\">" + bookName + "</A>";
```

By using other ActionScript variables and methods, you can apply specific text formatting to external data sources that have been loaded into the Flash movie, such as database records or lists. In the next section, you learn how to format text within text fields using the new `TextFormat` object in ActionScript.

On the CD-ROM You can find the completed **htmlText_dynamic.fla** document in the ch31 folder of the *Flash MX Bible* CD-ROM.

Formatting fields with the TextFormat object

Flash MX ActionScript has introduced a wide range of options for the `TextField` object. Many properties of the `MovieClip` object, such as `_x` and `_y`, can be controlled with `TextField` objects, too. One interesting method of the `TextField` object is the `setTextFormat()` method. This method allows you to control the formatting of text within a `TextField` object without relying on HTML tags. The `setTextFormat()` method works much like the `setTransform()` methods of the `Color` and `Sound` objects that we cover in Chapter 27, "Interacting with Movie Clips." Like `setTransform()`, `setTextFormat()` requires another object—a `TextFormat` object—that contains individual properties and values in order to adjust the targeted instance's text contents.

New Feature ActionScript in Flash MX can also create text fields on the fly using the `createTextField()` method of the `MovieClip` object.

In this section, you will create a Flash movie that makes a dynamic text field on the fly and applies formatting to the field with the `TextFormat` object. You will also use the `TextFormat` object to determine the dimensions of the `TextField` instance.

1. Create a new Flash document (Ctrl+N or ⌘+N).

2. Rename Layer 1 to **actions**. The entire contents of this movie will be created by ActionScript. You will not use any tools from the Toolbox to create the text.

3. Select frame 1 of the Actions layer and open the Actions panel. In Expert mode, type the following code into the Script pane:

```
titleStyle = new TextFormat();
titleStyle.font = "Verdana";
titleStyle.bold = true;
titleStyle.color = 0x0000FF;
titleStyle.url = "http://www.flashsupport.com/";
titleStyle.target = "_blank";
```

This code creates a new `TextFormat` object named `titleStyle` (line 1). This formatting will be used for site links displayed in the Flash movie. Within this object, properties of the site link text will be specified. Lines 2 through 6 assign the `font`, `bold`, `color`, `url` and `target` properties of the style. In later steps, we will apply this style to a `TextField` instance.

4. Within the same actions list shown in Step 3, add the following code:

```
site_1 = "Flash Support";
fieldSize = titleStyle.getTextExtent(site_1);
```

This code declares a `site_1` variable, which contains the text of the first site link the movie displays. `fieldSize` is an object created by the `getTextExtent()` method of the `TextFormat` object. This method allows you to determine the pixel dimensions of text with formatting applied to it before you actually create the `TextField` object displaying the text. `fieldSize` will have two properties: width and height. You will access these properties in the next step.

5. After the last line of code listed in Step 4, add the following code. Note the ⊃ character indicates a continuation of the same line of code:

```
_root.createTextField("siteList", 1, 10, 10, ⊃
  fieldSize.width, fieldSize.height);
siteList.html = true;
siteList.text = site_1;
siteList.setTextFormat(titleStyle);
```

The first line of code uses the `createTextField()` method of the `MovieClip` object to make a new Dynamic text field named `siteList` at a depth 1 on the Main Timeline (`_root`). The field is positioned at the X and Y coordinates of 10, 10, with a width and height specified by the `fieldSize` object created earlier.

The second line of code enables the `siteList` field to use HTML text.

The third line fills the text field with the value of the `site_1` variable, "Flash Support."

The fourth line applies the `titleStyle` `TextFormat` object to the entire contents of the `siteList` field.

6. Save the Flash document as **textFormat_100.fla** and test it (Ctrl+Enter or ⌘+Return). The `siteList` text field will appear in the top-left corner of the Stage. When you click the text, the default Web browser will open, displaying the URL for `flashsupport.com`.

You can find the completed **textFormat_100.fla** file in the ch31 folder of the *Flash MX Bible* CD-ROM.

You can continue to develop this Flash document, adding more sites to the `siteList` text field. You don't necessarily need to make more text fields — create more `site_` variables and add their expressions together as the contents of the `siteList` instance.

It is beyond the scope of this chapter to discuss all of the methods, properties, and event handlers for `TextField` and `TextFormat` objects. For more detailed information, read the *Macromedia Flash MX ActionScript Bible*.

Using asfunction in <A HREF> tags

Not only can you use HTML formatting in Flash text, but you can also execute Flash actions from your text fields using the <A> tag and a HREF attribute value of `asfunction:` `function,argument`. For example, if you wanted to link text to a function that loads a new Flash movie (SWF file) into a Movie Clip target, you can create a custom function that uses the `loadMovie()` action and reference that action from your <A HREF> tag for a text field. See the following code (note that the ⊃ indicates a continuation of the same line of code; do not insert this character into your actual code):

```
function myMovie(name){
   loadMovie(name, _root.mcHolder);
}
myText = "<A HREF=\"asfunction:myMovie,movie.swf\"> ⊃
   Click to load movie</A>";
```

In this code example, the text within the <A></A> tags will execute the `myMovie()` function, passing the string `movie.swf` as the `name` argument.

The `asfunction` can only pass one string value. You do not need to enclose the argument in quotes. If you need to pass another ActionScript variable for the value, then use the + operator to add it to the HTML text string.

If you need to pass more than one argument, then you will need to send all the values as one string separated by a comma (or preferred character). Then you would use the split method as follows (note that the ⊃ indicates a continuation of the same line of code; do not insert this character into your actual code):

```
function myMovie(name){
   var tempArgs = name.split(",");
   var mcTarget = tempArgs[0];
   var swfUrl = tempArgs[1];
   loadMovie(swfUrl, mcTarget);
}
myArgs = "_root.mcHolder,movie.swf";
myText = "<A HREF=\"asfunction:myMovie," + myArgs + "\"> ⊃
   Click to load movie</A>";
```

In this example, the myMovie() function takes the name argument and creates an array with the split method. This array's name is tempArgs. The elements of the tempArgs array are the two string values separated by a comma in the myArgs variable.

You can see examples of HTML-formatted Flash text and the asfunction in the ch30 folder of the *Flash MX Bible* CD-ROM.

Controlling Text Field Properties

Input and Dynamic text fields have several properties that are accessible with ActionScript. Two of these, scroll and maxscroll, control the viewable area of a text field that has more lines of text than the text field can show.

✦ scroll: This property can retrieve the current line number (from the top of the field), and it can also move to a new line number in a text field.

✦ maxscroll: This property returns the maximum value of the scroll property for a given text field. You can only retrieve this value — you cannot set it.

To understand how these properties work, you need to see how lines are enumerated in a text field. Suppose you had ten lines of text as a string value for a variable called myText. If you want to use this text in a Dynamic text field named article, which only has a viewable area of five lines, then the remaining five lines of the myText variable will not be seen in the text field. To make the text field "scroll" to the next line of text by showing lines 2 to 6 (instead of lines 1 to 5), you can create a Button instance, such as a down-arrow button, with ActionScript to advance the lines:

```
on(release){
   article.scroll = article.scroll + 1;
}
```

or

```
on(release){
   article.scroll += 1;
}
```

The maxscroll property will return the maximum value for the top line number in a text field. In our previous ten-line text value example, the maxscroll property would equal 6. If you had 20 lines of text in the article text field, then the .maxscroll property would return a value of 16.

Flash MX has a ScrollBar component that will automatically use the scroll and maxscroll properties to work with a TextField object. You can find more information on components in Chapter 29, "Using Components."

In the ch31 folder of the *Flash MX Bible* CD-ROM, you will find a Flash document named **scrollProp_simple.fla**. This movie demonstrates the use of the scroll property to view the entire Gettysburg Address within a text field. A more advanced scrolling mechanism can be found in the **scrollProp_advanced.fla**, which features a draggable scroll bar. We have also included a version of this document that uses the ScrollBar component, **scrollProp_component.fla**. Compare the file sizes of these Flash movies — the ScrollBar component, while incredibly handy and useful, takes up about 6K of file size alone within the Flash movie.

Manipulating Text with the Selection Object

The last text feature that we discuss in this chapter is the Selection object. The Selection object is similar to the Mouse object — you don't create instances of the Selection object as there can only be one active highlighted item at any given time.

Either Input or Dynamic text fields can use the Selection object. The Selection object uses a string reference to the text field's variable name to perform its methods. We discuss the methods of the Selection object in the following sections.

 Note   In Flash 4 movies, there is no way of checking which text field was active. You could turn off a focus rectangle for Flash 4 text fields and Button instances, but you can't control tab order or automatically set a text field active.

getBeginIndex()

This method detects and returns the starting position of a highlighted selection in a text field. The method returns –1 if there is no active text field and/or there is no selection inside the text field. As with the Array object, selection indexes start position values at 0. You do not need to specify a target path for this method — only one text field can have a selection at any given point. Therefore, as a variable startIndex, the getBeginIndex() method would look like:

```
_root.onMouseMove = function(){
startIndex = Selection.getBeginIndex();
trace("startIndex = " + startIndex);
};
```

In the Output window, the trace() action would reveal startIndex = -1 until you made a selection within a text field in the movie, as shown in Figure 31-3.

 On the CD-ROM   In the ch31/Selection_object folder of the *Flash MX Bible* CD-ROM, review the **getBeginIndex_trace.fla** to see how the getBeginIndex() method returns values for a text field. Each of the following sections also has a Flash document to demonstrate its respective method.

test **this** text field with a selection

Figure 31-3: A text field with a starting selection index of 3

getEndIndex()

Similar to the getBeginIndex() method, this method returns a number indicating the index position at the end of a highlighted selection in a text field, as shown in Figure 31-4. If there is no active selection, then a value of –1 will be returned.

test **this** text field with a selection

Figure 31-4: A text field with a starting selection index of 5 and an ending index of 9

getCaretIndex()

This method of the `Selection` object returns the current cursor position (as an index value) within an active text field, as shown in Figure 31-5. As with the two previous methods, if you use the `getCaretIndex()` method when there is no active cursor in a text field, it will return a –1.

test this text field with a selection

Figure 31-5: A text field with a caret index of 5

getFocus()

This method returns the current active text field's Var or instance name as an absolute path; that is, if you have selected or inserted the cursor position inside a text field instance named `myOutput` on the Main Timeline, then `Selection.getFocus()` returns `_level0.myOutput`. If there is no active text field, then this method returns `null`.

Note   If a text field does not have an instance name but does have a Var name, then the Var name and path will be returned. A text field's instance name, when available, will be returned by this method.

setFocus()

Perhaps the best enhancement to controlled text field activity is the `setFocus()` method. This method enables you to make a text field active automatically—the user doesn't need to click the mouse cursor inside the text field to start typing. To use this method, simply indicate the `setFocus()` method of the `Selection` object and the *absolute* path to the text field as its argument:

```
onClipEvent(load){
    Selection.setFocus("_root.testInput");
}
```

This code, when used on an empty Movie Clip instance, sets the current focus to the `testInput` text field. If any text exists in the text field, it will be highlighted as a selection. You can only use string data types as the `setFocus()` argument. If you try the following:

```
myTextField = _root.testInput;
Selection.setFocus(myTextField);
```

the `setFocus()` method will not work. Why? The first line of code sets `myTextField` equal to the *value* or the data type of `_root.testInput`, not to the text field's name itself. To remedy the situation, simply refer to the text field's name in quotes:

```
myTextField = "_root.testInput";
Selection.setFocus(myTextField);
```

Note   The same rule regarding Var and instance names for `getFocus()` applies for `setFocus()` as well.

setSelection()

Another method available for the `Selection` object is `setSelection()`. This method enables you make a specific selection within an active text field. The method takes two arguments: a start index and an end index. Using the same index numbering as `getBeginIndex()` and `getEndIndex()`. Note that this method will not work unless a text field is already active. The following code creates a selection span from index 5 to 9 of the `testInput` text field:

```
onClipEvent(load){
  Selection.setFocus("_root.testInput");
  Selection.setSelection(5,9);
}
```

On the CD-ROM   We have provided several examples of the `Selection` object methods. You can find these examples in the ch31/Selection_object folder of the *Flash MX Bible* CD-ROM.

Cross-Reference   Our coverage of the `Selection` object will get you on your way to selection and highlight control within your Flash movies. It is beyond the scope of this book to provide further explanations of `Selection` object methods and handlers. You can continue to read more about the Selection object in the *Macromedia Flash MX ActionScript Bible*. There, you will also find detailed information about the new `addListener()` and `removeListener()` methods of several ActionScript classes, including the `Selection` object.

Summary

✦ You can use HTML text formatting within Flash text fields. Only basic HTML text formatting is allowed.

✦ You can insert HTML tags into the values of ActionScript variables that refer to Input or Dynamic text fields. Any quotes used with HTML attributes should be preceded by a backward slash, \.

✦ The `TextFormat` object allows you to create object-based styles that can be applied to text within `TextField` objects.

✦ The `asfunction` parameter for the `HREF` attribute of the `<A>` tag enables you to execute ActionScript functions from text fields. You can pass one argument to the specified function.

✦ The `scroll` property of Input and Dynamic text fields enables you to control the portion of a text field value that is displayed within the text field. `maxscroll` returns the highest top line number for a given set of text in a text field.

✦ The new ScrollBar component removes the burden of creating your own custom scroll bars for text fields in Flash movies.

✦ The `Selection` object in Flash MX ActionScript enables you to control the focus and highlighted selection spans of text fields in a Flash movie.

✦   ✦   ✦

Creating a Portfolio Site in Flash MX

◆ ◆ ◆ ◆

In This Chapter

Evaluating and
organizing content

Creating an extensible
site structure

Establishing a
navigation system

Optimizing and
naming assets

Placing reusable
graphic elements

Loading content
with ActionScript

Using components
to add dynamic color
and scale effects

◆ ◆ ◆ ◆

There are probably as many different approaches to building a Flash project as there are designers, but getting insight into how other designers choose to work can help you to build your own best process. Whether you work independently or in larger teams, the fundamental pieces of a project that have to be put together will be similar.

This chapter will walk you through the production workflow that the authors used for building a sample portfolio site for artist/designer Daisy Reinhardt. The organizational principles and the basic structure of this project can be adapted to suit a variety of content. As a two-person core team with one more design-oriented partner and one more code-oriented partner, [the MAKERS] has addressed many of the issues that come up in any collaborative effort. Centralizing assets and approaching the site structure as a modular assembly of various individual files help to make the best use of both partners' skills while minimizing redundant effort.

The project development process described in this chapter will help you review and apply the Flash MX production techniques covered in earlier chapters of the book. The workflow progresses from the basic strategy of design to adding the ActionScript needed to load assets and control dynamic color and scale effects.

Each phase of the project will include a step-by-step workflow outline, but you should refer to the relevant chapters if you need a more detailed reminder of how to complete specific tasks.

Creating an Extensible Site Structure

Depending on the project, you may begin your planning by designing a structure and then sorting content to fit that structure; or more likely, you will first evaluate the content and then design a structure to accommodate it. For this portfolio project, we began with the basic premise of having a main page and some individual sections that would highlight different kinds of design work. Although the limited number of images that we are starting with could easily be accommodated in one page with an interface for navigating through the various items, we have decided to build a site that can accommodate more content in the future. As with most projects, it is helpful to look ahead and consider how new portfolio content will be integrated with the original site structure.

The goal is to create a site that will grow painlessly, without major overhaul of the navigation system or other core features. No matter what the content of your project might be, the features you should consider when designing an *extensible* site structure are similar:

✦ **Asset organization:** Create logical categories for content, even if you currently only have a limited number of assets.

✦ **Titles and graphic text:** Make site section titles and navigation text or icons descriptive, but keep them generic enough that they will not have to be changed as the site content is updated. For example, it would be better to have a site section titled "Company News" than to have a section titled "April Newsletter." In the portfolio site we are designing, we have titled a section simply "Costumes," rather than "Mermaid Costumes," because this will allow the designer to add other costumes in the future without having to modify the site structure.

✦ **Navigation:** Consider how your navigation interface will accommodate added content. It may be better to number assets and to create a generic Movie Clip that can load preview icons than to manually name assets and create thumbnails that will have to be modified whenever the content is updated. If you plan carefully, your interface will work equally well with 10 items or 100 items.

✦ **Consistency:** Although the site structure and layout should suit the content, it will make your life difficult if each asset has to be placed and aligned manually. Wherever possible, define a consistent area of the site for loaded assets and format the content to fit the site instead of changing the site to fit the content. Think of your site design as architecture rather than as window dressing. If you do your research and create a site that is appropriate for the content, than you shouldn't have to modify the site to accommodate additions or changes (at least on a regular basis). If you're planning an extensible site, create a layout and choose colors and fonts that will support a range of content rather than making a design that only "goes with" a very specific asset.

The files referred to in this chapter are in the ch32 folder of the *Flash MX Bible* CD-ROM. You will find the Flash MX project files as well as the various planning documents included for your reference.

Planning the basic site structure

It's not really surprising how many developers can't be bothered to make a formal plan before jumping in and putting valuable time into working out the visual aspects of a design—after all, that's the fun part, right? Unfortunately, this can easily put you in a situation where you waste initial enthusiasm, not to mention production time, working without perspective on how the whole project will come together. Doing a bit of groundwork before you start designing will empower you to focus your production efforts and help you to avoid the dreaded pitfalls of plan-as-you-go production: The animation you just spent three hours on doesn't fit into the site anywhere. The detailed menu graphics that you designed all have to be redone because it turns out the navigation has to be oriented vertically instead of horizontally, and the whole site has be finished by Monday and you're missing 15 photos and 3 product descriptions. Isn't this fun?

The two simple tools you can use to help you avoid haphazard and painful production scenarios are site flowcharts and the technical specification documents. You have probably seen examples of these at some point, but you may not have paid much attention or considered making them for yourself. Even if you aren't the most enthusiastic paper-pusher, you can probably find a way to make these tools work for you in some shape or form.

Cross-Reference There are many options for authoring your planning documents. You can make flowcharts and tables for technical specification documents in most basic text-editing programs or in your preferred graphics program (such as Illustrator or Fireworks). Some terrific specialized programs make the task of creating charts and tables much easier. The use of some of these programs is discussed in Chapter 3, "Planning Flash Projects."

Before getting too carried away with rough page layouts, it is helpful to establish the site "skeleton" or a flowchart of how the content will be organized. Flowcharts can range in complexity from thumbnail sketches on coffee-stained napkins to highly detailed and beautifully rendered presentation boards. Unless you're trying to sell a client on your designs, the beauty of your charts isn't as important as the basic logic that they represent.

The important thing to establish with a flowchart is how content will be accessed by visitors. Spending the time now to work out the hierarchy and navigation paths of the site will save a lot of confusion and potentially wasted effort down the road. This step is also important because it may be the first time that you can start to really see how the content can be broken down into balanced categories. Hopefully, you will also be able to identify missing elements or weaknesses in the plan early enough to make improvements without disrupting work that you've already completed.

The flowchart should, at the very least, identify basic site sections and navigation paths, but it can also be developed to a level of detail that describes all the individual elements on every page of the site. As shown in Figure 32-1, the flowchart we created for the portfolio site is a very simple "tree" that shows the navigation paths, the main category names, the background colors, and the numbering scheme for loaded images (SWF and JPEG files).

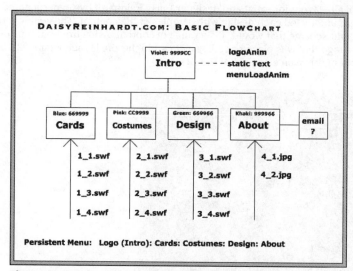

Figure 32-1: A basic flowchart is helpful for planning even small projects.

The next step in detailing the logic and structure of your site design is to begin compiling *functional specifications*. Like flowcharts, functional specs can be simple or highly detailed, but the main purpose is to itemize all the elements that will be put together to make your final site. The document should include the following information, regardless of how it is organized:

✦ A naming convention for assets and interface elements.

✦ A description of any special technique or content required to complete each element.

✦ An explanation of the purpose that each element serves in the site. (If you can't come up with a brief and compelling reason for including a particular element, than you may want to consider removing it from your design plan.)

If the term *functional specification* is too off-putting, you can think of this document in terms of a film script — name all the characters (who are they and why are they included?), explain the plot(what happens and in what order?), and list any special effects, locations, or props needed to complete the story (what skills and assets will be needed?).

On the CD-ROM   The functional specification document for the portfolio site described in this chapter is included in the ch32 folder of the *Flash MX Bible* CD-ROM in both Word and PDF format.

As work progresses on a project, both the flowchart and the functional specs will most likely need to be updated to reflect small changes or additions. These documents will only be as useful as you make them; if they are simply done as a convention and not tailored to your specific needs or kept up to date, then chances are these documents will simply get lost in the shuffle. If you make an ongoing effort to make these documents actually work for you and others on your team, it will make your production go more smoothly in almost every way. Honest!

Establishing key elements

To establish a visual site layout for artist and designer Daisy Reinhardt, we experimented with different designs and tested each design with samples of the content. The goal was to find a consistent layout scheme that would "fit" a range of content. Aside from bitmaps of her designs, Daisy had a logo that was placed as a key element in the site layout. Figure 32-2 shows a rough layout of the main elements of the site.

Figure 32-2: By roughly placing key elements and samples of the artwork, we can begin to establish a site layout.

If we were going to design this site with no consideration for extensibility, we would probably design each page of the site as a separate layout — perhaps even adding modifications to the layout to accommodate individual loaded assets. However, our goal with this project is to create a framework that will allow the loaded assets to change without having to modify any key elements. The first step toward establishing a framework is to convert the information we have gained from the rough layouts (shown in Figure 32-2) into a more simplified sketch that maps out the space in our page design. As shown in Figure 32-3, this "map" should indicate the approximate size and placement of key elements.

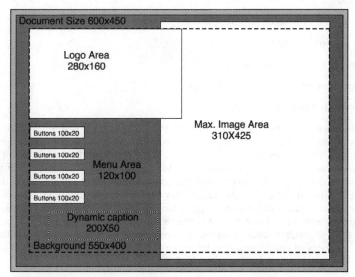

Figure 32-3: To create an extensible structure that will accommodate various loaded assets, it is important to define a consistent image area and to position navigation elements.

The most important thing to establish is the maximum size and the boundaries for loaded content — the layout should work visually when loaded assets of various sizes are aligned consistently. In our map, the loaded images will be aligned with ActionScript within the border of the image area as they are loaded. This will keep the layout balanced while accommodating smaller square images of cards and larger vertical images of costume designs.

To make it easy to update the content of the site without having to re-author the main Flash document, we're going to use loaded text for the image captions.

On the CD-ROM   The custom *description* component that Robert created to facilitate loading the caption text is included on the CD-ROM. You can reuse this component for any site structure that requires loaded text to be associated with specific assets.

Organizing the document

When you have a general map of the content and the layout, you can begin to organize and label your main Flash document. For this portfolio site, we have decided to use a document size of 600×450, with a medium-gray background color.

With all Flash projects, we always start with a basic layer structure that will make it easy to identify and edit content in the future. The layers in the document for the portfolio site are as follows:

✦ Layer 1: actions

✦ Layer 2: labels

✦ Layer 3: logo

✦ Layer 4: mainMenu

✦ Layer 5: secondMenu (forward and back arrows)

✦ Layer 6: caption (for loaded and static text)

✦ Layer 7: imageMC (for loaded images)

✦ Layer 8: bgTexture (for background patterns)

✦ Layer 9: bgColor (for background color tile)

Now that you have a layer structure, the next step is to start building a timeline structure. In the *Labels* layer, insert evenly spaced keyframes and use the frame label field in the Property inspector to add names for each section of your project. The spacing of the frames is not critical at this point, because we are using Movie Clips for animated elements and loading images dynamically. We don't need to worry about making space for a lot of content on the Main Timeline (just be sure to leave enough frames after each keyframe to keep the label names visible). The frame labels will be used to guide the navigation ActionScript, so it is helpful to use consistent and logical naming conventions for the labels. Otherwise, you will have to keep reminding yourself of what crazy label names you used while you are creating the scripts for various parts of your navigation interface. For this site, we made six labeled keyframe sections, about ten frames apart, on the Main Timeline:

✦ Label 1: preload

✦ Label 2: intro

✦ Label 3: cards

✦ Label 4: costumes

✦ Label 5: design

✦ Label 6: about

The last four sections are obvious, but the first two sections merit some explanation. (They are described in detail later in this chapter.) The *preload* keyframe will be used to hold a looping animation that plays while the interface loads. And what about *intro?* Don't we want to skip intro as a general rule? Although we don't condone forcing users to watch long animated sequences before they can make any other choices, they do have to start from somewhere; and obviously if they are dumped straight into one of the specific categories, it may be confusing. The intro section could also be considered the Home page or the Welcome page; it introduces visitors to the site and lets them decide what section they want to look at first. You will notice in our flowchart of the site that the mainMenu is persistent—visitors can move between sections without having to return to the intro page. In fact, we have "hidden" the link back to the intro page in the logo graphic because visitors are not likely to need to get back to the intro. The link just gives the logo a secondary purpose and rewards the user for exploring.

Preparing Graphics

We have now established the placement and approximate size of core elements, and we can move on to adding visual flair. The same principles of consistency and modular production should be kept in mind while creating visual elements. Wherever possible, we've reused symbols and kept the scale, color, and style of the graphics consistent from section to section.

For this project, we had multiple sources for the graphics, and the challenge was to try to unify the look of the images and then to optimize everything for use in Flash.

Acquiring original portfolio images

Daisy had high-quality photographs of some of her designs, but only snapshots (or even laser-printed *copies*) of snapshots for others. She also sent us actual samples of her card designs to include on the site. The challenge was to find the best way of getting all the images edited so that they would be as clean and consistent as possible.

Capturing images

The first step was to get all the assets digitized and saved as high-resolution source files. We used different methods for the various image sources:

✦ **High-quality photo prints:** 4-x-6-inch images scanned at actual size, millions of colors, and 100 dpi resolution. The scanned images were brought into Photoshop for cropping and saved in TIFF format with descriptive names.

Because the photo prints were already larger than we needed the final images to be — and for this project, we wanted to keep our resources streamlined for Web use only — we chose to scan at 100 dpi. If you are working with smaller originals or you plan to use details of the final images, than it is important to scan at a higher resolution setting. The final image scaled to the largest size you need it should be no less than 100 dpi resolution. If there is some chance that you will be using the images in printed graphics, then it is also important to have high-resolution source files (minimum 300 dpi at final size).

✦ **Rough copies of photos:** Some of the images were provided as low-resolution ink-jet prints. Instead of trying to smooth the pixel pattern that would have been exaggerated by scanning these images, we decided to "copy" them by shooting a digital still of the printed pages. The result was a digital image that had a less noticeable ink pattern and enough resolution for retouching and scaling to the final size.

✦ **Physical card samples:** We considered scanning the cards but decided that they would have more depth if we photographed them instead. We used a white background and even lighting to get consistent color. It was also important to get good separation between the colorful cards and the clean, monochrome background to make clipping paths easier to make later on. To keep the size and framing of each shot consistent, we used a "locked" tripod setup for the digital camera and were as precise as possible with positioning the cards in the same place for each shot. The captured images were saved on a Sony memory stick, so we were able to upload them directly to our server. These images were also brought into Photoshop for cropping and down-sampled from the original capture resolution to about 500×500 pixels.

Retouching images

In an ideal production environment, all the images for a given project would be delivered on Photo CD from the same source, with consistent lighting, resolution, and formatting. In reality, we're usually dealing with a motley collection of images gathered from various sources. The trick, especially when handling images that may not be as high quality as you would like, is to find a way of editing the images so that they're more consistent. If you're lucky, you'll be able to take a little bit of artistic license with the images to create whatever hybrid photo illustration looks best.

The card photos that we created in a controlled studio environment didn't require a lot of work to get them Web-ready. We used Photoshop 7 to clean up the images, size them, and add an alpha channel. Using the fixed-ratio option for the Photoshop Cropping tool made it easy to crop the images consistently to the same size and position within the frame (see Figure 32-4).

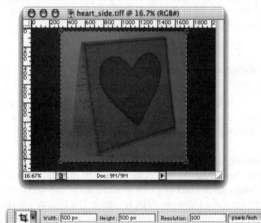

Figure 32-4: The constrained cropping feature in Photoshop ensures that the framing and resolution for each image in the series will be consistent.

The next step was to add a Levels layer to improve the contrast of the image, which was a little too dark originally. Finally, the Magnetic Lasso tool made it quick to create an accurate selection around the edges of the card. This selection was used to define a Mask for the card image, eliminating the background cleanly (see Figure 32-5).

 A step-by-step explanation of the process for creating mask layers in Adobe Photoshop is included in Chapter 37, "Working with Raster Graphics."

After saving the layered Photoshop file in PSD format (in case we need to make any changes later), the final step was to use the Save for Web command to choose the format and size of our final image (see Figure 32-6). We saved the images in PNG-24 format to preserve the alpha channel so that the mask we added would transport to Flash.

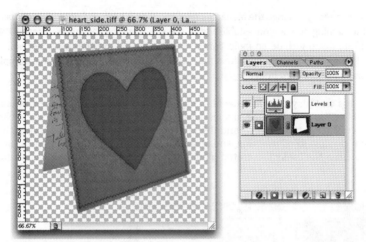

Figure 32-5: Using layers for levels adjustment and a mask to crop out the background allows *non-destructive* edits. (The original image is kept intact in its own layer.)

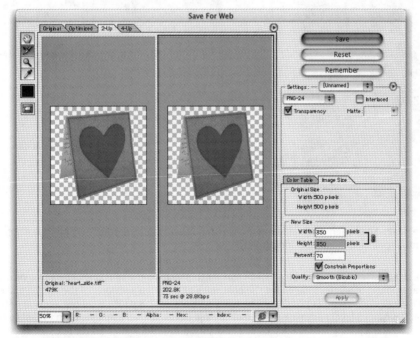

Figure 32-6: The Save for Web window in Adobe Photoshop provides a preview of the final image with the selected export settings

Tip   Although you can always change the filenames later, it will save time and potential confusion if you use the naming convention established in the site planning for the Web-ready PNG files. It is helpful if you include an indication of what section of the site these files will be used for and a number that relates to how they will be organized on the site (for example, you might name the first card image *1_1_card.png*).

For the design photos on Daisy's site, we decided that the focus should be on the clothes, not on the backgrounds or the people in the images. Using Photoshop, we made the same basic adjustments that were made to the cards and then did some additional work to stylize the images. After some cloning, filled masking, and selective application of the Watercolor art filter, the final image has the funky illustrated quality that suits the style of Daisy's designs (see Figure 32-7).

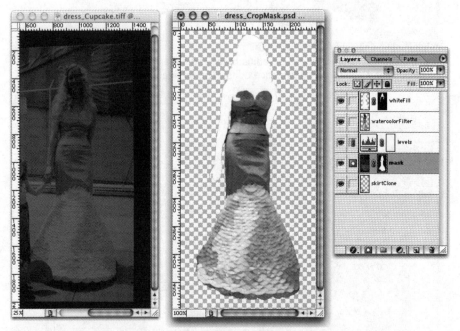

Figure 32-7: The rough original image (left) is modified with layered effects in Photoshop for a more polished illustrated look (right).

These images were also saved in PNG-24 format to preserve the masking. The same retouching was applied to all the images for the costumes and design sections of the site to make them look as consistent as possible. The two portraits of Daisy for the about section of the site only required levels adjustment and cropping. Because these images didn't need to have any transparency, they were saved out of Photoshop in JPEG format to reduce the file sizes.

Caution   When exporting JPEGs for use in Flash, *do not* use the Progressive option. The JPEG compression on files saved with progressive loading is not recognized by Flash, so you won't be able to use imported JPEG data, and the images will be double JPEG-ed when you export the final Flash movie (SWF).

Preparing image assets for loading

Placing all the PNG files directly into our final project file (FLA) would bloat the file size, making it a long and painful download even for users with fast Internet connections. The solution to this aspect of developing image-heavy sites is to structure the site so that images load individually when the visitor wants to view them. This way, the download doesn't have to happen all at once, and the user won't be forced to wait for images they may not even look at.

Flash MX now supports dynamic loading of JPEG images. This is a terrific option for sites that have large numbers of images or images that need to change often. The only restriction is that the JPEG format doesn't support transparency, so the image backgrounds can't be masked out. For the photos in the about section that are loaded into a graphic "frame," we can use loaded JPEGs; but the other portfolio images need to be loaded with masking intact. The best way to accomplish this is to use loaded SWF files. By placing the original PNG files into individual SWFs, we can load the images dynamically with masking preserved. The other advantage of creating SWF files for each image is that we can add any other graphic details or text that may go with the individual photos. This keeps our main project file uncluttered and makes it easy to modify the image files independently for updates or changes.

The process for creating the individual SWF files is straightforward. The only thing to keep in mind is that the SWFs should all have a consistent size, and the alignment and scale of the imported photos on the Stage should also be kept as consistent as possible from one image to the next. The process we used to generate a series of SWF files is as follows:

1. To export a Flash movie (SWF file), we obviously need to make a Flash document (FLA file) first. For the card images, we created a document sized to 310×300. The **Image** layer holds the placed bitmap image and the dashed line detail that frames the image (see Figure 32-8).

Figure 32-8: The first PNG image imported with a vector line added to frame it

2. The **Description** layer holds an instance of a custom component that will be used to enter variable text descriptions for each image. When the component is selected on the Stage, the Property inspector shows a Description field where the image caption can be entered (see Figure 32-9). The text won't be visible in the exported SWF file, but it will be attached information so that it can be loaded into our main project file (as described later in this chapter).

Figure 32-9: The description component allows a caption to be entered and stored with each image SWF file.

3. Save the Flash document (FLA) with a descriptive name, so that revisions can be made later if needed. We used the name **1_1_butterfly.fla** to indicate that this is the first image in the first portfolio category of the site and that it contains the butterfly card image.

4. To simplify the ActionScript needed for loading the images, we want to publish Flash movies (SWF files) that are identified with only the numbers that describe the section and sequence that they belong in. By default, the Flash movie will have the same name as the document (as noted in Step 3). The Flash movie can always be renamed manually after it has been published, but there is another way that you can control naming of exported files from Flash. In the Publish Settings dialog box (shown in Figure 32-10), you can clear the **Use default names** check box and modify the name shown in the Flash (SWF) field. Now when you publish your file, the Flash movie will have the name you've specified rather than the same name as the original document.

5. Instead of creating a new Flash document (FLA) from scratch for each image, it is much faster to work from one document with the correct size and layer structure to support any other text or graphic elements related to the images. To prepare the next image in our card series, keep the current document open and proceed to Step 6.

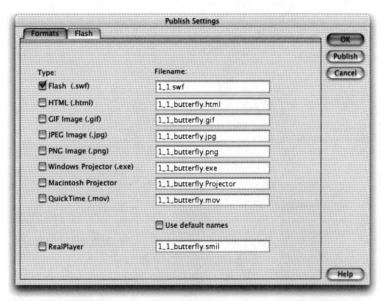

Figure 32-10: Clear the Use default names check box in Publish Settings to modify the name specified for the final Flash movie.

6. Use the Bitmap Properties dialog box to import the next image — "replacing" the first PNG with the second PNG in our series of card images. The benefit to using this method is that you will be certain that the import settings are consistent and that any sizing or alignment adjustments made with the first image will be applied to each new image. As shown in Figure 32-11, the new image that you select for import displays in the preview window of the Bitmap Properties dialog box, but the filename field still shows the name of the original PNG.

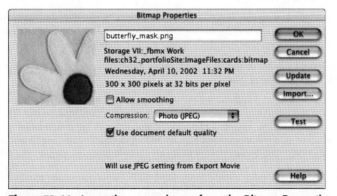

Figure 32-11: Importing a new image from the Bitmap Properties dialog box allows you to swap the original image with the next image in the series.

7. The new image will now be in the Library and on the Stage, with all the same attributes as the original image (see Figure 32-12). To make it less confusing when you come back to the files later on, you can change the bitmap name in the Library so that it is correct for the new image.

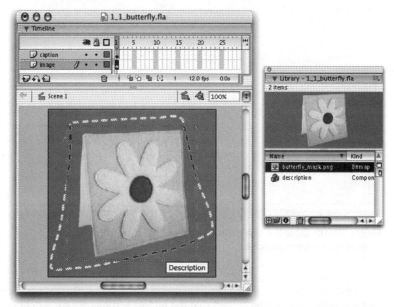

Figure 32-12: The new image will replace the original bitmap in the Library and will appear in your layout at the same scale and position as the original image.

8. Select the description component instance and modify the caption text to fit the new image.

9. Be cautious when saving the FLA file. If you accidentally use a direct save, the file you saved with the first image will be overwritten. Use **Save As** and assign a new name to the file that indicates its place in the sequence (**1_2_daisy.fla**).

10. Before publishing the Flash movie (SWF), make sure to change the name specified in the Publish Settings dialog box.

And that's it! Repeat Steps 6 through 10 for each of the images in the card sequence. If all of your image assets have the same aspect ratio, then you can continue to use the same document size. In this portfolio, the design and costume images are much taller than the card images, so we changed the document size to 310×425 before starting to import the PNG images for those sections. You'll also notice that the dashed line was consistent on each card image, but for the designs and costumes, we added a unique outline to fit each image. To ensure that the URLs used to locate the images for loading into the main project file will be logical, the final SWF files are placed in named category folders inside the main site folder. The FLA files should be archived in case you need to make changes in the future, but you don't need them in the main site folder.

Formatting logo graphics and other vector art

If you're creating all your artwork directly in Flash, then you don't need to worry about file compatibility and color consistency. However, it's common to receive graphic art created in other applications, and the best method for translating these files to Flash will depend on the original format and the content of the file.

Some of the most common workflows for integrating vector artwork in other formats with Flash MX projects are described in Chapter 38, "Working with Vector Graphics."

Using logo art created in Illustrator

For this project, the logo was originally designed as vector artwork in Adobe Illustrator (see Figure 32-13).

Figure 32-13: The original logo in Adobe Illustrator with paths describing the outlined shapes

The easiest way to get the vector artwork into Flash with all the color and outlines intact is to use the Illustrator **SWF export** option to create a file that can be imported directly to Flash. When the SWF is imported to the Flash authoring environment, it appears as a group of various vector shapes (see Figure 32-14).

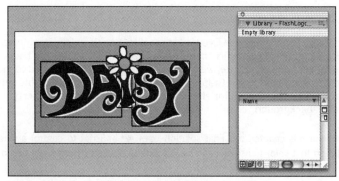

Figure 32-14: The imported SWF file comes into Flash as several grouped shapes.

To optimize the file for use in our project, the groups are reorganized and converted into logical Graphic symbols that can be nested inside animated Movie Clips and Button symbols (see Figure 32-15).

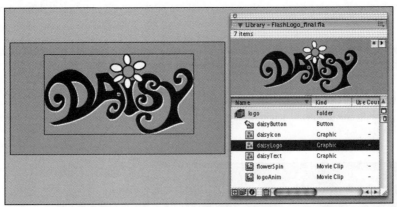

Figure 32-15: The basic shapes are converted into Graphic symbols used to build other animated elements.

Giving these symbols descriptive names and sorting them into a single labeled folder in the Library makes it easy to transfer them into other project files when they're needed. Note that all the animation is contained on symbol timelines rather than on the main movie timeline. Also, if you open the **FlashLogo_final.fla** (in the ch32 folder on the CD-ROM,) you can see that the animated symbols in the Library are all created by nesting and reusing other symbols wherever possible.

Cross-Reference For a review of how to convert primitive shapes into symbols for optimized Flash files, refer to Chapter 6, "Symbols, Instances, and the Library."

Creating backgrounds

To make the site lively and fun, we decided to give each section of the site a unique background color. The colors for the backgrounds were chosen to complement colors that Daisy uses in her designs; but to make them work with different artwork and to keep them from overpowering the loaded images, we used slightly muted tones.

To create a custom palette, you can use the Eyedropper tool to sample colors from images and then use the Color Mixer panel to modify the colors as needed. To change the background color in different sections of our site, we made a white filled rectangle sized to match our document (600 × 450) and saved it as a Graphic symbol. Instances of this Graphic symbol can then be reused and tinted using the color effects settings available in the Property inspector to change the "background" color for different sections of the site.

Note As described later in this chapter, our final solution uses ActionScript to control a single background "tile" so that color transitions can be animated between different site sections dynamically.

We also wanted to add some texture to the backgrounds but to make the designs as flexible and easy to update as possible, we created separate Graphic symbols and drew patterns in white. This allowed us to apply the textures as alpha overlays on any background color and to scale them as needed. Figure 32-16 shows the individual texture patterns and instances of these Graphic symbols placed onto the background colors with alpha and scaling applied.

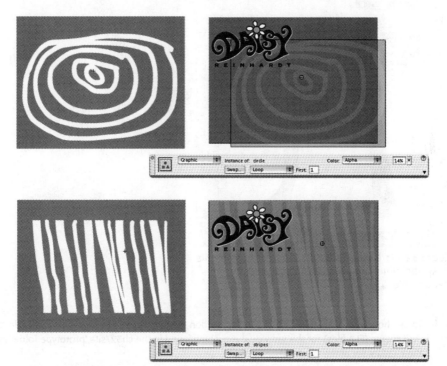

Figure 32-16: Graphic symbols in a neutral color (left) can be layered over different background colors and modified with color effects and scaling to suit the layout (right).

Cross-Reference   For a review of working with the color tools and panels, refer to Chapter 7, "Applying Color." For a review of using color effects on symbol instances, refer to Chapter 9, "Modifying Graphics."

Using symbols to organize graphic elements

The remaining vector artwork, for interface elements and decorative graphics are created with the Flash drawing tools and organized in symbol timelines. Even simple elements, such as the "photo frame" used in the *about* section of the Web site to frame loaded JPEG images, are built in layers to keep all the graphics as easy to modify as possible (see Figure 32-17). To keep the file structure manageable, elements that work together should also be nested inside symbols rather than stacked or grouped on the main project file timeline. For example, the *JpegFrame* Graphic symbol has the *JpegHolder* Movie Clip used as the target for loaded JPEGs nested under the frame art and above the white mat art.

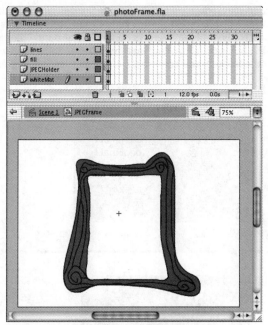

Figure 32-17: Nesting artwork and related elements on symbol timelines keeps files optimized and manageable.

On the CD-ROM To see how the elements described in this section are structured, you can look at the Flash documents (FLA files) for the individual examples found in the ch32/site/prototype folder in the ch32 folder of the CD-ROM.

Putting It All Together

While one designer is working on preparing the graphic elements, the coder on your team can be developing scripts for animation or other features of the site that will be controlled with ActionScript. As long as you're both working from the same plan, you should be able to make progress independently until it's time to start putting everything together. The first step toward assembling your project is usually to drop in any static graphic elements or persistent navigation elements that do not require scripting. The next step is to add the simple scripting needed to control the Main Timeline. When these elements are in place, we start putting in placeholders for the dynamic content. This should be a fairly quick and painless process if you've managed to stick to your original "map" of the various elements.

On the CD-ROM To see the various stages of the site as it is put together, refer to the incrementally numbered Flash documents in the **site** folder in the ch32 folder of the *Flash MX Bible* CD-ROM. Starting with **daisySite_100.fla** and finishing with **daisySite_107.fla**, you can scrub through the Timelines and check out the symbols stored in the Library for each document to see what elements are added as we work toward the finished site.

Placing static elements and text

We start assembling the site by opening up daisySite_100.fla (the file described earlier that has the basic folder and timeline labels in place). The first elements that we add to the project file are as follows:

✦ **Logo:** The first element to add is the animated symbol of the logo (logoAnimMC). As you can see in logoFinal.fla, the timeline of the animated symbol is set up with the final sized static logo on frame 1 before the logo animation starts on frame 2. This allows us to use the same symbol instance in all the site sections (instead of using one animated symbol for the intro and another static symbol for the other sections of the site). There are two ways that you can move the logo from the source file (logoFinal.fla) to the project file (daisySite_100.fla):

  • Open both files and copy and paste the symbol instance of logoAnimMC onto the Stage in the **intro** keyframe of the **logo** layer of daisySite_100.fla.

  • Open daisySite_100.fla and use the Open As Library command to open only the Library of logoFinal.fla. Drag the folder of logo symbols from the source library into the project library (daisySite_100.fla) before placing logoAnimMC onto the Stage in the **intro** keyframe of the **Logo** layer.

✦ **Background Textures:** The Graphic symbols for the various background patterns are placed into their respective **category keyframes** on the **bgTextures** layer. The Graphic symbol instances are each assigned an **alpha** value of **15** in the Property inspector so that they blend better with the background.

Tip

We could have used an alpha fill to create the original background patterns, but using a solid fill and then using Color Effect to change the alpha value of the symbol instances gives us more options. It is easier to preview how different alpha values look on the Stage and to quickly make adjustments in the Property inspector than to go back inside each symbol and modify the alpha value of the original fill color.

✦ **Static text:** The text for the **intro** and the **about** sections of the site is entered in Static text fields; but to keep track of these elements, we converted them to Graphic symbols. (Now they're stored in the Library.) An instance of the relevant text symbol is placed on the **Caption** layer of the **intro** keyframe and the **about** keyframe, respectively. The intro text is actually placed on a new keyframe that is a few frames ahead of the keyframe that marks the start of the intro section. This gives the logo animation time to start before the intro text pops up on screen.

The intro text symbol includes the decorative vector elements that dress up that text. Again, the goal is to make the project file easy to navigate and edit without having to dig through the items on the Stage in each area of the timeline. For now, the text is left editable; but before we save and publish the final version of the site, we will convert this text to outlines to avoid font display problems when the files are opened on other systems.

Note

Since Robert prefers to work in Windows XP for coding and Snow prefers to work in Mac OS X for design, the font display is sometimes inconsistent when Rob opens the files, but because he doesn't have to worry about editing the layout, he just views the file with a default substitute font while adding code. The final files are saved and published from the OS X machine.

✦ **JPEG frame:** As discussed earlier, we will not be using the same SWF image-loading convention for the photos in the **about** section of the site. For this section, we will be loading JPEG files directly into an empty Movie Clip. To add a bit of polish to the JPEGs (that will load with a flat white border,) the empty Movie Clip is nested inside a Movie Clip that contains vector artwork of a photo frame. This element was created and saved in a separate FLA file (photoFrame.fla). An instance of the final **JpegFrame** Movie Clip is placed on the **imageMC** layer of the **about** keyframe. To fit the layout, the instance is scaled down to 50 percent of the original symbol size. Option+drag (Alt+drag) the instance to create a second frame with the same scaling and position it in the layout.

To see the project file after these items are added, open **daisySite_101.fla** from the site folder on the CD-ROM. (Figure 32-18 shows a sample frame from the site at this stage.)

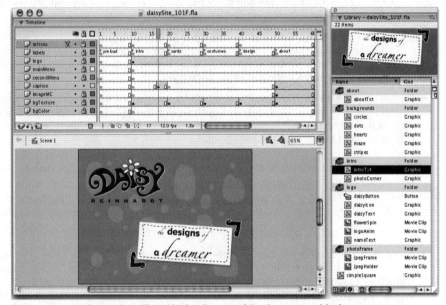

Figure 32-18: The project file with the first graphic elements added

Basic timeline navigation

Although some of the navigation will need to be finalized after the placeholders for dynamic content have been added, we can start building the navigation that will allow visitors to view each category that we have labeled on the Main Timeline.

✦ **mainMenuMC:** The text menu that is persistent throughout the site can be prebuilt in a separate Flash document. See **mainMenu.fla** in the ch32/site/prototype folder on the CD-ROM. The individual Button symbol instances are contained in a Movie Clip symbol and the actual text that appears in the buttons is converted into Graphic symbols so that any changes to the text style will propagate to each frame of the Button symbol timeline automatically. The nested file structure makes it easy to move or scale the menu as a single element while still allowing quick edits to the contents of each button at any time. (The hierarchy of menu elements is visible in the location label of the Document window shown in Figure 32-19.)

Figure 32-19: Clicking into the nested elements of mainMenuMC reveals the structure in the location label above the Stage.

Because we're using text as the only visible content of our buttons, it is important to remember to set the Hit state of the button as a solid filled rectangle, rather than using the Graphic symbol of the text box. There are often times when we need a basic filled rectangle to define elements of the site (such as invisible buttons, hit states, or masks). Instead of making a new shape each time you need a rectangle, it's better to create a single Graphic symbol of a rectangle that can be reused wherever it's needed. In this project, a black filled rectangle is stored in the Library as a Graphic symbol named "basicSquare."

To set up the buttons for navigating to the different site sections, make sure to include the following steps:

1. Place an instance of the mainMenuMC Movie Clip onto the **intro** keyframe of the **mainMenu** layer of the project file. Because the menu is consistent for all sections of the site, you don't need to make keyframes anywhere after the intro keyframe on the mainMenu layer.

2. Modify the ActionScript for each Button instance in the menu to correctly target the corresponding category frame label with a `goto` action, composed as follows:

```
on (release){
  _root.gotoAndStop("cards");
}
```

✦ **secondMenu:** At this stage of the project, we also added the Button instances of **arrowBN** and aligned them in the layout on the keyframes for each image category in the **menuSecond** layer. The rollOver and Down animation for the button is working now, but the ActionScript needed to control the loaded images will be added later.

✦ **Contact button:** A simple text button (**contactBN**) is added to the **about** keyframe on the **menuSecond** layer. The scripting needed to make this button launch an email window will be added later.

To see the project file after these navigation elements are added, open **daisySite_102.fla** on the CD-ROM. (Figure 32-20 shows a sample frame from the site at this stage.)

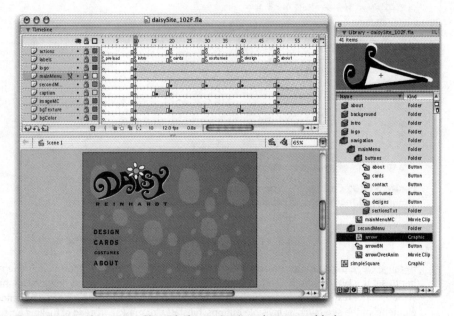

Figure 32-20: The project file with the navigation elements added

Load functions and intro animation

Although there aren't any images in the Main Timeline (that is, Scene 1) of our project, the graphic interface may still take a bit of time to load on a slow connection, so we have left room at the beginning of the timeline for a preloader (after the interface is loaded, the preloader will not appear again if the visitor returns to the intro section of the site). This same preloader is reused throughout the site, whenever a new asset is loaded into an empty Movie Clip.

Cross-Reference

For a review of building and using preloaders, refer to Chapter 28, "Sharing and Loading Assets."

The animation for the preloader (shown in Figure 32-21) was organized in a separate document (**loader_101.fla**). The only thing unique about the preloader used in this example is that the percent loaded is equated with a frame on the animation Timeline, rather than being equated with an increase in the X scale of a standard loader bar. The daisy graphic has ten petals and each petal represents 10 percent of the total site size. As the site loads, the petals are added until, at 100 percent, all ten are in place.

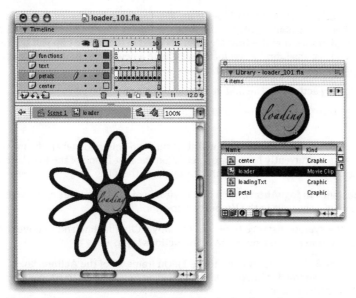

Figure 32-21: The Movie Clip timeline for the loader animation

We don't include the ActionScript as part of our discussion in this section, but if you want to see the timeline structure and code used for the loader, open loader_101.fla from the ch32/site/prototype folder and look at the ActionScript on the first frame of the Main Timeline and also on the first frame of the loader Movie Clip timeline.

The steps taken to integrate the loader with our main project file are as follows:

1. Create a new layer titled **functions** at the top of the layer stack (above the **Actions** layer,) on the Main Timeline of **daisySite_102.fla**.

2. Add the ActionScript on the first keyframe of the **Functions** layer that will monitor loading and control the loader animation. Because we aren't describing in detail how the code is structured in this example, you can auto-load the pre-authored ActionScript by adding just one line of code to the keyframe:

```
#include "scripts/addLoader.as"
```

Inside of this script file is an ActionScript function named addLoader(). When this function is executed, the code will create a Movie Clip named holder to hold the loaded Flash movies. The function will also grab a Movie Clip symbol named loader from the Library and place it on the movie's Stage — as the movie runs in the Flash Player. The addLoader() function tells the new loader instance which asset download it is monitoring. For this section, it will monitor the progress of the Main Timeline (_root), in the master movie (SWF file).

The ActionScript is not printed here, but it is included on the CD-ROM for you to review or reuse. You will find the code in the **scripts** folder.

3. Now you can add the actual loader Movie Clip. Use the Open As Library command to open the library for **loader_101.fla** and drag the **loader** Movie Clip into the main Library. You will notice that the Graphic symbols used in the Movie Clip will be transferred also. To keep the Library organized, we create a new folder named **preloader** and store all the loader assets together.

4. Add the following actions on the first keyframe of the **Actions** layer:

```
addLoader("main", _root, {x: 300, y: 225});
stop();
```

The next step is to add the ActionScript that will start the logo animation when the intro loads. Remember that we currently have a stop action on the first frame of the logoAnim Movie Clip, so the logo works as a static graphic throughout the site.

1. Select the instance of **logoAnim** on the first keyframe of the **Logo** layer and give it an instance name of logoAnim in the Property inspector.

2. Double-click the symbol instance to access the Movie Clip timeline and remove the stop(); action from the first keyframe of the Actions layer.

3. Go back to the Main Timeline (that is, Scene 1). On frame **10** of the **Actions** layer (above the first keyframe for **intro**), add the following ActionScript to trigger the logoAnim Movie Clip to play.

```
logoAnim.gotoAndPlay(2);
stop();
```

To see the project file after these navigation elements are added, open **daisySite_103.fla** on the CD-ROM. Because the changes we've made are not visible on the Stage unless the file is viewed in the Test Movie environment, Figure 32-22 shows the changes visible in the Timeline window and in the Library.

Navigation for loaded assets

The next step is to add the Dynamic text field to hold the image captions attached to the loaded SWF images. A function is called that will enable switching of loaded images. Next, actions on the secondMenu buttons and the Actions layer of the Main Timeline are edited to control navigation of the image sequences. We also set up a function to clear the Stage so that images don't accidentally overlap when the visitor moves from section to section. We will walk through the steps for the first portfolio section on the Main Timeline, marked by the keyframe label "cards."

Note   You may have noticed earlier that the order of the category keyframe labels doesn't match the order of the categories in the main menu list — design is the last portfolio keyframe label, but it's the first menu item — but we didn't! Aside from proving that even when you're really trying to be organized, little things can still go wrong, this anomaly illustrates clearly that the exact order of sections on the Main Timeline doesn't control how visitors will actually navigate through the site. Because the playback of the Main Timeline is completely subordinate to the actions on our buttons, the viewer will never know how the timeline is really organized. As long as all the ActionScript correctly references keyframe labels and Movie Clip instance names, the movie should function smoothly. The main reason to try and match up the order of the timeline with the navigation menu is to make it easier to find our way around while editing the project file (FLA).

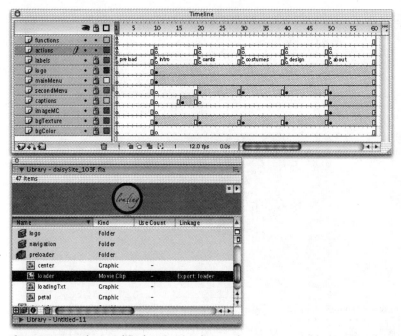

Figure 32-22: The modified Main Timeline and new assets added to the Library in daisySite_103.fla

Once you've followed these steps, you can repeat the same edits on the other two portfolio sections ("costumes" and "design").

1. **Create a caption field**: Add a Dynamic text field on the first keyframe of the **cards** section (frame 20) on the **Caption** layer and give it an instance name of caption in the Property inspector (see Figure 32-23).

2. **Bring in ActionScript for loading images**: In the first keyframe of the **Functions** layer add the following code to auto-load the pre-authored ActionScript (provided in the scripts folder on the CD-ROM):

```
#include "scripts/switchImage.as"
```

This #include directive will load and "store" the code in the Functions layer so that it can be called by the navigation elements when they need to load an image SWF.

3. **Note:** An update was also made to the ActionScript on the button nested inside the **logoAnim** Movie Clip, so that clicking on the daisy graphic of the logo would return visitors to the intro section. On the first frame of the **Daisy** layer on the Movie Clip timeline of **logoAnim**, select the instance of **daisyButton** and add the following ActionScript:

```
on (release) {
  _root.gotoAndStop("intro")
}
```

Figure 32-23: The settings in the Property inspector for the caption text field that will display the text variables attached to the loaded image SWFs

4. **Edit secondMenu:** In the cards section, name the Button instances of **arrowBN** on the **secondMenu** layer as `nextButton` (right-pointing arrow) and `prevButton` (left-pointing arrow), respectively. Next, add actions to each of these Button instances to call the relevant image load functions (imported to the function layer in step 2).

   On the `prevButton` instance add:

   ```
   on(release){
     prevImage();
   }
   ```

   On the `nextButton` instance add:

   ```
   on(release){
     nextImage();
   }
   ```

5. **Define the cards section with code:** Add the following Actions to frame 20 of the **Actions** layer to configure the cards section of the site. Note that the ⤸ should not appear in your actual code—it indicates a continuation of the same line of code:

   ```
   _global.sectionName = "cards";
   _global.sectionNum = 1;
   ```

```
_global.currentImage = 1;
_global.imageLimit = 4;
_global.holderPos = {x: 260, y: 75};
_global.loaderPos = {x: 445, y: 215};
addLoader(sectionName, currentImage, ↪
  {x: loaderPos.x, y: loaderPos.y});
checkButtons();
stop();
```

This code will set up the cards section to work properly with the `addLoader()` function you added previously. The new `_global` object in Flash MX ActionScript is used to store the current section's configuration, specifying its number (`sectionNum`), the starting image in the SWF sequence (`currentImage`), how many images are in the sequence (`imageLimit`), the position on the Stage where the SWF files will load (`holderPos`), and the position on the Stage where the loader instance will appear (`loaderPos`) while the SWF files are loading.

The `addLoader()` function is then passed this configuration data. The function will create a holder instance into which the first SWF file for this section, located in `cards/1_1.swf`, will load. The filename path is formed with the following expression inside the `addLoader()` function:

```
var file = section+"/"+sectionNum+"_"+currentImage+".swf";
```

6. **Add a function to remove content:** To avoid accidental overlap of images when a visitor moves to a new section, we define a function on the first frame of the **Functions** layer that can be referenced at any time to clear the Stage:

```
function clearStage(){
  masterHolder.holder.removeMovieClip();
}
```

7. **Execute `clearStage()` function:** On frame 10 of the Actions layer, add the following code to "activate" the `clearStage()` function for the cards section:

```
clearStage();
```

The project file with these changes is saved as **daisySite_104.fla**, and it is included on the CD-ROM for you to review.

Duplicating the functionality

Now that you have followed the step-by-step changes that were needed to develop the cards section of the site, you can use **daisySite_105.fla** (on the CD-ROM) as a guide to help you duplicate the same functionality on the other two portfolio sections of the site as follows:

1. Name the arrowBN instances (`prevButton` and `nextButton`) in the **secondMenu** layer for the **costumes** and **design** sections of the site.

We included a gap of four empty frames between each section's buttons to make sure that instances would be "refreshed" when the timeline jumps to the new frame. In our tests, we found that Button instances from previous sections would show up in new sections, overwriting the position of the placed instances there. By inserting empty keyframes between the instances, each section "clears" the old instances before the new ones load.

2. Add actions to all the buttons in the **secondMenu** layer for each section. Copy and paste the actions from the buttons in the **cards** section to make the work go faster and to reduce the margin of error (typing can be dangerous, especially when you get tired!).

3. Add actions to the **Actions** layer for each section. Copy and paste the code used for cards, but customize the code where needed to fit each section (section names, section numbers, and so on).

And that will complete the steps needed to create a functional navigation system for the portfolio images. Figure 32-24 shows a frame of the Flash movie as it should appear in the Test Movie environment with the loaded images.

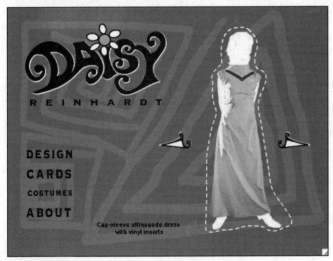

Figure 32-24: Dynamically loaded portfolio images will be visible only in the published SWF of the main project movie (or in the Test Movie environment).

Setting up placeholders for loaded JPEGs

Remember those photo frames that we placed in the about section of the site? It's finally time to get them ready to load the JPEG images dynamically.

1. Name the instances of the JpegFrame symbol on the **imageMC** layer in the **about** section to image_1 (top) and image_2 (bottom,) respectively, in the Property inspector.

2. In the first keyframe of the **Actions** layer for the **about** section (frame 50), add the ActionScript to load the JPEG images:

```
image_1.holder.loadMovie("about/4_1.jpg");
image_2.holder.loadMovie("about/4_2.jpg");
clearStage();
```

Note   The clearStage() action is only necessary for the **intro** and **about** sections because the holder instance is automatically replaced with new content in the other sections.

While we're working on the about section, we also add a getURL action to the **contact** Button symbol instance on the **menuSecond** layer:

```
on(release){
   getURL("mailto:daisy@isyReinhardt.com");
}
```

After these changes are made, the project file is saved as **daisySite_105.fla**. Figure 32-25 shows how the about section of the published SWF will appear with the dynamically loaded .jpeg images.

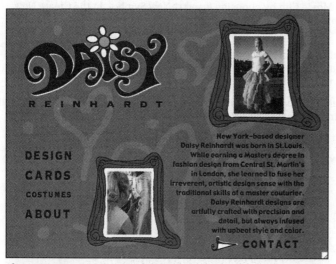

Figure 32-25: Jpeg images loaded into the frames on the about section of the main movie (SWF).

ActionScript for final functionality

Now that the basic asset loading is in place, we can move on to doing something about that dull gray background. Rather than placing static filled rectangles in each section (which would change abruptly), we're going to use ActionScript to control the color of a background color tile. Using the Color object in ActionScript, we can change the color of a dynamically added rectangle graphic, and gradually fade the color using the _alpha property of the Movie Clip object.

On the CD-ROM

To see how this effect works on the site, you can look at the Flash movie for the final project file (daisySite_107.swf), saved in the site folder of the ch32 folder on the CD-ROM.

Adding actions to change the background color

To give you a "shortcut" for developing the more complex features of this project, we have included some custom components that you can reuse in other projects too. The first component controls the color changes and is saved in a document titled bgFader_100.fla (in the prototypes folder). This fade component is nested inside of another symbol named bgTile.

Cross-Reference The fade component is described in more detail in Chapter 20, "Making Your First Flash MX Project."

To integrate the component with our current project, follow these steps:

1. With **daisySite_105.fla** active, open **bgFader_100.fla** as a Library and drag a copy of the **bgTile** Movie Clip symbol into the main document Library. When all the new assets were transferred, we moved them into the **background** folder in the main Library.

2. Rename the **bgColor** layer to **bgFader**.

3. Create an empty Movie Clip by choosing Insert ➪ New Symbol. In the Create New Symbol dialog box, name the symbol **emptyMC**, choose the Movie Clip behavior, and click **OK**.

4. Return to the Main Timeline. In frame **10** of the **bgFader** layer, place an instance of the emptyMC symbol in the top-left corner of the Stage (0,0). (You may need to unlock the layer.) Name the placed instance bgFader in the Property inspector.

5. To bring in the function that will change the color of the background tile, add the following code to the first keyframe of the **Functions** layer:

```
#include "scripts/changeColor.as"
```

6. In the **Actions** layer, add the following code to each category section to define their colors.

   For intro:

```
changeColor("purple",0x9999CC);
```

   For cards:

```
changeColor("blue",0x669999);
```

   For costumes:

```
changeColor("pink",0xCC9999);
```

   For design:

```
changeColor("green",0x669966);
```

   For about:

```
changeColor("khaki",0x999966);
```

Adding a scale effect to loaded images

Now that the background colors are changing more subtly, we need to make the transition from one loaded image to another a bit more polished. A setScale.as script is included in the scripts folder if you want to deconstruct how it was coded. Otherwise, just enjoy using the script wherever you want something to scale dynamically. To integrate the pre-authored script with our current project file, follow the same steps used to call functions in previous steps:

1. On the first keyframe of the **Functions** layer add the following code:

```
#include "scripts/setScale.as"
```

The setScale() function described in this .as file is already incorporated into the functions defined in the switchImage.as script file. You can cross-reference the functions in the script files to see how the loaded Flash movie is dynamically scaled.

2. Save the Flash document, and test it (Ctrl+Enter or ⌘+Return). Go into any section that loads external Flash movies (such as **cards**). When you click the **next** button, the current image will scale down and the next image will scale up.

Fixing details for final Flash movie

There are a few last-minute things that need to be taken care of before the Flash movie (SWF file) is published for the final project.

✦ Adjust the position of the `holder` instance for each section in the main document. The holder instance is targeted by the `addLoader()` function to display the loaded SWF files. You can adjust the position of the `holder` instance in the following line of code, found in each section's keyframe on the **Actions** layer:

```
_global.holderPos = {x: 260, y: 13};
```

Simply change the x and y numeric values to indicate the position of the top-left corner of the loaded assets for each section. With this method, it is possible to change the position for the assets for each section — but not for the individual images in a series. If any of the images in a series require unique adjustment, then you must open the Flash document that contains the imported PNG file and change the alignment or size of the bitmap on the Stage before republishing a new movie (SWF) to load into the Empty Movie Clip in the main project file (FLA). This can be a slightly tedious process of trial and error as you try to get the images just exactly right — you will have to keep publishing SWF files to test how the images align in the project layout.

✦ Adjust the position of the `loader` instance for each section in the main document. The same notes apply from the previous point. To change the position of the loader instance in each section, adjust the following line of code found in each section's keyframe on the **Actions** layer:

```
_global.loaderPos = {x: 445, y: 215};
```

✦ Make any last-minute changes to the graphics or effects used in the movie. For example, we decided that we wanted the introTxt graphic in the intro section to only display after the `logoAnim` instance was finished playing. So, we selected the introTxt graphic on the Stage, switched the instance's behavior to a Movie Clip, and named it `introTxt` in the Property inspector. We then added the following code to the Actions layer keyframe for the intro section:

```
introTxt._visible = false;
```

This code turns off the visibility of the `introTxt` instance. Then we went inside of the logoAnim symbol and inserted this action on its last keyframe:

```
_root.introTxt._visible = true;
```

This code will show the `introTxt` instance when the animation finishes.

✦ The other changes you will notice in our final version of the site layout are in the **about** section. We decided to make one of the photo frames (and the loaded .jpeg) larger and we added an instance of the **arrow** Graphic symbol to point out the **contact** button text.

To modify the size of the photo frame Movie Clip, select the `image_1` instance of JpegFrame and change the scale in the Transform panel from 50 percent to 60 percent size. In the **about** keyframe of the **Actions** layer, you will see the code added to modify the alignment and scale of the loaded .jpeg image so that it will align correctly with the new larger frame.

✦ Publish an index.html file for your main Flash document. Use the Publish Settings to specify the name of the .html file, and use the HTML tab to adjust the parameters for the <EMBED> and <OBJECT> tags that will be included in the published .html file.

You may need to publish a different filename for the main HTML document for your particular web server. For example, Microsoft IIS servers commonly use default.htm as the primary document in a Web server directory.

✦ Publish a final Flash movie for the main document. We usually use a generic name such as main.swf for the final "master" movie. Again, use the Publish Settings to specify this name.

In the final Flash document available on the CD-ROM, we converted any graphic text to outlines by using the Break Apart command. In this way, you can see the typeface we're using for the document. However, you should not break apart the text in your own Flash documents. Presumably, you'll always have access to the fonts you're using throughout the project.

Other than sorting out the files you will need to upload to the server, you should be home free. Hopefully, you're happy with your project and confident that you can reuse some of what you've learned on the next project you decide to tackle.

As we've mentioned throughout this chapter, all the files you will need in order to deconstruct the project and reuse the ActionScript or the components are included in the ch32 folder on the CD-ROM. Although the logo graphic and some of the source portfolio images are also included, we ask that you please respect the copyright on those elements of the project.

Uploading the final files to the Web server

After you've made any last-minute changes to the final document, you're ready to transfer the files to your site's Web server. Using Macromedia Dreamweaver MX or your preferred FTP client, upload the following files to the Web server:

✦ index.html (or equivalent)

✦ main.swf (the master movie file)

✦ A sub-folder named about, containing all of the numbered JPEG images

✦ A sub-folder named cards, containing all the numbered .swf files

✦ A sub-folder named costumes, containing all the numbered .swf files

✦ A sub-folder named design, containing all the numbered .swf files

You do not need to upload the .as script files because they're automatically included with the main movie (SWF file) when you publish it.

When you're finished uploading the files, test the site in a Web browser. Make sure the files load properly. **Remember:** UNIX servers are case-sensitive with filenames, so be certain to specify the same case in your folder and filenames that you used in your ActionScript code.

Cross-Reference You can also decide to add further functionality to the site by adding a Flash Player detection mechanism to the first HTML document that loads for your site. You can learn more about detection in Chapter 22, "Integrating Flash Content with HTML."

Summary

✦ The principles of extensible design can be applied to any project to reduce redundant production work as the content grows or changes.

✦ Site maps, technical specification sheets, and other design planning documents are useful tools for guiding development on projects of all sizes.

✦ Building a site from a series of smaller pieces that are brought together with ActionScript facilitates collaboration.

✦ Leveraging the strongest skill sets of different members of a production team and reducing redundant effort will make the work better and faster to create.

✦ Centralizing assets for dynamic loading and de-centralizing the structure of your site by breaking it down into smaller Flash documents (FLA files) makes it easier to delegate production tasks while maintaining design consistency.

✦ Custom components are a great way for developers to strategically "deploy" ActionScript in a format that will be manageable for less code-fluent designers (or clients who may want to take on more control of their own sites).

✦ Components are also a flexible way for coders to re-purpose custom ActionScript behaviors. Components are portable and easy to reuse, minimizing the need to re-architect solutions that may be useful in more than one project.

✦   ✦   ✦

Creating a Game in Flash

◆ ◆ ◆ ◆

In This Chapter

Thinking about
game plan logic

Using the break and
return functions

Asking questions
with conditionals

Using arrays

Writing code with the
new event model

Creating text fields
dynamically

Creating Movie Clips
dynamically

Using setInterval

Using SharedObject

◆ ◆ ◆ ◆

Creating a game requires much more than programming. It is a combination of many skills — game design, interaction design, visual and sound design, and scripting — that brings it all together. These skills also represent the different phases of game design and will be covered in this chapter. Attention must be given to all these aspects to produce a successful game.

To illustrate the different aspects of game design, we will build a simple game, the universally known Hangman.

On the CD-ROM

Before reading through this chapter, copy the hangman.fla and the hangman.swf files from the ch33 folder of the CD-ROM onto your hard drive. Double-click the SWF file to play the game and become acquainted with our project. Now, open the hangman.fla file and look at the three first frames on the movie. The third frame script is the game itself and will be addressed first. The first and second frame scripts collect and display the user's personal information and will be covered last.

The Game Plan: Four Phases of Game Design

Game development includes the four different phases introduced earlier. The following sections discuss those phases in detail.

Note

Many thanks to Jonathan Brzyski for contributing his illustrations to the Flash movie used in this chapter. You can learn more about Jonathan at www.humanface.com/brzyski.

Game design

Designing a game is creating a fantasy world, a story and characters with defined roles and goals. It establishes a structure with a clearly defined set of rules and a scoring system. In a single-player computer game, such as the one we create in this chapter, the computer acts both as the opponent and the referee.

This traditional Hangman game presents the user with a number of empty slots corresponding to the letters of a word. The player must guess the word, entering one letter at a time. A right guess, and the letter appears in the appropriate slot. A wrong guess, and the hangman is revealed, one body part at a time. It is clearly understood that the hangman is a representation of the state of the user in the game. Being hanged represents defeat, but no harm is done. If the user guesses the word before the body is complete, he or she wins the round; otherwise the man is hanged, and the round is lost.

Interaction design

Interaction design is creating the visual representation of the mechanisms of a game: It determines how to play the game and communicates the rules to the user.

The interaction of our game is very simple, and our design should be just as simple. To keep the interface to a minimum, the alphabet is used both to represent the choices and to display the user's selection. The character's physical state is a character representation of the user as well as an indication of the score within one round.

For the Hangman interface, we need

   ✦ A field to display the empty slots for the letters of the word to guess.

   ✦ A listing of the alphabet that indicates letters already selected as well as ones that remain. This listing is also the device by which the user can select a letter.

   ✦ A field for feedback from the computer referee.

   ✦ An area to display the score.

   ✦ The hangman character.

Visual and sound design

The visual design is essential because it is the first and longest lasting impression. It communicates the mood of the game. Ours is fun, colorful, and somewhat humorous.

This particular game is fairly limited with not much of a narrative. Nonetheless, the character drawing and animation should keep the user entertained: The hangman is now an alien character going back to the mother ship. Each round was designed with a different set of colors to give some visual diversity. The alien choice is meant to be humorous, both as a homage to the old computer games using such characters and as a spoof on the too many computer demonstrations and illustrations using aliens.

The alien character and the background, including the selection of color schemes, were created by Jonathan Brzyski, a talented artist with a sense of humor (see Figure 33-1).

Of course, good sound effects are an important complement to the visual. They translate a mood and are helpful to indicate a win or a loss. They also are crucial in supporting and reinforcing animation.

Figure 33-1: Our version of the hangman is a tribute to aliens and old computer games.

Programming

Programming a game is the task of asking a series of questions and making decisions, including asking new questions based on the answers, in a language and syntax that the computer can understand. Writing short and task-specific functions is helpful to break down the logic of the game into discrete elements.

The programmer must deconstruct the game in terms of a dialogue between the computer and the player. It must address every detail, no matter how obvious it seems. By thinking of the flow of events ahead of time, you will be able to write code that can handle several aspects of a problem at different times of your game cycle.

Finally, with every new update, Flash provides new functions to simplify our scripting task. Becoming acquainted with them will streamline this process and make your code easier to write and more elegant.

Building the Project

This section discusses the creation of the art and assets for the interface and then talks about assembling the game's mechanics.

In the tradition of character animation, the alien puppet is constructed of independent Movie Clips for each body part for maximum flexibility. (Figure 33-2 shows the Movie Clips for the alien's head.) Each Movie Clip is made of nine frames used for the nine rounds of the game. Each frame displays the same Movie Clip symbol with different advanced color effects. You can view the color settings by selecting the Movie Clip symbol, opening the Property inspector, and clicking the Settings button to the right of the Color menu. Note that by using the color effects, we can use the same symbols over and over, keep our file small, and still develop a very large visual vocabulary.

When the game is a loss and the alien is complete, an animation is triggered. This animation uses tweening in two ways. As shown in Figure 33-3, the first one is Motion tweening and applies to the light beam that moves down and up; the second one is alpha tweening and makes the alien disappear over time.

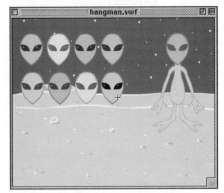

Figure 33-2: The head Movie Clip uses the head symbol and displays it with different color schemes.

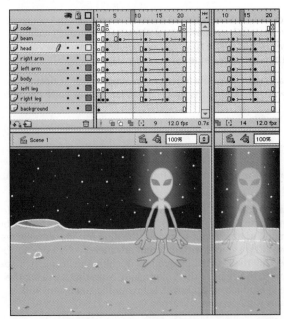

Figure 33-3: The end-of-round animation uses tweening for the light beam and the alien body parts.

Scripting the Game

The Hangman game consists of a series of rounds, corresponding to the number of available words to guess. In each round, the computer randomly chooses a word and generates slots as placeholders for the letters. The user attempts to guess the word one letter at a time. For each right guess, the letter appears. For each wrong guess, a piece of a character appears. After six wrong guesses, the alien character is completed, does a little animation for us, and the round is over. The score for each round appears on the screen.

The three steps to the game are the setup, user input, and interpretation of the user input. All the code for this aspect of the game is located on frame 3 of the hangman.fla document.

The game has an additional feature: The username and his or her score are saved on the local machine, and the data is available the next time the user plays the game. The code for this feature is located on frames 1 and 2. This feature, however, is covered last.

New Feature The SharedObject allows you to save data locally, similarly to the way a cookie saves data in a Web browser.

Initializing Variables and Creating Sound Objects

Before writing functions, a few variables are created:

The `wordSelection` array is an array containing the words to guess. For our game, the user must guess old computer games. Note that some of the words contain a ^ character, which will represent a carriage return and be used as an indicator to place words on multiple lines. This additional feature is to make the word easier to guess as well as create a more attractive layout.

```
var wordSelection = "Asteroids", "Defender", "Donkey^Kong",
   "Pac^Man", "Paddle", "Pong", "QBert", "Space^Invaders",
   "Tetris"];
```

The `lettersLeft` array will be populated by the letters of the alphabet. It is used to keep track of the selected letters.

```
var lettersLeft = new Array();
```

Two Sound objects, `soundWin` and `soundLoss`, are created for this project, and a sound is attached to each of them. These sounds provide audio feedback for the score.

```
var soundWin = new Sound(this);
var soundLoss = new Sound(this);
soundWin.attachSound("applause");
soundLoss.attachSound("error");
```

The `myDepth` variable determines which depth is available sequentially every time an object requiring a depth is created. It is initialized to 1 when the game starts.

The `roundNumber` variable keeps track of the round to inform the user at the beginning of every round. It is assigned a value of 0.

The `editedWord` variable stores the number of letters in a word (minus the ^) and determines when a word is complete.

The `delayCounter` variable gives a time delay between rounds in association with the `setInterval()` method. `setInterval()`, new to Flash MX, is used to call a function at a specific time interval.

The `win` and `loss` variables increment as the score changes. The `saveWinScore()` and `saveLossScore()` functions are created on the first frame of the movie. However, they will be discussed last in the "Added Feature: Storing User and Game Information" section of this chapter. For now, note that they are passed the value of `win` and `loss`.

```
var win = 0;
var loss = 0

saveWinScore(0);
saveLossScore(0);
```

Building the Interface

With Flash MX, it is now possible to create primitives and text fields via ActionScripting. We will take advantage of this feature to create the rest of our assets.

 New Feature You can now create text fields dynamically by using ActionScripting.

Creating text fields

The `createTextField()` method creates a new empty text field as a child of a Movie Clip object. Note that the `createTextField()` takes several parameters: the instance name, the depth, x position, y position, width, and height.

A `TextFormat` object can be also be created and applied to a text field. Let's create our first one here:

```
var fieldStyle = new TextFormat();
with (fieldStyle) {
  font = "Arial";
  size = 10;
  align = "left";
}
```

Now, we create the score text fields as well as the feedback text field. We then invoke the `setNewTextFormat()` method with the instance name of the TextFormat object to apply its settings. To target all the field dynamic text fields, we use the `for . . . in` action and search all instance names starting with the string `"field"`. The `myDepth` variable sets the text field's depth and gets incremented every time a new field is created.

```
this.createTextField("fieldWon", myDepth, 300, 255, 40, 15);
myDepth++;
this.createTextField("fieldLost", myDepth, 300, 268, 40, 15);
myDepth++;
this.createTextField("fieldFeedback", myDepth, 35, 259, 260, 20);
myDepth++;
for(name in this) {
```

```
if(name.indexOf("field") != -1){
  with(this[name]) {
    selectable = false;
    setNewTextFormat(fieldStyle);
  }
}
}
```

To create the content of the score text fields, we concatenate, respectively, the string "Win", the variable win, the string "Loss", and the variable loss:

```
fieldWon.text = "Win  " + win;
fieldLost.text = "Loss " + loss;
```

All the preceding code is part of the buildInterface() function. Figure 33-4 shows the comments throughout the first round and the opening comment of the second round.

Round 2	Win 0 Loss 1
You lost this round	Win 0 Loss 1
Sorry, that letter is not in this word. Try again	Win 0 Loss 0
Correct! K is in the word	Win 0 Loss 0
Round 1	Win 0 Loss 0

Figure 33-4: The fieldFeedback text field displays comments throughout the game. The fieldLost and the fieldWin text fields display the score.

Creating the alphabet

Movie Clips can be created dynamically using the createEmptyMovieClip() method. This method takes two parameters: an instance name and a depth. Furthermore, with Flash MX's new event model, Movie Clips can be used as buttons.

 New Feature You can now create Movie Clips dynamically using ActionScript.

We use the alphabet as both visual feedback of the user selection and input device for the user to make a selection. To take care of both aspects, we are going to create dynamic Movie Clips and then create text fields as their children.

Let's first define a text format for the text fields:

```
centeredStyle = new TextFormat();
with (centeredStyle) {
  font = "Arial";
  size = 10;
  align = "center";
}
```

ASCII characters can be created using the String.fromCharCode() method, which uses the number corresponding to a letter and returns its corresponding string (A=65, B=66, and so forth). Each letter of the alphabet is displayed in a dynamically created text field, as shown in Figure 33-5.

Note that we are also defining a function for each letter Movie Clip that will execute when the event is invoked. When the mouse is released, the letter will be checked for a match. The readyToPlay variable prevents the call to the function from being executed between rounds and at the end of the game.

New Feature

With the new event model, you can define a function for an object that will execute when an event, such as a mouse click, is triggered. And the script no longer needs to be on the object itself.

```
var objX = 35;
for (var i = 65; i<=90; i++) {
  fieldName = String.fromCharCode(i);
  this.createEmptyMovieClip(fieldName, myDepth);
  this[fieldName].createTextField("character", 1, objX, 225, 13, 15);
  with (this[fieldName].character) {
    selectable = false;
    setNewTextFormat(centeredStyle);
    background = true;
    text = fieldName;
  }
  this[fieldName].onRelease = function() {
   if (readyToPlay) {
    checkInput (this._name);
   }
  }
  objX += 12;
  myDepth++;
 }
}
```

The createAlphabet() function is called from the buildInterface() function. Both buildInterface() and createAlphabet() functions are invoked only once at the beginning of the game.

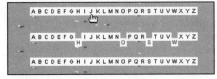

Figure 33-5: Our alphabet Movie Clips work as both text fields and buttons.

Starting the Game

The functions that we will cover next are built with the framework of the game in a circular fashion: All the functions are used within one game cycle and again within the next game cycle. This kind of flow is specific to games and must be kept in mind when writing code. In particular, variables need to be reset properly at the beginning of a new cycle.

At the beginning of each round, some of our assets need to be edited and some variables initialized. The `setRound()` function takes care of it by incrementing the variable `roundNumber`, setting the value of variable `editedWord` and `delayCounter` to 0 and setting `readyToPlay` to true.

```
roundNumber++;
editedWord = 0;
delayCounter = 0;
readyToPlay = true;
```

`setRound()` also prepares the alien character: The `hangMan` array is created to store the instance names of the body parts. A repeat loop hides these Movie Clips. These Movie Clips go to the frame number corresponding to the `roundNumber` to display a new color scheme.

```
background.gotoAndStop(roundNumber);
  hangMan = new Array(head, body, armL, armR, legL, legR);
  for (var i = 0; i < hangMan.length; i++) {
  hangMan[i]._visible = false;
  hangMan[i].gotoAndStop(roundNumber);
}
```

This line makes the Main Timeline go to frame 4 to reset the game in case the losing animation played.

```
    this.gotoAndStop(4);
```

Putting the Movie Clips' instance names in an array will come in handy during the game when we want to reveal the letters one at a time. We will also use it to check the status of the game.

Display the letters of the alphabet

The `setRound()` function also invokes the `positionAlphabet()` function.

This function stores each letter of the alphabet in the `lettersLeft` array. It also moves the vertical position of the Movie Clips by the same name. Note that the array is first emptied using the `splice()` method before being assigned elements again. This is used in the circular fashion mentioned earlier.

```
function positionAlphabet () {
  lettersLeft.splice(0);
  for (var i = 65; i<=90; i++) {
    lettersLeft[lettersLeft.length] = String.fromCharCode(i);
    fieldName = String.fromCharCode(i);
    this[fieldName]._y = 0;
    this[fieldName].character.textColor = 0x000000;
  }
}
```

Choose a random word

The selection of words is stored in an array called `wordSelection`, which is defined at the beginning of the game. A random number, generated using the `Math.random()` function, defines the index in the array and stores its element in the variable randomWord. Lastly, the selected word is removed from the array using the splice() method so that it doesn't get chosen again.

```
fieldFeedback.text = "Round " + roundNumber;
randomNumber = Math.floor(Math.random()*wordSelection.length);
randomWord = wordSelection[randomNumber];
wordSelection.splice(randomNumber, 1);
```

Note   In this version of the game, a word is randomly selected from a pool for each round. As such, the difficulty of each word (number of characters, number of words, and so on) is not ranked. You could modify the game to create a series of word arrays, each one varying in level of difficulty. As the player progressed to the next round, a word from another array could be chosen.

Create the slots for the letters of the word

The createWord() method sets the number of slots corresponding to the letters.

Using the for . . . in action is a convenient way to search for text fields with an instance name including the string "letter" and then remove them. Again, because we are working in a cycle between rounds, this would remove the letter text fields created in a previous round before creating new ones.

```
for(name in this){
  if(name.indexOf("letter_") != -1){
    this[name].removeTextField();
    myDepth--;
  }
}
```

Looking back at the wordSelection array, you will notice that some of the elements have a ^ character in the string (such as "Donkey^Kong"). We use this character to detect entries with multiple words and place them on several lines. When the system sees a ^ string, the repeat loop ignores the rest of the statement block and goes back to the top of the loop using the continue action.

In all other cases, a text field is created, using the objX and objY variables as coordinates. Flash assigns the text field a text format, and its text becomes a question mark as a cue to the user.

The variable editedWord is incremented. This variable keeps track of the number of letters in the word and will be used to check when the word is complete. Figure 33-6 shows a game in play with some letters already guessed.

```
var objX = 35;
var objY = 25;
for (var i = 0; i < word.length; i++) {
  if (word.substr(i, 1) == "^") {
    objX = 40;
    objY += 25;
    continue;
  }
  this.createTextField("letter_"+i, myDepth, objX, objY, 25, 25);
```

```
with (this["letter_"+i]) {
  border = true;
  background = true;
  backgroundColor = 0x99FFFF;
  setNewTextFormat(centeredStyle);
  text = "?";
}
myDepth++;
editedWord++;
objX += 25;
}
```

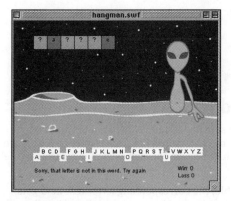

Figure 33-6: The slots correspond to the number of characters in the word to guess. At the beginning of a round, all slots display a question mark. When a selection is correct, the ? character is replaced by the letter.

The User Input

The user enters his or her selection by clicking one of the Movie Clip letters (remember how the Movie Clips now function as buttons).

On release, the checkInput() function is called, and the Movie Clip instance name is passed. Its instance name corresponds to the letter of the alphabet it represents.

Interpreting the User Input

This is the bigger part of our project. A series of questions are asked, and their answers determine the next step in the process.

```
function checkInput (guess) {
  if(isLeft(guess)){
    lookForMatch(guess);
  } else {
    fieldFeedback.text = "Sorry, you already tried that letter";
  }
}
```

The isLeft() function looks to see if the selected letter was already chosen, and the lookForMatch() function checks the letter against the word to guess.

Was the letter selected before?

Using a repeat loop, the isLeft() function compares the lettersLeft array to the chosen letter, one element at a time. If the letter is contained in the array, the vertical position of its corresponding Movie Clip is offset by 10 pixels, and the color of its text field is modified. The letter is deleted from the array, and the function returns true.

```
function isLeft (char) {
  for (var i = 0; i<lettersLeft.length; i++) {
    if (lettersLeft[i].toLowerCase() == char.toLowerCase()) {
      this[char]._y = 10;
      this[char].character.textColor = 0x003333
      lettersLeft.splice(i, 1);
      return true;
    }
  }
  return false;
}
```

Is the letter part of the word?

The lookForMatch() function compares the selected letter to the variable randomWord, one character at a time. The toLowerCase() method converts the character to lowercase so that the two compared elements would match if they are the same letter, regardless of their case.

If the letter is found in the randomWord variable, the corresponding letter text field gets assigned a new background color, and its text is changed to reveal the letter. Also, the variable match is assigned the value of true.

```
for (var i = 0; i <randomWord.length; i++) {
  if (randomWord.substr(i, 1).toLowerCase() == char.toLowerCase()) {
    this["letter_"+i].text = randomWord.substr(i, 1);
    this["letter_"+i].backgroundColor = 0x00FFFF;
    var match = true;
  }
}
```

For a match, we also want to start a sound and display a feedback message; but because we want to execute it only once, it is placed outside the repeat loop. The variable match keeps track of a match.

```
if (match) {
  soundWin.start();
  fieldFeedback.text = "Correct! " +fieldGuess.text+ " is in the word";
}
```

Tip   You could also construct a hangman Movie Clip symbol that uses several keyframes to animate the progression of the hangman. Instead of using an array, the Movie Clip instance could be told to advance one frame further with nextFrame() to proceed to the next stage of the hangman.

The letter is not part of the word

If the character is not contained in the array, the shift() method deletes the first element in the hangMan array and makes the corresponding Movie Clip visible to reveal a piece of the alien. It also displays a text message and starts the sound effect that corresponds to a wrong choice.

```
var hangPiece = hangMan.shift();
hangPiece._visible = true;
fieldFeedback.text = "Sorry, that letter is not in this word. Try again";
soundLoss.start();
```

Checking the Status of the Game

The last step in our process is to check the status of the game. More specifically, is the word complete, is the character complete, and/or is the game complete? The function gameStatus() asks all these questions. The following sections discuss questions and conditions that exist in the game and the programming logic behind their answers and actions.

Is the word complete?

To check whether the word is complete, we check for any remaining ? characters in the letter text fields. We use a repeat loop (with the length of the editedWord variable as the condition to exit the loop). Note how the Boolean variable allMatch is assigned the value of true if the word is complete and of false if the word is not complete.

```
for (var i = 0; i <= editedWord; i++) {
  if (this["letter_"+i].text == "?") {
    allMatch = false;
    break;
  } else {
    allMatch = true;
  }
}
```

The word is complete

If the word is complete (and allMatch has a value of true), the feedback text field displays the corresponding message. The variable win is incremented, and the new score displays on the screen.

```
if (allMatch) {
  fieldFeedback.text = "You won this round!";
  win++;
  fieldWon.text = "Win    " + win;
  saveWinScore(win)
  reset = true;
```

Is the alien complete?

If the word is not complete (and `allMatch` has a value of `false`), we need to check that the status of the alien: If it has all its parts, the round is lost. The `feedback` text field displays the corresponding message. The variable `loss` is incremented, and the new score displays on the screen. The movie moves forward on the timeline to play the losing animation.

```
} else if (hangMan.length <= 0) {
  fieldFeedback.text = "You lost this round";
  loss++;
  fieldLost.text = "Loss  " + loss;
  saveLossScore(loss);
  reset = true;
  this.play();
}
```

In both cases, the `reset` variable is set to `true`. This is a flag to indicate that this round is over and to proceed to the next step. Only if reset is true, the process continues. Otherwise, it is complete, and the game is ready for the next user input.

Is the word selection empty?

If the `wordSelection` array is empty, it is the end of the game, and the `feedback` text field displays a "thank you" message.

```
if(wordSelection.length == 0){
readyToPlay = false;
  fieldFeedback.text = "Thanks for playing!";
```

There are more words to guess

If it is the end of a round but not the end of the game, a delay is created before calling the next game.

```
else if (reset){
readyToPlay = false;
  delayNextRound = setInterval(createDelay, 10);
}
```

The `readyToPlay` variable prevents interactivity on the letters Movie Clips when it is set to `false`. This is to prevent the user from making selections between rounds or at the end of the game.

Adding a delay before the next round

Let's add a delay so the user has the time to view the result before moving on to the next round. Flash MX provides a new way to add a timer without having a script going between two frames or on an `enterFrame` event. The `setInterval()` method calls a function at the time increment you choose. It will keep running until you call the `clearInterval()` method, at which point the `startGame()` function is invoked again.

```
function createDelay() {
  delayCounter++;
  if (delayCounter > 150) {
```

```
        clearInterval(delayNextRound);
    reset = false;
      startGame();
    }
  }
```

Added Feature: Storing User and Game Information

Being able to save information opens new dimensions to game development. For example, users will particularly enjoy playing a multilevel game if they know the next time they visit the site, they can pick up where they left off because the computer remembers which level they last completed and their current score.

For our Hangman game, the following section demonstrates a very simple application of saving data onto the user's local hard drive and recalling it when the player returns to the game at a later time.

Flash MX introduces a new feature, the SharedObject, which allows you to save data locally, similarly to a Web browser cookie. The next time the user runs the game, it will display the saved information. The information can be saved in two ways: when the movie ends or as soon as the information is entered. For our game, the information is saved right away using the flush() method.

The SharedObject.getLocal() method creates a new object called localInfo.

```
  localInfo = SharedObject.getLocal("hangMan");
```

First, we check that the data was saved for the username and the win and loss scores. If any of this information is missing, the movie stops at frame 1

```
if (localInfo.data.winScore == undefined || localInfo.data.lossScore ==
undefined || localInfo.data.user == undefined) {
  gotoAndStop(1);
```

and two text fields are created dynamically, as shown in Figure 33-7. One is an input form for the user to enter his/her name, and the second is an instruction of what to do.

```
function fieldsFrame1() {
  this.createTextField("nameLabel", myDepth, 50, 232, 200, 20);
  with (nameLabel) {
    selectable = false;
    setNewTextFormat(openingStyle);
    text = "Please Enter Your Name";
  }
  myDepth++;
  this.createTextField("nameEntry", myDepth, 50, 250, 150, 18);
  with (nameEntry) {
    setNewTextFormat(openingStyle);
    nameEntry.background = true;
    nameEntry.type = "input";
  }
  myDepth -= 1;
}
```

Figure 33-7: The input form

Figure 33-7 shows the first frame you see when you first come to the game. Not unlike a registration form, you enter your name. Every time after that, your name and score are remembered and displayed.

After the user enters his/her name and clicks on the orange button on the screen, the data is saved by calling the `saveName( )` function:

```
function saveName(name) {
  _root.localInfo.data.user = name;
  localInfo.flush();
}
```

In the first frame of the movie, the function `showUserInfo( )` is also declared but will only be used on the second frame:

```
function showUserInfo() {
  _root.user.text = localInfo.data.user;
  _root.winText.text = localInfo.data.winScore;
  _root.lossText.text = localInfo.data.lossScore;
}
```

If the data is stored on the local drive, the movie goes to frame 2 and displays the information by calling the `showUserInfo( )` function. This function populates a text field, which is created dynamically. The field displays a message, including the user's name and score, as shown in Figure 33-8.

```
this.createTextField("displayData", myDepth, 50, 220, 150, 50);
displayData.setNewTextFormat(openingStyle);
displayData.text = localInfo.data.user + "," + newline + "This is your last
  score:" + newline + "you won " + localInfo.data.winScore + " rounds and
  lost " + localInfo.data.lossScore + "." + newline + "Good luck on your
  new game!";
```

The `saveWinScore()` function and the `saveLossScore()` function are called from within the game at the end of each round and store the win and loss scores.

```
function saveWinScore(win) {
  _root.localInfo.data.winScore = win;
  localInfo.flush();
}
function saveLossScore(loss) {
  _root.localInfo.data.lossScore = loss;
  localInfo.flush();
}
```

Figure 33-8: The second time you play the game and every time after that, the Playhead goes to this frame, where your name and previous score are displayed.

The next frame brings us to the game. Our game, shown in Figure 33-9, is complete!

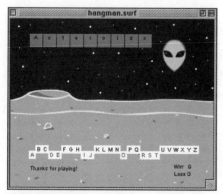

Figure 33-9: This chapter is an homage to old video games. Test your knowledge of them by playing the game.

Summary

✦ Creating a game is much more than programming. It involves other talents, such as game design, interaction design, and visual and sound design.

✦ Before writing code, it is helpful to deconstruct the game into small detailed steps.

✦ Scripting a game is asking a series of questions and responding to them appropriately, depending on the user input.

✦ Arrays are helpful to store, retrieve, and manipulate information. In our game, we use them for the selection of words to guess as well as for the alien character's body parts.

✦ Functions are essential to intelligent programming. Writing small, task-focused functions allows for greater flexibility, particularly for complex games.

✦ With the new event model, functions can be defined for objects and executed when events, such as a mouse event, are triggered. We are using this new model to create functions for the alphabet Movie Clips. Instead of writing the code on each Movie Clip, the functions are created within a repeat loop only once on a frame script. The code no longer needs to be on the object itself.

✦ Movie Clips and text fields can be created dynamically. Additionally, text fields' properties can be manipulated via ActionScript. In addition to adding flexibility, it reduces the weight of your movie.

✦ The new setInterval() action can be used as a timer to call a function over time without having the playhead move between frames. Here, we are using it to create a delay between rounds.

✦ A SharedObject is a great new feature to save data on the local drive. We are using it to store the user's name as well as the game's score.

✦   ✦   ✦

Optimizing and Troubleshooting Flash Movies

P A R T

VIII

✦ ✦ ✦ ✦

In This Part

Chapter 34
Optimizing Your
Flash Movies

Chapter 35
Getting Your Code
Under Control

Chapter 36
Solving Problems
in Your Movies

✦ ✦ ✦ ✦

When you've put all the pieces of your project together and realize you need to drastically reduce file size, Chapter 34 will give you a review of all the methods you can use to optimize your Flash projects. As your ActionScript gets more complex, Chapter 35 will provide some tips and tricks for keeping all that code organized, logical, and clean. When you run into trouble after following all the suggestions in other chapters of the book, Chapter 36 will walk you through some techniques for isolating and analyzing problems with your Flash movies.

To make room for all the other new content in this edition of the Flash MX Bible, we had to move this troubleshooting section to the CD-ROM. These chapters are intended as a summary of the tips and techniques that you will encounter in other chapters throughout the book, so if you work through other chapters and examples, you won't be missing anything. But, if you need some targeted, quick tips for optimization and troubleshooting, this section will be the best place to start.

On the CD-ROM

You will find these chapters of the book on the CD-ROM in the Bonus_Chapters PDF. The example files relevant to each chapter will be found in the ch34, ch35, and ch36 folders respectively.

Expanding Flash

If you've done nearly everything you can do in Flash and you're wondering what else is possible — this is the section that will give you an introduction to the best applications and workflow for expanding your projects beyond pure Flash. We could have called this section the "Working With" section because all of the chapters included here cover applications that work with Flash and the techniques you can use to work with these programs to enhance your multimedia project development.

In Parts 1 through VIII, you learned that Flash can tackle some of the most complex graphic, animation, sound, and interactive projects. But, as we all know, no one program can do it all (or do it all *best*). For optimum efficiency and creative options, most of us work with a toolbox of multiple programs that fit together in various ways. In an effort to help you find the best place for Flash among the other key applications that you might be using, we have included this section on "Expanding Flash."

With the help of expert contributors, we have compiled coverage of the best and most relevant applications that you can leverage for specialized tasks and use to discover new creative possibilities. From Macromedia FreeHand to SoundForge, from Discreet 3ds max to Dreamweaver, Director, ColdFusion, and QuickTime, you will learn new techniques and be introduced to some of the many programs that will push your Flash work as far as you want to go.

✦ ✦ ✦ ✦

In This Part

Chapter 37
Working with
Raster Graphics

Chapter 38
Working with
Vector Graphics

Chapter 39
Working with Audio
Applications

Chapter 40
Working with
3D Graphics

Chapter 41
Working with
QuickTime

Chapter 42
Working with
Dreamweaver MX

Chapter 43
Working with
Director

Chapter 44
Working with
ColdFusion MX

Chapter 45
Making Movies
for the Pocket PC

✦ ✦ ✦ ✦

Working with Raster Graphics

✦ ✦ ✦ ✦

In This Chapter

Preparing raster images for use in Flash projects

New features of Fireworks MX

Using Fireworks MX to streamline workflow

Moving files with multiple elements into Flash

Creating alpha channels in Photoshop

Exporting raster images from Flash MX

Using raster artwork in Flash animation

✦ ✦ ✦ ✦

Although Flash can generally hold its own for vector art creation, you need another application to acquire, finesse, and export bitmap images for use in your Flash projects. Flash MX is an amazingly versatile application that can import and export just about any raster (a.k.a. *bitmap*) image format. This chapter shows you how to create bitmaps for Flash in image-editing applications such as Macromedia Fireworks and Adobe Photoshop.

Preparing Bitmaps for Use in Flash MX

Regardless of the specific effects that you apply to your images in other programs, the key features to consider when preparing bitmaps for use in Flash are size, compression, and transparency.

✦ **Size:** It is important to know what the maximum image size will be in your final Flash layout. You may choose to size your bitmaps slightly larger than the final size to accommodate browser scaling. Although you can scale multiple instances of the same image to different sizes in Flash, if you intend to use many smaller thumbnails and only a single instance of the image at a larger size, it will be worthwhile to make a smaller copy of your image to import into Flash in addition to the original, larger image.

✦ **Compression:** Different compression schemes will work better on some images than on others. With experience, you will learn to select the most appropriate compression to maximize the quality of your images, while minimizing file size. For example, if you are working with a black-and-white photo that has high contrast or a bitmap image of a line-art illustration, you might find that GIF compression is actually more effective than JPEG compression.

Some images need to be very high-resolution to maintain details, while other images (such as abstract background images) can be downsampled significantly, while still serving their purpose in your design. Although you can always add additional compression to your images in Flash with the native JPEG options, it is helpful to decide on a baseline for an image and reduce it to the highest quality that you will actually need in your final presentation. If you choose to add JPEG compression to your images *before* importing them to Flash, make sure to select the Use Imported JPEG data check box when you import the files to Flash. The Launch and Edit functionality of Fireworks ensures that you will always have the option of making changes to your source image, even if you use a flattened JPEG version of the image for authoring in Flash.

✦ **Transparency:** There are many different ways of adding *transparency* to an image; you might need a very subtle fade of one image over another, or you might simply need to eliminate the white space around a central image. Deciding on the final effect that you need and then finding the best way to achieve this while keeping your file size small is the challenge. Bitmap file formats that support true transparency in Flash include PNG, PICT (Mac), BMP (Win), and TIFF. These file formats all have *lossless* native compression schemes, making them ideal for high-quality images. However, these benefits come with a high price to pay in file size. If you can achieve the effect that you need by applying a vector mask in Flash, or by cropping the original image, it is much better to take that approach.

Enhancing Web Production with Fireworks MX

The newest release of Macromedia Fireworks has upped the ante on what you can expect from a Web-imaging application. Many of the new features of Fireworks MX enable you to do more of your Web-image production from start to finish without ever going to another application.

With Fireworks, designers have the freedom to import work that they have created in Photoshop, Illustrator, FreeHand, Flash, Poser, After Effects, LiveMotion, or even 3ds Studio Max—while keeping the option of editing the files. Unlike other Web graphic design programs, Fireworks combines the ease of vector-based editing with the tools required for advanced bitmap editing.

Along with its advanced, yet familiar, tools Fireworks also sports a superior optimization engine for exporting files, and for the automation of custom command batch processing. It even has the ability to implement a Find and Replace for elements within a graphic project. For designers working in Flash, one of Fireworks' most powerful features is its capability to prepare (and optimally compress) huge quantities of bitmap files for import.

Perhaps the most important feature of Fireworks MX is that the native PNG formatted files can be imported directly to Flash MX without any other file export or format conversion required. All vectors, bitmaps, animations, and even multi-state button graphics will be preserved in the Flash authoring environment. This workflow finally breaks down the barrier between raster files and vector art or text, allowing you to take advantage of the best features of these different formats without having to switch modes or break your artwork up into multiple files. Going the other way, Fireworks is equally capable of receiving files from Flash and optimizing them for inclusion on HTML sites.

Here's a quick overview of some of the core features of Fireworks MX, which make it a preferred partner for Flash MX:

✦ **Macromedia common user interface (UI):** Just like Flash MX, Fireworks MX has a new streamlined interface (shown in Figure 37-1). All the tools and options are laid out in dockable panels that are distinguished by unique icons and names. Also, the new **Property inspector** provides intuitive, centralized information and controls relevant to the active tool or element. A new Select menu makes it easy to find all of the common selection commands in one place.

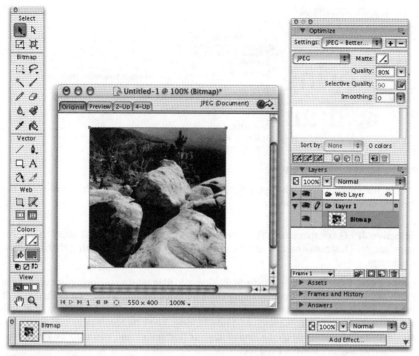

Figure 37-1: The sleek new interface for Fireworks MX is consistent with the changes you'll see in other Macromedia MX Studio programs.

✦ **Create and edit text directly:** In Fireworks MX you can now create and edit text directly on the canvas without having to use a separate Text Editor. You can modify text settings at any time directly in the Property inspector.

✦ **New Bitmap tools:** Fireworks MX flaunts a new set of bitmap-editing tools that will make designers requiring detailed image editing options very happy. These include, Blur, Sharpen, Dodge, Burn, and Smudge.

✦ **New Gradient tool:** Fireworks MX also has an improved Gradient tool that can be used to fill pixel selections, vector objects, and text.

✦ **Batch Processing:** The user interface for Batch Processing makes it easy to optimize large quantities of images. You can also run scripts during a batch process.

✦ **Quick Export button:** Fireworks MX gives developers a shortcut to their other Macromedia MX Studio programs. As shown in Figure 37-2, this new icon at the top of the Document window provides a drop-down menu of various options for file export or transfer to other core development programs.

✦ **Extend Fireworks with custom commands made in Flash:** Fireworks MX allows you to enhance the Fireworks JavaScript Extensibility API by combining pre-built or custom commands with interfaces created in Flash MX using ActionScript and components. Visit the Macromedia Exchange to download user-built commands.

Figure 37-2: The Fireworks Quick Export button provides a shortcut to other core programs and common file options.

✦ **Selective JPEG compression:** Fireworks enables you to add a JPEG Mask to an area of your image. This mask can have a different JPEG compression setting than the rest of the image.

✦ **Launch and Edit:** You can easily edit PNG image files while authoring documents in Flash MX or in Dreamweaver by using the Edit With option, as shown in Figure 37-3. When a PNG image is opened in Fireworks from another application, Fireworks will let you know that you're in "Launch and Edit" mode. The changes made in Fireworks will automatically be applied to the image in your document and can also be saved to update the original source PNG file.

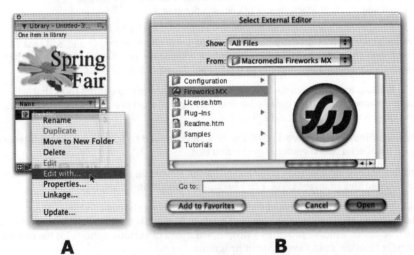

Figure 37-3: The Flash Edit With option allows you to choose an image editing application to modify raster images that you've placed in Flash.

✦ **Reconstitute image tables:** Fireworks MX will rebuild an editable source PNG file from an image table in an HTML file. Fireworks will import the slices with Web behaviors, such as rollovers or pop-ups, still attached. The graphic can be edited in Fireworks and then exported with all of the behaviors intact.

✦ **Streamline Web production tasks in Fireworks:** The new Fireworks MX Data-driven Graphics Wizard takes automated production a step further by supporting variable-assignment for graphic elements and Web objects in a Fireworks template document. This reduces repetitive production time for designers authoring multiple copies of the same elements. Also, Flash MX now offers instance-level button properties, making it easier than ever to make multi-button navigation bars or pop-up menus by assigning unique text and URLs in the Property inspector.

✦ **Director export:** Fireworks can export its files in a format suitable for Director use. This export requires an additional plug-in for Director.

✦ **FreeHand reader:** You can import or copy and paste FreeHand files from versions 7, 8, 9, and 10 into Fireworks MX.

Note

Although Fireworks supports the direct import of FreeHand files, if you plan to move vector artwork *from* Fireworks *to* FreeHand (or any vector graphics program other than Flash), you will need to export your files from Fireworks in Illustrator 7.0 format.

There's plenty more to Fireworks MX, and we get you on your way by introducing some solutions for Fireworks and Flash integration. Fireworks MX is an incredibly robust program that offers many features for Web production that go beyond the scope of this book.

Cross-Reference

For more detailed information on working with Fireworks MX (a core product in the Macromedia MX Studio), refer to the online help that is offered by Macromedia or the *Fireworks MX Bible* (Wiley Publishing).

Transferring Fireworks images with transparency to the Flash authoring environment

The Fireworks tools and options will be familiar to anyone who has some experience with photo-editing—we will have to leave you to explore all the possible effects on your own. To introduce you to the various export options available in Fireworks for images with bitmap or vector masking, we will walk through the steps for moving a logo with bitmap and vector elements into Flash MX from Fireworks.

On the CD-ROM

You can find the files used for this example in the "FireworksMask" folder in the ch37 folder on the CD-ROM.

1. You can add mask layers to your bitmap file in Fireworks to isolate the areas of the bitmap image that you want visible in the final image. As shown in Figure 37-4, text created in Fireworks is automatically "masked;" it will float on any background color without additional clipping paths or masking.

2. By saving the file in Fireworks' native PNG file format, you will preserve all masking, bitmap images, and editable text.

3. Open Flash MX and create a new document (or open an existing .fla file that you want to add a new element to).

4. Select the timeline and the frame that you want to import the artwork to. You may choose to create a new symbol before importing the artwork, or you can import directly to the Main Timeline and convert the graphic into a symbol later on.

Figure 37-4: In Fireworks you can easily add complex masks and editable text to your bitmap images.

5. Select File ➪ Import from the main application menu and find the Fireworks PNG file you saved in Step 2. When you select Open, the Fireworks PNG Import Settings dialog box will appear. To import our static graphic with masking, while preserving editable text, select the options as shown in Figure 37-5.

Figure 37-5: Import Settings for translating Fireworks PNG files to the Flash MX authoring environment

The various options will interpret the PNG file as follows:

- **File Structure:** The first option (**Import as movie clip and retain layers**), will automatically insert the content of the Fireworks PNG file into a Movie Clip symbol in Flash. All the layers from the original Fireworks file will be preserved as individual Flash layers. The second option (**Import into new layer in current scene**), will import all of the content of the Fireworks PNG file into a single new layer on the current Flash timeline — you can manually convert individual elements into symbols after the file has been imported.

- **Objects:** These options determine how Fireworks vector artwork is interpreted when imported to Flash. The first option (**Rasterize if necessary to maintain appearance**), will convert any special vector effects or fills that are not supported by Flash into raster images to preserve the visual look of the artwork, but you will no longer be able to modify the original vector elements in Flash. The second option (**Keep all paths editable**), will preserve vector artwork as editable elements, but any special effects or fills that are not supported by Flash will be lost when the file is imported.

- **Text:** If you are working with text that has special formatting that may not be supported by Flash, this is an important option to select. If the text will not require further editing in Flash — such as an illustrative text element or logo — then the first option (**Rasterize if necessary to maintain appearance**) will ensure that any special formatting is preserved, but the text may appear in Flash as a bitmap element and the resulting file size may be larger. If the priority is to maintain editable text then it is best to select the second option (**Keep all text editable**), even if special formatting that is not supported by Flash may be lost.

- **Flatten:** The final option listed at the bottom of the Import Settings dialog box (**Import as a single flattend bitmap**) will cancel all of the other options and simply flatten and rasterize all of the elements in the Flash PNG file. This option is useful if you want to simplify a complex graphic that you know will not require further editing. It will make the graphic easy to place and may produce a smaller final file size.

6. After choosing the settings that are appropriate for the content of your Fireworks file, select **OK** to import the graphics to your Flash document as specified. Presto! As shown in Figure 37-6, the example Fireworks file has been placed on a single layer on the Main Timeline in Flash. The editable text box is preserved and the bitmap (with masking applied) is automatically placed in the Library.

Figure 37-6: The masked bitmap and editable text block from the Fireworks PNG file are preserved in the Flash authoring environment.

It is also possible to copy and paste content from Fireworks to Flash MX with the following cautions:

✦ Standard copy (Ctrl+C or ⌘+C) and paste of content from a Fireworks file to a Flash MX document will render all of the copied graphics as a single flattened bitmap image in Flash. The visual appearance of the graphics will be maintained, but the image will not have any transparency.

✦ The **Copy as Vectors** command will allow you to preserve editable Fireworks text and vector artwork when it is pasted into Flash, but bitmap images may not be transferred correctly with this method.

Preparing other bitmap formats in Fireworks

Flash MX will accommodate most common raster formats without any difficulty. The process for optimizing files with the various compression settings available in Fireworks is straight-forward. The various View tabs in the Document window allow you to compare different image formats and compression settings that can be chosen in the Optimize panel (see Figure 37-7.)

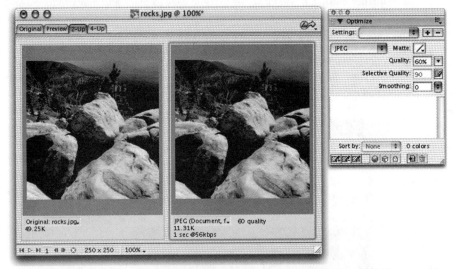

Figure 37-7: Preview tabs in the Fireworks Document window and the Optimize panel for choosing file formats and compression settings

The other option that can help you to preview the effect of different optimization settings is the Export Preview window that is invoked by selecting File ➪ Export Preview (Ctrl+Shift+X or ⌘+Shift+X.) As shown in Figure 37-8, this window also includes all the familiar settings that will affect how your final file displays when imported to other applications.

Figure 37-8: The Fireworks Export Preview window provides all the options you will need to decide on the settings to use for the final exported image.

Note the color swatches available from the Matte drop-down menu; these let you define the background color to match when complex clipping paths are exported. The only special consideration to keep in mind when exporting JPEGs for use in Flash is that JPEG files exported with the **Progressive** check box selected *won't* be recognized by Flash as optimized files. This means that you will not be able to select **Use imported JPEG data** in the Bitmap Properties dialog box and will be forced to allow additional JPEG compression to be applied to the image when the final .swf is exported from Flash. Compare Figures 37-9 and 37-10 to see the options available in the Flash MX Bitmap Properties dialog box for the same .jpeg file that was exported from Fireworks with Progressive selected and with Progressive deselected, respectively.

Figure 37-9: A .jpeg file imported to Flash that has been compressed to allow Progressive download (**Use imported JPEG data** option is *not* available)

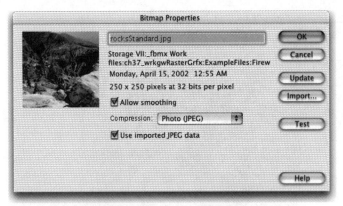

Figure 37-10: A .jpeg file imported to Flash that has been compressed *without* the Progressive download option (**Use imported JPEG data** option is available)

Leveraging Fireworks to Streamline Common Production Tasks, *by Scott Brown*

Fireworks is an essential production tool for Flash projects in which bitmaps are involved. Furthermore, if you're trying to get any kind of graphic out onto the Web, whether via Flash movies or GIFs and JPEGs for HTML Web pages, Fireworks is the optimal Web graphic processing center.

Optimizing a bitmap sequence for Flash

Consider a Flash project — a catalog or a portfolio, for example — that requires many bitmaps and bitmap animations. How do we get all those nicely rendered images into Flash? Suppose you have an animation created in a bitmap program such as Adobe After Effects, 3D StudioMax, QuickTime Pro, or Poser; all of these programs have an option to export the animation as a sequence of files, usually as a sequence of PICT, PNG, or BMP images. Often, this will be a sequence of `filename_01`, `filename_02`, `file-name_03`, and so on. The obvious challenge of working with such file sequences is that they have the potential to add up to hundreds of individual files, all needing to be prepared and optimized for Flash import. Often, in dealing with such a sequence, the files are the wrong dimension, or need to have other changes made! It's daunting to consider the laborious tedium of massaging so many files! Luckily, there is Fireworks. Fireworks, with its batch-processing capabilities coupled with its capability to run custom commands during such batch processes, easily saves the day (and your wrists).

On the CD-ROM You'll find all of the required assets for this project in the ch37 folder of the CD-ROM. To work through this example, copy the exported PNG sequence to a separate folder on your hard drive.

Setting up Fireworks to batch process

To batch process efficiently, we first need to consider the several changes that might be required to prep the file sequence for Flash:

1. All of the files are the wrong dimensions. For the animation to fit nicely into our Flash project, we need to change the dimensions from 500x300 to 300x200.

2. We also want to change the hue and saturation of those files to match the color scheme of the Flash project.

3. The art director decided to shake things up; he actually wants you to flip the animation horizontally.

4. Finally, we need to convert all those files from the PNG format to JPEG format, so that they will perform efficiently in Flash.

Let's get started. Open the first file of the sequence (ch37/scott_brown/sequence/ Original Files/video_test023.png) and make a copy. Then, working on just this one file, make all of the changes that need to be done, per your list (as explained previously). This will be your test file.

If you're familiar with the Actions Palette and the batch file feature in Photoshop, you might be thinking that you could do all those functions in Photoshop. Well, you would be right, but the truth is that Fireworks has the inside track for working with Flash. When a JPEG from Fireworks is imported into Flash, Flash recognizes the compression that was set in Fireworks and knows not to recompress it. However, when a JPEG that was made in Photoshop is imported into Flash, Flash doesn't automatically recognize the JPEG settings. Unless care is taken with the Flash JPEG compression settings — in both the Library and the Publish Settings — Flash will attempt to apply its own JPEG compression to the previously compressed file. And we all know that JPEGing a JPEG is bad practice: Hello, blocky graphic! So that's another reason for doing this batch processing in Fireworks.

Creating a Fireworks command

Let's assume that you found the perfect settings and are completely pleased with the results on your test file. If not, undo and repeat the process until it comes out just right. Then, the next step is to use the History panel to create a Fireworks command. To make this custom command we need to make the necessary changes to the sample file to get our desired final result:

1. Resize the image to 300 pixels wide.

2. Change the hue/saturation to a cool color.

3. Flip the image horizontally.

In case you didn't notice, the History panel has kept track of every action or event that's been done to the file. This is how Fireworks commands are created. However, here's a word of caution about the History panel: Not every step in Fireworks can be used in a command. When you select steps that cannot be translated into a command, Fireworks will notify you with a dialog box. Fireworks also gives you two visual clues for steps that cannot be applied as commands: One is the step icon with a red X over it, and the other is not so obvious — it's a horizontal line break in between steps. However, there are workarounds. To get around these glitches, we'll just make two commands for the batch process.

To create the first command:

1. In the History panel, select the first two steps (by Shift-clicking) and repeat.

2. Click the **Save** icon at the bottom of History panel.

3. Save the new command as **Resize & Colorize,** and click **OK.**

You've just made a custom command in Fireworks. The custom command can then be accessed in the Command menu for future use.

For the second command, while still in the History panel, select the last action applied to the image (flip horizontal), and save this command as **Flip.**

With these two custom commands saved, the next step is to customize the compression settings for the PNG sequence.

Creating custom export settings

Fireworks ships with two default preset quality options for exporting JPEGs: **better quality** (80 percent), and **smaller file** (60 percent). However, we need more compression than 60 percent. So, we simply create our own custom export setting:

1. Select the Preview View tab at the top of the document window and experiment with the JPEG compression settings in the Optimize panel, until you finally conclude that 50 percent is ideal for this project.

2. Set the JPEG quality to 50 percent.

3. Select the **Save** icon at the bottom of the Optimize panel.

4. Save this new custom setting as **JPEG 50.**

Launching the batch process

Now that we have two custom commands and a custom compression setting, we're ready to initiate the Fireworks batch process. Here's how:

1. Go to File ➪ Batch process and navigate to the folder that contains the (original) files to be processed.

2. Select the files to batch by opening the folder where all the images reside, clicking **Add All,** and then clicking **Next.**

3. This invokes the Batch Options dialog box. Here, we can choose what commands to apply to the selected files. A word of caution though: To get the desired effect, the commands need to be arranged in chronological order. The order of the commands should be (a) **Resize &Colorize,** (b) **Flip,** and (c) **Export.** Select each command in sequence and click the **Add** button.

Note More options become available in the bottom half of the window if you select the command on the right side. Although the two custom commands don't have any extra options, the **Export** command does. With the Export command selected, click the drop-down menu for Export Settings, and then select the **JPEG 50** setting that we created earlier. Click **Next**.

   4. This last step of the batch process asks where to place the new files and what to do with the originals. We also have the option to save these batch process settings, which is useful if there's even a remote possibility that there may be more than one set of files to batch. For now, just click the **Go** button. While batch processing, Fireworks opens a feedback window indicating how many files are completed and how many files have yet to be processed.

Now that we've sized, flipped, and optimized all of our files, we'll be ready to import them into Flash.

Tip It is usually best to import the image files to a Movie Clip symbol timeline so that they are easier to modify or move within your Flash project. Flash MX will auto-detect a numbered sequence and give you the option of importing all of the images in the sequence to individual frames on the current Flash timeline.

Creating Flash/GIF ad banners

Not only does Fireworks excel at preparing file sequences for Flash, but also it's equally capable of importing Flash animations. It really is a two-way street with these programs. So, if you're already comfortable creating animations in Flash, why waste time learning how to animate in any other program, when Fireworks can import anything you've done in Flash!

Flash banner ads continue to gain in popularity, however many clients still require animated GIF banners. Someday, we can hope to work in a world of pure Flash advertising and rich-media banners. Meanwhile, we'll be in a transitional period where we'll still need to turn Flash ad banners into animated GIFs.

New Feature The new Ad templates that come pre-built with Flash MX go a long way toward encouraging consistent standards for rich-media banners. To start your design with any of these templates as a guideline simply open Flash MX and chose Open ➪ New From Template to choose a template available in the Ads category.

Before we make a cool animated banner with Flash, we need to know the basic restrictions on banners. Here are some basic guidelines for animated banners: Target file size ranges from 12KB on the high end, to an acceptable 5KB, and on down to the ideal of a mere 3KB. Typical dimensions are 468x60, 392x72, and 125x125.

Now we need to create an exciting animated banner ad that will work on all browsers. (That means it has to be an animated GIF.) The dimensions of the movie are 468×60 and the file size limitation is that it can be no more than 12KB.

With these limitations in mind, we can begin designing our banner in Flash:

1. In the Document Properties dialog box (which is accessed from the Property inspector or from the application menu under Modify ➪ Document), set the movie size to the specified dimensions.

2. Also in the Document Properties, set the frame rate to no more than 10 fps. That's because we know we have to make this animation into an animated GIF and, to stay within our file size limit, the lower the frame rate, the better our chances.

3. While creating the animation, watch out for file size. Try to design a simple animation with few colors and few frames. Fewer colors with fewer frames make it more likely to land within our target file size.

Which format is best for export?

Once the animation works to your liking, the next step is to decide how to export it. If the animation has a lot of colors or images, then the best option is usually to export the animation as a PNG sequence with File ➪ Export Movie. But if the animation has very few colors, it's often best to export it as an animated GIF, either from the Publish Settings or with Export Movie.

Colorful animation export

Because the hypothetical animation is very colorful, we choose to export a PNG sequence. PNG is ideal for this, due to the amount of information that the format can hold, which is 24-bit color plus an alpha channel.

1. Still in Flash, choose File ➪ Export Movie.

2. In the Export Movie dialog box, choose **PNG Sequence** from the Format drop-down menu. Then, name the animation, choose a location for the exported file sequence, and click **Save.**

3. Now, open Fireworks and create a document that matches your Flash banner size. To import the PNG sequence as one file, choose File ➪ Open, and then navigate to the folder containing the PNG sequence. The next step is important.

4. If, at this point, we were to shift-click all the files that we want to open and then open them, Fireworks would open each file individually, which would make it more difficult to create our animated GIF. So, we need to make sure to check the **Open as Animation** option, *before* we click Open. With this option, Fireworks places each selected file in its own frame within a single Fireworks file, in numerical order. Now click **Open.**

5. This new Fireworks file should have the file sequence set for export as an **Animated GIF.** But we're not done yet. To reduce the file size, we still have to go to work with the color palette.

6. Select the Preview tab to see how our animation will look when exported. In preview mode, Fireworks indicates the file size that will result with the current compression settings. Now it's necessary to focus on the Optimize panel, which is where the file type is chosen.

7. Select Animated GIF in the Optimize panel. Once a file type is selected, various optimization options appear. For an animated GIF, we begin by editing the number of colors, either (a) choosing from a range of default color settings, with 128, 64, 32, 16, 8, 4, or 2 colors in the color palette, or (b) entering a specific number of colors. Note that with every change to the color range or adjustment to the Optimize panel, the preview window updates with the file size. To ease comparison, Fireworks gives the option to view compression schemes with the 2-up and 4-up preview modes, viewing either two or four settings side by side.

Cross-Reference To see an illustration of how the various GIF color settings will affect color range in an image, refer to the samples printed in the color insert pages.

The trick to compression is finding a balance between appearance and file size. Too much compression, and the graphic looks like dirt, although the file size is ideal; too little compression and, while the graphic looks beautiful, the file size threatens to choke the fastest connections. So what can you do after trying to find that balance between image quality and file size, without success? What to do when the image quality can't go any lower, but the file size is still way too large? As mentioned earlier, there is a second factor to the file size of animated GIFs: the number of frames. When image optimization fails, change your focus from the Optimize panel to the Frames panel.

The Fireworks Frames panel is used to control several animation playback settings. These are

✦ The number of frames in the animation.

✦ The frame delay for each frame — should this frame hold for a second or two or just breeze right through as quickly as possible?

✦ The loop settings for the animation. Will the animation loop ten times, five times, never, or forever?

To further reduce the file size of an animated GIF, remove some frames. To remove a frame, simply select the frame in the Fireworks Frames panel, and then click the trashcan icon at the bottom of the panel.

Keep deleting frames, judiciously, and continuously preview the animation, until you've brought the animation down to the required file size. Throughout this process, the preview mode will update its display of the file size every time a change is made. Unfortunately, you will find that, as you delete frames from the animation, the animation will not play back as smoothly as originally designed and intended. But that's just a limitation of animated GIFs and a compelling reason to start creating pure Flash banner ads!

When the file's been brought down to an acceptable size, the next step is to edit the timing of each frame. Each frame in the Frames panel has a name on the left and a number on the right. The number signifies the delay length for each frame, measured in 100ths of a second. The default setting is 20 — or 20/100 of a second. So, to pause a frame for 3 seconds, set the frame delay to 300.

The last adjustment to set is the looping of the animation. At the bottom left of the Frames panel is a loop icon. Select it and choose a loop setting. Finally, it's time to export this file as an animated GIF and send it off to the Web. Use File ➪ Export Preview. In the

Export Preview window, select **Animated GIF** from the format pull-down menu. Now press the **Export** button to name the file and place it within the desired location. Click **Save** and you will be ready to go.

Alternative workflow

If an animation is created in Flash with few colors, there's no need to export it as a PNG sequence. Instead, export the animation directly from Flash as an animated GIF. Use the application menu to select File ⇨ Export Movie, then choose **Animated GIF** from the Format drop-down menu; or use the Publish Settings dialog box, and first select the **GIF** check box, and then from the GIF tab, choose **Animated.** In either case, use the largest possible color palette in order to defer color crunching to Fireworks, where the controls over the color palette are generally more accurate and effective.

The exported animated GIF is easily imported into Fireworks by choosing File ⇨ Open, and then selecting the single animated GIF file. Fireworks imports each frame with the frame delay settings intact. From here, the animation may be optimized per the previous instructions, proceeding from the color palette, to the number of frames and loop settings.

Preparing Images for Flash with Photoshop 7

Adobe Photoshop 7 is an exciting upgrade to this premiere image-editing program. When you're preparing bitmaps for use in Flash, Photoshop 7 adds some extremely useful and powerful Web features that make saving high-quality JPEGs and PNGs a snap. The PNG-24 format is a great format to use with Flash, because this file format has lossless compression and can support an alpha channel (a.k.a. *transparency mask*). In this section, we show you how to export a Photoshop image (.psd file) as a PNG-24 image to use in Flash.

Creating alpha channels for PNG files

Photoshop has excellent selection and masking tools for the most complex images. Although some third-party plug-ins can make the task a littler simpler, some basic know-how with Photoshop tools can also go a long way toward completing your task with ease. In the following tutorial, we take an image of some houses along the beach and mask the background sky. This lesson assumes that you have a working knowledge of Photoshop layers and layer masks.

Use the sample image beachhouses.psd in the ch37 folder of the *Flash MX Bible* CD-ROM for this section. The completed PSD and PNG versions of the masked image titled beachhouses_masked.psd and beachhouses_masked.png are also on the CD-ROM.

1. Open the beachhouses.psd file from the CD-ROM. If you receive a message about a color profile mismatch, choose **Don't Convert**. For more information about color profiles and Flash, see the "Color Management in Photoshop" sidebar in this section.

2. To more easily separate the color tones of the sky from the foreground, add a separate Levels adjustment layer for the image on Layer 0. Do *not* use the regular Levels command, which permanently applies its effect to the image. We only need a temporary Levels effect to increase the contrast (see Figure 37-11).

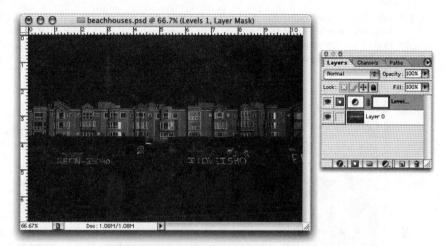

Figure 37-11: The image with a Levels adjustment layer

On the CD-ROM

You can achieve the correct level values in the Levels layer by loading the `separation.alv` file into the Levels dialog box, using the Load button when you first create the new Levels layer. This file is in the ch37 folder of the *Flash MX Bible* CD-ROM.

3. Select the Magic Wand tool in the Photoshop Tools palette. In the Magic Wand settings of the Option bar, enter **15** in the Tolerance field, and make sure **Anti-Aliased** and **Contiguous** are checked. Click the uppermost area of the now-darkened sky to select it. Shift+click additional areas with the Magic Wand tool until the entire sky is selected. If you grab anything in the foreground, either undo or start over (Select ➪ None). See Figure 37-12.

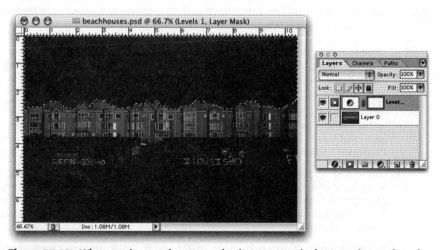

Figure 37-12: When you're creating your selection, pay particular attention to the edges of the rooftops.

4. With Layer 0 highlighted in the Layers window, Option+click (Mac) or Alt+click (Windows) the Add a mask icon at the bottom of the Layers window. This applies the current selection of the sky as a mask (see Figure 37-13). If the Add a mask icon was clicked without holding Alt or Option, then the foreground elements would have been masked instead.

Figure 37-13: Option+clicking (Mac) or Alt+clicking (Windows) the Add a mask icon uses the active selection as the black area of a layer mask.

5. Now that we have masked out the sky, we don't need the Levels effect anymore. Turn off the Levels adjustment layer, or delete it.

Caution   Make sure you double-check the layer mask by viewing it separately in the Channels window. If any faint gray lines appear along the top edges of the mask, paint over them with a black brush. If any gray appears in the black area of the mask, it shows up in the Flash movie as hints of the original image.

6. Before we save this image as a PNG-24 file, we should crop all unnecessary information from the image. In this example, the masked sky should be nearly eliminated. See Figure 37-14.

7. In Chapter 16, "Importing Artwork," the effects of larger-than-necessary bitmaps were discussed. Because the image width is currently larger than the default Flash movie width, we also use the Image ⇨ Image Size command to change the width from 755 pixels to 550 pixels. Be careful when using the Image Size command. For this example, the **Constrain Proportions** and **Resample Image: Bicubic** options should be checked.

8. We're ready to save the image as a PNG-24 file, using the Photoshop Save for Web command located in the File menu (Option+Shift+⌘+S or Ctrl+Shift+Alt+S.) After you've chosen this command, the image appears in Live Preview mode within the Save for Web dialog box (see Figure 37-15). Click the **2-Up** tab to view the original image with the optimized version.

In the Settings section, choose the PNG-24 preset. Make sure the **Transparency** option is checked—this exports the layer mask as an alpha channel in the PNG file. Do not use the Interlaced or Matte options for Flash import. Click **OK**; Photoshop will ask you to specify a location and filename for the PNG-24 image. **Images Only** should be chosen from the Format drop-down menu. You can leave the Settings option as **Default** and the Slices option as **All Slices**.

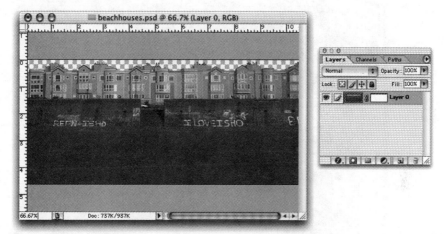

Figure 37-14: It's always a good idea to crop unnecessary information (especially if it's hidden by a mask) from the image before importing it into Flash.

Tip
The Save for Web dialog box has many other cool features. While the 4-Up preview is not necessary for PNG-24 files (there are no compression options to worry about), you can preview your original with three different JPEG or GIF versions, each at a different compression setting. You can use the Preview Menu to see the effect of 8-bit browser dither (by checking the Browser Dither option), and you can use color profiles using Photoshop Compensation or Uncompensated Color. For PNG-24 files, always use the Uncompensated Color preview, because it is the most accurate for Flash use. See the sidebar titled "Color Management in Photoshop" for more information on color compensation.

Note
You can also resize the optimized image in the Image Size tab, instead of performing this action as we did in Step 7.

9. We're ready to import the PNG file into Flash, which recognizes the alpha channel in the PNG-24 version of our image. Open a document in Flash (or create a new one), and choose File ➪ Import (⌘+R or Ctrl+R). Select the PNG image and Flash places the image on the current frame of the active layer. Remember that all bitmaps are stored in the Flash Library. If you delete the instance of the bitmap on the Stage, you can always replace it with the bitmap in the Library. That's it! You've successfully imported an image with an alpha channel into Flash (see Figure 37-16).

On the CD-ROM
Check out the finished sample Flash document, `alphabitmap.fla`, in the ch37 folder of the *Flash MX Bible* CD-ROM.

Cross-Reference
The various options for controlling Flash JPEG compression of imported bitmaps are discussed in Chapter 16, "Importing Artwork," and in Chapter 21, "Publishing Flash Movies."

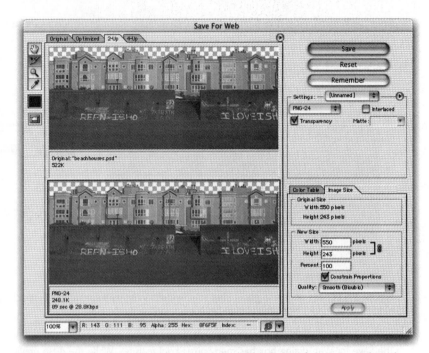

Figure 37-15: The Save for Web command enables fast Web image previews in Photoshop. You may need to resize this dialog box in order to display horizontal images on top of each other, as shown in this figure.

Figure 37-16: Using a bitmap with an alpha channel enables you to seamlessly place other elements behind the bitmap in a Flash movie.

Color Management in Photoshop

Many strategies exist for color calibration on desktop computer systems. Macintosh computers have had a leg up in this area of graphics creation and output ever since the development of ColorSync. Apple's ColorSync software provides one of the most complete system-level color management solutions for desktop publishing. Unfortunately, while Windows 98 and Windows ME do include ICC profile support, it's not as comprehensive as Apple's ColorSync system. Since the release of Photoshop 5.0, it has been possible to specify and attach ICC color profiles to most image file formats. In a nutshell, ICC profiles describe the color capabilities of a given input or output device, such as a computer monitor, printer, or scanner. When an ICC profile is attached to an image, the profile tells the application that is using the image how the colors in the image should be interpreted. If every program in your workflow supports ICC profiles, then, theoretically, this provides a consistent display and output of all graphics.

However, while Photoshop and most page-layout programs recognize ICC profiles, the majority of Web development applications do not. Some Web browsers do not support embedded image profiles, although Apple has proposed many ICC tags to make color management a reality for the Web (visit `www.apple.com/colorsync/benefits/web`). More importantly, Flash MX does not support ICC profiles. Neither does the current implementation of the PNG-24 format. The JPEG file format is the only current Web image format that supports embedded profiles. Moreover, ICC profiles typically add about 500 to 800 bytes to an image's file size.

This is why the Save for Web feature (introduced with Photoshop 6.0) and its Preview Menu are so invaluable. They enable you to see how the JPEG, GIF, or PNG looks without Photoshop Compensation.

If you work primarily with Web or screen graphics, then you should use Photoshop's new Color Settings presets (Photoshop 6 and Photoshop 7 only), to quickly switch color spaces. For Web work, always use Web Graphics Default. For ColorSync management on the Mac, choose ColorSync Workflow. On the PC, choose a setting that best matches your printing needs (ColorSync is an Apple-only management system).

In Photoshop 5.5, change your RGB working space to sRGB, or turn off Display Using Monitor Compensation if you continue to use other RGB spaces. Either method enables you to work with your images so that the Photoshop Compensation and Uncompensated Color settings render the image exactly the same within the Save for Web preview panes. Also, disable ICC profile embedding in the Profile Setup preferences (File ⇨ Color Settings ⇨ Profile Setup) by deselecting all the boxes under the Embed Profiles heading.

Exporting Raster Images from Flash

If you've been wondering how to use your artwork in Flash with other raster-based applications, then this section is for you. Many people prefer to use Flash as their primary drawing and illustration tool, thanks to Flash's uniquely intuitive set of vector drawing tools. Combined with a pressure-sensitive graphics tablet, Flash can indeed be a powerful illustration program.

Why would you want to export raster-based images from a vector-based application? The answer is quite simple: Some applications work better with raster (or bitmap) images than they do with vector images. Video-editing applications and other motion graphics programs intended for producing broadcast content usually prefer to work with bitmaps instead of vectors. If the application in which you want to use Flash artwork does support vector file formats such as EPS or AI, then you most likely want to use those instead of bitmap-based formats such as BMP or PCT.

Cross-Reference We discuss using external vector applications in Chapter 38, "Working with Vector Graphics." If you want the best quality vector artwork exported from Flash, jump to that chapter.

If you are unsure of the format to use in your graphics program, refer to Table 37-1. Afterward, we show you how to export a frame's artwork as a static raster image.

Table 37-1: Raster Image Formats for Flash Export

Flash Export Format	File Extension	Comments
BMP (Win only), Windows Bitmap	.bmp	Can be used with all Windows and some Mac applications. Variable bit depths and compression settings with support of alpha channels. Supports lossless compression. Ideal for high-quality graphics work.
CompuServe GIF, Graphics Interchange File	.gif	Limited to a 256-color (or less) palette .Not recommended as a high-quality Flash export format, even for Web use.
JPEG, Joint Photographic Experts Group	.jpg	Supports 24-bit RGB color. No alpha channel support. Recommended for most high-quality graphics work that will not need to be re-edited. Note that this format throws out color information due to its lossy compression method.
PICT (Mac only), Picture	.pct	Can be used with many Windows and all Mac applications. Variable bit depths and compression settings with support of alpha channels. Supports lossless compression. Can contain vector and raster graphics. Ideal for high-quality graphics work.
PNG, Portable Network Graphic	.png	Supports variable bit depth (PNG-8 and PNG-24) and compression settings with alpha channels. Lossless compression schemes make it an ideal candidate for any high-quality graphics work.

To export a raster image format from Flash MX:

1. Move the Playhead in the Flash timeline to the frame that contains the artwork that you wish to export.

2. Choose File ➪ Export Image.

3. Select a destination folder and enter a filename. Select your preferred raster image format in Format drop-down menu.

4. Depending on the file format you selected, you are presented with an export dialog box with options specific to that file format. We look at the general options and at some file-specific settings next.

General export options in raster formats

Every raster image format in Flash's Export Image dialog box has the same basic options. All of these pertain to the image size, resolution, and bit depth (or number of colors) for the exported image. You can also trim any unused stage area from the final exported image. As you will see in the next section, for each specific raster format there are other unique settings in addition to the main options described here.

✦ **Dimensions:** The Width and Height options control the image's width and height, respectively, in pixels. Note that the aspect ratio of these values is always locked. You cannot control the Width value independently of the Height value.

✦ **Resolution:** Measured in dpi (dots per inch), this setting controls the quality of the image in terms of how much information is present in the image. By default, this setting is 72 dpi. If you want to use Flash artwork in print or high-resolution graphics work, enter a higher value, such as 300 or 600. If you change this setting accidentally, pressing the Match Screen button reverts the value to 72 dpi, the resolution of most computer monitors. Note that changing the value for this setting also changes the Width and Height values in the Dimensions setting.

✦ **Include:** This drop-down menu determines what Flash content is included in the exported image.

• **Minimum Image Area:** When this option is selected, the image size (a.k.a. *dimensions*) is reduced to the boundary of Flash artwork currently on the Stage. This means that if you only have a circle in the middle of the Stage, then the dimensions of the exported image match those of the circle—the rest of the Flash Stage or background won't be included.

• **Full Document Size:** When this option is selected, the exported image looks exactly like the Flash stage. The entire frame dimensions and contents are exported.

✦ **Color Depth (or Colors):** This drop-down setting controls the color range of the raster image. The higher the bit depth, the wider the color range. Depending on the file format, not all options are identical. We define the most frequently occurring options here. This option is not available for the JPEG format, as that format must always be 24-bit. The options include

• **8-bit grayscale:** This option limits the image to 256 levels, or values, of gray. It is equivalent to a typical scan of a black-and-white photograph.

• **8-bit color:** This option reduces the image to 256 colors. You may notice unsightly dithering in the image as a result. See Chapter 21, "Publishing Flash Movies," for more information regarding dither.

• **24-bit color:** This option allows the image to include any of the 16.7 million colors available in true RGB color space. Use this option for the best color quality.

• **32-bit color w/ alpha:** This image enables the same range of colors as 24-bit color, but also adds an alpha channel using the Flash movie's background color as a matte. If your raster image program can read alpha channels, then the Flash background color is transparent.

Other raster file format options

Each specific file format Export dialog box will also have some additional export options. In this section, we look at the additional options available for BMP (Windows only), PCT or PICT (Mac only), and GIF. These options have not changed from the previous release of Flash. In fact, you may have more control with export file formats using the Export Image command than in the Publish Settings/Publish commands.

Cross-Reference

The JPEG, GIF, and PNG format options are discussed in Chapter 21, "Publishing Flash Movies." Because a problem exists with publishing adaptive GIFs in the Macintosh version of Flash, however, we explore the GIF export options here.

Export BMP (Windows only) options

The Windows Bitmap (.bmp) file format has numerous options. In addition to the general export settings (described previously), the BMP Export dialog box has an options setting containing a check box for Smooth. When this option is selected, Flash anti-aliases all Flash artwork, making the edges nice and smooth. If this option is unchecked, then Flash artwork is rendered in an aliased fashion, in which edges appear jagged and rough.

Caution

In most external graphics applications, the **32 bit w/ alpha** option in the Colors drop-down menu is not supported. You should use the 24-bit option if you experience difficulties using 32-bit BMP files. If you need to export an image with alpha channel support, use the PNG format in the Windows version of Flash.

Export PICT (Mac only) options

The PICT (short for Picture) format is a standard Macintosh graphic file format. Any Mac OS application that uses graphics can use it, and, with QuickTime, you can also use PICT (or PCT) files on Windows computers. PICT files can contain both vector and raster (bitmap) information. Usually, only raster-based .PICT files are truly cross-platform (see Figure 37-17).

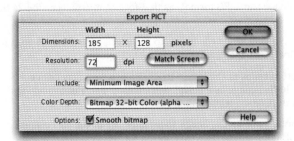

Figure 37-17: The PICT format has a unique Objects option (in the Color Depth drop-down menu) in addition to traditional raster-based options.

✦ **Color Depth:** This drop-down menu is the same as the Colors setting for other raster-image file formats. (It has a few peculiarities that are defined in the next section.)

- **Objects:** Because PICT files will support vector or raster information, you can specify Objects to export Flash artwork as vector-based images. Note that selecting this option enables you to select Use PostScript in the Options setting. Use PICT output that contains PostScript with caution, as it can produce undesirable results. If you need PostScript with your output, it is better to use Illustrator or EPS as the format.

- **Bitmap 1-bit B/W:** This option converts all colors to either black or white, with no intermediate values of gray. It is equivalent to the Bitmap image mode in Photoshop, and gives a fax document look to your Flash artwork.

- **Bitmap 8-bit Gray:** This option converts your Flash artwork colors to 256 values of gray.

- **Bitmap 8-bit Color:** This option creates an adaptive palette of 256 colors for the exported image.

- **Bitmap 24-bit Color:** This option produces the highest-quality raster-based PICT files, enabling any color in the RGB color space to be represented. This is usually the preferred color setting for images that will be used for graphics work in other applications.

- **Bitmap 32-bit Color (alpha channel):** This option has the same color depth as 24-bit color, with the addition of an alpha channel (or transparent mask). An unoccupied area of the Flash Stage is used to determine the transparent areas of the alpha channel.

✦ **Options:** The PICT Export dialog box displays only one other option. The options that are displayed vary depending on the Color Depth setting.

- **Smooth bitmap:** If you chose any of the Bitmap color options in Color Depth, then you have the option of anti-aliasing (or smoothing) Flash artwork. Smoothing produces cleaner edges on Flash vector-based artwork.

- **Include PostScript:** If you choose Objects from the Color Depth menu, then you can enable the Include PostScript option. This option optimizes the file's settings for output to a PostScript-compatible printer.

Export GIF options

The majority of the options listed in the Colors section of the GIF Export dialog box are discussed in the "Using the GIF settings" section in Chapter 21, "Publishing Flash Movies." The Colors drop-down menu is slightly different, however. Also, as mentioned in a previous note, the Publish settings in the Macintosh version of Flash MX do not create adaptive GIF images (even if you have selected the option to do so). You can, however, create suitable GIF images in both Windows and Macintosh versions of Flash using the Export Image command. See Figure 37-18.

On the CD-ROM

You can see the effect of each of these color options by looking at a series of GIF images created from a test Flash movie, gifcolors.fla, located in the ch37 folder of the *Flash MX Bible* CD-ROM. Each GIF color depth setting was applied to this movie, and saved as a separate GIF image. These images are also printed for your reference in the color insert pages of the book.

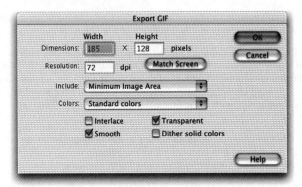

Figure 37-18: Export Options that are specific to the
GIF format.

✦ **Colors:** As stated in the discussion regarding general options, this setting controls the
range of colors contained in the exported image. GIF images can use a variety of bit
depths with the overall 8-bit color depth setting. The fewer colors, the smaller the
resulting GIF file.

- **Black & White:** This option is equivalent to a 2-bit color depth, and converts all
  Flash colors to one of three colors (Web hex in parentheses): black (#000000),
  middle gray (#808080), or white (#FFFFFF).

- **4, 8, 16, 32, 64, 128, or 256 colors:** These options create the respective color
  ranges within the GIF format. Flash determines which colors are used for each
  setting, similar to the adaptive palette type in Photoshop.

- **Standard Colors:** This option creates GIF images that use the 216 Web-Safe
  palette.

Using Raster Animation Tools

Although the main appeal of Flash is the sleekness of vector-based animation, there are occasions when you might want to try something a little different. Whether you choose to start
your animation in a raster program because you are more comfortable in the authoring environment or because you simply like the look of the artwork, you can easily integrate your
raster artwork with Flash projects. There are an increasing number of programs that natively
support export to the .swf format. However, the workflow described earlier in this chapter for
optimizing a bitmap sequence for Flash can be used to integrate raster image sequences from
any program that may not support direct export to the .swf format.

Painter 7 from Corel is one popular tool for creating organic raster artwork for use in Flash
animation. Arena Reed describes her process for recording a painting and then creating a
frame-by-frame sequence that animates her illustrations.

**On the
CD-ROM**

Arena Reed's tutorial, "Combining Flash with the Natural Beauty of Painter 7," is in the
Bonus_Tutorials folder on the *Flash MX Bible* CD-ROM. To see an example of the artwork she
will show you how to create in the tutorial, refer to the printed color insert pages.

Summary

✦ Flash MX is a vector artwork tool that does not support creation of bitmap images from scratch. You need to use an image-editing application such as Macromedia Fireworks to create, modify, and optimize bitmap images for Flash.

✦ Fireworks MX and Flash MX share a common user interface, making it simpler for Flash users to learn the tools in Fireworks. In addition to a consistent interface, Fireworks MX offers several powerful new features that make it easy to develop a streamlined workflow. By taking advantage of the strongest features of different programs, you can save time and enhance your Flash designs.

✦ Flash MX supports the direct import of Fireworks MX PNG files. This format allows you to preserve bitmap graphics, vector artwork, and editable text without having to change authoring modes or to export individual files.

✦ Either Macromedia Fireworks or Adobe Photoshop can be used to create a PNG-24 image with an alpha channel. Flash renders the black area of an alpha channel transparent (or semi-transparent) on the Flash Stage, which allows other elements in a Flash movie to show through the foreground bitmap.

✦ Flash MX can export a variety of raster image file formats, which enables you to transfer your Flash artwork to other graphics programs. You can specify the exported image's quality and size in the Export Image dialog box.

✦   ✦   ✦

Working with Vector Graphics

In This Chapter

Optimizing vector graphics for use in Flash projects

Converting rasters to vectors using Adobe Streamline and Macromedia FreeHand

Using Illustrator and FreeHand to create artwork for Flash projects

Adobe's Flash Writer plug-in for legacy versions of Illustrator

Planning Flash projects with FreeHand

Exporting vector graphics from Flash

As the Flash authoring environment has matured, more designers have realized that much (if not all) of their design and artwork for Web projects can easily be created directly in Flash. On the other hand, more designers have begun to integrate Flash as part of a streamlined production process to deliver consistent design to clients who have a presence in print and broadcast as well as on the Web.

Even if your designs are only going to be used on the Web, adding a few other programs to your toolkit allows you to take advantage of specialized features that can enhance your Flash projects and save production time.

Flash MX offers more options than ever for integrating preexisting artwork created in other authoring programs. With a few simple steps, the process of importing or exporting vector artwork between Flash MX and other professional graphics programs can be seamless. This chapter discusses some of the most common workflow options and gives you the background you need to keep artwork and page layouts consistent when moving from one program to another.

Optimizing Vector Graphics for Use in Flash

Macromedia FreeHand and Adobe Illustrator are two of the most commonly used vector programs, but there are many other programs that also offer tools or techniques that can add a special touch to your Flash designs. The best effects are often complex, and a detailed description of specific techniques in other programs is beyond the scope of this book. However, with an understanding of how Flash interprets imported vector files, you will be able to apply the information in this chapter to optimize your workflow, regardless of what specific programs you choose to work in.

Cross-Reference For coverage of how imported vector files can be modified in the Flash authoring environment, refer to Chapter 16, "Importing Artwork."

Converting text to outlines

Many of the designs you import from other programs may only consist of vector shapes, but there are usually times when you also need to handle text. An important aspect of vector graphics that you need to keep in mind — especially when working with other designers — is font linking and embedding. With most vector file formats, such as Illustrator, FreeHand, or EPS, you can link to fonts that are located on your system. However, if you give those files to someone else who doesn't have the same fonts installed, then he (or she) won't be able to work with or view your file as it was originally designed. Some formats (such as PDF) enable you to embed fonts into the document file, which circumvents this problem. However, whether the fonts are linked or embedded, you may be unnecessarily bloating the size of the vector graphic by including all of the font information.

You can convert any text into outlines (a.k.a. *paths*) in most drawing or illustration programs. In FreeHand 10, select the text as a text block (with the Arrow tool, not the Text tool) and choose Text ➪ Convert to Paths. In Illustrator 10, select the text as an object and choose Type ➪ Create Outlines.

Converting text to outlines is also discussed in more detail in Chapter 16, "Importing Artwork."

When importing files from FreeHand to Flash directly, any text with special formatting is automatically converted to outlines. If you use the FreeHand SWF export feature and then import the SWF into Flash, the text will be preserved as editable text, although it will be broken into smaller blocks to maintain the original FreeHand layout. For more detail on converting artwork from FreeHand to Flash, refer to the FreeHand section, later in this chapter.

If you have a lot of body text in the graphic, you may want to copy the text directly into a Flash text box and use a *sans, serif,* or *typewriter* device font. These fonts do not require any additional file information (unlike embedded fonts) when used in a Flash movie.

For more detailed information on optimizing and managing fonts in Flash projects, please refer to Chapter 8, "Working with Text."

Controlling color output

Flash can only use an RGB color space, meaning that it renders colors in an additive fashion — full red, green, and blue light added together produce white light. Whenever possible, you should use RGB color pickers in your preferred drawing application. If you use CMYK, then you will notice color shifts when the artwork is imported into Flash. If you're using FreeHand or Illustrator, be sure that you specify colors with the RGB color picker; so that both copied-and-pasted objects and exported files will appear as you see them in the original workspace. If you're using Macromedia FreeHand 9 or 10, then you have a wider range of clipboard options.

For more coverage of color issues related to Flash production, please refer to Chapter 7, "Applying Color."

Saving in the proper file format

Some vector file formats cannot save artwork color values in RGB space. If you're using Adobe Illustrator 8 or higher, be sure to specify Illustrator 7 in the Illustrator document options when saving. If you choose the Illustrator 6 or lower format, then RGB values will not be saved, and color shifts will result. If you're exporting EPS files from FreeHand 8, use the Setup (Win) or Options (Mac) button in the Export Document dialog box to access the same color options available in the FreeHand Preferences for more recent versions of FreeHand, (discussed later in this chapter). Because FreeHand 9 and 10 support export to SWF files, you should use this route, or direct import (instead of EPS files), to insure complete color compatibility with Flash. The various methods for importing FreeHand files into Flash are further discussed in the section on "Enhancing Flash Production with Macromedia FreeHand," later in this chapter.

For detailed discussion of some of the issues related to rendering imported artwork in Flash, refer to Chapter 16, "Importing Artwork."

Tracing to convert rasters to vectors

A handful of applications, including Flash MX, lets you trace raster artwork. In the following sections, we compare the tracing capabilities of Macromedia FreeHand, and Adobe Streamline.

For coverage of the Flash MX program's native Trace Bitmap command, refer to Chapter 16, "Importing Artwork."

With any tracing application, keep these points in mind:

✦ Higher resolution images always yield better "traced" vector artwork. With more pixels to define edges, the application can better detect shapes.

✦ Sharper images (such as clearly focused images) and higher contrast images produce better traced artwork. Applying Photoshop art filters to reduce the complexity of a photographic image can make it easier to trace.

✦ One-color images or scans, like those of hand-drawn sketches with pencil or ink, produce the best traced results.

Ironically, the results of some traced raster images can produce even larger vector images. Remember that vectors were designed for solid colors, limited blends, lines, and points. Every file format has its purpose, and sometimes raster images are smaller than their traced counterparts. With a little practice, you'll be able to judge what kind of images will produce small traced versions.

FreeHand's Trace tool

The Trace tool in Macromedia FreeHand works like a magic wand, allowing you to selectively trace areas of a bitmap based on color. You can access the Trace tool in the FreeHand toolbox; double-clicking the icon invokes the Trace tool settings dialog box. The FreeHand Trace tool offers numerous settings that control how imported bitmapped artwork will be modified (as shown in Figure 38-1).

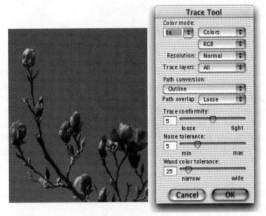

Figure 38-1: The FreeHand Trace tool offers an array of options for precise tracing.

When you're ready to trace the bitmap, you can do the trace in one of two ways: (a) selectively trace bitmap image areas or (b) trace the entire bitmap. To use the first method, click the desired area with the Trace tool wand. Once a selection is made, click inside the selection. FreeHand shows you the Wand options dialog box (as shown in Figure 38-2), and you can choose whether you want to trace everything inside the selection (Trace Selection) or just the edge of the selection (Convert Selection Edge). Click OK after you have chosen an option, and FreeHand traces the specified area. To use the second method of tracing, simply click-drag a marquee selection with the Trace tool active, and FreeHand traces everything in the selection area.

Figure 38-2: When you have selected an area with the Trace tool wand, the Wand Options dialog box lets you choose how the selection will be traced.

Tip   Use the Magic Wand method if you want to extract a traced image from a bitmap that contains multiple elements or an irregular shape. For example, if you have a picture of many people and you want to trace just one of them, the Magic Wand can help you isolate that one person. If you want to trace all the people as well as the background, trace the entire image using the method described previously.

Because the nature of bitmapped artwork varies by subject matter, finding the optimal settings for the FreeHand Trace tool may require a bit of trial and error. If the results are not satisfactory, then simply undo the trace and try a different setting.

FreeHand retains the original bitmapped artwork behind the traced vector artwork; to see the traced image, select it and move it to a new position on the page (as shown in Figure 38-3). If you no longer need the bitmapped version, delete the bitmap image after you have moved the traced objects to a new location. Group the traced objects for greater ease in moving them.

Figure 38-3: FreeHand preserves the original bitmap (left) beneath the traced graphic (right).

When you import a traced vector image into Flash directly from FreeHand (.fh 10), the file is brought in as multiple grouped shapes. To make it easier to edit the graphic as a single element, ungroup the imported items until you are able to select the graphic as a unified shape (see Figure 38-4).

FreeHand traced bitmap > Ungrouped in Flash

Figure 38-4: Traced vector graphics imported from FreeHand should be ungrouped in Flash, so that they can be edited as a unified shape.

Tracing with Adobe Streamline

Although you can trace images in Adobe Illustrator, Adobe has a stand-alone product that is specifically designed for tracing raster artwork—Streamline 4.0. With Streamline, you have the most extensive conversion options, and more importantly, you can optimize the results with smoothing commands. See Figure 38-5 for one example of the detailed conversion presets available in Streamline 4.0.

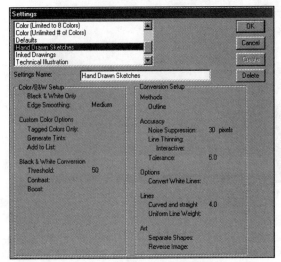

Figure 38-5: Streamline 4.0 includes a wide range of presets in the Settings dialog box.

After you have converted a bitmap image to vector artwork, you have the option of smoothing the results. *Smoothing* means eliminating redundant or excess points to create simpler shapes and curves. By reducing the complexity of points in vector artwork, you can reduce the overall file size dramatically.

In the Edit menu, you can access two types of smoothing: Smooth Paths and Smooth Direction Points. Smooth Paths eliminates anchor points within selected paths, and Smooth Direction Points changes hard-edged corners into rounded edges. Each command has a Minimum, Normal, and Maximum setting. For more exact information on these settings, refer to the Adobe online help for Streamline.

Caution   Be extremely careful of *oversmoothing*. While we all would like smaller file sizes, smoothing can have an adverse affect on image quality.

Reducing vector complexity

Although Flash MX provides robust tools for modifying the complexity of vector artwork, if you're creating artwork in other applications, you have some options for streamlining the artwork before bringing it into your Flash project.

For coverage of the Flash MX native tools for modifying artwork, refer to Chapter 9, "Modifying Graphics," and Chapter 16, "Importing Artwork."

Using the Pathfinder panel in Illustrator

You can use the Pathfinder panel (View ➪ Pathfinder) in Illustrator to control how overlapping paths are combined. Not only does this reduce the complexity of the path, but it also makes the graphic easier to edit or move. The Pathfinder panel offers several different options for combining overlapping paths, including merging or cropping specific sections to create custom shapes.

To apply the Pathfinder options, select the overlapping paths by Shift+clicking each object (or by dragging a selection box around all of the elements you want to modify). In the Pathfinder panel, select an option to combine the overlapping elements and create a single path shape. In Figure 38-6, the Merge option is used to combine the individual circle outlines (left) into one unified path (right) that describes the polygon.

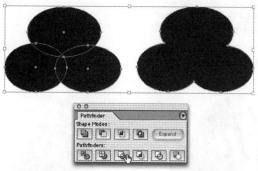

Figure 38-6: The Pathfinder panel in Illustrator offers a variety of options for simplifying overlapping paths.

Simplify paths in FreeHand

Complex artwork can be simplified in FreeHand. *Simplifying* reduces the number of points to describe a path (or a set of paths). To simplify any artwork, select the paths that describe the object and choose Modify ➪ Alter Path (or Xtras ➪ Cleanup). The Simplify option in either menu will invoke the Simplify dialog box that allows you to choose a level of smoothing to be applied to the graphic (as shown in Figure 38-7). As in Flash, simplifying a vector graphic in FreeHand reduces the number of the points that define the lines and curves to make the file smaller and easier to edit. FreeHand has ten different simplification levels, but it doesn't have a multipass option like Flash's native Optimize command.

As shown in Figure 38-8, the visual differences between the various levels of Simplify in FreeHand are not as drastic as the differences between levels of Optimize in Flash, but they can make a difference in the final size of your FreeHand file.

Figure 38-7: The Simplify dialog box for setting the level of cleanup to apply to a vector graphic in FreeHand

a) Original artwork   b) Simplify "5"   c) Simplify "8"

Figure 38-8: Compare the effects of the Simplify command at different settings.

If you are importing your artwork to Flash in FreeHand (.fh 10) format (or by copying and pasting), the file size saving achieved by simplifying the artwork in FreeHand will translate into smaller Flash movie (SWF) sizes. However, if you are exporting your artwork from FreeHand directly to SWF format, the various Simplify settings are less important to the size of your SWF files than the Path Compression settings chosen in the Export process. This setting controls the file size of artwork exported in SWF format from FreeHand and is found in the Movie Settings dialog box (accessed from the Setup button in the Export dialog box). The process for exporting SWF files directly from FreeHand is described later in this chapter.

Choosing the most effective workflow

With all of the software and tool options available to you, it can be difficult to keep track of all the variables. The most important thing to decide is how you want your final artwork to look. For example, if you want a minimal silhouetted vector look, then it may actually be better to create a clipping path from the bitmap and fill it with solid color manually than to use an auto-trace tool. On the other hand, if you are trying to maintain detail in an image and your goal is simply to reduce your file size, it may be best to import an optimized bitmap directly into Flash (where you can then apply the Break Apart command and erase any unnecessary parts of the image).

The two traps that you want to avoid in production are unnecessary file size and needless quality loss. There are certainly times when you will have to compromise on image size or resolution in order to keep your Flash movies streamlined, but don't make the mistake of assuming that the worse the image looks, the smaller your file will be — this is not always the case.

Figure 38-9 compares the same bitmap image in a series of different workflow options. As you can quickly see, the differences in file size do not always have the same relationship to image quality as you might expect.

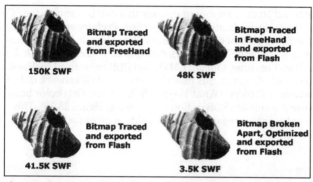

Figure 38-9: Even when the final image quality is similar, the file sizes that are achieved with different workflow options can vary widely.

In our production testing overall, Flash MX proves to be the first choice for achieving high image quality and small file sizes. The lesson we've learned is that unless we need a special effect that can't be created directly in Flash, it's best to import high-quality images (scaled appropriately for the movie size) directly to Flash and use the native Flash MX authoring tools to modify the image if needed.

Enhancing Flash Production with Macromedia FreeHand

Macromedia's print and design application, FreeHand 10, adds many features that make integration with Flash MX intuitive and hassle-free. Actually, as you'll see, Flash MX does most of the work by natively supporting FreeHand files as a direct import file type. If you're not familiar with FreeHand, take a look at the features that it offers:

✦ Blending effects that automatically produce intermediate steps between two pieces of artwork

✦ Powerful text tools for creating custom layouts — including curved paths, runarounds, and columns

✦ Spell-checking and Search and Replace capability for text and graphic elements

✦ A Perspective Grid that believably distorts the scale of artwork

✦ Color Mixer for creating subtle blends and complex gradients

✦ Trace tool and Cleanup tools for optimizing vector artwork

✦ Native SWF export

✦ Preview Flash files with anti-aliased display mode

✦ Transferable symbols and simple navigation that translate to Flash MX

✦ Release to Layers feature that exports drawings to Flash as animated frames

Setting up preferences in FreeHand

Both Macromedia FreeHand 9 and 10 offer clipboard options that can be customized. These settings are accessible from the main application menu via File ➪ Preferences. In the Windows version of FreeHand, click the Export tab of the Preferences dialog box. In the Mac version of FreeHand, click the Export Category of the Preferences dialog box. There, you find a Convert Colors To drop-down menu. If you're using a mix of CMYK and RGB color in a FreeHand document, then choose CMYK and RGB. However, this may still render CMYK artwork differently when imported to Flash. To have WYSIWYG (What You See Is What You Get) color between FreeHand and Flash, opt to use the solitary RGB option (as shown in Figure 38-10). This option converts all artwork to RGB color space, regardless of the original color picker used to fill the object(s).

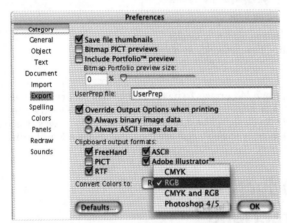

Figure 38-10: Setting the Convert Colors to preference in FreeHand to RGB will ensure color consistency when creating artwork for use in Flash.

FreeHand allows you to create more-complex gradients and blends than Flash, but when these elements are imported to Flash, they will be interpreted as graphic symbols with masks and clipping paths (see Figure 38-11). Although the visual translation of your custom gradient is fairly seamless, the graphic elements are difficult to edit after they have been converted to Flash, and you should be mindful of the effect they can have on your final SWF size. A raster version of the same gradient may produce smoother blends and smaller file sizes.

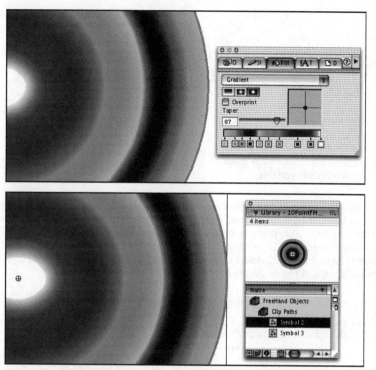

Figure 38-11: A ten-point gradient created in FreeHand (top) is interpreted by Flash as two separate graphic symbols with masking and complex clipping paths (bottom).

Cross-Reference
The process for replacing blends with editable Flash gradients is covered in Chapter 16, "Importing Artwork."

Creating custom type layouts in FreeHand

The FreeHand text-handling features alone can make this program an invaluable addition to your design tool kit. The tools and options available in FreeHand for controlling text will be familiar to designers who have worked in Quark, Adobe InDesign, or other professional page layout programs. Aside from precise settings for kerning and line spacing, FreeHand offers tools that make it easy to create custom text block shapes, curved type, runarounds, and multicolumn spreads.

Curved paths

If you've ever spent time manually placing individual text characters along a curved guide in Flash, you will appreciate how painless custom type paths are in FreeHand. Figure 38-12 shows type aligned on a curved path and the FreeHand Text toolbar with multiple options for creating type paths.

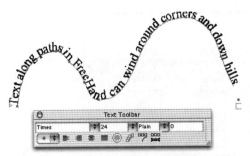

Figure 38-12: FreeHand text paths are quick to make and almost infinitely variable.

There are two ways of bringing a text path created in FreeHand into your Flash document. The specific steps for moving artwork from FreeHand to Flash are discussed in the next section, but the way that Flash interprets text paths will depend on the complexity of the path and how it is saved in FreeHand. If you import a FreeHand file (.fh10) directly into Flash MX, Flash will convert the text into individual outlines (shapes) to preserve the custom layout of the characters (as shown in Figure 38-13).

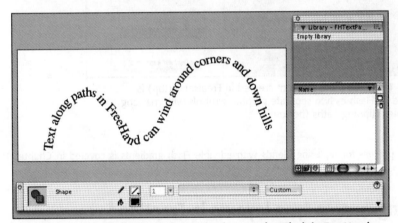

Figure 38-13: Text with custom formatting imported to Flash in FreeHand format (.fh 10) is converted automatically to individual outlines to preserve the design.

If you export a SWF file from FreeHand, the text will be converted to outlines, but the character shapes will be translated into graphic symbols so that your file is optimized. When you import the SWF into the Flash authoring environment (FLA), the symbols are loaded into the Library, and the type layout is preserved on the Stage (see Figure 38-14).

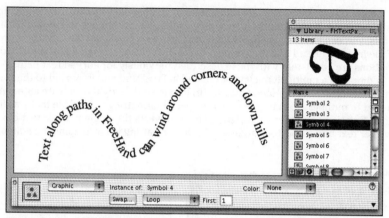

Figure 38-14: SWF files exported from FreeHand will optimize custom text as graphic symbols that are preserved when imported to the Flash authoring environment (FLA).

The FreeHand Text inspector

The FreeHand Text inspector is the central control for most of the text effects that you can create. As shown in Figure 38-15, this compact panel displays the options and settings relevant to five different kinds of text adjustment that you can select to work with. If the inspector is not available when you open a document in FreeHand, you can invoke it using the shortcut keys, Ctrl+T or ⌘+T, or find it in the application menu by selecting Window ➪ Inspectors ➪ Text.

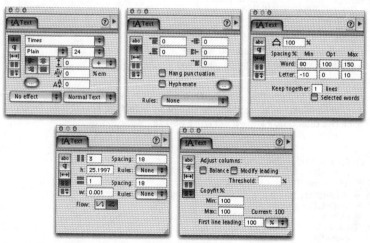

Figure 38-15: The Text inspector has five different display states for controlling different features of your text layout.

Two of the standard text effects that are difficult to create manually in Flash are multicolumn layouts and runarounds (or custom text wrapping). After you design text in FreeHand using these controls, you can either bring the layout into Flash as a FreeHand file (.fh 10) or export it as a SWF file from FreeHand and then import the SWF to Flash. The results of these two workflow options are consistent with those described previously for curved text paths. Figure 38-16 compares a multicolumn layout created in FreeHand and imported to the Flash MX authoring environment. FreeHand files (.fh 10) imported directly to Flash are automatically converted to outlines (top) to preserve the special formatting. A SWF file that was first exported from FreeHand and then imported to Flash converts the original single text box into multiple smaller text boxes (bottom) to preserve the formatting while keeping the editable text intact.

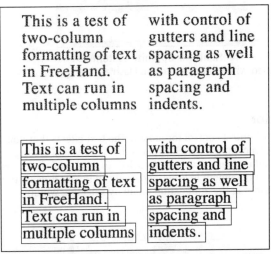

Figure 38-16: Multicolumn text created in FreeHand and imported to Flash MX will be interpreted as outlines (top) or as multiple editable text fields (bottom).

Fitting text blocks around images can be tedious to do manually in Flash. In FreeHand, you can precisely control how text wraps around an image by selecting Text ⇨ Run Around Selection to invoke the dialog box shown in Figure 38-17.

Figure 38-17: The Run Around Selection settings in FreeHand allow you to control how text wraps around other elements in your layout.

Whether you import the FreeHand file into Flash directly or export the file as a SWF from FreeHand, the bitmap will be included in your layout, and the text formatting will be preserved, as described previously for other FreeHand text treatments.

Moving artwork from FreeHand to Flash

Macromedia has invested a lot of development time in its quest to create a seamless workflow between FreeHand and Flash — and it shows! The result is that it's much easier and more efficient to use these applications together. The best example of this workflow is the ease of copy and paste and drag and drop between FreeHand and Flash. (These processes have worked seamlessly since FreeHand 9 and Flash 5.) You have a total of four ways to get your artwork from FreeHand to Flash: the SWF export feature from FreeHand, copy and paste, drag and drop, or opening the FreeHand files directly in Flash (Flash 5 and Flash MX only).

Opening FreeHand files directly into Flash MX

With the continuity between FreeHand and Flash available in the more recent versions, Flash development and concept design started in FreeHand is even more easily integrated with your final project. FreeHand 9 introduced symbols, which function much like Graphic symbols in Flash. Consequently, symbols that are created in FreeHand 9 or 10 will be maintained — along with their layers and guides — when the FreeHand file is opened in Flash. Let's take a look at the basic steps for importing a FreeHand file into Flash MX.

1. Open a new Flash file and set the movie size to match the page size of the FreeHand file that you will be importing.

2. Use File ⇨ Import to select your FreeHand 10 file.

3. A dialog box appears with a number of options specific to FreeHand import (see Figure 38-18) that control how you want your file translated. Select the desired options and click OK.

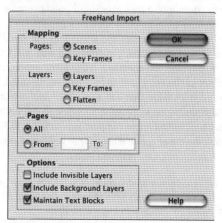

Figure 38-18: The Flash MX FreeHand Import dialog box

4. Some text or vector artwork may be translated from FreeHand to Flash as grouped elements. To edit individual shapes or text characters, simply ungroup the items in Flash until they can be isolated.

5. Now that you have your FreeHand artwork in Flash (intact and organized just as it was in FreeHand), you are ready to develop your Flash project.

Caution   If you plan to open your FreeHand files directly in Flash, be aware of the following issues while working in FreeHand: Use symbols in FreeHand to start the optimization process. Only use Type 1 PostScript fonts. You may have problems with TrueType Fonts. Only use image formats supported by Flash—JPG, PICT, BMP, and PNG.

Using FreeHand SWF export for layouts

Opening FreeHand files directly into Flash MX is very convenient because it retains a good deal of structure, including layers and guides. However, the FreeHand SWF Export feature is also an excellent method for translating FreeHand files into Flash movies, because it not only creates the most optimized result, it also does much of the tedious work for you. For example, exporting a SWF from FreeHand will automatically convert any custom text into smaller text blocks or into Graphic symbols to preserve the layout while optimizing the file and keeping editable text intact wherever possible.

Tip   If you prefer to manually select the typography elements in your layout and convert them to paths, simply select the text blocks that you want to change and apply the Text ⇨ Convert to Paths command.

Before you export a FreeHand document as a Flash file, you need to prepare the FreeHand artwork for optimal export. In the FreeHand file, select all the objects on a page that you want to export and *align the upper-left-hand extents of objects with the upper-left-hand extents of the page*. If you only need to export a few elements from a detailed FreeHand layout, it is best to select and copy those elements and paste them into a new FreeHand page before exporting.

Caution   When you export a SWF, the file will be sized to center the artwork in the middle of the movie. If you've been working on a vertical page layout in FreeHand with a lot of empty space above and below your artwork, the SWF will contain a lot of blank space too. If you align your artwork in the top-left corner of the FreeHand page, then the exported SWF will not have extra empty space. Alignment is an issue that will also affect your artwork when importing FreeHand files into the Flash authoring environment. Although the empty white space of the FreeHand page will not be visible when you import your artwork to Flash, you may find your artwork placed far below the Stage area because Flash will "read" and include the space that was above the artwork in the original FreeHand layout.

You can access the SWF Export feature by choosing File ⇨ Export (Ctrl+Shift+R or ⌘+Shift+R) and selecting Flash SWF (Windows) or Macromedia Flash SWF (Mac) in the Save as Type (Windows) or Format (Mac) drop-down menu (as shown in Figure 38-19).

Click the Setup button to access the Movie Settings used to convert the FreeHand file into a Flash SWF, as shown in Figure 38-19.

Note that, in FreeHand 10, you can now choose Flash 2, 3, 4, or 5 as the SWF version format, any of which is perfectly fine for Flash MX artwork. The Flash MX SWF format has not changed any artwork specifications that were used in earlier versions.

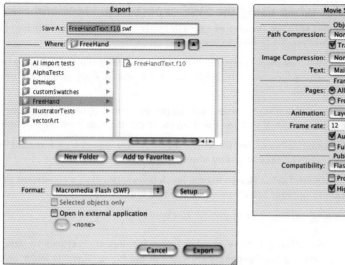

Figure 38-19: The Export dialog box (left) allows you to access the Movie Settings (right) with the Setup button.

To preserve editable text wherever possible, export with the Maintain Blocks option enabled in the Movie Settings dialog box. Text with custom FreeHand effects (such as columns, runarounds, or paths) will automatically be converted to smaller text blocks, individual characters, or letter-shape symbols as needed to preserve the layout in Flash. If you do *not* need to edit your text in Flash, set the text option of the SWF Export dialog to Convert to Paths. This converts all the text to paths and creates symbols of each character in the process.

Caution

FreeHand 10 automates text conversion when you export to the SWF format. It will automatically break apart text blocks that have custom alignment or spacing added and render them in the SWF as individual text blocks that still contain editable text. If you import files with special text formatting directly to Flash in FreeHand format (.fh 10), Flash converts the text to outlines to preserve the layout.

Because you are exporting a static layout, select None in the Animation drop-down menu. Because this export is a transition from FreeHand to Flash and *not* a final file, you will want to eliminate any file degradation by setting the Path Compression and Image Compression drop-down menus to None also. Click OK to close the Movie Settings dialog box and then choose Export from the Export dialog box. You will now have a Flash SWF that can be imported into your Flash document (FLA.).

Once in Flash, you will want to go through a process of organizing your file and optimizing the imported artwork. The objects exported from FreeHand come into Flash as a group — often, objects are in nested groups. You need to move key elements to separate Flash layers. As you do this, ungroup the objects and create logically named Flash symbols out of them. After the scene is organized with the objects regrouped and named as symbols and arranged on their own layers, you're ready to animate.

General guidelines when using the SWF export from FreeHand

After you become familiar with the process of exporting artwork to Flash, you'll discover that it's relatively simple. However, it's helpful to keep some guidelines in mind:

✦ When exporting SWF files from FreeHand, do not include large amounts of body text with custom formatting. Re-create the body text (for example, copy and paste the text into a text box) in Flash.

✦ Remember that elements from FreeHand will be put into groups, often stacked or nested within other groups. If you can't edit an element, ungroup it or break it apart.

✦ Any symbols automatically created by FreeHand when you export a SWF should be renamed in your Flash Library after you import the file.

✦ Organize your FreeHand artwork into logical Flash layers. Develop a consistent system that you and others on your team can recognize and implement.

✦ You must be using FreeHand 8.01 or greater to export Flash SWF files.

If you are interested in learning more about the new features of FreeHand 10, refer to Bentley Wolfe's tutorial, "Using Freehand with Flash" in the Bonus_Tutorials folder on the CD-ROM.

Streamlined Workflow: FreeHand and Flash, by *Todd Purgason*

Todd originally developed this tutorial for the Flash 5 Bible, *but the Juxt workflow translates seamlessly to Flash MX; and his insight on optimizing Web and print production is invaluable, so we have included it in this edition.*

Flash is a powerful tool for developing intelligent, sophisticated Web sites and interactive environments. But as most of us in the digital design arena know, no single tool does it all. We've all mastered many applications that enable us to design and produce the images and interfaces that are imagined in our mind's eye. The old cliché, "the right tool for the job," holds just as true in the digital arena as it does in your grandpappy's garage. By adding FreeHand to your Flash toolbox, you go from having four drawers of specialized tools to having eight drawers of specialized tools. FreeHand is a proven illustration and typography tool that brings more than ten years of research, design, and refinement to all your Flash projects. By tapping the strengths of FreeHand, your Flash applications can be that much more effective.

What advantages can FreeHand give to Flash projects?

For starters, familiarity: For some designers, Flash is a new tool with a new paradigm for creating vector-graphic artwork. Many of us have become quite proficient with programs, such as FreeHand and Illustrator, and setting these skills aside would be a terrible waste. But FreeHand brings much more than familiarity to the table. It has very powerful tools for illustration and — my personal favorite — typography.

A huge benefit of using FreeHand in the Flash design process is conceptualizing a design. By using the FreeHand multipage format, you can lay out moments in time or keyframes to visualize and study the interface and motion graphics that you will be executing in Flash. This is a big advantage of using FreeHand, instead of Illustrator, for your conceptualizing needs: Illustrator is limited to one-page documents. In addition, Macromedia has spent a great deal of time and effort on features, such as the Animate to Layer tool and SWF export in FreeHand, which enable FreeHand to live symbiotically in the same design space as Flash. Flash MX brings this synthesis to completion by allowing direct import of FreeHand files. You can preserve layers, guides, text, and even symbols that you have created in FreeHand when you import directly to Flash MX.

I think that the greatest asset that FreeHand brings to the Flash table is *print*. Ooooo . . . that nasty word: the old medium of print. Don't we live in the paperless society yet? Not quite. While developing your design in FreeHand, you're actually doing production and composition at the same time. After you have visualized an animation over several pages in FreeHand, it's a very simple task to bring those pages together onto a large format presentation board that you can output to a printer. These presentations blow the clients away! After you get approval, it's on to Flash, where you breathe life into the design that you've been carefully planning in FreeHand. If your clients are like mine, they'll come back and want you to do print promotions, ads, and even identity materials based on the Web site. You already have all the print assets developed in your page compositions. What a bonus! I just hate getting more billable work, don't you?

Developing a process model

Because the complexity of this process would require several chapters, I walk you through the key steps, using visuals from one of my recent projects, an in-house marketing project titled "The Process." It's a reflection of our creative philosophy at Juxt Interactive. Visit this project at www.juxinteractive.com/theprocess.

Design planning

Many Flash projects are orchestrated over one or more layouts that are called *scenes*. The term *scene* is appropriate because, oftentimes, they are just that — scenes in a Flash movie. After I've developed a concept in my head and scribbled sketches on paper, I go to FreeHand and start sketching out scenes. Figure 38-20 is an example of a scene.

Next, I start building moments in time — or keyframes — which bring elements (characters) into the scene to be laid out and experimented with. I typically start by developing a moment in time that is very heavy visually — often the end of the first major scene. Once I am happy with the scene and the way the elements or characters are working together, I duplicate the page in FreeHand. Then, working with the duplicated page(s), I experiment with the relationships of all the characters. During this step, I'm mindful of the motions that will get me to and from each moment in time. I continue to develop a number of keyframes that form the framework of what I intend to do. The renowned film title designer, Kyle Cooper, of Imaginary Forces, has been a great inspiration to me. He once said, "I think that, in the end, I should be able to pull any frame out of my title sequences, and it should be able to stand on its own as an effective illustration." By studying my design as snapshots in time in FreeHand, I hope to ensure that the motion won't destroy the concept but instead enhance its effectiveness.

Figure 38-20: The Process scene, as seen in a Web browser by using the Flash Player plug-in

Impact of presentation

Now, I have many pages that help me to understand just how to pull this project off. I take those keyframe pages and lay them out onto a large format sheet that will be printed on our large format HP Design Jet at roughly 30"x40". Many people ask me why I continue to print in this day and age. I will tell you why: Communication. Half of the job of design is selling the design you create, especially if you are asking the client to take risks pushing the envelope that they are accustomed to. A digital presentation has many advantages, but so does a good old tangible printed piece.

We have developed a presentation process at Juxt that I affectionately call the 2x4 approach. It is based on the old aphorism, "How do you get the attention of a donkey? Hit him over the head with a 2x4." Don't get me wrong—I'm not insulting any clients, but the point is to make an impact. When we go into a presentation, we intend to exceed the client's expectations. With a presentation board, I can show many keyframes or screens simultaneously as I walk the client through the animation, explaining the process of the motion or the interaction of the interface without, at this early stage, committing the resources to create an actual working prototype.

However, as a communication tool, the advantages are far greater than saving time. Here's why: The digital medium is abstract, whereas print is tangible and real. With a presentation board, the clients can absorb the design when it is all laid out for them. They can see how their brand is working across the piece. Because the print piece is so very tangible, they can grasp the wholeness of it—which means that they can take ownership of it emotionally. But most importantly, it communicates to the client that you are good at what you do. Consequently, they'll have more faith in the decisions that you'll make for them during the process of creating the project (see Figure 38-21).

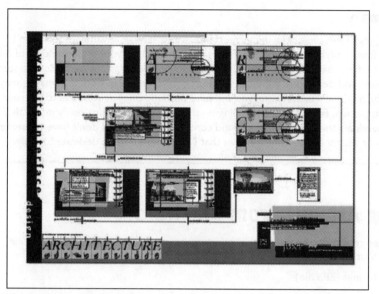

Figure 38-21: Here's an example of the presentation board, which is used as a printed presentation for clients.

Instant changeability

So you've finished presenting the project, your client is sold on your design, but then his partner walks in and says, "Eww . . . I just hate that green." You try to explain its purpose and the importance of that color to the design, but he won't budge. If you'd completed a prototype in Flash, you would have to go back and spend many hours tediously changing that green to tan. But because you laid it out in FreeHand, you can change that green to tan across the entire piece — in about 5 seconds. You simply select the new tan color in the FreeHand Web-Safe Color palette, drag and drop it on top of the banished green in the color list, and — voilà — every instance of the green is now tan. Anywhere there were green lines, files, patterns, text, or colored bitmaps, all are now tan.

Before you have time to gloat, the client's graphics guru tells you that you were given the old corporate design standards manual. Instead of Franklin Gothic (the font you used on 75 percent of the typography), you are supposed to be using Meta Plus. Well, because you still have all your pages in FreeHand, you can simply use the graphic search-and-replace feature to instantly change every bit of Franklin Gothic to Meta Plus. After a few minutes of double-checking kerning effects, you are back to where you started. Now go ahead and feel proud of yourself. Your client will love that these changes won't cost the company a dime.

Summary

Starting your Flash project by using FreeHand gives you huge advantages that won't detract from Flash as a tool. Instead, FreeHand can enhance your understanding of animation and interactive concepts. With FreeHand, you'll have a fast, powerful tool to study your design and develop it, without investing countless hours in work that may or may not make the final cut. Furthermore, you will have fantastic print deliverables to sell your design approach. For me, this is the icing on the cake — I have print-ready materials if the client needs anything from the FreeHand concepts. That means I don't have to create my artwork or designs twice — which means that I have more time to dedicate to design.

Exporting Artwork from Illustrator

You can also repurpose Adobe Illustrator artwork to use in Flash 5. If you use Adobe Illustrator 9 or 10, you can export your artwork for Flash as:

✦ EPS format (EPS file)

✦ Adobe Illustrator format (AI file)

✦ Flash format (SWF file)

Depending on the nature of your artwork, you may choose to use any of the three file formats listed previously. For most purposes, you will want to export directly to the SWF format from Illustrator and then import the SWF to Flash MX for final optimization, since this provides the most consistent translations of artwork from Illustrator to Flash.

To see examples of the different (not always great) results that can happen when using different methods of getting your Illustrator artwork into Flash, open the Flash files (FLA) in the Illustrator folder for ch38.

If you use Illustrator 8, then you can still export artwork as SWF files if you download and install Macromedia's free Flash Writer plug-in, which is available at `www.macromedia.com/support/flash/download`.

Using SWF Export from Illustrator 9 or 10

A feature that was introduced with Adobe Illustrator 9 is the capability to export SWF files without the use of an additional plug-in. The options for the Flash Format are nearly identical to the Macromedia Flash Writer plug-in, with some important additions. To export a SWF file directly from Illustrator, follow these steps:

1. In Illustrator 9 or 10, open your Illustrator (AI or EPS) file.

2. Select Export from the File menu and choose Flash (SWF) from the Format drop-down menu. Type a name for your new SWF file and choose a folder to store the file.

Using the Macromedia Flash Writer Plug-In

Shortly after Flash 4 was released, Macromedia wrote a Flash Writer plug-in for Illustrator 8 that enabled the direct export of SWF files. This free download from the Macromedia Web site bypasses many problems with using EPS and AI files in Flash 4 and 5. Notably, the Flash Writer plug-in can convert EPS blends into Flash gradients. After you download the plug-in from Macromedia, you'll receive an e-mail with a serial number so that you can run the installation on your system. To export SWF files in Illustrator 8, follow these steps:

1. Run the Illustrator application and open your artwork file.

2. Access the Export command in the File menu and select Flash Player SWF in the Format drop-down menu of the Export dialog box. Select a folder or directory to store your SWF file, and type a name for the file. Make sure you include the .swf extension at the end of the filename. Click Save.

3. In the Flash Writer dialog box, select the options for your SWF file. The dialog box contains these options:

   • **Image Settings:** These options control the compression of any placed bitmaps in your Illustrator file. We recommend setting the compression type to JPEG (lossy) at Medium or Medium-High quality and the dpi setting at 72 to reduce file size.

   • **File and Objects:** Use these options to set the target Flash version and to control how the artwork structures are mapped to Flash gradients and frames. If you're not planning to bring the SWF back into Flash for further editing, you'll want to enable the Export File as Protected option. You can also choose to export each layer of your Illustrator document as a unique SWF file, using the Export Layers as Separate Files option. The remaining options determine how Illustrator artwork translates into Flash. If you are using Gradient Meshes, Patterns and Brushes, Text Objects, or Chart Items, then enable these options as needed.

   • **Movie Size:** Usually, you'll want to export the SWF to match the size of the artwork on the page. By default, the Match to Content option is selected. To output the SWF with the dimensions of the page layout, select Preserve Artboard Bounds. If you want a border to appear around the edge of the Flash movie frame, then select Add Border to Content.

4. Click OK and you now have a new SWF file. You can import the SWF file into an existing Flash movie or publish it on your Web site.

Again, the Flash Writer plug-in is available only for Illustrator 8. If you want to export SWF files from Illustrator 9 or 10, proceed to the next section.

Be sure to read the help files that install with the Flash Writer plug-in. You can access these HTML files by clicking the Help button within the Flash Writer dialog box. Among other guidelines, the Help documents indicate that some text settings, such as leading, kerning, and tracking, will not export properly with the Flash Writer plug-in. You should convert your text to outlines before using the Flash Writer plug-in if you alter any of these text settings.

3. In the Flash (SWF) Format Options dialog box (shown in Figure 38-22), you can choose how you want your artwork to export. With the exception of choosing Baseline (Standard) or Baseline Optimized for JPEG compression, the Image Options are nearly identical to those of the Image Settings in the Flash Writer plug-in (see the "Using the Macromedia Flash Writer Plug-In" sidebar).

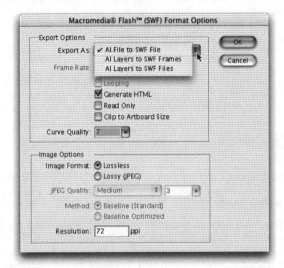

Figure 38-22: Flash Format Options in Illustrator 10

The Export Options dialog box has the following settings:

- **Export As:** If AI File to SWF File is selected, all of your artwork will appear on one keyframe and in one layer in the Flash movie. AI Layers to SWF Frames will export each layer as separate sequential keyframes on the Flash movie timeline. If this option is selected, then you can enter a Frame Rate as well. AI Layers to SWF Files exports a separate SWF file for each Illustrator layer.

- **Frame Rate:** As mentioned in the Export As section, you can specify a frame rate for your SWF animation if you chose the AI Layers to SWF Frames option. By default, this option is 12 fps. For faster animations, enter a higher frame rate.

- **Looping (AI 10 only):** If you are intending to place your SWF directly on the Web without any further editing in Flash, this option will control playback of the frames in the SWF file generated by Illustrator. If you want a multiframe sequence to repeat after it has finished playing through the first time, choose AI Layers to SWF Frames from the Export As drop-down menu and select the Looping check box before you export the file.

- **Generate HTML (AI 10 only):** Like the looping option, this option was added to the SWF Format Options for files that you intend to use on the Web without any further editing in Flash. This will create an HTML file that you can load into a browser to preview your SWF file.

- **Auto-create Symbols (AI 9 only):** This setting converts each piece (or group) of Illustrator artwork into a Flash symbol that can be accessed from the Flash Library. Use this setting if you want to import the SWF file into Flash for further editing and for reuse in other Flash movies. This feature will add a duplicate keyframe for each symbol when imported into Flash. As odd as this may seem, it's necessary for Flash to recognize the symbols on import. Make sure that you remove the second keyframe before you publish your final SWF from Flash.

* **Read Only:** To prevent your SWF file from being imported into the Flash authoring environment, select this check box.

* **Clip to Artboard Size:** This option forces the SWF's movie dimensions to match the page size of your Illustrator document, even if your artwork doesn't occupy the whole page.

* **Curve Quality:** This setting enables you to specify the accuracy of paths exported from Illustrator. Higher settings (up to 10) result in better accuracy but larger file sizes. Lower settings produce smaller file sizes, at the expense of line quality. We recommend that you use the default setting of 7.

* **Image Options:** These standard settings control how any placed bitmap images will be compressed when the SWF is exported from Illustrator.

4. Click OK, and Illustrator exports a new SWF file. You can import the new file into another Flash document (FLA) or publish it to the Web.

Illustrator 10 offers the handy option of using the File ➪ Save for Web command to invoke the Save for Web window (as shown in Figure 38-23). This allows you to preview how your file will appear with different export settings. Although the settings are not as extensive as those in the Export Options dialog box (described previously), the Save for Web dialog box does allow you to alter the file's dimensions and to see a preview of how the file size is affected by the different Curve Quality settings.

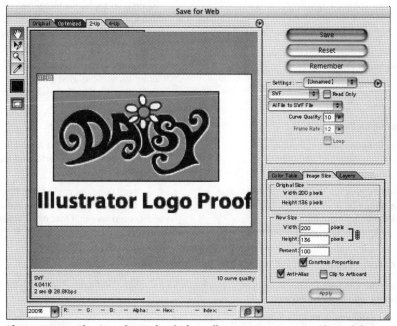

Figure 38-23: The Save for Web window allows you to see a preview of the file size and quality as you choose settings for the exported SWF.

For more information on importing and editing vector artwork from other applications in Flash, refer to Chapter 16, "Importing Artwork."

Exporting Vector Graphics from Flash

In the previous chapter, you learned to export raster image formats from Flash. If you've created artwork in Flash that you want to share with other drawing applications, then you can export any frame (or series of frames) from Flash — in any of the popular vector file formats.

Why would you want to export vector-based images from Flash? If you're a design or graphics professional, then you probably need to reuse your artwork in a number of different media for print, multimedia, or broadcast delivery. As such, you don't like wasting valuable time recreating the same artwork twice. Most Flash artwork exports flawlessly to the file formats listed in Table 38-1.

If you want to export a series of vector images from a Flash movie to use with video or other multiframe applications, check out Chapter 14, "Exporting Animation."

If you are unsure of the format to use in your graphics program, then refer to Table 38-1. Afterward, we show you how to export a Flash frame's artwork as a static vector image.

Table 38-1: Vector Image Formats for Flash Export

Flash Export Format	File Extension	Comments
EPS 3.0 (Encapsulated PostScript)	EPS	Universal vector format recognized by most applications. However, any gradients created in Flash will not export well with this format.
Illustrator (Adobe Illustrator)	AI	Proprietary file format mainly used by Adobe applications. However, any gradients created in Flash will not export well with this format.
DXF (Drawing eXchange Format)	DXF	AutoCAD 2D/3D file format.
PICT — Mac only (Picture)	PCT	Strange as it may seem, the Macintosh PICT format can contain vector and raster information.
WMF/EMF — PC only (Windows Meta File/ Extended Meta File)	WMF, EMF	Only some Windows applications support these formats. These formats are not widely used on either Mac or PC systems.

To export artwork as a vector file format from Flash MX, follow these steps:

1. Move the Current Frame Indicator in the Flash Timeline to the frame that contains the artwork you wish to export.

2. Choose the File ➪ Export Image command.

3. Select a destination folder and enter a filename. Select your preferred vector image format in the Save as Type drop-down menu.

4. Click Save and use the new vector file in your drawing or illustration program.

Unlike exported raster image formats from Flash, the exported vector file formats do not have any additional settings for image quality, contents, or size. This is due primarily to these settings not being necessary for vector file formats. By their nature, vector graphics can be scaled at any size.

For a complete listing of all the formats that can be imported or exported from Flash, refer to Appendix A, "Flash-Compatible Media Formats," in the Bonus_Appendixes PDF on the CD-ROM.

A word of caution: Using vector formats from Flash

Generally, the quality of exported vector files from Flash is less than desirable. Although it would seem that Flash's vector exports would be better than its raster exports, this simply isn't the case. Because RGB color space (as the end product) is relatively new to the world of print-based production, most vector file formats need to encode color information as CMYK. This presents a couple of problems, as you'll see in the following sections.

Color consistency

Flash works within an RGB color model, which means that all color is defined by three numbers, one assigned to each color channel of the image (for example, red, green, and blue). Most standard vector file formats do not encode the color information in this manner. Rather, they use CMYK (cyan, magenta, yellow, and black) colors that have a much more restricted color *gamut* (range) than RGB.

As such, most, if not all, of your Flash artwork will display quite differently when exported as a vector file format, such as EPS or AI. Is this yet another reason to start projects intended for multiple media formats in Macromedia FreeHand? Yes and no. While starting projects in FreeHand lends itself to greater flexibility for the reuse or repurposing of artwork, you do have another alternative to exporting vector files from Flash: good old copy and paste. If you select Flash artwork, choose Edit ⇨ Copy, switch to your illustration program, and choose Edit ⇨ Paste; the newly pasted artwork should match your original Flash artwork.

Why is this so? Most likely it is because the Flash export file formats (or the versions of these formats) don't seem to support RGB colors. However, the clipboard can support a multitude of data types, and Adobe Illustrator and FreeHand can recognize RGB colors. Therefore, the copied-and-pasted colors show up as RGB colors in these programs.

Interestingly, if you choose Adobe Illustrator (AI) as the export file format from Flash, you can only choose up to and including Illustrator 6 formats. RGB color support was first introduced to Adobe Illustrator in version 7. It is also likely that the EPS 3.0 format is an older version of the format that does not support RGB colors.

Flash gradients

Another troublesome spot for exported vector files from Flash is the re-rendering of Flash gradients as CMYK *blends*. Depending on the vibrancy of the original gradient in Flash, the exported vector equivalents might end up very muddy or brownish—especially in the middle range of the gradient. Again, you can avoid this color shifting by copying and pasting the Flash gradients directly between applications. Note that this still converts Flash gradients to blends, but it will retain the RGB color values of the original Flash gradient.

Tip If you need perfect exported material from Flash, you might consider exporting high-resolution bitmap (a.k.a. *raster*) files instead. For coverage of bitmap export from Flash, refer to Chapter 37, "Working with Raster Graphics."

On the CD-ROM CorelDRAW 10 Graphics Suite has many powerful tools to help you design and edit unique vector-based graphics. And with ready support for Macromedia Flash SWF files, CorelDRAW 10 makes it easy to create images and directly export them into Macromedia Flash for animation. For an introduction to the capabilities of CorelDRAW 10, refer to Doug Downey's tutorial in the Bonus_Tutorials PDF on the *Flash MX Bible* CD-ROM.

Summary

✦ You can use Flash MX to import and export many vector formats to support designs for print, broadcast, or other media.

✦ To maintain color consistency when you're creating artwork in other programs, it is important to work in RGB color whenever possible. This will avoid unexpected color shifts in the artwork when you import it to Flash.

✦ FreeHand 10 offers specialized tools for handling text and complex vector artwork, which can greatly enhance your Flash designs.

✦ FreeHand 10 is used by top designers, such as Todd Purgason, to plan and print high-impact presentations that help sell clients on Flash project proposals before production begins in the Flash authoring environment.

✦ Many vector programs offer tools for converting raster images into vector images, but the final artwork can result in larger file sizes than the original bitmaps imported directly to Flash MX.

✦ Finding the best workflow requires a balance between the visual effect and the final file size constraints. The most important factor to decide first is what look you are trying to achieve with your graphics. The next step is testing different format and compression options to find the best way of keeping the image quality high and the file size streamlined.

✦   ✦   ✦

Working with Audio Applications

◆ ◆ ◆ ◆

In This Chapter

Getting an overview
of audio programs

Building your own
recording studio

Basic functions
of audio editing

Normalizing and
optimizing sound

Step-by-step optimizing

Adding and creating
custom effects

Creating sound effects
in Rebirth

Making sound loops
for Flash

◆ ◆ ◆ ◆

Flash MX is one of the main applications of choice for showcasing bands and their music. You can find audio players, turntables, and interactive mixing boards created in Flash all over the Web. There is a behind-the-scenes process that involves various audio applications to capture and edit audio in a digital environment. Creating and editing your own sound will give you a unique and fresh approach to your projects. With audio-editing software, you might find that you gain some insight into the music world, even if you can't play an instrument!

In this chapter, you'll learn how to prepare multimedia sounds for use in Flash. Because of the limited number of options for editing audio in Flash, we recommend that you optimize and experiment with sound clips in an external application before importing them into the Library. When creating or editing audio for use in Flash, we cannot stress enough the importance of starting out with the highest sample and bit conversion rates possible. Remember that sound quality, in general, is simple to degrade but can be difficult or impossible to restore, so it's not a good idea to skimp from the beginning. Ideally, your original files are 16-bit 44.1 kHz stereo. From this point on, we assume that your audio clips are of reasonable quality and were captured or created from a good 16-bit source, such as an audio CD or a sound effects application, such as Propellerhead's Rebirth (which is discussed later in this chapter).

Sound-Editing and Creation Software

Just about every multimedia or video software package includes a sound-editing application. For the most part, you'll find limited edition (a.k.a. *LE*) versions of popular sound applications bundled with Macromedia Director or video application suites, such as Digital Origin's EditDV. For a price, you can upgrade these LE versions to full versions, or purchase them separately if you don't need or want a full multimedia production software package. While very few of the following applications are available on both Macintosh and Windows platforms, their functionality is virtually identical.

Several software companies produce excellent sound-editing software. Many of these companies offer a software suite of their flagship products bundled with several supporting products that specialize in different areas of audio editing and creation. The following is a list of some of the most popular software developers that offer audio creation and editing applications.

Note   You can perform the same basic functions described in this chapter in either the LE or fully featured versions of the sound-editing application. LE versions usually have less effects-oriented controls, such as sound filters and enhanced noise reduction.

Sonic Foundry's suite (PC only)

Sonic Foundry (www.sonicfoundry.com) provides the best-known sound-editing solutions for the Windows operating system. From simple editing to powerful looping effects, Sonic Foundry has a tool to work with any sound project.

Sound Forge

Sound Forge is a powerful, yet easy-to-use waveform sound editor for the PC environment. A great feature of Sound Forge is nondestructive editing. Sound Forge can also be integrated with Sonic Foundry's ACID software.

Sound Forge supports all three of the Flash-compatible audio import formats, AIFF, WAV, and MP3. In addition, it has the capability to save in the RealAudio G2 streaming format. You can open an existing sound file, edit it, and save it as WAV, MP3, or AIFF with several different options for sampling and bit rates.

ACID PRO

ACID is a powerful, loop-based sound-editing program that is ideal for use with Flash (see Figure 39-1). With ACID, you can very easily take loops created in other programs and arrange them on multiple tracks. One of the ACID program's great features is its capability to change the speed of the loop without changing the key. ACID PRO also comes with over 100 ready-to-use loops, so you can arrange an audio track in a pinch.

Syntrillium Software

Syntrillium Software (www.syntrillium.com) creates sound-editing applications for the Windows operating systems. Cool Edit 2000 offers an excellent alternative to Sound Forge as does Cool Edit Pro for digital multi-tracking.

Cool Edit 2000

Cool Edit 2000 is a waveform editor that has many similarities to Sonic Foundry's Sound Forge. It allows you to edit and convert your audio samples as well as enhance them with special effects, such as reverb, delay, chorus and many others. Cool Edit 2000 supports all three of the Flash-compatible audio import formats, AIFF, WAV, and MP3.It also has the capability to save in the RealAudio G2 streaming format.

Cool Edit Pro

Cool Edit Pro is a complete multitrack recording studio with up to 128 stereo tracks to record with. Utilizing multiple editing and mixing windows, you can also take advantage of real time effects and looping tools. Other features include MIDI playback support, CD ripping, and customizable interface configurations. Cool Edit Pro supports all three of the Flash-compatible audio import formats, AIFF, WAV, and MP3.

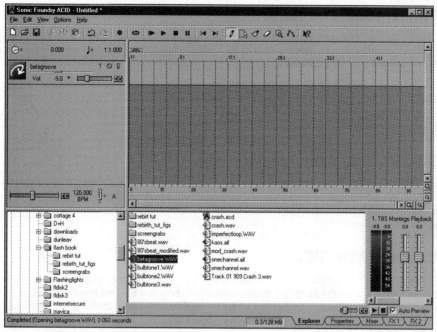

Figure 39-1: In ACID, you can very easily preview an audio clip, add it as a track, and move it around a timeline.

Bias suite (Mac only)

Bias (www.bias-inc.com) creates sound-editing applications for the Macintosh operating system. When Macromedia stopped developing SoundEdit 16 Deck, Bias picked up the products and started to fine-tune them for new Web technologies.

Peak

Peak is the tool for getting down and dirty with editing stereo tracks. It supports a large number of file formats and nondestructive editing. Some of the other features of Peak are its capability to execute batch file processing, burn CDs directly from a playlist, and export in RealAudio G2 streaming format. Peak is rapidly becoming one of the most widely used audio-editing applications for multimedia on the Macintosh. It is available in both full and LE versions.

Deck

Deck is a powerful nondestructive multitrack editor, for the Macintosh platform. In addition to being capable of playing back up to 64 tracks simultaneously, Deck can also function as a multitrack recorder, enabling you to create your own music or sound effects. It is less expensive than other similar software packages, and can be closely integrated with Bias Peak.

Cakewalk Pro suite (PC only)

Cakewalk (www.cakewalk.com) manufactures top-of-the-line audio software for the sound professional. The company's software is designed for serious users who need to master audio for broadcast and CD applications.

Sonar is a powerful multitrack editor and MIDI sequencer for the Windows platform. Sonar allows unlimited potential tracks, has an unlimited undo and redo history, and comes equipped with real-time effects. These features make this software an excellent option to Pro Tools and Cool Edit Pro.

Studio Vision Pro (Mac only)

Studio Vision Pro (www.opcode.com) is probably the best deal out there for anyone on a tight budget but who needs all the advanced features from the more expensive programs. Studio Vision Pro is a multitrack editor/recorder with the capability to work with MIDI information and digital audio.

Cubase (Mac/PC)

Cubase (www.us.steinberg.net) is one of the very few programs available on both platforms. Cubase is a top-of-the-line multitrack editor/recorder. Cubase has the capability to edit and print musical scores and to handle both MIDI and digital audio. It is capable of 16- to 24-bit audio and has a built-in virtual synthesizer.

Macromedia SoundEdit 16 (Mac only)

SoundEdit has had a relatively long history with Macintosh users as a sound-editing workhorse, especially for use with multimedia. Although still widely used, SoundEdit 16 is no longer being produced by Macromedia, and Mac users are slowly migrating to the more-robust, full-featured Peak.

Digidesign's Pro Tools (Mac/PC)

Last, but not least, is Pro Tools (www.protools.com), the industry standard. If we were to walk into just about any major recording studio, we would see Pro Tools displayed on their massive monitors. Naturally, the professionals will have more than just Pro Tools on their system. In fact, the audio engineers will usually have several of the programs mentioned earlier because they might require a feature or two that only another program supports. (In the same way that Flash can't do everything we want, so we use other programs to help get some effects.) But in the end, the reality is that the Pro Tools system is the primary professional tool for audio editing and mixing.

Not only do the makers of Pro Tools make software products, but they also make some of the hardware for sound studios, including computer peripherals. Once you bring hardware into the equation for setting up a system, the cost can go sky-high. Thankfully, Digidesign is aware of this fact and has developed two home studio kits for all those people who love to make music but don't have a major studio budget or a degree in audio engineering.

The four main systems in the Pro Tools shop are the Pro Tools HD, Pro tools 24MIX, Digi 001, and the Mbox. The HD and 24MIX are high-end systems (beyond the scope of this chapter). The Digi 001 and Mbox are very keen units. The Mbox is a stand-alone unit with two analog inputs and outputs, 24-bit stereo S/PDIF digital I/O, and built in mic preamps. This system is currently supported by Mac only, although a Windows version is on the way. The Digi 001 is a step up from the Mbox, with up to 18 inputs and outputs combined. Both units utilize Pro Tools LE software to organize and mix tracks. LE software gives you 24 audio tracks, 128 MIDI tracks, and editing and sequencing power. These units are perfect for anyone considering taking their recording to the next level.

Capturing Your Own Sound: Building Your Own Recording Studio

All the situations mentioned in this chapter assume that you already have digital audio files to work with. However, you might want to create some custom sound effects, voice-overs, or original music for your Flash movies. Let's take a brief look into what it takes to build your own home recording studio.

Instrument of choice

The first step in organizing your audio tools is asking yourself what type of audio you want to bring into the digital world. Whether you have a keyboard, guitar, drum set, or microphone, you'll need to capture that audio and digitize it to use in an audio application. The quality of your sound starts here, and certain mistakes in this step can ultimately ruin the final sound quality. Microphone position, quality instruments, and preamps all play an integral role in this process. If you're interested in taking sound recording to a more advanced level, it is worth seeking out some of the excellent books available specifically on this topic.

Choosing a sound card

Although some audio applications allow you to edit audio without a sound card, most computers come with a sound card preinstalled. You will have to determine if that card is sufficient to meet your audio requirements. Certain audio applications require a higher level of card (or even preamps and processors) to bring music to line level. You will have to evaluate the software requirements of the editing program that you choose as well as your own audio needs to determine if an upgrade from your existing sound card is necessary. One of the most important things to look for in a sound card is the bit rate—anywhere between 16 and 24 bit is acceptable. A standard audio CD is recorded at 16-bit, 44.1 kHz, stereo. The next feature to look for is the number of input and output modules. If you need to record more than one instrument at a time (or if you choose to record in stereo), you will need two or more inputs. Your output modules are important for playing back audio on a designated set of speakers. Another feature to look for is Digital Ins/Outs to hook up CD, DAT, and other digital players that have a coaxial output. Since most sound cards are compatible with a variety of audio applications, you have the option to shop for your own or purchase the specific card suggested by your preferred editing application.

Getting your sound in

Now that you've picked some type of instrument and have a sound card to digitize your audio, you need to prepare the sound for entry into the digital world. Depending on your equipment, you may not be able to plug your instruments directly into the sound card. If this is the case, your audio will need some sort of preamp to bring the signal up to an adequate level. Some sound cards do come with a built in preamp. But you also have the option to purchase an external unit with a built in preamp for the inputs, such as the Digi 001. Most amplifiers have a direct out, however your microphones and synthesizers need an external preamp. Your options are to purchase a mixing console with built in preamps or to purchase individual preamp units. Such units can run from under $100 into the thousands. This is an important step that you will get better at with experience. Don't be afraid to experiment with different preamp settings, microphone placements, and individual volume settings on your instruments to achieve the custom sound that you desire.

Getting your sound out

After you record your sound, you need to preview the digitized audio to ensure that your instruments, preamps, and sound card/computer are all working together. Your sound card will have some sort of output port, which can connect to an external set of speakers. You will often have the option to run the instrument internally through your computer directly out to your speakers. This step is important because it lets you check the digitized sound against the original sound of the instrument. This method also allows you to adjust your equipment to achieve a particular sound and even create presets to save time in setting up frequently used instruments.

Conclusion

Just remember to keep it simple at first. Learn and purchase enough to get started. You can always expand and add new equipment and hardware to your collection. If you start to get more involved, you might want to have a computer solely for audio purposes. You will need a processor that can handle streaming audio as well as the hard drive space to store it all.

Basic Functions of Audio Editing

The editing features of audio applications can range from basic to extremely advanced; many go well beyond the audio needs of most common users. In this section, we will discuss some common editing features, from basic to more advanced.

Making your audio selection

First, you will have to choose which portion of audio you want to use in your Flash application. Each audio clip has a cursor point that designates the point at which the audio will start playing or the selection will begin. You can change the location of this point by clicking your mouse at any position in the audio timeline. The cursor point also designates where your copying, or cutting and pasting, begin. Clicking and dragging your mouse from one point to another will highlight a particular section of the audio. You can now copy or cut this selection from the edit menu. Let's apply these methods in a real production situation.

Setting In and Out points

One of the first things you do with an audio file before bringing it into the Flash environment is set its In and Out points. These points, respectively, control where the sound will start and end. Removing any unwanted sound (or dead space), at the beginning and end of each audio file will help keep your audio in perfect synch with animations and loops. This also helps to minimize the sound's file size (see Figure 39-2), making it less cumbersome to move around and reducing the amount of time that you'll have to spend adjusting the sound in Flash. You can set In and Out points in most, if not all, audio applications.

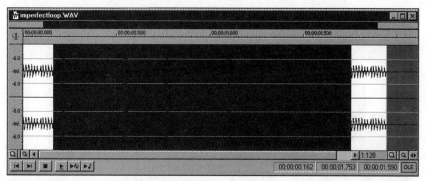

Figure 39-2: You can greatly reduce the file size of a Flash movie by limiting audio tracks to essential portions.

In Sound Forge, Peak, and SoundEdit 16, follow these steps to set the In and Out points of a sound:

1. Highlight the area you want to keep.

2. Test your selection by pressing the Play Loop or Play button (Sound Forge).

To create a new audio file with your selection:

1. Select File ➪ Copy (Ctrl+C or ⌘+C).

2. Select File ➪ New (Ctrl+N or ⌘+N).

3. A new window opens. Select Edit ➪ Paste (Ctrl+V or ⌘+V).

4. Your selection will now be a new audio file, containing only the part of the sound that you want to use.

Fade in and fade out

As discussed in Chapter 15, "Adding Sound," *fading in* means increasing the volume of a sound over time, and *fading out* means decreasing it. Most audio-editing applications have more sophisticated fading effects than Flash.

To fade audio in Sound Forge:

1. Select the part of the audio that you want to fade in or out.

2. Choose Process ➪ Fade ➪ Graphic.

3. The Graphic Fade Window appears (see Figure 39-3).

You should now see your selected sound as a *waveform* (that is, a graphic representation of sound waves). The interface for customizing your fade is similar to the one used in Flash. You create envelope handles by clicking points on the envelope line at the top of the waveform. Drag these handles around to create your desired volume/fading effects. The lines themselves show the volume level of the sound. Thus, when you drag an envelope handle down, the line slopes down, indicating a decrease in the volume level. Click Preview to hear your custom fade. Click OK when you are satisfied.

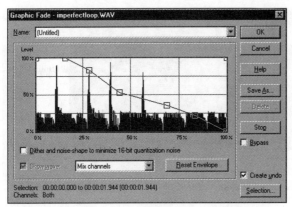

Figure 39-3: Sound Forge enables you to save custom fade effects to apply to other sounds.

To fade audio with Peak, follow these steps:

1. Select the section of audio that you want to fade in or out.

2. Choose Preferences ➪ Fade In Envelope or Fade Out Envelope. The Fade In Envelope or Fade Out Envelope Window appears.

3. You can use the default fade shape or create your own by using a similar technique to the one described previously for Sound Forge.

4. Choose DSP ➪ Fade Out. Peak will apply the fade to your selection.

5. To hear your Fade, press Option+spacebar.

To fade audio with SoundEdit, follow these steps:

1. Select the section of audio that you want to fade in or out.

2. Choose Effects ➪ Fade In or Effects ➪ Fade Out.

3. Create your fade using a similar technique to the one described for Sound Forge. SoundEdit also has Slow, Medium, or Fast fade presets. Click OK when finished.

Normalizing Audio Levels

Normalizing is a process applied to audio to gain equilibrium in the overall sound level. This function allows you to put a cap on how high the audio level can go to prevent *clipping*. Digital clipping occurs when audio is recorded at too high a level. When the upper levels of the sound are above the range of the recording or playback device, parts of the sound are clipped or distorted, resulting in an undesirable crackling or buzzing sound. The Normalize option is available in most audio applications and can also be used to boost levels when your audio file was recorded too low.

Tip If you're gathering sound samples from a number of different audio sources (such as audio CD, direct recordings with a computer microphone, DAT recordings, DV camcorder audio, and so on), it's best to normalize all of them to a consistent audio level.

To normalize in Sound Forge, follow these steps:

1. Select a specific part or all of the clip to be normalized.

2. Choose Process ➪ Normalize.

3. The Normalize window appears (see Figure 39-4). You can click Preview to see how the default settings will affect your sound levels.

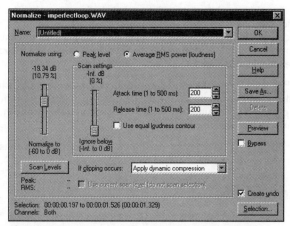

Figure 39-4: The Sound Forge Normalize window enables you to preview settings before you apply them to the audio clip.

Watch the Play Meter on the right side of the screen. If the levels seem high (constantly in the red), lower the levels with the slider bar on the left side of the Normalize dialog box. If your levels are too low, gradually raise the slider bar. Click OK, and your file will be normalized to the levels you have selected. Note that many other options exist in the Normalize Window; experiment with these settings to get the result you're looking for.

To normalize in Peak and SoundEdit, follow these steps:

1. Select part or all of the clip to be normalized.

2. In Peak, choose DSP ➪ Normalize; in SoundEdit, choose Effects ➪ Normalize.

In Peak's Normalize dialog box, you can move the slider bar back and forth to choose the normalization percentage. The number you choose will normalize the sound to a percentage of the maximum level. After you click OK, you can listen to the normalized selection by pressing Option+spacebar. Watch the levels for any clipping. The next section will go into more detail on normalizing and optimizing audio.

Caution
If you're recording sounds with a microphone attached to your computer's sound card, make sure that you have adjusted the microphone's volume level (or gain) in the sound-recording application. If the levels are too high during recording, you won't be able to normalize the sound — the resulting sound will be very distorted and "clip" on playback.

Optimizing Sound for Flash in Sound Forge

While we already explained how to perform basic normalization on sound files, we will now explain how and why to optimize sound levels and sampling within Sound Forge. Most of the sound-editing applications we mentioned earlier can perform similar operations as well. Refer to your sound-editing software manual for the specific menu commands that are necessary for normalization and sampling rate.

In a perfect Web world, we would be using stereo files at their highest sample rate. As the creator, you must decide which is more important: download time or sound quality. The settings discussed in this section can be used to decrease file size while maintaining decent sound quality. However, if your original sample sounds bad, these settings will make it sound worse. A little bit of sound advice: Bad in = Bad out!

Although it is true that MP3 offers the best sound compression, for ideal results it helps to know a few tricks that will enable you to reduce the file size before importing sounds into Flash — this will result in even smaller sound files with better sound quality. Another bit of sound advice: Smart sound = Better, smaller sound.

Although a number of excellent programs may be used for sound editing, we will use Sonic Foundry's Sound Forge to explain *normalizing* and *resampling*.

Normalizing a sound file

Normalizing is used to increase the volume of a sound file without fear of clipping. You can also set specific parameters so that certain areas can be ignored or intensified. Start by opening your sound file in Sound Forge. If you like, you can drag and drop the file right into the workspace. Make sure that your file is completely deselected; then choose Process ➪ Normalize. This applies the normalization process to the whole file. Don't be intimidated by all the settings. Here is a walk-through of each control in the Normalize dialog box.

✦ **Normalize using Peak level or Average RMS:** Choose Average RMS. This will enable you to save a setting so that if you have more than one sound file, you can maintain and compare volume between audio files.

✦ **Normalize to:** This sets the level of your normalized sound. A value of 16 to 20 percent is a good starting point. These settings mean that the sound volume will be reduced by a factor of 16 to 20 percent. Remember that when the final SWF is played, the Flash player will boost your gain by several decibels.

✦ **Scan settings:** The best feature of this is the Ignore below slider. This enables you to choose a level at which the normalization will bypass. Simply put, you might have sections of silence in your file. If you boost the gain in these sections, you might bring out unwanted frequencies (noise) that you couldn't hear previously. After you've scanned a selection, you can use the RMS calculations to gauge what level to set the slider at. In most cases, anything under 5 percent is a good starting point. Be careful though! If your file is already at a low decibel, these settings could bypass the whole normalization process. If you're uncertain, leave the slider at 0 percent. You can leave the default settings for attack and release time at 200 and leave the Use equal contour box checked.

✦ **If clipping occurs:** Select Apply dynamic compression. This is your safety net. Although you may have a situation in which the normalization settings are exactly where you need them to be, some sections may still peak. Applying dynamic compression prevents any peaks from exceeding the threshold.

After you've set the parameters, you can audition (preview) your selection. If you're using multiple audio files in a Flash project and want to maintain consistent volume throughout, use the Save as button to save a preset for future use.

Resampling

Most of the audio files you work with are probably set to stereo 44.1 kHz. This may be fine for CD-ROM applications, but the Web is a different area. If you plan to severely downgrade the original sampling rate of a particular sound file in the final Flash movie (SWF file), we recommend that you optimize your sound as mono 22.05 kHz before you import the file into Flash MX. After the sound is in a Flash document, you can then continue to decrease the file size with MP3 compression. A third-party sound editor, such as Sound Forge, gives you the advantage of higher-quality filters and high-end processing. Although Flash can resample PCM files, it will not process them with the same level of quality that a program such as Sound Forge offers. Furthermore, Flash prevents you from resampling in MP3 format. Your ideal situation is to resample while introducing as little audible change as possible. Again, your ear will be the best judge.

Note PCM stands for Pulse Code Modulation. It is a standard sound-sampling mechanism for audio — it is a digital representation of sound.

To begin resampling, with your sound open in Sound Forge, select Process ➪ Resample. Then make your choices from the settings that follow:

✦ **New Sample Rate:** Select a new sample rate from the New Sample Rate drop-down or else type the rate into the field yourself. The next two items are the most important. These filters maintain your sound quality.

✦ **Interpolation accuracy:** This determines the range of number crunching or the complexity of the calculations that will be used to resample the sound. A higher number results in a more accurate resample calculation. A setting of 4 takes longer to process than a setting of 1 but will come closer to your original sample. This setting will *not* change your file size; it only affects the *quality* of the resample.

✦ **Antialias filter:** When resampling sound, you might notice distortion or a loss in the high end. Applying an antialias filter helps prevent these high frequencies from distorting. Preview your sound and resample accordingly.

Final notes

You should always normalize your sound file before you resample, because this processing order preserves the best sound quality. We recommend that you keep the Create Undo box checked at all times, because this type of editing drastically alters your file, and it can be very nice to have that Undo available. Similarly, it can be advantageous to use the Save as command (and save to a new name) after you have made your changes. This procedure preserves the original file so that you can go back to it later.

Optimizing a Sound File Step by Step

The following exercise demonstrates how to optimize the file size and type prior to importing a sound to Flash. This example uses Sonic Foundry's Sound Forge. You can also follow similar steps with other audio editing applications. The order of the steps is important and should be applied, regardless of what editing application you're working in. Other applications may differ slightly from step to step, but the basic process remains the same.

1. Open the **DB_Loop.wav** file, located in the ch39 folder of the *Flash MX Bible* CD-ROM.

2. Note the file's info at the bottom right hand of the application window (see Figure 39-5).

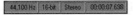 **Figure 39-5:** The sound file's information

3. Select File ➪ New (Ctrl+N) and choose settings to match the file info (shown in the previous step) for the sound that you want to edit (see Figure 39-6).

 **Figure 39-6:** The New Window dialog box is used to select settings for a new file.

4. Return to your source file (DB_Loop) and use Edit ➪ Select All (Ctrl+A).

5. Go to your new sound file window and paste the source selection in. You can now close the original DB_Loop.wav file.

   Now, let's increase the level of audio and cap the peaks so there is no clipping.

6. Select the new file, named sound2 by default. When no particular selection is highlighted, any process or effect you choose will be applied to the entire file.

7. Choose Process ➪ Normalize. The Normalize dialog box appears. You can click Preview to hear what your current settings are. We recommend -16.00 db as a starting point. Note that the Apply dynamic compression option is selected in the If clipping occurs field, as shown in Figure 39-7.

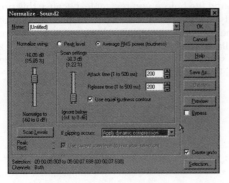 **Figure 39-7:** The Sound Forge Normalize dialog box

Now that you have the file levels set, you can start to optimize the file to a lower size. Converting the file to Mono will cut the file size in half.

8. Choose Process ➪ Channel Converter. The Channel Converter dialog box appears. Choose Mono from the Output channels radio buttons. Lower the levels to 70% to avoid clipping. See Figure 39-8 for these settings.

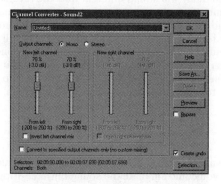

Figure 39-8: The Channel Converter dialog box

The last step in the optimization process is to resample your loop. This step will make noticeable changes to your sound quality. You can adjust this based upon the final quality and file size that your project requires.

9. Choose Process ➪ Resample. Select 22,050 from the New sample rate menu. Select 4 from the interpolation accuracy slider. Select the Apply an anti-alias filter during resample option. Refer to Figure 39-9. Click OK.

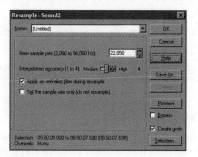

Figure 39-9: The Resample dialog box

10. Save your file. The sound is now ready to import into Flash.

You can use the MP3 settings in Flash to reduce the file size even more. Note the difference in file size between the original file and your new file—1,327 KB for the original and 332 KB for the optimized!

There are many possible variations in these steps. The previous steps were merely recommendations for the best optimization of file size while preserving sound quality. Each project will dictate it's own rules. Use your best judgment for file size and always use your ear. If it sounds really bad . . . try a different approach!

Effects

Audio applications come with effects that can be applied and customized for enhancements to your sounds. It is extremely important to know when to use effects and how they can work together. Special effects can have compound results, depending on the order in which you place them. Placing Reverb first and then Delay will sound different than the reverse order. Many effects can also push your levels into the red zone and cause clipping. You may have a selection normalized and ready to go and then decide to add a bit of reverb. This could cause clipping that would require a customized setting in the effects window to correct. If you're inexperienced, this may start to get confusing. Although many applications use nondestructive editing, there is often a specific order in which things can be removed. Say you cut, paste, normalize, and add reverb to a selection of audio in that order. If you wish to remove the normalization process you will have to remove the reverb first. For this reason, we highly recommend normalization as a final step.

Creating a reverb effect

Adding reverb to a sound file can create an interesting effect. Reverb creates the auditory illusion of acoustic space. For example, you could simulate the sound of water dripping in a cave.

To add a reverb to an audio sample in Sound Forge, follow these steps:

1. Select the section of sound that you want to add reverb to.

2. Choose Effects ⇨ Reverb.

3. The Reverb dialog box appears.

4. Select a Reverberation Mode from the drop-down menu. To create the dripping-water sound, choose Cavernous Space.

5. Press the Preview Button to hear how the effect sounds. Play with some of the sliders and other options until you achieve the desired effect. When done, click OK.

SoundEdit 16 has a similar effect to reverb called Echo. To add Echo to a selection, choose Effects ⇨ Echo.

Creating your own custom sound effects.

You might have the need for a sound effect that you cannot find on a library disk or that you don't have a budget to pay for. This will give you the chance to get creative and make your own sounds by utilizing everyday objects in conjunction with the effects processing available in Sound Forge. The following exercise shows how to create an explosion effect by recording a door closing. This example assumes that you already have access to a microphone and sound card and that you're set up to record your own sounds.

Let's add some space to the end of the file for the explosion effect:

1. Open the **door.wav** file, located in the ch32 folder of the *Flash MX Bible* CD-ROM.

2. You'll need to add some sound to the end of the file for the echo. Select Process ⇨ Insert Silence. Set the menu to End of File and add 2 seconds in the time area, as shown in Figure 39-10.

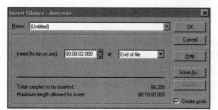

Figure 39-10: The Insert Silence dialog box

Now let's create an explosion.

3. Select the final portion of the sound waveform, as shown in Figure 39-11.

Figure 39-11: A selection from the sound file

4. Select Effect ⇨ Reverb. Choose the preset Cathedral from the Name menu at the top of the dialog box. Adjust the Reverb out to -9.0dB. Adjust the Early Out slider to –20.0. Adjust the Decay time slider to 3.5 seconds. Adjust the Pre-delay to 55. When you're finished, your settings should resemble those shown in Figure 39-12.

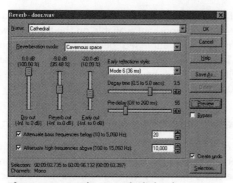

Figure 39-12: The Reverb dialog box

You can cut the opening of the door off or leave it on. That is up to you. This should give you some other ideas on making you own sound effects. All you really need to get started is a microphone and some imagination.

Other effects

Many other effects and processes are available in these audio-editing applications, and to list them all would be beyond the scope of this book. A great feature of many of these software packages is nondestructive editing. You can make as many changes to your audio clips as you like without destroying the original source files. Set aside some time to experiment and let your creativity take over.

If you don't have any source sound material for adding effects, you can create your own super-synth techno music with Propellerhead's Rebirth. The next tutorial by Justin Jamieson shows you how to create a soundtrack with Rebirth.

Using Propellerhead's Rebirth to Create Loops for Flash, *by Justin Jamieson*

If you don't want to invest time and money in audio hardware, you can use Rebirth to create electronic music. Justin's tutorial walks you through the basic process of mixing samples and beats in Rebirth.

Rebirth is an innovative sound-creation tool that accurately replicates vintage analog synthesizers and drum machines. Simply put, it enables you to easily create electronic music without investing tons of money in hardware.

With Rebirth, you can create looping music for Stream or Event sounds in Flash. You can also create some weird effects by tweaking the various knobs and adding distortion. Prepare yourself to spend long hours and sleepless nights experimenting with this program. That's not to say that it's extremely difficult — it's not. Rebirth is actually quite easy to get the hang of, but you'll soon be keeping the neighbors awake at night with heavy bass and spacey frequencies.

Rebirth emulates two synthesizers, Roland 303s, and two drum machines, a Roland 808 and a Roland 909. Countless Mods (modifications) are available on the Internet, with different graphics and sample sets. Some of these sample sets specialize in certain types of electronic music, such as drum and bass, dub, industrial, and so on. For the purposes of this tutorial, however, we use the default Mod, which has controls that are easy to use (and that provide that sought-after 1980s Electro sound.)

Getting started with Rebirth

First, familiarize yourself with some of the Rebirth controls. Refer to Figure 39-13 for the main Rebirth window. This interface offers a fair number of different audio control options, and the Rebirth manual describes them very well. You should have a basic knowledge of Rebirth for the purposes of this tutorial. When you open Rebirth, you see the main interface shown in Figure 39-13.

Although you can use the demo version of this software for the purposes of this tutorial, it lacks the capability to save any final audio files and shuts down after 15 minutes.

Figure 39-13: The main Rebirth window

Creating your first simple beat in Rebirth

In Pattern Mode, press Play and look at the 909 at the bottom of the screen. You'll notice red lights moving from left to right over the 16 step buttons. This represents one musical measure. To modify the beat that is playing, you can clear some or all of the buttons and add your own. You can also select pre-made beats by pressing the pattern buttons on the left side of the screen.

Note   To clear an entire pattern, move the red Focus Bar down to the bottom of the screen using the down-arrow key and then choose Edit ➪ Clear.

To begin creating your own beat, or to modify an existing one, you will want to "solo" the 909, so the other sections don't get in the way. To do this, click the Mix buttons to turn off the green lights in all but the 909 section. You should now only hear the 909. You can also select the number of beats per minute by altering the number on the BPM selector at the top left of the screen.

More advanced musicians may want to change the time signature by altering the number in the value display on the left side of the 909 (see Figure 39-14). When you change the number, you're altering the total of sixteenth notes within a bar. Thus, if you change it to 14, there will be 14 sixteenth notes between the beginning and end of a bar.

Figure 39-14: The 909 is "soloed" in the main Rebirth window.

To select different drum sounds to play, you can either use the rotary dial on the right side, or you can click the sound names above the 16 step buttons. Each step button also has two instance levels. The first time that you click a step button, a faint red light appears, indicating a lighter drum hit. The second time that you click the same step button, the heavier red light appears, indicating a heavier hit. The third time that you click the same button, you clear it. No sound is produced.

The 909 also has a Flam feature that simulates the sound of a percussionist hitting a drum with both sticks at slightly different intervals (see Figure 39-15). To use this feature, click the Flam button on the 909 and choose the step button that you want to hear the Flam on. The dial above the Flam button adjusts the "width" of the Flam — the actual time interval between the two simulated "stick hits."

Figure 39-15: This figure shows the various instance levels of the 909.

The faint light in Figure 39-15 indicates a "light hit." The heavier one indicates a "heavy hit." The green light indicates a "Flam," which is similar to the sound of a drummer hitting a drum with both sticks at slightly different intervals.

The process of creating your own beat involves clearing all or some of an existing drum pattern by manually clicking the step buttons for the various drum sounds and then clicking in new ones. After you've found a suitable bar of beats, at a suitable speed, you're ready to add some 303 synthesizer.

Adding sound from the 303

The two top sections are digital replications of the vintage Roland TB 303 analog synthesizer. These are a little bit more difficult to program than the 808s, and those new to Rebirth may find it a little frustrating. A good way to begin is to customize an existing pattern.

Use the up-arrow keys to move the focus bar to the 303 that you want to use. Solo it the same way that you solo the 808 (forthcoming). Press play, and begin the process of choosing a pattern.

You can choose the pattern, either by using the Pattern Selector on the left side of the 303 (see Figure 39-16), or by pressing Ctrl+R to randomly *surf* the patterns. After you find a suitable pattern, you can begin to modify it using the synthesizer sound controls.

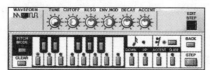

Figure 39-16: The various synthesizer sound controls on the 303

The synthesizer sound controls can create interesting results. For a detailed description of what each control does, consult the Rebirth manual. Keep in mind that experimentation is key. Set aside some time to create the perfect synthesizer lick by playing with these controls.

Using the 808

The 808 drum section, above the 909, is similar to the 909, but with several differences. For one, the drum sounds are different. Also, the controls aren't quite the same. When you are creating or editing beats in the 808, you only have one instance level on the key buttons. The 808 uses instead the Accent (AC) feature to create heavier beats. The Accent feature is located over the first key button, and when selected, this allows you to add accents just like you would add a sound or beat. When you add an accent to a key button, all other sounds that occur on the same key button are emphasized.

Other controls in Rebirth

Other effects and controls in Rebirth can help you find the sound you're looking for. Here are some of the basic ones:

✦ **Distortion (Dist):** *Distortion* is an effect similar to cranking up a guitar amplifier to full volume. It creates a harsher, louder sound. Clicking the Dist button on the right side of any of the four sections applies Distortion. Although distortion can be applied to any or all of the sections at the same time, only one master control exists for all sections. It is located on the right side of the Rebirth window.

✦ **Pattern Controlled Filter (PCF):** The PCF is a versatile filter that can be applied to one section at a time. It has a master control on the right side of the Rebirth window. The PCF radically modifies the sound, essentially by reshaping it. To experiment with the PCF controls, move the four slider bars up and down.

✦ **Compressor (Comp):** The Compressor evens up the audio signal, making it sound tighter. You can use the Compressor for one individual section or for the Master Output.

✦ **Delay:** The Delay creates an echo effect for a given sound. You'll find delay knobs on the right side of each section and one master control on the right side of the Rebirth window.

✦ **Level Controls:** You can control the sound levels that are going out to mix by using the mix slides to the right of each section. Remember that as discussed earlier in this chapter, Levels are important to consider before you import your final sound or music loop into Flash. A Master Output slide also exists that controls the Levels going out. Make sure that the meter isn't spending too much time in the red, or clipping will occur.

Preparation, mixing, and exporting Rebirth loops

At this point you should have a loop created that you want to export to AIF or WAV format. Before you do the final export, you should take a few steps to ensure good quality output.

✦ **Final Mixing:** Make sure that all the sections you want to mix are no longer soloed. To do this, make sure that all of your sections are set to go to the mix (green light on). Set the Levels on your sections individually to your liking by adjusting the Level Controls, as described previously. Bring them down if they are too *hot* (too much in the red), and set the Master Output Levels in a similar way.

✦ **Switch to Song Mode:** To export your Rebirth loop to AIFF or WAV, you need to switch to Song Mode. To do this, click Song Mode at the top of the application window. In Song Mode, choose Edit ➪ Initialize Song from Pattern Mode. Press Play to test your loop.

✦ **Exporting:** To export your loop, choose File ➪ Export Loop as Audio File. You'll be given the option to save your loop as a WAV or AIF file. The quality is automatically set to 44.1 kHz, 16-bit.

You should now have a one bar loop in AIF or WAV format. You can test it in another audio application, such as Peak or Sound Forge, and make any necessary changes, add additional effects, or import it directly into Flash.

Once you get the basics down, you will no doubt want to work on more-complex sounds. Creating a one-bar loop in Rebirth is just the beginning — you can use the Rebirth recording and loop features to make complex songs. Rebirth can also be integrated with other audio applications, such as Cubase VST. For more information on how to create a more-complex sound in Rebirth, refer to the very comprehensive Rebirth manual.

With the greatly improved MP3 compression available since Flash 5 and new MP3 import abilities in Flash MX, an incentive now exists to create complex, high-quality electronic music by using an application, such as Rebirth, without having to worry as much about file size. And the rewards for creating your own samples, loops, and songs are tremendous.

Rebirth is available for Macintosh and Windows platforms. You can download a demo version of Rebirth from the Propellerhead Web site at `www.propellerheads.se/demo`. You can also find information about Rebirth at `www.steinberg.net`.

ACID Loops to and from Flash

As in any creative field, there are certain basic guidelines for audio editing. At the same time, any truly creative person knows that creative ideas often come out of breaking these guidelines. This tutorial only presents some basic ideas to follow if you're looking for a starting point in using Sonic Foundry's ACID to make sound loops for use in Flash. The tutorial also assumes that you have at least beginner-level experience with ACID — you'll need to know how to use the basic ACID tools and must be familiar with the faders, tempo, and pitch functions.

About the library disks

Sonic Foundry ACID software comes with a disk titled Essential Sounds vol. 1. This disk contains enough loops to keep you busy for quite some time. You can purchase additional disks from Sonic Foundry. (For more information, check Sonic Foundry's Web site at `www.sonicfoundry.com/acid.html`).

Choosing the loops

Choosing the files for your loops is something everyone does differently. Although there is no right or wrong way to arrange a song, there are a few things to keep in mind. Not everyone has a subwoofer! If you decide to crank some serious bass and drums, be aware that it might sound awful coming through a tiny set of built-in speakers. You can also lose many high frequencies because of poor speakers.

Tempo and key changes

The tempo of a loop is up to the creator. However, some loops might seem to drag or speed up when played with other loops. Loops are usually best when placed within a limited range of beats per minute (BPM) above and below their original tempo. If the loop is pushed outside this range, it can lead to bad sound. Although there is no set rule for this threshold, it helps to know the original tempo when you are pushing a sound in this manner. Tempo is listed on the general ACID interface. The original tempo of a loop can also be found in the Properties dialog box. Just right-click/Control+click the file and choose Properties from the contextual menu. Speeding up and slowing down a loop will bring out human errors that aren't easily noticed at the original tempo. Don't assume that all Sonic Foundry loops are cut precisely either! Again, your ear is the best judge. As for key change, just be sure that you change all the tracks if you change one track. Otherwise, this might result in some disharmonious music. Yet, if that's your thing, by all means experiment.

Mixing

The key to mixing in ACID, or any environment, is consistency. Because each loop was probably recorded in a different environment, you will want to mix all the tracks smoothly to make it sound as if they were all playing together. Also, a combination of like instruments (such as four tracks of drums or two bass tracks) can lead to an overload in one particular frequency or a muddy mix. When mixing, test at least three different levels. If you only mix with your speakers cranked all the way up to 10, you will be inconsistent with the same mix at a lower level. Try to find a mix that sounds equally good at low, medium, and loud volume. This ensures that the listener has a pleasant experience with whatever speaker setting they're using.

Exporting

When you've finished mixing your loop, you can export it in a number of different formats. Make sure that your loop region is marked at the beginning and end of the selection you want to export. (To be safe, you may choose to erase all existing audio outside of the loop region.) From the File menu choose Save as and check the option to Save only the audio within the current loop region. The drop-down menu to the right of your new filename will give you a number of combinations for sample rates in both WAV and AIFF formats. Save your file to a new name (to avoid overwriting your original file) and then import the loop into the Flash Library.

Summary

✦ Remember the order in which the optimization process should follow: 1) Edit audio, 2) Normalize, 3) Convert to mono, 4) Resample.

✦ Always start with the highest quality audio possible. While it may be easy to reduce quality and file size, it is extremely hard to increase quality on an already poor file.

✦ Choosing a sound card appropriate for your project needs and paying attention to the output of your recorded audio are the best ways to ensure control over your final sound quality. The speakers on which you listen to your recorded audio can be just as important as the preamps and sound card you use to maintain that great sound quality. Shop around, talk to people with experience, and try to test equipment before buying it.

✦ Adding a small fade to the beginning and ending of loops can help remove unwanted skips and clips to your event loops in Flash. Make sure that the fade does not occur over too long of a gap, or the loop will appear to drop.

✦ Use programs like Propellerhead's Rebirth and Sonic Foundary's ACID to create your own custom loops and sound effects.

✦ Always save a backup copy of your original sound file. This is key in checking two files against each other, matching and comparing file sizes, as well as giving you a great place for starting over when you completely mess up!

✦   ✦   ✦

Working with 3D Graphics

◆ ◆ ◆ ◆

In This Chapter

Understanding 3D
terminology

Creating 3D effects
using Flash and 3D
sequences

Planning and Executing
a 3D based Flash
project

◆ ◆ ◆ ◆

Although Flash has no true 3D tools, it is possible to simulate 3D depth through a combination of layering and well-placed sequences of animation. With more 3D software companies creating programs with support for .swf output, Flash designers have a growing number of choices in ways to create 3D animations for import into Flash.

This chapter will explore the steps for creating a 3D animation in the Flash SWF format using one of the better-known professional 3D programs, Discreet's 3ds max. Because most 3D software programs have similar tools and layouts you can likely follow along using whichever program you're most comfortable with. This chapter assumes you have a rudimentary knowledge of 3D modeling and animation: X, Y, and Z-axes, splines, lights, and cameras, all of which we will be using in the examples that follow.

Note   Thanks to Kenn Brown (www.kontent-online.com) for all his help with concept and artwork for the Masters of the Game example discussed in this chapter.

Introduction to the 3D Environment

The world of 3D design is complex and diverse, and branches off into a variety of fields including modelers, animators, and specialists whose whole focus is creating incredibly detailed textures, lighting scenarios, and animations that span the life-like to the fantastic.

While the scope of this tutorial doesn't include complex animation techniques, a well-planned and designed 3D animation can add a level of professionalism and excitement to your Flash project that is hard to match.

In the examples that follow later in this chapter, you will create objects from scratch in a 3D environment using tools such as wire framing, texture-mapping, extruding, lathing, and lighting. Then you will animate these objects and export them in a format that can be brought into Flash.

3D basics

Computer monitors have only two dimensions, width and height, but 3D artwork occurs in what is called 3D space, a simulation of real space. As Figure 40-1 illustrates, three-dimensional space has three axes: X (width), Y (height), and Z (depth). While conceptualizing three dimensions may not be difficult, controlling views of objects and cameras, or rotating objects with a mouse and keyboard can prove to be an arduous task.

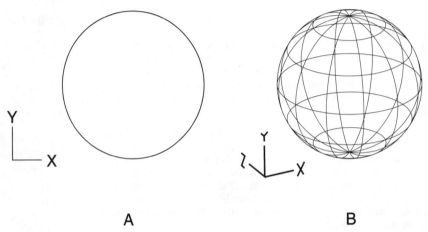

A   **B**

Figure 40-1: The left diagram (A) provides a two-dimensional representation of space and the right diagram (B) depicts three-dimensional space.

Most artwork achieves the appearance of depth through the use of perspective, wherein the proportion of the composition's foreground and background spaces lend a perceived depth. With linear perspective, parallel lines are drawn as converging lines, usually to a single vanishing point on a horizon line (picture train tracks), as shown in Figure 40-2. Objects closer to the viewer appear larger, while objects farther from the viewer appear smaller. Similarly, atmospheric perspective adds to a composition's sense of depth by reducing the visibility (detail and definition) of objects as they approach the horizon.

In most 3D computer applications, you can also choose a viewpoint known as orthographic perspective, in which objects and scenes are shown from a strict mathematical viewpoint—without any sense of depth (see Figure 40-3). Technically, because orthographic views do not use perspective, this viewpoint should be referred to as *orthographic projection*. This is because an orthographic view renders an object or scene with mathematical accuracy instead of perceptual perspective accuracy. Some applications may also have an *isometric* view. As far as 3D computer-drawing programs are concerned, *isometric* and *orthographic* views are the same.

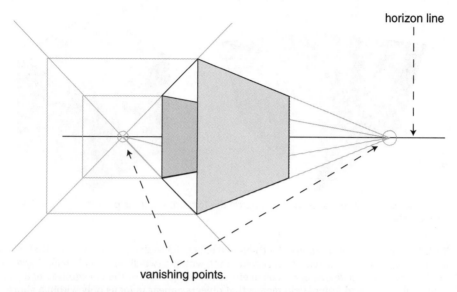

horizon line

vanishing points.

Figure 40-2: The line drawing (top) illustrates the concept of linear perspective. The image created in Corel Bryce 3D (bottom) shows linear and atmospheric perspective.

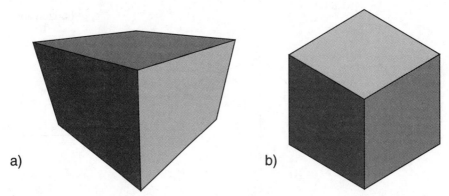

a)   b)

Figure 40-3: Linear perspective of a cube on the left; orthographic projection of a cube on the right

With the advent of photography, depth-of-field effects have also become factors that can be used to contribute to a sense of perceived depth within a two-dimensional plane. *Depth of field* refers to the range of clear focus in either the foreground or the background of a composition. A low depth of field means that objects appear in focus only within a short distance range from the viewer (see Figure 40-4). For example, if a camera lens is focused on a person with mountains in the distance, then the person is in focus, while the mountains are not. A high depth of field means that objects can be farther apart from one another while maintaining the same focus clarity. Using the same previous example, a high depth of field enables both the near person and the distant mountains to appear in focus.

Figure 40-4: Low depth of field on the left; high depth of field on the right

Most 3D-creation programs not only strive to render scenes with accurate perspective, but also strive for a sense of near-photographic realism. Given the nature of Flash's vector-based framework, most highly textured 3D artwork won't mesh well with small vector file sizes. Nevertheless, simpler 3D objects and animations can be imported into Flash while maintaining reasonable file sizes.

3D programs use the following processes or enhancements to add realism and depth to artwork:

✦ **Extruding:** This is the process of importing a two-dimensional vector graphics file (such as Illustrator EPS) into a 3D modeling program and giving depth to an otherwise flat object — usually by extending vertices or edges along the Z-axis (see Figure 40-5).

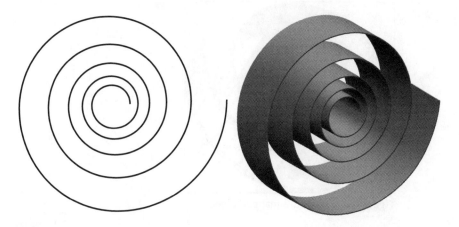

Figure 40-5: A flat 2D graphic on the left; an extruded 2D graphic on the right

✦ **Lighting:** The most important factor in creating the illusion of spatial depth is adding and positioning light sources. A well-lit 3D model emphasizes planar depth; poorly lit 3D objects look flat (see Figure 40-6).

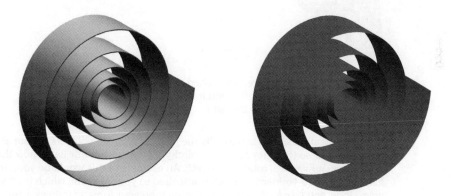

Figure 40-6: A well-lit 3D object on the left; a poorly lit object on the right

✦ **Texture Mapping:** Textures (images of patterns or surface materials) can be stretched across an object's surface(s) or faces (see Figure 40-7). Through the use of color contrast, pattern, and opacity, texture mapping gives an object unique, realistic attributes.

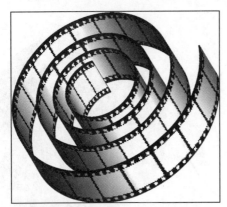

Figure 40-7: A texture-mapped object

✦ **Wireframe:** A wireframe is the most basic model structure of a 3D object. It renders objects using lines to represent the edges of polygons and faces (see Figure 40-8).

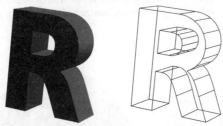

Figure 40-8: A fully rendered view of an extruded letter "R" on the left; a wireframe view of the same model on the right

✦ **Inverse Kinematics:** This is basically the process of linking objects in your 3D environment together so that they form a hierarchy that affects and/or limits how those objects can now move, rotate, bend, etc. An example of this would be your arm. Your hand is joined to your wrist, which is attached to your forearm, which is attached to your elbow and so on. If your hand is lifted then your forearm follows, your elbow bends and then eventually your whole arm is lifted.

Creating inverse kinematics is fairly advanced and outside the scope of this book, but you may want to explore it more fully on your own if you find yourself creating complex objects or reusing objects or characters in your animation. The more time and care you put into building these objects the more time you'll save yourself later animating them.

A more limited form of inverse kinematics can also be created in Flash using ActionScript to link objects together. To see such an example, check out www.vectorlounge.com/ 04_amsterdam/jam/wireframe.html.

File formats

Several cross-platform 3D file formats exist including DXF (AutoCAD), and VRML (Virtual Reality Modeling Language). The one we are going to be focusing on is 3ds (3D Studio) because of the following:

✦ It is supported by Flash-based 3D modeling programs such as Electric Rain's Swift 3D.

✦ There are free downloadable models available on Web sites such as www.3dcafe.com.

Flash MX does provide limited support for the DXF format, but only recognizes two-dimensional files such as those created by CAD programs. Consequently, we suggest that if your 3D program doesn't support outputting directly to Flash's SWF format you should then use one of the following 4 formats:

Raster formats

✦ **PICT:** A file format developed by Apple Computer in 1984. All graphics programs that run on Macintosh computers support it as well as most professional graphics programs for the PC.

✦ **PNG:** Designed for on-line viewing applications it is fully streamable with a progressive display option and can store extra data including alpha, gamma correction, and chromaticity data for improved color matching on heterogeneous platforms. Most commonly used if your images have an alpha channel (transparency).

Vector formats

✦ **EPS:** Encapsulated PostScript. Pronounced as separate letters, EPS is the graphics file format used by the PostScript language.

✦ **AI:** Adobe Illustrator's format, commonly supported by most 3D and graphics programs.

As a general rule we would suggest bringing your animations in using vector-based formats, as Flash is a vector-based program. Exceptions to this would be if your vector illustrations were quite complex or being displayed at such a small size that raster-based formats would actually cut down on file size while maintaining image quality.

There are a variety of 3D programs out there that vary in price and complexity. Higher-end packages such as Lightwave, 3ds max, and Maya offer the most control and flexibility to the 3D designer, whereas lower-end packages such as Swift 3D, Vecta 3D, and the soon-to-be-available (at the time of this writing) Plasma generally offer less control but are more focused towards the needs of Flash designers and have a smaller learning curve than the higher-end packages. There are also third-party plug-ins available such as Illustrate, Vecta 3D, and Swift 3D that allow higher-end packages to export directly to Flash's SWF format.

3D Exports and Imports

If you already own a 3D program and are creating objects that don't require perspective animation you likely don't need a middleware solution to prep the files for importing into Flash. Simply render the image out as an EPS or raster image for importing or tracing. When creating objects that animate in perspective, a 3D program/plug-in such as those listed earlier would prove valuable in creating detailed vector-based graphics with realistic perspectives.

A Flash designer could probably get by without these products for creating 3D animations, but there are definitely some benefits to having the right tools:

✦ Easier animation

✦ Quicker turnaround

✦ Higher level of precision and control

✦ Streamlining of process

✦ Provides a level of reality hard to attain by hand

EPS files, alpha channels, and image compression

Most 3D packages allow you to export your image as (vector-based) EPS files or as (raster-based) image sequences that have an alpha channel that Flash recognizes.

If you are exporting to EPS, you will likely need to spend time simplifying your vector graphics after import to remove unwanted points, objects, and remnants. Often shading will be lost, meaning the object would have the same (flat) shading for all the faces.

If you are exporting as raster images, then consider whether these require transparency (an area in the image that objects on another layer will be visible through). This requires exporting to a format where Flash recognizes the transparency. You will also want to consider image compression. A few bitmapped images may not be a concern but larger sequences of these images could cause problems with file size and playback speed.

There have been great developments in Flash and 3D, supported by third-party software allowing developers/animators to export their animations/objects directly into streamlined SWF format. Earlier software didn't allow the 3D animator to do much more than change line thickness and fill color. Newer versions of most Flash-friendly 3D software allow for shading, specular highlights (lighting hotspots), and the use of bitmaps for texture mapping. Earlier versions also rendered the entire object (including areas that you didn't see such as an object's back), causing unwanted lines and fills to be rendered. File size would be increased while the animation display quality suffered. Newer versions don't do this so much and are more concerned with keeping file size down, but you'll still find a fair bit of tweaking required after bringing your animations into Flash.

Flash and 3D

Although Flash math wizards are able to use manually animated shapes and ActionScript to simulate simple square and polygon shapes that users can manipulate in a 3D environment, this chapter is focused on creating or simulating 3D objects using more traditional methods such as modeling and frame-by-frame rendering. Flash and 3D programs have some similarities in their use of vectors but whereas 3D plug-ins like VRML and Shockwave use a 3D engine to display and allow manipulation of the objects/mesh in real time, Flash does not. A Flash designer has to simulate these elements using sequences of animation (possibly combined with ActionScript to detect user input). The most important thing to remember is that a user will not be able to manipulate objects on a 3D axis without each frame of this object's rotation first being created.

There are a few methods of using 3D in Flash, all of which can be combined to add realism to your animations.

✦ Using various perspectives in your design and scaling objects to match those perspectives. Example: A car coming towards you appears to grow bigger as it gets closer (see Figure 40-9 and Figure 40-10).

✦ Using layers to simulate depth. Layers in the background can be made to appear less vibrant or be blurred, while layers in the foreground are left crisp and vibrant. Layers can be animated to move at different speeds to simulate different distances from the viewer. Example: A car travels horizontally down a road. Both the car and the road are moving but because the car is moving faster it simulates depth. This was used a lot in early video games and lends itself well to Flash.

✦ Using a sequence of frames that have been rendered in a 3D program. This sequence of individual images shows the object appearing to rotate to a different position in each frame, giving the illusion that the object is doing so in 3D space (see Figure 40-11). This is generally the most realistic method and is what we'll be covering in the following exercise.

To illustrate some of the differences in these methods, we'll use an animation of a car illustrated in two different ways.

Figure 40-9: Simulated 3D using a single object and scaling. The car appears to be moving toward the viewer. Other methods involve masking, alpha tweens, and so on to give the illusion of depth in a 2D space.

Figure 40-10: Showing one of many limitations in the simulated 3D method using 2D tools

Note   For the animation shown in Figure 40-11, ten frames have been flipped horizontally and repeated to simulate the car moving 30 degrees in the opposite direction — a trick of using symmetric objects to reduce the amount of frames needed to simulate a rotation, reducing overall file size dramatically.

Things to consider before creating 3D models

Even though using 3D tools makes life easier, you must still be aware of some inherent limitations. Each unique frame rendered into SWF format is taking up bytes. You must consider this when planning the final piece. Complex shapes have more vector points and faces and require more bytes of information and processing power to smoothly animate. Consider the following items during the planning phase:

Reusing frames

An excellent way to reduce overall file size of your Flash movies is to reuse unique frames. This could mean reusing objects in your movie, using some of Flash's built-in effects, such as transparency or tinting, to give different instances of an object a different look, or reusing sequences of frames. A good example is the traditional 3D walk-cycle. A walk-cycle usually consists of 24-30 unique frames that can be repeated or "looped" to provide a complex animation at a small file size.

Symmetric objects

One of the advantages of using symmetric objects is that it limits the amount of unique frames needed in Flash to simulate 3D. Let's use a rotating cube as an example. It could take 36 unique frames to animate the cube rotating 360 degrees. But because a cube looks pretty much exactly the same on each side, you really only need to animate 90 degrees of the rotation and then loop that four times to simulate the full rotation. You could then even flip your looped animation to simulate a cube spinning in the opposite direction.

Figure 40-11: This example includes ten frames that show the car rotating 30 degrees, allowing us greater flexibility and a more realistic movement of the car.

Layering animations

By layering animations you can limit what needs to be created in 3D. Keep your animating and non-animating objects on different layers. Don't use unique frames for non-animating objects. A good example would be creating an animation of fish swimming in a tank. Only the fish need to be animated, as the tank doesn't move. You can chop off a lot of file size by rendering only the fish as an animation and rendering the tank separately as a single frame.

Using 3ds max to Create 3D Models

The examples in the remainder of this chapter cover the techniques of delivering 3D content (or the illusion of) with Flash. The software we'll be using on this project is Discreet's 3ds max R4.2, Electric Rain's Swift3D Max Exporter plug-in, and Macromedia Flash MX.

3ds max is an extremely flexible and powerful modeling and animation solution that can be the cornerstone of any interactive project. Swift3D Max is a plug-in application for 3ds max that allows you to render 3D scenes directly from the software to the most popular vector file formats, including .swf (Macromedia's native Flash format). The key feature of this software is its ability to translate complex geometry into compact vector-based content including lighting and shading. Electric Rain's Swift3D is also available as a stand-alone 3D modeling/animating product.

Note You can find demo versions of these programs at the following locations: Discreet 3ds max at www.discreet.com/products/3dsmax, Electric Rain's Swift3D Max Exporter plug-in at www.erain.com, and Macromedia Flash MX at macromedia.com/software/flash/.

To demonstrate the process of preparing 3D animation for Flash and then importing it and setting up an interface in the Flash authoring environment, we have created a sample promo or trailer for a fictional company called Masters of the Game, with a 3D animation of a chess set. In the remainder of this chapter, we will go through the various steps involved in creating the original elements in 3ds max and bringing them into Flash.

On the CD-ROM To see the final Flash animation with the 3D elements and the functional interface, open the MoTG.swf file from the ch40 folder on the CD-ROM. To see the file structure, open the MoTG.fla file from the ch40 folder. The .fla file is carefully commented and labeled to help you see how the project was put together.

There are several parts to this tutorial, covering storyboarding/planning, modeling, animating, and exporting via 3ds max and Swift 3D, plus some tips for optimizing your content before and after you bring it into Flash.

Planning and design

Although there are other simple 3D programs out there, 3ds max (combined with a SWF-exporting plug-in) gives the modelers/animators a complete toolbox that enables them to create complex and realistic animations well outside the scope of simple rotations and panning.

This tutorial is not meant to be a beginners guide to 3d studio max, but is instead intended to guide readers who have 3D experience through the process of integrating 3D content with Flash movies. It is meant to demonstrate 3D animation effects that can be used to spice up Flash movies and expects the reader to have at least rudimentary experience with the 3D tools available in 3ds max or other, similar 3D programs including X, Y, and Z-axes, splines, lights, cameras, and rendering.

There are several methods of storyboarding a project. 3ds max is an excellent tool for creating the initial storyboards as it provides a lot of flexibility and control in creating and displaying the storyboards and outputs professional quality images.

Planning for this tutorial began by identifying and writing out objectives and scribbling ideas on paper, then setting about to create a nice-looking storyboard that communicated what we were trying to accomplish. This was a simple matter of creating low poly (poly = polygon or a single 2D section or "face" of a 3D object) objects and placing them on the "stage" with various cameras indicating the POV (point of view) and transitions. Then draft renderings were created (see Figure 40-12 and Figure 40-13) and compiled into a word program with write-ups to explain action and function. This was printed out in black and white and kept for reference as construction on this project began.

To see the rough storyboard for the project described in this chapter, go to the ch40 folder on the *Flash MX Bible* CD-ROM and open Storyboard.doc.

The graphics shown in Figure 40-12 already look "finished" in the draft rendering because the surfaces of the chess set do not require any texturing on the surfaces. If this were a more detailed scene with organic shapes and textures, it would look less realistic at this stage than it would in the final renderings.

Having the storyboard was important to maintain the content and visual integrity of the tutorial goals. (Refer to Figure 40-13 to see some frames from the storyboard.)

Figure 40-12: Draft rendering of chess pieces and board

Initial Storyboard for Masters of the Game (rendered from 3ds max)

Stage #1
Camera begins to swing down
and to the left in a smooth and
steady arc.

Stage #2
Camera settles into final
orientation for interactive
movie 01, Chess pieces begin
to fade in...

Stage #3
Camera is fixed to a circular Path. Center of
circle/target is focused on the primary
interactive object. Chess pieces are all in place.
Camera control/HUD displays in the lower left
corner. Orientation of camera is controlled by
the left and right arrows and indicated by the
yellow arrow.

Figure 40-13: Storyboard graphics

Note   By comparing the storyboard (Figure 40-13), with the actual tutorial files you can see that the
overall scope of the project was cut back to fit time constraints.

Building your objects

The chess pieces for this tutorial were created with simple 2D splines, which were then lathed (rotated around an axis) into 3D objects. The chessboard is comprised of basic primitive objects — boxes that have been replicated using the Array function. We also address other basic principles such as detaching the faces of an object to create new objects, and using the Array function. The geometry in the chess pieces all have a budget of around 1,000 polys that determines the overall quality of the final output/renders.

Note
When using texture mapping, the Swift 3D engine does not precisely interpret bitmapped materials; instead, it attempts to approximate the overall color value of the object or polygon. For this reason it's always prudent to create basic materials in the Material/Map browser using the default setting (Blinn) with a semi-gloss surface and basic diffuse coloring. This will give you much more control over the final relationships between the objects in your scene after outputting.

To create the chess pieces, follow these steps:

1. Activate the front view port and press W on the keyboard to maximize this view port into a single large window.

2. In the Create panel, click the Shapes tab and then select Line.

3. Begin drawing the profile of the chess piece starting at the top, clicking to place your first point. Continue placing points along the length of the profile until you have created a general shape as shown. Right-click to finish the Line/profile creation. You can now edit the spline in the vertex sub select of the Modify menu. This will allow you to move the points around to clean up and refine your shape (see Figure 40-14).

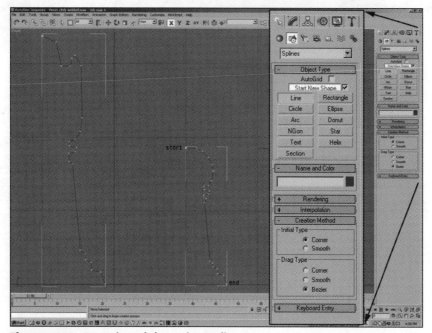

Figure 40-14: Front view of chess piece spline

4. With the spline selected, in the Modify panel ➪ Modifier List, choose Patch/Spline Editing ➪ Lathe. This will create the 3D shape of your chess piece. In the Parameters rollout you can affect the orientation by clicking Min, Max, or Center to influence the axis of rotation. Try clicking each one and view the results. If your object appears to be inside out, scroll to the bottom of the parameters menu and activate both Flip Normals and Weld Core (see Figure 40-15).

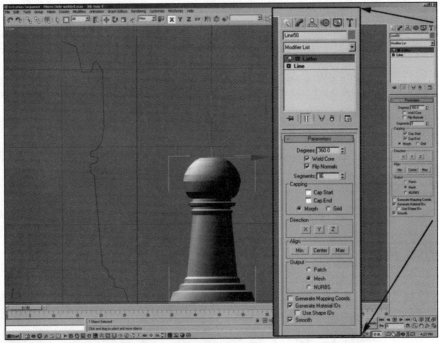

Figure 40-15: Rotation sequence using Flip Normals

5. Add additional detailing to the upper section by creating a cylinder using the Create ➪ Standard Primitives ➪ Cylinder, which is then adjusted based on the parameters available in the Modify panel.

6. Once the first cylinder has been put into position, hold the Shift key while dragging the object upward along its Y-axis. When it's in position, release the object and a dialog box will come up asking you whether you want to Copy, Instance, or Reference. Choose Instance and repeat this for the third and final ring (see Figure 40-16). (Although this detailing could have been added to the original spline of the Lathe object, these objects were originally intended to be animated.)

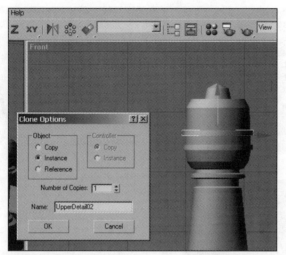

Figure 40-16: Instancing first cylinder to add detail to chess piece

Adding additional detail to the base

To add additional detail, follow these steps:

1. Create details for the Base by using the Create ➪ Standard Primitives ➪ Box. Once you have the approximate scale and orientation of the first box, move it into position (see Figure 40-17 #1).

2. Open the Hierarchy tab in the Command panel and making sure your box is selected, choose Affect Pivot Only. Your pivot will be displayed in your view port as arrows pointing on the three axes. If you have the Select and Move tool active, you can right-click on the axes and select Move from the Quad menu.

3. Move the pivot point to the center of your master object (see Figure 40-17 #1).

4. Replicate the object eight times around its central pivot using the Array function in the Array Flyout tool (see Figure 40-17 #2). 360 degrees divided by 8 equals 45 degrees. This means the array function will instance an object every 45 degrees around the Z-axis of the central pivot. Your final result should look like Figure 40-17 #3, with the arrayed boxes highlighted in green.

5. Select one of the boxes and use the Attach function in the Modify Panel. Attach the entire array of boxes to create a single object. This will allow us to animate the sub-objects (the individual blocks) as well as animate a rotation on the entire group, which we'll get into in more detail later in the tutorial.

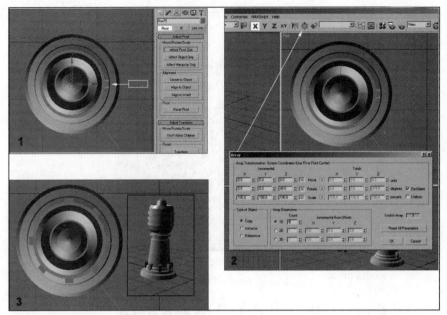

Figure 40-17: Array transformation using pivot center

Creating the chessboard

To create the chessboard, follow these steps:

1. In the Command panel select the Display tab, scroll mid-way down the menu, and select Hide by Hit. Click on your objects until they are all hidden. (Another alternative is to first select all of your objects and then click the Hide Selected button.)

2. Click the Create Tab ➪ Standard Primitives ➪ Box. Draw a box of any size/proportion (see Figure 40-18).

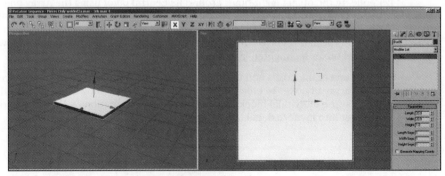

Figure 40-18: The initial pieces of the chessboard

3. Click the Modify tab. The box parameters are displayed. Enter the following values: 20 for length, 20 for width, and 1 for height.

4. Select your box and click the Array button. We will use the array function again to create an 8 x 8 grid that will become our chessboard. (See Figure 40-19). We will create eight boxes along the Y-axis with a distance of 2 units between each box. Activate the Copy radio button and click OK.

5. Select all eight boxes and click the array button again. Repeat the same process used in Step 4, only this time along the X-axis. You now have a standard 8 x 8 checkerboard (see Figure 40-19).

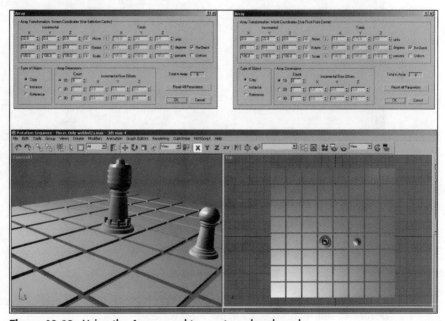

Figure 40-19: Using the Array panel to create a chessboard

Adding materials

Let's take a few moments to add *materials* to the chess objects. The surfaces of 3D objects are defined by the materials assigned to them; the materials determine the various surface properties of the objects. To add materials, follow these steps:

1. Open the Material Editor by pressing the M key or by clicking the Material Editor button in the menu bar (see Figure 40-20).

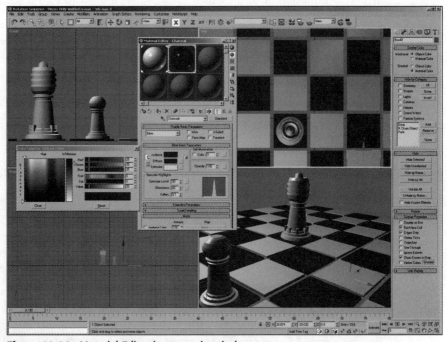

Figure 40-20: Material Editor in our main window.

2. In the Material Editor click the first slot (upper-left). It will now have a white border to show that it is the active slot (see Figure 40-21).

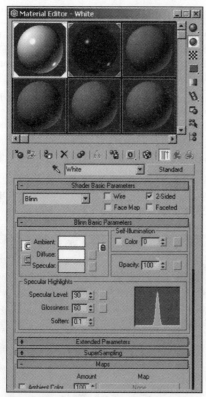

Figure 40-21: Material Editor window settings

3. In the material name field type **White** and press Return. Shader Basic parameters should be set to Blinn.

4. Click the diffuse color chip to open your color selector. In the Whiteness slider bar, drag the marker all the way to the bottom of the scale (R-255, G-255, B-255). Close the Selector box.

5. Set your Specular level to 90, and your Glossiness to 60. By default Soften should be set to 0.1.

6. Mouse down on the upper slot of the White material you have just created and drag it over the adjacent slot. You should now have two materials both named **White**.

7. Change the name of your second material to **Charcoal** and click the Diffuse color chip to open the color selector. Set your values to R-25, G-25, and B-25. You now have two materials in your Editor, called **White** and **Charcoal**.

8. Assign the materials to our chess pieces. You have the choice of dragging and dropping the material from the active slot onto your object or selecting your object and clicking the Assign Material to Selection button. Any selected objects will now be given the surface properties set by that material.

Preparing your object for animation

One of the key effects in this example is the exploding panel on the master chess object. Although the assembly and control mechanisms for this sequence are handled in Flash, you have to consider carefully your desired results and render your elements out accordingly via 3ds max for importing into your Flash file.

1. Convert the chess piece to an editable mesh. Because your object is a lathed spline, you will have to either convert it to an editable mesh by right-clicking and selecting Convert To: ⇨ Convert To Editable Mesh in the Quad Menu or by adding an edit Mesh Modifier to the objects stack.

2. You can now use the Editable Mesh function in the Modifier panel. Under Selection, choose Face and select the upper third of the master chess object.

3. Under Edit Geometry in the same panel, choose Detach. When you are prompted to name this object, type **Top** (see Figure 40-22).

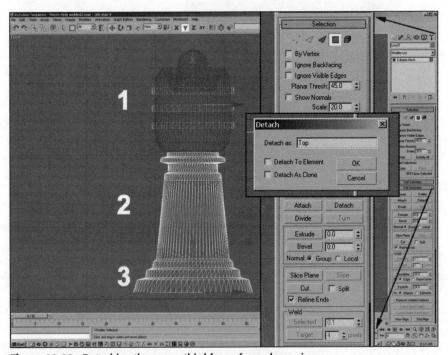

Figure 40-22: Detaching the upper third face of our chess piece

4. Repeat this process for the Middle and Base sections, naming the detached objects respectively.

The next step is to subdivide the vertical thirds into quarters. You want to follow the same process of selecting the **Top** object and using the Edit Mesh function in the Modifier panel:

1. Activate your Top View port and press the W key to Zoom Extents.

2. Under Selection choose Face and drag a selection box around the upper-right quad of the Top object as shown.

3. Make sure you have the entire 90 degrees of faces selected. Use the Detach button under Edit Geometry. This time, you want to Detach To Element (see Figure 40-23).

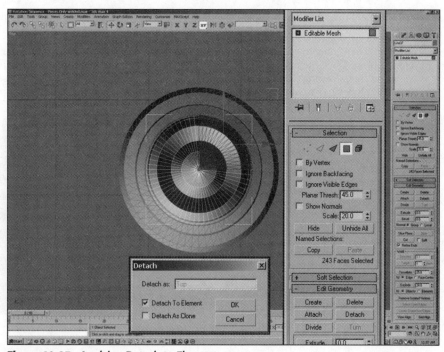

Figure 40-23: Applying Detach to Element

4. Repeat this process until the Top object is subdivided into four Quadrants within the object.

5. Repeat the same process for the Middle and Base sections.

Note   The reason we chose to Detach to Element (as opposed to creating entirely new objects) is dictated by how we want to handle the "exploding" animation. Detaching the elements allows us to animate the rotation(s) of the Top, Middle, or Base objects independent of the sub-object animations in which the slices or panels move out from the center to their final "exploded" position.

To animate the chess piece, follow these steps:

1. Select the top pieces.

2. Create a key frame at 45 on the timeline and another at 80.

   3. Animate the pieces outward.

   4. Repeat for the middle and bottom sections.

To create the Legman, follow these steps:

   1. Create the Legman's body using simple splines.

   2. Extrude or lathe the splines into a 3D character.

   3. Create the head and platform using simple primitives. Apply the same techniques used to build your chess objects.

The important thing to remember is that our Legman character has to fit within the master chess object. Once the master chess object is built, it's a simple process of setting up a front view and then drawing the splines to conform to the dimensions of the master chess object—which explodes to reveal our little character (see Figure 40-24).

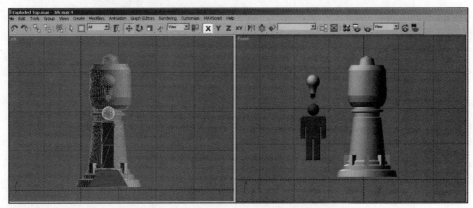

Figure 40-24: Our Legman as it fits inside the master chess object

Setting up your scene

We are first going to set up our camera to closely match the composition we chose in the storyboards. With the proper composition framed for our animation sequence, we can then concentrate on lighting placement. Most current vector packages take into account light sourcing and will create outputs that are based on flat or graduated shading with specular highlights and shadows as selectable options.

To set up your camera animation, follow these steps:

   1. Activate the Top view port and zoom out so you have all of your elements visible.

   2. Go to the Modify panel and click the Create tab. Now select the Cameras button (fourth from the left) and under Object Type select Free.

3. Click in the Top view port directly above the center of the chessboard. Activate the Perspective View port and press C on your keyboard to change it to the Camera View port. You should now be looking straight down onto your scene. This will become the first frame of our animated sequence.

4. Give the camera a lens setting of 43 mm, which will give you an FOV of 45.429 degrees.

5. Set your target distance to 195 units (see Figure 40-25).

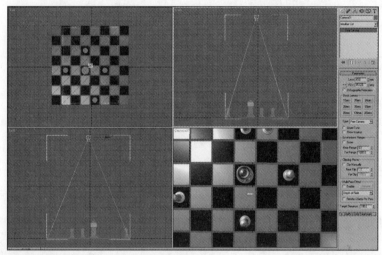

Figure 40-25: Setting up our camera

We also know that based on our storyboard we want the camera to arrive at a three-quarter view relative to the chessboard. We will deal with this later, but for now let's just go ahead to the next step and set a key at frame 45 for the arrival point of our camera in order to set up the composition.

6. Click on the Time Configuration Key and set your Frame Rate to 24 Frames Per Second (FPS). In the Animation Group set your End Time to 120 and click OK. These are just arbitrary settings to get you started (see Figure 40-26).

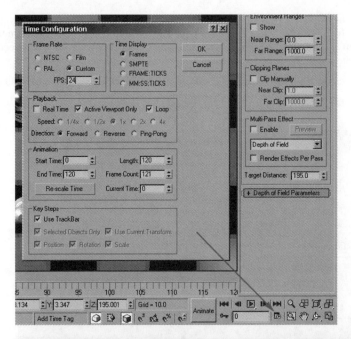

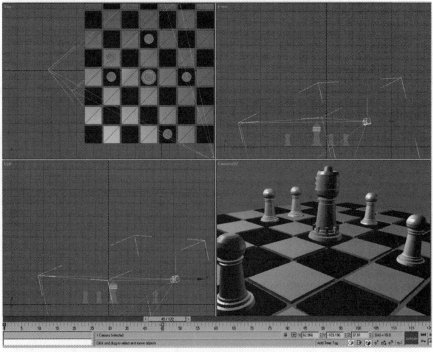

Figure 40-26: Configuring the timeline

7. Select Camera01 and turn on the Animate key.

8. Drag the time slider to frame 45 and use the Select and Move tool to position the camera around the lower-left corner of the chessboard, then use the Select and Rotate tool to roughly frame the scene. In order to refine the composition within the camera view you can use any of the tools available such as Truck, Pan, and Orbit (see Figure 40-27).

Figure 40-27: Truck, Pan, and Orbit tools

9. Once you are satisfied with your composition turn off the Animate key. The transition of your camera moving from above the board to a three-quarter view has been recorded as an animation across 45 frames. We will refine that sequence later.

It is worth noting that the pawn objects were instanced by selecting and holding down the Shift key while dragging the instance to its new position on the board. The pawns were arranged based on the final camera composition.

The correct use of lighting — in this case placement and color — can make or break your final rendered image. Because we are dealing with a stylistic representation of reality (our vector output) we are not as concerned with simulating real-world lighting (although a lot of the basic principles are very much applicable). For this situation we will use two default Omni lights with variance set only in the color and multiplier values. Omni01 is our main light source and has a source color of white and a default multiplier of 1. Omni02 is our secondary light source and has been given half the multiplier value of Omni01 as well as a Blue Hue:

1. Open the Modify Menu.

2. Select Create ➪ Lights ➪ Omni.

3. Click anywhere in the view ports to place lights in your scene.

The choice of Blue as a secondary light source is used to soften or "pick up" the shadowed areas of the chess pieces, and to offer variance to an otherwise mundane scene (see Figure 40-28).

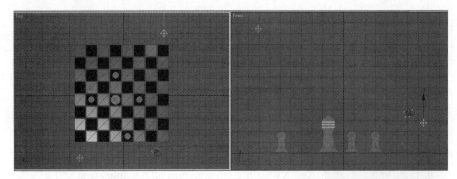

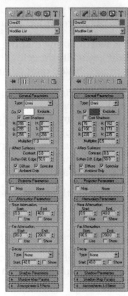

Figure 40-28: Configuring your lighting

The position you choose for your lights can enhance or weaken the overall impact of your scene. The type of light, quality, and position can be used to evoke mood or emotion. We've selected the main light source (Omni01) to present strong illumination from the upper left creating dramatic specular highlights on the upper surfaces of the chess pieces. The secondary light source (Omni02) is set opposite our main light source but is much lower and casts a softer blue glow to the non-illuminated sides of the chess pieces. This lighting solution also creates a nice variance in the surface of the chessboard for the animated intro sequence.

In preliminary tests it was decided that rendering would be done with Swift3D's Cartoon Average Color Fill and specular settings set to On. Shadow casting relative to our light sources is not a primary concern, but feel free to experiment. Be prepared to spend almost as much time lighting your scene as you spent constructing it — the time is well spent doing test renders while experimenting with different lighting solutions. A render of our scene with the final lighting in place is shown in Figure 40-29.

Figure 40-29: A render of the scene with lighting added

Swift 3D Animation and Rendering for Flash

Let's now deal with the issues of animation and how to handle the output based on the results you want to achieve in Flash. This section will show you how to deconstruct your scene in 3ds max and render with Swift 3D to create an optimized sequence for efficient authoring within the Flash environment.

Timing and rendering intro animation

The intro sequence in which we go from a head-on view of the chessboard to a three-quarter perspective is handled as a simple camera move. The big concern here is to decide how many frames you want to use to accomplish this introductory sequence. Because the animation is running at 24 frames per second, let's keep the camera move under 2 seconds and run the entire sequence across 45 frames. It was very convenient that our earlier guess of 45 frames for the intro was pretty much bang on.

Before you move forward, click the Zoom Extents All button in the lower-right-hand corner of your screen. Because you have already set the Start key and Finish key for the movement of the intro camera your task is now to review and refine it. When you play the animation, you will notice that the motion is overly even and mechanical. To make the sequence more dynamic, you need to slowly accelerate the camera at the beginning of the animation and then decelerate it as it comes to a stop (see Figure 40-30).

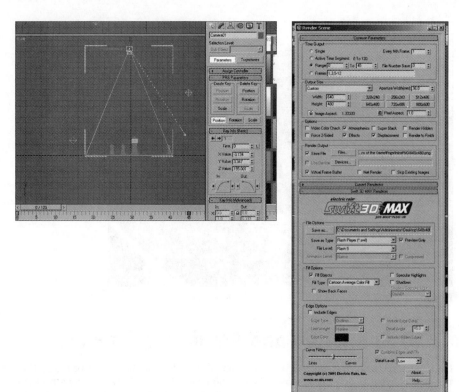

Figure 40-30: Setting the camera's acceleration and deceleration

To fine-tune your camera animation, follow these steps:

1. With the Camera object selected, click the Display tab in the Modify Menu and scroll down to the Display Properties group.

2. Activate the Show Trajectories radio button. Click the Motion tab (with Camera01 still selected) and scroll down to the Key Info (Basics) group. This group changes the animation value, time, and interpolation methods of one or more selected keys.

3. Click the IN interpolation Flyout and change the value to Slow-In.

4. Use the arrow key to select the second key at frame 45 and change the value to Slow-Out. You will notice that the white ticks (representing each frame) are much closer together at the start and finish. Keys for influencing the camera rotation can also be accessed here.

5. Remember to assign Swift 3D as your Production Renderer under the Current Renderers Group. With this sequence we'll turn off Specular Highlights and Shadows and dial down the detail to Low because of the overall simplicity of the objects being rendered. You can also see how the lighting setup combined with the glossy materials creates nice surface variation during the 45-frame intro sequence.

6. Save that sequence out as IntroAnim.swf or something similar.

Table 40-1 shows a comparison of the file size for our example, when rendered from Swift3D at Low Detail and High Detail settings, with the file size of the same sequence in bitmapped PNG format. Based on the comparison chart, it is not hard to see the value in vector-based 3D animation versus traditional bitmapped sequences.

Table 40-1: 45 Frame Intro Sequence

Setting	Size
Swift3D Low Detail	0160k
Swift3D High Detail	0460k
Bitmapped PNG files	2000k

Exporting the single pawn object

Now move your time slider to frame 50 and click Unhide All under the Display tab in your Modify menu. Select all the boxes associated with the checkerboard and hide those elements (see Figure 40-31).

If you were to now render out the just the chess pieces as a single frame, you would run into a problem—the master chess piece would be rendered with the cartoon average fill as separate objects. You can easily solve this problem by using either of the following two methods:

✦ **Method One:** Hide the master object and render only the pawn objects. Now hide everything except the master chess piece but this time around, use the Mesh Gradient setting to Render.

✦ **Method Two:** Do a Save-As on the 3ds max file and attach all the master chess pieces as a single object. Use the Weld vertices function to create a single seamless mesh and render out your single frame (pawns and master chess piece) using the Cartoon Average fill. You can then separate and edit those elements later within Flash.

We used method two for the final Flash project located on the CD-ROM (see Figure 40-32).

Figure 40-31: Hiding objects in our scene before rendering

Figure 40-32: Pawn objects rendered individually

The purpose of these stills is to create static objects that can be animated within Flash as transitions over time. We are also going to use the master chess object as a mask to reduce the amount of information per frame of animation.

Confused? Don't be. It will all make sense shortly.

Isolating exports for optimized animation

Animation is dependent on Flash's most basic yet powerful feature: *layers*. Employed by many graphics programs to improve their ability to handle complex drawings as well as add support for depth, layers serve as the ultimate organization tool in a program such as Flash where we place objects on top of one another and then animate them.

In this case, once the intro movie has finished, we have the last frame of the movie on its own layer. We then introduce the pawns on their own layer and the master chess piece on its own layer. We can then use transitional effects to introduce our elements at different times and modify them *individually* to respond to interactivity. This becomes extremely important when we are animating some objects but not others. Max/Swift 3D will output vector information for every object in *each* frame, which makes it even more important to isolate only those objects that are moving through 3D space so they can later be *composited* into Flash via layers. If all elements reside on a single layer, you would have a copy of them on every frame — dramatically reducing your movie's performance and increasing file size. (See the paragraph earlier on "Layering animations.")

The master chess piece animation that occurs on the frame following the intro (shown in Figure 40-33), only requires isolated items to move on top of the background.

The top reveal (or explode) animation was done from frames 45 to 85. As you can see, the light bulb, middle section, and base do not move, yet in the .swf output from 3ds max, the vector information appears in *every* frame. You are again faced with two choices. You can edit the 40 frames in Flash, deleting the unnecessary information within each frame on a per-frame analysis, or you can output only the animated object and composite it over the central object as a layer (see Figure 40-33). This will also entail some editing within Flash as objects overlap and you will have to create a series of foreground frames of the central non-animating object on a per-frame basis.

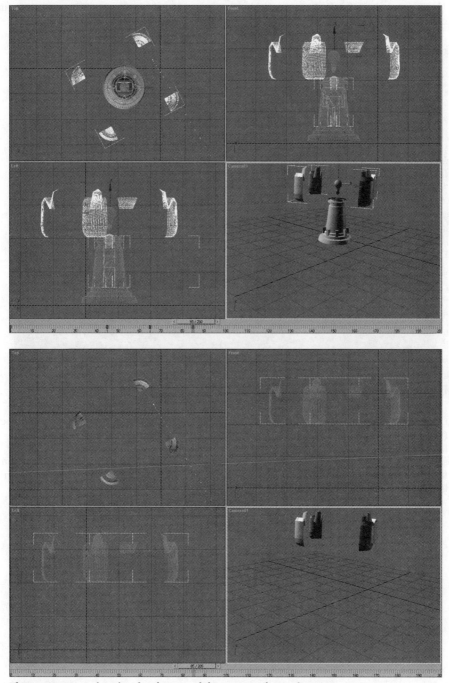

Figure 40-33: Animation for the top of the master chess piece

The Legman character that is revealed by the master chess piece animation poses the same challenge as the chess piece itself (see Figure 40-34 and Figure 40-35).

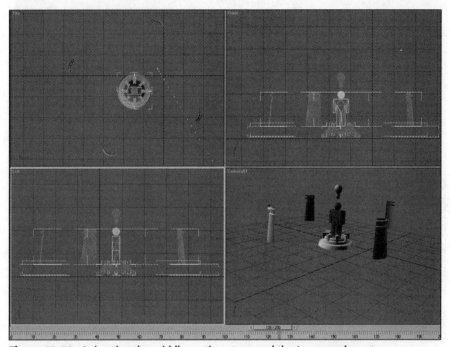

Figure 40-34: Animating the middle sections to reveal the Legman character

Once again, certain key elements (such as Legman) that interact with the animating objects (exploding corners) do not need to animate in the .swf output — at this point the vector information for the middle character appears in *every* frame. You are now faced with the same two choices: You can edit the frames in Flash, deleting the unnecessary information frame-by-frame, or you can output only the animated object(s) and composite it on Flash layers.

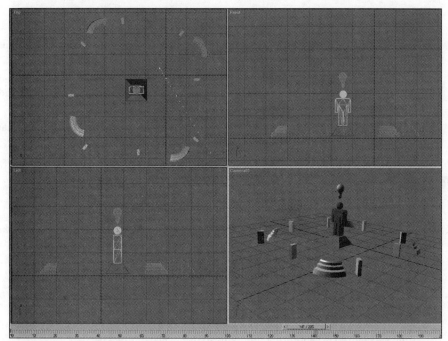

Figure 40-35: Animating the bottom sections to complete the reveal of the Legman character

Importing and Creating the Final Flash Piece

Once we've rendered out each of our objects and animated sequences to SWF format, we can then import them into our Flash file. After the animations are imported, you will need to set up the Flash file to create the final project.

To complete the project, within the Flash authoring environment, we will create a static intro screen, static backgrounds based on single keyframes of the imported 3D sequences, and buttons that allow the user to trigger the animation by controlling playback of the sequence on the Main Timeline.

On the CD-ROM

To see the final Flash animation with the 3D elements and the functional interface, open the MoTG.swf file from the ch40 folder on the CD-ROM. To see the file structure, open the MoTG.fla file from the ch40 folder. The .fla file is carefully commented and labeled to help you see how the project was put together.

✦ Create a Flash document with the dimensions 640×480, running at 24 frames per second

✦ Import your animated elements into separate layers. Place the foreground elements on upper layers and the background elements on lower layers.

✦ Organize the various layered elements along the Main Timeline to create the final animated sequence.

✦ For the Masters of the Game presentation, we created a prompt screen at the beginning of the timeline, asking the user to trigger the animation.

✦ Single-frame renders are used in the background layers for non-keyframed animated objects (like the chess pieces and the chessboard). These objects are made into individual symbols in Flash, so that they can be animated with Motion tweens.

✦ The final animation is placed inside a Movie Clip symbol, so that a Motion tween can be applied to add an animated alpha fade to the whole animation.

Summary

✦ Preplanning is crucial in creating effective 3D in Flash.

✦ The more aware you are of how a 3D object's complexity can affect processing power, file size, and the time that is needed to import and tweak these sequences, the better your 3D will look when integrated with other Flash elements.

✦ Isolating individual elements in a 3D animation and rendering them separately so that they can be composited after import to Flash is crucial for creating optimized sequences.

✦ Using a SWF export plug-in such as Swift 3D Max makes it possible to export elements from specialized 3D authoring programs to use in Flash projects.

✦ Take advantage of Flash's ability to reuse animations and organize objects in layers to ensure that your work displays professionalism and attention to detail while still animating as smoothly as possible.

✦   ✦   ✦

Working with QuickTime

In This Chapter

Defining QuickTime
and Flash tracks

Differentiating Linked
and Embedded Video

Making QuickTime
Flash movies

Creating QuickTime
Video movies from Flash

Extracting frames from
digital video

This chapter explains how to use QuickTime media with Flash MX. Apple and Macromedia have expanded the definition of desktop video by adding a Flash track type to QuickTime movies. We explore the integration of QuickTime movies with Flash interactivity, as well as distinguishing the different types of QuickTime movies (Flash, video, and VR).

QuickTime 4 introduced a new media track to QuickTime movies: the Flash track. A Flash track is just one of the many multimedia tracks available for use in QuickTime. Flash MX has the capability to import linked QuickTime movies, add Flash content on layers above or below the QuickTime movies, and to re-export the whole product as a QuickTime Flash movie. QuickTime Flash movies are basically the same file type (.mov file) as other QuickTime movies — QuickTime Flash movies simply have an internally stored or externally referenced Flash movie (.swf file).

Flash MX introduces the powerful capability of embedding video directly into Flash movies (as .swf files) that can be played back within Flash Player 6! QuickTime Flash movies can only be played within the QuickTime 4 or higher Player. Since Flash Player 6 can play video without additional video plug-ins, you may no longer find the need to use QuickTime Flash movies. However, the QuickTime architecture is very popular, especially for movie trailers on the Web. If video playback and quality is the priority for your project, you may want to consider using the QuickTime architecture, using Flash MX to add interactivity and vector elements like animation. For example, if you wanted to add a search utility at the end of a movie trailer that allowed the user to find other material related to the motion picture film, then you could use Flash MX to create the artwork and ActionScript necessary to send and receive live data from the QuickTime Flash movie.

Note   To reiterate, Flash Player 6 has its own video playback mechanism. Other video plug-ins do not need to be installed in order for video to work in the Flash movies and Flash Player 6. QuickTime Flash movies can not be played with Flash Player 6. Only the QuickTime 4 or higher Player can play QuickTime Flash movies.

QuickTime versus Windows AVI

Because QuickTime has the powerful capability to store a combination of multimedia tracks, Flash MX supports the QuickTime format with its Export and Publish commands. Although Flash developers on the Windows platform can also export Windows AVI (also known as Video for Windows) files, these files don't support a Flash track. The differences between these two formats are intricate. But before we talk about the intricacies, how do you recognize one from the other? The QuickTime file extension is .mov (from the Macintosh File Type MooV), while the file extension for Windows video is .avi (Audio-Video Interleaved format).

Video content is usually delivered in wrapper formats for distribution. Two primary system-level container formats or *wrappers* exist for video content on computer systems today: QuickTime and Windows AVI. Although both can be considered architectures for multimedia content, QuickTime has the most advanced architecture of the two. (Technically, RealSystems' RealOne is also a container format for multimedia, but it's only used for delivery — it cannot be used for editing and reediting material.) Before Windows 95, multimedia developers relied on the QuickTime architecture on the Macintosh to make their multimedia components work together harmoniously. That's because QuickTime for Windows lacked many of the Mac's QuickTime features until its 3.0 release, which finally delivered to Windows the same multitrack interactivity that Mac users had enjoyed from the start. With QuickTime 4, both Windows and Mac versions can play Flash 3 content — Flash 4 and 5 features are not supported by QuickTime 4. Flash 3 content can be embedded as an interface to control another QuickTime video or audio track, or even as an enhancement to Sprite animation. QuickTime 5 supports Flash 4 content, and the newly released QuickTime 6 supports Flash 5 content! You can now create Flash movies with dot syntax and ActionScript objects that work in QuickTime.

Caution   Unfortunately, Video for Windows (VfW) wasn't developed along the same lines as QuickTime. Video for Windows (or Windows AVI files) is just that — video that's designed to play on Windows machines. It can't contain other media tracks (such as Flash tracks) like QuickTime can. Luckily, newer versions of the Windows Media Player can play QuickTime content, and QuickTime 3.0 (or higher) can play Video for Windows movies, provided that the necessary codecs are installed. Both QuickTime and Video for Windows can read most of the software-based codecs, such as Cinepak or Indeo. When you get stuck, usually it's not difficult to translate a QuickTime file to a Video for Windows file using a video editing application such as the Windows version of Adobe Premiere, or vice versa with the Mac version.

The only difference between QuickTime files on the Mac and Windows is that movies made on the Macintosh can internally reference media content from either a resource or data fork, whereas movies made on Windows cannot. Because the two operating systems have different file and directory structures, this referencing system can't be carried over to Windows. Consequently, most Mac movies need to be *flattened* in order to work properly on Windows — *flattening* means that all material referenced in the resource fork of the Mac QuickTime is compiled into one data fork, which is then accessible by all operating systems. Usually, when you are rendering video content on the Mac, you are given an option to flatten (or not flatten) the final movie. A movie can also be flattened with QuickTime Player by selecting Make Movie Self-Contained when you save (or resave) the movie.

Since version 4 of QuickTime, Apple has renamed the MoviePlayer application to QuickTime Player. You need the professional version of QuickTime Player to edit or recompress QuickTime movies. Luckily, you only need to purchase an unlock key code from Apple's Web site to transform the regular player into the pro player, as well as download a few extra components using the QuickTime Updater. Use the QuickTime control panel to enter your unlock key. The application name, however, remains QuickTime Player. Even though we refer to QuickTime Player Pro, you won't see the Pro suffix in the application name.

The major limitation of Video for Windows is that it only supports two tracks of multimedia content: video and audio. QuickTime, however, supports multiple media tracks: video, audio, Flash, text, Sprite, and time code tracks. Furthermore, using QuickTime Player, you can set up many options for each movie's track, such as preloading into memory and enabling high quality. QuickTime 4 or higher also enables you to create reference movies specifically designed for the varying speeds of Internet connections. Using the free Apple utility, MakeRefMovie, you can create different versions of the same movie with a range of file sizes. Depending on the visitor's QuickTime plug-in settings, the proper movie downloads to the computer. For example, if the connection speed setting of the plug-in is set to ISDN, the visitor receives the ISDN-version of the movie, which is of better quality and — as you've learned in this introduction — also bigger in file size. (MakeRefMovie is available at `http://developer.apple.com/quicktime/quicktimeintro/tools/` along with many other QuickTime tools and utilities.)

Discreet Cleaner 5 (or higher) can take the guesswork out of video compression. It has optimized presets for CD-ROM and Web delivery. Find it at `www.discreet.com`. We also discuss video compression for Flash video in Chapter 17, "Embedding Video."

QuickTime Support in Flash

Flash MX can import QuickTime movie files into the Library. If you want to synch your Flash movie with a pre-existing QuickTime movie, you can bring the QuickTime movie into a Flash scene and play both movies simultaneously in the authoring environment of Flash. When you're finished, you can export the Flash movie as a QuickTime Flash movie, using either the Export or Publish commands. The result is a QuickTime movie with video, audio, and Flash tracks. At the time of this writing, you need QuickTime 4 or higher to pull off this stunt. As mentioned earlier, each version of QuickTime since version 4 has varying support for Flash features:

✦ QuickTime 4 can only interpret Flash 3 or earlier actions. This means that any dot syntax or ActionScript specific to Flash Players 4, 5, and 6 is not recognized.

✦ QuickTime 5 can recognize Flash 4 or earlier features. This means that you can use ActionScript like loadVariables, as long as you don't use dot syntax.

✦ QuickTime 6 can use Flash 5 or earlier features, giving you the power to open up QuickTime Flash movies to object-oriented programming in ActionScript. This is by far the biggest jump we've seen with Flash support in QuickTime.

At the time of this writing, QuickTime 6 had been publicly announced, but its release had been indefinitely delayed because of third-party codec licensing issues. The figures and steps in this chapter use QuickTime 5.0.2.

Remember, you can't export a Flash movie (.swf file) from Flash MX with both Flash content and imported QuickTime movies. To play QuickTime movies with Flash content, you need to use the QuickTime format (.mov).

Note Flash Player 6 can play embedded video that's encoded in the new Sorenson Spark codec.

When you import a QuickTime file into Flash, you need to keep your original QuickTime movie file independent of the Flash document (.fla file). Flash MX does not make a copy of the QuickTime file inside the movie. Rather, it links to the external QuickTime movie file for playback and rendering purposes.

Cross-Reference You can find a list of version-specific Flash actions in Bonus Appendix C, "Flash Player-Compatible Actions," located in the **bonus_appendixes.pdf** on the *Flash MX Bible* CD-ROM.

You should have the latest version of QuickTime installed. If you already installed QuickTime 4 or 5, you may want to check `www.apple.com/quicktime` for an update.

Importing QuickTime into Flash

To bring a QuickTime movie into Flash MX, use the File ➪ Import command (Ctrl+R or ⌘+R) and select a QuickTime movie from the Import dialog box. QuickTime movies usually have a QuickTime logo icon and end with the .mov extension, although they sometimes end with .qt. Prior to import, make sure you've selected the layer in which you wish to import the QuickTime. You should always create a new layer to hold the imported QuickTime, and nothing except the QuickTime movie should be on this layer. As soon as you click OK in the Import dialog box, you'll be presented with a dialog box new to Flash MX, shown in Figure 41-1. You will be asked whether you want to embed or link the video file. If you plan to export your movie as a QuickTime Flash movie (.mov file) rather than a regular Flash movie (.swf file), always choose the **Link to external video file** option (shown selected in Figure 41-1).

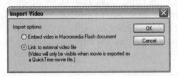

Figure 41-1: When you select a video file to import, you will be asked whether to embed or link the file.

Tip You can use the new File ➪ Import to Library command to put linked QuickTime video files directly into the Library panel.

If you are importing the video file into a new movie or a layer that only has one or a few frames, then you'll receive yet another dialog box new to Flash MX (shown in Figure 41-2), asking whether you want to auto-insert enough frames onto the current layer to accommodate the length of the video. Most likely, you'll want to click Yes to auto-expand the layer.

Figure 41-2: Flash MX has a new feature for video import that will add frames to the current layer in order to fit the length of the video in the Timeline window.

After you've imported the QuickTime movie, the first frame of the QuickTime movie displays in the current frame of the Flash document. You also see a specific asset type in the Library panel — this is a Linked Video (see Figure 41-3), not to be confused with the new Embedded Video icon. The Linked Video icon has a chain link attached to the bottom of the camera.

Figure 41-3: Imported QuickTime movies have a movie camera icon. This file, sleepyStella.mov, can be found in the ch41 folder of the CD-ROM.

The Timeline window in Flash MX displays the QuickTime's movie length relative to the duration (in time, *not* frames) of the Flash movie. Note that one second of the Flash movie equals one second of the QuickTime movie. This means that one frame of QuickTime video is *not* equivalent to one frame of a Flash movie — unless your Flash frame rate matches the QuickTime video frame rate. You can see this for yourself. After you have imported a QuickTime movie, use the F5 key to add more frames to the layer of the QuickTime movie (if you didn't click Yes to auto-expanding the frames of the layer on import). Then, scrub the timeline to preview the QuickTime movie. Stop on any discernable frame, and change the frame rate of the Flash movie via the Property inspector or the Modify ➪ Document command (Ctrl+M or ⌘+M). After you modify the frame rate, you notice that the QuickTime movie frame has changed even though the Flash frame marker is still on the same frame. How do you deal with this variability? Usually, if you intend to export the Flash movie as a QuickTime movie with a Flash track, you want to set the frame rate of your Flash movie to match the frame rate of your QT movie. If you have a Flash movie frame rate that's different from the video track of the QuickTime, you may run into slow or jerky playback.

QuickTime Flash movies can have theoretically any number of Flash scenes. If you have more than one scene, the QuickTime Player may continue to briefly play any running QuickTime movie from the previous scene. For this reason, you may want to add a few blank buffer frames at the beginning of any transition point (for example, going from one scene to the next). This seems to depend on how large the imported QuickTime movies are — the QuickTime Player needs to unload one movie before it proceeds with the next.

With regards to movie length, no built-in limitations exist. You can make the scene as long as you want in order to accommodate any range of interactivity or animation. If you plan to have continuously running Flash and video layers (for example, a Flash animation moving on top of the video track), add enough frames to view the entire length of the QuickTime movie within the Flash timeline. The problem to avoid is this: If you don't add enough frames to accommodate the entire QuickTime movie, then the duration of the Flash movie determines the duration of the video track. This means that your imported QuickTime movie may be arbitrarily cropped or trimmed to the length prescribed in the Flash document (.fla file).

Combining Flash and QuickTime Movies

After you've created a Flash movie synched to an imported QuickTime movie, you can export a fully self-contained QuickTime movie that stores both the Flash and imported QuickTime movie. However, you don't need to use Flash to put Flash content into QuickTime movies. If you want to layer Flash movies into pre-existing QuickTime movies, you can import .swf files directly into the QuickTime Player. But you need the latest Player that installs with QuickTime 4 or higher to import Flash material. Prior versions of the QuickTime Player cannot do this.

Creating QuickTime Flash movies

After you've created a Flash movie with an imported QuickTime movie, you can export or publish the entire Flash scene as a self-contained QuickTime Flash movie that can be played with the latest QuickTime Player.

To create a quick and simple QuickTime movie from Flash MX, choose File ➪ Export Movie (Ctrl+Alt+Shift+S or ⌘+Option+Shift+S). Browse to a folder where you want to save the QuickTime, type a filename, and click Save (see Figure 41-4). You are then presented with the Export QuickTime dialog box.

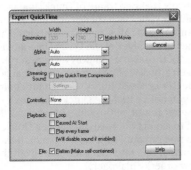

Figure 41-4: For a quick look at a QuickTime Flash movie equivalent of your Flash document, accept the defaults in the Export QuickTime dialog box.

To check out the quality of the QuickTime movie, open the new QuickTime movie with QuickTime Player.

Caution   Be careful with the controller type setting. If you select None, you won't even be able to stop the movie by using the space bar once it's started.

While you can use the Export Movie command to produce independent QuickTime movies, the Publish Settings command enables you to create QuickTime movies as well as other linked file formats. Go to the File menu, and choose Publish Settings (Ctrl+Shift+F12 or ⌘+Shift+F12).

In the Format tab, make sure that you have a checkmark next to the QuickTime option, and deselect the others. Each time you check or uncheck an option in the Publish Settings dialog, the corresponding Settings tab appears or disappears, respectively.

For the purpose of exporting QuickTime, you should only have the Format, Flash, and QuickTime tabs showing (see Figure 41-5). If the Use default names option is checked, the resulting QuickTime movie has the same name as the Flash document that is currently open in Flash MX. Otherwise, you can uncheck this option and specify a different name in the text fields next to the corresponding format types. You can't control the location of the new files that are generated via the Publish command — all files produced via Publish are saved to the same location as the .fla file.

Tip   You can use relative path notation to publish into parent or child folders, such as ../filename. swf. This will publish the Flash movie in the parent folder of the Flash document (.fla file). On the Mac, use ..:filename.swf for the parent folder.

Figure 41-5: The Publish Settings dialog box for QuickTime-only publishing. Click the QuickTime tab to access the movie's properties. The Flash tab is available to set the version to Flash 3, 4, or 5, which are the versions supported by QuickTime 6.

The following sections describe all of the QuickTime settings in the QuickTime tab of the Publish Settings and how each setting is used.

Dimensions

The Dimensions setting controls the size of the QuickTime Flash movie frame. Although you've probably already set the correct movie size in the Document Properties dialog box (Modify ➪ Document) to conform to your specific output needs, it's good to note here that you can resize your QuickTime movie with the Dimensions properties to export a movie at alternate dimensions.

Alpha

For the Alpha property, you can decide whether you want the Flash track's background to be transparent or opaque. If want your Flash material to display together with underlying QuickTime video content, choose Alpha-Transparent. If you don't want the underlying QuickTime video to show through the Flash track, choose Copy. The Auto setting makes the Flash background transparent if Flash artwork exists on top of other content. If a QuickTime movie is stacked above the Flash artwork, then Auto makes the Flash background opaque. If you export a QuickTime Flash movie with only Flash artwork, Auto uses an opaque background.

Layer

For the Layer property, you can decide whether you want the Flash track to be layered on top of or below the QuickTime content. If you want the Flash content to play on top of the QuickTime movie, choose Top. If you designed an interface or animation to appear underneath the QuickTime movie, choose Bottom. The Auto setting for the Layer property places the Flash track in front of QuickTime material if Flash artwork appears on top of the QuickTime anywhere in the Flash editor document. If you placed QuickTime movies on top of Flash artwork layers, then Auto places the Flash track behind the video track.

Streaming Sound

If you want Flash-enabled sounds to be converted to an additional QuickTime sound track, check the Use QuickTime Compression option for the Streaming Sound property. Any and all sounds that are used in the scenes are recompressed into a separate sound track. This sound track is separate from any other sound tracks that may be present in imported QuickTime movies. The Settings button enables you to define the parameters of the audio compression. You may want to match the audio characteristics of the imported QuickTime movie used in the Flash movie if you choose to use this option. Because this property converts Flash audio into QuickTime audio, you can use any sound compressor that is available to QuickTime. Refer to Tables 41-1 and 41-2 for an overview of the QuickTime audio codecs.

Table 41-1: QuickTime Audio Codecs

Popular Codecs	Best For	Description
Qdesign Music 2	Internet	Excellent compression ratio; great for music, streaming audio.
Qualcomm PureVoice	Internet	Excellent compression ratio. Very good for voice.
IMA	CD-ROM	Good quality; only encodes 16-bit audio. Inadvisable for low frequencies (booming bass) or Web use.

Table 41-2: Alternative Audio Codecs

Other Formats	Description
24-bit Integer, 32-bit Integer, 32-bit Floating Point, 64-bit Floating Point	Increases (or retains) bit depth to 32-bit and 64-bit, respectively. Note that dedicated sound applications (and hardware) are generally necessary to play back sound files higher than 16-bit.
ALaw 2:1	European standard compression scheme for digitizing telephone calls. Recommended for human speech.
MACE 3:1, MACE 6:1	Old Macintosh standards. Low quality, high file size. Forget about using these codecs.
>Law 2:1	Standard for compressing telephone calls in Japan and North America. Low quality, large file size. Downsamples 16-bit audio to 8-bit.
Uncompressed	Retains original quality of source audio, just as the Flash Raw audio setting does. High fidelity, large file size.

Controller

The Controller property determines whether a controller (control panel for playback) is shown with the movie in the QuickTime Player application, and if one is shown, what kind of a controller. None disables the display of a control panel, and, subsequently, it is the default setting for the Export Movie command. If you have created your own Flash buttons to play and stop the timeline, you may want to disable the display of the regular QuickTime controller. The Standard option presents the QuickTime movie with the standard QuickTime Player 4 interface, enabling play, pause, frame forward and backward, and volume level, among other controls. The QuickTime VR option displays the specialized control panel for QuickTime panorama or object movies. We discuss QTVR later in the "A Word about QuickTime VR Movies" section of this chapter. To compare the different controllers, see Figures 41-6 through 41-8.

Figure 41-6: A QuickTime movie with no controller: This was made with the Controller property set to None.

Figure 41-7: A QuickTime movie with the standard controller

Figure 41-8: The QuickTime VR controller used with a Flash-enabled QTVR panorama

Playback

The Playback property controls how the movie plays when it's first opened in the QuickTime Player. Check the Loop option if you want the QuickTime Player to automatically replay the movie when it's reached the end. Check the Paused at Start option if you don't want the QuickTime movie to automatically start playing as soon as it opens in the QuickTime Player. Note that if any controller (other than None) is specified, the movie is always paused when it loads in the QuickTime Player. The Play Every Frame option, when checked, overrides the frame rate setting to play back every frame contained in the video. Usually, this is not recommended because the QuickTime audio track is silenced.

File

The File property has only one option, Flatten (Make self-contained). Checking this option forces Flash to write one QuickTime movie that contains any and all referenced material. If you imported a 10MB QuickTime movie into Flash and created a few layers of Flash content to work with the QuickTime movie, flattening creates one QuickTime movie that copies the imported QuickTime movie and Flash material to video, audio, and Flash tracks, respectively. If you do not check Flatten, Flash MX creates a reference QuickTime movie that looks for (and requires the presence of) the Flash movie (.swf file) and other QuickTime file(s) on playback. While this reference movie has a very small file size, you need to make sure all the referenced material is readily available for playback. This means that the Formats tab of the Publish Settings dialog box should have a checkmark next to Flash (.swf) as well as QuickTime (.mov). Furthermore, you may run into linking problems over the Internet due to connection latency or if the referenced files aren't together in one location. For this reason, you may prefer to package everything into one flattened QuickTime movie.

Click OK to accept your current Publish Settings and return to the Flash document. Make any final adjustments to your movie. When you're ready to test drive your new QuickTime movie, you can preview the QuickTime movie by using the Publish Preview menu, and selecting QuickTime. QuickTime Player Pro should automatically start and load the movie. Note that Publish Preview actually creates the QuickTime Flash movie file(s).

Note   On some system configurations, Internet Explorer may open to play the QuickTime movie.

You can also publish the files by choosing File ➪ Publish (Shift+F12). Flash MX saves a QuickTime movie to the same directory where your Flash document (.fla file) has been saved. You can also publish the movie by using the Publish button directly in the Publish Settings dialog box.

Note   For those who want to maximize the built-in functions of QuickTime Player Pro, QuickTime video filters and graphics modes can be applied to Flash tracks.

So far, you've seen how to combine existing QuickTime movies with your Flash content. You don't need to import other QuickTime content into Flash MX in order to export QuickTime material from Flash MX. With QuickTime 4 or higher, you can create QuickTime movies that are essentially repackaged .swf files. Using Flash MX, Flash documents (.fla files) can be exported to QuickTime formats. To export QuickTime Flash movies from Flash MX, follow the same steps described previously without importing any external QuickTime movie files.

Export Movie or Publish?

Although the Export QuickTime dialog box is identical to the QuickTime tab of the Publish Settings dialog box, one important difference exists. The File property, which controls linking to external files, creates different results with each command.

If Flatten (Make self-contained) is unchecked in the Export QuickTime dialog box, then only the imported QuickTime movie is referenced externally — it is not stored in the new QuickTime Flash movie.

If you check both the Flash (.swf) and QuickTime (.mov) options in the Formats tab of the Publish Settings dialog box *and* uncheck the Flatten (Make self-contained) option in the QuickTime tab, then the Publish command creates a QuickTime Flash movie (.mov file) that links to the .swf file as well as the original imported QuickTime movie (.mov). Neither the Flash content nor the imported QuickTime movie is stored in the new QuickTime Flash movie — the QuickTime Flash movie, .swf file, and original QuickTime(s) need to be in the same location in order to play.

Creating QuickTime video with Flash

If you own the Macintosh version of Flash 4, 5, or MX, then you can also export QuickTime Video via the Export Movie command. QuickTime Video is raster- or bitmap-based animated movement. Remember, QuickTime Flash movies contain a new Flash media track, which is exactly the same file format as a Flash movie (.swf file). As such, the Flash track uses anti-aliased vector graphics to store and display information. QuickTime Video, however, uses only raster information — each frame in the movie is described as collection of pixels. This method of storage is much more byte intensive. For this reason, QuickTime Video files are usually several megabytes large, and time-consuming to download over slower Internet connections.

Tip   Why would you want to use QuickTime Video if it creates larger file sizes than QuickTime Flash? Unfortunately, QuickTime Flash movies can only be played with QuickTime 4.0 or greater. If you want to be sure that your QuickTime movies can be played with older versions of QuickTime, then the movies need to be QuickTime Video.

In the Mac version of Flash MX, you have the option of creating either QuickTime Video or QuickTime Flash movies. If you want to use your Flash animations in home videos or video-taped presentations, then you should export Flash movies as QuickTime Video movies. These movies can then be edited with your other digitally captured video.

Tip   Some digital video editing applications such as Adobe After Effects 5.5 can directly import Flash movies (.swf files) for non-linear editing with other video material. Be sure to export the Flash movie in a version that is compatible with your installed version of QuickTime. However, for the highest quality video output, we recommend that you use exported image sequences from Flash MX for video editing, as discussed in Chapter 14, "Exporting Animation."

To save a Flash movie as a QuickTime Video movie, choose File ➪ Export Movie and select QuickTime Video as the Format type. After you specify a filename and a location to save the movie, click Save. Next, you see the Export QuickTime dialog (Figure 41-9), where you can specify how Flash should rasterize the Flash movie.

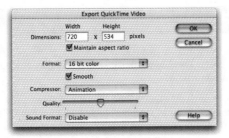

Figure 41-9: By using the Export QuickTime (Video) dialog, you can specify Dimensions, Format, Compressor, Quality, and Sound Format.

Dimensions

This property performs exactly the same way as the Dimensions property of QuickTime Flash movie exports. See our coverage of Publish Settings and QuickTime Flash earlier in this chapter. Because Flash vector can maintain high quality at any size, you can scale the dimensions of the QuickTime Video file to match the requirements of your video project. For example, if you want to use this QuickTime Video with DV format video, then scale the movie dimensions to 720×534.

Cross-Reference See Chapter 14, "Exporting Animation," for more detailed information on frame dimensions.

Format

Use the Format property to control the bit-depth of the QuickTime Video movie. For most high-quality video work, use 24-bit or 32-bit color formats. For Web distribution of QuickTime Video movies, lower color formats yield smaller file sizes. Refer to Table 41-3 for a quick breakdown of each color format. If the Smooth option of the Format property is checked, Flash artwork is converted to anti-aliased bitmap information. Otherwise, curved lines may exhibit the "jaggies" — jagged or staircased steps on curves or gradients.

Table 41-3: QuickTime Video Color Formats

Format	Number of Colors	Description/Use
Black and white	2	Fax-like image quality
4-bit color	16	Similar to the 16 system colors used by Windows in Safe mode
8-bit color	256	Indexed Color mode, like GIF
16-bit color	65,536	High Color in Windows 95/98 or Thousands of Colors on the Mac
24-bit color	16.7 million	True Color in Windows 95/98 or Millions of Colors on the Mac
32-bit color	16.7 million + 8-bit alpha channel	Same as 24-bit color; supports 256 levels of transparency

Note Even though QuickTime Video is only available as an export option in the Mac version of Flash MX, Table 41-3 compares video color settings to Windows color modes. Regardless of where QuickTime video files are created, the .mov files can be played on any system that has a QuickTime Player.

Compressor

This menu determines which video codec (*compressor-de*compressor) is used for the bitmap frames in the QuickTime Video movie. Because QuickTime Video is more bandwidth-intensive, bitmap information needs to be condensed in some manner. Compressors, or codecs, reduce the amount of information that needs to be stored for each frame. For general distribution, you may want to use Sorenson, Cinepak, or Intel Indeo Video codecs. For high-quality video output for editing or broadcast purposes, use the hardware codec used by your specific video capture card. Chapter 14, "Exporting Animation," explores codecs more deeply.

Quality

This unmarked slider (which apparently has no units) controls how the compressor selected in the previous menu works. As you drag the slider to the right, less compression is applied to the QuickTime Video, which results in higher-quality video. As you drag the slider to the left, more information is discarded from each frame of video (more compression, lower quality).

Sound format

If your Flash movie contains any audio, then you can choose to convert those audio samples to a QuickTime-compatible audio track. QuickTime can use any major sampling rate (such as 22 kHz), bit-depth (such as 8 or 16), or channel (such as mono or stereo). Usually, you won't want to use anything lower than 22 kHz 16-bit stereo for quality audio. If you don't need to use Flash audio in the QuickTime Video file, then choose Disable.

Cross-Reference See our coverage of QuickTime audio codecs that appears earlier in this chapter for more information.

A word about QuickTime VR movies

If you are familiar with QuickTime VR's amazing panorama and object movies, then you should be happy to know that Flash MX supports QuickTime VR (QTVR) movies as well. Because QTVR movies aren't strict linear playback video movies, you need to keep a few points in mind when you use QTVR movies in Flash MX. Note that you cannot create QTVR movies from scratch in Flash. You first need to create a QTVR movie with VR equipment and software, like Apple's QuickTime VR Authoring Studio. Flash MX can then import these movies and add Flash artwork and actions to them.

On the CD-ROM The QTVR folder of the ch41 folder on the *Flash MX Bible* CD-ROM contains sample Flash documents (.fla files) and QuickTime VR movies (.mov files) to use with this section. Paul Nykamp, a QTVR specialist in Toronto, Canada, provided the QTVR movies. He can be reached at paul@diginiche.com.

Panoramic movies

QuickTime panoramic movies enable you to view a physical or virtual space by stitching a series of images into a 360-degree view. You navigate the space by clicking and dragging the mouse inside the movie frame. When you import a QTVR panoramic movie (a.k.a. *pano*) into Flash, it only displays the first frame of the QTVR movie on the stage, regardless of the frame marker's position. It's very important to make sure that your Flash timeline's frame span doesn't extend beyond the length of the QTVR movie. Playback beyond the length of the QTVR causes the QTVR to disappear until the Flash frame playback loops back to the starting frame. The best solution, whenever possible, is to limit your timeline to the length of the imported QTVR movie, and use Movie Clips with tellTarget() actions (for Flash 4 compatibility in QuickTime 5) to provide longer frame length animations.

Caution   QuickTime VR panos are particularly sensitive to Flash movie frame rates. The default setting of 12 fps may result in incomplete panoramas with missing sections. If a problem occurs, try changing the Flash movie frame rate to 1 fps and then re-exporting the QuickTime VR movie.

Due to limitations of the QTVR controller, there's no way to rewind a movie or return to frame 1 of the Flash track. Technically, because each media track has its own timeline of frames, if the Flash track plays beyond the QTVR track, you lose the QTVR movie. You can prevent this from happening by ensuring that you can always view the QTVR's first frame within the Flash authoring environment. Another clue is this: If you go beyond the length of the QTVR movie, the extended area is represented by a struck-through rectangular box, as shown in Figure 41-10.

Tip   You can also nest longer timelines for Flash animation, artwork, and interactivity in a Movie Clip symbol, and place instances of the symbol on the Main Timeline along with the QuickTime movie.

Figure 41-10: If your Flash movie plays beyond the length of an imported QTVR panorama or object movie, it disappears from the stage and is replaced with a struck-through box.

To export or publish QTVR pano movies, specify the QuickTime VR Controller type in the Export QuickTime dialog box or in the Publish Settings' QuickTime tab.

Object movies

You can also make QTVR object movies in Flash MX. QTVR object movies let you rotate or spin an object — photographed or 3D modeled — by dragging the mouse inside the movie frame (see Figure 41-11). With Flash, you can expand the multimedia capabilities of object movies. Adding Flash buttons, audio, and artwork to an object movie can provide a different navigational interface for the object, and provide call-out information to the object movie.

Figure 41-11: QTVR object movies with Flash tracks can have more impact than regular QTVR movies.

Unlike QuickTime pano movies, object movies can be fully viewed within the Flash authoring environment. Each frame of the object movie shows a different viewing angle of the object. Again, like regular QuickTime movies, make sure you add enough frames to view the entire object movie. Keep adding frames until the stage displays the object movie with a struck-through box. Then, subtract any frames that show the movie as a struck-through box.

Our tests with object movies have also shown that the frame rate of the Flash movie is a critical setting. Most of our test exports with QTVR object movies played back very poorly — the object's rotation movement was not very smooth. However, when we specified a controller type of None and added a Flash button to provide a *play* action, the object movie played back very smoothly.

Tip For Flash-controlled playback of QTVR object movies, you need to add a `gotoAndPlay()` action to the last frame of the scene, which loops back to the first frame of the scene. However, the QuickTime Player does not recognize a Flash `stop()` action on the first frame. To start a QTVR Flash movie in a paused state, select the Paused at Start option in the Playback section of the Export QuickTime dialog or in the QuickTime tab of Publish Settings.

Using Bitmap Sequences from Video

Because the primary strength of Flash lies in its vector animation capabilities, it makes sense that Flash optimization works best with vector-based material. Most Web site visitors prefer quicker download speeds, and vector animations are much easier to store as small files than are raster graphics. As a result, Flash handles raster-based material with JPEG or lossless (a.k.a. PNG) compression schemes. In the past, Flash didn't let you import or embed digital video files into a Flash movie because they added too much to the file size, which prevented efficient compression and delivery on the Web. So, what do you do if you want to showcase your next blockbuster feature in your Flash movie? With Flash MX, you now have two options:

1. Embed (not link) your digital video movies. When you embed video in Flash MX documents, you actually make a new copy of the digital video, encoded with the Sorenson Spark codec. While this method is the preferred of the two, it will only work with Flash Player 6.

2. Import a series of still images that have been extracted from your original digital video movie. If you want visitors to get a taste of some raster-based animation, it's best to select a short section of the overall movie and extract frames from that selection. This method will work with any version of the Flash Player.

Read Chapter 17, "Embedding Video," for more information on the process to converting digital video movies to the new Sorenson Spark codec, used by Flash Player 6.

In this section, we talk about option 2, and describe how to create still image sequences and bring them into Flash. If you want to accommodate visitors who are willing to wait for larger full-length movies, then you can then link the preview in Flash to load the entire QuickTime movie (or QuickTime movie reference), via HTML and the QuickTime plug-in, into its own window or frame. Generally, though, this method of digital video integration into Flash is used for visual effects or just really cool raster content you snagged on video, such as water ripples or textures.

We explained earlier in this chapter the process of creating new QuickTime Flash movies. This is an alternative to adding Flash content to existing QuickTime movies, and, therefore, distributing Flash and QuickTime content simultaneously on the Web. In this section, we discuss the process of storing a series of still images derived from video into a Flash movie (.swf file), not into a QuickTime Flash movie (.mov file). This method is useful if you want to create video-like imagery in Flash 5 or earlier movies. If you want to use video frames in Flash 6 movies, read Chapter 17, "Embedding Video."

This section covers a basic method of converting digital video content into a Flash-friendly sequence of frames. If you want to recreate the movement of original video via the converted vector-based art in Flash, we recommend that you read this section first and then check out WebMonkey's tutorial on Converting Animations to Flash at `http://hotwired.lycos.com/webmonkey/98/42/index3a.html?tw=multimedia`.

If you want to embed frames from a QuickTime movie in your Flash movie for playback in Flash Player 5 or earlier, read the rest of the section. If you want to synchronize your Flash animations and interactivity with a QuickTime movie to use in a final QuickTime 4 movie, refer to "Importing QuickTime into Flash," earlier in this chapter.

Extracting frames from digital video clips

The premise of frame extraction is simple: Instead of downloading large video files with Flash content, reduce the video in frame size, rate, and length to something that Flash (and slow Internet connections) can handle. With this method, we can convert any video clip into a short sequence of still images that can play as an animation or Movie Clip in Flash.

The following exercise assumes that you have some working knowledge of the QuickTime Player. Also, you must have some existing digital video material; we do not create or edit any video in these tutorials.

We recommend that you have QuickTime 4 or higher installed on your computer. At the time this book went to press, QuickTime 6 had been announced by Apple. You don't need an expensive video-editing application to extract frames from video clips. In fact, you can do it for less than $30! Apple's QuickTime Player Pro (see Figure 41-12) can export any QuickTime movie as a series of individual still frames, which can then be imported to Flash MX. You need QuickTime 4 or higher to export image sequences. You can download the latest software at www.apple.com/quicktime.

Time Display

Show/Hide

Playhead   Sound Controls

Volume   Pause
          /Play   QuickTime TV channels

Go to Start   Go to End

Fast Rewind   Fast Forward

Figure 41-12: The QuickTime 5 Player interface

On the CD-ROM   If you want to use a sample QuickTime movie, choose a QuickTime movie from the ch41 folder on the *Flash MX Bible* CD-ROM.

After you have some QuickTime movie footage that you want to use in a Flash document, you can begin the process of selecting a range of frames and exporting them as a bitmap sequence. This sequence will then be imported into our Flash document.

Making a selection

First, decide how much of the QuickTime movie you want to import into Flash. Do this sparingly. Remember that raster animation is heavy on file sizes, and people generally like faster-loading content on Web pages. Restrict your selections to movie clips of very short duration, less than five seconds if possible. If you want the visitor to see more than that, consider linking to the entire QuickTime movie from the smaller clip that you import into the Flash .swf file.

Defining your selection

Use the In and Out markers to define your selection. Unfortunately, the QuickTime Player does not show frame numbers in the time code display. As a result, you need to eyeball your selection. You can also use the additional video controls to move through the video clip frame by frame. The selection is indicated by a gray bar between the In and Out points. By using Movie ➪ Get Movie Properties and selecting Time from the drop-down menu, you can view the time code of where your selection starts and its duration (see Figure 41-14). In Figure 41-13, a two-second selection is made from a QuickTime video clip.production.

In point   Out point

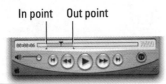

Figure 41-13: Keep your selections as short as possible. Longer selections add substantial weight to the file size of the Flash .swf file.

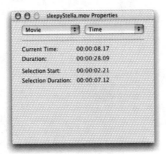

Figure 41-14: The Movie Properties allow you to view and change settings for the QuickTime movie.

Trimming the movie

After you've defined a selection, you need to delete the rest of the video track. If we don't delete it, QuickTime Player Pro exports the entire movie as an image sequence. Again, we only need the short selection for use in Flash. Choose Edit ➪ Trim from the QT Player Pro menu bar. This command discards everything but your selection from the movie clip. (Don't worry about losing this content. As long as you don't resave your QuickTime movie at this point, your video clip file won't be altered in any way, because we simply want to export this selection as an image sequence and then close the QuickTime movie *without saving*.) After you execute the Trim command, the In and Out markers automatically reset to encompass the entire remaining video, and the QuickTime movie only contains the selection that you defined previously.

Exporting an image sequence

Now you're ready to export the QuickTime selection as an image sequence:

1. Choose File ➪ Export (Ctrl+E or ⌘+E) to open the Save exported file as dialog box (see Figure 41-15).

2. Select a folder (or create a new one) to store your image sequence, specify a filename, and choose Movie to Image Sequence in the Export drop-down menu.

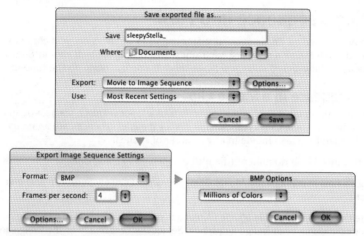

Figure 41-15: In the Save Exported File As dialog, choose Movie to Image Sequence as the Export type.

3. Click the Options button to define the format settings to be used for the image sequence. You see the Export Image Sequence Settings dialog box. If you are using the Windows version of Flash, choose BMP (Windows Bitmap) for the Format property. If you're using the Mac version of Flash, choose the PICT format.

   Note that Flash MX can use BMP, PICT, and PNG formats (among others) on either the Mac or Windows version. However, we recommend that you choose a lossless format, like the ones just mentioned.

4. For the Frames per second property, choose a value from the drop-down menu (or type one) that's appropriate to the length of the clip. For a two-second clip, a value of 4 or 5 is adequate, rendering a total of 8 or 10 frames.

5. Click the Options button to select a bit-depth for the BMP or PICT sequence. In the Export Image Sequence Settings, you can access the file type-specific settings, such as color depth or compression. Choose Millions of Colors (for BMP format) if you don't want to prematurely limit the Color palette used for the image sequence.

Note The Options dialog box displays the settings applicable for the file format chosen. Some file formats, such as JPEG, enable you to define compression levels in addition to bit-depth.

6. Click OK to the BMP or PICT Options dialog box, and then click OK again in the Export Image Sequence Settings dialog box.

7. Finally, click Save in the original Save exported file as dialog box to render your image sequence. QuickTime Player Pro adds consecutive numbers to the end of each filename generated in the sequence. Flash can recognize file sequences with this kind of numbering.

Now you have a collection of still images that can be imported into Flash. See the following "Importing a sequence into Flash" section for instructions on bringing the stills into Flash MX.

Importing a sequence into Flash

After you have created an image sequence from another application, you can import the sequence into Flash MX as a series of keyframes with bitmaps. Flash can auto-import an entire sequence of numbered stills and place them frame by frame on the timeline.

Storing a sequence in a Movie Clip

Rather than import an image sequence directly into a layer within a scene, you can import the sequence into a Movie Clip symbol. This makes it easier to duplicate an image-sequence animation through the Flash movie in any number of scenes.

1. Create a new Flash document (.fla file) or open an existing one.

2. Create a new symbol of the Movie Clip type (Insert ➪ New Symbol), and give it a descriptive name.

3. While the timeline for this Movie Clip is active, choose File ➪ Import and browse to the folder containing your image sequence. Select the first image of the image sequence, and click OK.

   You are presented with the message shown in Figure 41-16.

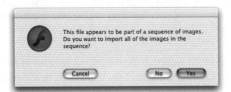

Figure 41-16: Whenever you import a file whose name contains a number, Flash MX asks you whether you want to import the entire numbered sequence of files.

4. Click Yes in the dialog shown in Figure 41-16 and Flash MX automatically imports every image in the numeric sequence.

5. Go back to the Scene 1 timeline (i.e. the Main Timeline) and drag an instance of the Movie Clip onto the Stage.

6. Use `tellTarget()` actions (for Flash 3 or 4 compatibility) or Movie Clip methods (in ActionScript Dots notation) to control the Movie Clip instance if necessary. For more information on intramovie interactivity, see Part V, "Adding Basic Interactivity to Flash Movies."

Optimizing bitmaps

Like any imported bitmap, you can trace each bitmap in the image sequence. Tracing effectively converts raster information into vector information. Depending on the complexity of the bitmap image, though, the efficiency of tracing can vary wildly. Refer to Chapter 16, "Importing Artwork," for more information on optimizing bitmap images in Flash MX.

Tip

If you plan to trace bitmaps in an imported image sequence, you may want to consider applying an art filter (for example, Extract, Posterize, or Solarize) to the original footage in Adobe Premiere or After Effects. Some art filters create more solid areas of color in the image, making the traced bitmaps in Flash less complex with smaller file sizes. Any filter that you can apply to reduce the number of colors in your footage will simplify the image and reduce the file size in Flash.

Summary

✦ QuickTime 4 or higher supports Flash tracks. With this feature, Flash MX can export QuickTime movies with Flash tracks that control playback of QuickTime movies.

✦ Flash tracks can provide a clean visual layer to a QuickTime presentation using vector graphics such as text and shape animations.

✦ You can export Flash movies as Flash-only QuickTime movies. As of this writing, the QuickTime 5 Player can currently play Flash 4 content only.

✦ Digital video needs many megabytes of disk storage. For this reason, there are some limitations and precautions involved when extracting frames from digital video for use in Flash movies.

✦ By extracting frames at low frame rates from digital video files such as QuickTime or AVI, you can import small video clips into Flash documents and play them back from Flash .swf files. The results can be of astonishingly high quality with relatively fast transmission. However, Flash MX now supports embedded video that can be viewed in Flash Player 6.

✦   ✦   ✦

Working with Dreamweaver MX

In This Chapter

Integrating Flash elements into Dreamweaver

Using the Flash Deployment Kit for Flash detection

Adding Flash buttons and text

Using the Link Checker

Adding Dreamweaver behaviors

Editing ActionScript in Dreamweaver MX

Macromedia Dreamweaver is the most popular HTML authoring tool for professional Web developers. This chapter teaches you how to integrate advanced Flash movies, created from lessons in other sections of this book, into final production as an integral part of a Web site.

Flash movies are rarely viewed as standalone objects. People point their browsers at HTML pages that contain .swf files; they will rarely navigate to a standalone Flash movie. Although Flash can generate basic HTML pages using the Publish feature, Macromedia Dreamweaver allows you to gain more control over the visual placement of your Flash movie, to customize plug-in settings and to manage your Web site more effectively.

Why Use Dreamweaver?

Dreamweaver is much more than an HTML authoring tool. It provides many options for site management; not only is it a great tool for HTML pages, but it's also excellent for keeping track of site assets such as images, source files, and Flash movies. The latest version, Dreamweaver MX, also supports database interaction using a variety of server-side scripting languages.

While there are many other site management and HTML authoring tools available, when it comes to integrating Flash with your Web site, there's no other tool that compares to the capabilities of Dreamweaver.

Cross-Reference You need to know how to export your Flash documents (.fla files) as Flash movies (.swf files). You may want to read Chapter 21, "Publishing Flash Movies," and Chapter 22, "Integrating Flash Content with HTML," before proceeding with this chapter.

Dreamweaver MX

Dreamweaver MX, as its name suggests, is designed with integration with the other Macromedia MX products in mind. The standard release of Dreamweaver MX now includes server-side scripting abilities previously only found in the Dreamweaver UltraDev release, and due to its improved integration with Flash we highly recommend it over previous versions.

Installing Dreamweaver MX

Building sites with Dreamweaver can vary in complexity. Developing database-driven sites always involves several other necessary components—a Web server and database, to name but two. In this chapter we're going to explore the simpler option of building basic sites with Dreamweaver. Additional information on the configuration and installation of more complex development environments can be found at www.macromedia.com.

What's new in Dreamweaver MX?

New features introduced in Dreamweaver MX include the following:

✦ **Database Interaction:** Previously only available in the Dreamweaver UltraDev edition, Dreamweaver MX has both greatly improved the options for building database-driven sites, and included all these functions in the standard edition.

✦ **MX Panel Management:** Dreamweaver MX now matches the layout of Flash MX and Fireworks MX.

✦ **Server-side Scripting**: Macromedia has included support for ColdFusion, ASP, ASP.NET, JSP, and PHP.

✦ **Site Setup Wizard:** Macromedia has greatly improved the mechanism for the initial configuration of a Web site.

✦ **Snippets:** The new Snippets panel allows you to easily store and reapply pieces of code that you want to use throughout your site. Dreamweaver comes with many built-in Snippets, including JavaScript functions, navigational elements and form elements.

✦ **Code Hinting:** Similar to the Actions panel in Flash, Dreamweaver MX now has code hinting when editing the Web page code.

✦ **Pre-built Layouts:** Many excellent sample page layouts are built-in to Dreamweaver. They include image placeholders and sample text for a range of common pages—from text layouts to registration forms to shopping carts—making page creation quick and easy.

You may like to create your pages visually, or prefer to get your hands dirty with the behind-the-scenes coding. Either way, Dreamweaver is a robust and powerful authoring tool, with vastly improved features in this latest version.

Dreamweaver MX and Flash MX integration

Of course, of all the elements improved or introduced in Dreamweaver MX, we are particularly interested in the new features that make our lives easier as Flash developers. These include:

✦ **Launch and edit Flash from within Dreamweaver:** If you used this feature with Fireworks 4 you'll realize how welcome this is. It's very easy to change a .swf file from a Dreamweaver page. By just clicking one button, Dreamweaver will open Flash with the correct .fla file, allow you to make your changes, then when you finish editing, one more click automatically exports the .swf, saves the .fla and takes you back to the updated page in Dreamweaver.

✦ **ActionScript editing:** The improved coding environment in Dreamweaver now has code hinting and editing abilites for creating ActionScript. This can come in especially useful when creating large ActionScript files, as the Actions panel within Flash can often seem a little small for comfort.

✦ **Link updates:** From within Dreamweaver, you can now change URL links within Flash movies, and have the change propogate to both the Flash movie (.swf file) and to the Flash document (.fla file).

Importing Flash into Dreamweaver

Although Flash MX's Publish feature takes a lot of the guesswork out of placing Flash movies into HTML pages, you might want to add HTML graphics and text to the page, too. Macromedia Dreamweaver has been a huge hit with Web designers — its roundtrip HTML feature keeps your HTML code just the way you like it. Roundtrip HTML refers to Dreamweaver's capability to transfer HTML code back and forth between applications, keeping your preferred formatting intact — Dreamweaver will not overwrite or reformat your own code, as many other HTML authoring tools are known to do.

In this section, we look at the fundamentals of using Flash movies with Dreamweaver and HTML.

Working with your Flash movie

After you've created an interactive animation and have exported the file into the SWF format, it's time to put the file into your HTML document.

Cross-Reference

For more information on using the Publish feature of Flash MX for exporting a Flash animation to the SWF format, see Chapter 21, "Publishing Flash Movies."

Let's get started. First, create a new document in Dreamweaver, using File ➪ New (Ctrl+N or ⌘+N). Select the Basic Page category and create a basic HTML page.

Next, insert the Flash file by selecting Insert ➪ Media ➪ Flash, or by clicking the Flash icon on the Insert bar as shown in Figure 42-1. If you prefer to use keyboard shortcuts, try Ctrl+Alt+F or Option+⌘+F. The Select File dialog box appears. Now, browse your folders until you find a Flash movie (.swf file) to import.

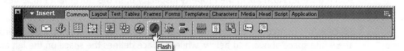

Figure 42-1: Click the Flash icon on the Insert bar to insert a Flash movie.

Choose a Flash movie (.swf file) and click Select. You should see a gray rectangle with a small Flash symbol in your Dreamweaver document, indicating that this is a Flash movie.

You should also notice that when your Flash movie is selected, its details appear in the Dreamweaver Property inspector, as shown in Figure 42-2, which displays the properties most commonly used in Dreamweaver (see Table 42-1 for a description of those properties). If the Property inspector is not visible, access it with Window ➪ Properties (Ctrl+F3 or ⌘+F3). If all of the properties are not displayed, click the expand arrow in the lower-right corner or double-click the inactive areas of the inspector. The inspector hosts many options and controls:

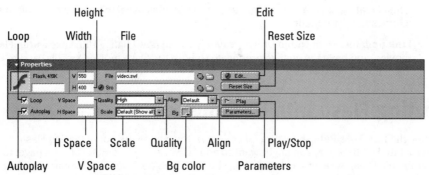

Figure 42-2: The Property inspector in Dreamweaver MX

Table 42-1: Flash Properties in the Property Inspector

Property	Description
Name	Identifies the movie for scripting purposes. As always, it is a good habit to name all your elements in Dreamweaver.
W and H	Represents the movies dimension in default pixels. The dimensions can also be set to pc (picas), pt (points), in (inches), mm (millimeters), cm (centimeters), or %. By default, this information is automatically set to the movie's original dimensions.
File	The file's path/location. The information for your current file should automatically appear in this field.
Src	Holds the source file (FLA) for the Flash movie. This is what allows the launch and edit feature to function from within Dreamweaver MX.
Align	Determines how the movie is aligned on the page (left, middle, right). The default is align left.
Bg	Specifies a background color for the movie area. This color also appears while the movie is not playing (while loading and after playing). This setting can also be selected within Flash MX in the Property inspector or in the Document Properties dialog box (Modify ➪ Document or shortcut keys Ctrl+J or ⌘+J).
V Space and H Space	Specifies the number of pixels for white space around the movie. V Space pertains to the white space above, and below, while H space defines the space on the left and right sides of the movie.
Quality	Sets the quality parameter for the object and embed tags that run the movie. The settings to choose from are Low, Auto Low, Auto High, and High.
Scale	Sets the scale parameter for the OBJECT and EMBED tags that place the movie. Scale defines how the movie is placed within the browser window when the width and height values are percentages.
Loop	Makes the Flash movie automatically loop if no stop actions occur on the Main Timeline.
Autoplay	Plays the movie's Main Timeline automatically when the page loads.
Parameters	Opens a dialog box for entering additional parameters to pass to the movie. The movie must be created in Flash to receive these parameters. These can be hard-coded, or they can be dynamic and drawn from a database.
Reset Size	Examines the SWF file and resets it to the original size it was created with in Flash.

Positioning your movie

The best way to center your Flash movie within the browser window is to surround the `<EMBED>` and/or `<OBJECT>` tags with the `<CENTER></CENTER>` tags. This method will preserve the original aspect ratio of your Flash movie and will not stretch or expand the size. This ensures that items outside the Stage area of the Flash movie will not be visible. There is, of course, another way to center the Flash movie in the browser—all you need to do is set the width and height dimensions to 100 percent in the Dreamweaver Property inspector. However, this method might cause some unwanted effects by altering how your movie is framed in the browser window. For example, if you had items in the Flash authoring environment that bled off the Stage area and into the Work area, those parts of the items off Stage would normally be "cropped" by the dimensions of the movie. When the Flash movie is imported to Dreamweaver, Dreamweaver adheres to the original dimensions, giving you the cropping and the clean edge that you expect. But when the width and height are set to 100 percent in Dreamweaver, items in the Flash work area that were meant to be cropped may be visible, creating a "sloppy" edge on the movie. Although most Web sites are viewed in full-screen capacity, some users scale their browser to their own desired size, which may adversely impact the aspect ratio (the height and width ratio) of your movie. The Dreamweaver scale options enable you to select from three display settings to achieve the desired perspective. These options are

✦ **Default (Show All):** Makes the entire movie visible in the specified area. The aspect ratio of the movie is maintained, and no distortion occurs. Borders may appear on two sides of the movie.

✦ **No Border:** Forces the movie to fill the specified area. The aspect ratio of the movie is maintained, and no distortion occurs—but portions of the movie may be cropped.

✦ **Exact Fit:** Forces the entire movie to fill the specified area. This option is rarely used because the aspect ratio of the movie is not maintained, and distortion may occur.

Specifying Window Mode

Chapter 21, "Publishing Flash Movies" describes how the Publish Settings dialog box within Flash MX has a Window Mode setting that is used to make Flash movies transparent and show DHTML content that would otherwise be hidden behind them. You may have noticed that there is no equivalent of the Window Mode option in the Dreamweaver Property inspector. If you want that option, you have to specify it a little more directly.

The Window Mode parameter for Flash movies currently only works with Windows 95 or later versions of Internet Explorer 4.0 or higher. The window mode parameter, `WMODE`, lets the background of a Flash movie drop out, so that HTML or DHTML content can appear in place of the Flash movie background. Because this option is not broadly supported, you are unlikely to find very many Web pages that use it. However, if you want to try it out, it's pretty simple.

The three options for Window Mode are

✦ **Window:** This is the "standard" player interface, in which the Flash movie plays as it would normally, in its own rectangular window on a Web page.

✦ **Opaque:** Use this option if you want the Flash movie to have an opaque background and have DHTML or HTML elements behind the Flash movie.

✦ **Transparent:** This option "knocks out" the Flash background color so that other HTML elements can show through. Note that the Flash movie's frame rate and performance may suffer on slower machines when this mode is used, because the Flash movie needs to composite itself over other non-Flash material.

If you want to animate other material behind or in front of the Flash movie, make sure that your Flash movie is on its own DHTML layer.

1. In your Dreamweaver page, select the Flash movie (.swf file).

2. Click the Parameters button in the Property inspector.

3. The Parameters dialog box appears. Enter WMODE for the Parameter and TRANSPARENT, OPAQUE, or WINDOW for the value, as shown in Figure 42-3.

Figure 42-3: Specifying Window Mode in Dreamweaver MX

4. Click OK. Preview your page by pressing F12 or by choosing File ➪ Preview In Browser.

Caution   Window Mode only works with the Flash ActiveX control on Internet Explorer for Windows 95/98/ME/NT/2000/XP. Therefore, it only applies to 32-bit Windows versions of Internet Explorer. If you intend to deliver to this browser, then you can animate Flash content on top of DHTML content. If you are using browser detection on your Web pages, you can divert visitors using these browsers to specialized Flash and DHTML Web pages, while routing visitors with older systems to standard pages that don't use Window Mode.

Cross-Reference   For more information on using browser detection, refer to Chapter 22, "Integrating Flash Content with HTML."

Using the Built-In Flash Functions

Dreamweaver includes some simple but useful options for creating Flash movies (.swf files) without having to use the Flash authoring tool. These options can be found on the Media tab of the Insert panel, shown in Figure 42-4.

Insert Flash

Insert Flash text

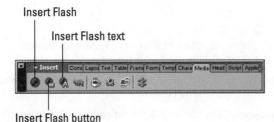

Insert Flash button

Figure 42-4: Flash options on the Media Tab of the Insert panel

Adding a Flash Button

Since version 4.0, Dreamweaver has had the capability to create Flash Button objects based on predetermined button styles. The styles available in Dreamweaver MX look much like the Button Library that ships with Flash MX. Dreamweaver actually lets you edit the text labels and links of these buttons. Dreamweaver will also create a Flash movie (.swf file) that is placed in the same directory as the current HTML document.

Note   You must save your document first before inserting a Flash Button or Text object. If you have not saved your document, Dreamweaver will prompt you to do so at that time. Dreamweaver needs to know where the HTML file resides before it can create the Flash movie (.swf file).

To create a Flash Button object in Dreamweaver follow these steps:

1. Select the Flash Button icon from the Media tab of the Insert Panel, or select Insert ➪ Interactive Images ➪ Flash Button. Alternatively, you can drag the Flash Button icon from the Insert panel into the document window. Using any of these methods will enable you to access the Insert Flash Button dialog box, shown in Figure 42-5.

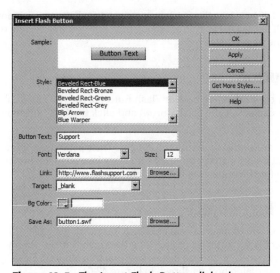

Figure 42-5: The Insert Flash Button dialog box

2. Now select a Button style from the list provided. Dreamweaver provides you with a preview of the Button style. You can also click and roll over the Button style in the sample window to preview how the button will behave. However, you will not be able to preview any changes to the text or Bg color in this window.

3. Next, in the Button text field, type the text that you would like to add. This field doesn't work for every button style, as VCR-style Play and Stop buttons don't have text. If the button preview has the words Button Text on the button, then you will be able to type in your own text. Also, the amount of text is limited to the width of the button.

4. For the Font field (optional), select a font for the text and the font size from their respective drop-down menus. Make sure this is not too small to read effectively.

5. For the Link field (optional), type a filename (or URL) or click the Browse button to locate the file to link to. The link can be either a document-relative or absolute link for the button.

6. The Target field (optional) enables you to choose a target frame or target window from the drop-down menu.

7. The Bg field (optional) enables you to choose a background color for your Flash button within a rectangular area. You can either type in a hexadecimal color value (for example, #0066FF) or use the color well to select a background color.

8. For the Save As field, type in a name to save your new Flash movie (.swf file) as, or accept the default button name. You could also choose a different location for the Flash movie to be saved by clicking the Browse button and then finding (or creating) the folder where you want to place your Flash button (for example, flash_assets/green_arrow.swf).

9. If you can't find a Button style that suits you, click Get More Styles to connect to the Macromedia Exchange site to download even more button styles.

10. Finally, click Apply or OK to insert the Flash button into the document window. If you clicked Apply, you will not leave the Button dialog box; but you will be able to preview your new button on the page.

Editing a Flash Button

There are two ways to open the Edit dialog box for Flash Buttons: (a) you can double-click the Flash Button, or (b) you can select the Flash Button and click the Edit button in the Property inspector.

More button editing options are available within the Property inspector. Bg color and File are the only two options that are repeated from the Edit dialog box. Also, no Src option is present, because the .fla file for the buttons is not available to you.

Inserting a Flash Text object

The Flash Text object enables you to insert a body of Flash Text with a simple rollover effect. Inserting the Flash Text object is very similar to inserting the Flash Button. Simply select the Flash Text icon in the Objects panel, or choose Insert ➪ Interactive Media ➪ Flash Text. This brings up the Insert Flash Text dialog box, as shown in Figure 42-6.

Using the Insert Flash Text dialog box, follow these steps to format and insert your text:

1. Select a font face from the Font drop-down menu.

2. Enter a font size (in points) in the Size field.

3. Select style attributes by clicking the Bold, Italic, and Text Alignment buttons.

4. Choose a text color by entering a hexadecimal color (for example, #0066FF) or by choosing a specific color from the color pop-up menu. You can also choose a separate rollover color for your text.

5. Type in your desired text in the Text field.

6. Enter a document-relative or absolute HTML link (optional).

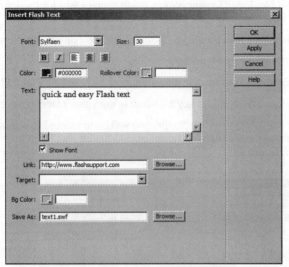

Figure 42-6: The Insert Flash Text dialog box.
Dreamweaver MX enables you to place anti-aliased
Flash Text within an HTML document. Dreamweaver
will create the necessary .swf file for the HTML document.

7. Choose an HTML target window or target frame (optional).

8. Choose a background color (optional).

9. Type in a file name for the Save as field or accept the default name (for example,
text1.swf).

10. To preview all of your settings, click Apply to insert the Flash Text without leaving the
dialog box.

11. To insert the Flash Text and exit the dialog box, click OK.

Editing a Flash Text object

There are two ways of opening the Edit dialog box for Flash Text: (a) you can double-click the
Flash Text object, or (b) select the Flash Text object and click Edit in the Property inspector.

Launch and edit Flash from Dreamweaver

You can't edit your Flash movies (.swf files) directly in the Dreamweaver authoring environment, so you must go to the Flash document (.fla file). Before Dreamweaver MX, this entailed
opening up Flash and navigating through your files to find the source Flash document, which
might even be in a different location than the Flash movie placed in Dreamweaver, with no
inherent mechanism for tying the two together. You'd edit in Flash, export the .swf file and
finally go back to Dreamweaver, hoping that you'd exported to the correct location. This
could be a surprisingly time-consuming task on a large site and even on simpler sites could
certainly interfere with workflow and add unnecessary steps to what should be an easy
routine. Fortunately, we now have a simpler method.

Dreamweaver MX can store related information about a Flash movie: most importantly, its associated .fla file. This can be viewed in the Src element of the Property inspector. The first time you decide to change a .swf file within Dreamweaver, it will prompt you for the location of the .fla file and remember it from that point on.

In your Dreamweaver page, select the Flash movie you want to edit. Do one of the following:

✦ Click the Edit button on the Property inspector.

✦ Right-click (Control-click) on the Flash movie placeholder and choose Edit with Flash.

✦ Hold down the Ctrl (Windows) or ⌘ (Mac) key and double-click the placeholder movie.

If Dreamweaver does not know the location of the .fla file, you will be prompted to supply it. Flash will then open, and make it apparent that you have decided to edit this Flash movie from Dreamweaver, as shown in Figure 42-7.

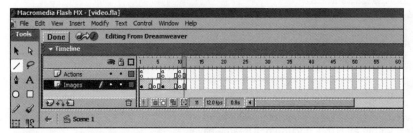

Figure 42-7: Editing a Flash MX file from Dreamweaver MX

When you are finished editing the Flash movie, click the Done button. Flash will export the Flash movie (.swf file), save the Flash document (.fla file) and return you to Dreamweaver MX.

Adding Dreamweaver Behaviors

Dreamweaver MX includes several pre-written JavaScript behaviors to supply a variety of different client-side interactions. These include routines to perform image rollovers and DHTML functions. There are two routines that are of particular interest to Flash developers: the Check Plugin behavior and the Control Shockwave or Flash behavior.

Check Plugin behavior

While this is not the most foolproof way of detecting Flash, it's quick and easy to use.

1. Create a new Dreamweaver document or open an existing one.

2. In the Behaviors panel (Window ⇨ Behaviors or Shift+F3) click the Plus button and select the Check Plugin behavior.

3. The Check Plugin dialog box opens, as shown in Figure 42-8. Select Flash from the drop-down list.

4. For If Found, Go To URL field, specify a page to go to if the visitor has the Flash Player. This can be a relative or absolute address.

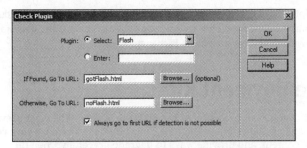

Figure 42-8: The Check Plugin behavior enables you to apply simple Flash detection easily.

5. For Otherwise, Go To URL field, specify an alternative page to go to if the visitor does not have the Flash Player. This can be a relative or absolute address.

6. Click OK. The Behaviors panel should show the Check Plugin behavior and the event on which it happens, typically the OnLoad event.

Control Shockwave or Flash behavior

This allows simple JavaScript control of a Flash movie, telling the movie to Play, Stop, Rewind, or Go To a certain frame. You can apply these behaviors to regular HTML images or hyperlinks and use them to control the timeline of your Flash movie.

1. Add a Flash movie to your Dreamweaver page.

2. Add a name for the Flash movie in the Properties inspector. Dreamweaver will not allow you to add the Control Shockwave or Flash behavior unless the .swf is named.

3. Typically, you'd use images or hyperlinks to control the Flash movie. If you want to use images, select the image. If you want to use a link, make sure you at least have # in the link section of the Property inspector.

4. In the Behaviors panel (Window ➪ Behaviors), Click the plus (+) button and choose Control Shockwave or Flash.The Control Shockwave or Flash dialog box appears, shown in Figure 42-9.

Figure 42-9: The Control Shockwave or Flash dialog box

5. If you have more than one movie on your page, choose the correct one from the drop-down list. Choose whether you want to Play, Stop, Rewind, or Go To a frame. If Go To Frame, enter the frame number.

6. Click OK. Check that the event (onMouseOver, onMouseDown) is correct.

Note   For more about JavaScript behaviors and events in Dreamweaver, check the documentation and Macromedia's Dreamweaver support area at www.macromedia.com. Other behaviors are also available for download at the Macromedia Exchange.

Using the Flash Deployment Kit

Flash detection is a vital part of any Flash Web site. Although Flash is one of the most prevalent browser plug-ins, it may still exclude some audiences. You should always make sure your audience is able to view your content, and provide ways to degrade gracefully when they don't have the required plug-ins or other special requirements. In the last section, we added a simple JavaScript behavior to check for the Flash Player plug-in, but that solution has limitations and is not the best way to check. For example, it only checks for the existence of the Flash Player plug-in, not for any specific version. This means someone with Flash Player 3 could be let in to areas of your site that are really only usable by those with Flash Player 6.

Exhaustive Flash Player detection is surprisingly involved, due to the huge number of possible configurations of browser, machine, and plug-in version — not to mention the issue of all the different possible security configurations — is ActiveX allowed? Is JavaScript turned off? In fact, most people involved with Flash Player detection would tell you that completely accurate detection is in fact impossible. But we can get 99 percent of the way there, with a helpful download from Macromedia.

Downloading and installing the Deployment Kit

In this exercise, you make menu buttons that will enable the user to navigate to the different areas of the Flash movie.

1. Point your browser to www.macromedia.com/software/flash/download/deployment_kit/ and download the version that's right for you.

2. The deployment kit files are zipped, so you'll need a tool like WinZip or StuffIt Expander to uncompress them.

3. After uncompressing the file, you should have a folder (Flash_Deployment_Kit) with several other folders inside it.

4. In the dreamweaver_behavior folder, find the file called FlashDispatcher.mxp. Double-click it.

5. This will open the Macromedia Extension Manager and prompt you to install the Flash Dispatcher behavior. Agree to the prompts to install it. After it is installed, you should see the behavior in the Extension Manager, as shown in Figure 42-10.

6. If Dreamweaver MX is open, close it. New behaviors require a restart of the application before they will become available.

7. Open Dreamweaver MX. Either save a new page or open an existing one that you want to use. What you're going to do here is add a behavior to this page that will redirect people to the correct content. Quite often, the page you would add this behavior to would be the home page of your site.

8. Make sure your cursor is on the page but you have not selected an object or image. From the Behaviors panel (Window ➪ Behaviors) select the Macromedia Flash Dispatcher behavior from the menu, as shown in Figure 42-11.

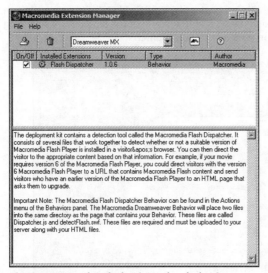

Figure 42-10: The Flash Dispatcher behavior installed

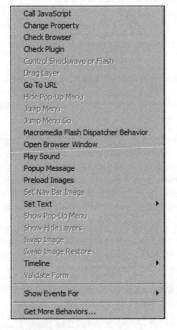

Figure 42-11: The Macromedia Flash Dispatcher behavior has been added to the behaviors list.

9. The Macromedia Flash Dispatcher behavior dialog box will open (see Figure 42-12). For Macromedia Flash Content URL, select the page the visitor should go to if he has the correct version of Flash.

10. For Alternate URL, select the page the visitor should go to if he doesn't have the correct version. This could be an HTML version of the site, or a page asking him to upgrade — it depends on your site demographic.

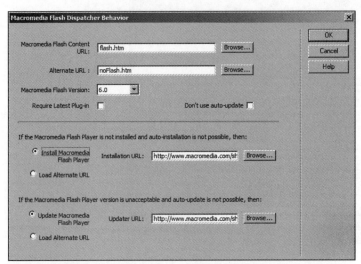

Figure 42-12: The Macromedia Flash Dispatcher behavior allows a great deal of control over the options available for different visitors.

11. You can click OK at this point or go on to change some of the other options detailed later.

The Macromedia Flash Dispatcher behavior will, by default, attempt to automatically upgrade the Flash Player if it detects the incorrect version. This usually only works with the Windows ActiveX control for Internet Explorer, but you can choose to turn this off by selecting the Don't Use Auto-Update check box.

The lower section of the dialog box deals with what to do if the player is not acceptable but automatic update is not possible. The first part asks what to do if the Flash Player is missing but can't be automatically installed. The default option is Install Macromedia Flash Player — this seems a little confusing, as we're only at this option if Flash *can't* be automatically installed. What this actually does is redirect the browser to the Macromedia Web site (or another link if you choose to specify one) and require the user to install the player manually.

The final section asks what to do if the Flash Player is an incorrect version but can't be automatically updated. The default option is Update Macromedia Flash Player. This option redirects the browser to the Macromedia Web site (or another link if you choose to specify one) and requires the user to install the latest version of the player manually.

You might notice that your site files in Dreamweaver seem to have changed. That's because adding the Macromedia Flash Dispatcher behavior adds two files to your site:

✦ **detectFlash.swf**: This is a tiny Flash file that sits in your detection page. If the visitor does have a recent version of the Flash Player, this can do a fair amount of detection very quickly by using ActionScript. If the visitor doesn't have Flash, this file won't be able to do anything, and we will need to use other means of evaluating the situation.

✦ **Dispatcher.js**: This is a JavaScript file that attempts to cope with every possible configuration available—including no Flash Player at all—and to redirect to the correct page for each situation.

Caution

As Dreamweaver needed to add the two files to provide all this functionality, you must make sure that when you upload your pages to your remote Web site, you also upload the detectFlash.swf and Dispatcher.js files.

Link Checker

One of the most common—and often most tedious—tasks in site management is keeping links updated and changing out-of-date URLs. Dreamweaver has long supplied many Find/Replace options for searching entire sites of HTML pages and changing one link to become a different link, but when your site consists of both Flash and HTML content, it was always a manual process to change all the links within the Flash movies.

With Dreamweaver MX, this is no longer a limitation. You can change links even in Flash movies (.swf files). View the Site Map (Alt+F8 or Option+F8, or choose Map view in the Site panel). You can also click the Expand/Collapse button in the Site panel to view the full size Site Map. See Figure 42-13.

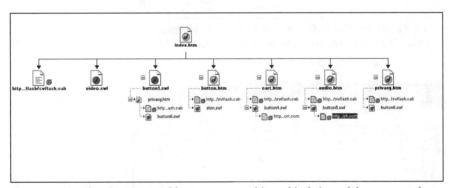

Figure 42-13: The Site Map enables you to see a hierarchical view of the pages and links in your site, including links from Flash movies.

To be able to see this level of detail in the Site Map, you must have a page defined as your Home page in your site definition, and also be able to view any dependent files. You can specify this in the site definition as shown in Figure 42-14, or choose View ⇨ Show Dependent Files.

When a link is visible in a Flash movie in the Site Map, you can change it by right-clicking (Control+clicking) and choosing Change Link. This will allow you to either browse to a relative file or enter an absolute address.

You can also check all the links in the site, including links within Flash movies, by right-clicking in the Site Map and choosing Check Links. You can then check the entire site or just a subset of folders.

The results of this check will appear in the Results panel (refer to Figure 42-15). You can then view them by category—broken links, external links and orphaned files—and even change the links from this window simply by typing over the old value.

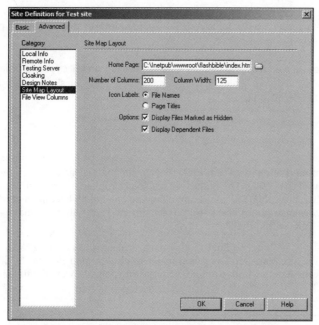

Figure 42-14: The Site Definition Site Map Layout is where you select a Home page and choose to Show Dependent Files.

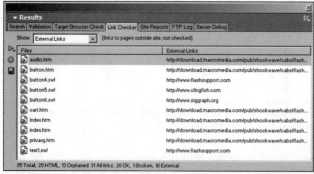

Figure 42-15: The Results panel enables you to view and change the links within your site, even within Flash movies (.swf files).

Writing ActionScript with Dreamweaver

When creating large Flash movies, many programmers choose to keep their ActionScript in external text files—typically ending in .as. There are many benefits to this method:

✦ You can start building libraries of code external to your .fla files, making it easier to reuse code in Flash movies which share common routines.

✦ You can avoid the ActionScript window in Flash, which can often be cramped and difficult to navigate, especially when writing large amounts of code.

✦ You can modularize your code files, allowing different developers to work on different parts of the same Flash movie simultaneously.

✦ When code files are stored externally, you can use a version control system to track changes.

New in Dreamweaver MX is the ability to create external ActionScript files with full syntax coloring and code hinting features, as shown in Figure 42-16. This is very similar to using the ActionScript panel in Flash MX.

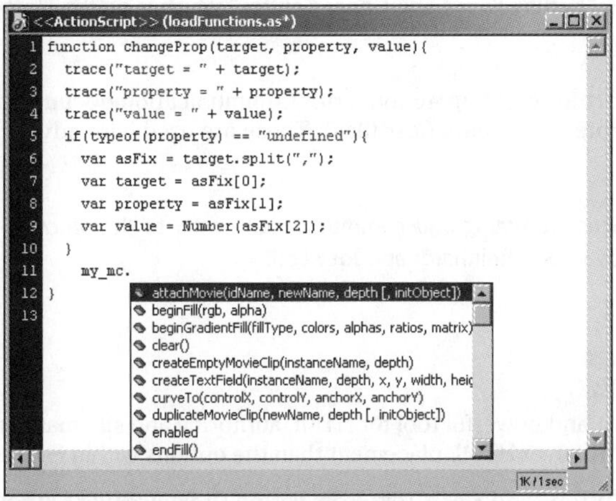

Figure 42-16: Dreamweaver MX supports full ActionScript editing, including syntax coloring and code hinting.

This makes the process of creating code files much less error-prone than it was in previous versions of Dreamweaver, where most methods of editing external ActionScript didn't offer any means of syntax checking.

Code hinting in Dreamweaver MX creates pop-up menus that automatically appear when typing the name of an object, as in the ActionScript panel in Flash MX. For example, if your object name ends in _mc, the code hint menu will show the methods and properties for a movieClip object. If your object name ends in _xmlsocket, you see the methods and properties for an XMLSocket object. If you aren't using the suggested suffixes and want to force code hints to appear, press Ctrl+Spacebar (⌘+Spacebar).

To create an ActionScript .as file in Dreamweaver MX, follow these steps:

1. In Dreamweaver MX, select File ➪ New to open the New Document window.

2. In the Other category, select the ActionScript entry and click the Create button.

3. A new page will open in code view with a comment at the start to indicate an ActionScript file. You can begin writing ActionScript.

Some ActionScript is well suited to being written in external files—long routines, groups of functions, and object definitions, for example. Though it may seem counter-intuitive, it's practical to have more—rather than fewer—external files when writing code. A common method is to use a separate .as file for each object definition within your Flash movie.

You use the #include command in your Flash movie to load the code from an external file. External ActionScript is only included in the Flash movie when the .swf is published. If you change any code in the external file, you need to publish your Flash movie again to include the changed ActionScript.

> **Cross-Reference**
>
> You need to know how to use the #include directive to use external ActionScript files (.as files). The #include directive is covered in more detail in Chapter 32, "Creating a Portfolio Site in Flash" and Chapter 35 "Getting Your Code Under Control," which is on the *Flash MX Bible* CD-ROM.

Dreamweaver MX also has support for creating ActionScript Communication documents (.asc files) and ActionScript Remote documents (.asr files). These are used with advanced ActionScripting features.

> **Cross-Reference**
>
> For more details on ActionScript remoting and communications, refer to the *Macromedia Flash MX ActionScript Bible* by Robert Reinhardt and Joey Lott.

Summary

✦ Dreamweaver MX is a robust and powerful tool for HTML authoring and site management, and allows much more control over HTML placement than the options within Flash.

✦ You can easily add Flash Buttons and Flash Text from within Dreamweaver without ever opening Flash.

✦ Dreamweaver comes with many built-in JavaScript behaviors that are easy to apply, including methods for detecting plug-ins and simple control of Flash movies.

✦ Macromedia supplies the Flash Deployment Kit for free download. This allows a simple yet powerful creation of Flash detection within your site, by adding the Flash Dispatcher Behavior.

✦ Dreamweaver MX now includes full ActionScript code editing abilities, including code hinting and syntax coloring.

✦ URL links in Flash movies can be checked and edited within the Dreamweaver environment without opening Flash.

✦ You can launch Flash and edit Flash movies from within Dreamweaver MX, making the process of updating your Flash files much simpler within an HTML site environment.

✦   ✦   ✦

Working with Director

In This Chapter

Advantages of Director
over Flash

Benefits of Flash assets
in Director

Controlling Director
with Flash

Controlling Flash
with Director

Macromedia Director has been the industry standard multi-media authoring application for DVD-ROMs, CD-ROMs, kiosk presentations, and Shockwave game development on the Web. After version 6.5 of Director, you can import Flash movies (.swf files) via the Flash Asset Xtra. With version 8.5, you can take even more control of your Flash movies in Director. Moreover, the latest versions of the Shockwave plug-in automatically install the Flash Asset Xtra on Web browsers. That means that you can count on Shockwave-enabled visitors being able to view your Flash-Director Shockwave content.

Why would you want to use Director in combination with Flash? With any multimedia project, you should use the technology that will allow you to accomplish your goals. Flash MX has greatly expanded the capabilities of Flash movies, but the application (and the Flash Player) does have a few limitations. Macromedia Director can augment the toolset of Flash MX, and allow you to take your multimedia projects to a higher plane of interactive experiences.

Caution   As of this writing, Macromedia Director 8.5 could import only Flash 5 or earlier movies (.swf files). If you want to use Flash MX to create Flash movies for Director movies, make sure you export Flash 5 or earlier movies. Director 7.02 and 8.0 can use Flash 4 or earlier movies. You can set the version of the Flash movie in the Version menu of the Publish Settings' Flash tab. You can find the most up-to-date information about Director at www.macromedia.com/software/director.

Advantages of Director over Flash

Flash MX has added many improvements upon its predecessor, Flash 5. With the continuing growth (and maturity) of the ActionScript language and the added support for embedded video, it may seem that a tool such as Director is no longer necessary. The following list reviews some of the current benefits of Director movies and its authoring environment.

✦ **Xtra Architecture:** The functionality of Director can be expanded with the use of Xtras. Xtras are similar to Flash MX components in the sense that both allow you to expand the capabilities of your movies. However, Xtras are much more integrated with the actual playback engine of Director movies. Many of Director's standard features, such as importing Flash movies (.swf files), are controlled by Xtras. Third-party Xtras can add additional file support to your Director movies (such as MIDI and PDF files) or allow custom data types or server connections to be employed by your Director movies. You can find more information on Xtras at `www.macromedia.com/software/xtras/director/`.

✦ **Faster Playback Engine:** The Shockwave Player (and Director projectors), while only available on Windows and Macintosh platforms, outperforms the playback speed of the Flash Player. Director movies usually have faster screen redraws and process data much more quickly than Flash movies in Flash Player 6.

✦ **Extended Drawing API:** In Director 8, a new `image` object was introduced to Lingo, the scripting language used within the Director authoring environment. The `image` object allows you to control, at a pixel level, lines and fills on the Director stage. Flash MX ActionScript also allows you to create artwork with code, but Lingo's implementation of the image object allows you to create visual effects not easily achieved (or possible) with ActionScript.

✦ **Built-in 3D Engine:** Director 8.5 introduced the ability to use high-impact, textured, 3D graphics and models. Flash movies can not import true 3D models — you can only simulate 3D effects with Flash artwork and animation. Using Lingo, you can manipulate 3D models and apply lighting effects. Check out Flash pioneer Yugo Nakamura's site `www.yugop.com` for an extensive collection of inspiring Shockwave 3D movies.

To learn more about the new drawing features of Flash MX ActionScript, read the *Macromedia Flash MX ActionScript Bible* by Robert Reinhardt and Joey Lott.

Advantages of Flash MX over Director

Of course, you're reading the *Flash MX Bible* instead of the Director *Bible* — clearly, something's drawn you to Flash MX. Flash is slowing taking on more features that used to be strictly Director's domain. Let's take a quick look at the benefits of Flash MX development.

✦ **Flash Player penetration:** Simply put, the Flash Player dominates the Web. While the Flash Player is available for several operating systems and mobile devices, Director movies can only be viewed on Windows and Macintosh desktop computers. The Flash Player is also a much smaller download than the Shockwave Player — even with its new video capabilities, Flash Player 6 is still under 1MB! You can develop Flash movies that deliver high-quality content over the Internet to a wide audience.

✦ **Superior drawing and animation tools:** Flash started as a vector-based animation tool. Everyone from traditional animators to interactive designers can easily learn how to use the drawing toolset in Flash MX to create animated content.

✦ **Leaner file sizes:** While you can create small Director movies (.dcr files) for distribution on the Web, Flash movies by and large tend to be much smaller for equivalent use of graphics and interactive elements. Because most artwork in Flash movies is vector-based, file sizes remain quite small.

✦ **Broad range of support options:** Many Flash developers are surprised at the lack of Director resources on the Web. You won't find equivalents to ultrashock.com, flashkit.com, and were-here.com for Director developers. These sites offer hundreds (if not thousands!) of Flash tutorials and example files. While there is a Director community on the Web, the number of Flash developers sharing information with one another far exceeds the number of Director developers doing so.

Benefits and Limitations of Flash Assets in Director

Flash MX has been another monumental leap forward for Flash interactivity. With the ever-growing scope of the ActionScript language and the improved media handling capabilities that Flash movies can now employ, many of the previous Flash-Director scenarios or workarounds are no longer needed. However, if you're already familiar with Director and Lingo (Director's scripting language), then you may find integrating Flash movies into Director projects easier than learning advanced scripting with ActionScript in Flash MX. The following list describes some of the benefits and drawbacks of using Flash movies in Director projects.

✦ **Vector control:** Even though Director has vector shape-drawing tools, it doesn't use the same intuitive drawing mechanism that Flash does. Use Flash for any complex vector drawing and animation, and then bring it into your Director project.

✦ **Implement existing projects:** With the ability to use Flash movies in Director, you need not duplicate efforts if material already exists in one format or the other. Therefore, if you've already developed some cool animations in Flash for your company's Web site, you can reuse the same Flash .swf files in your Director projects.

✦ **Similar scripting environments:** Both Flash and Director use a form of dot syntax for their scripting languages. Flash ActionScript resembles JavaScript much more closely than Director Lingo does. Director Lingo uses a different model of command and event control than Flash MX does.

Flash and Director both have means to communicate with each other. Data can be sent from Flash to Director, or Director to Flash, via Lingo. Just as Flash Movie Clips can be self-contained interactive modules within one overall Flash movie (.swf file), Flash movies can be elements of a much larger and media rich Director movie. To get you started with Director-Flash interactivity, the next section shows you how to send events from Flash movies to Director movies.

Cross-Reference   The following sections are intended for readers who already know the basics of Director movie production. If you need more information on the Director authoring environment, please refer to the *Director 8 Bible*. You can also find more advanced Flash-Director integration coverage in the *Macromedia Flash MX ActionScript Bible*.

Creating Director-Specific Actions in Flash

You can use Flash movies (.swf files) in any number of ways with Director. If you simply want to use a Flash animation for graphic content within a Director presentation, you can simply use the same Flash movie (.swf file) you generated for the Web. Use the Flash Asset Xtra import box (see the more in-depth discussion later in this section) to set the parameters of playback without needing any Lingo. However, if you want Flash actions (in frames or on buttons) to do something in your Director movies, then you need to know how to get Lingo's attention. The drawback to this type of "dual" interactivity is that you need to plan ahead with both your Flash and Director movies. As with any project, you should outline a storyboard before embarking on a task such as this.

Cross-Reference Use a project planner such as Microsoft Visio to plan an interactive project. By creating interactive hierarchies and flow-charts (for example, determining which scenes will link to other scenes), you can manage projects with greater ease. We discussed the importance of interactive project planning in Chapter 3, "Planning Flash Projects."

You have three methods to use within the Flash authoring environment, all involving the getURL() action. You can assign any of these methods the same way you would with any other Flash interactivity — attach these actions to buttons, frames, or ActionScript conditions.

Caution If you experience crashes in Director using any of the getURL() commands listed in this section, please see the sidebar "Quirks with Flash Sprites and Lingo go Commands" later in this chapter.

Standard getURL command

On a Flash Button or frame, open the Actions panel and assign a getURL() action. This is the preferred method of sending information to Director movies because you can deal with the result of the action in Director — you do not need to specify what Director does with the string from Flash. When a Button instance is selected and the Actions panel is in Normal mode, Flash MX automatically creates a default on (release) action to contain the getURL() action. In the URL setting, create a string to be passed to an event handler in Lingo. In Figure 43-1, a getURL() action is assigned to a frame in Flash. The string ProjectOne is entered in the URL text field. This string, in turn, is received by Lingo.

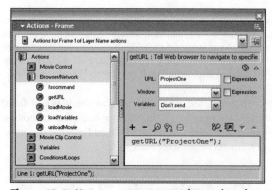

Figure 43-1: You can enter any word or series of characters (that is, a string) in the URL field. This string is then passed to Lingo.

In Director, you need to attach a behavior script to the Flash Sprite so that the `getURL()` action and string can be received by Lingo. We discuss the actual implementation of this example later in the "Controlling Flash Movies in Director" section. In Figure 43-1, the string `ProjectOne` was assigned to `getURL()`. In Director, we could tell Lingo to go to the frame marker called `ProjectOne`:

```
on getURL me, FlashString
   go to frame FlashString
end
```

When the Flash Sprite plays in Director and the `getURL()` action is executed, the `ProjectOne` value of `getURL` is passed as the `FlashString` argument of the Lingo event handler, on `getURL`. Lingo will direct the playback of the Director movie to the frame marker `ProjectOne`.

event: command

You can also specify an `event:` handler in the URL field of the `getURL()` action. This method is useful if you would like to describe an event that is repeatedly used in Flash, but needs customized settings with each use. For example, if you want to add a mouse click to go to a different Director frame depending on which button was clicked, you could use the following URL in the `getURL()` action:

```
event: FClick "ProjectOne"
```

In Director, you then write a behavior that would receive the `FClick` event:

```
on FClick me FlashString
   go to frame FlashString
end
```

How is this different from the last example? If you want to have several events in one script that perform different Lingo commands, you need to label each one with a separate event, such as:

```
on FClickButton01 me FlashString
   go to frame FlashString
end

on FClickButton02 me FlashString
   quit
end
```

In the preceding example, we have two defined Flash events, `FClickButton01` and `FClickButton02`, which do different things. If we had used the standard `getURL()` action, we could only pass the string to one Lingo command.

Tip With a bit more programming in Lingo, you could pass one argument string to multiple Lingo commands by testing the string with `if...else` statements.

Quirks with Flash Sprites and Lingo go Commands

In Director 6.5, you may experience crashes if you send Flash events to Lingo that make a Director movie go to a frame where the Flash Sprite is no longer on the Stage. For example, if you start a Director movie with a Flash animation, and you have a frame action on the last frame of the Flash animation that directs playback to a new section of the Director score, the Flash Sprite duration needs to be extended all the way to the frame that the Director movie is jumping to. Use a Lingo command such as:

```
set the visible of sprite X to false
```

(where X designates the Flash Sprite number) to make the Flash Sprite invisible on that frame if necessary. If you don't want to extend the Sprite to that frame and/or you are jumping to a new movie, see the advanced workarounds at www.macromedia.com/support/director/ts/documents/flash_asset_xtra_go_issue.htm.

lingo: command

The last getURL() method of sending events to Lingo is the most direct method of communicating with Director movies. In the URL field, a lingo: handler is used to specify a Lingo statement. This is the most inflexible method of sending events to Director — insofar as you cannot do anything in Director to modify or direct the event. For example, if you added the following code to an on (release), getURL() button event in Flash:

```
lingo: quit
```

then the Director movie quits (or the Director projector closes) when that button was clicked.

With lingo: statements in getURL() actions, you do not need to specify any further Lingo in the Director movie, unless you are setting the value of prescripted variable or executing an event described in the Director movie script.

Controlling Flash Movies in Director

You can import and use Flash movies (.swf files) into Director just as you would any other cast member. Director controls Flash movies with the Flash Asset Xtra. This section shows you how to import Flash movies and use them in the Director Score window. You should already be familiar with the Director authoring environment and basic Behavior use.

The Flash Asset Xtra: Importing Flash movies

Since Director 6.5, the Flash Asset Xtra has enabled Flash movies to play within a Director movie. Again, make sure you have Director 8.5 in order to use Flash 5 movies. If you have Director 8.0 or 7.0.2, you'll need to export your Flash 4 movies from Flash MX. Director 7.0.1 supports Flash 3 or earlier movies. If you have Director 6.5, you need to export your Flash movies as Flash 2 movies.

Note

As we mentioned earlier in this chapter, you can not currently use Flash 6 movies in Director 8.5. You must publish your Flash MX documents as Flash 5 or earlier movies for use in Director. By the time this book is published, it's highly likely that a new Flash Asset Xtra will be available for Flash 6 movies.

Caution

If you are using a version of Director earlier than 7.0.2, then be extremely careful with the use of Flash audio. In older versions of Director that support Flash movies, Flash audio cannot play simultaneously with Director score sounds. Macromedia's tech notes advise turning sound off when using earlier versions of the Flash Asset Xtra.

On the CD-ROM

You can use any of the Flash movies (.swf files) on the Flash MX Bible CD-ROM for this example. For this section, we use the crossButton.swf file, which is located in the ch43 folder on the *Flash MX Bible* CD-ROM.

To import a Flash movie (.swf file), do the following:

1. Start a new Director movie (.dir file) or open an existing movie.

2. Use the File ➪ Import command (Ctrl+R or ⌘+R) to select a Flash movie (.swf file). Double-click the filename in the upper portion of the Import dialog box (see Figure 43-2), or select the filename and choose Add. You can select several files of different types and import them all at once. When you are done adding files, click Import to bring the Flash movie(s) into the Internal Cast.

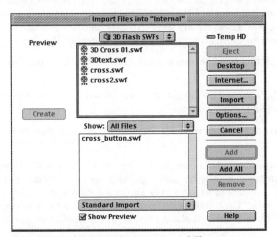

Figure 43-2: You can import several files at once with the Import command. (The Mac version is shown here.)

3. Open the Cast window (Ctrl+3 or ⌘+3). Double-click the Flash movie that was imported. This brings up the Flash Asset Properties dialog box (see Figure 43-3). The top section of the dialog box is used to link to external or remote Flash movies (see following tip and sidebar), while the lower section sets the playback attributes:

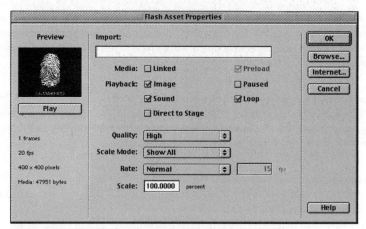

Figure 43-3: The Flash Asset Properties dialog box enables you to specify how the Flash movie functions in the Director movie.

- **Media:** This setting has two options, Linked and Preload. If you don't want to store a Flash movie within the Director movie, check Link and specify the path to the Flash movie. Unless you want to link to a Flash movie on the Internet, you should store the Flash movie in the Director movie — Flash movies are usually very small due to their vector structure. If Link is checked, then you can also enable Preload. Preloading will force Director to load (or download) the entire SWF file before it starts playing the Flash movie. Otherwise, Director will start playing the Flash movie as soon as it starts to stream the Flash cast member. See the sidebar at the end of this section for more information on linked Internet files.

- **Playback:** This setting has five options that control how Director displays the Flash movie.

  The Image option, checked by default, determines whether Director shows the graphic content of a Flash movie.

  The Sound option determines whether Director plays the audio content of a Flash movie.

  The Direct to Stage option tells Director to give priority to the Flash movie Sprite over all other Sprites currently on the Stage. Although this option may enable Flash movies to playback more smoothly, Director ignores any ink effects applied to the Sprite (see the "Flash movies as Sprites" section for more information on ink effects), and the Flash movie always displays on top of other Sprites.

  The Paused option is akin to adding a stop( ) Flash action to the first frame of the Flash movie — you can force Director to display the movie in a paused state.

  The Loop option enables continuous playback of the Flash movie. If this option is checked, the Flash movie repeats as soon as it reaches the last frame unless the last frame has a stop( ) Flash action. It continues to repeat while the Flash Sprite is present in the Director Score, or until it is paused by a Lingo command.

- **Quality:** This setting has a drop-down menu with the some of the same Quality settings found in the Flash MX Publish Settings. By default, this setting is High. For more information on the Quality property of a Flash movie, see Chapter 21, "Publishing Flash Movies."

- **Scale mode:** By default, this setting uses Auto-Size, which enables Director to automatically resize the Flash movie's width and height according to the Sprite's bounding box on the Director stage. Meaning, if you resize the Sprite, then the Flash movie should fit the size of the Sprite box. Auto-Size automatically sets the Scale setting to 100 percent. Conversely, No Scale keeps the Flash movie at the size specified by the Scale setting (covered in a moment) and any subsequent resizing of the Sprite bounding box may crop the Flash movie. The remaining options, Show All, No Border, and Exact Fit operate the same as the Publish Settings options in Flash MX (see Chapter 21, "Publishing Flash Movies").

- **Rate:** Perhaps one of the most powerful settings in the Flash Asset Properties dialog box, Rate controls how fast or slow the Flash movie plays in a Director Scores — irrespective of the Tempo setting used in the Score. The Flash Asset Properties' Rate setting has two options: a drop-down menu and an fps text field. If Normal or Lock-Step is selected, then the fps text field is disabled. Normal plays the Flash movie at its native frame rate, as set in the Flash application via the Modify ⇨ Document dialog box.

  Lock-Step plays one Flash movie frame for every Director frame that its Sprite occupies (for example, if the Flash movie occupies four frames of the Director score, then only the first four frames of the animation plays back in Director). Therefore, Lock-Step inherits the frame rate of the Director movie as established in the Tempo setting in the Score.

  Fixed Rate enables you to specify a new frame rate for the Flash movie, independent of the original frame rate specified in Flash MX (via Modify ⇨ Document) or the Director Tempo setting in the Score.

- **Scale:** This setting works hand-in-hand with the Scale mode setting. If anything other than Auto-Size is selected in Scale mode, you can specify what percentage of the original Flash movie is used for the Flash Sprite. If 50 percent is used for the Scale of a 550×400 Flash movie and Exact Fit is chosen in Scale mode, then the movie displays at 225×200 in the original placed Flash Sprite on the Stage. If you resize the Sprite box, then it continues to maintain a 50 percent portion of the Sprite box area.

Tip
You can also use the Insert ⇨ Media Element ⇨ Flash Movie command to import Flash movies via the Flash Asset Properties dialog box. Simply click the Browse button and select a Flash movie (.swf file). Both the File ⇨ Import and Flash Asset Property dialog boxes enable you to enter Internet URLs for the filename path.

After specifying the settings you wish to use for your Flash movie, you can then place the Flash cast member as a Sprite on to the Director Stage.

Using Lingo to Preload Flash Movies

Like other Director Cast Members, you can control how a Flash movie Cast Member is loaded into a Shockwave movie or stand-alone Director projector. While you author a Director movie with a Flash movie Cast Member, it's useful to have a linked .swf file included in the Internal Cast. However, when you launch a Shockwave movie on the Web, you may want to make changes to the .swf file only and leave the Director .dcr file unchanged. Moreover, the path of a locally linked file is different from a file linked remotely over the Internet. This problem is easy to fix with a little Director Lingo.

For any Director movie that uses .swf files that you intend to update on a regular basis, you should dynamically set the filename property of the Flash Cast Member with Lingo. The following steps show you how to detect where the Director movie is being played (for example, from a standalone projector or from the Shockwave Player), and how to change the source of a linked Flash Cast Member:

1. Create or add the following Lingo to the Movie Script for your Director movie (note that the ⊃ indicates a continuation of the same line of code):

```
on prepareMovie
    global URLRootPath
    global shockPlayer
    if (the runMode contains "Projector") OR (the ⊃
    runMode contains "Author") then
        shockPlayer = false
    else
        shockPlayer = true
        URLRootPath = "http://theMakers.com/flash5/"
    end if
end prepareMovie

on initLoad me
    global URLRootPath
    global myNetID
    global flashPath
    flashPath = URLRootPath & "sliders.swf"
    set myNetID = preloadNetThing(flashPath)
end initLoad
```

For the variable URLRootPath, change the value to the path to your Flash files on your Web server. Don't forget the ending forward slash character, as a filename is appended to this path in the initLoad handler. In the initLoad handler, change the flashPath variable to specify the filename of the Flash movie (.swf file) that you want to load into the Director movie.

2. In the Director Score window, reserve a section of ten frames at the very beginning of the Score. Create a frame marker named initPreload on frame 1, and on frame 5, create a marker named loadLoop. Also, make sure that you have a marker on the frame where your Director movie's first interactivity takes place (for example, wherever the movie starts beyond these first ten frames for the preload sequence). In this example, we use the name intro.

3. On frame 1, add the following Frame Script:

```
on enterFrame
    global shockPlayer
    if shockPlayer = true then
        initLoad
    else
        go to "intro"
    end if
end
```

Here, we check whether the `prepareMovie` handler returned a `true` or `false` value for the `shockPlayer` variable. If the movie is being played in a Web browser, then `shockPlayer` will equal true. If that's the case, then execute the `initLoad` handler (in the Movie Script). Incidentally, handlers in Lingo work much like functions in ActionScript and JavaScript.

If the movie is being played in the authoring environment or a projector, then `shockPlayer` will equal `false`. Therefore, the `else` condition will execute, moving the Director Playhead to the `intro` marker.

4. On frame 10, add the following Frame Script:

```
on exitFrame
    global myNetID, flashPath
    if netDone(myNetID) = true then
        member("sliders").fileName = flashPath
        go to "intro"
    else
        go to "loadLoop"
    end if
end
```

Here, we check whether the `preloadNetThing` command that was executed in the `initLoad` handler has finished loading the Flash movie (.swf file). If it has, then the path of the linked (or stored) Cast Member sliders is changed to the Internet path described in `flashPath`. Then, the Director Playhead moves to the `intro` frame marker to start the movie. If the Flash movie file isn't finished loading, then the Director Playhead moves back to the `loadLoop` frame marker. The playhead will continue looping the frames between `loadLoop` and frame 10 until the Flash movie loads.

You will want to change the name of the Cast Member sliders to the name of your Flash movie Cast Number that was used in your Director movie.

These are the basic steps to preloading and changing the source file for Flash Cast Members. We didn't include error handling in the frame 10 script. As you may well know, Web servers can crash, Internet connections may falter, or a file is deleted or moved to another location. Refer to the Lingo Dictionary included with Director 8.5 to see the various `netDone` and `netError` return values.

Using Director's Property Inspector

Director 8.0 introduced a new look-and-feel to the authoring environment. In addition to a resizable Stage window, you can change the Cast window to view by list or thumbnail, and you can quickly modify Sprite, Cast Member, and Movie attributes (among others) with the Property Inspector.

The Property Inspector (shown in Figure 43-4) enables you to quickly change all of the Flash Asset Properties for any Flash Cast Member. You can click the More Options button on the Property Inspector to access the traditional Flash Asset Properties dialog box, which enables you to change Import (the path to remotely or locally linked Flash movies) and Media (Linked and Preload) properties. You cannot preview Flash movies in the Property Inspector.

Figure 43-4: Director's Property Inspector

Tip   You may have noticed that the Flash Asset Properties dialog box takes a few seconds to load, as it requires the entire Flash Asset Options Xtra to load into memory. Why? In order to use the Play button in the Flash Asset Properties dialog box, the Flash Player contained within the Flash Asset Options Xtra must be loaded. Because the Property Inspector doesn't include a preview/play option, you can change Flash movie settings much more quickly in the Inspector.

Flash movies as Sprites

In Director, any item that is used in a movie becomes part of a Cast, and is referred to as a Cast Member. When a Cast Member is placed on the Stage, it becomes a Sprite. A Sprite is an instance of the Cast Member used in the Score. The relationship between a Flash Symbol and a Symbol instance is similar to the relationship between a Director Cast Member and its Sprite(s).

To place a Flash Cast Member on the Director Stage, simply click and drag its Cast Member icon (or thumbnail) from the Internal Cast window to the Stage or the Score. If you drag a Cast Member to the Stage (see Figure 43-5), it automatically becomes a Sprite on the first Sprite channel. If you drag a Sprite to the Score (see Figure 43-5), it is automatically centered on the Stage.

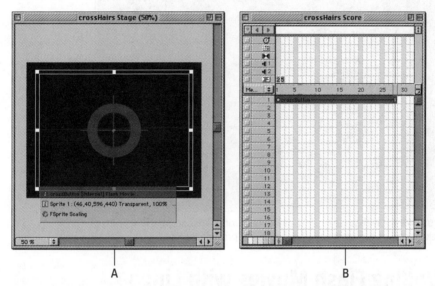

Figure 43-5: (A) A Flash Sprite on the Director Stage. (B) A Flash Sprite in the Director Score.

Although Flash Sprites perform almost the same as other Director Sprites, you should be aware of certain Sprite properties before proceeding with Lingo Behaviors and Flash Sprites.

Cross-Reference

> For more information on basic animation features of Director, please consult the *Macromedia Using Director 8.5 Shockwave Studio* manual that comes with the Director software.

✦ **Sprite Duration:** The duration of a Sprite appears in the Score. By default, the duration of every Sprite that is dragged to the Score or Stage is 28 frames. Like digital video and sound Sprites, Flash Sprites only play for as long as their frame duration allows them. For example, if a Flash movie that is 30 Flash frames long (and has a Lock-Step rate) is inserted as a 15-frame Flash Sprite in Director, then Director only shows the first half of the Flash movie.

✦ **Sprite Inks:** Of all the inks available to Sprites, only Copy, Transparent, and Background Transparent have any noticeable effect on Flash Sprites. Copy makes the Flash movie background opaque, in the same color that you specified in the Flash authoring environment. Transparent or Background Transparent (see Figure 43-6) hide the background of a Flash movie, so that the Director movie background (and other Director Sprites) show through.

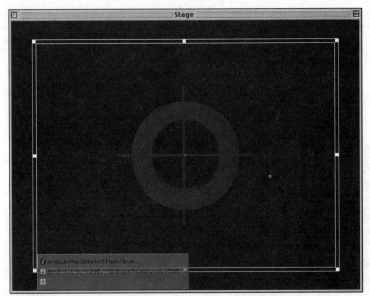

Figure 43-6: With an ink effect of Background Transparent, the white background of the crosshairsButton Flash Sprite drops out.

Controlling Flash Movies with Lingo

Not only can you send events from Flash movies to Director movies, but you can also control Flash movies from Director with Lingo. More than 70 Lingo commands exist that are specific for Flash movie assets in a Director movie. Unfortunately, it is beyond the scope of this book to explore so many different commands. This section provides an overview of the new Lingo commands for Flash movie, and shows you how to alter the size and rotation of Flash Sprites.

Lingo and ActionScript

For a complete listing of Flash-specific Lingo commands that can be used with Flash Cast Members and Sprites, access the Help ⇨ Lingo Dictionary in Director 8.5 and search for Flash. Some of the more powerful Lingo commands are `getVariable` and `setVariable`, which give you access to any variables inside a Flash 4 or 5 movie. Make sure that you specify the variable name as a string in Director Lingo (unless it's also the name of a Lingo variable), as in:

```
on beginSprite me
  sprite(me.spriteNum).setVariable("/globals:currentURL", ⊃
    "http://www.theMakers.com")
end
```

This Lingo code will give the variable `currentURL` in the `globals` Movie Clip instance of the current Sprite (`me.spriteNum`) the value of `http://www.theMakers.com`. Therefore, you can use Slashes notation to access nested variables in Movie Clip instances.

Note   Notice the similarities of Director's Dots syntax to Flash MX's ActionScript syntax. Both Director and Flash can use Object references followed by methods or properties.

Similarly, the `getFlashProperty` and `setFlashProperty` Lingo commands can use Slashes notation to access Movie Clip or Main Timeline properties:

```
on enterFrame me
   global dog_ScaleX
   dog_ScaleX = sprite(1).getFlashProperty("/dog_1", #scaleX)
end
```

This Lingo code will retrieve the current X scale of the `_root.dog_1` Movie Clip instance and make it the value of a global Director variable named `dog_ScaleX`. Table 43-1 details the Flash Movie Clip and Main Timeline properties that can be retrieved and set by Lingo.

Table 43-1: Lingo and ActionScript Property Conversion Chart

Lingo	ActionScript	Definition
#posX	_x	The current X coordinate of the specified Flash target.
#posY	_y	The current Y coordinate of the specified Flash target.
#scaleX	_xscale	The current percent value of the target's X scale.
#scaleY	_yscale	The current percent value of the target's Y scale.
#visible	_visible	Determines whether the target is shown or hidden.
#rotate	_rotation	The current degree value of the target's rotation.
#alpha	_alpha	The current percent value of the target's opacity.
#name	_name	The name given to the Movie Clip instance in the Instance Panel or with a `duplicateMovieClip` (or `attachMovie`) Flash action.
#width	_width	The current width (in pixels) of the specified Flash target.
#height	_height	The current height (in pixels) of the specified Flash target.
#target	_target	The full Flash path (in Slashes notation) to the specified Flash target. The path starts from the root (Main Timeline) and ends with the Instance name.
#dropTarget	_droptarget	The full Flash path (in Slashes notation) of a dragged-over Flash target. See Chapter 25 for more information on `_droptarget`.

Continued

Table 43-1: *(continued)*

Lingo	ActionScript	Definition
#url	_url	The full location path of the Flash target, in HTTP syntax (for example, `http://www.theMakers.com/flash5/sliders.swf` or `file://Macintosh%20HD/Internet/Shared/load.swf`).
#totalFrames	_totalFrames	The total number of Flash frames in the specified Flash instance.
#currentFrame	_currentFrame	The current position (frame number) of the Playhead in the Flash instance's timeline.
#lastframeLoaded	_framesLoaded	The number of the last frame (of the specified target) to have fully loaded into the Director movie.
#focusRect	_focusRect	This global property controls the visibility of focus rectangles for Flash Button instances. The target should be specified as an empty string (" ").
#spriteSoundBufferTime	_soundbuftime	This global property controls how much audio should stream from a Flash movie before playback begins. The target should be specified as an empty string (" ").

Macromedia has expanded the Lingo hitTest method (which can be used to detect whether an arbitrary point in the Flash movie is the transparent background area, a normal "fill" area, or a Flash button) to include an #editTest return value to detect Flash 4 and 5 editable text fields. The Lingo hitTest method works much like the hitTest() ActionScript method. For more information on Director's hitTest method, refer to the Help ⇨ Lingo Dictionary. Refer to Chapter 27, "Interacting with Movie Clips," for more information on Flash's hitTest() method.

Finally, Director 8.5 adds five new Lingo commands to work with Flash movies:

✦ call: This command works just like the call() action in Flash ActionScript. It executes the actions on the specified Flash timeline keyframe.

✦ print **and** printAsBitmap: These commands print the contents of a target Flash timeline. See Chapter 27, "Interacting with Movie Clips," for more information on the print actions.

✦ sendXML: This is a event handler in Director 8.5 that catches any sendXML events from a Flash 5 movie. You can define an on sendXML handler on a Flash Sprite that will execute whenever a sendXML action is executed in the Flash movie. For more information on the XML Object in Flash MX, see Chapter 30, "Sending Data In and Out of Flash."

✦ `tellTarget` **and** `endTellTarget`: These commands work like the Flash 4 equivalent actions. However, in Lingo, you nest the actions in a slightly different manner. Also, you can only use the following actions within a `tellTarget` Lingo group: `stop`, `play`, `gotoFrame`, `call(frame)`, `find(label)`, `getFlashProperty`, and `setFlashProperty`. You use a `tellTarget` Lingo action in the following way:

```
on exitFrame me
  sprite(1).tellTarget("/nestedMovie")
  sprite(1).setFlashProperty("",#ScaleX,200)
  sprite(1).setFlashProperty("", #ScaleY, 200)
  sprite(1).goToFrame(2)
  sprite(1).endtellTarget()
  go to frame 5
end
```

This Lingo code targets the `nestedMovie` Movie Clip instance located on the Main Timeline and sets its scale to 200 percent and moves its Playhead to frame 2. Then, Director's Score moves to frame 5.

Changing the size and rotation of Flash Sprites

The previous section listed the properties of internal Flash Movie Clips that can be manipulated with Lingo. You can also control the Flash Sprite properties with Lingo, which will affect everything in the Flash movie. With the crossButton.swf example used earlier, we can rotate and zoom the Flash movie in Director. Because the crossButton Sprite is a Flash button that already plays a 3D rotation sequence, we disable the Flash button by using a Lingo script in the first frame of the score:

```
on enterFrame
  sprite(1).buttonsEnabled = false
end

on exitFrame
  go the frame
end
```

The `sprite(1)` line of code refers to the Sprite occupying the first Sprite channel, which in our example is the crosshairs_button Flash Sprite. Adding the `.buttonsEnabled` property lets Director know what property we want to change with the Sprite — in this case, Flash button activity. Setting this property to `false` means it is being turned off.

Next, add the following behavior script to the Flash Sprite:

```
on mouseEnter me
  repeat while sprite(1).rotation < 720
    sprite(1).rotation = sprite(1).rotation + 10
    updateStage
  end repeat
end

on mouseLeave me
  sprite(1).rotation = 0
end
```

This Behavior causes the Flash Sprite to rotate a full 720 degrees — two revolutions — when the mouse enters the Flash Sprite. Here, the `.rotation` property is called and manipulated. Notice that when the mouse leaves the Sprite, the rotation is reset to 0.

To change this to a zooming behavior, simply change the script to the following:

```
on mouseEnter me
  repeat while sprite(1).scale < 800
    sprite(1).scale = sprite(1).scale + 10
    updateStage
  end repeat
end

on mouseLeave me
  sprite(1).scale = 100
end
```

For a cool effect, re-enable the Flash button by removing the `on enterFrame` section, containing the `sprite(1).buttonsEnabled` line, from the frame 1 script. Now, as the Flash movie zooms, the button continues to rotate on a 3D axis.

To view the current Flash Sprite properties in Director's Message window, you can add the following line of Lingo to the Frame Script:

```
on exitFrame
    sprite(1).showProps()
    go to frame 2
end
```

Then, on frame 2, create the following Frame Script:

```
on exitFrame
    go the frame
end
```

The `showProps()` command shows you the current properties of the Flash Sprite and Cast Member, as shown in Figure 43-7.

Figure 43-7: Director's Message window, displaying the current Flash Sprite properties

On the CD-ROM Open the **crossHairs.dir** file in the ch43 folder of the *Flash MX Bible* CD-ROM to see the rotation and scaling Lingo actions.

Summary

✦ Macromedia Director 8.5 has traditionally been used for more advanced multimedia projects for CD-ROMs, DVD-ROMS, and presentations that don't require network connections.

✦ Director 8.5 can integrate most multimedia file formats and play them within a Shockwave movie over the Web.

✦ Carefully weigh the goals of a multimedia project to determine which technology (or combination of technologies) will most effectively fulfill the requirements. While Flash MX can create rich media presentations, you may need the extended functionality of Director for more advanced projects.

✦ Flash and Director movies can communicate with one another via Lingo (Director's scripting language) or ActionScript (Flash's scripting language). You can control Flash movie playback from Director movies, or send commands from Flash movies to control the interactivity of a Director movie.

✦   ✦   ✦

Working with ColdFusion MX

In This Chapter

Overview of ColdFusion

What's new in
ColdFusion MX

Installing and working
with ColdFusion

Sending mail using
ColdFusion and Flash

Working with databases

Creating a guestbook

Creating a Flash login

ColdFusion is becoming increasingly important in the Flash environment with the added support and integration we see in newly released software. ColdFusion is a diverse and useful tool for developers, which can be used to enhance the dynamic nature of Flash Web sites. It is also one of the easiest languages you can learn to create server-side scripts. ColdFusion can be used to create simple to advanced applications, including: feedback forms, guestbooks, logins, polls, content management systems, image galleries, and message boards. You will be able to develop some of these applications by using this chapter, and then make them fully integrated with a Flash interface.

An Overview of ColdFusion

ColdFusion is aimed at developers who are looking to create dynamic Web applications and introduce some interactivity in their Web sites. It basically consists of two components: an application server and a markup language called "ColdFusion Markup Language" or "CFML."

ColdFusion was the first in the field of Web application servers. It is designed to work alongside your HTTP server, so whenever a ColdFusion page is requested, the application server executes the page and returns the processed page to the client. Since all processing is done on the server, your source code is not visible to the end user. ColdFusion will also work the same way on the browser of every client.

Why ColdFusion?

ColdFusion is an easy language to learn and implement due to its small learning curve, and it can greatly enhance the dynamic nature of your Flash. CFML is a tag-based language similar to HTML, which minimizes the learning curve and allows users to pick up the language particularly easily if they have previous HTML experience. Because of this, ColdFusion is usually considered easier to learn than other languages that sometimes perform similar functions, such as PHP, ASP and Perl/CGI.

The Development of ColdFusion

The ColdFusion Server and language has been around for much longer than is sometimes realized. Let's take a quick look at how it has developed over the years.

✦ **May 1995:** Allaire Corporation is formed.

✦ **July 1995:** Allaire Corporation is founded and *ColdFusion 1.0* is launched.

✦ **November 1996**: *ColdFusion 2.0* begins shipping with a customer base of roughly 10,000 people.

✦ **March 1997:** Allaire acquires *HomeSite*, a HTML editing tool, from Bradbury Software.

✦ **July 1997:** *ColdFusion 3.0* ships with a customer base of roughly 30,000 developers.

✦ **November 1997:** *ColdFusion 3.1* is released for NT and Solaris and is bundled with *ColdFusion Studio. HomeSite 3.0* begins shipping.

✦ **November 1998:** Allaire ships *HomeSite 4* and *ColdFusion 4.*

✦ **November 1999:** Allaire announced the launch of *ColdFusion 4.5.*

✦ **March 2001:** Macromedia announced the completion of its merger with Allaire Corporation.

✦ **June 2001:** Macromedia announces availability of Macromedia *ColdFusion Server 5.*

✦ **Mid 2002:** As of writing, *ColdFusion MX* is scheduled to be released at this time.

ColdFusion MX marks the most significant version the history of the application, due to the increasing integration across a broad spectrum of technologies. This proves Macromedia is completely committed to the continued and inevitable success of ColdFusion.

ColdFusion MX is very easy to use with Flash, and several new and exciting pieces of software are using ColdFusion to integrate with Flash MX for added functionality. As is usually true with most software, using these tools generally becomes more automated. The advantages to this automation are two-fold: it helps a wider range of developers create content using this language and the server, and also makes work faster and easier. Of course, it also allows more time spent on developing increasingly complex applications of a higher quality. You will find added support and integration in new Macromedia software, as well as new features in established software such as Dreamweaver.

Another good reason to use ColdFusion in your Web development is the wider acceptance and support of the language since Macromedia acquired the technology from Allaire. Increased attention and support of any language is a great reason to learn it, because wider support means it is easier to find hosting, and clients who want you to use the technology in their Web sites.

What's new in ColdFusion MX?

New features introduced in ColdFusion MX include the following:

✦ **ColdFusion Components:** Allows developers to create reusable code components, which are accessible from ColdFusion templates, Web services and even Flash clients.

✦ **XML Handling:** XML documents can be imported, queried, modified and manipulated in ColdFusion using syntax familiar to anyone who has used ColdFusion arrays and structures.

✦ **Web Services:** Integrate external SOAP based Web services into your applications or publish your own Web services using a completely standards-based Web services engine.

✦ **Flash Application Services:** Allows developers to integrate ColdFusion and Flash without having to use XML or URL variables. Data is encoded and decoded and handled automatically by ColdFusion MX and the Flash player. It uses a secure HTTP-based protocol and new binary message format named AMF (Action Message Format).

✦ **Improved Security:** Allows hosting companies to secure access to tags, functions, and Data Sources in a shared hosting environment.

✦ **Improved Internationalization:** Extended support for character-based languages such as Chinese, Japanese, or Korean with support for UNICODE encodings.

✦ **Flash Remoting:** Through the use of Server-Side ActionScript (SSAS), Flash developers can easily integrate ColdFusion with their productions through the use of components. Support for Remoting exists both in ColdFusion and Flash to facilitate this interaction. Server-Side ActionScript is essentially the same as Server-Side JavaScript.

 More information on using Flash Remoting can be found in the *Macromedia Flash MX ActionScript Bible* by Robert Reinhardt and Joey Lott.

A trial version is also available online, which has the full functionality of the Enterprise Edition of ColdFusion and lasts for 30 days after which time it reverts to a Developer Edition that only accepts requests from one IP address. This chapter uses Macromedia ColdFusion Server MX with Flash MX. At the time of writing, ColdFusion MX had been released in a preview version to the public. For the latest information on ColdFusion MX, please visit `www.macromedia.com/software/coldfusion/`.

Installing and configuring ColdFusion Server

Understanding how to properly install and configure ColdFusion Server is important due to the complexity of the software. At the time of writing, the install procedure in the latest edition of ColdFusion Server was limited. Therefore, we recommend you refer to the installation instructions online at `www.macromedia.com`.

 Please check the online resource, `www.flashmxbible.com`, for more information on custom installation procedures for ColdFusion Server, how to best set up the software for use with this chapter, and troubleshooting.

How Does ColdFusion Work?

The ColdFusion server can run along side of Microsoft IIS, Microsoft Personal Web Server (PWS), Apache, and several other Web servers. ColdFusion MX has added the option to install ColdFusion using a standalone server, which includes its own Web server and embedded Java server based on JRun technology. ColdFusion Server has an impressive list of supported operating systems, including support for Windows, Linux, Solaris, and HP-UX. There are currently no versions available for the Macintosh.

Let's look at how ColdFusion works. When the Web server receives a request for a ColdFusion template (your .cfm page), ColdFusion Server intercepts the request and parses the CFML code and returns it back as HTML to the user's browser. Refer to Figure 44-1 to see how this process works.

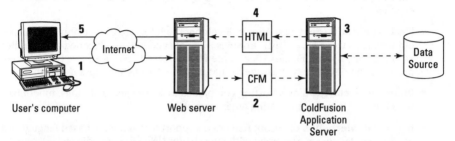

Figure 44-1: The ColdFusion Server works in the following way: 1) A user requests a ColdFusion template to be displayed. 2) This request is sent to the Web server. 3). The Web server delegates the request to the ColdFusion Server, which processes the template. 4). The Web server returns the generated HTML to the end user. 5). It is now displayed as an HTML page.

How does ColdFusion work with Flash?

Now that you understand how ColdFusion works with a server, it should be easy to apply this to how it works with Flash. The basic progression of events is as follows:

Flash MX ➪ ColdFusion template ➪ ColdFusion Server ➪ ColdFusion template ➪ Flash MX

Essentially what is happening here is that Flash is calling out to a ColdFusion template (using the LoadVars object and methods), which then executes queries, transforms data and/or performs calculations. Then, the results of these actions are sent back to Flash MX.

HTML text editors and CFML

Macromedia HomeSite and ColdFusion Studio are text editors designed to assist in writing and developing code. These programs are very similar to one another, although ColdFusion Studio is tailored to suit ColdFusion developers by adding documentation and shortcuts specific to CFML. These programs are obviously quite different from your typical WYSIWYG/graphical editors such as Dreamweaver, as Web developers using these programs must know how to hand-code. ColdFusion Studio and HomeSite are designed to speed up and simplify the hand-coding process. Many useful features are built into both these, such as Remote Development Services (RDS), debugging tools and tag auto completion, tag hints, as well as ColdFusion Server documentation (Studio only).

HomeSite+ is the latest version of Macromedia's editing software. It combines Homesite and ColdFusion Studio into one software package, and plans as of writing are to also bundle it with Dreamweaver MX. Dreamweaver MX contains thorough support for ColdFusion authoring, including support of ActionScript unique to Flash Remoting.

Remote development services

RDS is an excellent tool to speed up the process of developing and updating your Web pages. It allows developers to directly modify code on remote servers without having to use an FTP program in conjunction with your editor. This feature is available in several code and Web authoring programs.

Follow these steps to get RDS to connect to your server using HomeSite or ColdFusion Studio 5:

1. Open either ColdFusion Studio or HomeSite. Make sure the Files tab is activated in the Resource Window. If your Resource Window isn't visible, choose View ➪ Resource Window.

2. At the top of the Files pane you should see a drop-down list of all your drives. Select **Macromedia FTP & RDS** from the list. Then, right-click Macromedia FTP & RDS and choose **Add RDS Server** in the contextual menu.

Note   Connecting to your server by FTP is done in almost the same way. The only difference is that instead of choosing Add RDS Server in Step 2, choose **Add FTP Server**.

3. In the Description field enter a label for this connection. In the Host name field, type in the IP/URL of the server that you wish to connect to. Then, fill in the User Name and Password for this connection and press OK.

Your server will now appear as Macromedia FTP & RDS in the drop-down list (see Figure 44-2) and you can browse, edit, and open files, and save in the folders on any added servers. You can create new files and add them directly to the server. When you edit a file, it is immediately updated live on the server each time the file is saved. Using this feature should immensely increase your productivity and efficiency of Web development.

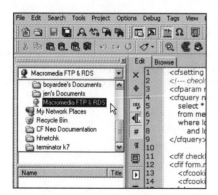

Figure 44-2: This menu is where you can find your FTP and RDS link.

You can also right-click the new connection and select **Administer** from the contextual menu. A Web browser window will launch and take you to the ColdFusion Server login page.

Note   RDS is also available in Dreamweaver MX, although is configured somewhat differently. RDS can be found in the Advanced tab of the Site definition dialog box, by clicking the Remote info category. From the Access menu, select RDS and click the Settings box. Your configurations can be made in the dialog box, which appears.

For more information on Macromedia Dreamweaver MX, refer to Chapter 42, "Working with Dreamweaver MX."

Using ColdFusion

Now that you know about the main features of ColdFusion and how it works, it is time to create a document using ColdFusion Markup Language, or CFML. ColdFusion templates end in a .cfm extension — any pages you write including CFML such as `<cfoutput>` must end in this extension in order for the server to read and parse them. You can also name your file with a .cfm extension even if it does not have CFML within your code, which you will find true in some of the following examples.

If you want to save time typing out the following pieces of code, the source files can be found in the ch44 folder on the *Flash MX Bible* CD-ROM.

Your First ColdFusion page

Let's begin with a simple exercise to test if your ColdFusion installation was successful, and to illustrate what a basic .cfm file looks like. Launch your preferred HTML editor, or even a basic text program such as Notepad, and type the following:

```
<!---helloworld1.cfm--->
<html>
<body>
Hello world.  My name is Jane Doe.
</body>
</html>
```

Save your file as **helloworld1.cfm**, open a browser and load the page into it. As you can hopefully see, it does exactly what you would expect since all the code in this template is HTML. We could easily rename this page helloworld1.html and it would still continue to function in exactly the same way. Let's try adding some CFML now:

```
<!---helloworld2.cfm--->
<cfset name = "jane doe">
<html>
<body>
Hello world. My name is #name#.
</body>
</html>
```

Save this file as **helloworld2.cfm** and view it in your browser. As you can now see, there is a slight problem. Instead of it displaying the value of the variable called name it displays the string #name#. When you are trying to output ColdFusion variables to a page, you need to wrap the ColdFusion variables in a `<cfoutput>` tag. Let's go back to the text editor and try again:

```
<!---helloworld3.cfm--->
<cfset name = "jane doe">
<html>
<body>
```

```
Hello world.  My name is <cfoutput>#name#</cfoutput>.
</body>
</html>
```

Save this as **helloworld3.cfm** and view it in your browser. Much better! You have now completed your first page using ColdFusion.

As we already know, and have just witnessed, ColdFusion is a tag-based language. We have had an opportunity to use two CFML tags so far (`<cfset>` and `<cfoutput>`), and as you may have noticed all ColdFusion tags start with the prefix `cf`. In this chapter, we see many more ColdFusion tags as well as some ColdFusion functions, which are quite similar to ActionScript functions. Some of the ColdFusion functions we will be using in this chapter include `#Now( )#` which simply returns the current date and time. The functions `#DateFormat( )#` and `#TimeFormat( )#` take date objects as parameters and format them using a mask that you specify. Finally, we also cover `#isDefined( )#` which checks to see if a variable exists or not.

A simple feedback form

Next we're going to build a simple feedback form, and hook it up to Flash MX. We will start by creating a form in HTML. Open your favorite text or HTML editor and create a file named **feedbackform.html**. Type the following code:

```
<!--- feedbackform.html --->
<html>
<body>
<form action="sendfeedback.cfm" method="post">
<table>
<tr>
<td>Name:</td>
<td><input type="text" name="username"></td>
</tr>
<tr>
<td>Email:</td>
<td><input type="text" name="email"></td>
</tr>
<tr>
<td>Comments:</td>
<td><textarea cols="40" rows="8" wrap="soft"
name="comments"></textarea></td>
</tr>
<tr>
<td colspan="2" align="center"><input type="submit" value="Send
feedback"></td>
</tr>
</table>
</form>
</body>
</html>
```

So far we have simply created a feedback form in HTML, in order to troubleshoot our ColdFusion code before we begin incorporating it into our Flash movie. The main reason for doing this is to avoid debugging both the CFML code and the Flash ActionScript code all at the same time.

Now we need another file to send the e-mail. Let's create a file called **sendfeedback.cfm**:

```
<!--- sendfeedback.cfm --->
<cfmail from="#form.email#" to="you@yourdomain.com" subject="feedback
from your site." server="mail">
name : #form.username#
email : #form.email#
comments : #form.comments#
```

There are a few very important concepts we have not touched on yet, and now need to address. First, you will notice we are referencing a variable named `#form.email#`. In our feedbackform.html template, we created a text input box in HTML named `email`. Since we submitted the form to sendfeedback.cfm using the `POST` method all of our variables are passed as form fields, and we have to reference them using the `form` prefix in CFML. If we try submitting our form using the `GET` method, then all our variables would be passed along the query string in the address bar and we would refer to them as `url.username` (i.e.: `sendfeedback.cfm?username=Robert+Reinhardt`).

ColdFusion provides access to several different scopes such as `form`, `url` and `cookie`, all of which we will be looking at in this chapter. However, there are a few more "scopes" available to us in ColdFusion. Perhaps the simplest way to think of scopes is as objects: for instance, the "form object" which has several variables contained within it. This is similar to referring to a variable in ActionScript in the `_root.email` syntax.

Now let's go back to our code and look at the `<cfmail>` tag and see if we can understand exactly what it is doing.

```
<cfmail from="#form.email#" to="you@yourdomain.com" subject="feedback
from your site." server="mail">
```

ColdFusion will send an e-mail from the email address that was supplied by the user in the feedbackform.html template and send it to `you@yourdomain.com`. Obviously you will want to replace that e-mail address with another e-mail address so the messages will be directed to the right place. Next we have a `subject`, which is simply the text that will be displayed in the subject area of your e-mail client. Finally we see the `server` parameter, which is the outgoing mail server the ColdFusion server will use to send e-mail messages. This value can be either an IP address or a domain name. We will use `mail` as our outgoing SMTP mail address in our examples. If `mail` does not work for you, try `smtp`, or another server listed in your preferred e-mail client (such as Microsoft Outlook or Outlook Express) for outgoing mail.

Both the `from` and `to` fields must contain valid e-mail addresses — otherwise, ColdFusion may not send the e-mail. When ColdFusion goes to send the e-mail message it will replace `#form.email#` with the value that the user has entered into our feedbackform.cfm template.

That is all the code required to send an e-mail using ColdFusion. Remember to change `you@yourdomain.com` to the e-mail address you want the feedback sent to. We could also extend this example and send the e-mail as HTML by adding `type = "HTML"` to the `<cfmail>` tag.

Now we will see how we can use this code in conjunction with an interface built in Flash MX.

Integrating your feedback form with Flash MX

Using ColdFusion to send messages from a Web site to a recipient is a very useful method to integrate into your Flash sites. First of all, you can use it instead of the `getURL()` action with the `mailto:` tag, thus negating the need for an e-mail client to be actively and properly set up on the end users computer when browsing your site. By using ColdFusion, anyone at any location, such as a library or school, can easily send feedback or messages from your Web site.

Using ColdFusion to send mail from your movie requires much less code than using other methods, such as CGI or ASP. In its simplest form, Flash requires very few steps and not a large amount of ActionScript to get the application working on this end. Not to mention, you can add many design elements to your interface not possible by using HTML only. So now let's get started on an interface in Flash.

The source file for this example, **feedback.fla**, is in the ch44 folder on the *Flash MX Bible* CD-ROM for your reference.

To begin, let's create a simple form in Flash MX. Open Flash MX, and save it as **feedback.fla** in the same folder as the sendfeedback.cfm file you just created in the previous section. Then follow these steps:

1. The first step is to create Static text labels for "name," "e-mail," and "comments" anywhere on the Stage of your new movie's Main Timeline. Add a keyframe on frame 3, and add the Static text "sending" anywhere on your Stage. Finally on frame 5, add a message to the user indicating that the e-mail has been sent. You can also refer to his or her name, by adding a Dynamic text field with the instance name username. Also, you may want to add a back button to take the user away from this page to another part of the movie.

2. Create a new layer named **actions** and add keyframes on frame 1 and 5. Add the stop(); frame action on frame 1 and then _root.username.text = cfData.username; on frame 5. This code will add the username entered by your visitor in the form on frame 1 into the Dynamic text field you just created on frame 5.

3. Create a new layer for your Input text fields. Somewhere beside each of these Static fields, create Input text fields. You will want to size them large enough to contain a name or comments. Therefore, you will probably want your comment box to be taller than your name and e-mail fields. In the Property inspector, be sure to select **Single Line** in the Line Type menu for the name and e-mail fields, and **Multiline** for your comments field if this is the case. You may wish to limit the name and e-mail fields to 64 characters (add 64 to the Maximum Characters field.) In the <Instance Name> field of the Property inspector, you need to name each Input text instance with **username**, **email**, and **comments**, respectively, so ColdFusion knows what to reference in your movie. Refer to Figure 44-3 for the Property inspector settings for the comments field.

Figure 44-3: This is how your settings in the Property inspector may look with after you are finished this step.

4. Create a button (Insert ➪ New Symbol), or grab one from the Buttons Library (Window ➪ Common Libraries ➪ Buttons). This button will be used to send the information in the feedback form by e-mail.

5. Now you will want to add labels to your frames. When you are finished, your document's Stage should resemble Figure 44-4.

- **Label frame 1:** feedbackform

- **Label frame 3:** wait

- **Label frame 5:** results

Figure 44-4: This is an example of a very simple feedback form made using Flash MX.

Now you're ready to add ActionScript to the Stage, layers, and timeline to connect your .cfm to the interface. Let's start with the ActionScript for your submit button. Select your submit button, and add the following code to the Script pane in the Actions panel. Make sure you are in Expert mode (Ctrl+Shift+E, or ⌘+Shift+E):

```
on (release) {
  if (username.text == "" || email.text == "" || comments.text == "") {
    getURL("javascript:alert('name, email and comments are needed');");
    gotoAndStop("feedbackform");
  } else {
    cfData = new LoadVars();
    cfData.onLoad = function() {
      _root.gotoAndStop("results");
    };
    cfData.username = _root.username.text;
    cfData.email = _root.email.text;
    cfData.comments = _root.comments.text;
    cfData.sendAndLoad("sendfeedback.cfm", cfData, "POST");
    _root.gotoAndStop("wait");
  }
}
```

The methodology for performing this action in Flash has changed somewhat from Flash 5, and although the end result is similar, the processing in MX using the new LoadVars object is more effective and efficient than before.

Let's step through the code, which is performing a few different actions. First of all, in if (username.text == "" || email.text == "" || comments.text == ""), the code is validating that the user has entered information into all of the input boxes. If the user tries to pass this form without entering information in one of the fields, Flash displays a JavaScript alert.

If all of the fields are filled in, the information from the text input fields is sent to the server using the LoadVars object. You will see this functionality used throughout the rest of the chapter, so let's take a look at what it does. The cfData is what we chose to set as our variable name, and the form fields are placed into an object structure. This information then moves to the sendAndLoad() method, which sends the LoadVars object to the server. Now your movie will then proceed to the wait frame while the e-mail is being sent. When the data is finished loading back to the movie from ColdFusion, the onLoad function is triggered and executed which moves the movie to the results frame. Using this method verifies data has actually been sent to and received by the server.

Cross-Reference

For more information using the LoadVars object in Flash MX, please refer to Chapter 30, "Sending Data In and Out of Flash."

Publish your Flash document (Shift+F12) and upload feedback.swf, feedback.html and sendfeedback.cfm to your server, placing them in the same folder. With ColdFusion Server installed, this movie will send you an e-mail to the e-mail address you designated in your .cfm document. This is a very useful method for sending information from a Web site to a recipient. It can be modified in many ways to suit your needs; for instance, you can verify that proper e-mail syntax has been entered into the email text field . Also, the code and format can be modified into a guestbook with relative ease, which we will try in the following section.

Note

You will not be able to test your movie simply by using Publish preview. You will need to upload your .swf, .cfm, and database files (if applicable) to your server with ColdFusion Server installed, and actively test the results.

Turning Your Feedback Form into a Guestbook

For our next example we'll modify our feedback form and turn it into a very simple guestbook. This is where ColdFusion's interaction with a database comes into action, which is an extremely important part of working with this technology.

Working with databases

A database is a collection of related data. There are many database solutions available on the market ranging from basic personal databases such as Microsoft Access to enterprise level solutions such as Oracle and Microsoft SQL Server. Every database allows you to organize your data into tables and then insert, update, delete, or select data. When you are selecting data, you can filter the results so only items matching a certain criteria will be returned (i.e., only members with the name "Robert" will be returned to by the query).

Microsoft Access is one of the simplest and most widespread database solutions available today. It is adequate enough for small Web sites, but if you have a medium to large Web site with a lot of traffic then you would want a more scalable database such as SQL Server or Oracle. These robust databases can handle more data and concurrent connections than Microsoft Access.

Tables are the most important aspect of a database. They organize data into rows and columns, and if you are familiar with a spreadsheet then you will find tables quite similar. A typical database in MS Access can be seen in Figure 44-5.

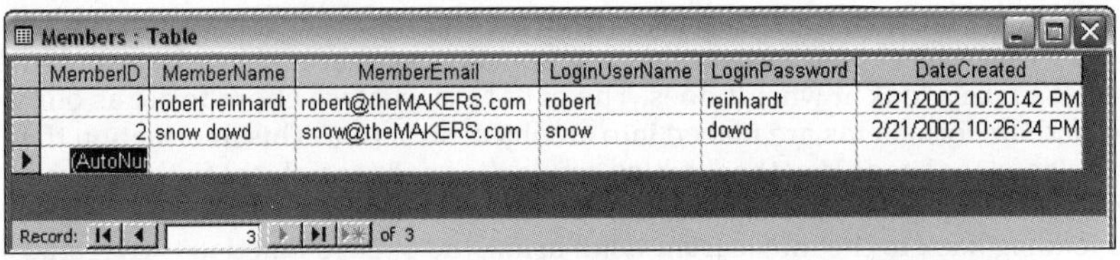

Members : Table

MemberID	MemberName	MemberEmail	LoginUserName	LoginPassword	DateCreated
1	robert reinhardt	robert@theMAKERS.com	robert	reinhardt	2/21/2002 10:20:42 PM
2	snow dowd	snow@theMAKERS.com	snow	dowd	2/21/2002 10:26:24 PM
(AutoNur					

Record: 3 of 3

Figure 44-5: This is an example of a simple database in Microsoft Access.

Now let's build our database. We will be using Microsoft (MS) Access to construct our database, which saves a file with a .mdb file extension. We will construct a simple table consisting of the person's ID, name, e-mail, username, password, and the date the member was created. By looking at this table we can see how each row in the table relates to a single member for our Web site. Our Members table has 6 columns; the first one is `MemberID` which is simply a unique number generated by Access allowing us to identify a single row of data, or a single member from our table. The next column is `MemberName` which tells us the full name of the member, as well as columns for the member's e-mail address, login username, login password, and the date the member joined the site. We could easily add more columns if necessary to track the Member's birth date, number of times they have logged on to the site, the latest date the person logged on to the site.

To create the database with MS Access, follow these steps:

1. In MS Access, select File ➪ New and select **Blank Database**. (It will prompt you to select a location and filename for the new Access database.)
2. Name the database **mysite.mdb** and click the Create button to save the database.
3. Click **Create table** in Design View. For our simple guestbook, we will include five columns:
   - GuestbookID (Data Type = AutoNumber, Primary Key)
   - GuestbookName (Text, Field Size: 64)
   - GuestbookEmail (Text, Field Size: 128)
   - GuestbookMessage (Memo)
   - GuestbookDate (Date/Time)

   To create the primary key for GuestbookID, right-click on that row and select **Primary Key** from the contextual menu and a little key should appear to the left of the Field Name.
4. Save the table as **guestbook**.
5. To create our Members table click **Create table** in Design View again and type in the following six columns:
   - MemberID (Data Type = AutoNumber, Primary Key)
   - MemberName (Text, Field Size: 64)
   - MemberEmail (Text, Field Size: 128)

- LoginUserName (Text, Field Size: 32)

- LoginPassword (Text, Field Size: 32)

- DateCreated (Date/Time)

6. Save the table as **members** and close MS Access. An example of this Access database is seen in Figure 44-6.

A copy of this database, called **mysite.mdb**, is available in the ch44 folder of the *Flash MX Bible* CD-ROM.

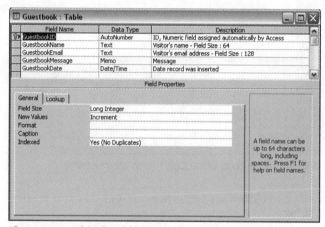

Figure 44-6: This should look similar to the database you have just created in MS Access.

Setting up a Data Source

Now that we have created a database, the next step is to create a *Data Source*. A Data Source is an alias for a database. Data Source ODBC is used to access data from a number of management systems. ***ODBC*** stands for *O*pen *D*ata*b*ase *C*onnectivity.

In order for ColdFusion to connect to this database that we have created, we will have to set up the Data Source. To do so we use the ColdFusion administrator which can be found by going to Start ➪ Programs ➪ Macromedia ColdFusion MX ➪ Administrator or by typing the following into a browser:

```
http://<your IP or localhost>/CFIDE/administrator/index.cfm
```

1. Go to your ColdFusion administrator and click the Data Sources link under the DATA & SERVICES section. Type in the name of the Data Source that you would like to set up, which in this case will be **flashbible**. Refer to Figure 44-7 for the Data Source settings look like in the ColdFusion administrator.

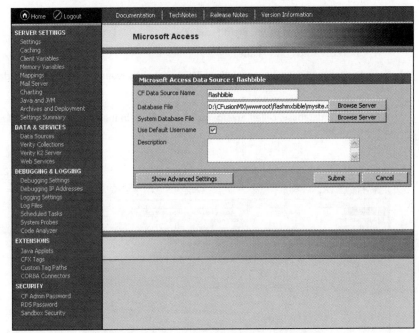

Figure 44-7: Data Source settings in the ColdFusion administrator

2. The next step is to select **Microsoft Access** from the drop-down list of drivers then press the **Add** button.

3. On the next page we can see that ColdFusion has entered `flashbible` into the CF Data Source Name for us already. So click the Browse Server button next to the Database File text box. ColdFusion then allows us to browse for our mysite.mdb file which we saved onto the hard drive.

4. Once you locate the Access database file, select the mysite.mdb file and click **Apply**. You will be taken back to the previous screen.

5. Now make sure that the **Use Default Username** check box is selected, and press the Submit button at the bottom. You will be taken back to the Data Sources page. If the Data Source was successfully created then you will see "ok" in the Status column beside the newly created Data Source. This can be seen in Figure 44-8.

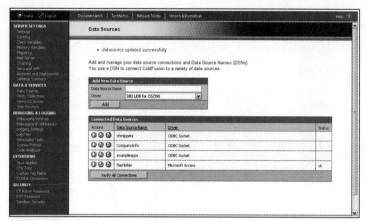

Figure 44-8: A successfully created Data Source, as seen in the status column of the Data Sources page

Creating the Guestbook

Now that a Data Source and database are set up, we are ready to start building the guestbook.

Tip   Again, we will do our troubleshooting in HTML before dealing with Flash MX. This is a wise practice to adopt, as it will inevitably help you avoid future headaches. It is much easier to debug the page in HTML rather than trying to troubleshoot both the ColdFusion and Flash simultaneously. If you do choose to work in Flash, you can temporarily change the `sendAndLoad()` method to a `getURL()` action with the target set to "`_blank`". Now when you submit the form, the ColdFusion page opens in a new window and you then see if it is working, or if you have problems. Try both methods, and see which one is most appropriate for your project.

First, create a new file named **guestbookform.html** and enter the following code into any text or HTML editor:.

```
<!--- guestbookform.html --->
<html>
<body>

<form action="addguestbook.cfm" method="post">
<table>
<tr>
<td>Name:</td>
<td><input type="text" name="username"></td>
</tr>
```

```
<tr>
<td>Email:</td>
<td><input type="text" name="email"></td>
</tr>
<tr>
<td>Comments:</td>
<td><textarea cols="40" rows="8" wrap="soft"
name="entry"></textarea></td>
</tr>
<tr>
<td colspan="2" align="center"><input type="submit" value="Add
Comments"></td>
</tr>
</table>
</form>

</body>
</html>
```

You will notice our guestbook.html is very similar to our feedbackform.html with the following subtle changes: We changed the form `action` value as well the label on the submit button.

Next, we need to create **addguestbook.cfm** with the following code. In the following code, do not type the ⊃ symbol in your actual code — this indicates the continuation of the same line of code.

```
<!--- addguestbook.cfm --->
<cfquery name="insertfeedback" datasource="flashbible">
  insert into Guestbook (GuestbookName, GuestbookEmail, ⊃
    GuestbookMessage, GuestbookDate)
  values ('#form.UserName#', '#form.Email#', '#form.entry#', ⊃
    #createODBCDateTime(Now())#)
</cfquery>
```

Understanding the code

This is a fair amount of code in just a few lines, so let's try to go through this carefully. The first line is a query, which basically lets you execute SQL commands and talk directly to a database. You will notice the query has both a `name` and a `datasource` defined. The query name is required, and it allows you to reference the recordset (the results) of the query. We have also defined a Data Source pointing to the database we created earlier. The next line of code is the query itself. It inserts a record into the guestbook table of our Access database. We are explicitly telling the query which columns we want inserted into the database. The following line tells the query the values of the columns to insert into the newly formed record. Essentially, the query is talking to the database and telling Access to insert a new record into the guestbook table, and assign the columns these specific values. It is very important when inserting data into your databases that you take care to match up the columns with their proper values. The order of the values must match the column names specified, or else you will either get errors or incorrect data. The format of the query is

```
insert into <tablename> (<columns>)
values (<column values>)
```

You can even insert the code from our previous exercise, sendfeedback.cfm, into our current file addguestbook.cfm. This will use the ColdFusion server to e-mail the user's comments directly into your inbox at the same time as it inserts the values into the database. Or you could simply send yourself an e-mail notifying you a comment has been made in the guestbook.

One of the biggest strengths of ColdFusion is how quickly and easily it allows you to interact with a database. In four short lines of code, we are able to add a new record into our Access database. We could extend upon this code and build a more complex form allowing us to collect information on members, or to save a user's preferences into a database and then retrieve their preferences when they return to our site. The possibilities are almost limitless with ColdFusion!

Retrieving comments from the guestbook

Let's build a ColdFusion template that retrieves the comments from the guestbook and displays them in a simple HTML page.

Create a new file called **getcomments.cfm** and type the following code:

```
<cfsetting enablecfoutputonly="Yes">
<!--- getcomments.cfm --->
<cfparam name="form.currentnum" default="1">

<cfquery name="getfeedback" datasource="flashbible">
     select *
     from guestbook
     order by guestbookdate
</cfquery>

<cfoutput query="getfeedback" startrow="#form.currentnum#"
maxrows="1">&name=#urlencodedformat(guestbookname)#&email=#urlencodedformat
(guestbookemail)#&comments=#urlencodedformat(GuestbookMessage)#&dt=#urlenco
dedformat(dateformat(GuestbookDate) & "  " &
timeformat(GuestbookDate))#&totalrecs=#getfeedback.recordcount#&</cfoutput>
```

Understanding the code

The first new code we see is `<cfsetting enablecfoutputonly="Yes">`. This tag ensures that the only content returned to the user's browser is HTML that is enclosed in a `<cfoutput>` block. The next tag we encounter is the `<cfparam name="form.currentnum" default="1">` tag, which essentially checks whether or not a variable has already been set or not. The `<cfparam>` checks to see if `form.currentnum` has already been declared or passed to this page. If ColdFusion cannot find a variable called `form.currentnum`, it will declare it for us, and assign it the default value that we specified (in this case it will be "1"). If the value has been already been set, then ColdFusion simply will ignore this tag and continue processing this page. Next, we execute a query, which retrieves all entries from our guestbook. Then it sorts them according to the date the entry was posted as. By default, records are sorted in ascending order (smallest to highest), so when we sort by date we are receiving the oldest records first and the newest records will be returned last. If you would like to return the newest posts first, then you can simply add `desc` (short for descending) after the `order by guestbookdate` line and ColdFusion will reverse the sort order.

Here is where it gets more complex. We have already seen the `<cfoutput>` tag in our earlier examples, and we know that it simply outputs the values of our variables. But by supplying a `query` attribute to the `<cfoutput>` tag, ColdFusion automatically will loop over each row of the query and output our code. By adding a `startrow` and `maxrow` parameter to our `<cfoutput>` we can tell ColdFusion which row to begin the loop from, as well as how many records to display at a time. For our example we are only displaying one record at a time, but by setting our `startrow` as a variable we are able to tell ColdFusion to start looping at any arbitrary point in the query results.

The next unfamiliar ColdFusion function we see is the `#urlencodedformat( )#` function. This tag automatically encodes a string and escapes all non-alphanumeric characters so they are safe to import into Flash. Basically this function replaces all spaces with %20, all ampersands (&) as %26, and so on.

Our final two variables that we are passing back into Flash are `dt` and a variable called `totalrecs`. DT is simply the date and time the user submitted their comments. You will notice the two ColdFusion functions called `#DateFormat( )#` and `#TimeFormat( )#` which allow us to format a date and time to a specified format. By default, the date is formatted displayed using a mask of `dd-mmm-yy`, which would display in the following manner: 09-Mar-02. By specifying our own mask we are able to format this date in almost any way we want. For example, if you wanted to display the full name of the month, the day as an integer, and a 4 digit year, then we would be able to use the a mask of `mmmm d, yyyy` and rewrite the `#DateFormat()#` function as `#DateFormat(GuestbookDate, "mmmm d, yyyy")#`. This would display as "March 9, 2002". ColdFusion also has a `#TimeFormat()#` function which operates much in the same way as `#DateFormat()#` although obviously it has different masks.

Integrate your guestbook with a Flash interface

You will notice there are two distinct areas to our guestbook: the input area and the area where you can view entries in the guestbook. In this Flash document, you will also notice both areas are simultaneously put onto the Stage. Of course, by now it will be easy for you format your guestbook in any number of ways, depending on your own requirements. You may even wish to reuse and modify the feedback form we finished earlier in this chapter, and turn it into a guestbook.

On the CD-ROM   The source file, **guestbook.fla**, and all associated .cfm files are available in the ch44 folder on the *Flash MX Bible* CD-ROM.

Our guestbook shares many of the same attributes as our previous example. For instance, the `name`, `email` and `comments` text fields are exactly the same. The submit button has very similar ActionScript on it as well. The main difference we will see in this example is what happens to the data when it is sent using the submit button, and the buttons controlling the area where you view entries submitted by visitors to the guestbook. Now let's build the guestbook.

1. The first step is to again create Static text labels for displaying **name**, **email**, **guestbook entry** in frame 1. On the Stage in the same frame, create a submit button as well. You may want to reuse your feedback form for this step. Now add a Dynamic text field on the Stage, which is where we will view entries. You may wish to add a ScrollBar component onto the view entries area, and perhaps your entry input area. Next to the Dynamic text field, you will need a button for next, previous, first and last in order to navigate through entries submitted. You can see an example of these buttons in Figure 44-9. Assign the following names to your instances:

- **name (Input text field):** name
- **email (Input text field):** email
- **guestbook (Input text field):** entry
- **view guestbook (Dynamic text field):** comments
- **first button:** firstb
- **previous button:** prevb
- **next button:** nextb
- **last button:** lastb

After you are finished, go to frame 15 on each layer you have created, and press the F5 key so these layers cover the entire length of our timeline. Your Stage should resemble Figure 44-9.

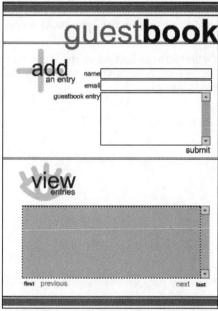

Figure 44-9: A typical guestbook setup, with all the elements we need to put ours together

2. We will use frames 1, 5, 10 and 15. Apply ActionScript, and show status messages to our users. Let's add the following labels to these frames, which of course you type into the <Frame Label> field in the Property inspector:

- **Frame 1:** init
- **Frame 5:** sending
- **Frame 10:** wait
- **Frame 15:** viewcomment

After you are finished, your timeline will look much like the one in Figure 44-10.

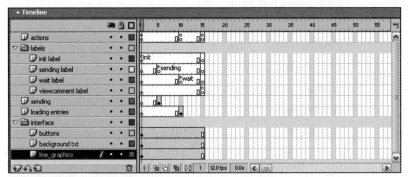

Figure 44-10: Your timeline will look similar to this by now.

3. On frame 5 you will want to add Static text notifying the end user their guestbook entry is being sent. On frame 10, add Static text notifying guestbook entries are being retrieved.

4. In this next step, we will add ActionScript to the buttons on the Stage. The code in the submit button for adding entries is very much like what we used in the feedback form, except a different ColdFusion file is being used.

```
on (release) {
  if (username.text == "" || email.text == "" || ⊃
  entry.text == "") {

    getURL("javascript:alert('name, email and an entry ⊃
    are needed');");

    gotoAndStop(1);

  } else {

    cfData = new LoadVars();
    cfData.onLoad = function() {
      _root.gotoAndStop("init");
    };
    cfData.username = _root.username.text;
    cfData.email = _root.email.text;
    cfData.entry = _root.entry.text;

    cfData.sendAndLoad("addguestbook.cfm", cfData, ⊃
    "POST");

    _root.gotoAndStop("sending");
  }
}
```

Now let's add some code to the buttons controlling the view guestbook area of our Flash document. On the \first button, we added to the Stage we need to add the following code:

```
on (release) {
  _root.mynum = 1;
  gotoAndPlay("init");
}
```

Add this code to the "previous" button:

```
on (release) {
  _root.mynum--;
  gotoAndPlay("init");
}
```

You need to add the following code to your "next" button:

```
on (release) {
  _root.mynum++;
  gotoAndPlay("init");
}
```

On the "last" button, the following code is required:

```
on (release) {
  _root.mynum = cfData.totalrecs;
  gotoAndPlay("init");
}
```

On each of these buttons, which are controlling the guestbook, we are setting a Flash variable which will be used by the Flash movie to tell ColdFusion which record we want to see.

5. Now it's time to create the main part of our ActionScript, which is placed in frame actions. The first step is to create a new layer named **actions**. On frame 1 add the following ActionScript. Do not insert the ⟁ symbol in your actual code—this indicates a continuation of the same line of code.

```
stop();
_root.username.text = "";
_root.email.text = "";
_root.entry.text = "";
if (typeof (_root.mynum) == "undefined") {
  mynum = 1;
}
cfData = new LoadVars();
cfData.onLoad = function() {
  gotoAndStop("viewcomment");
};
cfData.currentnum = _root.mynum;

cfData.currentnum = ⟁
cfData.sendAndLoad("getcomments.cfm", cfData, "POST");

_root.gotoAndStop("wait");
```

This ActionScript begins by ensuring the email, entry, and comments fields remain empty. The next section of ActionScript is sending a request to ColdFusion for a specific record from the guestbook database. When the buttons are pressed to control the guestbook, it changes the value of the ActionScript variable called `mynum` and passes it to ColdFusion. ColdFusion then returns the specific record we requested.

6. On frame 10 of the Actions layer, add a `stop()`; action.

7. On frame 15 of the Actions layer, add the following ActionScript. Type lines with a ⤶ symbol as one line of code:

```
showprev = _root.mynum<=1;
shownext = _root.mynum>=cfData.totalrecs;

_root.comments.text = cfData.name + "\n" ⤶
+ cfData.email + "\n" + cfData.dt + "\n" ⤶
+ cfData.comments;

_root.firstb._visible = !showprev;
_root.prevb._visible = !showprev;
_root.nextb._visible = !shownext;
_root.lastb._visible = !shownext;
stop();
```

This code will control the visibility of the next, previous, first and last buttons depending on which record is being viewed. If your user reaches the end of the guestbook, the next and last buttons will disappear because they are no longer applicable. Similarly, at the beginning of the guestbook, there is no point to the previous or first buttons, so they will be hidden. Checking the record number of the entry, and altering the visibility accordingly accomplishes this task. Because Flash understands the total number of records in the guestbook database (`cfData.totalrecs`), and its current record index (`_root.mynum`), it is able to dynamically toggle the visibility of our navigation buttons. This code also includes the input and formatting within your Dynamic text field.

8. Now that your ActionScript has been added to the timeline, you are ready to publish and test your guestbook. Publish your movie (Shift+F12), and upload guestbook.swf and guestbook.html along with the getcomments.cfm and addguestbook.cfm files you created earlier into the same folder on your server. Now you will be able to add some comments to your guestbook, and they will dynamically load after you press the submit button, as shown in Figure 44-11.

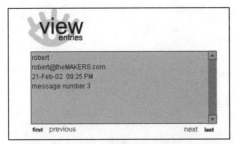

Figure 44-11: Your dynamic guestbook viewing box should look similar. Modifying the ActionScript can enhance the formatting of the entries.

Now that you have completed a more complicated version of the feedback form, you are ready to move onto an even more involved project.

Creating the Login Form

Another useful example of ColdFusion would be to create a simple user login form. This example allows you to password protect parts of your site to the general public, but allow registered members to log in and gain access. We'll also use cookies created in ColdFusion in this example to store information on the end users computer, so returning members entered in the database do not have to log in repeatedly.

Let's begin with a very simple login and expand it as we move along. Create a new text document named **loginform1.cfm** and type in the following text:

```
<!--- loginform1.cfm --->
<html>
<body>

<form action="dologin1.cfm" method="post">
<table>
<tr>
<td>Username:</td>
<td><input type="text" name="username" size="20" maxlength="64"></td>
</tr>
<tr>
<td>Password:</td>
<td><input type="password" name="password" size="20"
maxlength="64"></td>
</tr>
<tr>
<td colspan="2" align="center"><input type="submit"↵
value="Login!"></td>
</tr>
</table>
</form>

</body>
</html>
```

The page is a fairly straightforward HTML form that simply collects the user's username and password and submits the data to dologin1.cfm. So we will now create the **dologin1.cfm** page with the following code:

```
<cfsetting enablecfoutputonly="Yes">
<!--- dologin1.cfm --->
<cfif form.username eq "robert" and form.password eq "reinhardt">
<cfoutput>&success=1&loaded=1</cfoutput>
<cfelse>
<cfoutput>&success=0&loaded=1</cfoutput>
</cfif>
```

This simple login only has one username and password for all users, so the usefulness to you may be somewhat limited. Let's modify this code to get it working with our database.

Create a new file named **loginform2.cfm** and type the following code:

```
<!--- loginform2.cfm --->
<html>
<body>

<form action="dologin2.cfm" method="post">
<table>
<tr>
<td>Username:</td>
<td><input type="Text" name="username" size="20" maxlength="32"></td>
</tr>
<tr>
<td>Password:</td>
<td><input type="Password" name="password" size="20"
maxlength="32"></td>
</tr>
<tr>
<td colspan="2" align="center"><input type="Submit"
value="Login"></td>
</tr>
</table>
</form>

</body>
</html>
```

Since this code is almost identical to our previous login form we will continue onto the next step which is to create a file named **dologin2.cfm** with the following code:

```
<cfsetting enablecfoutputonly="Yes">
<!--- dologin2.cfm --->
<cfquery name="CheckUser" datasource="flashbible">
  SELECT MemberName
  FROM members
  WHERE loginusername = '#form.username#'
    AND loginpassword = '#form.password#'
</cfquery>

<cfif checkuser.recordcount eq 0>
<cfoutput>&success=0&loaded=1</cfoutput>
<cfelse>
<cfoutput>&success=1&loaded=1</cfoutput>
</cfif>
```

First, we execute a query and select all members from our table, which have a username and password that match the ones supplied by the user. Next, we check the recordcount (number of matching records returned) of the query. If there are zero matching records found, display a status of 0; otherwise, we successfully found a matching member in the database so we return a success code.

Using cookies with ColdFusion and Flash MX

Cookies are pieces of information stored on an end users hard drive about a Web site, so upon returning the site can refer to this information again. For example, cookies can remember your personal site preferences, uniquely identify you while you are shopping online, or store your `memberid` so a site can uniquely identify you after you have logged in. Cookies are not the only way to save information on the end users computer. We can now use a new object in Flash MX called a `SharedObject` to store information locally on a hard drive. In our case, however, we will use ColdFusion to create a cookie to store login information our end user inputs into our Flash movie.

Let's take this example a little bit further and add cookies to the code so we can track a user throughout the site, and also provide the option for this user to allow the site to remember who they are on subsequent visits so he or she can bypass the login form.

Create a new file named **loginform3.cfm**, and type the following text:

```
<!--- loginform3.cfm --->
<cfif isdefined("cookie.Remember_Me")>
  <cflocation url="dologin3.cfm">
</cfif>

<html>
<body>

<form action="dologin3.cfm" method="post">
<table>
<tr>
<td>Username:</td>
<td><input type="Text" name="username" size="20"
maxlength="32"></td>
</tr>
<tr>
<td>Password:</td>
<td><input type="Password" name="password" size="20"
maxlength="32"></td>
</tr>
<tr>
<td> </td>
<td><input type="Checkbox" name="Remember_Me" value="1">
Remember Me</td>
</tr>
<tr>
<td colspan="2" align="center"><input type="Submit"
value="Login"></td>
</tr>
</table>
</form>

</body>
</html>
```

Let's carefully go through this code as there are a few things here we haven't seen before.

First, we have the line of code

```
<cfif isdefined("cookie.Remember_Me")>.
```

This tests to see if a cookie called Remember_Me has already been defined. If the cookie does not exist, the <cfif> block is skipped and the user will see a login form.

The next new tag we see is a <cflocation> tag. This tag is fairly simple, because it simply redirects the browser to the supplied URL. In our case, it is dologin3.cfm. This page checks to see if the user has a cookie called Remember_Me and if so, it redirects the user to dologin3.cfm. Otherwise, it will prompt the user to log in.

Let's check out **dologin3.cfm**:

```
<cfsetting enablecfoutputonly="Yes">
<!--- dologin3.cfm --->
<!--- if the user has accessed this page through the login form. --->
<cfif isdefined("form.username") and isdefined("form.password")>
  <cfquery name="CheckUser" datasource="flashbible">
    SELECT *
    FROM members
    WHERE loginusername = '#form.username#'
      AND loginpassword = '#form.password#'
  </cfquery>
  <cfif CheckUser.RecordCount gt 0>
    <cfif isdefined("form.remember_me")>
      <cfcookie name="Remember_Me" value="1" expires="NEVER">
      <cfcookie name="MemberID" value="#CheckUser.MemberID#" ⤵
      expires="NEVER">
    <cfelse>
      <cfcookie name="MemberID" value="#CheckUser.MemberID#">
    </cfif>
    <cfoutput>&success=1&membername=#urlencodedformat⤵
    (checkuser.membername)#&loaded=1</cfoutput>
  </cfif>
<!-- if this user was already logged in and has a cookie planted. -->
<cfelseif isdefined("Cookie.MemberID")>
  <cfquery name="CheckUser" datasource="flashbible">
    SELECT *
    FROM Members
    WHERE MemberID = #Cookie.MemberID#
  </cfquery>
  <cfoutput>&success=1&membername=#urlencodedformat⤵
  (checkuser.membername)#&loaded=1</cfoutput>
<!-- user didnt supply a username and password, or have the required
cookie, so redirect them to the login page. -->
<cfelse>
  <cfoutput>&success=0&loaded=1</cfoutput>
</cfif>
```

Okay, there is a lot happening on this page so we'll carefully step through this information. First of all, we check to see if two form fields, form.username and form.password, exist. If they are defined, then we will try and validate the user's information against the data in the database. If the query finds a match, then we check to see if the user checked the box for "Remember Me."

Note   Check boxes and radio controls work a little differently in CFML than in most HTML form objects. If a user doesn't check the box, then the check will not be passed to the next page. So in our example, if the user checked the "Remember Me" check box, then the check box's value would be passed to the next page, but if the check box was NOT selected then the check box would not be passed at all. Because of this, we have to check to see if the check box is defined on the dologin3.cfm page or else we may get a ColdFusion error when we try and reference `form.rememberme`.

If they selected "Remember Me," we will set two cookies, `Remember_Me` and `MemberID`. Both of these cookies will have no expiry date which means that the user should be able to close their browser down and go back to loginform3.cfm and have it redirect them to dologin3.cfm without having to login. If the user did ***not*** choose "Remember Me," a single cookie is set with their `MemberID`, which expires when the user closes their browser. If no username and password were passed to this page, we check to see if a cookie named `MemberID` exists. If this variable is already defined, we can assume the user has already logged in. We will simply retrieve their information from the database. If the necessary form variables or cookies were not supplied to the page, we would redirect the user to the login form.

Let's quickly create a page that will log the user out of the Web site so we can fully test our application:

```
<!--- logout3.cfm --->
<cfcookie name="MemberID" value="0" expires="NOW">
<cfcookie name="RememberMe" value="0" expires="NOW">
<meta http-equiv="Refresh" content="0; url=loginform3.cfm">
```

The first two lines make the users cookies expire, so we can no longer track this user through the site and he or she will be forced to log back in to the system.

The last line is an HTML meta-refresh that redirects the user's browser back to the login form. This may seem a little strange since we have been using the `<cflocation>` tag to do the redirection thus far. There is one rule in ColdFusion about setting cookies and using `<cflocation>` on the same page. The `<cflocation>` tag redirects the user's browser to a new URL, but the cookies will not be sent to the user's browser. To accomplish this, we have to use a meta-refresh or you can also use `<cfheader name="refresh" value="0; url=loginform3.cfm">` which does the same thing. The general rule is the `<cflocation>` is executed at the server before any data is sent back to the user. Since cookies are stored on the client's machine, the server will redirect the user to the new URL before the cookies have a chance to get cleared, and are therefore never expired. By using a meta-refresh, ColdFusion is able to return the code to the user's computer and the cookies successfully get deleted. The browser is then able to redirect safely.

Now let's rewrite this slightly to work with our Flash movie. First we have to break up the ColdFusion into two separate pages. The first page will simply check for the `Remember_Me` cookie. If the cookie exists, ColdFusion will return a `success` variable to Flash along with the member's full name. If the cookie variable doesn't exist then ColdFusion will simply return an `errorcode`, and let Flash handle the logging in and redirection. Create a new file called `checkrememberme.cfm` and type the following code:

```
<cfsetting enablecfoutputonly="Yes">
<!--- checkrememberme.cfm --->
<cfif isdefined("cookie.Remember_Me")>
<cfquery name="getusername" datasource="flashbible">
  select *
  from members
```

```
   where memberid = #Cookie.MemberID#
</cfquery>
<cfoutput>&remember_me=1&membername=#urlencodedformat⏎
(getusername.membername)#&</cfoutput>
<cfelse>
<cfoutput>&remember_me=0&</cfoutput>
</cfif>
```

Our next template will handle the logging in. Let's go back to our HTML editor, type the following code, and save it as checklogin.cfm:

```
<cfsetting enablecfoutputonly="Yes">
<!--- checklogin.cfm --->
<cfparam name="form.rememberme" default="0">
<cfquery name="checklogin" datasource="flashbible">
   select *
   from members
   where loginusername = '#form.loginname#'
      and loginpassword = '#form.password#'
</cfquery>

<cfif checklogin.recordcount gt 0>
<cfif form.rememberme eq 1>
   <cfcookie name="Remember_Me" value="1" expires="NEVER">
   <cfcookie name="MemberID" value="#checklogin.MemberID#" ⏎
   expires="NEVER">
<cfelse>
   <cfcookie name="MemberID" value="#checklogin.MemberID#">
</cfif>
<cfoutput>&success=1&membername=#urlencodedformat⏎
(checklogin.membername)#&</cfoutput>
<cfelse>
<cfoutput>&success=0</cfoutput>
</cfif>
```

First, we notice that we set a default value for form.rememberme. That way if a value was never passed for form.rememberme, we can assume the user didn't want to have a persistent cookie. Next we run our query and check if any users in the database have a matching username and password. If we find a match in our query and the user selected rememberme, we set our two non-expiring cookies (Remember_Me, and MemberID). Otherwise, we just set the one cookie with only the MemberID value. Lastly we return a success flag to Flash, and also return the user's full name from the database. If we weren't able to find a matching record in the database, we return an error code to Flash and again let Flash decide how to deal with this user.

Finally, we have to slightly modify our logout code and remove the <meta http-equiv="Refresh"... since we won't need that when working with Flash. Create a file named **logout.cfm** and type the following code:

```
<!--- logout.cfm --->
<cfcookie name="MemberID" value="0" expires="NOW">
<cfcookie name="Remember_Me" value="0" expires="NOW">
```

The next step is to create a Flash interface and connect it to our ColdFusion files.

Connecting your login to a Flash interface

The login form is only slightly different from the guestbook that we created in the earlier exercise. This section is very useful if you want to protect a certain part of your all-Flash site from the general public.

On the CD-ROM

To help you get started faster this time, open the file **login_start.fla** from the ch44 folder on the *Flash MX Bible* CD-ROM.

1. As you will see, there are several elements already set up on the Stage. There are four areas involved in this file. First of all you check for a cookie on the end user's computer. This is followed by a "wait" page, which is shown when information is being sent from the server. Finally, you will find a standard login input text field, and with a button Movie Clip check box, which will store a cookie locally on the user's computer if it is selected (see Figure 44-12). Lastly, you have the main content area signifying a successful login.

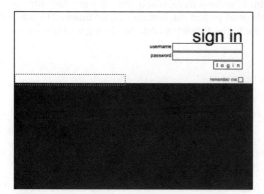

Figure 44-12: This is our login user interface.

2. The first thing you will want to do is add the proper instance names to all of the elements on the Stage. Begin with the frame 10, or "login." Find the input text boxes and give the one next to username an instance name of `loginname` and the one next to password an instance name of `passwd`. Provide an instance name of `myVar` for the Dynamic text field on the Stage.

3. The next step is to add some ActionScript to the login button. You will need to add the following code:

```
on (release) {
  cfData = new LoadVars();
  cfData.onLoad = function() {
    if (cfData.success == "1") {
      _root.gotoAndStop("results");
    } else {
      _root.passwd.text = "";

      _root.myvar.text = "hey, "+_root.loginname.text ⤾
      + ", please try again.\n ";
```

```
        _root.gotoAndStop("login");
    }
  };
  cfData.loginname = _root.loginname.text;
  cfData.password = _root.passwd.text;
  cfData.rememberme = _root.rememberme;
  cfData.sendAndLoad("checklogin.cfm", cfData, "POST");
}
```

You should notice by now that all of this is very similar what we have used in the past. In the checklogin.cfm file we created, you may recall that values are being sent to Flash. This is where those values are checked — and depending on what is returned will affect what happens in our movie. If it returns an unsuccessful result (0), it will return a message to our Dynamic text box myvar, asking the user to try again. If it returns successful (1), the movie will direct the user to the "results" page, or the main content of the movie.

4. The following step is to set up our final page, where the user is taken after successfully logging in. On this page, you need to add the instance name uname2 to the Dynamic text box. The next step is to add the following code to the logout button on this page:

```
on (release) {
  cfData = new LoadVars();
  cfData.onLoad = function() {
    _root.gotoAndStop("check");
  };
  cfData.sendAndLoad("logout.cfm", cfData, "POST");
}
```

This code should be very familiar to you by now. It is referring to the logout.cfm, which in turn expires the cookie from the system.

5. Now we need to add some frame actions for three of the four areas. First of all, add a new layer and name it **actions**. On frame 1, add the following ActionScript:

```
cfData = new LoadVars();
cfData.onLoad = function() {
  if (cfData.remember_me == "1") {
    gotoAndStop("results");
  } else {
    gotoAndStop("login");
  }
};
cfData.sendAndLoad("checkrememberme.cfm", cfData, "POST");
_root.gotoAndStop("wait");
```

This is the first thing that happens when your movie is loaded. What it is doing is calling for the checkrememberme.cfm file we created earlier, which checks for our cookie on the user's computer. If it detects our cookie, it will return a successful result (1) and then skip past the login and straight to the results frame. When it is checking the server, it holds on the "wait" frame. If it does not detect a cookie, it will go to the login page on frame 10.

6. On frame 10 of the Actions layer (the "login" frame), add the following code:

```
loginname.text = "";
passwd.text = "";
```

All this does is makes sure the login and password text fields remain empty when the user accesses this page.

7. On frame 15 of the Actions layer, add the following code:

```
uname2.text = cfData.membername;
stop();
```

This makes sure the username of our logged in user is returned and put into our Dynamic text field named `uname2` on this page.

8. Now we are ready to upload and test our login document. Publish login_start.fla, and upload the .swf, .html and .cfm files you created earlier (checkrememberme.cfm, checklogin.cfm and logout.cfm) to your server. Grab a username and password from your Access document you already completed in the previous section, and try it out. You should be able to login, and bypass your login page by using the "Rememember Me" check box, until you log out.

On the CD-ROM You can check out a completed version of this file, **login.fla**, located in the ch44 folder of the *Flash MX Bible* CD-ROM.

Hopefully, by now you can see how easy it is to get started with ColdFusion and then incorporate it into Flash. After you grasp these easy concepts, you are well on your way to creating dynamic and useful applications for yourself or your clients.

Summary

✦ ColdFusion is a combination of an application server (ColdFusion Server) and a language, CFML. CFML is a user-friendly, tag-based language.

✦ ColdFusion MX has many new features that integrate other software, including increased support of Flash MX. Integration will increase in future software, thus expanding the user base and ease of development with ColdFusion.

✦ It is not difficult to connect your dynamic Flash interfaces with ColdFusion in order to create more complex applications, using ActionScript such as the `LoadVars` object.

✦   ✦   ✦

Making Movies for the Pocket PC

✦ ✦ ✦ ✦

In This Chapter

The Pocket PC

Flash on the Pocket PC

Pocket PC and
Flash Resources

Flash content on your
Pocket PC

Mac users and
Pocket PCs

✦ ✦ ✦ ✦

Are you ready to learn more about a new way to utilize your skills in Macromedia Flash MX? Are you also ready to take your Flash content out into the wireless and mobile arena? Are you ready for a way to expand your client base and bring more value to the projects you create with Flash MX? Then this chapter is for you. In this chapter we will cover a brief overview of what a Pocket PC is and why you would want to use it to deliver Flash content, the basics of how Flash can be deployed on the Microsoft Pocket PC 2002 platform and tips for working with Flash MX to develop content for use on Pocket PCs.

What Is a Pocket PC?

We will not delve too deeply into the technical specifications and many capabilities of the various Pocket PC devices, which in and of itself could fill an entire book. Rather, we will focus on the basics you will need to know to get you started developing Flash content for the Pocket PC. For those of you who do not yet have your hands on one of these devices and are curious about the platform in general, a brief introduction to the Pocket PC platform is warranted. In this chapter we will discuss and refer specifically to Microsoft Windows Pocket PC 2002 based devices. Therefore, whenever you see Pocket PC we will be referring to a Pocket PC 2002 capable device unless specifically noted. There are other types of PDAs or Personal Digital Assistants on the market such as Palm, Handspring, and others, but none of them are currently capable of displaying Flash content.

Note   You can convert Flash movies into QuickTime Video (.mov files) or Windows AVI files, and then convert these video files into gMovie files (.pdb files) that play on Palm and Visor devices. You can learn more about gMovie Maker at www.genericmovie.com. You cannot make interactive movies with this software—only linear Flash animations can benefit from this technology.

Basic information about the Pocket PC

It is important to understand the general specifications and capabilities of a Pocket PC before you start developing Flash content for these devices. Let's take a look at some of the main attributes of typical Pocket PCs:

✦ Pocket PCs rely on Microsoft Windows CE for their core operating system. For more information about this operating system, visit `www.microsoft.com/windowsce/`

✦ A Pocket PC is considered a PDA or Personal Digital Assistant. For a brief overview of the qualities that define a PDA, visit `www.microsoft.com/mobile/pocketpc/pdainfo.asp`

✦ There are three basic processor types powering the Pocket PC platform: ARM, MIPS, and SH3. At the time of this writing, the ARM processor running at 206 MHz is the fastest processor in any currently available Pocket PC. ARM Limited is the designer of the chip, while Intel is the company responsible for actually manufacturing and distributing its StrongARM SA-1110 chip. MIPS Technologies licenses its MIPS design to Pocket PC manufacturers for use in their devices. The high-end speed for current MIPS chips is 150Mhz. The last processor, the SH3, is designed and produced by Hitachi. It currently zips along at 133Mhz.

✦ There are many companies on the market manufacturing Pocket PC 2002 devices, and they typically use one of the previously mentioned processors. Casio, Compaq, Hewlett-Packard, NEC, and Toshiba all make various models. As this book was going to press another global company, Fujitsu, announced that it would soon be releasing the fastest Pocket PC yet. The Pocket LOOX, a 400mhz Intel PXA250 powered device. An up-to-date list of various manufacturers and comparisons of popular Pocket PC devices is available directly from Microsoft at `www.microsoft.com/mobile/pocketpc/hardware/default.asp`

Note   Why the focus on processors in an introduction to the platform? The speed at which a Pocket PC device operates directly affects the performance of the Flash player. You will need to keep this in mind as you develop your Flash content.

✦ Pocket PCs are typically rechargeable battery powered devices. They have 240×320 pixel, touch-sensitive displays. They are operated with a stylus (or finger if yours is slender enough) as opposed to a mouse. Therefore, the screen real estate you have for displaying content is much smaller than a typical desktop machine.

✦ Navigating on a Pocket PC is very similar to working with a standard Microsoft Windows based desktop machine. There is a Start Menu equivalent and even a File Explorer to root around in the file structure.

✦ A Pocket PC can be thought of as a miniature, portable version of your desktop PC. The main focus of a Pocket PC is to give users freedom by providing the means to be productive while on the go, thus freeing you from your desktop. The Pocket PC also allows you to stay connected to your e-mail and other services while away from the home or office. Pocket PCs even come with smaller stripped down "Pocket" versions of Microsoft Word, Excel, and even Internet Explorer. For many workers, these are the only programs necessary to do their job.

✦ In addition to providing specific workplace staples, a Pocket PC also contains personal information manager (PIM) features like an address book, contacts, task lists, calendar and scheduling functions, e-mail capabilities — pretty much everything you would need to stay on top of things while away from your home or office. All of those features come with the ability to easily synchronize the data on your desktop with your device. Those are just the basic features. The fun comes when you start to add in the other capabilities of the Pocket PC, like support for: wireless internet and data services, voice annotation, speech recognition, Microsoft Reader, Adobe Acrobat, MSN Messenger, Terminal

Services client, Real Media, and Windows Media Players with full audio and video capabilities, third party software for specialty tasks and applications. There is also a significant amount of hardware support, such as: Compact Flash storage devices, Secure Digital media, portable keyboards, bar code scanners, digital cameras, GPS navigation systems, wireless LAN cards, Bluetooth connectivity, the list goes on and on.

✦ The foremost reason why we like Pocket PCs: the ability to play Macromedia Flash content.

If this has not yet whet your appetite sufficiently, point your Web browser to the Microsoft official site for information about Pocket PCs, `www.pocketpc.com/` and read up on the other capabilities and features that make this platform unique. You might also take a trip to your nearest electronics boutique for an hour and play around with the various models to see what strikes your fancy. If you would rather not leave your office, Microsoft recently released an excellent demonstration application showing off the many features of the Pocket PC platform most appealing to the enterprise environment. The best part about this demonstration is that the content was created and delivered using Macromedia Flash, and it is a perfect example of what you can do with Flash on the Pocket PC. In addition, it works on your desktop and on your device. Take a peak at `www.microsoft.com/mobile/enterprise/ interactivedemo/default.asp`

Why Flash on the Pocket PC?

Now that you know a bit about the basics of what a Pocket PC device is, why would you want to put Flash content on it? Let's go through the most compelling reasons and break each one down with a small explanation and examples where appropriate:

Small file size

Flash content is ideal for Pocket PCs, where the memory and file size requirements are more stringent than desktop PC's. A typical Pocket PC without add-on memory has anywhere between 32 and 64MB of RAM available to the system for storage and application use. The vector-based graphics of Flash, and its built-in compression of assets and media, lend a hand toward staying within the confines of the platform. The small file size also increases the efficiency of wireless connectivity. Right now, many of you enjoy high-speed access at your home and office thanks to broadband services, such as Cable and DSL. The wireless world is still in its infancy when it comes to high-speed data services; cellular carrier-based data services are not comparable to wireless 802.11b LAN services. In the past year alone, several major players in the high-speed data service for Pocket PCs including Metricom Inc. Ricochet, Omnisky and a few others, all filed for Chapter 11 bankruptcy protection. Hopefully, they may re-emerge to offer their services again. Major carriers like Verizon, AT&T, Sprint, Voicestream and Cingular are now starting to offer near-broadband speed services for devices based on new networks being established as you read this. Right now, most data-capable cellular services clip along at a paltry FAX-like speed of 14.4 Kbps, with some services only capable of maxing out at a snails pace of 9.6 Kbps. If you are lucky you might be able to get 19.2 Kbps from your wireless carrier. With these items in mind, you can see the benefit of the small file sizes Flash content offers when working with portable devices. Even better is the ability of the larger chunks of your application to play locally while the dynamic data that may change over time can be pulled into your Flash application on demand. At the same time, small chunks are served from middleware and server-side technologies, so bandwidth requirements are reduced.

Recycle, Repurpose, and Redeploy — the three R's of Flash

This is the mantra that emanates from Macromedia and is, in fact, included in its "What We Do" statement on its Web site: "enable Web professionals to efficiently and cost effectively design and develop dynamic content that can be delivered to multiple platforms and devices."

It couldn't have been stated better. If you look at the press releases and partnerships that Macromedia has announced over the past few years, you will see one of their main goals shine through: allowing the Flash developer to author content once and deploy it on any device under the sun. Content created for one device can be quickly redeveloped for another device — using the "Three R's." This is ideal for companies desiring to maintain a consistent look and feel, usability, and branding across their entire product line.

Rapid development time and low barrier to entry

Macromedia has taken all the hard work and done it for you. They have completed the task of making sure that content created with Flash works on various devices. As a content and application developer, you will not need to spend your time learning the ins and outs of the low-level APIs and specifics of the devices and platforms you need to deploy on. Simply make your Flash content by following the guidelines for your target platform and size, and it will work. Flash MX makes your job even easier by using the new templates feature, which we cover later in this chapter. The learning curve of Flash reduces potential barriers, so even a designer who is just beginning to learn the basics of programming can dive in head first and crank work out in a relatively short amount time. Compared to traditional device specific languages and development methods this is an incredibly attractive feature of Flash. Imagine handing a book on C++ to a traditional graphic designer with no fundamental programming experience and asking him or her to build an application in a few days. They would be hard pressed to come up with a working program for one targeted platform in a short amount of time, let alone multiple platforms.

Real-World Example of the Three R's in Use

To see a real-world example of the Three R's of Flash in use, point your desktop browser to: www.usabancshares.com/broadband/demo/ and then your Pocket PC or another desktop browser to: https://broadband.usabancshares.com/pocketbank/demo/. These are demo versions for non-account holders.

This project was the world's first 100% Macromedia Flash and Generator-driven online banking experience developed for USABancShares.com. The site was launched in June of 2000. When this project was being developed Generator 2 had only been around for a few months and the whole thing was built around Flash 4. About 8 months later, the very day that Macromedia announced the availability of the Flash 4 Player Developer Release for the Pocket PC platform in February of 2001, developers were able to release a Recycled, Repurposed and Redeployed version specifically for the Pocket PC platform. Microsoft announced just prior to this, the availability of the 128-bit High Encryption pack for the Pocket PC, enabling Pocket Internet Explorer to support SSL (Secure Sockets Layer) 128-bit encrypted connections. This was the final key ingredient for allowing a Pocket PC to access a Web-based banking site securely. The "Three R's" process did not involve the lengthy development time that the original project's scope entailed. The architecture did not have to change, simple optimization of the assets and a bit of reworking to account for the limited screen size and localizing portions of the content so only data chunks needed to be sent back and forth during its use. The branding and look and feel were retained, thus allowing users familiar with one version to be just as at home with the smaller Pocket PC version.

By now you should be able to see the benefits of using Flash as your application development tool of choice for deploying content on Pocket PCs.

Pocket PC and Flash resources

One of the unique aspects of developing Flash-based content is the incredible community of developers and resources available to get you going and answer any questions you might have along the way. This section provides you with a good base of resources to which you can refer as you begin to work with Pocket PCs and Flash:

✦ The first resource for support and information is of course the Macromedia Flash support area on Macromedia's site. There is even a section containing white papers, and various kits and documents relating directly to the Pocket PC and other devices beyond the desktop that are capable of playing Flash content. This area is available at www.macromedia.com/software/flashplayer/resources/devices/. It includes links to download and install the Flash 4 and Flash 5 Players for Pocket PCs, along with a good set of FAQs (Frequently Asked Questions).

✦ Just before this book was going to press, Macromedia announced and released a CDK (Content Developer Kit) for Flash Player 5 for the Nokia Communicator 9200 series of wireless handsets. More information about this unique platform is also available from the same site we mentioned previously. The CDK available at this site has many tips, guidelines and best practices for working with Flash 5 content on the Pocket PC. At the time of this writing, Macromedia had recently announced the availability of Flash Player 5 for the Pocket PC through OEM partnerships, Casio being the first. Casio owners can download Flash Player 5 by visiting: www.mycasio.com/ and registering. The rest of us can visit www.macromedia.com/software/flashplayer/pocketpc/download/ where Macromedia keeps an up to date list of the OEMs that have licensed and released versions of Flash Player 5 for their respective devices.

Note

Currently, Flash Player 6 is not available for the Pocket PC to coincide with many of the new features available in Flash MX, but you can still use Flash MX to author your content. (Macromedia did indicate in a press release and in a column in their Designer Developer area: www.macromedia.com/desdev/ that later in 2002 the Flash Player 6 SDK (Software Development Kit) would be available to device manufacturers for licensing. This will allow those manufacturers willing to participate to port Flash Player 6 to their respective devices. Until February of 2002 all that was officially available from Macromedia for the Pocket PC was the Flash Player 4 Developer Release. This version worked only on color models of Compaq's iPaq, Casio's Cassiopeia and Hewlett Packard's Jornada devices. The Flash Player 4 Developer download is still available from Macromedia's Web site but the SDK for version 4 is more difficult to find. It has been replaced by the more up to date Flash 5 CDK, but it does have a few extra examples. You can still find the version 4 SDK while it lasts at: www.macromedia.com/software/flashplayer/pocketpc/authoring/.

✦ Macromedia also has a newsgroup macromedia.flash.handhelds that contains a wealth of information about Pocket PCs, and newbies and experts alike can get together to discuss Flash and devices. This area can be accessed via a regular newsgroup reader application (including Outlook Express) by subscribing to forums.macromedia.com or via the new Web-based interface available at www.macromedia.com/support/forums/.

✦ This list would not be complete without including the following two sites that are the best online third party sites for info about Pocket PCs and Flash: Bill Perry's excellent `www.pocketpcflash.net` and Phillip Torrone's amazing `www.flashenabled.com`. Both of these sites feature news and updates concerning devices and Flash, reviews of products, peaks at inspiring commercial products, new fangled devices, tutorials, and excellent links to other sites covering Pocket PC specifics.

✦ Two additional sites for general Pocket PC news and information: Jason Dunn's `www.pocketpcthoughts.com` and Dale Coffing's `www.pocketpcpassion.com`. If you want news and information about Pocket PC's these two sites will get you off to a great start. The amount of time these guys spend going to conferences, attending industry events and posting news items is unbelievable. If there is something new for the Pocket PC platform you'll find it here first.

Getting Flash Content onto Your Device

Now that we have covered the basics of what a Pocket PC device is, why you would want one, reasons for developing Flash content for one, and the places and resources you can visit to ask questions and seek help as you learn about your device and develop content, you probably want to know how to get your content onto a device and test these applications as you work. The previously mentioned Flash 5 for Pocket PC 2002 CDK is a great resource for getting started with Flash and Pocket PCs. If you haven't already downloaded it, then it is recommended you do so before going any further. It covers all of the most important best practices, known issues, and information you will need to author content. So rather than repeat what is already available for free from experts on this subject, our focus will be on items that were left out of the CDK, especially concerning development workflow with the Pocket PC and the authoring environment. We will also include information for users who develop their content on Apple Macintosh systems who are left out in the cold without native connectivity for syncing, testing and installing applications on their Pocket PCs.

The most often asked question about developing content for Pocket PCs is, "Do I need a Pocket PC to develop Flash content for use on a Pocket PC?" No, it is not necessary that you have a device in order to develop content for the Pocket PC. You can reasonably build simple Flash movies that will playback just fine on a Pocket PC without testing the content on a real Pocket PC device. However, owning a Pocket PC makes your job a lot easier, shortens the development time, and gives you the peace of mind that your content is working smoothly and correctly. For any large or advanced Flash project, you will have to do testing with an actual device or you may never know if your application is functioning properly.

Caution   You may be tempted to test Flash content on the Pocket PC 2002 emulator that Microsoft has available as part of the free Pocket PC 2002 SDK at: `www.microsoft.com/mobile/developer/downloads/`.

While the emulator (which requires Microsoft eMbedded Visual Basic 3.0, also a free download) does allow you test applications on a Windows desktop operating system, you cannot test Flash movies on the emulator. Part of the problem lies in the inability to install the Flash Player on the emulator version. For updates on Pocket PC and Flash developments, check out the Using Flash with Devices forum at `www.flashsupport.com`.

There is no standalone player on the Pocket PC — all of your content needs to be viewed as an embedded object in an HTML file. You cannot simply click on a .swf file, or pull one in directly to a browser like you can from a desktop PC. The Pocket PC must have an accompanying .html file.

Note Some Casio devices and Nokia devices do not use Pocket Internet Explorer to play content, as they use a custom Web application for certain models of their devices.

Flash MX and the Pocket PC

In Flash MX, there is a great new feature called templates. These are Flash files that have been preconfigured for a particular type of presentation. They are available to help you format your movies for deployment to several different kinds of devices. Let's take a look at how we can get started on a movie that is intended for a device by using templates in Flash MX.

Cross-Reference You can find more coverage of templates in the QuickStart section of this book.

1. Open Flash MX, and choose File ➪ New From Template. A New File dialog box will appear. Select MobileDevices from the left column named Category. You will notice several options then appear in the Category Items column — templates for the Nokia Communicator and the Pocket PC 2002 platform. You are off to a good start with Flash MX already!

2. Select the Pocket PC template, and press the Create button. You will now have by default a 230×250 size document, just right for the Pocket PC. A temporary Guide layer will provide you some instructions about this template.

3. Now select File ➪ Publish Settings. The Flash SWF settings should default to Flash 5 format for this template. HTML publishing should be checked by default as well. Click on the HTML tab. The Template menu should be set to the Flash Only template. There is a new template in this menu called Flash Only for Pocket PC 2002. For now press OK and save the Flash document (.fla file) with an appropriate name to a folder on your hard drive.

4. Now try making some content on a layer. Drop in a button or import your favorite logo. After you have done this, go ahead and publish your file. The following is a peek at the source HTML code generated from that HTML template:

Listing 45-1: **Example Output from Pocket PC .html Template**

```
<HEAD>
<TITLE>example</TITLE>
</HEAD>
<BODY bgcolor="#FFFFFF" LEFTMARGIN="0" TOPMARGIN="0">
<!-- URL's used in the movie-->
<!-- text used in the movie-->
<!--
This template contains both <OBJECT> and <EMBED> tags so that HTML pages
generated
can be deployed in both Pocket IE and desktop IE and Netscape browsers.
If the Flash content is targeted for only local Pocket IE use, the codebase
attribute in the <OBJECT> tag can be deleted, and the <EMBED></EMBED> section
can be deleted.
-->
<OBJECT classid="clsid:D27CDB6E-AE6D-11cf-96B8-444553540000"
codebase="http://download.macromedia.com/pub/shockwave/cabs/flash/⤵
swflash.cab#version=5,0,0,0"
```

Continued

Listing 45-1: *(continued)*

```
WIDTH="230" HEIGHT="250" id="example" ALIGN="">
<PARAM NAME=movie VALUE="example.swf">
<PARAM NAME=quality VALUE=high>
<PARAM NAME=bgcolor VALUE=#FFFFFF>
<EMBED src="example.swf" quality=high bgcolor=#FFFFFF
WIDTH="230" HEIGHT="250" NAME="example" ALIGN=""
      TYPE="application/x-shockwave-flash"
      PLUGINSPAGE="http://www.macromedia.com/go/getflashplayer">
      </EMBED>
</OBJECT>
</BODY>
</HTML>
```

Now take a look at the published .swf and .html file in a Web browser. If everything looks right up to this point, now is the time to grab your friend who has a Pocket PC. Have him or her test it on the device for you. These are going to be the steps you will have to repeat over and over again: Publish, upload, nag your friend, test, repeat. This is not ideal, but it will work. In the next section we will take a look at testing your movie on a Pocket PC.

Testing your movie

Once you have a Flash movie or two to test, you need to have access to a Pocket PC with the right software and connections. Make sure your friend with the Pocket PC has correctly installed the proper Flash Player. Now, you have several methods to get the content into the device for testing. The first method we will discuss involves viewing your production directly from the device by using Microsoft ActiveSync to synchronize it with their Pocket PC. ActiveSync is the software Microsoft developed allowing you to synchronize a device with your desktop. It also allows you to browse the device and any storage cards attached to it you may be using for expansion. With the Pocket PC 2002, ActiveSync 3.5 also allows you to share your desktop's internet connection with your Pocket PC when it is either "cradled" or hooked up with a sync cable (there are a few other methods for network syncing if you have a wireless LAN card or IR port on your desktop computer), which in essence turns your desktop machine into a Proxy server. You can now browse the Web with the built-in Pocket Internet Explorer, or PIE, simply by entering in the URL and pulling up the site. PIE also happens to be the environment in which Flash Player 5 for Pocket PC lives. ActiveSync typically comes with all Pocket PCs but you will need to make sure you have version 3.5 as some of the features we are going to use are only available with that specific version. If you are using Windows XP you will also need version 3.5 for compatibility reasons.

Note   To obtain a copy or update your current version, ActiveSync 3.5 (or higher) is available from `www.microsoft.com/mobile/pocketpc/downloads/`.

Instructions for installing and configuring this software and creating a partnership between the host PC and the target device come with the software. This software will only work on machines running a Microsoft-based operating system. Mac users fear not, we have a solution for you further into the chapter.

Once ActiveSync 3.5 is installed and a relationship with the device has been established, and you can successfully sync content with your Pocket PC by cradling the device or by cabling the Pocket PC and desktop PC together with a sync cable, you are ready to move the content onto the device. Just follow these steps:

1. Grab the .swf and .html files you created and transfer them to the desktop PC that has ActiveSync installed. You can transfer the files in several ways, including the use of a floppy or CD, file-sharing or LAN. Once the files are on the desktop PC, open ActiveSync on the desktop PC if it is not already open.

2. Click the Explore icon in the ActiveSync application toolbar. Alternately, once a device is connected via ActiveSync, it should also appear as a new icon named Mobile Device under My Computer. You can double-click the Mobile Device icon there to access the files on the Pocket PC.

3. Either method described in Step 2 will take you to the My Documents folder on the Pocket PC. Now you may simply copy the .swf and .html files into an appropriate folder. We recommend you create a special folder named Flash in the root of My Documents. This folder can contain all Flash applications. If you have an expansion pack for your device allowing you to have additional storage space via Compact Flash memory cards, Secure Digital card, Microdrive, and so on, then you may navigate to that specific area by clicking the My Pocket PC icon that is in the currently open window. Within the folder that opens next, you will see another folder corresponding with your expansion device — in our case, a folder named Storage Card corresponding with a 128MB Compact Flash card. Your .swf and .html file may also be placed there in order to save your system memory for other applications and files.

Tip   Create a folder called My Documents at the root level of the storage card. Then, other programs on your device will be able to easily access documents and files from this area on your storage card.

4. Once the copy operation is complete, launch the File Explorer application from the Start menu on your Pocket PC.

5. Navigate to the location on the device where you placed the copies of the .swf and .html files. Tap the .html file to launch Pocket Internet Explorer. The Flash movie (.swf file) will begin playing in the browser. If the browser does not show the Flash content, double-check to make sure you have installed the correct Flash Player for your device. Also make sure you have published the .swf file in a Flash 5 or lower format.

Note   Prior to publication of this book, certain Casio devices are the only Pocket PCs with a publicly available Flash Player 5. Other Pocket PC devices are capable of Flash 4 files only. The authors of this book have it on good authority that by the time this book hits store shelves this situation should be resolved in some fashion.

If everything worked properly you have just completed moving and storing content onto a device. At this point you are well on your way!

Note   The procedure you just went through would be the same if you had ActiveSync and a Pocket PC device on the machine you are running Flash MX on and doing the actual development work from. You would simply publish your SWF and HTML files and follow the same steps again.

Now that you can see the content on the device, you should go step by step through the CDK for Flash 5 on the Pocket PC that was covered in the "Pocket PC and Flash resources" section of this chapter to see if you followed the guidelines and tips presented. A general rule of thumb would be to make sure your app functions as desired, and with the same visual representation you intended. Also check for playback speed and memory use.

You can also check to see how much memory your Flash application and Pocket Internet Explorer are utilizing on your device with the following steps:

1. Completely close all other Pocket PC applications.

2. Select Settings from the Start menu.

3. Click the Memory icon.

4. You should be in the Main tab, which shows how much total memory your device has built in, how much is being used for Storage (files and documents) on the device, and how much is being used for Programs (running applications). In our case we have a Compaq iPaq with 64MB of built-in RAM. We have allocated half for storage and half for Programs. The Pocket PC allows you to adjust this slider based on your usage and needs. This is something for you to consider when developing your movies. Many users with older devices may only have 32MB of RAM.

5. The Storage Card tab appears if you have an Expansion Pack installed with a device inserted, in our case a 128MB Compact Flash card.

6. To confirm you only have PIE (Pocket Internet Explorer) running, switch to the Running Programs tab. If there are other programs running besides Internet Explorer you can stop them from this screen as well.

7. Once nothing but Internet Explorer is running, click back to the Main tab. Make a note of how much memory is in use for Programs. Then switch to the Running Programs tab and Stop Internet Explorer. Again, switch back to the Main tab and note how much memory is in use for Programs.

8. One final step to accurately gauge how much memory was being used by your Flash content in the Internet Explorer application is to launch Internet Explorer and open an HTML file containing no content (simply a blank HTML document). Now go back to the Memory Settings and see how much is being used by Internet Explorer.

By comparing all the usage settings you noted and comparing them you should have a good idea how much memory your Flash application is consuming. If you have a section of ActionScript in your application that is particularly heavy with attaching sounds (or Movie Clips) and duplicating Movie Clips, you should navigate to the corresponding section of your Flash application and compare the memory settings at that point. This is important since memory usage climbs as Flash has to duplicate and control additional Movie Clips. If you are loading in additional movies with a `loadMovie()` command or data with a `loadVariables()`, then your memory use will also climb during that portion of your application. If at all possible, unload Movie Clips when they are no longer necessary. All the steps you would normally take to decrease memory usage for a desktop deployed Flash application are even more crucial when deploying content on the Pocket PC.

There is another way to get content onto your device using ActiveSync 3.5. One of the new features of 3.5 and Pocket PC 2002 is that when your device is cradled to your PC it can share your desktop's Internet connection. Your PC effectively becomes a proxy server for your Pocket PC. You can simply launch Pocket Internet Explorer, type in the URL of your Web site and view your Flash content. For content that will end up on the Web, this is an ideal method of final stage testing. Do keep in mind that the connection speed of a Pocket PC using a wireless service may be drastically slower than the connection speeds you will experience in this cradled proxy mode. Therefore, the final test should always be via a low speed data connection to see if your application is still usable.

Tip

Try to chunk your application into sections. Any content that can be distributed once to the end user via an installer or .zip file of your main .swf and .html files is ideal. In turn, those files can pull in dynamic data or additional Flash movies from your server at runtime. This is a great usage for shared libraries. Distribute a main file to end users via a .zip file that is installed locally on the device. This file would contain all your large assets and sounds while the interface and updates may be tiny Flash movie or `loadVariable()` files pulled from your server on demand.

Mac Users and Pocket PCs

Now you may say, "That's all great information, but I use my iMac and my G4 tower to run Flash MX as my development environment of choice and they don't support ActiveSync. I don't have any spare PCs to run ActiveSync with anyway. What are my options?"

You have several options from which to choose:

✦ Wireless connectivity

✦ Storage Card readers

✦ PocketMac

✦ Connectix Virtual PC

Go through each of these items and lay out the options and methods that are available.

Wireless connectivity

In this section we will cover a couple wireless capabilities for your device that will allow you to move content to it while doing your development work on a Mac.

An 802.11b wireless LAN card and network

By installing an 802.11b wireless LAN adapter into your Pocket PC, such as Symbols Compact Flash Wireless Networker, found at:

```
www.symbol.com/products/wireless/wirelessflash.html
```

you will be able to connect to and share the network created by an Apple Airport base station or other similar 802.11b wireless access points.

With this setup you can use the wireless LAN to share the Internet connection on the Airport network. You can also use the Web sharing feature of Mac OS X on your development Mac that's running Flash MX; simply drag and drop files into the folder that is served up by the robust Apache Web server that is built into every copy of Mac OS X. The Sites folder that is found under each individual user's home folder is the location from which Mac OS X serves your files. Once your Pocket PC is connected to your wireless LAN, point Pocket Internet Explorer to the IP address of your Mac:

```
http://xxx.xxx.xxx.xxx/~your_username_here
```

where `xxx.xxx.xxx.xxx` is replaced by the IP address of your Mac, and `your_username_here` is replaced by your short login name of your account on the Mac OS X machine. From there you will be able to preview content directly. Alternatively, by compressing your files into .zip archives with a program like Stuffit Deluxe, you can download and save the compressed files to your Pocket PC. On the Pocket PC side you can then use a program such as HandyZIP from `www.cnetx.com` to uncompress files on Pocket PCs.

Note PC users with a wireless LAN card in a device and the desktop PC connected to this network, will be able to use the previously mentioned ActiveSync wirelessly without having to cradle the device.

Wireless data carriers

The next wireless method for pulling in files you author on your Mac workstation involves using a wireless data carrier, such as a cellular service provider, to allow the Pocket PC to pull in files from a Mac workstation or your Web site hosted at an ISP. The drawbacks of this are a slower connection speed, and typically this will be more expensive in the long run. You would need to sign up with a service provider and also purchase the appropriate hardware to enable your Pocket PC to use the service if it is not already built in. If you already own a cell phone, then it may be worth looking into the following Web site: `www.thesupplynet.com`. The SupplyNet sells cables allowing various Pocket PC devices to be connected to a variety of data-capable cell phones. SupplyNet ships their cables with complete instructions for connecting the cable to your device and the settings you will need to configure on your Pocket PC.

Many Pocket PCs and phone manufacturers also support Bluetooth short-range wireless connectivity allowing them to connect, sync, and share information without cables. Apple announced in April 2002 the availability of a tiny USB-based Bluetooth adapter and software for Mac OS X.

You should check with your preferred cellular carrier for package deals and the type of connections, phones and platforms that they carry and support.

Note Microsoft has recently announced the Pocket PC 2002 Phone Edition that is capable of supporting enhanced data and wireless connectivity for devices that have built-in hardware for utilizing such services.

Storage cards

Now that we have covered several methods taking advantage of wireless connectivity to move Flash content from your development environment to your Pocket PC, let's cover one of the easiest methods — using Storage Cards. Most Pocket PC devices have support for accepting a variety of storage media through built-in slots or via expansion sleeves such as the Compaq iPaq line. There is CF (Compact Flash), MMC (MultiMedia Card), SD (Secure Digital) available, and for devices like the Compaq iPAQ which support PCMCIA adapter sleeves, there are even more options. These are all solid-state memory devices, available in a variety of capacities. You may already be familiar with these technologies as they are popular for use with digital cameras, printers, and other consumer devices. IBM even has miniature hard drives in the Compact Flash form factor called the MicroDrive, in 340MB and 1GB capacities. More information can be found at:

```
www.storage.ibm.com/hdd/micro/datasheet.htm
```

We mentioned earlier that if your device is cradled on a PC, the storage card simply appears as a folder named Storage Card on your device. You can browse through this like any other folder, and move and copy files to it directly from your PC. On a Mac not supporting

ActiveSync, you will need a way to read the card. If you happen to have a Mac laptop, then you can use a PCMCIA adapter sleeve to slide the storage card into your Mac and mount it like a hard drive. If you are using a desktop-based Mac or one that does not have PCMCIA slots, you will need to use a card reader. There are many available that support systems as old as Mac OS 8.5 and as new as Mac OS X. Typically they connect via the USB port on your Mac. Readers that connect via Firewire are also available. One of the most versatile and portable readers available that works with most PCs and Macs is the Imation FlashGo! It is unique in that by using included adapter sleeves it can read all types of Compact Flash media, IBM MicroDrives, Secure Digital, MMC, and even Sony Memory Sticks. Apple even lists this product in their online store because OS X has built-in native support for this card reader. If you go with another manufacturer, make sure the reader you purchase can support your specific OS. Many readers do not yet support OS X.

All of these storage types appear as hard disks on your desktop when inserted into a reader. Simply treat them as you would any other drive. Make sure to follow the manufacturer's instructions for ejecting the media from your reader before removing it to prevent corruption of data. Mac users should note that the cards will typically be formatted with the PC FAT file system, and you should be aware of filename issues, which may arise during use. Once you have copied your Flash content onto the Storage Card, simply eject and remove it from your reader and re-insert the card into your Pocket PC. The content can then be accessed via the File Explorer.

PocketMac

This is a fairly new program, and is available from www.pocketmac.net. PocketMac provides a way to use several brands of Pocket PCs directly with Mac OS 9 and OS X. There are still some rough edges to the interface, but it improves with every new release. A professional version is also underway that will allow Mac users to sync their contacts, calendar and task data from Microsoft Entourage, Microsoft Exchange 2000 Server and even the Mac OS X address book application. The regular version allows you to sync a documents folder, or simply drag and drop files in either direction. The software works via the USB cradle, sync cable, or even via your local LAN if your Pocket PC has a wired or wireless LAN card. Another helpful application from PocketMac is currently in beta and is free to purchasers of PocketMac. It is called CabExtractor. This application allows Mac users to extract CAB files from Pocket PC application installers thus helping Mac users install many third party applications. PocketMac also just released a version of PocketMac called PocketMac Ir 2002 that allows you to use the Ir port on your Pocket PC or any Mac with an Ir port (such as the Titanium Powerbook G4) to beam files back and forth between the devices.

Note   For PC users, ActiveSync also supports Ir syncing if your PC has an Ir port (which many laptops come equipped with.) No cables or cradles are involved: simply aim, point, and click.

Connectix Virtual PC

Connectix recently released version 5.0.2 of their popular emulation software, allowing Mac users to run multiple operating systems typically found on Intel processor based PCs. Their product is fairly solid, however, their support for USB-based syncing of Pocket PC devices through ActiveSync has been spotty. A few configurations of Virtual PC 5.0.2 have been tested on Mac OS X 10.1.3 running on a dual 500 MHz G4. The tests were done with Virtual PC running Windows 98, Windows 2000 and Windows XP. Windows 98 and Windows 2000 worked with ActiveSync and a Compaq iPAQ over USB rather well. The installation procedure was identical to that of a regular PC. The Windows XP test on the other hand, was unable to see the device after initially working fine. Connectix confirms on their Web site that this is indeed an open issue of compatibility with Pocket PC devices. More information can be found at:

```
www.connectix.com/products/vpc5m_usb_list_dec01.html
```

If you already have Virtual PC, then this may be a viable route to transfer files between your Mac and a Pocket PC. However, it is quite slow compared to the other methods for moving content onto your device.

Summary

✦ Many manufacturers are developing Pocket PCs, which are increasingly becoming a viable option for Flash movie deployment. You should consider the specifications and features of these devices carefully before you start making content in Flash MX.

✦ Macromedia provides up-to-date resources and development kits that cover best practices and methodology for working with the latest Flash player release on the Pocket PC platform.

✦ Flash MX contains templates that will help you get a head start in developing properly formatted content for the Pocket PC and other devices capable of displaying Flash content.

✦ Testing your Flash content on the targeted device throughout the development process, while considering the current limitations of the platform and specific Flash Player versions, is key to developing and successfully deploying content on Pocket PC devices.

✦ There are many alternative methods of working with Pocket PC devices while developing Flash content on Macintosh operating systems. If you are a Flash developer working on a Macintosh, look into third-party software and hardware to assist you.

P A R T

✦ ✦ ✦ ✦

In This Part

Appendix A
Keyboard Shortcuts

Appendix B
Digital Sound Basics

Appendix C
Using the CD-ROM

Appendix D
Contact and
Bibliography
Information

✦ ✦ ✦ ✦

Keyboard Shortcuts

It is surprising how long some developers will go before learning shortcut keys, but after you begin to make them a part of your workflow, you will realize how much time you can save. Not only will your Flash production be more efficient, but you may just save yourself the pain of getting *carpal tunnel syndrome* — a chronic condition that can result from overusing your "mouse arm."

In order to make Flash shortcut keys more consistent with other Macromedia programs, there have been some shortcut changes in Flash MX. Tables A-1 through A-5 are intended to serve as a quick reference for the shortcut keys used for common tasks.

Table A-1: Tool Shortcut Keys

Toolbox Item	Shortcut	Toolbox Item	Shortcut
Arrow tool	V	Subselect Arrow tool	A
Line tool	N	Lasso tool	L
Pen tool	P	Text tool	T
Oval tool	O	Rectangle	R
Pencil tool	Y	Paintbrush tool	B
Free Transform	Q	Transform Fill	F
Ink Bottle	S	Paint Bucket	K
Eyedropper	I	Eraser	E
Hand tool	H (Spacebar)	Zoom (magnifier)	Z (M)

Table A-2: View Shortcut Keys

Menu Item	Windows Shortcut	Macintosh Shortcut
100 percent View scale	Ctrl+1	⌘+1
Show Frame	Ctrl+2	⌘+2
Show All	Ctrl+3	⌘+3
Zoom In	Ctrl+= (equal key)	⌘+= (equal key)
Zoom Out	Ctrl+- (minus key)	⌘+- (minus key)
Hide Edges (Mesh)	Ctrl+Shift+E	⌘+Shift+E
Grid (Show/Hide)	Ctrl+' (quote key)	⌘+' (quote key)
Guides (Show/Hide)	Ctrl+; (semicolon key)	⌘+; (semicolon key)
Rulers (Show/Hide)	Ctrl+Shift+Alt+R	⌘+Shift+Option+R
Outlines	Ctrl+Shift+Alt+O	⌘+Shift+Option+O
Work Area (On/Off)	Ctrl+Shift+W	⌘+Shift+W

Table A-3: Panel and Window Shortcut Keys

Menu Item	Windows Shortcut	Macintosh Shortcut
Actions panel	F9	F9
Accessibility panel	Alt+F2	Option+F2
Align panel	Ctrl+K	⌘+K
Answers panel	Alt+F1	Option+F1
Color Mixer panel	Shift+F9	Shift+F9
Color Swatches panel	Ctrl+F9	⌘+F9
Components panel	Ctrl+F7	⌘+F7
Component Parameters panel	Alt+F7	Option+F7
Debugger window	Shift+F4	Shift+F4
Document properties	Ctrl+J	⌘+J
Movie Explorer panel	Alt+F3	Option+F3
Hide/Show panels	F4	F4
Info panel	Ctrl+I	⌘+I
Library panel	F11	F11
New Document	Ctrl+N	⌘+N
New window	Ctrl+Alt+N	⌘+Option+N
Output window	F2	F2
Preview in browser	F12	F12
Property inspector	Ctrl+F3	⌘+F3
Publish Flash Movie	Shift+F12	Shift+F12
Publish Settings	Ctrl+Shift+F12	Shift+Option+F12
Reference (AS booklets)	Shift+F1	Shift+F1
Scene panel	Shift+F2	Shift+F2
Test Movie	Ctrl+Enter	⌘+Return
Timeline window	Ctrl+Alt+T	⌘+Option+T
Toolbox	Ctrl+F2	⌘+F2
Transform panel	Ctrl+T	⌘+T
Using Flash MX (Help)	F1	F1

Table A-4: Edit and Modify Shortcut Keys

Menu Item	Windows Shortcut	Macintosh Shortcut
Break Apart	Ctrl+B	⌘+B
Copy	Ctrl+C	⌘+C
Copy Frames	Ctrl+Alt+C	⌘+Option+C
Cut	Ctrl+X	⌘+X
Cut Frames	Ctrl+Alt+X	⌘+Option+X
Clear Frames	Alt+Delete	Option+Delete
Distribute to Layers	Ctrl+Shift+D	⌘+Shift+D
Duplicate	Ctrl+D	⌘+D
Edit Symbols	Ctrl+E	⌘+E
Group	Ctrl+G	⌘+G
Ungroup	Ctrl+Shift+G	⌘+Shift+G
Import File	Ctrl+R	⌘+R
Open	Ctrl+O	⌘+O
Optimize	Ctrl+Shift+Alt+C	⌘+Shift+Option+C
Paste	Ctrl+V	⌘+V
Paste Frames	Ctrl+Alt+V	⌘+Option+V
Paste in Place	Ctrl+Shift+V	⌘+Shift+V
Save	Ctrl+S	⌘+S
Save As	Ctrl+Shift+S	⌘+Shift+S
Select All	Ctrl+A	⌘+A
Deselect All	Ctrl+Shift+A	⌘+Shift+A
Insert Frame	F5	F5
Remove Frame	Shift+F5	Shift+F5
Convert to Keyframe	F6	F6
Remove Keyframe	Shift+F6	Shift+F6
Convert to Blank Keyframe	Shift+F7	Shift+F7
Convert to Symbol	F8	F8
Create New Symbol	Ctrl+F8	⌘+F8
Scale & Rotate	Ctrl+Alt+S	⌘+Option+S
Remove Transform	Ctrl+Shift+Z	⌘+Shift+Z
Undo	Ctrl+Z	⌘+Z
Redo	Ctrl+Y	⌘+Y

Table A-5: Align and Arrange Shortcut Keys

Menu Item	Windows Shortcut	Macintosh Shortcut
Rotate 90 degrees CW	Ctrl+9	⌘+9
Rotate 90 degrees CCW	Ctrl+7	⌘+7
Align Left	Ctrl+Alt+1	⌘+Option+1
Align Center Vertical	Ctrl+Alt+2	⌘+Option+2
Align Right	Ctrl+Alt+3	⌘+Option+3
Align Top	Ctrl+Alt+4	⌘+Option+4
Align Center Horizontal	Ctrl+Alt+5	⌘+Option+5
Align Bottom	Ctrl+Alt+6	⌘+Option+6
Align Distribute Widths	Ctrl+Alt+7	⌘+Option+7
Align Make Same Width	Ctrl+Shift+Alt+7	⌘+Shift+Option+7
Align to Stage	Ctrl+Alt+8	⌘+Option+8
Align Distribute Heights	Ctrl+Alt+9	⌘+Option+9
Align Make Same Height	Ctrl+Shift+Alt+9	⌘+Shift+Option+9
Send to Back	Shift+Alt+↓	Shift+Option+↓
Bring to Front	Shift+Alt+↑	Shift+Option+↑
Send Backward	Ctrl+↓	⌘+↓
Bring Forward	Ctrl+↑	⌘+↑

✦　　✦　　✦

Digital Sound Basics

If you plan carefully and pay attention to technical detail, sound can add dimension to your Flash projects. That's because sound introduces another mode of sensory perception. Coordinated with visual form and motion, sound deepens the impact and can even enhance the ease of use of your Flash creation.

Cross-Reference
For detailed information on adding sound to your Flash productions, refer to Chapter 15, "Adding Sound." This chapter fully explains how to work with imported sound in Flash MX, covering topics from codecs and compression to syncing.

The Basics of Sampling and Quality

Before you begin integrating sound with your Flash project, it's important to understand the basics of digital audio. To help you with this, we've dedicated this appendix to sampling, bit resolution, and file size.

What is sound?

When you hear a sound, the volume of the sound is determined by the intensity of the vibrations, or sound waves. The *pitch* that you hear—meaning how high (treble) or low (bass)—is determined by the frequency of those vibrations (waves). The frequency of sound is measured in hertz (abbreviated as Hz). Theoretically, most humans have the ability to hear frequencies that range from 20 to 20,000 Hz. The frequency of the sound is a measure of the range of the sound—from the highest high to the lowest low. It's important to note here that, when starting to work with sound, the most common error is confusing the frequency of the sound with the recording sample.

The quality and size of sound files

When you add sound to a Flash movie, a number of factors affect the final quality of the sound and the size of the sound file. The quality of the sound is important because it determines the aesthetic experience of the sound. The file size is important because it determines how quickly (or slowly) the sound will arrive at the end user's computer. The primary factors that determine the quality and size of a sound file are sample rate and bit resolution.

Sample rate

The sample rate, measured in hertz (Hz), describes the number of times an audio signal is sampled when it is recorded digitally. In the late 1940s, Harry Nyquist and Claude Shannon developed a theorem. The theorem said that, for optimal sound quality, a sampling rate must be twice the value of the highest frequency of a signal. Thus, the higher the sample rate, the better the audio range. Generally, higher sample rates result in a richer, more complete sound. According to Nyquist and Shannon, in order for the audible range of 20 to 20,000 Hz to be sampled correctly, the audio source needs to be sampled at a frequency no lower than 40,000 Hz, or 40 kHz. This explains why CD audio — which closely resembles the source sound — is sampled at 44.1 kHz.

> **Note**   A sound *sample* refers to one "analysis" of a recorded sound, whereas a sound *file* refers to the entire collection of samples recorded, which comprise a digital recording.

The less a sound is sampled, the further the recording will deviate from the original sound. However, this tendency toward loss of the original quality of the sound yields one advantage: When the sample rate of a sound file is decreased, the file size drops proportionately. For example, a 300KB, 44.1 kHz sound file would be 150KB when saved as a 22.05 kHz file. See Table B-1 for more details on how sample rate affects quality.

Table B-1: Audio Sample Rates and Quality

Sample Rate	Quality Level	Possible Uses
48 kHz	Studio quality	Sound or music recorded to digital medium such as miniDV, DAT, DVCam, and so on
44.1 kHz	CD quality	High-fidelity sound and music
32 kHz	Near-CD quality	Professional/consumer digital camcorders
22.050 kHz	FM radio quality	Short, high-quality music clips
11.025 kHz	Acceptable for music	Longer music clips; high-quality voice; sound effects
5 kHz	Acceptable for speech	"Flat" speech; simple button sounds

Because the native playback rate of all audio cards is 44.1 kHz, sound that is destined for playback on any computer should be a multiple of 44.1. Thus, we recommend sample rates of 44.1 kHz, 22.05 kHz, and 11.025 kHz for *any* use on computers. (Although sample rates that deviate from the rule of 44.1 may sound fine on your development platform, and may sound fine on many other computers, some may have problems. This simple rule will go a long way toward reducing complaints of popping and distorted sound.) This becomes more important with Flash. When Flash imports sounds that are not multiples of 11.025, the sound file is resampled, which causes the sound to play at a lower or higher pitch than the original recording. This same logic applies to sound export, which is discussed in Chapter 15. Finally, although Flash menus list sample rates as 11, 22, and 44, these are abbreviations for the truly precise sample rates of 11.025, 22.05, and 44.1 kHz.

Bit resolution

The second key factor that influences audio quality is bit resolution (or bit depth). Bit resolution describes the number of bits used to record each audio sample. Bit resolution is increased exponentially, meaning that an 8-bit sound sample has a range of 2^8, or 256, levels, while a 16-bit sound sample has a range of 2^{16}, or 65,536, levels. Thus, a 16-bit sound is recorded with far more information than an 8-bit sound of equal length. The result of this additional information in a 16-bit sound is that background hiss is minimized, while the sound itself is clearer. The same sound recorded at 8 bits will be noisy and washed out.

A 16-bit sound file is twice the size of the same file saved at 8-bit quality. This is due to the increase in the amount of information taken to record the higher quality file. So, if your sound is too big, what can you do? Well, a sound that's been recorded at a higher bit resolution can be converted to a lower bit resolution, and a sound with a high sample rate can be converted to a lower sample rate. Although a professional studio might perform such conversions with hardware, either of these conversions can also be done with software.

For more information on down sampling and conversion, refer to Chapter 39, "Working with Audio Applications."

If you're having difficulty understanding the significance of bit depths yet are familiar with the intricacies of scanning photographic images, consider the difference between an 8-bit grayscale image and a 24-bit color image of equivalent dimensions. The file size for the 8-bit grayscale image (such as a black-and-white photograph) is much smaller than the 24-bit color image (such as a color photograph). The grayscale image doesn't have as much tonal information — only 256 levels of gray — yet the 24-bit color image records a range of 16.7 million colors. Unlike photographs, sound samples don't require anything close to a range of 16.7 million values. Sixteen-bit sound samples deliver a dynamic range of over 64,000 values, which is more than the human ear can detect.

Table B-2 lists the various bit depths of sound along with their quality level and possible uses.

Table B-2: Audio Bit Resolution and Quality

Bit Depth	Quality Level	Possible Uses
16-bit	CD quality	High-fidelity sound and music
12-bit	Near-CD quality	Professional/consumer digital camcorder audio
8-bit	FM radio quality	Short, high-quality music clips
4-bit	Acceptable for music	Longer music clips; high-quality voice; sound effects

Refer to Figures B-1 and B-2 for a comparison of the differences between sounds at different sample rates and bit depths. Both figures show a wave form derived from the same original sound file, differing only in their sample rates and bit depths. The waveform of the 16-bit 44.1 kHz sound has twice as many "points" — or samples of information — as the 8-bit 11.025 kHz sound. Because the 16-bit 44.1 kHz sound has more samples, the gap between each sample isn't as large as the gaps of the 8-bit 11.025 kHz sound. More samples result in a much smoother, cleaner sound.

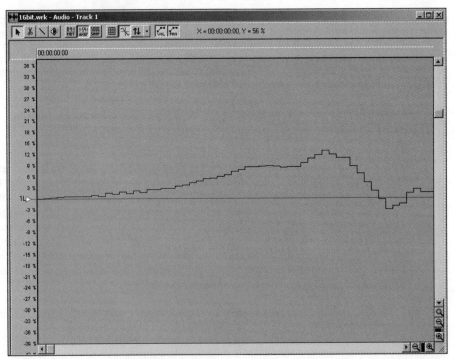

Figure B-1: This is a waveform of a sound sampled at 44.100 kHz with a 16-bit resolution, as displayed in a high-end sound application.

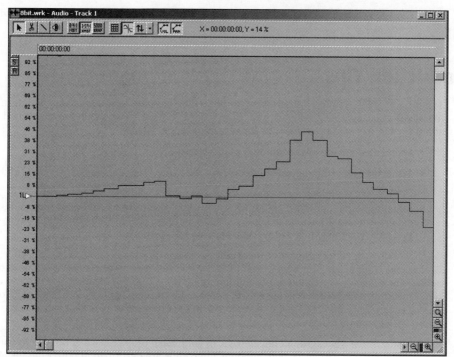

Figure B-2: Here's the same sound as shown in Figure B-1, but down-sampled to 11.025 kHz with an 8-bit resolution.

Tip

A common mistake novices make with sound is the assumption that 8-bit audio is acceptable, especially because it ought to result in a much smaller file size than 16-bit sound. This is wrong for at least two reasons. First, 8-bit is unacceptable because it sounds incredibly worse than 16-bit sound. Second, the horrible sound will not pay for itself in diminished file size because most compression codecs won't work on 8-bit sound.

Channels

Audio files are either mono (single channel) or stereo (dual channel: left and right). Stereo files are twice the size of mono files because they have twice the information. Most audio-editing applications offer the option to mix the two stereo channels together and either save or export a stereo sound to a one-channel mono sound. Most audio applications also have the ability to save the right or left channel of a stereo sound separately as a WAV or AIF file.

With the more robust, multitrack-editing applications, such as Deck 3.5, ProTools, Sound Forge, or Cool Edit, it's not unusual to work with eight or more audio tracks — limited only by your system configuration. As you may imagine, these applications give the sound artist greater control over the final sound mix. For use in Flash, these multitrack audio project files need to be "bounced" or mixed down to a stereo or mono file in order to be saved as WAV or AIF files.

Cross-Reference

For a more detailed description of this process, refer to Chapter 39, "Working with Audio Applications."

Production Tips

The primary goal of sound optimization for limited delivery networks (such as the Internet) is to deliver an acceptable quality without a large file size "cost". You should be concerned about the file size of your audio clips for several reasons.

✦ Sound files require a large amount of drive space.

✦ Managing large sound files and importing them into Flash can be cumbersome and slow.

✦ Download times for large, elaborate sound clips (even when heavily compressed upon export from Flash) can be detrimental to the appreciation of your Flash project, even if you have what may be considered a high-speed Internet connection.

When working with audio clips, it's important to create the shortest audio clips possible. That means trimming off any excess sound that you don't need, especially any blank lead-in or lead-out *handles* (also called in and out points) at the either the beginning or the end of a clip. This procedure is discussed briefly in Chapter 15, "Adding Sound," with reference to Flash's sound tools, and then again in greater detail in Chapter 39, "Working with Audio Applications," where external audio applications are introduced.

If you plan to have a background music track in your Flash project, it's a good idea to use a small audio clip that can be looped. Looping audio clips are described in both Chapter 15, "Adding Sound," and in Chapter 39, "Working with Audio Applications."

Here is a simple formula to determine the file size, in bytes of a given audio clip:

Seconds of audio × sample rate* × # of channels × (bit depth ÷ 8**) = file size

*Expressed in hertz, not kilohertz.

**There are eight bits per byte.

Thus, a 20-second stereo audio loop at 8 bits, 11 kHz would be calculated like this:

20 sec × 11,025 Hz × 2 channels × (8 bits ÷ 8 bits/byte) = 441,000 bytes = 430 KB

There are two schools of thought regarding the ideal quality of sound files for import into Flash. These schools are pretty much divided into those who have high-end sound-editing tools and those who don't. In an effort to delineate the best path for each group, we've noted the following:

✦ If you *don't* have high-end sound tools available, then you may be among those who *always* prefer to start with audio source files of the highest possible quality (16 bit, 44.1 kHz is ideal), and then use the Flash sound settings to obtain optimal compression upon export.

Cross-Reference

See Chapter 15, "Adding Sound," for detailed information on the sound export settings for Flash movies.

✦ If you *do* have high-end sound tools available, then you may prefer to compose most of your clients' music from scratch and you rarely work with the MP3 format before importing into Flash. You may also disagree with those who advise that one should bring their sound into Flash at the highest quality before optimizing. This workflow difference is attributable to the plethora of options that are available to those with high-end sound tools. We know of one sound engineer who converts all of his audio to 16-bit 22.1 kHz mono files, "with major bass reduction," *before* importing into Flash.

Cross-Reference   For more information on high-end sound tools, refer to Chapter 39, "Working with Audio Applications."

✦   ✦   ✦

Using the CD-ROM

This appendix provides you with information on the contents of the CD that accompanies this book.

Note For the latest version of this appendix, please refer to the ReadMe file, including any late-breaking updates, located in the main directory of the CD-ROM.

Here is what you will find on the CD-ROM:

✦ Explanation of System

✦ Reference to bonus chapters, tutorials, and appendixes

✦ Notes on reviewing SWF and FLA files

✦ Tips for installing and using plug-ins and applications

✦ Steps for installing and using the sendmail scripts

✦ Listing of applications and software trials

✦ Troubleshooting information and support

Before loading up the CD-ROM, you should ou must first make sure that your computer meets the minimum system requirements listed in this section. If your computer doesn't match up to most of these requirements, you may have a problem using the contents of the CD-ROM.

For Windows 9*x*, Windows 2000, Windows NT4 (with SP 4 or later), Windows Me, or Windows XP:

✦ PC with a Pentium II processor running at 300 Mhz or faster

✦ At least 96 MB of total RAM installed on your computer; for best performance, we recommend at least 128 MB. Note that additional RAM is needed to open other programs with Flash.

✦ 16-bit color monitor capable of 1024x768 (millions of colors) or better

✦ A CD-ROM drive

For Macintosh:

- ✦ Power Mac G3 running OS 9.1 or higher, or OS X 10.1 and higher

- ✦ At least 96 MB of total RAM installed on your computer; for best performance, we recommend at least 128 MB

- ✦ 16-bit color monitor capable of 1024x768 (millions of colors) or better

- ✦ A CD-ROM drive

Bonus Chapters, Tutorials, and Appendixes

The scope of updates to the core content of the *Flash MX Bible* necessitated moving some of the chapters and expert tutorials onto the CD-ROM. To help tie-in this content, cross-references were added in relevant chapters. Appendix G lists all of the chapter contributors and guest experts in alphabetical order with notes on where to find their content—in the book or on the CD-ROM. You will find PDF files on the CD-ROM for Bonus Chapters, Bonus Tutorials, and Bonus Appendixes.

Reviewing Example SWF and FLA Files

Many of the examples discussed in the text and in step-by-step tutorials are included in the relevant chapter folder on the CD-ROM. Opening the Flash movie (.swf file) is the quickest way to see how the finished example is supposed to look. The fonts should display correctly, and as long as you haven't moved the file to a new location, any loaded assets should also work.

When you open a Flash document (.fla file), you may get a warning about missing fonts. This warning simply means that you do not have the same fonts installed on your machine as the original author of the file. Select a default font and you will be able to review and edit the Flash document on your machine. Without the proper fonts installed, the layout may not appear as it was originally designed.

Note The only font files included on the CD-ROM are Craig Kroeger's vector-based miniml fonts, described in Chapter 8. Other fonts are copyrighted material, and, as such, can not be distributed on this CD-ROM.

Installing and Using Plug-Ins and Applications

In the software folder of the CD-ROM, you'll find the trial versions of many of the applications discussed in this book, particularly those from Part IX.

On a Macintosh, go to the specific application's folder and double-click the installation file. Then follow the installer's instructions to proceed.

On a PC, go to the specific application's folder and either unzip the installation ZIP file or double-click the installation EXE file.

Installing and Using the sendmail Scripts

Chapter 30, "Sending Data In and Out of Flash," introduces the concept of creating Flash forms that interact with server-side scripts. These scripts need to be installed on a live Web server in order to work properly with the Flash movies created in the lesson. You may need the assistance of your Web server administrator to get the appropriate script working correctly.

sendmail.asp

This script is written in ASP (Active Server Page) for use on a Microsoft IIS Web server (or equivalent). This script works in conjunction with a free version of the w3 JMail server component. While the sendmail.asp script file is in the ch30 folder of the CD-ROM, you will need to download the latest version of the w3 JMail component at

```
http://tech.dimac.net/websites/dimac/website/products/w3JMail
```

Download the free personal edition of this software if you are using this example for educational or personal use. Follow the standard installation steps for the JMail component, and place the sendmail.asp script in a directory on the IIS server where ASP scripts have permission to run and execute.

In a text editor such as Notepad, BBEdit, or Macromedia Dreamweaver MX, you will need to change the location of the SMTP server information in the sendmail.asp script. In lines 3 and 4 of the sendmail.asp file, you will see

```
smtpServer = "flaction.com"
smtpPort = 25
```

Change the value of `smtpServer` to the SMTP server for your Web hosting provider or ISP (Internet Service Provider). Most SMTP servers use port 25 — if your SMTP server requires a different port number, specify it for the `smtpPort` value.

Caution   Do not leave the flaction.com server address as the default SMTP server. You will not be able to access this SMTP from another Web server.

Once the script and the component are installed on your IIS server, you will be able to create your own custom Flash form as described in Chapter 30.

sendmail.pl

To use Joey Lott's sendmail.pl Perl script, you need to have Perl 5 installed on your Web server. You may need the assistance and permission of the system administrator of your Internet service provider (ISP) or Internet presence provider (IPP) to install (or use) Perl 5. After it is installed, upload the script file, sendmail.pl, to a directory or folder that is accessible by Perl. This folder may need to have proper permissions in order for Web users to execute the script file.

In a text editor such as Notepad, BBEdit, or Macromedia Dreamweaver MX, you may need to edit the first line of the script to indicate the path to the Perl files on your server. On line 19, you can remove the comment code (#) and specify a default e-mail to which output from the script will be sent. Meaning, if you wish to omit a variable in the Flash movie ActionScript, then you can specify an e-mail address on line 19. If you are receiving errors from the script during trials, you may need to adjust the location parameter of the Web server's `sendmail` program (*not* the script file, but the actual program the server uses to send e-mail), specified in line 24.

After you have the script installed, follow the "Creating a Flash Form" section in Chapter 30 to create a fully functional form in your Flash movies.

Note   You need to modify the `LoadVars` object actions to refer to your script's URL instead of the `flashmxbible.com` script URL.

Applications

The CD-ROM included with this book aids you with many examples and tutorials by providing relevant files and software trials, including the following:

✦ Trial versions (Macintosh and Windows) of Macromedia Flash MX.

✦ Limited edition versions of Craig Kroeger's vector-based fonts from miniml.com, as described in Chapter 8.

✦ Evaluation versions of some SWF-compatible applications and helpful color utilities, including Swift3D from Electric Rain, Inc., ColorSafe from BoxTop Software, and Color Schemer from Digital Studios, LLC.

✦ Limited-edition version of the new sendmail.asp script used for the Flash form lesson in Chapter 30. This ASP script requires Microsoft IIS (Internet Information Server) or equivalent. You can also find the original sendmail.pl script (written in Perl) that Joey Lott created for the *Flash 5 Bible*. Please refer to the explanation of how to use these scripts, included in the previous section of this appendix.

✦ Pre-built components for alpha effects and text loading, scripted by Robert Reinhardt and integrated with project examples in Chapters 20 and 32.

✦ Just about every FLA and SWF file that is discussed in the book, including those shown in examples from guest experts.

Tip   Other applications or utilities discussed in the book can be found online. For a list of relevant Web links, refer to the **links.html** document included in the main directory of the CD-ROM.

Shareware programs are fully functional, trial versions of copyrighted programs. If you like particular programs, register with their authors for a nominal fee and receive licenses, enhanced versions, and technical support. *Freeware programs* are copyrighted games, applications, and utilities that are free for personal use. Unlike shareware, these programs do not require a fee or provide technical support. *GNU software* is governed by its own license, which is included inside the folder of the GNU product. See the GNU license for more details.

Trial, demo, or evaluation versions are usually limited either by time or functionality (such as not allowing you to save projects). Some trial versions are very sensitive to system date changes. If you alter your computer's date, the programs may "time out" and will no longer be functional.

Troubleshooting

If you have difficulty installing or using any of the materials on the companion CD, try the following solutions:

✦ **Turn off any anti-virus software that you may have running.** Installers sometimes mimic virus activity and can make your computer incorrectly believe that it is being infected by a virus. (Be sure to turn the anti-virus software back on later.)

✦ **Close all running programs.** The more programs you're running, the less memory is available to other programs. Installers also typically update files and programs; if you keep other programs running, installation may not work properly.

✦ **Reference the ReadMe:** Please refer to the ReadMe file located at the root of the CD-ROM for the latest product information at the time of publication.

If you still have trouble with the CD-ROM, please call the Wiley Customer Care phone number: (800) 762-2974. Outside the United States, call 1 (317) 572-3994. You can also contact Wiley Customer Service by e-mail at techsupdum@wiley.com. Wiley Publishing, Inc. will provide technical support only for installation and other general quality control items; for technical support on the applications themselves, consult the program's vendor or author.

✦   ✦   ✦

Contact and Bibliography Information

Chapter Contributors

Allardice, Simon
Scottsdale, AZ, USA
simon@clingfish.com
www.clingfish.com
✦ Chapter 42, "Working with Dreamweaver MX"

⇨ A Web developer, trainer + writer ⇨ with seventeen years programming experience, he has pretty much done everything you can do with a computer ⇨ created the inaugural Web Graphics program for SIGGRAPH 2002 ⇨ Simon currently works on www.clingfish.com, creating extensions that make it easier, faster and smoother to build database-driven Web sites.;

Bazar, Andrew (with Lee, David)
Sidney, NSW, Australia
andrewb@spike.com.au
www.spike.com.au
✦ Chapter 34, "Optimizing Your Flash Movies," on the CD-ROM

⇨ Senior Multimedia Designer for Spike ⇨ rated the top interactive agency in Australia by B&T Weekly magazine ⇨ winner of the IDN "best entertainment Web site '99 - '00" + an ATOM award for the flashed lemonruski site ⇨ Andrew has lectured on Flash at the KvB Institute of Technology in North Sydney for the last year and a half.

Brossier, Véronique
New York, NY, USA
veronique@v-ro.com
www.v-ro.com
✦ Chapter 33, "Creating a Game in Flash"

⇨ Currently programs and designs games + interaction design for Web sites + museum exhibitions ⇨ teaches "Interactivity in Flash" at the Interactive Telecommunications Program at New York University ⇨ Véronique is equally interested in art + technology.

deHaan, Jen & Peter
Vancouver, BC, Canada
jepo@ejepo.com
peter@mosaicinternet.com
www.flash-mx.com
✦ Chapter 44, "Working with ColdFusion MX"

⇨ Jen + Peter combine their knowledge to create effective, streamlined + engaging productions ⇨ they focus on the integration of Flash with server-side technology, using ColdFusion PHP + XML ⇨ Peter has been a Web developer since 1998, working on the backend of many large-scale sites + is currently a lead programmer at Mosiac Media Inc ⇨ Jen has a BFA in developmental art + recently graduated from the Vancouver Film School with top honors.

Glennon, Dermot
Vancouver, BC, Canada
dermot@toque.ca
www.toque.ca
✦ Chapter 40, "Working with 3D Graphics"

⇨ Founder + Interactive Director of toque industries ⇨ toque is a small company of fearless, thoughtful image-makers who focus within the graphic realms of print + new media design ⇨ Dermot's goal is to create high-caliber work that is both innovative + client-centered.

Lee, David (with Bazar, Andrew)
Sidney, NSW, Australia
fretgrinder@comcen.com.au
www.url.com
✦ Chapter 34, "Optimizing Your Flash Movies," on the CD-ROM

Mebberson, Scott
Adelaide, SA, Australia
scott@pixelogic.org
www.pixelogic.org
✦ QuickStart
✦ Chapter 35,"Getting Your Code Under Control," on the CD-ROM
✦ Chapter 36, "Solving Problems in Your Movies," on the CD-ROM

⇨ A Flash developer based in Adelaide, Australia ⇨ works for himself writing chapters for Flash books, editing Flash books + developing Flash-based applications ⇨ pixelogic.org is his home on the Web, where he shares his wares with the community ⇨ Pixelogic is a Flash experimental site, offering Scott's source code + interesting experiments.

Moschella, William
Hartford, CT, USA
bill@timeritemedia.com
www.timeritemedia.com
www.deluxesounds.com
✦ Chapter 39, "Working with Audio Applications"

⇨ After acquiring a degree in 20th Century music theory + composition, he opened his own recording studio where he applied his engineering techniques to sound for digital environments ⇨ scored music for radio + television advertising before discovering Flash ⇨ Bill now works on sound for CD-ROMs + Web sites, including www.deluxesounds.com, and www.step2production.com.

Guest Experts

Bazley, Richard
Bazley Films
Corsham, England, UK
richard@bazleyfilms.com
www.bazleyfilms.com
✦ Tutorial: "2D Character Animation," on the CD-ROM: XRef in ch13

➪ Was a Lead Animator on such films as Disney's *Hercules* + Warner Bros. *The Iron Giant* ➪ now heads a studio that can deliver top-notch animation in 2D or 3D for film + broadcast ➪ clients include the BBC, Channel 5, High Eagle Ent., Telemagination, 4:2:2, Grove International, Mousepower Productions, The ALKEMI Group, Future Publishing, Varga, Hahn Film, Bermuda Shorts and Hart TV ➪ Richard was one of the first to use Flash for a theatrically released animated short, *The Journal of Edwin Carp,* sponsored by Macromedia + Wacom + featuring the voice of Hugh Laurie (*Stuart Little, 101 Dalmatians*).

Brown, Scott
Los Angeles, CA, USA
sbrown@artcenter.edu
www.spicybrown.com
✦ Tutorial: "Designing for Usability," in Chapter 3
✦ Tutorial: "Leveraging Fireworks to Streamline Production," in Chapter 37

➪ Graduated from Art Center College of Design with a degree in product design ➪ has worked in new media development for guess.com + did interface design for rampt.com ➪ teaches Flash classes for Art Center College of Design ➪ Scott currently does Web development for tekniondna.com, an office-furniture design company in Pasadena.

Corsaro, Sandro
sandro corsaro animation
Hermosa Beach, California, USA
info@sandrocorsaro.com
www.sandrocorsaro.com
✦ Tutorial: "The Strategy of Character Design," in Chapter 13

➪ A pure Flash animation specialist trained in traditional animation ➪ has created projects for Intel, McDonalds, MCA Records, Nestle, + E Music ➪ Recently completed a book entitled *The Flash Animator*, for New Riders Publishing ➪ invited to speak at SIGGRAPH 2002 on the future of Flash for broadcast ➪ Sandro has taught Flash animation seminars for Art Center of Pasadena + for lynda.com's Ojai Digital Art Center.

deChristopher, Brock
Providence, RI, USA
brock@guitaryoga.com
www.guitaryoga.net
✦ Tutorial: "Dynamic Sound Design," on the CD-ROM: XRef in ch27

➪ Son of a painter + grandson of a graphic designer ➪ studied music with Pozzi Escot + Hal Crook ➪ has performed on HBO, opened for the Village People + played on the helipad of the World Trade Center ➪ has conducted flash workshops for RISD + Fraunhofer CRCG ➪ is a member of the 2002 SIGGRAPH Web graphics jury ➪ maintains www.guitaryoga.com as an experimental site ➪ Brock is currently working on www.wernerdesign.net.

deHaan, Jen
Vancouver, BC, Canada
jepo@ejepo.ca
www.ejepo.com
✦ Tutorial: "Comparing Video Compression," on the CD-ROM: XRef in ch17
✦ Tutorial: "Using Embedded Fonts with Components," in Chapter 29

⇨ Working full time in the new media field is a dream for this aspiring motion graphics designer ⇨ Flash MX has inspired her to focus on this software above all others on her hard drive ⇨ lives for compression, loves Cleaner 5 + After Effects just about as much as coffee, but not as much as Flash ⇨ Jen thinks components are cool.

Downey, Doug
Freshink Image Design
Stratford, ON, Canada
design@freshink.net
www.freshink.net
✦ Tutorial: "Animation in CorelDRAW 10 Graphics Suite," on the CD-ROM: XRef in ch38

⇨ Started in the sign making industry ⇨ now focuses purely on design ⇨ when he found a program to take the vectors he created + make them move, he fell in love again ⇨ (Doug's wife, Jane, + 5 children are his other loves) ⇨ took up the challenge of doing a Flash project for a local company + never looked back ⇨ Doug's motto is "learn to do, by doing!"

Dundon, MD
Flash411
Oakland, CA, USA
info@flash411.com
http://www.flash411.com
✦ Tutorial: "Storyboarding and Planning Interactivity," on the CD-ROM: XRef in ch3

⇨ A filmmaker and experience designer ⇨ found Flash when it was still known as FutureSplash, while working in Director doing interface design + CD-ROMs ⇨ credited with having taught the first Flash classes in the world ⇨ has a new tutorial CD-ROM, *Inside Flash MX: Production Essentials* ⇨ MD is founder of Paradox Productions (film) + Flash411, an ui and prototype design business.

Elliott, Shane
Timberfish
Studio City, CA, USA
shane@timberfish.com
www.timberfish.com
✦ Tutorial: "Using XML Sockets with a Flash Movie," in Chapter 30

⇨ A designer, programmer, teacher + writer with nine years of online design + web experience ⇨ worked with TBWA\Chiat\Day to deliver online Flash ads that are less intrusive + more compelling ⇨ continues to work on projects with companies such as Infiniti, Toyota + Siebel ⇨ currently developing an online University-level Flash course with education2Go. com ⇨ Shane now focuses on www.timberfish.com to bring artistic communities together under one domain to share + learn from one another.

Honselaar, Chris
HTMwell Holistic Multimedia
Groningen, the Netherlands
flash@htmwell.com
www.htmwell.com
✦ Tutorial: "Introduction to XML and Flash," in Chapter 30

⇨ An academic educational programmer ⇨ develops multimedia apps in C++ and for the Web platform ⇨ htmwell is a company that develops informative software and Web sites ⇨ discovered Flash while experimenting with digital video overlay ⇨ after immediately finding bugs with Flash and QuickTime and through no end of complaining to Macromedia, began his relationship with Flash ⇨ Chris claims to like danger.

Jamieson, Justin
mediumLarge
Toronto, ON, Canada
justin@mediumLarge.com
www.mediumLarge.com
✦ Tutorial: "Using Propellerhead's Rebirth to Create Loops for Flash," in Chapter 39

⇨ Cofounder of mediumLarge ⇨ starting using his first computer when he was eight years old ⇨ years later, after studying design + cinematography, combined his training with his computing knowledge to work in new media design ⇨ Justin's dream is to create an old-school MP3 ghetto blaster.

Jordan, Eric
President and Chief Creative Officer
2Advanced Studios
Aliso Viejo, California, USA
ejordan@2advanced.com
www.designinsites.com
www.2advanced.com
✦ Tutorial: "Interface Design," in Chapter 3

⇨ President, Founding Partner + Creative Visionary behind 2advanced Studios ⇨ leads a team of accomplished designers + developers to build unique + compelling Web sites ⇨ 2advanced has been recognized as a finalist in two FlashForward conference exhibitions ⇨ Eric has served as a contributing author in multiple book publications, including: *New Masters of Flash, Flash 5 Bible, Flash 5 Creative Web Animation + Flash MX Magic.*

Kroeger, Craig
Miniml Fonts
Somewhere, USA
craig@miniml.com
www.miniml.com
✦ Sidebar: "Using Miniml Fonts," in Chapter 8

⇨ Creates Flash-friendly, vector-based pixel fonts perfect for large or small screen applications available at www.miniml.com ⇨ The purpose behind miniml is to encourage functional + beautiful design by providing inspiration + resources ⇨ Craig's miniml fonts are also featured in *Flash Enabled*, released by New Riders in 2002.

Lo, Timothy
Vancouver, BC, Canada
design@meatcleavermedia.com
www.meatcleavermedia.com
✦ Tutorial: "Interfacing Miva with Flash Movies," on the CD-ROM: XRef in ch30

⇨ His interests sparked from a simple Commodore 64, a "pen" program + a few plottable points ⇨ with healthy mix of creative exploration + formal education, he creates innovative work ⇨ years of experimenting with Flash + Miva led him to come up with solutions to help Miva developers use Flash with as much ease as users of other server-side programming languages ⇨ Tim continually strives to become a true "A-List" Flash Guru.

Lott, Joey
North Hollywood, CA, USA
joey@cleardigital.com
www.person13.com
✦ sendmail.pl script on the CD-ROM: XRef in ch30

⇨ Co-author of the *Macromedia Flash MX ActionScript Bible* ⇨ runs Person13, an Internet consulting company based in Los Angeles specializing in J2EE solutions ⇨ Joey is an independent thinker, a self-described genius, and a real nice guy.

Moock, Colin
Toronto, ON, Canada
colin@moock.org
www.moock.org
www.moock.org/unity
✦ Tutorial: "Filling the Browser Window by Using the <FRAMESET> Tag," on the CD-ROM: XRef in ch22
✦ Tutorial: "Unify the Web: Multiuser Flash Content," in Chapter 30

⇨ An independent Web guru with a passion for networked creativity + expression ⇨ author of the world-renowned guide to Flash programming, *ActionScript: The Definitive Guide* (O'Reilly & Associates, 2001 www.oreilly.com/catalog/actscript) ⇨ runs one of the Web's most venerable Flash developer sites ⇨ Colin's latest project is Unity, a Flash socket server for multi-user content.

Nisinson, Dorian
Dorian Nisinson Design
New York, NY, USA
dorian@nisinson.com
www.nisinson.com
www.flashcentral.com
✦ Tutorial, "Creating Faux 3D," on the CD-ROM: XRef in ch9

⇨ Has her own motion graphics company, Dorian Nisinson Design ⇨ when asked how near she lives to New York City, replied, "You couldn't get any closer, I was born and raised and live there — right uptown." ⇨ discovered Flash when it was still Future Splash, just before MM bought it ⇨ Dorian is cofounder of www.FlashCentral.com + designed the graphic intro for www.flashability.org.

Nisselson, Jane
Virtual Beauty
New York, NY, USA
vb@vbnyc.com
www.vbnyc.com
✦ Tutorial: "The Human Interface," on the CD-ROM: XRef in ch8

⇨ Founder of Virtual Beauty, a company that designs motion-based media to represent each client's voice consistently for all marketing purposes ⇨ clients include Fairchild Publications, Condé Nast, Chanel, Barneys NY, Clinique, MAC, Advance Media Group, the American Museum of the Moving Image + the United Nations Population Fund ⇨ Jane is a graduate of MIT Media Lab + worked at the New York Institute of Technology as a software developer + animator before launching her own company.

Parameswaran, Viswanath (Vish)
CTO
FastCurve
Singapore
vnath@pacific.net.sg
www.fastcurve.com
✦ Appendix B: "Multilingual Content in Flash," on the CD-ROM: XRef in ch8

⇨ Creates Web-based + standalone multilingual applications using Flash ⇨ Vish has shared his knowledge of multilingual content management for Flash development with audiences at the Flashforward conferences in San Francisco + Amsterdam, and at the Flash Kit Singapore conference in 2001.

Plant, Darrel
Moshofsky/Plant
Portland, OR, USA
dplant@moshplant.com
www.moshplant.com
✦ Tutorial: "Animation on Bézier Curves," on CD-ROM: XRef in ch27

⇨ Designer, publisher, editor, writer, electronic prepress specialist, multimedia geek + politician ⇨ has written for magazines including *The Dragon*, *Step-by-Step*, *WIRED*, *The Net*, *Lingo Users Journal*, *Macromedia User Journal* + *Macworld* ⇨ author + contributor for several books including *Special Edition Using Flash 5* (Que, 2001) + *Director 8.5 Studio* (Friends of Ed 2001) ⇨ Plant received 23 percent of the vote in the 1994 Democratic primary for Oregon State House of Representatives District 14.

Purgason, Todd
JUXT Interactive
Newport Beach, CA, USA
toddhead@juxtinteractive.com
www.juxtinteractive.com
www.juxtinteractive.com/deconstruction
www.juxtinteractive.com/toddhead
✦ Tutorial: "Streamlined Workflow: FreeHand and Flash," in Chapter 38

⇨ Creative Director for JUXT Interactive ⇨ cited as one of today's top ten Web designers in the world by Create Online Magazine + the Internet Professional Publishers Association (IPPA) ⇨ an author + international speaker on the subject of interactive Web design ⇨ completed a book titled *Flash deCONSTRUCTION* (New Riders, 2001) ⇨ Todd has led Juxt in creating innovative work for clients like Sketchers, Billabong, Macromedia, Kawasaki, Reef, Red Bull, OmniSky, Nortel, Toshiba, Fujitsu, J.F.Shea Companies, TBWA\Chiat\Day, FCB + many others.

Reed, Arena
Santa Cruz, CA, USA
arena@visualarena.com
www.visualarena.com
✦ Tutorial: "Combining Flash with the Natural Beauty of Painter 7," on the CD-ROM: XRef in ch37

⇨ An artist + designer who uses traditional + digital tools ⇨ has been a member of the Painter development team since version 4 ⇨ When she isn't in the studio, Arena enjoys bicycling, gardening + field sketching.

Richards, Mike
Macromedia
San Francisco, CA, USA
miker@macromedia.com
www.macromedia.com
✦ Tutorial: "Creating Printable Paper Airplanes," in Chapter 27

⇨ Originally from Cleveland, Ohio ⇨ developed his Flash prowess creating animated Flash cards and games at American Greetings (www.americangreetings.com) ⇨ in his free time, Mike continues to develop www.hipid.com.

Robertson, James
EDesign.uk.com Ltd
Crowborough, England, UK
james@edesign.uk.com
www.edesign.uk.com
✦ Tutorial: "Complex Hit Detection on the Z Axis," on the CD-ROM

Spiridellis, Gregg
JibJab Media, Inc.
Raleigh Studios
Manhattan Beach, CA, USA
getinfo@jibjab.com
www.JibJab.com
✦ Tutorial: "JibJab.com's Collage Animation Workflow," in Chapter 13

⇨ JibJab Media creates + produces original Internet + broadcast animation ⇨ Gregg + Evan Spiridellis founded JibJab in November 1999, seizing the opportunity to broadcast their creative productions directly to a worldwide audience ⇨ since then, millions of people have visited JibJab.com ⇨ JibJab's productions have been broadcast on FOX, ABC, CNN, WB, Noggin + Nickelodeon.

Turner, Bill
Turnertoons Productions, Inc.
Melbourne, FL, USA
bill@turnertoons.com
www.turnertoons.com
✦ Tutorial: "Lip-Synching Cartoons," in Chapter 13

⇨ Author of a new book titled *Flash 5 Cartoons and Games FX/Design* (Coriolis, 2001) ⇨ co-author of *Flash the Future,* a book on the subject of graphics and games specific to dealing with Pocket PCs ⇨ Bill created one of the first interactive animated cartoon sites, "Dubes," in early 1996.

Wolfe, Bentley
Macromedia
Richardson, TX, USA
bwolfe@macromedia.com
www.macromedia.com/support
✦ Tutorial: "Using FreeHand with Flash," on the CD-ROM: XRef in Chapter 38

⇨ Flash found him while he was working on the tech support teams for FreeHand + Director when Macromedia bought FutureSplash ⇨ become an online support evangelist, focusing only on Flash ⇨ has made contributions to thousands of Flash sites by helping Flash users online ⇨ Bentley is the full-time single father of three girls who like to ride motorcycles as much as he does.

Wolter, Sascha
Duesseldorf, Germany
wolter@flashforum.de
www.saschawolter.de
www.flashforum.de
✦ Tutorial: "Scriptless Flash Player Detection," on the CD-ROM

⇨ A professional multimedia developer and consultant for online and offline media ⇨ also a freelance author who has contributed articles to a number of German magazines ⇨ his books are the best-selling publications on Flash in Germany ⇨ has been giving lectures and training on these topics for many years ⇨ part of the first German TV-series on Flash ⇨ Sascha is the founder of the German Macromedia User Group and the most-visited German Flash support site, www.flashforum.de.

✦   ✦   ✦

Index

Symbols & Numerics

& (ampersand) variable name/value pair separator, 687

&& (ampersands) logical AND operator, 690, 692

* (asterisk) multiplication operator, 689

| | (bars) logical OR operator, 690, 692

{} (braces, curly) action delimiters, 544

^ (caret) carriage return escape, 923, 928

: (colon) subroutine prefix, 699

= (equals sign) assignment operator, 681, 684, 689

== (equals signs) equality operator, 690, 691

===(F6) (equals signs, F6) equality operator, 690

! (exclamation mark) logical NOT operator, 690

!= (exclamation mark, equals sign) inequality operator, 690, CDBC 49

> (greater than sign)
  alphabetically after operator, 690
  greater than operator, 690

>= (greater than sign, equals sign)
  alphabetically after or same as operator, 690
  greater than or equal to operator, 690

< (less than sign)
  alphabetically before operator, 690
  less than operator, 690

<= (less than sign, equals sign)
  alphabetically before or same as operator, 690
  less than or equal to operator, 690

<> (less than sign, greater than sign) inequality operator, 690, CDBA 25

- (minus sign) subtraction operator, 689

( ) (parentheses)
  function argument delimiters, 747, 756
  operator group delimiters, 690

.. (periods) path notation characters, 564

+ (plus sign)
  addition operator, 689
  concatenation operator, 690, 743
  variable name/value pair separator, 687

" " (quotation marks)
  parameter name/value delimiters, 640
  string delimiters, 683, 690

; (semicolon) action line suffix, 544

/ (slash)
  division operator, 689
  path notation character, 564

// (slashes) comment prefix, 113

_ (underscore)
  movie level prefix, 809
  property prefix, 706

3D CAFE Web site, 1025

3D graphics
  animation, 302, 387–388, 1026–1030, 1042–1045, 1047–1055
  array transformation, 1035–1036, 1037
  atmosphere, simulating depth using, 1020, 1021
  axes, 1020, CDBT 57–60
  camera movement, 1042–1045, 1047–1049
  cylinder object, 1034–1035
  depth-of-field effect, 1022
  Director 3D engine, 1098
  explosion effect, 1040–1042, 1054
  exporting, 1025–1030
  extrusion effect, 1022–1023
  file format, 1025
  file size considerations, 1022
  Flash, creating using, 264–265, 290, 1026–1028, CDBT 19–28
  focus, simulating depth using, 1022
  frame effects, 1027, 1028, 1029
  glossiness, 1039
  gradient, simulating depth using, 264–265, 290, CDBT 24–27
  horizon, 1020, 1021
  importing, 42, 1025–1030, 1055–1056
  kinematics, inverse, 1024
  lathing, creating 3D object via, 1033–1035
  layers, simulating depth using, 1027, 1030
  lighting, 264–265, 1023, 1045–1047
  material (object surface property), 1038–1039
  mesh, working with, 1040

Continued

3D graphics *(continued)*
  perspective, 1020–1022, 1026, CDBT 57–58,
      CDBT 102
  planning, 1031
  POV (point of view), 1031
  projection, isometric, 1020
  projection, orthographic, 1020
  rotation, using, 1027, 1028, 1029, 1045
  scaling, simulating depth using, 1026, 1027,
      CDBT 57–59
  shadow, 264, 269, 1042, 1045–1046, 1049
  software, specialized, 1025, 1030
  specular level, 1039
  sphere object, 264–265
  spline, creating 3D object via lathing,
      1033–1035
  storyboarding, 1031–1032
  symmetry, advantages of using, 1028
  texture mapping, 1023–1024, 1033
  vanishing point, 1021, CDBT 57–58
  wireframe, 1024
3Dgraphic.eps (on the CD), 485
3ds format, 1025
3ds max software
  Animate key, 1045
  array function, 1035, 1037
  Attach feature, 1035
  Box feature, 1036–1037
  Camera View, 1043
  Cameras button, 1042
  Command panel, 1035, 1036
  Convert To Editable Mesh feature, 1040
  Copy button, 1037
  Create tab, 1033, 1042
  Cylinder feature, 1034
  demo, downloading, 1030
  Detach button, 1041
  Display tab, 1036, 1048
  Edit Geometry feature, 1040, 1041
  Editable Mesh function, 1040
  exporting content to Flash, 1031, 1049,
      1055–1056
  Flip Normals feature, 1034
  Glossiness control, 1039
  Hide by Hit feature, 1036
  Hierarchy tab, 1035
  IN interpolation flyout, 1048
  Lathe feature, 1034
  lighting features, 1045–1046
  Material Editor, 1038–1039
  Mesh Gradient feature, 1049
  Modify panel, 1033, 1035, 1040–1041, 1048
  Motion tab, 1048
  Orbit tool, 1045
  Pan tool, 1045
  Parameters rollout, 1034
  Perspective View, 1043
  Quad Menu, 1040
  Renderer options, 1049
  Shader Basic parameters, 1039
  Shapes tab, 1033
  Show Trajectories button, 1048
  Soften control, 1039
  Specular level, 1039
  storyboarding, using, 1031–1032
  Swift3D integration with, 1030, 1049, 1052
  Time Configuration Key, 1043
  time slider, 1045, 1049
  Truck tool, 1045
  vertex sub select feature, 1033
  Weld Core feature, 1034
  Weld vertices function, 1049
  Whiteness slider bar, 1039
  Zoom features, 1041, 1047
2advanced Studios, 64–72
2D Character Animation tutorial (Bazley),
      CDBT 29–35

A

A HREF HTML tag, 646, 651, 880–881
About.com Graphics Software page, 669
acceleration, conveying in animation, 307, 321,
      1047–1049
Access database software, 1127–1130
accessibility
  browser considerations, 43
  button text, 604–605
  Flash Player, 33
  MSAA specification, 582
  screen reader, 45, 582, 602–605
Accessibility panel, 90, 603
ACID PRO software, 998, 999, 1017–1018

.act files, 204

Action Script Viewer utility, 619

action/reaction, conveying in animation,
308–309

actions. *See also specific actions*
authoring modes, 533–534
backwards compatibility, 535
CGI script, using remote, 610
conflict, 536, CDBC 65
deleting, 534
deprecated, 535
described, 531
Director, calling from, 1112
Director Lingo, interactivity with, 1099–1102
event handler, combining with, 542–544
expression, assigning using, 539, 682–683
Flash version 6, recognized by, CDBA 28–38
Flash version 5, recognized by, CDBA 28–36
Flash version 4, recognized by, CDBA 26–27
Flash version 3, recognized by, CDBA 26
Flash version 2, recognized by, CDBA 25
Flash version 1, recognized by, CDBA 25
interactivity, relation to, 531
keyframe, association with, 547–548
loop, adding to actions list, 697
method, relation to, 707
movie control, 534
nesting, 695, 721
placement confusion, CDBC 64
preview, 610
Script pane, adding to, 534
Test Movie environment, in, 610
text field, executing from, 880–881

Actions ⇨Conditions/Loops, 691

Actions ⇨Miscellaneous Actions, 562

Actions ⇨Movie Control, 543

Actions ⇨Movie Control ⇨Stop, 549

Actions panel
accessing, 532
actions list organization, 678
Actions pane, 533, 678
Auto Format option, CDBC 27
booklet access from, 534
breakpoint controls, CDBC 55–57
Check Syntax button, 678
code hinting feature, 560, 563, 1080, 1095,
CDBC 29–30
customizing, 15–16
described, 15–16, 37
Esc shortcut key definition, CDBC 28–29
Expert mode, 533–534, 562, 677, CDBC 26–27
Expression field, 576
introduced, 15–16
line number display, 771
Normal mode, 533–534, 677, CDBC 26
Parameters area, 537
Script pane, 534
Status bar, 536
title, 532

ActionScript. *See also* expressions; functions;
methods; variables
acceptance as programming language, 36, 40
Auto Format option, CDBC 27
breakpoint, 697, CDBC 55–59, CDBC 60
Button instance, adding to, 181
code, centralized, CDBC 37
code, including descriptive definition in,
CDBC 38–40
code, placing, CDBC 36–37
code, reusable, CDBC 37
code, stepping through, CDBC 57–59
code, storing in external file, 680, 909, 1096,
CDBC 31–34, CDBC 39
code hinting, 560, 563, 1080, 1095, CDBC
29–30
coding, importance of planning, CDBC 23–24
color, syntax, CDBC 30–31
commenting, CDBC 38, CDBC 63
condition, checking, 690–695, 696, 697, 743
described, 532
dot syntax, 557–559, 707, 1059
Dreamweaver MX, writing in, 1081, 1094–1096
ECMA-262 specification conformance, 558
editor, 37
either/or situation, 743
equation, 683, 738
error message display in Output window,
CDBC 46
event model, 24–26, 37
history, 40
HTML integration, 33
indentation, CDBC 27, CDBC 29

Continued

ActionScript *(continued)*
   JavaScript similarity, 40
   layer order, effect on execution order, CDBC 66
   library, storing code in, CDBC 34
   line number display, 771, CDBC 28
   Lingo compared, 1099
   Lingo/ActionScript property conversion chart, 1111–1112
   loop statements, 694–698
   math operations, 689, 742–743
   Movie Explorer, filtering using, 188
   object definition in separate `.as` file, 1096
   object model, 37
   operators, 689–690
   procedure, 746
   QuickTime programming, 1059
   Remote document, 1096
   search and replace within code, CDBC 35–36
   SSAS, 1119
   subroutine, 698–699
   .swf file, extracting from, 619
   syntax, checking, 678, CDBC 46
   system capability checking, 36
   text field scripting, 23–24, 877–878
   text file, inserting in code, 680
   timeline, controlling using, 335, 336
   XML integration, 33
ActionScript Dictionary, 86, 87, 675, 676
Active Server Pages. *See* ASP
ActiveSync software, 1156–1157, 1158
ActiveX
   Flash Player control detection, 46, 622, 645, 646
   Flash Player control download, 643
   Flash Player control versus plug-in, 642–643
   ID code, specifying in HTML page, 636
   location, specifying in HTML page, 636
ad banners, 622, 953–956
`add` concatenation operator, 690
`addListener` method, 719, 842
`addLoader` function, 907–908, 911
Adobe TypeManager. *See* ATM
Adobe Web site, 44, 409

ADPCM (Adaptive Differential Pulse-Code Modulation), 422, 423, 440
Advanced Effect dialog box, 288, 773
.aep files, 410
After Effects
   art filters, 1077
   exporting Flash content from, CDBT 40–41
   importing image sequence into, 409–415
   importing movie into, 1067
   trial version download, 409
   video compression, CDBT 40–41
Aftershock software, CDBT 49
AI image. *See also* Illustrator
   exporting from Flash, 404, 994, 995
   exporting from Illustrator, 990
   importing, 454, 478–480
   3D graphic format, as, 1025
AICC (Ausingtion Industry CBT Committee), 622–623
AIF file import, 420
AIGA Professional Practices in Graphic Design (Crawford), 56
ALaw 2:1 codec, 1064
alienzone.com, 669
Align panel, 155, 157–158, 276
alignment
   button, 182
   color fill, 258
   drawing element, 155, 156, 157–158
   FreeHand SWF export, considerations in, 984
   Motion tweening, in, 328
   movie on HTML page, 625–626, 637, 638, 1082
   text, 228, 230, 231
Allaire Corporation, 1118
Allardice, Simon (Web developer), 1185
`#alpha` Director Lingo property, 1111
alpha effects. *See* transparency
`_alpha` property, 709, 1111
`alphabitmap.fla` (on the CD), 959
American Standard Code for Information Interchange character encoding. *See* ASCII
ampersand (&) variable name/value pair separator, 687

ampersands (&&) logical AND operator, 690, 692

anchor point, drawing, 135, 144, 145, 147

anchors, named
> browser back/forward buttons, interacting with using, 17–18, 512, 601
>
> browser support, 17, 601
>
> described, 512
>
> Flash Player support, 512
>
> frame label as, 513
>
> keyframe, automatic assignment to first, 102
>
> movie timeline, adding to, 601–602
>
> naming, 103
>
> publishing using Named Anchors template, 18, 623
>
> video timeline, adding to, 512–513

Anim name suffix, 556

animation
> acceleration effect, 307, 321, 1047–1049
>
> action overlap, 367
>
> action/reaction, conveying, 308–309
>
> algorithm, using, CDBT 63
>
> anime, 30
>
> anticipation, use of, 300, 304–305, 367
>
> artist, role of, CDBT 35
>
> background, 384–388, CDBT 81–82
>
> background layer, techniques using, CDBT 31–32, CDBT 33
>
> backup, importance of, 362
>
> Bézier curve, on, 790, CDBT 63–67
>
> bitmap, using in, 361, 385
>
> blur, 300–301, 368, 387–388
>
> bounce, conveying, 308–309
>
> breaking object into parts, facilitating via, 373–376, 554, 560–564, 921, 1040–1042
>
> broadcast quality, 361, 365, 380, 385, 396
>
> business, CDBT 35
>
> button, animating, 181–187
>
> camera movement, panning, 377, 384, 386–387
>
> camera movement, storyboarding, 1032, 1042, 1043
>
> camera movement, 3D animation, 1042–1045, 1047–1049
>
> camera movement, truck-in effect, CDBT 31–32
>
> camera movement, zoom in/out, 384
>
> character, conveying, 299–300, 365, 369, 372, 920

classical, CDBT 30

collage, 362–364

collision of moving objects, CDBT 59–60

color, 296, 299, 372–373

consistency, 300, 312

CorelDraw10 Graphics Suite, using, CDBT 83–92

deceleration effect, 321, 1047–1049

depth, calculating, CDBT 60

design strategy, 295–296, 373–376

dialog diagram, CDBT 35

emotion, conveying, 366–367

exaggeration, use of, 300

explosion effect, 1040–1042, 1054

facial expression, 379, 380

file size, 361–362, 363

flip, movement using, CDBT 30–31

frame rate, 366, 1043, CDBT 30

frame-by-frame, creating using Director, 42

frame-by-frame, creating using Flash, 314

frame-by-frame, creating using Painter 7, CDBT 79–82

frame-by-frame, described, 112, 311

frame-by-frame, inbetweening, 368–372

frame-by-frame, key, 368

frame-by-frame, keyframe in, 312, 313

frame-by-frame, mixing with tweened, 306

frame-by-frame, repeater frame in, 313, 314, 371

frame-by-frame, reversing sequence, 337

frame-by-frame, uses for, 306, 312

framing, 303

full, CDBT 30

hardware considerations, 361–362

illusion, 300–306

importing, 1055–1056

inertia, conveying, 307

irregularity, 300

limited, CDBT 30

lip-syncing, 378–383, 430

look and feel, 296–299

looping, 315, 334, 337–338, 386, 554

motion, choosing appropriate, 296, 297, 298–299

Continued

animation (continued)
    motion, conveying, 306–309, 366–367, 368
    motion, secondary, 305–306
    movie preload, showing during, 890, 906–907
    music, 300, 380
    nesting structures, 330
    pacing using repeater frame, 313, 314, 371
    Painter 7 painting, creating from, CDBT 75–82
    panning, 377, 384, 386–387
    path, moving object on, 113, 328
    perception, manipulating, 300–306
    phrasing, CDBT 34–35
    playback, 314, 330, 388
    post-production, 364
    potential of Flash, 361
    preproduction, 362–364
    QuickTime, designing for, 385
    random movement, CDBT 63, CDBT 66
    raster graphic animation, 361, 385, 966
    resolution, 363
    reuse of element, CDBT 30
    reversing, 337–338
    rhythm, 300
    rotoscope, CDBT 34
    scalability, 361
    scaling, simulating depth using, 1026, 1027,
        CDBT 57–59
    scene, 365
    scenery, 384–388
    sequence length, changing, 314
    sequences, integrating multiple, 330–333
    shot, 365
    sound, 296, 365–366, 380
    stagger movement, CDBT 33–34
    storyboarding, 362–366, 1032, 1042, 1043,
        CDBT 5–6
    straight-ahead, CDBT 32–33
    structure, determining, 296
    surprise, use of, 300
    symbol, techniques using, 183–184, 330–339
    talent necessary for, 295
    texture, CDBT 34–35
    3D, 302, 387–388, 1026–1030, 1042–1045,
        1047–1055
    timeline, on Main, 312, 330, 1041, 1044
    timeline, on multiple, 330–333, 554

    timeline-based, replacing with scripting,
        CDBC 18–19
    timing, 300, 1047–1049, CDBT 30,
        CDBT 34–35
    tweening, using, 376–378, CDBT 31,
        CDBT 32
    2D, CDBT 29–35
    viewpoint, 301–302
    voice, 365
    walking, conveying, 369–372
    weight, conveying, 367
Animation in CorelDRAW 10 Graphics Suite
    tutorial (Downey), CDBT 83–92
Animation on Bézier Curves tutorial (Plant),
    CDBT 63–67
anime, 30
Answers panel, 87
anti-aliasing, sound, 1007, 1009
anti-aliasing, visual
    display options, 103
    font, 221, 234, 235, 238
    image, 452, 463, 465, 965
anticipation, use of, 300, 304–305, 367
Apple Airport base station, 1159
Apple Web site, 394, 961, 1059, 1060, 1073
AquaServer, 872
Arabic character set, CDBA 12, CDBA 22–23
arithmetic operations, 689, 742–743
Array constructor, 749
arrays
    creating, 749, 751, 927
    data, removing from, 928, 930
    data, replacing in, 749
    data, returning from, 749
    data, setting in, 749, 757, 927
    deleting, 757
    Flash 4, emulating in, 750
    for loop, iterating through using, 754, 930
    index number, 749
    length, returning, 749, 751
    menu, creating dynamic using, 750–755
    sound, working with in, 760, 779–782
    string, splitting into, 757
    3D graphic array transformation, 1035–1036,
        1037
Arrow tool, 97, 135–139, 142, 226, 254
.as files, 680, 1094, CDBC 33

ASCII (American Standard Code for Information Interchange) character encoding, 926, CDBA 11
.asf files, 498
asfunction parameter, 511, 880–881
ASP (Active Server Pages) script, form processing by, 855–859
.asr files, 1096
asterisk (*) multiplication operator, 689
ATM (Adobe TypeManager), 236
atmospheres_1 files (on the CD), 18, 427
attachMovie method, 713, 717, 766, 818, 829–830
attachSound method, 775
.au files, CDBA 9
audience, designing for, 50, 51, 57–58
audio. *See* sound
Ausingtion Industry CBT Committee. *See* AICC
authoring environment, 35, 609, 610, 1097–1099
Authorware, 44
Auto Format Options dialog box, CDBC 27
AVI video
    color, 407
    compression, 407–408
    exporting from Flash, 406–408
    frame rate, 406
    importing, 497
    QuickTime versus, 1058–1059
    sound, 407
axis point, 272

B

background, animation, 384–388, CDBT 81–82
background color
    ActionScript, controlling using, 913–914
    composition, 413
    contrast, 146, 373
    Director Sprite, 1109–1110
    fade effect, 913–914
    HTML page, 639, 641, 651–655
    movie, 639, 647, 1063, 1082, 1083–1084
    painting, 127
    printing, 121
    sniffer movie, 647
    stage, 121, 639, 801
    temporary, 373

background image
    bitmap, 456–457
    scaling, 901
    sizing, 456–457
    texture, 901, 903
    transparency, 901, 903
background noise, 493
background sound, 427–428, 429, 437
backup, 362
backward compatibility, 30, 41
Baltic character set, CDBA 22–23
bandwidth
    bit rate table, 447
    emulating, 613–614, CDBC 6, CDBC 44, CDBC 46
    sniffer script, CDBC 19–20
Bandwidth Profiler, 245, 611, 612–615, CDBC 5–8, CDBC 45
bandwidth report.txt (on the CD), 616
bandwidth.fla (on the CD), 612
banner ad, 622, 953–956
|| (bars) logical OR operator, 690, 692
Basic Actions booklet, 534
Bazar, Andrew (multimedia designer), 1185
Bazley, Richard (2D Character Animation tutorial), 302–303, 384, 1187, CDBT 29
beachhouses files (on the CD), 956
Bézier curve, 135, 790, CDBT 63–67, CDBT 87
Bias suite software, 999
bit depth
    QuickTime video, 1068
    raster graphic, 457, 631–632, 1173
    sound, 492, 1173–1175, CDBC 11
bitmap, 452. *See also* raster graphics
Bitmap Properties dialog box, 459, 462, 897, 949
bitmap shift, 466
Black, Roger (*Don't Make Me Think: A Common Sense Approach to Web Usability*), 62
Blackwell, Lewis (*The End of Print*), 220
blur
    depth, conveying using, 387–388
    fill edge, softening using, 268–269
    motion, conveying using, 300–301, 368
BMP image
    exporting from Flash, 405, 962, 964
    exporting from QuickTime, 1075

Continued

BMP image *(continued)*
    importing, 454
    32-bit, 964
`Bonus_Tutorials.pdf` (on the CD), 81
booklets
    Basic Actions, 534
    Conditions/Loops, 691
    Deprecated, 535
    Miscellaneous Actions, 562
    Movie Control, 534, 543
`boolean` data type, 743
Da Boss cartoon (on the CD), 374–376
bounce, conveying in animation, 308–309
`bounce50percent.swf` (on the CD), 308
Bourg, David M. (*Physics for Game Developers*),
    309
BoxTop software, 195
braces, curly ({}) action delimiters, 544
breadcrumb, 101
`break` action, 692, 696–697
Break apart feature
    font, CDBC 4
    groups, 277
    introduced, 4
    raster graphic, 11, 280–281, 471–472
    symbol, 277
    text, 9–10, 248–249, 277–279, 284, 483–484
    vector graphic, 485
breakpoint, 697, CDBC 55–59, CDBC 60
Bright Lights Film Journal Web site, 298
Bringhurst, Robert (*The Elements of Typographic
    Style*), 220
broadband connection rate, simulating, 46
Broadcast Colors filter, 415
broadcast templates, 398–400
Brossier, Véronique (game designer), 1185
Brown, Scott (Designing for Usability tutorial),
    57, 1187
browser
    accessibility, 43
    caching, 619
    DHTML support, 43
    discrepancy, smoothing, 61
    DOM (document object model) support, 656,
        657
    Flash Player plug-in support, 665
    `fscommand` support, 650, 651

graphic display consistency, 466
history feature, 512
interface design for compatibility, 67
LiveConnect support, 641
movie interaction with back/forward
    buttons, 17–18, 512, 601
named anchor support, 17, 601
`<OBJECT>` tag support, 642
path considerations for older, 803
PNG support, 631
redirection if Player not installed, 42, 63, 642,
    667, 1092
redirection in ColdFusion MX, 1142, 1143
testing target browsers, 62
Bruce Conner Web site, 298
Brush tool, 98, 127–133, 151, 373
brzyski.com, 919
`buildInterface` function, 926
buraks.com, 619
business, CDBT 35
Button library, 164, 426, 543, 722
buttons
    accessibility, 604–605
    action target, as, 36
    ActionScript, adding to Button instance, 181
    aligning, 182
    animating, 181–187
    ColdFusion MX interaction with, 1136–1138
    color, 181, 185–186, 845, 1086
    Director movie, working with Flash button in,
        1100–1102, 1113–1114
    disabling, 543
    Down state, 172, 182
    drag-and-drop functionality, adding via
        button instance in Movie Clip symbol,
        725–726
    Dreamweaver MX, creating using, 1085–1086
    Dreamweaver MX, editing using, 1086
    event handling, 542–546, 548–552
    font, 845–846, 1086
    form, button instance on, 838–839, 858, 1125
    `getURL` action, adding to, 550, 552, 853–854,
        913
    graphic symbol, using in, 181–183
    guestbook application, in, 1134–1135,
        1136–1138
    Hit state, 172, 182, 591–592, 905

invisible, 548–552

Mask layer considerations, 349, 352

Movie Clip, adding to button symbol, 184–185

Movie Clip rotation button, 724–725

Movie Clip scaling button, 723–724

Movie Explorer, filtering using, 188

navigation system, creating for, 591–593, 905–906, 909–910, 911

Over state, 172, 182

play button, 431–432, 505

preview, 592

PushButton component, 770–772, 835, 838, 843–846, 858

RadioButton component, 835–836, 838

sound association with, 425–427, 431–432

state, 172

stop button, 431–432, 505, 543–544

style, 842–843, 845, 1086

symbol, button, 172, 180–187, 426–427

text, descriptive, 594, 604–605, 1085–1086

text buttons, 591–593

timeline, 172, 181

Up state, 172, 182

video playback, 21, 505–506, 593–595

button_sound_100.fla (on the CD), 427

C

CabExtractor software, 1161

Cakewalk Pro suite software, 1000

call action

Director, 1112

Flash, 699, 747

camera, video, 491–492, 493, 494–495

camera movement

panning, 377, 384, 386–387

storyboarding, 1032, 1042, 1043

3D animation, in, 1042–1045, 1047–1049

truck-in effect, CDBT 31–32

zoom in/out, 384

caption custom description component (on the CD), 889

cardemo files (on the CD), CDBT 59, CDBT 60

caret (^) carriage return escape, 923, 928

Carson, David (*The End of Print*), 220

cartoon. *See* animation

case action, 692, 694

case (upper/lower)

conversion, 742, 930

sensitivity, 547, 916

caseIn keyword, 692

Casio Web site, 1153

CBR (constant bit rate) encoding, 514

CD-ROM, distributing stand-alone on, 662–664

CD-ROM with this book

alphabitmap.fla, 959

animation examples, 301, 312, 334, 337

Animation in CorelDRAW 10 Graphics Suite tutorial (Downey), CDBT 83–92

Animation on Bézier Curves tutorial (Plant), CDBT 63–67

atmospheres_1 files, 18, 427

bandwidth report.txt, 616

bandwidth.fla, 612

beachhouses files, 956

blur line examples, 368

bounce50percent.swf, 308

button_sound_100.fla, 427

caption custom description component, 889

cardemo files, CDBT 59, CDBT 60

characterAnim.fla, 402, 408

ColdFusion MX source files, 1122

Color Schemer trial version, 199

color table example, 204

ColorSafe demo, 195

Combining Flash with the Natural Beauty of Painter 7 tutorial (Reed), CDBT 75–82

Comparing Video Compression tutorial (deHaan), CDBT 37–41

Complex Hit Detection on the Z Axis tutorial (Robertson), CDBT 57–60

component_definition files, CDBC 35, CDBC 39

components, 1182

components files, 12, 15

component_start.fla, 838

content overview, 1180, 1182–1183

countdown files, 651, 655, 657

createmenu files, 755, 759

Creating Faux 3D tutorial (Nisinson), CDBT 19–28

crossButton.swf, 1103

Continued

CD-ROM with this book *(continued)*

crossHairs.dir, 1115

Da Boss cartoon, 374–376

daisyLogo files, 481

daisySite files, 902, 904, 911, 913

DB_Loop.wav, 1008

debugging_code.fla, CDBC 52

Digital Video Production sample project, 581–582

dogColor files, 770, 772, 773

door.wav, 1010

doppler*.swf files, CDBT 61, CDBT 62

download.html, 650

Dynamic Sound Design tutorial (deChristopher), CDBT 61–62

enhanced_view.fla, 429

externalActions.as, CDBC 32

feedback.fla, 1125

Filling the Browser Window by Using the <FRAMESET> Tag tutorial (Moock), CDBT 43–46

Fireworks MX examples, 945

Flash MX trial version, 1182

Flash Player detection examples, 644

flash*.html files, 650

FlashLogo_final.fla, 900

flowchart examples, 76, 79

fontEmbed files, 244

font_finish.fla, 846

fontLink files, 244, 246

fontSource files, 244

font_start.fla, 845

frames_example.fla, 115

FreeHand drawing examples, CDBT 95

function_definition.as, CDBC 39

gifcolors.fla, 965

graphics_*.fla files, 841, 843, 844

guestbook.fla, 1134

hangman.fla, 919

hitTest files, 765, 766

htmlText_ files, 877, 878

The Human Interface tutorial (Nisselson), CDBT 11–17

Illustrator export examples, 990

image1.jpg, 18

images folder, 5

Interfacing Flash with Miva Movies tutorial (Lo), CDBT 69–73

introduction.rtf, 602

item_ RTF files, 596, 599

The Journal of Edwin Carp, 302–303, 384, CDBT 29

links.html, 1182

lip-sync files, 380

loader_100.fla, 818

loadfile.as, 818

loadMovie.fla, CDBC 12

loadMovie_100.fla, 804, 806

loadMovie_200.fla, 808

loadMovie_201.fla, 810

loadMovie_202.fla, 810, 813

loadMovie_300.fla, 814, 815

loadSound_100.fla, 816, 818

loadVideo.swf, 520

login.fla, 1147

login_100.fla, 702

login_start.fla, 1145

main_800.fla, 605

main_500.fla, 599

main_400.fla, 595

main.html, 581

main_100.fla, 585

main_700.fla, 602

main_600.fla, 601

main_starter.fla, 583

main_300.fla, 593

main_200.fla, 590

Using FreeHand with Flash tutorial (Wolfe), CDBT 93–102

Mask layer examples, 349, 352

MCAnimMask.swf, 358

menuarray_100.fla, 754

metalType.fla, 277

Miniml font, 238, 239

Miva examples, CDBT 73

modifyText.fla, 248

MoTG files, 1030, 1055

Motion Guide examples, 344

mouse_hitTest.fla, 768

movevariables.fla, 745

movieclip_droptarget.fla, 730

mysite.mdb, 1129

named_anchors files, 17, 18
object_definition.as, CDBC 39
orbit.swf, CDBT 61
Painter 7 examples, CDBT 75
paperplane_starter.fla, 786
pianokeys files, 565, 578, 777
plug-in, installing from, 1180
poemclip files, 863
portfolio site files, 886
preloader files, 794, 819
profiler_starter.fla, CDBC 5
property_inspector.fla, 706
quick_animation files, 12
QuickTime movies, 1073
reuseWalk.swf, 376
rotatingCube files, 542
sampleButton.fla, 180
sample_48kf_50qu.swf, 501
sample_high.avi, 495, 525
sample_high_import.mov, 500, 502
sample_low.mpg, 494
sample_mid.avi, 494
sample_1kf_50qu.swf, 501
sampleVideo_400.fla, 512
sampleVideo_100.fla, 504
sampleVideo_300.fla, 508, 510
sampleVideo_200.fla, 507
sampleVideo_Broadband files, 527
sample_0kf_50qu.swf, 501
scriptDetection.html, 644
Scriptless Flash Player Detection tutorial
        (Wolter), CDBT 47–55
scrollProp files, 881
Selection object method examples, 884
sendmail files, 855, 859, 1181–1182
separation.alv, 957
sharedFont_starter.fla, CDBC 16
sharedLib files, 823
sleepyStella.mov, 1061
slider_basic files, 730, 733, 736, 738, 739
sniffer*.fla files, CDBC 20
sniffer.html, 650
SoftenEdges.fla, 269
software, installing from, 1180
Sorenson Squeeze demo, 515
soundLib_ActionScript.fla, 782

soundObjects.fla, 759
soundSlider_100.fla, 785
SphereLighting.fla, 264
stella files, 560, 564, 1061
stop_sound_100.fls, 432
storyboard resources, 365, CDBT 4
Storyboard.doc, 1031
Storyboarding and Planning Interactivity
        tutorial (Dundon), CDBT 1–10
surpriseButton.fla, 187, 189
Swift3D software trial version, 1182
symbolMask.fla, 352
system requirement, 1179–1180
textFormat_100.fla, 880
textSamples.fla, 221
themakers_ad_starter.fla, 548
3Dgraphic.eps, 485
tracker_eventmodel.fla, 716
trashCanMX.swf, CDBT 19
troubleshooting, 1183
tweening examples, 319
typeof files, 745
video_anchors files, 512, 513, 801
video.swf, 520
walk cycle examples, 369
XML document load examples, 862
XML_SignIn.fla, 870
Central Processing Unit sniffer script. See CPU
        sniffer script
<cfheader> ColdFusion MX tag, 1143
<cfif> ColdFusion MX tag, 1142
<cflocation> ColdFusion MX tag, 1142, 1143
.cfm files, 1120, 1122. See also ColdFusion MX
<cfmail> ColdFusion MX tag, 1124
CFML (ColdFusion Markup Language), 1117. See
        also ColdFusion MX
<cfoutput> ColdFusion MX tag, 1122, 1133,
        1134
<cfparam> ColdFusion MX tag, 1133
<cfset> ColdFusion MX tag, 1122
<cfsetting> ColdFusion MX tag, 1133
CGI (Common Gateway Interface)
        form processing script, 688, 855
        remote script, action using, 610
changeColor function, 770, 771, 773–774
changeCursor function, CDBC 36

changeDrawingTool function, CDBC 36
character, conveying in animation, 299–300, 365, 369, 372, 920
character encoding, CDBA 11–14
Character Options dialog box, 8, 233
Character panel, 224
characterAnim.fla (on the CD), 402, 408
chat client, creating, 870–871
Check Plugin Dreamweaver MX behavior, 1088–1089
CheckBox component, 833
checkInput function, 929
checkLoad function, 817
Chinese
　　character encoding, CDBA 12, CDBA 14, CDBA 18–20
　　variable, assigning character string to, CDBA 13
clearInterval function, 817
clearMenu
　　function, 757
　　method, 757
clearStage
　　action, 912
　　function, 911
client, working with
　　budget approval, 56
　　change, dealing with last minute, 188, 989
　　concept approval, 56
　　consensus, 58
　　contract, CDBT 3–4
　　copyright, CDBT 3
　　goal, determining with, 51–52
　　ideas, documenting, 50
　　problem, defining with, 50
　　questions to ask, 50, 51, CDBT 3
　　rate, 56, CDBT 3
　　sign off, 56
　　time schedule, 52, 56
clingfish.com, 1185
Clips. See Movie Clips
.clr files, 202, 207
CNetX Web site, 1160
Code Complete: A Practical Handbook of Software Construction (McConnell), CDBC 41

code hinting
　　Dreamweaver MX, 1080, 1095
　　Flash, 560, 563, 1080, 1095, CDBC 29–30
codecs. See also compression
　　ALaw 2:1 codec, 1064
　　Floating Point, 1064
　　Fraunhofer MP3, 445, 521
　　IMA, 1064
　　Integer, 1064
　　Law 2:1, 1064
　　Nellymoser, 422
　　PureVoice, 1064
　　Qdesign Music 2, 1064
　　Qualcomm PureVoice, 1064
coding. See ActionScript
ColdFusion MX
　　administrator, 1129–1130
　　browser redirection, 1142, 1143
　　<cfheader> tag, 1143
　　<cfif> tag, 1142
　　<cflocation> tag, 1142, 1143
　　<cfmail> tag, 1124
　　CFML, 1117
　　<cfoutput> tag, 1122, 1133, 1134
　　<cfparam> tag, 1133
　　<cfset> tag, 1122
　　<cfsetting> tag, 1133
　　character escaping, 1134
　　check box handling, 1143
　　code, writing in HTML text editor, 1120–1121
　　components, 828, 1118
　　cookies, using with, 1141–1144
　　data source settings, 1129–1130
　　database, querying, 1132, 1133–1134, 1140
　　date, working with, 1123, 1134
　　#DateFormat function, 1123, 1134
　　described, 1117–1119
　　driver, adding, 1130
　　e-mail, sending via, 1124–1125
　　field existence, checking, 1142–1143
　　file extension, 1122
　　Flash Application Services, 1119
　　Flash button, interacting with, 1136–1138
　　Flash remoting, 1119, 1120–1121

form, using in, 1123–1124, 1139–1147
functions, 1123
guestbook application using, 1131–1139
history, 1118
HTML, returning from, 1133
HTML, troubleshooting in, 1131
language support, non-Roman, 1119
LoadVars object, working with, 1126–1127
meta-refresh operation, 1143
#Now function, 1123
operating systems supported, 1120
page, creating, 1122–1123
radio control handling, 1143
RDS, 1120, 1121
request handling, 1120
scopes, 1124
security, 1119
server, 1117
server, connecting to via FTP, 1121
server, installing, 1119
server, running alongside other Web servers,
    1119–1120
server-side scripting support, 1080
SSAS, use of, 1119
string encoding for import to Flash, 1134
tags, 1123
template, 1120, 1122, 1124, 1133, 1144
time, working with, 1123, 1134
#TimeFormat function, 1123, 1134
#urlencodedformat function, 1134
username, default, 1130
variable, working with, 1122, 1124,
    1126–1127, 1133–1134, 1138
Web service integration using, 1119
XML handling, 1119
ColdFusion Studio, 1120, 1121
colon (:) subroutine prefix, 699
color. See also fill; gradient; transparency
ActionScript syntax coloring, CDBC 30–31
adjustment, subtractive, 289
animation artwork, in, 296, 299, 372–373
AVI video, in, 407
background, composition, 413
background, contrast considerations, 146,
    373
background, controlling using ActionScript,
    913–914

background, Director Sprite, 1109–1110
background, fade effect, 913–914
background, HTML page, 639, 641, 651–655
background, movie, 639, 647, 1063, 1082,
    1083–1084
background, painting, 127
background, printing, 121
background, sniffer movie, 647
background, stage, 121, 639, 801
background, temporary, 373
banding, 194
bitmap shift, 466
brightness, 178
button, 181, 185–186, 845, 1086
clearing, 202
CMYK shift, 481
component color, changing, 831, 832
contrast, 146, 197
control, absolute, 289–290
control, relative, 289
custom, saving, 202, 207
data type, 744
design choices, 66, 67, 146, 196–200
Director ink, 1109–1110
dithering, 103, 194, 628, 629
8-bit, 194
export operation, setting in, 963
file format, problems when switching
    between, 194
gamut, 194
GIF image, 196, 628–629, 965–966
grayscale, converting to, 197–198
grid, 104
hexadecimal, 195
HSB, 205
ICC profile, 961
Illustrator, considerations when importing
    from, 971
importing, 196, 202
importing from FreeHand, 474, 477, 970–971,
    978, CDBT 99
importing from Illustrator, 971
importing palette, 203–205
indexed, 194, 204
intermediate, 194

Continued

color *(continued)*
layer outline color, 108, 110
line color, 124, 152, 201, 256
Macintosh versus Windows, 194, 961
methods related to, 769, 772–775
model sheet, 372
monitor screen handling of, 193–194
Movie Clip attribute manipulation, 770–772
NTSC, 399, 400–401, 415
palette, adaptive, 629
palette, custom, 203–205
palette, default, 200, 202
palette, importing, 203–205
palette, saving, 202
palette, sorting, 202–203
palette, storyboard, CDBT 4
palette, Web 216, 629
palette, Web snap adaptive, 629
permutation, 299
PICT format color depth, 965
PNG format, 632
printing, 121, 721, 786
properties, appearance-related, 709
QuickTime video color quality, 1068–1069
relative nature of, 197
replacing, 202
RGB (Red, Green, Blue), 193–194, 769,
    772–775
RGBA (Red, Green, Blue, Alpha), 156, 205
sampling using dropper tools, 207, 216,
    254–260, 280
selecting range in bitmap, 144, 281–282
shortcuts for applying, 373
16-bit, 194
stroke, 149–151
swatch, 149–151, 194, 200–205, 206–207
symbol instance, 177–178, 193, 288–290
table, creating, 204–205
table, loading, 204
text, 228, 249, 874
32-bit, 964, 965
tint, 178, 208
Toolbox, chip display on, 201
tweening, in, 193, 194, 326
24-bit, 194
vector graphic limitation, 473, 477, 970–971,
    978, 995

video, 397–398, 399–401
Web-safe, 194–196, 202
WebTV-safe, 397–398
Color Mixer panel
Alpha control, 208, 213
Color bar, 205
Color Pointer, 210
Color Proxy chip, 211
Color Selection field, 205, 207
Color Swatches panel, using in conjunction
    with, 205, 206–207
Control Pointer, 211
gradient controls, 210, 212
hex value field, 207
Macintosh layout, 92
Options menu, 205–206
Preview area, 209, 215–216
Swatches pop-up, 207, 208, 210, 211
Tint slider, 205, 207
color object, 721, 744, 768–775
Color property, 709
Color Schemer trial version (on the CD), 199
Color Swatches panel, 149–151, 194, 200–205,
    206–207
ColorMix utility, 195
ColorSafe plug-in (on the CD), 195
ColorSync software, 961
colorTransformObject object, 772–775
Combining Flash with the Natural Beauty
    of Painter 7 tutorial (Reed),
    CDBT 75–82
ComboBox component, 12–15, 833–834, 839
commenting
    code, CDBC 38, CDBC 63
    frame, 113, 549, 585
Common Gateway Interface. *See* CGI
Compaq iPAQ storage card, 1160
Comparing Video Compression tutorial
    (deHaan), CDBT 37–41
comparison operators, 689, 690
Complex Hit Detection on the Z Axis tutorial
    (Robertson), CDBT 57–60
Component Definition dialog box, 830, 831
Component panel, 168, 829–830
Component Parameters panel, 830
component_definition files (on the CD),
    CDBC 35, CDBC 39

components
    ActionScript, controlling using, 831
    assets belonging to, 829
    built-in, 8, 832–840
    CD-ROM with this book, included on, 1182
    CheckBox, 833
    ColdFusion MX components, 828, 1118
    color, changing, 831, 832
    ComboBox, 12–15, 833–834, 839
    creating custom, 847
    definition, accompanying code with
            descriptive, CDBC 38–40
    described, 827–828
    distributing, 847
    downloading, 828, 829
    Fade, 599–600, 913–914
    file size considerations, 828
    folders, arranging in, 602, 829
    font, changing, 842, 843–846
    font, working with embedded in, 845–846
    Generator versus, 827
    graphic in, changing, 841–842
    instance, 829
    instance, adding additional, 829
    instance, copying from one Clip to another,
            841
    instance, swapping, 831
    interface predictability, 828
    layer containing, 845
    library, adding to, 831
    library, defining from, 168
    ListBox, 16, 834
    Live Preview feature, 847
    movie, adding to, 829–830, 837–840
    movie, removing from, 832
    parameter, adding/removing, 830
    parameter value, setting, 830–831
    PushButton, 770–772, 835, 838, 843–846, 858
    RadioButton, 835–836, 838
    reusing assets, 41
    ScrollBar, 8–9, 595–599, 836–838, 881, 1134
    ScrollPane, 837, 840, 845–846
    set, 828
    sizing, 842
    skinning, 829, 841
    Smart Clip compared, 827, 828
    Stage, adding to, 829

    style format, 842–843
    symbol, Component, 172
    third-party, trustability of, 829
    w3 JMail Personal ASP component, 855, 1181
components files (on the CD), 12, 15
Components panel, 8, 13
component_start.fla (on the CD), 838
Composition ⇨Add to Render Queue, 413
Composition ⇨Background Color, 413
Composition ⇨New Composition, 412
compression. *See also* Sorenson Squeeze
    ADPCM, 422, 440
    After Effects video compression, CDBT 40–41
    AVI video, 407–408
    CBR (constant bit rate) encoding, 514
    default, overriding, 462, 463, 465
    Discreet Cleaner video compression, CDBT
            39
    file size/quality balance, 955, CDBT 38
    importing graphic, considerations when, 457,
            459, 462, 467–471
    interframe, 500
    intraframe, 500
    JPEG, 454
    JPEG, applying selectively via Mask, 944
    JPEG, applying to 8-bit files, 470
    JPEG, avoiding doubling, 459, 463, 464, 470
    JPEG, Fireworks MX options, 944, 949, 952
    JPEG, for progressive download, 470, 812,
            894, 949–950
    JPEG, Illustrator options, 991, 992
    JPEG, overriding, 462, 463, 465
    JPEG, setting, 468
    JPEG, setting before import to Flash, 942
    lossless, 457, 459, 468–470
    lossy, 470–471
    MJPEG, 393, 396
    PNG, 632
    publishing options, 32, 620
    QuickTime, 497, 1059, 1069, CDBT 38, CDBT
            39
    QuickTime codec support, 1058, 1060, 1064,
            1069
    raster graphic, 941–942
    raster graphic, export
            considerations, 1026

                                        Continued

compression *(continued)*
    raster graphic, imported, 457, 459, 462
    raster graphic, previewing, 948
    raster graphic, setting, 463, 465, 468
    raster graphic, source file considerations,
        468–471
    raster graphic, updating information, 463
    recompression, 498
    sound, artifact creation in, CDBC 11
    sound, dynamic, 1006
    sound, event, 439, 443, 620–621
    sound, MP3, 421, 440–441, 448, 521, CDBC 11
    sound, QuickTime codec support, 1064
    sound, raw format, 422, 441
    sound, setting, 439–441, 443–444, 447
    sound, Shockwave, 421
    sound, Sorenson Squeeze options, 521, 527
    sound, speech, 421, 422, 423, 441
    sound, stream, 439, 620
    sound, VBR MP3, 445–446
    sound default, 445
    sound track of video, 497, 502
    temporal, 500
    video compression file output comparison,
        CDBT 37–40
    Wildform Flix video compression, CDBT 37,
        CDBT 38, CDBT 39
Compression Settings dialog box, 415, 520
concatenation, 690, 743
condition checking, 690–695, 696, 697, 743
Conditions/Loops booklet, 691
Connectix Virtual PC, 1161–1162
Conner, Bruce (artist), 298
constant bit rate encoding. *See* CBR
continue action, 697
contract with client, CDBT 3–4
Control ⇨Debug Movie, CDBC 51
Control ⇨Disable Keyboard Shortcuts, 702
Control ⇨Enable Simple Buttons, 6
Control ⇨Play, 321
Control Shockwave or Flash Dreamweaver MX
        behavior, 1089
Control ⇨Test Movie, 245
Control ⇨Test Scene, 428
Controller, 88, 89, 106–107
Convert to Symbol dialog box, 10, 173, 181

cookies, 1141–1144
Cool Edit software, 998
copy/paste operations. *See also* sampling
        element attributes
    component instance from one Clip to
        another, 841
    described, 160
    drawing elements, 136, 159
    duplication versus, 160
    Fireworks MX content into Flash, 948
    frames, 108, 115, 322
    layer name retention, 333
    library asset, 165, 167
    Movie Explorer, 190
    raster graphic into Flash, 461
    scenes, 102
    text, 226, CDBA 14–15
    transparency considerations, 453
    vector graphic into Flash, 475
copyright, 56, CDBT 3
CorelDRAW 10 Graphics Suite
    Artistic Media tool, CDBT 87
    Basic Shapes tool, CDBT 88
    Bézier tool, CDBT 87
    bitmap, converting graphic to, CDBT 91
    Blend effect, CDBT 89
    Color palette, CDBT 84
    Contour effect, CDBT 89
    Dimension tool, CDBT 87
    Effects menu, CDBT 89–90
    Ellipse tool, CDBT 87
    exporting from, CDBT 91, CDBT 92
    Eyedropper tool, CDBT 90, CDBT 91
    font menu, CDBT 89
    Freehand tool, CDBT 87
    Graph Paper tool, CDBT 88
    Interactive Distortion effect, CDBT 89
    Interactive Drop Shadow tool, CDBT 90
    Interactive Envelope tool, CDBT 89
    Interactive Extrude tool, CDBT 90
    interface, customizing, CDBT 84–85
    introduced, 996
    Options dialog box, CDBT 84, CDBT 85
    Outline tool, CDBT 87, CDBT 90
    page layout, CDBT 85
    page order, changing, CDBT 85

page size, CDBT 84
Paintbucket tool, CDBT 91
Pick tool, CDBT 84, CDBT 87
Polygon tool, CDBT 87, CDBT 88
Property Bar, CDBT 86
Rectangle tool, CDBT 87, CDBT 91
Shape tool, CDBT 87
Spiral tool, CDBT 87
Text tool, CDBT 88, CDBT 92
toolbars, CDBT 84, CDBT 86
Transparency tool, CDBT 90, CDBT 91
Zoom tool, CDBT 87
Corsaro, Sandro (Flash Character Design
    Strategies tutorial), 1187
countdown files (on the CD), 651, 655, 657
CPU (Central Processing Unit) sniffer script,
    CDBC 19–20
Crawford, Tad (AIGA Professional Practices in
    Graphic Design), 56
Create New Symbol dialog box, 181
createAlphabet function, 926
createEmptyMovieClip method, 713, 756, 761,
    925
createLib function, 760
createmenu files (on the CD), 755, 759
createMenu function, 756, 757
createTextField method, 878, 879, 924
createWord method, 928
Creating Faux 3D tutorial (Nisinson), CDBT
    19–28
Creating Printable Paper Airplanes tutorial
    (Richards), 786–790
crossButton.swf (on the CD), 1103
crosshair cursor, 135, 147
crossHairs.dir (on the CD), 1115
Cubase software, 1000
#currentFrame Director Lingo property, 1112
_currentframe property, 710, 1112
cursor
    Arrow tool, 137, 138
    changing, CDBC 36
    crosshair, 135, 147
    Pen tool, 146, 147
    Subselection tool, 144
    text entry, 74
    text field, returning position in, 883

curves
    Bézier, 135, 790, CDBT 63–67, CDBT 87
    corner point, converting to, 145–146, 149
    end point, converting to, 149
    optimizing, 134, 135, 484, CDBC 9–10
    Pen tool, drawing using, 148–149
    Pencil tool, drawing using, 126, 127
    reshaping, 135, 137–138, 145
    simplifying, 138
    smoothing, 126, 127, 128, 138, 146
    tangent handle, 145, 149
Custom Modem Settings dialog box, CDBC 46
Cut operations, 160, 190
Cyrillic character set, CDBA 12, CDBA 14–17,
    CDBA 18, CDBA 22–23

D

Da Boss cartoon (on the CD), 374–376
daisyLogo files (on the CD), 481
daisySite files (on the CD), 902, 904, 911, 913
Data event, 720
data type
    boolean, 743
    checking using typeof, 745
    color, 744
    described, 705, 741
    function, 744
    movieclip, 744
    number, 742–743
    object, 744
    sound, 744
    string, 741–742
    text field, considerations in, 742
    undefined, 744–745
database
    application, data-driven, 47
    capability overview, 36
    column name, 1132
    guestbook application, setup for, 1128–1134
    image loading from, 41
    key, primary, 1128
    Miva, interacting with using, CDBT 70, CDBT
        72
    movie, loading from, 41
    movie, sending to, 41

                                        Continued

database *(continued)*
  MS Access, building using, 1127–1130
  ODBC, 1129
  presentation, data-driven, 47
  querying in ColdFusion MX, 1132, 1133–1134,
    1140
  table, creating, 1127–1128
  text, loading from, 41
date, working with in ColdFusion MX, 1123, 1134
#DateFormat ColdFusion MX function, 1123, 1134
DB_Loop.wav (on the CD), 1008
.dcr files, 1098. *See also* Director
de los Reyes, August (*Flash Design for Mobile
    Devices*), 446
Debreuil, Robin and Sandy (Graphic Symbols
    versus Movie Clips tutorial), 174
Debug ⇨List Variables, 615
Debugger panel, 619, 620, CDBC 51–55, CDBC 57
debugging. *See also* testing
  Bandwidth Profiler Debug menu, using, 615
  breakpoint, using, 697, CDBC 55–59, CDBC 60
  code, stepping through, CDBC 57–59
  download time, emulating, 615
  expressions, CDBC 48
  HTML tags in use, listing, 877
  loop, 697
  movie, streaming, CDBC 43–45
  movie properties, displaying in Debug mode,
    CDBC 54–55
  movie properties, editing in Debug mode,
    CDBC 55
  objects, listing, 781, CDBC 50–51
  Output window, using in, CDBC 46–51
  passwording debug access in Publish
    settings, 619–620, CDBC 60
  remote, CDBC 59–62
  text fields, listing, 850
  text file, saving debugging data to, 697
  trace action, using, CDBC 46–49
  variable, modifying from Debugger panel,
    CDBC 52
  variable, monitoring in Watch list, CDBC
    53–54
  variables, listing, 615, 684, CDBC 50, CDBC 52
debugging_code.fla (on the CD), CDBC 52
deceleration, conveying in animation, 321,
    1047–1049

deChristopher, Brock (Dynamic Sound Design
    tutorial), 1187, CDBT 61
Deck software, 999
default action, 692, 694
deHaan, Jen (Comparing Video Compression
    tutorial), 1186, 1188, CDBT 37
deHaan, Peter (Web developer), 1186
Deprecated booklet, 535
Designer panel set, 155
Designing for Usability tutorial (Brown), 57–61
Designing Interactive Digital Media (Iuppa), 56
desktop, synchronizing Pocket PC with,
    1156–1157, 1158
detectFlash.swf, 1092
DHTML (Dynamic Hypertext Markup Language).
    See also HTML (Hypertext Markup
    Language)
  browser support, 43
  introduced, 43
  JavaScript/Flash interactivity involving,
    650–657
  movie, showing DHTML content behind, 639,
    1083–1084
  movie, showing DHTML content in front of,
    639
dialog diagram, CDBT 35
.dib files, 454
Digidesign Pro Tools software, 1000–1001
Digital Video Production sample project (on the
    CD), 581–582
Dimac Intranet, Internet & Extranet portal, 855
.dir files, 1103. *See also* Director
Director. *See also* Shockwave Player
  action on Flash timeline, calling, 1112
  ActionScript, Lingo compared, 1099
  ActionScript/Lingo property conversion
    chart, 1111–1112
  #alpha property, 1111
  argument string, passing to multiple Lingo
    commands, 1101
  behavior, writing, 1101
  call action, 1112
  cast, 1103, 1108
  crash, experiencing when sending Flash
    event to Lingo, 1102
  #currentFrame property, 1112
  described, 43

dot syntax, 1099, 1110
Drawing API, 1098
#dropTarget property, 1111
endTellTarget command, 1113
event handling, 1100, 1101–1102, 1112
Fireworks MX Director export feature, 945
Flash action, Lingo interactivity with,
    1099–1102
Flash Asset Properties dialog box, 1104, 1105,
    1108
Flash Asset Xtra, 669, 1097, 1099,
    1102–1105
Flash audio considerations, 1103
Flash authoring environment versus,
    1097–1099
Flash button, working with in Director movie,
    1100–1102, 1113–1114
Flash movie, integrating in Director project,
    669, 1099
Flash movie within Director movie
    frame rate, 1105
    looping, 1104, 1107
    placing on Stage, 1109
    playing, 1102–1103, 1104
    preloading, 1104, 1106–1107
    quality setting, 1105
    sizing, 1105
    Sprite bounding box, 1105
    script to, 1101, 1102
#focusRect property, 1112
frame in Director movie, assigning Flash
    action to, 1100–1102
frame-by-frame animation, 42
getFlashProperty command, 1111
getURL action, using in Director/Flash
    interaction, 1100–1102
getVariable command, 1110
#height property, 1111
if...else statement, 1101
image object, 1098
Import dialog box, 1103
importing Flash movie into, 669, 1097, 1099,
    1103–1105
ink, 1109–1110
#lastframeLoaded property, 1112
Lingo, 1098
Lingo Dictionary, 1110

Message window, 1114
multimedia authoring using, 43
#name property, 1111
playback engine, 1098
#posX property, 1111
#posY property, 1111
printing, 1112
properties, 1111–1112, 1114
Property Inspector, 1108
#rotate property, 1111
#scaleX property, 1111
#scaleY property, 1111
Score window, 1102, 1106
sendXML command, 1112
setFlashProperty command, 1111
setVariable command, 1110
Slash notation, 1110–1111
sound-editing software bundled with, 997
Sprite, 1108
Sprite, rotating, 1113–1114
Sprite, sizing, 1113–1114
Sprite duration, 1109
Sprite properties, viewing, 1114
#spriteSoundBufferTime property, 1112
Stage, placing Flash cast member on, 1109
#target property, 1111
3D engine, 1098
#totalFrames property, 1112
transparency, 1109–1110, 1112
#url property, 1112
variable, working with, 1102, 1106–1107,
    1110–1111
vector drawing, using for, 1099
#visible property, 1111
#width property, 1111
Xtras, 1098
Director 8 Bible, 1099
Discreet Cleaner utility, 498, 514, 1059, CDBT 39
Dispatcher.js file, 1092
distortion transformation, 273–274
Distribute to Layers command, 10
dithering, 103, 194, 628, 629. *See also* color
do ... while loop, 695
document
    active, 98
    creating, 98

Continued

document *(continued)*
   default, 100
   file extension, 30
   file size, movie versus, 609
   library, relation to, 165
   movie, exporting to, 402–404, 616
   movie, relation to, 30
   playback speed, 107
   predefined, 98
   saving, 30
   scene, relation to, 30
   sound, extracting from, 449–450
   sound relation to, 423, 425
Document dialog box, 93
Document Properties dialog box, 111
Document window, 98–105, 176
dogColor files (on the CD), 770, 772, 773
DOM (document object model), 656, 657, 865
Don't Make Me Think: A Common Sense
       Approach to Web Usability (Krug and
       Black), 62
door.wav (on the CD), 1010
doppler*.swf files (on the CD), CDBT 61,
       CDBT 62
dot syntax
   Director, 1099, 1110
   Flash, 557–559, 707, 1059
Downey, Doug (Animation in CorelDraw10
       Graphics Suite tutorial), 1188, CDBT 83
download
   frame download status, checking, 794
   movie download, progressive, 793, CDBC 2
   movie download status, checking, 494
   movie download status, displaying in
       progress bar, 795–799
   streaming technology versus progressive,
       CDBC 2, CDBC 43
   time needed, emulating, 615
download.html (on the CD), 650
drag-and-drop functionality
   button instance in Movie Clip symbol, adding
       via, 725–726
   described, 725
   drop position, detecting, 727–730
   lock mouse to center option, 726
   rectangle, constraining to, 726–727
   slider, using in, 730–739

dragOut event, 546
dragOver event, 546
draw function, CDBC 36
drawing
   alignment, 155, 156, 157–158
   anchor point, 135, 144, 145, 147
   area, selecting, 142–144
   aspect ratio, 155
   click accuracy, setting, 128
   corner point, 145–146, 148, 149
   corner sharpening, 266–267
   curve, Bézier, 135, 790, CDBT 63–67, CDBT 87
   curve, optimizing, 134, 135, 484, CDBC 9–10
   curve, reshaping, 135, 137–138, 145
   curve, simplifying, 138
   curve, smoothing, 126, 127, 128, 138, 146
   curve, using Pen tool, 148–149
   curve, using Pencil tool, 126, 127
   curve point, converting corner point to,
       145–146, 149
   curve point, converting end point to, 149
   curve tangent handle, 145, 149
   distribution, horizontal/vertical, 157
   edge, hiding, 105
   element, copying, 159
   element, deselecting, 136
   element, duplicating, 136, 160
   element, moving, 135, 137–138
   element, selecting, 135–139, 142, 160
   endpoint, 147, 149
   erasing, 133–134, 258
   freehand, 126–133
   FreeHand versus Flash as drawing tool,
       CDBT 94
   hairline, 153
   ink mode, 126–127, 135
   interface design, tools used in, 67
   introduced, 24–25
   line, connect setting, 128, 140
   line, converting to fill, 265–267
   line, dashed, 154, CDBT 102
   line, dotted, 154
   line, hatched, 154
   line, height (thickness), 124, 151–152, 256
   line, optimizing, 146
   line, pulling, 135
   line, ragged, 154

line, recognition, 128
line, reshaping, 135, 138
line, sampling, 216, 254–256
line, selecting, 135, 136, 137, 144–146, 286–287
line, selecting portion of, 142
line, simplifying, 128
line, smallest displayable, 266
line, softening edge, 268
line, solid, 153
line, stacking order, 275
line, stippled, 154
line, style, 151–154, 254, 255–256
line, using Line tool, 124
line, using Pen tool, 146–149
line, using Pencil tool, 126–127
optimizing, 134, 135
outline, displaying shape as, 103
outline, layer, 108, 110
outline, moving, 137
outline, onion skin, 111
outline, reshaping, 137
oval, 98, 124–125, 151
Paintbrush, using, 127–133, 151
positioning, 155, 156–157, 158
rectangle, 125–126, 151, 213–215, 266–267
regularizing, 155
reshaping, 135, 137, 145
shape, compound, 286–288
shape, geometric, 124–126
shape, recognition, 128
shape, splitting, 142
shape, using Pen tool, 146
sizing, 155, 156, 157, 158, 159
slant, 155
smoothing, 128, 134, 138–139
straightening, 127, 128, 138–139, CDBC 9
stroke, 151
subselection, 135, 144–146
symbol editing mode, 160
tablet, using, 127, 129, 380, CDBT 29, CDBT 82
text boxes, 137
Drawing Toolbox. *See* Toolbox
Dreamweaver MX. *See also* HTML (Hypertext Markup Language)
ActionScript, writing in, 1081, 1094–1096
behaviors, 1088–1091

code hinting feature, 1080, 1095
database interaction, 1080
described, 1079
file upload, using for, 634, 916
Flash, launching from, 1087–1088
Flash button, creating using, 1085–1086
Flash button, editing using, 1086
Flash Deployment Kit, 1090–1093
Flash Dispatcher behavior, 1090–1092
Flash functions, built-in, 1084–1088
Flash MX, integration with, 1080–1081
Flash Player detection behavior, 1088–1089, 1090–1093, CDBT 50
Flash Text object, editing, 1087
Flash Text object, inserting, 1086–1087
importing Flash content into, 1081–1084
Insert panel, 1084
installing, 1080
layouts, pre-built, 1080
link update feature, 1081, 1093–1094
Map view, 1093
Media Tab, 1084
movie, controlling using Control Shockwave or Flash behavior, 1089
movie, editing from, 1087–1088
movie in HTML page, aligning, 1082
movie in HTML page, autoplay, 1082
movie in HTML page, background color, 1082, 1083–1084
movie in HTML page, border, 1082, 1083
movie in HTML page, inserting, 1081
movie in HTML page, looping, 1082
movie in HTML page, naming, 1082
movie in HTML page, passing parameter to, 1082
movie in HTML page, positioning, 1083
movie in HTML page, quality setting, 1082
movie in HTML page, sizing, 1082
panel similarity to other MX products, 1080
plug-in detection using Check Plugin behavior, 1088–1089
plug-in detection using Flash Deployment Kit, 1090–1093
Property inspector, 1081–1082
RDS, 1121
Results panel, 1093, 1094

Continued

Dreamweaver MX *(continued)*
    roundtrip HTML feature, 1081
    scripting support, 1080
    Site definition dialog box, 1121
    Site Map feature, 1093–1094
    Site Setup Wizard, 1080
    Snippets panel, 1080
    UltraDev, CDBT 50
    window mode parameter, 1083–1084
Dropper tool. *See* Eyedropper tool (Flash)
#dropTarget Director Lingo property, 1111
_droptarget property, 709, 727–730, 763–764,
    1111
Dundon, MD (Storyboarding and Planning
    Interactivity tutorial), 1188, CDBT 1
Duplicate dialog box, 95
duplicateMovieClip
    action, 737
    method, 713, 717, 730–732
duplication
    color swatch, 201
    copy versus, 160
    drawing element, 136, 160
    library asset, 167
.dv files, 497
DXF image
    exporting from Flash, 405, 994
    importing, 454
    support for, 1025
    3D file format, as, 1025
Dynamic Hypertext Markup Language. *See* DHTML
Dynamic Sound Design tutorial (deChristopher),
    CDBT 61–62

E
ECMA-262 specification conformance, 558
Edit ⇨Compression Settings, 520
Edit ⇨Copy Frames, 108
Edit ⇨Deselect All, 136
Edit ⇨Edit All, 276
Edit ⇨Edit in Place, 175
Edit ⇨Edit Movie, 176
Edit ⇨Edit Selected, 134
Edit ⇨Edit Symbols, 175
Edit Envelope dialog box, 428, 434–436
Edit ⇨Filter Settings, 524
Edit ⇨Font Mapping, 238

Edit ⇨Keyboard Shortcuts, 95
Edit menu, 159–160
Edit ⇨Paste Frames, 115
Edit ⇨Preferences, 106
Edit ⇨Preferences ⇨Editing, 128
Edit ⇨Preferences ⇨General ⇨Printing Options,
    121
Edit ⇨Print Margins, 121
Effect menu, 428
Electric Rain Swift 3D. *See* Swift3D software
Electric Rain Web site, 1030
The Elements of Typographic Style (Bringhurst),
    220
elitevideo.com, 491
Elliott, Shane (Using XML Sockets with a Flash
    Movie tutorial), 1188
else if statement, 691
e-mail
    attachment, printing to, 121, 785
    ColdFusion MX, sending via, 1124–1125
    form data, e-mailing, 855–859, 1124–1125
    guestbook, e-mailing comment from, 1133
    mailto link, 552, 853–854, 875–876, 913
<EMBED> tag, inserting movie in HTML page
    using, 635, 640–642, 643, 688, 1083
EMF image
    exporting from Flash, 402, 405, 994
    importing, 454
emotion, conveying in animation, 366–367
Encapsulated PostScript image format.
    See EPS
The End of Print (Blackwell and Carson), 220
endTellTarget Director Lingo command, 1113
enhanced_view.fla (on the CD), 429
*Enough Rope to Shoot Yourself in the Foot: Rules
    for C and C++ Programming* (Holub),
    CDBC 41
enterFrame event, 717
Envelope Modifier tool, 4, 9–10, 274–275
EPS (Encapsulated PostScript) image
    blend, 485–486
    exporting from Flash, 404, 994
    exporting from Illustrator, 990
    exporting from 3D application, 1026
    importing, 454, 477, 478–480
    3D graphic format, as, 1025
eq equality operator, 690

equals sign (=) assignment operator, 681, 684, 689

equals signs (==) equality operator, 690, 691

equals signs, F6 (===) equality operator, 690

equations, 683, 738

Eraser tool, 98, 133–134, 249–250, 258

Esc shortcut key definition, CDBC 28–29

eval function, 683–684

evaluate action, 562

event handlers

    on, 534, 543–544

    onClipEvent, 711, 717–720, 789

    onData, 720

    onEnterFrame, 717, 722, 736–738, 739, CDBC 40

    onKeyDown, 719

    onKeyUp, 719

    onLoad, 717

    onMouseDown, 718

    onMouseMove, 718, 764, 767, 784

    onMouseUp, 719

    onUnload, 717

event handling

    action, combining, 542–544

    ActionScript event model, 24–26, 37

    button event, 542–546, 548–552

    data event, 532, 867–868

    described, 531

    Director, in, 1100, 1101–1102, 1112

    drag event, 546

    external input event, 720

    Flash 5 versus Flash MX, CDBC 40

    frame event, 717, 722, 736–738, 739, CDBC 40

    game application, in, 921, 926

    interactivity, relation to, 531

    keystroke event, 544, 546–547, 719

    LoadVars object, related to, 858

    methods related to, 716

    mouse event, 532, 545–546, 718–719, 764, 767

    Movie Clip, 711, 717–720

    playback event, 532, 717

    system-based event, 532

    time event, 532, 547–548

    timeline event, 544

    user input event, 532, 718–719

    XML data event, 867–868, 1112

event sound. See also sound

    background, 429

    compression, 439, 443, 620–621

    dynamic, 777

    exporting, 438, 443

    frames, skipping starting, CDBC 19

    loading, 429

    looping, 429, 437, 1012

    movie, storage in, 425

    playback, 429, 431, CDBC 3

    publishing, 445

    reusing, 425

    start sound as, 430

    stopping, 431–432

    stream sound, doubling as, CDBC 3

    streaming mode, kicking into, 446

    uses of, CDBC 2–3

exaggeration, using in animation, 300

exclamation mark (!) logical NOT operator, 690

exclamation mark, equals sign (!=) inequality operator, 690, CDBC 49

Expand Fill command, 267–268

expert tutorials

    Animation in CorelDRAW 10 Graphics Suite (Downey), CDBT 83–92

    Animation on Bézier Curves (Plant), CDBT 63–67

    Combining Flash with the Natural Beauty of Painter 7 (Reed), CDBT 75–82

    Comparing Video Compression (deHaan), CDBT 37–41

    Complex Hit Detection on the Z Axis (Robertson), CDBT 57–60

    Creating Faux 3D (Nisinson), CDBT 19–28

    Creating Printable Paper Airplanes (Richards), 786–790

    Designing for Usability (Brown), 57–61

    Dynamic Sound Design (deChristopher), CDBT 61–62

    Filling the Browser Window by Using the <FRAMESET> Tag (Moock), CDBT 43–46

    Flash Character Design Strategies (Corsaro), 373–376

Continued

expert tutorials *(continued)*
 Graphic Symbols versus Movie Clips
  (Debreuil and Debreuil), 174
 The Human Interface (Nisselson), CDBT
  11–17
 Interface Design (Jordan), 64–72
 Interfacing Flash with Miva Movies (Lo),
  CDBT 69–73
 Introduction to XML and Flash (Honselaar),
  862–865
 JibJab.com's Collage Animation Workflow
  (Spiridellis), 362–364
 Leveraging Fireworks to Streamline Common
  Production Tasks (Brown), 950–956
 Lip-syncing Cartoons (Turner), 380–383
 Using FreeHand wiht Flash (Wolfe), CDBT
  93–102
 Scriptless Flash Player Detection (Wolter),
  CDBT 47–55
 Storyboarding and Planning Interactivity
  (Dundon), CDBT 1–10
 Streamlined Workflow: FreeHand and Flash
  (Purgason), 986–990
 2D Character Animation (Bazley), CDBT
  29–35
 Unifying the Web: Multiuser Flash Content
  (Moock), 870–872
 Using Embedded Fonts with Components
  (deHaan), 845–846
 Using Miniml fonts in Flash MX (Kroeger),
  238–240
 Using Propellerhead's Rebirth to Create
  Loops for Flash (Jamieson), 1012–1017
 Using XML Sockets with a Flash Movie
  (Elliott), 865–870
experts
 Bazley, Richard, 302–303, 384, 1187, CDBT 29
 Brown, Scott, 57, 1187
 Corsaro, Sandro, 1187
 Debreuil, Robin, 174
 Debreuil, Sandy, 174
 deChristopher, Brock, 1187, CDBT 61
 deHaan, Jen, 1186, 1188, CDBT 37
 Downey, Doug, 1188, CDBT 83
 Dundon, MD, 1188, CDBT 1
 Elliott, Shane, 1188
 Honselaar, Chris, 1188–1189

 Jamieson, Justin, 1189
 Jordan, Eric, 1189
 Kroeger, Craig, 1189
 Lo, Timothy, 1189, CDBT 69
 Moock, Colin, 1190, CDBT 43, CDBT 48
 Nisinson, Dorian, 1190, CDBT 19
 Nisselson, Jane, 1190, CDBT 11
 Parameswaran, Viswanath, 1191
 Plant, Darrel, 1191, CDBT 63
 Purgason, Todd, 1191
 Reed, Arena, 1191, CDBT 75
 Richards, Mike, 1192
 Robertson, James, 1192, CDBT 57
 Spiridellis, Gregg, 1192
 Turner, Bill, 1192
 Wolfe, Bentley, 1192, CDBT 93
 Wolter, Sascha, 1193, CDBT 47
explosion effect
 animation, 1040–1042, 1052, 1054
 sound, 1010–1011
Export AVI Settings dialog box, 406
Export Image dialog box, 963
Export Movie command, 402, 616–617
Export Movie dialog box, 402
export operations. *See also* publishing
 ActionScript code to external file, CDBC
  33–34
 After Effects, Flash content from, CDBT 40–41
 AI image from Flash, 404, 994, 995
 AI image from Illustrator, 990
 AVI video from Flash, 406–408
 BMP image from Flash, 405, 962, 964
 BMP image from QuickTime, 1075
 color depth setting, 963
 CorelDRAW 10 Graphics Suite, from,
  CDBT 91, CDBT 92
 to Director from Fireworks MX, 945
 document to movie, 402–404, 616
 DXF image from Flash, 405, 994
 EMF image from Flash, 402, 405, 994
 EPS image from Flash, 404, 994
 EPS image from Illustrator, 990
 EPS image from 3D application, 1026
 font, 233–234
 FreeHand SWF export feature, 970, 976,
  980–981, 982, 984–986
 GIF animation from Fireworks MX, 953–956

GIF image from Flash, 405, 456, 962, 965–966
gradient considerations, 410
Illustrator, from, 990, 992–994
to Illustrator from Fireworks MX, 945
to Illustrator from Flash, 404, 990, 994, 995
JPEG from Fireworks MX, 949, 951, 952, 953
JPEG image from Flash, 406, 962
layer flattening in, 30
Mask layer considerations, 405
Motion Guide layer, graphic from, 344
Painter 7, from, CDBT 78, CDBT 81
PICT image from Flash, 405, 962, 964–965, 994
PICT image from QuickTime, 1075
PNG image from Flash, 406, 962
PNG sequence from Fireworks MX, 950, 954–956
projector, 633
QuickTime, image sequence from, 1074–1075
QuickTime, to, 385, 391, 1059, 1062, 1067–1069
raster image from Flash, 404, 405–406, 961–966
resolution, setting, 963
runtime sharing, for, 822
Shared library considerations, 820
sizing image, 963
sound, 408–409, 421–423, 443–444
sound stream export quality, 438
3D graphic, 1025–1030
3ds max, from, 1031, 1049, 1055–1056
transparency considerations, 1026
vector graphic from Flash, 404–405, 994–996
video from Flash, 174, 395–398, 402–404
WMF image from Flash, 402, 405, 994
Export PICT dialog box, 403
Export QuickTime dialog box, 1062
Export QuickTime Video dialog box, 409, 1068
Export Windows WAV dialog box, 409
expressions
    action assignment using, 539, 682–683
    conditional, 682
    creating, 688–698
    debugging, CDBC 48
    described, 682
    numeric, 682
    Output window, sending to, CDBC 48
    string, using in, 683

string expression, 682
string versus, CDBC 66
variable, referencing in, 683
variable, specifying as, 684
extensibility, planning for, 886, 889, CDBC 24
extensible Markup Language. *See* XML
eXtensible Stylesheet Language. *See* XSL
externalActions.as (on the CD), CDBC 32
Eyedropper tool (CorelDRAW 10 Graphics Suite), CDBT 90, CDBT 91
Eyedropper tool (Flash)
    application, sampling from external, 207
    Arrow tool eyedropper, 254
    bitmap sampling, 280, 284
    Color Mixer panel eyedropper, 207–208
    color sampling, 207, 216, 254–260, 280
    fill sampling, 216, 254–256
    Ink Bottle, transferring sampled attribute to, 216, 254–255
    Paint Bucket, transferring sampled attribute to, 216, 254–255
    stroke sampling, 216, 254–256
    text sampling, 249
    Toolbox eyedropper, 98, 254

F

facial expression, 379, 380
Fade component, 599–600, 913–914
FCheckBox methods, 833
FComboBox methods, 834
feedback form, 73, 76, 77, 855–859, 1123–1127
feedback.fla (on the CD), 1125
FezGuys Web site, 446
.fh_ files, 454, 476. *See also* FreeHand
fieldSize object, 879
Fig Leaf Software, 872
File ⇨Close, 3
File ⇨Create Projector, 661–662
File ⇨Export Image, 627
File ⇨Export Movie, 402
file formats compatible with Flash, CDBA 6–9
File ⇨Import, 424
File ⇨Import to Library, 424
File ⇨Interpret Footage ⇨Main, 411
File menu, CDBA 1–4
File ⇨New, CDBA 1
File ⇨New From Template, 98

File ⇨Open, CDBA 1
File ⇨Open as Library, 165
File ⇨Open Recent, CDBA 2
File ⇨Page Setup, 121
File ⇨Print, 121
File ⇨Print Margins, 121
File ⇨Print Preview, 121
File ⇨Publish Preview, 633
File ⇨Publish Settings, 438
File ⇨Revert, CDBA 4
File ⇨Save, 30
File ⇨Save As, 30
File ⇨Save As Template, 98
file size
    animation, 361–362, 363
    Bandwidth Profiler, checking using, 245
    component, 828
    compression file size/quality balance, 955,
        CDBT 38
    curve, 363
    Flash advantages, 41
    Flash Player, 1098
    font effect on, 229, 234, 244, 247–248, CDBC 4
    interface design considerations, 68
    .jpg file, 630, 812
    layer number effect on, 276
    library asset sharing, reducing through, 170,
        171, 820
    line editing, reducing through, 146
    of movie, displaying, 613
    of movie in stand-alone distribution, 664
    movie versus document, 609
    MP3 file, 448, 814
    projector, 660
    QuickTime movie, 1059
    QuickTime video, 1067
    raster graphic, 451, 453
    Size Report, 616, CDBC 5
    sound, 448, 1002–1003, 1006–1009, 1172
    sound, estimating, 444, 1176
    symbol, reducing through using, 163
    text, CDBC 3
    3D graphic, 1022
    tweening, reducing through, 318
    vector graphic, 451, 453, 974–977
    video quality versus, CDBT 38

FileIO Xtra utility, 663
fill. *See also* color; gradient
    adjustment handle, 260–261
    alignment, 258
    bitmap, 193, 210, 257–258, 259–261, 262–263
    center point, 210, 258, 261, 262
    deleting, 201
    edge softening, 268–269
    expanding, 267–268
    gap treatment options, 259, 373
    line conversion to, 265–267
    lock option, 128, 259–260
    Mask layer using, 349
    painting behind, 131
    painting over, 131, 132
    rotating, 210, 262
    sampling, 216, 254–256
    scaling, 210, 262–263, 265–266
    selecting, 132, 137, 215–216, 286–287
    skewing, 210, 263
    style, custom, 258
    tools, 98, 124–125, 127, 201
    transparency, 208–209
Fill Transform tool, 98
Filling the Browser Window by Using the
    <FRAMESET> Tag tutorial (Moock),
    CDBT 43–46
Filter Settings dialog box, 524
Fireworks MX
    ad banner, creating using, 953–956
    batch processing, 943, 950–951, 952–953
    Bitmap Properties dialog box, 949
    color tables, 204
    command, creating custom, 951–952
    copying/pasting into Flash, 948
    described, 942–943
    Document window, 948
    Export Movie dialog box, 954
    Export Preview window, 948–949
    exporting to animated GIF, 953–956
    exporting to Director, 945
    exporting to Illustrator, 945
    exporting to JPEG, 949, 951, 952, 953
    exporting to PNG sequence, 950, 954–956
    file sequence, optimizing for Flash, 950
    FreeHand file, importing into, 945

GIF, creating animated, 627–628, 953–956
Gradient tool, 943
History panel, 951–952
image table, image reconstitution from, 944
Import Settings dialog box, 947
importing from, 455, 469, 476, 945–948
JavaScript Extensibility API, 943
JPEG compression options, 944, 949, 952
keyboard shortcut set in Flash, 95
Launch and Edit mode, 944
masking, 945–946, 947
Matte drop-down menu, 949
Optimize panel, 948, 954–955
PNG format, working with, 469, 942, 944,
     945–946, 954
PNG Import Settings dialog box, 946
Property inspector, 942
Publish Settings dialog box, 956
Quick Export button, 943, 944
text, working with, 943, 947, 948
transparency, 945–948
user interface, 942
variable assignment, 945
Web production features, 945
FirstRun folder, 622
.fla files, 29, 30–31
Flash Asset Xtra, 669, 1097, 1099, 1102–1105
Flash Bible Web site, 1119
Flash Character Design Strategies tutorial
     (Corsaro), 373–376
Flash Debug Player, 619–620, CDBC 61
Flash Design for Mobile Devices (de los Reyes),
     446
Flash Dispatcher Dreamweaver MX behavior,
     1090–1092
Flash Exchange, 86, 87
Flash ⇨Keyboard Shortcuts, 95
Flash Player
   accessibility, 33
   ActiveX control versus plug-in, 642–643
   browser redirection if not installed, 42, 63,
        642, 667, 1092
   browser support, 665
   closing, 663
   Debug version, 619–620, CDBC 61
   deleting, 54

detection, brute force method, CDBT 47,
     CDBT 48
detection, forcing content without, 642–643
detection, forgoing, CDBT 47
detection, scriptless, CDBT 47, CDBT 50–55
detection of ActiveX control, 46, 622,
     645, 646
detection using Dreamweaver MX behavior,
     1088–1089, 1090–1093, CDBT 50
detection using gateway page, CDBT 47
detection using JavaScript, 622, 644–645, 667,
     CDBT 48–50, CDBT 54–55
detection using sniffer movie, 646–650,
     CDBT 50–53
detection using template, 622, 644, 645, 667,
     CDBT 49–50
detection using VBScript, 46, 622, 644, 645,
     CDBT 48–50
distributing stand-alone, 662–664, 666
downloading, 42, 619, 636–637, 665, 666
executable, opening from, 663
file size, 1098
font, limiting number found by, 235
font interpretation, 236
full-screen mode, 663
HTML document, opening from, 663–664
HTML plug-in detection page, 63, 622,
     642–650, 667
installation, automatic, 636–637, 643, 1092
key press capture, 663
licensing, 661, 666
Macintosh, 33
menu bar visibility, 625, 637–638, 661, 663
mobile device support, 666
movie, scaling in, 663
MP3 support, 422, 423, 442
MSAA integration, 33
named anchor support, 512
OEM (Original Equipment Manufacturer)
     partnership, 1153
operating systems supported, 665
platforms available for, 42
plug-in, 42, 665–667
Pocket PC support, 666, 1151–1154
prevalence of, CDBT 47

Continued

Flash Player *(continued)*
    projector, creating using stand-alone, 661–662
    QuickTime Flash movie playback on, 1057
    Shockwave Player versus, 1098
    sound playback, frame drop to keep up with, CDBC 3
    stand-alone, 659, 661–664
    stand-alone, movie testing in, 609
    Unicode support, CDBA 14
    version detection, CDBT 48
    version detection using JavaScript, 645, 667, CDBT 49, CDBT 55
    version detection using sniffer movie, 647–648, CDBT 50, CDBT 52–53
    version detection using template, 622, 667
    version detection using VBScript, CDBT 49
    version numbering convention, 33
    video, handling of embedded, 801
    XML integration, 33, 36
Flash ⇨Preferences, 106
Flash ⇨Preferences ⇨Editing, 128
Flash Support Center, 86, 87
Flash UI Components folder, 602, 829
Flash Writer Illustrator plug-in, 990, 991
FlashDispatcher.mxp file, 1090
flashenabled Web site, 1154
FlashForge software, 669
Flashforum Web site, 1193, CDBT 48
FlashGo software, 1161
flash*.html files (on the CD), 650
FlashJester Web site, 669
FlashKit Web site, 1099, CDBC 67
FlashLogo_final.fla (on the CD), 900
Flashmagazine.com, 669
FlashMXBible Web site, 633, 794
FlashNow server, 872
FlashPlanet Web site, CDBC 67
FlashSupport.com Web site, 45, 633, 1154, CDBA 15, CDBC 67
flattening
    export operation, layer flattening in, 30
    QuickTime movie, 1058, 1066, 1067
flipping object, 270, CDBT 30–31
FListBox functions, 834
Floating Point codec, 1064

floppy disk, distributing stand-alone on, 662–664
flowchart.html (on the CD), 79
flowcharting
    interface design, 53–54, 76–78
    layout flowchart, 53
    movies, 556
    navigation flowchart, 53
    organizational flowchart, 53, 72–76, 583, 887
    portfolio site, 53–54, 887
    preproduction, CDBT 2
    process flowchart, 53, 76–79
    shapes used in, 73–74
    site flowchart, 53
    storyboard flowchart, CDBT 8–10
    Visio, creating using, 72–81
flush method, 933
.flv files, CDBA 8. *See also* video
focus JavaScript method, 547
#focusRect Director Lingo property, 1112
_focusrect property, 710, 1112
followMouse function, CDBC 36
font. *See also* font, embedded; text
    antialiasing, 221, 234, 235, 238
    bitmap font, 236, 250
    bold, 228, 230, 242, 874
    breaking apart, CDBC 4
    button font, 845–846, 1086
    changing, 226, 227–228, 230, 874
    component font, changing, 842, 843–846
    current, displaying, 227
    device font, 229, 234–235, 625, 639, 641
    display troubleshooting, 235–236
    exporting, 233–234
    file size, effect on, 229, 234, 244, 247–248, CDBC 4
    Flash Player, limiting number found by, 235
    Flash Player interpretation process, 236
    FreeHand, considerations when using, 984
    HTML styles, 874
    importing, 173
    italic, 228, 230, 242
    Library, shared, 166, 170, 240–248, 821–822, CDBC 16–17
    linkage, 240–241, 244, 245–247, 970
    Mac/Windows confusion, 236–237
    Miniml (on the CD), 238–240

missing, 237–238
non-Roman, 18
optimizing, CDBC 3–4
outline, 221, 233, 235
outline, missing, 236
PostScript, 236, 250
publishing options, 625
_sans, 234
_serif, 234
sizing Miniml font, 239
sizing using application Text menu, 230
sizing using HTML, 874
sizing using Movie Explorer, 226, 228
sizing using Property inspector, 227
storage location, 240–241, 245
subscript, 230
substitution, 233, 236–238
superscript, 230
symbol, font, 166, 167, 173, 240–248, CDBC 4
text field, 173, 239
TrueType, 236
_typewriter, 234
virtual, CDBA 22–24
font, embedded
    anti-aliasing, 234, 235
    auto-embedding, default, 221, 233–234
    component, working with in, 845–846
    device font versus, 234–235
    file size, effect on, 234, 244, 247–248
    font symbol, storing in, 242
    Miniml font, 239
    naming, 821
    options, setting in Character Options dialog
        box, 233
    outline, converting to, 483–484
    PDF (Portable Document Format) file, in, 970
    Shared library, in, 821
    vector graphic, in, 473, 483–484
Font Mapping dialog box, 237
Font Symbol Properties dialog box, 166, 242
fontEmbed files (on the CD), 244
font_finish.fla (on the CD), 846
fontLink files (on the CD), 244, 246
fontSource files (on the CD), 244
font_start.fla (on the CD), 845
for loop, 695

for ... in loop, 695–696
formats compatible with Flash, CDBA 6–9
form.cgi, 688
forms
    ASP script, processing by remote, 855–859
    button instance on, 838–839, 858, 1125
    CGI script, processing by, 688, 855
    ColdFusion MX, in, 1123–1124, 1139–1147
    creating, 855–859
    described, 855
    e-mailing data collected by, 855–859,
        1124–1125
    feedback form, 73, 76, 77, 855–859, 1123–1127
    getURL action, role in form submission, 540,
        541, 688
    guestbook HTML form, creating, 1131–1132
    login, 699–702, 1139–1147
    percent loaded information, displaying in
        HTML form, 651, 655–656
    text, descriptive, 856
    text field for user input, 699–700, 856
    time form data received by server,
        displaying, 856–857
    variables in, 699–702, 855, 857–858
Fortress server, 872
forums, Internet, 45
FPushButton methods, 835
FRadioButton methods, 536
frame rate. See also frames
    alpha value effect on, 326
    animation, 366, 1043, CDBT 30
    AVI format, 406
    CD-ROM, 394
    default, 100
    Director movie, of Flash movie within, 1105
    displaying, 111, 613
    Illustrator, specifying when exporting SWF
        from, 992
    maximum, 111
    optimizing, CDBC 5
    preview accuracy using Play, 610
    QuickTime, 1061, 1070, 1075
    setting, 111
    Sorenson Squeeze, in, 515, 516, 520, 521, 527
    sound, effect on, 429
    video, 393, 395, 496, 501, 515

Frame View options menu, 119–120
frame-by-frame animation. *See also* animation
   described, 112, 311
   Director, creating using, 42
   Flash, creating using, 314
   inbetweening, 368–372
   key, 368
   keyframe in, 312, 313
   Painter 7, creating using, CDBT 79–82
   repeater frame, 313, 314, 371
   sequence, reversing, 337
   tween animation, mixing with, 306
   uses for, 306, 312
frames. *See also* frame rate; keyframes; timeline
   auto-insert feature, 1060–1061
   Bandwidth Profiler, representation in, CDBC
      45
   blending, 412
   byte limit, 613
   clearing, 116
   commenting, 113, 549, 585
   content, editing, 116
   copying/pasting, 108, 115, 322
   current, displaying ID number, 111
   cutting, 116
   deleting content from, 110
   in Director movie, assigning Flash action to,
      1100–1102
   download status, checking, 794
   dragging, 114–115
   empty, 112, 113
   endframe, 112, 113
   event handling, 717, 722, 736–738, 739, CDBC
      40
   filled, 112
   going to specific, 536–539, 1089
   introduced, 35
   keyframe creation from, 115, 313
   label, 113, 513, 584, 890
   label naming convention, 890, CDBC 65
   layer visibility in, 35
   library asset loading into, 30
   looping, 337–338
   Movie Clip symbol, replacing with, 395
   Movie Explorer, filtering using, 188
   moving, 114, 314, 315

   multiple, editing, 111, 315–316
   named anchor, frame label as, 513
   naming, 113
   number, going to specific, 538
   number of, returning total, 794
   number supported, maximum, 107
   Playhead, relation to, 35
   preview, 120
   printing, 121, 721, 786
   property display, 108
   QuickTime video, extracting from, 1072–1073
   removing, 116
   repeater frames, 313, 314, 371
   reusing, 1028
   reversing, 337–338
   selecting, 113–114, 116
   size in bytes, streaming considerations, 613,
      614
   size on screen, 393–394, 395, 396–397, 496,
      501
   span, 112, 113–114, 116, 313
   statistics, viewing, CDBC 45
   3D effect using, 1027, 1028, 1029
   time elapsed, measuring in, 111
   timeline, centering on, 110
   timeline, deleting from, 108, 116
   timeline, display on, 106, 107, 110
   timeline, inserting on, 115
   timeline, ordering on, 108
   tinting, 120
`<FRAMESET>` tag, CDBT 43–46
`frames_example.fla` (on the CD), 115
`_framesloaded` property, 710, 794, 1112
framing animation, 303
Fraunhofer MP3 codec, 445, 521
Free Transform tool, 98, 248, 271–275, 348
FreeHand
   advantages of using, 977–978, 986–990
   Animate to Layer tool, 987
   Blend feature, CDBT 95
   clipping paths, CDBT 101
   design, conceptualizing using, 987
   exporting from, 970, 976, 980–981, 982,
      984–986
   features, 977–978
   Flash versus as drawing tool, CDBT 94

font considerations, 984
gradient, 978–979
Illustrator versus, 987
importing content into Fireworks MX, 945
importing content into Flash, 454, 476–477,
    983–986
    alignment considerations, 984
    clipping path considerations, CDBT 101
    color considerations, 474, 477, 970–971,
        978, CDBT 99
    compression options, 985
    Convert Editable EPS option, 477
    dashed line handling, CDBT 102
    EPS file considerations, 477, 478, 481,
        CDBT 94
    fill considerations, CDBT 93–94
    gradient considerations, 474, 477
    keeping overlapping elements intact, 477
    layer preservation during, 476, CDBT 96,
        CDBT 100
    via opening file, 983–984, CDBT 94
    rasterizing vector graphic during, 476
    stroke square cap conversion during, 477
    symbol considerations, CDBT 98–100
    text considerations, 477, 970, 980,
        984–985, CDBT 101–102
layout using, 66, 984–985, 989
Lens fill, CDBT 101
Object Inspector, CDBT 95
page sizing, CDBT 94
path, simplifying using, 975–976
Perspective Grid, CDBT 102
planning using, 987
preferences setup, 978
presentation production, role in, 987,
    988–989
printing, 987, 988–989
Release to Layers feature, CDBT 96
Rotation tool, CDBT 95
spiral tool, CDBT 95
Symbol Editing mode, CDBT 96
text, converting to outline using, 484, 970,
    980, 982, 985
text considerations when exporting from,
    984, 985, 986
text effects, 979–983

Text inspector feature, 981–983
Trace tool, 971–973
Transform dialog box, CDBT 95
FreeHand Import dialog box, 476, CDBT 97
Freshink Image and Graphic Design Web site,
    CDBT 92
fromCharCode method, 926
fscommand action, 512, 623, 650–655, 662–663
FScrollBar methods, 837
FScrollPane methods, 837
FStyleFormat object, 843, 845
FStyleMethod
    object, 842
    property, 842
function
    action, 744
    constructor, 698
    data type, 744
functional specification document, 54–55,
    887–888, CDBT 3
function_definition.as (on the CD), CDBC
    39
functions
    addLoader, 907–908, 911
    argument, 746
    buildInterface, 926
    built-in, 698
    chain, CDBC 36
    changeColor, 770, 771, 773–774
    changeCursor, CDBC 36
    changeDrawingTool, CDBC 36
    checkInput, 929
    checkLoad, 817
    clearInterval, 817
    code centralization, using for, CDBC 37
    ColdFusion MX, 1123
    createAlphabet, 926
    createLib, 760
    createMenu, 756, 757
    #DateFormat ColdFusion MX function, 1123,
        1134
    defining, 747–748
    definition, accompanying function code with
        descriptive, CDBC 38–40
    described, 746–747

                                        Continued

functions *(continued)*
draw, CDBC 36
Dreamweaver MX Flash built-in functions, 1084–1088
eval, 683–684
executing, 748
FListBox functions, 834
followMouse, CDBC 36
game application, in, 921, 924, 926–927, 931
gameStatus, 931
getColour, CDBC 36
isLeft, 929, 930
keyframe, dependence on, 748
keyframe, placing in, 747
loadArticles, 861–862
loadFile, 818
loadMP3, 816
loadSWF, 802–803, 804
lookForMatch, 929, 930
method, as, 755–759
modifyOptions, CDBC 36
MovieClip object, dependent on, 721
multipurpose, CDBC 36
naming, 746–747, 748
new constructor, using with, 759–761
#Now ColdFusion MX function, 1123
object, creating using, 759–761
positionAlphabet, 927
print, 721, 785, 786
printAsBitmap, 785, 786
printAsBitmapNum, 786
printing-related, 786
printNum, 786
random, 927–928
saveLossScore, 934–935
saveName, 934
setRound, 927
showUserInfo, 934
situations calling for, 747
sound library, creating using, 759–761
startDrawing, CDBC 36
text field, executing from, 880–881
#TimeFormat ColdFusion MX function, 1123, 1134
unloadSWF, 815
#urlencodedformat ColdFusion MX function, 1134
FutureSplash compatibility with Flash, CDBA 6

G
game application
character, conveying, 920
design, 919–921
event handling, 921, 926
feedback to user, displaying, 925, 931–932
functions in, 921, 924, 926–927, 931
interaction design, 920
interface, 920, 924–926
randomness, generating, 927–928
round, asset resetting at beginning of each, 926–927, 928, 932
round, keeping track of, 923
rounds, setting delay between, 932–933
rounds, storing information between, 933–935
score handling, 920, 923–924, 925, 931–932, 933–935
skill required, 919
sound, 920, 923
status, checking, 931–933
text, working with in, 924–926, 927–931, 934
user input, handling, 929–931, 933
username, displaying, 923, 934
username, inputting, 933–934
variable initialization/reinitialization, 923–924, 927, 928, 932
variable value comparison, 930
visual design, 920
gameStatus function, 931
ge alphabetically after or same as operator, 690
Generator
component versus, 827
history, 39–40
introduced, 36
template, 624, 673
genericmovie.com, 1149
Get Info dialog box, 670
getBeginIndex method, 882
getBytesLoaded method, 494, 715, 777
getBytesTotal method, 715, 777, 794
getCaretIndex method, 883
getCode method, 719
getColour function, CDBC 36
getDepth method, 714
getEndIndex method, 882
getFlashProperty Director Lingo command, 1111

getFocus method, 883
getLocal method, 933
getPan method, 776
getProperty action, 706
getRGB method, 769, 771
getTextExtent method, 879
getTimer keyword, 683
getTransform method
    color object, 769, 772, 775
    sound object, 776, 782–783
getURL action
    button, adding to, 550, 552, 853–854, 913
    described, 540, 853
    Director/Flash interaction, using in,
        1100–1102
    form submission, role in, 540, 541, 688
    HTML document, opening using, 647,
        663–664
    link types possible using, 540
    mailto link using, 552, 853–854, 913
    Movie Clip timeline, using on, 688
    URL parameter, 540, 683
    variable, sending to URL using, 687–688
    Variables parameter, 541, 681, 683
    Window parameter, 541
getVariable Director Lingo command, 1110
getVolume method, 776
Ghostwriters Radio Mall Web site, 365
GIF Export dialog box, 965–966
GIF (Graphics Interchange File) image
    animated, 627–628, 953–956
    color, 196, 628–629, 965–966
    exporting, 405, 456, 962, 965–966
    gradient, removing from during publishing,
        628
    importing, 454, 463
    interlacing, 628
    JavaScript/VBScript, displaying in HTML
        page using, 645–646
    JPEG compared, 630
    Photoshop image preview in GIF format, 959
    publishing settings, 627–630
    smoothing, 628
    transparency, 470, 628–629
gifcolors.fla (on the CD), 965
Glennon, Dermot (founder/interactive director,
    toque industries), 1186

_global namespace, 745
Global Skins folder, 829
glossiness, 1039
gMovie Maker, 1149
goals, establishing, 51–52, 57, 674
Goldshell Digital Media, 669
Goodman, Danny (*JavaScript Bible*), 46
goto action, 536–539
gotoAndPlay
    action, 537, 542, 576, 1071, CDBA 25
    method, 712
gotoAndStop
    action, 506, 536, 542, CDBA 25
    method, 712
gradient. *See also* color; fill
    adjustment handle, 260–261
    alpha setting, 213–215, CDBC 8
    blend, replacing with, 485–487
    center point, 210, 258, 261, 262
    color, 150–151, 210–213
    custom, 210–215
    export considerations, 410
    Fireworks MX Gradient tool, 943
    FreeHand, in, 978–979
    GIF, removing from during publishing, 628
    Illustrator, considerations when exporting
        from, 996
    importing graphic, considerations when, 202,
        474, 477, 485–487
    lighting effect using, 264–265
    linear, 205, 209–210, 261, 262–263
    lock fill option, 259–260
    pre-built, 201, 210
    radial, 205, 209–210, 212, 261, 262–263
    rotating, 210, 262
    scaling, 210, 262–263
    skewing, 210, 263
    swatches, gradient, 201
    3D effect, using, 264–265, 290, CDBT 24–27
    24-bit color required for smooth, 194
    vector graphic, 474
*Graphic Artists Guild Handbook of Pricing and
        Ethical Guidelines*, 56
Graphic Symbols versus Movie Clips
        (Debreuil and Debreuil), 174
graphics. *See* drawing; raster graphics; 3D
        graphics; vector graphics

Graphics Interchange File format. *See* GIF

`graphics_*.fla` files (on the CD), 841, 843, 844

greater than sign (>)
    alphabetically after operator, 690
    greater than operator, 690

greater than sign, equals sign (>=)
    alphabetically after or same as operator, 690
    greater than or equal to operator, 690

Greek character set, CDBA 12, CDBA 14, CDBA 22–23

grid
    color, 104
    Document window display options, 104
    hiding/showing, 104
    Info panel alignment grid, 156
    measurement units, changing, 104
    Snap to, 104, 140–141
    spacing, 104

Grid dialog box, 104

group
    breaking apart, 277
    creating, 137, 276
    data, raw, 171
    drawing elements, of, 135–136, 137, 276
    editing, 160, 276
    erasing, 134
    graphic elements, of, 137
    importing grouped vector graphics, 474–475, 476–480
    library, group information in, 171
    Mask layer using, 349, 351
    moving, 137
    selecting, 135–136
    stacking order, 275
    Stage, moving to, 136
    symbols versus, 171
    text block, 137
    transformation applied to, resetting, 155, 159
    tweening, 318
    ungrouping, 134, 276

`gt` alphabetically after operator, 690

guestbook application
    buttons, 1134–1135, 1136–1138
    ColdFusion MX, using, 1131–1139
    comment, inserting, 1132
    comment, retrieving, 1133–1134, 1138
    comment sorting, 1133

comment time/date, retrieving, 1134
database, inserting record in, 1132
database, querying, 1132, 1133–1134
database, setting up, 1128–1131
e-mailing comment from, 1133
Flash interface, integrating with, 1134–1139
HTML form, creating, 1131–1132
login setup, 1128–1129
publishing, 1138
ScrollBar, 1134
status message display, 1135–1136
string encoding for import to Flash, 1134

`guestbook.fla` (on the CD), 1134

Guide layers, 118, 342–344

guides, 105, 141, CDBT 20

Guides dialog box, 105

GW Micro Web site, 602

H

Hand tool, 98, 101

HandyZIP utility, 1160

`hangman.fla` (on the CD), 919

The Hard Truth About Resolution Web Page at elitevideo.com, 491

Harold, Elliotte Rusty (*XML Bible*), 860

Hebrew character set, CDBA 12, CDBA 22–23

`#height` Director Lingo property, 1111

`_height` property, 709, 725, 1111

Help menu, 86–87

Help ⇨ Using Flash, 602

`hide` method, 766

history of Flash products, 39–40

`hitTest` files (on the CD), 765, 766

`hitTest` method
    Director Lingo, 1112
    Flash, 718, 764–766, 768

`holder` object, 810

Holub, Allen (*Enough Rope to Shoot Yourself in the Foot: Rules for C and C++ Programming*), CDBC 41

Homesite, 1120, 1121

Honselaar, Chris (Introduction to XML and Flash tutorial), 1188–1189

Hot Door Harmony plug-in, 199–200

How to Boss Your Fonts Around (Williams), 236

HREF HTML attribute, 646, 651, 880–881

HTML (Hypertext Markup Language). *See also* DHTML (Dynamic Hypertext Markup Language)
  ActionScript, integration with, 33
  ActiveX control attributes, 636
  background color, 639, 641, 651–655
  browser redirection if Player not installed, 642
  ColdFusion MX, returning from, 1133
  ColdFusion MX troubleshooting in, 1131
  device font option, 639, 641
  display quality, specifying, 638, 641
  enabling when displaying Dynamic text, 232
  Flash integration overview, 45
  Flash Player, opening HTML document from, 663–664
  Flash Player detection, 63, 622, 642–650, 667
  Flash Player menu visibility, specifying, 637–638
  font style, 874
  frameset, 63
  `getURL` action, opening HTML document using, 647, 663–664
  Illustrator, creating HTML page when exporting SWF from, 992
  image map, 623
  JavaScript identifier assignment, 637, 641
  JavaScript/Flash interactivity involving, 650–657
  linking, 875
  LiveConnect feature, enabling, 641
  MIME type designation, 642
  movie in HTML page, aligning, 625–626, 637, 638, 1082
  movie in HTML page, border size, 638, 641, 1082, 1083
  movie in HTML page, inserting using Dreamweaver MX, 1081
  movie in HTML page, inserting using `<EMBED>` tag, 635, 640–642, 643, 688, 1083
  movie in HTML page, inserting using link, 636
  movie in HTML page, inserting using `<OBJECT>` tag, 635–640, 643, 688, 1083
  movie in HTML page, inserting using template, 621–624
  movie in HTML page, looping, 637, 641, 1082

  movie in HTML page, naming, 1082
  movie in HTML page, passing parameter to, 1082
  movie in HTML page, playback during download option, 637, 1082
  movie in HTML page, positioning, 625–626, 637, 638, 641, 1083
  movie in HTML page, quality setting, 1082
  movie in HTML page, sizing, 624, 626, 637, 641, 1082
  page production overview, 63
  paragraph style, 874
  percent loaded information, displaying in HTML form, 651, 655–656
  Pocket PC content, 1155–1156
  projector, opening HTML document from, 663–664
  publishing to, 512–513, 617, 621–627
  sniffer movie, integrating into HTML document, 649–650
  tags in use, listing, 877
  tags supported, 873–874
  templates, 621–624, 644, 645, 667, 668
  text field, 511
  text field, HTML formatting within, 873–881
  text field, inserting using ActionScript, 877–878
  variable declaration, 688
  variable declaration upon movie loading, 639–640
Htmlscript. *See* Miva script
`htmlText_` files (on the CD), 877, 878
`htmlText` property, 874
HTTP (Hypertext Transfer Protocol) request handling, 811
The Human Interface tutorial (Nisselson), CDBT 11–17
human vision considerations in interface design, 220, CDBT 11–15
humanface.com, 919
hyperlinks
  Dreamweaver MX, update using, 1081, 1093–1094
  HTML, 875
  image map, 623
  `mailto`, 552, 853–854, 875–876, 913

Continued

hyperlinks *(continued)*
    SSL (Secure Socket Layer) connection, 540
    text, adding to, 230
    Web page from movie, 540–541, 550
Hypertext Markup Language. *See* HTML

I

IBM Microdrive, 1160
ICC (International Color Consortium) profile,
    961
IconBuilder utility, 669
Iconfactory Web site, 669
`if. . .else` statement
    ActionScript, 690–694
    Director Lingo, 1101
`if` statement, 691
`ifFrameLoaded` action, 794
illusion, manipulating, 300–306
Illustrator
    color, 971
    curve quality, 993
    exporting from, 990, 992–994
    exporting to from Fireworks MX, 945
    exporting to from Flash, 404, 990, 994, 995
    Flash Writer plug-in, 990, 991
    FreeHand versus, 987
    gradient considerations, 996
    importing content from, 454, 478–481, 971
    JPEG compression options, 991, 992
    keyboard shortcut set in Flash, 95
    logo graphic, creating in, 899
    Pathfinder panel, 975
    Save for Web feature, 993
    text, converting to outline using, 484, 970
IMA codec, 1064
Image Map template, 623
Image ⇨Mode ⇨Indexed Color, 204
image scanning, 891
`image1.jpg` (on the CD), 18
Imation FlashGo, 1161
Import Color Swatch dialog box, 204
Import dialog box, 424, 474, CDBA 4–5
import operations
    ActionScript code in external file, CDBC 33,
        CDBC 39
    After Effects, image sequence to, 409–415

After Effects, movie to, 1067
AI image, 454, 478–480
animating imported vector graphic, 481
animation, 1055–1056
.asf file, 498
.avi file, 497
.bmp file, 454
color, 196, 202
color from FreeHand, 474, 477, 970–971, 978,
    CDBT 99
color from Illustrator, 971
color palette, 203–205
compression considerations, 457, 459, 462,
    467–471
Director, Flash movie into, 669, 1097, 1099,
    1103–1105
Dreamweaver MX, Flash content into,
    1081–1084
.dv file, 497
.dxf file, 454
EMF image, 454
EPS image, 454, 477, 478–480
.fh_ file, 454, 476
file formats importable, 41, 42, 453–456
Fireworks MX, from, 455, 469, 476, 945–948
font symbol, 173
FreeHand into Fireworks MX, 945
FreeHand into Flash, 454, 476–477, 983–986
    alignment considerations, 984
    clipping path considerations, CDBT 101
    compression options, 985
    Convert Editable EPS option, 477
    dashed line handling, CDBT 102
    EPS file considerations, 477, 478, 481,
        CDBT 94
    fill considerations, CDBT 93–94
    gradient considerations, 474, 477
    keeping overlapping elements intact, 477
    layer preservation during, 476, CDBT 96,
        CDBT 100
    via opening file, 983–984, CDBT 94
    rasterizing vector graphic during, 476
    stroke square cap conversion during, 477
    symbol considerations, CDBT 98–100
    text considerations, 477, 970, 980,
        984–985, CDBT 101–102

gradient considerations, 202, 474, 477, 485–487
group, 474–475, 476–480
Illustrator, from, 454, 478–481, 971
layer preservation, 476, CDBT 96, CDBT 100
library, to, 173, 424, 460, 566, 821
library storage of imported element, 172–173, 196
Mac Paint, from, 454
Mask layer considerations, 458
.mov file, 498
movie, import-protecting, 30, 619
.mpeg file, 497, 498
.mp3 file, 419–420, 421, 423, 612
Painter 7, from, CDBT 78, CDBT 81
Photoshop, from, 455, 461
.pict file, 455
.png file, 460, 895–898
.png file from Fireworks, 455, 469, 946
.png file from Photoshop, 959
.psd file, 455
QuickTime audio, 420
QuickTime graphic, 455
QuickTime image sequence, 1076–1077
QuickTime movie, 1059, 1060–1062, 1073–1076
QuickTime video, 498
raster graphic, 172–173, 456–457, 458–461, 462
Shared library, from external, 823
sound, 173, 419–421, 423–425, 444
symbol conversion, 173
text, 224
3D graphic, 42, 1025–1030, 1055–1056
transparency considerations, 453, 461
vector graphic, 173, 473–481
video, 20, 497–504
WMF images, 455
.wmv file, 498
Import to Library dialog box, 215
Import Video dialog box, 499
Import Video Settings dialog box, 20, 500
inbetweening, 368–372
#include action, 680, 909, 1096, CDBC 32–33
indexOf method, 742
inertia, conveying in animation, 307

Info panel, 155–157
information architecture, 51
Ink Bottle tool, 153, 201, 216, 254–255, 256–257
input state, 853
Insert ⇨Blank Keyframe, 115
Insert ⇨Convert to Symbol, 10
Insert ⇨Create Motion Tween, 11
Insert ⇨Create Symbol, 332
Insert ⇨Frame, 115
Insert ⇨Keyframe, 115
Insert ⇨New Symbol, 181
Insert ⇨Remove Frames, 116
Insert ⇨Remove Scene, 102
Insert ⇨Scene, 102
Insert Target Path dialog box, 562–563
Inset ⇨Motion Guide, 344
Install Flash Player 6 AX.exe, 620
Install Flash Player 6 OSX file, 620
Install Flash Player 6.exe, 620
Install Flash 6 Player file, 620
instanceof operator, 745–746
Integer codec, 1064
interactivity
    action relation to, 531
    check box, 836
    event handling relation to, 531
    fscommand interactivity, 651
    game interaction design, 920
    Input text field, 685
    introduced, 41
    mapping in visual symbols, CDBT 8
    planning, 673–676, CDBT 1–10
    presentation, interactive, 46
    problem, defining, 674
    process, breaking down into language, 675–677, CDBT 7
    radio button, 836
    storyboarding, CDBT 6–8
    video, lost in, 392, 395
interface design
    aesthetics, 65–66
    backtracking difficulty, 65
    browser compatibility, 67
    build-out phase, 70–71
    color, 66, 67
    comprehensive phase, 68–70

Continued

interface design *(continued)*
    drawing tools used, 67
    drop-down menu, 66, 71
    file size considerations, 68
    flowcharting, 53–54, 76–78
    game interface, 920, 924–926
    human vision considerations, 220,
        CDBT 11–15
    layout, conceptual, 66–67
    modules, swappable, 66
    movement, CDBT 13
    navigation system, 55, 59, 67
    peak moment, 68
    predictability through using component, 828
    presentationalist approach, 64
    resolution target, 67
    roughs, 65, 67–68
    structuralist approach, 64
    text, screen versus print presentation,
        CDBT 14–16
    timeline, 68–70
    usability, 595
    working model, 65
Interface Design tutorial (Jordan), 64–72
Interfacing Flash Movies with Miva tutorial (Lo),
        CDBT 69–73
International Color Consortium profile. *See* ICC
Interpret Footage dialog box, 411
Introduction to XML and Flash tutorial
        (Honselaar), 862–865
introduction.rtf (on the CD), 602
irregularity, using in animation, 300
isLeft function, 929, 930
ISO (International Standards Organization)
        character encoding standards, CDBA 12
item_ RTF files (on the CD), 596, 599
Iuppa, Nicholas (*Designing Interactive Digital
        Media*), 56

J

Jack's Page Web site, 309
Jamieson, Justin (Using Propellerhead's Rebirth
        to Create Loops for Flash tutorial), 1189
Jan Tschichold: A Life in Typography (McLean),
        220
Japanese character encoding, CDBA 12, CDBA
        14, CDBA 18–20

JavaScript
    ActionScript similarity to, 40
    client-side scripting, 45–46
    Dreamweaver MX JavaScript behaviors,
        1088–1091
    Flash, using in conjunction with, 45–46
    Flash Player detection using, 622, 644–645,
        667, CDBT 48–50, CDBT 54–55
    GIF image, displaying in HTML page using,
        645–646
    loading progress display using, 655–657
    movie, working with in, 637, 641, 650–657
    movie identifier assignment, 637, 641
JavaScript Bible (Goodman), 46, 651
JibJab.com's Collage Animation Workflow
        tutorial (Spiridellis), 362–364
Jordan, Eric (Interface Design tutorial), 1189
Jordan, Lawrence (animator), 298
The Journal of Edwin Carp (on the CD), 302–303,
        384, CDBT 29
JPEG compression
    doubling, avoiding, 459, 463, 464, 470
    8-bit file, applying to, 470
    Fireworks MX options, 944, 949, 952
    Illustrator options, 991, 992
    introduced, 454
    Mask, applying selectively via, 944
    overriding, 462, 463, 465
    progressive download, 470, 812, 894, 949–950
    setting, 468
    setting before import, 942
JPEG (Joint Photographic Experts Group)
        image. *See also* MJPEG (Motion JPEG);
        raster graphics
    exporting from Fireworks MX, 949, 951, 952,
        953
    exporting from Flash, 406, 962
    file size, 630, 812
    GIF format compared, 630
    importing, 454, 463–465
    loading, 36, 714, 811–814, 895, 912–913
    Photoshop image preview in JPEG format,
        959
    placeholder, 912–913, 915
    preloading, 816–820
    publish settings, 620, 630

rotation distortion, 466
unloading, 813
JTools utility, 669

K

Key object, 547
keyboard shortcuts, 94–96, 677, 702, 1165–1169,
    CDBC 28–29
KeyDown event, 719
keyframes
    action association with, 547–548
    animation, in, 112, 312, 313–315
    blank, 111, 313, 315
    described, 111
    frame, creating from, 115, 313
    fscommand action, adding to, 652
    function, placing in, 747
    function dependence on, 748
    label, 113, 584
    label, goto action targeting of, 538–539
    named anchor assignment to, automatic, 102
    naming, 113
    presentation mapping to, 584–585, 988
    preview, 120
    scene, relation to, 30
    scene versus, 590
    Sorenson Squeeze, creation in, 522–523
    sound, assigning to, 423–424, 427
    sound object versus keyframe sound, 777
    time event, capturing using, 547–548
    timeline, inserting on, 9, 115
    timeline, moving on, 113
    tween beginning/ending keyframes,
        specifying, 35
    variable declaration in, 684
    video keyframe, 500, 501
keyPress event, 546–547
keys (motion drawings), 368–372
keystroke event handling, 544, 546–547, 719
KeyUp event, 719
kinematics, inverse, 1024. See also 3D graphics
Kontent-Online Web site, 1019
Korean character encoding, CDBA 12, CDBA 14,
    CDBA 18–20
Kroeger, Craig (Using Miniml fonts in Flash MX
    tutorial), 1189

Krug, Steve (Don't Make Me Think: A Common
    Sense Approach to Web Usability), 62

L

language support, non-English
    Arabic, CDBA 12, CDBA 22–23
    Baltic languages, CDBA 22–23
    character encoding, CDBA 11–14
    Chinese, CDBA 12, CDBA 13, CDBA 14, CDBA
        18–20
    content character set, changing, CDBA 17–18
    Cyrillic-alphabet languages, CDBA 12, CDBA
        14–17, CDBA 18, CDBA 22–23
    font, non-Roman, 18
    Greek, CDBA 12, CDBA 14, CDBA 22–23
    Hebrew, CDBA 12, CDBA 22–23
    Japanese, CDBA 12, CDBA 14, CDBA 18–20
    Korean, CDBA 12, CDBA 14, CDBA 18–20
    showing multiple languages simultaneously,
        CDBA 20
    system character set, changing, CDBA 15–17
    text, dynamic, CDBA 20–22
    text, static, CDBA 14–18
    Turkish, CDBA 12, CDBA 14, CDBA 22–23
Lasso tool, 98, 142–144, 281–282
#lastframeLoaded Director Lingo property,
    1112
Latin character set, CDBA 11, CDBA 12
Launcher Bar, 90
Law 2:1 codec, 1064
Layer Properties dialog box, 93, 119
Layer ⇨Switches ⇨Frame Blending, 412
Layer ⇨Switches ⇨Video, 412
layers. See also Mask layer; Motion Guide layer
    Actions layer, 113
    active, 109
    adding, 108, 110, 118
    animation techniques using background
        layer, CDBT 31–32, CDBT 33
    bottom level objects, 275
    component layer, 845
    contextual menu, 118–119
    deleting, 108, 110, 118
    depth, 108
    displaying, 118

                                    Continued

layers *(continued)*
distributing to, 4, 10, 284–286
export, flattening in, 30
file size, effect on, 276
Guide, 118, 342–344
importing, 476, CDBT 96, CDBT 100
introduced, 29
locking/unlocking, 108, 110, 118, 317, CDBC 64
Movie Explorer, filtering using, 188
moving, 108
name retention in copy/paste operation, 333
naming/renaming, 108, 117, 284–285
order, 108, 118, 275–276, 284, CDBC 66
outline display, 108, 110
overlay level objects, 275
performance, effect on, 276
planning, 117, 889–890
QuickTime Flash movie, 1064
scrolling through, 109
sound layers, 113, 424, 426, 428–429
3D effect, using, 1027, 1030
tweening, using in, 318, 319, 323, 325, 329
vector graphic, 474
visibility, 35, 108, 110, 118, 358
layers folders
creating, 110, 113, 118
deleting, 110, 119
described, 3, 35, 108
expanding/collapsing, 113, 119
importance of, 117
moving, 110
naming/renaming, 110
sound, organizing in, 429
subfolders, 113
timeline, display in, 113
layout consistency, 41
1e alphabetically before or same as operator, 690
Learning Interactions library, 164, 622–623
Lee, David (Flash developer), 1185
less than sign (<)
alphabetically before operator, 690
less than operator, 690

less than sign, equals sign (<=)
alphabetically before or same as operator, 690
less than or equal to operator, 690
less than sign, greater than sign (<>) inequality operator, 690, CDBA 25
level, storing movie in, 801, 803–804, 805
Leveraging Fireworks to Streamline Common Production Tasks tutorial (Brown), 950–956
libraries. *See also* libraries, shared
ActionScript library, storing code in, CDBC 34
active, 165
asset, accessing from application menu, 165
asset, accessing from Library panel, 164
asset, adding to, 164, 166
asset, deleting from, 170
asset, duplicating, 167
asset, naming/renaming, 166, 169
asset, opening for editing, 167
asset, selecting unused, 168
asset, storage in publishing, 30
bitmap storage in, 215–216
Button library, 164, 426, 543, 722
Common, 164
component, adding to, 831
component, defining from, 168
conflict, 169
copy/paste operations, 165, 167
default, 164
described, 3, 163–164
document, relation to, 165
file size, reducing through use of, 170, 171
folders, 166, 167, 168, 169
frame, asset loading into, 30
group information in, 171
import element storage in, 172–173, 196
importing to, 173, 424, 460, 566, 821
instance definition, role in, 171
Learning Interactions library, 164, 622–623
linkage, 165, 167
opening, 164
preview from, 166, 168
QuickTime video, adding to, 1060, 1061
raw data in, 171

sorting, 165
Sound library, adding sound to, 164
Sound library, creating using ActionScript,
   759–761, 777–782
Sound library, customizing sound in, 443–445
Sound library, Movie Clip, 565, 566–574,
   777–782
Sound library, previewing sound from, 424
Sound library, retrieving sound from, 173,
   426
Sound library, storing sound in, 173, 423–425,
   434
symbol, accessing from, 163, 165, 167
symbol, adding, 164, 166
symbol, editing in, 175
symbol, linking from, 167
symbol, storing in, 29, 163, 171–172
symbol usage from, counting, 168
update after asset edit, 168
Video object, adding to, 166, 504
libraries, shared
   accessing item in, 820
   asset, naming, 822
   asset, updating shared, 824–825
   author-time sharing, 170, CDBC 15,
      CDBC 16
   creating, 820–821
   described, 165, 170, 820
   export considerations, 820
   file size considerations, 820
   font, 166, 170, 240–248, 821–822, CDBC 16–17
   importing from, 823
   linkage, 167, 821, 823
   location, specifying, 822
   optimizing, CDBC 15–17
   properties, accessing, 168
   publishing movie file in, 822–823
   run-time sharing, 170, 821, 822, CDBC 16
   symbol updating, 170, CDBC 17
Library panel
   audio settings, 443
   Linkage settings, 823, 824
   loader symbol, 816
   narrow state view, 164
   New Font option, 241
   New Symbol button, 181

Play button, 431
preview pane, 424
Shared library Properties, 822
Stage, dragging object from, 10
waveform display, 424
wide state view, 164
Library window, 164, 166–168
licensing, 661, 666
lighting, 264–265, 1023, 1045–1047
line break, 225
Line Style dialog box, 152
Line tool, 98, 124, 201
lines. See also drawing
   connect setting, 128, 140
   dashed, 154, CDBT 102
   dotted, 154
   edge, softening, 268
   fill, converting to, 265–267
   hairline, 153
   hatched, 154
   height (thickness), 124, 151–152, 256
   Line tool, drawing using, 124
   optimizing, 146
   Pen tool, drawing using, 146–149
   Pencil tool, drawing using, 126–127
   pulling, 135
   ragged, 154
   recognition, 128
   reshaping, 135, 138
   sampling, 216, 254–256
   selecting, 135, 136, 137, 144–146, 286–287
   selecting portion of, 142
   simplifying, 128
   smallest displayable, 266
   solid, 153
   stacking order, 275
   stippled, 154
   style, 151–154, 254, 255–256
Lines to Fills command, 265–267
Lingo. See also Director
   ActionScript, Lingo compared, 1099
   ActionScript/Lingo property conversion
      chart, 1111–1112
   argument string, passing to multiple Lingo
      commands, 1101

Continued

Lingo *(continued)*
    crash, experiencing when sending Flash
        event to, 1102
    described, 1098
    Dictionary, 1110
    Flash action, interactivity with, 1099–1102
Linkage Properties dialog box, 245
`links.html` (on the CD), 1182
lip-syncing, 378–383, 430
Lip-Syncing Cartoons tutorial (Turner), 380–383
`lip_track` files (on the CD), 380
List Objects command, CDBC 50–51
List Variables command, 615, 684
ListBox component, 16, 834
`listener` object, 719
Live Preview feature, 847
LiveConnect feature, 641, 651
LiveMotion software, 44
Lo, Timothy (Interfacing Flash with Miva Movies
        tutorial), 1189, CDBT 69
`load`
    event, 717
    method, 853, 861
`loadArticles` function, 861–862
`loader_100.fla` (on the CD), 818
`loadFile` function, 818
`loadfile.as` (on the CD), 818
loading progress display, 655–657
`loadMovie` action
    JPEG loading, 811–814
    movie loading, 511, 799–800, 805, 807–810,
        CDBC 11–13
`loadMovie` method, 714, 806, 810, 853
`loadMovie.fla` (on the CD), CDBC 12
`loadMovie_100.fla` (on the CD), 804, 806
`loadMovie_200.fla` (on the CD), 808
`loadMovie_201.fla` (on the CD), 810
`loadMovie_202.fla` (on the CD), 810, 813
`loadMovie_300.fla` (on the CD), 814, 815
`loadMovieNum` action, 679, 803, 809
`loadMP3` function, 816
`loadScrollContent` method, 837
`loadSound` method, 775, 815, 816
`loadSound_100.fla` (on the CD), 816, 818
`loadSWF` function, 802–803, 804
`loadVariables`
    action, 36, 686–687, 865–866
    method, 715, 853

`LoadVars` object. *See also* variables
    ColdFusion MX, working with in, 1126–1127
    data transfer to/from, 857–858, 1126–1127
    defining, 23, 858
    e-mailing form data, in, 1126–1127
    event handling, 858
    `load` method, 853
    `loadVariables` action versus, 36
    Miva document, loading variable from using,
        CDBT 71–73
    `send` method, 853
    `sendAndLoad` method, 853, 858, 1127, 1131
    terminal tag, avoiding through, 854
    variable data loading, detecting using, 855
`loadVideo.swf` (on the CD), 520
logical operators, 689
login form, 699–702, 1139–1147
`login_100.fla` (on the CD), 702
`login.fla` (on the CD), 1147
`login_start.fla` (on the CD), 1145
`lookForMatch` function, 929, 930
`Loop While` action, 694
looping
    actions list, adding to, 697
    ActionScript statements, 694–698
    animation, 315, 334, 337–338, 386, 554
    counter, 694, 695, 697
    debugging, 697
    exiting using `break` action, 696–697
    Flash movie, 624, 817, 992
    Flash Movie Clip, 386, 539
    Flash movie in Director movie, 1104, 1107
    Flash movie in HTML page, 637, 641, 1082
    frames, 337–338
    Illustrator, specifying when exporting SWF
        from, 992
    Miva, in, CDBT 70
    QuickTime Flash movie, 1066
    sound, event sound, 429, 437, 1012
    sound, from Edit Envelope, 428, 437
    sound, from Property inspector, 428, 437
    sound, music, CDBC 3
    sound, stream sound, 430, 1012, CDBC 11
    sound, using ACID PRO, 998, 1017–1018
    sound, using Cool Edit Pro, 998
    sound, using Rebirth, 1016–1017
    sound, using Sound Forge, 1008
    video, 508

Lott, Joey (*Macromedia Flash MX ActionScript Bible*), 442, 1190

lt alphabetically before operator, 690

M

Mac Paint
    Flash, compatibility with, 454, CDBA 9
    importing from, 454
Macintosh Flash interface, 87–89, 96
Macromedia Authorware. *See* Authorware
Macromedia Dashboard, 87
Macromedia Director. *See* Director
Macromedia Extension Manager, 1090
Macromedia Flash MX ActionScript Bible
    (Reinhardt and Lott), 422
Macromedia SoundEdit software, 1000, 1003, 1005
Macromedia Web site
    ActionScript Dictionary, 676
    browser support tech note, 665
    ColdFusion MX resources, 1119
    component resources, 8
    Director resources, 1097, 1098, 1102
    Dreamweaver MX resources, 1080, 1090
    feedback, 670
    Flash Player debug version, CDBC 61
    Flash Player download, 42, 619, 665, 666
    Flash Player survey, CDBT 47
    Flash Player technotes, CDBT 48
    Flash Player web browser differences list,
        CDBT 48
    Flash Player Web version checking
        resources, CDBT 50, CDBT 54
    Flash Writer Illustrator plug-in download, 990
    JavaScript Flash Player detection tech note,
        667
    JavaScript tech support page, 655
    license download, 662
    Live Preview information, 847
    logo download, 662, 666
    Macintosh Internet Explorer issues tech
        note, 803
    Pocket PC resources, 1153
    Swift3D Max Exporter download, 1030
    Transparency Support in Flash TechNote,
        461, 470
    Usability pages, 595
Magic Wand tool
    Flash, 142–143, 144, 281–282
    Photoshop, 957

mailto link, 552, 853–854, 875–876, 913
main_100.fla (on the CD), 585
main_200.fla (on the CD), 590
main_300.fla (on the CD), 593
main_400.fla (on the CD), 595
main_500.fla (on the CD), 599
main_600.fla (on the CD), 601
main_700.fla (on the CD), 602
main_800.fla (on the CD), 605
main.html (on the CD), 581
main_starter.fla (on the CD), 583
MakeRefMovie utility, 1059
Using FreeHand with Flash tutorial (Wolfe),
    CDBT 93–102
Mask layer
    animated, 4, 349, 352
    animation background using, 386
    aperture, 349
    button considerations, 349, 352
    creating, 118, 349–351, 355–357
    described, 113, 348–349
    elements ignored in, 349
    export considerations, 405
    fill, using, 349
    Fireworks MX, working with in, 945–946, 947
    group, using, 349, 351
    import considerations, 458
    JPEG compression, applying selectively
        using, 944
    line, using, 349
    locking/unlocking, 350–351
    Mask layer, masking another, 349
    Motion Guide-controlled element, containing,
        355–358
    Movie Clip, using, 349, 355–358
    Photoshop, masking in, 892, 956, 958
    shape, using filled, 349–351
    shape, using tweened, 353
    static, 349
    symbol instance, using, 351–352, 355
    text, masking, 352–355
material (object surface property), 1038–1039.
    See also 3D graphics
math operations, 689, 742–743
maxscroll property, 881
MCAnimMask.swf (on the CD), 358
McConnell, Steve (*Code Complete: A Practical
    Handbook of Software Construction*),
    CDBC 41

McLean, Ruari (*Jan Tschichold: A Life in Typography*), 220

.mdb files, 1128. *See also* Microsoft Access

measurement units
  changing, 104
  grid, 104
  points, 152
  ruler, 104, 229
  text, 229

Mebberson, Scott (Flash developer), 1186

menu
  creating dynamic using array, 750–755
  creating using function, 755–759
  instance, deleting, 757
  registration point, 758

Menu ⇨Save Panel Layout, 91

`menuarray_100.fla` (on the CD), 754

`metalType.fla` (on the CD), 277

methods
  action, relation to, 707
  `addListener`, 719, 842
  asset-related, 713–715
  `attachMovie`, 713, 717, 766, 818, 829–830
  `attachSound`, 775
  color-related, 769, 772–775
  `createEmptyMovieClip`, 713, 756, 761, 925
  `createTextField`, 878, 879, 924
  `createWord`, 928
  defined, 558
  event-related, 716
  `FCheckBox` methods, 833
  `FComboBox` methods, 834
  `flush`, 933
  focus JavaScript method, 547
  `FPushButton` methods, 835
  `FRadioButton` methods, 536
  `fromCharCode`, 926
  `FScrollBar` methods, 837
  `FScrollPane` methods, 837
  function as method of object, 755–759
  `getBeginIndex`, 882
  `getBytesLoaded`, 494, 715, 777
  `getBytesTotal`, 715, 777, 794
  `getCaretIndex`, 883
  `getCode`, 719
  `getDepth`, 714
  `getEndIndex`, 882

`getFocus`, 883
`getLocal`, 933
`getPan`, 776
`getRGB`, 769, 771
`getTextExtent`, 879
`getTransform` (color object method), 769, 772, 775
`getTransform` (sound object method), 776, 782–783
`getVolume`, 776
`hide`, 766
`hitTest` (Director Lingo method), 1112
`hitTest` (Flash method), 718, 764–766, 768
`indexOf`, 742
`loadMovie`, 714, 806, 810, 853
`loadScrollContent`, 837
`loadSound`, 775, 815, 816
Movie Clip-related, 707–711
naming, 756
object, defining for, 756
`onClose`, 867
`onConnect`, 867
`onLoad`, 861–862
`onPress`, 729, 734–735
`onRelease`, 729, 734–735
`onXML`, 867
`PercentLoaded` JavaScript method, 655–657
playback-related, 712
position-related, 712
`removeMovieClip`, 713, 730
`send`, 853
`sendAndLoad`, 853, 858, 1127, 1131
`setFocus`, 883
`setPan`, 776
`setRGB`, 769, 771, 774–775
`setSelection`, 884
`setSize`, 842
`setStyleProperty`, 842, 845
`setTextFormat`, 878
`setTransform` (color object method), 769, 772–775
`setTransform` (sound object method), 776, 782–783
`setVolume`, 761, 776, 782
`setWidth`, 842
`shift`, 931
`show`, 766

slice, 742
sound-related, 760–761, 775–776
splice, 927, 928
split, 757
start, 775
stopDrag, 712, 739
swapDepths, 714
toLowerCase, 930
toUpperCase, 742
MicroDrive miniature hard drive, 1160
microphone, 366, 492, 1005
Microsoft Access, 1127–1130. *See also* database
Microsoft Active Accessibility. *See* MSAA
Microsoft Web site
    ActiveSync download, 1156
    Pocket PC resources, 1150, 1151, 1154, 1156
    Visio download, 72
MIME (Multipurpose Internet Mail Extension)
    type designation, 642
Miniml font (on the CD), 238–240
minus sign (–) subtraction operator, 689
Miscellaneous Actions booklet, 562
Missing Fonts alert box, 237, 238
Miva script, CDBT 69–73
MJPEG (Motion JPEG), 393, 396
model sheet, 372
Modify ⇨Arrange ⇨Bring Forward, 275
Modify ⇨Arrange ⇨Bring to Front, 275
Modify ⇨Arrange ⇨Send Backward, 275
Modify ⇨Arrange ⇨Send to Back, 275
Modify ⇨Break apart, 250
Modify ⇨Distribute to Layers, 10
Modify ⇨Document, 104
Modify ⇨Frames ⇨Convert to Blank Keyframes, 313
Modify ⇨Frames ⇨Convert to Keyframes, 313
Modify ⇨Frames ⇨Synchronize Symbols, 328
Modify ⇨Group, 276
Modify ⇨Layer, 119
Modify ⇨Movie, 229
Modify ⇨Optimize, 473
Modify ⇨Reverse Frames, 337
Modify ⇨Shape, 265
Modify ⇨Shape ⇨Add Shape Hint, 323
Modify ⇨Shape ⇨Expand Fill, 267
Modify ⇨Shape ⇨Lines to Fills, 265
Modify ⇨Shape ⇨Remove All Hints, 324

Modify ⇨Smooth, 138
Modify ⇨Straighten, 138
Modify ⇨Trace Bitmap, 283
Modify ⇨Transform, 270
Modify ⇨Transform ⇨Distort, 273
Modify ⇨Transform ⇨Envelope, 274
Modify ⇨Transform ⇨Remove Transform, 270
Modify ⇨Transform ⇨Rotate and Skew, 272
Modify ⇨Transform ⇨Scale, 273
Modify ⇨Ungroup, 134
modifyOptions function, CDBC 36
modifyText.fla (on the CD), 248
Moock, Colin (Unify the Web: Multiuser Flash
    Content tutorial), 1190, CDBT 43, CDBT
    48
moock commServer, 872
moock.org Web site, 871, CDBC 67, CDBT 48
MooV files, 1058
morphemes, 378
morphing shape. *See* tweening, Shape
Moschella, William (sound designer), 1186
Moshofsky/Plant Web site, CDBT 64
MoTG files (on the CD), 1030, 1055
motion, conveying in animation, 306–309,
    366–367, 368
Motion Guide layer
    adding, 110, 113, 118, 344–347, 355–358
    graphic export from, 344
    Guide layer conversion to, 345
    Mask layer containing element controlled by,
        355–358
    path definition, 344–347
    registration point considerations, 345–346,
        347–348
    tween, working with, 328, 345–347, 378
Motion JPEG. *See* MJPEG
mouse. *See also* cursor
    event handling, 532, 545–546, 718–719, 764,
        767
    methods related to, 716
    pointer, hiding/unhiding, 766
    pointer, moving Movie Clip with, 711
    pointer graphic, changing, 766–768
    position, testing, 708, 711, 766–768
    properties related to, 708
mouse object, 721, 766–768
mouseDown event, 718

`mouse_hitTest.fla` (on the CD), 768

`mouseMove` event, 718, 764

`MouseUp` event, 719

.mov files, 498, CDBA 7. *See also* QuickTime

move arrow, 271

`movevariables.fla` (on the CD), 745

Movie Clips. *See also* movies

  background, playing in, 863

  button symbol, adding to, 184–185

  collision detection, 763–766

  color attribute manipulation, 770–772

  depth, returning, 714

  depth, swapping, 714

  drag-and-drop functionality, 725

  drag-and-drop functionality, constraining to rectangle, 726–727

  drag-and-drop functionality, drop position detection, 727–730

  drag-and-drop functionality, lock mouse to center option, 726

  drag-and-drop functionality, slider creation using, 730–739

  duplicating using `duplicateMovieClip`, 713, 717, 730–732, 737

  empty, 713, 756, 761

  event handling, 711, 717–720

  frame, replacing Clip symbol with, 395

  frame graphic, displaying in, 904

  functions dependent on `MovieClip` object, 721

  Graphic symbol animation in, 183–184, 330

  Graphic symbol versus, 174

  holder, 806–808

  instance, 174

  instance, modifying, 185–187

  instance, replacing tween sequence with on Main timeline, 334–335

  instance, variable attachment to, 681

  intersection, testing for, 764

  library component definition, 168

  loading movie into Clip instance, 805–806

  looping, 386, 539

  Mask layer using Clip symbol, 349, 355–358

  methods, 707–711

  mouse pointer, moving with, 711

  movie, interaction with, 554–555

  Movie Explorer, filtering using, 188

  naming, 556, 561

  nesting, 330, 557, 565, 572–574, 696

  objects dependent on `MovieClip` object, 721

  path, 557, 559, 564

  positioning, 722–723, 730–732

  preview, 609–610

  printing content from, 788–789

  properties, 706–707, 721–725

  QuickTime image sequence, storing in, 1076

  removing duplicated, 713, 738–739

  rotating, 724–725

  scaling, 723–724, 733–735, 808

  sequence, replacing with Clip symbol, 334, 335

  sound library Movie Clip, 565, 566–574, 777–782

  Stage, timeline appearance on, 554, 555–556

  symbol, identifier string assignment to, 167

  targeting, 556–564, 810

  `TextField` object in Clip symbol, 682

  timeline, 172, 174, 554

  timeline, adding Motion Guide to, 355–358

  timeline, `getURL` action on, 688

  timeline, moving tween onto, 330–333, 335–336

  timeline, nesting, 1070

  timeline, organizing on Main, 555–556

  timeline, placing on using `attachMovie` method, 713

  timeline, replacing tween sequence with Clip instance on Main, 334–335

  video, placing in Clip symbol, 507–508

  XML, controlling using, 863

Movie Control booklet, 534, 543

Movie Explorer panel, 188–191, 226

Movie Properties dialog box, 229

movie streaming

  bandwidth, emulating, 613–614, CDBC 6, CDBC 44, CDBC 46

  bandwidth, profiling, CDBC 6

  debugging, CDBC 43–45

  described, 793–794

  download status, checking, 494

  frame size considerations, 613, 614

  message shown while loading, 794

preloading to specified point before
playback, 613, 794–799

progressive download versus, CDBC 2, CDBC
43

`movieclip` data type, 744

`MovieClip` object, 705–706, 721

`movieclip_droptarget.fla` (on the CD), 730

movies. *See also* Movie Clips; movie streaming

actions, movie control, 534

After Effects, importing into, 1067

browser back/forward button interaction,
17–18, 512, 601

browser window, filling, CDBT 43–46

closing, CDBA 3

component, adding to, 829–830, 837–840

component, removing from, 832

container movie, 41

database, loading from, 41

database, sending to, 41

DHTML content, showing behind, 639,
1083–1084

DHTML content, showing in front of, 639

Director, importing into, 669, 1097, 1099,
1103–1105

Director movie

frame rate of Flash movie within, 1105

integrating Flash movie in, 669, 1099

looping Flash movie within, 1104, 1107

placing Flash movie on Stage of, 1109

playing Flash movie within, 1102–1103,
1104

preloading Flash movie within, 1104,
1106–1107

quality setting of Flash movie within, 1105

sizing Flash movie within, 1105

Sprite bounding box of Flash movie
within, 1105

document, relation to, 30

document export to, 402–404, 616

download, progressive, 793, CDBC 2

download status, checking, 494

download status, displaying in progress bar,
795–799

Dreamweaver MX, editing from, 1087–1088

Dreamweaver MX Control Shockwave or
Flash behavior, controlling using, 1089

duration, displaying, 613

exporting to AVI, 406–408

exporting to sequence, 402–404

file extension, 30

file size, displaying, 613

file size, document versus, 609

file size in stand-alone distribution, 664

flowcharting, 556

format overview, 32

frameset, displaying in, 63

FreeHand SWF export feature, 970, 976,
980–981, 982, 984–986

`fscommand` action, adding to, 651–653

in HTML page, aligning, 625–626, 637, 638,
1082

in HTML page, background color, 1082,
1083–1084

in HTML page, border size, 638, 641, 1082,
1083

in HTML page, inserting using `<EMBED>`, 635,
640–642, 643, 688, 1083

in HTML page, inserting using link, 636

in HTML page, inserting using `<OBJECT>`,
635–640, 643, 688, 1083

in HTML page, inserting using template,
621–624

in HTML page, looping, 637, 641, 1082

in HTML page, naming, 1082

in HTML page, passing parameter to, 1082

in HTML page, playback during download,
637, 1082

in HTML page, positioning, 625–626, 637, 638,
641, 1083

in HTML page, quality setting, 1082

in HTML page, sizing, 624, 626, 637, 641, 1082

JavaScript, working with in, 637, 641, 650–657

level, communicating with movie on
different, 809

level, storing in, 801, 803–804, 805

linking to asset from another movie, 167, 823

loading external, 801–808

loading into Clip instance, 805–806

loading multiple, 801, 803

loading multiple of varying dimension, 805

loading progress display, 655–657

loading section of, 799–800

loading through proxy server, 811

Continued

movies (*continued*)
    loading using `loadMovie` action, 511,
        799–800, 805, 807–810, CDBC 11–13
    loading using `loadMovie` method, 511, 714,
        799–800, 805
    loading using `loadSWF` function, 802–803, 804
    looping, 624, 817, 992
    looping Flash movie in Director movie, 1104,
        1107
    looping in HTML page, 637, 641, 1082
    looping QuickTime Flash movie, 1066
    Movie Clip interaction with, 554–555
    MP3, loading into, 775, 777, 814–816
    naming, 610, 1082
    optimizing, CDBC 1, CDBC 4–8, CDBC 18
    path considerations, 803
    playback, publishing options, 624–625
    playback, stopping using `stop` action, 540
    playback during download, 637, 1082
    playback speed, 107
    playback speed, altering by changing display
        quality, CDBC 12–13
    playback using Dreamweaver MX behavior,
        1089
    playback using `play` action, 539
    preloader, creating, 794–799, CDBC 14–15
    preloader role in optimization, CDBC 4–5
    preloading, 794
    preloading, animation display during, 890,
        906–907
    preloading, bandwidth profiling, 613
    preloading, checking download status
        during, 794
    preloading, displaying download status
        during, 794, 796–799
    preloading, judging need for, CDBC 47
    preloading, optimizing, CDBC 13–15
    preloading, symbol placement
        considerations, CDBC 13–14
    preloading, testing, 63, 657
    preloading external, 816–819
    preloading Flash movie within Director
        movie, 1104, 1106–1107
    preloading initial frames, CDBC 14–15
    printing content from, 42, 789–790
    properties, displaying in Debug Mode, CDBC
        54–55

    properties, editing in Debug Mode, CDBC 55
    properties, planning, 583–584
    QuickTime Flash movie, checking quality,
        1062
    QuickTime Flash movie, creating, 1062–1067
    QuickTime Flash movie, file settings, 1066
    QuickTime Flash movie, layering, 1064
    QuickTime Flash movie, looping, 1066
    QuickTime Flash movie, playback, 1057,
        1060, 1062, 1066
    QuickTime Flash movie, self-contained, 1058,
        1066
    QuickTime Flash movie, sizing, 1063
    QuickTime Flash movie, sound streaming,
        1064
    QuickTime Flash movie, transparency, 1063
    QuickTime video frame, embedding in Flash
        movie, 1072
    read-only option when exporting from
        Illustrator, 993
    rotating externally loaded, 806
    sample movies available from Help menu, 87
    saving, CDBA 3
    saving, incremental, CDBC 63
    scaling in stand-alone player, 663
    scaling on Stage, 624, 805–808
    sections, breaking into using `loadMovie`
        action, 799–800
    sniffer movie, 646–650, CDBT 50–53
    Sorenson Squeeze output to, 516
    sound storage in, 423, 425
    stand-alone, distribution as, 659, 661–664
    text, loading into at runtime, 838
    timelines, on multiple, 555–556
    troubleshooting guidelines, CDBC 62–66
    unloading, 534, 714, 810
    variable, declaring when loading, 639–640
    VBScript identifier, assigning, 637
    video, exporting to, 174, 395–398, 402–404
    video sequence creation from, 401–406
    viewing in Test Movie environment, 185
    Web page linking, 540–541, 550
    XML document, loading into, 861–862
MP3 files
    bit rate, 441–442, 815
    compression, 421, 440–441, 448, 521,
        CDBC 11

decoder, checking if installed, 442
encoding, testing, 814–815
export, 422, 423, 440–441
file size, 448, 814
Flash Player support, 422, 423, 442
import, 419–420, 421, 423, 612
loading, 775, 777, 814–816
memory considerations, 815
movie containing, publishing, 611–612
preloading, 816–820
streaming, 815
VBR (Variable Bit Rate), 445–446
.mpeg files
importing, 497, 498
resolution, 490–491
MS Access, 1127–1130. *See also* database
MSAA (Microsoft Active Accessibility), 33, 582
Multipurpose Internet Mail Extension. *See* MIME
MultiServer, 872
Multiuser Server, 669
music
animation, in, 300, 380
looping, CDBC 3
Muybridge, Eadweard (photographer), 298
mysite.mdb (on the CD), 1129

N

#name Director Lingo property, 1111
_name property, 709, 1111
named anchors. *See* anchors, named
named_anchors files (on the CD), 17, 18
namespace conflict, CDBC 65
naming
conflict, 169, CDBC 64
font, embedded, 821
frame, 113
frame label, 890, CDBC 65
function, 746–747, 748
keyframe, 113
layer, 108, 117, 284–285
layer folder, 110
library asset, 166, 169, 822
method, 756
Movie Clip, 556, 561
movie in HTML page, 1082
named anchor, 103
raster graphic, 462

scene, 36, 102
sound, 566, 778
symbol, 168
text field, 15, 223
variable, 223, 680, CDBC 35
naming convention
acronym usage, CDBC 38
capitalization, CDBC 37, CDBC 38
descriptiveness, CDBC 37
file, 54, 894, CDBC 63
folder, 54
frame label, 890, CDBC 65
functional specification document, defining
in, 888
importance of, 566, CDBC 63, CDBC 65
item ID, 54
layer, 117
length of name, CDBC 37
Movie Clip element, 566
planning, 54, 117, 894
sound, 566
text field, 223
variable, 223
version increment, CDBC 63
National Television Standards Committee. *See*
NTSC
navigation system. *See also* interface design
buttons, 591–593, 905–906, 909–910, 911
consistency, 59
designing, 55, 59, 67, 886
timeline, organizing on, 591–595, 904–906,
908
navigator.mimeTypes JavaScript array, 644
ne inequality operator, 690
Nellymoser audio codec, 422
new constructor, 759–761
nextFrame
action, 506, 539, 542, 594, CDBA 25
method, 712
nextScene action, 542
Nisinson, Dorian (Creating Faux 3D tutorial),
1190, CDBT 19
Nisselson, Jane (The Human Interface tutorial),
1190, CDBT 11
noise, background, 493
Nokia Communicator 9200 series CDK (Content
Developer Kit), 1153

The Non-Designer's Type Book (Williams), 220
not logical comparison operator, 690
#Now ColdFusion MX function, 1123
NowMedia FlashNow server, 872
NPSWF32.dll, CDBT 54
NTSC (National Television Standards
       Committee)
    color standards, 399, 400–401, 415
    video standards, 395
"null sound" tutorial Web site, 446
number
    data type, 742–743
    function, 743
number generation, random, 927–928, CDBT 66
numeric operators, 689

O

object data type, 744
<OBJECT> tag, inserting movie in HTML page
       using, 635–640, 643, 688, 1083
object_definition.as (on the CD), CDBC 39
objects, listing, 781, CDBC 50–51
ODBC (Open Database Connectivity), 1129
Official Flash Bible Web site, 1119
on event handler, 534, 543–544
onClipEvent
    action, 535
    event handler, 711, 717–720, 789
onClose method, 867
onConnect method, 867
onData event handler, 720
onEnterFrame event handler, 717, 722, 736–738,
       739, CDBC 40
onion skinning, 111, 316–317, 346, 371, CDBT
       79–80
onKeyDown event handler, 719
onKeyUp event handler, 719
onLoad
    event, 547
    event handler, 717
onload method, 861–862
onMouseDown event handler, 718
onMouseMove
    event handler, 718, 764, 767, 784
    method, 716
onMouseUp event handler, 719
onPress method, 729, 734–735

onRelease method, 729, 734–735
onUnload event handler, 717
onXML method, 867
Open as Library dialog box, CDBA 2
Open Database Connectivity. *See* ODBC
Open dialog box, CDBA 1–2
operators, 689–690
Optimize command, 473
Optimize Curves dialog box, 134
Optimizing Streaming Sounds in Flash
       whitepaper, 446
or logical comparison operator, 690
orbit.swf (on the CD), CDBT 61
org_chart.vsd (on the CD), 76
outline
    font, 221, 236
    layer, 108, 110
    moving, 137
    onion skin, 111
    reshaping, 137
    shape display as, 103
    Stage outline view, 103
    text, converting to, 483–484, 970, 980, 982, 985
Output Module Settings dialog box, 415
output state, 853, 855, 857
Output window, CDBC 46–51
Oval tool, 98, 124–125, 151

P

Page Setup dialog box, 121
Paint Bucket tool (Flash), 98, 151, 216, 254–255,
       257–260
Paintbrush tool, 98, 127–133, 151, 373
Paintbucket tool (CorelDRAW 10 Graphics
       Suite), CDBT 91
Painter 7
    animation tool, as, CDBT 75–82
    background painting, CDBT 81–82
    Brush tool, CDBT 80
    Detail airbrush, CDBT 82
    exporting from, CDBT 78, CDBT 81
    Fine Spray airbrush, CDBT 82
    importing from, CDBT 78, CDBT 81
    Movie panel, CDBT 80–81
    New Frame Stack dialog box, CDBT 80
    Objects palette, CDBT 77
    onion skinning, CDBT 79–80

painting process, playing back as frame
  stack, CDBT 77–78
painting process, recording, CDBT 76–77
Pencil brush, CDBT 82
Save As dialog box, CDBT 78
Save Frames on Playback option, CDBT
  77–78
text effects, CDBT 82
Tracing Paper feature, CDBT 81
Painter 7 WOW Book (Threinen-Pendarvis),
  CDBT 82
palette, color
  adaptive, 629
  custom, 203–205
  default, 200, 202
  importing, 203–205
  saving, 202
  sorting, 202–203
  storyboard, CDBT 4
  Web 216, 629
  Web snap adaptive, 629
Palm device Flash support, 1149
Panel Layouts menu, 87
Panel Sets menu, 87, 91
panels. *See also specific panels*
  default, 87–89
  deleting, 91
  dual-monitor workstation, 99
  expanding/collapsing, 91
  focus, 93–94
  hiding/showing, 96, 105
  layout, customizing, 86, 87, 91, CDBC 24–26
  Mac/Windows differences, 87–89
  menu items versus, 93
  windows versus, 92–93
panning
  animation, 377, 384, 386–387
  sound, 428, 436, 776, 777, CDBT 62
paperplane_starter.fla (on the CD), 786
Paragraph Format options dialog box, 229
Paragraph panel, 224
Parameswaran, Viswanath (Multilingual Content
  in Flash appendix), 1191
parentheses (( ))
  function argument delimiters, 747, 756
  operator group delimiters, 690

password
  debug access, 619–620, CDBC 60
  login sequence, asking for in, 699–700
  script, verifying using server-side, 619
  source file, avoiding storage in, 619
paste. *See* copy/paste operations
paths
  Illustrator, curve quality when exporting SWF
    from, 993
  Illustrator Pathfinder panel, 975
  Motion Guide, defining using, 344–347
  moving, 145
  object, moving along, 113, 328
  orientation on, 347
  overlapping, combining using Illustrator, 975
  simplifying, 974–977
  smoothing, 974
  text, converting to outline, 483–484, 970
  text path, 979–981
  tween element, moving along, 345, 347–348
PCM (Pulse Code Modulation), 421, 422, 423, 441
.pct files, 405
PDA (Personal Digital Assistant) Flash support,
  1149. *See also* Pocket PC
.pdb files, 1149
PDL (Program Design Language), CDBT 7
Peak software, 999, 1003, 1005
Pen tool, 98, 146–149, 201
Pencil tool, 98, 126–127, 201
PercentLoaded JavaScript method, 655–657
perception, manipulating, 300–306
performance
  bitmap effect on, 456
  layer number effect on, 276
  transparency effect on, 209, CDBC 7
  tweening considerations, 326, 329
periods (..) path notation characters, 564
personality, conveying in animation, 299–300,
  365, 369, 372, 920
perspective, 1020–1022, 1026, CDBT 57–58,
  CDBT 102. *See also* 3D graphics
phonemes, 378, 382–383
Photoshop
  animation background, layered, 385–386
  color profile mismatch, 956

Continued

Photoshop *(continued)*
  color tables, 202, 204–205
  ColorSafe plug-in, 195
  cropping feature, 892
  GIF format, viewing image in, 959
  Hot Door Harmony plug-in, 199
  ICC color profile support, 961
  image preparation using, 892–894
  importing from, 455, 461
  JPEG format, viewing image in, 959
  keyboard shortcut set, using in Flash, 95
  Layers window, 958
  layout creation using, 55, 66
  Levels adjustment, 956–957, 958
  Magic Wand tool, 957
  Magnetic Lasso tool, 892
  masking, 892, 956, 958
  Profile Setup, 961
  Save for Web feature, 893, 959, 960, 961
  sizing image, 958, 959
  transparency, working with in PNG format,
      956–960
  transparency ignored when pasting from, 461
  Watercolor filter, 894
PhotoSlideshow template, 5–7
phrasing, CDBT 34–35
Physics for Game Developers (Bourg), 309
pianokeys files (on the CD), 565, 578, 777
PICT Export dialog box, 965
PICT image
  anti-aliasing, 965
  color depth, 965
  exporting from Flash, 405, 962, 964–965, 994
  exporting from QuickTime, 1075
  importing, 455
  Include PostScript option, 965
  3D graphic format, as, 1025
  transparency, 468, 965
PIE (Pocket Internet Explorer), 1152, 1155, 1156
pixel size, adjusting for video, 395–396
planning
  advantages/disadvantages of using
      Flash, weighing, 40–43, 51, CDBC 24,
      CDBC 41
  asset organization, 886
  comp, 55
  competitors, studying, 50, 52, 58
  concept, establishing, 50–51
  consensus, reaching, 58
  consistency, 59, 886, 895
  cost, 52, 56
  element boundary, establishing maximum,
      889
  element size, establishing maximum, 889
  extensibility, for, 886, 889, CDBC 24
  file versioning, CDBC 24
  flowcharting, 52–54, 72–81, 556, 583, 887
  FreeHand, using, 987
  functional specification document, 54–55,
      887–888, CDBT 3
  game design, 919–921
  goals, establishing, 51–52, 57, 674
  ideas, documenting, 50
  importance of, 29, CDBC 23–24, CDBC 63
  interactivity, 673–676, CDBT 1–10
  key elements, establishing, 888–889
  layer structure, 117, 889–890
  mission, establishing, 57
  mockup, using, 61
  movie properties, 583–584
  naming convention, 54, 117, 894
  navigation system, 55, 59, 67, 886
  problem, defining, 50–51
  scenario, 58
  site structure, 53, 58, 885–890, CDBC 23
  support considerations, 51
  team, dividing work between, CDBC 34
  technology decisions, 40–43, 51, CDBC 24,
      CDBC 41
  text, onscreen, 59–60
  3D graphic, 1031
  titles, 886
Plant, Darrel (Animation on Bézier Curves
      tutorial), 1191, CDBT 63
play
  action, 505, 539, CDBA 25
  method, 712
Play command, 321, 609–610
playback speed, 107
Player. *See* Flash Player
Playhead
  Controller, 88, 89, 106–107
  frame, relation to, 35
  Timeline window, accessing from, 108

plus sign (+)
    addition operator, 689
    concatenation operator, 690, 743
    variable name/value pair separator, 687
PNG image
    alpha channel support, 460, 468
    animation sequence, 950, 954–956
    bit-depth, 631–632
    browser support, 631
    color, 632
    compression, 632
    exporting from Flash, 406, 962
    filtering, 632
    Fireworks MX, working with in, 469, 942, 944,
        945–946, 954
    importing, 460, 895–898
    importing from Fireworks MX, 455, 469, 946
    importing from Photoshop, 959
    Photoshop, working with transparency in,
        956–960
    PNG-8 format, 460
    PNG-24 format, 460, 468, 892, 956
    publishing settings, 631–632
    3D graphic format, as, 1025
    transparency, 460, 468, 892, 956–960, CDBC 7
.pntg files, 454, CDBA 9
Pocket Internet Explorer. *See* PIE
Pocket PC
    audio capability, 1151
    bandwidth, 1151
    banking using, 1152
    battery, 1150
    Casio devices, 1153, 1155, 1157
    CDKs (Content Developer Kits), 1153, 1154
    content development for, 1154–1156, 1159
    desktop, synchronizing with, 1156–1157, 1158
    emulator, 1154
    encryption, 1152
    Excel for, 1150, 1156
    Flash Player support, 666, 1151–1154
    forums, 1153, 1154
    hardware support, 1151
    HTML content, 1155–1156
    Internet Explorer for, 1150, 1156
    Macintosh, interfacing with, 1159–1162
    manufacturers, 1150, 1153
    memory, 1151, 1157–1158, 1160–1161
    navigation system, 1150
    network, connecting to using wireless,
        1159–1160
    newsgroups, 1153
    Nokia devices, 1153, 1155
    operating system, 1150
    Phone Edition, 1160
    PIM (personal information manager)
        features, 1150–1151
    playback speed on, 1157
    processor, 1150
    publishing for, 1155
    screen size, 1155
    speed, 1150
    storage media, 1160–1161
    tasks performed by, 1150
    template, 623, 1155–1156
    testing content, 1154, 1156–1159
    video capability, 1151
    Word for, 1150, 1156
Pocket PC Flash.net, 1154
Pocket PC Passion Web site, 1154
Pocket PC Thoughts Web site, 1154
Pocket PC Web site, 1151
PocketMac, 1161
poemclip files (on the CD), 863
point of view. *See* POV
pop-up windows
    Flash contextual menu, 93
    JavaScript, using, 46
    usability, designing for, 60–61
portfolio site
    asset organization, 886
    background, 900–901, 903, 913–914
    captioning, 889, 908, 909
    consistency, 886, 895
    element boundary, establishing maximum,
        889
    element size, establishing maximum, 889
    extensibility, 886, 889
    flowcharting, 53–54, 887
    functional specification document, 887–888
    image capture, 891–892
    image preparation for loading, 895–898
    image retouching, 893–894
    image transition, 914–915

Continued

portfolio site *(continued)*
  key elements, establishing, 888–889
  label design, 890, 908
  layout scheme, 888
  logo, 899–900, 903
  navigation system, 886, 904–906, 908–911
  preloader, 906–908
  static element placement, 903–904
  structure, designing, 885–890
  text, static, 903–904
  titles, 886
positionAlphabet function, 927
#posX Director Lingo property, 1111
#posY Director Lingo property, 1111
POV (point of view), 1031. *See also* 3D graphics
PowerPoint, multimedia authoring using, 44
Preferences dialog box
  ActionScript Editor tab, CDBC 29–30, CDBC
      31
  Drawing options, 128
  Named Anchor options, 601
  Pen tool options, 147
  Printing options, 121
  selection options, 135, 136
  Snap to options, 140
  text options, 223
  Timeline options, 106, 114
preloader files (on the CD), 794, 819
preloading JPEG, 816–820
preloading movie
  animation, displaying during, 890, 906–907
  bandwidth profiling, 613
  described, 794
  Director movie, preloading Flash movie
      within, 1104, 1106–1107
  download status, checking, 794
  download status, displaying, 794, 796–799
  external movie, 816–819
  frames, initial, CDBC 14–15
  optimization, preloader role in, CDBC 4–5
  optimizing, CDBC 13–15
  preloader, creating, 794–799, CDBC 14–15
  symbol placement considerations, CDBC
      13–14
  testing, 63, 657
preloading sound, 710, 816–820

preloading symbol, CDBC 13–14
presentations
  2×4 approach, 988
  concept presentation, CDBT 5
  data-driven, 47
  FreeHand role in, 987, 988–989
  interactive, 46
  interface design, presentationalist approach
      to, 64
  keyframes, mapping to, 584–585, 988
  layout storyboard, CDBT 4
  linear, 46
  PowerPoint, 44
  print, using in, 987, 988–989
  production process overview, 62–64
  slide shows, 588
  testing, 62, 63–64
Press event, 545
prevFrame
  action, 506, 539, 542, 594, CDBA 25
  method, 712
prevScene action, 542
primitive shape, 124, 171
print action
  Director, 1112
  Flash, 787–788
print function, 721, 785, 786
Print Margins dialog box, 121
printAsBitmap action
  Director, 1112
  Flash, 788–789
printAsBitmap function, 785, 786
printAsBitmapNum function, 786
printing
  ActionScript, using, 785–790
  color, 121, 721, 786
  contact information page, 785
  coupon, 785
  Director, from, 1112
  e-mail attachment, to, 121, 785
  frame, 121, 721, 786
  FreeHand, using, 987, 988–989
  functions related to, 786
  images, 785
  invoice/receipt, 785
  Main Timeline, content from, 787–788

margins, 121

movie, content from, 42, 789–790

Movie Clip instance, content from, 788–789

Movie Explorer, from, 191

page setup, 121

PostScript versus non-PostScript printer, 785

presentation, using print in, 987, 988–989

preview, 121

Reference panel description, 679

sizing, 121

storyboard, 121

transparency (alpha value) considerations, 786

printNum function, 786

Pro Tools software, 1000–1001

procedures, 746. *See also* functions

procreate.com, CDBT 82

profiler_starter.fla (on the CD), CDBC 5

Program Design Language. *See* PDL

projector

    closing, 663

    creating, 660–662

    described, 42

    distributing, 662–664

    executable, opening from, 663

    export, 633

    file size, 660

    Flash Player, using stand-alone, 661–662

    full-screen mode, 663

    HTML document, opening from, 663–664

    icon image, replacing, 670

    key press capture, 663

    licensing, 661

    Macintosh, 633

    menu bar visibility, 661, 663

    movie, scaling in, 663

    publishing as, 633, 660–661

    stand-alone, 659–661, 662–664

    Windows, 633

projects. *See also* client, working with; planning

    application, data-driven, 47

    architecture design, 52–54, 62, 79–81, 800–801

    assets, assembling, 62

    audience, designing for, 50, 51, 57–58

    budget approval, 56

    concept, establishing, 50–51

    concept approval, 56

    flowcharting, 52–54, 72–81, 556, 583, 887

    functional specification document, 54–55, 887–888, CDBT 3

    goals, establishing, 51–52, 57

    mission, establishing, 57

    page production phase, 63

    preproduction process, CDBT 2

    presentation, 46–47

    QA, 63–64

    scene, organizing by, 102

    time schedule, 52, 56

    types, 46–47

    usability, designing for, 59–61

    Web production process, 49–50

Propellerhead Rebirth software, 1012–1017

Propellerhead Web site, 1017

properties

    appearance-related, 709

    defined, 558

    global, 710

    Movie Clip, 706–707, 721–725

    path-related, 709–710

    position-related, 708, 722–723, 731, 737

    size-related, 708–709, 723–724, 733

    timeline-related, 710

    variable, storing value in, 698

Property Inspector (Director), 1108

Property inspector (Dreamweaver MX), 1081–1082

Property inspector (Flash)

    Auto Kern check box, 229, 231

    Baseline shift menu, 229

    bitmap options, 467

    Bold button, 228

    Change Handler setting, 833

    Character button, 8

    Character embedding options button, 233

    Character spacing menu, 228

    color options, 149–150, 178, 193, 200, 211

    component options, 13, 598, 831, 832, 833

    described, 4, 90–91

    Enable HTML button, 232

    Font field/menu, 227

Continued

Property inspector (Flash) *(continued)*
    Font Size controls, 228
    Format button, 229, 231
    frame options, 108
    Italic button, 228
    line style options, 8, 151–152, 256
    Link entry option, 230
    Movie Clip options, 556, 560–561
    Named Anchor check box, 17
    Paragraph Format options, 229, 231–232
    path options, 347
    Properties tab, 831
    Render text as HTML button, 224, 875
    Rotate button, 231
    Selectable button, 229
    Show border check box, 232
    sound options, 426, 428, 435–438
    Stroke Style menu, 254, 256
    symbol behavior options, 179–180
    Target menu, 230
    Text Align options, 228, 231
    Text field instance name field, 232
    text options, basic, 221
    text options, static, 227–230
    Text Orientation menu, 228
    Text type menu, 8, 227, 875
    Text Wrap menu, 232
    tween options, 318, 320–321
    URL field, 875–876
    Use Device Fonts check box, 229
    Variable field, 233
property_inspector.fla (on the CD), 706
prototyping, 52, CDBT 10
proxy server, 811
.psd files, 455, CDBA 7. *See also* Photoshop
pseudocode, CDBT 7
Publish command, 617
Publish Preview, 513, 550, 601, 609, 633–634
Publish Settings command, 438, 617
Publish Settings dialog box
    debug settings, 619–620, CDBC 60
    Flash tab, 618–621, CDBC 60
    Formats tab, 18, 633, 660–661
    GIF tab, 627–629
    HTML tab, 18, 621–627
    JPEG tab, 630
    PNG tab, 631–632

QuickTime tab, 623, 1063
    Template menu, 18
    Use default names check box, 649, 896–897
    Window Mode option, 625
publishing. *See also* export operations
    alignment of movie, specifying, 625–626
    bandwidth calculation, 612–615
    compression options, 32, 620
    debug access, passwording in Publish
        settings, 619–620, CDBC 60
    device font option, 625
    display quality, specifying, 625
    file location, 634
    file optimization, 30
    Flash Player menu access, specifying, 625
    format, default, 618
    format, selecting, 617–618
    GIF settings, 627–630
    guestbook application, 1138
    HTML, to, 512–513, 617, 621–627
    import-protecting movie, 30, 619
    JPEG settings, 620, 630
    layer flattening, 30
    library asset storage, 30
    load order, specifying, 619
    name default option, 618, 649, 896–897
    named anchor, page with, 18, 623
    playback options, specifying, 624–625
    PNG settings, 631–632
    Pocket PC, for, 1155
    preview, 513, 550, 601, 634
    projector, as, 633, 660–661
    QuickTime, to, 623, 633, 1062–1067
    RealPlayer, to, 633, 668
    Shared library movie file, 822–823
    Size Report, 616, CDBC 5
    sound settings, 438–442, 445, 620–621
    testing prior to, 609–611
    trace action options, 619
    variable considerations, 682
    version option, 618
    video, movie with embedded, 508–513
    warning messages, 626–627
    Window Mode option, 625, 1083–1084
Pulse Code Modulation. *See* PCM
PureVoice codec, 1064

Purgason, Todd (Streamlined Workflow: FreeHand and Flash tutorial), 1191
PushButton component, 770–772, 835, 838, 843–846, 858

Q

QA (quality assurance), 63–64
Qdesign Music 2 codec, 1064
.qt files, 1060. *See also* QuickTime
.qtif files, 391, 455, CDBA 7. *See also* QuickTime
QTVR (QuickTime VR), 1065, 1069–1071
Qualcomm PureVoice codec, 1064
_quality property, 710
quick_animation files (on the CD), 12
QuickTime
    ActionScript, programming for, 1059
    animation, designing for, 385
    AVI video versus, 1058–1059
    bit-depth, video, 1068
    bitmap sequence from video, using, 1071–1077
    BMP Options dialog box, 1075
    codec support, 1058, 1060, 1064, 1069
    color quality, video, 1068–1069
    compression, 497, 1059, 1069, CDBT 38, CDBT 39
    controller display during playback, 1065
    creating QuickTime Flash movie, 1062–1067
    dot syntax support, 1059
    exporting image sequence from, 1074–1075
    exporting to, 385, 391, 1059, 1062, 1067–1069
    file extension, 1058, 1060
    file settings, QuickTime Flash movie, 1066
    file size, movie, 1059
    file size, video, 1067
    Flash content, playing in, 1057, 1058
    Flash interface with, 44, 391–392, 1057
    Flash layer vector format, 33
    Flash support, 1059–1060
    Flash track, 1057
    flattening movie, 1058, 1066, 1067
    frame, extracting from video, 1072–1073
    frame rate, 1061, 1070, 1075
    importing audio from, 420
    importing graphic from, 455
    importing image sequence from, 1076–1077
    importing movie from, 1059, 1060–1062, 1073–1076

    importing video from, 498
    layering QuickTime Flash movie, 1064
    length of movie, maximum, 1062
    library, adding video to, 1060, 1061
    linking imported video, 1060, 1061
    looping QuickTime Flash movie, 1066
    Macintosh considerations, 1058–1059
    Movie Properties dialog box, 1074
    object movie, QTVR, 1071
    panorama movie, QTVR, 1065, 1070–1071
    PICT Options dialog box, 1075
    playback of QuickTime Flash movie, 1057, 1060, 1062, 1066
    Player, distributing for, 668–669
    publishing to, 623, 633, 1062–1067
    QTVR (QuickTime VR), 1065, 1069–1071
    quality of QuickTime Flash movie, checking, 1062
    quality of video, setting, 1069
    Save exported file as dialog box, 1074–1075
    scenes, working with multiple, 1061
    self-contained QuickTime Flash movie, 1058, 1066
    sizing QuickTime Flash movie, 1063
    sizing video, 1068
    Sorenson Squeeze output to QuickTime video, 516–517
    sound format of video, setting, 1069
    sound streaming, QuickTime Flash movie, 1064
    timeline, working with QuickTime movie on, 1061
    transparency settings, QuickTime Flash movie, 1063
    unlock key, 1059
    Windows considerations, 1058–1059
    wrapper, 1058
QuickTime VR. *See* QTVR
quotation marks ("")
    parameter name/value delimiters, 640
    string delimiters, 683, 690

R

Radio Mall Web site, 365
RadioButton component, 835–836, 838
random function, 927–928
random number generation, 927–928, CDBT 66

raster graphics. *See also specific file types*
    animation, 361, 385, 966
    background image, bitmap, 456–457
    bit depth, 457, 631–632, 1173
    bitmap shift, 466
    breaking apart, 11, 280–281, 471–472
    browser consistency, 466
    color range in bitmap, selecting, 144, 281–282
    compression, 941–942
    compression, export considerations, 1026
    compression, previewing, 948
    compression, setting, 463, 465, 468
    compression, source file considerations,
        468–471
    compression information, updating, 463
    compression to apply to imported, 457, 459,
        462
    copying bitmap into Flash, 461
    CorelDRAW 10 Graphics Suite, converting
        image to bitmap in, CDBT 91
    editing outside Flash, 467
    Envelope Modifier tool, using on bitmap, 11
    exporting to, 404, 405–406, 961–966
    file information, viewing, 462
    file size, 451, 453
    fill, bitmap, 193, 210, 257–258, 259–261,
        262–263
    handler, bitmap, 34
    importing, 172–173, 456–457, 458–461, 462
    library, bitmap storage in, 215–216
    loading, dynamic, 18–19
    Movie Explorer, filtering using, 188
    naming, 462
    optimizing, CDBC 10
    performance, minimizing bitmap effect on,
        456
    placed bitmap, 478
    preparing for use in Flash, 941–942, 948–950
    preview, 462
    properties, setting, 462–464
    QuickTime video, using bitmap sequence
        from, 1071–1077
    resolution, 457, 458
    rotating, 466
    sampling bitmap attributes, 280, 284
    scaling, 452, 458–459
    sequence, bitmap, 461

    sizing, 458, 459, 941, 958, 959
    smoothing, 452, 463, 465, 628
    swapping, 467
    3D file formats, 1025
    transparency, 461, 942, 1026, CDBC 7
    vector graphic, converting to, 280, 282–284,
        471–473, 971–974
    vector graphic, rasterizing, 410, 471–473, 475,
        482
    vector graphic compared, 451–453, 996
raw PCM (Pulse Code Modulation) audio format,
    421, 422, 423, 441
RDS (Remote Development Services), 1120, 1121
RealOne Player, 44, 1058
RealPlayer, publishing to, 633, 668
Rebirth software
    AC (Accent) feature, 1015
    BPM selector, 1013
    Compressor feature, 1016
    Delay feature, 1016
    Distortion feature, 1015
    drum sound, 1014
    Flam feature, 1014
    Focus Bar, 1013
    level controls, 1016
    looping sound, 1016–1017
    Mix buttons, 1013
    modifications available on Internet, 1012
    Pattern Mode, 1013
    Pattern Selector, 1015
    PCF (Pattern Controlled Filter), 1015–1016
    Solo feature, 1015
    Song Mode, 1016
    synthesizer emulation, 1012, 1015
recording sound
    capture device, 366
    microphone, 366, 492, 1005
    software related to, 998, 999, 1000, 1001
    sound effect, 366
    studio, 1001–1002
recording video, 489–495
Rectangle tool
    CorelDRAW 10 Graphics Suite, CDBT 87,
        CDBT 91
    Flash, 98, 125–126, 151
Recycle, Repurpose, Redeploy. *See* RRR
Redo operations, 160

Reed, Arena (Combining Flash with the Natural Beauty of Painter 7 tutorial), 1191, CDBT 75
Reference panel, 678–679, CDBC 25
registration point, 345–346, 347–348, 758
Reinhardt, Daisy (designer), 885
Reinhardt, Robert (*Macromedia Flash MX ActionScript Bible*), 442, 446
release event, 543–544, 545
releaseOutside event, 545
Remote Debug dialog box, CDBC 60–61
Remote Development Services. *See* RDS
removeMovieClip method, 713, 730
Render Queue window, 413–414
Render Settings dialog box, 414
render speed sniffer script, CDBC 20
resolution
    animation, for, 363
    export operation, setting in, 963
    interface design resolution target, 67
    raster graphic, 457, 458
    Stage view percentage, 100
    tracing, considerations when, 971
    video, 392, 394, 490–491
Resolution Test Patterns Web page, 491
restoreLook object, 774
reuseWalk.swf (on the CD), 376
Revert feature, CDBA 4
Richards, Mike (Creating Printable Paper Airplanes tutorial), 786
Robertson, James (Complex Hit Detection on the Z Axis tutorial), 1192, CDBT 57
rollOut event, 546
rollOver event, 546
#rotate Director Lingo property, 1111
rotatingCube files (on the CD), 542
rotation
    Director Sprite, 1113–1114
    fill, 210, 262
    gradient, 210, 262
    Motion tweening, using, 327–328
    movie, externally loaded, 806
    Movie Clip, 724–725
    object, 158, 159, 270, 272
    raster graphic, 466
    text, 222, 224, 231, 250
    3D effect using, 1027, 1028, 1029, 1045

_rotation property, 708, 724, 1111
rotoscope, CDBT 34
RRR (Recycle, Repurpose, Redeploy), 1152
rulers, 104, 141, 229, CDBT 20
runtime asset sharing, 243

S

sampleButton.fla (on the CD), 180
sample_48kf_50qu.swf (on the CD), 501
sample_high.avi (on the CD), 495, 525
sample_high_import.mov (on the CD), 500, 502
sample_low.mpg (on the CD), 494
sample_mid.avi (on the CD), 494
sample_1kf_50qu.swf (on the CD), 501
sampleVideo_100.fla (on the CD), 504
sampleVideo_200.fla (on the CD), 507
sampleVideo_300.fla (on the CD), 508, 510
sampleVideo_400.fla (on the CD), 512
sampleVideo_Broadband files (on the CD), 527
sample_0kf_50qu.swf (on the CD), 501
sampling element attributes
    bitmap, 280, 284
    color, 207, 216, 254–260, 280
    fill, 216, 254–256
    Ink Bottle, dumping sampled attribute from, 256
    Ink Bottle, transferring sampled attribute to, 216, 254–255
    Paint Bucket, dumping sampled attribute from, 257–260
    Paint Bucket, transferring sampled attribute to, 216, 254–255
    stroke, 216, 254–256
    text, 249
Save As dialog box
    Flash, CDBA 3
    Painter 7, CDBT 78
saveLossScore function, 934–935
saveName function, 934
Scalable Vector Graphics. *See* SVG
#scaleX Director Lingo property, 1111
#scaleY Director Lingo property, 1111
scaling
    background image, 901
    depth, simulating using, 1026, 1027, CDBT 57–59

Continued

scaling *(continued)*
    fill, 210, 262–263, 265–266
    gradient, 210, 262–263
    image transition using, 914–915
    line, 265–266
    Motion tweening, using, 325, 329
    Movie Clip, 723–724, 733–735, 808
    movie in stand-alone player, 663
    movie on HTML page, 624, 626, 637, 641, 1082
    movie on Stage, 624, 805–808
    object, 157, 158, 159, 265–266, 272–273
    properties, size-related, 708–709, 723–724
    raster graphic, 452, 458–459
    slider, creating for, 733–735
    symbol, 180, 273, 377
    text, 249
    vector graphic, 452
scanning images, 891
Scene panel, 101–102
scenes
    adding, 102
    cartoon, 365
    copying, 102
    deleting, 102
    document, relation to, 30
    frame in specific, going to, 537
    introduced, 36
    keyframe, relation to, 30
    keyframe versus, 590
    library folder, organizing in, 169
    naming, 36, 102
    navigating, 102–103
    ordering, 36, 101, 103
    project, organizing by, 102
    QuickTime, working with in, 1061
    testing, 428, 610, 611
    timeline, relation to, 103
SCORM (Shareable Content Object Reference
    Model), 623
screen reader, 45, 582, 602–605
ScreenTime Media Web site, 669
Screenweaver Web site, 669
`scriptDetection.html` (on the CD), 644
scripting. *See* ActionScript; JavaScript; VBScript
Scriptless Flash Player Detection tutorial
    (Wolter), CDBT 47–55

`scroll` property, 881
ScrollBar component, 8–9, 595–599, 836–838,
    881, 1134
scrolling, text, 231, 248, 595–599, 881
ScrollPane component, 837, 840, 845–846
`scrollProp` files (on the CD), 881
.sd2 files, CDBA 9
search engine indexing of Flash text, 42,
    CDBC 3
Secure Socket Layer. *See* SSL
security
    ActionScript extraction from .swf file, 619
    browser caching, 619
    ColdFusion MX, 1119
    Illustrator, read-only option when exporting
        SWF from, 993
    login sequence, 699
    movie, import-protecting, 30, 619
    object extraction from .swf file, 619
    Pocket PC encryption, 1152
    SSL connection, 540
Select External Editor dialog box, 467
`Selection` object, 882–884
semicolon (;) action line suffix, 544
`send` method, 853
send state, 853–854
`sendAndLoad` method, 853, 858, 1127, 1131
`sendmail` files (on the CD), 855, 859, 1181–1182
`sendXML` Director Lingo command, 1112
`separation.alv` file (on the CD), 957
sequences
    bitmap, 461
    described, 401
    exporting from QuickTime, 1074–1075
    exporting PNG sequence from Fireworks MX,
        950, 954–956
    format comparison, 404–406
    importing into After Effects, 409–415
    integration of multiple, 330–333
    length, changing, 314
    multiple, integrating, 330–333
    reversing in frame-by-frame animation, 337
    tween sequence, replacing with Clip instance
        on Main timeline, 334–335
    video sequence, creating from movie,
        401–406

server
proxy, 811
socket, 33, 41, 865–872
Web, 634, 916
Server-Side ActionScript. *See* SSAS
Set Variable action, 684
setFlashProperty Director Lingo command, 1111
setFocus method, 883
setInterval
function, 817
method, 924, 932
setPan method, 776
setRGB method, 769, 771, 774–775
setRound function, 927
setSelection method, 884
setSize method, 842
setStyleProperty method, 842, 845
setTextFormat method, 878
setTransform method
color object, 769, 772–775
sound object, 776, 782–783
setVariable Director Lingo command, 1110
setVolume method, 761, 776, 782
setWidth method, 842
.sgi files, 455
shadow, 264, 269, 1042, 1045–1046, 1049. *See also* 3D graphics
shape hints, 105, 322–325
Shareable Content Object Reference Model. *See* SCORM
Shared library
accessing item in, 820
asset, naming, 822
asset, updating shared, 824–825
author-time sharing, 170, CDBC 15, CDBC 16
creating, 820–821
described, 165, 170, 820
export considerations, 820
file size considerations, 820
font, 166, 170, 240–248, 821–822, CDBC 16–17
importing from, 823
linkage, 167, 821, 823
location, specifying, 822
optimizing, CDBC 15–17
properties, accessing, 168

publishing movie file in, 822–823
runtime sharing, 170, 821, 822, CDBC 16
symbol updating, 170, CDBC 17
Shared Properties dialog box, 168
sharedFont_starter.fla (on the CD), CDBC 16
sharedLib files (on the CD), 823
SharedObject feature, 663, 933
shift method, 931
Shift-JIS character set, CDBA 13
ShockFusion Web site, CDBC 67
Shockwave Player. *See also* Director
compression, sound, 421
Flash Asset Xtra, 669, 1097
Flash Player versus, 1098
Shockwave-Flash-NP-PPC file, CDBT 54
Shockwave-Flash-NP-68 file, CDBT 54
shovemedia.com, 872
Show Info dialog box, 670
show method, 766
showProps Director Lingo action, 1114
ShowTime Screen Saver Web site, 669
showUserInfo function, 934
site architecture, 52–54, 62, 79–81, 800–801
Size Report, 616, CDBC 5
skew
fill, 210, 263
gradient, 210, 263
object, 158, 159, 270, 272
text, 223, 248
Slash notation
Director, 1110–1111
Flash, 564
slash (/)
division operator, 689
path notation character, 564
slashes (//) comment prefix, 113
sleepyStella.mov (on the CD), 1061
slice method, 742
slide show, 588
slider, creating
scaling control, for, 733–735
sound control, for, 783–785
transparency control, for, 730, 733, 735–736
slider_basic files (on the CD), 730, 733, 736, 738, 739

Slideshow template, 5–7

Smart Clip, 29, 138, 164, 827, 828

SMIL (Synchronized Multimedia Integration
        Language), 44

smoothing
    drawing, 128, 134, 138–139
    paths, 974
    raster graphic, 452, 463, 465, 628
    Sorenson Squeeze, in, 523
    vector graphic, 452, 974, 975

Snap to feature
    to grid, 104, 140–141
    to guide, 105, 141
    magnet strength setting, 140
    to object, 105, 140
    to pixel, 105, 141–142

sniffer movie, 646–650, CDBT 50–53

sniffer script, CDBC 19–20

sniffer*.fla files (on the CD), CDBC 20

sniffer.html (on the CD), 650

socket server, 33, 41, 865–872

Soften Fill Edges dialog box, 268

SoftenEdges.fla (on the CD), 269

Sonic Foundry ACID PRO software, 998, 999,
        1017–1018

Sonic Foundry software suite, 998

Sorenson Squeeze
    2-pass VBR encoding, 514
    batch processing, 514
    black restore control, 524
    brightness control, 524
    compression presets, 515, 517–519
    compression presets, changing, 520
    contrast control, 524, 525–526
    de-interlacing, 515, 524
    demo (on the CD), 515
    described, 514
    DV capture, 515
    editions available, 514
    encoding, 514
    fade effects, 525
    filters, 515, 524–525
    Flash movie, output to, 516
    Flash MX native compressor, 34, 514
    Flash video, output to, 515–516
    frame dropping, 522, 523

    frame rate, 515, 516, 520, 521, 527
    frame size, setting, 521
    gamma control, 524
    image cropping, 525
    image quality, setting minimum, 523
    image smoothing, 523
    keyframe creation, automatic, 522–523
    Output File queue, 517, 526
    output formats, 515
    playback, 523
    Quick Compress option, 522
    QuickTime video, output to, 516–517
    sound compression, 521, 527
    sound normalization, 525
    sound volume, 524, 525
    Spark, 34, 499–502, 518, CDBT 38
    video compression, 521, 525–527, CDBT
        38–39
    video noise reduction, 525
    white restore control, 524

sound. See also sound, event; sound, streaming
    ActionScript, working with in, 759–761
    antialias filter, 1007, 1009
    array, working with in, 760, 779–782
    audio output, checking if present, 442
    AVI, in, 407
    background, 427–428, 429, 437
    background noise, 493
    balance, creating slider control for, 783–785
    balancing, 492
    bandwidth/bit rate table, 447
    bit-depth, 492, 1173–1175, CDBC 11
    button, association with, 425–427, 431–432
    chance, using in sound design, CDBT 62
    channels, 1175
    channels, combining for mono playback, 440,
        441, 521, 1009
    channels, editing separately, 434–435
    channels, pan effect using, 436, 776
    channels, playing separately, 436
    channels, volume control for individual, 776,
        782, 783–785
    clipping, 388, 1004, 1006, 1008
    compression, artifact creation in, CDBC 11
    compression, default, 445
    compression, dynamic, 1006

compression, event sound, 439, 443, 620–621
compression, MP3, 421, 440–441, 448, 521,
    CDBC 11
compression, QuickTime codec support,
    1064
compression, raw format, 422, 441
compression, setting, 439–441, 443–444, 447
compression, Shockwave, 421
compression, Sorenson Squeeze options,
    521, 527
compression, speech, 421, 422, 423, 441
compression, video sound track, 497, 502
cross-platform environment, 420
data type, 744
dead space, 1002
design, dynamic, CDBT 61–62
Director, considerations when using Flash
    audio in, 1103
disabling, 440
document, extracting from, 449–450
document, relation to, 423, 425
doppler effect, CDBT 61
echo effect, 1010
editing overview, 1002–1004
editing software, third-party, 997–1001
editing using Flash, 434–437
effects, 365–366, 380, 1010–1012
explosion effect, 1010–1011
exporting, 408–409, 421–423, 443–444
fading, 436, 1003–1004
file size, 448, 1002–1003, 1006–1009, 1172
file size, estimating, 444, 1176
filename, displaying, 428
.fla file, extracting from, 449–450
Flash Player frame drop to keep up with,
    CDBC 3
frame rate effect on, 429
frequency, 1171
game sound, 920, 923
handle, 1176
import, 173, 419–421, 423–425, 444
in point, 1002–1003, 1176
instance, 425, 775
interpolation accuracy, 1007
keyframe, assigning to, 423–424, 427
keyframe, sound object versus, 777

label, applying to, 567–568
latency, 421
layer, sound, 113, 424, 426, 428–429
length, CDBC 11
linkage, 760, 778
lip-syncing, 378–383, 430
listing sound objects, 781
loading, dynamic, 18–19
looping event sound, 429, 437, 1012
looping from Edit Envelope, 428, 437
looping from Property inspector, 428, 437
looping music, CDBC 3
looping stream sound, 430, 1012, CDBC 11
looping using ACID PRO, 998, 1017–1018
looping using Cool Edit Pro, 998
looping using Rebirth, 1016–1017
looping using Sound Forge, 1008
memory requirements, 425
methods related to, 760–761, 775–776
mono, 440, 441, 521, 1009
movie, storage in, 423, 425, 443
Movie Explorer, filtering using, 188
muting, 578–579
naming, 566, 778
normalizing, 1004–1005, 1006–1007, 1008
null, 446
optimizing, 437, 446–448, 1006–1009, CDBC
    2–3, CDBC 10–11
out point, 1002–1003, 1176
overlapping, 429, 432, 567–568
overriding settings, 438, 440, 621
panning, 428, 436, 776, 777, CDBT 62
PCM format, storage in, 421, 422, 423, 441
pitch, 1171
Play button, creating, 431–432
playing, decompression process in, 421
playing channels separately, 436
playing using start method, 775
playing using Start Sync option, 430
Pocket PC audio capability, 1151
preamp, 1001–1002
preloading, 710, 816–820
preview from Edit Envelope dialog box, 435
publish settings, 438–442, 445, 620–621

Continued

sound *(continued)*
    quality, 492–493, 997, 1001, 1006, 1172–1177
    QuickTime video sound format, setting, 1069
    raw format, 422, 423
    recording, capture device, 366
    recording, microphone, 366, 492, 1005
    recording, sound effect, 366
    recording software, 998, 999, 1000, 1001
    recording studio, 1001–1002
    reusing, 425, CDBC 11
    reverb effect, 1010
    sample rate, 492, 1006, 1007, 1009, 1172–1173
    scrubbing, 430
    simultaneous, effect on performance,
        CDBC 11
    slider control, creating, 783–785
    software, audio-editing, 997–1001
    Sorenson Squeeze settings, 521, 524, 527
    speech, 365, 421, 422, 423, 441
    start sound, 430
    state, 567
    stopping, 431–434, 444, 540, 567–569, 776
    symbol, as, 168
    synchronization, 379, 382, 409, 428, 429–430
    synthesizer emulation software, 1012–1017
    targeting, 574–578
    testing, 422, 428, 444
    timeline, adding to, 427–428
    timeline, display on, 113, 1002
    timeline, organizing on, 428–429
    update of audio file, checking for, 444
    volume, controlling for individual channel,
        776, 782, 783–785
    volume, controlling using setVolume
        method, 761, 776, 782
    volume, creating slider control for, 783–785
    volume, Edit Envelope settings, 434, 436
    volume, returning, 776
    volume, Sorenson Squeeze settings, 524, 525
    waveform display, 113, 382
    zoom effect, 436
sound, event
    background, 429
    compression, 439, 443, 620–621
    dynamic, 777
    exporting, 438, 443

    frames, skipping starting, CDBC 19
    loading, 429
    looping, 429, 437, 1012
    movie, storage in, 425
    playback, 429, 431, CDBC 3
    publishing, 445
    reusing, 425
    start sound as, 430
    stopping, 431–432
    stream sound, doubling as, CDBC 3
    streaming mode, kicking into, 446
    uses of, CDBC 2–3
sound, streaming
    animation, pacing in sync with, 430
    broadcast animation, in, 380
    buffer time setting, 710, 1112
    compression, 439, 620
    event sound, doubling as stream sound,
        CDBC 3
    event sound, kicking into streaming mode, 446
    export quality, 438
    exporting audio as separate file, 408–409
    lip-sync, using for, 430
    looping, 430, 1012, CDBC 11
    movie, sound storage in, 423, 425, 443
    MP3, 815
    Playhead, dragging over, 379, 428, 430
    QuickTime Flash movie, 1064
    stopping instance of, 433
    Sync option, choosing as, 428
    testing, 428
    timeline, relationship to, 430
    visual content, priority over, 430
sound card, 1001, 1002
Sound Designer II file import, 420
Sound Forge software
    ACID software, integration with, 998
    Channel Converter dialog box, 1009
    echo feature, 1010
    editing, nondestructive, 998
    Fade In/Out envelopes, 1004
    file formats supported, 998
    Graphic Fade window, 1003–1004
    In/Out point, setting, 1003
    Insert Silence dialog box, 1010–1011
    looping, 1008

New Window dialog box, 1008
Normalize dialog box, 1005, 1006–1007,
    1008–1009
Resample dialog box, 1007, 1009
Reverb dialog box, 1010, 1011
Sound library
    adding asset to, 164
    creating using ActionScript, 759–761, 777–782
    customizing sound in, 443–445
    Movie Clip sound library, 565, 566–574,
        777–782
    previewing sound from, 424
    retrieving sound from, 173, 426
    storing sound in, 173, 423–425, 434
sound object, 721, 744, 760–761, 775–777
Sound Properties dialog box, 168, 443–444, 447
Sound Settings dialog box, 439
_soundbuftime property, 710, 1112
SoundEdit software, 1000, 1003, 1005
soundLib_ActionScript.fla (on the CD), 782
soundObjects.fla (on the CD), 759
soundSlider_100.fla (on the CD), 785
soundTransformObject object, 782–783
.spa files, CDBA 6
Spark codec. See Sorenson Squeeze
spell-check, 226
SphereLighting.fla (on the CD), 264
Spiridellis, Gregg (JibJab.com's Collage
        Animation Workflow tutorial), 1192
.spl files, CDBA 6
splice method, 927, 928
split method, 757
#spriteSoundBufferTime Director Lingo
        property, 1112
SSAS (Server-Side ActionScript), 1119
.ssk files, CDBA 9
SSL (Secure Socket Layer) connection, 540
Stage
    background color, 121, 639, 801
    clearing using clearStage function, 911
    component, adding to, 829
    Document window Stage area, 100–101
    dragging objects on, 101
    drawing object, positioning in relation to, 158
    group, moving to, 136
    library asset copy/paste operations, 165

Library panel, dragging object to, 10
magnification, 100–101, 103
Movie Clip timeline appearance on, 554,
    555–556
movie scaling on, 624, 805–808
object, 624, 636
outline view, 103
symbol, working with on, 163, 165, 167, 175,
    177
stand-alone distribution
    CD-ROM, on, 662–664
    file size, 664
    Flash Player, 659, 661–664
    floppy disk, on, 662–664
    projector, 659–661, 662–664
    scaling movie in stand-alone player, 663
    utilities for working with, 669
start method, 775
startDrag
    action, 725–726, 727, 735
    method, 712, 764
startDrawing function, CDBC 36
states
    button state, 172
    data process, defining using, 852–855
    input state, 853
    output state, 853, 855, 857
    send state, 853–854
    sound state, 567
    wait state, 853, 854
Steinberg Media Technologies Web site, 1017
stella files (on the CD), 560, 564, 1061
stop
    action, 505, 508, 539, 540, CDBA 25
    method, 712, 776
stopAllSounds action, 433–434, 540
stopDrag method, 712, 739
stop_sound_100.fls (on the CD), 432
storyboard
    animation storyboard, 362–366, 1032, 1042,
        1043, CDBT 5–6
    camera movement, 1032, 1042, 1043
    Color palette, CDBT 4
    creating, 362–363
    flowchart storyboard, CDBT 8–10

Continued

storyboard (continued)
 functionality testing, CDBT 10
 interaction storyboard, CDBT 6–8
 layout storyboard, CDBT 4–5
 presentation tool, CDBT 4–5
 printing, 121
 template (on the CD), 365
 3D storyboard, 1031–1032
 3ds max, using, 1031–1032
Storyboard.doc (on the CD), 1031
Storyboarding and Planning Interactivity
  tutorial (Dundon), CDBT 1–10
streaming movies
 bandwidth, emulating, 613–614, CDBC 6,
  CDBC 44, CDBC 46
 bandwidth, profiling, CDBC 6
 debugging, CDBC 43–45
 described, 793–794
 download status, checking, 494
 frame size in bytes, streaming
  considerations, 613, 614
 message shown while loading, 794
 preloading to specified point before starting
  playback, 613, 794–799
 progressive download versus, CDBC 2,
  CDBC 43
streaming sound
 animation, pacing in sync with, 430
 broadcast animation, in, 380
 buffer time setting, 710, 1112
 compression, 439, 620
 event sound, doubling as stream sound,
  CDBC 3
 event sound, kicking into streaming mode,
  446
 export quality, 438
 exporting audio as separate file, 408–409
 lip-sync, using for, 430
 looping, 430, 1012, CDBC 11
 movie, sound storage in, 423, 425, 443
 MP3, 815
 Playhead, dragging over, 379, 428, 430
 QuickTime Flash movie, 1064
 stopping instance of, 433
 Sync option, choosing as, 428
 testing, 428

 timeline, relationship to, 430
 visual content, priority over, 430
streaming video, 19–22, 509
Streamline, tracing raster image using, 974
Streamlined Workflow: FreeHand and Flash
  tutorial (Purgason), 986–990
string data type, 741–742
string literals, 682, 683
String object, 742. See also text
string operators, 689
Stroke Height numeric entry box, 151
Stroke panel, 126
Stroke Style dialog box, 152–153
Studio Vision Pro software, 1000
Stuffit Deluxe utility, 1160
subroutine, 698–699
Subselection tool, 98, 135, 144–146
Sun AU file import, 420
SupplyNet Web site, 1160
Support Center, 86, 87
surprise, use of, 300
surpriseButton.fla (on the CD), 187, 189
SVG (Scalable Vector Graphics), 44
Swap Bitmap dialog box, 467
Swap Symbol dialog box, 179–180
swapDepths method, 714
Swatches panel, 149–151, 194, 200–205, 206–207
Swatches pop-up, 200
.swd files, 620
.swf files, 29
SWF-Browser utility, 619
swflash.inf file, CDBT 54
swflash.ocx file, CDBT 54
SwiffTOOLS Web site, 619, 669
Swift3D software
 Cartoon Average Color Fill feature, 1046
 Material/Map browser, 1033
 Max Exporter plug-in, 1030
 optimizing vector artwork using, 483
 texture mapping, 1033
 3ds format support, 1025
 3ds max software, integration with, 1030,
  1049, 1052
 trial version (on the CD), 1182
switch action, 692, 693, 839